Athletic Training
and Sports Medicine

An Integrated Approach

Fifth Edition

Edited by
Chad Starkey, PhD, AT, FNATA
Professor
Division of Athletic Training
College of Health Sciences
   and Professions
Ohio University

JONES & BARTLETT
LEARNING

AMERICAN ACADEMY OF ORTHOPAEDIC SURGEONS

World Headquarters
Jones & Bartlett Learning
5 Wall Street
Burlington, MA 01803
978-443-5000
info@jblearning.com
www.jblearning.com

Editorial Credits
Chief Education Officer: Mark W. Wieting
Director, Department of Publications:
    Marilyn L. Fox, PhD
Managing Editor: Barbara A. Scotese
Associate Senior Editor: Gayle Murray
AAOS Board of Directors, 2011–2012
President: Daniel J. Berry, MD
First Vice-President: John R. Tongue, MD
Second Vice-President: Joshua J. Jacobs, MD
Past President: John J. Callaghan, MD
Treasurer: Frederick M. Azar, MD
Treasurer-elect (ex officio): Andrew N. Pollak, MD

Jeffrey O. Anglen, MD
William J. Best
Kevin P. Black, MD
Wilford K. Gibson, MD
Mininder S. Kocher, MD, MPH
Gregory A. Mencio, MD
Fred C. Redfern, MD
Steven D.K. Ross, MD
Naomi N. Shields, MD
David D. Teuscher, MD
Daniel W. White, MD, LTC, MC
Karen L. Hackett, FACHE, CAE *(ex officio)*

Jones & Bartlett Learning books and products are available through most bookstores and online booksellers. To contact Jones & Bartlett Learning directly, call 800-832-0034, fax 978-443-8000, or visit our website, www.jblearning.com.

Substantial discounts on bulk quantities of Jones & Bartlett Learning publications are available to corporations, professional associations, and other qualified organizations. For details and specific discount information, contact the special sales department at Jones & Bartlett Learning via the above contact information or send an email to specialsales@jblearning.com.

The authors, editor, and publisher have made every effort to provide accurate information. However, they are not responsible for errors, omissions, or for any outcomes related to the use of the contents of this book and take no responsibility for the use of the products and procedures described. Treatments and side effects described in this book may not be applicable to all people; likewise, some people may require a dose or experience a side effect that is not described herein. Drugs and medical devices are discussed that may have limited availability controlled by the Food and Drug Administration (FDA) for use only in a research study or clinical trial. Research, clinical practice, and government regulations often change the accepted standard in this field. When consideration is being given to use of any drug in the clinical setting, the health care provider or reader is responsible for determining FDA status of the drug, reading the package insert, and reviewing prescribing information for the most up-to-date recommendations on dose, precautions, and contraindications, and determining the appropriate usage for the product. This is especially important in the case of drugs that are new or seldom used.

Production Credits
Publisher: Cathleen Sether
Executive Acquisitions Editor: Shoshanna Goldberg
Editorial Assistant: Agnes Burt
Production Manager: Julie Champagne Bolduc
Production Editor: Jessica Steele Newfell
Marketing Manager: Jody Yeskey

VP, Manufacturing and Inventory Control: Therese Connell
Composition: Circle Graphics
Cover Design: Kate Ternullo/Kristin Parker
Cover and Title Page Image: © Shawn Pecor/ShutterStock, Inc.
Printing and Binding: Malloy, Inc.
Cover Printing: Malloy, Inc.

Some images in this book feature models. These models do not necessarily endorse, represent, or participate in the activities represented in the images.

Library of Congress Cataloging-in-Publication Data
Athletic training and sports medicine : an integrated approach / edited by Chad Starkey. — 5th ed.
    p. cm.
 Includes bibliographical references and index.
 ISBN 978-0-7637-9609-9 (casebound : alk. paper)
 1. Sports medicine. 2. Physical education and training. I. Starkey, Chad, 1959–
 RC1210.A84 2013
 617.1'027—dc23
                            2011040745

6048

Printed in the United States of America
16 15 14 13 12   10 9 8 7 6 5 4 3 2 1

CONTENTS

PREFACE

First published in 1984, *Athletic Training and Sports Medicine* is now one of the longest, most durable, and continually updated textbooks dedicated to the physical medicine and rehabilitation of musculoskeletal injuries. The 28 years in which *Athletic Training and Sports Medicine* has been published have seen remarkable advances in the diagnosis, management, and rehabilitation of orthopaedic injuries. The fifth edition of the retitled *Athletic Training and Sports Medicine: An Integrated Approach* reflects these developments.

This new edition focuses on the integration of immediate management, diagnosis, surgical and nonsurgical management, and rehabilitation of common orthopaedic pathologies and other conditions experienced by athletes. "Integration" occurs by synthesizing the various steps in the injury process, from the initial management to the patient's return to play. To meet this end, this text incorporates the following user-friendly features:

- Description of the pathology
- Pathomechanics and functional limitations
- Imaging techniques
- Post-injury and post-surgery management
- Commonly prescribed medications
- Surgical techniques and their implications for rehabilitation
- Progressive treatment and rehabilitation guidelines
- Return-to-play guidelines
- Best practices highlights

The *Fifth Edition* was written for the reader who has a good understanding of human anatomy and clinical diagnostic skills and who is familiar with the basic principles of acute injury management, therapeutic modalities, and therapeutic exercise.

Chapters 1 through 3 describe the concept of integrated injury management, the basic patholog-

ical response and management of soft tissue and bony injuries, and the role of therapeutic medications in the management of these conditions. Subsequent chapters present important considerations for the immediate management, surgical/medical interventions, and follow-up management (such as short-term bracing or immobilization) for such conditions as well as relevant considerations influencing the patient's care. The medical techniques described in this text are not a "how-to" guide for injury management. Rather, they provide a "how, what, when, and why" approach regarding the medical procedures that are used to return athletes and other patients to activity and describe the implications of these procedures on the treatment and rehabilitation protocol.

This text will help students tie together the content of various courses. Practicing clinicians will find this a useful clinical resource. This text will be a valuable tool for nonorthopaedic team physicians in their management of orthopaedic conditions and their interaction with the sports medicine team.

The team at Jones & Bartlett Learning has dedicated countless hours in seeing this project from conception to completion. Thanks to Shoshanna Goldberg, Executive Acquisitions Editor; Amy L. Bloom, Managing Editor; Agnes Burt, Editorial Assistant; Jody Yeskey, Marketing Manager; Jess Newfell, Production Editor; and Sarah Cebulski, Photo Researcher.

A special note of thanks to the editor of the *First Edition*, Arthur E. Ellison, MD; the editor of the *Second Edition*, Letha "Etty" Griffin, MD; the editor of the *Third Edition*, Robert C. Schenck, MD; and their Editorial Boards. These individuals laid the framework for a remarkable and long-lasting resource for athletic trainers, physical therapists, and physicians who are involved in orthopaedic medicine.

—*Chad Starkey, PhD, AT, FNATA*

CONTRIBUTORS

AAOS Reviewer
Letha Y. Griffin, MD
Peachtree Orthopaedic Clinic
Atlanta, Georgia

Joel W. Beam, EdD, LAT, ATC
University of North Florida
Jacksonville, Florida

Jeff Bechler, MD
University of Orthopaedic Associates
New Brunswick, New Jersey

Fred Beck, MD
University of North Florida
    Student Health Services
Jacksonville, Florida

Anthony Beutler, MD
Uniformed Services University
Bethesda, Maryland

Michelle C. Boling, PhD, LAT
University of North Florida
Jacksonville, Florida

Derrick Brown, ATC, PA-C
Hinsdale Orthopaedic Association
Westmont, Illinois

Sean T. Bryan, MD, FAAFP
Turley Family Health Center
Clearwater, Florida

Douglas J. Casa, PhD, ATC, FACSM, FNATA
University of Connecticut
Storrs, Connecticut

A. Bobby Chhabra, MD
University of Virginia
Charlottesville, Virginia

Benjamin Domb, MD
Hinsdale Orthopaedic Association
Clearwater, Illinois

Jay Hertel, PhD, ATC, FNATA
University of Virginia
Charlottesville, Virginia

Jeff G. Konin, PhD, ATC, PT, FACSM, FNATA
University of South Florida
Tampa, Florida

Frank C. McCue III, MD
Professor Emeritus, University of Virginia
Charlottesville, Virginia

Brendon P. McDermott, PhD, ATC
University of Tennessee at Chattanooga
Chattanooga, Tennessee

Michael Moser, MD
University of Florida, Orthopaedics and
    Rehabilitation
Gainesville, Florida

Anh-Dung Nguyen, PhD, ATC
College of Charleston
Charleston, South Carolina

Jason Reed, DO
Orthopedics of Southeast Ohio
Athens, Ohio

Jake E. Resch, PhD, ATC
University of Texas, Arlington
Arlington, Texas

Erin M. Rosenberg, MS, ATC
Concord, North Carolina

William Rosenberg, MD
The Sports Medicine and Injury Center
Concord, North Carolina

Susan Saliba, PhD, PT, ATC
University of Virginia
Charlottesville, Virginia

Robert J. Schoderbeck, Jr., MD
Orthopaedic Specialists of Charleston
Charleston, South Carolina

Adam Shimer, MD
University of Virginia
Charlottesville, Virginia

Lauren J. Stephenson, MA, AT
Stony Brook University
Stony Brook, New York

Charles Thompson, MS, AT
Princeton University
Princeton, New Jersey

Brady L. Tripp, PhD, ATC
University of Florida
Gainesville, Florida

Contributors to the *Fourth Edition*

Soft-Tissue Injury Management
Christopher D. Ingersoll, PhD, ATC, FACSM
Dilaawar J. Mistry, MD, MS, ATC

Fractures: Diagnosis and Management
Christopher D. Ingersoll, PhD, ATC, FACSM
David M. Kahler, MD

Foot, Ankle, and Leg Injuries
Peggy A. Houglum, PhD, ATC, PT
David A. Porter, MD, PhD

Knee Injuries
Jeff Ryan, PT, ATC
Peter F. DeLuca, MD

Patellofemoral Injuries
Jeff Ryan, PT, ATC
Paul A. Marchetto, MD

Femur, Hip, and Pelvis Injuries
Peggy A. Houglum, PhD, ATC, PT
Glen Johnson, MD

Shoulder Injuries
Ned Bergert, PTA, ATC
Bick Harmon, PT, ATC
Lewis Yocum, MD

Elbow Injuries
Jeff Ryan, PT, ATC
John P. Salvo, MD

Lumbar Spine Injuries
Peggy A. Houglum, PhD, ATC, PT
Brett A. Taylor, MD

Abdominal and Thorax Injuries
Allen E. Mathieu, PAC, MS, ATC
L. Michael Brunt, MD

Cervical Spine Injuries
Katie Walsh, EdD, ATC
K. Stuart Lee, MD, FACS

Head Injuries
Kevin M. Guskiewicz, PhD, ATC
Michael McCrea, PhD, ABPP

Face and Related Structures Pathologies
Christine Heilman, MS, L/ATC, CSCS
Michael Ellerbush, MD

Exertional Heat Illnesses, FNATA
Douglas J. Casa, PhD, ATC, FACSM, FNATA
E. Randy Eichner, MD, FACSM

Reviewers of the *Fourth Edition*

Kristen M. Agena, MS, LAT, ATC, CSCS
Luther College
Decorah, Iowa

Sara D. Brown, MS, ATC
Boston University
Boston, Massachusetts

Derek J. Port, MBA, MS, ATC
Campbellsville University
Campbellsville, Kentucky

Daniel Sedory, MS, ATC, N.H. LAT
University of New Hampshire
Durham, New Hampshire

Adam J. Thompson, PhD, LAT, ATC
Indiana Wesleyan University
Marion, Indiana

Michael Scott Zema, MEd, ATC
Slippery Rock University
Slippery Rock, Pennsylvania

Overview

Integrated Injury Management

Musculoskeletal trauma can be an unfortunate consequence of physical activity. When tissues are traumatized, a series of events are triggered that influence the patient's return to activity. Although the primary tissue destruction has already occurred, the initial and follow-up management affect the healing process.

The proper course of postinjury management depends on obtaining a correct diagnosis. The initial diagnosis—which is often made immediately after the traumatic event—has two purposes: (1) to determine whether the patient requires immediate transportation to a medical facility and (2) to decide which procedures will be required to protect the injured body part while the patient is moved, so a more thorough evaluation can be conducted. Furthermore, in catastrophic instances, emergency medical procedures may need to be performed to preserve the patient's life, limbs, or neurologic function.

A definitive diagnosis is based on careful analysis of the findings of the clinical evaluation, imaging studies, and, when applicable, medical diagnostic tests. Some conditions are readily apparent on simple visual inspection, whereas further diagnostic testing may be needed to identify confounding structural defects, rule out concomitant trauma, and determine the functional integrity of the surrounding tissues. When definitive findings are present, the final diagnosis may be established by excluding other possible conditions, the differential diagnosis.

Discerning a differential diagnosis comprises a systematic method of examining a condition that lacks unique signs or symptoms, has signs and symptoms that closely resemble multiple conditions, or has signs and symptoms that can mask another injury. Due diligence mandates that all other possible maladies be considered and ruled out before the final, definitive diagnosis is reached. Similarly, if an injury does not respond to treatment as anticipated, a complete reexamination should be conducted and the patient referred to an appropriate specialist if applicable.

Between the initial diagnosis of the condition to the full return to activity, several different providers—physicians, athletic trainers, physical therapists, and strength and conditioning specialists—may be involved in the patient's care. The size and composition of the caregiving team will depend on the nature of the injury, geographic barriers to care, and the patient's ability to pay for these services (i.e., healthcare insurance). The efforts of these various providers must be part of a coherent and coordinated plan, with each understanding the patient's pathology, functional limitations, and level of function, as well as the other providers' roles in this process.[1]

Pathomechanics and Functional Limitations After Injury

Traumatized or improperly healed tissues can lead to the alteration of a joint's normal biomechanics (pathomechanics). With time, this pathomechanical change may disrupt the normal function of other joints and muscle groups along the kinetic chain, leading to disability.

Injury to ligaments and joint capsular structures can produce instability during movement as the joint fails to maintain its optimal position, causing weakness and inhibiting normal biomechanics. Prolonged alterations of normal range of motion (ROM) result in compensatory postures, increasing the amount of stress placed on the other joints and muscles. The ensuing biomechanical changes lead to functional shortening of some tissues and elongation of others, creating imbalances in muscle length and strength. Subsequent pathomechanical changes may include muscular compensation or substitution.

Imaging Techniques

The role of diagnostic imaging in the evaluation process has significantly increased during the past decade. Diagnostic imaging was once primarily limited to the inclusion or exclusion of bony defects (including joint malalignment). More recently, advances in radiographic imaging techniques, nuclear medicine, and computer technology have expanded the imaging modalities available to physicians, including magnetic resonance imaging (MRI) and computed tomography (CT) (see **Figure 1.1**). Diagnostic ultrasound is a useful diagnostic tool for identifying tendinous lesions and soft-tissue masses and cysts.

The views obtained for each body area are relatively consistent for each imaging modality (see **Table 1.1**). Limitations do exist and multiple views—or multiple imaging devices—are often required to obtain accurate images of the involved area.

■ Radiographs

Radiographic images are obtained by passing an x-ray beam through the tissues. The x-ray energy is collected on a film cassette or digitally (digital

kinetic chain A series of body parts linked together by joints and muscles through which action/reaction forces are transmitted.

compensation Changes in biomechanical function to overcome muscular weakness or joint dysfunction.

substitution A secondary muscle or muscle group performing the action that would otherwise be performed by a primary muscle.

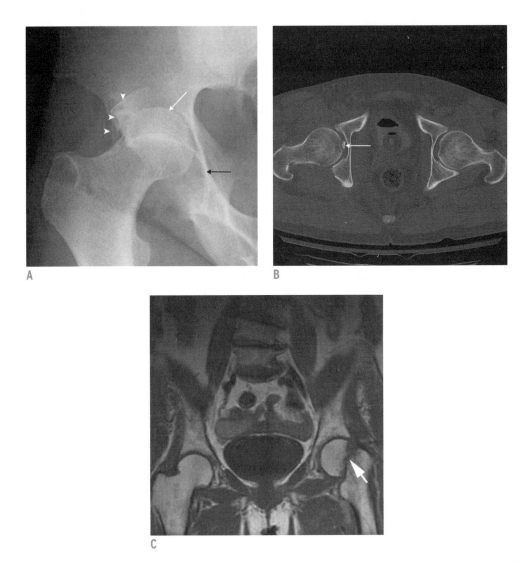

Figure 1.1   Comparison of imaging types. (**A**) Anteroposterior radiograph of a posterior hip dislocation (white arrow). The black arrow indicates the acetabulum; the white arrowheads identify fracture segments. (**B**) An axial CT scan of the hip shows an intra-articular fracture (white arrow) that was not visible on the radiograph in (A). This scan can be "windowed" to better illustrate soft tissue but at the expense of bony images. (**C**) Coronal T1-weighted MRI of a femoral neck fracture.

or computed radiography). On a gray-scale continuum, radiographic images are white in areas of high x-ray uptake (primarily bone), filtering down to black in areas where no x-ray energy is absorbed by the tissues. Although skin, adipose tissues, some degree of soft tissue, and, in certain cases, edema or hemorrhage can be identified on radiographs, their quality and contrast resolution are often insufficient to make a definitive diagnosis. For bony defects, however, radiographs are the most sensitive imaging modality, capable of detecting objects as small as 0.05 to 0.1 millimeter (depending on the equipment used), compared with 0.4 to 1 millimeter on high-resolution CT scans.[2] Another limitation of radiographs is their two-dimensional views. Fluoroscopy is the process of obtaining radiographic images in real time, allowing for visu-

alization of joint kinematics and guidance during surgical procedures.

■ Magnetic Resonance Imaging

In MRI, a strong static magnetic field with intermittent radiofrequency (RF) pulses is delivered to the tissues to form an image of the internal tissues. A powerful magnetic generator affects the hydrogen atoms that are found in all tissues. Similar to what happens in a compass, these atoms align with the magnetic field. When a brief (millisecond) RF pulse is introduced, the atoms are deflected from their axis. When the RF pulse terminates, the atoms wobble as they become realigned with the magnetic field, in the process emitting weak RF signals of their own. Atoms in different types and densities of tissues realign themselves at different rates,

Table 1.1

Routine Imaging Views by Body Area

Upper Extremity

Fingers	PA, lateral, oblique (fingers should be separated)
Hand	PA, oblique, lateral
Wrist	PA, lateral (both with neutral positioning)
Forearm	AP, lateral
Elbow	AP (supinated), lateral (90° flexed); oblique views may be added for trauma patients
Humerus	AP, lateral
Glenohumeral joint	AP in internal and external rotation, true AP of the scapula, axillary; a 30° caudal tilt view is added for suspected impingement; a transscapular view is helpful in assessing glenohumeral dislocation and acromion morphology
Acromioclavicular joint	AP, 10° cephalad AP (Zanca view)

Lower Extremity

Hip	AP internal rotation, frog lateral (or cross-table lateral)
Femur	AP, lateral
Knee	AP, lateral (30° flexion)
Knee: arthritis	Add AP weight-bearing views or PA flexed weight-bearing views, lateral weight-bearing views, and occasionally Merchant axial views
Knee: intercondylar notch	Tunnel view (angulated PA or AP 45° flexed)
Patellofemoral joint	Merchant view
Lower leg	AP, lateral
Ankle	AP, lateral, mortise
Foot	AP, lateral, medial (internal) oblique (weight-bearing AP and lateral for foot alignment abnormality)
Subtalar joint	Lateral view, posterior tangential
Calcaneus	Lateral, AP, axial
Toes	AP, lateral, AP oblique

Axial Skeleton

Cervical spine	AP and lateral views; a lateral flexion-extension view can be added in patients with rheumatoid arthritis and suspected instability; a trauma spine series should include an open mouth odontoid view and a swimmer's view if C7 is not visualized
Thoracic spine	AP, lateral
Lumbar spine	AP, lateral
Sacrum	30° cephalad angulated AP, lateral
Coccyx	10° caudal angulated AP lateral
Sacroiliac joint	30° cephalad angulated AP (Ferguson view)
Pelvis	AP (Judet view and/or inlet/outlet views for pelvic ring fractures)

PA indicates posteroanterior (ie, beam of x-ray originates from the patient's posterior and travels to the anterior); AP, anteroposterior (ie, beam of x-ray originates from the patient's anterior and travels to the posterior).

Source: Reprinted with permission from Johnson TR, Steinbach LS (eds), *Essentials of Musculoskeletal Imaging*, Rosemont, IL: American Academy of Orthopaedic Surgeons: 2004:6.

producing a magnetic resonance signal. These signals are collected by the unit and reconstructed into relatively high-resolution, high-contrast images by a computer and its software.

MRI excels in imaging soft tissue and is sensitive enough to detect stress fractures more acutely than radiographs. This imaging technique is clearly superior in detailing soft tissue such as ligaments, cartilage, tendons, and muscles. In some instances, a contrast medium may be injected into the tissues to improve the quality of the image. The individual RF properties (spin echo) of different tissue types can be filtered to accentuate different tissue types (see **Table 1.2**). Depending on the weighting used—T1, proton density, or T2—the tissue resolution is altered for more or less prominence (see Figure 1.2).

Most MRI scans take 20 to 60 minutes. In addition, a potential complication exists if the patient

Table 1.2

Relative Signal Intensities of Selected Structures on Spin Echo in Musculoskeletal Magnetic Resonance Imaging

	Sequence		
Structure	T1-Weighted	Proton Density	T2-Weighted
Fat*	Bright	Bright	Intermediate
Fluid†	Dark	Intermediate	Bright
Fibrocartilage‡	Dark	Dark	Dark
Ligaments, tendon§	Dark	Dark	Dark
Muscle	Intermediate	Intermediate	Dark
Bone marrow	Bright	Intermediate	Dark
Nerve	Intermediate	Intermediate	Intermediate

*Includes bone marrow.

†Includes edema, most tears, and most cysts.

‡Includes labrum, menisci, triangular fibrocartilage.

§Signal may be increased because of artifacts.

Source: Reprinted with permission from Johnson TR, Steinbach LS (eds), *Essentials of Musculoskeletal Imaging.* Rosemont, IL: American Academy of Orthopaedic Surgeons; 2004:12.

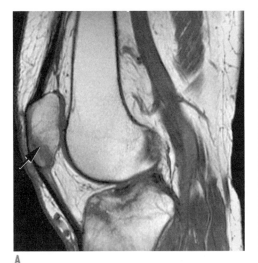
A

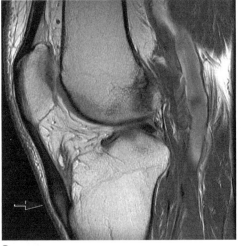
B

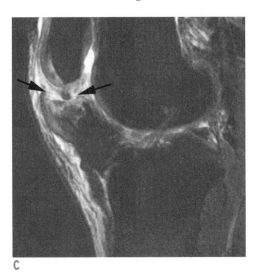
C

Figure 1.2   MRI tissue weighting. (**A**) A sagittal T1-weighted image demonstrating bone marrow edema (arrow) consistent with a stress fracture. (**B**) A sagittal proton-density-weighted image demonstrating thickening of the patellar tendon (arrow) consistent with patellar tendinitis. (**C**) A sagittal T2-weighted, fat-suppressed image demonstrating a tear within the proximal patellar tendon (arrows). The altered signal intensity above the arrows indicates edema.

is claustrophobic and a closed (tubelike) scanner is being used. Metal within the magnetic field is of particular concern. Most implanted metal is MRI compatible, but other metals can be affected by—and violently pulled toward—the magnet. MRI of areas with certain tattoo inks that contain metal can cause burns.[3]

Computed Tomography

CT scans use thin x-ray beams that are passed through the body and read by multiple detectors. Similar to radiographs, the amount of x-ray energy received by the detector is a function of the tissue density through which the beam passes, but the CT scan also detects the amount of energy scattered by the tissue. Selected soft tissues such as joint spaces and vasculature can be imaged by injecting a contrast medium.

The final image is formed by computer analysis and manipulation of the energy collected by the detector. Contrast resolution is superior to that obtained via plain-film radiographs, and the gray-scale continuum can be digitally altered to display only those tissues that fall within a defined density range ("windowing"). Different views, or slices, can be extracted to create an image of the body part in various planes. Some CT scanners can construct three-dimensional images.

CT scans are primarily used to identify cortical bone, bony lesions that are not normally visible on radiographs, and (using a contrast medium) joints. This technology, however, lacks the contrast needed to image most soft tissues.

Diagnostic Ultrasound

Diagnostic ultrasound transmits high-frequency sound waves into the tissues. Diagnostic ultrasound uses a lower frequency than therapeutic ultrasound, however, and it does not heat the tissues. Depending on the density and consistency of the underlying tissues, the sound waves then are reflected back at different speeds and amplitudes. This information is collected by a receiver and transmitted to a computer, where it is reconstructed to form an image. Doppler ultrasound is used to detect motion, particularly in vascular studies.

Dense, highly reflective tissues appear white on the ultrasonic image, whereas less reflective tissues appear darker (see **Figure 1.3**). False-positive readings of tendon lesions may occur if the ultrasonic energy does not strike the tissue at a right angle.[4] Although ultrasonic images allow for better spatial resolution than CT or MRI, the interpretation of these images

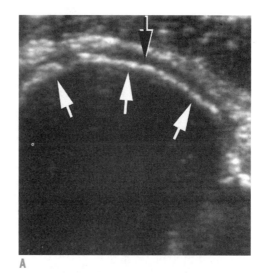

A

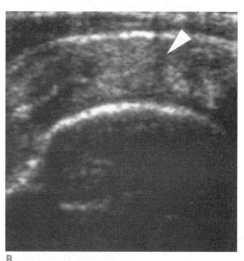

B

Figure 1.3 Ultrasonic images of a glenohumeral rotator cuff tear. This transverse bilateral view demonstrates a massive rotator cuff tear of the right shoulder (black arrow). The supraspinatus tendon is not visible on the upper image (**A**) but is visible on the lower (**B**) (white arrowhead). Also note that the humeral head on the upper image (white arrows) is riding higher than that on the lower image.

depends more on the skill and experience of the individual reading them.

Therapeutic Medications

Both prescription and nonprescription medications are useful during the short- and long-term care of patients with musculoskeletal injury. These medications alter the inflammatory response, control pain, prevent infection, and reduce muscle spasm. Anti-inflammatory agents, analgesics, anesthetics, antibiotics, and antiseptics are among the medications most commonly used in orthopaedics and sports medicine. Considering the frequency with which these agents

analgesic Pain-relieving without the loss of consciousness.
anesthetic Loss of sensation; may be local or general (body-wide).
antibiotic Used to kill bacteria that cause infection.
antiseptic Inhibits the growth of disease-producing microorganisms.

are used and the potential harm that can occur if they are used inappropriately, an understanding of their mechanisms of action, common adverse effects, and potential drug interactions is essential.

Medications presented in this text include both prescription and over-the-counter (OTC) products. Prescription medications also are called "legend drugs" because they carry the following federal warning (or legend) on the package:

> CAUTION: Federal law prohibits dispensing without a prescription.

A comprehensive resource for commonly used medications should be available to every healthcare provider. Among the more commonly used drug references are *The Physicians' Desk Reference* (PDR), *American Hospital Formulary Service Drug Information,* and *Drug Facts and Comparisons.* These references should be consulted whenever questions arise about drug interactions, contraindications for use, adverse effects, and instructions for administration. In addition, all sports medicine personnel should have on hand the most current lists of banned medications maintained by the various sport-regulating bodies, such as the National Collegiate Athletic Association, the U.S. Olympic Committee, and the International Olympic Committee. These lists can be accessed via the Internet and should be reviewed frequently so updates are not missed.

Medication administration is the direct application of a single dose of a drug, whereas dispensing a drug is the "preparing, packaging, and labeling of a drug or device" for patient use.[5] Most states have strict regulations for drug administration and dispensing. Box 2.1 (in Chapter 2) describes commonly used anti-inflammatory and analgesic medications while Box 2.2 describes commonly used antibiotic medications.

■ Routes of Drug Administration

The primary routes for delivering drugs to the body include enteral, parenteral, and topical administration (see **Table 1.3**). Drug delivery through the skin can be enhanced by application of a low-level electric current (iontophoresis) or ultrasound (phonophoresis). Although these clinical techniques are widely used, their efficacy has not been substantiated.

Iontophoresis uses a low-amperage direct current to drive ions from drug solution into tissue. This technique is used to treat musculoskeletal inflammatory disorders with nonsteroidal anti-inflammatory drugs (NSAIDs), corticosteroids, and other medications. Iontophoresis treatment regimens (measured

Table 1.3	
Methods of Drug Delivery into the Body	
Route	**Method**
Enteral	Oral.
	Sublingual (under the tongue).
	Rectal.
Parenteral	*Subcutaneous* injection into the subcutaneous tissue under the skin that overlies muscle. The medication is absorbed slowly via this delivery method, thereby delaying the onset of drug action.
	Intramuscular injection directly into muscle tissue.
	Intravenous injection in the form of an intravenous bolus or a slower intravenous infusion. Medications delivered via this route have a rapid onset of action.
Topical	Applied to the skin and absorbed into the underlying tissues. This method reduces the risk for systemic side effects and focuses the agent's effects at the site of inflammation.

in milliampere-seconds of current) vary depending on the medication used and the condition being treated (see **Figure 1.4**).[6]

Phonophoresis is the application of therapeutic ultrasound to increase drug delivery through the skin.[7] In this technique, ultrasonic energy is transferred through a medium capable of transmission. The ultrasonic waves have two primary physical consequences within the skin—heating and cavitation. The overall result is increased skin permeability, which enhances drug diffusion through the skin. Although a variety of medicinal agents have been administered via phonophoresis, hydrocortisone and dexamethasone are the agents most frequently used for treating musculoskeletal injuries.

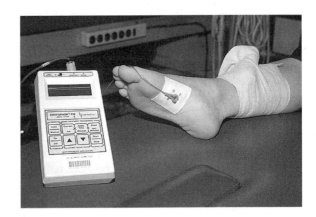

Figure 1.4 The iontophoresis technique uses a low-amperage direct current to introduce NSAIDs or corticosteroids into the subcutaneous tissues.

Postinjury Management

Postinjury management encompasses the nonsurgical, preoperative, and prerehabilitation injury care that occurs after the immediate management of the injury and after acquiring a working diagnosis of the injury. Examples of postinjury management include suturing and the closed reduction of fractures and dislocations (see Chapters 2 and 3).

Most postinjury management involves the continued use of ice, compression, and elevation. If indicated, an immobilization device is obtained and applied, splinting the extremity in a specific position and/or restricting a certain ROM.

Crutches

Crutches and, on occasion, canes are used to reduce or eliminate lower extremity weight-bearing forces. The two primary forms of crutches used in orthopaedic medicine are full-length and forearm crutches. Forearm crutches run only to the forearm, but require greater upper extremity strength and better balance than full-length crutches.

Full-length crutches are fitted by placing the tips 4 to 6 inches anterior and lateral to the foot and adjusting the length to allow 2 to 3 inches of clearance between the axilla and the top of each crutch. The hand grips are adjusted so that the elbows are flexed to approximately 30°. The body weight should be borne on the hands rather than the axillae. Improper crutch mechanics that place the body weight on the axillae can result in axillary nerve neuropathy.

Crutches can be used for either non-weight-bearing (NWB) mobility or partial-weight-bearing (PWB) mobility. When the patient is instructed to remain NWB, the crutch and injured extremity move in unison during normal ambulation. When ascending stairs, the patient leads with the good leg; when descending stairs, the involved leg leads (remembered by "up with the good, down with the bad"). When the patient engages in PWB behavior, the involved extremity and crutches move together, but the patient bears as much weight as tolerable on the injured leg. The amount of pressure used must still allow for a proper heel–toe walking gait. If the gait is improper, the patient should be instructed to decrease the amount of pressure on the involved leg.

A cane should be held in the hand opposite the side of the injury, and the length should be adjusted so the elbow is flexed to 20° to 30° when the tip is placed 6 inches in front and 6 inches to the side of the foot. When the patient is walking, the cane moves forward with the involved extremity. If the patient leans or places too much weight on the cane, then two crutches should be used.

Prehabilitation

Prehabilitation is the use of rehabilitation exercises prior to surgery. The goal of prehabilitation is to maximize the strength of the surrounding muscles and increase joint ROM within tolerable limits before the patient undergoes the physical stress of surgery. Because the patient goes into the surgery with the involved extremity strong and with increased ROM, the postsurgical rehabilitation starts at an advanced point (relative to the patient with no prior conditioning) and prevents postoperative complications. Prehabilitation that addresses ROM normalization in patients with acute anterior cruciate ligament injuries, for example, significantly decreases the incidence of arthrofibrosis after reconstruction.

Bracing

A variety of braces are commercially available and can be found for virtually every joint of the body. Braces are classified into three categories: rehabilitative, functional, and prophylactic.[8] Rehabilitative braces are designed to provide protection and control motion during the healing and rehabilitative phases after injury or surgery. Functional braces allow motion and support the joint as the patient is returning to activity. These braces, which provide protection to the injury without hindering motion, include derotation braces, patellar stabilization braces, and ankle braces. Prophylactic braces are intended to provide protection against potentially injurious forces. Other forms of support include specific pads and orthotic devices that can help protect injured structures or shield them from injury.

Splinting and Casting

Made of plaster, moldable plastics, or fiberglass, splints cover only two or three sides of the extremity, are used for relatively short-term immobilization, and can be easily removed for treatment or evaluation. Braces and immobilizers also can be used to splint a body part. Casts completely surround the joint and are worn for extended periods.

The following general considerations are important in the application of splints and casts:[9]

1. Clothing should be removed from the area of any suspected fracture or dislocation to inspect the extremity for open wounds, deformity, swelling, and ecchymosis.
2. Any jewelry items are removed immediately if possible, including finger and toe rings.
3. The pulse, capillary refill, and neurologic status distal to the site of injury are noted and recorded. If pulses are compromised, reduction should be attempted and the patient immediately transported to an emergency care facility.
4. All wounds should be covered with a dry sterile dressing before a splint is applied. The physician should be informed of all open wounds in case further evaluation is necessary.
5. The splint should immobilize the joints above and below the suspected fracture.
6. With injuries in and around the joint, the splint should immobilize the bones above and below the injured joint.
7. All rigid splints should be padded to prevent local pressure.
8. Clinicians should use their hands to minimize limb movement and support the injury site until the splint has been placed and the limb is completely immobilized.
9. A severely deformed limb should be aligned with constant, gentle manual traction so that it can be placed in a splint.
10. Check the pulses and neurologic status after the alignment.
11. If resistance to limb alignment is encountered when applying traction, the limb should be splinted in the position of deformity.
12. When in doubt, splint the limb, monitor neurovascular status, and arrange for transportation to an emergency care facility.

Surgical Intervention

Surgical intervention is indicated when an injury will leave lasting consequences of functional deficits and restoration of the anatomy will improve the prognosis and functional outcome. Although surgery is a restorative process, the scalpel's contact with the tissues creates additional trauma. The fact that this trauma is created in a controlled environment does not negate the ensuing inflammatory response and the short- and long-term functional limitations associated with surgery. The choice of timing of the surgical intervention, the surgical procedure used, the severity of the condition, and the surgeon's skill all influence the postoperative care, rehabilitation protocol, and long-term outcomes, as do the patient's ability and willingness to comply with the postoperative program.

Most orthopaedic surgical procedures have very specific influences on activity progression and functional limitations that must be adhered to when designing the rehabilitation program. These limitations are highly individualized and can vary even with similar procedures; they can be surgeon-specific, procedure-specific, and injury-specific. If questions exist regarding the indications and contraindications of rehabilitation techniques, clarification should be obtained from the physician to facilitate complete commitment to the postoperative protocol.

Postoperative Management

The immediate postoperative care involves protection of the repair and care of the surgical wound. Protecting the repair (including reconstructions and fixations) includes limiting the stress on the skin closure by immobilization with bracing, casting, splinting, or wrapping. After lower extremity surgery, NWB or PWB crutch ambulation is often necessary to protect the surgical site.

Basic postoperative wound care is directed at preventing contamination of the incision and optimizing the tissues' healing environment by limiting swelling and inflammation. Basic ice, compression, and elevation principles are employed. Clean wound care techniques and dressing changes help prevent contamination. The incision should be kept dry to avoid skin maceration and contamination. Sutures or staples are removed only after adequate healing has been demonstrated, usually a minimum of 7 to 14 days after surgery.

As healing progresses and it becomes safe to start mobilization, controlled passive and active ROM exercises are started. Once motion has been normalized, a comprehensive progressive resistance exercise program is begun. This program is accompanied in the later phases of postoperative care by cardiovascular conditioning activities. Functional evaluations determine progression to the next phase of rehabilitation and return to play.

Table 1.4

General Rehabilitation Goals

Control inflammation, swelling, and pain.

Restore range of motion.

Restore strength.

Restore neuromuscular function.

Restore power and endurance.

Regain full function.

Return to pain-free activity.

Injury-Specific Treatment and Rehabilitation Concerns

The principles of rehabilitation are founded on an understanding of anatomy, pathophysiology, biomechanics, and tissue healing. Better incorporation of biomechanics and improvements and changes in postinjury and surgical techniques have allowed for accelerated rehabilitation programs. These changes have been made possible through sound scientific studies and continual reevaluation of the outcomes.

General rehabilitation goals appear in **Table 1.4**. Most injuries have specific concerns that must be addressed during the rehabilitation program. Similarly, surgical procedures place short- and long-term limitations on the rehabilitation techniques that can be employed with specific patients.

Although rehabilitation goals are presented sequentially in Table 1.4, in practice there is considerable overlap of goals and the specific rehabilitation protocols used to address the problems within each area (see **Figure 1.5**). The physiologic ability of the patient to properly and completely perform any given exercise should be the criterion applied to progress through that activity. The exercises should be performed without compensation or the risk of injuring the healing tissues. Use of criterion-based progression allows patients to advance, if activity can be tolerated, yet protects patients who are not physically ready to move forward in the rehabilitation program.

If permitted by the physician during the convalescence period, the patient should exercise the uninvolved extremities. A stationary bicycle, stair stepper, or elliptical trainer can be used if the upper extremity is involved (and for certain lower extremity injuries). If the patient is unable to bicycle or bear weight, an upper body ergometer can be used to maintain cardiovascular endurance.

Amount of Time Lost

The estimated amount of time lost is an average of the time loss for patients with similar conditions. Although the minimum amount of time required to recover from an injury is more easily predicted, the maximum recovery time is affected by numerous other variables, such as the severity of the injury, the patient's age, the vascular integrity in the healing tissues, nutrition, medication, and steroid use. Older patients with reduced cardiac function require a longer time for recovery. Poor nutrition or anabolic steroid use also may delay healing.

Another factor influencing the recovery time is patient compliance. With regard to the rehabilitation program, home-care instructions and activities to avoid should be carefully identified. Noncompliant patients can increase the amount of time needed to return to activity if they do not follow through with home rehabilitation instructions, thereby delaying the anticipated progression. Failure to adhere to activity limitations, such as avoiding weight bearing, can further injure the tissues and delay the healing process.

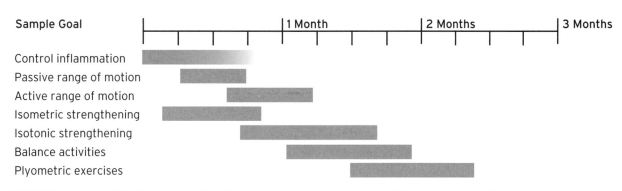

Figure 1.5 A sample rehabilitation sequence. The individual components (goals) of the rehabilitation progression often overlap.

Return-to-Play Criteria

Before returning to sports participation or other strenuous activity, the patient should be pain free; demonstrate bilaterally equal strength, ROM, and proprioception; and be able to perform sport-specific or work-specific tasks. Muscle strength should be at least 85% to 90% of that in the uninvolved extremity.

The athlete should be able to perform all sport activities such that an observer would be unable to identify the extremity that had been injured, and the athlete should display confidence in himself or herself and the injured segment. Athletes should also be psychologically prepared to return to activity, demonstrating confidence in their ability to perform appropriately. Once all of these factors are satisfied, return to activity may be allowed. Return to play should start in controlled situations with the athlete's own team and in friendly confines in a practice and scrimmage situation.

References

1. Kraemer W, Denegar C, Flanagan S. Recovery from injury in sport: considerations in the transition from medical care to performance care. *Sports Health.* 2009;1:392–395.

2. Curry TS III, Dowdey JE, Murry RC Jr. *Christensen's Physics of Diagnostic Radiology,* ed 4. Malvern, PA: Lea & Febiger; 1990.

3. Wagle WA, Smith M. Tattoo-induced skin burn during MR imaging. *Am J Roentgenol.* 2000;174:1795.

4. Chang A, Miller TT. Imaging of tendons. *Sports Health.* 2009;1:293–300.

5. Klossner D (ed). Prescription medication, in *2010–11 NCAA Sports Medicine Handbook.* Indianapolis, IN: National Collegiate Athletic Association; 2010:18. Available at: http://www.ncaapublications.com/productdownloads /MD11.pdf. Accessed December 25, 2010.

6. Kanikkannan N. Iontophoresis-based transdermal delivery systems. *Biodrugs.* 2002;16:339–347.

7. Machet L, Boucaud A. Phonophoresis: efficiency, mechanisms and skin tolerance. *Intl J Pharm.* 2002;243:1–15.

8. France EP, Paulos LE. Knee bracing. *J Am Acad Orthop Surg.* 1994;2:281–287.

9. Lucas GL (ed). General orthopaedics: splinting principles, in Greene WB (ed), *Essentials of Musculoskeletal Care,* ed 2. Rosemont, IL: American Academy of Orthopaedic Surgeons; 2001:81–87.

Soft-Tissue Injury Management

Joel W. Beam, EdD, LAT, ATC
Fred Beck, MD

Soft tissue is classified into four types—epithelial, muscle, connective, and nervous—that are differentiated by histology and function. This chapter addresses epithelial, muscle, and connective tissues, which are collectively referred to as "soft tissue." Topics include the qualities of tissue, inflammation, and injuries to skin, muscle, ligaments, fascia, and synovial tissue.

Qualities of Soft Tissue

Connective tissues are composed of cells and extracellular matrix, but the proportions of each vary in different types of tissues. In tendon, ligament, and cartilage, cells account for 20% of the total tissue volume. The response of these tissues to injury relies on the migration of reparative cells to the injured area. By contrast, muscle contains pluripotential cells that initiate the repair process. The extracellular matrix, which is 70% water and 30% solid, determines the form and function of connective tissue and may modulate protein synthesis by cells in response to loading or use. The two most abundant solid components of the extracellular matrix are collagen and proteoglycans.

Collagen consists of stiff, helical, insoluble protein macromolecules that provide scaffolding and tensile strength in fibrous tissues. Collagen is differentiated into various types depending on its histologic composition. Type I collagen—the most common type—is a component of tendon, ligament, and muscle.

Proteoglycans function to retain water within the tissues, thereby making the matrix a gel-like substance rather than an amorphous solution. Proteoglycans enhance the strength of tissues by serving as a kind of "cement" between collagen fibers. Their presence helps stabilize the collagenous skeleton and improves the strength of the tissue.

Response to Loading

The soft tissues that make up tendons, ligaments, and joint capsules exhibit specific types of behavior under loading. When a load is applied to a ligament, microtrauma occurs before the yield point is reached. When the yield point is reached, the ligament begins to plastically deform and becomes abnormally displaced (see Figure 2.1). If the load continues to be applied, plastic deformation will continue until the failure point is reached. Surrounding structures, such as the joint capsule and other ligaments, may also be damaged.

Soft tissues exhibit viscoelastic behavior, including stress relaxation, creep, and hysteresis. Stress relaxation is the decrease in force required to maintain the tissue over time when it is subject to constant deformation. Creep is characterized by continued deformation in response to a maintained load (see Figure 2.2). The hysteresis response is the amount of relaxation, or variation in the load–deformation relationship, that occurs within a single cycle of loading and unloading. The shape of the load–deformation curve for viscoelastic soft tissues depends on the previous loading and unloading history and the tissue's histology.

When tendons and ligaments are not being stretched, the collagen fibers display crimp—that is, a regular undulation or wave-type pattern of cells and matrix. Crimp provides a buffer or shock absorber that protects the tissue from damage during elongation. Under loading, the tendon or ligament straightens out and the crimp disappears, similar to what happens when a rubber band is extended. When a rubber band is "relaxed," curves can be seen throughout its length. When the band is stretched, the curves (crimps) disappear. When the tension is released from the band, the crimps reappear.

Inflammation

A process common to all trauma, inflammation is a localized response initiated by injury to or destruction of vascularized tissues that are exposed to excessive mechanical load or antagonistic agents (see Table 2.1). This time-dependent, evolving process is characterized by complex but orderly vascular, chemical, and cellular events that ultimately lead to tissue repair, regeneration, or scar formation. The inflammatory response may progress to resolution of the injury and repair of the damaged tissue, or it may persist as chronic inflammation.

When significant tissue damage has occurred, inflammation is a necessary element of wound repair. The inflammatory process is initiated by tissue cell death, or necrosis, which results from damage and hypoxia at the site of injury. This nonspecific response to physical trauma resembles the body's response to infection and chemical or thermal injury. Inflammation is the body's attempt to limit the extent of injury, remove devitalized tissue from the wound, and initiate tissue repair. Inflammation protects healthy tissue through three primary functions: (1) It provides the inflamed area with an exudate that contains proteins and immune cells

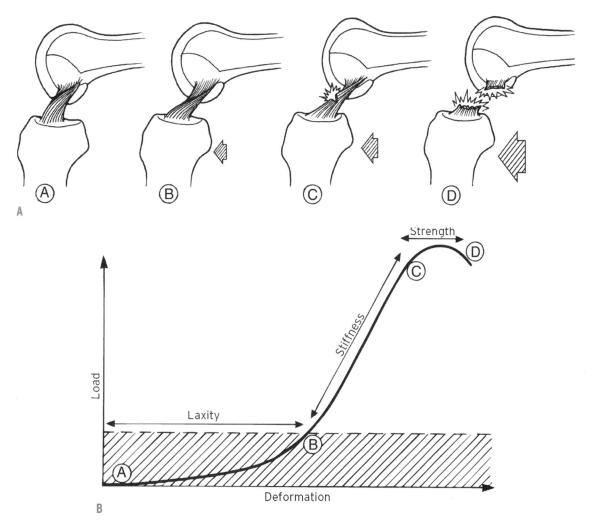

Figure 2.1 Schematic and graphic descriptions of laxity, stiffness, and strength. (**A**) Mechanisms of joint failure. A = flexion (some fiber recruitment), B = Lachman end point (100% fiber recruitment), C = sprain (microfailure), D = rupture (catastrophic failure). (**B**) The graph depicts the load deformation behaviors of a ligament with mechanisms defined. The hatched area represents the range of loads experienced during normal daily activities. *Source:* Reproduced with permission from Frank CB. Ligament healing: current knowledge and clinical applications. *J Am Acad Orthop Surg.* 1996;4:74-83.

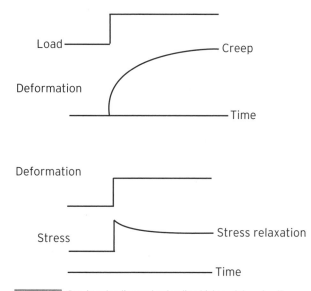

Figure 2.2 Previous loading and unloading history determine the shape of the load–deformation curve for viscoelastic soft tissues.

(neutrophils, macrophages) to boost local defense mechanisms and destroy infective agents (viruses, bacteria, fungi); (2) it purges the body of necrotic debris; and (3) it repairs, regenerates, revitalizes, and strengthens affected tissue.

Pathophysiology

The inflammatory response is not dose related. In fact, severe local inflammation can result from relatively minor trauma. The sudden swelling of a bursa or tendon is a good example of a disproportionate inflammatory reaction. The inability to precisely regulate the inflammatory process may further damage local tissues. Anti-inflammatory medications are administered to modulate the severity and duration of the inflammatory response (see **Box 2.1**).

Table 2.1

Inflammatory Tissue Responses

Source	Effect	Examples
Physical and environmental agents	Tissue is directly injured as the result of physical contact	Sunburn via exposure to ultraviolet radiation
		Frostbite via excessive tissue cooling
		Burns
		Extended physical activities at high altitude
Inadequate tissue oxygenation	Inadequate cellular adenosine triphosphate (ATP) causing decreased protein synthesis and/or disordered membrane transport	Ischemia secondary to swelling
		Arterial compromise
Microbes	Microbes cause an inflammatory response by releasing toxins (bacteria), intracellular reproduction (virus), or local multiplication (fungus)	Bacterial, viral, or fungal infection
Hypersensitivity	Erroneous and disproportionate immune responsiveness can induce inflammation via various cellular or chemical mediators	Foreign substances (antigens)
		Microbes and allergens (dust, pollen, cat dander)
		Human tissue and cellular elements (autoimmune)
Chemical damage	Inflammation as the result of gross tissue damage	Acids and liquid nitrogen (used commonly to freeze warts)
		Contact dermatitis (e.g., poison ivy)

Box 2.1

Anti-Inflammatory and Analgesic Medications

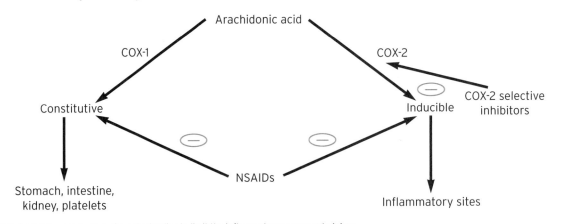

NSAIDs inhibit the production of prostaglandins to limit the inflammatory response to injury.

Several medication options exist for management of inflammation and pain, including acetaminophen (inflammation only), nonsteroidal anti-inflammatory drugs (NSAIDs), steroidal anti-inflammatory drugs, and the opioid analgesics. Acetaminophen is used for its analgesic effects in mild pain situations; this medication also has antipyretic properties. The NSAIDs include both salicylates, such as acetylsalicylic acid (aspirin), and nonsalicylates, such as ibuprofen, that exhibit anti-inflammatory and analgesic properties. NSAIDs are routinely used for relieving mild to moderate pain associated with acute or chronic inflammatory conditions.

NSAIDs act by inhibiting two cyclooxygenase enzymes, COX-1 and COX-2. The anti-inflammatory and analgesic effects of NSAIDs are mediated through the COX-2 isoenzyme, which, when inhibited, results in a blockade of prostaglandin production.[1-3] The prostaglandins sensitize nerves to painful stimuli and are produced from arachidonic acid, which is released when an injury occurs.

Both COX-1 and COX-2 inhibitors interfere with the process by which arachidonic acid is converted to prostaglandin. COX-1 is found in most tissues and is responsible for helping to maintain homeostatic functions such as gastric, renal, and platelet function. In the care of musculoskeletal injuries, COX-1 inhibitors affect platelet aggregation, thereby inhibiting blood clotting and prolonging bleeding. COX-2 inhibitors act directly on the inflammatory sites and do not have the unwanted effects on platelets or other homeostatic functions that are influenced by COX-1 inhibitors.

Inflammation is an essential element of the injury response process. Some physicians will delay prescribing anti-inflammatory medications for 5 to 7 days following the initial injury to allow the body to initiate the acute inflammatory process.

Inflammatory Cells

Leukocytes, also known as white blood cells, are the primary buttress of the immune system that protects the body after a disruption in homeostasis. Five types of white blood cells exist.

Neutrophils

After tissue injury, neutrophils—the pivotal cells of the acute inflammatory response—are released from the bone marrow in response to various chemical mediators present at the site of tissue injury. Subsequently, neutrophils traverse the intravascular space and migrate through blood vessel walls (emigration) to arrive at the site of inflammation in the extravascular tissue within 12 hours of release from the bone marrow. Their main function is to ingest (phagocytose) and destroy microbes by means of various intracellular mechanisms.

Monocytes

The largest of the leukocytes, monocytes mature to macrophages after their release from bone marrow into the bloodstream. Subsequently, macrophages emigrate into tissue spaces, where they may reside for several weeks or even years. At the site of inflammation, macrophages phagocytose particulate matter and process and present immune information from foreign proteins (antigens) to B and T lymphocytes, a crucial step in the future recognition of offending agents.

Lymphocytes

Lymphocytes are classified into B lymphocytes and T lymphocytes. B lymphocytes have immunoglobulins on their surfaces. After antigenic stimulation, these white blood cells are transformed into plasma cells that secrete antibodies. Antibody production is a vital immune mechanism that allows the human body to counteract future antigenic stimuli. Unlike B lymphocytes, T lymphocytes participate in the cell-mediated immune response, which occurs independent of the production of circulating antibodies.

Eosinophils

Similar to the action of neutrophils and macrophages, eosinophils emigrate into extravascular tissues, where they can survive for several weeks and phagocytose particulate matter. They also exert toxic effects on microbes.

Basophils

Basophils are analogous to neutrophils and eosinophils. These motile cells emigrate into extravascular tissues. After stimulation by immunoglobulins, they phagocytose microbes and particulate matter.

▨ The Phases of Inflammation

Inflammation proceeds through three well-defined phases—acute inflammatory response, proliferation, and remodeling. Inflammation has both beneficial and harmful effects on the body. The beneficial effects include stimulating the immune system, producing antibodies, diminishing the strength of toxins, and providing nutrition to the tissues. Harmful effects include destroying otherwise viable tissues and impairing tissue function. The magnitude of the inflammatory response is marked by the cardinal (clinical) signs and symptoms of inflammation (see **Table 2.2**).

Acute Inflammatory Phase

During the acute inflammatory phase, as a result of sequential processes, leukocytes arrive at the site of injury and destroy abnormal agents, permitting healing to progress. The inflammatory phase comprises a chronology of events beginning with blood stasis and ending with the onset of the proliferation phase. It may be active for a matter of hours or for a month or more depending on the severity and magnitude of the injury and the tissues involved.

stasis Slowing or blockage of blood flow.

Blood Stasis

Chronologic alterations in the microcirculation adjacent to the injured area after injury are readily apparent and play a pivotal role in tissue healing. During the first 15 minutes after injury, arterioles contract—an action that has little relevance to inflammation. When the arterioles subsequently dilate, blood flow to the injured area first increases (hyperemia) and then slows dramatically (stasis).[4] This process eventually allows leukocytes to migrate to injured tissues and promote healing.

Increased Vascular Permeability

The walls of the smallest blood vessels are lined by a sheet of a single layer of cells (endothelium).

Table 2.2

The Cardinal (Clinical) Signs and Symptoms of Inflammation

Sign/Symptom	Cause
Redness (rubor)	Produced by dilation of small blood vessels
Heat (calor)	Secondary to increased blood supply (hyperemia)
Swelling (tumor)	Caused by increased fluid in the tissue space (edema)
Pain (dolor)	From stimulation of free nerve endings produced by tissue distortion and local chemical mediators of inflammation
Loss of function	Result of reflex inhibition of the inflamed area

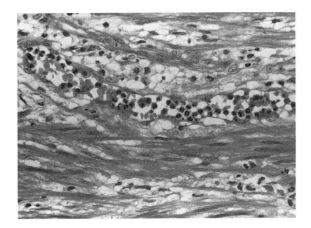

Figure 2.3 Electron micrograph showing margination of leukocytes.

Normally the endothelium is intact and acts as a highly selective microfilter that prevents the escape of blood cells and excess fluid into the surrounding tissues. After injury, however, the endothelium is damaged by toxins and physical agents, and the endothelial cells contract. As a result, the endothelium becomes porous, leading to increased vascular permeability that allows passage of protein-rich fluid (exudate) and blood cells.

Margination

As a consequence of blood stasis and increased vascular permeability, leukocytes that are generally present in the central portion of blood flow begin to flow adjacent to the vascular endothelium. Subsequently, influenced by inflammatory mediators released by tissues at the site of injury,[5-7] leuko-

cytes aggregate and adhere to the endothelium, a process called margination (see **Figure 2.3**).

Emigration

After margination, neutrophils, eosinophils, and macrophages initially introduce extensions of cytoplasm (pseudopodia) into the breaches between constricted endothelial cells of small veins (venules) and, in some instances, arterioles. Using active amoeboid movement, they move through the walls of blood vessels into the tissues surrounding blood vessels (extravascular space) in a process termed emigration. These temporary defects induced in the vessel walls are self-limiting, and endothelial cells are not damaged during this process.

Chemotaxis

After arriving in the extravascular space, leukocytes are directed to the site of injury by chemical mediators in a process called chemotaxis (*chemo*: "chemical;" *taxis*: "movement") (see **Figure 2.4**). The focused movement of leukocytes follows a concentration gradient of chemical inflammatory mediators (chemotactic factors). These factors bind to receptors on the surface of leukocytes, increase the concentration of calcium in the cytoplasm, and, by a complex mechanism, induce the formation of pseudopodia that are critical to amoeboid movement toward the site of injury.

Chemotactic factors that specifically attract neutrophils include components of bacteria, histamine, lymphokines, prostaglandins, leukotrienes, serotonin, and lysosomal compounds. Other phys-

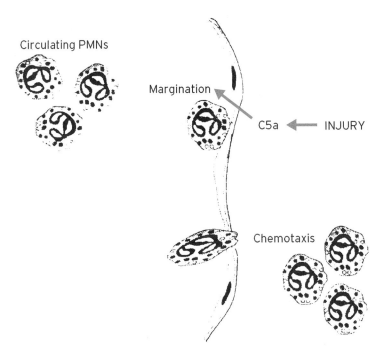

Figure 2.4 A schematic of inflammation. In chemotaxis, leukocytes migrate unidirectionally toward concentrations of mediators at the injury site. *Abbreviation:* PMN, polymorphonuclear neutrophils.

iologic mechanisms present in the plasma that serve as chemotactic factors include the complement,[8] kinin, coagulation, and fibrinolytic systems.[4]

Adhesion and Phagocytosis

After arriving at the site of injury, leukocytes first attach themselves to microbes and other tissue debris (adhesion) using receptors on their surface, a process that makes the microbes more suitable for ingestion (see **Figure 2.5**). Adhesion is accomplished by the formation of pseudopodia that engulf microbes and debris. The pseudopodia subsequently fuse, thereby entrapping microbes and debris within the cytoplasm of leukocytes.

Intracellular Killing of Microorganisms

The entrapped microbes and debris are exposed to several toxic chemicals and enzymes within the leukocyte cytoplasm, which eventually results in microbial death and digestion of debris. The mechanisms responsible for this process include production of antimicrobial substances by neutrophils that combine hydrogen peroxide with myeloperoxidase, and release of potent enzymes stored in small sacs (lysosomes) in the cytoplasm of leukocytes. Release of lysosomal products then damages the injured tissue further. The same process also activates chemotactic factors such as the coagulation system, resulting in enhanced vascular permeability, margination, and emigration of leukocytes. Thus the intracellular killing of organisms, via a feedback mechanism, serves to further the process of acute inflammation.

Proliferation Phase

The proliferation phase (fibroblastic phase) lasts 3 to 4 weeks and represents a continuum of several distinct, yet overlapping processes. Within 5 to 7 days of injury, the number of fibroblasts increases substantially (fibroplasia). Fibroblasts initially synthesize the protein tropocollagen. Three strands of tropocollagen linked together by chemical bonds form procollagen, which is secreted into the extracellular space between fibroblasts to form collagen. Fibroblasts also secrete heparin sulfate, hyaluronic acid, chondroitin sulfate, keratin sulfate, and proteoglycans, which collectively contribute to matrix deposition—a critical step in increasing the tensile strength of the healing tissue. Steered by growth factors, endothelial cells finally migrate, divide, and mature, leading to the formation of new blood vessels (angiogenesis) (see **Figure 2.6**). This process promotes the delivery of vital nutrients and oxygen to the healing tissues.

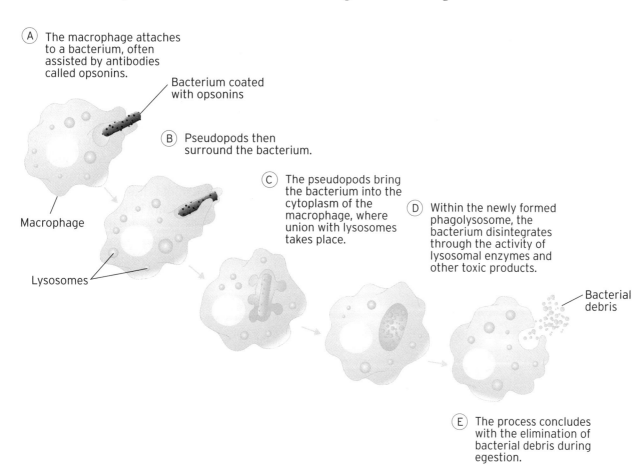

A The macrophage attaches to a bacterium, often assisted by antibodies called opsonins.

Bacterium coated with opsonins

B Pseudopods then surround the bacterium.

C The pseudopods bring the bacterium into the cytoplasm of the macrophage, where union with lysosomes takes place.

D Within the newly formed phagolysosome, the bacterium disintegrates through the activity of lysosomal enzymes and other toxic products.

Macrophage

Lysosomes

Bacterial debris

E The process concludes with the elimination of bacterial debris during egestion.

Figure 2.5 Phagocytosis.

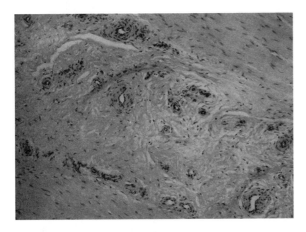

Figure 2.6 Proliferation of fibroblasts and new capillaries often are found in areas of tendon degeneration.

Remodeling Phase

After the third week, inflamed tissue undergoes steady modifications that can persist for several years after the initial injury. Collagen is broken down (lysis) and subsequently deposited (synthesis) in a cyclic fashion without any change in the net magnitude of collagen. Concurrently, myofibroblast proliferation produces a contraction of healing tissue and is supported by collagen alignment. Maximal tensile strength of the wound is achieved by week 12 after the initial injury.

Skin Injuries

The skin is more than just a covering for the body: It provides structure, form, and protection, and also helps regulate temperature. The skin is composed of various layers, each serving a well-defined purpose (see **Table 2.3**). Any of the skin components can be injured and produce a local inflammatory response. The most commonly encountered traumatic injuries to the skin are abrasions, avulsions, blisters, incisions/lacerations, punctures, and contusions.

Table 2.3

Skin Layers and Function

Layer	Function
Stratum corneum	Barrier to noxious substances
Epidermis	Protects against ultraviolet damage
	Provides cutaneous immunity
Dermis	Provides the skin with elasticity and strength
Subcutaneous adipose tissue	Insulates and protects the body

> **Practice Tip**
>
> Sterile 0.9% saline and potable tap water are the preferred cleansing solutions for acute wounds. There are no differences in infection rates and damage to tissues with their use as cleansing solutions among various acute wounds.[15,16] While questions remain, most sources agree that povidone-iodine, acetic acid, hydrogen peroxide, and sodium hypochlorite are cytotoxic to human fibroblasts and macrophages and should not be used for cleansing of the wound bed, although they can be used on periwound tissues.[12,17,18]

■ Abrasions

Abrasions result from shearing forces, typically in one direction, along a rough surface. Superficial abrasions involve injury to the superficial epidermis, partial-thickness injury to the epidermis or superficial dermis (or both), and full-thickness injury down to and possibly extending into the subcutaneous adipose tissue.

Pathophysiology

The wound bed and periwound tissues undergo normal inflammatory processes. Contamination with microorganisms leading to critical colonization and possible infection can delay and prevent healing.[9]

Symptoms

Abrasions produce capillary bleeding and can contain debris in the wound bed such as dirt, grass, or sand. Mild erythema of the periwound tissues is common.

Immediate Management

Abrasions should be thoroughly cleansed and debrided with saline or tap water irrigation to remove all debris and nonviable tissue (see **CT** 2.1). Periwound tissues can be cleansed with irrigation or scrubbing/swabbing using sterile gauze. Antiseptics used on the periwound tissues should not make contact with the wound bed. Apply a film, foam, hydrogel, or hydrocolloid dressing based on the wound depth (see **CT** 2.2 and **Table 2.4**). A secondary dressing may be used to secure this dressing and protect the area against further trauma. Ice may be applied to the area to reduce the formation of a contusion secondary to the injurious mechanical force.

> **Practice Tip**
>
> Irrigation has been shown to effectively remove contaminants, loose tissue, and debris and to reduce bacterial colonization of the acute wound bed without damage to granulation and epithelial tissues.[11] A 35-mL syringe and 19-gauge needle hub or plastic cannula will deliver a solution at a pressure between 7 and 11 pounds per square inch (psi), with 8 psi being the optimal pressure.[12] Scrubbing and swabbing are not indicated for cleansing of the wound bed because these practices spread bacteria over the wound rather than removing it and can cause mechanical damage to tissues.[13,14]

CT Clinical Technique 2.1

Wound Irrigation

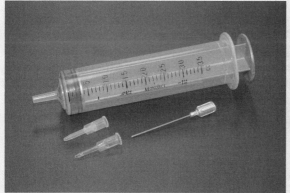
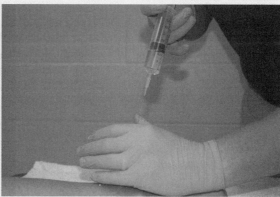

A   B

1. Place the patient in a seated, supine, or prone position. Drape the area with towels to catch body fluids and irrigation drainage.
2. Using a 35-mL syringe and 19-gauge needle hub or plastic cannula, fill the syringe with sterile 0.9% saline or potable tap water (**A**).
3. Position the syringe 4 to 6 inches above the wound bed.
4. Depress the plunger and move the syringe back and forth over the wound. Concentrate the stream over visible debris and nonviable tissue (**B**).
5. Use of universal precautions[10] is imperative during this technique. Commercial syringe splash guards and eye shields are recommended to lessen splash-back and cross-contamination. A gloved, cupped hand placed above the wound bed during irrigation will also protect against exposure to bodily fluids.
6. Continue irrigation until all visible debris and nonviable tissue is removed.
7. Following OSHA standards, dispose of and clean all supplies and equipment.

CT Clinical Technique 2.2

Application of Film, Foam, Hydrogel, and Hydrocolloid Dressings

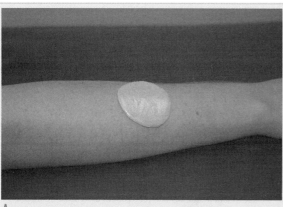
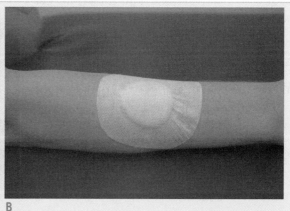

A   B

1. Based on the wound type and depth, body location, and needs and activity level of the patient, choose the appropriate dressing.
2. If necessary, cut the dressing with sterile scissors to cover the wound bed and extend a minimum of 2 centimeters over the periwound tissues.
3. Center the dressing over the wound bed and allow it to adhere to the periwound tissues (**A**).
4. For active patients, apply Cover-Roll (BSN-Jobst, Inc., Charlotte, North Carolina) to further secure the dressing to the skin (**B**).

Table 2.4

Guidelines for Semi-Occlusive and Occlusive Dressings

Dressing	Uses
Film (Bioclusive, Tegaderm, Polyskin)	Superficial to partial-thickness abrasions, blisters, lacerations, and incisions; small punctures; minor burns; wounds with minimal exudate
Foam (PolyMem, Curafoam, Allevyn)	Partial- to full-thickness abrasions, blisters, lacerations, and incisions; small punctures; wounds with heavy exudate
Hydrogel (Curagel, 2nd Skin, More Skin)	Partial- to full-thickness abrasions, blisters; minor lacerations and incisions; first- and second-degree burns; small punctures; wounds with moderate to heavy exudate
Hydrocolloid (DuoDerm, Ultec, Tegasorb)	Superficial to full-thickness abrasions, blisters, lacerations, and incisions; small punctures; wounds with moderate exudate
Dermal Adhesives (Dermabond, Histocryl)	Easily approximated wound edges from surgical incisions and traumatic lacerations

Practice Tip

Semi-occlusive and occlusive dressings promote a moist wound environment and have demonstrated increased healing rates and decreased rates of infection and pain compared with non-occlusive dressings (i.e., sterile gauze, adhesive strips, or patches) and no dressings. Although the exact mechanisms underlying this effect are unclear, semi-occlusive and occlusive dressings appear to enhance fibroblast and keratinocyte proliferation and migration,[19-23] the inflammatory response,[24] and autolytic debridement[25]; stimulate angiogenesis and collagen synthesis[26-28]; increase the rate of wound contraction[29,30]; provide a physical barrier to the external environment[31-36]; provide thermal insulation[37,38]; prevent tissue necrosis and wound desiccation[39]; lower rates of cross-contamination and infection[38]; and reduce levels of pain.[37]

Medical Management

Monitor the patient daily for signs of dressing leakage, adverse reactions, and infection. Leakage of exudate, contact dermatitis, folliculitis, or maceration of the periwound tissues warrants a dressing change. The presence of abscess, purulent discharge, abnormal heat, excessive edema, erythema, discharge, unexpected pain or tenderness, or abnormal smell can indicate infection,[40] for which the patient may require oral or intravenous antibiotic therapy (see Box 2.2). In the absence of complications, allow the dressing to remain on the wound bed for the recommended time to avoid unnecessary changes.

■ Tissue Avulsions

Tissue avulsions occur as a result of a tensile load presented to the tissue. The tissue undergoes ultimate failure and separates from its normal anatomical location.

Box 2.2

Antibiotic Medications

Antibiotics are used to treat a variety of infections, including cellulitis and infected wounds. Antibiotics should only be used to treat bacterial infections, and the patient must complete the entire course of therapy as prescribed by a physician. Failure to completely eradicate the organisms causing an infection can result in a relapse of the infection and the patient's development of resistance to the antibiotic. Bacteria that are resistant to the effects of antibiotics are emerging as a major concern for today's healthcare providers.

Penicillin and its derivatives are called beta-lactam agents because of their chemical structure. These agents disrupt the cell walls of bacteria, resulting in a bacteriocidal effect. Penicillin has generally been viewed as the drug of choice for the treatment of streptococcal infections. Unfortunately, in recent decades, bacteria have become increasingly resistant to the effects of penicillin and its derivatives. Among the more commonly prescribed penicillins are dicloxacillin, ampicillin, amoxicillin, and amoxicillin/clavulanate. Dicloxacillin is active against the microorganism *Staphylococcus aureus* and is often used for the treatment of skin infections resulting from these bacteria.

Quinolone antibiotics have become increasingly popular since the emergence of bacterial resistance to penicillins, cephalosporins, and macrolides. The wide spectrum of their coverage makes quinolones appropriate for treating many types of infection, but these agents are contraindicated in children because of concerns over their potential for causing detrimental effects on skeletal growth and development. In addition, when quinolone antibiotics are orally administered, they should not be given concurrently with antacids or calcium or iron supplements. The quinolone antibiotics are usually well tolerated but have the potential to induce arrhythmias in susceptible individuals; they may also lead to development of tendon disorders, especially those affecting the Achilles tendon.[41]

Tetracycline antibiotics are used for a variety of infections but should not be administered to children age 8 years and younger because they can cause enamel hypoplasia and tooth discoloration in developing teeth. Medication interactions can also be a problem with these agents. Antacids containing aluminum, calcium, or magnesium and laxatives containing magnesium, when given concurrently with tetracyclines, interfere with tetracycline absorption. Iron products should also not be given concurrently with tetracycline antibiotics.

Pathophysiology

Contamination of tissue flaps and tissue completely removed from the body can lead to infection.

Symptoms

Tissue avulsions can result in venous or arterial bleeding, deformity, and pain. Completely avulsed tissue can contain debris based on the mechanism of injury and location of tissue recovery.

Immediate Management

The avulsed area should be cleansed and debrided with saline irrigation. If completely avulsed tissue is heavily contaminated, gently irrigate the tissue with saline. Wrap saline-soaked gauze around the avulsed tissue and place it in a watertight bag. Insert the bag into ice water or place it on top of an ice bag. Do not allow direct contact of the tissue with the ice. Apply saline-soaked sterile gauze over the avulsed area. It is imperative that wounds of this nature receive further evaluation for consideration of excision of devitalized tissue.

Practice Tip

The elapsed time from the avulsion to medical management is critical. However, the exact time avulsed tissue remains viable for revascularization or reattachment is unknown.[42] The patient and avulsed tissue should be sent for medical management as soon as possible.

Medical Management

Avulsed tissue may need to be approximated with sutures, staples, or dermal adhesives to attain hemostasis. Sutures, staples, and dermal adhesives are discussed in conjunction with tissue lacerations and incisions later in this chapter. Heavily contaminated tissue may warrant surgical debridement and cleansing. Small flaps (less than 1.0 cm^2) that do not have a dusky discoloration—which is a sign of compromised blood flow—do not require sutures and can be closed with skin tapes (see **CT** 2.3) or dermal adhesives (see **CT** 2.4). In contrast, large flaps require sutures, staples, or dermal adhesives for tissue approximation and hemostasis.

CT Clinical Technique 2.3

Application of Skin Tapes

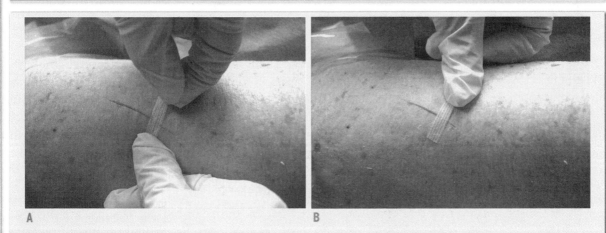

A   B

1. Following cleansing, dry the periwound tissues with sterile gauze.
2. Apply a thin coat of tape adhesive or benzoin tincture along the periwound tissues to increase the adherence of the strips.
3. Anchor the strips below the wound on the periwound tissues (**A**).
4. Approximate the wound edges and pull the strips with minimal tension across the wound.
5. Anchor the strips on the periwound tissues above the wound (**B**).
6. Continue to apply strips approximately 3 mm apart across the wound to achieve approximation.
7. Maintain adherence of the strips on the periwound tissues for a minimum of 5 to 7 days or until the strips have separated from the skin.
8. Monitor the patient daily for signs of infection and dehiscence.

CT Clinical Technique 2.4

Application of Dermal Adhesives

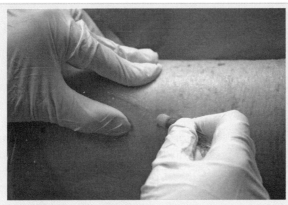

A

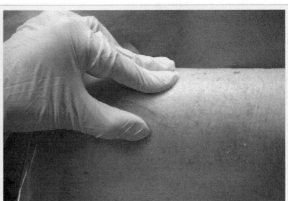

B

1. Following cleansing, dry the periwound tissues with sterile gauze.
2. Hold the ampule and crush it at its midpoint.
3. Gently squeeze the ampule and push the adhesive into the applicator tip.
4. Approximate the wound edges. Apply a thin layer of adhesive with a brush stroke onto the wound edges (**A**).
5. After 15 to 20 seconds, apply a second layer of adhesive.
6. Maintain tissue approximation throughout the application and for 60 seconds following application of the second layer of adhesive (**B**).
7. Maximum adhesion of the wound edges should be achieved at 2 1/2 minutes following application of the second layer.
8. After the adhesive is no longer tacky (approximately 5 minutes post application), a secondary dressing of sterile gauze or nonadherent pads can be applied.
9. Keep the wound dry until the adhesive separates from the wound edges, approximately 5 to 10 days after application. Gentle washing of the area can be performed during this time.
10. Monitor the patient daily for signs of infection and dehiscence.

---

dehiscence Opening of the wound.

Practice Tip

The Advisory Committee on Immunization Practices[43] has issued the following schedule for tetanus, diphtheria, and acellular pertussis (Tdap) vaccination for adults (19-64 years). Adults with unknown or incomplete history of vaccinations should begin or complete a primary vaccination series. A primary series consists of three doses of tetanus and diphtheria (Td) toxoid-containing vaccines. Doses 1 and 2 should be administered at least 4 weeks apart; dose 3 should be given 6 to 12 months after dose 2. In this three-dose series, Tdap can be given to replace any one of the doses of Td. A booster of Td should be administered to those with a completed primary series every 10 years. Tdap can be used to substitute for Td boosters in those who have not received a dose of Tdap previously.

In cases of skin injury with possible contamination among athletes with a completed primary series, a Td or Tdap booster should be administered if the previous inoculation was administered more than 5 years earlier. Skin injury with possible contamination in athletes with unknown or incomplete history of vaccinations should be administered a Td or Tdap vaccine and tetanus immune globulin (TIG) inoculation as soon as possible. Most cases of tetanus occur in those persons who have never received a primary series or those who received the series but did not receive a booster in the subsequent 10 years.

Following closure of the wound, immobilization of joints may be required to protect the flap and prevent dehiscence. Tetanus prophylaxis should be administered and oral antibiotics considered depending on the degree of contamination and elapsed time to closure.

■ Blisters

Blisters (bullae or bullous lesions) are the result of repeated, unidirectional or multidirectional friction forces with the presence of moisture on the skin. Blisters are common on the hands and feet from contact with athletic equipment in baseball, softball, rowing, and weight lifting activities and with the use of new or improperly fitted footwear, respectively. Prevention methods include keeping the skin dry, gradually increasing exercise intensity to allow skin adaptation to stresses, and wearing appropriate footwear, socks, and gloves. Lubricants and drying agents can be used, but most are effective for less than 1 hour of exercise.

Pathophysiology

Blisters occur as extracellular fluid extravasates into a closed space between the epidermis and the dermis at the site of friction.

Symptoms

Erythema, pain, and a burning sensation are present at the site of the blister or forming blister. A fluid-filled sac of varying size forms at the site of friction.

Immediate Management

If the blister is closed and does not affect activity, leave the roof intact and apply a hydrogel dressing over the roof to reduce friction. A foam "doughnut pad" can be placed over the dressing for additional protection.

Closed blisters affecting activities, containing cloudy fluid, or with impending rupture near a joint require cleansing and debridement. Cleanse the roof and periwound tissues by scrubbing with sterile gauze soaked with povidone-iodine. Using a sharp, sterile instrument, puncture the roof and allow the blister to drain. With sharp debridement, remove the roof. Irrigate the wound bed with saline or tap water. Apply a film, foam, hydrogel, or hydro-colloid dressing based on wound depth.

If the blister is open, debride the roof and cleanse it with irrigation. Apply a semi-occlusive or occlusive dressing. Application of a secondary dressing is recommended to secure the dressing. A hydrogel dressing or foam doughnut can be applied over the dressing to lessen friction.

Medical Management

The roof of a blister is nonviable tissue and can serve as a culture medium for microorganisms.[44] Removal of this tissue should be performed as soon as possible. Monitor the patient daily for dressing leakage, adverse reactions, and infection.

▇ Tissue Lacerations and Incisions

A laceration is an irregular tear in the skin caused by the application of tension and shear. An incision is produced by a sharp tensile force resulting in a clean or regular tear in the skin.

Pathophysiology

Debris and contaminants can be present in the wound. To lessen the risk of infection, the wound should be thoroughly cleansed and debrided prior to closure.

Symptoms

Lacerations and incisions may produce venous or arterial bleeding and local pain.

Immediate Management

Lacerations and incisions should be thoroughly cleansed and debrided with saline irrigation. Periwound tissues can be cleansed with saline irrigation, or antiseptic scrubbing and swabbing in cases of

heavy contamination. Ice can be used to diminish secondary injury and reduce pain.

Medical Management

Wound length, width, depth, and location will determine the appropriate method of tissue approximation and closure. Deep lacerations or incisions that allow the tissue to spread, potentially exposing the underlying subcutaneous adipose tissues, require sutures, staples, or dermal adhesives to approximate the wound edges to promote healing. Closure of facial and neck wounds should be guided by long-term cosmetic outcomes (see **Figure 2.7**). Lacerations

extravasate To escape from the blood or lymph vessels into the tissues.

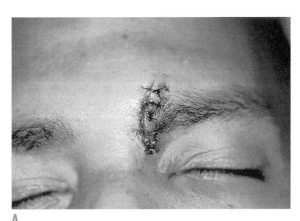

A

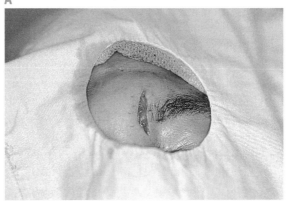

B

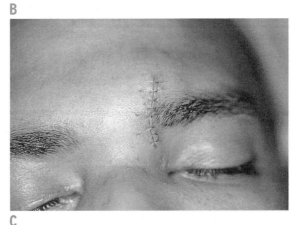

C

Figure 2.7 Monofilament sutures are used to approximate the epidermis. (**A**) A hastily repaired laceration illustrating overlapping and jagged skin margins. (**B**) Wound edges should be cleaned and sharply debrided. (**C**) Precise layered repair allows for better healing and a more acceptable cosmetic outcome.

and incisions over areas where healing may be impaired by poor blood supply, bony prominences, or high tension often require the use of sutures and, possibly, immobilization of the joint to prevent dehiscence. Film, foam, hydrogel, or hydrocolloid dressings may be used if tissue approximation can be achieved.

Dermal adhesives, including cyanoacrylate and octylcyanoacrylate derivative tissue glues, can be used to replace standard wound closure techniques (sutures, staples, skin tapes) for traumatic and surgical lacerations and incisions in areas of low tension (see CT 2.4). The adhesives can be used with, but should not replace, subcutaneous sutures.

> ### Practice Tip
>
> Dermal adhesives have been shown to produce acceptable cosmetic outcomes, hasten wound closure, lower levels of pain, and decrease erythema; unfortunately, they have also been associated with a higher risk of dehiscence when compared with standard wound closure (i.e., sutures, staples, adhesive strips).[45] Dermal adhesives should not be used in animal bites; in stellate wounds; in wounds with infection, gangrene, or ulceration; in mucosal surfaces or across mucocutaneous junctions; in areas of high moisture or dense hair; and in areas of high tension.[46]

Staples are an option for closure of wounds under high tension on the extremities, trunk, and scalp but are not appropriate for use on the hands, feet, neck, or face. Compared with other closure techniques, staples can be applied more quickly and result in fewer adverse reactions such as infection. Their relatively high cost and less precise tissue approximation are disadvantages of their use.

Suturing for primary closure should occur within 12 hours for an uncontaminated wound. With lacerations, the wound margins may need trimming to obtain good approximation of the skin flaps (see **Figure 2.8**). Contaminated wounds should be allowed to heal via secondary intention, with the patient making regular follow-up visits to allow the provider to change dressings, assess healing, and check for latent infection.

Once the decision to suture is made, the type of suture must be selected (see **Table 2.5**). Subcutaneous sutures are usually bioabsorbable and can be either monofilament or braided. If prolonged strength is needed because of tension placed on tissues, nonabsorbable sutures are recommended. Skin sutures can be either monofilament or braided bioabsorbable. Nonabsorbable sutures can also be

secondary intention Healing that occurs secondary to the formation of a scar or other indirect union.

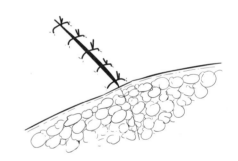

Figure 2.8 Contused, jagged wound edges should be sharply debrided to allow for better and faster healing of the laceration.

used but need to be removed after the healing is well under way, with the timing varying depending on anatomical location. Sutures are named for their constituent material and the size of the needle and suture: 0 is larger than 00 (2-0), which is larger than 000 (3-0), and so on.

A variety of suture techniques can be employed by the physician. The decision of which to use is based on the amount of tension on the closure during the healing process, the location of the wound, and the blood supply available for healing. Facial injuries are closed with very fine sutures (5-0 or 6-0), using a small needle, and removed quite early (approximately 5 to 7 days later) to prevent scarring. Extensor surfaces generally are under more

Table 2.5		
Suturing Guidelines for Skin Avulsions		
Site of Injury	**Suture Gauge and Material**	**Suture Removal**
Mouth	4.0 Vicryl* absorbable	Absorbed
Extremities	4.0-5.0 Ethilon*, Prolene*	12 to 14 days
Trunk	4.0-5.0 Ethilon, Prolene	8 to 10 days
Scalp	5.0 Ethilon, Prolene	6 to 8 days
Face	6.0 Ethilon, Prolene	3 to 5 days
*Vicryl, Ethilon, Prolene, Ethicon, Somerville, NJ.		

tension than flexor surfaces and, therefore, require lower suture grades (stronger suture material). The type of surface may influence suture type, suture technique, and suture healing time.

■ Tissue Punctures

A puncture is a hole or wound made by a sharp, cylindrical object that disrupts tissue with tensile loading.

Pathophysiology

Puncture wounds are subject to normal inflammatory processes. These wounds carry an increased risk of infection, because microorganisms such as *Clostridium tetani* spores, *Pseudomonas,* staphylococci, or streptococci can be introduced and may not be removed with typical cleansing and debridement techniques.

Symptoms

Pain and bleeding are present at the entry site of the wound. The offending object may be embedded and visible in the wound.

Immediate Management

The puncture site should be examined for embedded objects and residual foreign bodies. Embedded objects that are large and intact or broken off in the wound should not be removed. Instead, apply sterile gauze around the object and immobilize the object and involved joint. Surgical debridement and cleansing are required.

Embedded objects that are small and visible can be removed with sterile instruments. Avoid forcing the object deeper into the cavity. With removal of the object, bleeding serves to self-cleanse the wound. To control venous or arterial bleeding, the clinician should apply pressure. Irrigate the wound and periwound tissues with saline or tap water. Forceful irrigation is not warranted to prevent pushing debris and contaminants into the cavity.

Dress small puncture wounds with a semi-occlusive or occlusive dressing. Large cavity wounds require advanced dressings and follow-up care.

Medical Management

Puncture wounds can be difficult to manage. The offending object, its environmental location, and the substances it passed through on its path to penetrating the skin will all determine the level of concern for contamination. Puncture wounds sustained in contaminated water, on grass or dirt fields, or from footwear are often contaminated and require surgical debridement and cleansing. Punctures through damp tennis shoes can predispose an individual to *Pseudomonas* infection, which may potentially lead to more serious conditions such as osteomyelitis or septic arthritis. Based on the uncertain tissue damage and contaminant entry into the wound, closely monitor the patient and wound daily for signs of infection. Oral or intravenous antibiotics and a tetanus booster should be considered.

■ Traumatic Injuries to Muscle

All skeletal muscles are supplied with arteries, veins, and nerves. Blood carries oxygen and nutrients to muscles; it also carries away the wastes produced by muscle contractions. Muscle **morphology** depends on the fibrous connective-tissue framework that is present in addition to the arrangement of the muscle fibers. Connective tissue surrounds whole muscle (epimysium), each fascicle or bundle of fibers (perimysium), and individual muscle fibers (endomysium). This connective-tissue framework attaches to tendons and is essential for the efficient generation of force. Disruption of any of these processes decreases the strength of the muscle and/or range of motion (ROM) of the joint. Muscles are subject to traumatic injuries and inflammatory

morphology Pertaining to a tissue's structure and form without regard to function.

conditions and, because of their contractile properties, are prone to hypotonic and hypertonic conditions.

Contusions

A contusion, or bruise, is an injury in which the skin is not broken secondary to compressive forces. A muscle contusion differs from a skin contusion in that the blood extravasates into muscle tissue, not into the skin.

Pathophysiology
A muscle contusion is created by extravasation of blood into the muscle as a result of trauma.

Symptoms
Localized tenderness, pain, swelling, and ecchymosis are present.

Immediate Management
Contusions are first treated with ice, compression, elevation, and protection.

Medical Management
Treatment with ice, compression, elevation, and protection should be continued while the inflammatory response is still active. Thermotherapy, massage, and overzealous rehabilitation are contraindicated early in the healing process to prevent the development of heterotopic ossification. Radiographs may be required early to rule out underlying fractures and later to rule out ossification within muscle if healing of contusions leads to a loss of strength and muscle contracture. Major muscle contusions can magnify the potential risk of rhabdomyolysis.

Additionally, significant soft-tissue trauma in the extremities, with swelling restricted by fascial planes, may result in elevated compartmental pressures. Elevated pressures can cause an acute compartment syndrome, in which the viability of tissue is compromised. Pain seemingly out of proportion to the observed injury, numbness and tingling in the region, and diminished distal pulses heighten the concern for this important diagnosis. Seek consultation immediately if compartment syndrome is suspected.

Hematomas

A hematoma is a swelling or mass of blood (usually clotted) confined to an organ, tissue, or space. It is caused by a break in a blood vessel as the result of a compressive force.

Pathophysiology
A hematoma is caused by extravasation of blood and lymph fluid into a localized region, usually encapsulated by a connective-tissue membrane.

ecchymosis A bluish discoloration of the skin caused by bleeding under the skin; a bruise.

Symptoms
Localized tenderness, pain, swelling, and ecchymosis are present.

Immediate Management
Initial treatment for hematomas includes ice, compression, elevation, and protection.

Medical Management
Treatment with ice, compression, elevation, and protection should be continued while the inflammatory response is still active. A hematoma that does not produce neurovascular compromise should not be aspirated. If neurovascular compromise is present, the patient should be referred for aspiration. Aspiration of a large hematoma may serve to diminish the patient's discomfort and may significantly reduce the time necessary for resolution. It may also lessen the risk of complications such as a calcified hematoma or myositis ossificans. Aspiration of a hematoma is not without controversy: Even with very cautious, sterile techniques, aspiration potentially provides a portal of entry for microorganisms.

Strains

A strain consists of trauma to the muscle or the musculotendinous unit from violent contraction or excessive forcible stretch. Strains occur as a result of tensile forces on the muscle. When stretched to failure, most muscle fails near the proximal musculotendinous junction. Failure occurs in the Z-disks when the muscle is not stimulated; conversely, it occurs external to the membrane of the myotendinous junction in stimulated muscle (see **Figure 2.9**). Damaged tissue is subject to the inflammatory process.

Muscle strains are graded based on the amount of damage to the muscle fibers and the ability to palpate defects in the muscle. A grade I strain is an overstretching of the muscle fibers, with less than 10% of the muscle fibers tearing; no defect is palpable. A grade II strain is a partial tear of the muscle, usually involving 10% to 50% of the muscle fibers, with a palpable defect in the muscle belly. A grade III muscle strain is an extensive tear or a complete rupture of the muscle fibers, affecting 50% to 100% of the muscle fibers. A large defect in the muscle is palpable, and normal contraction is impossible with this type of strain.

Symptoms
The severity of symptoms depends on the magnitude of injury. Symptoms generally include local pain, strength loss, possibly ROM loss, mild swelling, ecchymosis, and local tenderness.

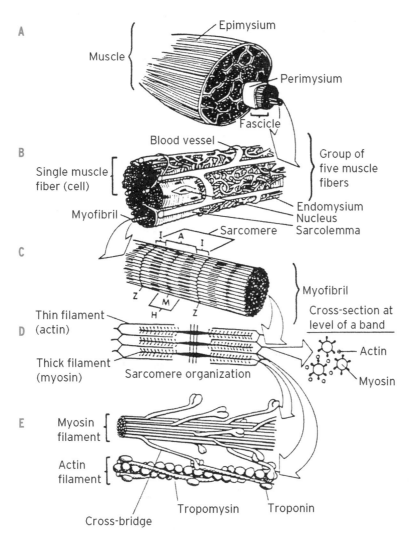

Figure 2.9 The structural organization of muscle consists of a connective-tissue framework and arranged muscle fibers. (**A** and **B**) Connective tissue surrounds the epimysium, perimysium, and endomysium. (**C**) Intricately arranged thick and thin filaments allow fibers to slide past each other in the sarcomere. Z-lines represent the ends of a sarcomere. (**D**) Thick filaments are made up of a protein aggregate that consists of myosin; thin filaments are made up of a protein aggregate that consists of actin, troponin, and tropomyosin. (**E**) Bands and zones make up the sarcomere, enabling effective and efficient muscle contraction at the subcellular or molecular level. *Source:* Reproduced with permission from Pitman MI, Peterson L. Biomechanics of skeletal muscle, in Frankel VH, Nordin M (eds), *Basic Biomechanics of the Skeletal System*, ed 2. Philadelphia: Lea & Febiger; 1989:90.

Clinically, grade III strains (muscle ruptures) present with muscle irregularity, a palpable defect, significant weakness, and loss of function. Patients describe the feeling during injury as a "pop;" pain and swelling occur acutely, secondary to intramuscular hemorrhage.

Differential Diagnosis

It may be necessary to differentiate a strain from a sprain, which can be done by assessing pain during ROM. Active and resisted ROM exercises may cause pain with a strain but not necessarily with a sprain.

Imaging Techniques

Muscle strains (including grade III ruptures) can be identified using axial T2-weighted MRI views (see **Figure 2.10**). Strains are not visible on plain radiographs.

Immediate Management

Strains are first treated with ice, compression, elevation, and protection.

Medical Management

A severe strain may be associated with the formation of a hematoma. Thermotherapy and massage are contraindicated early in the healing process to prevent the development of heterotopic ossification (discussed in the next section).

Grade III strains may require surgical intervention for full recovery and optimal musculoskeletal performance. Grade III tendinous injuries

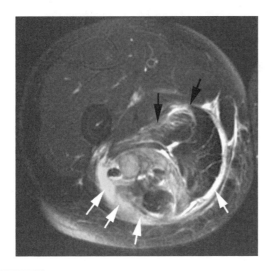

Figure 2.10 Magnetic resonance image of a hamstring strain showing increased fluids in the fascial planes (white arrows) and high signal intensity consistent with a strain of the hamstring muscles (black arrows).

are more amenable to surgical repair than intramuscular ruptures.

Inflammatory Conditions of Muscle and Tendon

Heterotopic Ossification

Myositis is an inflammation of muscle tissue as the result of infection (infectious myositis), trauma (traumatic myositis/heterotopic ossification), idiopathic inflammatory myopathy (polymyositis, dermatomyositis, and inclusion body myositis), or infestation by parasites (parasitic myositis). Heterotopic ossification is the most common type seen in athletes. Through a metaplastic process similar to fracture callus formation, chondroid and osteoid scars form rather than the expected fibroblastic scar; this results in heterotopic ossification, marked by ossification of the muscle.

Pathophysiology

Inflammation of the connective tissue within a muscle.

Symptoms

Muscle weakness, heat, swelling, and pain are present. With heterotopic ossification, a mass may be palpable. An ossified mass may be detectable radiographically after 2 to 3 weeks of persistent symptoms.

Imaging Techniques

Typically, heterotopic ossification takes approximately 6 to 12 months to mature, and three-phase bone scans have been shown to be helpful in determining the maturity of the lesion. Computed tomography scans (CTs) are useful for identifying subacute myositis (see **Figure 2.11**). Mature (hardened) masses eventually become apparent on plain radiographs.

Immediate Management

Heterotopic ossification (and the associated contusion) is first treated with ice, compression, elevation, and protection.

Medical Management

Surgical management of heterotopic ossification is controversial. Early surgical intervention has been associated with deterioration of the condition, resulting in recurrence of ossification and a longer period of disability. Surgical excision may be recommended for persistent muscle atrophy, decreased ROM, and worsening pain when radiographic evidence shows that the lesion has matured.[47,48] Delayed surgical intervention of symptomatic heterotopic ossification has been associated with recurrence rates as high as 67%.

Tendinopathy

Tendinopathy is an inflammation or degeneration of a tendon or its surrounding structures that is most commonly caused by overuse; however, trauma can also produce acute tendinopathy. Pathologic changes consistent with chronic inflammation are usually observed. Tissue degeneration, characterized by cell atrophy, may also be noted. Calcium can be deposited along the course of the tendon (calcific tendinopathy), with the shoulder being the site most commonly affected.

Histologically, tendon injury is characterized by mucoid degeneration, which is the loss of the normal cellularity and organized, crimped collagen fiber architecture that characterizes healthy tendon. Granulation tissue may also form, but

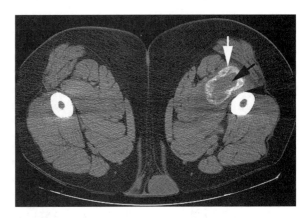

Figure 2.11 Computed tomographic scan of traumatic quadriceps heterotopic ossification showing a well-bounded mass with an ossified rim (white arrow) and a central unaffected area (black arrow). Note that the mass is not in contact with the femur (black arrowhead).

inflammatory cells are usually absent unless the tendon is torn. The inflammation that characterizes tendinopathy and tenosynovitis with tendinosis may result from associated local vascular disruption. The mechanism of tendon failure is believed to be inadequate production of maintenance collagen and matrix in response to increased loading. In addition, diminished vascularity contributes to tendon failure by leading first to decreased cellularity and consequently to decreased collagen production.

Tendinosis

Tendinosis is an intratendinous avascular degeneration that results in collagen disorientation, disorganization, and fiber separation because of an increase in mucoid ground substance, increased prominence of cells and vascular spaces with or without neovascularization, and focal necrosis or calcification. Tendinosis can refer to degeneration of a tendon from repetitive microtrauma, tendinopathy without inflammation, or collagen degeneration.

Tenosynovitis

Tenosynovitis is inflammation of a tendon within its sheath. It may occur when the sheath is subjected to repeated pressure and friction.

Symptoms

Tendinopathy causes pain over the affected tendon close to its insertion into the muscle. The pain is usually worsened by repetitive motion but can also be present at rest. Mild swelling may be seen over the tendon, accompanied by warmth and possible crepitus. Tendinosis produces pain with ROM, swelling, and stiffness; it may present with a nontender, palpable nodule as well. Tenosynovitis is characterized by pain, swelling, and crepitus within the tendon sheath.

Immediate Management

Initial treatment of tendinopathy consists of ice, compression, elevation, protection, and rest.

Medical Management

Anti-inflammatory medications, as described in Box 2.1, often are prescribed for both acute and chronic tendinopathies. Extracorporeal shockwave therapy and ultrasound have shown good results as treatments for calcific tendinopathy but remain under study for this indication. Extracorporeal shockwave therapy is currently approved by the U.S. Food and Drug Administration only for treatment of plantar fasciitis and lateral epicondylitis. Use of this therapy for patellar tendinopathy and fracture nonunion is awaiting approval.

Hypotonic and Hypertonic Conditions

Muscle Cramps

Muscle cramps are painful, involuntary contractions of muscles. Exercise-associated muscle cramps are the type generally encountered in sports medicine settings. Such cramps comprise painful, spasmodic, involuntary contractions that occur during or immediately after muscular exercise.

Muscles cannot function properly without both a continuous supply of nutrients and the continuous removal of cellular wastes. Cramps result when insufficient amounts of oxygen or nutrients are available or when waste products, such as lactic acid, accumulate. This condition may result from dehydration and electrolyte imbalance or an abnormal, sustained increase in α-motoneuron activity.

Symptoms

Muscle cramp symptoms include painful, sudden, involuntary contraction of the muscle, with visible or palpable localized knotting of the muscle.

Immediate Management

For mild cases, oral replenishment of fluids and electrolytes, stretching, ice, and gentle massage should suffice to eliminate the cramps.

Medical Management

For more severe cramps, intravenous rehydration is indicated to prevent the more serious forms of heat illness. A variety of intravenous solutions are used for this purpose, including lactated Ringer's solution, normal saline, and several different combinations of dextrose with saline. Athletes are apt to develop hyponatremia during prolonged exercise if their fluid consumption exceeds their fluid losses, thereby lowering the concentration of sodium in their blood. In addition, use of hypotonic solutions for intravenous rehydration of individuals with muscle cramps can exacerbate hyponatremia, leading to respiratory distress and mental status changes. Accordingly, hypotonic solutions for rehydration should be avoided. Chapter 19 discusses the management of heat-related muscle cramps in more detail.

Muscle Spasms

A spasm is an involuntary, sudden movement or muscular contraction that occurs as a result of an irritant, muscle injury, overuse, stress, dehydration, electrolyte imbalance, or poor posture.

Symptoms

Muscle spasms are characterized by restricted motion and painful or "tight" muscles that are tender to the touch.

Immediate Management

Oral replenishment of fluids and electrolytes, stretching, ice, and gentle massage can eliminate muscle spasms.

Medical Management

Antispasmodic medications may be treatment options for athletes. Such muscle relaxants tend to be sedating, however, and their use should be deferred pending use of other modalities and non-pharmacologic therapies such as massage, acupressure, tissue mobilization, and electric muscle stimulation.

Contractures

Contractures may be caused by muscle imbalance, pain, prolonged bed rest, or immobilization that results in a fibrosis of connective tissue in skin, fascia, muscle, or a joint capsule that prevents normal mobility of the related tissue or joint.

Symptoms

Loss of joint motion with contractures is significant, resulting in immobility. Pain without any voluntary joint movement may be present in severe cases.

Immediate Management

Joint mobilization, soft-tissue stretching, continuous passive motion, or some combination of these treatments should be instituted.

Medical Management

In severe cases, surgery or joint manipulation under general anesthesia may be necessary. These approaches are rarely used in sports medicine, however.

Arthrogenic Muscle Inhibition

Arthrogenic muscle inhibition is a presynaptic, ongoing reflex inhibition of the musculature surrounding a joint after distention or damage to structures of that joint.[49] Arthrogenic muscle inhibition is caused by presynaptic and postsynaptic inhibition at the motoneuron.

Symptoms

Arthrogenic muscle inhibition is characterized by diminished force output and control of the muscle.

Immediate Management

Early exercise after joint injury, particularly cryokinetics programs, and transcutaneous electric nerve stimulation may overcome the inhibitory response.

Medical Management

Medical management of arthrogenic muscle inhibition is largely undefined. Persistent arthrogenic muscle inhibition is not thought to be amenable to treatment.

Atrophy

Atrophy is synonymous with wasting—it is a decrease in the size of an organ or tissue as a result of disuse, aging, or disease. In orthopaedics, atrophy most commonly refers to muscular atrophy. When atrophy occurs, cell size and function decrease in response to an environmental signal. Protein synthesis decreases, as does cell division, energy production, energy storage, and contractility. Immobilization is one cause of muscle cell atrophy. Other causes include denervation, inadequate oxygen supply or nutrition, hormonal deficiency, chronic inflammation, and aging.

Tissue degeneration implies the existence of a weaker structure. With this type of deterioration, tissues become more vulnerable to sudden dynamic overload or cyclic overloading, which in turn may lead to fatigue and failure. Traumatic disruption can cause vascular injury and initiate a renewed inflammation repair process.

Symptoms

Atrophy is characterized by loss of muscle mass and force-producing capabilities.

Immediate Management

The first line of treatment is active exercise, possibly augmented by submotor neuromuscular electric stimulation.

Medical Management

The most commonly encountered form of atrophy following musculoskeletal trauma is disuse atrophy. Recovery of an atrophied cell requires a balance of rest and physical stimulation. Returning to activity after prolonged inactivity without substantially improved tissue integrity increases the risk of reinjury of the involved tissue. For this reason, protected activity or controlled therapeutic exercise is usually a better treatment for injuries than complete rest to maintain musculoskeletal integrity.

The following general principles should be addressed to prevent disuse atrophy and to restore form and function:

- Encourage early mobilization activities.
- Reduce pain (pain can cause muscle inhibition during rehabilitation).
- Restore muscle flexibility, endurance, and strength with a graded program.
- Return the patient to sport- and position-specific training.
- Protect the area of atrophy against further injury.
- Restore cardiovascular endurance.

- Optimize nutrition by emphasizing a moderate increase in protein intake without compromising nutritional balance.

Ligament Injuries

Ligaments and joint capsules connect bone to bone and augment the mechanical stability of joints, guide joint motion, and prevent abnormal motion. Type I collagen is the major structural component of ligaments, accounting for 70% of their dry weight.[50] Ligaments and tendons share a similar ultrastructure with comparable fascicular arrangements of highly oriented, highly packed collagen fibers that provide tensile strength and flexibility.[51] Ligaments also have much lower thickness-to-width ratios, and their fiber orientation varies more. In addition, ligaments contain less collagen, more glycosaminoglycans, and more elastin than tendons.

Some ligaments are composed of more than one band of fibrils or bundles. As the joint moves through its ROM, different bands of fibrils become taut to allow for greater flexibility. For example, the anteromedial bundle of the anterior cruciate ligament becomes tight as the knee flexes, and the posterolateral bundle becomes taut during knee extension. Ligaments receive their blood supply from their insertion site on bone. They house mechanoreceptors that provide proprioceptive feedback and initiate protective reflexes.

Sprains

A sprain occurs when trauma from tensile or shear forces (or both) is delivered to a joint, causing pain and disability, depending on the degree of injury to the ligaments. The collagen fibers within the ligament lose their crimp and progressively fail as these forces increase. In sports medicine, a sprain is typically defined as any disruption to the integrity of a ligament.

Sprains are graded according to the magnitude of the tear and resultant joint instability. A grade I sprain is a stretch to the ligament with no joint opening during a stress maneuver. A grade II sprain is a partial tear with moderate instability and opening of the joint during a stress maneuver. A grade III sprain is a complete tear of the ligament with gross opening of the joint during a stress maneuver.

Pathophysiology
Damaged ligaments are subject to inflammation.

Symptoms
Local tenderness, swelling, ecchymosis, and impaired function are present.

Differential Diagnosis
Sprains may need to be differentiated from avulsion fractures or muscle strains. Muscle strain can be identified by assessing pain during ROM; active and resisted ROM exercises may cause pain with a strain but not necessarily with a sprain.

Imaging Techniques
Plain radiographs may be ordered to rule out an avulsion fracture. MRI or CT scans can identify complete or partial tearing of the ligament.

Immediate Management
Initial treatment includes ice, compression, elevation, and protection to avoid further injury.

Medical Management
General indications for surgical repair of sprains include the following:

- Persistent dysfunction despite conservative management
- Associated bony avulsion
- Most injuries with multidirectional instability
- Ankle sprains in prepubescent individuals with Salter-Harris type III–V fractures
- Displaced osteochondral avulsion of the talar dome

Although most grade III sprains are not amenable to medical management, many exceptions to this rule exist. For example, isolated medial collateral ligament sprains in athletes are rarely repaired surgically because of the equivocal results, both from conservative management and from surgical intervention.

Fascia

Fascia is a flat band of tissue below the skin that covers underlying tissues and separates different layers of tissue; fascia also encloses muscle. The most commonly encountered injuries to the fascia are myofascial pain syndrome and fasciitis.

Myofascial Pain Syndrome (Fibromyalgia)

Specific definitions of myofascial pain syndrome vary in the literature. This condition is generally characterized as a painful musculoskeletal response after muscle trauma involving sensory, motor, and autonomic phenomena.[52] The key feature of myofascial pain syndrome is the presence of trigger points, which may be caused by any of the following:

- Sudden trauma to the musculoskeletal tissues
- Generalized fatigue
- Repetitive motion, excessive exercise, or muscle strain due to overactivity
- Inactivity
- Nervous tension or stress
- Chilling of specific areas of the body (e.g., sitting under an air-conditioning duct, sleeping in front of an air conditioner)

Symptoms

Myofascial pain syndrome is distinguished by the development of myofascial trigger points that are locally tender when active and that refer pain through specific patterns to other areas of the body. A trigger point may develop from any number of causes and is usually associated with a taut band—that is, a rope-like thickening of the muscle tissue. Pressing on a trigger point typically causes referred pain.

Immediate Management

Stretch and spray (in which a vapocoolant is sprayed on the trigger point to lessen the pain and then the muscle is stretched), massage, and strengthening exercises are used in the early management of myofascial pain.

Medical Management

Therapeutic massage seems to be the most effective treatment for myofascial pain syndrome. Chronic pain modulation with analgesics can be detrimental to the patient's long-term health. Trigger points can be injected with a local anesthetic.

Fasciitis

Fasciitis—that is, inflammation of the fascia—results from repetitive trauma to the fascia. Often, the fascia is exposed to repetitive tensile loads that result in an inflammatory process. This repeated trauma frequently causes microscopic tearing of the fascia at or near the point of attachment of the tissue. The result of the damage and inflammation is pain.

Symptoms

Fasciitis is characterized by dull, aching pain that may improve with rest.

Immediate Management

Initial treatment is ice and rest.

Medical Management

Treatment may be enhanced by use of ultrasound, phonophoresis, transverse friction and deep tissue massage, or augmented soft-tissue mobilization.

Synovial Tissue

The synovium is a thin, weak layer of tissue (only a few cells thick) that lines the joint space. The synovium controls the environment within the joint in two ways. First, it acts as a membrane to determine what can pass into the joint space and what stays outside. Second, the synovial cells produce substances such as hyaluronan, which is a component of joint fluid. The most common injuries to the synovium are synovitis and bursitis.

Synovitis

Synovitis is inflammation of a synovial membrane (see **Figure 2.12**).

Pathophysiology

Inflammation occurs by the collection of synovial fluid within the membranes.

Symptoms

Pain, particularly with movement, and swelling are present.

Immediate Management

Initial management of synovitis consists of application of ice and rest.

Medical Management

The management of synovitis is based on the cause. Rheumatologic causes of synovitis must be ruled out using comprehensive blood tests. A synovial biopsy may be needed to determine the exact cause (i.e., inflammatory, infectious, or posttraumatic).

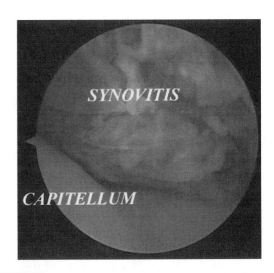

Figure 2.12 Synovitis of the elbow. This arthroscopic view shows the anterior aspect of the elbow joint as seen from the anterolateral portal. Proliferative synovial tissue is visible over the capitellum. *Source:* Reproduced with permission from Horiuchi K, Momohara S, Tomatsu T, et al. Arthroscopic synovectomy of the elbow in rheumatoid arthritis. *J Bone Joint Surg Am.* 2002;84:342-347.

Bursitis

Bursitis is an inflammation of a bursa as a result of repetitive movement or direct trauma to the bursal sac.

Pathophysiology

Inflammation of the bursal sac occurs as a result of repetitive movement or trauma.

Symptoms

Bursitis is characterized by a dull ache or stiffness, pain worsening with movement or pressure, swelling, palpable warmth, and occasionally redness of the skin overlying the bursa.

Immediate Management

Initial treatment is with ice, compression, elevation, and protection.

Medical Management

The goal of medical management is to treat the cause of the bursitis, such as leg-length discrepancy, exaggerated Q angle, or overuse issues.

References

1. *American Hospital Formulary Science Drug Information,* ed 2003. Bethesda, MD: American Society of Health-System Pharmacists; 2003.

2. Dipiro JT, Talbert RL, Yee GC, et al (eds). *Pharmacotherapy: A Pathophysiologic Approach,* ed 5. New York: McGraw-Hill Medical Publishing Division; 2002.

3. *Physician's Desk Reference 2010,* ed 64. Montvale, NJ: Medical Economics; 2010.

4. Guyton AC, Hall JE. *Textbook of Medical Physiology,* ed 11. Philadelphia: WB Saunders; 2005.

5. Luster AD. Chemokines: chemotactic cytokines that mediate inflammation. *N Engl J Med.* 1998;338:436–445.

6. Efron DT, Barbul A. Modulation of inflammation and immunity by arginine supplements. *Curr Opin Clin Nutr Metab Care.* 1998;1:531–538.

7. Polla BS, Bachelet M, Elia G, Santoro MG. Stress proteins in inflammation. *Ann N Y Acad Sci.* 1998;851:75–85.

8. Malm C, Nyberg P, Engstrom M, et al. Immunological changes in human skeletal muscle and blood after eccentric exercise and multiple biopsies. *J Physiol.* 2000;529:243–262.

9. Myers BA. *Wound Management: Principles and Practice,* ed 2. Upper Saddle River, NJ: Pearson Prentice Hall; 2008:95.

10. U.S. Department of Labor Occupational Safety and Health Administration. Bloodborne pathogens and needlestick prevention standards. Available at: http://www.osha.gov/SLTC/bloodbornepathogens/index.html. Accessed May 22, 2010.

11. Goldsmith SP. Wound care: combining three classification systems to select dressings. *Home Health Care Manage Prac.* 1996;8:17–27.

12. Bergstrom N, Allamn R, Alvarez O, et al. *Treatment of Pressure Ulcers.* Clinical Practice Guidelines No. 15 [AHCPR Publication No. 95-052]. Rockville, MD: U.S. Department of Health and Human Services; 1994.

13. Thomlinson D. To clean or not to clean? *Nurs Times.* 1987;83:71–75.

14. Rodeheaver GT, Smith SL, Thacker JG, et al. Mechanical cleansing of contaminated wounds with a surfactant. *Am J Surg.* 1975;129:241–245.

15. Fernandez R, Griffiths R, Ussia C. Water for wound cleansing. *Cochrane Database Syst Rev.* 2002;2:CD003861.

16. Fernandez R, Griffiths R, Ussia C. Wound cleansing: which solution, what technique. *Primary Intention.* 2001;9:51–58.

17. Cohen KI, Diegelmann R, Yager D, et al. Wound care and wound healing, in Spencer S, Galloway D (eds), *Principles of Surgery, International.* New York: McGraw-Hill; 1999:269–290.

18. Lineaweaver W, Howard R, Soucy D, et al. Topical antimicrobial toxicity. *Arch Surg.* 1985;120:267–270.

19. Winter GD. Formation of the scab and the rate of epithelization of superficial wounds in the skin of the young domestic pig. *Nature.* 1962;193:293–294.

20. Alper JC, Tibbetts LL, Sarazen AA Jr. The in vitro response of fibroblasts to the fluid that accumulates under a vapor-permeable membrane. *J Invest Dermatol.* 1985;84:513–515.

21. Katz MH, Alvarez AF, Kirsner RS, et al. Human wound fluid from acute wounds stimulates fibroblast and endothelial cell growth. *J Am Acad Dermatol.* 1991;25:1054–1058.

22. Madden MR, Nolan E, Finkelstein JL, et al. Comparison of an occlusive and a semi-occlusive dressing and the effect of the wound exudate upon keratinocyte proliferation. *J Trauma.* 1989;29:924–930.

23. Eaglstein WH, Mertz PM. New method for assessing epidermal wound healing: the effects of triamcinolone acetonide and polyethylene film occlusion. *J Invest Dermatol.* 1978;71:382–384.

24. Rovee D, Kurowsky C, Labun J, Downes A. Effect of local wound environment on epidermal healing, in Maibaich H, Rovee D (eds), *Epidermal Wound Healing.* Chicago, IL: Yearbook Publishers; 1972:159–184.

25. Baxter CR. Immunologic reactions in chronic wounds. *Am J Surg.* 1994;167:12S–14S.

26. Lydon M, Hutchinson J, Rippon M, et al. Dissolution of wound coagulum and promotion of granulation tissue under DuoDerm. *Wounds.* 1989;1:95–106.

27. Knighton DR, Silver J, Hunt T. Regulation of wound-healing angiogenesis: effect of oxygen gradients and inspired oxygen concentration. *Surgery.* 1981;90:262–270.

28. Bolton L, Johnson C, Rijswijk L. Occlusive dressings: therapeutic agents and effects on drug delivery. *Clinics Dermatol.* 1992;9:573–583.

29. Beam JW. Occlusive dressings and the healing of standardized abrasions. *J Athl Train.* 2008;43:600–607.

30. Claus EE, Fusco CF, Ingram T, et al. Comparison of the effects of selected dressings on the healing of standardized abrasions. *J Athl Train.* 1998;33:145–149.

31. Ameen H, Moore K, Lawrence JC. Investigating the bacterial barrier properties of four contemporary wound dressings. *J Wound Care.* 2000;9:385–388.

32. Bowler P, Delargy H, Prince D, Fondberg L. The viral barrier properties of some occlusive dressings and their role in infection control. *Wounds: Compendium Clin Res Pract.* 1993;5:1–8.

33. Dunn LJ, Wilson P. Evaluating the permeability of hydrocolloid dressings to multi-resistant *Staphylococcus aureus. Pharm J.* 1990;248:248–250.

34. Lawrence JC, Lilly HA. Are hydrocolloid dressings bacteria-proof? *Pharm J.* 1987;184.

35. Mertz PM, Marshall DA, Eaglstein WH. Occlusive wound dressings to prevent bacterial invasion and wound infection. *J Am Acad Dermatol.* 1985;12:662–668.

36. Wilson P, Burroughs D, Dunn J. Methicillin-resistant *Staphylococcus aureus* and hydrocolloid dressings. *Pharm J.* 1998;241:787–788.

37. Myer A. Dressings, in Kloth LC, McCulloch JM (eds), *Wound Healing Alternatives in Management,* ed 3. Philadelphia: FA Davis Company; 2002:232–270.

38. Turner T. Which dressing and why? *Nurs Times.* 1982;78:1–3.

39. Linsky C, Rovee D, Dow T. Effects of dressings on wound inflammation and scar tissue, in Dineen P, Hildick-Smith G (eds), *The Surgical Wound.* Philadelphia: Lea & Febiger; 1981:191–205.

40. Cutting KF, White RJ. Criteria for identifying wound infection-revisited. *Ostomy Wound Manage.* 2005;51:28–34.

41. Casparian JM, Luchi M, Moffat RE, Hinthorn D. Quinolones and tendon ruptures. *South Med J.* 2000;93:488–491.

42. Pons P, Markovchick V. *Prehospital Emergency Care Secrets.* Philadelphia: Hanley & Belfus; 1998.

43. Centers for Disease Control and Prevention. Recommended adult immunization schedule—United States. *MMWR.* 2010;59(1).

44. Attinger CE, Bulan EJ. Debridement: the key initial first step in wound healing. *Foot Ankle Clin.* 2001;6: 627–660.

45. Farion K, Osmond MH, Hartling L, et al. Tissue adhesives for traumatic lacerations in children and adults. *Cochrane Database Syst Rev.* 2001;4:CD003326.

46. Bruns TB, Worthington JM. Using tissue adhesive for wound repair: a practical guide to Dermabond. *Am Fam Physician.* 2000;61:1383–1388.

47. Jackson DW. Quadriceps contusions in young athletes. *J Bone Joint Surg Am.* 1973;55:95–105.

48. Ryan JB, Wheeler JH, Hopkinson WJ, et al. Quadriceps contusions: West Point update. *Am J Sports Med.* 1991;19: 299–304.

49. Starkey C. *Therapeutic Modalities,* ed 3. Philadelphia: FA Davis; 2004:24.

50. Fu FH, Harner CD, Vince KG (eds). *Knee Surgery.* Baltimore, MD: Lippincott Williams & Wilkins; 1994.

51. Hopkins JT, Ingersoll CD. Arthrogenic muscle inhibition: a limiting factor in joint rehabilitation. *J Sport Rehabil.* 2000;9:135–159.

52. Simons D, Travell J, Simons L. *Myofascial Pain and Dysfunction: The Trigger Point Manual. Volume 1: Upper Half of Body,* ed 2. Baltimore, MD: Lippincott Williams & Wilkins; 1998.

Fractures: Diagnosis and Management

After injury, most soft tissues heal by replacing the injured tissue with a dense collagen scar. Bone is unique as the only tissue that can completely restore itself to its original form after injury via inflammatory, early reparative, late reparative, and remodeling phases. Through the process of fracture healing and remodeling, bone eventually assumes its original microscopic structure and form, ultimately regaining the same resistance to further stress as the original, uninjured structure. The goal of fracture management is to restore form and function. The rigid, biphasic composition of bone allows use of treatment options that are not available for soft tissue.

Many fractures will heal without surgery. In general, surgical intervention to stabilize a fractured bone actually slows down the normal healing process. The treatment goals for osseous injuries are to maintain anatomic length and alignment during the healing process, while doing as little as possible to disturb the normal biology of fracture healing. For particular fracture patterns in certain locations, optimal preservation of form and function is provided by early surgical fixation of the fracture; this treatment allows early motion of adjacent joints while preserving anatomic length and alignment. A fracture in a high-performance athlete may be treated more aggressively than a fracture in a more sedentary person to expedite the athlete's return to function and participation.

Low-intensity pulsed ultrasound (LIPUS—output frequency: 1.5 MHz; burst width: 200 microseconds; intensity: 30 mW/cm^2) has demonstrated the ability to improve the rate and quality of fracture repair (see **Figure 3.1**).[1–3] The ultrasonic energy causes microdisplacement of the fracture segments that signals osteogenic cells to produce fibrocartilage; when applied early in the healing process, it results in a stronger bony callus.[4,5] The efficacy of this technique is based on the location and stability of the fracture site and the amount of time since the onset of the fracture (the more quickly it is applied following the trauma, the better the results).[6]

> **Practice Tip**
>
> When applied early in the healing process, ultrasonic bone growth stimulators produce accelerated healing relative to no treatment or electromagnetic bone growth generators.[1,3,6]

Qualities of Bone Tissue

Bone is designed to provide support and protection. A biphasic composite material, it provides rigidity, yet also allows flexibility.[7] Like other tissues, bone contains an organic extracellular matrix of fibers and a ground substance. However, bone is unique because of its high content of inorganic materials. Mineral salts combine with organic components to make bone both hard and rigid while providing for flexibility and resilience. The mineral portion of bone is primarily calcium and phosphate; these minerals account for 65% to 70% of the dry weight of bone.

Protein collagen—the fibrous portion of the extracellular matrix—is tough and pliable, but resists stretching and has little extensibility. This collagen accounts for 95% of the extracellular matrix and 25% to 30% of the dry weight of bone.

Ground substance is a gelatinous material that surrounds the mineralized collagen fibers. It is composed primarily of protein polysaccharides called glycosaminoglycans (GAGs), which serve as a glue between the layers of the mineralized collagen fibers. Ground substance accounts for approximately 5% of the extracellular matrix.

Water also is abundant in bone, accounting for as much as 25% of live bone weight. Most (85%) of the water is found in the organic matrix, with the remaining 15% being found in various canals and cavities throughout the bone.

The osteon (also called the haversian system) is the fundamental structural unit of bone. It consists of concentric layers of mineralized matrix, called lamellae, surrounding a central haversian canal (see **Figure 3.2**). The outer edges of the lamellae

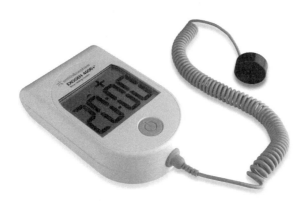

Figure 3.1 Ultrasonic bone growth stimulator. This device uses low-intensity, pulsed ultrasonic energy to promote osteogenesis. When it is applied once per day for 20 minutes, several systematic reviews support the efficacy of this technique. Note that clinical therapeutic ultrasound units cannot be used for this purpose.

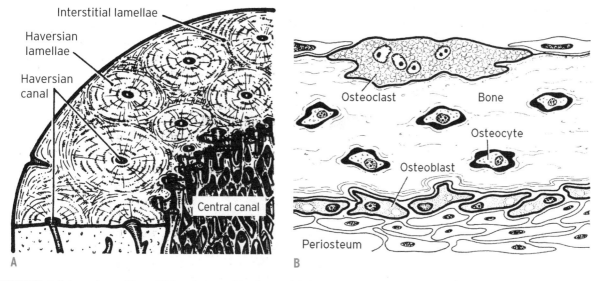

Interstitial lamellae

Haversian lamellae

Haversian canal

Central canal

A

Osteoclast   Bone

Osteocyte

Osteoblast

Periosteum

B

Figure 3.2 Cellular anatomy of bone. (**A**) An osteon consists of concentric layers of mineralized matrix around a central canal. The haversian canal is found at the center of the osteon. (**B**) Bone cells are composed of osteoclasts, osteoblasts, and osteocytes.

contain small cavities called lacunae. A single osteocyte is contained within the lacunae. Small channels called canaliculi radiate out from each lacuna, connecting lacunae in adjacent lamellae. This interconnecting network of canaliculi ultimately contacts the haversian canal, allowing nutrients to reach the osteocytes.

Osteons, which are approximately 200 millimeters in diameter, usually run longitudinally but can branch and **anastomose** with one another. The haversian canals of individual osteons are interconnected to one another via Volkmann canals.

Osteons form two types of osseous tissue—cortical bone and cancellous bone. Cortical, or compact, bone forms the hard, outer shell of the bone. Also called the cortex, cortical bone has a dense structure similar to ivory (see **Figure 3.3**). Cancellous, or trabecular, bone is contained within the cortical shell. It is formed of thin plates called trabeculae, organized within a loose mesh structure. Red marrow is contained within the trabeculae. Cancellous bone is arranged in lamellae but does not contain haversian canals. Nutrients pass through the red marrow to the canaliculi. The percentage of cortical and cancellous bone varies among individual bones, depending on the functional requirements of that bone.

Bones are classified according to their morphology into three groups—long, short, and flat. They are further described according to certain anatomic characteristics. Long bones, for example, have a diaphysis (shaft), metaphyses (flares at the ends), and epiphyses (rounded ends at a joint). A physis separates the epiphysis from the metaphysis and serves as the growth center for a long bone. Other areas on bones are described based on their shape, function, or both.

■ Biomechanical Properties

Bone is an anisotropic material,[8] which means that it exhibits different mechanical properties when loaded along different axes. A classic example of anisotropic bone is the proximal femur just below the lesser trochanter. All human bone is stronger in compression than in tension. The subtrochanteric region of the femur is placed in pure compressive load on the medial cortex and pure tensile load on the lateral cortex during normal ambulation or running. Its anatomic structure is well designed to withstand these stresses. If the pattern of stresses is reversed, or if a severe torsional load is applied to this area, the proximal femur may fail by fracturing. Because this area of bone is never subjected to expansile forces from within, insertion of an implant into the canal of the femur may result in increased barrel or hoop stresses and cause a longitudinal fracture. The term *anisotropy* is used to describe how bone behaves differently when stressed in directions other than those usually encountered during physiologic loading.

Bone also has the unique ability to remodel itself along lines of stress. In immature bone in the very young and in new bone formation after a fracture, the bone trabeculae and osteons are not aligned along lines of stress. During the healing

anastomose To join or connect two structures such as blood vessels.

3

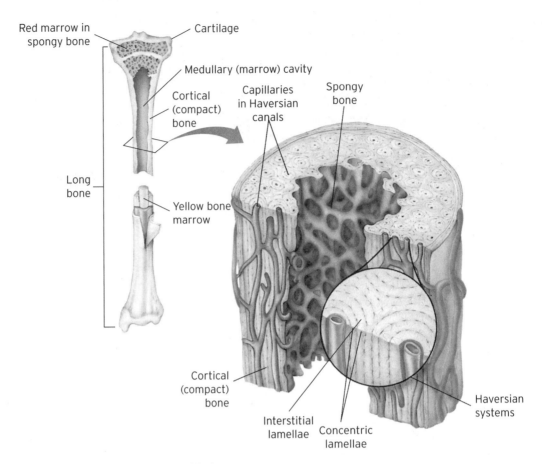

Figure 3.3 Cortical bone forms the hard, outer shell of the bone.

and remodeling process, the bony architecture is gradually remodeled into a form that best resists stresses applied to the bone. During normal growth, bone is subjected to various tensile and compressive stresses during daily activities, and the immature bone is remodeled into a structure ideally suited to withstand these stresses. If new stresses are applied—whether from growth, a new conditioning drill, or a new sport—the bone may gradually be remodeled to accommodate the new lines of stress. When this remodeling process is too slow to accommodate a rapid change in stress applied to the bone, a stress fracture may occur. After injury, the architecture of the bone is gradually remodeled into a form that best resists the applied stresses. For this reason, rehabilitation of acute fractures and stress fractures requires that stresses be gradually applied to the bone during the healing process to avoid refracture.

The stress–strain curve (see **Figure 3.4**) provides a key to understanding the mechanical properties of bone. The various forces and torques that may be presented to bone result in tension, compression, bending, and shear (see **Figure 3.5**). Combinations of these loads can also occur.[9]

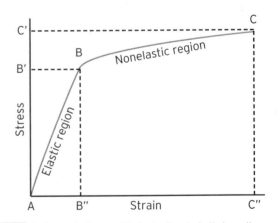

Figure 3.4 A stress-strain curve illustrates the strain that results from placing a standard specimen of tissue in a testing device and loading it to the point of failure. Yield point B represents the point past which some permanent deformation of bone occurs, yield stress B′ represents the load per unit area that the bone sample sustained before nonelastic deformation, and yield strain B″ represents the total amount of deformation the sample sustained before nonelastic deformation. Ultimate failure point C is the point past which the sample failed, ultimate stress C′ is the load per unit area that the sample sustained before failure, and ultimate strain C″ shows the amount of deformation that the sample sustained before failure. *Source:* Reproduced with permission from Frankel VH, Nordin M (eds). *Basic Biomechanics of the Skeletal System,* ed 2. Philadelphia, PA: Lea & Febiger; 1989.

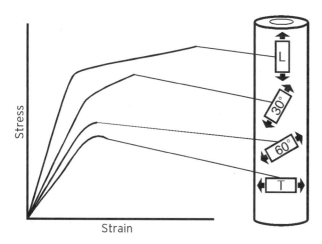

Figure 3.5 Forces and moments applied to bone in various directions produce tension, compression, bending, shear, torsion, and combined loading. *Source:* Reproduced with permission from Frankel VH, Nordin M (eds). *Basic Biomechanics of the Skeletal System*, ed 2. Philadelphia, PA: Lea & Febiger; 1989.

Fracture Categories

Fractures are characterized according to the injured bone, the location of the fracture in that bone, the amount of fracture displacement or malalignment, and the condition of the soft-tissue envelope about the injured bone[10] (see **Table 3.1**).

Fractures are generally categorized using a mechanistic classification that describes both the orientation of the fracture line and the degree of displacement. The initial clinical examination, however, separates fractures into closed fractures, which

are associated with varying degrees of soft-tissue injury, and open fractures, in which either the bone has protruded through the skin or a penetrating injury has caused the fracture. The descriptive terms "open" and "closed" are now preferred to the older traditional terms "compound" and "simple." Further classification includes differentiation between nondisplaced fractures, in which a radiographic cleft can be seen but no gap exists between the fracture fragments, and displaced fractures, in which a gap or malalignment can be seen on radiographs (see **Figure 3.6**).

Fracture displacement is described as distracted, shortened, translated, or angulated. Distracted displacement (in which there is a visible gap at the fracture site) generally occurs due to the weight of an unsupported, injured limb. This condition often is seen in a midshaft humeral fracture. Oblique and spiral fractures of long bones frequently become shortened due to muscular forces, and the degree of shortening can often be estimated by measuring the radiographic displacement. Translational displacement occurs when traumatic or muscular forces cause malalignment, with or without angulation of the fracture fragments; in other words, a fracture may be well aligned (axes of the bone are parallel) but translationally displaced in any direction.

Table 3.1

Basic Fracture Categories

Fracture Type	Description
Nondisplaced	Bone fragments are in anatomic alignment
Displaced	Bone fragments are no longer in their usual anatomic alignment
	Malaligned fragments: angulated displacement
	Distal fragment longitudinally overlaps the proximal fragment: bayonetted displacement
	Distal fragment separated from the proximal fragment by a gap: distracted displacement
Closed	A fracture with no associated penetrating skin wound
Open	Fragments of bone protrude through the skin, or an external wound leads to the fracture site

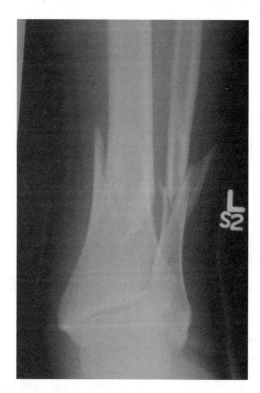

Figure 3.6 A radiograph demonstrates displaced fractures of the shaft of the tibia and fibula. The displaced fractures show translational displacement, shortening, and angulation. The spiral pattern of the fractures suggests a twisting mechanism combined with axial loading.

Angulation is described based on the apex of angulation, which may be described as medial, lateral, anterior, or posterior in any extremity. For example, a midshaft femoral fracture that has assumed a flexed position has the apex of angulation directed anteriorly. In the forearm, the apex of angulation is frequently described as toward the radius or ulna, or the volar or dorsal direction. Specific orthopaedic terms used to describe angulation in the coronal plane are varus (away from the midline) or valgus (toward the midline).

Radiologic Techniques

Plain radiographs, fluoroscopy, computed tomography (CT), and magnetic resonance imaging (MRI) are used to definitively diagnose fractures. Plain radiography is often the only radiologic technique required to confirm the presence, shape, and severity of a fracture. Fractures involving the articular surface may require the use of CT or MRI to confirm the diagnosis. MRI also is useful in identifying intra-articular loose bodies, skeletal malformations, and associated soft-tissue lesions.

Scintigraphy (bone scans) is a type of nuclear medicine used to image increased bone-related metabolic activity associated with stress fractures or diseases. With this technique, a radioisotope such as technetium (Tc-99m) is injected into the patient's body. Once enough time has been allotted to allow the isotope to be absorbed, the body part is imaged. Areas of increased uptake of the isotope may be indicative of a stress fracture. Scintigraphy has some shortcomings, however: It indicates only the area of increased metabolic activity, lacks the precise anatomic detail of other imaging techniques, and does not definitively diagnose the presence of a stress fracture.

Evaluation of a Suspected Fracture

The typical signs and symptoms of a suspected fracture are pain, swelling, tenderness, loss of function, and occasionally crepitus or deformity.[10] The diagnosis is obvious when angulation is severe. Nonetheless, with a deformity near the end of a long bone, ligament injury, joint dislocation, and growth plate injury must be included in the differential diagnosis. A deformed extremity such as a protruding bone is always a dramatic physical finding that can distract from other, potentially

more serious trauma such as chest, abdominal, or brain injury.

The initial evaluation of a suspected fracture should always include a careful neurologic and vascular examination distal to the injury. The presence and symmetry of pulses and motor and sensory function for all major nerves crossing the injured site must be documented. The initial examination is extremely important because a worsening neurologic presentation usually warrants aggressive intervention.

Radiographic evaluation of a suspected fracture should include two views taken 90° from each other and encompassing both adjacent joints. If a fracture is suspected but not seen on initial radiographs, additional special views may be taken, or CT or MRI studies may be considered.

Fracture Types

Greenstick Fracture

A greenstick fracture occurs in response to a bending force (see **Figure 3.7**). With this type of injury, the side that experiences tension will fracture. The cortex on the side experiencing compression remains intact but undergoes plastic deformation. Thus bone fails on the weaker tension side, and the stronger compression side maintains its integrity, despite bending through plastic deformation. The resultant fracture appears as a transverse fracture into the midsubstance of the bone, intersecting with a longitudinal fracture. Bones in children tend to have a relatively low content of inorganic material and higher extracellular matrix content compared with adults; as a consequence, children's bones are more pliable and more likely to bend without break-

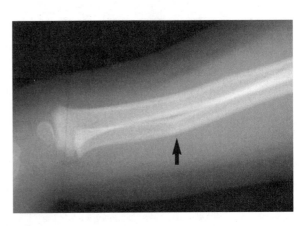

Figure 3.7   Greenstick fracture. This type of fracture is prevalent in children because of their pliable bones.

ing. If untreated, greenstick fractures may continue to displace for up to 2 weeks following the injury.

Differential Diagnosis

Because greenstick fractures occur exclusively in children, the differential diagnosis for any deformity near the end of a long bone must include injury to the growth plate or ligaments. Greenstick fractures must be differentiated from buckle fractures, which are stable and are managed more conservatively.[11] However, greenstick fractures usually occur in the diaphysis or metadiaphysis and typically remain significantly angulated after injury, leaving little doubt as to the diagnosis.

Prognosis

The prognosis for a greenstick fracture depends on the degree of initial displacement. In nearly every greenstick fracture involving a long bone in a growing patient, 10° of angulation may be acceptable. In certain patients (those with varus angulation of the tibia, for example), more precise restoration is required. Angulation of as much as 10° in the diaphysis of a long bone is usually readily remodeled to normal alignment during the healing process. In contrast, a greenstick fracture near the end of the long bone may sometimes develop progressive angulation, particularly in the proximal tibia, requiring long-term follow-up.

Although a greenstick fracture can often be partially reduced by applying external forces and a cast, it is sometimes necessary to anesthetize the patient and complete the fracture on the compression side to adequately reduce the malalignment. This reduction of the malalignment without a skin incision is termed a closed reduction. Greenstick fractures are almost always treated with closed reduction rather than open surgical reduction, and reduction is maintained by external means such as a cast or splint rather than internal fixation.

Remodeling is generally far more rapid in children than in adults. Remodeling of angular deformities is particularly rapid when the deformity occurs in the same plane of motion as the nearest joint or when the deformity is found near a rapidly growing physis. Remodeling of rotational deformities is less reliable and should not be expected to provide an acceptable result. Closed reduction for rotational deformities is recommended.

■ Transverse Fracture

Transverse fractures result from a direct blow or pure bending forces, which produce a fracture line that is perpendicular to the long axis of the bone (see **Figure 3.8**). The weaker tension side of the bone fails before the compression side. If an

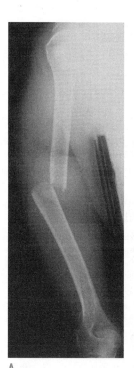 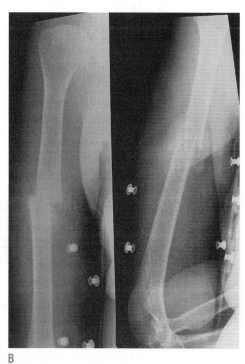 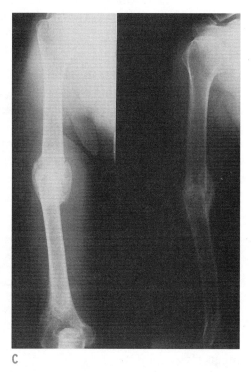

A   B   C

Figure 3.8 This transverse fracture of the humeral shaft was treated with application of an external fracture brace. (**A**) Initial radiograph. (**B**) Radiographs at 4 weeks demonstrate the formation of early peripheral callus. (**C**) Radiographs at 4 months. The fracture healed with minimal varus angulation.

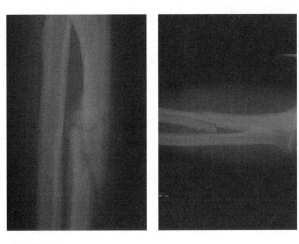

Figure 3.9 Radiographs showing nightstick, or tapping, fractures of the ulna.

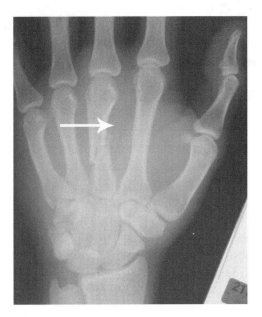

Figure 3.10 Radiograph showing an oblique fracture of the third metacarpal (arrow).

axial load is applied to the bone at the time of the bending force, the bone typically fails with a "butterfly" fragment on the concave side of the bending forces.

An example of a typical transverse fracture is a "nightstick" fracture of the ulna, which is caused by a direct blow to the subcutaneous surface of the ulna. Sometimes called a "tapping" fracture, this type of injury is often seen in lacrosse players (see **Figure 3.9**).

Prognosis
These low-energy injuries can often be treated nonsurgically. The prognosis is generally good if there is no displacement and the fracture is closed.

Oblique Fracture

Oblique fractures occur in response to compressive (axial) loads. In this type of injury, the bone fails through shear forces, producing a fracture line approximately 45° to the long axis (see **Figure 3.10**). The failure mechanism usually involves oblique breaking of the osteons, and these fractures tend to occur in the metaphysis.

Differential Diagnosis
Oblique fractures typically demonstrate some shortening due to the mechanism of injury (longitudinal or axial loading) and angulation at the fracture site. These fractures may be differentiated from spiral fractures by their radiographic appearance: Oblique fractures appear to have blunt ends, whereas spiral fractures usually have sharp ends like the nib of a fountain pen.

Prognosis
The prognosis for an oblique fracture depends on the amount of initial displacement. Minimally displaced fractures are frequently treated nonsurgi-

cally. Fractures that have significantly shortened the bones disrupt the blood supply to the bone ends and often require surgery. The amount of initial displacement has also been correlated with the time required for bone healing. Severely displaced oblique fractures may require bone grafting to obtain bony union.

Spiral Fracture

Spiral fractures occur as a result of torsion, a twisting about the long axis of the bone that produces a helical fracture line (see **Figure 3.11**). A spiral fracture is characterized by a fracture line that twists around the bone and is connected by a longitudinal fracture line. Shear, compressive, and tension loads occur during torsion. The fracture occurs due to failure in shear followed by failure in tension.

Prognosis
Internal fixation, either with an intramedullary rod for a midshaft fracture or with a plate and screws near the end of a bone, is often the treatment of choice for severely displaced spiral fractures.

Avulsion Fracture

Avulsion fractures occur from tensile loading at the site of ligament or tendon insertion (see **Figure 3.12**). A sudden traction load applied to the ligament or tendon pulls, or avulses, a fragment of bone away from the epiphysis or metaphysis. Common sites for avulsion fractures include the greater tuberosity of the humerus, the various apophyses about the pelvis,

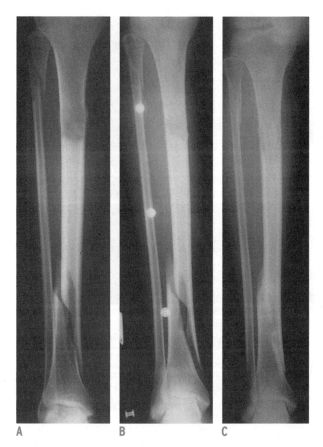

Figure 3.11 A spiral fracture of the distal tibia and proximal fibula. (**A**) Initial radiograph. (**B**) Radiograph 10 days later (taken through a brace). (**C**) Radiograph at 1 year.

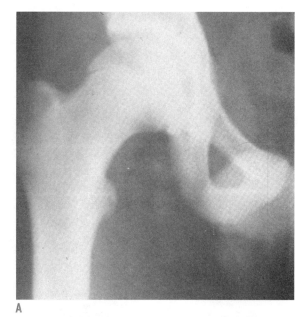

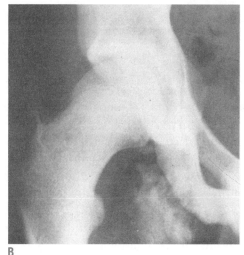

Figure 3.12 Radiographs of an avulsion fracture of the ischial tuberosity. (**A**) Anterior view. (**B**) Posterior view.

the tibial tubercle, and the styloid process of the fifth metatarsal.[12]

Prognosis

The prognosis for an avulsion fracture depends on the location and amount of displacement. As little as 5 millimeters of displacement in a greater tuberosity fracture may warrant surgical reduction and fixation to restore normal rotator cuff function. Conversely, avulsions of the ischial apophysis or anterior-superior iliac spine of the pelvis are often widely displaced but rarely require surgical management. In general, avulsion fractures are treated surgically if they occur very close to a joint or if the degree of displacement suggests they may not heal in a position allowing restoration of normal function.

■ Comminuted Fracture

A comminuted fracture involves failure of the bone at two or more sites (see **Figure 3.13**). Such a fracture is the result of compression, tensile, or shearing forces or some combination of these forces. Comminution at a fracture site indicates that the bone has absorbed a large quantity of energy before failure (fracture) and significant soft-tissue injury may have occurred to the nerves, muscles, and blood vessels around the fracture site. The term *segmental fracture* is used to describe a fracture of the bony diaphysis in two separate places—a pattern seen exclusively in high-energy injuries such as violent collisions. Another common type of comminuted fracture is a shattering injury to either the tibial plateau or tibial plafond or the distal radius, in which the joint surfaces are broken into multiple pieces by a sudden, violent axial load.

Prognosis

The goals of treatment for comminuted fractures are generally the same as for other fracture patterns. However, because these fractures are high-energy

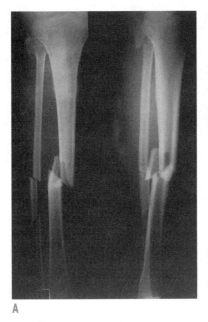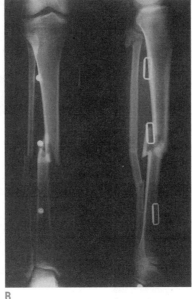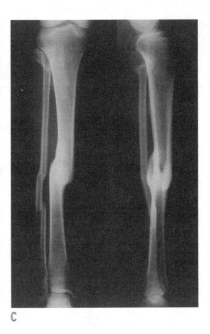

Figure 3.13 A comminuted fracture associated with a two-segment fibular fracture. (**A**) Initial radiographs. (**B**) Radiographs at 2 weeks (taken through a brace). (**C**) Radiographs at 11 months.

injuries, it is usually more difficult to maintain anatomic length and alignment with closed methods, and surgery is often indicated. Fractures involving the articular surface usually require open reduction to restore normal alignment of the joint surface, followed by internal fixation using screws and buttress plates or, occasionally, an external fixator. Even if the fracture heals in the correct anatomic position, joint stiffness, pain, and posttraumatic arthritis are common outcomes.

Epiphyseal Fracture

Epiphyseal fractures involve the separation of the epiphysis from the bone between the shaft and its growing end. Epiphyseal fractures can occur as a result of shearing, avulsion, splitting, or crush mechanisms.

The Salter-Harris classification describes damage to the epiphyseal plate, with or without a fracture (see **Figure 3.14**). A type I injury has no bony fracture, but the epiphysis separates at the level of the entire physeal plate. Type II injuries, which are the most common pediatric fractures, involve separation of part of the epiphysis from the metaphysis through the physeal plate, plus a metaphyseal fracture. In type III injuries (which rarely occur), the fracture line extends from the joint space to the physeal plate and then laterally to the edge of the plate, separating the fractured epiphysis from the metaphysis. Type IV fractures extend from the

joint space through the growth plate and across the metaphysis. A type V fracture is a severe crush injury of the physeal plate itself. Displacement is unusual, and the injury may go unnoticed.

Prognosis

When adequately reduced by closed reduction, type I and II Salter-Harris epiphyseal fractures usually have a good prognosis, even if they are less than perfectly reduced. Type II injuries, however, lead to growth disturbances in 5% of children. Type III fractures must be reduced perfectly, potentially requiring an open technique and wire fixation; even when this technique is used, however, the prognosis is usually poor. Type IV fractures almost always require open reduction and smooth wire fixation. The prognosis is poor for type IV and V fractures. Interruption of growth of the epiphyseal growth plate often accompanies type V fractures.

The significance of a fracture involving the epiphysis or physis is that a subsequent disturbance in growth may occur. Early fusion of the epiphysis may lead to a growth disturbance, and asymmetric fusion through a fracture line may result in progressive angulatory deformity as the uninjured portion of the physis grows while the injured portion does not. In skeletally immature patients, physeal and epiphyseal injuries should be followed by a pediatric orthopaedic surgeon to identify potential growth disturbances.

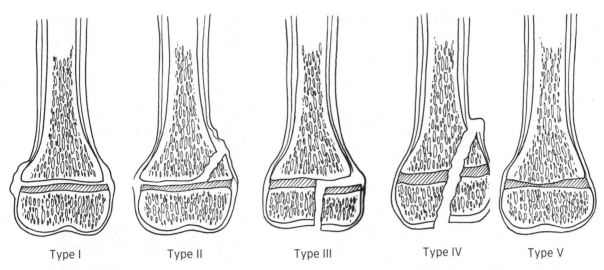

Figure 3.14 Salter-Harris classification of fractures. Type I is characterized by physeal separation; type II by a fracture line that extends transversely through the physis and exits through the metaphysis; type III by a fracture that traverses the physis and exits through the epiphysis; and type IV by a fracture line that passes through the epiphysis, across the physis, and out the metaphysis. Type V is a crush injury to the physis.
Source: Reproduced with permission from Kay RM, Matthys GA. Pediatric ankle fractures: evaluation and treatment. *J Am Acad Orthop Surg.* 2001;9:268-278.

▨ Impacted Fracture

A result of compressive forces, impacted fractures have one side of the fracture wedged into the interior of the other end of the bone (see **Figure 3.15**). Impacted fractures generally occur in the metaphyseal regions because of axial loading: The more rigid cortical diaphysis is typically forced into the cancellous metaphysis. These types of fractures occur most frequently in aging individuals with osteoporosis. Many impacted fractures can be treated nonsurgically, provided there is no worrisome angulation through the fracture site or significant (more than 5 mm) intra-articular depression.

Prognosis

The prognosis for impacted fractures is generally good unless the fracture extends into the joint and causes articular irregularities. Severe impaction leading to angulation of the metaphysis or articular surface also may require open reduction to restore normal joint range of motion. In general, the cancellous bone surfaces in impacted fractures heal very rapidly. Therapeutic motion may be started immediately because these fractures are usually stable.

▨ Intra-articular Fracture

Intra-articular fractures involve a portion of the articular surface of the joint and are frequently caused by severe axial loads or combined axial loading and angular deviation (see **Figure 3.16**). The articular cartilage and underlying bone are typically fractured. Intra-articular fractures involve the joint surfaces at the ends of the bone and often require surgical management to restore articular congruity.

Differential Diagnosis

Pain, swelling, significant joint effusion, and severe restriction of joint motion occur as the result of an intra-articular fracture. A lipohemarthrosis is essentially always present in articular fractures because of leakage of the bone marrow contents into the articular space. Lipohemarthrosis is sometimes visible on plain radiographs as the fat layers above the blood in the joint. Occasionally, the fracture line is not visible, but lipohemarthrosis confirms the diagnosis, either radiographically or with aspiration of the affected joint. Intra-articular fractures commonly affect the tibial plateau of the knee, the articular surface of the ankle, and the radial head in the elbow joint.

lipohemarthrosis
Fatty cells within the synovial membrane.

> **Practice Tip**
> Intra-articular fractures are best identified using multidetector CT scans rather than film radiographs.[13]

Prognosis

Articular fractures can occasionally be treated nonsurgically if displacement is minimal. In general, fractures with less than 1 millimeter of articular displacement can be managed nonsurgically, but any step displacement greater than this distance usually mandates open reduction to restore a smooth joint surface. Fractures of the tibial plateau

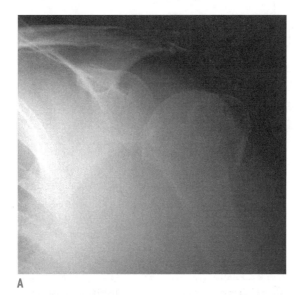

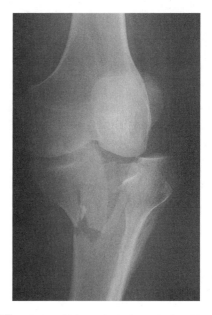

Figure 3.16 A displaced intra-articular fracture of the tibial plateau.

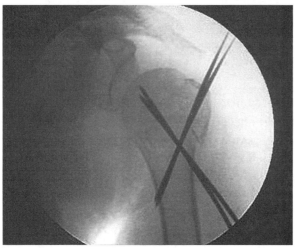

Figure 3.15 Impacted fracture of the humerus. (**A**) Anteroposterior view demonstrating a nondisplaced four-part fracture of the humeral shaft. (**B**) Radiograph obtained after open reduction and fixation using Kirschner wires and transosseous sutures.

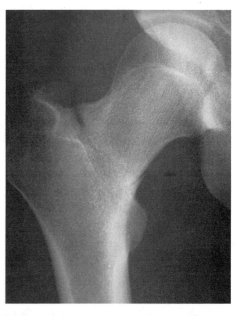

Figure 3.17 Anteroposterior radiograph of the proximal femur of a 19-year-old Marine recruit reveals a fatigue fracture on the superior portion of the femoral neck.

may have a smooth depression in the center of the articular surface; in these cases, as much as 5 millimeters of depression can be managed nonsurgically. Occasionally, external fixation with pins and a frame can be used to stabilize the fracture. As long as stable fixation can be achieved, early motion of articular injuries can result in excellent function, although the risk of posttraumatic arthritis remains increased.

■ Stress Fracture

Stress fractures occur in bone that is actively remodeling because of the application of new or unfamiliar stresses to the bone (see **Figure 3.17**). When a runner suddenly increases mileage or an athlete

adds a conditioning technique such as plyometric squats, for example, new stresses are applied to normal bone. The bone responds by reabsorbing some of the existing bone and laying down new osteons along the lines of the new stress. During this period of remodeling, the bone temporarily becomes weaker and may be unable to withstand the new stresses. This weakening often occurs about 3 weeks after a new activity is initiated and manifests itself as a stress reaction or stress fracture.

Insufficiency fractures—a subset of stress fractures—occur in abnormal bone that is unable to withstand the normal stresses of daily activity. These fractures are common in elderly osteoporotic women and frequently occur about the hip or knee.

The signs and symptoms of a stress fracture are pain and tenderness without deformity. Tibial shaft stress fractures typically present with little pain at rest, but pain is experienced when the individual arises and takes the first few steps in the morning. This pain generally subsides with modest activity such as walking, and the patient may even be able to run a short distance before progressively acute pain limits activity. In severe or neglected stress fractures, the symptoms may progress to the point that weight bearing is not possible and pain is experienced even at rest.

Most stress fractures are treated nonsurgically, with restriction of painful activity and a gradual return to weight-bearing exercise within the limits of pain. Radiographs are usually obtained at intervals during healing to ensure that a fracture line has not developed and that the injury is healing. Surgical management is generally reserved for fractures that persist for a long period or develop a nonhealing fracture line. Stress fractures that are usually treated surgically include the Jones fracture of the proximal fifth metatarsal and the tibial fracture that develops the "dreaded black line," indicating a fracture with poor potential for healing.

A stress fracture of the femoral neck is a special case. The consequences of undertreating a stress fracture of the femoral neck are potentially more dire than those for fractures in other anatomic locations: A complete fracture of the femoral neck may result in loss of the blood supply to the femoral head and subsequent need for hip replacement. Athletes with stress fractures of the femoral neck are typically runners who present with groin pain approximately 3 weeks after adding mileage or changing their running surface or shoe type. A change in activity almost always precedes the development of a stress fracture; the only exception is the distance runner with osteoporosis who develops an insufficiency fracture without a change in activity. Pain is generally relieved by modest activity but builds up during the course of a run and eventually necessitates a cessation of activity. Initial radiographs of the hip are usually normal. Any patient with a suspected femoral neck stress fracture should be immediately placed on restricted weight bearing with crutches until a confirmatory test such as a bone scan or MRI can be obtained.

Stress fractures of the femoral neck are classified into two types that differ radiologically and in clinical outcome. The first is the tension stress fracture, which originates at the superior surface of the femoral neck and results in a transverse fracture directed perpendicular to the line of force transmitted in the femoral neck. Such injuries carry the risk of further advancement of the fracture line superiorly and eventual displacement, leading to nonunion and osteonecrosis. Hence, early diagnosis and treatment of a tension stress fracture are essential.

The second type is a femoral neck compression stress fracture, which is evidenced by internal callus formation in radiographs. The fracture is usually located at the inferior margin of the femoral neck without cortical discontinuity and is thought to be mechanically stable. This type of compression fracture occurs mostly in younger patients, and continued stress typically does not cause displacement. The earliest radiographic evidence of a compression stress fracture is a haze of internal callus in the inferior cortex of the femoral neck. Eventually, a small fracture line appears in this area and gradually scleroses.

Differential Diagnosis

Initial radiographs are generally negative in the evaluation of a suspected stress fracture; consequently, other potential differential diagnoses must be ruled out. With tibial pain, these possibilities include medial tibial stress syndrome and compartment syndrome. For suspected stress fractures of the femoral neck, differential diagnoses include iliopsoas bursitis and referred pain from the low back. Additional imaging, such as a bone scan or MRI, often is required to confirm the diagnosis of a stress fracture.

Imaging Techniques

Plain radiographs, scintigraphy, CT scans, and magnetic resonance images (or MRI scans) have been used to identify stress fractures, but each has certain limitations. Radiographs are only 15% accurate on the initial (early) image and 50% accurate on the subsequent follow-up. Scintigraphy images are nonspecific for stress fractures, and other pathologies, including tumors, infections, and inflammation, may produce false-positive results. CT scans provide the best detail of the osseous structures but lack sensitivity. The use of this technology is indicated for specific conditions and as a follow-up to positive findings on other imaging modalities. Research indicates that MRI provides the best sensitivity and specificity for most types of stress fractures. Early stress fractures

nonunion Failure of a bone to heal within 9 months following the initial fracture.
osteonecrosis Bone death secondary to a decreased blood supply; avascular necrosis.

are best identified by using short tau inversion recovery (STIR) or T2-weighted images; more developed stress fractures are best identified using T2- or T1-weighted images.[14]

> **Practice Tip**
>
> When available, MRI is the imaging modality of choice for the early identification of stress fractures.[14]

Prognosis

High-risk stress fractures may progress to a complete fracture, nonunion, malunion, and/or osteonecrosis (see **Table 3.2**).[15] Early diagnosis and treatment are essential to prevent these sequelae. Stress fractures due to compression are generally thought to be mechanically stable. After the internal callus develops, a small fracture line appears and gradually scleroses.

sequelae Conditions resulting from an injury or disease.

Fracture Management

Fracture management consists of seven elements (see **Table 3.3**). In general, fractures in athletes are treated more aggressively than the same injuries in the general population, to allow for early motion of the adjacent joints, preserve muscle tone and mass, and expedite return to activity. Although internal fixation of a fracture does not speed healing, it may allow accelerated rehabilitation. Considerations differ depending on the nature of the fracture and the stability of the fracture site. Unique requirements of nondisplaced, displaced, and angulated closed and open fractures must be considered.[16]

Table 3.2

High-Risk Stress Fracture Sites

Femoral neck (tension side)

Patella

Anterior cortex of the tibia

Medial malleolus

Talus

Navicular

Fifth metatarsal

First metatarsophalangeal joint sesamoids

Source: Adapted from Boden BP, Osbahr DC. High-risk stress fractures: evaluation and treatment. *J Am Acad Orthop Surg.* 2000;8:344.

Table 3.3

Basic Steps in Fracture Management

Step 1: History.

Step 2: Physical examination.

Step 3: Laboratory and radiographic investigations.

Step 4: Obtain reduction if the fracture is not in an acceptable position (closed reduction by manipulation or surgical open reduction).

Step 5: Maintain reduction (application of external immobilization using an external splint, cast, or brace, or surgical internal fixation using a plate and screws, intramedullary rod, or external fixator).

Step 6: Systemic therapeutic exercise such as cardiovascular exercise to maintain conditioning level; therapeutic exercise can also be performed on the uninvolved extremities.

Step 7: Rehabilitation of the involved body part once healing has occurred.

■ Nondisplaced Fracture

Nondisplaced fractures often require little treatment beyond immobilization, analgesics, and time to heal. If the fracture is stable and nondisplaced, all that may be required is protection (a cast or a splint), along with measures to decrease swelling and pain (ice; elevation; and analgesics, nonsteroidal anti-inflammatory drugs [NSAIDs], or both) for 24 to 48 hours, followed by progressive mobilization with weight bearing as comfort permits. An appropriate rehabilitation program should be carried out as the fracture heals.

■ Displaced and Angulated Fracture

Angulated and displaced fractures may not be in acceptable positions. Angulation often can be corrected by manipulation under anesthesia. Displaced fractures can occasionally be treated with closed reduction under anesthesia followed by placement of a cast, but more often they require surgery. Unstable fractures are at risk of shifting during healing; consequently, patients with these injuries usually need surgery for stabilization and realignment. Many fixation constructs are available for surgical intervention. These devices, which can be used individually or in combination, include screws, a variety of fracture-specific plates, intramedullary nails, wires, and external fixators. The device selection depends on the type of fracture and the surgeon's preference.[17]

3

In general, fracture treatment attempts to preserve the biology of fracture healing while restoring the anatomy. Although open application of plates and screws provides excellent and immediate stability, stripping the periosteum and removing the normal fracture hematoma often slows the healing process. Contemporary techniques of percutaneous fixation and intramedullary nailing help to preserve the normal fracture biology and speed healing.

Closed Fracture

Closed fractures are managed based on their angulation and displacement (as described previously).

Open Fracture

Open fractures are a surgical emergency requiring immediate evaluation and treatment. Appropriate management includes early surgical debridement and irrigation of the fracture site. These fractures are usually stabilized acutely with internal or external fixation so as to splint the soft tissues and allow wound management. Although excellent results can be expected with lower-grade open fractures, fractures involving extensive stripping of the periosteum, contamination, or vascular injury often require multiple surgical procedures to prevent infection and obtain bony union. Even in the best of settings, open fractures with compromised blood supplies have an ominous prognosis. Fractures associated with vascular injuries that compromise the perfusion of the distal limb result in a 50% amputation rate.

Complications

Complications with fractures can be grouped into three categories—life-threatening complications, limb-threatening complications, and complications having local effects (see **Table 3.4**).

Rehabilitation Implications

The goal of surgical management of any fracture is to provide an anatomic reduction and enough stability to allow accelerated rehabilitation. If the limb needs to be immobilized after surgical treatment of a fracture, surgical management is generally considered to have been a failure. The exceptions are segmental fractures, significantly comminuted fractures, and fractures involving vascular injuries.

Stable fracture patterns (transverse, short oblique, and minimally displaced) can generally be treated with aggressive mobilization of adjacent joints and partial weight bearing. Full weight bearing is allowed as soon as fracture healing is apparent on follow-up radiographs. Unstable fracture patterns (comminuted, long oblique, and most spiral fractures) are generally treated surgically and then with protected weight bearing, whereas adjacent joints are mobilized. Weight bearing is restricted until fracture healing is documented.

Therapeutic modalities have also been used as adjuncts to therapy. For example, low-intensity ultrasound has been approved by the U.S. Food and Drug Administration to accelerate healing in new

---

Table 3.4

Fracture Complications

Life-Threatening	Limb-Threatening	Local Effects
Fat-embolism syndrome	Compartment syndrome	Delayed union
Shock	Joint contracture	Malunion
Sepsis (cellulitis, gas gangrene, necrotizing fasciitis)	Chronic osteomyelitis	Nonunion
Pulmonary embolism	Chronic vascular insufficiency	Chronic nerve damage
Acute compartment syndrome	Reflex sympathetic dystrophy (complex regional pain syndrome)	Osteonecrosis
Vascular damage		

malunion Healing of a bone in a faulty position, creating an imperfect union.

sepsis The spread of an infection into the bloodstream, creating a systemic condition.

fractures and to treat nonunions. Electric bone stimulation has been used for traumatic fractures of long bones, failed joint fusion, infantile pseudarthrosis, and pseudarthrosis of the spine. In addition, some practitioners have begun using low-power lasers to promote healing in stress fractures. Other interventions claimed to promote bone healing include growth hormone, thyroid hormones, calcitonin, insulin, vitamin A, vitamin D, anabolic steroids, chondroitin sulfate, hyaluronidase, hyperbaric oxygen, growth factors, demineralized bone matrix, and bone marrow cells.

Healing times vary greatly, but bone is generally stable in 6 to 8 weeks. Age, nutrition, smoking, type of bone, and location of fracture are all factors that influence fracture healing time.

Communication forms the foundation of developing a rehabilitation plan. The perceived compliance of the patient and the fracture pattern dictate the amount of activity allowed. Most surgeons approve an accelerated rehabilitation protocol performed under the strict supervision of an athletic trainer or physical therapist. Such a protocol is also predicated on stable internal fixation and a compliant patient. A prescription for prolonged immobilization should be questioned, because the long-term deleterious consequences of immobility have been well documented.

References

1. Walker NA, Denegar CR, Preische J. Low-intensity pulsed ultrasound and pulsed electromagnetic field in the treatment of tibial fractures: a systematic review. *J Athl Train.* 2007;42:530–535.

2. Della Rocca GJ. The science of ultrasound therapy for fracture healing. *Indian J Orthop.* 2009;43:121–126.

3. Busse JW, Bhandari M, Kulkarni AV, Tunks E. The effect of low-intensity pulsed ultrasound therapy on time to fracture healing: a meta-analysis. *CMAJ.* 2002;166:437–441.

4. Dijkman BG, Sprague S, Bhandari M. Low-intensity pulsed ultrasound: nonunions. *Indian J Orthop.* 2009;43:141–148.

5. ter Haar G. Therapeutic applications of ultrasound. *Prog Biophys Mol Biol.* 2007;93:111–129.

6. Romano CL, Romano D, Logoluso N. Low-intensity pulsed ultrasound for the treatment of bone delayed union or nonunion: a review. *Ultrasound Med Biol.* 2009;35:529–536.

7. Bassett CAL. Electrical effects in bone. *Sci Am.* 1965; 213:18–25.

8. Frankel VH, Burstein AH. *Orthopaedic Biomechanics.* Philadelphia, PA: Lea & Febiger; 1970.

9. Frankel VH, Nordin M (eds). *Basic Biomechanics of the Musculoskeletal System,* ed 2. Philadelphia, PA: Lea & Febiger; 1989.

10. Harkness JW, Ramsey WC, Harkness JW. Principles of fractures and dislocations, in Rockwood CA, Green DP, Buchholz RW (eds): *Rockwood and Green's Fractures in Adults,* ed 3. Philadelphia, PA: JB Lippincott; 1991.

11. Randsborg PH, Sivertsen EA. Distal radius fractures in children: substantial difference in stability between buckle and greenstick fractures. *Acta Orthop.* 2009;5:585–589.

12. Heineck J, Wolz M, Haupt C, et al. Fifth metatarsal avulsion fracture: a rational basis for postoperative treatment. *Arch Orthop Trauma Surg.* 2009;129:1089.

13. Arora S, Grover SB, Batra S, Sharma VK. Comparative evaluation of postreduction intra-articular distal radial fractures by radiographs and multidetector computed tomography. *J Bone Joint Surg.* 2010;92A:2523–2532.

14. Moran DS, Evans RK, Hadad E. Imaging of lower extremity stress fracture injuries. *Sports Med.* 2008;38:345–356.

15. Boden BP, Osbahr DC. High-risk stress fractures: Evaluation and treatment. *J Am Acad Orthop Surg.* 2000;8:344–353.

16. Cherubino P, Bini A, Marcolli D. Management of distal radius fractures: treatment protocol and functional results. *Injury.* 2010;41:1120–1126.

17. Busse JW, Morton E, Lacchetti C, Guyatt GH, Bhandari M. Current management of tibial shaft fractures: a survey of 450 Canadian orthopedic trauma surgeons. *Acta Orthop.* 2008;79:689–694.

18. Boutis K, Willan A, Babyn P, et al. Cast versus splint in children with minimally angulated fractures of the distal radius: a randomized controlled trial. *CMAJ.* 2010;182: 1507–1512.

3

II Lower Extremity

Foot, Ankle, and Leg Pathologies

Jay Hertel, PhD, ATC,
FNATA

TOE INJURIES

First Metatarsophalangeal Joint Sprain

CLINICAL PRESENTATION

History
Hyperextension of the first MTP joint.
First MTP joint pain.

Observation
Swelling and possible discoloration of the first MTP joint.

Functional Status
Antalgic gait with toe off shifted laterally to the lesser toes.

Physical Examination Findings
Tenderness over the first MTP joint line.
Reduced or painful first MTP joint range of motion.
Exacerbation of pain with valgus stress and/or hyperextension of the first MTP joint.
Pain and difficulty with heel raises (pushing up onto toes).

Traumatic injuries to the first metatarsophalangeal (MTP) joint are common in field and court sports that require athletes to make quick changes of direction. Collectively, injuries to this joint often are referred to as "turf toe," although the injuries can actually occur on any surface. Sprain of the joint capsule of the first MTP joint is often caused by hyperextension of the joint as the athlete changes direction. The addition of varus or valgus forces coupled with hyperextension may cause injury to the first MTP joint capsule. Injury to the fibrocartilaginous plantar plate may also occur in some cases. In severe cases, the first MTP joint may be dislocated.

Even minor injuries to the first MTP joint may be disabling because a large proportion of body weight is transferred through this joint during the push-off phase of gait. Severe or unresolved injuries to this joint may result in hallux rigidus or hallux valgus deformities and lead to altered gait patterns and disability.

Differential Diagnosis
First MTP joint sprain, first MTP joint dislocation, sesamoid fracture, sesamoiditis, fracture of the first metatarsal, fracture of the first proximal phalanx, hallux rigidus, hallux valgus.

Imaging Techniques
Anteroposterior (AP) and lateral imaging may be ordered to rule out bony injury and evaluate joint alignment. Degenerative changes, such as hallux rigidus, may be noted in chronic cases. Magnetic resonance imaging (MRI) may prove useful in determining the extent of ligamentous damage and plantar plate involvement. In addition, diagnostic imaging should rule out sesamoid fracture and bipartite sesamoids (see **Figure 4.1**).[1]

> **bipartite** A congenital or traumatic splitting of a structure into two parts.

4

Definitive Diagnosis
The definitive diagnosis is based on the patient's history, clinical findings, and the absence of evidence of acute trauma on radiographs.

Pathomechanics and Functional Limitations
Normal foot mechanics place a significant amount of stress on the first MTP joint. When a person walks, 30% to 50% of the body weight is transferred to this joint. During activities such as running and jumping, the forces applied to the first MTP joint are magnified to three to eight times body weight. Stresses applied to an injured MTP joint must be limited until healing is sufficient to tolerate even the relatively low-level forces experienced during walking. Prolonged injury can result in hallux rigidus, hallux valgus, or both.

■ Immediate Management
Immediate treatment includes the usual course of rest, ice bag, compression, and elevation.

■ Medications
Nonsteroidal anti-inflammatory drugs (NSAIDs) may be prescribed in the early postinjury phase of rehabilitation. In higher-level athletes, the physician may inject the joint directly with a combination of anti-inflammatory and analgesic medications.

■ Surgical Intervention
Surgery is indicated if an MTP joint dislocation cannot be reduced. In contrast, surgery is unnecessary for routine turf toe conditions unless the plantar plate is ruptured.

■ Postinjury/Postoperative Management
Treatment of first MTP joint injuries is typically conservative. Nevertheless, in cases of first MTP joint dislocation, severe ligamentous disruption, or chronic joint degradation, surgery may be indicated.[2] Initial management of acute injury should include the usual course of rest, ice, compression, and elevation. NSAIDs may be prescribed to assist in limiting inflammation and pain early in the treatment process. Use of a rigid shoe insert, often consisting of a flat steel plate, is recommended, as is the wearing of a firm-soled shoe. If the patient is unable to execute a normal gait pattern without

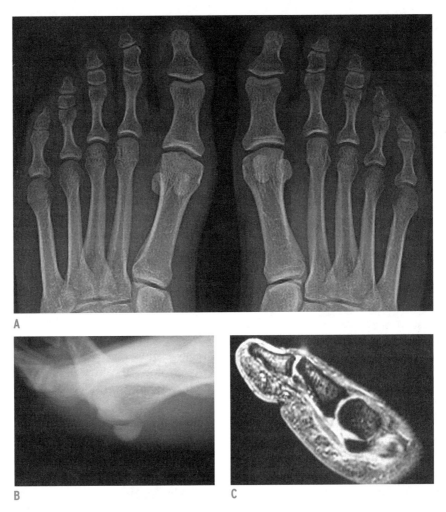

Figure 4.1   Imaging of "turf toe" injury. **(A)** Radiograph demonstrating retraction of the sesamoids (left image) relative to the uninvolved side. **(B)** Lateral view showing sesamoid retraction. **(C)** Sagittal T2-weighted MRI scan that identifies disruption of the plantar plate just distal to the sesamoids.

limping, assistive devices such as crutches or a cane should be used. The wearing of high-heeled shoes should be avoided completely during recovery from this injury because of the increased stress placed on the first MTP joint with an elevated heel.

Injury-Specific Treatment and Rehabilitation Concerns

> **Specific Concerns**
>
> Limit first MTP joint extension.
> Encourage early, pain-free ROM.
> Control inflammation.
> Restore joint motion.

During rehabilitation, emphasis should be placed on restoring normal joint motion in both non-weight-bearing and weight-bearing conditions. The use of joint mobilizations may be useful in restoring normal ROM. Strengthening of the intrinsic and extrinsic muscles of the foot through exercises such as towel curls, marble pickups, and the short-foot exercise is encouraged. Weight-bearing exercises such as heel raises should be added in a graduated manner, with care being taken not to aggravate the first MTP joint during such maneuvers. A return to normal walking and running mechanics may be assisted with underwater gait exercises. Cutting exercises should be introduced cautiously, and protective taping and a rigid shoe insert should be used initially to protect the first MTP joint (see **CT** 4.1). Return to play should be allowed once full range of motion (ROM) of the first MTP joint has been restored, a normal gait pattern has been achieved, and the athlete is able to spring, cut, jump, and land without pain.

Estimated Amount of Time Lost

If normal ambulation and running are possible with a grade I sprain, the patient may continue sport participation with shoe modifications and toe

CT **Clinical Technique** 4.1

Turf Toe Taping

A   B   C

D   E   F

Application

1. Cut a 2-in.-wide piece of moleskin (**A**).
2. Place the great toe in a neutral position. Place anchors around the distal phalanx of the great toe and one around the midfoot (**B**).
3. Using the moleskin, apply a checkrein that spans the plantar surface of the foot and toe between the anchors (**C**).
4. Use 1-in. tape to connect the anchors, taping from the toe to the foot. Apply strips on the plantar surface to prevent hyperextension, on the dorsal surface to restrict hyperflexion, or on both surfaces to keep the toe immobile (**D**).
5. Spica wraps may be applied to further support the joint (**E**).
6. Complete the taping by repeating the anchor strips around the distal toe and midfoot (**F**).

taping. A grade II sprain can restrict participation for 2 to 4 weeks, whereas a grade III sprain can result in 6 to 8 weeks lost from activity.[3] Although a properly treated turf toe may heal in 2 to 8 weeks, disability may be prolonged because of the secondary effects of injury and the MTP joint stress applied during normal activity. If the condition is chronic or has not been treated appropriately, even lengthier disability may ensue. Chronic turf toe delays the return to normal participation. Older patients with compromised distal lower extremity circulation will require a longer recovery period.

■ Return-to-Play Criteria

Full ROM (70° to 90° of extension) and strength of the intrinsic foot muscles, especially the first digit flexors and abductors, must be restored to preinjury levels. The patient should be able to push off from each foot, jump and land, cut and stop suddenly, sprint forward and laterally, and run posteriorly on the involved foot without difficulty.

Functional Bracing

A stiff-soled shoe or a stiff insert such as a steel foot plate placed in the shoe will reduce pain during ambulation.[1] Such a modification should be continued once the athlete has returned to activity to further protect the toe and reduce stresses applied to it. Graphite or rolled steel insoles can be manufactured and inserted in any shoe. Toe-spica taping to restrict extension can also allow the patient to return to full function more comfortably (see CT 4.1).

Sesamoiditis

CLINICAL PRESENTATION

History
Insidious onset of pain on the plantar aspect of the first MTP joint.
Pain is exacerbated with great toe hyperextension during weight bearing, as in the terminal stance during gait.

Observation
Swelling and/or calluses may be localized under the first MTP joint.
Reduced first MTP flexion and extension may be noted.
Pes cavus or a plantar-flexed first ray may be observed.

Functional Status
Antalgic gait with toe-off shifted laterally to the lesser toes.

Physical Examination Findings
Tenderness over the sesamoids and plantar aspect of the first MTP joint.
Decreased first MTP joint extension.
Pain and difficulty with heel raises (pushing up onto the toes).

The two sesamoid bones are embedded within the tendon of the flexor hallucis brevis and are stabilized by strong intrinsic ligaments (see **Figure 4.2**). These bones are lined with hyaline cartilage and are interconnected with the plantar plate of the first MTP joint. The sesamoids slide proximally (during flexion) and distally during extension; they provide an increased mechanical advantage to the flexor hallucis brevis during flexion. Repetitive tensile forces applied to the sesamoids during weight bearing, especially when the first MTP joint is hyperextended, can lead to irritation of the sesamoids. Although the larger medial sesamoid receives more stress than the lateral sesamoid, sesamoiditis may occur in either bone. Sesamoiditis is characterized by inflammation of the hyaline cartilage, periosteum, and subchondral bone. If it is unresolved, deterioration of the sesamoid joint surfaces may occur and lead to chronic conditions such as hallux rigidus or hallux valgus.

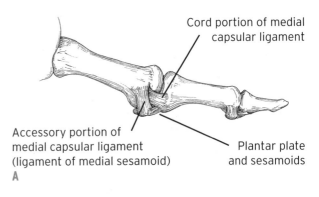

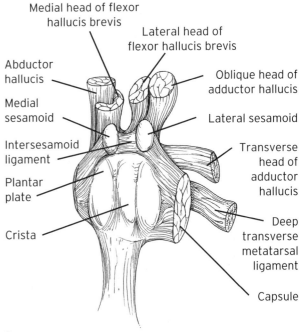

Figure 4.2   Anatomy of the hallux. (**A**) Components of the medial capsular ligament. (**B**) Intrinsic muscles and ligaments surrounding the sesamoids. The intrinsic muscles have been dissected and moved distally to show the plantar aspect of the first metatarsophalangeal joint. *Source:* Adapted from Richardson EG. Injuries to the hallucal sesamoids in the athlete. *Foot Ankle.* 1987;7:228-244.

Differential Diagnosis
Acute sesamoid fracture, sesamoid stress fracture, first MTP joint sprain, hallux rigidus, hallux valgus, medial plantar neuropathy.

Imaging Techniques
Standard AP views of the sesamoids should be augmented by medial oblique and lateral oblique views in an effort to identify fractures or degeneration of the sesamoids (see **Figure 4.3**). Some individuals may develop congenital bipartite sesamoids, in which one of the sesamoids is formed in two distinct pieces. The presence of bipartite sesamoids does not indicate pathology. A bone scan can be helpful in revealing increased metabolism consistent with periosteal inflammation at the site of the sesamoids.

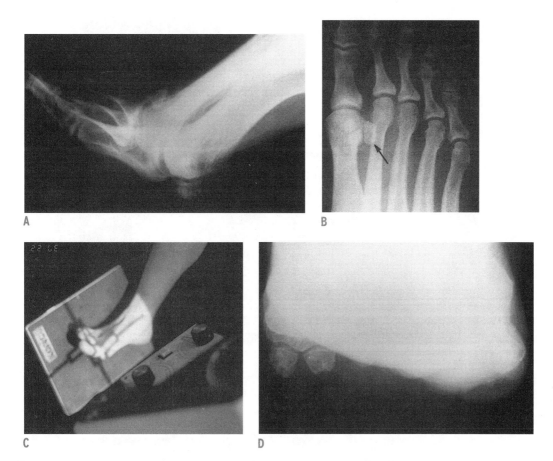

Figure 4.3   Radiographic imaging techniques for the sesamoids. (**A**) Medial oblique view. (**B**) Lateral oblique view (arrow highlights sesamoids). (**C**) Technique for posteroanterior axial view. (**D**) Axial view demonstrating medial sesamoid degeneration.

Definitive Diagnosis

Diagnosis is confirmed through a thorough physical examination, radiographic findings, and elimination of other possible diagnoses.

Pathomechanics and Functional Limitations

Pain is the primary factor limiting activity. If weight-bearing stresses under the first metatarsal head are not reduced, the inflammatory process will continue, further limiting function. With time, pain, muscular compensation, and deterioration of the joint surfaces may alter the first MTP joint biomechanics and lead to other conditions such as hallux rigidus or hallux valgus.

▇ Immediate Management

Ultimately, pain will dictate the activity tolerance. As a treatment for acute symptoms, ice and NSAIDs may be used to decrease pain and inflammation. Additionally, the use of customized padding on the plantar surface of the foot may reduce pressure under the sesamoids (see **Figure 4.4**). Efforts should be made to avoid hyperextension of the first MTP joint. Wearing high-heeled shoes should be avoided, as they increase the loading on the first MTP joint.

If symptoms are so severe that they do not allow the individual to achieve a pain-free gait, an assistive device should be used. In more chronic cases, corticosteroid injection at the site of injury may be warranted.

▇ Medications

An NSAID in conjunction with the immediate management can help to control pain and inflammation. Corticosteroids also can aid in treating this problem; an injection resolves pain more quickly than oral medication.

▇ Surgical Intervention

If conservative treatment fails, open excision of a chronically injured sesamoid may be required (see **Figure 4.5** and **Figure 4.6**). In this procedure, all or part of the sesamoid is removed, with great care being taken to not damage the flexor hallucis brevis tendon or surrounding ligaments. After surgery, the patient is initially restricted from first MTP joint extension. Soft-tissue mobilization will be useful if adhesions are palpated postoperatively. Restoration of the mobility of the remaining sesamoid is an

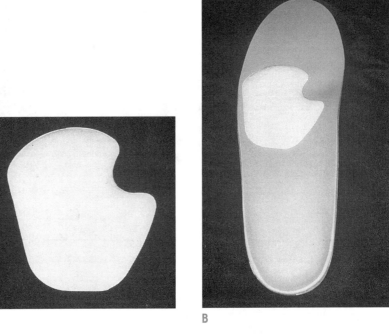

Figure 4.4   Padding to reduce weight-bearing forces on the sesamoids. **(A)** Pad cut from felt or similar material with a cutout for the sesamoids (upper right). **(B)** The pad is affixed to the patient's orthosis or shoe insert. Note the added dimple under the weight-bearing area of the sesamoids.

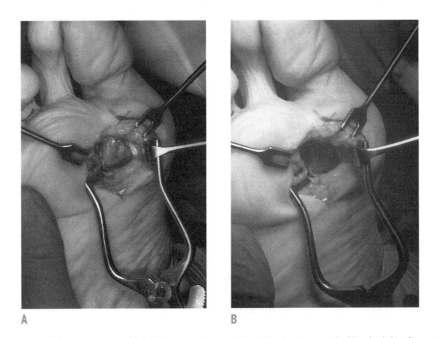

Figure 4.5   Surgical excision of the lateral sesamoid. **(A)** The incision is made from the plantar aspect of the foot. The flexor hallucis longus tendon and neurovascular bundle must be identified and protected. **(B)** View after sesamoid removal.

important treatment goal. Rehabilitation focuses on pain-free restoration of first MTP motion and strengthening of the great toe flexors.

Postoperative Management

Postoperatively, the tendon and incision are protected by limiting weight bearing and MTP joint hyperextension. Instruct patients to avoid wearing high-heeled shoes, as they extend the great toe and focus weight-bearing forces on the sesamoids. Taping and padding may assist the athlete in returning to sport participation sooner, but should not be used after surgery to shorten the recovery process.

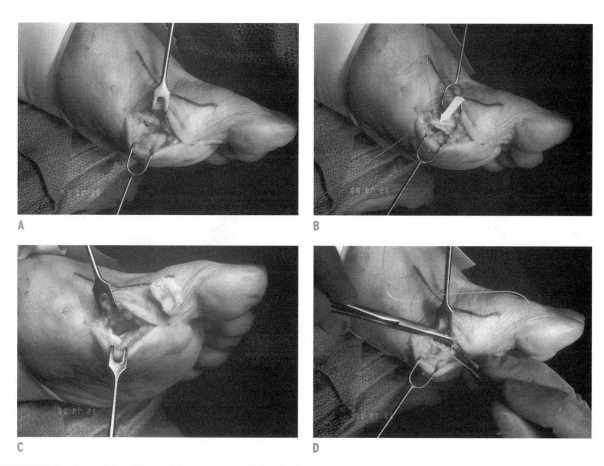

Figure 4.6 Surgical excision of the medial sesamoid. (**A**) This incision is made along the medial joint line. (**B**) The plantar medial hallucal nerve is identified and avoided. (**C**) The medial sesamoid is excised. (**D**) The joint capsule is sutured closed, and the flexor hallucis brevis tendon is repaired.

▦ Injury-Specific Treatment and Rehabilitation Concerns

> **Specific Concerns**
>
> Reduce weight-bearing forces on the sesamoids.
> Limit great toe extension, especially during weight bearing, in the early stages of treatment.
> Progress to flexion-extension ROM exercises.
> Strengthen the toe flexors.

Accommodative changes in footwear can help to relieve symptoms of sesamoiditis[4,5] (see **Table 4.1**). If footwear alterations do not sufficiently reduce pain, then use of crutches, a short leg cast, or a brace may be necessary.[5]

If palpation reveals scar-tissue adhesions, soft-tissue mobilization techniques may improve the mobility of the sesamoids and permit their movement during toe flexion and extension. If the MTP and interphalangeal joints have lost their normal accessory movement, grade III and IV AP, posteroanterior, and lateral glides and rotational joint mobilization can aid in restoring mobility once inflammation has subsided.

If these techniques are not successful, the athlete may need to wear a below-knee, non-weight-bearing brace or cast for 4 to 8 weeks to accomplish the desired goals. If symptoms persist despite this conservative approach, surgical excision may be necessary.

Table 4.1

Footwear Modifications to Relieve Sesamoiditis

Lower heels of the shoes.

Use a shoe with a thick, medium to firm outer sole.

Use a stiff-soled shoe to decrease first MTP joint extension.

Insert a pad with a soft insole.

Insert a pad that extends just proximal to the head of the first metatarsal to decrease weight-bearing loads on the sesamoids.

Carve a depression in the insole of the shoe to accommodate the sesamoids.

Use a custom-made orthotic.

Estimated Amount of Time Lost

If adequate stress reduction can be accomplished with footwear modifications, no time from competition may be lost. In contrast, if pain is severe, the patient may need to restrict the pressure applied to the area by reducing or halting the offending activity until inflammation subsides. If surgical excision is the treatment, an extended recovery time will be necessary, lasting perhaps 3 to 4 months.

Return-to-Play Criteria

Return to play should be allowed once full ROM of the first MTP joint has been restored, a normal gait pattern has been achieved, and the athlete is able to sprint, cut, jump, and land without pain.

Functional Bracing

Use of a stiff shoe insert and/or continued padding to relieve pressure on the sesamoids may be used when athletes return to sport.

Hallux Valgus

CLINICAL PRESENTATION

History

Insidious onset of deformity and pain of the first MTP joint.

Observation

Obvious valgus deformation of the first MTP joint.
Medial prominence of the first MTP joint, often called a bunion, which may be obviously irritated from rubbing against the interior of the shoe.
Pes planus.

Functional Status

Full weight bearing is possible but symptoms are often exacerbated during the terminal stance.
Patient is more comfortable without shoes.

Physical Examination Findings

Tenderness on the medial aspect of the first MTP joint.

Hallux valgus is a term that can refer to both a malalignment of the first MTP joint and chronic pathology at this joint. The malalignment occurs when the first metatarsal head angles excessively toward the medial border of the foot and the first proximal phalanx angles laterally toward the midline of the foot (see **Figure 4.7**). A prominent exostosis, or bunion, often forms on the medial aspect of the joint. This deformity, which is more common in women than in men, can become a source of pain and discomfort.

exostosis A bone spur or bony overgrowth.

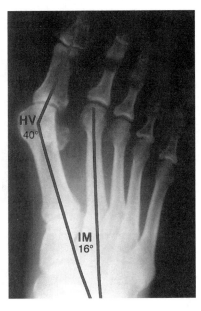

Figure 4.7 The hallux valgus (HV) angle is formed by the intersection of lines bisecting the first metatarsal and the first phalanx of the great toe. The normal angle is approximately 15°. (The radiograph demonstrates a 40° angle.) The angle between the first and second metatarsals (intermetatarsal [IM] angle) should be less than 9°.

Symptoms will occur insidiously and may become worse if the foot is not treated appropriately. If the malalignment is allowed to progress, the medial aspect of the joint capsule can become chronically inflamed and the surfaces may begin to degenerate. In addition to arthrosis developing in the first MTP joint, the mechanical efficiency of the great toe flexor mechanism may become more inefficient with increasing malalignment. As the joint surfaces shift medially, the flexor hallucis brevis tendons and the sesamoids often do not migrate concurrently. The subsequent loss of alignment between the sesamoid complex and the first MTP joint will alter mechanics during the push-off phase of gait. The medial protrusion of the first MTP joint may rub against the inside of shoes, particularly those with narrow toe boxes, and further exacerbate symptoms. Lastly, the second MTP joint may become symptomatic in advanced cases as the first and second metatarsal heads separate and the second MTP joint loses medial stability.

Differential Diagnosis

Hallux rigidus, sesamoiditis, rheumatoid arthritis, gout.

Imaging Techniques

Weight-bearing radiographs are helpful to quantify the amount of deformation and the amount of joint surface degeneration. A valgus angle of greater

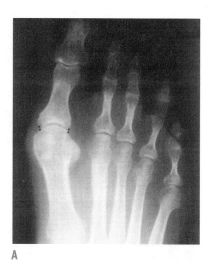
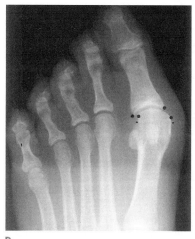

A   B

Figure 4.8   Congruency of joint surfaces in the presence of hallux valgus. (**A**) Congruent joint surfaces. The surfaces are parallel, and there is no lateral subluxation of the metatarsal head. (**B**) Subluxation associated with hallux valgus. The joint surfaces are not parallel, and the proximal phalanx is subluxated laterally relative to the metatarsal head.

than 15° is considered diagnostic (see **Figure 4.8**). The divergence between the first and second metatarsal heads should also be examined to assess for pathology at both joints.

Definitive Diagnosis

The hallmark of hallux valgus is an angle greater than 15° between the proximal phalanx and first metatarsal. Positive physical findings and confirmatory radiographic findings are diagnostic.

Pathomechanics and Functional Limitations

When the joint is altered, normal function is impaired. Notably, during the movement from a terminal stance to pre-swing, the foot passively rolls over the lateral metatarsal heads rather than over the first MTP joint. A hallux valgus deformity commonly develops in a hypomobile foot as the forefoot remains pronated during the last half of stance, when it should be supinating. As the heel is raised from the ground in the terminal stance and the foot remains pronated, the forces are directed to the medial aspect of the great toe, with little force being distributed to the lateral aspect of the foot. Over time, repetitive great toe stress first causes a callus buildup over the medial aspect of the toe, and then the MTP joint and the sesamoid bones subluxate, resulting in medial capsule stretching and stress to the great toe tendons and the second toe.

▥ Medications

NSAIDs may be prescribed to control the acute local inflammatory process. Although not commonly used, a corticosteroid injection may be con-

sidered with severe pain and associated MTP joint degeneration.

▥ Management

Hallux valgus is a self-limiting condition. When it is symptomatic, patients may be treated with cryotherapy and NSAIDs in an effort to control pain and inflammation. A felt spacer can be placed between the first and second toes, and the first toe can also be pulled medially with a medial checkrein in an effort to straighten the alignment of the first ray (see **Figure 4.9**). In addition, a doughnut pad may be used directly over the bunion to reduce rubbing against the inside of the shoes. Patients must be advised to avoid the wearing of shoes with narrow toe boxes, especially high-heeled shoes. Foot orthotics may be useful in patients with considerable pes planus. If conservative treatments fail and a patient's symptoms, malalignment, and joint degradation continue, surgical management should be considered.

▥ Surgical Intervention

Several surgical techniques can be used to correct a hallux valgus deformity. The nature and cause of the deformity, the patient's complaints, the radiographic findings, and the surgeon's preference will all factor into the decision-making process.[6] In competitive athletes, hallux valgus surgery is indicated only after the career is completed or when shoe modifications, inserts, and NSAIDs have failed and the patient is unable to compete because of pain.

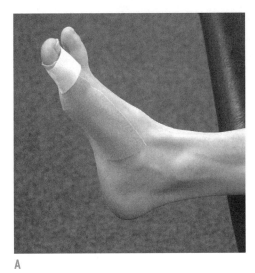
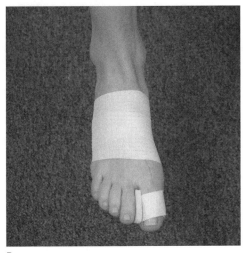

A

B

Figure 4.9 Taping for hallux valgus. (**A**) Moleskin is used to apply a mild varus force to the great toe. (**B**) Padding between the first and second toes assists in discouraging the valgus alignment.

A distal osteotomy with a soft-tissue procedure and occasionally a proximal phalanx osteotomy is most often performed on competitive athletes[7] (see (ST) 4.1). If hallux rigidus is concurrent, the dorsal 25% to 35% of the first metatarsal head and spurs are removed. Some surgeons include a dorsal closing-wedge osteotomy of the proximal phalanx. The goal is to obtain 90% of MTP joint extension at surgery.

Postoperative Management

The patient is instructed to wear shoes that have adequate forefoot width and a low heel. Avoid high-heeled and pointed-toe shoes, as they place high compressive forces on the first MTP joint. Although orthotics designed to correct pes planus do not correct the hallux valgus, they may nevertheless reduce the rate of deformity progression.

The toe can be taped with a medial checkrein to reduce the valgus deformity. A felt or soft rubber insert can be placed between the first and second toes to further reduce the angulation. A doughnut pad reduces pain caused by a bunion.

Injury-Specific Treatment and Rehabilitation Concerns

Specific Concerns

Wear proper footwear to decrease external forces on the deformity.

If a bunion is present, protect it with a doughnut pad.

Correct foot biomechanics with an orthotic if indicated.

Rehabilitation of nonsurgical hallux valgus is founded in identifying the possible causes of the deformity and reducing the pain associated with it. Individuals with concurrent pes planus may benefit from use of orthotics, as they may stop the degenerative progression linked to hallux valgus. Altering footwear assists in reducing pain. Shoes with rigid or leather uppers are more irritating to hallux valgus than shoes with soft uppers made of cloth or nylon mesh. MTP joint padding to reduce pressure on the tender area may also reduce pain. Shoes should have a toe box of adequate width into which the forefoot fits comfortably.

After surgical correction, graduated ROM activities, joint mobilization, and gradual return to activities as pain allows are sufficient for the patient to resume a normal level of function. Strengthening the intrinsic foot muscles is necessary. Gait training may be necessary if the patient reverts to the previous gait style.

Estimated Amount of Time Lost

Hallux valgus is a self-limiting condition. If the patient can wear a shoe that does not irritate the bunion, normal activities may be possible. If surgery is required, 3 to 6 months of recovery may be needed before full return to participation is possible, primarily because of the time required to relieve pain, wear shoes, and run without pain after surgery.

Return-to-Play Criteria

The patient must be able to wear the appropriate athletic shoe and run, cut, and jump without pain. The MTP joint must have near full ROM (at least

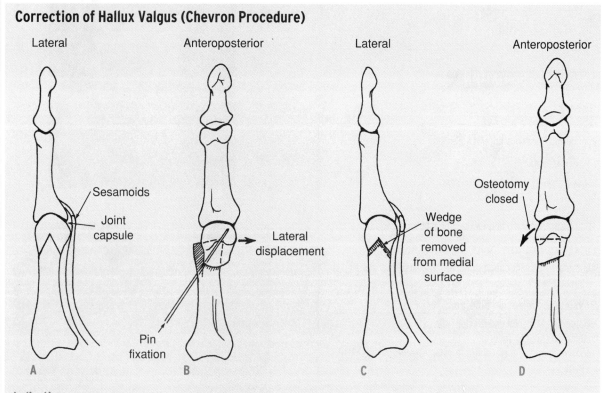

S|T Surgical Technique **4.1**

Correction of Hallux Valgus (Chevron Procedure)

Lateral   Anteroposterior   Lateral   Anteroposterior

Sesamoids

Joint capsule

Lateral displacement

Pin fixation

Wedge of bone removed from medial surface

Osteotomy closed

A   B   C   D

Indications

Hallux valgus angle less than 30° and an intermetatarsal angle of less than 13° that fail to respond to conservative treatment.

Procedure Overview

1. An incision is made over the medial aspect of the joint.
2. A chevron (V-shaped) wedge is cut into the distal metatarsal (**A**) and (**B**).
3. The head is translated laterally 4 to 5 mm. Occasionally a 1- to 3-mm wedge of bone is removed to correct the distal metatarsal articular angle (**C**).
4. The osteotomy is closed and fixated with a pin (**D**).

Functional Limitations

Great toe extension is often limited. Appropriate early great toe passive and active-assisted exercise can maximize extension. First ray shortening often results from this procedure.

Implications for Rehabilitation

High-impact activity must be avoided after osteotomy until radiographically proven healing occurs. MTP joint extension is emphasized, and tight-fitting shoes should be avoided.

Potential Complications

If the valgus deformity is too great, correction may be incomplete. Loss of internal fixation and osteonecrosis are also possible.

Source: Reproduced with permission from Mann RA. Disorders of the first metatarsophalangeal joint. *J Am Acad Orthop Surg.* 1995;3:34-43.

60° of dorsiflexion), full intrinsic muscle strength of the great toe muscles, and restored joint proprioception, balance, and agility.

Functional Bracing

Taping and protective inserts may help to support the first MTP joint; a doughnut pad under the medial aspect of the great toe can relieve pressure. Realigning the toe with anchor tape (as in taping for turf toe) may be helpful. The tape strips between the two anchors are applied to the medial side of the toe from the interphalangeal joint anchor to the midarch anchor while the toe is passively positioned in normal alignment. Once the toe tape strips maintain the toe in proper alignment, closing anchors are applied.

Hallux Rigidus

CLINICAL PRESENTATION

History

Previous history of first MTP joint pathology.
Pain during terminal stance of gait.

Observation

Gross deformity is not always present.
Dorsal or medial prominence on the first MTP joint may be present.
Triceps surae atrophy may be present in chronic conditions.

Functional Status

Abnormal mechanics during terminal stance lead to a more lateral toe-off.

Physical Examination Findings

Limited first MTP joint dorsiflexion ROM.
Inability to stand on toes.
Tenderness on the dorsal and/or medial aspect of the first MTP joint.

Hallux rigidus describes a degenerated first MTP joint that is characterized by limited dorsiflexion of the joint. Because at least 60° of first MTP joint dorsiflexion is needed for normal gait, a substantial dorsiflexion ROM will lead to abnormal terminal stance. Specifically, the patient with hallux rigidus will tend to hypersupinate and toe-off more on the lateral aspect of the foot as opposed to the medial side. Atrophy of the triceps surae may occur due to altered gait mechanics. Arthrosis of the joint often—but not always—occurs secondary to other pathologies such as hallux valgus, turf toe, or intra-articular fracture. A dorsal or medial osteophyte is often present (see **Figure 4.10**).

Differential Diagnosis

Hallux valgus, sesamoiditis, rheumatoid arthritis, gout.

Imaging Techniques

Radiographs will show degenerative changes at the first MTP joint. Particular attention should be paid to the presence of dorsal or medial osteophytes (see **Figure 4.11**).

Definitive Diagnosis

The diagnosis of hallux rigidus is confirmed by a physical examination demonstrating limited ROM in dorsiflexion and positive radiographic studies.

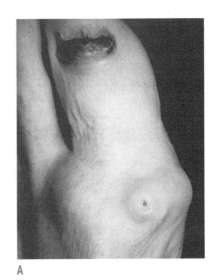

A

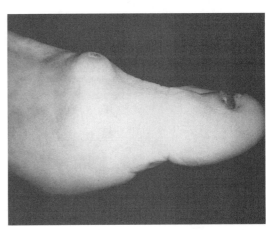

B

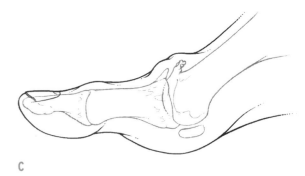

C

Figure 4.10   Osteophytes of the first metatarsophalangeal joint. **(A)** Dorsal view. **(B)** Lateral view. **(C)** Illustration of osteophyte. *Source:* (C) Reproduced with permission from *The Foot: Examination and Diagnosis.* New York: Churchill Livingstone; 1990:65.

Pathomechanics and Functional Limitations

Normal gait requires 60° to 75° of first MTP joint extension. When dorsiflexion is limited, the patient may ambulate with the foot supinated, vault over the toe during the terminal stance and pre-swing phases of gait,[2] or walk on the lateral foot border. Because the patient does not extend the first MTP or have a normal heel-off to toe-off gait, atrophy

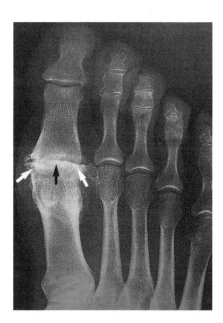

Figure 4.11 Anteroposterior view of hallux rigidus. A weight-bearing view demonstrates narrowing of the joint space (black arrow) and medial and lateral osteophytes (white arrows).

may be present in the involved calf.[8] Compensatory conditions at the knee or hip may occur secondary to gait alteration.

■ Immediate Management

Ice and immobilization are initiated for pain relief. Firm-soled shoes or rigid inserts to prevent excessive MTP joint motion are recommended.

■ Medications

Although NSAIDs are helpful in decreasing inflammation, they do little to resolve the overall problem. In severe cases, a corticosteroid injection may be helpful to control pain.

■ Surgical Intervention

Hallux rigidus is common, but the optimal surgical treatment remains unclear.[8–11] Surgery is indicated in competitive athletes for debilitating pain or when shoe modifications, taping, inserts, and NSAIDs have failed and the athlete cannot compete because of the pain.

Surgical techniques that may be potentially used include cheilectomy, proximal phalanx osteotomy, and arthroplasty, with excision of the phalanx or metatarsal or a prosthetic replacement sometimes being necessary.[8] A cheilectomy is the surgical technique recommended for athletes.[12] Proximal osteotomies, in which the base of the proximal phalanx is resected, are not used on athletes because they would disrupt the plantar plate and flexor hallucis attachments, resulting in decreased push-off strength.[12]

A more technically demanding procedure—distal osteotomy of the head of the first metatarsal with soft-tissue procedures—is often used to treat competitive athletes with hallux rigidus. Hallux rigidus surgery involves removing the dorsal 25% to 35% of the first metatarsal head and spurs. The goal is to achieve 90% of great toe MTP joint extension at surgery.

Great toe extension is often limited after surgery, but appropriate early great toe passive and active-assisted exercises can minimize this limitation. High-impact activity must be avoided after osteotomy surgery until radiographically proven healing occurs. Pain-free extension of the MTP joint should be emphasized. After hallux valgus surgery, tight-fitting shoes should be avoided, and the use of orthotics to limit or protect extension can be helpful.

■ Postinjury/Postoperative Management

Postinjury management is directed toward preventing reinjury, which is accomplished with rigid inserts to limit MTP joint motion and irritation and a wide toe box to prevent metatarsal head compression. Shoe modifications, including rigid inserts or firm-soled shoes, are recommended.

Postoperative care includes routine incision care, limited weight bearing, and an initial restriction of great toe extension and impact activities for several weeks. Following this period, passive and active ROM exercises should be employed in an effort to restore extension. A gradual return to functional activities may occur after 6 to 8 weeks. Shoes with narrow toe boxes and high heels should be permanently avoided.

■ Injury-Specific Treatment and Rehabilitation Concerns

> **Specific Concerns**
>
> Remove compressive MTP joint forces with appropriate footwear modifications.
> Limit forced MTP extension.
> Restore pain-free ROM into MTP extension.

Primary nonsurgical management for hallux rigidus includes reducing first MTP joint stress. This can be accomplished with shoe modifications, such as use of a rocker-soled shoe, stiff insert, or custom orthosis. If an osteophyte is present, a shoe that has an extra-deep or extra-wide toe box may be necessary. Doughnut pads may also assist in reducing pressure on the osteophyte. Rest and use of an NSAIDs should reduce any inflammation.

cheilectomy Surgical removal of bone spurs.

arthroplasty Joint replacement surgery.

Weight bearing is permitted in a wooden-soled or other stiff-soled shoe for 6 weeks postoperatively. At 1 to 2 weeks after surgery, when type I collagen begins to form in earnest at the operative site, MTP joint dorsiflexion exercises are initiated to encourage the newly forming collagen to align for optimal strength. As the athlete continues to heal and achieves adequate flexibility, strength gains are followed by the normal progression of therapeutic exercises for balance, coordination, and agility. Grade II joint mobilization may be used for initial pain relief, advancing to grade III and IV mobilizations after the surgical site is healed.

Estimated Amount of Time Lost

Patients treated nonsurgically are self-restricted by pain. Those who undergo surgical correction have recovery times ranging from 2 to 12 months, although the average time is less than 6 months.[10]

Return-to-Play Criteria

The patient must be able to wear the appropriate athletic shoe; run, cut, and jump without pain; and have full MTP joint ROM (at least 60° of dorsiflexion), full intrinsic muscle strength of the great toe muscles, and restored joint proprioception, balance, and agility.

Functional Bracing

Rigid inserts can protect against excessive MTP joint motion and prevent recurrence. Footwear modifications may be necessary, depending on whether osteophytes are present

FOOT INJURIES

Plantar Fasciitis

CLINICAL PRESENTATION

History

Insidious onset of plantar heel pain that may extend into the arch of the foot.
Pain with the first steps in the morning.
Pain with prolonged standing.

Observation

No obvious deformity, although swelling may be present at the calcaneal origin.

Functional Status

Antalgic gait and pain with prolonged standing.

Physical Examination Findings

Tenderness on the medial calcaneal tubercle.
Limited ankle dorsiflexion ROM (equinus foot).

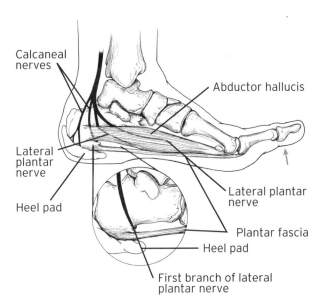

Figure 4.12 Location of nerves in proximity to the heel. The arrow indicates dorsiflexion. Inset: Windlass mechanism involving fascial attachment at the base of the proximal phalanges. *Source:* Reproduced with permission from Gill LH. Plantar fasciitis: Diagnosis and conservative management. *J Am Acad Orthop Surg.* 1997;5:109–117.

Inflammation of the plantar fascia near its insertion on the plantar medial aspect of the calcaneus is termed plantar fasciitis (see **Figure 4.12**). The plantar fascia is critical to providing tension to the medial longitudinal arch during weight bearing. This is particularly true during the propulsive phase of gait, as the windlass mechanism increases plantar fascia tension when the first MTP joint is extended. As the Achilles tendon simultaneously pulls on the posterior aspect of the calcaneus during the terminal stance, the plantar fascia can be subjected to further tension. With repetitive stress, the plantar fascia can become irritated and inflamed. In prolonged cases, an exostosis, or heel spur, may form on the calcaneal insertion (see **Figure 4.13**). Individuals with pes planus

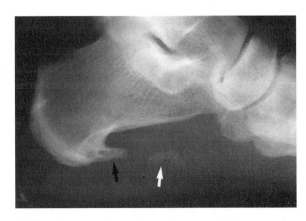

Figure 4.13 Lateral view of a heel spur. The black arrow highlights a large spur emanating from the distal calcaneal tubercle. Calcification is also seen distal to the spur (white arrow), representing calcification within the plantar fascia or a fracture of a preexisting spur.

or pes cavus may be at increased risk of developing plantar fasciitis. In some cases, the plantar fascia may be completely ruptured.

Plantar Fascia Rupture

Patients who have a plantar fascia rupture experience effects similar to those who opt for surgical release to relieve the pain. However, the long-term effects include a variety of possible injuries and deformities, such as longitudinal arch sprain, midfoot sprain, lateral plantar nerve dysfunction, stress fracture, hammer toe deformity, swelling, lateral column pain, and antalgic gait.[13] Many patients who experience a plantar fascia rupture have received corticosteroid injections. For this reason, corticosteroid injections and surgery as treatment options should be carefully considered.

Differential Diagnosis

Tarsal tunnel syndrome, contusion to the plantar surface of the foot, calcaneal stress fracture, plantar fascia rupture, seronegative spondyloarthropathy.

Imaging Techniques

Although radiographs may show development of a bone spur at the origin of the plantar fascia, neither the presence or absence of spurring is required for a diagnosis of plantar fasciitis. MRI may show thickening of the plantar fascia and other signal uptake indicative of inflammation and/or degradation of the fascia (see **Figure 4.14**).

Medical Diagnostic Tests

Nerve conduction velocity and electromyography exams are often used to rule out neurologic involvement.

Definitive Diagnosis

The diagnosis of plantar fasciitis is frequently one of exclusion: negative imaging studies, negative

electromyography and nerve conduction testing for tarsal tunnel syndrome, and negative bone scan for calcaneal stress fracture. Radiographs may reveal a bone spur, but this is not necessarily the cause of the plantar fasciitis. Often the diagnosis is based on the classic history and area of tenderness. In 10% of patients, another diagnosis, such as tarsal tunnel syndrome, also is present.[13]

Pathomechanics and Functional Limitations

Loss of normal foot flexibility and decreased dorsiflexion ROM redistribute the weight-bearing loads across the foot. Altered foot and ankle biomechanics can affect lower extremity biomechanics and predispose the patient to other repetitive stress injuries. Excessive plantar fascia load can be induced by barefoot walking, excessive or prolonged pronation, and being overweight.

Immediate Management

Ice and stretching with plantar fascia support are the foundations of treatment.

Medications

Initially, a course of an NSAID in conjunction with aggressive Achilles tendon stretching is indicated. If NSAIDs are ineffective, phonophoresis or iontophoresis may be performed. Although corticosteroid injections may provide immediate relief, they should be used cautiously because they predispose the patient to plantar fascia rupture and fat pad atrophy.[14]

Surgical Intervention

In patients who fail to respond adequately to an extended course of conservative intervention, surgery to release the plantar fascia may be considered.[15] Arthroscopic or open techniques are used

seronegative spondyloarthropathy An inflammatory condition of the spine that progresses to affect tendinous insertions throughout the body.

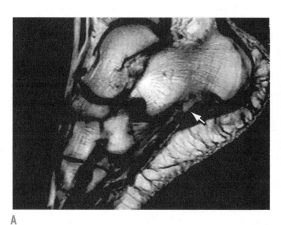
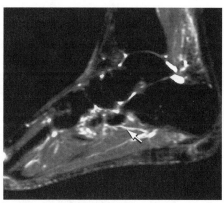

Figure 4.14 MRI of plantar fasciitis. (**A**) T1-weighted sagittal image demonstrating thickening of the plantar fascia at its origin from the medial calcaneal tubercle (arrow). (**B**) Sagittal short-tau inversion recovery (STIR) image showing high signal intensity in the deep plantar fascia (arrow).

to surgically release the inflamed medial band of the plantar fascia (see **ST** 4.2). When tarsal tunnel syndrome has also been documented, a simultaneous tarsal tunnel release is performed. While care must be taken to avoid damaging the lateral plantar nerve, fascia around this nerve is often released. The plantar fascia itself should not be completely severed in an effort to avoid complete arch collapse.

Patients should be immobilized in a boot or cast postoperatively. A gradual return to weight-bearing and gait activities must be undertaken. Return to sport typically takes several months postoperatively.

■ Postinjury/Postoperative Management

Therapeutic modalities and medications should be used to reduce pain and inflammation in patients with plantar fasciitis.[15] Although corticosteroid injections often prove helpful, caution must be exercised because the risk of plantar fascia rupture is increased after such an injection. In resistant cases, the use of extracorporeal shock-wave therapy may be used in an effort to break up bone spurs at the plantar fascia origin.[16]

Because barefoot walking is often bothersome in patients with plantar fasciitis, care should be taken to avoid this situation. Patients often complain of extreme pain with the first few steps of the day, so they should be encouraged to wear shoes even first thing in the morning. Use of a night splint that holds the ankle in dorsiflexion is often helpful in relieving symptoms. The use of orthotics may prove helpful in providing additional arch support to patients, particularly in those who hyperpronate. A heel cup or heel pad may provide better relief in some patients. Taping of the plantar fascia may be useful in controlling symptoms during athletic participation (see **CT** 4.2). Any weakness of muscle groups in the lower extremity should be assessed for and addressed with appropriate strengthening exercises.

S|T   Surgical Technique   4.2

Plantar Fascia Release

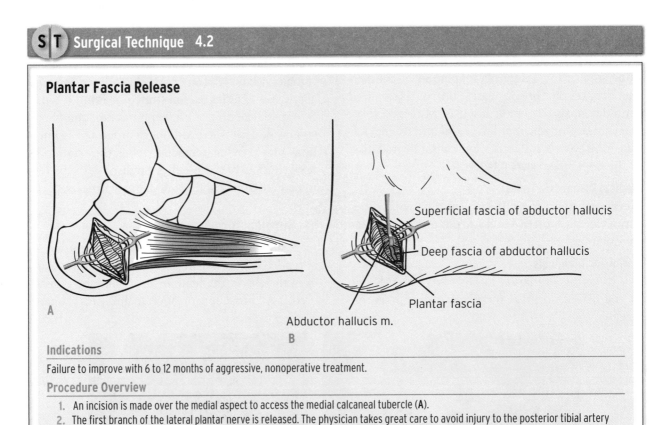

Indications

Failure to improve with 6 to 12 months of aggressive, nonoperative treatment.

Procedure Overview

1. An incision is made over the medial aspect to access the medial calcaneal tubercle (**A**).
2. The first branch of the lateral plantar nerve is released. The physician takes great care to avoid injury to the posterior tibial artery and nerve and the first and calcaneal branches of the lateral plantar nerve.
3. The medial 50% to 75% of the proximal plantar fascia is released, leaving the lateral band intact to decrease the risk of arch collapse.
4. The superficial and deep fascia of the abductor hallucis muscle are released (**B**).

Functional Limitations

Occasionally, patients will develop painful scarring and nerve pain. To minimize this risk, desensitization massage is started immediately.

Implications for Rehabilitation

Initially, protection (boot or cast) is needed, and high-impact activity is restricted for 2 to 3 months to avoid excessive arch collapse. Orthoses are used to support the remaining tissue and prevent excessive medial stresses.

CT Clinical Technique 4.2

Taping for Plantar Fasciitis

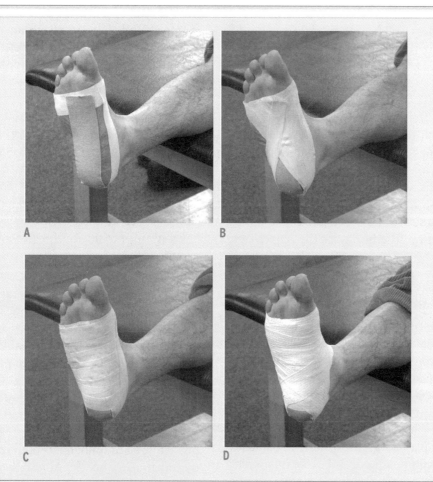

Application

1. Apply anchor strips over the plantar surface of the metatarsal heads, spanning from the lateral aspect of the fifth MTP joint to the medial aspect of the first MTP joint (do not cross the dorsal aspect of the foot). Another anchor runs from the lateral aspect of the fifth MTP joint to the medial aspect of the first MTP joint, crossing the midportion of the posterior calcaneus.
2. Pulling snugly, apply a 2- or 3-in.-wide piece of moleskin from the posterior anchor on the calcaneus to the metatarsal anchor (**A**).
3. Using 1-in. adhesive tape, apply "X" strips from lateral to medial, circling behind the calcaneus, starting with the fifth MTP joint. Repeat this process, moving the starting point medially with each strip (**B**).
4. To ensure calcaneal inversion and support the bone with a thicker fat pad beneath it, starting distally on the foot, apply stirrups from the lateral to medial anchors, overlapping half of the tape's width each time (1- or 1.5-in. tape may be used) (**C**).
5. End the procedure using 1.5-in. stretch tape (**D**).

■ Injury-Specific Treatment and Rehabilitation Concerns

Specific Concerns

Stretch the Achilles tendon complex.
Elongate the plantar fascia.
Strengthen the supporting musculature.
Control inflammation.
Correct the biomechanical causes contributing to the condition.

Plantar fasciitis is a chronic condition that frequently goes unattended for several months after onset, and 10% to 20% of patients may not experience complete pain relief even with treatment.[13,17] If pain levels can be controlled with conservative treatment, patients may be willing to endure occasional bouts of pain rather than undergo surgery. Avoiding unsupported weight bearing (e.g., bare feet, stocking feet, flip-flops) may prevent further aggravation of the inflammatory condition.

An aggressive stretching program for the Achilles tendon should be implemented in an effort to reduce stress on the plantar fascia.[14] Because of the amount of collagen in both the plantar fascia and the Achilles tendon, prolonged stretches that affect the plastic qualities of these structures provide the most benefit. Heating modalities should be applied before the stretches to optimize the tissues' viscoelastic properties.

Standing on an incline board with the heel down and the knee straight for 10 to 15 minutes can provide sufficient Achilles complex stretching. The patient can stretch the plantar fascia by passively extending the toes or, if pain and strength permit, standing on the toes. Each of these mechanisms relies on the windlass effect to stretch the fascia. The patient may also roll the arch over a rolling pin, bottle, or ball to stretch the fascia. To prevent discomfort, do not roll the heel over the object (see Figure 4.15).

In addition to a night splint and orthosis, taping the heel and plantar surface to stabilize and centralize the calcaneal fat pad under the calcaneus may provide more cushioning for ambulation. A semi-rigid or rigid orthosis to reduce overpronation or an accommodative orthosis for a rigid foot can decrease the torque or impact forces placed on the plantar fascia. A cast is sometimes used for 2 weeks in an attempt to reduce heel pain.

If the patient has a foot deformity that is contributing to the plantar fasciitis problem, orthoses may provide symptomatic control of the inflammatory process. If lower extremity strength is deficient, the muscles affected by the antalgic gait should be strengthened using a variety of exercises. Although any lower extremity muscle group can be affected by an antalgic gait, the hip abductors, hip extensors, and knee extensors are most often involved. If the patient has developed a habitual antalgic gait, gait correction should be included in the treatment program. An antalgic gait also results in muscle imbalances and weakness; thus, once an assessment of the entire lower extremity has been made, strengthening exercises for the affected muscles are undertaken.

Once the proper orthoses are provided, if needed, running mechanics should be assessed to ensure proper execution. The primary site of concern is rear-foot mechanics. Heel movement from inversion or an erect position just before initial contact, moving rapidly into eversion in the first half of weight bearing, with the heel moving into inversion or an erect position in the last half of weight bearing in preparation for pre-swing, should be examined.

Extracorporeal Shock-Wave Therapy

Extracorporeal shock-wave therapy has been used to treat plantar fasciitis in Europe for several years. In 2000, the Food and Drug Administration approved the use of extracorporeal shock-wave therapy devices for the treatment of plantar fasciitis in the United States.

Some controversy exists concerning the efficacy of extracorporeal shock-wave treatments. In contradictory reports, this approach has been reported to be of no benefit[18] and to be a successful treatment modality.[16,19] Although the therapy is not recommended as the first procedure for recalcitrant heel pain, significant improvements have been noted with its use.[20] Even so, the researchers who obtained these favorable results caution that pain is difficult to measure, their subjects had other procedures that might have contributed to the overall effects, and patients with heel pain often experience resolution without treatment.

■ Estimated Amount of Time Lost

In the case of plantar fasciitis, pain is self-limiting. Rupture of the plantar fascia may result in a minimum of 6 to 8 weeks' time lost from competition.

■ Return-to-Play Criteria

If foot biomechanics are abnormal (e.g., a very mobile foot with excessive pronation, a rigid foot with no pronation), an orthosis or taping may relieve the excessive stresses otherwise placed on the plantar fascia. Only patients with severe pain need to modify or restrict their activities. Pain reduction

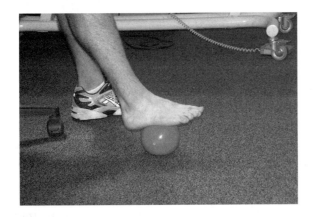

Figure 4.15 A ball, glass bottle, or roller can be used to stretch the plantar fascia. The patient presses down against the object and rolls it back and forth along the fascia, increasing pressure as tolerated. To prevent discomfort, instruct the patient to avoid placing pressure on the heel.

may occur with the use of orthoses, but some pain may still be present; however, this level is not sufficient to decrease the ability to perform.

Functional Bracing

Support for the fascia starts with not walking barefoot or in stocking feet or slippers, and using tape, heel cups, orthoses, or cross-trainer footwear. An accommodative orthosis may benefit patients with rigid arches. In contrast, individuals with a flexible foot will benefit from a rigid or semirigid orthosis that supports the arch and corrects excessive or early pronation.

Interdigital Neuroma (Morton's Neuroma)

CLINICAL PRESENTATION

History

Insidious onset of pain and numbness in the area of the metatarsal heads.
Radiation of symptoms distally into the toes and less often proximally into the foot.

Observation

No obvious deformity.
Antalgic gait.

Functional Status

Antalgic gait and pain with standing on the toes.

Physical Examination Findings

Intense pain with palpation of the neuroma or squeezing of the foot (Mulder sign).[21]

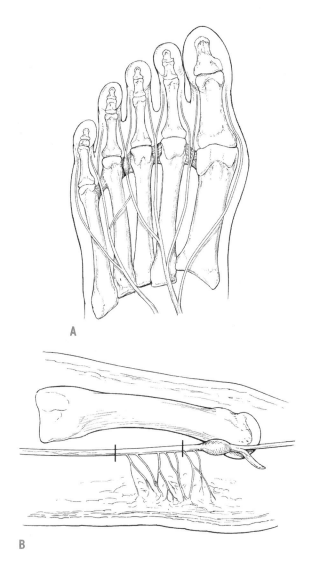

A

B

Figure 4.16 Anatomy of the interdigital nerves. (**A**) Normal anatomy of the plantar aspect of the foot. (**B**) Lateral view of the plantar branches of the digital nerve. *Source:* Reproduced with permission from Weinfled SB. Interdigital neuritis: Diagnosis and treatment. *J Am Acad Orthop Surg.* 1996;4:328-335.

Interdigital neuroma, frequently called Morton's neuroma or intermetatarsal neuroma, represents a compression of the interdigital nerve between the metatarsal heads.[22] This condition occurs most often between the second and third metatarsal heads or between the third and fourth metatarsal heads (see **Figure 4.16**). Repetitive irritation can result in development of a neuroma—that is, scar tissue around the nerve.

Each interdigital nerve innervates two toes. Although interdigital neuroma was initially thought to result from digital nerve compression, the condition is now believed to be potentially more complex. Increased fibrotic connective tissue, arteriosclerosis, and other changes in the arterial wall leading to ischemia, inflammation of nearby bursae that leads to secondary fibrosis, tethering of the nerve by restricted soft tissue, and digital nerve compression during weight bearing have all been identified as fac-

tors that may lead to a neuroma.[23] Interdigital nerve compression can also occur from wearing tight shoes, using inappropriate shoes for athletic workouts, and wearing high heels.[12]

Weight bearing exacerbates the symptoms of pain and numbness. Perhaps because of the type of footwear associated with interdigital neuroma, women are much more susceptible to developing this condition. Specifically, the wearing of shoes with narrow toe boxes or high-heeled shoes is often associated with the development of an interdigital neuroma.

Differential Diagnosis

Osteochondritis of the metatarsal head (Freiberg's infarction), metatarsal head stress fracture, MTP joint synovitis, arthritis, metatarsalgia, transverse metatarsal arch sprain.

Imaging Techniques

Although the diagnosis of interdigital neuroma is primarily based on the clinical symptoms, MRI with gadolinium can identify the lesion. Ultrasonic imaging has also been successfully used to identify the presence and location of an interdigital neuroma. Plain radiographs may be ordered to rule out MTP joint changes, arthritis, and fracture.

Medical Diagnostic Tests

The diagnosis of interdigital neuroma is based on the history and physical examination. Resolution of symptoms with a lidocaine injection in the distal web space can help confirm the diagnosis.

Definitive Diagnosis

Interdigital neuroma pain arises from between the metatarsal heads rather than from the metatarsal or the MTP joint. Burning and numbness are classic symptoms of nerve irritation that are not reported with other possible diagnoses.

Pathomechanics and Functional Limitations

Repetitive digital nerve compression or irritation causes interdigital neuroma. Weight bearing is painful, and the increased stresses of impact can exacerbate pain, numbness, and eventual paralysis in the nerve distribution. The interdigital nerve injury affects two toes because of the branching of the common interdigital nerve. Altered biomechanics—representing an attempt to reduce pain—can lead to stress-related lower extremity injury from muscular compensation and the redistribution of weight-bearing forces.

■ Immediate Management

Remove the patient from activity and treat the area with ice. If normal weight-bearing activities produce pain, fit the patient for crutches.

■ Medications

Inflammation can be relieved with NSAIDs. Persistent symptoms may respond to a corticosteroid injection. No more than one or two injections should be given, because they may cause fat pad atrophy, thereby worsening the problem.

■ Postinjury Management

Therapeutic modalities and medications should be used to reduce pain and inflammation in patients with an interdigital neuroma. Use of felt or foam padding or orthotics may be useful in relieving pressure in the area of the neuroma and lead to a re-

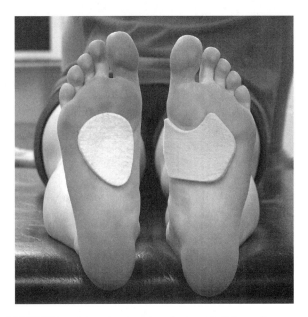

Figure 4.17 Metatarsal pads. A "teardrop" pad (left) is used to support the transverse metatarsal arch. A "moon pad" (right) is used to support and/or protect the first metatarsophalangeal joint.

duction in symptoms (see **Figure 4.17**). Reduced weight bearing and the avoidance of irritating footwear should also be implemented to reduce irritation. Continue with crutch walking as indicated. Proper footwear (i.e., shoes with a wide toe box with a cushioned forefoot and a low heel) should be instituted, and impact activities limited.

■ Surgical Intervention

Surgery is a treatment of last resort, performed only if the patient's symptoms fail to respond to conservative treatment and pain continues for as long as 1 year or significantly affects activity. In this procedure, the interdigital nerve is excised; thus, after surgery, numbness occurs in the area of skin innervated by the excised nerve (see **ST 4.3**). The ensuing numbness is not typically a major complaint if only the interdigital nerve is excised.

■ Postoperative Management

Following surgery, immediate weight bearing is typically allowed, and standard incision care is performed. Deep tissue massage may be helpful. Foot and toe ROM exercises should be undertaken, in addition to balance and gait training exercises. Padding to the plantar surface of the foot may aid in recovery. Wearing of proper footwear—that is, shoes with wide toe boxes and low heels—should be encouraged. Complete recovery, including a return to sport participation, typically occurs within 1 to 2 months.

4

S|T Surgical Technique 4.3

Excision of an Interdigital Neuroma

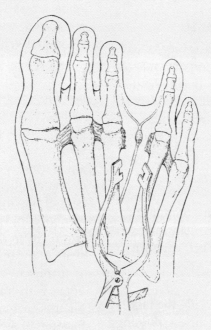

Indications

Recalcitrant pain despite properly sized shoes.

Procedure Overview

1. A dorsal incision is made to expose the nerve.
2. The nerve is resected at least 1 cm distal to its bifurcation.
3. The plantar-directed branch is cauterized.
4. The nerve is resected proximally in the foot to allow the stump to be clear of the weight-bearing surface of the plantar foot.
5. Typically the transverse metatarsal ligament is cut to expose the nerve. In some elite athletes, the ligament is only partially cut to reduce postoperative spreading of the metatarsals and reduce pain.

Functional Limitations

The patient has permanent numbness between the adjacent toes (e.g., between the third and fourth toes with intermetatarsal resection between toes three and four).

Implications for Rehabilitation

Early desensitization massage assists in recovery from nerve pain. After the wound is well healed (2 to 4 weeks), rehabilitation can be aggressive.

Source: Figure reproduced with permission from Weinfled SB. Interdigital neuritis: Diagnosis and treatment. *J Am Acad Orthop Surg.* 1996;4:328-335.

cauterized Sealed off by using heat.

■ **Injury-Specific Treatment and Rehabilitation Concerns**

Specific Concerns

Relieve pressure on and irritation to the nerve.
Prevent pressure on the nerve during activities with a pad, orthotic inserts, and/or shoe modifications.

The initial treatment for interdigital neuroma is designed to relieve inflammation and reduce stress on the neuroma. The patient should wear shoes with a thicker outer sole for added shock absorption, a wide toe box to relieve lateral compression, and a low heel to relieve downward pressure on the neuroma. A neuroma pad inserted in the shoe can spread the metatarsal heads and relieve nerve pressure. Modalities to relieve inflammation may be indicated, depending on the source of irritation. If the nerve tethering is caused by scar tissue or soft-tissue adhesions, deep tissue mobilization is needed.

Estimated Amount of Time Lost

Because the interdigital neuroma injury is self-limiting, time lost from competition depends on the pain level, specific sport activity (how much stress is applied to the foot), and the ability to achieve sufficient pain relief with treatment.

Return-to-Play Criteria

Return to full sport participation is permitted when the patient can don athletic shoes and perform sport activities without pain. The cause of irritation (e.g., soft-tissue restriction, narrow shoes, plantar-flexed ray) should be relieved or removed before return to participation.

Functional Bracing

Wearing proper footwear with a wide toe box is more important than bracing. Nevertheless, padding properly placed behind the metatarsal heads can help relieve interdigital nerve pressure.

Fifth Metatarsal Fractures

CLINICAL PRESENTATION

History
Acute fractures will have a distinct mechanism resulting in immediate lateral foot pain.
Stress fractures will typically have an insidious onset of lateral foot pain that is exacerbated with weight-bearing exercise.

Observation
Acute fractures will present with swelling, and obvious deformity may be present.
Stress fractures will often present with no obvious deformity, although swelling may be noted at the site of fracture.

Functional Status
An antalgic gait is often observed and will be exacerbated with running and cutting.

Physical Examination Findings
Tenderness to palpation at the site of the injury is noted.
Compression of the fifth metatarsal will cause pain.

The fifth metatarsal is the most mobile of the metatarsals and is the most likely of the metatarsals to be fractured.[24] Similar to other stress fractures, metatarsal stress fractures occur most often from a rapidly increased activity level or a dramatic change in sport with repetitive bone overloading and insufficient recovery time. Metatarsal stress fractures can be oblique, longitudinal, or transverse. Transverse stress fractures are common in the fifth metatarsal, whereas compression stress fractures are more likely in the first metatarsal.[25]

Although fractures typically occur to the proximal end of the fifth metatarsal, three distinct pathologies are possible (see **Figure 4.18**). Clinical management of a fifth metatarsal fracture will depend on the location of the fracture. First, an avulsion fracture may occur in conjunction with a lateral ankle sprain at the site of the peroneus brevis tendon attachment on the most distal portion of the base of the fifth metatarsal. Second, a "Jones fracture" occurs as the base of the fifth metatarsal transitions from the metaphysis to the diaphysis, or shaft, of the bone. Jones fractures typically have an acute onset. A high preponderance of nonunion is noted with Jones fractures, and surgical management is recommended for athletes. Third, stress fractures of the fifth metatarsal typically occur in the proximal portion of the fifth metatarsal.

Pes cavus, genu varum, and chronic ankle instability may increase the risk of fifth metatarsal stress fractures. Such injury is thought to result from increased adduction forces placed on the fifth metatarsal by proximal instability or medially directed forces placed on this site from foot or knee malalignment. A cavus foot tends to absorb stress in the metatarsal rather than transferring it to the tibia and fibula.[25]

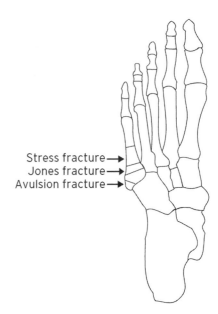

Stress fracture →
Jones fracture →
Avulsion fracture →

Figure 4.18 Common fracture locations of the fifth metatarsal.

Caution must be exercised when treating athletes with a stress fracture to ensure that healing occurs and a full fracture does not develop. Fifth metatarsal fractures can be particularly problematic for athletes who participate in field and court sports that require high-intensity change-of-direction maneuvers such as cutting.

Differential Diagnosis

Lateral ankle sprain, tarsometatarsal joint sprain, cuboid fracture.

Imaging Techniques

Plain radiographs are useful in identifying acute fractures but will not identify stress fractures until they begin to heal. A bone scan will reveal a more acute stress fracture. Serial radiographs may be used to document the healing of conservatively treated fractures.

Definitive Diagnosis

Positive radiographs, bone scan, computed tomography (CT) scan, or MRI is necessary to make a definitive diagnosis. Notably, fifth metatarsal stress fractures tend to remain relatively asymptomatic until a complete fracture suddenly occurs.

Pathomechanics and Functional Limitations

The loss of bony integrity or pain redistributes the weight-bearing surfaces of the foot, altering foot and, therefore, gait biomechanics. Such modifications increase the likelihood of new stress fractures or lower extremity overuse conditions. The athlete's ability to perform sport-specific activities, such as explosive starts, cutting, jumping, and landing, may also be impaired. Metatarsal stress fractures are generally the result of overuse. Adequate healing time before returning to activities can help prevent their recurrence.

■ Immediate Management

A high suspicion of stress fracture should prompt a workup for this condition. Symptomatic treatment is indicated when it is identified, as application of ice, elevation, and protective weight bearing with crutches can limit the symptoms.

■ Medications

The use of NSAIDs for pain relief is helpful.

■ Other Metatarsal Fractures

The other metatarsals may be subjected to acute fractures and stress fractures, although such injuries do not occur as frequently as fifth metatarsal injuries. Acute fractures to the first metatarsal de-

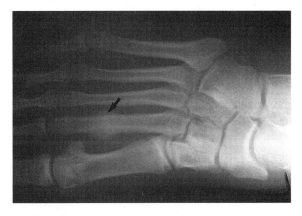

Figure 4.19 Late-stage stress fracture of the second metatarsal. The arrow indicates callus formation.

serve special consideration because of the large amount of force transferred through the first ray during gait. A prolonged period of non-weight-bearing immobilization is typically needed to treat these injuries. Although stress fractures may occur to any of the metatarsals, the most common site of stress fracture is the second metatarsal (see **Figure 4.19**). Stress fractures will typically respond well to immobilization and reduced weight bearing.

A cavus or planus foot may predispose an individual to metatarsal stress fractures, with a planus foot having with a higher risk than a cavus foot, particularly in the first and second metatarsals.[25] The hyperpronation associated with pes planus increases forces on the medial aspect of the foot. A short first metatarsal and a long second metatarsal have also been implicated as factors contributing to second metatarsal stress fractures. With such a configuration, an increased load is applied more laterally to the foot, increasing second metatarsal stress. This condition is particularly problematic if the hallux is rigid or abducted.

■ Surgical Intervention

Surgical intervention is common in failed union or nonunion of a fifth metatarsal Jones fracture. Intervention during the competitive season may allow the athlete to return before the season ends. Because the fifth metatarsal is at increased risk of a nonunion in response to conservative treatment, many physicians elect to surgically repair the fracture once it is diagnosed. The two predominant surgical techniques are a bone graft and an intermedullary screw. Although internal screw fixation allows for a more rapid return to participation, it can also cause soft-tissue irritation.[26] To decrease the likelihood of refracture, the screw is normally left in place for the remainder of the athlete's competitive life. With bone grafting, complications are usually rare, but recovery is slower.[26]

After surgery, hardware failure or nonunion may still occur. Successful surgeries do not result in long-term functional limitations, although an orthosis may be prescribed before return to activity to minimize the refracture risk.

■ Postinjury Management

Avulsion fractures of the fifth metatarsal often heal well with conservative management, consisting of immobilization of the foot and ankle for several weeks. Rehabilitation will be similar to that described for a lateral ankle sprain, with an emphasis on restoring ROM, strengthening of the peroneal muscles, balance and coordination training, and restoration of normal gait patterns.

Jones fractures may be treated conservatively with a lengthy period of immobilization—as long as 16 weeks. Because of the high rate of nonunion fractures, however, surgical management of such an injury is recommended for athletes. An open reduction and internal fixation (ORIF) procedure is performed to provide a stable healing environment. The fracture site is stabilized using a Kirscher wire (K-wire) and an intermedullary screw inserted longitudinally from proximal to distal. Likewise, diaphyseal stress fractures may be treated conservatively, but surgical stabilization with an intermedullary screw should be considered in high-level athletes.

Postoperative management includes 4 to 8 weeks of immobilization followed by rehabilitation as outlined previously and a gradual return to functional activities.

■ Injury-Specific Treatment and Rehabilitation Concerns

Specific Concerns

Relieve stress on the metatarsal.
Stabilize and protect the fracture site.

Second, third, and fourth metatarsal stress fractures should heal with rest and conservative care. First metatarsal stress fractures are managed with reduced activity and shoe modifications; they result in the least amount of time lost.[27] Fifth metatarsal fractures do not respond as well to conservative treatment as do other metatarsal stress fractures.

■ Estimated Amount of Time Lost

On average, the athlete is restricted from normal activity for 4 to 8 weeks, which does not include the time necessary for rehabilitation and a gradual return to full participation. Depending on the individual's response to treatment and rehabilitation, full recovery may take 6 to 12 weeks.

■ Return-to-Play Criteria

The patient with a metatarsal fracture should be able to perform all activities without pain before returning to play. To receive clearance for a return to competition, the athlete is tested on sport-specific activities and drills and must demonstrate normal performance without favoring or hesitating to use the foot. The foot should be in a stable, supportive shoe, and the causative factors that initially led to a stress fracture should be resolved.

Functional Bracing

A shoe with a stiff sole or rigid insert reduces metatarsal stress. A rocker-bottom shoe also decreases metatarsal stress during the last half of the stance phase. A stiff foot plate insert with a viscoelastic insole covering the stiff foot plate may also be used; the former device splints the metatarsal, while the latter attenuates impact force.

Tarsometatarsal Injuries (Lisfranc Injuries)

CLINICAL PRESENTATION

History

A distinct mechanism of injury involving a twisting of the foot during axial loading, resulting in immediate medial foot pain.

Observation

Moderate to severe swelling present at the tarsometatarsal joint. Plantar ecchymosis.

Functional Status

Antalgic gait, especially during the propulsive phase of gait.

Physical Examination Findings

Tenderness to palpation at the site of the injury.
Pain with passive pronation and abduction of the forefoot on the midfoot.

The tarsometatarsal joint is also referred to as the Lisfranc joint. The articulation between the medial cuneiform and first and second metatarsal bases is a frequent site of severe foot injury. This joint may be sprained or dislocated with or without associated fractures. The mechanism of injury often involves a fall from a height or excessive pronation (eversion) and abduction of the forefoot on the midfoot. These injuries have a high probability of prolonged disability if not treated appropriately. Of particular concern is the development of diastasis between the first and second metatarsal bases. Surgical management is often necessary to ensure proper alignment and stabilization of the tarsometatarsal complex.

Differential Diagnosis

Tarsal or metatarsal fractures, compartment syndrome.

Imaging Techniques

Anteroposterior, lateral, and oblique radiographs taken during standing are needed to identify diastasis of the metatarsals. Non-weight-bearing radiographs may reveal fractures but are not sufficient to visualize the extent of joint instability. A *fleck sign* is used to identify avulsion of the Lisfranc ligament from the base of the second metatarsal (see Figure 4.20). A computed tomography (CT) scan can be performed to identify osteochondral fractures that are often missed on radiographs.

▪ Management

Stable fractures that do not involve diastasis may be treated with 6 weeks of immobilization. In contrast, any Lisfranc injuries that involve diastasis should be treated surgically with ORIF to realign the tarsometatarsal and intermetatarsal joints. Post-

operative management requires immobilization and non-weight-bearing restrictions for approximately 6 weeks, followed by another several months in a controlled ankle motion (CAM) walker. A gradual return to functional activities may be initiated 6 months after surgery. Screws or other hardware that cause continuous irritation may be removed after 4 months. Foot orthotics with considerable medial arch support often are helpful in providing relief.

Navicular Stress Fractures

CLINICAL PRESENTATION

History

Insidious onset of diffuse pain on the dorsal and medial aspects of the midfoot.
Pain that increases with weight-bearing activity and diminishes with rest.

Observation

Deformity is rarely observed with a stress fracture.
An unusually pronounced navicular tuberosity may indicate the presence of an accessory navicular.

Functional Status

Antalgic gait.

Physical Examination Findings

Tenderness to palpation at the site of the injury.

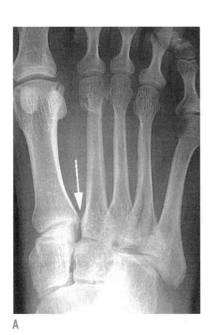
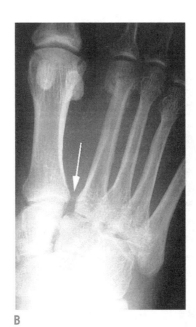
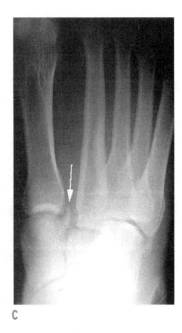

Figure 4.20 Radiographs of a Lisfranc injury. (**A**) Non-weight-bearing radiograph demonstrating widening between the bases of the first and second metatarsals (arrow). (**B**) Standing view of the same foot. Note the increased space between the first and second metatarsals (arrow). (**C**) Avulsion of the Lisfranc ligament, also known as the fleck sign (arrow).

Stress fractures to the tarsal navicular often present as vague medial foot pain. Because this bone has distinct areas of avascularity, healing may be compromised and a nonunion fracture may develop over time. Navicular stress fractures can be disabling because of the considerable weight-bearing forces exerted along the medial column of the foot. The stress is magnified when dynamic weight-bearing loads increase during activities such as sprinting, running, and jumping. The combination of the contractile forces applied by the muscles during forceful activities and the compressive forces is thought to contribute to overstressing the navicular.[28] Clinicians should maintain a high level of suspicion for navicular stress fracture in athletes presenting with complaints of medial midfoot pain. Morton toe, hallux valgus, limited dorsiflexion, and restricted subtalar motion may also contribute to navicular stress fractures.[29]

Another injury of concern may be attributable to the presence of an accessory navicular bone. An accessory navicular is a congenital condition that results in a secondary ossification protuberance involving the insertion of the tibialis posterior tendon (see Figure 4.21). Although the presence of an accessory navicular does not automatically indicate pathology, it should be considered as a site of potential injury when it is identified on radiographs.

Differential Diagnosis
Tarsal tunnel syndrome, tibialis posterior tendinopathy, medial ankle sprain, synovitis.

Imaging Techniques
Acute stress fractures will not be visible on plain radiographs, but they will be visible on a CT scan, MRI scan, and bone scan (see Figure 4.22). Healing stress fractures, nonunion fractures, and the presence of an accessory navicular will be identifiable on radiographs.

Definitive Diagnosis
A positive bone scan with CT scan or MRI can confirm a navicular stress fracture.

Pathomechanics and Functional Limitations
As the fracture matures, pain occurs earlier in the workout and persists longer after the activity. Unstable muscular and ligamentous attachment sites for the medial longitudinal arch decrease the arch's

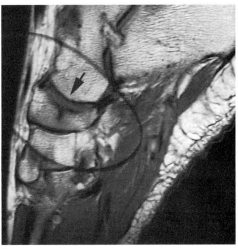

A

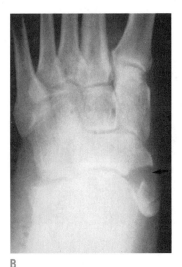

B

Figure 4.22 Radiographic views of the navicular. (A) Magnetic resonance image indicating a stress fracture of the navicular midsection (arrow). (B) Anteroposterior radiograph demonstrating an avulsion fracture of the accessory navicular. Contraction of the tibialis posterior muscle has caused proximal migration of the fragment.

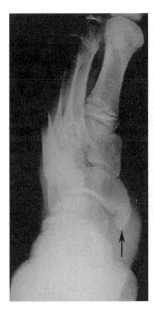

Figure 4.21 Oblique radiograph of an accessory navicular (arrow).

stability and alter the biomechanics during foot pronation and supination. If stress continues, the fracture may become a nonunion or become displaced and require surgical fixation.

Immediate Management

Protected weight bearing based on symptoms displayed during the workup will help limit the pain and inflammatory response. Ice and NSAIDs also are helpful in the immediate management of a navicular stress fracture. Immobilization may be indicated in certain situations, such as with acute trauma or intense pain.

Medications

An NSAID is helpful for pain relief. With extreme trauma or pain, oral narcotics are indicated.

Surgical Intervention

Navicular stress fractures that demonstrate nonunion or do not heal with prolonged immobilization should be treated with ORIF in an effort to prevent fragmentation of the fracture site. A bone graft may also be used in an effort to augment fracture healing. In high-level athletes, surgery may be considered initially in lieu of an initial treatment with immobilization.

Most patients require 6 weeks of non-weight-bearing restrictions after surgery. The most common postoperative complications include recurrent stress fracture, nonunion, and degenerative arthritis. Motion can be initiated early as long as the wound is healing well and the patient maintains non-weight-bearing status.

Postinjury/Postoperative Management

A stress fracture of the navicular is initially treated with 6 to 8 weeks of non-weight-bearing immobilization. Serial diagnostic imaging is needed to determine whether the stress fracture is healing properly. If adequate healing does occur, athletes may be transitioned into a gradual return to functional activities, with caution being exercised to be sure that symptoms do not return.

Postoperative management entails a 6- to 8-week period of immobilization. Partial weight bearing with a CAM walker is used as a transition to full weight bearing. A gradual and cautious return to functional activities may be initiated 4 to 6 months after surgery. Use of a foot orthosis that provides medial arch support may be helpful.

Injury-Specific Treatment and Rehabilitation Concerns

Specific Concerns
Prevent the application of excessive stress to the navicular. Restore function as healing progresses.

Weight bearing is restricted for 6 to 8 weeks, whether or not the patient has a cast. The patient is reexamined at 3 weeks and again at 6 weeks. If tenderness persists at 6 weeks, the cast (if used) and non-weight-bearing status are continued for another 2 weeks. Once the cast is removed, the patient may experience generalized foot discomfort with weight bearing and paresthesia, but these complaints differ from the initial complaints. Because non-weight-bearing restrictions and immobilization may be prolonged, soft-tissue and joint-mobilization techniques may be required to restore the athlete's motion and function. These techniques may be utilized during the non-weight-bearing period if the foot is not in a cast. If a cast was applied, these techniques are applied once the cast is removed. When weight bearing is permitted, progressive rehabilitation for strength, balance, coordination, agility, and functional activities is instituted, using the patient's pain as a guide for advancement.

Estimated Amount of Time Lost

In nonsurgical cases, the patient is restricted to non-weight-bearing status for 6 to 8 weeks. This period may be followed by an additional 2 to 6 weeks of rehabilitation before return to full participation in the athlete's sport is feasible. After surgery, 4 to 6 months of activity may be lost.

Return-to-Play Criteria

Once the fracture demonstrates radiographic healing and no point tenderness to palpation or pain during activities, the patient may return to full participation. In addition, the patient's gait should be normal, in both walking and running, and he or she should be able to perform all required sport activities while remaining pain free upon return to full participation.

Functional Bracing

Because a navicular stress fracture may occur secondary to a shortened first metatarsal, a firm, full-length insert that extends under the first ray may reduce the stress on the bone. If the predisposing factor was reduced navicular or subtalar motion, a flexible orthotic insert may limit forces applied to the navicular. A heel insert relieves stresses by reducing dorsiflexion.

ANKLE INJURIES

Lateral Ankle Sprains

CLINICAL PRESENTATION

History

Distinct mechanism of injury involving excessive inversion and plantar flexion of the rearfoot.
A history of previous ankle sprain.

Observation

Swelling in the sinus tarsi and around the lateral malleolus.
Ecchymosis on the lateral aspect of the ankle a few days after the original injury.

Functional Status

Antalgic gait.
Inability to run, cut, and land from a jump.

Physical Examination Findings

Tenderness to palpation over the involved ligaments.
An increase in pain during the first two weeks after sprain.[30]
Laxity noted with the anterior drawer and inversion talar tilt special tests.
Peroneal muscle weakness.

Sprains to the lateral ankle ligaments are the most common injuries suffered during competitive and recreational athletics. The mechanism of injury is typically supination (inversion, plantar flexion, and internal rotation) of the rearfoot coupled with external rotation of the lower leg. These injuries frequently occur when landing for a jump on the foot of an opponent or when changing direction in field or court sports. The anterior talofibular ligament is the ligament most frequently injured, followed by the calcaneofibular ligament (see **Figure 4.23**). Injuries to the posterior talofibular ligament are rare.

While ankle sprains often are considered innocuous injuries, in many cases they are actually associated with long-term consequences. Recurrent sprains are extremely common, as are residual symptoms including pain and the sensation of the ankle "giving way" during functional activities. As many as one-third of individuals suffering first-time ankle sprains will go on to develop chronic ankle instability, a condition characterized by repetitive ankle sprains, frequent episodes of the ankle giving way, prolonged symptoms, and diminished self-reported function.

Lateral ankle sprains typically present with swelling in the sinus tarsi and around the lateral malleolus. Ecchymosis frequently develops on the lateral aspect of the ankle and may spread proximally and distally. The severity of the ankle sprain is graded based on the extent of ligamentous damage. A first-degree ankle sprain typically involves a stretching, but not complete disruption, of the anterior talofibular ligament. A second-degree sprain is characterized by moderate laxity due to injury to the anterior talofibular and calcaneofibular ligaments, whereas a third-degree sprain represents complete disruption of both ligaments. The extent

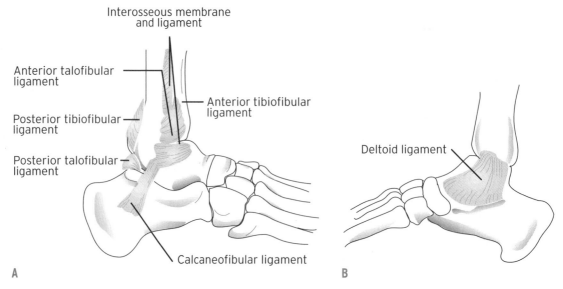

Figure 4.23 Ligaments maintaining the relationship of the distal tibia, fibula, and talus. **(A)** Lateral view. **(B)** Medial view.

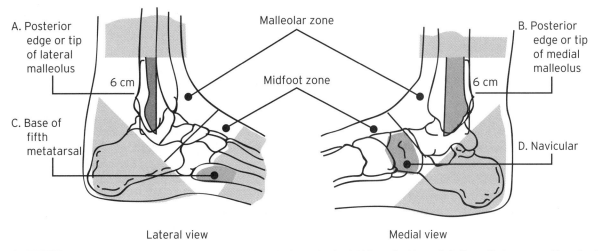

Figure 4.24 The Ottawa Ankle Rules. An ankle radiographic series is required only if the patient has pain in the malleolar zone and bone tenderness in zones A or B or if the patient is unable to bear weight either immediately or while in the emergency department. A foot radiographic series is needed if the patient has pain in the midfoot zone or bone tenderness in zones C or D or if the patient is unable to bear weight either immediately or while in the emergency department. *Source:* Stiel IG, Greenbuerg GH, McKnight RD, Wells GA. The "real" Ottawa Ankle Rules. *Ann Emerg Med.* 1996;27:103-104.

of ligament damage is determined based on physical examination tests, including the anterior drawer and inversion talar tilt tests, with the assessment potentially being augmented by stress radiographs or ultrasonography.

Associated lesions to other structures in the ankle are common in patients with lateral ankle sprains. Such injuries include, but are not limited to, fibular fractures, peroneus brevis avulsion fractures at the base of the fifth metatarsal, split lesions of the peroneus longus tendon, osteochondral injuries to the talus, and sinus tarsi syndrome (a hypertrophic synovitis of the subtalar joint). Clinicians need to be cognizant of these associated pathologies and not rush to the conclusion that injured patients have "just an ankle sprain."

Differential Diagnosis
Fibula fracture, fifth metatarsal fracture, tibia fracture, osteochondral injuries to the talus, syndesmosis ankle sprain.

Imaging Techniques
Although imaging techniques are not needed to make a diagnosis of lateral ankle sprain, plain radiographs should be ordered whenever a patient is suspected of having a fracture. The Ottawa Ankle Rules serve as a useful clinical prediction rule to aid in this decision (see **Figure 4.24**). Stress radiographs or stress ultrasonography may be used to assess the extent of ligamentous damage by taking images in anterior drawer and inversion talar tilt stress (see **Figure 4.25**). In addition, MRI or CT scan may be used to identify osteochondral lesions.

Definitive Diagnosis
The history of an inversion injury and positive physical examination provide the basis for a definitive diagnosis of a lateral ankle sprain. Concomitant injuries, such as malleolar avulsion fracture, medial ankle injury, syndesmosis sprain, peroneal tendon subluxation, and peroneal avulsion fracture, often go unnoticed, especially with moderate and severe ankle sprains, so all areas of pain must be investigated.

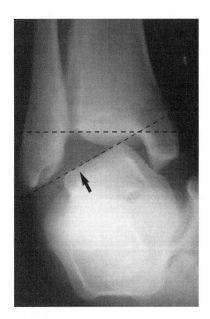

Figure 4.25 Ankle inversion stress radiograph. The ankle is passively inverted (i.e., talar tilt test) during the radiograph. The angle formed between the superior border of the ankle mortise and the talus demonstrates the amount of laxity (arrow).

Table 4.2

Possible Factors Contributing to Recurring Ankle Sprains

The ligaments heal in a lengthened and stretched position, so support becomes deficient.

Scar tissue replacing the ligament is never as strong as the original ligament and lacks sufficient strength to restrict motion.

Peroneal muscles are not properly rehabilitated after a sprain and may, therefore, be too weak to provide active protection.

Instability of the distal tibiofibular joint.

Genetic ligamentous laxity.

Loss of proprioception after the original injury to the ligaments.

Impingement of the distal fascicle of the anterior talofibular ligament.

The damaged capsule's scar tissue is impinged in the talofibular joint.

Tight Achilles tendon.

Tarsal coalition.

Source: Adapted from Safran MR, Zachazewski JE, Benedetti RS, et al. Lateral ankle sprains: A comprehensive review (part 2). Treatment and rehabilitation with an emphasis on the athlete. *Med Sci Sports Exerc.* 1999;31(suppl 7):S438-S447.

Pathomechanics and Functional Limitations

Several factors contribute to the high rate of ankle ligament reinjury (see **Table 4.2**). Functional ankle instability is a frequent byproduct of lateral ankle sprains, occurring in 29% to 42% of sprains[31]; however, mechanical ankle instability is much less common. Functional ankle instability is a perceived instability by the patient and includes a sensation of the ankle giving way.

Recurrent or severe inversion ankle sprains can result in osteochondral injury to the talus or distal tibia. In this scenario, the patient complains of pain arising from the medial aspect of the ankle, especially during inversion and dorsiflexion.

Practice Tip

Pain and subjective instability have been reported after 1 year in a large percentage of patients who suffered a lateral ankle sprain. In one study, approximately one-third of patients reported at least one reinjury of the affected ankle within 3 years of the initial injury; approximately two-thirds reported full recovery at the end of 3 years.[30]

■ Immediate Management

Rest or immediate immobilization with tape, wrap, or splint; ice; compression; and elevation are components of the initial treatment of ankle sprains. Focal compression with a horseshoe or circular pad can further reduce edema (see **Figure 4.26**).[32]

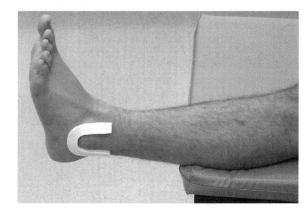

Figure 4.26   A U-shaped focal compression pad. This pad prevents excess fluid accumulation within the ankle joint capsule by forcing it to move over the fibula and proximally on the lower leg.

■ Medications

The early use of NSAIDs can help limit the inflammatory response and speed recovery. Nevertheless, the decision whether to use NSAIDs during the first 24 to 48 hours after injury or withhold them for the anticoagulation effect (which may increase swelling) remains controversial. During the immediate care of severe ankle sprains, narcotic analgesics may be necessary to help control pain.

■ Postinjury Management

The standard of care for the management of lateral ankle sprains is functional treatment, as opposed to an extended period of immobilization, although some clinicians advocate maintaining 10 days of immobilization in severe ankle sprains. A compression bandage with a horseshoe pad around the lateral malleolus should be applied from the forefoot to the lower leg. This measure is often complemented by a pneumatic brace that allows plantar flexion and dorsiflexion motion but restricts inversion and eversion. Walking boots should also be considered as a treatment option. If the patient has an antalgic gait, assistive devices such as crutches or a cane should be used until a pain-free gait pattern is restored.

■ Surgical Intervention

In cases of third-degree ankle sprains or chronically unstable ankles with extreme laxity, surgical stabilization of the lateral ankle ligaments should be considered. Primary repair of the ruptured ligaments is the preferred surgical treatment, although this procedure is often not feasible due to the extent of ligament damage (see **ST 4.4**). In such cases, reconstruction of the lateral ankle ligaments is performed using a portion of the peroneus brevis tendon to reconstruct the lateral ligaments (see **Figure 4.27**).

Nonaugmented Lateral Ankle Reconstruction

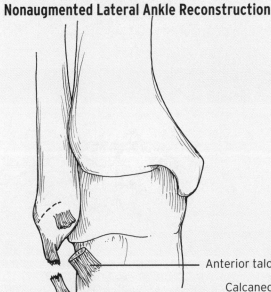
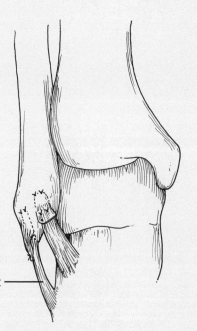
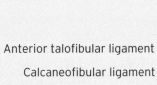

Anterior talofibular ligament

Calcaneofibular ligament

Indications

Chronic instability of the lateral aspect of the ankle requires surgery when rehabilitation or ankle bracing fails or when instability occurs with daily activity and/or with use of a brace and/or limits activity level.

Procedure Overview

Nonaugmented lateral reconstruction (Bröstrom and modified Bröstrom, pictured here):
1. A curvilinear incision is made to expose the distal fibula, lateral ligaments, and calcaneus.
2. The repair is completed, with the torn ligaments and inferior extensor retinaculum being reflected and sutured in place.
3. If a tenodesis is performed, the tendon is harvested and routed through drill holes or held in position with suture anchors to reproduce the lateral ligamentous structures.

Augmented lateral reconstructions (Evans, Watson-Jones, Elmslie-Trillat, Chrisman-Snook; see Figure 4.27)
1. The tendon (often the peroneal brevis) is identified and harvested, retaining as much length of the tendon as possible.
2. Often the tendon is left attached distally.
3. The tendon is then rerouted with various combinations of soft-tissue tunnels, bone tunnels, and suture anchors.
4. Retinacula are repaired, and tissues are closed.

In all techniques, the ankle is immobilized postoperatively to protect the repair or reconstruction.

> **tenodesis** The surgical relocation and fixation of a tendon.

Functional Limitations

Tenodesis (augmented) surgery has relatively poor long-term results, with degenerative changes and restricted subtalar motion being noted postoperatively. Tenodesis techniques cross the subtalar joint, thereby limiting that joint's motion, and subsequent pathomechanics can occur. Anatomic reconstruction (nonaugmented) can provide full ROM after surgery because the procedure does not cross the subtalar joint, but degenerative ankle changes can still occur postoperatively. The ligament repair and extensor retinaculum reflection (nonaugmented) are more anatomic and less restrictive with this technique.

Implications for Rehabilitation

The repair is protected with immobilization during the early healing phase. After 3 to 4 weeks, the ankle can be moved through a gentle ROM exercise program and bear partial weight. Generally, the athlete must avoid plantar flexion and inversion for 4 weeks after surgery (some surgeons allow dorsiflexion and eversion after 1 week). After 6 weeks, the patient can bear weight as tolerated, with brace support for the repair being implemented. Early progressive resistance exercises with plantar flexion and dorsiflexion can begin. Gradual progression occurs through the next 8 weeks. The lateral repair continues to be protected during this period with a lace-up or lateral stabilizer brace.

Comments

Return to sport is allowed after 3 months. Many physicians require the use of an ankle brace for the first full season after the athlete's return to competition. Nonaugmented repairs are preferred by most specialists.

Source: Figures reproduced with permission from Colville MR. Surgical treatment of the unstable ankle. *J Am Acad Orthop Surg.* 1998;6:368-377.

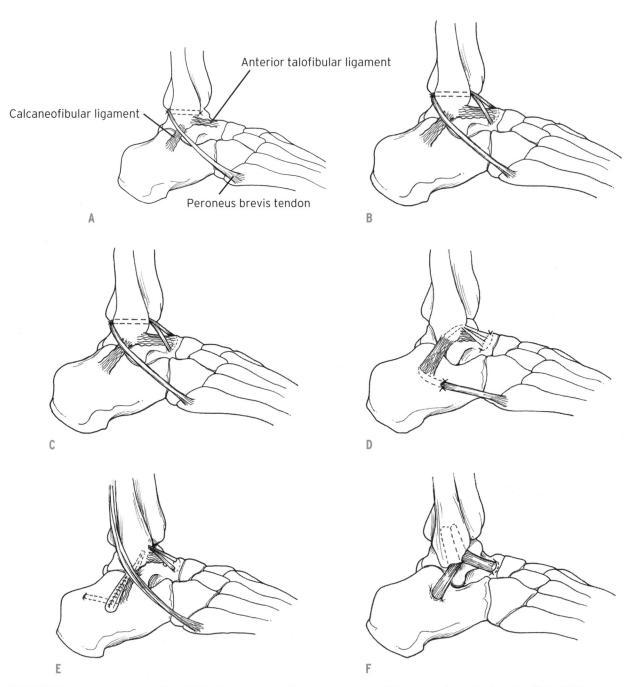

Anterior talofibular ligament

Calcaneofibular ligament

Peroneus brevis tendon

A

B

C

D

E

F

Figure 4.27   Augmented reconstructions. (**A**) The Evans reconstruction uses a tenodesis of the peroneus brevis tendon to the fibula. (**B**) The Watson-Jones procedure reconstructs the anterior talofibular ligament in addition to providing tenodesis of the peroneus brevis tendon. (**C**) The Chrisman-Snook procedure uses a split peroneus brevis tendon to reconstruct the anterior talofibular and calcaneofibular ligaments. (**D**) The Colville procedure also uses a split peroneus brevis tendon to reconstruct the anterior talofibular and calcaneofibular ligaments in an anatomic manner without limiting subtalar motion. (**E**) The Anderson procedure uses the plantaris tendon to anatomically reconstruct both lateral ligaments without limiting subtalar motion. (**F**) The Sjølin technique uses periosteal flaps to augment an anatomic repair. *Source:* Reproduced with permission from Colville MR. Surgical treatment of the unstable ankle. *J Am Acad Orthop Surg.* 1998;6:368-377.

Postoperative Management

Postoperative immobilization typically involves 4 to 6 weeks of immobilization, followed by a rehabilitation program similar to that described previously for conservative management of lateral ankle sprains.

Injury-Specific Treatment and Rehabilitation Concerns

> **Specific Concerns**
>
> Prevent unwanted stresses on the healing ligament.
> Control edema formation.
> Maintain weight bearing and ROM within limits of pain.

Early active ROM exercises should be encouraged, along with stretching of the triceps surae musculature. Passive joint mobilizations aimed at restoring posterior glide of the talus on the tibia and anteroposterior gliding of the fibula at the distal and proximal tibiofibular joints should also be incorporated to restore full ROM. A wobble board may be used initially with the patient seated in a chair; the patient may use this setup to perform partial weight-bearing ROM exercises. Strengthening exercises in all four directions of ankle motion should be gradually added to the rehabilitation program and progressed from isometric to isotonic contractions. The use of elastic bands or tubing is particularly helpful in performing both concentric and eccentric strengthening exercises.

A key component of ankle sprain rehabilitation is balance and coordination training. Progressions may be made by imposing added constraints on balance exercises. These constraints include manipulation of vision (eyes open to closed), surface (firm surface to foam pad), and arm position (arms abducted at 90° to across chest). Low-level plyometrics consisting of controlled hopping exercises can be advanced to activities requiring longer and faster jumps. Pain-free gait activities should be progressed from walking to jogging to sprinting. Performing gait activities in aquatic settings may be possible before dry-land training begins. Lastly, agility exercises should be added prior to allowing athletes to return to full sport participation.

Estimated Amount of Time Lost

The amount of pain, swelling, and disability and the time requirements for recovery are related to the severity and recurrence of injury, the patient's response to and compliance with treatment, and the clinician's ability to manage the injury. A patient with a grade II sprain may recover in 2 to 6 weeks, whereas a patient with a grade III rupture may require 6 to 8 weeks or more for full recovery.

Return-to-Play Criteria

Care must be taken to ensure that soft-tissue and joint mobility is restored, especially if the ankle has been immobilized. An antalgic gait can cause muscle imbalances to develop between the left and right lower extremities; thus, examination prior to the return to competition should reveal full strength restoration throughout the involved extremity. Return of proprioceptive function is evaluated by comparing balance, coordination, and agility between the extremities.

Functional Bracing

Upon their return to competition, athletes should be taped or fitted with a semi-rigid or lace-up prophylactic ankle brace. Taping and bracing have been found to significantly reduce the risk of recurrent ankle sprain.

Syndesmosis Ankle Sprains (High Ankle Sprains)

CLINICAL PRESENTATION

History

Distinct mechanism of injury involving excessive eversion/external rotation, inversion, dorsiflexion, or plantar flexion of the ankle.

Observation

Swelling over the anterior aspect of the distal tibiofibular joint in an area that is distinctly proximal to the talocrural joint line.
Ecchymosis on the anterior aspect of the ankle occurring a few days after the original injury.

Functional Status

Antalgic gait.
Inability to run, cut, and land from a jump.

Physical Examination Findings

Tenderness to palpation over the AITFL may or may not extend proximally over the interosseous membrane.
Special tests such as the squeeze test or external rotation (Kleiger's) test that stress the AITFL may cause distinct pain over the injured ligament.
Passive dorsiflexion may exacerbate symptoms.
Clinicians must be cognizant that AITFL injuries may occur concurrently with lateral ankle sprains, medial ankle sprains, and fibula fractures.

4

Injuries to the distal tibiofibular syndesmosis, also known as high ankle sprains, are a different clinical entity than lateral ankle sprains. The tibia and fibula are held together distally by the interosseous membrane and the anterior and posterior inferior tibiofibular ligaments. The anterior inferior tibiofibular ligament (AITFL) is the most commonly injured structure at this joint. In more severe injuries, the interosseous membrane may be affected and a diastasis (widening) of the syndesmosis may occur. Fractures to the fibula sometimes accompany high ankle sprains as well, so particular suspicion should be paid to identifying a proximal fibular fracture (Maisonneuve fracture).

> **Practice Tip**
>
> The incidence of injury to the distal tibiofibular syndesmosis is higher in those activities where the ankle is rigidly immobilized, such as in sports requiring a hockey or ski boot.[33]

Several potential mechanisms for this injury exist. Although syndesmosis ankle sprains sometimes occur simultaneously with lateral ankle sprains due to a hyperinversion mechanism, they more often occur with a mechanism that involves excessive external rotation and eversion of the foot coupled with internal rotation of the lower leg.[34] This mechanism can also lead to concurrent injury of the deltoid ligament (medial ankle sprain). In addition, syndesmosis ankle sprains frequently occur with a hyperplantar flexion mechanism, such as when a football player is tackled from behind and the dorsum of the foot is on the ground. Lastly, hyperdorsiflexion of a weight-bearing ankle can result in injury to the distal tibiofibular syndesmosis.

Regardless of the specific mechanism involved, injury to the AITFL will result in instability of the syndesmosis. A stable tibiofibular syndesmosis is needed to allow normal motion of the talus within the tibiofibular mortise during talocrural plantar and dorsiflexion. When the distal tibiofibular joint is unstable, the mechanics of the entire ankle complex are altered. With each step taken, the talus pushes superiorly into the tibiofibular syndesmosis, thereby stretching the AITFL and interosseous membrane. If restricted weight bearing is not included as part of the treatment regimen, the injured ligaments will not have an opportunity to heal. Because of these factors, return to sport is typically much longer for syndesmosis injuries compared to lateral ankle sprains.

Differential Diagnosis

Fibula fracture, tibia fracture, talus fracture, lateral ankle sprain, medial ankle sprain.

Imaging Techniques

As with lateral ankle sprains, the Ottawa Ankle Rules should be used to help guide decisions regarding the need for radiographs. If a severe syndesmosis injury is suspected, AP, mortise, and lateral radiographs should be taken to assess the entire length of the fibula fracture and to assess for the amount of diastasis of the tibiofibular syndesmosis (see **Figure 4.28**).[34] CT scan and MRI both provide accurate diagnostic information.[34]

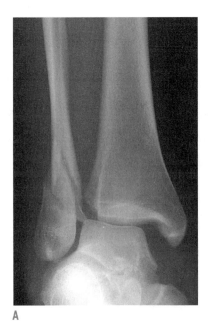

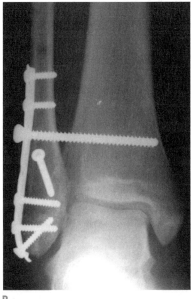

A   B

Figure 4.28   Distal tibiofibular syndesmosis sprain with associated fracture. **(A)** Preoperative radiograph demonstrating widening of the tibiofibular joint with associated fracture of the lateral malleolus and distal fibula. **(B)** Postoperative radiograph showing fixation of the syndesmosis and fracture repair.

Definitive Diagnosis

The definitive diagnosis is based on the mechanism of injury and clinical examination and confirmed with diagnostic imaging.[34]

> **Practice Tip**
>
> MRI is both highly sensitive (1.0) and highly specific (0.93) in diagnosing rupture of the AITFL.[34]

Pathomechanics and Functional Limitations

The distal syndesmosis provides secondary support of the ankle mortise.[34] Instability of the distal syndesmosis allows the talus to shift within the ankle mortise. Lateral and/or rotational translation reduces function of the ankle joint. Pressure from the talus causes the fibula to separate from the tibia, resulting in pain and disability.

■ Immediate Management

The standard immediate treatment protocol of ice, compression, and elevation should be followed. If a fracture can be ruled out, placing a compressive pad over the distal fibula can assist in maintaining congruity of the syndesmosis. The athlete should be fitted for crutches.

■ Medications

As in lateral ankle sprains, the early use of NSAIDs can help limit the inflammatory response and speed recovery from high ankle sprains. Narcotic analgesics may be necessary to help control pain.

■ Postinjury/Postoperative Management

Even mild syndesmosis ankle sprains must be treated more conservatively than lateral ankle sprains. Immobilization of the ankle in a high walking boot or Aircast and restricted weight bearing are integral to the treatment of these injuries. The principles of ice, compression, and elevation should also be applied. If associated fractures and frank diastasis have been ruled out, the immobilization and restricted weight bearing period should last a minimum of 7 to 10 days prior to progression to full weight bearing. In more severe sprains, the length of immobilization and restricted weight bearing should extend from 14 to 21 days.

■ Surgical Intervention

Surgical stabilization of the syndesmosis via ORIF is indicated when frank diastasis of the syndesmosis is evident. There are no hard-and-fast criteria that can be applied in making this decision, but the amount of medial clear space between the talus and medial malleolus, the amount of tibiofibular overlap, and the syndesmotic clear space should all be assessed on AP or mortise view radiographs. Surgical stabilization is also indicated in the presence of medial malleolus or fibular fractures that accompany syndesmosis diastasis.

Stabilization of the syndesmosis is typically performed with a syndesmosis fixation screw that is directed medially through the fibula and well into the tibia (see ⓈⓉ 4.5). The fixation screw is often removed after 6 to 12 weeks. Postoperative management should follow the same principles as conservative managements of syndesmosis injuries.

■ Injury-Specific Treatment and Rehabilitation Concerns

> **Specific Concerns**
>
> Prevent unwanted stresses on the syndesmosis.
> Control edema formation.
> Maintain weight bearing and ROM within limits of pain.

Upon return to full weight bearing, it is essential that the patient execute a pain-free gait. If the patient has pain in the syndesmosis during gait, the individual should be restricted to partial weight bearing. Rehabilitation should emphasize restoration of ROM, strength, endurance, and proprioception. The athlete may find that circumferential taping around the distal tibiofibular joint provides relief of discomfort. A slow and deliberate return to more functional activities should be taken in comparison to recovery from lateral ankle sprain.

■ Estimated Amount of Time Lost

Following surgical repair of the syndesmosis, return to full activity may require 4 to 6 months.[35]

■ Return-to-Play Criteria

The athlete should be able to demonstrate sport-specific skills (running, cutting, jumping, backpeddling) without pain or weakness.

Functional Bracing

Overly restrictive footwear (e.g., ice hockey boots) can place increased forces on the syndesmosis.[33] The literature is inconclusive regarding the optimal functional bracing for this condition.

frank Clearly or visibly evident.

S|T Surgical Technique 4.5

Repair of a Distal Tibiofibular Syndesmosis Disruption

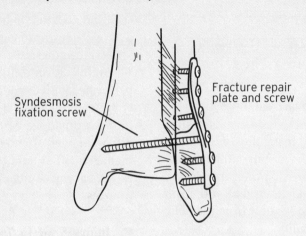

Syndesmosis fixation screw

Fracture repair plate and screw

Indications

A deltoid ligament (medial) sprain is often associated with syndesmosis injury and may require surgical intervention. If any mortise widening is seen on radiographs, surgery is required to repair the deltoid ligament and syndesmosis.

Overview

1. A curvilinear incision is made medially over the medial malleolus, and the injury is identified and repaired with sutures. Care is taken to protect the distal tendons and posterior tibial artery that pass inferiorly to the medial malleolus.
2. Laterally, the fibula is approached just above the tibial plafond. If a concurrent fracture is present, it is fixated using a plate and screws. A syndesmosis screw is placed across from the fibula into the tibia with the ankle dorsiflexed.
3. Reduction of the syndesmosis is visualized under fluoroscopy.

Functional Limitations

The patient is maintained on non-weight-bearing status while the syndesmosis screw is in place.

Potential Complications

Similar to nonoperative treatment, calcification of the syndesmosis and associated interosseous membrane is a concern.[33]

Implications for Rehabilitation

The placement of a syndesmosis screw necessitates postoperative non-weight-bearing restrictions to prevent screw breakage.[34] Once the screw is removed (in an outpatient procedure) 6 to 12 weeks after the initial surgery, ambulation can begin. ROM exercises and light resistance exercises can be introduced after the immobilization period.

Medial Ankle Sprains

The deltoid (medial) ligament is sprained less frequently than the lateral ligaments. The injury mechanism in the former case involves extreme subtalar joint eversion, and the extent of injury is directly proportional to the amount of stress applied to the ligament. With the subtalar joint in an everted position, the ankle may be in plantar flexion, a neutral position, or dorsiflexion at the time of the stress application. Because of the deltoid ligament strength, when a sprain occurs, a distal tibial avulsion fracture should be suspected until ruled out with radiographs.

Practice Tip

The medial (deltoid) ligaments serve as the primary stabilizer of the ankle. Disruption of these ligaments (by either a sprain or fractures of the medial malleolus) results in talar instabilty.[36]

Differential Diagnosis

Potential differential diagnoses include avulsion fracture, lateral malleolar fracture, fifth metatarsal fracture, osteochondral talar dome fracture, syndesmosis sprain, subtalar ligament lesion, peroneal strain, and subluxating peroneal tendons. Additional differential diagnoses for syndesmosis

CLINICAL PRESENTATION

History

Subtalar eversion or talocrural rotation.
Pain arising from the medial malleolus.

Observation

Immediately postinjury, swelling is localized to the medial malleolus.
Acute injuries may be associated with swelling and ecchymosis throughout the foot.

Functional Status

Pain and dysfunction are usually proportional to the trauma severity.
The patient is unable to bear weight, or an antalgic gait may be noted.

Physical Examination Findings

Pain occurs with palpation of the deltoid ligament; pain at a bony insertion site may indicate a fracture.
To complete the physical examination, palpation over the proximal fibula is necessary to fully evaluate syndesmosis integrity.
Decreased ROM is noted in all planes of motion.
The following tests are positive:

- Eversion stress test
- External rotation test (Kleigler test)

sprains include extensor digitorum longus strain, extensor hallucis longus strain, and Maisonneuve fracture.

Imaging Techniques

If pain occurs over the bony structures, radiographs are necessary to rule out a fracture.

Definitive Diagnosis

The definitive diagnosis is based on the mechanism of injury and clinical examination findings and is supported by diagnostic images. Concurrent injury to the distal tibiofibular syndesmosis should also be ruled out.

Pathomechanics and Functional Limitations

The deltoid ligament is the primary stabilizer of the ankle mortise and supports the medial longitudinal arch.[36] Injury to this ligament may result in prolonged disability because of these requirements and stress. If the athlete has a preinjury condition such as pes planus or excessive pronation, chronic instability of the medial aspect of the ankle can result.

Immediate Management

Rest or immediate immobilization with tape, wrap, or splint; ice; compression; and elevation are included in the initial treatment of ankle sprains.

Medications

NSAIDs may be prescribed with caution, especially during the first 24 to 48 hours after injury. During the immediate care of severe ankle sprains, narcotic analgesics may be necessary to help control pain.

Surgical Intervention

Deltoid ligament repair often requires concurrent repair of the distal syndesmosis (see ST 4.5). If a syndesmosis screw has been placed, some surgeons restrict weight bearing until the screw is removed at 6 to 12 weeks postoperatively. Strength and ROM exercises with partial weight bearing are then initiated. Full weight bearing is allowed after 8 weeks, and impact activities are permitted after 12 weeks.

Postinjury/Postoperative Management

Protecting the injured ligaments during the healing process is necessary to optimize healing. Postoperative management begins with immobilization and non-weight-bearing restrictions. Partial weight bearing and ROM exercises are started after the initial healing response. Refer to the Functional Limitations and the Implications for Rehabilitation (in ST 4.5) for the specific surgery that was performed.

Pain and edema control are important. The most effective methods to achieve these goals are compression, elevation, and minimization of stress to the damaged structures. Weight bearing may occur to the patient's tolerance level; a general rule of thumb is if the athlete is unable to ambulate normally, crutches or other assistive devices to allow normal gait are necessary.

Injury-Specific Treatment and Rehabilitation Concerns

Specific Concerns

Prevent unwanted stresses on the healing ligament.
Control edema formation.
Maintain weight bearing and ROM within the limits of pain.

For both surgically repaired and conservatively treated ankle sprains, timing of the healing process and the patient's response are the primary factors pacing the rehabilitation progression. Active ROM exercises are initiated when the injury is in the proliferation phase of healing. When surgical repairs are undertaken, active ROM exercises may begin after the first postoperative week. The point at which active ROM exercises for conservatively treated ankles are initiated depends on the severity of the injury—it ranges anywhere from day 2 for very minor injuries to days 3 to 5 for moderate injuries. If the ankle is immobilized, soft-tissue adhesions and joint restrictions will have likely developed secondary to edema, tissue damage, and immobilization. These problems must be treated with soft-tissue and joint mobilization before full ankle and foot motion are restored. Taken together, the mobilization techniques and active and passive motion exercises have the potential to restore normal mobility of the segment.

When the patient is in the mid- to late proliferation phase of healing, more aggressive strengthening exercises can be started. Once the athlete is bearing full weight on the involved extremity, strength is increased with closed kinetic chain activities. Proprioceptive exercises begin with balance activities and progress to coordination and then agility activities in preparation for plyometric and finally functional and sport-specific activities.

Estimated Amount of Time Lost

The amount of pain, swelling, and disability and the time requirements for recovery are related to the severity and recurrence of injury, the patient's response to and compliance with treatment, and the clinician's ability to manage the injury. A patient with a grade II sprain may recover in 2 to 6 weeks, whereas a patient with a grade III rupture may require 6 to 8 weeks or more for full recovery.

Return-to-Play Criteria

Because of the deltoid ligament's primary stabilizing role in the ankle mortise, healing of this type of sprain must be demonstrated prior to return to activity. Return of proprioceptive function is evaluated by comparing balance, coordination, and agility between the extremities.

Functional Bracing

Athletes should be taped or fitted with a semi-rigid or lace-up prophylactic ankle brace.

Tarsal Tunnel Syndrome

Just posterior to the medial malleolus, the tarsal tunnel provides the passageway for the tibial nerve, tibial artery, and tendons from the deep posterior compartment muscles to pass from the leg to the foot (see **Figure 4.29**). The roof of the tunnel is formed by the medial flexor retinaculum.

CLINICAL PRESENTATION

History

The onset of symptoms may follow distinct trauma to the medial ankle or rearfoot, or it may be insidious in nature.

The patient complains of intermittent pain, burning, tingling, or numbness on the medial aspect of the ankle and rearfoot.

Observation

Edema may be observed posterior to the medial malleolus.

Abnormal foot posture, either pes planus or pes cavus, may be noted when the onset is insidious.

Functional Status

The patient's function is self-limited by pain.

An antalgic gait may be present with more severe cases.

Physical Examination Findings

Passive ankle dorsiflexion and eversion may increase symptoms.

A positive Tinel's sign may be present along the tibial nerve.

Weakness and atrophy of the plantar intrinsic foot muscles may be present.

Tarsal tunnel syndrome is characterized by tension, stress, or pressure on the tibial nerve as it passes through the tarsal tunnel, or on its medial or lateral plantar nerve branches more distally. Space may become compromised in the tarsal tunnel following medial ankle trauma (such as medial malleolus fracture) and result in a distinct onset of tarsal tunnel syndrome symptoms. More frequently, however, an insidious onset of symptoms is noted. Hyperpronation of the rearfoot, often associated with pes planus and rearfoot valgus, can place the tibial and medial plantar nerves in a condition char-

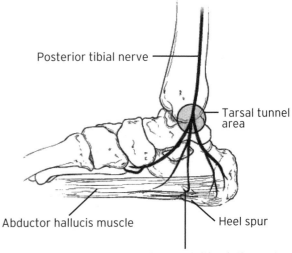

Posterior tibial nerve

Tarsal tunnel area

Abductor hallucis muscle

Heel spur

Nerve to abductor digiti quinti muscle

Figure 4.29 Anatomy of the tarsal tunnel. *Source:* Reproduced with permission from Greene WB (ed). *Essentials of Musculoskeletal Care*, ed 2. Rosemont, IL: American Academy of Orthopaedic Surgeons; 2000:511.

Table 4.3

Causes of Tarsal Tunnel Syndrome

Trauma	Space-occupying Lesions	Foot Deformities
Fracture of the distal tibia	Varicosities	Rearfoot valgus
Fracture of the calcaneus	Lipoma	Pes planus
Medial ankle sprain	Edema	Rearfoot varus
Posterior tibial injury	Exostosis	Pes cavus
Flexor digitorum longus trauma	Weight gain	
Flexor hallucis longus trauma	Ganglion cyst	
Secondary soft-tissue scarring		
Medial capsular adhesions		

acterized by excessive stretch (see **Table 4.3**). Conversely, a pes cavus foot type may be associated with a shortened abductor hallucis muscle that places pressure on the tibial nerve.

Regardless of etiology, the symptoms typically involve pain and numbness that can radiate both proximally and distally from the tarsal tunnel. In prolonged cases, weakness and atrophy of the plantar intrinsic foot muscles may also occur.

Differential Diagnosis

Lumbar disk herniation (radiculopathy), plantar fasciitis, posterior tibialis tendinopathy, flexor hallucis longus tendinopathy, flexor digitorum tendinopathy, diabetic neuropathy.

Imaging Techniques

Radiographs may show bony impingement of the tarsal tunnel, while MRI may demonstrate soft-tissue structural impingement such as a cyst in the tarsal tunnel (see **Figure 4.30**).

Medical Diagnostic Tests

Diagnostic electromyography and nerve conduction velocity tests are useful in confirming peripheral neuropathy (as opposed to radiculopathy). Anesthetic injection into the tarsal tunnel may also be used to verify the source of pathology as the tibial nerve or one of its plantar branches.

Definitive Diagnosis

Diagnosis is confirmed by positive electromyography and nerve conduction velocity test results for tarsal tunnel or pain relief with bupivacaine injection (or both).

Pathomechanics and Functional Limitations

A valgus foot deformity is a common predisposing element of tarsal tunnel syndrome. The posterior tibial nerve is subjected to ongoing tension—a condition that increases during ambulation. Lesions occupying the space in the tarsal tunnel, such as a nodule or swelling from an injury, reduce the space within the tunnel, applying pressure to the nerve. Abductor hallucis hypertrophy may also be a source of the problem if it pushes the lateral plantar nerve against the navicular tuberosity.

The patient's function is self-limited by pain. In severe cases, the patient may be unable to run for the time or intensity required for sport because of pain. Identifying the cause of the lesion and correcting

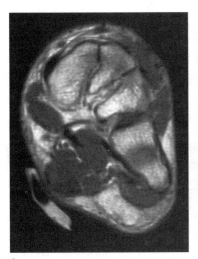
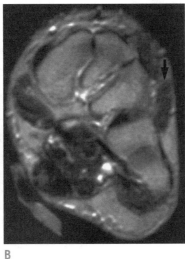
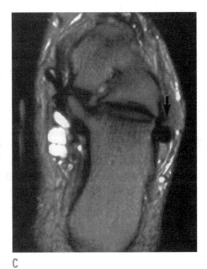

A   B   C

Figure 4.30 MRI image of tarsal tunnel impingement. (**A**) Normal view. (**B**) T1 weighted image showing a mass in the tarsal tunnel (arrow). (**C**) T2 weighted image demonstrating a ganglion in the tarsal tunnel (arrow).

the problem or eliminating the nerve pressure allows resumption of pain-free activity.

Immediate Management

Relieving nerve pressure eliminates the patient's pain. Most patients report reduced symptoms with rest. For permanent relief, the underlying cause must be identified and resolved (e.g., foot deformity, space-occupying lesion, intrinsic muscle hypertrophy, tight retinaculum).

Medications

Initially, NSAIDs are used to decrease the inflammatory process. However, the cause of the problem may limit NSAID effectiveness. Corticosteroid injections or nerve-desensitizing medications such as gabapentin (Neurontin) may also be used to treat patients with recalcitrant symptoms.

Surgical Intervention

Surgical intervention may be necessary in patients with space-occupying lesions, with surgical decompression of the tarsal tunnel being the most commonly employed approach. This procedure typically involves release of the medial flexor retinaculum and the medial plantar nerve distal to the navicular.

Postinjury/Postoperative Management

Rest coupled with analgesic and anti-inflammatory modalities and medications may serve to limit symptoms. Ultimately, however, the source of the pathology must be identified and mitigated to permanently resolve the symptoms. Patients with postural foot deformities should be fitted with appropriate foot orthotics to address necessary malalignment and motion control needs. Appropriate footwear prescriptions should also be made.

Postoperatively, the patient's ankle is typically immobilized and placed on non-weight-bearing restrictions for 7 to 10 days. A CAM boot is utilized during the transition to partial weight bearing. Rehabilitation should focus on restoration of foot and ankle ROM and strengthening of the plantar intrinsic foot musculature and the extrinsic ankle muscles.

Injury-Specific Treatment and Rehabilitation Concerns

> **Specific Concerns**
> Avoid dorsiflexion and eversion early in the rehabilitation program.
> Prevent denervation atrophy.

Modalities such as ice, heat, and ultrasound may be used to relieve inflammation; electrical stimulation can be used for neuromuscular reeducation. Orthotic appliances can reduce the nerve stresses caused by some foot deformities. Once pain and inflammation are under control, stretching and strengthening exercises can be beneficial in preparing the athlete to return to sport participation.

After 7 to 10 days, weight bearing to tolerance is permitted and exercises for stretching and strengthening are initiated. Once the patient is bearing full weight, swelling has subsided, and muscle strength and function are restored, the patient should be measured for orthotic appliances. Closed kinetic chain exercises should be performed while the patient is wearing the orthotic appliances. A progression of strengthening exercises for the intrinsic and extrinsic foot muscles is introduced, with steady advancement to agility, plyometric, functional, and sport-specific activities before the athlete returns to full participation.

After 2 weeks, mild isometric exercises of the ankle and subtalar joint can start. By the end of the third week, resistive toe exercises such as marble pickups can begin, along with isotonic ankle and subtalar exercises. Once the patient is bearing full weight, balance activities to restore proprioception are initiated, followed by a progression of activities leading to coordination and then agility skills. Because the athlete will be restricted from normal activity for a time, exercises for the uninvolved extremities and cardiovascular conditioning activities that do not stress the injured foot are necessary. A progressive return to full activity can begin once the athlete's agility skills reflect appropriate performance.

Estimated Amount of Time Lost

In nonsurgical cases, the patient may be restricted to no or limited activity for as long as 4 weeks. If surgery is the treatment of choice, a period of 3 months may be required before return to activity is possible.[37]

Return-to-Play Criteria

Because pain is the primary limiting factor, pain-free activities are the goal before return to competition occurs. If surgery has been performed, the soft tissue surrounding the scar and adjacent tissue must be mobile. The cause of the problem must be identified and resolved. Balance, coordination, agility, motion, and strength must be restored if the athlete has been unable to participate for a time. The athlete must demonstrate the ability to perform sport-specific activities without hesitation or favoring the affected side.

Functional Bracing

Orthotic appliances to relieve nerve pressure by correcting a valgus or varus foot deformity may be required. Care should be taken in shoe selection to prevent rubbing the medial aspect of the heel, especially if surgery has been part of the treatment. Shoe modifications may be needed if pressure on the surgical site is uncomfortable.

Ankle Fractures and Dislocations

CLINICAL PRESENTATION

History

High-force impact to the ankle, often involving inversion and plantar flexion.
Exquisite pain.

Observation

In most cases, gross joint deformity and malalignment are noted.
Some talar dislocations may present more subtly.

Functional Status

Loss of ROM secondary to disrupted joint alignment.
Inability to bear weight on the extremity.

Physical Evaluation Findings

Obvious joint disruption.
Fracture of the lateral and/or medial malleolus.

Talocrural dislocations often occur with accompanying fracture to the medial or lateral malleolus (or both). An isolated talocrural dislocation without concomitant fracture of the malleoli or posterior tibia is rare.[38] Ankle fractures can involve the lateral malleolus, medial malleolus, collateral ligament structures, posterior tibia (posterior malleolus), and talar dome. Among the most serious ankle fractures are those that involve the tibial weight-bearing articular surface or the adjacent tibial metaphysis, or both.[39]

Fractures involving one side of the ankle are stable and can be successfully treated symptomatically. A bimalleolar fracture includes the tibial and fibular malleoli or a distal fibular fracture with deltoid ligament disruption. A trimalleolar fracture involves the posterior tibia and a bimalleolar fracture. Because both of these fractures occur on the medial and lateral aspects of the ankle, they are considered unstable, and surgical repair is the treatment that ensures the best outcome. In addition, a fracture of the posterior tibia or talus (talotibial osteochondral defect) can occur with a dislocation. Because of the proximity to the bones, the skin covering the malleoli can be disrupted, causing an open fracture-dislocation.

Combined ankle plantar flexion and forced subtalar inversion or eversion can result in the fractures described previously and a posterior talar dislocation. If inversion occurs, the displacement is posteromedial; an eversion force produces a posterolateral displacement. Posteromedial dislocations occur more frequently because the ankle tends to be in an inverted and plantar-flexed position when an athlete lands from a jump. Ankle dislocations may also occur from a severe rotation or twisting mechanism while the foot is planted.

Predisposing factors for ankle dislocations include ligamentous laxity, medial malleolus hypoplasia, a history of ankle sprains, and peroneal muscle weakness.[38] Support for the ankle region is primarily medial-lateral rather than anterior-posterior, the direction in which ankle dislocations occur. If the angle of force application causes a dislocation, osteochondral defects of the posterior tibia and talus may arise, but are frequently overlooked because of the more obvious dislocation.

Differential Diagnosis

Syndesmosis sprain, talar dome fracture.

Imaging Techniques

Radiographs will confirm the presence of the fracture-dislocation suggested by the deformity. A CT scan or MRI may be required to define the fracture configuration and possible presence of soft-tissue injury or bone bruises (see **Figure 4.31**).

Definitive Diagnosis

Positive radiographic findings confirm the diagnosis of ankle dislocation or fracture.

Pathomechanics and Functional Limitations

A pure dislocation without fracture, although rare, can result in a good outcome when treated by closed reduction, followed by immobilization and a progressive rehabilitation program.[38] Some motion may be lost, but the ankle will be functional.

In an ankle with a fracture-dislocation, the effects are more profound. If the medial malleolus fracture occurs proximal to the deltoid ligament, the ankle is unstable and requires surgical fixation. Displaced fractures of any bone also need open reduction and internal fixation. Talar fractures are more complex and demand removal of osteochondral fragments and prolonged non-weight-bearing restrictions.

An open fracture requires surgical debridement to reduce the risk of osteomyelitis. Such an injury produces extensive damage to soft tissue, bone, and joints. Recovery may occur with proper treatment and rehabilitation, but eventual posttraumatic arthritis is common.

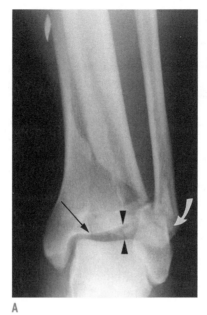
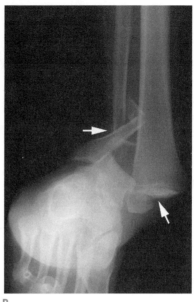

A   B

Figure 4.31 (**A**) Radiograph of an ankle mortise fracture. The black arrow highlights an intra-articular pilon fracture; the white arrow highlights a distal fibular fracture. The mortise is unstable and marked by widening of the lateral joint line (arrowheads). (**B**) Bimalleolar fracture-dislocation of the ankle mortise. The arrows demonstrate the fractures of the malleoli.

Immediate Management

In the patient with an ankle dislocation, immobilization in the position of dislocation, application of ice and elevation, and transport to an emergency department are necessary, especially when the injury is accompanied by an open fracture or suspected bimalleolar, trimalleolar, or talar dome fracture. Neurovascular examination should always be performed before immediate treatment. Continued periodic examinations should take place until emergency department treatment is provided.

Medications

Oral or injectable narcotic analgesics are used for pain relief because of the traumatic nature of the injury. Massive damage occurs to the ankle and subtalar soft tissues from this high-energy injury.

Surgical Intervention

All dislocations require immediate closed or open reduction and documentation of congruent joint alignment. Surgery might be required to obtain acceptable anatomic joint and bony alignment. **Table 4.4** lists other conditions warranting surgery after ankle mortise fracture. The surgical technique depends on the fracture type and requires rigid fixation, anatomic alignment, and restoration of joint surfaces.

Rigid internal fixation allows near-immediate ROM (see **Figure 4.32**). Weight bearing is limited or delayed in articular surface injuries, however.

Arthritis, stiffness, and pain are common after these injuries.

Postinjury/Postoperative Management

Immobilization in the neutral position following surgical reconstruction is necessary to allow soft-tissue and bone healing. Allowances for motion depend on the presence of associated fractures and degree of soft-tissue injury.

> **Practice Tip**
>
> When the distal tibial fibular syndesmosis remains intact, surgical and nonsurgical management of lateral malleolus offer equivalent long-term outcomes. Surgical reduction and stabilization of bimalleolar fractures yield superior outcomes.[36]

Table 4.4

Indications for Surgery After a Talocrural Fracture or Dislocation

Bimalleolar fracture

Trimalleolar fracture

Lateral malleolar fracture with concomitant medial (deltoid) ligament rupture

Displaced or angulated tibial fracture

Unstable syndesmosis injury

Fracture of the weight-bearing articular surface 1 mm or larger

Dislocation that cannot be reduced by closed means

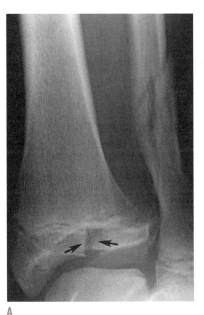

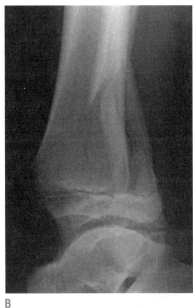

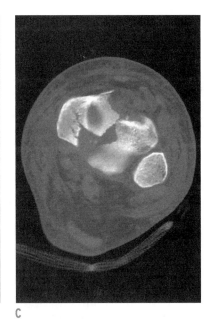

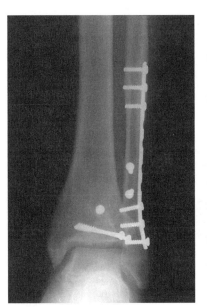

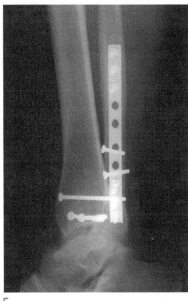

Figure 4.32 (**A**) Anteroposterior radiograph of a two-part lateral triplane fracture (arrows) and a comminuted fracture of the distal fibula. (**B**) Lateral radiograph of A. (**C**) CT scan demonstrating marked external rotation of the lateral portion of the distal fibula, fracture displacement, and comminution of the distal tibia. (**D**) Anteroposterior view of subsequent repair. (**E**) Lateral view of repair.

▣ Injury-Specific Treatment and Rehabilitation Concerns

> **Specific Concerns**
>
> Protect the bones from unwanted stresses.
> Delay the onset of atrophy.
> If applicable, protect traumatized ligaments and surgical repair sites.
> Restore soft-tissue mobility.
> Restore joint ROM.
> Restore muscular strength.

After surgery, the ankle is usually placed in a CAM boot with a brief period of no or partial weight bearing to tolerance at the outset of recovery. The ankle may be removed from the boot after approximately 7 days for mild passive or active ROM exercises. After 2 to 3 weeks, isometric exercises within the patient's pain-free range may be initiated.

Once the surgical site is well healed, soft tissue around the site and the scar itself should be examined for adhesions. If the tissue is restricted, soft-tissue mobility techniques are used to restore movement. Care should be taken, however, because the tissue is new and will tear very easily. Aggressive mobilization of the involved joints should be avoided for the first 6 to 8 weeks postoperatively. After that time, if examination reveals tightness in any of the joints of the unaffected foot, mobility should be increased.

While the patient is restricted in activities, it is important to maintain cardiovascular fitness and maintain or develop muscle strength in the uninvolved extremities. Open kinetic chain exercises for the hip, knee, and foot of the involved extremity can also be included during the non-weight-bearing phase of rehabilitation.

■ Estimated Amount of Time Lost

Time lost from competition may range from 3 months in uncomplicated cases to 12 months or longer in severe cases. Complicating factors such as neurovascular compromise and talar dome or tibial osteochondral defects can also prolong recovery.

■ Return-to-Play Criteria

Patients with this type of injury will participate in rehabilitation programs for extended periods. Thus a thorough examination of the athlete's abilities must be performed before return to athletic participation. With immobilization and swelling, soft tissue in the ankle commonly becomes restricted; these restrictions must be released to restore full motion and function. Joint mobility and ROM should be fully regained. Muscle strength of the entire lower extremity can be significantly affected by prolonged inactivity and needs to be normal before the athlete returns to play.

Functional Bracing

The athlete may feel more confident during activities if the ankle is taped or an ankle brace is applied. Neither measure offers real protection against a repeated injury, but proprioception may benefit from such a technique or device.

Achilles Tendinopathy

The Achilles tendon serves as the common tendon of insertion for the gastrocnemius and soleus muscles into the posterior aspect of the calcaneus. This tendon is covered with a paratenon—a sheath lined with synovial-like fluid. Tremendous force is transferred through this tendon with every step, as these muscles concentrically contract to plantar-flex the

CLINICAL PRESENTATION

History

Insidious onset of pain.
Increased symptoms with weight-bearing activities.

Observation

Redness, edema, and/or thickening around the Achilles tendon.

Functional Status

The patient's function is self-limited by pain.
An antalgic gait may be present with more severe cases.

Physical Examination Findings

A palpable nodule may be present in the midsubstance of the tendon.
Passive ankle dorsiflexion places the Achilles tendon on stretch and is often bothersome.
Weakness of the plantar flexor musculature may be noted.

ankle and propel the body forward during gait. Additionally, the tendon is stressed eccentrically as the ankle dorsiflexes during the loading response of gait. While overuse of the tendon can result in symptoms occurring anywhere from its myotendinous junction proximally to its insertion into the calcaneus, the most common site of irritation is in the tendon's midsubstance.[40]

Although the term "tendinitis" is often used to describe pathology of the Achilles tendon, this term is truly accurate only when an active inflammatory process is present. While inflammation may be present in the sheath around the Achilles tendon early in the course of injury, chronic tendinopathy is not associated with active inflammation. Thus the more widely accepted term to describe longstanding Achilles tendon pathology is Achilles tendinosis—a nomenclature that indicates a degenerative pathology of the tendon. This process involves the replacement of the normal type I collagen with the less elastic type III collagen. In addition, areas of increased vascularity and hypercellularity develop during this deterioration of the Achilles tendon (see **Figure 4.33**).[32,41] Although these features might sound as if they would be positive events, they actually result in a weakened tendon. The new tenocytes often differ morphologically from the typical tenocytes, and the new vascular structures are not exact replicas of the normal blood vessels supplying the healthy tendon. The result is often a thickening of the tendon and its sheath at the site of pathology (see **Figure 4.34** and **Figure 4.35**). Over time, the tendon becomes weaker and less efficient in transferring and absorbing forces.

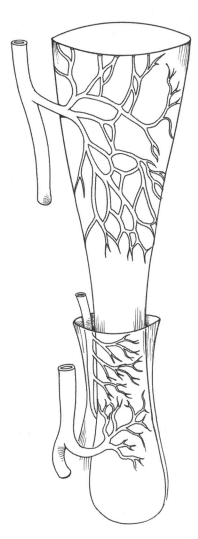

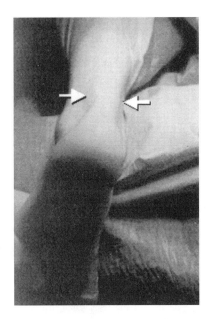

Figure 4.35 Photograph of chronic Achilles tendinopathy. A tender, nodular swelling (arrows) can be seen moving as the ankle is plantar-flexed and dorsiflexed. *Source:* Reproduced with permission from Paavola MP, et al. Current concepts review: Achilles tendinopathy. *J. Bone Joint Surg Am.* 2002;84:2062-2076.

Figure 4.33 Blood supply to the Achilles tendon. Note that longitudinal vessels supply the tendon proximally and distally, whereas transverse vessels supply the middle portion. *Source:* Reproduced with permission from Jones DC. Tendon disorders of the foot and ankle. *J Am Acad Orthop Surg.* 1993;1:87-94.

Patients with Achilles tendinosis will complain of a gradual worsening of pain as the condition progresses. With insertional tendinopathy, a Haglund deformity (pump bump) may form as an exostosis on the posterior calcaneus. The retrocalcaneal bursa may also become inflamed.

Differential Diagnosis
Retrocalcaneal bursitis, calcaneal stress fracture, tibial stress fracture, symptomatic os trigonum, posterior tibialis tendinitis, tarsal tunnel syndrome.

Imaging Techniques
Radiographs can show bony pathology such as a Haglund's deformity, whereas MRI can identify pathology in the tendon itself and the paratenon sheath (see **Figure 4.36**).

Definitive Diagnosis
Clinical symptoms are often sufficient to make the diagnosis of Achilles tendinopathy, once other possible diagnoses have been ruled out. The diagnosis is further confirmed through radiographic findings. In some cases, an Achilles tendon nodule is palpated as the patient plantar-flexes and dorsiflexes the ankle.

Pathomechanics and Functional Limitations
Pain can decrease triceps surae strength, leading to a weak toe-off phase of gait and diminishing the patient's ability to perform functional activities such as jumping. If the condition is advanced, the athlete is unable to perform normal workouts or has pain during workouts. The patient may also report

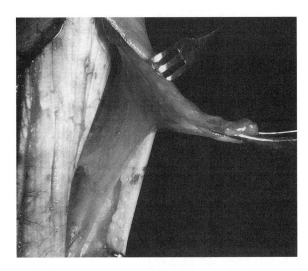

Figure 4.34 Thickening of the Achilles paratenon as the result of inflammation.

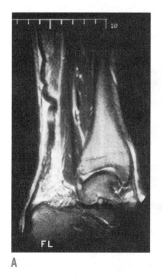
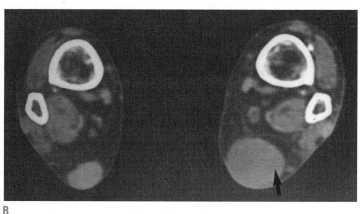

Figure 4.36   Imaging of the Achilles tendon. (**A**) MRI demonstrating a partial longitudinal tear of the Achilles tendon associated with tendinopathy. (**B**) Axial CT scan of both legs. The Achilles tendon of the right leg is notably thicker than the left.

sleep disturbances. Over time, a longitudinal tendon tear may develop.

Medications

Anti-inflammatory modalities and medications should be used when acute inflammation is suspected. Their use in patients with tendinosis, however, is likely to produce only analgesic effects because inflammation is not present. In recalcitrant cases, a corticosteroid injection may be considered; caution must be exercise following such an injection, however, as it is associated with an increased risk for Achilles tendon rupture. Repeated corticosteroid injections are contraindicated.

Surgical Intervention

Surgical intervention is indicated when pain and dysfunction persist despite 3 to 6 months of aggressive Achilles tendon stretching and eccentric strengthening and/or a 1- to 2-month trial of immobilization. Via a medial incision, the tendon sheath is dissected and a tenosynovectomy is performed, removing the nonviable degenerative tissue and bone spurs (see **Figure 4.37**). If the inflammation involves the tendon insertion, the superior calcaneus prominence may be removed as well.

After surgery, return to activity is anticipated in 3 to 4 months, but the surgical results are highly variable. If the calcaneus was debrided, 6 weeks of

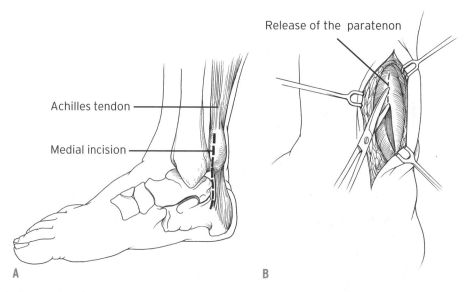

Figure 4.37   Surgical intervention of Achilles tendon inflammation. (**A**) A medial longitudinal incision minimizes cutting of the sural nerve and short saphenous venous system. (**B**) After full-thickness flaps are created, the paratenon is released and any thickened areas are excised. *Source:* Reproduced with permission from Saltzman CL, Tearse DS. Achilles tendon injuries. *J Am Acad Orthop Surg.* 1998;6:316-325.

immobilization is warranted. After paratenonitis surgery, the patient remains on non-weight-bearing status for 7 to 10 days, progressing to full weight bearing as tolerated. With tendinosis, the patient can bear full weight, albeit while protecting the tissues using a rocker boot with an adjustable heel for 2 to 4 weeks. During this time, ROM exercises can be performed.

◼ Postinjury Management

Patients with Achilles tendinopathy should be treated conservatively. Rest is critical in this overuse condition to limit the amount of new stress placed on the tendon. The use of a heel lift may be considered initially to limit stretching of the injured tendon. Likewise, the prescription of appropriate foot orthotics should be considered in patients who have a foot malalignment, such as pes planus and rearfoot valgus, that may be exacerbating the strain placed on the Achilles tendon. As symptoms diminish, a progressive stretching and strengthening program should be implemented. The use of a progressive eccentric exercise program has been found to be particularly effective in the rehabilitation of patients with Achilles tendinopathy.

◼ Injury-Specific Treatment and Rehabilitation Concerns

> **Specific Concerns**
>
> Decrease Achilles tendon stress.
> Improve Achilles tendon, ankle, and hamstring flexibility.
> Restore Achilles tendon soft-tissue mobility.

The primary goal with Achilles tendinopathy is to identify and correct (as much as possible) the causative factors. As a consequence, changes in the athlete's workout may be required. The athlete who is restricted in activities can maintain cardiovascular fitness and preserve or develop muscle strength in the uninvolved extremities. Pool running may be possible if it does not irritate the Achilles tendon. Open kinetic chain exercises for the involved extremity's hip, knee, and foot can also be included during the non-weight-bearing phase of rehabilitation. Once inflammation is alleviated, a gradual progression of eccentric exercises effectively treats tendinitis.[42]

Heel lifts can be inserted in the shoes to relieve Achilles tendon stress; arch supports or orthotic appliances should be used to correct biomechanical or structural deviations. Stretching exercises

may be implemented to improve Achilles, ankle, and hamstring flexibility. Ice, ultrasound, cross-friction massage, and NSAIDs may all assist in relieving inflammation. A progressive program of eccentric exercises is initiated once the inflammation is manageable—for example, when the athlete can performs 3 sets of 10 heel raises at a moderate eccentric pace without pain.

◼ Estimated Amount of Time Lost

The patient's activity is limited primarily by pain. The time lost from activity varies greatly; the condition is self-limiting, but return is also governed by the degree of inflammation, the individual's tolerance, and the success of efforts to reduce inflammation. Reduced activity is recommended until the inflammation can be controlled and causative factors resolved.

◼ Return-to-Play Criteria

The causative factors involved in the athlete's tendinopathy must be identified and corrected or diminished. To avoid pain during activity, inflammation should be resolved before the athlete is allowed to fully resume sport participation.

Functional Bracing

Orthoses may be necessary to correct biomechanical or structural deviations contributing to Achilles tendinopathy. If calf flexibility remains a problem, inserting heel lifts into the shoes may reduce some of the Achilles stress.

Achilles Tendon Rupture

CLINICAL PRESENTATION

History

Sudden onset of pain and disability.
A report of being kicked or hit in the back of the leg.

Observation

Edema over the distal aspect of the posterior calf.
Obvious deformity.

Functional Status

Inability to ambulate normally.

Physical Examination Findings

A palpable defect in the Achilles tendon.
Marked decrease in plantar flexion strength.
A positive Thompson test.

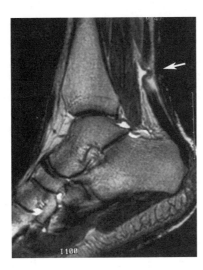

Figure 4.38 Sagittal MRI demonstrating an acute, incomplete tear of the Achilles tendon.

Rupture to the Achilles tendon typically occurs 5 to 7 cm from the tendon's insertion point (see Figure 4.38). This injury is most often seen in male athletes between 30 and 40 years of age, although it may also occur in younger athletes and females.[40] The mechanism typically consists of power-producing movements such as a jump, sprint, or rapid change-of-direction maneuver. The athlete may or may not have complained of prodromal Achilles tendinopathy. At the time of injury, the patient will report a sudden "pop" and immediate pain in the calf. The sensation is often described as being kicked or hit in the back of the leg. Immediate disability will be present. Referral to an orthopaedic surgeon should occur as soon as the injury is diagnosed.

Differential Diagnosis

Achilles tendinosis, gastrocnemius strain, plantaris strain, deep vein thrombosis.

Imaging Techniques

A clinical diagnosis can typically be made without imaging. Even so, MRI may prove useful in determining whether there is a complete or incomplete rupture of the Achilles tendon (see Figure 4.38).

Definitive Diagnosis

A clinical diagnosis of a complete Achilles tendon rupture can be made based on a positive Thompson test result, in which squeezing of the triceps surae group fails to produce plantar flexion. Partial tendon tears are diagnosed based on the findings of MRI studies.

Pathomechanics and Functional Limitations

The athlete is unable to ambulate or does so with difficulty and cannot stand on the toes of the involved leg.

■ Immediate Management

On-field management of an Achilles tendon rupture should consist of rest, ice, compression, and elevation. The ankle should be immobilized in slight plantar flexion, and the patient should use crutches for non-weight-bearing ambulation. The athlete should be referred to an orthopeadic surgeon for medical management.

■ Medications

Narcotic pain medication may be used to control severe pain. However, pain is often not an overriding problem.

■ Postinjury Management

The ankle is immobilized in a position that approximates the Achilles tendon, with approximately 20° or less of plantar flexion. (If this position does not appropriately realign the tendon, surgical repair should be performed.) Immobilization and non-weight-bearing restrictions are maintained for at least 2 weeks. The patient next progresses to a short leg cast or boot for an additional 6 to 8 weeks and then is gradually weaned from it. When normal footwear is introduced, a ½- to ¾-in. heel lift is used for 1 month, followed by 1 month of a 1-cm lift. Progressive resistance exercises can be started at 8 to 10 weeks after injury.

■ Surgical Intervention

While conservative treatment consisting of 6 to 8 weeks of immobilization in slight plantar flexion may be used for sedentary patients with Achilles tendon ruptures, surgical repair is typically indicated in athletes. Surgical reapproximation of the tendon ends reestablishes "normal" gastrocnemius-soleus tendon length (see **ST** 4.6). Surgical repair of the ruptured tendon should be performed within a few days of injury.

■ Postoperative Management

Postoperatively, the patient is immobilized in slight plantar flexion in a removable boot and weight bearing is not allowed for 2 to 3 weeks. A CAM walking boot fitted with a heel lift is then used for 6 weeks postoperatively, with the amount of dorsiflexion allowed being gradually increased over time. Gentle ROM exercises may begin 3 to 7 days after surgery, but aggressive stretching and

S|T **Surgical Technique** 4.6

Achilles Tendon Repair

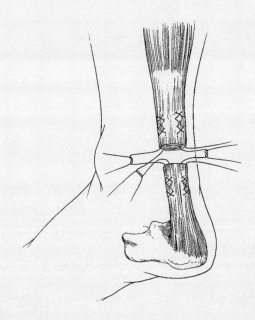

Indication

Ruptured Achilles tendon.

Procedure Overview

1. A medial incision is made over the Achilles tendon to expose the stumps.
2. The stumps are approximated using two to four sutures. If the rupture occurred at the bony attachment, suture anchors are required.
3. Some surgeons also advocate repair of the paratenon.
4. If Achilles tendinitis is present, the nonviable degenerative tissue is debrided, and the bone spurs and prominence of the posterior superior calcaneus are removed.
5. The ankle is immobilized in 20° of plantar flexion.

Functional Limitations

Calf size following this procedure is smaller; thus the involved extremity must be isolated to regain full strength and size. The tendon is thicker after surgery.

Implications for Rehabilitation

Achilles stretching is avoided for 3 to 6 weeks after surgery to protect the tendon from "stretching out." Plantar flexion mobility and strengthening can begin early (2 to 4 weeks postoperatively).

Comments

After Achilles repair, return to sport requires 6 to 12 months.

Source: Figure reproduced with permission from Saltzman CL, Tearse DS. Achilles tendon injuries. *J Am Acad Orthop Surg.* 1998;6:316-325.

---

strengthening exercises should not be performed until at least 3 weeks after surgery. Gait retraining will be necessary after the discontinuation of ambulatory devices. Use of a heel lift may be required for several months. Rehabilitation should also emphasize muscular strength, endurance, proprioceptive, and agility exercises. Return to sport will typically take at least 6 months with surgical intervention.

▪ Injury-Specific Treatment and Rehabilitation Concerns

Specific Concerns

Avoid forceful motion for the first 8 to 12 weeks.
Restore Achilles tendon length.
Restore triceps surae strength.

With conservative management, the athlete begins rehabilitation in a cast or CAM boot in plantar flexion; the cast is changed or the CAM boot is adjusted monthly to gradually increase dorsiflexion to reach the neutral position by 3 months. A foot orthotic appliance that restricts dorsiflexion to neutral is then worn for an additional 4 to 8 weeks.

Because surgical repair of a ruptured Achilles tendon offers quicker recovery and a lower rerupture rate than nonsurgical management, athletes usually undergo surgical treatment for this condition. Different surgical techniques are available; the athlete's recovery depends on the surgical technique and the postoperative protocol. A more liberal protocol uses a postoperative posterior splint that is removed on the third day to allow early passive ROM within a pain-free range throughout the day.[43] Early weight bearing is permitted after the sutures are removed during the second or third week postoperatively. A CAM boot that allows full plantar flexion but limits dorsiflexion to −10° is used for the next 2 weeks. At week 4, neutral dorsiflexion is permitted.

A more conservative postoperative protocol requires the patient to have a below-knee cast, with progressive decreases in ankle plantar flexion occurring every 3 weeks for 6 weeks.[44] At 6 weeks, the cast is removed, and active ankle exercises, including strengthening and full weight bearing, are allowed. Jogging can begin in a pool; it is permitted on land at 3 months postoperatively. Provided the athlete has fully recovered in all areas, unrestricted activity is allowed at 6 months.

Two extremes of care exist, and most surgeons opt for a postoperative protocol that lies in between the two. The patient's foot is placed in a boot with the ankle positioned in 15° to 30° of plantar flexion, and no weight bearing is permitted for 1 to 3 weeks. During this time, the athlete can perform toe exercises and active ankle and foot ROM exercises within the boot. Knee and hip exercises can also be performed as long as the boot is worn. After the third week, toe-touch weight bearing is started; by week 6, the athlete begins progressing to full weight bearing as tolerated. During the toe-touch weight-bearing period, slow isometric exercises can be initiated with the foot in the boot. Starting in the third week, the plantar flexion angle of the boot is decreased 5° each week until the patient can wear a shoe with a heel lift by week 8. Gentle active ROM moving into dorsiflexion can also begin in the third week. At 6 weeks, slow, progressive, passive Achilles stretching can start, along with intrinsic muscle strengthening and stationary bicycling, with push-off only from the heel, not the toes. In aggressive rehabilitation, the patient engages in stationary bicycling while wearing a boot at 2 weeks and full weight bearing at 3 weeks.

When full weight bearing is permitted, gait training is required. After week 8, a gradual progression of resistive exercises is started, beginning with light resistance and limited excursion, which gradually increase to tolerance. Running activities are delayed until about 6 months.

■ Estimated Amount of Time Lost

The amount of time lost from activity depends on the treatment technique selected. It ranges from 6 to 12 months for surgical repair to more than a year for conservative care.

■ Return-to-Play Criteria

If the Achilles remains tight, a heel lift in the shoes may relieve some tendon stress. Rehabilitation after an Achilles repair is prolonged, and significant deficiencies occur in motion, strength, proprioception, and sport performance for several months, so these factors must be restored before the athlete can safely return to full sport participation.

Functional Bracing
A heel lift may be required if full ROM into dorsiflexion is not present.

Retrocalcaneal Bursitis

CLINICAL PRESENTATION

History

Pain arising from the posterior calcaneus.

Observation

Retrocalcaneal exostosis (pump bump).
Swelling.

Functional Status

Plantar flexion compresses the soft tissues, resulting in pain.
Pain may be decreased when walking barefoot.
Walking on the toes or in high heels may increase pain.

Physical Examination Findings

Pain occurs when pressure is applied to the soft tissue anterior to the Achilles tendon. The tendon itself is not painful.
Increased tissue temperature and swelling may be noted lateral to the Achilles tendon.

Retrocalcaneal bursa inflammation is also known as Haglund disease, "pump bump," and tendo-Achilles bursitis. Mechanical disorders such as repetitive retrocalcaneal compression or friction can lead to this condition.[45]

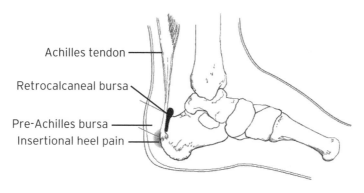

Achilles tendon
Retrocalcaneal bursa
Pre-Achilles bursa
Insertional heel pain

Figure 4.39 Sites of posterior heel pain. *Source:* Reproduced with permission from Greene WB (ed). *Essentials of Musculoskeletal Care*, ed 2. Rosemont, IL: American Academy of Orthopaedic Surgeons; 2000:493.

The bursa's anterior wall lies against the calcaneus, and its posterior wall merges with the epitenon of the Achilles tendon[46] (see **Figure 4.39**). Its fluid is highly viscous. Thus, when the bursa becomes inflamed, its walls become thickened and edematous. During normal ambulation, the enlarged bursa is compressed between the calcaneus and the Achilles, a condition that is intensified when shoes are worn.

Foot pathomechanics resulting from excessive pronation contribute to this condition. Wearing negative-heeled shoes can increase the bursal compression by stretching the Achilles tendon during initial contact and midstance. A shortened Achilles also increases the compression force on the bursa.

Differential Diagnosis
Achilles tendinitis, plantar fasciitis, calcaneal stress fracture.

Imaging Techniques
Bursography differentiates between retrocalcaneal bursitis and insertional Achilles tendinitis.[46] An enlarged Haglund process can be noted on lateral radiographs. Sagittal MRI can demonstrate an enlarged retrocalcaneal bursa (see **Figure 4.40**).

Definitive Diagnosis
Diagnosis of retrocalcaneal bursitis is made through positive physical examination and exclusion of other conditions.

Pathomechanics and Functional Limitations
Alteration of the patient's gait secondary to Achilles tendon tightening or foot overpronation can redistribute forces along the foot and lower extremity. Retrocalcaneal bursitis can, therefore, lead to Achilles tendinitis, metatarsal stress fractures, and lower extremity inflammatory conditions.

epitenon A glistening, synovial-like membrane that envelops the tendon surface.

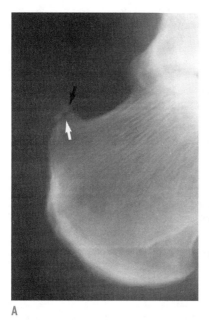

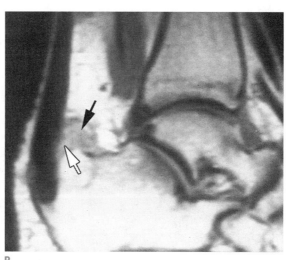

A   B

Figure 4.40 Imaging of retrocalcaneal bursitis. (**A**) Lateral radiograph of the calcaneus demonstrating an enlarged Haglund process (white arrow). The exostosis has fragmented (black arrow). The clouding around the structure indicates soft-tissue inflammation. (**B**) Sagittal MRI demonstrating enlargement of the retrocalcaneal bursa (black arrow) and inflammation of the Achilles tendon insertion on the Haglund process (white arrow).

Immediate Management

Ice and immobilization may help to decrease the inflammatory process. Relief of external pressure from shoes or heel straps is also helpful.

Medications

Pain and inflammation can be controlled by the use of NSAIDs. With recalcitrant symptoms, corticosteroid injections can be used in an attempt to decrease the inflammatory reaction.

Postinjury Management

The three primary concerns are to (1) identify and correct the cause of retrocalcaneal bursitis, (2) reduce the inflammation, and (3) restore all deficiencies to allow the individual to return to full participation.

A doughnut pad can be placed over the bursa to reduce friction. During peak inflammation, however, the patient will likely prefer to wear a slipper or sandal without a back or back strap. A heel lift may reduce the biomechanical forces on the Achilles tendon.

Surgical Intervention

Surgery for retrocalcaneal bursitis is rarely indicated. Surgery involves excision of the exostosis and the superior border of the calcaneal tuberosity. If the Achilles tendon is calcified, the involved portion may be removed through a longitudinal incision. After surgery, a padded short leg cast or brace is applied with the ankle maintained in approximately 20° of plantar flexion for 3 weeks.

Postoperative Management

The patient remains on non-weight-bearing status for approximately 3 weeks after surgery and then uses a walker boot. Active plantar flexion and dorsiflexion exercises can be initiated once the patient transitions to the boot.

Injury-Specific Treatment and Rehabilitation Concerns

Specific Concerns

Decrease compressive forces on the calcaneus and Achilles tendon caused by footwear.
If present, protect the exostosis with a doughnut pad.
Correct improper foot mechanics.
Increase Achilles tendon flexibility.

Resolving this condition is rooted in correcting the underlying cause and reducing inflammation. Two factors that often contribute to retrocalcaneal bursitis are a tight Achilles tendon and a flaccid foot that promotes excessive pronation. When the foot is pronated during the gait phase as it should be supinating, a medial torque is applied to the Achilles tendon; this torque increases pressure on the bursa. Placing a lift in the shoe heel can reduce the stretching stress on the Achilles and compression on the bursa. (Both shoes should have the same-size lift to prevent lumbosacral injury.) Custom orthotic appliances may correct foot alignment to place less pressure on the bursa and also can lift the heel. Ice, whirlpool treatment, and ultrasound can be used to reduce the inflammation.

Estimated Amount of Time Lost

At least 4 to 6 weeks may be required for the condition to resolve.

Return-to-Play Criteria

Return to full sport participation is permitted once inflammation has subsided and the causes of the condition have been resolved. At this point, the patient should be able to wear an athletic shoe without discomfort.

Functional Bracing

If the patient has a flaccid, excessively flexible, or planus foot, orthotic appliances should be provided and used for all activities.

Peroneal Tendon Subluxations and Dislocations

CLINICAL PRESENTATION

History

Mechanism of sudden, strong peroneal contractions, especially when the ankle is dorsiflexed.
Pain arising from the posterior aspect of the lateral malleolus.
A "snap" or "pop" as the tendon dislocated from the groove.

Observation

Swelling posterior to the lateral malleolus.

Functional Status

If the tendon remains dislocated, ambulation is difficult or impossible.
Complaints of the ankle "giving way" as the tendon dislocates are common in chronic conditions.

Physical Examination Findings

Motion into plantar flexion and inversion is normal.
An avulsed segment of the superior peroneal retinaculum may be palpated.
Resisted eversion causes pain and may reproduce the symptoms.
Crepitus may be palpated over the tendons as they pass behind the lateral malleolus.

Most peroneal tendon subluxations and dislocations primarily involve the peroneus brevis tendon (PBT). The least severe injury occurs when the PBT displaces anterior to the lateral malleolus but remains within the peroneal retinaculum. In more severe cases, the retinaculum tears and a bony segment avulses from its posterior attachment, such that the retinaculum lies posterior to the PBT.

The mechanism of injury is a sudden, severe contraction of the peroneals while the ankle is dorsiflexed. Snow skiers are susceptible to this type of injury when the ski tips dig into the snow and the skier falls forward or digs the inner ski borders into the snow during a turn. Peroneal tendon subluxations and dislocations are also seen in skating, water skiing, gymnastics, basketball, football, tennis, and dancing.

Peroneal dislocations can be acute or chronic. Acute injuries may be misdiagnosed as lateral ankle sprains. The dislocated tendons often relocate spontaneously, so the actual injury remains undiagnosed. Patients with a history of recurrent ankle sprains should be evaluated for peroneal tendon subluxation or dislocation.

Predisposing anatomic conditions that may contribute to this injury include the following: (1) a shallow fibular groove for the peroneal tendons, (2) a prominent calcaneofibular ligament, (3) congenital absence of the peroneal retinaculum, (4) acquired or congenital laxity of the peroneal retinaculum, and (5) a low peroneus brevis muscle belly that crowds the fibular malleolar groove.[47]

Differential Diagnosis

Lateral ankle sprain, chronic ankle instability, anterolateral impingement syndrome, nerve injury, osteochondral lesions, arthritis.

Imaging Techniques

A CT scan or MRI with axial views may assist in diagnosing peroneal inflammation, tendon disruption, or dislocation. A superior peroneal retinaculum avulsion can result in a bony fragment being laterally displaced—a condition which can be identified through a "fleck sign"[48] (see **Figure 4.41**).

Definitive Diagnosis

The definitive diagnosis is based on a positive history of complaints indicating that the tendon is slipping out of its groove, such as snapping and popping, and is confirmed by visualization or palpation of the dislocating tendon.

Pathomechanics and Functional Limitations

In addition to pain and swelling affecting normal function, repeated PBT subluxation against the fibula can cause a longitudinal tear or shredding of the tendon. Chronic ankle instability is another complication of chronic PBT subluxation. If left untreated, adaptive tendon shortening occurs, resulting in reduced power and function during ambulation.

Gait is also mechanically altered when the tendon dislocates from the peroneal groove. When the tendons are displaced anteriorly, their mechanical angle of pull changes from that of a plantar flexor to a dorsiflexor with a strong eversion component.

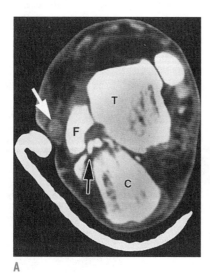 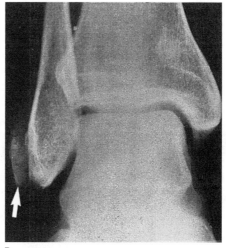

A   B

Figure 4.41 Radiographic images of peroneal tendon dislocations. (**A**) CT scan showing lateral displacement of the peroneal tendon (white arrow). There is also an associated subluxation of the subtalar joint (black arrow). (**B**) The "fleck sign" associated with a rupture of the superior peroneal retinaculum. As the retinaculum avulses from the anterior fibula, a piece (fleck) of bone may be displaced (white arrow).

Immediate Management

Acute injuries are managed using ice, compression, and elevation.

Medications

Pain and the inflammatory process that can accompany a dislocating or subluxating tendon can be limited by the use of NSAIDs.

Postinjury Management

Successful conservative treatment can occur but is rare. Conservative attempts to maintain the tendon in place may include adhesive strapping with a pad to restrict subluxation, J-shaped pads that anchor in front of the fibula and wrap around laterally and posteriorly to hold the tendon in place, and non-weight-bearing restrictions maintained for 3 weeks (see Figure 4.42). If the foot is kept relatively stable and the tape restricts the tendon's movement, scar-tissue formation may allow the tendon to be managed without surgery.

If an acute injury is treated conservatively with a non-weight-bearing short leg cast for 6 weeks and results are successful, the time lost may be an additional 3 to 6 weeks, depending on the individual's response to treatment. Although most reports of conservative management indicate poor success rates with this approach,[49,50] some physicians attempt conservative treatment in acute cases.

Surgical Intervention

Chronic peroneal tendon subluxations and dislocations are universally treated with surgical repair.[49,51,52] The surgery typically involves deepening the posterior fibular groove and reconstructing the superior retinaculum. After surgery, concomitant dorsiflexion and eversion are avoided to remove stress from the retinacular reconstruction, but plantar flexion and inversion actively create smooth tendon excursion. Return to athletic competition is expected after 3 to 4 months of rehabilitation.

Postoperative Management

After surgery, the ankle is maintained for 4 weeks in a non-weight-bearing cast, followed by 2 weeks in a weight-bearing cast. Active and resisted dorsiflexion and eversion are prevented during the early rehabilitation phase (approximately 6 to 8 weeks). This is followed by progressive resistance and ROM exercises within 2 weeks.

Injury-Specific Treatment and Rehabilitation Concerns

> **Specific Concerns**
>
> Avoid eversion and dorsiflexion motions to reduce stress on the superior retinaculum.
> Restrict motion, especially dorsiflexion with eversion, for the first 6 to 8 weeks.

Early in the rehabilitation process, superior peroneal retinaculum stresses are reduced by avoiding dorsiflexion and eversion. Once the patient begins partial weight bearing in a CAM boot, active plantar flexion and inversion can begin, but the return to the starting position (the motion of dorsiflexion and eversion) must be passive. Talar mobilization exercises and active dorsiflexion and eversion begin when the patient can bear weight without pain.

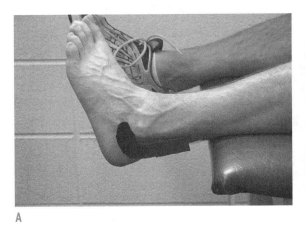
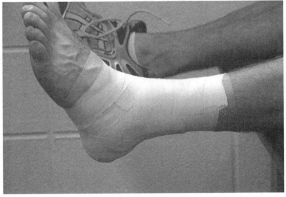

A   B

Figure 4.42 Use of a J-pad to control peroneal subluxations. (**A**) A foam or felt pad is cut to conform to the path of the peroneal tendons as they pass around the lateral malleolus. (**B**) The pad is secured using athletic or elastic tape.

The progression of resisted strengthening, proprioception, and agility exercises is initiated when the patient can bear weight without pain when not wearing a brace. As strength and proprioception improve, the patient can progress through plyometric and functional activities that lead to a return to competition.

Estimated Amount of Time Lost

Conservative approaches to management may result in 6 to 12 weeks of time lost from competition. After surgical repair, the patient may be withheld from competition for 2 to 4 months.

Return-to-Play Criteria

Before returning to full participation, the patient must have full motion without pain or tendon subluxation during functional activities.

Functional Bracing

A J-pad may be used in an attempt to decrease the forces on the superior peroneal retinaculum (see Figure 4.42).

LEG INJURIES

Acute Compartment Syndrome

The leg consists of four distinct muscular compartments that are separated fascia and, in some cases, the two bones of the lower leg and their interosseous

CLINICAL PRESENTATION

History

Initial trauma to the lower leg such as a contusion or fracture.
Gradually worsening symptoms that are often disproportionate to the initial injury.

Observation

The skin over the involved compartment is distended and may be pale.

Functional Status

Extreme pain limits the patient's ability to walk.

Physical Examination Findings

Pain with passive stretching of the muscles in the involved compartment.
Diminished sensation distal to the site of injury.
Diminished distal pulses may be present.

membrane (see Figure 4.43). In addition to muscles, these compartments contain neurovascular structures. While the elasticity of the fascia allows for increases in fluid volume within each compartment, such as occur with exercise, trauma can sometimes result in massive swelling that creates neurovascular compromise within a compartment. Injuries such as fractures, contusions, and muscle strains can trigger a compartment syndrome.

As the amount of swelling accumulates within a given compartment, increased pressure is placed on vascular structures. Of particular concern is the increased pressure placed on veins. Normal blood flow to and from the extremities requires an arteriovenous gradient with more pressure in the arteries than in

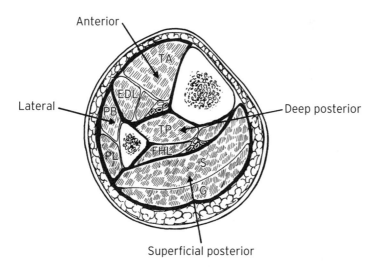

Figure 4.43 Cross-section of the proximal half of the leg shows the direction of needle insertion for testing each compartment. EDL, extensor digitorum longus; FHL, flexor hallucis longus; G, gastrocnemius; PB, peroneus brevis; S, soleus; TA, tibialis anterior; TP, tibialis posterior. *Source:* Reproduced with permission from Whitesides TE, Heckman MM. Acute compartment syndrome: Update on diagnosis and treatment. *J Am Acad Orthop Surg.* 1996;4:209-218.

the veins. As swelling increases pressure equally throughout a closed compartment, the gradient between arteries and veins equalizes, stagnating the return of blood to the heart via veins and limiting the flow of oxygenated blood into the compartment. The resulting effect is ischemia to the tissues within the compartment. Prolonged ischemia will result in necrosis of the muscles and nerves; thus acute compartment syndrome is a limb-threatening emergency.

A patient with acute compartment syndrome will present with a swollen and distended leg that may exhibit pallor. The patient's pain is often out of proportion to the extent of the underlying injury. Passive stretching of the involved muscle group produces extreme pain (e.g., passive plantar flexion of the ankle will be extremely painful in a patient with acute anterior compartment syndrome) and may be the most reliable symptom of compartment syndrome.[53] Paresthesia distal to the site of injury may be a sign of compartment syndrome, as may a diminished distal pulse. Patients suspected of having acute compartment syndrome should be referred to a hospital emergency department for prompt treatment.

Differential Diagnosis

Deep vein thrombosis, popliteal artery claudication, peripheral nerve entrapment, tibial fracture, fibular fracture, muscle strain, muscle contusion.

Imaging Techniques

Radiographs may be used to identify associated fractures, and MRI may be used to identify intracompartmental swelling. Neither imaging modality, however, is essential to the diagnosis of acute compartment syndrome.

Medical Diagnostic Tests

Measurement of intracompartmental pressure is needed to confirm the presence of compartment syndrome. In certain cases, such as concurrent tibial fractures, time-series pressure measurements may be ordered.[53]

Definitive Diagnosis

A clinical diagnosis of acute compartment syndrome can be made based on the injury history and the patient's signs and symptoms. If intracompartmental pressure measurements are taken, the diagnosis is confirmed if the diastolic pressure minus the intracompartmental pressure is less than or equal to 30 mm Hg.

Pathomechanics and Functional Limitations

The patient is unable to bear weight on the involved limb. As pressure increases within the compartment, the neurovascular structures become compressed, increasing pain and decreasing the distal

fasciotomy
Surgical incision of the fascia.

blood supply and innervation. The distal extremity may swell secondary to impaired venous return. In the worst-case scenario, vascular and neurologic compromise can lead to permanent disability of the distal extremity.

■ Immediate Management

Acute compartment syndrome is a medical emergency, and an athlete suspected of having this condition should be immediately transported to a hospital emergency department. Ice and elevation may be used in an attempt to limit swelling, but external compression should not be applied to the leg.

■ Medications

Intravenous, intramuscular, or oral narcotic medications may be administered for short-term pain relief, but it is inappropriate to use them to delay the need for surgical intervention. The failure to control pain with narcotics should be a warning of potential acute compartment syndrome.

■ Surgical Intervention

Patients with acute compartment syndrome are almost always treated surgically with a fasciotomy (see **Figure 4.44**). All four compartments must be released. An anterior incision is made from the proximal tibia to the distal tibia to identify the intermuscular septum that separates the anterior and lateral compartments, taking care to avoid the superficial peroneal nerve. These two compartments can be released through this single incision. The deep posterior and posterior compartments are released through a medial incision, avoiding the saphenous vein and nerve. The deep posterior compartment is approached through a medial tibial periosteal approach. The incisions are typically left open for several days to allow the inflammatory process of the initial injury to run its course.

■ Postinjury/Postoperative Management

Great care must be taken to keep the surgical wounds clean postoperatively to prevent infections. Repeated wash-out procedures and secondary closures are required. Tissue jacks have become popular means to close the wounds after repetitive wash-out procedures once tissue viability is assured. These devices can speed the healing process, as they enable the surgeon to avoid performing split-thickness skin grafts. The wounds are closed after several days.

The extremity should be elevated to decrease interstitial pressures and to encourage venous

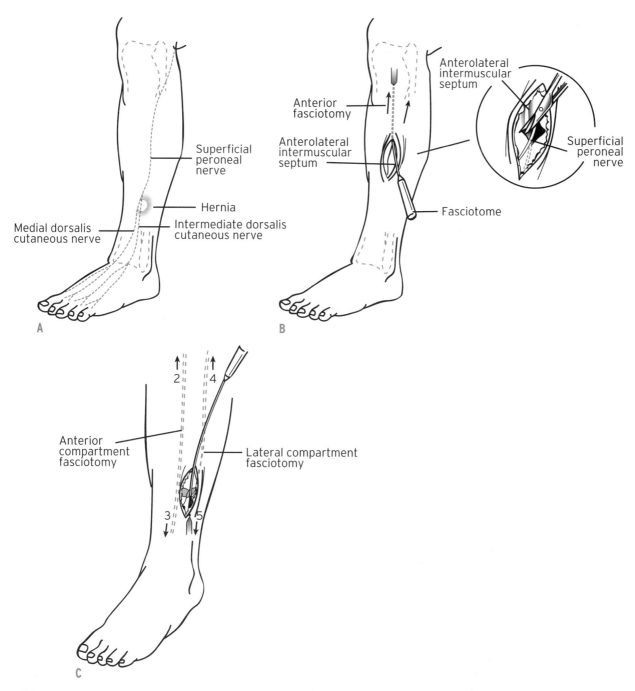

Figure 4.44 Single-incision release of the anterior compartment. (**A**) The compartment's neurovascular structures are identified and avoided during the procedure. The incision is made directly over the defect, if one is present. Otherwise, the incision is made between the tibial crest and fibular shaft. (**B**) The fasciotome is first passed superiorly. (**C**) A second pass is made to release the fascia.

and lymphatic return. Ice packs placed on the extremity can minimize swelling and limit secondary hypoxic injury. A compression wrap should not be applied until permitted by the attending physician. Crutch use is often indicated. Once wound healing occurs, a progressive rehabilitation program may be instituted and the athlete typically can return to play a few months after initial injury.

Injury-Specific Treatment and Rehabilitation Concerns

Specific Concerns

Monitor and change dressings to prevent infection.
Prevent unwanted pressure increases within the compartment.
Stretch compartmental muscles as tolerated.

Once healing of the surgical incisions has been deemed to have progressed to an appropriate point by the physician, ankle ROM and strengthening exercises can begin. The rehabilitation program progresses as described for ankle sprains.

Estimated Amount of Time Lost

Approximately 12 weeks is required after surgery for complete recovery.[54] Posterior compartment release requires more time for recovery than anterior or lateral compartment release because of the more extensive dissection and healing of a larger muscle mass.

Return-to-Play Criteria

Even after the surgical sites are healed, the tissue remains relatively fragile for several months. Thus, if the patient participates in contact or collision sports, protective padding over the wounds may be necessary to prevent skin breakdown. If the surgical release was performed in a timely manner, the patient may have no deleterious effect on motor or sensory innervation. If permanent sensory deficit has occurred, return to sport participation may still be possible, but this decision depends on the extent of the deficit and the sport.

Functional Bracing

Protective covering of the healed surgical sites may be indicated if there is a risk of damaging the cutaneous scar tissue. Once healing is complete (approximately 12 weeks postoperatively), protective padding is no longer needed.

Exercise-Related Lower Leg Pain

Overuse injury to the lower leg is a common occurrence in athletes and others participating in exercise and physical activity. Many nonspecific terms such as "shin splints" and "medial tibial stress syndrome" have been used to describe a collection of symptoms without identifying a specific pain generator or source of pathology. The equally vague term "exercise-related lower leg pain" (ERLLP) has become the diagnosis of choice in recent years.

Athletes with ERLLP typically present with areas of pain on the posteromedial aspect of the tibia,

CLINICAL PRESENTATION

	Tibial Periostitis	Tibial Stress Fracture	Chronic Exertional Compartment Syndrome
History	Insidious onset of ERLLP. Diffuse pain during and after exercise.	Insidious onset of ERLLP. Sharp and distinct point of pain during and after exercise.	Insidious onset of ERLLP. Intense pain and paresthesia present only during exercise. Symptoms resolve quickly after exercise is ceased.
Observation	No obvious deformity at site of injury. Malalignment associated with hyperpronation often is present.	No obvious deformity at site of injury. Malalignment associated with hyperpronation often is present.	No obvious deformity at site of injury.
Functional Status	Pain may limit the ability to perform weight-bearing exercise.	Pain may limit the ability to perform weight-bearing exercise.	Intense pain prevents the athlete from participating in prolonged weight-bearing exercise.
Physical Examination	Diffuse tenderness extending several centimeters on the posteromedial aspect of the tibia. Pain and weakness with resisted contraction of involved muscles	Sharp point tenderness on the posteromedial aspect of the tibia. Palpation of a bony callus may present after several weeks of symptoms	Examination is unremarkable when performed while the athlete is at rest

ERLLP, exercise-related lower leg pain.

with the pain being exacerbated during and after weight-bearing exercise. Although the exact pathology is not always fully understood, potential specific diagnoses include tibial periostitis, tibial stress fracture, and chronic exertional compartment syndrome. These conditions should not be viewed as residing along a continuum, but instead should be viewed as distinct injuries to specific tissues. Each diagnosis has specific characteristics and treatment approaches.

■ Tibial Periostitis

Tibial periostitis is characterized by diffuse pain along the posterior medial aspect of the lower two-thirds of the tibia. Areas of tenderness may range from a few to several centimeters in length. The pain is typically worse during and after weight-bearing exercise and may become persistent during walking as well. The source of pathology is thought to be an inflammation of the periosteum at the origins of the soleus and/or one or more of the deep posterior compartment muscles (tibialis posterior, flexor digitorum longus, flexor hallucis longus). The origins of all of these muscles are placed under tension with pronation of the foot during the loading response of gait. Hyperpronation—like that commonly exhibited in patients with foot malalignment such as rearfoot valgus, pes planus, plantarflexed first ray, and forefoot varus—will increase the tension placed on these tendons of origin. This tension is thought to cause inflammation of the periosteum at the site of tendon attachment along the posteromedial tibia. Overtraining allows microtrauma to outpace tissue remodeling and can lead to chronic inflammation of the periosteum. If left unresolved, continued overuse via weight-bearing exercise may lead to tibial stress fracture, although this outcome is not inevitable.

■ Tibial Stress Fracture

One of the most common sites of stress fracture is in the lower two-thirds of the tibia. If bone reabsorption occurs at a faster rate than bone repair and remodeling, a stress fracture will occur. Clinical suspicion of a stress fracture should be high when an athlete presents with point tenderness less than a centimeter in length along the posteromedial aspect of the tibia. Palpation of a bony callus may occur once the stress fracture has begun to heal, although such a callus typically takes several weeks to develop. Radiographs taken in the first few weeks after the onset of pain are often negative with stress fractures. A bone scan, however, will show areas of increased bony metabolism associated with stress fracture.

Female athletes with menstrual irregularities such as amenorrhea and oligomenorrhea are predisposed to stress fractures because of hypoestrogenism. Observe for all aspects of the female athlete triad—disordered eating, abnormal menstruation, and osteopenia—when working with these athletes.

■ Chronic Exertional Compartment Syndrome

Chronic exertional compartment syndrome (CECS) is the third and final distinct pathology that falls under the umbrella of ERLLP. CECS has some similarities in symptom presentation to acute compartment syndrome, but the inciting event with CECS is exercise rather than macrotrauma. With CECS, the increased blood flow associated with exercise causes an increase in fluid volume within the compartments of the exercising muscles. Normally, the fascia surrounding each compartment will expand in response to exercise. With CECS, however, inadequate expansion of the fascia occurs; in turn, the increased fluid volume due to exercise places pressure on the vascular structures, resulting in ischemia within the involved compartments. The intense ischemic pain forces the athlete to stop exercising.

The unique presentation of CECS is that patients are typically symptomatic only when they are exercising. Once they stop exercising, the symptoms quickly resolve. This pattern can be used in making a diagnosis of CECS—patients will usually present for evaluation when they are asymptomatic. When athletes complain of ERLLP that is very intense and is present only during (and never after) weight-bearing exercise, the professional should maintain a high suspicion of CECS. CECS may affect any of the four compartments of the lower leg and often occurs in more than one compartment simultaneously.

Differential Diagnosis

Periostitis, fibular stress fracture, tibial stress fracture, tibial stress reaction, medial tibial syndrome, tenosynovitis, tarsal tunnel syndrome, muscle disorders, infection, popliteal artery claudication, peripheral nerve entrapment, tumor.

Imaging Techniques

Radiographs are often unremarkable until the patient is symptomatic for several weeks. Bone scan show increased bony metabolism at the stress fracture site earlier than MRI, although MRI is occasionally used to rule out stress reactions (see **Figure 4.45**).

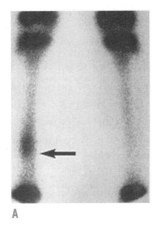
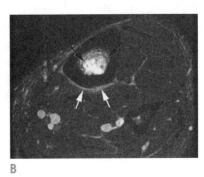

Figure 4.45 Imaging of tibial stress fractures. (**A**) Bone scan demonstrating focal uptake characteristic of a stress fracture (arrow). (**B**) MRI indicating bone marrow edema (black arrows) and periosteal edema (white arrows) indicative of a stress fracture.

Medical Diagnostic Tests

Diagnostic studies are undertaken when there is a clinical suspicion of chronic exertional compartment syndrome. Such tests involve compartment pressure measurements taken before and after exercise activity after onset of symptoms, using commercially available slit catheters. Elevated pressures preactivity (more than 15 mm Hg) and/or postactivity (more than 30 mm Hg) aid in the diagnosis.

Definitive Diagnosis

The definitive diagnosis of tibial stress fracture is based on the results of diagnostic imaging, medical diagnostic tests, and/or clinical signs and symptoms. Diagnosis of CECS is made based on the results of intracompartmental pressures before and during weight-bearing exercise. The diagnosis of tibial periostitis is often one of exclusion.

Pathomechanics and Functional Limitations

Pain and/or increased compartmental pressure limit functional performance.

■ Immediate Management

Ice, rest, and stretching as tolerated will provide pain relief.

■ Medications

Pain can be reduced and the patient can safely return to activity with the assistance of NSAIDs.

■ Surgical Intervention

In the case of CECS, the elevated compartmental pressures and symptoms experienced during exercise, although not a medical emergency, may nevertheless require surgical release of the fascia. Most symptoms arise from elevated anterior and lateral compartment pressures. Rarely do pressures become high enough to produce symptoms in the posterior compartments. Surgical release for the anterior and lateral compartments can be accomplished with a single incision.

If the involved fascia has herniated, a small (3- to 5-cm) incision is made directly over the defect; otherwise, the incision is made midway between the tibial crest and fibular shaft. The intermuscular septum and nearby superficial peroneal nerve are identified. A fasciotome is passed superiorly and inferiorly, 1 cm medial and 1 cm lateral to the intermuscular septum, to release the anterior and lateral compartments, respectively. If necessary, the posterior compartments are easily released through a second incision made along the medial border, in the middle one-third of the tibia. Following the procedure, the skin incisions are closed and a pressure dressing is applied.

■ Postinjury/Postoperative Management

Tibial Periostitis

Management of tibial periostitis should be conservative, with emphasis being placed on treating the cause of the pathology and not just the symptoms. The most important aspect of treatment should be rest. Analgesic and anti-inflammatory modalities and medications may be used to control symptoms initially. A thorough lower-quarter biomechanical evaluation should be performed to identify potential causes such as structural malalignment, musculotendinous inflexibility, inadequate muscle strength, and gait abnormalities. An appropriate therapeutic exercise program should be implemented and the use of foot orthotics should be considered as appropriate.

Tibial Stress Fracture

Tibial stress fractures must be treated with rest that includes a prolonged cessation of weight-bearing exercise and a very gradual pain-free return to the

fasciotome A device used to split subcutaneous or intramuscular fascia.

activities that led to the stress fracture. Complete withdrawal from weight-bearing exercise should occur for a minimum of 4 weeks. Non-weight-bearing exercise may be performed provided it does not aggravate the stress fracture site. The use of a pneumatic splint or walking boot should be seriously considered in an effort to unload the injured limb. As described previously, a full lower-quarter screening should be performed and appropriate actions taken when designing a rehabilitation and return-to-sport plan. Return to weight-bearing exercise must be performed in a slow and deliberate manner. Emphasis must be placed on the athlete achieving pain-free exercise.

Minimizing stresses during the pre-swing and initial contact phases of gait by wearing stress-reducing shoes or running on a firm yet giving surface such as a composite may allow the athlete to continue workouts in a relatively pain-free manner. If these modifications are not possible, alternative workouts may be required until the pain is resolved. If the pain becomes too intense, the athlete may have to stop activity until the pain becomes manageable or resolves.

Chronic Exertional Compartment Syndrome

After surgical release, the patient usually bears weight to tolerance, but activities causing swelling must be avoided. Crutch weight bearing as tolerated, stretching, and stationary bicycling with progressive walking are advanced for the first 2 weeks after surgery. Active ROM and stretching exercises can be started immediately postoperatively. Monitoring the dressings and preventing wound infections are important considerations during the first week. As the skin heals, active motion and mild massage may assist in maintaining good soft-tissue mobility. Care must be taken to avoid excessive friction on new scar formation that will tear or shear the immature tissue; massage should not be performed until at least week 6, and even then emphasis should be more on the adjacent tissue than directly over the new scar tissue. The patient normally has only mild postoperative pain and experiences a rapid recovery, with resumption of full sport participation within 3 to 6 weeks.

■ Injury-Specific Treatment and Rehabilitation Concerns

> **Specific Concerns**
>
> In the case of surgical correction, prevent infection of fasciotomy wounds.
> Encourage a progressive return to activity to prevent reoccurrence of symptoms.

The rehabilitation program for ERLLP injuries is similar to that for ankle sprains or acute compartment syndrome. Care must be taken to gradually reintroduce the patient to activity to prevent exacerbation of symptoms.

■ Estimated Amount of Time Lost

In the case of tibial periostitis, the athlete can exercise at full intensity once symptoms decrease, with this period usually being measured in days or weeks. Tibial stress fractures must show radiographic resolution of the fracture before full activity resumes, which requires at least 4 to 6 weeks of recovery but often longer. The larger the fracture line, the longer the recovery period. Athletes with CECS may begin a progressive return to sport after approximately 3 to 6 weeks.

■ Return-to-Play Criteria

The athlete should not experience symptoms during or after activity.

Functional Bracing

Taping, orthotic appliances, and shoe modifications can help by allowing the athlete to continue participation. However, relief with immediate management is variable and often does not persist over the long term.[22]

Fibula Fractures

CLINICAL PRESENTATION

History

Distinct mechanism of injury consisting of a rotational (twisting) force on the lower leg or direct trauma to the lateral aspect of the lower leg.

Observation

Displaced fractures: obvious deformity.
Nondisplaced fractures: no deformity.
Edema over the fracture site.

Functional Status

Weight-bearing gait may be possible.
Pain is likely to present with higher-intensity activities such as cutting and landing from a jump.

Physical Examination Findings

Point tenderness upon palpation of the fracture site.
Pain at the fracture site with compression of the lower leg.

Fractures may occur along the entire length of the fibula. Regardless of the precise fracture site, concern for integrity of the tibiofibular syndesmosis must be heeded. Because the fibula is not a primary weight-bearing bone, athletes with acute fibular fractures may not present with gross gait abnormalities. A thorough history and physical examination are needed to not miss these injuries.

A Dupuytren fracture involves the lower fibular shaft just proximal to the tibiofibular syndesmosis. A fracture in the midshaft is termed a Hugier or high Dupuytren fracture. A fracture of the proximal fibular neck with disruption of the interosseous ligament is called a Maisonneuve fracture.[55] With a fracture of the fibular shaft, the distal tibiofibular syndesmosis and interosseous ligament up to the fracture site can also be injured.[56]

Differential Diagnosis
Lateral ankle sprain, syndesmosis ankle sprain, contusion, muscle strain.

Imaging Techniques
Lateral and AP radiographs will provide the definitive diagnosis of fracture. Structural integrity of the distal tibiofibular syndesmosis must be assessed regardless of the location of the fibula fracture (see **Figure 4.46**). When possible, weight-bearing radiographs should be performed; they utilize a physiologic stress on the ankle that allows for better

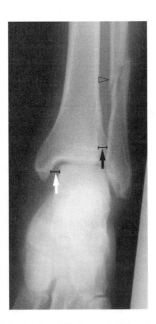

Figure 4.46 Fibular fracture. This non-weight-bearing anteroposterior view shows a fibular fracture caused by pronation and eversion. Note the increased space between the medial malleolus and talus and the medial clear space (white arrow), indicating a deltoid ligament rupture. The space between the distal tibia and fibula (the tibiofibular clear space) is widened (black arrow). For this condition to occur, the anterior tibiofibular ligament and the syndesmosis must be ruptured. An oblique fracture of the fibula (arrowhead) is seen above the level of the syndesmosis.

assessment of the ankle ligaments—in particular, the syndesmosis and deltoid ligament.

Definitive Diagnosis
The definitive diagnosis is based on positive radiographic findings.

Pathomechanics and Functional Limitations
If the fracture is isolated to the fibula, weight bearing may be possible because only approximately 6% of the body weight is distributed over the fibula during the stance phase of gait. The fibula bears essentially no weight, so aggravation during weight bearing is unlikely. Laypersons commonly think fractures do not exist if weight bearing is possible, but walking is feasible when the fibula is fractured. With an isolated fibular fracture, a CAM boot or walking cast can be used to minimize the pressure on this area. If the injury involves ligament or bony structures, initial weight bearing may be limited.

■ Immediate Management

Suspected fractures should be immobilized in the position in which they are found, with ice and compression applied, and the athlete transported for further medical assessment and radiographs.

■ Medications

Pain relief can be obtained using NSAIDs or narcotics. Avoid NSAIDs if surgery is contemplated.

■ Surgical Intervention

Fractures to the distal half of the fibula and more proximal fractures that have concomitant syndesmosis diastasis are typically treated surgically with ORIF. Surgically repaired fractures are typically immobilized, with the patient placed on non-weight-bearing status for as long as 6 weeks. The screw stabilizing the syndesmosis is often removed prior to the beginning of weight bearing. Displaced distal fractures are repaired with ORIF using plates and screws. Fibular shaft (midshaft and higher) fractures are generally left to heal without fixation.

■ Postinjury/Postoperative Management

Although there is some dispute over this management approach, many physicians remove the syndesmotic screw before the patient is allowed full weight bearing on the extremity without a boot or splint.[55] This relatively minor procedure should not delay the rehabilitation process because it does not require any specific postoperative concerns except for observation and management of the new wound.

Uncomplicated fractures to the proximal fibular shaft are generally treated nonoperatively with several weeks of immobilization. Rehabilitation commences when evidence of fracture healing is present

▪ Injury-Specific Treatment and Rehabilitation Concerns

> **Specific Concerns**
>
> Reduce stiffness and fibrosis by reestablishing ROM.
> Strengthen the foot, ankle, and lower leg.
> Retrain gait.

While restricted in activities, the athlete can maintain cardiovascular fitness and preserve or develop muscle strength in the uninvolved extremities. Open kinetic chain exercises for the hip, knee, and foot of the involved extremity can also be included during the non-weight-bearing phase of rehabilitation.

Once weight bearing is permitted, the patient can perform balance activities and closed kinetic chain strength exercises. Rehabilitation from this point follows a normal process with advances in mobility, strength, coordination, agility, and functional activities.

▪ Estimated Amount of Time Lost

Surgically repaired fractures may require as long as 6 weeks of non-weight-bearing restrictions after surgery. An additional 2 to 4 months of time lost from competition is necessary for rehabilitation. Complications after surgery, such as nonunion and infection, can prolong recovery. Nonsurgical management requires 2 to 3 months for healing.

▪ Return-to-Play Criteria

Whether the injury is treated conservatively or surgically, test results for strength and agility should be normal compared with the uninvolved leg before the patient is cleared to resume full activity. If surgery was performed, the site should be well healed and full motion regained in the foot and ankle before the athlete returns to participation. The sport-specific activities pursued during rehabilitation can be used to test the athlete's readiness for return to full participation. The athlete should perform equally with the left and right lower extremities and display confidence in his or her own performance. The surgical hardware for syndesmosis injuries is likely to have been removed by this time,

and the physician should have indicated that the fracture site is healed satisfactorily and cleared the athlete for return to participation.

Functional Bracing

Ankle taping or a brace may be used for return to participation, although use of such aids is optional. If the athlete is involved in a collision or contact sport, a pad or wrap may offer the healed surgical site some protection.

Tibia Fractures

CLINICAL PRESENTATION

History

Distinct mechanism of injury consisting of significant force to the tibia.

Observation

Displaced fractures present with obvious deformity.
Edema and muscle spasm develop soon after the injury.

Functional Status

Weight bearing is not possible on the involved leg.

Physical Examination Findings

The presence of an obvious deformity does not require further on-field examination; immobilize the entire injured leg and refer the patient immediately to the hospital emergency department. Nondisplaced fractures present with tenderness and crepitus at the fracture site.

Fractures to the tibia may occur in collision sports and high-velocity sports such as skiing and motor sports. Most tibial fractures are closed and involve the distal two-thirds of the bone. A significant impact or torsional force is required to fracture the tibia. Because the tibia is the primary weight-bearing bone of the lower leg, any fracture of this bone will be disabling and immediate medical management is necessary. Fractures that involve the tibial plafond or medial malleolus can disrupt the congruity of the talocrural joint and must be treated appropriately to ensure a functional ankle joint (see **Figure 4.47**). Care must be taken to ensure that a nonunion does not occur during the healing of tibia fractures.

Differential Diagnosis

Fibula fracture, talocrural dislocation, tibiofemoral dislocation, severe contusion.

Imaging Techniques

Lateral and AP radiographs will provide the definitive diagnosis of fracture. CT scan of intra-articular

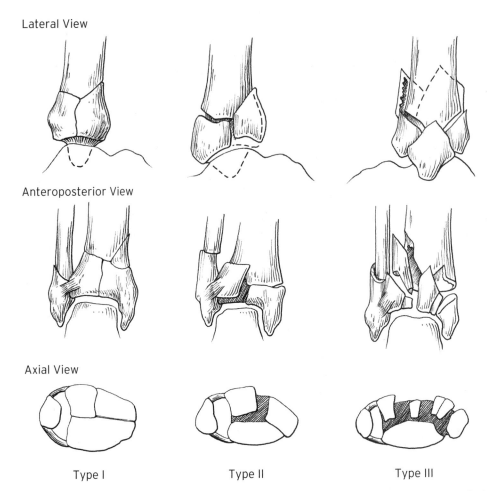

Lateral View

Anteroposterior View

Axial View

Type I   Type II   Type III

Figure 4.47 Rüedi-Allgöwer classification of tibial pilon fractures. Type I is a cleavage fracture of the distal tibia, with a nondisplaced articular surface. Type II is characterized by mild to moderate displacement of the articular surface but minimal to no comminution of the joint surface or adjacent metaphysis. Type III shows comminution of the articular surface and metaphysis with significant impaction of the metaphysis. *Source:* Adapted from Mueller ME, Allgower M, Schneider R, Willenegger H (eds). *Manual of Internal Fixation: Techniques Recommended by the AO-ASIF Group*, ed 3. New York: Springer-Verlag; 1991:279.

fractures is required to assess the congruity of the articulation (see **Figure 4.48**).

Definitive Diagnosis

Positive radiographic findings will confirm the diagnosis and type of tibial fracture.

Pathomechanics and Functional Limitations

A tibial fracture disrupts normal weight bearing, so ambulation is not possible. The patient is reluctant to move the extremity because of the associated pain. The rapid onset of muscle spasm also makes movement painful and limits the patient's desire to move the leg. Delayed union of an isolated tibial fracture is a risk. More successful outcomes with fewer complications have been achieved with internal fixation of tibial fractures.[57]

Functional limitations are often related to the fracture configuration. More unstable fractures require increased attentiveness and patient compliance to remain on non-weight-bearing status. Nonsurgical management can involve long leg or short leg casting and non-weight-bearing

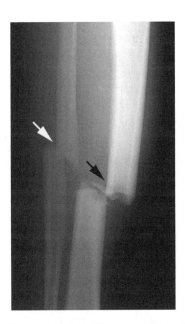

Figure 4.48 Tibial shaft fracture. This anteroposterior view of the tibia and fibula demonstrates a transverse fracture through the mid-diaphysis of the tibia (black arrow). Note also the transverse fracture through the midshaft of the fibula (white arrow) with lateral displacement of the distal fragments.

restrictions. Surgical fixation of the fracture may avoid the necessity of a cast and non-weight-bearing restrictions, but the limitations required ultimately depend on the construct stability and the fracture configuration.

Immediate Management

Immobilization of the fracture in the position in which it is found, monitoring for neurovascular integrity throughout the extremity, applying ice to the site, and immediate transport to the emergency room for radiographs and care are important. In case of an open fracture, a loose dressing should be applied to protect the wound during immediate care and the patient should be promptly transported to a medical facility for further treatment of this medical emergency.

Medications

Oral and injectable narcotic analgesics decrease the pain produced by the injury.

Surgical Intervention

The appropriate management of a tibial fracture depends on the location of the fracture, displacement, and associated injuries (see Chapter 3). Surgical repair is indicated when the fracture involves 1 mm or more of the articular surface, the syndesmosis is unstable, or the fracture is displaced or angulated. Care must be taken to ensure that alignment of the talocrural joint and the tibiofibular syndesmosis is achieved. Almost all bimalleolar and trimalleolar fractures require surgery, as do lateral malleolar fractures with concomitant medial (deltoid) ligament rupture.

Postinjury/Postoperative Management

Postinjury and postoperative management is determined by the stability of the fracture and the surgical construct. Less complex fractures permit a faster return of function. If the fracture is stable and does not involve multiple sites or the joint, it is likely to heal without complications and the athlete is likely to experience a more rapid recovery.

Non-weight-bearing immobilization will last a minimum of 3 weeks, but may be much longer depending on the site of fracture. A period of partial weight-bearing immobilization is often common as well. Complete healing of the tibia fracture may take several months. Once evidence of complete healing is present, a progressive rehabilitation program may be commenced. Return

to sport may take anywhere from 3 to 12 months depending on the fracture site and the severity of the injury.

Injury-Specific Treatment and Rehabilitation Concerns

> **Specific Concerns**
> Obtain anatomic fracture union.
> Ensure stabilization of the fracture site.
> Avoid infection of the surgical site (if applicable).

With tibial fractures, rehabilitation concerns are multifactorial and often conflicting. Early motion is desired, but if the fracture is unstable, this may not be possible. Generally speaking, intra-articular fractures need adequate stabilization so the construct tolerates early motion, but weight bearing must be avoided to prevent loss of reduction. Intramedullary nailing is the most stable construct, allowing for the earliest weight bearing and fastest functional progression. By comparison, open fractures carry a much higher risk of nonunion and infection and may be very slow to heal. Muscle strengthening of the entire closed kinetic chain is important during the rehabilitation process.

Estimated Amount of Time Lost

Without postinjury complications, recovery from a tibial fracture requires 3 to 6 weeks of non-weight-bearing restrictions, followed by a period of partial weight bearing before full weight bearing on the extremity is permitted. Disability can last 3 to 12 months. Complications such as delayed healing, nonunion, osteoporosis, compartment syndrome, and ankle pain will extend the time of disability.

Return-to-Play Criteria

The fracture site must be adequately healed before return to participation can be considered. Because of the long-term disability associated with tibial fractures, many of the standard elements of conditioning (e.g., motion, strength, proprioception) will be deficient and require sustained rehabilitation before the athlete can compete again. All aspects must be restored to normal limits before return to play is permitted.

Functional Bracing

A protective shin guard or pad may be necessary once the athlete returns to play. An ankle brace may aid a distal fracture, whereas a knee brace may help protect a proximal fracture.

Rehabilitation

While maintaining non-weight-bearing restrictions, the patient should maintain cardiovascular conditioning and strength of the upper extremities, contralateral lower extremity, and other involved extremity segments. A number of activities can be used to maintain these conditioning levels. For example, an upper body ergometer, single-leg stationary bicycling, running on crutches, or wheelchair activities can assist in maintaining cardiovascular conditioning. If the cast is waterproof, aquatic exercises can be used for both cardiovascular and lower extremity fitness. Upper and lower body resistance exercises will preserve strength and muscle endurance levels.

Gait training may require progressive advancement from no weight bearing to full weight bearing. This may entail moving from two crutches without weight on the involved extremity, to two crutches with partial weight, and then to one crutch with partial weight, before the athlete discards the crutches and walks unassisted.

Therapeutic modalities initially may consist of a whirlpool to warm the foot and prepare the skin for treatment. Grade I and II joint mobilizations to relieve pain during the first week after injury may be necessary, followed by grade III and IV mobilizations to increase joint mobility if the patient has acquired a capsular pattern or joint restriction with immobilization. Massage to reduce postcast edema and open lymph vessels may be needed for the first few days after injury. After the first week or two, passive modalities such as whirlpool and electric stimulation for pain or edema should not be necessary, because the pain and edema should be resolved. Once the athlete performs active flexibility and strengthening exercises, ice may be necessary to calm any irritation that may have occurred because of the stress of the exercises.

Flexibility Exercises

Each stretch is held for at least 15 to 20 seconds and repeated three or four times unless otherwise noted.

Dorsiflexion Stretch for the Gastrocnemius

Leaning against the table or wall, the patient stands in a lunge position with the stretch leg behind and the support leg forward. With the back heel remaining on the ground and the knee straight, the patient leans forward to put weight on the front leg and arms (see **Figure 4.49**).

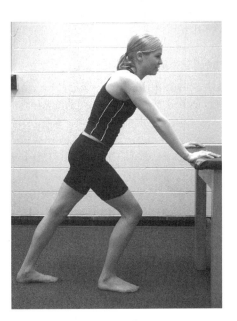

Figure 4.49 Dorsiflexion stretch for the gastrocnemius.

Dorsiflexion Stretch for the Soleus

Leaning against the table or wall, the patient stands in a lunge position with the stretch leg behind and the support leg forward. With the back heel remaining on the ground and the knee flexed, the patient leans forward to put weight on the front leg and arms (see **Figure 4.50**).

Prolonged Dorsiflexion Stretch

This exercise addresses tightness in the Achilles tendon or rigid scar tissue in the posterior calf. The

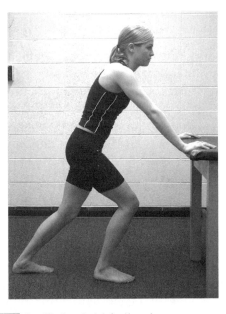

Figure 4.50 Dorsiflexion stretch for the soleus.

patient stands with the back to the wall, with a rolled-up towel placed behind the knees to prevent knee hyperextension, and the feet on an incline board with the heels on the floor and no more than 1 in. from the wall. This position is maintained for 5 to 15 minutes as tolerated.

Plantar Flexion Stretch
The patient sits on the heels with the knees fully flexed and feet in plantar flexion and attempts to push the dorsum of the feet to lie flat on floor.

Strengthening Exercises

Isometrics

Plantar Flexion
Sitting with the involved distal foot on top of the dorsum of the uninvolved foot, the patient points the involved foot downward as the movement is resisted by the opposite foot dorsiflexing. The patient holds this position for 10 seconds, and repeats the exercise 10 times.

Dorsiflexion
Sitting with the uninvolved heel on top of the dorsum of the involved foot, the patient pushes the involved foot up as the movement is resisted by the opposite foot plantar flexing. The patient holds this position for 10 seconds, and repeats the exercise 10 times.

Inversion
Sitting with the inside of the involved ankle against a doorway or table leg, the patient pushes the foot into the stable object, holding the position for 10 seconds. Repeat 10 times.

Eversion
Sitting with the outside of the involved ankle against a doorway or table leg, the patient pushes the foot into the stable object, holding the position for 10 seconds. Repeat 10 times.

Rubber-Tubing Exercises
Early isotonic foot and ankle exercises can be performed using rubber tubing, starting with light resistance and increasing as strength is developed (see Figure 4.51).

Intrinsic Foot Exercises

Towel Roll
A towel is placed on the floor in front of the seated patient. The heel of the involved foot is placed on the floor near the towel and the forefoot on the towel. Keeping the heel in place, the patient rolls the towel toward the foot, curling the toes to move the

towel. A weight can be added at the distal end of the towel to make the exercise more difficult (see Figure 4.52).

Marble Pickup
Marbles are placed on the floor, and the patient uses the toes to pick them up, one at a time. The marbles can be placed beside the opposite foot or lifted to the hand.

Short Foot Exercise
The short foot exercise is performed with the foot flat on the ground. The patient pulls their metatarsal heads towards their calcaneus while keeping their toes flat on the ground. As they do this, the medial longitudinal arch rises and the foot "shortens." Short foot exercises are initially performed while seated and later in standing positions.

Body Resistance Exercises

Heel Raises
Standing on the floor and keeping the knees extended, the patient raises up on the toes, lifting the heels off the floor. Progression for this exercise includes beginning with both feet, advancing to one foot, moving from the floor to an incline, and adding weights.

Toe Raises
Standing on the floor, the patient lifts the toes and forefoot off the floor, keeping weight on the heels. This exercise can be progressed to standing on a decline, with the heels higher than the toes.

Ankle Weights
With a cuff weight wrapped around the forefoot, the patient is placed in an antigravity position for the motion being resisted. For inversion, the patient lies on the involved side; for eversion, the patient lies on the opposite side; for dorsiflexion, the patient sits with the leg hanging off the table. These exercises can also be performed against manual resistance or progressively increased weights.

Balance Progression
The stork stand, balance beam, vestibular board, and proprioception/strength exercises described on pages 263 to 266 in Chapter 8 should be introduced into the rehabilitation program.

Orthotic Corrections

During gait, the foot initially contacts the ground in supination and immediately moves into pronation. At midstance, the rearfoot moves from pronation to a neutral position and continues to move into supination. Thus, at pre-swing, the foot has changed from being a force absorber in the first half of weight bearing to being a force deliverer during the propulsion

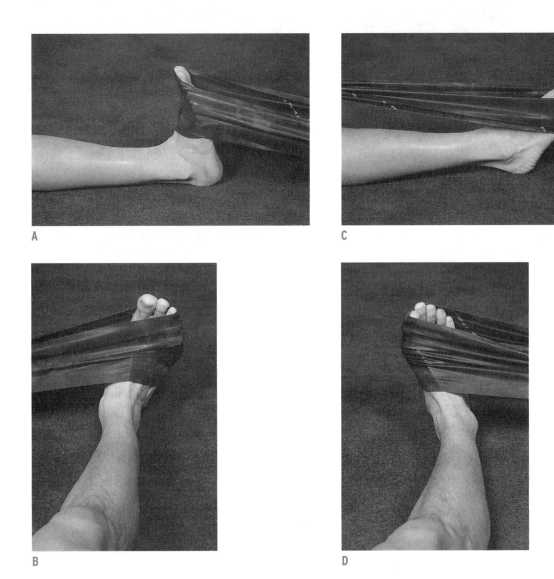

Figure 4.51 Rubber-tubing exercises. (**A**) Dorsiflexion. With the tubing anchored in a door jamb, the patient faces the door jamb and wraps the tubing around the forefoot of the involved ankle, so the resistance occurs when the foot is dorsiflexed. (**B**) Eversion. With the tubing anchored in a door jamb, the patient wraps the tubing around the forefoot of the involved ankle, so the resistance occurs when the foot is everted. (**C**) Plantar flexion. The patient grasps the tubing in both hands and loops the tubing around the plantar foot with the knee in extension. Taking slack out of the tubing, the foot is moved into plantar flexion against the tubing resistance. This exercise can be repeated with the knee flexed to emphasize the soleus muscle. (**D**) Inversion. With the tubing anchored in a door jamb, the patient wraps the tubing around the medial aspect of the involved ankle, so the resistance occurs when the patient inverts the foot.

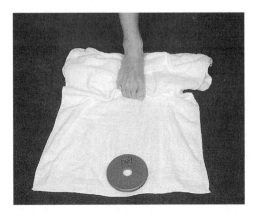

Figure 4.52 Towel roll.

phase at the end of weight bearing. The foot serves three functions during the weight-bearing phase of gait: It adapts and dissipates stresses at initial contact, it provides balance and stability by serving as the contact between the moving body and the ground, and it acts as a rigid lever to provide propulsion just before the non-weight-bearing phase.[58]

Although the description in the previous paragraph sounds fairly simple, the mechanics occurring because of these changes in the foot are anything but simple. When pronation occurs in weight bearing, calcaneal eversion, talar medial rotation, tibial medial rotation, forefoot abduction on the rearfoot, and depression of the medial longitudinal arch also occur. These changes cause the body's center of gravity to move medially to the foot, resulting in knee valgus with an increased Q angle and greater lateral quadriceps pull.

If joint tightness or muscle inflexibility is present, abnormal mechanics can result. Over time and with repetitive or exaggerated stress application, tissue breakdown may occur. Orthotic corrections can be the logical "fix" to alter these abnormal mechanics.

Purposes of Orthotic Corrections

Orthotics are used to accommodate a foot deformity or compensate for abnormal function and biomechanics during gait. These abnormalities increase forces on the foot and other segments up the chain, increasing the individual's risk of injury or creating cumulative stress to weaken and break down normal tissue. The ultimate purposes of orthotic appliances, then, are to accommodate or correct alignment to relieve pain, to reduce stress and injury risk, and to facilitate optimal function.

Foot Orthotic Corrections

Foot orthoses can be applied to or inserted in the shoe. Some athletic shoes have external adaptations to accommodate the patient's increased risk or to reduce stresses applied by the athlete's sport. For example, heel flares on running shoes increase heel stability at initial contact and may reduce valgus stresses experienced during running. An elevated heel placed in a running shoe reduces Achilles tendon stress during running. The outer sole of a tennis shoe has a squared edge rather than a rounded edge to provide more stability and prevent ankle rollover during sudden lateral direction changes. An anterior-posterior rocker bottom on an outer sole reduces ankle forces at initial impact and forces to the toes and forefoot during preparation for toe-off.

Orthotic inserts for shoes can be made of a variety of substances. Felt or foam pads, for example, can be used to correct alignment or absorb forces. More rigid substances help to improve alignment.

If more support is needed, various prefabricated orthotic appliances are available. They come in different styles and compositions and are designed for different functions. Some are composed of stiff materials and offer corrective assistance; others are composed of softer materials and provide accommodation, rather than correction.

Custom orthoses are more expensive than over-the-counter models, but they may be necessary to relieve pain or correct the deformity sufficiently to allow normal athletic performance. Custom or-

thoses can also be accommodative or correctional (sometimes called functional). The purpose is determined by the constituent substance. Semirigid materials such as cork, rubber, and light-density foam provide accommodative orthoses. Appliances made of rigid or semirigid substances that do not easily give or lose their shape when weight is applied are correctional or functional orthoses. To determine whether an orthotic appliance is accommodative or functional, apply pressure to the mold or attempt to twist the device. If it easily gives to stress application, then it is accommodative. The more rigid the orthotic appliance, the less room for error in device construction. The individual taking measurements of the patient's feet must be as precise as possible when rigid and semirigid orthoses are to be fabricated.

Custom orthoses are designed for a specific individual. To construct them, an impression of the patient's feet is taken, and the orthosis is then formed around that impression. Custom orthoses may also be fabricated from low-temperature thermoplastic materials molded through direct contact with the foot. Typically, an impression of the patient's feet is made by using plaster-of-Paris casts or by having the patient step into a box of foam similar to the green foam used by florists. The foam gives to the pressure of the foot in it and retains the shape when the foot is removed. The orthotist then builds an orthosis based on the impressions and the information provided by the clinician on factors that may alter the orthotic requirements. For example, if the patient has limited dorsiflexion, the orthotist may build heel lifts into the orthoses to reduce Achilles tendon stress.

Types of Orthotic Corrections

Valgus Pad

A valgus pad can be placed along the medial aspect of the shoe to reduce pronation stress by decreasing the amount of pronation and compensated forefoot varus, or it can be accommodative by supporting a supinated foot (see **Figure 4.53**).

Metatarsal Pad

A metatarsal pad can be used if pressure over the distal metatarsals is painful. Modifications of this pad can be made to relieve weight bearing around the first ray by cutting out that portion or improve weight bearing by cutting out the pad from the other metatarsal areas (see **Figure 4.54**).

Calcaneal Pads

A variety of calcaneal pads can relieve pressure over a calcaneal spur or reduce pronation with a medial wedge (see **Figure 4.55**).

Figure 4.55 Calcaneal pads.

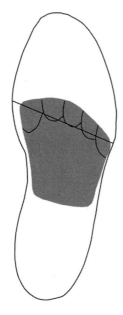

Figure 4.53 Valgus pad for the longitudinal arch.

Figure 4.54 Metatarsal pad.

Footwear

Shoes have an important role in foot mechanics. Their primary purpose is to protect the foot's soft tissue from the insults it would otherwise encounter without protection. Shoes also help to distribute force, absorb stress, provide traction, and support foot structures. They come in many styles, models, and colors. Ultimately, the shoe's function—not its color or style—should be the most important determinant in selection.

Athletic shoe selection should be a marriage of the shoe's function with the patient's sport demands and the foot's biomechanical and structural deviations. The clinician should inspect the patient's worn shoes and the patient's feet to obtain an idea of the abnormal biomechanical stresses created. A collapsed medial heel counter reflects pronation. Blood under the toenail indicates the toe box is too short. An unequal wear pattern of the shoes may be a sign of a leg-length discrepancy. A patient who has excessive or prolonged pronation should use a shoe with increased medial rearfoot midsole density or a medial wedge, a strong or reinforced heel counter, and a board last. A patient with a painful or rigid first ray should wear a rigid-soled shoe with a rocker bottom, especially in the forefoot, and the midsole should be thicker than normal to absorb more stress.

▨ References

1. Anderson RB, Hunt KJ, McCormick JJ. Management of common sports-related injuries about the foot and ankle. *J Am Acad Orthop Surg.* 2010;18(9):546–556.
2. Nihal A, Trepman E, Nag D. First ray disorders in athletes. *Sports Med Arthrosc.* 2009;17(3):160–166.
3. Clanton TO, Ford JJ. Turf toe injury. *Clin Sports Med.* 1994;13:731–741.
4. Jahss MH. The sesamoids of the hallux. *Clin Orthop Relat Res.* 1981;157:88–97.
5. Dietzen CJ. Great toe sesamoid injuries in the athlete. *Orthop Rev.* 1990;19:966–972.
6. Mann RA. Disorders of the first metatarsophalangeal joint. *J Am Acad Orthop Surg.* 1995;3:34–43.
7. Moberg E. A simple operation for hallux rigidus. *Clin Orthop Relat Res.* 1979;142:55–56.
8. Anderson RJ. Hallux rigidus and atrophy of calf muscles. *N Engl J Med.* 1999;340:1123.
9. Grady JF, Axe TM, Zager EJ, Sheldon LA. A retrospective analysis of 772 patients with hallux limitus. *J Am Podiatr Med Assoc.* 2002;92:102–108.
10. Thomas PJ, Smith RW. Proximal phalanx osteotomy for the surgical treatment of hallux rigidus. *Foot Ankle Int.* 1999;20:3–12.
11. Lau JTC, Daniels TR. Outcomes following cheilectomy and interpositional arthroplasty in hallux rigidus. *Foot Ankle Int.* 2001;22:462–470.

12. Hockenbury RT. Forefoot problems in athletes. *Med Sci Sports Exerc.* 1999;31(suppl 7):S448–S458.

13. Ogden JA, Alvarez R, Levitt R, et al. Shock wave therapy for chronic proximal plantar fasciitis. *Clin Orthop Relat Res.* 2001;387:47–59.

14. Gill LH. Plantar fasciitis: Diagnosis and conservative management. *J Am Acad Orthop Surg.* 1997;5:109–117.

15. Neufeld SK, Cerrato R. Plantar fasciitis: Evaluation and treatment. *J Am Acad Orthop Surg.* 2008;16(6):338–346.

16. Malay DS, Pressman MM, Assili A, et al. Extracorporeal shockwave therapy versus placebo for the treatment of chronic proximal plantar fasciitis: Results of a randomized, placebo-controlled, double-blinded, multicenter intervention trial. *J Foot Ankle Surg.* 2006;45(4):196–210.

17. Acevedo JI, Beskin JL. Complications of plantar fascia rupture associated with corticosteroid injection. *Foot Ankle Int.* 1998;19:91–97.

18. Richardson EG. Hallucal sesamoid pain: Causes and surgical treatment. *J Am Acad Orthop Surg.* 1999;7:270–278.

19. Helbig K, Herbert C, Schostok T, et al. Correlations between the duration of pain and the success of shock wave therapy. *Clin Orthop Relat Res.* 2001;387:68–71.

20. Rompe JD, Schoellner C, Nafe B. Evaluation of low-energy extracorporeal shock-wave application for treatment of chronic plantar fasciitis. *J Bone Joint Surg Am.* 2002; 84:335–341.

21. van Wyngarden TM. The painful foot, part I: Common forefoot deformities. *Am Fam Physician.* 1997;55:1866–1876.

22. Weinfeld SB, Myerson MS. Interdigital neuritis: Diagnosis and treatment. *J Am Acad Orthop Surg.* 1996;4:328–335.

23. Evans A. Podiatric medical applications of posterior night stretch splinting. *J Am Podiatr Med Assoc.* 2001;91:356–360.

24. Zwitser EW, Breederveld RS. Fractures of the fifth metatarsal: Diagnosis and treatment. *Injury.* 2010;41(6): 555–562.

25. Weinfeld SB, Haddad SL, Myerson MS. Metatarsal stress fractures. *Clin Sports Med.* 1997;16:319–338.

26. Lawrence SJ, Botte MJ. Jones' fractures and related fractures of the proximal fifth metatarsal. *Foot Ankle.* 1993;14: 358–365.

27. Lucas MJ, Baxter DE. Stress fracture of the first metatarsal. *Foot Ankle Int.* 1997;18:373–374.

28. Khan KM, Brukner PD, Kearney C, et al. Tarsal navicular stress fracture in athletes. *Sports Med.* 1994;17:65–76.

29. Omey ML, Micheli LJ. Foot and ankle problems in the young athlete. *Med Sci Sports Exerc.* 1999;31(suppl 7): S470–S486.

30. van Rijn RM, van Os AG, Bernsen RM, et al. What is the clinical course of acute ankle sprains? A systematic literature review. *Am J Med.* 2008;121(4):324–331.

31. Gerber JP, Williams GN, Scoville CR, et al. Persistent disability associated with ankle sprains: A prospective examination of an athletic population. *Foot Ankle Int.* 1998; 19:653–660.

32. Wilkerson GB, Horn-Kingery HM. Treatment of the inversion ankle sprain: Comparison of different modes of compression and cryotherapy. *J Orthop Sports Phys Ther.* 1993;17:240–246.

33. Williams GN, Jones MH, Amendola A. Syndesmotic ankle sprains in athletes. *Am J Sports Med.* 2007;35(7):1197–1207.

34. Zalavaras C, Thordarson D. Ankle syndesmotic injury. *J Am Acad Orthop Surg.* 2007;15(6):330–339.

35. Jelinek JA, Porter DA. Management of unstable ankle fractures and syndesmosis injuries in athletes. *Foot Ankle Clin.* 2009;14(2):277–298.

36. Michelson JD. Ankle fractures resulting from rotational injuries. *J Am Acad Orthop Surg.* 2003;11(6):403–412.

37. Kuper BC. Tarsal tunnel syndrome. *Orthop Nurs.* 1998; 17:9–17.

38. Rivera F, Bertone C, De Martino M, et al. Pure dislocation of the ankle: Three case reports and literature review. *Clin Orthop Relat Res.* 2001;382:179–184.

39. Thordarson DB. Complications after treatment of tibial pilon fractures: Prevention and management strategies. *J Am Acad Orthop Surg.* 2000;8:253–265.

40. Heckman DS, Gluck GS, Parekh SG. Tendon disorders of the foot and ankle, part 2: Achilles tendon disorders. *Am J Sports Med.* 2009;37(6):1223–1234.

41. Irwin TA. Current concepts review: Insertional Achilles tendinopathy. *Foot Ankle Int.* 2010;31(10):933–939.

42. Stanish WD, Curwin S, Mandel S. *Tendinitis: Its Etiology and Treatment.* New York: Oxford University Press; 2000.

43. Myerson MS. Injuries in the athlete, in Helal B, Rowley DI, Cracchiolo AR, Myerson MS (eds), *Surgery of Disorders of the Foot and Ankle.* Philadelphia: Lippincott-Raven; 1996:793–809.

44. Leppilahti J, Forsman K, Puranen J, Orava S. Outcome and prognostic factors of Achilles rupture repair using a new scoring method. *Clin Orthop Relat Res.* 1998;346.152–161.

45. Watson AD, Anderson RB, Davis WH. Comparison of results of retrocalcaneal decompression for retrocalcaneal bursitis and insertional Achilles tendinosis with calcific spur. *Foot Ankle Int.* 2000;21:638–642.

46. Frey C, Rosenberg Z, Shereff MJ, Kim H. The retrocalcaneal bursa: Anatomy and bursography. *Foot Ankle.* 1992;13: 203–207.

47. Diaz GC, van Holsbeeck M, Jacobson JA. Longitudinal split of the peroneus longus and peroneus brevis tendons with disruption of the superior peroneal retinaculum. *J Ultrasound Med.* 1998;17:525–529.

48. Frey C. Foot and ankle, in Johnson TR, Steinbach LS (eds), *Essentials of Musculoskeletal Imaging.* Rosemont, IL: American Academy of Orthopaedic Surgeons; 2004:650.

49. Brage ME, Hansen ST Jr. Traumatic subluxation/dislocation of the peroneal tendons. *Foot Ankle.* 1992;13:423–431.

50. Forman ES, Micheli LJ, Backe LM. Chronic recurrent subluxation of the peroneal tendons in a pediatric patient: Surgical recommendations. *Foot Ankle Int.* 2000;21:51–53.

51. Krause JO, Brodsky JW. Peroneus brevis tendon tears: Pathophysiology, surgical reconstruction, and clinical results. *Foot Ankle Int.* 1998;19:271–279.

52. Mendicino RW, Orsini RC, Whitman SE, Catanzariti AR. Fibular groove deepening for recurrent peroneal subluxation. *J Foot Ankle Surg.* 2001;40:252–263.

53. Whitesides TE, Heckman MM. Acute compartment syndrome: Update on diagnosis and treatment. *J Am Acad Orthop Surg.* 1996;4:209–218.

54. Schepsis AA, Lynch G. Exertional compartment syndromes of the lower extremity. *Curr Opin Rheumatol.* 1996;8: 143–147.

55. Yablon I, Forman ES. Ankle fractures, in Helal B, Rowley DI, Cracchiolo AR, Myerson MS (eds), *Surgery of Disorders of the Foot and Ankle.* Philadelphia: Lippincott-Raven; 1996:679–696.

56. Ebraheim NA, Mekhail AO, Gargasz SS. Ankle fractures involving the fibula proximal to the distal tibiofibular syndesmosis. *Foot Ankle Int.* 1997;18:513–521.

57. Wilkerson GB. Biomechanical and neuromuscular effects of ankle taping and bracing. *J Athl Train.* 2002;37: 436–445.

58. Subotnick SI. Conservative treatment for the foot in sport, in Helal B, Rowley DI, Cracchiolo AR, Myerson MS (eds), *Surgery of Disorders of the Foot and Ankle.* Philadelphia: Lippincott-Raven; 1996:867–869.

Knee Injuries

Anh-Dung Nguyen, PhD, ATC
Robert J. Schoderbeck, Jr., MD

Anterior Cruciate Ligament Sprain

CLINICAL PRESENTATION

History

Mechanism of injury:
- Acute tensile load from knee rotation and anterior tibial shear force with the foot planted
- Knee hyperextension
- Contact injury

A "pop" may be associated with the injury.

The initial pain may subside.

Swelling occurs within hours of the injury.

Observation

Joint effusion.

Patient postures the knee in slight flexion due to effusion or to reduce ACL stress.

Functional Status

Weight bearing may be limited by pain and instability.

Active and passive range of motion (ROM) is decreased by joint effusion and inflammation.

The quadriceps musculature may be inhibited by pain and joint effusion.

The patient avoids complete knee extension.

Physical Examination Findings

The following special tests may be positive:
- Lachman
- Anterior drawer
- Alternate Lachman
- Pivot shift

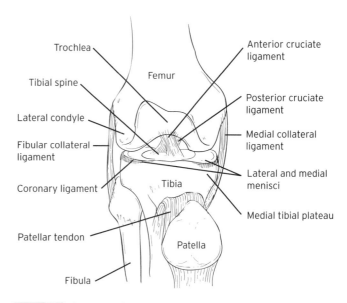

Figure 5.1   Illustration of knee anatomy.

Anterior cruciate ligament (ACL) sprains frequently occur secondary to noncontact forces associated with "cutting/twisting" on a planted foot and either externally or internally rotating the lower leg. This position, when combined with a valgus force, can place a tensile force on the ACL that exceeds the tissue strength (see **Figure 5.1**). ACL injury can also occur when changing direction or cutting while decelerating, landing, or planting the foot with the knee near full extension—a mechanism of injury commonly noted in sports such as basketball, gymnastics, and volleyball. These motions involve frontal plane and rotational moments along with anterior translation forces at the knee. Anterior translation force is thought to be the primary force that contributes to ACL injury.[1] However, cadaveric evidence suggests that the combination of an anteriorly directed force along with frontal plane or rotational forces produces higher strain on the ACL.[2,3] Noncontact ACL injuries account for 70% to 80% of all

ACL injuries where no physical contact occurs with other individuals at the time of injury.[1,4,5]

A contact-related ACL sprain commonly occurs with contact to the posterolateral knee. This load causes anterior tibial shear and creates the possibility of a medial collateral ligament (MCL) sprain and medial meniscal injury from a valgus load. Lateral knee compression might cause a lateral meniscal injury.

Specific types of meniscal injuries are associated with ACL injuries. For example, the lateral meniscus is more commonly torn in acute ACL injuries. The medial meniscus is more commonly injured in the chronically ACL-deficient knee.[6] Articular surface changes and osteochondral defects also can occur after ACL injury.[6] The incidence of chondral surface changes with chronic ACL tears is at least twice that associated with acute injuries.

Differential Diagnosis

Patellar dislocation, patellar subluxation, posterior cruciate ligament (PCL) injury, tibiofemoral dislocation, osteochondral defect, meniscal tear.

Medical Diagnostic Tests

Aspiration of a hemarthrosis limits the differential diagnosis to structures with a vascular supply. This procedure also relieves pain caused by joint distention. The lateral knee is cleansed with betadine or chlorhexadine gluconate (CHG), and the skin is numbed with a topical or local anesthetic. The physician inserts the needle below the patella at the lateral joint line or, if knee flexion is limited, a suprapatellar approach is used. One hand applies

hemarthrosis A collection of blood within a joint.

pressure to the medial aspect of the knee, pushing on the joint effusion, and the plunger is then slowly withdrawn in the syringe, siphoning out the fluid.

Imaging Techniques

Standard anteroposterior (AP) and lateral radiographs are helpful to rule out an avulsion fracture. Evaluate the radiographs for a Segond fracture—that is, an avulsion-type fracture of the soft-tissue attachment of the capsule off the lateral tibial plateau, which is occasionally seen with injuries to the ACL (see **Figure 5.2**). Magnetic resonance imaging (MRI) may demonstrate several signs indicating a tear—poor visualization or nonvisualization of the ligament with sagittal images, irregular contour of fibers, interrupted fibers, and/or a focally increased signal reflecting edema within the ligament (see **Figure 5.3**). Bone bruises, which may lead to long-term lateral knee pain and be clinically significant as osteochondritis dissecans, are more common in the lateral compartment. Such bruises are often visualized in the midlateral femoral condyle and the posterior lateral tibial plateau after an acute ACL injury. The long-term clinical significance of these bone bruises has not been determined (see **Figure 5.4**).

> **Practice Tip**
>
> Standard anteroposterior (AP) and lateral radiographs should be performed to evaluate the presence of an avulsion fracture. Radiographs should pay particular attention to the soft-tissue attachment of the capsule off the lateral tibial plateau (Segond fracture), which is occasionally damaged with injuries to the ACL.

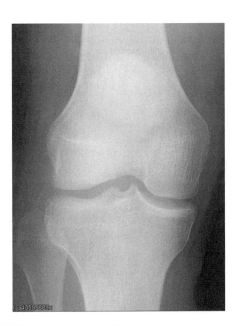

Figure 5.2 Avulsion fracture of the lateral tibial plateau (Segond fracture) at the soft-tissue capsular attachment; such a fracture is associated with ACL injuries.

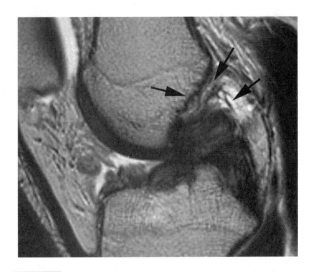

Figure 5.3 MRI sagittal view of an ACL tear. The arrows show tears in the proximal fibers from the femoral attachment, and the ligament stump is seen doubled over onto itself.

Definitive Diagnosis

Definitive diagnosis of an ACL sprain is made by positive Lachman test, positive findings on MRI, and a knee arthrometer (i.e., KT-1000, KT-2000) manual maximum test that shows more than 3 mm of laxity on the injured side compared with the uninjured side.

Pathomechanics and Functional Limitations

In the setting of an ACL sprain, most patients are unable to continue activity secondary to pain and instability. Joint effusion causes loss of full knee extension and flexion. Ambulation is impaired by pain, quadriceps inhibition due to the joint effusion, and the lack of full extension.

Patients with a chronic ACL-deficient knee may not experience dysfunction with normal activities of daily living (ADLs) and sports activities that do

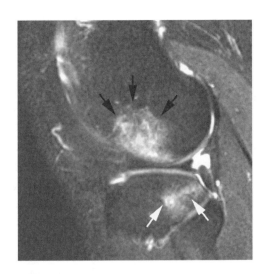

Figure 5.4 Femoral and tibial bone bruises. The black arrows indicate marrow edema in the anterolateral femur. The white arrows indicate tibial marrow edema.

not involve cutting, pivoting, or sudden starting and stopping. With repeated giving-way episodes, however, these patients may have increased instability, even with low-level function. Most are unable to participate in activities that require pivoting on the planted foot. Joint instability is common, creating actual giving way during these activities or a sensation that the knee will give way or shift. Often patients demonstrate the sensation of the shift phenomenon by wringing their hands.

■ Immediate Management

The patient is removed from activity, and ice is applied to the knee. The patient is placed in an immobilizer in slight flexion for comfort and fitted with crutches until further clinical workup is completed and the extent of injury determined.

■ Medications

Nonsteroidal anti-inflammatory drugs (NSAIDs) are useful in relieving pain in lower-grade injuries. With grade II and III injuries, acute pain management with narcotic analgesics may be used to allow patients to participate in the rehabilitation program and sleep more comfortably.

■ Postinjury Management

Most patients benefit from using crutches until full ROM and quadriceps activity have been restored. Patients with a concurrent collateral ligament sprain may benefit from use of a hinged knee brace (see Figure 5.5). Aspirating the joint effusion decreases

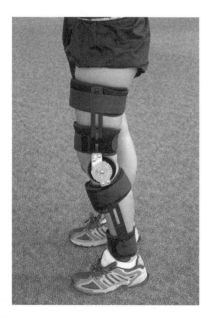

Figure 5.5   Hinged knee brace. This type of brace, which controls the range of motion, may be used for most types of knee sprains. The available range of motion can be adjusted by the clinician.

pressure within the joint, reducing pain, promoting restoration of ROM, preventing arthrogenic muscle inhibition, and allowing muscle activity through exercise.

In some patients, a conservative approach to treating the ACL injury may be chosen. These patients are generally less active individuals, especially in sports requiring cutting and pivoting. Some in-season athletes attempt to conservatively rehabilitate the ACL injury to return to activity that season, and then opt for reconstruction at season's end. A course of prehabilitation can decrease joint inflammation and restore ROM and muscle activity in the lower extremity before reconstruction.[7] Thorough knee examination should be performed for associated injuries (e.g., meniscal or other ligamentous injury) that would eliminate the possibility of a quick return to activity. MRI findings must rule out other injuries including meniscal abnormality.

■ Surgical Intervention

Proper timing of ACL reconstruction is important to minimize the risk of postsurgical arthrofibrosis.[8] The initial inflammatory reaction should subside, full extension and near full flexion should be obtained, and quadriceps tone should be restored before surgery (approximately 21 days) for an isolated ACL injury and 4 to 6 weeks with an associated MCL sprain.[8] Patients who also have sustained a locked bucket-handle meniscal tear causing a fixed flexion contracture—usually a chronic condition—need to undergo a staged surgical procedure to prevent the development of arthrofibrosis. In this case, the meniscus is repaired first, with ACL reconstruction occurring later.

Arthroscopic ACL reconstruction is the preferred (and gold standard) treatment technique for ACL reconstruction (ST 5.1). The surgical goal is to place the graft in a position that replicates the original anatomic position of the ACL and recreate a functionally stable knee.

> **Practice Tip**
>
> Proper timing of ACL reconstruction is important to minimize the risk of postsurgical arthrofibrosis.[8] The initial inflammatory reaction should subside, full extension and near full flexion should be obtained, and quadriceps tone should be restored before surgery.

Graft Choice

Several autogenic graft and allogenic graft options are available, each of which has both advantages and shortcomings (see **Table 5.1**).[9] Autograft options include bone–patellar tendon–bone, quadrupled

arthrofibrosis Abnormal formation of fibrous tissue within a joint.

autogenic graft Graft tissue transplanted from one part of the patient's body to another part.

allogenic graft Graft tissue obtained from the same species but not from the patient (e.g., from a cadaver).

S|T Surgical Technique 5.1

ACL Reconstruction

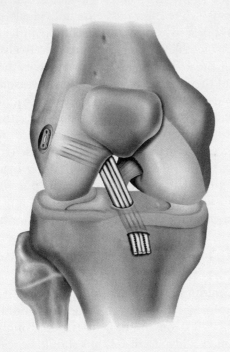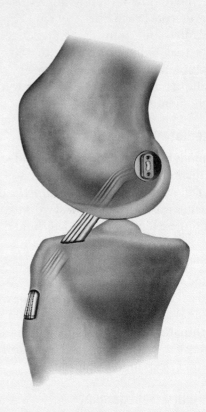

Indications

Failure to control giving way by limiting twisting activities or continual giving way with ADLs; individuals involved in high-risk activities that lead to giving-way episodes.

Procedure Overview

1. The knee is visually inspected and physically examined to assess the injury.
2. Routine arthroscopy portals are developed. If autogenous grafts are chosen, a medial parapatellar tendon incision is made and the patellar tendon is identified. If a hamstring graft is used, a short medial incision is made over the insertion extending along the medial hamstrings.
3. If an autograft is chosen, it is harvested from the knee.
4. Any additional procedures such as meniscal repair or resection are performed.
5. The knee is prepared to accept the graft with a notchplasty, and tunnels are drilled through the femur and tibia to reproduce the anatomy. An attempt is made to place the graft through the tunnels in the original ACL footprint.
6. The graft is passed into position and then fixated into the tunnels. Various fixation options exist, depending on the specific graft choice and the surgeon's preference.
7. Full motion and negative Lachman and pivot-shift tests should be demonstrated as part of the final phase of surgery.

notchplasty A surgical enlargement of the intercondylar notch to increase the space available to the ACL.

Functional Limitations

Functional limitations are dictated by the surgical procedure, graft source, and associated concomitant surgeries or comorbid conditions. Partial weight bearing (until quadriceps control is sufficient), avoidance of weight bearing and weight-loaded deep flexion (with meniscal repair), and restricted lateral movements are usually implemented postoperatively.

Implications for Rehabilitation

Accelerated rehabilitation focuses on regaining motion and full weight bearing in the early postoperative phase. Strengthening exercises are then instituted to regain function.

Potential Complications

The most feared complication is the development of arthrofibrosis, which limits the patient's functional ability. Other potential complications include graft failure, meniscal repair failure, donor-site injury (with autogenous graft harvest), infection, deep vein thrombosis, and tibial or femoral fracture.

Source: © 1995 American Academy of Orthopaedic Surgeons. Reprinted from the *Journal of the American Academy of Orthopaedic Surgeons*, Volume 3 (3), pp. 146–158 with permission.

Table 5.1

Advantages of Autografts and Allografts

Autograft	Allograft
Higher normal stability rate and lower graft failure rate	Less postoperative pain
No risk of disease transmission	No donor-site morbidity
Faster graft incorporation/ faster return to full activities	Larger grafts available for double-bundle reconstruction
Lower cost	Improved cosmesis
No risk of immune reaction	Faster immediate post-operative recovery

semitendinosus/gracilis tendons, and quadriceps tendon. Allograft choices include the Achilles tendon with calcaneal bone, bone–patellar tendon–bone, anterior tibial tendon, and posterior tibial tendon.

Surgeon experience and preference, graft availability, and tolerance to harvest morbidity determine which graft will be used (see (ST) 5.2). The patient's graft choice can also factor into the decision-making process. Some patients may choose an allograft to potentially decrease postoperative pain because there is no donor site. Other patients may choose not to have an allograft because they do not want cadaveric tissue implanted into their body for an elective procedure such as ACL reconstruction.

Certain conditions may favor the use of one type of graft over another. An autogenous bone–patellar tendon–bone (BPTB) graft may be excluded in patients with a history of patellofemoral disease or a significant history of Osgood-Schlatter disease because of the possibility of a weakened tibial tuberosity bone plug. In general, however, the autogenous BPTB graft offers a strong graft with bone-to-bone fixation points that make fixation stronger early in rehabilitation; this choice is seen as the "gold standard" graft choice for ACL reconstruction.

Autogenous soft-tissue grafts may be ruled out for larger males because the available graft may not offer a large enough construct. Although hamstring grafts tend to be more lax after reconstruction, this finding has not proved to be clinically significant, and hamstring muscle function is not disrupted. A double-looped tendon of gracilis and semitendinosus offers a good graft construct and is seen as

harvest morbidity The death, failure, or rejection of implanted tissue.

S|T   Surgical Technique   5.2

Harvesting an Autograft

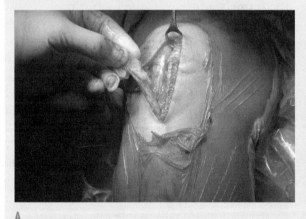

A

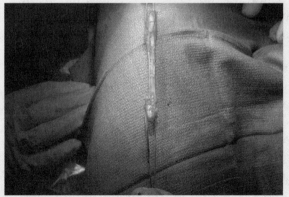

B

Bone–Patellar Tendon–Bone (A)

Through an anterior incision, the central one-third (9 to 10 mm) of the patellar tendon is harvested with a scalpel. Associated bone plugs from the inferior aspects of the patella and superior aspect of the tibial tubercle are obtained with a saw.

Semitendinosus and Gracilis (B)

Through an anteromedial incision, a long harvesting instrument slides along the tendon and separates it from its muscular attachment and the semimembranosus tendon/muscle unit. Once the semitendinosus and gracilis tendons are identified, the harvesting instrument is placed around the tendons and run up the medial hamstring group, amputating it at the proximal extent. Most physicians leave the distal attachment to the pes anserine and deliver the graft into the tibial and femoral tunnels after appropriate preparation.

being twice as strong as the native ACL graft. Modern fixation methods with soft-tissue screws and cross-pin transfixation provide effective fixation that is closer to the joint surfaces, thereby decreasing graft slippage within the bone tunnels and making this a highly favorable graft choice.

Allograft tissue is a safe choice for graft selection. With stringent testing and preoperative care, allografts have minimal potential for disease transmission. Tissue rejection with allografts is typically not as problematic as that seen during vital organ transplantation. Allografts can be larger than autografts, significantly increasing tensile strength. Given that they avoid donor-site morbidity, allografts tend to produce less postoperative pain, and exercise may begin earlier. Allografts can also be used in multiple-ligament reconstruction where graft choice is limited and in revision ACL surgery so that a second donor site is not created around the knee.

The primary issue with allograft tissue is that maturation of the inserted allograft tissue is slower than that for autograft tissue, suggesting that postoperative rehabilitation should not be as vigorous to allow appropriate graft incorporation and to make sure that graft compromise does not occur. Allografts recellularize more slowly and less completely than do autografts, which is why many surgeons will delay aggressive rehabilitation and return to full activities for their patients who receive allograft tissue for ACL reconstruction.[10]

Clinical series studies have shown varying stability outcomes for both autografts and allografts. Meta-analyses have demonstrated that allografts are less stabile than tendon autografts and have a roughly three times greater failure rate compared to autografts.[11,12] BPTB allografts have failure rates two to three times greater than BPTB autografts.[11] In one study, more than 20% of patients required revision ACL reconstruction after a initial allograft reconstruction.[13]

Graft Reconstruction Technique

The ACL consists of two bundles: anteromedial (AM) and posterolateral (PL). Each bundle makes a unique contribution to the knee kinematics at different flexion angles, with the AM bundle being tight in flexion and the PL bundle tight in extension.

Understanding the complex anatomy of the ACL is important to determine the best technique for reconstruction. Correct placement of the femoral and tibial tunnels that replicate the anatomic position of the ACL without roof impingement and a stable graft fixation are two of the most important

factors to achieve the best outcomes after ACL reconstruction. Single-bundle and double-bundle techniques for ACL reconstruction assist in positioning the graft to replicate the original anatomic position of the ACL.

The single-bundle technique has traditionally been the primary technique used for ACL reconstruction. This technique yields fewer complications, shorter surgical time, better technical ease of performing, less tunnel widening, and lower graft and implant cost, and it has proved to be a successful technique if the tunnels are placed in the anatomic position.[11] Single-bundle reconstruction has a 10% to 30% postsurgical incidence of persistent instability, with only 60% to 70% of patients returning to sports.[11,14] Correct tunnel placement is necessary to re-create normal knee kinematics. An oblique trajectory of the femoral tunnel aids in a single bundle restoring anteroposterior stability but is less effective in aiding in rotational stability.

Anatomic double-bundle techniques were developed to improve rotational stability.[11] Use of this technique is supported by biomechanical cadaver studies suggesting that it effectively restores functional anteroposterior and rotational knee stability.[11] This technique is technically more difficult to perform than the single-bundle technique, and it requires a longer surgical time. In addition, with the double-bundle technique, limited fixation options are available due to the proximity of the tunnels. Moreover, the footprint of the tunnels offers greater potential for notch impingement and tunnel failure, making surgical revisions more difficult due to the larger overall size of the tunnels.

Both the single-bundle and double-bundle techniques, if performed by an experienced surgeon, can produce outcomes that would allow an athlete to return to a functional level. The key to either technique is correct graft placement, with a goal of placing the graft in a position that replicates the original anatomic position of the ACL, thereby re-creating a functionally stable knee. Treatment of other menisco-ligament injuries also is important in determining the functional outcome of the knee during ACL reconstruction.

■ Postoperative Management

After surgery, the patient's wounds are covered with a sterile dressing; a compressive bandage is applied from the toes to the proximal thigh; and the leg is often placed in a postoperative, long leg, hinged knee brace. Dressings are changed several days later, and any bulky, compressive cotton dressings are removed. The elastic bandage is continued.

Continuous cold therapy can be applied over the dressings. Although patients subjectively favor continuous cold application, evidence is limited that the use of continuous cold is advantageous immediately postoperatively.[15] Similarly, patients may subjectively report increased comfort with the use of continuous passive motion (CPM), but long-term efficacy of this technique has not been substantiated.[16–18] Patients are instructed to bear weight as tolerated with the brace locked in full extension. The brace can be unlocked for ambulation once extension is full, flexion is greater than 120°, and adequate muscle control is demonstrated by a straight-leg raise without a lag and a normal gait pattern.

Quadriceps setting with the knee in full extension and straight-leg raises with the brace locked in extension begin on the second postoperative day. Patients start formal rehabilitation at 5 to 7 days postoperatively.

Injury-Specific Treatment and Rehabilitation Concerns

Specific Concerns

Protect the graft.
Restore full patellar motion and knee ROM.
Prevent early rotation forces on the knee.
Avoid early weight-bearing flexion (with associated meniscal tears).

Patients should begin weight bearing as tolerated with the knee fully extended in a locked knee brace as soon as possible. The goal is to bear full weight without assistance 1 week after surgery. Patients should sleep with the knee locked in extension until full, active extension can be maintained. The brace can be removed for rehabilitation. When good muscular control of the leg and full extension to flexion past 90° are achieved, the brace can be unlocked for ambulation. The brace can be discontinued when flexion is 120°.

To restore tibiofemoral motion, the patella is mobilized until it is moving normally compared with the contralateral knee. Patients who have had a BPTB graft are closely monitored for patellar mobility, especially a superior glide.

ROM exercises are started immediately using various active-assisted and passive ROM techniques. To restore full extension, the patient engages in

prone hanging or sitting with the knee in an extended position while the ankle is supported. The patient should have at least 90° of flexion by 2 weeks and 120° of motion by 4 weeks postoperatively. If these goals are not met, passive motion should be performed more aggressively. Bicycles are not recommended to regain ROM, as they tend to place high-load, low-duration stretches on the knee; the hip and ankle are likely to compensate for these stresses.

Early quadriceps muscle reeducation is also emphasized. In addition to active quadriceps setting and exercises, motor-level electrical stimulation is applied to the quadriceps with the knee fully extended. In full extension, the vector forces of the contracting quadriceps tendon should be more compressive than translatory. Counterweights can be applied to the proximal tibia to reduce or eliminate any unwanted translatory forces (see **Figure 5.6**).

Good quadriceps firing is emphasized during all exercises. Biofeedback may be helpful in reinforcing quadriceps muscle recruitment. The patient begins a partial or mini-squat program as soon as weight bearing is full and joint effusion is controlled. Weights can be held in the hands and increased as tolerated. One-leg mini-squats or step-up exercises begin when the patient's control is adequate to enable the individual to perform the exercise smoothly and maintain the knee in a straight plane.

Open-chain quadriceps exercises are initiated from 90° to 45° of motion 4 weeks after surgery, with extension increasing by 15° every 2 weeks until full extension is achieved. This protocol is followed not just to protect the graft but, more important,

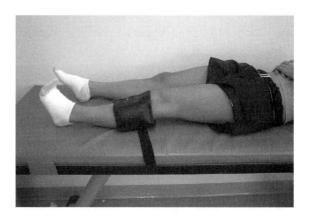

Figure 5.6 Use of tibial counterweights to reduce anterior translation of the knee during electrical stimulation. *Note:* The electrodes have not yet been applied.

to protect the patellofemoral joint. Early on, when an effusion is present, the vastus medialis obliquus (VMO) may be inhibited. Quadriceps exercises are performed in a range in which patellar control is not as dependent on the VMO.

Hamstring exercises can begin as soon as tolerated. In patients who undergo a hamstring tendon graft, the donor site may be sore for several weeks. Active or very light resistance exercises are performed when the soreness diminishes. Hamstring activity is increased as tolerated. Open- and closed-chain exercises for the hip and ankle also begin early in the rehabilitative process.

Bicycling activity is initiated when the patient has adequate ROM to cycle without any compensation in the hip, knee, or ankle. Stair-stepper machines can be introduced when the patient begins unilateral mini-squats, emphasizing shorter arcs of motion with a great deal of quadriceps activity. Use of an elliptical glider or ski machine and treadmill walking begin when the patient can ambulate without a brace with a normal gait pattern. None of these repetitive exercises should be started in the presence of active inflammation.

Balance and proprioception exercises are essential to develop a functionally stable knee. Weight-shifting exercises are begun early in the process to prepare the knee to accept full weight-bearing stresses. Simple exercises with a straight leg on a hard, stationary surface can start as soon as the patient is walking without a brace. These activities are done in a controlled, protected environment. More challenging situations, such as walking on soft or moving surfaces, can be introduced approximately 6 to 8 weeks after surgery if leg control is good. More challenging dynamic activities with perturbations or simultaneous upper extremity and trunk activities are started at 12 weeks postoperatively.

A straight-ahead running program can begin at 8 weeks postoperatively if the patient's strength and endurance are adequate to permit running without any deviations. At 12 weeks after surgery, gentle cutting and pivoting activities can be initiated, progressing to more acute angles of cutting, shuttle drills, and pivoting. Plyometrics are added for further challenge. Additional agility drills should be designed to challenge the patient in a manner similar to the activities encountered in returning to sports participation. This program is a general guideline for rehabilitation that may need to be modified depending on the graft used, the age of the patient, and other factors.

Estimated Amount of Time Lost

Some patients may try to rehabilitate and complete the sport season. Attempts to cope with the injury through rehabilitation and bracing may require at least 4 to 6 weeks of time lost. Surgical reconstruction typically sidelines the patient from full sport or strenuous work activities for 4 to 9 months.[19,20] Good results with return to activity as soon as 8 weeks postoperatively have been reported,[21] but some experts recommend that the return to full activity should not occur until 1 year postoperatively.[22]

An accelerated rehabilitation program focusing on early restoration of motion, quadriceps muscle activity, and full weight bearing may have the greatest influence on decreasing time lost after reconstruction.[21] Fewer complications after surgery, including patellofemoral pain, have also been demonstrated.[23]

Return-to-Play Criteria

There are multiple factors that need to be considered prior to determining whether the patient may return to competition. These factors include, but are not limited to, no pain, full ROM, and restored strength and neuromuscular control of the hip and lower extremity. The individual also should successfully complete functional tests for the lower extremity and an agility program with activities similar to the sport activities. Additional considerations include ample healing of the graft and the patient's confidence in completing sport-specific activities.

Functional Bracing

The patient may be fitted with a functional knee brace designed for ACL injuries or use an off-the-shelf brace. Individuals who need a streamlined brace for an activity such as gymnastics may prefer a custom brace (see **Figure 5.7**). Some physicians choose not to prescribe a brace because of the paucity of scientific evidence proving that bracing is effective in preventing future knee injury or improving functional performance.

Risk Factors for ACL Injury

Multiple factors, either individually or in combination, may contribute to noncontact ACL injuries. These risk factors are commonly divided into extrinsic (those external to the body) and intrinsic (those within the body) factors. A more descriptive grouping of risk factors classifies them into en-

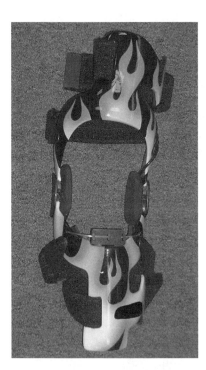

Figure 5.7 A custom ACL brace. These braces are designed to fit the contour of the patient's femur and tibia and allow for precise alignment of the knee joint. As the patient grows, or as muscle mass increases, the brace should be rechecked for fit and replaced if necessary.

vironmental, anatomical, hormonal, neuromuscular, and biomechanical factors.[24]

Environmental Risk Factors

Environmental (external) risk factors include weather conditions, the type of playing surface, the type of footwear, and protective equipment. The influence of weather conditions on ACL injury has not been extensively examined. Drier conditions resulting in a harder ground may increase the friction and torsional resistance at the shoe–surface interface, increasing the risk of ACL injury.[25] Nevertheless, other biomechanical and neuromuscular confounding factors have not been considered when examining the contributions of weather to ACL injury.

Artificial flooring and turf increase the coefficient of friction, leading to increased shoe–surface traction. The interaction of the increased traction and intrinsic neuromuscular and biomechanical factors may increase the risk of ACL injury. A retrospective examination of ACL injuries found an increased risk of ACL injury on artificial floors, relative to natural wood floors.[26] Some evidence also suggests that artificial turf reduces the risk of ACL injury compared to natural grass.[27] Unfortunately, no

definitive conclusions have been reached regarding the influence of playing surface on ACL injury, as studies have reported conflicting data related to the incidence, severity, nature, and cause of injuries when comparing injuries on artificial turf versus natural grass.

The use of protective equipment, particularly prophylactic knee braces, in the prevention of ACL injury has been an area of great debate. A body of prospective evidence suggests that prophylactic knee brace use is associated with a reduced rate of knee injury.[28] However, this conclusion is based on a small number of ACL injuries, leaving the question of whether prophylactic knee braces are more widely effective in preventing ACL injury unanswered.

Anatomical Risk Factors

Lower extremity anatomy and alignment are consistently included among the factors that have been suggested to increase risk of ACL injury. However, even the most updated consensus on ACL injury risk and prevention suggests that the relationship between lower extremity anatomical factors and ACL injury remains unclear.[29] A limited number of studies have examined the contributions of lower extremity anatomy and alignment to neuromuscular and biomechanical function of the knee joint. Reasons for the lack of empirical data may be attributed to an increased focus on neuromuscular risk factors, which are considered to be modifiable through training. Lower extremity anatomy and alignment are commonly considered to be nonmodifiable risk factors, as they are structural in nature. This may not be entirely true, however: Anatomical factors may be modified through interventions such as orthotics, bracing, and functional training. Furthermore, understanding the potential underlying causes for dynamic knee joint dysfunction leading to injury is necessary so that those persons at greatest risk of injury can be identified. This understanding would mark an important step toward the continuous effort in developing effective and accurate intervention strategies.

Femoral Notch Size and Tibial Geometry

A smaller width of the femoral intercondylar notch has been associated with increased risk of ACL injury in the athletic population. However, conflicting evidence has been gathered on this issue: Some studies suggest that a decreased femoral notch width is associated with increased risk of ACL injury,[30–32] whereas others[33] report that intercondylar femoral notch width cannot be used to identify an athlete at risk for an ACL tear.

Recent evidence suggests that tibial geometry may play a role in ACL injury. In particular, a greater posterior slope of the medial tibia,[34,35] reduced condylar depth on the medial plateau,[34] and presence of an anterior medial ridge on the intercondylar notch[36] have been observed in individuals who have injured their ACL compared to uninjured individuals.

Generalized Joint Laxity

Little is known about the biomechanical and neuromuscular relationship between generalized joint laxity (GJL) and ACL injury. The most comprehensive study was conducted by Uhorchak et al.,[37] who performed a prospective study of the relationship between intrinsic risk factors and ACL injury in athletes attending the U.S. Military Academy. They reported that those individuals with increased GJL had a 2.8 times increased risk of suffering an ACL injury.

A retrospective, matched-control study by Ramesh et al.[38] also supports a relationship between GJL and ACL injury. In this study, GJL was measured using the Beighton score—a score greater than 6 defined hypermobility. These researchers' results revealed a significantly greater proportion of subjects with GJL in the ACL-injured group (42.6%) compared to the control group (21.5%).

Anterior Knee Laxity

The ACL serves as a primary static stabilizer of the knee, providing the majority of restraint to anterior translation of the tibia relative to the femur.[39–45] Mechanoreceptors in the ACL[46,47] enable the ligament to provide sensory feedback regarding ligament length and tension, thereby modifying neuromuscular strategies.[48,49] As a consequence, the ACL plays an important role in knee joint stability as both a primary restraint to anterior tibial translation and a means to regulate and maintain neuromuscular and biomechanical control of the knee. The potential mechanisms by which anterior knee laxity influence ACL injury risk include reduced proprioceptive sensitivity to joint displacements and loads[50,51] and altered biomechanics during weight bearing.[52]

Research studies comparing uninjured individuals and those with ACL-deficient knees suggest that the ACL plays a major sensory role, in that ACL-deficient knees have been found to have reduced proprioception,[53,54] increased reflex delays,[39,55] and altered neuromuscular control strategies during cutting[56] and landing maneuvers[57,58] when compared to uninjured knees. These find-

ings suggest that increased knee laxity may allow greater joint displacement and loads before the body mounts a neuromuscular response to protect the knee.

Knee laxity has been cited as a potential risk factor for ACL injury;[50,59–62] however, limited research has examined knee laxity as an independent ACL injury risk factor. Increased knee laxity and increased pronation were found to predict ACL injury status in a retrospective examination of ACL-injured males and females.[63] When data were reviewed prospectively, anterior knee laxity, narrow femoral notch width, higher than average body mass index, and GJL were predictive of ACL injury in males and females in a military population.[30]

The relationship between anterior knee laxity and ACL injury remains unclear because studies that have examined this relationship included very few ACL-injured subjects. To better understand this relationship, prospective studies in a larger cohort of active individuals who generate a larger number of ACL injuries are needed.

Static Lower Extremity Alignment

While a standing posture of greater anterior pelvic tilt, internal femoral rotation, knee hyperextension, knee valgus, and foot pronation is thought to be associated with lower extremity dysfunction and biomechanical abnormalities,[64–66] it is unknown whether this posture increases the risk of ACL injury. The alignment characteristic most consistently linked to ACL injury risk is foot pronation.[63,66–68] Nevertheless, it appears that pronation alone is not independently related to ACL injury, as navicular drop has been found to be a predictor of ACL injury risk in combination with pelvic tilt,[68] genu recurvatum,[66] and knee laxity.[63]

"Functional valgus collapse" has been described as a common mechanism for ACL injury.[69,70] This event is characterized by valgus and either internal or external rotation of the tibia relative to the femur, as the lower limb transitions from no weight bearing to full weight bearing.[70] Research suggests that postural malalignments may also have the potential to significantly alter biomechanical function, internal–external rotation, and laxity of the knee joint.[64,66,67,71–75] These changes may further influence proprioceptive orientation and/or feedback from the hip and knee[64,66] as well as the mechanical efficiency and relative contribution of a muscle to control knee motion. Understanding how postural factors may influence dynamic control and biomechanical function of the knee is essential for understanding and preventing ACL injuries. The following sections discuss how various anatomic alignment variables may influence dynamic control of the knee and contribute to components of functional valgus collapse.

Subtalar Pronation

Subtalar joint pronation has been a variable of particular interest for ACL injury because of the compensatory increase in internal tibial rotation on the foot that occurs with excessive pronation. Increased internal tibial rotation at the foot is thought to be coupled with increased internal tibial rotation at the knee,[66,67,72] which has been shown to increase ACL strain values during weight bearing.[76]

As noted earlier, subtalar pronation may combine with other alignment factors to increase biomechanical stresses at the knee. An additional consequence of pronation and internal tibial rotation at the knee is the potential for increased internal femoral rotation and valgus angulation at the knee.[77] Therefore, individuals who have a propensity for increased femoral rotation (e.g., excessive hip anteversion, excessive anterior pelvic tilt) may increase the effects of subtalar pronation, further accentuating a valgus collapse of the knee.

Quadriceps Angle

The quadriceps angle reflects a composite measure of pelvic angle, hip rotation, tibial rotation, patella position, and foot position.[64,74,77] It is defined clinically as the angle in the frontal plane that is formed by intersecting lines from the center of the patella to the anterior superior iliac spine (ASIS) and the center of the patella to the tibial tuberosity.

Given the anatomical landmarks associated with this measure, the quadriceps angle can be greatly influenced by abnormal tibia and femur positions in the transverse and frontal planes. Depending on the relative contribution and interactions of these various malalignments, excessive quadriceps angle may contribute to dynamic knee valgus and increased torsion on the knee during weight bearing. However, because the quadriceps angle can be increased or decreased by changes in any one of these variables, this complex interaction creates challenges when trying to ascertain its relationship to at-risk knee motions and ACL injury risk. To clarify the effects of excessive quadriceps angle on neuromuscular and biomechanical function of the knee, it may be necessary to classify the quadriceps angle based on the relative contribution of the various soft-tissue, structural, or functional abnormalities that define the measure.[77] This relationship further supports the need to consider alignment of the entire lower extremity, rather than a single alignment variable, when assessing the risk of ACL injury.

Pelvic Angle

Anterior pelvic tilt has been hypothesized to be a predictor of ACL injury because excessive anterior tilt of the pelvis is thought to lead to an internal rotation and medial collapse of the extremities.[64,66,78] While two retrospective case-controlled studies identified a relationship between ACL injury and excessive anterior pelvic tilt,[66,68] it is not clear whether pelvic tilt itself or the distal functional malalignments it creates (i.e., knee recurvatum, navicular drop, knee laxity[30,63,66–68]) are most predictive of ACL injury risk. While one study found pelvic tilt and navicular drop combined to predict injury risk,[68] the other found pelvic tilt to be a predictor of risk only when examined independently, as it did not contribute to the multivariate model of injury risk based on genu recurvatum, rearfoot angle, and navicular drop.[66,68]

Femoral Anteversion

Femoral torsion is defined as the angle formed between the axis of the femoral neck and a transverse line through the femoral condyles.[79,80] Femoral anteversion results from a forward projection of the femoral neck from the transcondylar plane, which is manifested clinically as internal femoral rotation and a toe-in gait. In theory, increased femoral anteversion would seem to decrease the internal moment arm of the gluteus medius, thereby increasing the abduction force necessary to maintain stability of the pelvis. This theory is supported by work that examined muscle forces of the hip using a simulated hip model in which an internally rotated femur, as the case with femoral anteversion, required an increase in gluteus medius force to maintain a level pelvis compared to a neutral alignment of the femur.[81] Further, decreased activation of the gluteus medius as measured by electromyography (EMG) amplitude has been demonstrated in individuals with increased relative femoral anteversion.[82] Therefore, increased femoral anteversion may lead to decreased frontal and transverse plane hip control as a result of decreased gluteus medius activation.

Summary

Females differ from males with regard to neuromuscular and biomechanical function of the knee because of a variety of factors that may include structural influences. As yet, however, the extent to which sex differences in postural alignment impair neuromuscular and biomechanical function and explain the increased risk of ACL injury in females remains largely theoretical. Although females have been found to have greater anterior pelvic tilt, hip anteversion, knee valgus, and recurvatum,[83] studies examining these factors' potential to contribute to functional valgus collapse and increased knee loading during dynamic activity are limited. The interdependency that exists between independent alignment factors[84] further complicates this relationship, as one segment or joint may profoundly influence the alignment of other segments or joints, and ultimately the loads produced across the knee and ACL. Future studies should consider postural alignment of the entire lower extremity kinetic chain, from the pelvis to the foot, to determine the relationship between anatomic alignment, knee joint function, and ACL injury risk.

Hormonal Risk Factors

It has been suggested that sex hormones are related to knee joint laxity,[85–87] ligament tensile strength,[88] and injury risk.[89–91] The area that has received the most attention in this regard is the relationship between sex hormones and knee laxity, as females have greater knee laxity values compared to males,[50,59–61,92] and these differences appear to depend on the different phases of the female menstrual cycle.[85,86,92] While epidemiological studies have reported a relationship between ACL injury and menstrual cycle phase,[89,91,93] the precise nature of the relationship among sex hormones, knee laxity, and dynamic knee motion remains unknown. It has been suggested that cyclic increases in knee laxity during a female's menstrual cycle may further compromise the dynamic biomechanical response of the knee, especially during the postovulatory and early luteal days of the menstrual cycle.

Biomechanical Risk Factors

As mentioned earlier, one common mechanism for ACL injury has been described as functional valgus collapse of the knee,[69,70] with the hip in adduction and internal rotation along with the knee in a valgus and either internal or external rotation of the tibia.[70] This position has been prospectively found to predict ACL injury risk in adolescent female athletes[94] and is known to strain the ACL.[76] Although research in this area has yet to confirm those factors that contribute to this "at risk" position, neuromuscular deficits of the lower extremity are thought to be the main contributor to controlling knee motion.[94,95]

Medial Collateral Ligament Sprain

CLINICAL PRESENTATION

History

Valgus stress is exerted on the knee on a loaded extremity.
External rotation may also be reported.
Pain is described along the MCL.
Pain may extend distally to the medial tibial flare and proximally to the medial epicondyle.

Observation

The initial observation may not reveal significant findings. With time, swelling may develop over the medial knee.

Functional Status

Functional status depends on injury severity:
- Grade I: little to no loss of ROM or ability to bear weight
- Grade II: difficulty bearing weight due to pain and loss of ROM, especially at the end ranges
- Grade III: severe functional limitations

If the MCL is torn proximal to the joint line, motion loss is greater.[96]

Physical Examination Findings

The following special tests are positive:
- Valgus stress at 25° to 30°: MCL injury
- Valgus stress at 0°: damage to the MCL, medial joint capsule, and possibly the cruciate ligaments
- Slocum drawer

Tests for cruciate ligament stability may be positive if the valgus stress test at 0° is positive.
Tests for meniscal tears are less reliable in the presence of an acute MCL injury.

MCL sprains occur from a direct valgus force across the knee while the foot remains planted or, less frequently, by an indirect force as the knee is forced into valgus during an activity such as skiing. Indirect injuries are also seen in soccer when two players simultaneously contact the ball from opposite sides (a "50–50 ball").

After an indirect injury mechanism, a purely valgus force must be differentiated from a torsional force. Noncontact torsional injuries may result in a combined MCL–ACL injury and have a higher incidence of meniscal damage.[97,98] Although such an occurrence is less frequent, a valgus force to the knee while the tibia is externally rotated may result in trauma to the MCL and PCL.[99] In this mechanism, the unloaded foot contacts the ground; contact to the leg (but not necessarily the knee) then forces the knee into valgus and external rotation.

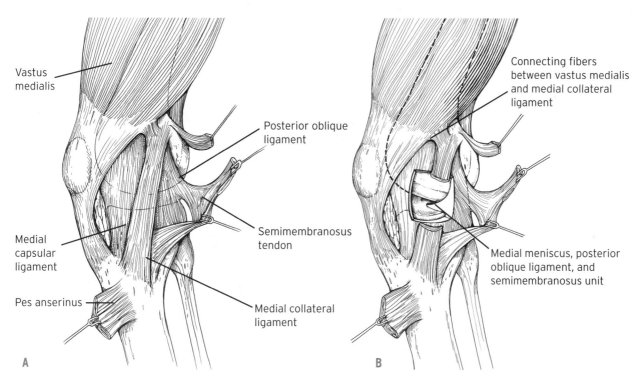

Vastus medialis

Posterior oblique ligament

Medial capsular ligament

Pes anserinus

Semimembranosus tendon

Medial collateral ligament

A

Connecting fibers between vastus medialis and medial collateral ligament

Medial meniscus, posterior oblique ligament, and semimembranosus unit

B

Figure 5.8 The medial structures of the knee. (**A**) The medial capsuloligamentous complex. (**B**) The MCL is dynamized by the connecting fibers of the vastus medialis, and the posterior oblique ligament is dynamized by the semimembranosus. *Source:* Reproduced with permission from Indelicato PA. Isolated medial collateral ligament injuries in the knee. *J Am Acad Orthop Surg.* 1995;3:9-14.

The medial-side structures form three distinct layers[100] (see **Figure 5.8**). The first layer, the superficial layer, is the deep fascia encompassing the patellar tendon anteriorly and the popliteal fossa, including the medial hamstrings, posteriorly. The second layer, the MCL, blends with the third layer, the posteromedial capsule, forming the posterior oblique ligament.

The tissues involved and the extent of injury depend on the knee position and the applied stresses. When the knee is extended, valgus forces are absorbed by the entire complex. If the knee is flexed beyond 20°, the superficial tissues are most responsible for dissipating forces.

The MCL deep layers communicate with the medial joint capsule and the medial meniscus. Damage to these structures should be suspected if the deep layer of the MCL is injured by the valgus force. A bone bruise or osteochondral trauma may occur in the lateral joint secondary to compressive forces.

Differential Diagnosis

Meniscal tear, ACL sprain, patellar retinaculum sprain, patellar dislocation, epiphyseal fracture (pediatric patients), medial hamstring strain, pes anserinus strain.

Imaging Techniques

Radiographs are obtained to rule out avulsion fracture, intra-articular fracture, and patellar injury.

MRI is used to identify MCL trauma and rule out damage to other ligaments and the menisci (see **Figure 5.9**).

Definitive Diagnosis

Definitive diagnosis of MCL sprain is made based on pain elicited on valgus stress with or without the presence of laxity in the acute setting, point tenderness over the MCL, and a positive MRI finding for MCL injury. If the examination is delayed by a few days, extension may be limited secondary to edema, making it difficult to perform a clinical examination.

Pathomechanics and Functional Limitations

MCL disruption results in pain and possible joint instability. Grade I injuries are marked by pain with activity, no instability, and minimal loss of ROM. Patients typically have minimal limitations in normal ADLs. Grade II MCL sprains produce increased pain, swelling, loss of ROM, and an inability to perform low-intensity activities without pain. Although knee laxity is increased and an end point can still be identified, valgus instability often results. Grade III sprains are painful and produce significant limitations in ROM, especially toward the end ranges. Complete ligament disruption causes significant instability during activity.

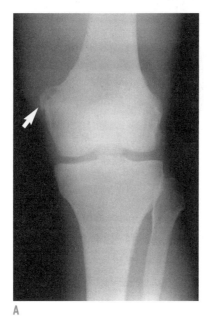
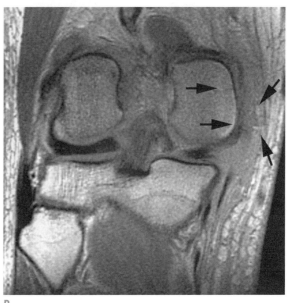

A   B

Figure 5.9   Imaging techniques for MCL sprains. (**A**) AP radiograph demonstrates a Pellegrini-Stieda lesion (arrow), indicating a chronic MCL injury. (**B**) Coronal MRI scan of an MCL tear. The arrows indicate a complete tear of the MCL.

Immediate Management

An acute MCL injury should be protected until the full extent of injury is appreciated. Initially, the knee may be more comfortable immobilized in slight flexion, especially with more severe injuries. The patient should use crutches to decrease stress through the knee. Ice, compression, and elevation control early inflammation and limit edema formation.

Medications

NSAIDs are useful for alleviating pain in lower-grade injuries, but keep in mind that long-term use inhibits healing. With grade II and III injuries, acute pain management with narcotic analgesics may be used to allow the patient to participate in the rehabilitation program and sleep more comfortably.

Surgical Intervention

Primary repair of an isolated MCL injury is typically not needed but may be considered in a combined MCL–ACL injury; the decision to repair the MCL is made during the ACL surgery.[101,102] The ACL is reconstructed first, and then the knee is reexamined in full extension. If the knee is still unstable while in or near full extension, the MCL is repaired (see **ST** 5.3). If valgus laxity is restored to grade I after ACL reconstruction alone, primary MCL repair is not performed.

> **Practice Tip**
>
> Primary surgical repair of an isolated MCL injury is typically not needed but may be considered in a combined MCL–ACL injury.[101,102] The ACL is reconstructed first, and then the knee is reexamined in full extension. If the knee is still unstable while in or near full extension, the MCL is repaired.

Surgical treatment of the MCL is prone to high complication rates, including stiffness and patellofemoral dysfunction.[103] These issues must be addressed early in the rehabilitation program.

Postinjury/Postoperative Management

Isolated MCL injuries are usually successfully treated with a conservative program of rest from aggravating activities, NSAIDs, and functional rehabilitation. At the same time, such injuries must be protected against recurrent valgus stress, including repetitive valgus stress testing. A hinged knee brace can protect this joint from injurious forces while allowing the patient to perform ROM exercises. Some grade III injuries may require a brief period of immobilization until pain subsides. A hinged brace can be initially locked in a comfortable position and then unlocked as the ligament heals. Use of the brace continues until the patient has at least 100° of motion, demonstrates good muscular control of the leg, and walks without a limp.

Patients with grade II or III MCL injuries should ambulate with crutches initially, increasing weight bearing as tolerated. Patients should

Surgical Technique 5.3

MCL Repair

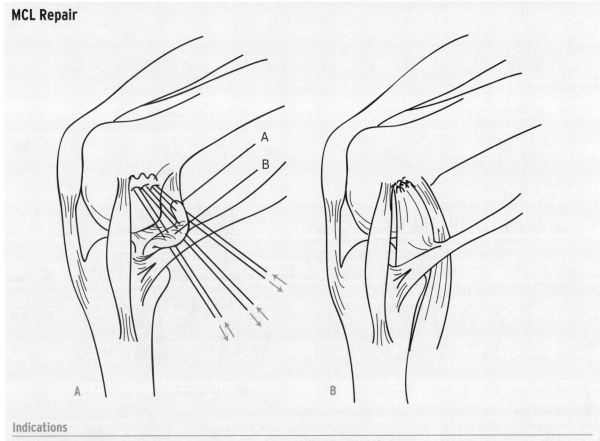

Indications

Persistent laxity with symptoms of valgus laxity and failure of conservative management.

Procedure Overview

Acute Combined MCL-ACL Injuries

1. ACL reconstruction is performed (see ST 5.1), and valgus laxity is reassessed. If the knee remains unstable in near or full extension, primary repair is performed.
2. The incision site is the same one used for the ACL reconstruction and autogenous graft harvest. With an allograft, a limited medial incision can be used.
3. The MCL and posterior oblique ligament are exposed.
4. Sutures are inserted into the stump of the posterior oblique ligament (POL) on the adductor tubercle (**A**).
5. With the knee in 60° of flexion, the POL is tied to the adductor tubercle (**B**).
6. The MCL is repaired, and the tibial end of the POL is attached to the tibia (**C**).
7. The anterior border of the POL is sutured over the posterior portion of the MCL (**D**).

(continues)

begin a formal rehabilitation program to restore ROM, strength, and function as soon as tolerable.

Injury-Specific Treatment and Rehabilitation Concerns

Specific Concerns

Maintain patellar mobility.
Encourage early strengthening.
Emphasize early, pain-free ROM.

All patients with isolated MCL injuries undergo a similar course of rehabilitation, but they progress at different rates depending on the extent of injury. The progression of rehabilitation exercises and activities is based on ability rather than set time periods.

Patients with grade I and II injuries can begin ROM exercises within a pain-free range as soon as tolerated. Simple quadriceps-setting exercises and leg raises may start immediately if tolerated. Other strengthening exercises can begin once pain and

S|T Surgical Technique **5.3 (Continued)**

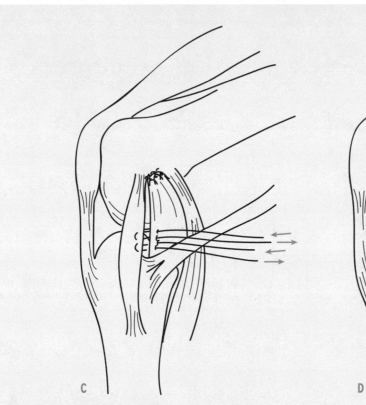
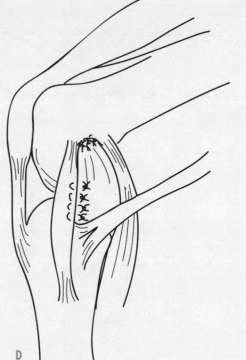

C   D

Chronic Instability of the MCL Despite an Adequate Healing Period
1. The MCL and POL are exposed.
2. The medial capsular is **reefed** or advanced to restore medial stability.

reef (reefing) A folding or tucking of tissues.

Functional Limitations

MCL repairs may result in some postoperative stiffness. Care should be taken to mobilize the joint without injuring the repair.

Implications for Rehabilitation

ROM and strengthening exercises are implemented early to prevent arthrofibrosis. The repair is protected with a brace, and valgus stress is limited to prevent injury to the repair.

Potential Complications

Arthrofibrosis, repair failure, and other surgical complications such as deep vein thrombosis and infection are possible.

Source: Reproduced with permission from Hughston JC, Eilers AF. The role of the posterior oblique ligament in repairs of acute medial (collateral) ligament tears of the knee. *J Bone Joint Surg Am.* 1973;55:923-940.

swelling begin to subside. The knee must not incur any valgus forces at any point during the early rehabilitation period, however. A valgus brace should be worn during adduction leg-raising exercises along with external weight applied to the proximal tibia.

When full, pain-free ROM is obtained and no pain is elicited on clinical examination, proprioceptive exercises are instituted. These exercises should stress the knee in full extension as well as some flexion. Activities that place limited, con-

trolled stress on the medial knee should be added to the program. These exercises include cup pickups and standard proprioceptive exercises with multiplanar activities and functions such as ball catching while balancing (see Chapter 8).

Once the clinical examination is pain free, ROM is full, and strength is adequate, straight-ahead activities such as jogging and straight up-and-down jumping may begin, followed by nonlinear agility activities as tolerated. Patients with grade II or III injuries should wear braces during agility activities.

Estimated Amount of Time Lost

Time lost to MCL injury varies with the grade of the sprain. Grade I sprains may result in loss of 1 to 2 weeks of sports participation. Grade II sprains may lead to loss of 2 to 4 weeks of sports activity, whereas grade III sprains may require 2 to 3 months until full return to activity is possible.

Return-to-Play Criteria

The patient may return to competition when there is no pain, full ROM, restored strength to the quadriceps and hamstrings, and normal balance. The patient also should successfully complete an agility program featuring activities similar to the sport activities.

Functional Bracing

A hinged knee brace with medial and lateral stays designed for MCL injuries is used with grade II and III sprains. This device may also be used in a grade I injury if the risk of reinjury is increased, as in a football lineman, or if the patient feels more confident returning to activity with the knee braced. An off-the-shelf brace designed for ACL instability is most suitable for grade III injuries and patients with grade II sprains requiring added protection (see **Figure 5.10**). The brace is used only until the season is completed and is not required in subsequent seasons.

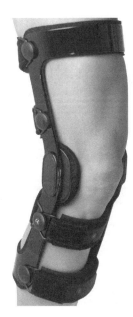

Figure 5.10 A collateral ligament brace. These off-the-shelf braces are used to protect and provide stability to the medial and lateral collateral ligaments.

Posterolateral Complex Injuries

CLINICAL PRESENTATION

History

Traumatic contact to the anteromedial knee, hyperextension, or a noncontact varus force to the knee.[104]
Lateral knee pain with instability.[105]
Patients with a concomitant peroneal nerve injury may describe paresthesia along the lateral foot.

Observation

Swelling, especially along the lateral knee.
Possible lateral thrust during ambulation.

Functional Status

Weight bearing is limited by pain and a sensation of instability.
ROM is decreased both actively and passively by pain.

Physical Examination Findings

A manual muscle test of ankle dorsiflexors or great toe extension is performed to document peroneal nerve function. Peroneal nerve injury has been reported in 15% to 56% of patients with grade III LCL injuries.[105,106]
The following special tests may be positive:
- Varus stress at 30°: isolated LCL injury
- Varus stress at 0°: concomitant tear of ACL or ACL and PCL
- External-rotation recurvatum
- Posterolateral rotation
- Lachman
- Anterior drawer
- Alternate Lachman
- Pivot shift
- Posterior drawer
- Slocum drawer

The posterolateral complex (PLC) is divided into three anatomic areas. The first layer consists of the prepatellar bursa, iliotibial tract, and biceps tendon; the second layer consists of the patellar retinaculum and the lateral collateral ligament; and the third layer includes the joint capsule and arcuate and fabellafibular ligaments (see **Figure 5.11**). Isolated lateral collateral ligament (LCL) sprains are rare. Forces that would otherwise be applied to the medial knee are usually deflected as the contralateral extremity is contacted first.

Most injuries involving the LCL also affect other tissues that form the PLC. Injuries to these tissues can be debilitating to the patient, even during regular gait, creating a varus thrust.[104] PLC injuries also may affect the cruciate ligaments.[107]

Differential Diagnosis

Fibular head avulsion fracture, lateral meniscal injury, ACL sprain, PCL sprain, tibiofemoral dislocation, physeal fracture in the pediatric patient.

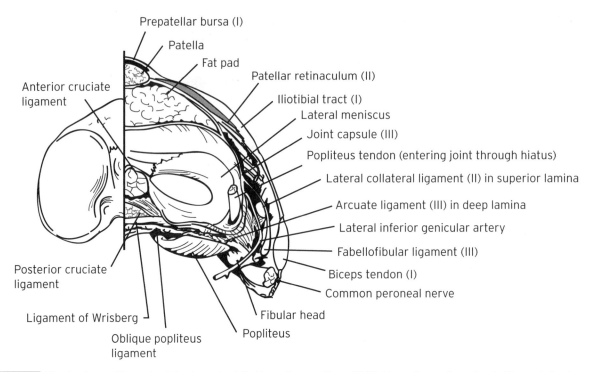

Prepatellar bursa (I)

Patella

Fat pad

Patellar retinaculum (II)

Iliotibial tract (I)

Lateral meniscus

Joint capsule (III)

Popliteus tendon (entering joint through hiatus)

Lateral collateral ligament (II) in superior lamina

Arcuate ligament (III) in deep lamina

Lateral inferior genicular artery

Fabellofibular ligament (III)

Biceps tendon (I)

Common peroneal nerve

Fibular head

Popliteus

Anterior cruciate ligament

Posterior cruciate ligament

Ligament of Wrisberg

Oblique popliteus ligament

Figure 5.11 The structures of the posterolateral complex. I, first layer; II, second layer; III, third layer. *Source:* Reproduced with permission from Seebacher JR, Inglis AE, Marshall JL, Warren RF. The structure of the posterolateral aspect of the knee. *J Bone Joint Surg Am.* 1982;64:536-541.

Imaging Techniques

AP radiographs are helpful to rule out a fibular head avulsion fracture (see **Figure 5.12**). An AP view while varus thrust is applied may be useful in determining the extent of lateral compartment joint-line opening.[108] With chronic instability, the amount of medial compartment arthritis must be assessed. A bilateral standing posteroanterior view with the knee flexed at 45° assesses tibiofemoral joint-space narrowing.[109]

MRI is used to confirm the extent of injury to the PLC, cruciates, and menisci. Standard coronal, sagittal, and axial cuts are obtained. If a PLC injury is suspected, thin-sliced (2-mm), proton-density, coronal oblique images including the entire fibular head and styloid are useful[110] (see **Figure 5.13**).

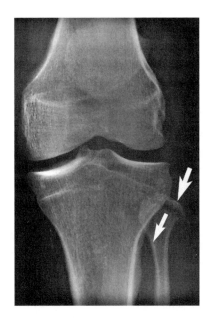

Figure 5.12 AP radiograph demonstrating an avulsion fracture of the fibular head (arrow) in a patient with combined PCL, posterolateral corner, and LCL injuries.

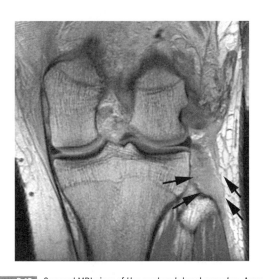

Figure 5.13 Coronal MRI view of the posterolateral complex. Arrows point to an avulsion of the LCL and biceps femoris tendon from the fibular head.

An **arteriogram** is obtained to assess vascular injury if clinically indicated or if a tibiofemoral dislocation is suspected.

Definitive Diagnosis

After evaluating a knee injury, understanding the clinical findings—particularly for athletic trainers who often are the first to evaluated injured individuals—is important to meet the accurate diagnosis of PCL. The definitive diagnosis of a PLC is based on positive findings of the varus stress test at 30° (isolated LCL), varus stress test at 0° (concomitant tear of ACL or ACL–PCL), external-rotation recurvatum test, and posterolateral rotation test. Passive knee extension results in hyperextension and external rotation of the involved leg. In chronic cases, a varus-thrust gait may be demonstrated. A posterior dynamic pivot shift also may be present.

MRI findings are used to confirm the clinical findings. Peroneal nerve damage is confirmed by electromyographic studies and nerve conduction tests, but it may take 3 to 4 weeks for these tests to become diagnostic.

Pathomechanics and Functional Limitations

Isolated PLC injuries result in varus laxity. Combined LCL and cruciate ligament injuries create a complex pattern of laxity leading to instability. Patients with isolated grade I LCL injuries present with ADL limitations secondary to pain. Patients with grade II and III injuries and combined cruciate ligament tears are limited in all weight-bearing activities due to instability.

■ Immediate Management

Acute PLC injuries should initially be protected until the extent of the injury is determined. The patient may be more comfortable with the knee immobilized in slight flexion, especially with a severe LCL injury. Use of crutches decreases stress through the knee. Ice, compression, and elevation are used to control early inflammation and limit edema formation.

■ Medications

NSAIDs are useful in alleviating pain with lower-grade injuries, but keep in mind that long-term use inhibits healing. In grade II and III injuries, acute pain management with narcotic analgesics may be used to allow the patient to participate in the rehabilitation program and sleep more comfortably.

■ Postinjury Management

Early recognition of the structures involved and injury severity forms the basis for successful treatment.[105,107,111] Isolated grade I and II injuries to the LCL or PLC can be treated conservatively. Patients with grade II injuries must be followed closely with a period of rehabilitation. Those with continued complaints of pain and instability may require surgical repair. Because of the high success rate with acute repair, some physicians elect to surgically repair all grade II PLC injuries to more adequately restore normal anatomy and function.

Patients with PLC and cruciate ligament injuries should have angiographic studies to rule out vascular injury.[112] If present, vascular injury should be assessed by a vascular surgeon for immediate repair of the injured vessel.

■ Surgical Intervention

Symptomatic grade II and III injuries require surgical anatomic repair of the tissues within 10 to 14 days.[107,111,113] After this time, retraction of the injured tissues may prevent an adequate anatomic restoration via primary repair. Failing to recognize the injury or the degree of laxity in the early postinjury period (2 weeks) dictates a late reconstruction with a graft or tissue advancement rather than primary repair of the injured structures. Late reconstruction yields results inferior to primary repair. Patients with chronic insufficiency require late reconstruction and/or high tibial osteotomy, which should be considered salvage procedures.

Primary tissue repair is favored over late reconstruction because of its ability to provide better restoration of normal knee biomechanics. Optimal techniques for repairing PLC injuries include direct repair back to bone and side-to-side suturing of soft tissues (see **S T** 5.4). Restoring the normal anatomic position with secure fixation allows ROM to be pursued early and safely postoperatively.[108] Any concurrent reconstructions of the ACL and PCL are performed at the time of the primary repair of the PLC.

■ Postoperative Management

If secure repair of the PLC tissues is performed to restore anatomic position, the patient can commence ROM immediately after surgery. The physician determines the limits of early ROM in a safe zone during surgery. With complex injuries, a 1- to 2-week immobilization period may be warranted. Delayed signs of neuropathy should be followed with serial electromyographic and nerve conduction tests.

arteriogram A radiograph of a blood vessel after the injection of a radiopaque dye into the bloodstream.

5

S|T Surgical Technique 5.4

Repair of the Posterolateral Complex

Primary Repair   Secondary Repair

A   B   C

Indications

Injury to the posterolateral structures with lateral instability.

Procedure Overview

Primary Repair

1. A curvilinear incision is made midway between the Gerdy tubercle and fibular head and extended up to the lateral femoral epicondyle in the midportion of the iliotibial band.
2. Dissection is carried through the iliotibial band, and the injury is identified.
3. If the injury involves the fibular head or peroneal nerve, the peroneal nerve is identified and moved out of the surgical field.
4. The tissue is repaired back to bone.
5. Sutures are placed through the tissue. If the tissue has been torn off the fibular head, a suture anchor may be passed to fixate it back to the fibular head.
6. A curette is used to produce a fresh bony bed to accept the tissue.
7. The tissue is advanced to the prepared bony bed and fixated (**A**).

Secondary Repair

1. The incision is similar to that used for a primary repair.
2. The graft tissue (such as the patellar tendon) is harvested.
3. A tunnel is bored through the lateral femoral condyle.
4. A bifurcated graft is fixated distally via tunnels bored through the proximal tibia and fibular head and fixated using anchors (**B**).
5. An isolated reconstruction involves fixation through a tunnel bored through the fibular head (**C**).

Functional Limitations

Postoperative motion limitations are determined by the surgical procedure, structures repaired, and fixation strength. Other limitations may be dictated by associated neurovascular injuries.

Implications for Rehabilitation

Avoidance of varus stress through weight bearing is required to prevent excessive stresses to the repair. Motion limitations may also be necessary, especially with secondary reconstructions.

Potential Complications

Repair failure and continued varus instability can limit the patient's functional outcome.

Source: Figures reproduced with permission from Veltri DM, Warren RF. Operative treatment of posterolateral instability of the knee. *Clin Sports Med.* 1994; 13:625.

curette A scoop-shaped surgical instrument used to remove tissue.

bifurcated Made up of, or divided into, two parts.

Injury-Specific Treatment and Rehabilitation Concerns

> **Specific Concerns**
>
> Encourage pain-free ROM within the limits established by the physician.
>
> Avoid knee hyperextension, external rotation, and varus forces.
>
> Maintain patellar mobility.

Nonsurgical Treatment of Grade I and II Injuries

Patients are initially protected in a knee immobilizer in full extension for 3 to 4 weeks with no weight bearing. Patellar mobilizations may be conducted. Quadriceps-setting and straight-leg raising into hip flexion exercises are performed while the patient is in the immobilizer.

After the initial immobilization period, the patient is placed in a hinged brace while ROM, strength, and weight bearing progress as tolerated. The brace can be discontinued when full ROM is achieved and control of the leg is adequate, as demonstrated by a normal gait pattern and straight-leg raising without a lag. No specific limitations are placed on restoration of ROM, which is advanced as tolerated. Hip-muscle strengthening with flexion and abduction exercises is progressed. Adduction and hip-extension exercises are introduced after 6 weeks, when tissue healing is more advanced. Quadriceps strengthening can begin with both open- and closed-chain activities. Hamstring activity starts at 6 weeks, as adequate tissue healing is achieved.

Primary Repair to the Posterolateral Complex

PLC injuries are associated with greater morbidity than PCL injuries. With a concurrent LCL–PCL reconstruction, ROM restrictions for the posterolateral complex override the PCL guidelines presented here and in the PCL section.

The patient bears no weight for 2 weeks. Partial weight bearing with the knee locked in extension for 2 weeks is then initiated. If sufficient leg control is established, the patient may bear weight as tolerated in an open-hinged brace for 2 more weeks. As long as adequate anatomic repair has been accomplished, the patient can immediately begin passive ROM exercises, avoiding knee hyperextension. Any motion restrictions required because of tension placed on the primary repair noted during surgery must be strictly followed. Active hamstring motion must be limited.

Straight-leg raises for hip flexion and adduction can begin after 1 week. Abduction and exten-sion exercises start after adequate healing of the primary repair, at approximately 6 to 8 weeks postoperatively. Quadriceps activity may begin with leg-extension exercises at 4 weeks. Initially, these exercises are performed from 90° to 30°, with extension being increased 15° every 2 weeks until full ROM is obtained. Closed-chain activities can begin at approximately 4 to 6 weeks postoperatively. Isolated hamstring activity is delayed until 4 months postoperatively.

The patient can begin proprioception exercises on a stable surface as soon as full weight bearing is achieved. At approximately 12 weeks, less stable and more challenging exercises may be introduced. Walking, swimming, and cycling may start 8 to 12 weeks after surgery. Running straight ahead on level surfaces can begin at 6 months, followed by agility and sport-specific drills if the patient demonstrates adequate strength and balance. Full return to activity may take 9 to 12 months.

Estimated Amount of Time Lost

Isolated grade I injuries require 2 to 4 weeks of rehabilitation. Grade II and III injuries and those involving the cruciate ligaments require surgical intervention and 6 to 9 months of rehabilitation, similar to isolated cruciate reconstruction. Surgical intervention and acute versus chronic surgical treatment of the PLC increase the time lost, possibly to as long as 1 year.

Return-to-Play Criteria

The patient must have grade I or less laxity of the lateral knee; full restoration of ROM, strength, and proprioception; and the ability to compete in sport-specific activities without instability.

Functional Bracing

Patients use a hinged knee brace for isolated lateral-side injuries. Patients with concomitant cruciate injuries use a functional knee brace designed to stabilize anterior or posterior laxity, as dictated by the involved structures.

Posterior Cruciate Ligament Sprain

PCL tears, although less common than ACL and MCL tears, are more prevalent than previously thought. A literature review demonstrated PCL tears in as many as 44% of patients with acute knee injuries.[114] The under-recognition of PCL tears is due, in part, to the asymptomatic nature of most of these injuries.

CLINICAL PRESENTATION

History

Knee hyperflexion.

A fall onto a flexed knee.

A posteriorly directed force to the anterior tibia with a flexed knee.

Mechanisms involving cutting, pivoting, or hyperextension could lead to multiple-ligament injury.

Patients may report minimal or no pain in acute injuries.

Over time, patients may complain of vague symptoms related to the patellofemoral joint.

Observation

Swelling is slight to moderate.

Ecchymosis may be present in the popliteal space.

A posterior sag may be noted.

Functional Status

Isolated grade I or II tears may initially be overlooked by the patient.

Gait may be normal or antalgic.

ROM may be normal.

Terminal flexion may be limited secondary to pain, especially with a partially torn PCL.

Concomitant injuries to other ligaments cause greater motion loss.

Physical Examination Findings

Any or all of the following special tests may be positive:
- Posterior drawer
- Godfrey
- External rotation
- Reverse pivot shift

The PCL is the primary restraint to posterior translation of the tibia on the femur (see **Figure 5.14**). The MCL, LCL, and posterolateral corner of the knee all form secondary restraints to this motion.[113]

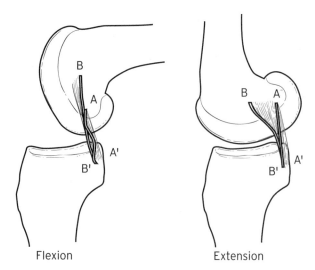

Flexion   Extension

Figure 5.14   The insertion of the PCL extends 2 cm below the surface of the posterior aspect of the tibial plateau. With flexion, the bulk of the ligament (B-B') becomes taut. The posterior band (A-A') becomes taut in extension.

In knees with an intact PCL, these secondary restraints play a minimal role in preventing posterior translation. In contrast, in the PCL-injured knee, the secondary restraints play a vital role in maintaining stability.[113]

An isolated PCL tear increases posterior translation of the tibia on the femur. Concomitant tearing of the MCL, LCL, or posterolateral corner can significantly increase posterior translation. The PCL also acts as a secondary restraint to external rotation, with the posterolateral corner of the knee providing the primary restraint. When the posterolateral corner is injured but the PCL remains intact, forces on the PCL increase.[113]

Differential Diagnosis

Posterior capsular sprain; meniscal tear; ACL sprain; symptomatic or ruptured Baker cyst; hamstring, gastrocnemius, popliteus, or plantaris muscle strain.

Imaging Techniques

Radiographic evaluation should include AP, lateral, tunnel, and patellofemoral views. MRI is highly accurate for diagnosing the location of PCL tears and aids in assessing possible posterolateral corner injury[113] (see **Figure 5.15**). This information may influence the treatment approach; femoral attachment injuries may be more amenable to surgical repair.[113]

Definitive Diagnosis

Definitive diagnosis of PCL sprain is based on positive orthopaedic tests demonstrating posterior laxity and conclusive findings on MRI.

Pathomechanics and Functional Limitations

Patients with an isolated PCL tear may have few functional limitations. The types and descriptions of these limitations differ depending on the extent of the injury. In the acute stage of injury, patients may be unable to perform activities due to pain and swelling. Because instability is not always present, however, they may not seek immediate treatment. In chronic PCL tears, functional limitations tend to be similar to those associated with patellofemoral disease, including generalized discomfort, pain on descending stairs, and the sensation of giving way during activity. Particular difficulty may occur when slowing down while running, as the hamstrings contract more forcefully and displace the tibia.

Anterior shear forces of the femur on the tibia produce pain and instability. When the foot is fixed on the ground and the femur decelerates, such as in a basketball jump-stop or a gymnastics dismount, the femur is displaced anteriorly relative to the tibia.

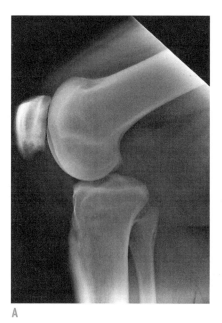 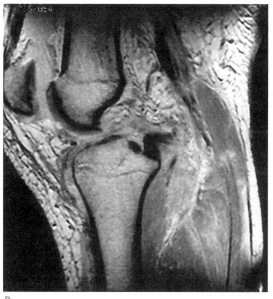

A   B

Figure 5.15 Imaging of PCL tears. (**A**) Posterior subluxation of the tibia seen on a lateral view of a posterior stress radiograph of a patient with combined grade III PCL-MCL injury. (**B**) MRI demonstrating an acute complete tear of the PCL.

Immediate Management

The patient should be placed in a hinged, controlled-motion brace as close to full extension as pain allows until a thorough assessment is conducted to rule out concomitant posterolateral corner injury. Keeping the leg near full extension removes stress from the injured structures by properly aligning the tibia. Ice, compression, and elevation control the early inflammatory process and limit edema formation.

Medications

NSAIDs are helpful in relieving pain in lower-grade injuries. In grade II and III injuries, acute pain management with narcotic analgesics may be used to enable the patient to participate in the rehabilitation program and sleep more comfortably.

Postinjury Management

Patients with isolated grade I and II PCL injuries are treated with protected weight bearing until pain and swelling are eliminated. Rehabilitation can begin immediately. With a conservative treatment approach, isolated grade III injuries are immobilized for 2 to 4 weeks in a hinged-motion brace as close to full extension as pain allows. Partial weight bearing to tolerance is permitted. Quadriceps setting and straight-leg raises should be performed.

Surgical Intervention

Immediate PCL reconstruction for an isolated grade III injury is indicated with a "peel-off" injury that

can be replaced in its bony attachment and in young, active patients. Failure to improve with conservative treatment of grade III sprains may also warrant PCL reconstruction. In addition, surgical intervention may be appropriate if symptoms occur in the medial compartment of the knee and the patellofemoral joint or if the PCL is injured along with other ligaments or the posterolateral corner. If the posterolateral corner must be repaired, surgery should be performed within 2 weeks of the initial injury.

Techniques to reconstruct the ligament are controversial. PCL reconstruction may be attempted arthroscopically or performed with an open technique. When the procedure is performed arthroscopically, fluid may extravasate into the lower leg. If this complication occurs, the arthroscopy must be abandoned and the surgery completed through an open technique.

Surgical techniques have focused on reconstructing just the larger anterolateral bundle of the PCL (one-bundle technique) or both bundles (two- or double-bundle technique) (see **Figure 5.16**). The one-bundle technique reduces but does not eliminate the laxity. Recent cadaveric studies of the double-bundle technique have demonstrated that it offers better restoration of joint biomechanics,[115] but long-term, in vivo studies of stability and function with this technique have not been performed as of yet.

The other controversy in PCL reconstruction involves tibial graft placement. The traditional technique places the graft through a tibial tunnel; the

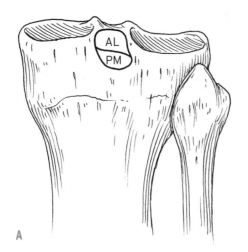 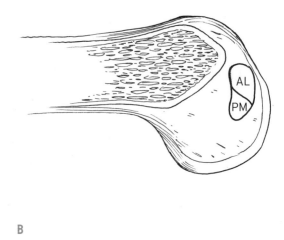

Figure 5.16   Anatomy of the PCL insertion. (**A**) Outline of the anterolateral bundle (AL) and posteromedial bundle (PM) of the tibial insertion. (**B**) Femoral origin. *Source:* Adapted from Harner CD, Hoher J. Evaluation and treatment of posterior cruciate ligament injuries. *Am J Sports Med.* 1998;26:471-482.

major disadvantage of this approach is that the graft exits the tibial tunnel just below the posterior tibial plateau and bends around ("killer turn") toward its eventual insertion into the femur (see 🅢🅣 5.5). The reconstructed graft also encounters a graft–femoral tunnel angle ("critical corner") that can be a site of increased shear stress and internal tendon pressures. This procedure is technically challenging, and the graft–tunnel interfaces at the tibia and femur may place unwanted forces on the graft, resulting in its eventual failure.

A tibial inlay technique has been previously described (see 🅢🅣 5.6).[116] With this method of repair, a bone trough is created at the PCL footprint. Bone attached to the graft is then inlaid in the trough and fixated, creating a more natural graft attachment and eliminating the bend that occurs with the tibial tunnel technique.

Many graft options are available, including patellar tendon autograft, quadriceps tendon autograft, hamstring autograft, patellar tendon allograft, and Achilles tendon allograft. If the tibial inlay technique is used, the graft must have a bone block attached.

■ Postoperative Management

The knee is immobilized in full extension for 4 weeks. The patient is carefully followed for signs and symptoms of arthrofibrosis, including increasing stiffness or pain and decreasing function. If any of these conditions are detected, knee mobility becomes more aggressive. The patient is allowed to weight bear as tolerated with the knee extended. Quadriceps-setting exercises and straight-leg raises are performed during this period. The brace is un-locked at 4 weeks for ambulation and discontinued at 8 weeks if the patient has good leg muscle control and at least 100° of flexion.

■ Injury-Specific Treatment and Rehabilitation Concerns

> **Specific Concerns**
>
> Protect the injury/graft from unwanted stresses.
> Avoid hamstring contractions.
> Emphasize quadriceps reeducation.
> Encourage weight bearing and ROM as tolerated.

Nonsurgical Rehabilitation

Rehabilitation of isolated grade I and II PCL injuries focuses on quadriceps muscle strengthening initiated with leg raises, open-chain knee extension from 60° to 0°, and mini-squats. As tolerated, the patient can begin proprioceptive training, progressing to straight-ahead running, agility skills, and sport-specific activities, and finally to full activity. Typically, patients return to full activity in 2 to 4 weeks.

Four weeks after their initial injury, patients with grade III PCL injuries progress to full weight-bearing and ROM exercises. Strengthening of the quadriceps musculature is initiated with open knee extension from 60° to 0° and mini-squats. At 8 weeks after injury, strengthening exercises can advance to 90° of motion and hamstring exercises can begin. The patient can begin proprioceptive training as tolerated, progressing to straight-ahead running, agility skills, and sport-specific activities, and finally to full activity. Typically, patients return to full activity in approximately 3 months.

S T **Surgical Technique** 5.5

Tibial Tunnel ("Killer Turn") Technique for PCL Reconstruction

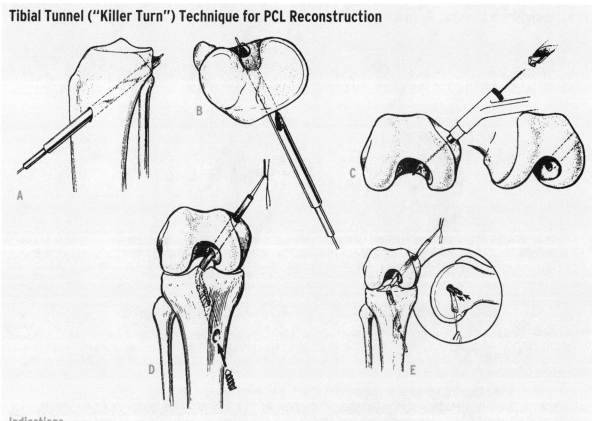

Indications

Patients with grade III PCL injuries who remain symptomatic after a course of formal rehabilitation.

Procedure Overview

1. The knee is examined; PCL remnants are identified and debrided.
2. The course of the tibial tunnel is identified, a guidewire is placed, and correct placement is confirmed with a radiograph before the tunnel is drilled.
3. A tibial tunnel from the anteromedial tibia to the tibial attachment footprint is created (**A** and **B**).
4. The femoral tunnels are then identified and drilled (**C**).
5. If a single bundle is used, it is placed, tensioned, and fixated.
6. With a double bundle, a semitendinosus autograft is harvested and prepared with an Achilles tendon allograft.
7. The graft is placed through the tibial tunnel and into the femoral tunnel. In double bundles, the allograft is typically used for the anterolateral bundle and the autograft for the posteromedial bundle (**D**).
8. The bundles are fixated at the femoral side (**E**).
9. The knee is cycled, and the graft is tensioned and fixated at the tibia. (If a single bundle is used, the graft is fixated at 90°. If a double bundle is used, the anterolateral bundle graft is fixated at 90°, whereas the posteromedial graft is fixated at 30°.)

Functional Limitations

Repaired isolated PCL tears rarely create functional limitations. When they are combined with other ligament injuries, however, multi-directional instability of the knee may result.

Implications for Rehabilitation

The graft sustains the greatest tension at 90° of flexion. This position should be avoided until healing is adequate.

Potential Complications

Potential complications include graft loosening and typical surgical complications such as deep vein thrombosis and infection. The tibial tunnel approach may create excess stress along the graft as it makes the "killer turn" around the posterior tibia, but no conclusive evidence demonstrates that this technique significantly affects the surgical outcome.

Source: Reproduced with permission from Miller MD, Harner CD, Koshiwaguchi S. Acute posterior cruciate ligament injuries, in Fu FH, Harner CD, Vince KG (eds), *Knee Surgery.* Philadelphia, PA: Williams & Wilkins; 1994:749–767.

S|T Surgical Technique 5.6

Tibial Inlay Method of PCL Reconstruction

 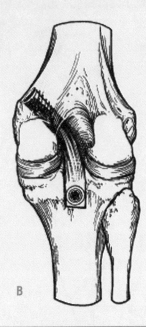

A   B

Indications

Patients with grade III PCL injuries who remain symptomatic after a course of formal rehabilitation.

Procedure Overview

1. The patient is placed prone or in the lateral decubitus position with the operative leg up.
2. A single- or double-bundle technique can be used. If a single bundle is chosen, it is placed in a position to replicate the anterolateral bundle of the original PCL.
3. The PCL remnants are identified and debrided.
4. The femoral tunnels are drilled to simulate the double bundle's footprints of the PCL in the anteromedial notch (**A**).
5. The leg is extended, and an oblique incision is made at the medial gastrocnemius head, exposing the area between the medial head and the semimembranosus tendon.
6. The neurovascular structures are retracted.
7. The posterior capsule is incised, and the PCL attachment is visualized.
8. An inlay window is prepared in the tibia to accept the bone block of the allograft tissue.
9. The graft is placed and fixated in the tibial inlay with one or two screws (**B**).
10. The graft is placed, tensioned, and fixated in the femoral tunnel.

Implications for Rehabilitation

The graft sustains the greatest tension at 90° of flexion. This position should be avoided until healing is adequate.

Potential Complications

Graft loosening and typical surgical complications, such as deep vein thrombosis and infection, are potential complications.

Comments

The tibial inlay technique is technically demanding. The lateral decubitus or prone position is necessary for this procedure; other surgical procedures for multiple-ligament injuries require the patient to be in a supine position. The position change extends surgical time and can be burdensome to the surgeon and operative team.

Source: Reproduced with permission from Bergfeld J, McAllister DR, Parker RD, et al. A biomechanical comparison of posterior cruciate ligament reconstruction techniques. *Am J Sports Med.* 2001;29:129-136.

Postoperative Rehabilitation

Two weeks after PCL reconstruction, patients can begin formal rehabilitation. Patellar mobilization is important because of the prolonged period of immobility. ROM exercises are commenced with the clinician or patient applying an anterior translatory force to the posterior tibia while the knee is flexed. The anterior translation force decreases or eliminates tensile stress that may be placed on the PCL graft with flexion and is used until approximately 8 weeks after surgery. Initially, ROM is progressed to 60°. Full extension should be obtained as soon as possible. At 6 weeks, ROM can advance as tolerated.

Strengthening focuses on the quadriceps and initially includes high-intensity electrical stimulation, straight-leg raising, and manual resistance from 60° to 0° while a manual anterior translatory force is applied to the posterior tibia. Closed-chain exercises, such as wall slides in a 0° to 60° range, can begin at 4 weeks. Hip flexion should be minimized during closed-chain exercises to decrease activity in the hamstring musculature. No active hamstring contractions are allowed until at least 8 weeks after surgery, at which time hamstring exercises begin with simple cuff weights. The patient can progress ROM during quadriceps strengthening exercises from 90° to 0° and increase exercise intensity as tolerated. Proprioceptive and balance exercises are begun at 8 weeks, when the graft can start to accept posterior translation forces from hamstring contractions. These activities are progressed as tolerated.

Stationary bicycling, swimming, and treadmill walking can be initiated 8 weeks after surgery. Running is allowed at 6 months, and agility and sport-specific drills start as tolerated. The patient must be able to perform these activities without any compensation before advancing to more challenging levels. Sports activities can begin at 9 months, but it may take as long as 12 months before the patient can participate successfully.

■ Estimated Amount of Time Lost

The amount of time lost to injury is 2 to 4 weeks after an isolated grade I or II injury. Grade III injuries are less predictable; conservative treatment may include prolonged rehabilitation of approximately 3 months, with PCL reconstruction taking 9 to 12 months before return to full activity.

The greatest influences on time lost are whether the PCL tear is isolated or part of a multiple-ligament injury and the severity of the tear. Isolated injuries can often be treated nonsurgically, whereas patients with grade III isolated injuries and PCL tears with concomitant ligamentous injuries are good candidates for surgical repair.

■ Return-to-Play Criteria

The patient may return to competition when there is no pain, full ROM, and restored quadriceps and hamstrings strength. The athlete should also successfully complete lower extremity functional tests and an agility program consisting of activities similar to the sport activities.

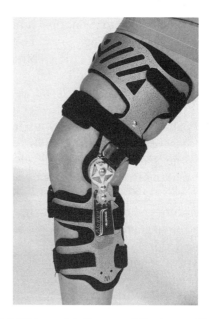

Figure 5.17 PCL brace. Note the suprapatellar strap used to stabilize the femur and prevent posterior displacement on the tibia.

Functional Bracing

The patient may be fitted with a functional knee brace designed for PCL injuries (see **Figure 5.17**).

Meniscal Tears

CLINICAL PRESENTATION

History

Shearing or torsional forces through the knee.
Pain along the joint line.
The patient may describe giving way or locking of the joint.
Meniscal tears should be suspected with an acute ACL injury.

Observation

A joint effusion is common with a medial meniscal tear but less common with a lateral meniscal tear.
The patient with a locked knee lies on the examination table with the knee flexed.

Functional Status

Weight bearing may be limited by pain and the sensation of instability.
ROM may not be limited unless the knee is locked.
Full flexion is usually painful, as the meniscus is compressed between the articular surfaces.

Physical Examination Findings

The joint line is painful to palpation. Typically, posterior joint-line pain on the medial side reflects a medial meniscal tear, and middle joint-line pain on the lateral side indicates a lateral meniscal tear. Pain along the anterior joint line may be related to patellofemoral injury.[117,118]
The McMurray test is positive; however, this test's reliability is low.
The Apley compression/distraction test is positive.

The menisci are integral to the normal function and long-term health of the knee joint. These fibro-cartilaginous structures provide stability, shock absorption, and joint lubrication. The blood supply to each meniscal portion determines whether a tear will heal spontaneously or whether it requires surgical repair. The peripheral 20% to 30% of the medial meniscus and 10% to 25% of the lateral meniscus—the "red zones"—are relatively well vascularized, making these areas more conducive to healing and repair.[119,120] The avascular (white) zone is the inner third and not conducive to healing. The red–white zone, which may have some blood supply, has limited healing potential (see **Figure 5.18**).

The type of meniscal injury experienced is affected by age. Younger patients tend to tear the meniscus and injure the ACL. Such a tear is likely to occur in the red and red–white zones, making those injuries more conducive to surgical repair. Older patients who have degenerated menisci may be more prone to acute, isolated tears in the white zone and through degenerative intrameniscal tissue. The type of tear sustained by the meniscus is the major determinant of the surgical procedure used (see **Figure 5.19**). The tear configuration also dictates the physician's choice of repair method. Complex tears, or tears that occur in multiple planes, are not generally conducive to repair.

Medial meniscal injuries tend to cause more symptoms than injuries affecting the lateral menis-

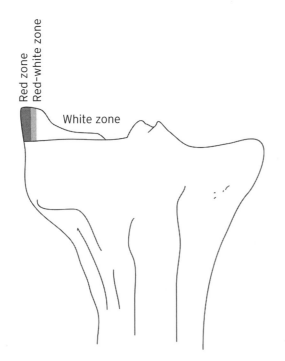

Figure 5.18 Vascular zones of the meniscus. The red zone formed by the outer 10% to 30% of the meniscus has sufficient blood supply to permit healing. The large white zone is avascular, and healing is not possible. The red-white zone is partially vascularized and has limited healing potential.

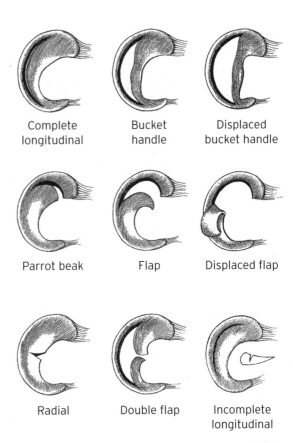

Figure 5.19 Types of meniscal tears. *Source:* Reproduced with permission from Tria AJ, Klein KS. *An Illustrated Guide to the Knee.* New York: Churchill Livingstone; 1992.

cus.[117] Most medial meniscal tears occur in the posterior portion, leading to pain with weight bearing. Medial meniscal tears are more common in chronic ACL-deficient knees and are more amenable to repair.[117,121] Lateral meniscal tears are more common in acute ACL injuries.[121] The lateral meniscus is more mobile than the medial meniscus, making it vulnerable to an increased number of insidious-onset tears.

Because of the important role played by the meniscus, tissue preservation is attempted whenever possible. Loss of meniscal tissue decreases the contact surface area and increases the peak local contact stress on the joint surfaces.[122] Over time, loss of meniscal tissue can lead to an earlier onset of arthritis.

Differential Diagnosis
Patellofemoral syndrome, symptomatic synovial plica, osteochondritis dissecans, loose body, chondral fracture, ligamentous injury.

Medical Diagnostic Tests
Positive MRI findings are diagnostic for meniscal tears.

Imaging Techniques
Standard radiographs should be obtained to rule out osteochondral fracture or osteochondritis dis-

secans. Narrowed joint space—the Fairbank sign—may be associated with osteophyte formation.[123] MRI is more than 90% accurate in detecting acute meniscal tears but less reliable in detecting degenerative tears.[124,125] This imaging modality is not accurate in determining repair potential, however: False-negative findings are most common in smaller peripheral tears that are conducive to repair.[122] MRI can also detect asymptomatic tears that do not require surgery (see **Figure 5.20**).

Definitive Diagnosis

The definitive diagnosis is based on the history and mechanism considered with other signs, such as joint-line pain with palpation, pain with flexion, and a positive McMurray test with associated clinical findings. MRI is helpful in the conclusive diagnosis of meniscal injury.

A sensation of giving way may be related to quadriceps inhibition or weakness from a variety of knee ailments. A meniscal tear should be suspected when true giving way or buckling of the knee is described. Although many patients may describe locking, true locking is the inability to completely extend the knee. This effect may be transient and related to a bucket-handle tear of the meniscus that wedges between the articular surfaces.

Pathomechanics and Functional Limitations

Patients complain of pain with weight-bearing and squatting activities. Acute meniscal tears may be more functionally limiting due to the associated pain and joint effusion. Pain occurs with deep flexion and twisting activities.

▦ Immediate Management

The patient should cease athletic activity, and ice should be applied to the knee. If the patient cannot tolerate weight bearing, crutches are needed until further clinical workup is completed and the extent of the injury is ascertained.

▦ Medications

NSAIDs are useful in pain management and controlling inflammation.

▦ Postinjury Management

If the knee is locked or unstable, the patient needs the protection afforded by using crutches. A locked knee requires immediate surgery so that no further damage is sustained. If a meniscal tear is suspected but the knee is not locked, the patient should be allowed pain-free function with normal ADLs. If pain or a sensation of giving way is experienced, crutches are helpful until the knee becomes asymptomatic.

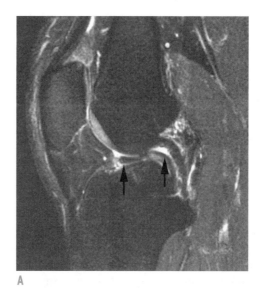

A

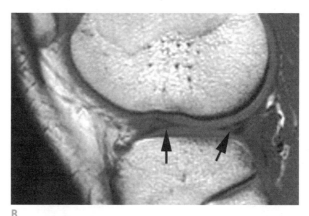

B

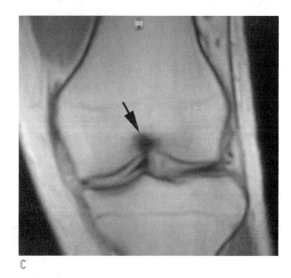

C

Figure 5.20   MRI of meniscal tears. (**A**) The darkened areas of the meniscus (arrows) are consistent with a displaced bucket-handle tear on a sagittal MRI. (**B**) Sagittal view demonstrating tears of the anterior and posterior horns of the lateral meniscus. (**C**) Coronal view of a bucket-handle tear.

Conservative treatment is usually indicated in the patient with an intact ACL and a stable meniscal tear. Treatment includes rehabilitation to strengthen the entire lower extremity, followed by a progressive return to more stressful weight-bearing activities. Patients who begin or continue to experience mechanical symptoms are candidates for surgery.

Surgical Intervention

Partial meniscectomy involves arthroscopic removal of unstable or symptomatic torn tissues (see ST 5.7). Tears within the avascular zone that are more complex, involve numerous cleavages within the tear, change the contour of the meniscal body, or are degenerative may not be repairable.[122] These tears are removed so that a smooth surface is left for femoral condyle contact. The surgeon preserves as much tissue as possible to decrease the risk of joint degeneration.

Tears in the outer third of the meniscus and some tears in the middle third of the meniscus may be nonrepairable—especially a complex tear that extends into the avascular zone in patients younger than 20 years.[126] Partial meniscectomy would necessitate removal of a large portion of the meniscus, resulting in loss of meniscal function and a greater risk of arthritis. In this scenario, a variety of techniques are available for the surgeon based on the location and extent of the repair (see ST 5.8).

In an unstable knee, the rate of successful meniscal repair along with ACL reconstruction is higher than that of isolated meniscal repair.[127,128] The stability provided by the reconstruction and the hemarthrosis created by the ACL reconstruction may produce a more conducive healing environment for the meniscal repair.[129,130]

Meniscal transplantations are being used on a limited basis, and the surgical techniques for this procedure are still being refined. They are technically demanding and not routinely offered as surgical options. Nevertheless, in patients who have had a subtotal to total meniscectomy, this option is attractive in preventing degenerative changes. Cadaver menisci must be matched in size to ensure appropriate function. The meniscal allograft is harvested and implanted with bone plugs attaching to the anterior and posterior meniscal horns. The allograft is then firmly sutured along its periphery to ensure stability.

Postoperative Management

The meniscal repair must be protected in the early healing phases. The patient is placed in a hinged brace, with no weight bearing, for 1 week. The individual is then progressed to full weight bearing with the brace locked in extension. The brace is discontinued when the patient has full ROM and demonstrates normal leg control by being able to straight-leg raise without a lag, walk normally, and perform stair climbing in a normal step-over-step manner.

Injury-Specific Treatment and Rehabilitation Concerns

> **Specific Concerns**
> Avoid early weight-bearing flexion.
> Emphasize early low-impact activities.

Nonsurgical Rehabilitation
Initial treatment focuses on controlling inflammation with ice and therapeutic exercise. Active or active-assisted ROM exercises such as heel slides are used. When adequate ROM is obtained, low-impact activity such as bicycling, elliptical gliding, and aquatic exercise can be initiated. The hip, quadriceps, and hamstrings are strengthened. At first, these exercises are performed in an open chain, but then progress to weight-bearing strengthening exercises when pain abates. Weight-bearing activities such as the stair stepper and treadmill can be added gradually.

When strength is within normal limits, the patient can complete agility drills, beginning with controlled tasks such as forward and backward running and side shuffling. More complex activities such as figure-of-eight exercises and jumping and cutting drills are introduced as tolerated.

Partial Meniscectomy
Using crutches, the patient bears partial weight until pain and inflammation are controlled, typically in 3 to 4 days. Subsequent treatment is similar to nonsurgical rehabilitation for meniscal tears. Flexion is not forced early in rehabilitation so that residual soreness does not worsen.

Meniscal Repair
The knee is immobilized, with no weight bearing being allowed. Passive ROM begins immediately, with a limit of 90° of flexion imposed until approximately 4 weeks after surgery to avoid compressing the meniscal repair; it then progresses to full flexion. Full, immediate motion and weight bearing have also demonstrated good results.[131–133]

Motor-level electrical stimulation and concurrent voluntary exercise are used for reeducating the

S T Surgical Technique 5.7

Surgical Menisectomy: Partial Menisectomy

Indications

A meniscal tear location and configuration not conducive to repair; therefore, the unattached segment must be removed.

Procedure Overview

1. Arthroscopic portals are made anteromedial and anterolateral to the patellar tendon at joint line. The inflow portal is superomedial or superolateral to the patella.
2. The meniscus is visualized, and a nonrepairable tear (a tear within the white zone or a radial tear communicating with the free edge of the meniscus) is identified (**A**).
3. The tear is debrided to a smooth margin using various biters and shavers (**B**).
4. A smooth, stable rim margin is made, sculpting the borders of the tear to form a smooth transition within the remaining portion of the meniscus (**C**).
5. The excised portion of the meniscus is removed (**D**).

Functional Limitations

Early motion limitations are secondary to the trauma of the arthroscopy and swelling. Early strength deficits are secondary to VMO inhibition from the joint distention and arthroscopic trauma.

Implications for Rehabilitation

The more tissue removed, the more compromised the shock absorption, and the greater the stresses that will be transferred to the articular surfaces. Early motion and progressive resistance exercises allow the patient to regain function quickly.

Source: Reproduced with permission from Canale ST (ed). *Campbell's Operative Orthopaedics*, ed 9. St. Louis, MO: Mosby-Year Book; 1998.

ST Surgical Technique 5.8

Meniscal Repair

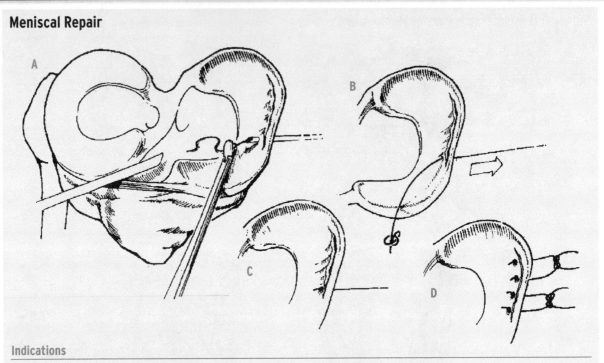

Indications

Mechanical symptoms of a meniscal tear, positive clinical examination, and positive findings on MRI.

Procedure Overview

Several methods are available for meniscal repair. In all methods, the rim of the tear should be abraded to create bleeding and an environment more conducive to healing.

Inside-Out Meniscal Repair

1. A small posteromedial or posterolateral incision is made.
2. Sutures are placed through the inner rim of the tear and out through the outer tear rim and the joint capsule.
3. The sutures are tensioned, and the tear is probed. If it can be stably reduced, the sutures are tied over the joint capsule.

Outside-In Meniscal Repair (shown)

1. A small posteromedial or posterolateral incision is made.
2. A spinal needle is placed through the joint capsule and across the tear (**A** and **B**).
3. Sutures are passed through the needle and tied down to secure the tear (**C** and **D**).
4. The outside-in technique may be preferred when the surgeon wants better control passing needles and sutures near the neurovascular bundles. These structures can be retracted and the needles and sutures passed.

All-Inside Repair

The all-inside technique is used specifically to repair posterior horn tears.

1. The all-inside technique is used to treat meniscal body and posterior horn tears.
2. Various orthopaedic instrument supply companies manufacture meniscal repair systems that allow fixation of repairable meniscal tears using the standard portals.
3. The meniscal repair systems are preloaded implants with a pre-tied self-sliding knot that allow the user to deploy two implants vertically or horizontally, tighten the suture, and trim the excess.

Functional Limitations

Limitations in weight bearing and deep flexion are often prescribed postoperatively to protect the repair. No impact activities should be permitted during the healing of the meniscal repair.

Implications for Rehabilitation

Protected motion and weight bearing naturally slow the rehabilitation process.

Comments

Biodegradable surgical "darts" and "arrows" have been used in place of sutures to repair the meniscus. However, these materials can become dislodged and float in the joint, causing pain and dysfunction.

Source: Reproduced with permission from Hanks GA, Kalenek A. Alternative arthroscopic techniques for meniscal repair: A review. *Orthop Rev.* 1990;19:541-548.

quadriceps. Straight-leg raises are performed in all planes except extension. Quadriceps exercises start when the patient can fully recruit the muscle and perform straight-leg raises without a lag. Light hamstring exercises with cuff weights do not begin until 4 weeks after surgery. The patient can transition to heavier weights with machines at 6 weeks as the repair heals further. Light closed-chain activities such as mini-squats and wall slides start when full weight bearing is achieved. More stressful activities such as leg presses and deeper squatting to 60° can be introduced at 8 weeks. Bicycling exercises may commence when ROM is adequate. Other activities that include weight bearing start at 8 weeks, with running and a progression of functional activities instituted at 10 weeks. Activities involving jumping and cutting are allowed at 12 weeks and are advanced carefully.

Estimated Amount of Time Lost

Conservative treatment of smaller peripheral tears may require 2 to 6 weeks before activity can be resumed. A patient with a partial meniscectomy may miss 4 to 6 weeks of activity. The amount of time lost after meniscal repair ranges from 10 weeks[132] to 6 months.[134]

With conservative treatment, smaller peripheral tears on the medial side quickly become asymptomatic relative to the lateral side. The aggressiveness of the rehabilitation program for a repaired meniscus is the determining factor that dictates the amount of time lost after surgery.[132]

Return-to-Play Criteria

The patient can return to play when sport-specific drills can be completed and the knee is relatively asymptomatic. Both good function and confident use of the knee should be demonstrated before the athlete returns to full competition. A knee sleeve may be helpful in the management of meniscal injuries to enhance joint warmth.

Distal Femur and Proximal Tibia Fractures

Fractures of the distal femur or proximal tibia rarely occur in sports because high-velocity forces are required to cause these injuries in young, healthy individuals. These fractures can be extra- or intra-articular in nature. In skeletally immature patients, lower-velocity forces can fracture the growth plate.

CLINICAL PRESENTATION

History

The mechanism of injury is usually a high-energy force.
Distal femur and tibial plateau fractures are usually the result of axial compression with varus or valgus force.
Medial tibial plateau fractures usually involve a varus force, whereas lateral tibial plateau fractures usually involve a valgus force.
The individual experiences immediate pain.

Observation

Joint effusion may occur with intra-articular fractures.
More generalized swelling is noted with extra-articular fractures.
Deformity may be noted in severe fractures.
Skin integrity should be checked to rule out an open fracture.

Functional Status

The patient is immediately unable to bear weight due to pain.
Depending on fracture severity and displacement, partial ROM may be possible.

Physical Examination Findings

Although ligaments may be concurrently injured, a thorough examination may be contraindicated by the presence of the fracture.
Distal pulses and nerve function should be thoroughly assessed.

Distal femur fractures are classified as supracondylar, intercondylar, or a combination of the two (see **Figure 5.21**). Proximal tibia fractures are commonly described as fractures of the medial or lateral tibial plateau with a fracture through the bone or a depressed fracture in the tibial plateau. Tibial plateau fractures are described using the Schatzker classification. Types I through III are associated with low-velocity forces, whereas types IV through VI are associated with high-energy forces (see **Figure 5.22**).

Intra-articular fractures must be treated to minimize the long-term effects on the articular surfaces. Restoring a normal articular surface is essential for ensuring proper joint function and minimizing early posttraumatic arthritic changes. Soft-tissue injuries should be suspected in fractures about the knee. Ligamentous injuries occur in approximately 20% of tibial plateau fractures, with the ACL and lateral meniscus most often involved.[135,136]

Differential Diagnosis
Ligament disruption, extensor-mechanism disruption, tibiofemoral dislocation.

Medical Diagnostic Tests
Fat droplets within the hemarthrosis confirm the breach of the bony cortex (see pages 129–130 for a description of the aspiration technique).

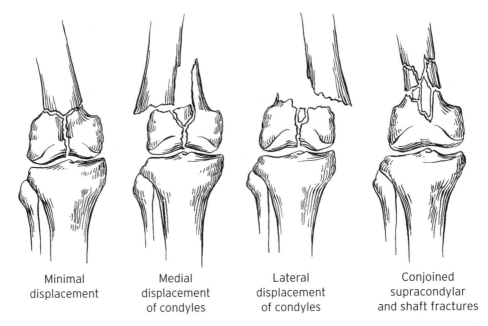

Minimal
displacement

Medial
displacement
of condyles

Lateral
displacement
of condyles

Conjoined
supracondylar
and shaft fractures

Figure 5.21 Classification of femoral condyle fractures. *Source:* Reproduced with permission from Greene WB (ed). *Essentials of Musculoskeletal Care*, ed 2. Rosemont, IL: American Academy of Orthopaedic Surgeons; 2000:376.

Imaging Techniques

Standard AP and lateral radiographs are obtained to determine the presence and extent of the fracture configuration. Radiographs taken at internal and external oblique angles of 40° are used to profile the condyles[137] (see **Figure 5.23**). Computed tomography is used to assess the extent of articular depression and/or fracture lines and for surgical planning. MRI is helpful in imaging suspected soft-tissue injury.

Definitive Diagnosis

Radiologic findings confirm the diagnosis of distal femur and proximal tibia fractures.

Pathomechanics and Functional Limitations

Most patients experience an immediate inability to ambulate secondary to pain and instability. With the accumulation of the joint effusion, extension and flexion are lost.

■ Immediate Management

The extremity should be splinted in the position in which it is found and the patient immediately transported to the emergency room. Distal pulses are checked and serially monitored. Motor and sensory function of the tibial and peroneal branches of the sciatic nerve should be assessed. The patient is evaluated for the presence or threat of an acute compartment syndrome. In addition, other trauma should be ruled out.

■ Medications

These injuries require acute pain management with narcotic analgesics and NSAIDs. Deep vein throm-

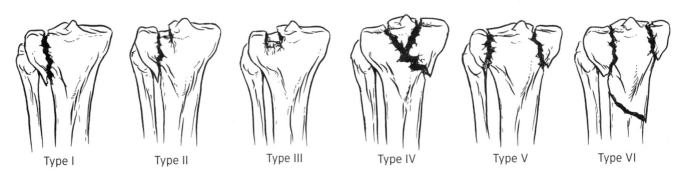

Type I   Type II   Type III   Type IV   Type V   Type VI

Figure 5.22 The Schatzker classification of tibial plateau fractures. Type I, wedge (split) fracture of the lateral tibial plateau; type II, split depression fracture of the lateral plateau; type III, pure central-depression fracture of the lateral plateau without an associated split; type IV, fracture of the medial tibial plateau, usually involving the entire condyle; type V, bicondylar fracture, consisting of split fractures of both the medial and lateral plateaus without articular depression; type VI, tibial plateau fracture with an associated proximal shaft fracture. *Source:* Reproduced with permission from Koval KJ, Helfet DL. Tibial plateau fractures: Evaluation and treatment. *J Am Acad Orthop Surg.* 1995;3:86–94.

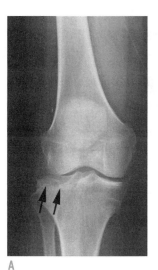
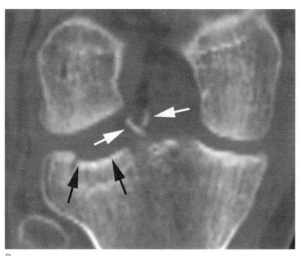
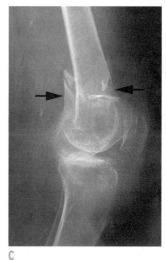

Figure 5.23 Imaging of fractures about the knee. (**A**) Radiograph of a depressed fracture of the lateral tibial plateau. (**B**) Computed tomographic scan of a depressed fracture of the lateral tibial plateau and associated tibial spine avulsion (white arrows) suggesting an associated cruciate ligament injury. (**C**) Lateral radiograph of a supracondylar fracture of the femur.

bosis prophylaxis may need to be considered, especially in patients who require extended periods of immobilization and activity restrictions.

Postinjury Management

Nondisplaced or minimally displaced and stable tibial plateau fractures can be treated nonsurgically in a controlled-motion brace, and placed on strict non-weight-bearing status. The fracture should be radiographically assessed weekly for the first 3 weeks to ensure that it has remained reduced and stable.

Surgical Intervention

Displaced fractures may require open reduction and internal fixation to restore joint alignment and congruity.[137,138] The amount of articular depression that requires surgical intervention is controversial; surgical intervention for depressions greater than 3 mm has been recommended in athletes.[139]

Arthroscopically assisted reduction of depressed tibial plateau fractures is an effective treatment method in athletes.[136,140,141] The fracture and concomitant soft-tissue damage can be better visualized intra-articularly without a large incision and dissection of soft tissues around the knee. Depressed fractures are reduced through a small incision over the tibia. Using guides placed arthroscopically, the surgeon can then elevate the depressed fracture with bone tamps placed through the small distal incision. Once elevated, the defect is packed with corticocancellous bone chips.

Distal femur fractures, usually angulated with joint congruity disrupted, require open reduction

with internal fixation. The fracture is fixated with intermedullary nails or a supracondylar plate with interfragmentary screws.

Postoperative Management

Patients with nondisplaced and minimally displaced tibial plateau fractures or arthroscopically assisted reductions of depressed tibial plateau fractures can initially be placed in a locked, hinged knee brace. After 3 to 4 weeks, the brace can be unlocked for ROM exercises. The patient remains on non-weight-bearing restrictions for 4 to 6 weeks.

The patient with stable internal fixation may begin CPM immediately. Active quadriceps and hamstrings exercises can start approximately 2 days after surgery. Minimal weight bearing can commence at 3 to 5 days, depending on fixation stability. Toe-touch weight bearing continues for 2 to 3 months, until radiographs demonstrate adequate healing. Weight bearing is progressively increased until solid union is achieved. External support is not required unless concomitant ligamentous injury is present or questions arise about fixation stability.

Injury-Specific Treatment and Rehabilitation Concerns

Specific Concerns
_____

Achieve adequate fracture healing in the correct anatomic position with maintenance of articular congruity.

Protect the healing bone.

Restore full patellar motion and knee ROM.

---

corticocancellous graft An autograft of bone, usually harvested from the iliac crest, that consists of both cortical bone and bony callus.

Although fractures about the knee must be protected, the benefits of early joint motion are taken into consideration in the rehabilitation process. Fracture management needs to provide stabilization so that passive motion can be introduced as soon as possible. Patellar mobilization is performed to restore normal joint biomechanics. Scar massage and mobilization are implemented after distal femur fracture surgery, because many times soft-tissue trauma and/or surgical scars cause soft-tissue contractures. Quadriceps and hamstrings stretching is important. Prone quadriceps stretching enhances normal knee flexion with internally fixated distal femur fractures; the quadriceps may have been disrupted by the fracture trauma, the surgical procedure, or the fixation plate lying underneath the quadriceps. If the quadriceps was disrupted during the surgical fixation, however, it must be allowed to heal adequately before tissue stretching begins.

Active lower extremity exercises are begun as early as possible—3 to 4 weeks after the initial injury for nonsurgically treated tibial plateau fractures. The ability to begin active exercises is actually enhanced by stable internal fixation. Heavy progressive resistance exercises are not introduced until adequate clinical and radiographic healing is demonstrated. As the patient advances to full weight bearing, proprioception exercises are instituted.

Estimated Amount of Time Lost

Patients with tibial plateau fractures may be able to return to activity approximately 3 months after the injury if the fracture was minimally displaced. Tibial plateau fractures that required open reduction and internal fixation will require a longer recovery period because of the prolonged weight-bearing restrictions associated with their repair. With distal femur fractures, typically 6 to 12 months recovery is required before patients can return to full participation in sports.[139] Surgical fixation of some fractures may shorten the injury recovery time. Once stabilized, these fractures can be more aggressively rehabilitated with protected weight bearing.

Return-to-Play Criteria

Complete fracture healing must be demonstrated radiographically. The knee must be pain free, with the patient demonstrating functional ROM and adequate return of strength. The patient should be able to successfully perform lower extremity functional tests.

Tibiofemoral Dislocation

CLINICAL PRESENTATION

History

A common sport mechanism involves a posteriorly directed force through the tibia, similar to that noted with a PCL injury.
Extreme pain is experienced, with immediate inability to move the leg.
A cold sensation in the foot is reported if lower leg blood flow is compromised.
Paresthesia in the associated nerve distribution may be noted with a peroneal or tibial nerve injury.

Observation

Gross malalignment of, and swelling in, the dislocated knee.
A large amount of swelling in the spontaneously relocated knee.

Functional Status

Immediate inability to move the leg secondary to the dislocation and pain.
Inability to bear weight.

Physical Examination Findings

Positive ligamentous tests in the spontaneously reduced knee.
Absence of dorsalis pedus and/or posterior tibial pulse with vascular injury. Initially present pulses need to be serially checked for changes.
Diminished function of the peroneal (toe extension) and/or tibial (toe flexion) branches of the sciatic nerve. Nerve function should be serially examined for several days after the injury.

The tibiofemoral, or knee, dislocation is arguably the most serious knee injury in athletics, posing significant risk of injury to the popliteal artery and peroneal nerve that could lead to the loss of the lower leg. Fortunately, this type of injury is rare in athletes. Knee dislocations also present challenges to rehabilitation. They can occur from either high- or low-velocity forces. Low-velocity injuries are more common in sports; high-velocity injuries are typically seen in motor vehicle, industrial, and water-skiing accidents.

Although knee dislocations can occur in any direction, most occur posteriorly. In some cases, the knee may spontaneously relocate, making timely recognition of the injury more difficult. Any injury to three or more of the knee's major ligaments (ACL, PCL, MCL, LCL) should be regarded as a knee dislocation, even if the joint surfaces are aligned at the initial examination.[142,143] While different combinations of ligamentous injury may occur, the ACL and PCL are always torn when the knee dislocates.[143] Knee dislocations often produce concurrent damage to the joint capsule, menisci, articular surfaces, and muscles and tendons surrounding the knee and threaten the neurovascular structures that cross the joint.

Vascular injury has been estimated to occur in 32% of all knee dislocations; this rate is slightly higher (40%) with anterior or posterior dislocations.[144] The popliteal artery is vulnerable to injury from knee dislocation because of its close proximity to the posterior tibia and its limited mobility.[142] Specifically, the artery is subject to a tension mechanism with an anterior dislocation or direct trauma from the tibial plateau during a posterior dislocation. Arterial injury can range from an intimal flap tear to total disruption. Careful assessment of the vascular supply is essential, because distal extremity circulation must be restored within 6 to 8 hours. Amputation rates as high as 85% have been reported when vascular damage was not treated within this time frame.[144]

The peroneal nerve is also at risk of injury with a knee dislocation. The incidence of this type of damage has been estimated at approximately 25% with knee dislocations.[142] The nerve may be more at risk with lateral or posterolateral injuries. The tibial nerve also may be injured. Acute compartment syndrome must be considered. Prolonged dislocation or transection of the popliteal artery further complicates this medical emergency.

Differential Diagnosis

Displaced femur or tibia fracture, dislocated patella, isolated ligament injury.

Medical Diagnostic Tests

Doppler pressure measurements are more accurate in assessing vascular status than the physical examination, and correlate well with arteriographic findings.[142] False-negative results may occur with intimal tears, however.

Imaging Techniques

Standard radiographic views confirm the dislocation and document intra-articular or periarticular fractures (see Figure 5.24). Arteriograms must be performed in all suspected and known knee dislocations (see Figure 5.25). MRI should be obtained to assess the associated soft-tissue structures after the patient's vascular status has been adequately evaluated and immediately treated.

Definitive Diagnosis

Definitive diagnosis of knee dislocation is made based on obvious visible signs of dislocation, positive radiographic findings, and three or more positive major ligamentous tests on clinical examination.

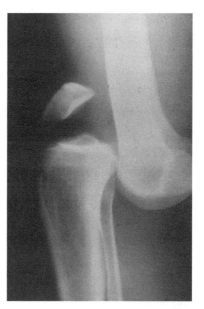

Figure 5.24 Lateral view of a typical anterior dislocation of the knee.

intimal Relating to the innermost membrane of the vessel.

Pathomechanics and Functional Limitations

Patients are immediately limited in function due to gross ligamentous instability.

Immediate Management

The leg should be splinted before the patient is moved, and the patient should be transported to the hospital as quickly as possible. While awaiting transport to the hospital, a physician may attempt a single, immediate reduction unless there is a suspected posterolateral dislocation.[145,146] These dislocations have a high incidence of medial joint-capsule

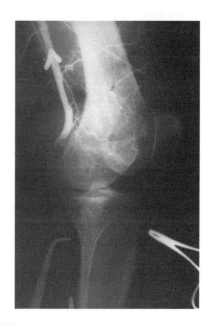

Figure 5.25 An intraoperative arteriogram demonstrates disruption of the popliteal artery just above the knee after a posterior dislocation.

interposition and should be reduced surgically to minimize the risk of skin necrosis.[145,146] If the reduction attempt fails on the first try, the leg should be splinted and the patient immediately transported. Monitor the patient for shock.

> ### Practice Tip
>
> As part of acute management of tibiofemoral dislocations, the leg should be splinted and the patient transported to the hospital as quickly as possible. A single, immediate reduction should only be attempted by a physician unless there is a suspected posterolateral dislocation.[145,146] If the reduction attempt fails, the leg should be splinted and the patient immediately transported. The patient is monitored for the onset of shock.

Medications

Tibiofemoral dislocations are painful; consequently, patients require administration of narcotic analgesics such as morphine or meperidine via intramuscular injection or intravenously. Later, NSAIDs may be indicated. Muscle relaxants may be employed to counteract significant muscle disruption.

Surgical Intervention

Arterial injury, a dislocation that will not reduce, an open dislocation, or acute compartment syndrome are indications for immediate surgery. Addressing vascular disruption or a compartment syndrome takes precedence over the surgical reconstruction of other aspects of the knee. The additional trauma from the ligament surgery could increase compartment swelling, and the fasciotomy could pose a higher risk of infection. The risk of infection with open dislocation is too high to warrant inserting foreign material into the knee at an early stage after injury.

After vascular repair, the repair should not be moved or stretched. With an intact vascular status and no open dislocation or risk of acute compartment syndrome, thorough examination of the ligaments and nerves is mandated. The aggressiveness of rehabilitation is determined on a case-by-case basis by the vascular and orthopaedic surgeons. If immediate surgical intervention is not needed, many experts believe that a delayed surgical approach to restore knee stability is preferable to conservative treatment of a knee dislocation.[143,147,148] However, the exact surgical procedure to perform and the timing of surgery are subjects of considerable controversy.

Some authors have proposed not reconstructing the ACL, whereas others recommend reconstructing the cruciates as essential to a functional, stable knee.[143,148] Although the concern over developing arthrofibrosis is real and favors delaying surgery at least 3 weeks, adequate repair of the medial, lateral, and posterolateral structures becomes increasingly difficult more than 2 weeks after injury. Reestablishing posterolateral corner continuity has the highest priority and must be undertaken in a timely manner. In the absence of overwhelming evidence to support increased symptoms related to arthrofibrosis when concomitant repairs and reconstructions are performed, surgical repair or reconstruction should be considered for all torn ligaments.[142] To minimize additional knee trauma, allografts should be considered. Because the lateral and posterolateral structures must be repaired to establish a stable joint, the surgical procedure should be performed after 2 weeks but no more than 3 weeks from the time of the initial injury.

The treatment of nerve injuries in dislocated knees remains controversial. If possible, a surgeon with expertise in nerve grafting should be available. A macroscopically intact nerve should not be treated except by careful serial assessments of function. If needed, nerve grafting using the sural nerve may be attempted, or the nerve may be tagged for later exploration if appropriate.

The patient should be prepared for a staged procedure, in which a series of surgeries is performed to address the neurologic, vascular, and musculoskeletal trauma. If the lateral corner is being addressed with nerve grafting, further surgery may be conducted after the lateral structures heal.

Postinjury/Postoperative Management

Postoperative management depends on secure fixation of repaired or reconstructed tissues. Mild instability is often preferred to an overly stiff knee; therefore, early motion is encouraged even if it might result in some instability. In the presence of stable surgical treatment, bracing and mobilization should be as aggressive as possible to decrease the likelihood of stiffness. A hinged knee brace and CPM are advocated for this purpose. The patient should keep the brace locked for ambulation until adequate quadriceps strength has returned and ROM is restored. Vascular and/or nerve grafting may require prolonged motion protection with a locked brace to ensure healing and prevent traction on the repairs.

If fixation security is in question, the brace may be locked in extension and ROM advanced after healing progresses. Arthrofibrosis is the primary postsurgical complication, and measures to decrease stiffness should be undertaken as soon as it is recognized.

Injury-Specific Treatment and Rehabilitation Concerns

> **Specific Concerns**
>
> Protect vascular and nerve graft repairs.
> Minimize arthrofibrosis.
> Reestablish joint stability.
> Restore patellar mobility.
> Regain ROM.
> Restore motor function.

After a knee dislocation, the return to sports activities, while still possible, is secondary to less aggressive goals such as the return to normal ADLs. The patient with a knee dislocation is at great risk for arthrofibrosis, which may ultimately lead to significant loss of ROM.

Edema about the knee also affects ROM. Intermittent compression devices should be used only if the possibility of compartment syndrome has been ruled out. Elevation and active exercise through muscle pumping and edema-reduction massage are helpful. Use of a compression stocking or elastic wrap helps to control edema between treatment sessions.

Early motion is advocated to minimize arthrofibrosis. Patellar mobilizations in all directions and passive and active-assisted ROM are beneficial in this regard. The surgeon should establish the safe ROM for the early rehabilitation stages. Less aggressive motion in certain ranges may be preferred, depending on the patient's tissue strength at the time of surgical repair or reconstruction. Significant loss of quadriceps function should be anticipated. Motor-level electrical stimulation can be used to stimulate the quadriceps muscles until volitional contractions produce sufficient tension.

The surgical procedure dictates the manner in which rehabilitation proceeds. If the ACL was reconstructed, a timeline similar to that for isolated ACL reconstruction can be instituted for strengthening exercises. If the PCL was also reconstructed, isolated PCL reconstruction guidelines should take precedence.

Proprioceptive exercises are essential for the patient with a knee dislocation. Simple proprioceptive exercises, such as single-leg stance on a hard stationary surface, can begin as soon as the patient is bearing full weight and has adequate leg control. The patient may initially benefit from wearing a functional knee brace while performing these exercises. More dynamic proprioceptive exercises can be introduced as the patient demonstrates adequate muscular control to safely perform these exercises with minimal risk to the surgical repair.

Estimated Amount of Time Lost

With knee dislocations, substantial time is lost from sports activity. The rehabilitation process may take 6 to 12 months or more, depending on injury severity, vascular involvement, and neurologic status. Vascular injury, compartment syndrome, and impaired neurologic status increase the time lost from activity. Return to competition may not be practical for many patients.

Return-to-Play Criteria

A full return to playing sports at preparticipation levels is difficult secondary to loss of ROM, possible instability, and dysfunction from nerve injury. Patients must demonstrate sufficient ROM, strength, and proprioception to perform at adequate competitive levels without placing themselves at risk for further injury. A custom functional knee brace designed to accommodate the patient's specific injury pattern is typically used.

Iliotibial Band Friction Syndrome

CLINICAL PRESENTATION

History

Insidious onset:
Repetitive activity causes the ITB to rub over the lateral femoral condyle between 20° and 30° of knee flexion as the foot strikes the ground.[149]
Downhill running exacerbates the syndrome.

Observation

Genu varum and hyperpronation may be predisposing lower extremity postures.

Functional Status

A stiff knee gait may be assumed to avoid rubbing the ITB over the condyle.
Active and passive ROM is normal.
Resisted knee extension may elicit pain at 20° to 30°.

Physical Examination Findings

Positive Noble compression test.
Positive Ober test.
True leg-length discrepancy may be present.

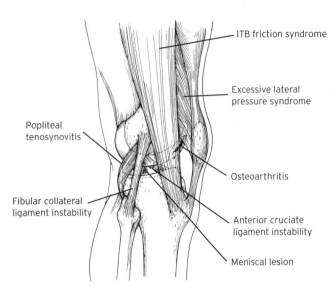

Popliteal
tenosynovitis

ITB friction syndrome

Excessive lateral
pressure syndrome

Osteoarthritis

Fibular collateral
ligament instability

Anterior cruciate
ligament instability

Meniscal lesion

Figure 5.26 Lateral view. Inflammation of the ITB where it passes over the lateral femoral condyle and can cause ITB friction syndrome. Other causes of lateral knee pain also are indicated. *Source:* Reproduced with permission from James SL. Running injuries to the knee. *J Am Acad Orthop Surg.* 1995;3:309-318.

Iliotibial band (ITB) friction syndrome is a localized inflammation of the ITB fascia or the knee joint capsule synovium. The inflammation results from friction that is created as the ITB passes over the lateral femoral condyle during repetitive activities (see **Figure 5.26**). This syndrome is most commonly seen in runners and cyclists.[150–152] Pain is localized over the lateral femoral condyle and may present at a specific distance or duration of the causative activity.

Differential Diagnosis
Symptomatic synovial plica, lateral meniscal tear, patellofemoral syndrome, popliteal tendinopathy.

Imaging Techniques
Imaging is not usually required.

Definitive Diagnosis
ITB syndrome is diagnosed based on pain at or near the lateral femoral epicondyle during foot strike relieved with activity cessation; the Noble compression test will also be positive.

Pathomechanics and Functional Limitations
Pain usually begins predictably after a specific time or distance into running and is localized over the lateral femoral condyle. The pain significantly improves when the patient stops the activity but returns quickly if the activity is resumed.

■ Immediate Management
The patient should cease all activity and apply ice over the ITB.

■ Medications
Oral NSAIDs are useful for management of pain and inflammation. Patients with symptoms that are initially resistant to NSAIDs, therapeutic modalities, and exercise may require a corticosteroid injection. Iontophoresis with dexamethasone (4 mg in 1-cm³ suspension) and lidocaine (4% in 2-cm³ suspension) can also be helpful in the early management of ITB friction syndrome.

■ Surgical Intervention
Surgical intervention, which is rarely necessary, entails surgical resection of only the portion of the ITB that impinges on the femoral condyle—typically the posterior 2 cm of the ITB at the condyle level.[150,151,153]

■ Postinjury/Postoperative Management
Nonsurgical management consists of oral NSAIDs, rehabilitation, and avoidance of aggravating activities. Ice and ITB and hamstring stretching are indicated. Patients with genu varum, true leg-length discrepancy, and hyperpronation may benefit from use of orthotics. Strengthening exercises for the trunk, pelvis, and extremity ensure proper biomechanics during activity.[151]

Immediate postsurgical concerns center on initiating knee ROM and ITB stretching to minimize scar tissue formation. The patient should perform early passive knee ROM and may resume an aggressive stretching program once wound healing is adequate.

■ Injury-Specific Treatment and Rehabilitation Concerns

> **Specific Concerns**
>
> Eliminate the localized inflammatory process.
> Correct abnormal biomechanics.
> Encourage ITB stretching.

Initial rehabilitation focuses on decreasing inflammation. Iontophoresis, ice, and pain-free flexibility exercises may be used. As the inflammatory process diminishes, rehabilitation addresses restoration of normal length to the tensor fascia latae/ITB complex. Deep friction massage and stretching of the complex are required. Preheating the area enhances the viscoelastic properties of the tissues. Localized adhesions (approximately 10 to 15 cm²) can be heated using 3-MHz ultrasound at continuous output and sufficient output intensity. Because of the relatively subcutaneous location of the ITB, larger areas can be adequately heated using a moist heat pack.

The ITB is partially inserted into the lateral patellar soft tissues. Combining medial patellar mobilization with ITB stretching or electrically induced ITB contractions may prove helpful in decreasing tension throughout this area. Nonaggravating aerobic activities such as bicycling, upper body ergometry, or swimming may be used to maintain cardiovascular conditioning.

A complete lower extremity strengthening program to address the pelvis and thigh musculature is instituted. Functional activities such as step-ups, lunges, and side lunges are essential. Activities focus on proper neuromuscular control of the lower extremity, including eliminating postures that may cause the ITB to rub over the lateral femoral condyle. Such activities include proper pelvic stabilization, which seeks to eliminate any contralateral drop of the pelvis as the weight is borne on the affected leg, and effectively stretching the ITB over the condyle.

Control of internal tibial rotation to prevent recurrence may be aided by limiting compensatory pronation through the use of orthotics. Postsurgical therapeutic interventions can begin in a similar fashion to conservative treatment once wound healing is adequate.

■ Estimated Amount of Time Lost

Initially, the patient must cease aggravating activities for 1 to 2 weeks while rehabilitating. Symptoms resistant to rehabilitation may require extended periods of time lost from competition, but this course is preferable to surgery. The patient may continue other nonaggravating activities such as bicycling or swimming to maintain cardiovascular conditioning. Activities such as tennis and basketball that involve more starting and stopping may be tolerated and can continue as long as the patient remains free of symptoms. Failure to improve with conservative measures may require surgical release of the ITB, extending the rehabilitation period. After surgery, patients can usually resume running after 4 weeks.[153]

■ Return-to-Play Criteria

The patient can begin return-to-play activities when symptoms are completely resolved on physical examination, beginning with low mileage and progressing to the desired distance as tolerated. Orthotics should continue to be used even after return to full activity.

Popliteal Tendinopathy

CLINICAL PRESENTATION

History

Insidious onset.
Mechanism of repetitive stress, such as running.
Pain in the posterolateral knee.

Observation

Foot hyperpronation may be present.
An antalgic gait may occur during the aggravating activity.

Functional Status

Active and passive ROM is normal.
Resisted leg flexion, especially as flexion is initiated from the fully extended position and the tibia is "unscrewed," may cause pain.

Physical Examination Findings

Pain during palpation of the popliteus tendon, posterior to the LCL.

The popliteal tendon often becomes inflamed concurrently with other knee injuries.[154,155] Because it produces pain over the posterolateral knee, popliteal tendinopathy must be differentiated from ITB friction syndrome and lateral meniscal injury. Isolated popliteal tendinopathy can occur from repetitive stress, such as running, and may worsen when running downhill.

Differential Diagnosis

ITB friction syndrome, lateral meniscal tear, symptomatic Baker cyst, lateral hamstring tendinopathy.

Imaging Techniques

MRI is helpful in differentiating between popliteal tendinopathy and lateral meniscal derangement if the clinical history and examination are nonspecific.

Definitive Diagnosis

Definitive diagnosis is based on identification of pain over the popliteus tendon, posterior to the LCL, with palpation.

Pathomechanics and Functional Limitations

Pain may limit the patient's ability to perform repetitive activities such as running, particularly running downhill.

■ Medications

Oral NSAIDs are useful for management of pain and inflammation. Phonophoresis or iontophoresis may be used in patients with recalcitrant symptoms.

Postinjury Management

Conservative management consists of oral NSAIDs, rehabilitation, and avoidance of aggravating activities. Compensatory pronation may be controlled with the use of foot orthotics. A heel lift may be employed to relieve the acute symptoms and allow inflammation to resolve. Ice and hamstring stretching are also indicated. Strengthening exercises for the trunk, pelvis, and extremities ensure proper biomechanics during activity.

Injury-Specific Treatment and Rehabilitation Concerns

Specific Concerns
Eliminate the localized inflammatory process. Correct abnormal biomechanics.

Initial rehabilitation focuses on decreasing the inflammation. Iontophoresis with an anti-inflammatory agent, ice applications, and pain-free flexibility exercises may be used. Normal flexibility and strength of the lower extremities should be restored before the patient begins activities (e.g., running) that place repetitive stresses on the tendon. Patients should continue with nonaggravating aerobic activities such as use of the upper body ergometer to maintain cardiovascular conditioning. A heel lift or orthotics may also relieve pain.

Estimated Amount of Time Lost

Initially, the patient may need to cease the aggravating activities for 1 to 2 weeks while rehabilitating. Failure to improve with conservative treatment may increase the amount of competitive time lost.

Return-to-Play Criteria

The patient can begin return-to-play activities when symptoms are completely resolved. Return to activity begins with low intensity and short time periods of activity and progresses to desired distances and durations as tolerated.

Osteochondral Defect

Chondral and osteochondral injuries can range from a simple contusion to the chondral surface and underlying bone to fractures of these structures.[157] Although other joints can sustain osteo-

CLINICAL PRESENTATION

History

Traumatic Mechanism
Shearing forces are caused by knee translation or rotation.
A compressive force is translated through the joint during landing or falling.
A combination of these forces may be reported.
Repetitive microtraumatic forces placed across the knee might also create an osteochondral lesion,[156] known as osteochondritis dissecans.
The patient may describe sudden pain.
Instability may be reported, especially if the osteochondral injury occurs in tandem with an ACL rupture.

Nontraumatic Onset
A history of repetitive activities.
Diffuse knee soreness.
Increasing pain over time.
Intermittent swelling.
Usually the patient notes that rest greatly improves symptoms. Pain and swelling return with resumption of activities.

Observation
Joint effusion is possible.
In chronic nontraumatic cases, quadriceps atrophy may be noted.

Functional Status
Depending on the injury location, an antalgic gait may be exhibited.

Physical Examination Findings
Positive Wilson sign.
Positive ligamentous tests if ligamentous injury is also present.
Area of the lesion may be tender to palpation.

chondral injury, the knee is most commonly affected.[156] The mechanism of injury is usually related to trauma, but the trauma may be so minor that it is not recognized at the time of injury. In more severe traumatic incidents of osteochondral injury, an acute hemarthrosis may develop. The osteochondral injury often occurs concomitantly with meniscal or ligamentous injury.

Differential Diagnosis
Meniscal injury, patellofemoral joint dysfunction, ligament sprain, tibial plateau fracture, soft-tissue overuse syndrome, degenerative joint disease.

Imaging Techniques
Standard AP and lateral knee radiographs and axial views of the patellofemoral joint can be sensitive enough to diagnose osteochondral injuries. A notch view has been advocated to visualize the lateral aspect of the medial femoral condyle, which is the most typical lesion location[158,159] (see **Figure 5.27**).

Tomograms have been recommended as the best method for diagnosis and follow-up management of osteochondral defects.[159] They assess the

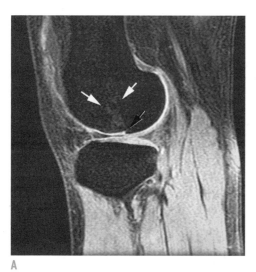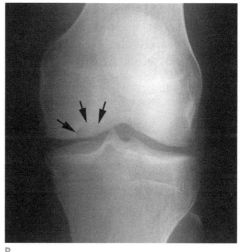

A   B

Figure 5.27 Knee osteochondral defects. (**A**) Sagittal MRI demonstrating injury to the articular cartilage (black arrow) and marrow edema (white arrows). The patient has an associated ACL lesion (not shown). (**B**) AP radiograph demonstrating the crescent-shaped area (black arrows) in the medial femoral condyle characteristic of osteochondritis dissecans.

bony contour and amount of cortical bone present on the osteochondral lesion. The amount of bone on the fragment predicts the healing response. Follow-up tomograms aid in determining the healing response to treatment.

MRI can also be used to diagnose osteochondral defects. An added benefit of this imaging modality is its ability to detect concomitant meniscal and ligamentous injuries. Although MRI may be sensitive enough to determine the size and degree of displacement of the lesion, it may not be sensitive enough to determine the prognosis for healing.

Bone scintigraphy may be helpful in diagnosing and following up osteochondral injuries. It predicts the prognosis of nonsurgical treatment in patients with open physes but is less reliable in patients with closed physes.[160]

Definitive Diagnosis
Clinical symptoms may be vague, and the defect should be confirmed with radiographs or MRI.

Pathomechanics and Functional Limitations
The osteochondral lesion creates pain with activity that is relieved with rest. ROM may be limited by pain and inflammation. A defect that becomes a loose body can create a mechanical block to motion. The patient may experience a sensation of giving way due to pain inhibition during activity or quadriceps weakness.

■ Immediate Management
Immediate management usually consists solely of ice, because the injury is not recognized as anything more than a contusion. In the instances where a large defect is created acutely, the patient may be

more comfortable in an immobilizer with crutches to unload the knee.

■ Medications
NSAIDs are used for management of pain and inflammation.

■ Postinjury Management
For children with osteochondral lesions, conservative treatment is recommended unless a fragment is detached or the patient is within 8 months of physis closure.[161] Conservative treatment may be attempted for small lesions in patients with closed physes but is not normally recommended for adults.

During conservative treatment of an osteochondral defect, the patient must cease all stressful activities but may bear weight as tolerated without pain. Crutches decrease the load through the joint. If ROM is painful, a knee immobilizer is used, and the patient can perform ROM exercises. This initial treatment period lasts 6 to 8 weeks and is followed by repeat imaging to assess the lesion status. Strengthening exercises and sport-specific activities progress as the patient's condition improves.

■ Surgical Intervention
Several surgical interventions can be used to repair osteochondral defects, including arthroscopic drilling with fixation. The drilling causes bleeding in the tissue, which creates a healing environment for the fragment. Mechanically fixating the fragment should improve the likelihood that

bone scintigraphy
A nuclear bone scan in which a radioactive substance is injected into the patient's body and the amount of absorption is identified. Increased absorption may indicate a stress fracture or periosteal inflammation.

the fragment will be held in place during healing, thereby enabling joint congruity to be restored.[159] The fragment can be fixated with Kirschner-wires, compressive screws, cannulated screws, bone pegs, or absorbable pins.[159]

Practice Tip

Several surgical interventions can be used to repair osteochondral defects, including arthroscopic drilling with fixation, abrasion chondroplasty, autologous chondrocyte transplantation, and osteochondral autograft transplantation. Regardless of the surgical intervention undertaken, protected weight bearing for an extended period is required to allow healing to proceed without aggravation. ROM is encouraged but not axial loading.

Abrasion chondroplasty and microfracture techniques penetrate the subchondral bone, causing bleeding and fibrin clot and primitive stem-cell formation (see ⓈⓉ 5.9).[162,163] These primitive stem cells then differentiate into chondrocytes, which repair the defect. The defect is filled with a mix of fibrocartilage and hyaline cartilage. Although the resulting mechanical properties are not identical to those of normal hyaline cartilage, the outcome is still a better alternative than exposed bone. Autologous chondrocyte transplantation uses chondrocyte cells that are harvested from the knee arthroscopically and then grown in a laboratory setting. These cells are then transplanted into the chondral defect during a second procedure performed approximately 4 weeks later. The cells are held in place by a periosteal flap until they mature. This procedure may be beneficial in pure chondral defects but not when bone loss is significant.

Osteochondral autograft transplantation may be useful in focal osteochondral lesions. The size of the defect that can be treated with this approach is partially determined by the amount of hyaline cartilage that can be harvested. In this procedure, harvest "plugs" are taken from non-weight-bearing areas of the knee and placed into the defect to form a mosaicplasty.[83] The mosaicplasty consists of a mosaic of hyaline cartilage plugs; interplug spaces are filled in with fibrocartilage "grout." Most management methods require protected weight bearing for an extended period to allow healing to proceed without aggravation. ROM is encouraged, but not axial loading.

fibrocartilage A mesh of collagen fibers, proteoglycans, and glycoproteins, interspersed with fibrochondrocytes.

◼ Postoperative Management

Postoperative care focuses on protection of the surgical site. Initially, the patient is placed on crutches, with no weight bearing allowed, for 6 to 8 weeks unless the lesion is located in a non-weight-bearing portion, such as the trochlear groove. In the latter case, the patient can bear weight as tolerated in a locked, hinged knee brace. The brace also protects the knee from unwanted torsional or shearing forces on the leg. Passive ROM, either with a CPM machine or through therapeutic exercises, is performed to aid in cartilage healing.

◼ Injury-Specific Treatment and Rehabilitation Concerns

Specific Concerns

Avoid painful weight-bearing exercise.
Avoid axial loads on the knee.
Maintain ROM.

After the initial 6- to 8-week healing period, the conservative or postsurgical management of osteochondral defects progresses to restoration of full ROM, strength, and function. Low-load aerobic exercises are beneficial. In addition to its cardiovascular benefits, such exercise physiologically warms the surrounding soft tissues before the knee is moved through ROM. The low loads, which provide intermittent compression to the healing cartilage, aid in bringing nutrition to the area.

Active, active-assisted, and passive ROM exercises can all be incorporated into the rehabilitation plan. Strengthening exercises are advanced for the entire extremity. Initially, open-chain exercises are beneficial within a pain-free ROM. Closed-chain exercises can progress if the knee remains asymptomatic. The physician determines which type of ROM will place the greatest stress across the defect, and this position is avoided until the defect is healed. Weight-bearing exercises are added carefully.

The patient also will benefit from proprioceptive exercises. Initial attempts at balance and proprioception should minimize the risk of producing shearing or torsional forces across the area of the defect. The patient can begin these activities once full weight bearing is achieved. Exercises that create a higher risk of shearing or torsional forces should not be initiated until 12 weeks after treatment has commenced. The patient can then progress as tolerated.

◼ Estimated Amount of Time Lost

Conservative treatment of young patients with osteochondritis dissecans can last 9 to 12 months,

S|T Surgical Technique 5.9

Microfracture Repair

Indications

Loss of articular cartilage (chondral defect based on physical examination and confirmed by MRI) in the weight-bearing areas of the femur and/or tibia with relatively normal alignment of the tibiofemoral joint.

Procedure Overview

1. Routine arthroscopy portals are developed for visual assessment of the defect.
2. Any unstable cartilage is removed from the exposed bone. Any additional loose cartilage surrounding the defect is removed to create a stable edge around the defect.
3. Multiple holes, or microfractures, are made with an arthroscopic awl in the exposed subchondral bone immediately adjacent to the healthy cartilage rim and move toward the center of the defect.
4. Holes are made about 3 to 4 mm. apart and at a depth of about 3 to 4 mm.

Functional Limitations

Postoperative limitations are dictated by pain, effusion, and restoration of range of motion. Conservative progression toward partial and full weight bearing is necessary to protect the microfracture areas.

Implications for Rehabilitation

Use of a continuous passive motion (CPM) machine immediately following surgery is recommended and exercises to regain full range of motion is imperative. Conservative strength training should progress through the first 16 weeks after surgery. Sport-specific activities that involve pivoting, cutting, and jumping should begin 4 to 6 months after a microfracture procedure. Return to sports activity should only occur following approval of the physician.

Potential Complications

Symptoms of "catching" or "locking" can occur until the area of the microfracture heals. These symptoms usually dissipate within 3 months. Typically, swelling and joint *effusion* disappear within 8 weeks after a microfracture procedure. Occasionally, a recurrent effusion develops between 6 and 8 weeks after surgery for a defect on the femur, usually when a patient begins to put weight on the injured leg. This effusion may mimic the preoperative or immediate postoperative effusion, although it is usually painless. It usually resolves within several weeks.

5

whereas surgical repair requires 6 to 9 months' recovery. Children who have demonstrable healing upon imaging and an asymptomatic knee may return to sports activities sooner with close follow-up. Some patients undergoing surgery may return at 4 to 5 months if the knee is asymptomatic; these are usually more competitive athletes.

Adults with osteochondral lesions may attempt a period of 2 to 3 months of conservative rehabilitation, followed by return to normal activities. Many times, the patient selectively modifies these activities based on symptoms. Surgical treatment options in the adult all require 6 to 9 months of rehabilitation to ensure healing of the donor graft into the osteochondral defect.

■ Return-to-Play Criteria

The patient can return to full activity when the clinical examination is normal, especially for pain and swelling. Healing should also be demonstrated on imaging studies. The patient must have adequate ROM, strength, and balance and must successfully complete a program of agility and function similar to the required sport activities.

Functional Bracing

Bracing is not needed unless the patient undergoes a concomitant ACL or PCL reconstruction. A knee sleeve may benefit the patient by warming the joint during activities.

Osteoarthritis

Arthritis of the knee may be caused by either osteoarthritis or rheumatoid arthritis. This condition is characterized by degeneration of the articular cartilage in the medial and/or lateral compartment, patellofemoral joint, or a combination of these areas. The medial compartment is most often affected.

Arthritis may occur from progressive articular cartilage degeneration or trauma from fractures, meniscal damage, or ligamentous insufficiencies.

Decreased meniscal load-bearing ability after subtotal or total meniscectomy correlates with arthritis development.[109] Various rheumatologic conditions can cause cartilage destruction and are usually associated with systemic symptoms as well. Osteoarthritis—the focus of this section—involves a loss of articular-cartilage integrity and biochemical and histologic changes. If the arthritis progresses, the underlying bone is eventually affected.

Differential Diagnosis

Meniscal tear, patellofemoral pain syndrome, gout, rheumatologic disorders, neoplastic synovitis, osteonecrosis, osteochondral defects, loose bodies.

Medical Diagnostic Tests

Aspiration of the effusion may reveal inflammatory synovitis. Laboratory analysis of this fluid may also lead to a diagnosis of rheumatic arthritis, which may alter the treatment course. Because other joints may be affected, medications specific to rheumatic disease may be used, and the patient may require follow-up with a rheumatologist to coordinate the total medical care of the disease, including its systemic effects.

Imaging Techniques

AP, lateral, and Merchant views of both knees are required (see **Figure 5.28**). Additionally, 45° posteroanterior, standing bilateral radiographs with the body weight evenly distributed over both legs demonstrate joint-space narrowing.

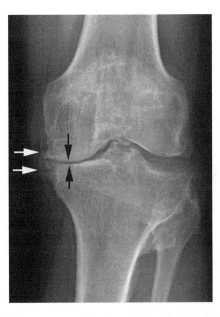

Figure 5.28 AP radiograph of osteoarthritis of the knee. Note the narrowing of the medial joint line (black arrows) and osteophytes along the medial joint line (white arrows).

History

Primary Osteoarthritis
Insidious onset.
Cartilage degeneration is more prevalent in patients older than 50 years of age.[109]
Increased body weight may increase the likelihood of primary osteoarthritis.
Localized joint pain becomes more diffuse as the disease progresses.
Pain initially is described with activity but may become more constant.
Chronic joint swelling is noted.
Pain leads to a decreased activity level.
Complaints of mechanical symptoms such as catching or locking may indicate an unstable meniscal injury, loose body, or gross articular-surface changes such as osteophyte formation.
Instability complaints should be further defined as either a sensation of giving way, which may result from muscle weakness and pain inhibition, or true instability from ligamentous insufficiency.

Secondary Osteoarthritis
Previous knee trauma is noted.
Because this type of arthritis is secondary to an established injury, it is more prevalent than primary osteoarthritis in younger populations. The patient may have a history of intra-articular fracture, meniscal injury, or ligamentous instability.[164]
Complaints are similar to those of patients with primary osteoarthritis.

Observation

Joint effusion is usually present.
The joint may be warm to the touch.
Medial compartment degeneration may create a varus (bow-legged) deformity.
Lateral compartment degeneration may create a valgus (knock-kneed) deformity.

Functional Status

Gait may be antalgic.
Patients with medial compartment arthritis and varus deformity may stretch the soft tissues on the lateral aspect of the knee, causing a lateral thrust of the knee when ambulating.
ROM is decreased both actively and passively by the joint effusion and inflammation in the early stages.
Osteophytes and irregular joint surfaces may create a mechanical block to motion.

Physical Examination Findings

Findings may suggest an unstable meniscal tear.
Ligamentous tests may be positive from previous injuries.
Varus instability may occur with medial compartment degeneration.
Valgus instability may occur with lateral compartment degeneration.

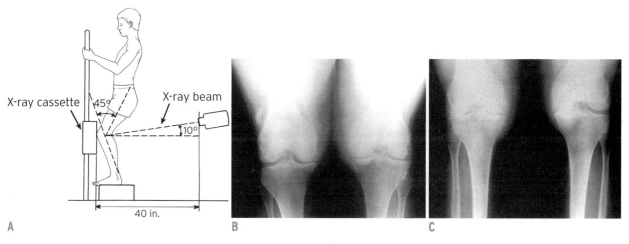

Figure 5.29 Radiographic imaging for knee arthritis. (**A**) Patient positioning. (**B**) Joint spacing appears normal with the knee extended. (**C**) When the same patient is positioned as in A, decreased joint space is apparent. *Source:* Figure A adapted from Rosenberg TD, Paulos LE, Parker RD, et al. The forty-five degree posteroanterior flexion weight bearing radiograph of the knee. *J Bone Joint Surg Am.* 1988;70:1479-1483.

Because the earliest cartilage loss usually occurs between 30° and 60° of flexion, routine weight-bearing AP radiographs may not be sensitive to early arthritic changes.[109] A weight-bearing, 45° flexed, posteroanterior radiograph may demonstrate subtle joint-space loss[165] (see Figure 5.29).

In patients with an angular deformity, especially those who will undergo surgical intervention, weight-bearing AP radiographs from the hips to the ankles should be obtained to accurately identify the angular deformity of the limb. MRI is most often indicated in the patient with minimal radiographic changes, localized pain, and complaints more consistent with meniscal injury. This type of imaging is also useful in assessing osteochondral fracture, osteonecrosis, or an isolated osteochondral defect.[109] In patients with suspected osteoarthritis, two radiographic views should be taken—an AP view and a posteroanterior 45°-flexed view. Radiographic sensitivity can vary dramatically with these views.

Definitive Diagnosis

Diagnosis of osteoarthritis is made when degenerative changes in the symptomatic knee are noted on radiographs.

Pathomechanics and Functional Limitations

In the early stages of osteoarthritis, patients may have transient symptoms that limit function to only a minor extent. Symptoms are usually reversible with minimal interventions such as over-the-counter NSAIDs, rest, and ice, with resultant return to activity. As the disease progresses, however, symptoms recur more often and more intensely and are more resistant to previously tried treatments. Functional activities are increasingly affected. Sports and occupational activities that place large weight-bearing stresses across the knee joint become limited, followed by progressive limitation of ADLs such as walking and normal stair climbing. This functional loss is often correlated with loss of motion and strength and increased frequency of inflammatory exacerbations.

■ Medications

Because patients most often complain of pain, especially in the early stages of arthritis, acetaminophen may be indicated, especially when swelling is minimal to absent. Although renal and hepatic toxicity can occur when recommended dosages are exceeded, acetaminophen offers efficient pain relief with minimal side effects when taken as recommended.[166] These dosages consist of 650 mg every 4 to 6 hours as needed, with a maximal daily dosage of 4000 mg. Because of its potential for inducing renal and hepatic toxicity, acetaminophen must be taken with caution when consuming alcoholic beverages.

NSAIDs offer both inflammatory control and analgesia. Over-the-counter or prescription NSAIDs are the pharmacologic options of choice when swelling is a persistent problem. By inhibiting the cyclooxygenase and lipooxygenase portions of arachidonic acid metabolism, these agents block inflammatory mediators such as prostaglandins and leukotrienes.

Prostaglandins also have many beneficial effects in the body. Notably, their protective effects on the gastric mucosal lining, renal blood flow, and sodium balance can all be affected by prostaglandin inhibition. The most common side effect of prostaglandin inhibition is dyspepsia. A history of gastrointestinal disorders or renal or liver disease and ongoing anticoagulation therapy are all contraindications to the use of NSAIDs.[167]

Glucosamine and chondroitin sulfate have become popular supplements in the treatment of arthritis. Glucosamine is thought to stimulate chondrocyte and synoviocyte metabolism, whereas chondroitin sulfate is proposed to inhibit the enzymes that cause cartilage degradation and prevent the formation of fibrin thrombi in periarticular tissues.[168,169] Recommended dosages of these agents are a minimum of 1 g of glucosamine and 1200 mg of chondroitin sulfate per day.[170]

Other pharmacologic agents that can be used for osteoarthritis include corticosteroid injections and viscosupplementation agents such as hyaluronate therapy. Corticosteroid injections may be useful in patients who fail to obtain relief from oral medications and those with contraindications to the use of NSAIDs. The corticosteroid injection is a strong anti-inflammatory medication that offers the benefit of direct delivery to the involved tissues without systemic effects. Only 3 to 4 injections per year are typically recommended, and even then should be given only as needed.

Patients with osteoarthritis have reduced concentrations of hyaluronate and, therefore, reduced viscoelasticity of their synovial fluid. Hyaluronate therapies should improve the viscoelastic properties of synovial fluid, making it more effective in absorbing joint loads and lubricating joint surfaces. Viscosupplements are injected weekly for a period of 3 to 5 weeks.

■ Postinjury Management

Nonsurgical treatment for osteoarthritis focuses on rest, pharmacologic agents, therapeutic exercise, and avoidance of high-impact activities.

■ Surgical Intervention

Arthroscopic **lavage** and debridement may be suitable for some patients. Indications warranting these interventions include a history of mechanical symptoms, symptoms for 6 or fewer months, normal knee alignment, and mild to moderate radiographic

changes.[171–173] Pain relief is reported in 50% to 70% of patients who undergo lavage and debridement, with the effect's duration ranging from several months to several years. To be most efficacious in this population, arthroscopy should be used to treat unstable meniscal tears, significant motion-limiting osteophyte formations, and loose or unstable chondral flaps.[109,174]

High tibial osteotomy may be prudent in patients with valgus or varus alignment and subsequent medial or lateral unicompartmental arthrosis. If the contribution of arthritic disease in the other compartment or the patellofemoral joint is in question, an offset (medially for a valgus deformity and laterally for a varus deformity), short leg walking cast may be used for 3 days to assess the level of pain reduction. Patients whose pain is not reduced may be having symptoms from several compartments of the knee, for which an osteotomy would not be useful.[175]

In the high tibial osteotomy, a wedge of bone is removed (closed wedge) or a wedge is created (open wedge) and filled in with iliac crest bone graft to correct knee alignment and unload the diseased compartment. The surgeon determines the proper amount of wedge that must be created to correct the alignment preoperatively, through the use of ankle-to-hip radiographs. Once the alignment is corrected, the bone must be fixated until it heals. Staples, plates, and external fixators can be used for this purpose.

An alternative for medial or lateral compartment disease without malalignment is a unicompartmental arthroplasty. In this procedure, only the diseased compartment is addressed. Surgical benefits of this method include a smaller incision, less bone loss, good function, and ease in revising the procedure to a total knee arthroplasty if needed. Both the high tibial osteotomy and unicompartmental surgical procedures require an intact ACL.

Total knee arthroplasty remains an excellent option for active patients, provided they are willing to modify their joint-loading activities. The arthroplasty replaces the tibiofemoral joint surfaces and may include the patellofemoral joint if it is involved. Although arthroplasty has always been a good alternative for patients older than 60 years of age, improved materials and surgical techniques have now made it an option for younger patients. Good results without a high risk of failure have been achieved in patients younger than 55 years.[176–178]

lavage The washing or cleansing of a hollow tissue space with water.

Postinjury/Postoperative Management

Patients undergoing an arthroscopic procedure begin rehabilitation with ROM and strengthening exercises immediately. They may use crutches for several days to increase their level of comfort. Postoperative management of a patient who has undergone a high tibial osteotomy varies depending on the type of fixation used. A plate allows for immediate ROM and weight bearing.

A patient with a total knee arthroplasty spends 3 to 5 days in the hospital. During this time, the focus is on wound healing, ROM, early weight bearing, and basic strengthening exercises. CPM is used in the hospital. The patient can typically bear weight as tolerated with either crutches or a walker. Quadriceps-setting exercises and straight-leg raises are performed for strengthening. The patient then undergoes formal rehabilitation at least 3 days per week in conjunction with an extensive home-based program.

Injury-Specific Treatment and Rehabilitation Concerns

> **Specific Concerns**
>
> Control pain and inflammation.
> Maintain ROM.
> Correct biomechanics and other predisposing factors.
> Minimize weight-bearing forces through the joint during activity.

The conservative or postoperative rehabilitation of the arthritic patient focuses on maximizing function while decreasing the load-bearing forces through the joint. Stiffness and loss of motion increase stress on the joint and pain. Patellar mobilization is especially important for restoring motion after total knee arthroplasty. Active-assisted and passive ROM exercises can be used to improve ROM. The end feel experienced while performing ROM exercises, especially in the conservative treatment of osteoarthritis, can indicate the functional status of the knee. Patients with arthritic changes, including osteophyte formation, may experience a hard end feel of bone hitting bone. This motion should not be forced. In addition, the flexion limitations of particular total joint replacement systems must be recognized. Exceeding the flexion limits may cause loosening of the prosthesis and result in its premature failure.

Strengthening exercises focus on the gravity-resisting muscles in the lower extremity. Strengthening the gluteals, quadriceps, and gastrocnemius–soleus complex helps reduce the fatigue that might otherwise lead to abnormal biomechanics during activity. Proper, efficient function of these muscle groups also assists in dampening forces through the lower extremity joints. Heavy weight-bearing exercises are not recommended. Pain-free open-chain and low-load, high-endurance closed-chain exercises are instituted.

Pain, loss of motion, aging, and ligamentous insufficiency may all affect balance in this patient population. Proprioceptive exercises are vital to improve function and decrease the incidence of falls. The patient's goals regarding the type and intensity of desired activity should be considered when designing a proprioceptive program.

Aerobic exercise is important for its cardiovascular benefits and to control the patient's body weight. Controlling body weight decreases the load-bearing forces through the joint or joint replacement. Exercises such as swimming, bicycling, elliptical gliding, ski machine, and walking are recommended.

Estimated Amount of Time Lost

Osteoarthritis is a progressive, degenerative disease. The amount of time lost from activity depends on the level of symptoms and the treatment interventions used. Patients with minimal symptoms may not miss any time from activity. Other patients may need several weeks of rehabilitation before returning to activity. Still others may be advised not to return to their previous activities or naturally tend to alter their activities to decrease joint stress by adopting different activities and activity levels. The amount of articular cartilage destruction, the patient's symptoms and willingness to adapt the lifestyle, and the treatment course chosen all influence the amount of time lost.

Return-to-Play Criteria

In the conservatively treated, active osteoarthritic population and patients undergoing arthroscopic or osteotomy procedures, pain is the most significant return-to-play criterion. The patient's inflammatory process should not be active, and pain should be minimal and controllable with medications, rest, and exercise. The patient must have adequate ROM and strength to perform activities without risk of acute injury. A knee sleeve may provide warmth to the joint, making activity more comfortable. Braces ("unloader" braces) designed to unload one of the knee compartments can be used but tend to be bulky; active patients may find them too restrictive for certain sports activities (see Figure 5.30).

The patient should consider engaging in activities that minimize joint loads. Some weight-bearing stresses cannot be avoided, such as those associated with tennis or basketball. Whenever possible, less stressful activities should be pursued for fitness. For example, the patient may choose swimming or bicycling over running for cardiovascular exercise.

Patients who have undergone a total knee arthroplasty must make activity changes to limit joint loading. Unrestricted golfing is allowed, and some surgeons may permit a return to limited amounts of doubles tennis. Walking, swimming, and bicycling are encouraged as fitness activities. No brace is needed after arthroplasty.

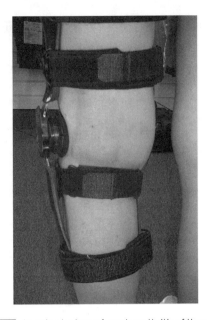

Figure 5.30 An unloader brace for osteoarthritis of the medial knee. This brace uses adjustable tension to create a valgus force on the knee, thereby reducing weight-bearing pressures on the medial joint surfaces.

Rehabilitation

A knee rehabilitation program must address trunk, pelvis, and lower extremity stability. Although isolated exercises are beneficial early in rehabilitation, functional therapeutic exercises must be included in the late stages of this program. Synergistic kinetic chain activity should be encouraged as soon as allowed. Proprioceptive and functional progression exercises for the knee and lower extremity are described in Chapter 8.

Range of Motion

Other relevant patellar mobilization activities and range of motion activities can be found in Chapters 6 and 8.

Continuous Passive Motion

A CPM device can increase early motion, but it is often better to involve the patient in active rehabilitation as soon as possible. CPM should not be used as a substitute for active or active-assisted ROM unless the specific diagnosis requires this course of action or postsurgical restrictions are imposed by the surgeon. Although a CPM device may promote early motion, it typically does not maintain full extension or achieve full flexion.

CPM is indicated when its use will decrease postinjury or postsurgery morbidity. The CPM device can increase motion and decrease pain and swelling; it may also aid in healing by promoting fibrocartilage or hyaline-cartilage growth. CPM is contraindicated in unstable fractures. It does not adequately stress full extension and is usually less effective once knee flexion has increased past 90°.

Heel Slide

In the heel slide, the patient lies supine or sits on a table with the back supported and the involved lower extremity kept straight. For the passive technique, the patient uses a towel to slide the heel toward the hip, moving the knee into flexion until a pulling or restriction in motion is experienced (see Figure 5.31). The active technique relies on hamstring contractions to move the foot. The position is held for 20 seconds. The patient then performs a slow, controlled return to the starting position. The patient may use a stretching strap, belt, or towel to assist the motion.

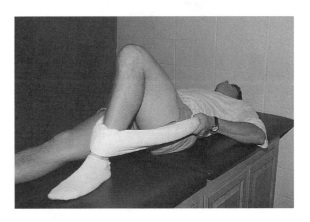

Figure 5.31 Heel slide.

Wall Slide

In the wall slide, the patient lies supine on a table placed perpendicular to the wall, with the involved lower extremity supported by the wall. The patient allows gravity to slowly pull the foot down the wall until a pulling or restriction in motion is experienced (see Figure 5.32). The terminal position is held for 20 seconds. The foot is then returned to the starting position.

Prone Hangs

In prone hangs, the patient lies prone on a table with the thighs supported just proximal to the patella. Gravity pulls the tibia into extension as the patient relaxes (see Figure 5.33). Light cuff weights can be added to increase the stretch. Higher loads should be avoided because patient guarding may occur. The patient can start at 5 minutes and work up to 10 minutes of continuous stretching, or may intermittently stretch for 1 minute and relax for 1 minute.

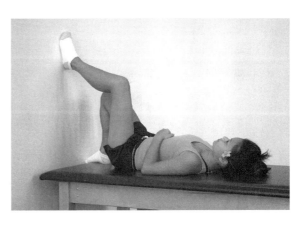

Figure 5.32 Wall slide.

5

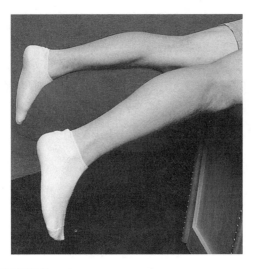

Figure 5.33   Prone hangs.

Prone Flexion

If a flexion restriction is determined to be caused by the extensor mechanism alone or in combination with the joint capsule, a prone stretch may be indicated. Lying prone on the table, the patient loops a strap around the ankle and pulls the knee into flexion (see Figure 5.34). The stretch is held for 20 seconds. The leg is then returned to extension.

Towel Propping

In towel propping, the patient sits on the table with a towel roll under the ankle of the involved extremity. Gravity pulls the unsupported knee into extension. The patient can manually assist the extension by gently pressing the thigh toward the table (see Figure 5.35). An active quadriceps set can also be performed in this position. For a prolonged stretch, weights may be placed proximal to the patella. For a flexion contracture, heat placed behind the knee may promote further relaxation and stretch.

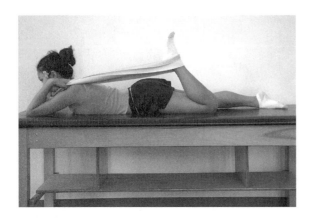

Figure 5.34   Prone flexion.

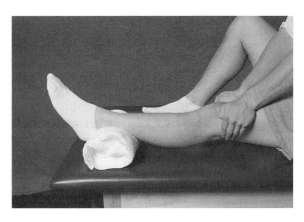

Figure 5.35   Towel propping.

Strengthening Techniques

Specific knee ROM exercises have both advantages and disadvantages, based on the injury being treated. For example, closed kinetic chain exercises develop high tibiofemoral joint contact forces but low shearing forces because of compression and the cocontractions of the quadriceps and hamstring muscles. In contrast, open kinetic chain exercises result in lower tibiofemoral compression, higher anterior shearing forces with quadriceps activity, and higher posterior shearing forces with hamstring activity. **Table 5.2** provides the results of analyses of joint forces in various positions and ranges.[179,180] See Chapter 8 for more on lower extremity strengthening exercises.

Isometric Exercises

Quadriceps Sets

In quadriceps sets, the patient lies supine, sits, or stands with the involved knee in full extension. The quadriceps are then maximally contracted, "setting" the muscle, and held for 10 seconds. Motor-level electrical stimulation can aid the patient in recruiting motor units and holding the contraction. Biofeedback can be used to recruit motor units and aid the patient in developing and sustaining an enhanced contraction. The patient should be monitored for proper muscle activation patterns, to prevent the gluteals and hamstrings from substituting for quadriceps activity.

Reverse Quadriceps Sets

In reverse quadriceps sets, the patient lies prone with the toes of the involved leg on the table. The patient then straightens the leg to lift the femur off the table (see Figure 5.36).

Table 5.2

Analysis of Joint Forces

Knee Position	Forces
0° (Full extension)	Minimal stress on the ACL and PCL
	Minimal PFJ contact forces and stability
	Marked quadriceps activity with isometrics and moderate activity with single-leg raising
0° to 30° (Terminal knee extension)	High anterior shear forces with quadriceps activity in both OKC and CKC
	Increased PFJ stability at 20°
	Greatest quadriceps EMG activity with OKC (all groups)
	Minimal PCL stress as a result of posterior shear forces with quadriceps activity in both OKC and CKC
0° to 60°	Low ACL stress as a result of anterior shear forces with hamstring activity in OKC
	Low PCL stress as a result of posterior shear forces with hamstring activity
60° to 90°	No ACL stress as a result of anterior shear forces from quadriceps or hamstring activity in OKC or CKC
	Good PFJ stability
	High PFJ contact forces
	High PCL stress as a result of posterior shearing forces with hamstring activity in OKC or CKC
90° to 105°	Highest posterior shearing forces in both OKC and CKC
	Highest tibiofemoral compressive forces
	Greatest quadriceps EMG activity in CKC

PFJ = patellofemoral joint; OKC = open kinetic chain; CKC = closed kinetic chain

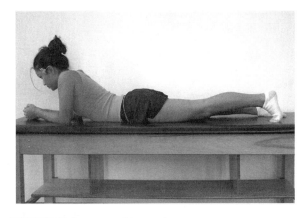

Figure 5.37 Reverse quadriceps sets.

Hamstring Sets

In hamstring sets, the patient sits or lies supine and presses the heel of the involved extremity into the supporting surface using the hamstring muscles. The patient should be monitored so that gluteal substitution patterns are avoided (see **Figure 5.37**).

Quadriceps and Hamstrings Cocontraction

In quadriceps and hamstrings cocontraction, the patient sits or lies supine with the involved extremity in full extension. The patient contracts or sets the quadriceps and simultaneously uses the hamstrings to press the involved heel into the supporting surface.

Multiangle Isometrics

The quadriceps and hamstrings can be exercised isometrically at various degrees of knee flexion. These angles are determined by the patient's diagnosis, postsurgical precautions, and tolerance. The level of shearing forces on the ACL and PCL, the patellofemoral joint reaction forces, and the levels of patellar stability vary with different positions.

◼ Isotonic Exercises

Straight-Leg Raises

Initially, straight-leg raises are performed using only the extremity weight. As the patient's strength improves, cuff weights can be added to the thigh, knee, or ankle. The patient should perform a quadriceps set during all planes of these motions to develop synergistic activity between the hip and thigh muscles (see **Figure 5.38**).

Closed-Chain Terminal Knee Extension

In closed-chain terminal knee extension, the patient stands with the involved knee in approximately 30° of flexion. Resistance is placed behind the knee proximal to the popliteal fossa, and the patient straightens the knee by setting the quadriceps (see

Figure 5.36 Hamstring sets.

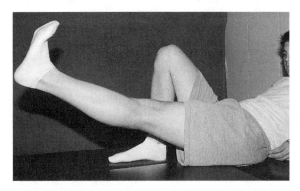

Flexion: The patient lies supine, with the uninvolved extremity flexed and the involved extremity fully extended. The patient first sets the involved quadriceps and then lifts the heel from the table. The leg is lifted only until the heel is 1 to 1.5 feet off the table. It is then slowly lowered, attempting to touch the calf before the heel. The quadriceps is then relaxed.

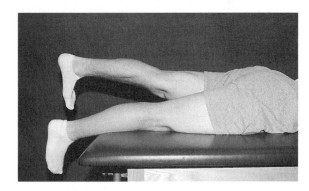

Extension: The patient lies prone with the knees fully extended. The patient first sets the involved quadriceps and then lifts the involved extremity away from the table.

Abduction: The patient lies on the uninvolved side, with the uninvolved knee flexed and the involved extremity fully extended. The patient first sets the quadriceps and then lifts the involved extremity away from the table.

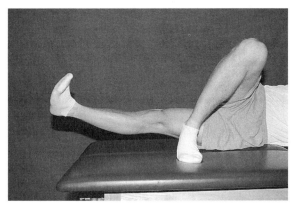

Adduction: The patient lies on the involved side, with the involved knee fully extended and the uninvolved extremity crossed over the involved extremity. The patient first sets the involved quadriceps, and then lifts the involved extremity away from the table.

Figure 5.38   Straight-leg raises.

Figure 5.39). The patient should be monitored during this exercise to prevent gluteal substitution.

Leg Curl

In the leg curl, the patient lies prone, and resistance is placed proximal to the ankle posteriorly. Limited arcs of motion can be used (see **Figure 5.40**).

Leg Extension

In leg extension exercises, the patient is seated, and resistance is placed proximal to the ankle anteriorly. Limited arcs of motion can be used (see **Figure 5.41**). If attempting a full arc, the quadriceps should be volitionally set as forcefully as possible at terminal extension to enhance recruitment.

Isokinetics

Isokinetics provides a useful strengthening and testing modality for speed-specific training, but requires the use of a computerized, electromechanical device that is not always readily available because of its prohibitive cost. With this rehabilitation tool, exercise velocity and volume, contraction type (concentric, eccentric, isometric, and isotonic), and ROM can be varied according to the needs of the patient. Although isokinetics exercise is versatile, it is not a panacea or replacement for a comprehensive rehabilitation progression.

5

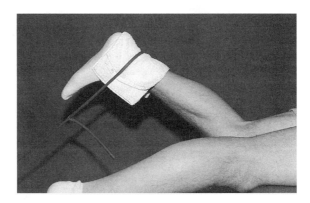

Figure 5.40   Leg curl.

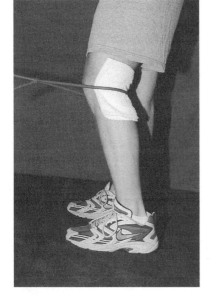

Figure 5.39   Knee extension.

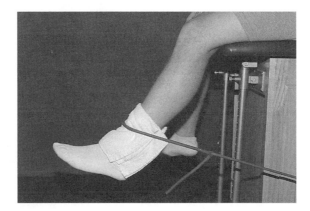

Figure 5.41   Leg extension.

References

1. Boden BP, Dean GS, Feagin JA, Garrett WE. Mechanisms of anterior cruciate ligament injury. *Orthopedics.* 2000;23(6):573–578.

2. Berns GS, Hull ML, Patterson HA. Strain in the anterior-medial bundle of the anterior cruciate ligament under combined loading. *J Orthop Res.* 1992;10:167–176.

3. Markolf KL, Burchfield DM, Shapiro MM, et al. Combined knee loading states that generate high anterior cruciate ligament forces. *J Orthop Res.* 1995;13(6):930–935.

4. Noyes F, Matthews D, Mooar P, Grood ES. The symptomatic ACL-deficient knee. Part II: The results of rehabilitation, activity modification, and counseling on functional disability. *J Bone Joint Surg Am.* 1983;65:163–174.

5. Noyes F, Mooar P, Matthews D, Butler DL. The symptomatic ACL-deficient knee. Part I: The long-term functional disability in athletically active individuals. *J Bone Joint Surg Am.* 1983;65:154–162.

6. Fithian DC, Paxton LW, Goltz DH. Fate of the anterior cruciate ligament–injured knee. *Orthop Clin North Am.* 2002;33:621–636.

7. Shelbourne KD, Trumper RV. Preventing anterior knee pain after anterior cruciate ligament reconstruction. *Am J Sports Med.* 1997;25:41–47.

8. Shelbourne KD, Wilckens JH, Mollabashy A, DeCarlo M. Arthrofibrosis in acute anterior cruciate ligament reconstruction: The effect of timing of reconstruction and rehabilitation. *Am J Sports Med.* 1991;19:332–336.

9. Miller SL, Gladstone JN. Graft selection in anterior cruciate ligament reconstruction. *Orthop Clin North Am.* 2002;33:675–683.

10. Malinin TI, Levitt RL, Bashore C, et al. A study of retrieved allografts used to replace anterior cruciate ligaments. *Arthroscopy.* 2002;18:163–170.

11. Prodromas CC, Fu FH, Howell SM, et al. Controversies in soft-tissue anterior cruciate ligament reconstruction: Grafts, bundles, tunnels, fixation, and harvest. *J Am Acad Orthop Surg.* 2008;16(7):376–384.

12. Prodromos CC, Joyce BT, Shi K, Keller BL. A meta-analysis of stability of autografts compared to allografts after anterior cruciate ligament reconstruction. *Knee Surg Sports Traumatol Arthrosc.* 2007;15:851–856.

13. Singhal MC, Gardiner JR, Johnson DL. Failure of primary anterior cruciate ligament surgery using anterior tibialis allograft. *Arthroscopy.* 2007;23:469–475.

14. Freedman KB, D'Amato MJ, Nedeff DD, et al. Arthroscopic anterior cruciate ligament reconstruction: A meta-analysis comparing patellar tendon and hamstring tendon autografts. *Am J Sports Med.* 2003;31:2–11.

15. Barber FA, McGuire DA, Click S. Continuous-flow cold therapy for outpatient anterior cruciate ligament reconstruction. *Arthroscopy.* 1998;14:130–135.

16. Richmond JC, Gladstone J, MacGillivray J. Continuous passive motion after arthroscopically assisted anterior cruciate ligament reconstruction: Comparison of short- versus long-term use. *Arthroscopy.* 1991;7:39–44.

17. Noyes FR, Mangine RE, Barber SD. The early treatment of motion complications after reconstruction of the anterior cruciate ligament. *Clin Orthop Relat Res.* 1992;277:217–228.

18. Rosen MA, Jackson DW, Atwell EA. The efficacy of continuous passive motion in the rehabilitation of anterior cruciate ligament reconstructions. *Am J Sports Med.* 1992;20:122–127.

19. Howell SM, Taylor MA. Brace-free rehabilitation, with early return to activity, for knees reconstructed with a double-looped semitendinosus and gracilis graft. *J Bone Joint Surg Am.* 1996;78:814–825.

20. Glasgow SG, Gabriel JP, Sapega AA, et al. The effect of early versus late return to vigorous activities on the outcome of anterior cruciate reconstruction. *Am J Sports Med.* 1993;21:243–248.

21. Shelbourne KD, Nitz P. Accelerated rehabilitation after anterior cruciate ligament reconstruction. *Am J Sports Med.* 1990;18:292–299.

22. Bynum EB, Barrack RL, Alexander AH. Open versus closed chain kinetic exercises after anterior cruciate ligament reconstruction: A prospective randomized study. *Am J Sports Med.* 1995;23:401–406.

23. Tyler TF, McHugh MP, Gleim GW, Nicholas SJ. The effect of immediate weightbearing after anterior cruciate ligament reconstruction. *Clin Orthop Relat Res.* 1998;357:141–148.

24. Griffin LY, Albohm MJ, Arendt EA, et al. Understanding and preventing noncontact anterior cruciate ligament injuries: A review of the Hunt Valley II meeting, January 2005. *Am J Sports Med.* 2006;34(9):1512–1532.

25. Orchard JW, Powell JW. Risk of knee and ankle sprains under various weather conditions in American football. *Med Sci Sports Exerc.* 2003;35:1118–1123.

26. Olsen OE, Myklebust G, Engebretsen L, et al. Relationship between floor type and risk of ACL injury in team handball. *Scand J Med Sci Sports.* 2003;13:299–304.

27. Meyers MC, Barnhill BS. Incidence, causes, and severity of high school football injuries on FieldTurf versus natural grass: A 5-year prospective study. *Am J Sport Med.* 2004;32:1626–1638.

28. Sitler M, Ryan J, Hopkinson W, et al. The efficacy of a prophylactic knee brace to reduce knee injuries in football: A prospective, randomized study at West Point. *Am J Sports Med.* 1990;18:310–315.

29. Shultz SJ, Schmitz RJ, Nguyen AD, et al. ACL Research Retreat V: An update on ACL injury risk and prevention, Greensboro, NC, March 25–27, 2010. *J Athl Train.* 2010;45(5):499–508.

30. Uhorchak JM, Scoville CR, Williams GN, et al. Risk factors associated with non-contact injury of the anterior cruciate ligament. *Am J Sports Med.* 2003;31(6):831–842.

31. Lund-Hanssen H, Gannon J, Engebretsen L, et al. Intercondylar notch width and the risk for anterior cruciate ligament rupture. A case-control study in 46 female handball players. *Acta Orthop Scand.* 1994;65(5):529–532.

32. Ireland ML, Ballantyne BT, Little K, McClay IS. A radiographic analysis of the relationship between the size and shape of the intercondylar notch and anterior cruciate ligament injury. *Knee Surg Sports Traumatol Arthrosc.* 2001;9:200–205.

33. Lombardo S, Sethi P, Starkey C. Intercondylar notch senosis is not a risk factor for anterior cruciate ligament tears in professional male basketball players. *Am J Sports Med.* 2005;33:29–34.

34. Hashemi J, Chandrashekar N, Mansouri H, et al. Shallow medial tibial plateau and steep medial and lateral tibial slopes: New risk factors for anterior cruciate ligament injuries. *Am J Sports Med.* 2010;38(1):54–62.

35. Simon RA, Everhart JS, Nagaraja HN, Chaudhari AM. A case-control study of anterior cruciate ligament volume, tibial plateau slopes and intercondylar notch dimensions in ACL-injured knees. *J Biomechanics.* 2010;43(9):1702–1707.

36. Everhart JS, Flanigan DC, Simon RA, Chaudhari AM. Association of noncontact anterior cruciate ligament injury with presence and thickness of a bony ridge on the

anteromedial aspect of the femoral intercondylar notch. *Am J Sports Med.* 2010;38(8):1667–1673.

37. Uhorchak JM, Scoville CR, Williams GN, et al. Risk factors associated with noncontact injury of the anterior cruciate ligament: A prospective four-year evaluation of 859 West Point cadets. *Am J Sports Med.* 2003;31(6):831–842.

38. Ramesh R, VonArx O, Azzopardi T, Schranz PJ. The risk of anterior cruciate ligament rupture with generalised joint laxity. *J Bone Joint Surg Br.* 2005;87-B:800–803.

39. Beard DJ, Kyberd PJ, Fergusson CM, Dodd CA. Proprioception after rupture of the anterior cruciate ligament: An objective indication for the need for surgery? *J Bone Joint Surg Br.* 1993;75-B:311–315.

40. Beynnon BD, Fleming BC, Labovitch R, Parsons B. Chronic anterior cruciate ligament deficiency is associated with increased anterior translation of the tibia during the transition from non-weightbearing to weightbearing. *J Orthop Res.* 2002;20:332–337.

41. Brask B, Lueke RH, Soderberg GL. Electromyographic analysis of selected muscles during the lateral step-up exercise. *Phys Ther.* 1984;64(3):324–329.

42. Butler DL, Noyes FR, Grood ES. Ligamentous restraints to anterior-posterior drawer in the human knee. *J Bone Joint Surg Am.* 1980;62(2):259–270.

43. Hsieh H-H, Walker PS. Stabilizing mechanisms of the loaded and unloaded knee joint. *J Bone Joint Surg Am.* 1976;58(1):87–93.

44. Lofvenberg R, Karrholm J, Sundelin G, Ahlgren O. Prolonged reaction time in patients with chronic lateral instability of the ankle. *Am J Sports Med.* 1995;23(4):414–417.

45. Smith BA, Livesay GA, Woo SLY. Biology and biomechanics of the anterior cruciate ligament. *Clin Sports Med.* 1993;12(4):637–670.

46. Schultz RA, Miller DC, Kerr CS, Micheli L. Mechanoreceptors in human cruciate ligaments. *J Bone Joint Surg Am.* 1984;66(7):1072–1076.

47. Zimny ML, Schutte M, Dabezies E. Mechanoreceptors in the human anterior cruciate ligament. *Anatomical Rec.* 1986;214:204–209.

48. Barrack RL, Lund PJ, Skinner HB. Knee joint proprioception revisited. *J Sport Rehab.* 1994;3:18–42.

49. Solomonow M, Baratta R, Shou BH, et al. The synergistic action of the anterior cruciate ligament and thigh muscles in maintaining joint stability. *Am J Sports Med.* 1987;15(3):207–213.

50. Rozzi SL, Lephart SM, Gear WS, Fu FH. Knee joint laxity and neuromuscular characteristics of male and female soccer and basketball players. *Am J Sports Med.* 1999;27(3):312–319.

51. Shultz SJ, Carcia CR, Perrin DH. Knee joint laxity affects muscle activation patterns in the healthy knee. *J Electromyography Kinesiol.* 2004;14:475–483.

52. Shultz SJ, Shimokochi Y, Nguyen A, et al. Non-weight bearing anterior knee laxity is related to anterior tibial translation during transition from non-weight bearing to weight bearing. *J Orthop Res.* 2006;24(3):516–523.

53. Mizuta H, Shiraishi M, Kubota K, et al. A stabilometric technique for evaluation of functional instability in anterior cruciate ligament–deficient knee. *Clin J Sports Med.* 1992;2(4):235–239.

54. Roberts D, Andersson G, Friden T. Knee joint proprioception in ACL-deficient knees is related to cartilage injury, laxity and age. *Acta Orthop Scand.* 2004;75(1):78–83.

55. Wojtys EM, Huston LJ. Neuromuscular performance in normal and anterior cruciate ligament–deficient lower extremities. *Am J Sports Med.* 1994;22(1):89–104.

56. Branch TP, Hunter R, Donath M. Dynamic EMG analysis of anterior cruciate deficient legs with and without bracing during cutting. *Am J Sports Med.* 1989;17(1):35–41.

57. Gauffin H, Tropp H. Altered movement and muscular-activation patterns during the one-legged jump in patients with an old anterior cruciate ligament rupture. *Am J Sports Med.* 1992;20(2):182–192.

58. McNair PJ, Marshall RN. Landing characteristics in subjects with normal and anterior cruciate ligament deficient knee joints. *Arch Phys Med Rehab.* 1994;75:584–589.

59. Grana WA, Moretz JA. Ligamentous laxity in secondary school athletes. *JAMA.* 1978;240:1975–1976.

60. Larsson LG, Baum J, Mudholkar GS. Hypermobility: Features and differential incidence between the sexes. *Arthritis Rheumatism.* 1987;30:1426–1430.

61. Rosene JM, Fogarty TD. Anterior tibial translation in collegiate athletes with normal anterior cruciate ligament integrity. *J Athl Train.* 1999;34(2):93–98.

62. Shultz SJ, Kirk SE, Sander TC, Perrin DH. Sex differences in knee laxity change across the female menstrual cycle. *J Sports Med Phys Fitness.* 2005;45(4):594–603.

63. Woodford-Rogers B, Cyphert L, Denegar CR. Risk factors for anterior cruciate ligament injury in high school and college athletes. *J Athl Train.* 1994;29(4):343–346.

64. Hruska R. Pelvic stability influences lower extremity kinematics. *Biomechanics.* 1998;6:23–29.

65. Hutchinson MR, Ireland ML. Knee injuries in female athletes. *Sports Med.* 1995;19(4):288–302.

66. Loudon JK, Jenkins W, Loudon KL. The relationship between static posture and ACL injury in female athletes. *J Orthop Sports Phys Ther.* 1996;24(2):91–97.

67. Beckett ME, Massie DL, Bowers KD, Stoll DA. Incidence of hyperpronation in the ACL injured knee: A clinical perspective. *J Athl Train.* 1992;27(1):58–60.

68. Hertel JN, Dorfman JH, Braham RA. Lower extremity malalignments and anterior cruciate ligament injury history. *J Sports Sci Med.* 2004;3:220–225.

69. Ireland ML. Anterior cruciate ligament injury in female athletes: Epidemiology. *J Athl Train.* 1999;34(2):150–154.

70. Olsen O, Myklebust G, Engebretsen L, Bahr R. Injury mechanisms for anterior cruciate ligament injuries in team handball. *Am J Sports Med.* 2004;32(4):1002–1012.

71. Bates BT, Osternig LR, Mason B, James LS. Foot orthotic devices to modify selected aspects of lower extremity mechanics. *Am J Sports Med.* 1979;7(6):338–342.

72. Coplan JA. Rotational motion of the knee: A comparison of normal and pronating subjects. *J Orthop Sports Phys Ther.* 1989;10:366–369.

73. Cornwall MW, McPoil TG. Footwear and foot orthotic effectiveness research: A new approach. *J Orthop Sports Phys Ther.* 1995;21(6):337–344.

74. Ilahi OA, Kohl HW. Lower extremity morphology and alignment and risk of overuse injury. *Clin J Sports Med.* 1998;8:38–42.

75. Krivickas LS. Anatomical factors associated with overuse sports injuries. *Sports Med.* 1997;24(2):132–146.

76. Fleming BC, Renstrom PA, Beynnon BD, et al. The effect of weightbearing and external loading on anterior cruciate ligament strain. *J Biomechanics.* 2001;34(3):163–170.

77. Powers CM. The influence of altered lower-extremity kinematics on patellofemoral joint dysfunction: A theoretical perspective. *J Orthop Sports Phys Ther.* 2003;33:639–646.

78. Chaitow L, DeLany JW. The pelvis, in *Clinical Application of Neuromuscular Techniques.* Vol 2. New York: Churchill Livingstone; 2000:301–386.

79. Crane L. Femoral torsion and its relation to toeing-in and toeing-out. *J Bone Joint Surg Am.* 1959;41(3):421–428.

80. Norkin CC, Levangie PK. *Joint Structure and Function: A Comprehensive Analysis.* ed 2. Philadelphia: F. A. Davis; 1992:312–313.

81. Merchant AC. Hip abductor muscle force: An experimental study of the influence of hip position with particular reference to rotation. *J Bone Joint Surg Am.* 1965;47:462–476.

82. Nyland J, Kuzemchek S, Parks M, Caborn DN. Femoral anteversion influences vastus medialis and gluteus medius EMG amplitude: Composite hip abductor EMG amplitude ratios during isometric combined hip abduction--external rotation. *J Electromyography Kinesiol.* 2004; 14(2):255–261.

83. Nguyen AD, Shultz SJ. Sex differences in clinical measures of lower extremity alignment. *J Orthop Sports Phys Ther.* 2007;37(7):389–398.

84. Nguyen A, Shultz SJ. Identifying postural relationships among lower extremity alignment characteristics. *J Athl Train.* 2009;44(5):511–518.

85. Deie M, Sakamaki Y, Sumen Y, et al. Anterior knee laxity in young women varies with their menstrual cycle. *Intl Orthop.* 2002;26:154–156.

86. Heitz NA. Hormonal changes throughout the menstrual cycle and increased anterior cruciate ligament laxity in females. *J Athl Train.* 1999;343(2):144–149.

87. Shultz SJ, Sander TC, Kirk SE, et al. Relationship between sex hormones and anterior knee laxity across the menstrual cycle. *Med Sci Sport Exerc.* 2004;36(7):1165–1174.

88. Slauterbeck J, Clevenger C, Lundberg W, Burchfield DM. Estrogen level alters the failure load of the rabbit anterior cruciate ligament. *J Orthop Res.* 1999;17:405–408.

89. Beynnon BD, Johnson RJ, Braun S, et al. The relationship between menstrual cycle phase and anterior cruciate ligament injury: A case-control study of recreational alpine skiers. *Am J Sports Med.* 2006;34(5):757–764.

90. Slauterbeck JR, Hardy DM. Sex hormones and knee ligament injuries in female athletes. *Am J Med Sci.* 2001; 322(4):196–199.

91. Wojtys EM, Huston L, Boynton MD, et al. The effect of menstrual cycle on anterior cruciate ligament in women as determined by hormone levels. *Am J Sports Med.* 2002;30(2):182–188.

92. Shultz SJ, Kirk SE, Sander TC, Perrin DH. Sex differences in knee laxity change across the female menstrual cycle. *J Sports Med Phys Fitness.* 2005;45(4):594–603.

93. Slauterbeck JR, Fuzie SF, Smith MP, et al. The menstrual cycle, sex hormones, and anterior cruciate ligament injury. *J Athl Train.* 2002;37(3):275–280.

94. Hewett TE, Myer GD, Ford KR, et al. Biomechanical measures of neuromuscular control and valgus loading of the knee predict anterior cruciate ligament injury risk in female athletes: A prospective study. *Am J Sports Med.* 2005;33(4):492–501.

95. Hewett TE, Stroupe AL, Noyes FR. Plyometric training in female athletes: Decreased impact forces and increased hamstring torques. *Am J Sports Med.* 1996;24(6):765–773.

96. Robins AJ, Newman AP, Burks RT. Postoperative return of motion in anterior cruciate ligament and medial collateral ligament injuries: The effects of medial collateral ligament rupture location. *Am J Sports Med.* 1993;21:20–25.

97. Indelicato PA. Non-operative treatment of complete tears of the medial collateral ligament of the knee. *J Bone Joint Surg Am.* 1983;65:323–329.

98. Shelbourne KD, Patel DV. Management of combined injuries of the anterior cruciate and medial collateral ligaments. *Instr Course Lect.* 1996;45:275–280.

99. Shelbourne KD, Mesko JW, McCarroll JR, et al. Combined medial collateral ligament–posterior cruciate rupture: Mechanism of injury. *Am J Knee Surg.* 1990;3:41–44.

100. Warren LF, Marshall JL. The supporting structures and layers on the medial side of the knee: An anatomical analysis. *J Bone Joint Surg Am.* 1979;61:56–62.

101. Ellsasser JC, Reynolds FC, Omohundro JR. The non-operative treatment of collateral ligament injuries of the knee in professional football players: An analysis of seventy-four injuries treated non-operatively and twenty-four injuries treated surgically. *J Bone Joint Surg Am.* 1974;56:1185–1190.

102. Indelicato PA. Isolated medial collateral ligament injuries in the knee. *J Am Acad Orthop Surg.* 1995;3:9–14.

103. Noyes FR, Barber-Westin SD. The treatment of acute combined ruptures of the anterior cruciate and medial ligaments of the knee. *Am J Sports Med.* 1995;23:380–389.

104. LaPrade RF, Wentorf F. Diagnosis and treatment of posterolateral knee injuries. *Clin Orthop Relat Res.* 2002;402: 110–121.

105. DeLee JC, Riley MB, Rockwood CAJ. Acute straight lateral instability of the knee. *Am J Sports Med.* 1983;11: 404–411.

106. LaPrade RF, Terry GC. Injuries to the posterolateral aspect of the knee: Association of injuries with clinical instability. *Am J Sports Med.* 1997;25:433–438.

107. Krukhaug Y, Molster A, Rodt A, Strand T. Lateral ligament injuries of the knee. *Knee Surg Sports Traumatol Arthrosc.* 1998;6:21–25.

108. LaPrade RF. The medial collateral ligament complex and the posterolateral aspect of the knee, in Arendt EA (ed), *Orthopaedic Knowledge Update: Sports Medicine.* Ed. Rosemont, IL: American Academy of Orthopaedic Surgeons 1999:327–340.

109. Cole BJ, Harner CD. Degenerative arthritis of the knee in active patients: Evaluation and management. *J Am Acad Orthop Surg.* 1999;7:389–402.

110. LaPrade RF, Gilbert TJ, Bollom TS, et al. The MRI appearance of individual structures of the posterolateral knee: A prospective study of normal and knees with surgically verified grade III injuries. *Am J Sports Med.* 2000; 28:191–199.

111. Rettig AC, Rubinstein RA. Medial and lateral ligament injuries of the knee, in Scott WN (ed), *The Knee.* St. Louis, MO: Mosby-Year Book; 1994:803–822.

112. Harner CD, Hoher J. Evaluation and treatment of posterior cruciate ligament injuries. *Am J Sports Med.* 1998;26: 471–482.

113. Kannus P. Nonoperative treatment of grade II and III sprains of the lateral ligament compartment of the knee. *Am J Sports Med.* 1989;17:83–88.

114. Shelbourne KD, Davis TJ, Patel DV. The natural history of acute, isolated, nonoperatively treated posterior cruciate ligament injuries: A prospective study. *Am J Sports Med.* 1999;27:276–283.

115. Harner CD, Janaushek MA, Kanamori A, et al. Biomechanical analysis of a double-bundle posterior cruciate ligament reconstruction. *Am J Sports Med.* 2000;28:144–151.

116. Berg EE. Posterior cruciate ligament tibial inlay reconstruction. *Arthroscopy.* 1995;11:69–76.

117. Fitzgibbons RE, Shelbourne KD. "Aggressive" nontreatment of lateral meniscus tears seen during anterior cruciate ligament reconstruction. *Am J Sports Med.* 1995;23: 156–159.

118. Steiner ME, Grana WA. The young athlete's knee: Recent advances. *Clin Sports Med.* 1988;7:527–546.

119. Arnoczky SP, Warren RF. Microvasculature of the human meniscus. *Am J Sports Med.* 1982;10:90–95.

120. Arnoczky SP, Warren RF. The microvasculature of the meniscus and its response to injury: An experimental study in the dog. *Am J Sports Med.* 1983;11:131–141.

121. Bellabarba C, Bush-Joseph CA, Bach BRJ. Patterns of meniscal injury in the anterior cruciate–deficient knee: A review of the literature. *Am J Orthop.* 1997;26:18–23.

122. McCarty EC, Marx RG, DeHaven KE. Meniscus repair: Considerations in treatment and update of clinical results. *Clin Orthop Relat Res.* 2002;402:122–134.

123. Brindle T, Nyland J, Johnson DL. The meniscus: Review of basic principles with application to surgery and rehabilitation. *J Athl Train.* 2001;36:160–169.

124. Reicher MA, Hartzman S, Duckweiler GR, et al. Meniscal injuries: Detection using MR imaging. *Radiology.* 1986;159:753–757.

125. Mink JH, Levy T, Crues JVI. Tears of the anterior cruciate ligament and menisci on MR imaging evaluation. *Radiology.* 1988;167:769–774.

126. Noyes FR, Barber-Westin SD. Arthroscopic repair of meniscal tears extending into the avascular zone in patients younger than twenty years of age. *Am J Sports Med.* 2002;30:589–600.

127. Greis PE, Holmstrom MC, Bardanna DD, Burks RT. Meniscal injury: II. Management. *J Am Acad Orthop Surg.* 2002;10:177–187.

128. DeHaven KE. Decision-making factors in the treatment of meniscal lesions. *Clin Orthop.* 1990;252:49–54.

129. Cannon WJJ, Vittori JM. The incidence of healing in arthroscopic meniscal repairs in anterior cruciate ligament–reconstructed knees versus stable knees. *Am J Sports Med.* 1992;20:176–181.

130. Morgan CD, Wojtys EM, Casscells CD, Casscells SW. Arthroscopic meniscal repair evaluated by second-look arthroscopy. *Am J Sports Med.* 1991;19:632–638.

131. Barber FA. Accelerated rehabilitation for meniscus repairs. *Arthroscopy.* 1994;10:206–210.

132. Shelbourne KD, Patel DV, Adsit WS, Porter DA. Rehabilitation after meniscal repair. *Clin Sports Med.* 1996;15:595–612.

133. Barber FA, Click SD. Meniscus repair rehabilitation with concurrent anterior cruciate reconstruction. *Arthroscopy.* 1997;13:433–437.

134. DeHaven KE, Lohrer WA, Lovelock JE. Long-term results of open meniscal repair. *Am J Sports Med.* 1995;23:524–530.

135. Delamarter RB, Hohl M, Hopp EJ. Ligament injuries associated with tibial plateau fractures. *Clin Orthop Relat Res.* 1990;250:226–233.

136. Gill TJ, Moezzi DM, Oates KM, Sterett WI. Arthroscopic reduction and internal fixation of tibial plateau fractures in skiing. *Clin Orthop Relat Res.* 2001;383:243–249.

137. Bharam S, Vrahas MS, Fu FH. Knee fractures in the athlete. *Orthop Clin North Am.* 2002;33:565–574.

138. Hohl M, Johnson EE, Wiss DA. Fractures of the knee, in Green DP, Bucholz RW (eds), *Fractures in Adults*, ed 3. Philadelphia, PA: JB Lippincott; 1991:1725–1797.

139. Cohn SL, Sotta RP, Bergfeld JA. Fractures about the knee in sports. *Clin Sports Med.* 1990;9:121–139.

140. Buchko GM, Johnson DH. Arthroscopy assisted operative management of tibial plateau fractures. *Clin Orthop Relat Res.* 1996;332:29–36.

141. Mazoue CG, Guanche CA, Vrahas MS. Arthroscopic management of tibial plateau fractures: An unselected series. *Am J Orthop.* 1999;28:508–515.

142. Good L, Johnson RJ. The dislocated knee. *J Am Acad Orthop Surg.* 1995;3:284–292.

143. Shelbourne KD, Porter DA, Clingman JA, et al. Low-velocity knee dislocation. *Orthop Rev.* 1991;20:995–1004.

144. Green NE, Allen BL. Vascular injuries associated with dislocation of the knee. *J Bone Joint Surg Am.* 1977;59:236–239.

145. Quinlan AG, Sharrad WJW. Posterolateral dislocation of the knee with capsular interposition. *J Bone Joint Surg Br.* 1958;40:660–663.

146. Hill JA, Rana NA. Complications of posterolateral dislocation of the knee: Case report and literature review. *Clin Orthop.* 1981;154:212–215.

147. Dedmond BT, Almekinders LC. Operative versus nonoperative treatment of knee dislocations: A meta-analysis. *Am J Knee Surg.* 2001;14:33–38.

148. Richter M, Bosch U, Wippermann B, et al. Comparison of surgical repair or reconstruction of the cruciate ligaments versus nonsurgical treatment in patients with traumatic knee dislocations. *Am J Sports Med.* 2002;30:718–727.

149. Orchard JW, Fricker PA, Abud AT, Mason BR. Biomechanics of iliotibial band friction syndrome in runners. *Am J Sports Med.* 1996;24:375–379.

150. Noble CA. Iliotibial band friction syndrome in runners. *Am J Sports Med.* 1980;8:232–234.

151. Kirk KL, Kuklo T, Klemme W. Iliotibial band friction syndrome in runners. *Orthopedics.* 2000;23:1209–1214.

152. Taunton JE, Ryan MB, Clement DB, et al. A retrospective case-control analysis of 2002 running injuries. *Br J Sports Med.* 2002;36:95–101.

153. James SL. Running injuries to the knee. *J Am Acad Orthop Surg.* 1995;3:309–318.

154. Forbes JR, Helms CA, Janzen DL. Acute pes anserine bursitis: MR imaging. *Radiology.* 1995;194:525–527.

155. Brown TR, Quinn SF, Wensel JP, et al. Diagnosis of popliteus injuries with MR imaging. *Skel Radiol.* 1995;24:511–514.

156. Birk GT, DeLee JC. Osteochondral lesions: Clinical findings. *Clin Sports Med.* 2001;20:279–286.

157. Farmer JM, Martin DF, Boles CA. Chondral and osteochondral injuries: Diagnosis and management. *Clin Sports Med.* 2001;20:299–319.

158. Minas T, Peterson L. Advanced techniques in autologous chondrocyte transplantation. *Clin Sports Med.* 1999;18:13–44.

159. Cain EL, Clancy WG. Treatment algorithm for osteochondral injuries of the knee. *Clin Sports Med.* 2001;20:321–342.

160. Paletta GAJ, Bednarz PA, Stanitski CL, et al. The prognostic value of quantitative bone scan in knee osteochondritis dissecans: A preliminary experience. *Am J Sports Med.* 1998;26:7–14.

161. Cahill BR. Osteochondritis dessicans of the knee: Treatment of juvenile and adult forms. *J Am Acad Orthop Surg.* 1995;3:237–247.

162. Johnson LL. Arthroscopic abrasion arthroplasty: A review. *Clin Orthop Relat Res.* 2001;391:S306–S317.

163. Steadman JR, Rodkey WG, Rodrigo JJ. Microfracture: Surgical technique and rehabilitation to treat chondral defects. *Clin Orthop Relat Res.* 2001(391):S362–S369.

164. Daniel DM, Stone ML, Dobson BE, et al. Fate of the ACL-injured patient: A prospective outcome study. *Am J Sports Med.* 1994;22:632–644.

165. Rosenberg TD, Paulos LE, Parker RD, et al. The forty-five–degree posteroanterior flexion weight-bearing radiograph of the knee. *J Bone Joint Surg Am.* 1988;70:1479–1483.

166. Bradley JD, Brandt KD, Katz BP, et al. Comparison of an antiinflammatory dose of ibuprofen, an analgesic dose of ibuprofen, and acetaminophen in the treatment of patients with osteoarthritis of the knee. *N Engl J Med.* 1991;325:1716–1725.

167. Berger RG. Nonsteroidal anti-inflammatory drugs: Making the right choices. *J Am Acad Orthop Surg.* 1994;2:255–260.

168. Ghosh P, Smith M, Wells C. Second-line agents in osteoarthritis, in Dixon JS, Furst DE (eds), *Second Line Agents in the Treatment of Rheumatic Diseases.* New York: Marcel Dekker; 1992:363–427.

169. Muller-Fassbender H, Bach GL, Haase W, et al. Glucosamine sulfate compared to ibuprofen in osteoarthritis of the knee. *Osteoarthritis Cartilage.* 1994;2:61–69.

170. Bougeois P, Chales G, DeHais J, et al. Efficacy and tolerability of chondroitin sulfate 1200 mg/day vs chondroitin sulfate 3 × 400 mg/day vs placebo. *Osteoarthr Cartilage.* 1998;6:525–530.

171. Merchan ECR, Galindo E. Arthroscope-guided surgery versus nonoperative treatment for limited degenerative osteoarthritis of the femorotibial joint in patients over 50 years of age: A prospective comparative study. *Arthroscopy.* 1993;9:663–667.

172. Wouters E, Bassett FHI, Hardaker WJ, Garrett WEJ. An algorithm for arthroscopy in the over-50 age group. *Am J Sports Med.* 1992;20:141–145.

173. Yang SS, Nisonson B. Arthroscopic surgery of the knee in the geriatric patient. *Clin Orthop Relat Res.* 1995;316:50–58.

174. Dervin GF, Stiell IG, Rody K, Grabowski J. Effect of arthroscopic debridement for osteoarthritis of the knee on health-related quality of life. *J Bone Joint Surg Am.* 2003;85:10–19.

175. Krackow KA, Galloway EJ. A preoperative technique for predicting success after varus or valgus osteotomy at the knee. *Am J Knee Surg.* 1989;2:164–170.

176. Gill GS, Chan KC, Mills DM. 5- to 18-year follow-up study of cemented total knee arthroplasty for patients 55 years old or younger. *J Arthroplasty.* 1997;12:49–54.

177. Stern SH, Bowen MK, Insall JN, Scuderi GR. Cemented total knee arthroplasty for gonarthrosis in patients 55 years old or younger. *Clin Orthop Relat Res.* 1990;260:124–129.

178. Diduch DR, Insall JN, Scott WN, et al. Total knee replacement in young, active patients: Long-term follow-up and functional outcome. *J Bone Joint Surg Am.* 1997;79:575–582.

179. Fox E, Bowers R, Foss M. *The Physiological Basis for Exercise and Sport,* ed 5. Madison, WI: Brown and Benchmark; 1993.

180. Henning CE, Lynch MA, Glick KR. An in vivo strain gage study of elongation of the anterior cruciate ligament. *Am J Sports Med.* 1985;13:22–26.

CHAPTER 6

Patellofemoral Injuries

Michelle C. Boling, PhD, LAT
Anthony Beutler, MD

Patellofemoral Pain Syndrome

CLINICAL PRESENTATION

History

Chronic or overuse mechanism.
Increase or changes in activity may be reported.
Achy, diffuse pain in the anterior knee.

Observation

Gross observation is often unremarkable.
Patellar malposition (e.g., baja, alta, or squinting positions) and/or increased quadriceps angle, femoral anteversion, and/or hyperpronation may be noted.

Functional Status

Activities that increase patellofemoral joint reaction forces, such as running, squatting, jumping, and stair climbing, may be impaired.
Prolonged flexion of the knee may increase pain (theater sign).

Physical Examination Findings

Crepitation may be present.
No definitive, reliable special or ligamentous tests exist.

anteversion The femoral neck is anterior relative to the long axis of the femur.

Patellofemoral pain syndrome (PFPS) is characterized by diffuse, achy pain in the anterior knee that is accentuated by actions that increase the pressure of the patella against the femoral condyles (e.g., squatting, stair climbing, running). PFPS is some-times referred to as anterior knee pain. The main theorized cause of PFPS is patellar malalignment, which is characterized by the improper tracking of the patella within the femoral trochlea. Normal patellar tracking requires proper balance in the strength and contraction timing of the medial and lateral quadriceps muscles of the knee. The soft-tissue restraints must be pliable enough to allow the patella to track freely through the femoral trochlea but without allowing the patella to drift too far laterally (see **Figure 6.1**). Additionally, in a weight-bearing stance, internal rotation of the femur can occur independent of the patella; as a consequence, rotation of the femur may lead to dynamic patellar malalignment.[1]

Pathomechanics at the foot, ankle, knee, hip, and trunk can influence patellar biomechanics. In the setting of PFPS, the complete kinetic chain should be analyzed, including static and dynamic postures of the entire lower extremity.

While the patient assumes a static posture, assess the patient's posture, including the position of the subtalar joint, quadriceps angle (Q angle), and femoral **anteversion** (this will present with toeing in posture and femoral internal rotation) (see **Figure 6.2**). Increased pronation, Q angle, and femoral anteversion may alter the position of the patella within the femoral trochlea, leading to changes in patellofemoral contact pressures and the development

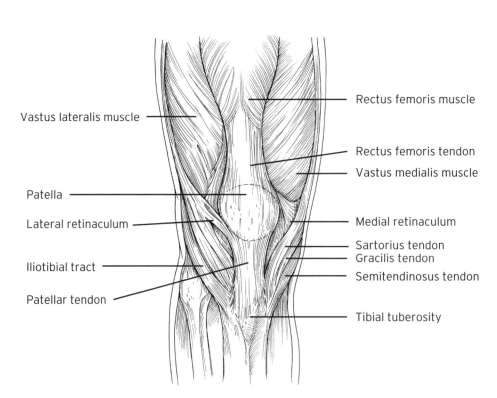

Figure 6.1   Normal anatomy of the knee's extensor mechanism. *Source:* Reproduced with permission from Matava MJ. Patellar tendon ruptures. *J Am Acad Orthop Surg.* 1996;4:287-296.

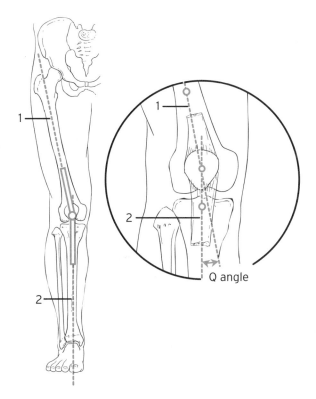

Figure 6.2 Measuring the Q angle. Three points (the anterior superior iliac spine, center of the patella, and the center of the tibial tubercle) form the Q angle. The line of pull of the quadriceps (1) is approximated by a line extending from the anterior superior iliac spine through the center of the patella and (2) from the tibial tubercle to the center of the patella.

of PFPS.[2,3] A leg-length difference may exist if one foot is pronated and the other foot is supinated (with the pronated foot representing the longer leg); in general, a pronated foot increases the Q angle.

During the clinical examination identify muscle tightness or weakness of the foot, ankle, knee, and hip. Tightness of the gastrocnemius–soleus complex, for example, may produce compensatory foot pronation. Tightness of the hip muscles can alter the biomechanical relationship between the femur and the patella. Tight quadriceps, tight hamstrings, or a tight iliotibial band can also affect patellofemoral pressure during normal movements. Decreased strength of the quadriceps musculature may lead to malalignment due to its role as the main dynamic stabilizer of the patella. Weak hip muscles, especially the gluteus maximus and gluteus medius, may allow the femur to drift into adduction and internal rotation during weight bearing activities, effectively increasing the dynamic Q angle.

Pelvic instability—particularly an anterior position of the pelvis—also has been implicated in PFPS. The anterior tilt of the pelvis can internally rotate the femur, increasing lateral compression of the patella, especially when the knee is loaded in the flexed position. The position of the pelvis and the biomechanical causes of improper positioning, such as weak trunk stabilizers and pelvic muscle inflexibility, should be evaluated.

"Chondromalacia patella"—a term that literally means softening of the patellofemoral articular cartilage—is sometimes incorrectly used as a synonym for PFPS. Chondromalacia patella is actually an arthroscopic diagnosis that is not synonymous with or **pathognomonic** for PFPS. Many patients with PFPS do not have cartilage softening; conversely, many with cartilage softening have no symptoms of PFPS. Thus this term is not preferred because it does not accurately describe either the patient or the clinical syndrome of PFPS.

pathognomonic
Specifically distinctive for some disease or disease process; absolutely diagnostic.

Differential Diagnosis
Patellar or quadriceps tendinopathy, patellar osteoarthritis, meniscal tear, plica syndrome.

Imaging Techniques
Anteroposterior (AP), lateral, and bilateral axial radiographs are obtained to rule out a fracture or bipartite patella and to assess malalignment (see **Figure 6.3**). Axial computed tomography (CT) scans provide a more sensitive imaging technique for identifying patellar malalignment and are recommended if surgical intervention is being considered.[4] This modality allows for imaging of the patella within the femoral trochlea from 20° of flexion to full extension, where the joint relies more on soft-tissue structures for stability. A CT scan can also be used to identify a laterally positioned tibial tubercle (see **Figure 6.4**).[5]

The surrounding soft tissues are well visualized on magnetic resonance imaging (MRI). Dynamic axial MRI scans have been proposed to

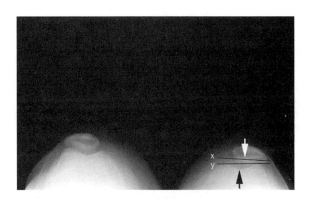

Figure 6.3 Axial view of patellar malalignment. The median ridge of the patella (white arrow) is located lateral to the most concave portion of the femoral trochlea (black arrow), indicating a patellar subluxation. The angle formed by the lateral patellar facet (**x**) and the line drawn across the femoral condyles (**y**) indicates an abnormal patellar tilt.

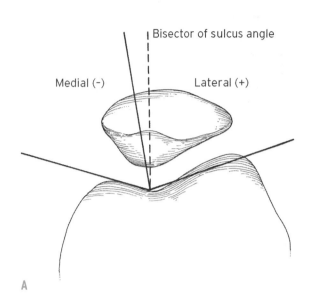

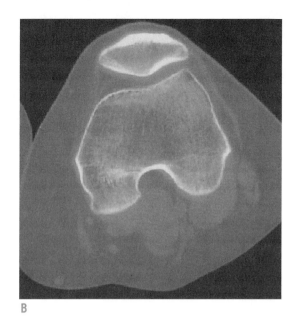

Figure 6.4 Imaging techniques for patellar maltracking and subluxation. **(A)** The congruence angle obtained from a standard Merchant view should demonstrate that the patellar apex is medial to the bisected femoral trochlea. **(B)** Computed tomography scans are useful for determining patellofemoral alignment. *Source:* Reproduced with permission from Fulkerson JP. Patellofemoral pain disorders: evaluation and management. *J Am Acad Orthop Surg.* 1994;2:124-132.

characterize the influence of the soft tissues on the patella.[6] These images can demonstrate the degree of knee flexion at which patellar malalignment is greatest.

MRIs also may be helpful if other soft-tissue injury in the knee is suspected. However, positive findings may be present on MRI in the absence of clinically significant symptoms. For example, a torn meniscus may be visible on MRI, even though the patient does not have meniscal symptoms.

PFPS is a clinical syndrome; thus its diagnosis is made based on clinical findings. Most patients with PFPS have no discrete CT or MRI findings. Advanced imaging is not required for the diagnosis of PFPS.

Definitive Diagnosis

Findings on the clinical examination (pain on posterior side of patella and surrounding the patella) and the exclusion of other possible pathologic findings warrant the diagnosis of PFPS.

Pathomechanics and Functional Limitations

Decreased extensor-mechanism efficiency and pain with patellar tendon function can produce significant changes in lower extremity biomechanics. As the condition of the patellofemoral joint deteriorates, running, squatting, and jumping become impaired. Eventually, pain interferes with activities of daily living, such as stair climbing and walking.

Medications

A nonsteroidal anti-inflammatory drug (NSAID) to control the acute inflammatory response is often recommended. Rarely, patients may receive an intra-articular injection of hydrocortisone. While short courses of NSAIDs, steroids, and other injectable drugs may be appropriate for acute flares, long-term use of these medicines is not warranted in chronic PFPS.

Surgical Intervention

Surgical intervention is not usually recommended to correct malalignment. In patients with severe, persistent symptoms despite 6 to 12 months of conservative management, surgery for concomitant conditions may be warranted.

Surgical options for PFPS patients with cartilage abnormalities include debridement or abrasion chondroplasty. Microfracture techniques can be used to penetrate the subchondral bone, causing bleeding and the formation of a fibrin clot and primitive stem cells.[7,8] These primitive stem cells differentiate into chondrocytes to repair the defect, which then heals with fibrocartilage or a mix of fibrocartilage and hyaline cartilage. Although the mechanical properties of the repaired knee are not those of normal hyaline cartilage, the result is still a better alternative than exposed nonarticular bone. Surgical treatment to restore proper patellar alignment may also be indicated if conservative management is unsuccessful.

■ Postinjury/Postoperative Management

If the patient has an antalgic gait, crutches or a cane should be used while ambulating. The patient should avoid activities that produce pain. If surgical microfracture techniques were performed, the patient may be maintained on a non-weight-bearing regimen, with passive range of motion (ROM) continuing for 6 to 8 weeks to allow the maturation of the chondrocytes. If surgery was performed to restore alignment of the patellofemoral joint, postsurgical treatment is the same as for the surgical procedures described in the treatment of patellar subluxation and dislocation.

■ Injury-Specific Treatment and Rehabilitation Concerns

> **Specific Concerns**
> Control pain and inflammation.
> Restore normal lower extremity biomechanics.

The initial treatment of PFPS focuses on controlling pain and inflammation with cryotherapy and therapeutic exercise. A thorough evaluation of trunk, pelvis, and lower extremity static and dynamic posture, flexibility, and muscle activation should be performed. If hyperpronation is thought to contribute to PFPS, the patient should be fitted for a corrective foot orthotic device. Flexibility exercises for the hip, quadriceps, hamstrings, iliotibial band, and gastrocnemius–soleus muscle groups are instituted as needed.

Studies provide conflicting evidence regarding the role of bracing in PFPS. Notably, McConnell taping has been shown to provide significant pain benefits for certain individuals with PFPS.[9] McConnell taping may also predict which patients are likely to respond to bracing and assist in determining the brace configuration of maximal benefit. (See the "Patellar Taping" section later in this chapter.)

Synergistic activity between the quadriceps and other lower extremity muscles must be emphasized. The quadriceps muscles are responsible for dynamic patellar stability, but work synergistically with the hip musculature and triceps surae. Initial quadriceps reeducation can begin in isolation with

motor-level electrical stimulation. Strengthening exercises for the quadriceps should focus on restoring synergistic control of the patella during extremity movement. Strengthening of the hip and core musculature provides stability to the trunk and maintains proper lower extremity alignment during functional tasks. Leg-raising activities are begun. The quadriceps and vastus medialis obliquus (VMO) are simultaneously contracted with the hip muscles during hip exercises. The patient progresses through open and closed kinetic chain strengthening, which is performed through the pain-free ROM only. As strength of the musculature and control of the patella are restored, the patient advances through proprioception exercises and agility and sport-specific drills.

chondrocyte A cell that forms the matrix of bone cartilage.

> **Practice Tip**
> Both weight-bearing and non-weight-bearing exercises are effective in reducing pain and improving function in the rehabilitation of individuals with PFPS.[10]

■ Estimated Amount of Time Lost

The patient may not lose any time from normal activities. In general, if pain is tolerable, no swelling is present, and the knee and lower extremity muscles function normally, activity may continue. If continued activity is impossible, however, a period of "relative rest" for approximately 4 weeks is warranted. In relative rest, the patient reduces activities to a pain-free level, focuses on rehabilitative exercise, and cross-trains using exercise modalities that do not cause pain. Relative rest ends as the patient progressively returns to full activity. Nevertheless, it is advisable that the patient continues rehabilitation exercises even after returning to full activity.

Patients who do not respond to 4 weeks of conservative rehabilitation, including relative rest, require further examination to rule out other conditions. In the absence of additional findings, formal rehabilitation exercise should continue.

■ Return-to-Play Criteria

The patient may return to competition when pain does not impair the athlete's ability to successfully complete lower extremity functional tests, agility tests, and sport-specific activities.

Functional Bracing
A knee sleeve with a patellar cutout may be used to increase warmth to the area, although the benefit of

this therapy on pain control or healing is unsubstantiated. A Drytex or elastic material is preferred to neoprene to avoid skin breakdown.

Patellar Subluxation and Dislocation

Patellar subluxation and dislocation are the most extreme forms of patellar instability. The patient may have a history of patellar malalignment, but acute patellar subluxation or dislocation (which is most frequently lateral) is often caused by rotational, pivoting movements (see **Figure 6.5**). Medial dislocation is rare but occurs secondary to a contact injury while large forces are being exerted on the patella or, more commonly, due to overcorrection following a realignment procedure.

When the patella laterally subluxes or dislocates, the medial retinaculum and medial patellofemoral ligament are injured (see **Figure 6.6**). An osteochondral defect or fracture of the medial patella may also be associated with the dislocation. As the quadriceps muscles contract to extend the knee and relocate the patella, the medial patellar facet is forcefully driven into and shears across the lateral femoral condyle, potentially causing bony bruises and chondral injury.

Anatomic deviations may predispose an individual to patellar dislocations. For example, patella alta, shallow femoral trochlea, increased Q angle, tight lateral retinaculum, genu valgum, femoral anteversion, pronated feet, and general laxity have all been implicated in a high rate of patellar dislocations.[11] The injury may result from contact or from the combination of malalignment of the extensor mechanism and laterally directed forces on the patella from the contraction of the quadriceps muscles. The knee is usually in some degree of valgus,

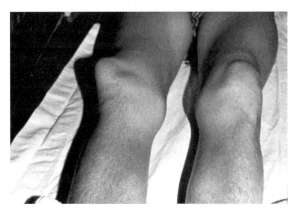

Figure 6.5 Acute lateral patellar dislocation.

CLINICAL PRESENTATION

History

Strong quadriceps contraction is observed.
A valgus force to the knee may be described.
Pain radiates from the knee and the surrounding restraints.
A "pop" may be reported.
The patient may describe the patella dislocating and, possibly, relocating ("subluxating").
The patient may have a history of patella alta, genu valgum, femoral anteversion, pronated feet, or a large Q angle.

Observation

If the patella remains dislocated, obvious deformity is noted, including the contour of the medial femoral condyle being visible under the skin.
The patient maintains the knee in flexion because full extension allows the patella to relocate.

Functional Status

If the patella dislocated with spontaneous reduction, decreased ROM, especially in flexion, is noted.
Weight bearing is decreased.
Inhibition of the quadriceps mechanism is noted as an inability to produce force.
If the patella remains dislocated, weight bearing is not possible.

Physical Examination Findings

The physical examination should not be performed while the patella remains dislocated (see the "Immediate Management" section for relocation maneuvers).
A relocated patellar dislocation will show a positive patellar apprehension test and a hypermobile lateral patellar glide.

such as planting or cutting on the planted foot, when the quadriceps forcefully contract.

Differential Diagnosis

Medial collateral ligament sprain, anterior cruciate ligament sprain, patellar fracture, chondral fracture.

Imaging Techniques

If the patella remains dislocated, AP and lateral radiographs of the knee are obtained. If the patella has been relocated, AP, lateral, tunnel, and axial radiographs are taken to determine the relationship of the patella to the femoral trochlea and to identify whether any osteochondral defects or fractures occurred during the dislocation.

The surrounding soft tissues are well visualized on MRI, and an MRI scan can reliably identify when the medial retinaculum is torn (see **Figure 6.7**). Dynamic axial MRI images may characterize the influence of the soft tissues on the patella, displaying the degree of knee flexion at which patellar malalignment is greatest and indicating whether the patella reduces.[6]

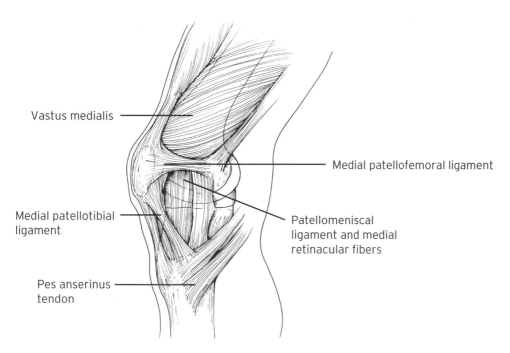

Vastus medialis

Medial patellofemoral ligament

Medial patellotibial
ligament

Patellomeniscal
ligament and medial
retinacular fibers

Pes anserinus
tendon

6

Figure 6.6 Anatomy of the medial aspect of the knee. The medial patellofemoral ligament provides 53% of the restraining force in preventing lateral displacement of the patella; the patellomeniscal ligament and medial retinacular fibers, on average, provide 22% of this force. *Source:* Reproduced with permission from Boden BP, Pearsall AW, Garrett WE, Feagin JA Jr. Patellofemoral instability: evaluation and management. *J Am Acad Orthop Surg.* 1997;5:47-57.

An axial CT scan is obtained to better determine the relationship of the patella to the femoral trochlea, particularly if surgical treatment is being considered. In particular, patellar malalignment can be more sensitively detected with a CT scan.[4] This modality allows imaging of the relationship of the patella to the femoral trochlea from 20° of flexion to full extension, when the joint relies more on the soft-tissue structures. The axial CT scan can also be used to demonstrate a laterally positioned tibial tubercle.[5]

Definitive Diagnosis

The definitive diagnosis is based on a history of the patella subluxating and subsequently being reduced, direct visualization of the dislocated patella, radiographic findings, and/or the finding of patellar instability causing apprehension. Medial retinacular tearing evident on MRI is helpful in diagnosing dislocation if the patella spontaneously reduced.

Pathomechanics and Functional Limitations

Tearing of the medial retinacular tissues can lead to chronic instability of the patellofemoral joint,

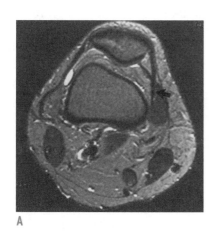
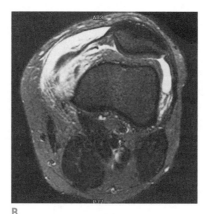

A

B

Figure 6.7 Axial magnetic resonance images of the patellofemoral joint. (**A**) Normal medial patellofemoral ligament. (**B**) Avulsion of the ligament off the medial femoral epicondyle.

potentially causing recurrent subluxations or dislocations. Patients with patellar instability may also experience quadriceps inhibition as a feeling that the leg is "giving way." Knee effusion may inhibit contraction of the VMO, thereby increasing patellar instability.

Immediate Management

Immediate management is to attempt to relocate the patella, either actively or passively. Active reduction is performed by having the patient try to extend the knee by contracting the quadriceps while a slight lateral to medial pressure is exerted on the patella. For a passive reduction, the patient should be as relaxed as possible, lying supine. The distal thigh is stabilized with one of the clinician's hands, while the other hand passively extends the leg. The patella relocation is recognized by the "clunk" as it goes back into the trochlear groove.

If an initial attempt to relocate the patella is unsuccessful, the leg should be immobilized in the current position and the patient transported to the hospital. Further attempts to relocate the patella can then be attempted after radiographs and the administration of oral or injectable pain medication. In the interim, ice and compression are applied to minimize muscle spasm and pain.

Medications

Narcotic analgesics may be prescribed to control the initial pain. A rapid-onset, short-acting intravenous muscle relaxant is used if the first attempt at reducing the dislocation is unsuccessful. The patient may then be prescribed a course of NSAIDs to control inflammation and relieve pain.

Postinjury Management

Joint aspiration may be used to alleviate a tense effusion caused by tearing of the medial structures. Fat droplets in the aspirate may indicate an osteochondral lesion.

The initial treatment is to immobilize the knee in full extension with a compressive dressing along the lateral aspect of the patella, approximating the torn medial patellar structures. The patient is evaluated every 2 weeks and can begin formal rehabilitation when the tenderness over the medial patellar structures has decreased. A patient with minimal effusion and no signs of malalignment is advanced through a course of conservative care.[11,12] The length of immobilization varies depending on patient's age, anatomy, and history of previous dislocations.

Longer immobilization times allow optimal healing of medial soft-tissue structures, but at the expense of more quadriceps atrophy.

> **Practice Tip**
>
> In the absence of congenital patellar abnormalities, conservative treatment of patellar dislocations can provide good to excellent results.[12]

Surgical Intervention

Surgical treatment should be considered if conservative management fails to restore patellofemoral joint function; surgical treatment for pain alone is rarely recommended. If the soft tissues around the joint are thought to be clinically affecting joint alignment, soft-tissue realignment is an option. This procedure may consist of a lateral release for tight lateral structures, repair or reconstruction of the medial stabilizing tissues for a relaxed or torn medial retinaculum, or a combination of these procedures.

Arthroscopy is indicated if an osteochondral lesion has created a loose body within the joint. The physician can visualize the site of the lesion to determine the course of treatment. A small loose body may be removed; a larger lesion may be surgically fixated to restore the joint surfaces. During arthroscopy, patellar tracking and patellar tilt can also be observed.[13]

Lateral release is most effective in patients with a documented patellar tilt but is seldom performed as an isolated procedure (see ⓢⓣ 6.1).[14] This surgery entails sectioning the lateral retinaculum from the vastus lateralis tendon distally, including the lateral patellofemoral and patellotibial ligaments from the superior pole of the patella to the tibial tubercle. Although the lateral release is thought to allow the patella to move medially, the surgery is actually more effective in reducing the posterolateral forces on the patella. Unfortunately, results of the lateral release for patellar instability tend to deteriorate over time.[15–17]

Repair of the medial stabilizing structures should be reserved for younger active athletes who have sustained a patellar dislocation through an indirect mechanism.[18] Surgical repair or reconstruction can also be performed after traumatic injury in athletes with incomplete healing of the medial stabilizing structures and recurrent instability.[15] Most often, the medial structures are tightened with a medial-reefing procedure (see ⓢⓣ 6.2). The medial patellofemoral ligament is identified through a medial incision and repaired.

Lateral Release

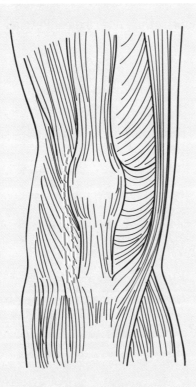

- - - - - - Retinacular release
- - - - Skin incision (open procedure)

Indications

Patellar tilt and failure of conservative management to decrease patellar dislocations.

Procedure Overview

Two methods are available for lateral retinacular release.

Arthroscopic

1. Anteromedial and anterolateral peripatellar tendon arthroscopic portals and a superolateral arthroscopic portal are created.
2. The retinaculum is bisected using electrocautery.
3. A needle is placed and visualized to mark the superior pole of the patella.
4. The retinaculum is released from the superior pole of the patella to the inferior aspect of the joint capsule with electrocautery.

Open Procedure

Arthroscopy is performed to visualize the patella and femoral trochlea. Thorough inspection of the joint is conducted to look for loose osteochondral or chondral fragments that were knocked off at the time of the dislocation.

1. A small lateral incision is made over the lateral retinaculum.
2. The lateral retinaculum is incised using electrocautery, without encroaching into the joint capsule.
3. The proximal extent of the release is from the superior patellar pole, but now the release can safely be extended to the level of the tibial tubercle if necessary.

After both procedures, a compressive dressing is applied to control swelling and place medially directed pressure on the patella, thereby keeping the edges of the newly released tissues unopposed.

Functional Limitations

Early return to functional activity is encouraged. Functional limitations following these procedures are minimal.

Implications for Rehabilitation

Patellar mobilization to avoid scar retraction of the release is necessary. Also, aggressive VMO strengthening encourages medialization and correction of the patellar tilt.

Potential Complications

If the lateral release is extended proximally, the vastus lateralis tendon can be separated from the extensor mechanism to the extent that medial dislocation of the patella can occur. Bleeding from the lateral geniculate artery can cause a postoperative hematoma, excessive swelling, and VMO shutdown.

Comments

Usually this procedure is combined with a distal realignment procedure and/or a proximal reefing of the VMO or medial retinaculum.

Medial-Reefing Procedure, Medial Imbrication, or Proximal Patellar Realignment

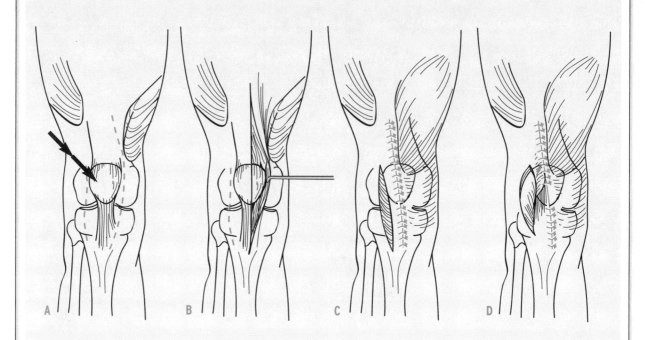

Indications

Acute injury with a documented tear of the medial retinacular structures. In a patient with chronic symptomatic patellar instability in whom conservative management has failed, a medial-reefing procedure can be performed in conjunction with a distal realignment procedure and/or a lateral retinacular release.

Procedure Overview

Acute Injury

1. An incision is made around the medial patella.
2. The injury is identified, which is usually easy in the acute setting because visible evidence of palpable defects helps direct the surgeon in the repair.
3. The torn borders of the defect are sutured with an absorbable material.
4. If the medial patellofemoral ligament has been torn from the femoral attachment, suture anchors may be used to repair the damage.

Chronic Injury

1. Dynamic tracking is visualized to observe the maltracking of the patella.
2. A lateral retinacular release is performed (**A**).
3. The tissue borders are freshened with a sharp incision (**B**).
4. Depending on the quality of tissue present for repair, the surgeon must decide whether to excise a wedge of tissue or to overlap the tissues and suture one over the other. Recently, these repairs have been augmented with porcine grafts to provide collagen scaffolding for tissue ingrowth, which strengthens the repair (**C** and **D**).

Functional Limitations

The extremity is immobilized while the repair heals. Gradually advancing flexion is allowed over time.

Implications for Rehabilitation

The knee is immobilized near extension for 2 weeks. The motion allowed depends on the repair and the quality of the tissue the surgeon encountered during the procedure. The porcine scaffolding graft is absorbed in 6 weeks. Open kinetic chain straight-leg raises and short-arc quadriceps exercises are initiated at week 2 and advanced to closed kinetic chain exercises by week 6.

Potential Complications

Failure of the repair can occur with time, resulting in increased patellar instability symptoms. Overcorrection can cause the patella to subluxate or dislocate medially, which results in significant extensor-mechanism dysfunction.

Comments

For a patient with chronic symptoms, an aggressive rehabilitation program precedes any surgical intervention.

Many times, the ligamentous injury involves an avulsion from the femoral attachment, which can be repaired with suture anchors.

The VMO distalization is an older surgical procedure that is no longer routinely performed for patellar dislocation.[15]

Lateral-release and medial-reefing procedures are commonly performed together for patellar instability. Indeed, a recent review found much better results when both procedures are performed than when just a lateral release alone is undertaken.[19] If the lateral tissues are tight and create abnormal mechanics and patellar tilt, release or lengthening of these tissues should be considered. In the absence of tight lateral structures, medial reefing should be considered as an isolated procedure.

A medialization procedure of the tibial tubercle should be considered for skeletally mature patients with an increased Q angle and recurrent subluxations or dislocations.[20] Medialization or medialization combined with moving the tibial tubercle distally (Hauser procedure) has been performed to treat recurrent patellar instability.[21] The Roux-Elmslie-Trillat procedure combines tibial tubercle transfer with lateral release and medial reefing.[22] Anteriorization procedures (e.g., Macquet procedure) have also been advocated to decompress the patellofemoral joint in patients with chronic PFPS (see ⑤Ⓣ 6.3). These procedures are primarily used for patients with patellar malalignment who also have patellofemoral pain. The final decision on the type of surgery performed depends on the patient's anatomic abnormality and physician preference.

More recently, the Fulkerson procedure has been used to correct patellar instability. A modification of earlier medialization procedures, this technique involves an oblique osteotomy of the tibial tubercle. The tubercle is moved medially and anteriorly, effectively decreasing the Q angle and decompressing the joint. This procedure can be combined with soft-tissue surgeries as necessary. One drawback associated with this surgery is that an increased incidence of proximal tibial fractures has been identified after Fulkerson procedures.[23]

▇ Postoperative Management

Cold packs are administered to reduce pain and control inflammation. Quadriceps-setting exercises are begun within the limits of pain while the patient is wearing the immobilizer. Crutch walking, with the patient bearing weight as tolerated, begins

immediately. If a tense effusion is present, joint aspiration may help control pain and prevent VMO inhibition. Conservative management to restore proper patellar alignment follows the regimen used for PFPS.

After arthroscopic debridement of a loose body or a lateral release without a realignment procedure, the patient is treated with a compressive dressing, a lateral buttress, and an elastic bandage (see **Figure 6.8**). Formal rehabilitation for strengthening and restoring function begins after 5 to 7 days.

After repair of the medial patellofemoral ligament, the knee is immobilized for 1 to 2 weeks. A compressive dressing with a lateral buttress is applied to push the patella medially and take stress off the repaired tissues. The patient is initially put on a non-weight-bearing plan. After 2 weeks, formal rehabilitation can begin.

After a tibial tubercle transfer procedure, the patient is fitted with a hinged knee brace that is locked in full extension. Wound healing over the tibial tubercle is a concern, especially with the Macquet procedure, and the immobilization period is required to ensure better wound healing. After 10 to 14 days of adequate healing, the patient can usually begin rehabilitation. The hinged knee brace remains locked for ambulation until the patient has more than 90° of motion and adequate quadriceps control. After the initial period of non-weight-bearing activity, the patient can progress to weight bearing as tolerated.

▇ Injury-Specific Treatment and Rehabilitation Concerns

> ### Specific Concerns
> Minimize early stresses on the medial patellar restraints.
> Control inflammation.
> Encourage proper realignment of healing tissues.
> Tighten lax tissues.
> Lengthen shortened tissues.
> Restore normal patellar mobility.

Conservative Management

The initial conservative treatment of patellar dislocation involves controlling inflammation with various modalities, medication, and therapeutic exercise. As the peripatellar soft tissues heal, patellar mobilization is used to restore normal medial patellar glide and patellar tilt. The patient can progress knee ROM as tolerated with active-assisted or passive exercises. Following a thorough evaluation of lower

Surgical Technique 6.3

Fulkerson, Roux-Elmslie-Trillat, and Macquet Distal-Realignment Procedures

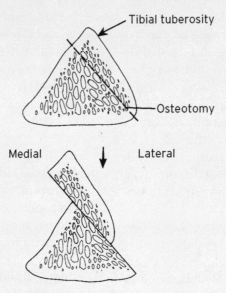

Indications

Failure of conservative management in chronic PFPS and chronic patellar dislocation.

Procedures Overview

1. Before the distal-realignment procedure, arthroscopy is performed to evaluate the position of the patella, the extent of the articular surface damage, and the presence of loose bodies.
2. Lateral retinacular release and proximal reefing may be done in conjunction with the distal-realignment procedure and are performed first.
3. A lateral peripatellar tendon incision is made, and the tibial tubercle attachment of the patellar tendon is identified. The proximal lateral tibia is cleaned off the periosteum, and an osteotomy is made with a saw or an osteotome.

Individual differences in procedures from this point follow.

Macquet Procedure

1. A long, horizontally oriented osteotomy extending at least one-third the length of the tibia is made.
2. The fragment of bone is mobilized and elevated using a bone graft from the iliac crest or allograft bone stock. The elevation unloads the patella to decrease the joint reaction forces.
3. The fragment and bone graft are held in position with one or two screws through the fragment into the proximal tibia.

Roux-Elmslie-Trillat Procedure

1. A shorter horizontal osteotomy is performed and medialized with a horizontal slide of 5 to 10 mm.
2. The extent of the medialization depends on the degree of correction anticipated by the preoperative planning and the visualization of patellar tracking intraoperatively.
3. One or two screws are placed through the fragment into the underlying tibia to hold it in the medialized position.

Fulkerson Procedure

1. An oblique osteotomy is performed through the tibial tubercle and directed from posterolateral to anteromedial.
2. The osteotomy is slid medially in an oblique manner, following the contour of the osteotomy. This oblique slide causes the tubercle to be medialized and elevated. Elevation of the extensor mechanism unloads the joint reaction forces, as in the Macquet procedure, and the medial slide corrects the maltracking, as in the Roux-Elmslie-Trillat procedure.
3. One or two screws are placed through the fragment into the underlying tibia to hold it in the elevated, medialized position.

Functional Limitations

Weight bearing is restricted and motion is protected during the early healing phases.

Implications for Rehabilitation

After surgery, the patient wears an immobilizer locked in extension, and weight bearing is limited for the first 2 weeks. Allowed motion and weight bearing progress during the next 4 weeks. At 6 weeks, the patient is out of the brace, performing rehabilitation and bearing weight as tolerated.

After a Macquet procedure, the osteotomy requires an extended time of healing to prevent complications and fracture. The healing time, as determined by radiographic examination, may delay the progression of ROM and weight bearing.

Potential Complications

Macquet: This procedure has a higher rate of nonunion because of the elevated anterior cortex. The very prominent anterior tibial cortex is cosmetically unappealing to some patients.

Fulkerson: A higher incidence of proximal tibia fractures *may* be related to the use of this procedure.

Comments

The purpose of this family of procedures is to realign the force vectors pulling on the patella or decrease the joint reaction forces on the patella.

Source: Figure reproduced with permission from Fulkerson JP. Patellofemoral pain disorders: evaluation and management. *J Am Acad Orthop Surg.* 1994;2:124-132.

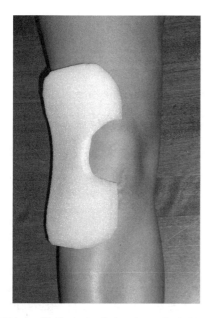

Figure 6.8 Lateral buttress. Applied postoperatively, this felt or foam pad prevents the patella from moving laterally, thereby reducing stress on the healing surgical tissues.

extremity flexibility, flexibility exercises for the hip, quadriceps, hamstrings, and gastrocnemius–soleus muscle groups are usually instituted.

The strength and proper muscular activation patterns of the pelvis and lower extremity must be restored. The trunk and pelvic muscles provide a stable base for the lower extremity muscles and must be incorporated into a comprehensive rehabilitation program. The quadriceps muscles provide dynamic stability of the patella but work synergistically with the hip and calf muscles. Except for quadriceps-setting exercises, other strengthening exercises for the lower extremity should focus on restoring synergistic control of the patella during extremity movement. The patient should simultaneously contract the quadriceps mechanism to stabilize the patella while performing all other lower extremity exercises. Early on, trunk- and pelvic-stabilization exercises and leg-raising activities are begun in all directions. The quadriceps and VMO are contracted simultaneously with the hip muscles during hip exercises. The patient progresses through open and closed kinetic chain strengthening.

As muscle strength and patellar control are restored, the patient advances through proprioception exercises and agility and sport-specific drills.

Postsurgical Rehabilitation

Lateral Release

After a lateral release, medial patellar mobilizations are initiated as soon as possible to maintain the length of the lateral structures and decrease any contracted scar formation within the tissues. A side-lying position is often helpful for the mobilization effort, as it stretches the lateral thigh musculature. Trunk, pelvis, quadriceps, and lower extremity strengthening are begun immediately.

Medial-Reefing Procedure

Following a medial-reefing procedure, medial patellar mobilization and ROM exercises can begin after 2 weeks of healing. The ROM and aggressiveness of the progression should be discussed with the surgeon and are determined by the degree of flexion tension placed across the repair.

As healing occurs, the strengthening program progresses. Submaximal quadriceps setting and electrical stimulation can begin at 3 to 4 weeks postoperatively. Active exercises can be advanced at 6 to 8 weeks. Maximal quadriceps contractions should not begin until approximately 10 to 12 weeks after surgery. The patient then proceeds through proprioception exercises and agility and sport-specific drills.

Distal-Realignment Procedure

With a distal-realignment procedure, after the initial period of immobilization for wound healing, the patient with a stable fixation of the tibial tubercle can progress knee ROM. Passive motion is used at first; flexion past 120° is not pursued until adequate bone healing is demonstrated on radiographs.

Strengthening is advanced once the osteotomy is adequately healed. Submaximal quadriceps exercises can commence at 3 to 4 weeks after the surgery, with more active exercises beginning at 4 to 6 weeks. Maximal contractions are not progressed until adequate bone healing is demonstrated radiographically, usually by 8 to 10 weeks postoperatively. The patient then proceeds through proprioception exercises and agility and sport-specific drills.

■ Estimated Amount of Time Lost

Time lost to the injury varies. Three to six weeks of rehabilitation is often needed for a patient who cannot perform exercises because of symptoms. A first-time patellar dislocation requires approximately 3 weeks of immobilization, followed by 3 to 6 weeks of rehabilitation before the athlete begins to return to activity. The degree of tearing of the medial patellar-stabilizing structures has the greatest influence on the amount of time lost from activity. If the patella is grossly unstable and requires surgical repair, the time lost can amount to 4 to 6 months. The surgical procedure ultimately influences the amount of time lost.

■ Return-to-Play Criteria

The patient may return to competition when pain is absent, ROM is full, quadriceps strength has been restored, and functional tests and agility programs with sport-specific activities for the lower extremity are successfully completed.

Functional Bracing

Patellar taping may be helpful in the patient who had a dislocation but now has symptoms more typical of PFPS. A knee sleeve designed to place a medially directed force on the patella may be used for the return to activity.

Quadriceps and Patellar Tendinopathy

Patellar tendinopathy is much more common than quadriceps tendinopathy in athletes.[24] Both quadriceps and patellar tendinopathy are overuse injuries of the knee's extensor mechanism. These conditions are characterized by pain in the anterior aspect of the knee; close inspection usually pinpoints the inflammatory process at the superior (quadriceps tendinopathy) or inferior (patellar tendinopathy)

patellar pole. Often generically termed "jumper's knee," these injuries are more common in basketball, volleyball, and soccer players and in dancers. The forceful extension exerted during jumping and eccentric forces during landing create microtrauma in the quadriceps or patellar tendon.[25] Tendinopathies can be classified using a six-stage scale modified from the work of Blazina[26,27] (see **Table 6.1**).

CLINICAL PRESENTATION

History

Repetitive running, jumping, or other activities that produce large concentric and eccentric forces from the extensor mechanism.

Pain is located at the superior (quadriceps tendinopathy) or inferior pole (patellar tendinopathy) of the patella.

Pain begins after exercising for a period and then subsides with rest.

Pain may become constant and is classically worsened by prolonged sitting and ascending/descending stairs.

Observation

Swelling and redness may be present at the quadriceps or patellar tendons.

Functional Status

Gait may be antalgic.

Usually, ROM is full but may be painful with active and resisted extension and/or passive flexion.

Physical Examination Findings

Pain with resisted extension.

Pain with passive stretch of the extensor mechanism.

Pain with palpation of the superior or inferior pole of the patella.

Table 6.1

Classification of Patellar Tendinopathy According to Symptoms

Stage	Symptoms
0	No pain
1	Pain only after intense sport activity; no undue functional impairment
2	Pain at the beginning and after sport activity; still able to perform at a satisfactory level
3	Pain during sport activity; increasing difficulty performing at a satisfactory level
4	Pain during sport activity; unable to participate in sport at a satisfactory level
5	Pain during daily activity; unable to participate in sport at any level

Source: Adapted from Ferretti A, Conteduca F, Camerucci E, Morelli F. Patellar tendinosis: a follow-up study of surgical treatment. *J Bone Joint Surg Am.* 2002;84:2179-2185.

Osgood-Schlatter disease is a traction apophysitis that causes tibial osteochondrosis from the pull of the patellar tendon. It occurs in children with active growth plates, usually while they are going through growth spurts, and is typified by pain at the tibial tubercle. Sinding-Larsen-Johansson syndrome is a traction injury that causes a patellar osteochondrosis at the origin of the patellar tendon into the inferior pole of the patella.

Differential Diagnosis
Partial patellar tendon rupture, patellar bursitis, Osgood-Schlatter disease, Sinding-Larsen-Johansson syndrome.

Imaging Techniques
Lateral and AP radiographs may be obtained to assess osteophyte formation at the superior or inferior pole of the patella and calcification within the quadriceps or patellar tendons. MRI is reserved for patients with recalcitrant symptoms and those in whom surgical intervention is being considered (see Figure 6.9).

Definitive Diagnosis
Diagnosis is made based on pain in the extensor mechanism during activity, resisted knee extension, and passive stretch of the extensor mechanism; pain with palpation of the quadriceps or patellar tendons; and pain with palpation of the superior or inferior poles of the patella.

Pathomechanics and Functional Limitations
Physical activity in patients is limited by pain from the tendinopathic process. Jumping activities are among the first to be limited, followed by running, ascending and descending stairs, and walking. Weakness of the knee extensor mechanism or patellar maltracking can alter the individual's lower extremity biomechanics and cause overuse injuries anywhere along the kinetic chain.

■ Immediate Management
Quadriceps and patellar tendinopathy do not occur acutely. If the pain affects the patient's ability to function normally during an activity, ceasing activity and applying ice are warranted.

■ Medications
Initially, NSAIDs, phonophoresis, or iontophoresis may be attempted for recalcitrant symptoms; the efficacy of these techniques has not been substantiated through clinical trials, however. Corticosteroid injection is contraindicated because of the increased risk of tendon rupture.

■ Postinjury Management
Acute tendinopathy is treated with relative rest, gentle quadriceps stretching, ice, and other modalities. Nevertheless, evidence demonstrating the effectiveness of these early-phase treatments is limited. If gait is painful, an assistive device such as crutches, a cane, or an immobilizer may be used.

If tendinopathy symptoms persist for more than 6 weeks, an eccentric quadriceps exercise treatment program is the preferred first-line treatment.

■ Surgical Intervention
Surgical intervention is rarely needed. In patients with advanced tendinopathy, the surgeon may debride the patella near the insertion of the quadriceps or patellar tendon to reinitiate the healing process (see (ST) 6.4).

Practice Tip

Surgical intervention for quadriceps or patellar tendinopathy should not be performed until consistent conservative management, including an eccentric exercise program, has been implemented and deemed unsuccessful.[28]

■ Postoperative Management
The patient's knee is placed in a hinged knee brace locked in full extension, and the patient may bear weight as tolerated for the first 2 weeks of healing.

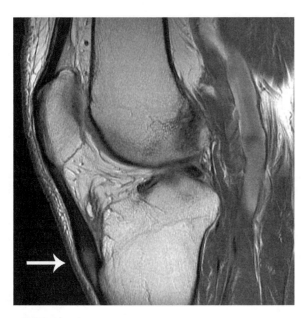

Figure 6.9 MRI demonstrating patellar tendinosis. The arrow illustrates a thickening of the patellar tendon, indicative of patellar tendinopathy.

Debridement of the Patellar or Quadriceps Tendon

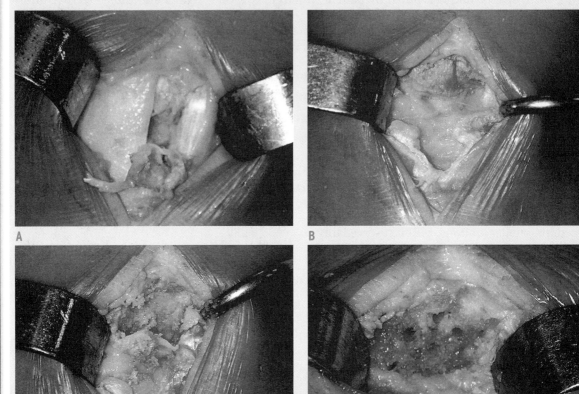

A

B

C

D

Indications

Failed conservative management.

Procedure Overview

1. An incision is made over the anterior tendon (**A**).
2. The paratenon and proximal portion of the tendon are split longitudinally (**B**).
3. The diseased areas of the tendon are identified. Gross inspection often reveals an outwardly normal appearance, however.[26]
4. The inferior pole of the patella is exposed, and a small cortical bone block is removed, along with the proximal central portion of the tendon (**C**).
5. The inferior pole of the patella is drilled to create a bleeding tissue bed conducive to healing (**D**).
6. Only the paratenon is closed.

Functional Limitations

The patient is restricted from weight bearing and motion is protected during the early healing phases.

Implications for Rehabilitation

After the initial non-weight-bearing period, the patient is permitted to ambulate in a locked brace with limited weight bearing as tolerated.

Potential Complications

Inadequate wound healing is a potential complication. Rarely, the patellar tendon may avulse or rupture after the patient returns to activity.

Comments

This procedure is reserved for patients whose symptoms do not respond to adequate conservative management.

Source: Figures reproduced with permission from Ferretti A, Conteduca F, Camerucci E, Morelli F. Patellar tendinosis: a follow-up study of surgical treatment. *J Bone Joint Surg Am.* 2002;84:2179-2185.

The patient may begin ROM exercises immediately, but extremes of flexion are avoided until the skin has healed adequately.

The patient can discontinue the brace after 4 weeks if knee flexion is at least 120°, adequate leg control is demonstrated by a normal leg raise, and the gait pattern is normal.

■ Injury-Specific Treatment and Rehabilitation Concerns

> **Specific Concerns**
>
> Control inflammation.
> Restore the normal muscle firing pattern.
> Restore the strength of the quadriceps and hamstrings.
> Emphasize proper biomechanics.

Initial rehabilitation focuses on controlling the inflammatory process. Iontophoresis using dexamethasone, with or without lidocaine, may be prescribed. Because of the superficial nature of the tissue, ice is used judiciously.

Gentle stretching exercises are begun as soon as possible; the sensation of stretch within the muscle group should be elicited. Pain at the inflamed tendon warrants modifying stretch positioning (prone with assistance from a strap versus standing) or passive stretching to eliminate this sensation. Cross-friction massage may be administered before the stretch to decrease pain and improve blood flow. Beginning with light but deep massage perpendicular to the tendon, greater pressure can be applied as the area becomes less sensitive to the applied force.

The quadriceps mechanism and the hip flexor groups are the focus of the rehabilitation effort. A generalized stretching program for both lower extremities should also be implemented. A progressive strengthening program is instituted to the patient's tolerance. In patients with severe, longstanding patellar or quadriceps tendinopathy, moderate to severe atrophy may be present.

Although the focus is on open and closed kinetic chain exercises for the quadriceps mechanism, a complete trunk, pelvic, and lower extremity program should be included. Proximal stabilization is essential, and eccentric control of the quadriceps musculature needs to be emphasized. Isokinetics may also be helpful in strengthening the quadriceps under conditions that better replicate the higher-speed contractions needed during jumping and landing from a jump.

When the patient is pain free and has adequate flexibility and strength, plyometric training is beneficial in preparing for the return to competitive activities. Initially, the focus must be on proper technique, progressing to endurance training for the athlete who must jump repetitively. On successful completion of a plyometric program, sport-specific drills can begin.

> **Practice Tip**
>
> Eccentric strengthening exercises for the quadriceps musculature are a key component of successful rehabilitation programs for patellar and quadriceps tendinopathy.[29,30]

■ Estimated Amount of Time Lost

Decreased or restricted activity for 1 to 4 weeks is required for conservative treatment, which should be tried for at least 6 months before surgery is considered. For minor symptoms, activity modification is favored over surgical treatment.

Patients whose symptoms interfere with their normal sports and daily activities and who fail to respond to conservative measures may require surgery.[31] Time lost after surgery can vary from 3 to 6 months, depending on the patient's ability to reverse the effects of previous inactivity and postsurgical morbidity.

■ Return-to-Play Criteria

The patient may return to competition when pain is absent, ROM is full, lower extremity and particularly quadriceps strength has been restored, and functional, agility, and sport-specific tests are successfully completed.

Functional Bracing

A patellar strap may be worn, but the success of and patients' tolerance for this device vary widely. A simple knee sleeve with a patellar cutout may be useful in increasing warmth within the quadriceps or patellar tendons, although evidence for its effectiveness in pain relief or healing is lacking.

Patellar Tendon Rupture

The patellar tendon is placed under high tensile forces during athletic activities, especially when the quadriceps femoris muscles are contracting eccentrically. This force becomes magnified if a fall is sustained on the patella while the quadriceps muscles are contracting eccentrically. The result-

CLINICAL PRESENTATION

History

Forceful contraction of the quadriceps, especially when the knee is flexed.
Immediate pain and disability.

Observation

Obvious defect at the rupture site.
Swelling from hemarthrosis.

Functional Status

Inability to straighten the leg against gravity or resistance.
Inability to bear weight.
Some knee extension may be possible if the patellar retinaculum is intact.

Physical Examination Findings

Passive flexion is limited by pain and swelling.
The patient is unable to maintain a passively extended knee against gravity.
A palpable defect is present in a complete rupture.

ing force can overwhelm the tendon and lead to a patellar tendon rupture or patellar fracture.

Although tendon ruptures are classified as suprapatellar or infrapatellar, complete tendon ruptures are rare (see **Figure 6.10**). Suprapatellar tendon ruptures are also known as quadriceps tendon ruptures. Both types of ruptures tend to occur in athletic patients who are 30 to 50 years old and are often the end result of long-term tendinopathy but may occur with a maximal eccentric quadriceps contraction in a person who has had no prior symptoms. Patellar tendon rupture also is a potential complication after anterior cruciate ligament reconstruction when the middle third of the patellar tendon is harvested as donor tissue, although rates of this complication are extremely low.

The course of treatment for a partial tendon tear depends on the severity of the injury. A low-grade, partial tear may be treated conservatively

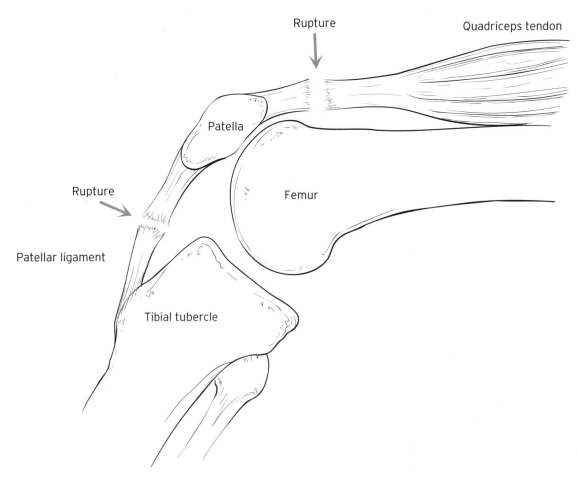

Figure 6.10   Common areas of ruptures in the extensor mechanism. *Source:* Reproduced with permission from Greene WB (ed). *Essentials of Musculoskeletal Care*, ed 2. Rosemont, IL: American Academy of Orthopaedic Surgeons; 2000: 404.

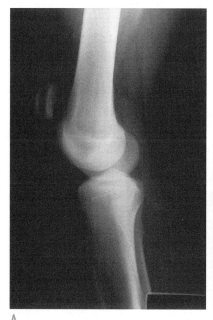
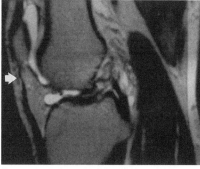
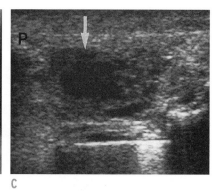

A   B   C

Figure 6.11 Imaging modalities for patellar tendon ruptures. (**A**) A lateral radiograph of the knee indicates a high-riding patella (patella alta). The entire patella is superior to the Blumensaat line (a line drawn parallel to the intercondylar notch). (**B**) A sagittal magnetic resonance image of the patellar tendon demonstrates a rupture near the infrapatellar pole (arrow). (**C**) A sagittal ultrasonic image indicates an acute tear of the mid-substance of the tendon (arrow) (P, patella).

with rehabilitation. If most of the tendon is rup- tured, however, the tear may need to be treated surgically.

Differential Diagnosis

Patellar fracture, patellar dislocation.

Imaging Techniques

Lateral and AP views are obtained to rule out bone injury. Secondary patella alta from complete ten- don rupture is easily identified using lateral radio- graphs. MRI is helpful if there is any question about the extent of the injury or if a concomitant injury to surrounding tissues is suspected (see Figure 6.11). Diagnostic ultrasound can also be used to visualize a tendon rupture.

Definitive Diagnosis

A partial tear is characterized by pain and extensor- mechanism weakness. The partial defect may be palpable, and the patient can hold the knee in a passively extended position. With a complete tear, the patient may be unable to actively maintain the passively extended knee against gravity; if the reti- naculum is also torn, the patient cannot extend the knee against gravity. A defect may be palpable at the rupture site. In all cases, the extent of the rup- ture can be confirmed by MRI.

Pathomechanics and Functional Limitations

Acutely, the patient with a partial tear is unable to bear weight without pain and has the sensation of

the knee "giving way." With a complete rupture, the patient is immediately unable to generate forces in the quadriceps mechanism and cannot maintain body weight against gravity.

▦ Immediate Management

The knee should be placed in a straight-leg immo- bilizer and the patient given crutches. Ice can be applied. The foot should be placed on the ground with minimal weight bearing—a stance that gives the patient greater stability while standing.

▦ Medications

Analgesic medications are helpful in controlling pain.

▦ Postinjury Management

The knee is placed in a hinged knee brace locked in extension until a decision on surgery versus conservative rehabilitation is reached. Aspiration of the hemarthrosis can make the patient more comfortable.

▦ Surgical Intervention

Patellar tendon rupture is best treated with surgical repair, to be undertaken within 7 to 10 days after the injury. Simple end-to-end suturing of the patellar de- fect alone or in conjunction with a cerclage suture is most commonly performed (see ⓈⓉ 6.5).[32] Suture

cerclage Encircling a structure with a ring or loop.

Repair of a Patellar Tendon Rupture

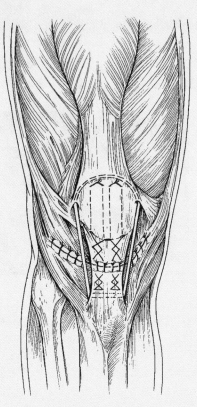

Indications

Definitive diagnosis of a patellar tendon rupture.

Procedure Overview

1. The tendon is exposed through a horseshoe midline incision.
2. The frayed tendon ends are debrided to yield a bed of viable tissue.
3. Three holes are drilled through the longitudinal length of the patella.
4. Sutures are woven through the distal tendon across the defect into the proximal portion of the tendon and then passed through the transpatellar holes. Suture anchors can replace these two steps and provide excellent fixation during the healing phase.
5. If a cerclage suture or tape is to be used, a hole is drilled transversely through the tibial tubercle posterior to the tendon insertion. The suture or surgical tape is placed through this hole, taken up over the patella, and passed posterior to the quadriceps tendon.
6. The sutures are clamped but not tied.
7. A lateral radiograph is obtained to determine whether the height of the patella is similar to that of the patella in the contralateral leg. Next, the sutures are tightened or loosened until the tension is adequate to restore normal tendon length. The sutures are then tied over the superior pole of the patella, and the cerclage suture or tape is tied off.
8. If the patellar tendon is avulsed from the inferior pole of the patella, suture anchors can be used with the suture woven through the tendon stump distally and tied as the tendon is reduced onto the patella.

Functional Limitations

Limitations are related to the severity of the injury and the speed of recovery from surgical repair.

Implications for Rehabilitation

During rehabilitation, it is important to protect the extensor mechanism with a hinged knee brace so as to limit ROM.

Potential Complications

Failure of the fixation is a potential complication. Difficulty regaining flexion may necessitate manipulation under anesthesia to break up fibrosis once the extensor mechanism has adequate healing.

Comments

A fine line exists between healing the extensor mechanism and regaining functional ROM. More problems tend to develop in quadriceps tendon repairs than in patellar tendon repairs.

Source: Figure reproduced with permission from Matava MJ. Patellar tendon ruptures. *J Am Acad Orthop Surg.* 1996;4:287-296.

anchors are being used more frequently, and the use of porcine scaffolding graft is also gaining acceptance as a means to augment the surgical repair.

Postoperative Management

A compressive dressing is applied to the knee, which is placed in extension in a locked hinged knee brace. The patient can bear weight by toe-touch during crutch-assisted walking. Active quadriceps isometrics should be performed on the first postoperative day. At 2 weeks after surgery, the skin sutures are removed, and formal rehabilitation begins.

Injury-Specific Treatment and Rehabilitation Concerns

> **Specific Concerns**
> Control loads placed on the extensor mechanism.
> Minimize quadriceps atrophy.
> Prevent arthrofibrosis secondary to decreased ROM during the immobilization period.

The patient continues to wear the locked brace for ambulation. Weight bearing is progressed at 4 weeks after surgery, with the goal of achieving full weight bearing in the locked brace by 6 weeks. During this time, the patient can perform gait training with the brace unlocked. The brace can be discontinued when flexion is at least 120°, control of the extensor mechanism without an extensor lag on straight-leg raise is adequate, and normal gait is possible.

Passive ROM exercises are initiated from full extension to 45°. Increasing flexion by approximately 30° per week is appropriate; greater flexion should not be forced. At approximately 6 weeks after surgery, the patient can begin prone stretching to activate the quadriceps mechanism. Patellar mobilization can be performed, but superior glides should be performed only out of necessity and with caution. Superior glides are not recommended until at least 4 to 6 weeks postoperatively.

At approximately 2 weeks after surgery, the patient begins leg raising in all planes, performed with active quadriceps setting during the exercise; leg raises can be performed with the brace on until adequate leg control is attained. Active knee extension begins at 3 weeks through the available ROM. If an extensor lag is present, the leg can be passively extended, and the patient can first work on eccentric contrac-

tions of the muscle group. Heavy loads are not added until at least 8 weeks postoperatively. Closed kinetic chain strengthening exercises can begin as soon as the patient is bearing at least 50% weight on the injured leg. Single-leg closed kinetic chain activities can progress when the patient is bearing full weight.

The patient may begin stationary bicycle riding as soon as sufficient ROM is available without any compensatory movements at other joints. Walking on a treadmill or elliptical glider or exercising on a ski machine can begin when the patient is capable of bearing full weight. However, these exercises must be performed without compensation or deviation. As the patient tires, especially early in the course of the rehabilitation program, the exercise should be halted for that session.

Aquatic therapy can be an excellent choice for this patient population. Exercises for ROM and strengthening can begin as the wound is healed, and actual swimming can begin at about 6 to 8 weeks. The patient can return to running at 4 months if no gait deviations are noted.

Estimated Amount of Time Lost

Estimated rehabilitation time is 4 to 6 months after surgical repair. Postoperative complications—including arthrofibrosis, patella baja, or patella alta—that affect the ability of the quadriceps mechanism to produce force can delay the rehabilitation process.

Return-to-Play Criteria

The patient may return to competition when pain is absent, full ROM is achieved, quadriceps strength is restored, and functional tests for the lower extremity are completed successfully. Typically, this point is reached 6 months after the repair.

Functional Bracing
A neoprene knee sleeve may be used for comfort.

Patellar Fracture

The primary mechanism of patellar fractures is similar to that of a patellar tendon rupture—namely, falling on the patella when the quadriceps is contracting eccentrically. A patellar fracture associated only with quadriceps muscle contraction is rare and usually results from a preexisting patellar stress fracture.[33]

Patellar fractures are classified as shown in **Figure 6.12**. After injury, articular surface congruency

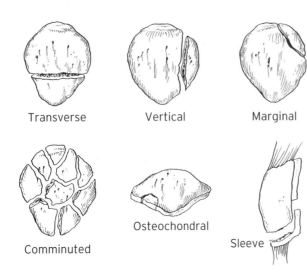

Transverse   Vertical   Marginal

Comminuted   Osteochondral   Sleeve

Figure 6.12 Classification of patellar fractures based on the configuration of the fracture lines. *Source:* Reproduced with permission from Cramer KE, Moed BR. Patellar fractures: contemporary approach to treatment. *J Am Acad Orthop Surg.* 1997;5:323-331.

must be restored to prevent decreased torque production from the extensor mechanism and to limit abnormal joint reaction force patterns at the patellofemoral articulation.

Differential Diagnosis

Patellar tendon rupture, quadriceps tendon rupture, patellar dislocation, bipartite patella.

Imaging Techniques

Lateral and AP radiographs are taken to determine the status of the fracture, including the number of fragments present and their positions (see **Figure 6.13**). If axial views are attainable, they can be helpful in

---

CLINICAL PRESENTATION

History

A fall or direct blow to the patella.
Pain arising from the patella.

Observation

Swelling over and around the patella.
Acute hemarthrosis.
Deformity of the patella may be noted, although it may be masked by edema.

Functional Status

The patient is unable to bear weight on the involved leg.
During flexion and extension, ROM is decreased; extension lags at least 10° to 30°.[33]
Inhibition of the quadriceps mechanism is evidenced by an inability to produce force.

Physical Examination Findings

Inability to generate force across the extensor mechanism to perform a straight-leg raise.

---

determining the congruity of the articular surface of the patella.

Definitive Diagnosis

Radiographic findings will demonstrate the presence of the fracture.

Pathomechanics and Functional Limitations

Fracturing the patella disrupts the ability of the extensor mechanism to generate forces across the knee. Both activities of daily living and sport

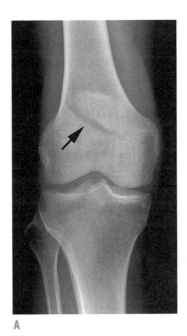
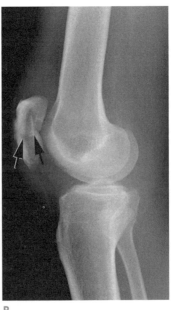

A   B

Figure 6.13 Radiographs of patellar fractures. (**A**) AP view demonstrating an oblique fracture through the superior patella (arrow). (**B**) Lateral view demonstrating a fracture of the body of the patella (left arrow) and a step-off of the articular surface (right arrow).

activities are severely limited with this injury. Occasionally, if the fracture is nondisplaced or vertical, enough integrity may remain in the extensor mechanism to allow a weak straight-leg raise. However, with displacement, the extensor-mechanism disruption limits the ability to perform a straight-leg raise.

Immediate Management

The knee is immobilized in a position of comfort; full extension is preferred if possible. Ice can be applied, and crutches are used for non-weight-bearing ambulation.

Medications

Narcotic analgesics can be used to control the initial pain. NSAIDs should be avoided, as these agents may inhibit bony healing. Acetaminophen can be used for longer-term pain control as needed.

Postinjury Management

A tense effusion can be aspirated to provide pain relief. Lacerations and abrasions must be actively managed with a wound-care program of cleaning and proper dressings. Adequate healing of any wounds is essential to minimize a surgical delay because of wound problems. The presence of surface wounds may constitute an open fracture—an injury that should be managed surgically.[34,35] The knee is placed in an immobilizer in full extension to minimize stress across the extensor mechanism. Ice can continue to be used before surgery.

Surgical Intervention

Except when the patellar fracture is a small avulsion, this type of injury almost always requires fixation using various techniques, including screw fixation or Kirschner wires and tension-band loops (see **ST** 6.6). Soft-tissue repairs to the retinaculum and quadriceps muscle can be performed as well.

The arthroscopically assisted surgical approach has been advocated as a means of avoiding skin problems, allowing early rehabilitation, and achieving better cosmesis.[36] With this technique, the surgical fixation is similar to that obtained from an open technique but is guided by an arthroscope and fluoroscopy.

Postoperative Management

The leg is placed in a compressive dressing and locked in extension in a hinged knee brace. Diligent attention must be directed toward wound care and adequate wound healing. After 3 to 4 days, the bulky dressing is removed and the wound assessed. At 1 week, the patient begins submaximal quadriceps setting and passive ROM that does not stress the wound.

Initially the patient is restricted from weight bearing and on crutches for 3 to 4 weeks. Partial weight bearing is then permitted until adequate fracture healing is demonstrated on radiographs, at about 6 to 8 weeks.

Injury-Specific Treatment and Rehabilitation Concerns

> **Specific Concerns**
> Control stresses across the healing fracture site.
> Encourage the healing of articular cartilage.

As the fracture heals, the patient can progress knee ROM, albeit limiting the amount of stress placed on the wound. Initially, this type of exercise is performed with passive ROM and then advanced to active-assisted ROM. Flexion past 90° is not pursued until adequate bone healing has occurred, usually 6 to 8 weeks after fixation. However, tension-band wiring may allow for mobilization at 4 to 6 weeks. Patellar mobilization is not performed until adequate fracture healing is demonstrated.

Submaximal quadriceps setting and electrical stimulation can begin at 2 to 3 weeks postoperatively. Early on, leg-raising activities are begun in all directions. The quadriceps and VMO are contracted simultaneously with the hip musculature during hip exercises. Active exercises for strengthening the quadriceps are progressed at 6 to 8 weeks. Maximal quadriceps contractions should not begin until the fracture has fully healed, at approximately 8 weeks after surgery. The patient proceeds through open and closed kinetic chain strengthening for the entire lower extremity.

Flexibility exercises for the hip musculature, hamstrings, and triceps surae groups are performed as tolerated. Quadriceps muscle flexibility exercises are not begun until the fracture has healed adequately.

Estimated Amount of Time Lost

Return to full activity may be possible at 4 to 6 months. Participation in sports requiring heavy

Surgical Technique 6.6

Open Reduction and Internal Fixation of Patellar Fractures

A   B

Indications

Fracture of the patella. The fixation technique varies according to the type and orientation of the fracture line.

Procedure Overview

1. A vertical incision is made, and the fracture is identified.
2. The joint is inspected through the defect to visualize the femoral condyles and trochlear groove and identify all defects and damage.
3. The patellar articular surface is palpated.
4. Thorough irrigation and probing are undertaken to extract any fragments.
5. The fracture configuration is determined by direct visualization. The fragment borders are cleaned to aid in the fracture reduction.
6. Fragments are drilled and Kirschner wires placed to hold the fragments in place for fixation.
7. Cannulated-screw systems have become popular because the fixation screw is placed directly over the temporary wire fixation. The fracture configuration dictates the fixation technique to be used.
8. Figure-of-eight **cerclage** wiring can augment the fixation. If comminution is severe, it may be the only option.
9. Often, capsular defects medially and laterally accompany a transverse patellar fracture and must be sutured and repaired.

Functional Limitations

Healing must occur before aggressive ROM and strengthening exercises can be initiated.

Implications for Rehabilitation

After surgery, the knee is placed in a controlled-motion brace and the patient is limited in weight bearing. Early open kinetic chain exercises are initiated when pain allows. As healing is documented, ROM and progressive resistance exercises are advanced. Complete healing takes place in 6 to 8 weeks.

Potential Complications

Failure or loss of fixation and posttraumatic arthritis are the most common complications. Also, retained hardware can become painful postoperatively.

Comments

Patellar fractures should be managed acutely. Skin defects should be thoroughly probed to determine whether the defect extends into the fracture. Although reestablishing the articular surface to limit posttraumatic arthritis is preferred, the fracture configuration ultimately dictates the fixation options. High degrees of comminution (which usually occurs in the distal pole of the patella) may require excision of some of the fragments.

Source: Figures reproduced with permission from Boden BP, Pearsall AW, Garrett WE, Feagin JA. Patellofemoral instability: evaluation and management. *J Am Acad Orthop Surg.* 1997;5:47–57.

quadriceps loads, such as jumping, is associated with increased time required to return to full activity.

■ Return-to-Play Criteria

The patient may return to competition when pain is resolved, full ROM is achieved, quadriceps strength is restored, and functional, agility, and sport-specific tests are successfully completed.

Functional Bracing

A knee sleeve with a patellar cutout may be used to increase warmth to the area. A Drytex or elastic material is preferred over neoprene to avoid skin breakdown.

Rehabilitation

This section presents treatment techniques that are unique to the patellofemoral articulation. Refer to the knee rehabilitation section in Chapter 5 and Chapter 8 for therapeutic exercises for the patellofemoral joint, knee, and lower extremity.

Patellar Mobilization

Patellar mobilization may be indicated for conditions of the interrelated patellofemoral joint and knee. An injury to one joint can adversely affect the other joint. To perform patellar mobilization, the patient should be supine or sitting off the edge of the table. While the patient is in the supine po-

sition, an adjustable bolster can be placed under the knee to modify the amount of extension. Having the patient sitting off the edge of the table assists in performing mobilizations with the knee in varying degrees of flexion. The patient's leg can then be placed over the clinician's leg to alter the amount of flexion.

Mobilization routines may be performed more easily if an interface between the clinician's hand and the patient's skin is used to better grasp the patella. Gauze pads, a damp towel, or a rubber material such as a jar opener can be used for this purpose. The patella is moved inferiorly, superiorly, medially, or laterally until resistance is felt, and the position is held for at least 30 seconds to attain a low-load, prolonged stretch (see **Figure 6.14**).

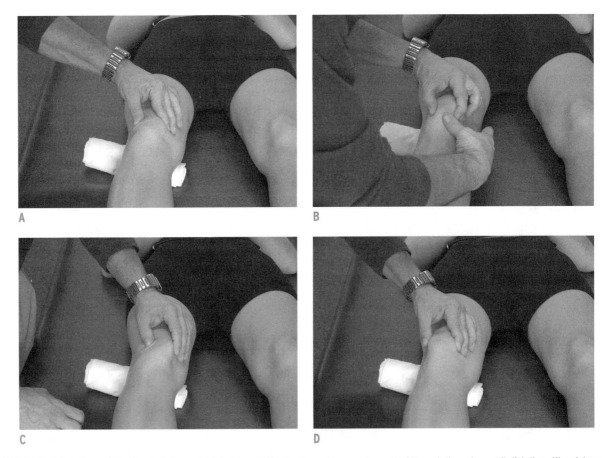

A

B

C

D

Figure 6.14   Patellar mobilization techniques. (**A**) *Inferior mobilization.* Grasp the superior pole of the patella and move it distally until resistance is felt. (**B**) *Superior mobilization.* Grasp the inferior patellar pole and move the patella proximally until resistance is felt. (**C**) *Medial mobilization.* Grasp the patella with the thumbs on the lateral side and the forefingers on the medial side. Glide the patella medially until resistance is felt. (**D**) *Lateral mobilization.* Grasp the patella firmly between the thumbs on the lateral side and the forefingers on the medial side.

Extra caution is required when performing lateral patellar mobilization. This technique is similar to the apprehension test and may result in patient anxiety. At minimum, a set of 5 repetitions should be performed, although the amount of mobilization should be tailored to each patient. As with any stretching of soft tissues, two to three sets of the mobilization should be performed throughout the day.

Patellar Tendon Cross-Friction Massage

With this technique, the patient is supine with the knee on a bolster or sitting over the edge of the table. The clinician's forefinger and middle finger deliver massage strokes perpendicularly to the patellar tendon. As the tendon becomes less sensitive, the pressure being applied should be increased.

Iliotibial Band Trigger-Point Massage

Numerous trigger points may form within the length of the iliotibial band as the result of patellofemoral dysfunction. Trigger-point massage is performed with the patient lying on the side opposite the injury. Positioning a pillow or towels between the patient's legs enhances the relaxation.

With the thumb or a commercially available device, start with light but deep pressure to the trigger point. The pressure is then increased to the patient's tolerance, and the massage is performed for about 30 to 60 seconds. The iliotibial band should be stretched immediately after the massage.

Patellar Taping

Patellar taping as developed by McConnell has become a popular adjunct to the treatment of patellofemoral conditions.[37] This taping pattern focuses on creating a more appropriate alignment of the patella as it tracks within the femoral trochlea, thereby decreasing pain and improving function (see **Figure 6.15**).

> **Practice Tip**
>
> Research on the effectiveness of McConnell taping has provided positive results for significantly reducing pain and increasing function specifically in patients with PFPS.[38-41]

After a thorough examination, patellar taping can be used as an adjunct to rehabilitation. The specific applications of the McConnell taping techniques are beyond the scope of this text, but in general the techniques attempt to correct patellar glide, tilt, and rotation (see **Table 6.2**).

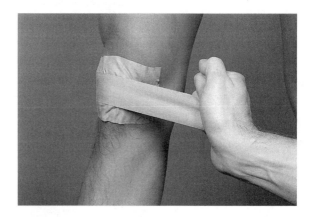

Figure 6.15 The McConnell taping technique. This figure shows the patella being moved medially.

Table 6.2

Patellar Taping

Position	Findings	Technique
Glide: the medial or lateral displacement of the patella	The critical test: The clinician manually blocks the patella into a medial glide as the patient performs isometric quadriceps contractions throughout the ROM. Decreased pain indicates a laterally gliding patella.	Tape is secured at the lateral border of the patella. The clinician applies a medial manual glide, takes up soft tissue along the medial aspect of the thigh, and secures the tape along the medial femoral condyle.
Tilt: (1) the anterior-posterior orientation with respect to the medial and lateral facet orientation to the femur or (2) the superior-inferior orientation with respect to the superior and inferior pole orientation to the femur	The clinician places the thumb and index finger along the medial and lateral borders of the patella, with the patient's knee extended and the quadriceps relaxed. The orientation of the patellar borders is assessed. (Tight lateral structures are presumed to cause the lateral border to rest lower than the medial border.) This process is repeated with the superior and inferior poles of the patella.	To correct a tilt, tape is placed opposite the tilt and secured to correct the alignment. For example, to correct a lateral tilt, the tape is placed along the medial aspect of the patella. The clinician applies a medial manual tilt, takes up soft tissue along the medial aspect of the thigh, and secures the tape along the medial femoral condyle.
Rotation: a comparison of the longitudinal axis of the patella with the longitudinal axis of the femur	The clinician determines the longitudinal axis of the patella by palpating the midpoint of the superior and inferior poles of the patella. The line formed by these two points is considered the axis of the patella and is compared with the axis of the femur. With an externally rotated patella, the inferior patellar pole sits laterally compared with the femur's longitudinal axis. With an internally rotated patella, the inferior patellar pole sits medially compared with the femur's longitudinal axis.	Correction of an externally rotated patella: Tape is secured laterally along the inferior border of the patella. The inferior pole of the patella is manually rotated into a neutral position, and the tape is secured superiorly along the medial aspect of the femoral condyle. Correction of an internally rotated patella: The tape is secured superiorly along the lateral border of the patella. The patella is manually corrected, and the tape is secured inferiorly along the medial aspect of the femoral condyle.

References

1. Powers CM, Ward SR, Fredericson M, et al. Patello-femoral kinematics during weight-bearing and non-weight-bearing knee extension in persons with lateral subluxation of the patella: a preliminary study. *J Orthop Sports Physl Ther.* 2003;33(11):677–685.

2. Lee T, Morris G, Csintalan R. The influence of tibial and femoral rotation on patellofemoral contact area and pressure. *J Orthop Sports Physl Ther.* 2003;33(11):686–693.

3. Huberti HH, Hayes WC. Patellofemoral contact pressures: the influence of Q angle and tendofemoral contact. *J Bone Joint Surg.* 1984;66A(5):715–724.

4. Inoue M, Shino K, Hirose H, et al. Sub-luxation of the patella: Computed tomography analysis of patellofemoral congruence. *J Bone Joint Surg Am.* 1988;70:1331–1337.

5. Jones RB, Barlett EC, Vainright JR, Carroll RG. CT determination of tibial tubercle lateralization in patients presenting with anterior knee pain. *Skeletal Radiol.* 1995;24:505–509.

6. Witonski D. Dynamic magnetic resonance imaging. *Clin Sports Med.* 2002;21:403–415.

7. Johnson LL. Arthroscopic abrasion arthroplasty: a review. *Clin Orthop.* 2001;391(suppl):S306–S317.

8. Steadman JR, Rodkey WG, Rodrigo JJ. Microfracture: surgical technique and rehabilitation to treat chondral defects. *Clin Orthop.* 2001;391(suppl):S362–S369.

9. Aminaka N, Gribble PA. A systematic review of the effects of therapeutic taping on patellofemoral pain syndrome. *J Athl Train.* 2005;40(4):341–351.

10. Witvrouw E, Lysens R, Bellemans J, et al. Open versus closed kinetic chain exercises for patellofemoral pain. *Am J Sports Med.* 2000;28(5):687–694.

11. Micheli LJ. Patellofemoral disorders in children, in Fox JM, Del Pizzo W (eds), *The Patellofemoral Joint.* New York, NY: McGraw-Hill; 1993:105–121.

12. Cash JD, Hughston JC. Treatment of acute patellar dislocation. *Am J Sports Med.* 1988;16:244–249.

13. Schreiber SN. Proximal superomedial portal in arthroscopy of the knee. *Arthroscopy.* 1991;7:246–251.

14. Kolowich PA, Paulos LE, Rosenberg TD, Farnsworth S. Lateral release of the patella: indications and contraindications. *Am J Sports Med.* 1990;18:359–365.

15. Post WR, Teitge R, Amis A. Patellofemoral malalignment: looking beyond the viewbox. *Clin Sports Med.* 2002; 21:521–546.

16. Metcalf RW. An arthroscopic method for lateral release of subluxating or dislocating patella. *Clin Orthop.* 1982; 167:9–18.

17. Betz RR, Magill JT III, Lonergan RP. The percutaneous lateral retinacular release. *Am J Sports Med.* 1987; 15:477–482.

18. Boden BP, Pearsall AW, Garrett WE, Feagin JA Jr. Patellofemoral instability: evaluation and management. *J Am Acad Orthop Surg.* 1997;5:47–57.

19. Ricchetti ET, Mehta S, Sennett BJ, Huffman GR. Comparison of lateral release versus lateral release with medial soft-tissue realignment for the treatment of recurrent patellar instability: a systematic review. *Arthroscopy.* 2007;23(5):463–468.

20. Fulkerson JP. Patellofemoral pain disorders: evaluation and management. *J Am Acad Orthop Surg.* 1994;2:124–132.

21. Hauser EW. Total tendon transplant for slipping patella. *Surg Gynecol Obstet.* 1938;66:199–214.

22. Cox JS. Evaluation of the Roux-Elmslie-Trillat procedure for knee extensor realignment. *Am J Sports Med.* 1982; 10:303–310.

23. Fulkerson JP. Fracture of the proximal tibia after Fulkerson anteromedial tibial tubercle transfer: a report of four cases. *Am J Sports Med.* 1999;27:265.

24. Maffulli N, Wong J, Almekinders L. Types and epidemiology of tendinopathy. *Clin Sports Med.* 2003;22:675–692.

25. Richards DP, Ajemian SV, Wiley JP, Zernicke RF. Knee joint dynamics predict patellar tendonitis in elite volleyball players. *Am J Sports Med.* 1996;24:676–683.

26. Ferretti A, Conteduca F, Camerucci E, Morelli F. Patellar tendinosis: a follow-up study of surgical treatment. *J Bone Joint Surg Am.* 2002;84:2179–2185.

27. Blazina ME, Kerlan RK, Jobe FW, et al. Jumper's knee. *Orthop Clin North Am.* 1973;4:665–678.

28. Panni AS, Tartarone M, Maffulli N. Patellar tendinopathy in athletes: outcome of nonoperative and operative management. *Am J Sports Med.* 2000;28(3):392–397.

29. Jonsson P, Alfredson H. Superior results with eccentric compared to concentric quadriceps training in patients with jumper's knee: a prospective randomised study. *Br J Sports Med.* 2005;39:847–850.

30. Purdam C, Jonsson P, Alfredson H, et al. A pilot study of the eccentric decline squat in the management of painful chronic patellar tendinopathy. *Br J Sports Med.* 2004; 38:395–397.

31. Popp JE, Yu JS, Kaeding CC. Recalcitrant patellar tendinitis: magnetic resonance imaging, histologic evaluation, and surgical treatment. *Am J Sports Med.* 1997;25: 218–222.

32. Matava M. Patellar tendon ruptures. *J Am Acad Orthop Surg.* 1996;4:287–296.

33. Hohl M, Johnson EE, Wiss DA. Fractures of the knee, in Rockwood CA, Green DP, Buchholz RW (eds), *Rockwood and Green's Fractures in Adults,* ed 3. Philadelphia, PA: JB Lippincott; 1991:1725–1797.

34. Johnson EE. Fractures of the patella, in Rockwood CA Jr, Green DP, Heckman JD (eds), *Rockwood and Green's Fractures in Adults,* ed 4. Philadelphia, PA: Lippincott-Raven; 1996:1956–1972.

35. Whittle AP. Fractures of the lower extremity, in Canale ST (ed), *Campbell's Operative Orthopedics.* St. Louis, MO: Mosby; 1998:2042–2179.

36. Turgut A, Gunal I, Acar S, et al. Arthroscopic-assisted percutaneous stabilization of patellar fractures. *Clin Orthop.* 2001;389:57–61.

37. McConnell J. The management of chondromalacia patellae: a long-term solution. *Aust J Physiother.* 1986;32:215–223.

38. Whittingham M, Palmer S, Macmillan F. Effects of taping on pain and function in patellofemoral pain syndrome: a randomized controlled trial. *J Orthop Sports Phys Ther.* 2004;34(9):504–510.

39. Crossley KM, Bennell KL, Green S, et al. Physical therapy for patellofemoral pain: a randomized, double-blinded, placebo-controlled trial. *Am J Sports Med.* 2002;30(6): 857–865.

40. Clark DI, Downing N, Mitchell J, et al. Physiotherapy for anterior knee pain: a randomised controlled trial. *Ann Rheumat Dis.* 2000;59:700–704.

41. Harrison EI, Sheppard MS, McQuarrie AM. A randomized controlled trial of physical therapy treatment programs in patellofemoral pain syndrome. *Physiother Can.* 1999;51(2):93–100.

CHAPTER 7

Femur, Hip, and Pelvis Injuries

Benjamin Domb, MD
Derrick Brown, ATC, PA-C

Strains

CLINICAL PRESENTATION

Adductor Strains	Hamstring Strains	Quadriceps Strains
History		
Sudden eccentric contraction of the adductor muscles. Sudden pain and tenderness at the site of injury.	Sudden, powerful eccentric contraction of the hamstring muscles. Risk increases when the hamstring muscles are fatigued or weak.	Sudden contraction of the quadriceps muscle. A sudden sprint or change of direction, a fall down the steps, or a clean-and-jerk maneuver when lifting weights.
Observation		
Secondary muscle spasm. Gradual onset of swelling and discoloration.	Secondary spasm develops quickly. Ecchymosis may occur within 2 days. A defect in the muscle contour may be palpated in a grade II or III injury.	A defect in the distal quadriceps may be apparent. Significant swelling. Muscle spasm. Ecchymosis.
Functional Status		
The patient may walk with an antalgic gait. Adduction against resistance is painful. Abduction in the terminal range of motion (ROM) may be deficient secondary to pain.	The patient may walk with an antalgic gait. Knee extension with hip flexion against resistance is painful, as are straight-leg raises. Full hip extension with concomitant knee flexion ROM may be less than on the injured side secondary to pain and spasm.	Grade I and II strains: · Decreased strength in the affected leg · Antalgic gait Grade III strain: · Inability to bear weight on the extremity · Inability to lift the leg · A stiff-legged gait is possible
Physical Examination Findings		
A palpable defect may be noted. Moving the leg into full abduction to stretch the injured muscle results in pain.	Muscle palpation and resistance testing produce pain. Muscle stretching produces pain. During resisted ROM, the foot rotates away from the involved portion of the muscle.	Grade I and II strains: · Limited flexion ROM · Manual muscle tests demonstrate weakness in the involved leg for knee extension and, possibly, hip flexion (if the rectus femoris is involved) Grade III strain: · Lack of active knee extension, especially against gravity

7

Adductor Strains

Adductor strains occur in sports that require strong eccentric muscle action of the adductors, such as hockey, fencing, handball, hurdling, high jumping, cross-country skiing, and especially soccer.[1,2] The adductor longus is the most frequently injured, possibly because of its relatively poor mechanical advantage.[1] This muscle tends to be injured at the musculotendinous junction. The mechanism of injury is usually a sudden, passive lengthening with a simultaneous active muscle contraction. The risk of adductor strains increases if the strength ratio between the adductors and abductors is less than 80%.[3] A history of previous adductor strains is also predictive of future episodes.[3]

Hamstring Strains

Hamstring muscle (semimembranosus, semitendinosus, and biceps femoris) strains are common in athletes who rely on the hamstring muscle group to decelerate the quadriceps during explosive activities, such as sprinting, jumping, and kicking. Hamstring strains are frequently noted in athletes participating in sprinting sports such as soccer, baseball, track sprinting, football, basketball, and rugby.[4] Avulsion injuries typically occur during activities such as ice skating, weight lifting, and water skiing, when sudden stress loads are placed on the isometrically contracting muscle group.[5]

Because the hamstring group comprises two-joint muscles that act concentrically at the hip and eccentrically at the knee during activity, it is at greater risk of injury. In addition, the biceps femoris has two heads originating from two different locations—one on the ischium and the other on the femoral shaft. Muscles with this type of compound origin and different innervations for the two heads are termed "hybrid muscles." The sudden change in function from concentric to eccentric motion during activity makes the hamstring group susceptible to injury. Hamstring strains tend to occur between the musculotendinous junction, either proximally near the tendon insertion onto the ischial tuberosity or more toward the midbelly of the muscle, where tendon slips extend (see **Figure 7.1**).[5]

The rate of reinjury is high when the quadriceps-to-hamstring strength ratio, left-to-right strength comparisons, and flexibility are not restored before returning to participation. The strength of the left and right hamstring groups should not differ by more than 10%. Ratios between the quadriceps and hamstring can be determined using isokinetic equipment. Although expected ratios vary by sport, a normal isokinetic range for the hamstring is 50% to 60% of quadriceps strength.

> **sports hernia** The combination of an adductor strain, abdominal strain, and osteitis pubis.

■ Quadriceps Strains

One of the quadriceps group's muscles, the rectus femoris, has a two-joint configuration, predisposing it to injury. The rectus femoris frequently works simultaneously at the hip and knee, with one end performing a concentric activity and the other end performing an eccentric contraction. A severe rectus femoris strain can result in an avulsion fracture at the proximal insertion on the anterior inferior iliac spine. The large amount of torque produced by the quadriceps muscle group and the dynamic forces placed on the lower extremity predispose the muscles to rupture (grade III strain). A rupture between

> **baja** An unexpectedly low position.

the patella and distal insertion is a patellar tendon rupture. A rupture that occurs between the origin of the individual muscles of the quadriceps group and the patella is a quadriceps tendon rupture. Both injuries disrupt the knee extensor mechanism. Individuals sustaining these injuries are usually older, between 30 and 60 years, with no history of quadriceps muscle or tendon injury. Long-term use of anabolic steroids may increase the risk of rupture.[6] In grade II and III strains, the patient should be evaluated for concurrent trauma of the cruciate ligaments, collateral ligaments, and menisci of the knee.

Differential Diagnosis
Adductors

For adductor strains, differential diagnoses include intra-abdominal trauma, genitourinary abnormalities, osteitis pubis, referred lumbosacral disorders, and hip injuries (see **Box 7.1**).[2] The possibility of hamstring or iliopsoas strain, avulsion fracture, or femoral tumor should also be considered if the injury does not respond to treatment. Adductor muscle strains may be part of a triad seen with abdominal sports hernia (see Chapter 14).

Hamstrings

For hamstring strains, differential diagnoses include adductor strains, avulsion fracture, hip injury, femoral stress fracture, lumbosacral referred pain syndrome, piriformis syndrome, sacroiliac dysfunction, sciatica, ischial bursitis, and hamstring tendinitis.

Quadriceps

For quadriceps strains, differential diagnoses include patellar fracture, patellar tendon rupture, and meniscal involvement.

Imaging Techniques

Plain radiographs are helpful in visualizing avulsion fractures (see **Figure 7.2**). In suspected adductor strains, radiographs may show evidence of osteitis pubis. In quadriceps injuries, radiographs can reveal patellar fractures, and patellar retraction can also be seen with a patellar tendon rupture as the patella rides in a baja position on lateral radiograph. Magnetic resonance imaging (MRI) is the most sensitive technique to identify midsubstance defects in a muscle or tendon.

Definitive Diagnosis

The physical examination findings noted in the "Clinical Presentation" feature, positive finding on MRI, or the exclusion of other conditions confirms the diagnosis. An adductor strain presents with pain along the muscle group that intensifies with passive

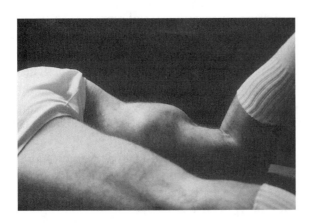

Figure 7.1 Third degree strain (rupture) of the hamstring muscle group.

Osteitis Pubis

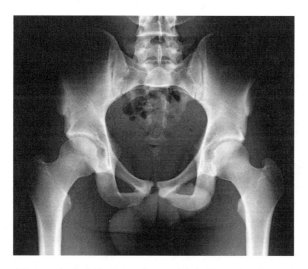

Osteitis pubis—that is, inflammation of the symphysis pubis—is usually associated with erosion of one, or potentially both, joint margins. Occurring more commonly in male athletes than in female athletes, osteitis pubis is frequently seen in individuals participating in tennis, soccer, wrestling, football, rugby, and ice hockey.[7]

Standard radiographs may demonstrate cystic changes at one or both of the margins of the symphysis. In addition, there may be associated widening of the joint. Unilateral and bilateral symphyseal joint narrowing and sclerosis are other radiographic features of osteitis pubis. Definitive diagnosis may be confirmed by a bone scan. Findings of increased uptake at the inferior margin of the symphysis pubis are characteristic of osteitis pubis as well.

Initial treatment includes rest, with cessation of the precipitating activity for a minimum of 6 weeks. Nonsteroidal anti-inflammatory drugs (NSAIDs) are used in the early treatment of this condition. If symptoms do not adequately resolve with rest and use of oral NSAIDs, a local corticosteroid injection may be considered.[7]

Rehabilitation should initially be directed at maintaining the aerobic fitness of the athlete. Once symptoms are controlled, stretching and strengthening of the hip adductors should be incorporated.

If conservative measures do not alleviate the athlete's symptoms, referral to an orthopaedic surgeon should be considered. Surgical exploration for excision of a bony fragment and local inflammatory granulation tissue may be indicated in refractory cases.

stretching into abduction and with resistive muscle action into adduction. Pain upon palpation may be difficult to elicit in minor strains, especially with high adductor strains. In a quadriceps strain with extensor mechanism disruption, the patient will have difficulty performing or may be unable to perform a straight-leg raise. A palpable defect accompanies the disruption and indicates retraction.

Pathomechanics and Functional Limitations
Premorbid Conditions

Weakness or muscle imbalance, rather than reduced flexibility, is the best predictor and a major predisposing factor for muscle strains.[8,9] A history of previous strains also plays a large role in predicting future strains.[10] The strain produces an antalgic gait, weakness, and inability to function at a normal level of sport participation.

Adductors

When a muscle imbalance and decreased flexibility develop concurrently, the probability of injury (or reinjury) increases significantly. Initial functional limitations of adductor strains include a pathologic gait, weakness, and inability to function at a normal level of sport participation. Because the adductors stabilize the hip during hip and trunk activities, loss of adductor strength can create an imbalance between these muscles and the hip abductors. If left

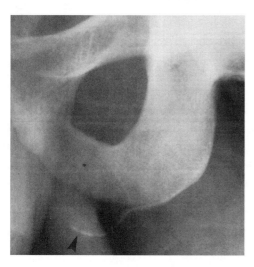

Figure 7.2 Avulsion of the origin of the common hamstring tendon from the ischial tuberosity (note the arrowhead in the lower left corner).

uncorrected, this imbalance can lead to other hip and knee injuries.

Hamstrings

Functional limitations include a pathologic gait with the knee held in slight flexion, reduced hip motion in both flexion (stretching the hamstring) and extension (activating the hamstring), and reduced stride length. Weakness and a reduced ability to use the hamstring in both concentric and eccentric activities are other common functional limitations.

Quadriceps

Significant extensor mechanism disruption results in the loss of knee control. The body compensates for the knee's insufficient contribution to gait through changes in the body's center of gravity relative to the knee joint and the use of other muscles to maintain knee extension during weight bearing. The knee is kept posterior to the body's center of gravity to maintain it locked in extension. The normal medial, or external, rotation of the tibia during knee flexion and extension is diminished and affects foot pronation and supination.

The knee is unstable, and the patient reports an inability to bear weight, actively move the knee, or control it. In essence, the knee is nonfunctional. Swelling is usually profound, which limits the possible knee ROM. The knee is maintained at approximately 30° of flexion, a position allowing maximum joint-capsule distortion by the fluid.

■ Immediate Management

Immediate management consists of ice, compression, elevation, and mild stretching to minimize inflammation and spasm.

■ Medications

Analgesic medications are commonly used for pain and NSAIDs may be prescribed for acute injuries.

■ Postinjury/Postoperative Management

If the patient cannot walk normally, crutch walking with weight bearing to tolerance is necessary.

■ Surgical Intervention

Adductor and Hamstring Strains

Surgery is indicated in proximal hamstring tendinous avulsion injuries with significant retraction but not for intrasubstance tears.[5] The surgery requires deep, tedious dissection into the tissues. To prevent scar tissue from hindering the repair, surgery should be performed as soon as possible once the retraction has been identified (see (s)(t) 7.1).

Quadriceps Strains

Complete extensor mechanism disruption requires reapproximation to reestablish function. The surgical approach consists of a direct midline incision and direct visualization of the injury. Primary repair yields superior results over late reconstruction. Various repair techniques are possible, with the appropriate procedure being chosen based on the tear location (see (s)(t) 7.2).

■ Injury-Specific Treatment and Rehabilitation Concerns

> **Specific Concerns**
> Control inflammation.
> Avoid early eccentric contractions of the healing muscle.
> Promote tissue elongation.
> Prevent contracture formation.

With a grade I or II thigh muscle strain, the patient should be examined for possible underlying causes of the injury. Biomechanical abnormalities such as leg malalignment, muscle-strength imbalances, or leg-length discrepancy should be assessed.[2] If the patient reports prior strains, the amount of old scar tissue and subsequent restrictions should be assessed.

While participation in activities is limited, the patient can maintain cardiovascular fitness and maintain or develop muscle strength in the uninvolved extremities. Open kinetic chain exercises for the hip, knee, and foot can be included if weight-bearing exercises cause pain. Abdominal exercises should be incorporated early in the program. Hip exercises for the other motions and knee-extension exercises can be performed against resistance if pain free.

Adductors

The adductors also are hip rotators, so rotator and adductor strengthening is necessary once pain and spasm are under control. After the inflammation phase has passed, ROM should be restored. Exercises to strengthen the weakened adductors are also included in the rehabilitation program. Scar-tissue management is incorporated into the program after the tissue has reached its remodeling phase and can tolerate tissue-mobilization techniques. Abdominal exercises are incorporated early in the program and focus on stabilization activities for the core muscles.

Hamstrings

If an avulsed tendon has been surgically repaired, the rehabilitation process will be prolonged, with

---

core muscles The muscles closest to the center of the body in the trunk that provide stability of the spine during movement, including the lower internal obliques, transverse abdominis, and multifidus.

Primary Repair of a Proximal Hamstring Avulsion

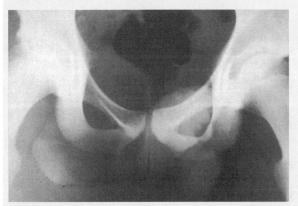
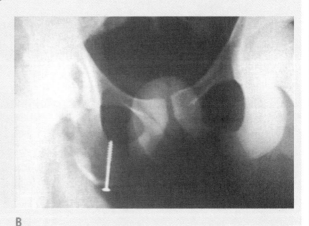

A   B

Indications

MRI demonstrating bony or tendinous avulsion from the ischial origin with more than 2 cm of retraction.

Procedure Overview

1. The patient is positioned prone for a posterior approach to the ischium.
2. A curvilinear (hockey stick) incision is made along the gluteal fold and extended down the medial leg.
3. The inferior border of the gluteus maximus is identified and retracted superiorly.
4. The hamstring group is identified and followed back to the avulsed ischium (**A**).
5. Care is taken not to damage the sciatic nerve, which is found under the biceps femoris and laterally as the nerve tracks proximally.
6. The avulsed tendon is fixed back to the ischium with the surgeon's choice of suture anchors or hardware (**B**).

Functional Limitations

The patient may experience pain and stiffness with hamstring stretching or contraction. The location of the scar is such that it can be tender or a neuroma may develop if the patient sits on hard surfaces. Some residual weakness may exist.

Implications for Rehabilitation

The repair should be protected by preventing simultaneous knee extension and hip flexion during the healing process. A knee immobilizer to restrict extension is used early in the recovery process. As healing progresses, the knee is allowed more extension with hip flexion.

Comments

Because of the muscle strength and the limited surface for reattachment of the avulsed tendon, an extended period of healing and rehabilitation is required. The patient may never return to the preinjury functional status.

---

slow progression to weight bearing and muscle activity. A fine balance must be attained between exerting sufficient stress to allow optimal healing and exerting excessive stress that hinders healing.

Postoperative bracing with a motion-controlled knee brace may assist in protecting a proximal repair from excessive tension. The knee is placed in flexion; with time and healing, progressive extension is allowed.

Quadriceps

After a severe or surgically repaired strain, the leg is immobilized, with no weight bearing allowed, for 3 to 6 weeks. Knee exercises are initially limited to quadriceps isometrics, active or active-assisted flexion ROM, and hamstring resistance in a limited range. Tibiofemoral joint mobilization can be used to reduce pain and maintain joint mobility. Patellofemoral joint mobilization may start with grade I and II methods for pain control at 10 days to 2 weeks; after week 3 or 4, depending on the surgeon's recommendation, grade III techniques may be used.

One of the concerns after a repair is the potential for wound contracture and scarring, which might cause patella baja or patella alta. Another issue is the risk of incomplete active knee extension, which results from dehiscing when stress is applied too early. Caution, common sense, knowledge of healing, and careful observation of treatment results must be used to gauge the appropriate amount and progression

alta An abnormally high position.

dehiscing Tearing of the repaired tissue.

S|T Surgical Technique 7.2

Extensor Mechanism Repair

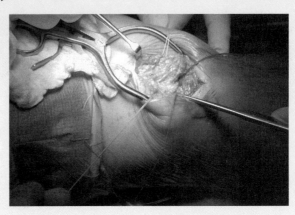

Indications

Extensor mechanism disruption demonstrated by functional evaluation and MRI.

Procedure Overview

1. The patient is placed in the supine position.
2. A midline incision is made, and dissection to the fascial plane overlying the extensor mechanism is performed, followed by peri-incisional blunt dissection.
3. The defect is identified, and the tear borders are trimmed and cleaned in preparation for the primary repair.
4. Using the surgeon's choice of suture anchors and/or locking tendon suture techniques, the ends are reapproximated and reinforced with extensor-retinaculum repair.

Functional Limitations

With healthy tissue for repair, few functional limitations are expected.

Implications for Rehabilitation

Protected flexion and weight bearing are necessary in the early postoperative period. Gradual weight bearing, flexion, and active quadriceps contractions are allowed as healing progresses.

Comments

Tears in close approximation to bony attachments can be firmly fixed to the patella or tibial tubercle with suture anchors. Some partial tears are amenable to surgical repair with similar techniques. MRI demonstrating a partial disruption and defect may reflect an injury that will respond more rapidly to surgical reapproximation of the torn tissues.

---

of stresses applied to the healing structures. If an extensor lag exists with active knee extension, the lag must be identified as secondary to either tightness, weakness, or overstretching of the repaired tendon. Joint mobilization, especially in the last few degrees of knee extension with rotation (i.e., screw-home mechanism), and scar-tissue mobilization may be necessary if the extensor lag is caused by tightness. A lag caused by weakness can be reduced by emphasizing terminal knee strength with electrical stimulation, biofeedback, and end-range facilitation. If the lag is the result of overstretching the repaired

tendon, the knee must be kept fully extended without attempts at stretching until the scar tissue can "take hold" and reduce the lag. If the lag occurs secondary to dehiscing and is not detected early, it may be uncorrectable.

▮ Estimated Amount of Time Lost

The amount of time lost from competition varies significantly, based on the injury severity and the quality and timing of early treatment. Mild strains may result in only a few days of decreased activity or inactivity. With a moderate strain,

3 to 12 weeks of recovery may be needed. Full recovery from a quadriceps rupture requires 6 to 12 months.

A history of prior strains prolongs the recovery phase, as does a more proximal site of injury. Steroid use, increased age, and poor general health are other factors that delay recovery. Failure of an adductor strain to improve in the expected time may merit further investigation for an abdominal sports hernia.

■ Return-to-Play Criteria

If adhesions are present, they should be pliable and not place tension on adjacent muscles or other structures during activity. Hip ROM should be normal compared with the contralateral leg. Agility activities—especially side-to-side maneuvers and sudden changes in direction—should be performed normally, with the athlete showing no hesitation or difficulty using the involved extremity during any explosive or lateral moves.

Functional Bracing

A thigh wrap may feel more secure for the athlete but is not necessary once sport participation has resumed (see **CT** 7.1 and see **CT** 7.2). Compression shorts may provide some support for high adductor strains (see Figure 7.3).

Quadriceps Femoris Heterotopic Ossification

CLINICAL PRESENTATION

History

The patient develops an unresolved contusion to the anterior thigh.
Within 2 to 4 weeks, the ossification can be seen on radiographs.

Observation

Point tenderness and swelling may be apparent over the site.
Knee effusion is noted.
If the contusion occurred long ago, discoloration may be absent.

Functional Status

Loss of full knee flexion is common.

Physical Examination Findings

A hard, palpable mass is usually noted in the anterior thigh.
Knee-flexion ROM is less on the affected side than on the contralateral side.

Heterotopic ossification occurs as a result of a muscle contusion. Although it can occur anywhere in the body, such a lesion is most often found in

CT Clinical Technique 7.1

Protective Hip Wrapping for Return to Competition

1. The spica wrap is begun at the proximal thigh.
2. The wrap is angled diagonally, proceeding to the distal lateral aspect of the quadriceps.
3. Above the knee, the wrap is spiraled upward, with each layer overlapping by half of its width.
4. At the proximal end of the thigh, the wrap continues around the waist, pulling laterally and posteriorly.
5. After circling the waist, the wrap is brought downward and around the thigh two or three times.
6. The wrap returns to the waist and back down to the thigh in a figure-of-eight pattern.
7. The wrap ends on the thigh, anchored with a strip of adhesive tape or stretch-elastic tape.

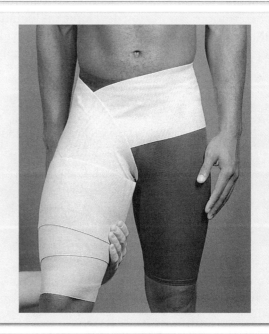

CT Clinical Technique 7.2

Protective Thigh Wrapping for Return to Competition

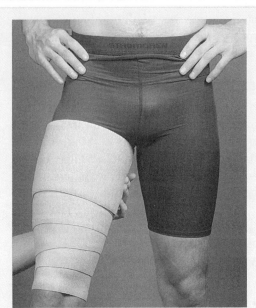
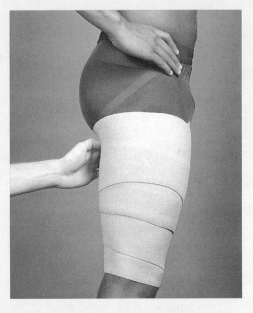

1. Begin the wrap at the distal portion of the thigh.
2. Angle the wrap diagonally toward the proximal portion of the muscle group.
3. Turn the wrap to begin an upward spiral, overlapping each layer by half its width.
4. End at the proximal portion of the thigh.
5. Secure the wrap using white tape or stretch-elastic tape.

ectopic A structure that is in an anatomically incorrect place.

the quadriceps and brachialis muscles. Ectopic bone forms within the muscle as an outgrowth of the hematoma after a contusion. Risk factors for heterotopic ossification development include ROM less than 120°, history of a previous quadriceps injury, treatment onset delayed by more than 72 hours, and sympathetic ipsilateral knee effusion.[11]

Differential Diagnosis
Periosteal or bone tumors, muscle spasm, muscle rupture.

Imaging Techniques
Radiographs or computed tomography (CT) scans 2 to 4 weeks after injury may show early signs of heterotopic ossification (see **Figure 7.4**). The lateral radiograph merits special attention. Serial films are helpful in documenting mass maturation.

Definitive Diagnosis
The definitive diagnosis is based on the history of trauma and the presence of heterotopic ossification on radiographs.

Pathomechanics and Functional Limitations
The mass restricts muscle elongation and decreases the amount of tension that can be generated. Adhesions of the calcific mass within the muscle

Figure 7.3 Compression shorts.

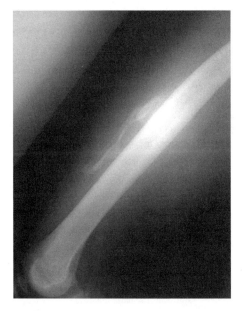

Figure 7.4 Imaging technique for femoral heterotopic ossification.

restrict its ability to contract, thereby limiting the force the muscle can produce. As a result, lower extremity function is inhibited. Reduced knee flexion may result in biomechanical changes during the swing phase of gait, characterized by hip abduction and pelvic elevation to allow the foot to clear the ground. Other functional limitations arise from decreased muscle strength.

Immediate Management

To prevent heterotopic ossification after a deep quadriceps contusion, treatment consists of ice to minimize hemorrhage, rest, quadriceps stretching, compression, and elevation. Depending on injury severity, this initial treatment may continue until hemorrhage ceases.[11]

Medications

Limited evidence suggests that treatment consisting of iontophoresis using a 2% acetic solution followed by 8 minutes of pulsed ultrasound at 1.5 W/cm^2 can be beneficial in resolving myositis ossificans.[12] NSAIDs or acetaminophen are often used to reduce pain and increase function.

Postinjury/Postoperative Management

Crutches are used until the knee can be flexed to at least 90°, pain is diminished, and the patient can walk normally with good quadriceps control.[11] Ice and quadriceps stretching are continued. When the patient is pain free, additional exercises may begin.

Surgical Intervention

Surgical intervention is not recommended because of the extensive dissection and tissue removal required and the high risk of recurrence.

Injury-Specific Treatment and Rehabilitation Concerns

Specific Concerns
Encourage hematoma resolution.
Maintain ROM.

Whirlpool treatments during the first week may promote ROM activities with less discomfort. Other modalities such as electrical stimulation (for pain relief, edema reduction, and muscle facilitation), heat, ice, or ultrasound may also be beneficial.

Gait training for normal ambulation may be required. Along with gait correction, progressive exercises for ROM and strengthening are incorporated early in the rehabilitation program. Before stretching and strengthening exercises, a brief period (10 to 15 minutes) of a cardiovascular activity such as stationary bicycling or upper body ergometry enhances the effects of exercise and joint mobilization. Gentle flexibility exercises should be performed for the first several days. Once the patient resumes full weight bearing, proprioceptive and balance exercises such as the Romberg, tandem stance, and stork stand on different surfaces (moving from stable to unstable) can be initiated. From these static exercises, the patient advances to more dynamic exercises that evolve into coordination work, and finally to agility activities and sport-specific drills.

Estimated Amount of Time Lost

A large hematoma can resolve within 3 weeks, but the formation of a large heterotopic ossification lesion can significantly increase the amount of time lost from competition.[13]

Return-to-Play Criteria

The patient should be able to perform all activities without pain, and radiographs should show resolution of the hematoma. Strength, ROM, proprioception, agility, and sport performance should all be within normal limits and allow the athlete to perform sport-specific activities at the preinjury level.

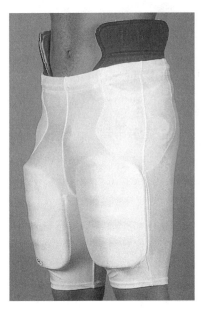

Figure 7.5 Compression girdle with fitted anterior thigh pads and iliac crest protection.

Functional Bracing

Bracing, taping, or padding (anterior thigh pad) protects the area from further impact injury and reduces the risk of reinjury (see **Figure 7.5**).

Trochanteric Bursitis

Trochanteric bursitis can be caused by friction between the bursa and trochanter or result from direct trauma, such as landing on the lateral hip or a direct blow. Idiopathic trochanteric bursitis is often related to other factors, including osteoarthritis of the hip or lumbar spine, degenerative disk disease, obesity, leg-length discrepancy, fibromyalgia, and pes planus.[14] Because bursae form in response to areas of friction, bursitis can occur in a number of possible sites; however, three or four areas around the greater trochanter area are primarily affected.[14]

idiopathic Of unknown cause or origin.

Proximal Iliotibial Band Syndrome

Proximal iliotibial band (ITB) syndrome is a possible cause of "snapping hip." This condition often occurs concurrently with trochanteric bursitis, although the cause-and-effect relationship between the two is unclear. The snapping results as the ITB moves over the greater trochanter.[15,16]

In other cases, the gluteus maximus snaps over the greater trochanter to produce the symptoms

CLINICAL PRESENTATION

History

Gradual onset of intermittent lateral hip pain is noted, with the pain being aggravated by hip external rotation and abduction.
Some patients may report direct trauma to the area of the greater trochanter.
Proximal iliotibial band (ITB) syndrome may result in reports of a "snapping" sensation in the lateral hip during activity.

Observation

No deformity or swelling is usually noted unless trauma has been acute, in which case ecchymosis and swelling may be present.
During static weight bearing, the patient may rotate the femur to clear the ITB from the greater trochanter.

Functional Status

The patient can ambulate, but end ranges of motion may be uncomfortable.
When standing statically, the patient may lean away from the involved leg, placing most of the weight on the uninvolved extremity.
Pain and associated weakness may be described as the ITB passes over the greater trochanter.

Physical Examination Findings

Resisted external rotation is often painful.
Deep palpation of the area around the greater trochanter reproduces pain.
Pain is elicited during passive stretching.
Pain is elicited if the patient lies on the involved side.
Snapping may be palpated in the hip as the hip is flexed, extended, and rotated.
Symptoms are exacerbated with ITB stretching and passive hip and knee motion.

(see **Figure 7.6**).[17] Other conditions are also called snapping hip, but they involve either intra-articular factors (e.g., a loose body) or internal factors (e.g., an iliopsoas tendon abnormality)[15] (see the "Iliopsoas Bursitis" section later in this chapter).

Differential Diagnosis

Osteoarthritis, femoral head osteonecrosis, femoral neck stress fracture, lumbar disk herniation, lumbar facet syndrome, lumbar spine compression fracture, abductor muscle strain, ischial or iliopectineal bursitis, tendinitis, bursitis, sciatica, tumor.[18–20]

Imaging Techniques

Radiographs are negative, and MRI often is not helpful.

Definitive Diagnosis

The definitive diagnosis is based on the clinical examination findings and the exclusion of conditions described in the "Differential Diagnosis" section.

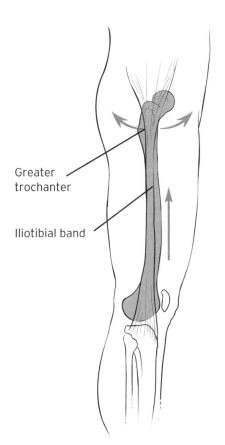

Greater
trochanter

Iliotibial band

Figure 7.6 Snapping hip syndrome. The iliotibial band slides anteriorly and posteriorly over the greater trochanter as the hip moves from flexion to extension and back. *Source:* Reproduced with permission from Greene WB (ed). *Essentials of Musculoskeletal Care*, ed 2. Rosemont, IL: American Academy of Orthopaedic Surgeons; 2000:325.

Pathomechanics and Functional Limitations

Pressure from the greater trochanter and the overlying muscles compresses the bursa into the trochanter, causing irritation and discomfort. Side-lying on the hip increases the pressure against the inflamed bursa, further aggravating the inflammation. If a leg-length discrepancy exists, the longer leg receives increased lateral stress on the soft tissues as the individual stands with a lateral shift toward the longer leg in an attempt to equalize the leg lengths.

Pain is the primary limiting factor to activity. Untreated conditions can develop into calcific bursitis. Snapping hip or proximal ITB syndrome often is a pain-free condition.

■ Medications

Acetaminophen or NSAIDs may be used to reduce pain and increase function. Phonophoresis and iontophoresis with anti-inflammatory medications have also been attempted, but the efficacy of these techniques remains controversial. Corticosteroid

injections may be necessary in patients with advanced conditions.

■ Postinjury Management

Any adaptable causative factors should be identified and corrected. If a leg-length discrepancy is responsible for the proximal ITB syndrome, a heel lift on the unaffected side reduces lateral stress on the affected hip. NSAIDs or corticosteroid injections (or both) help to relieve inflammation. If the condition is not acute or painful, cross-friction massage to loosen adhesions formed secondary to the bursal inflammation may help relieve pain and improve mobility. The condition is self-limiting, but crutches are seldom needed.

■ Surgical Intervention

Surgical excision of the trochanteric bursae or release of the tight ITB (or both) is indicated only in those patients whose symptoms cause disabling pain that is recalcitrant after conservative treatment (see **ST** 7.3).

■ Injury-Specific Treatment and Rehabilitation Concerns

Specific Concerns
Correct biomechanics.
Lengthen the ITB.

Therapeutic modalities are used to provide pain relief. Disability time is rarely prolonged; accordingly, loss of strength and other conditioning is not an issue. When the patient must be reintegrated into activity, early weight-bearing and ROM exercises are instituted, with functional progression occurring as tolerated. Exercises are included in the rehabilitation program only if strength and ROM deficiencies are found during the examination. If deficiencies are realized, the same sequence outlined for other injuries is followed. If the bursitis has been present for a while, reduced motion may result from pain and weakness caused by stance and gait deviations.

Stretching exercises for the hip abductors and adductors and ITB can reduce the tension stress on the area. Soft-tissue mobilization of the lateral thigh with a foam roller or manual therapy techniques softens and reduces tightness in the lateral thigh and hip (see **Figure 7.7**).

7

Surgical Technique 7.3

Proximal Release of ITB and Bursectomy

Indications

Disabling pain that fails to improve with conservative treatment.

Procedure Overview

1. The patient is placed in the lateral decubitus position to permit a direct approach to the greater trochanter laterally.
2. The surgical incision is directly lateral and just anterior or posterior to the landmark of the greater trochanter.
3. Blunt dissection to the ITB is performed.
4. The band is incised, and the bursa is excised.
5. Two techniques have been described to release the ITB:
   - The band is split such that it separates anterior and posterior to the greater trochanter.
   - A window is cut in the band, and this window is removed, allowing the greater trochanter to be uncovered by the band.

Functional Limitations

No functional limitations are expected. Full resolution is the rule, and relief of pain is immediate.

Implications for Rehabilitation

Early ROM and weight bearing are allowed to prevent scar tissue from forming in a retracted position.

■ Estimated Amount of Time Lost

Pain is the primary factor dictating the amount of time lost from competition.

■ Return-to-Play Criteria

The athlete should be able to participate in all activities without pain, and running gait should be normal.

Functional Bracing

A heel lift for the uninvolved leg helps reduce lateral stress on the hip. If the athlete participates in a collision or contact sport, use of a protective pad over the bursa may reduce the risk of reinjury from direct contact.

Figure 7.7 Stretching the iliotibial band. To stretch the band, the patient lies on a foam roller and rolls the leg over the length of the band.

Iliopsoas Bursitis

CLINICAL PRESENTATION

History

An insidious, gradual onset of progressive groin or anterior hip pain is described.
Pain, especially during hip extension, may be the only symptom.[21]

Observation

No outward signs are noted.

Functional Status

Stride may be shortened during ambulation to reduce hip extension.
In later stages of disease, the hip may be held in flexion, adduction, and external rotation to relieve pressure over the bursa.

Physical Examination Findings

Palpation of the bursa just distal to the inguinal ligament and lateral to the femoral artery reveals tenderness.

The iliopsoas bursa is the largest bursa in the body, averaging 6 cm × 3 cm in area.[21] Because of its proximity to the iliopsoas tendon, tendinitis or bursitis in one structure can develop secondary to tendinitis or bursitis in the other structure, making the conditions difficult to differentiate (see **Figure 7.8**). Causes of iliopsoas bursitis include rheumatoid arthritis, acute trauma, and overuse injury.[22] Acute trauma in sports can occur with vigorous hip flexion and extension. Overuse trauma is seen in athletes

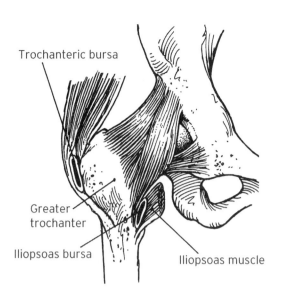

Figure 7.8 The trochanteric and iliopsoas bursae are located around the coxofemoral joint.

with hip weakness or tightness who participate in repetitive activities. Individuals involved in uphill running, track and field, rowing, strength training, and ballet are also susceptible to iliopsoas bursitis.

Internal Snapping Hip Syndrome

Iliopsoas tendon displacement as it passes the pelvic pectineal eminence, femoral head, or lesser trochanter may be a cause of snapping hip syndrome (see the "Trochanteric Bursitis" section earlier in this chapter).[16] Chronic pain, snapping, or both in the femoral triangle is reported, especially in the area over the inguinal ligament (see Figure 7.9). Symptoms develop during exercise and may persist for some time afterward. Passively extending the hip from a position of flexion, abduction, and external rotation reproduces the pain and will often reproduce an audible and palpable snap.[16]

Differential Diagnosis

Lymphadenopathy, tumor, inguinal hernia, hematoma, femoral artery aneurysm.

Imaging Techniques

Radiographs are negative, and MRI is often inconclusive.

Definitive Diagnosis

The definitive diagnosis is based on bursal inflammation, findings on clinical examination, and the exclusion of conditions described in the "Differential Diagnosis" section.

Pathomechanics and Functional Limitations

Hip hyperextension is uncomfortable and avoided during gait. Walking and running stride lengths are reduced to avoid hip extension. Sitting is more comfortable than standing, and side-lying is more comfortable than lying prone.

Immediate Management

Rest with limitation of hip motion—especially limitation of extension by using an elastic wrap—relieves pain. Ice may be used to reduce inflammation.

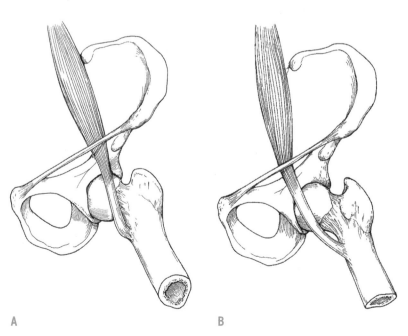

A   B

Figure 7.9 The iliopsoas in snapping hip syndrome. **(A)** With hip flexion, the iliopsoas tendon shifts laterally in relation to the center of the femoral head. **(B)** With hip extension, the tendon shifts medially in relation to the center of the femoral head. *Source:* Reproduced with permission from Allen WC, Cope R. Coxa saltans: The snapping hip revisited. *J Am Acad Orthop Surg.* 1995;3:303–308.

■ Medications

NSAIDs reduce inflammation. Corticosteroid injections into the bursa, when performed under ultrasound guidance, have also produced successful results.[16]

■ Postinjury Management

Inflammation is decreased and followed with stretching and strengthening exercises. Any gait or anatomic abnormalities should be corrected to prevent recurrence.

■ Injury-Specific Treatment and Rehabilitation Concerns

> **Specific Concerns**
> Limit hip extension early in the program.
> Strengthen the hip musculature.

Hip extension is avoided until inflammation and pain are under control. However, during this time and beyond, the hip muscles should be strengthened. Medial and lateral rotator strengthening can begin early in the course of rehabilitation.[23] Hip abduction and adduction strengthening also are necessary. Once strength is improved in these motions, combined-plane motions can be performed to strengthen the hip muscles in more functional planes. Hip-flexor stretches should also be included in the program, because tightness of the hip-flexor muscles correlates with the incidence of iliopsoas bursitis.[23]

Deep-tissue, cross-friction massage may be beneficial in relieving adhesions within the bursa if the patient can tolerate this treatment. Ultrasound and heat can also be helpful in relieving inflammation.

Proprioceptive and balance exercises such as the Romberg, tandem stance, and stork stand on different surfaces (moving from stable to unstable) are initiated when pain is resolved and hip strength is restored. From these static exercises, the patient progresses to more dynamic exercises that evolve first into coordination activities and finally into agility activities. Functional activities are started before the final phase of the rehabilitation program, in which sport-specific drills and skills are performed.

■ Estimated Amount of Time Lost

Because pain is the primary limiting factor, the amount of time lost from competition varies; activity modification can range from simple modification to complete cessation for several weeks. If the patient has delayed reporting the injury and bursitis is extensive, time lost may be several weeks.

■ Return-to-Play Criteria

Pain during activities reflects inflammation; consequently, the patient should be able to perform all activities without pain before returning to full participation. If the time away from full participation has been brief, pain relief may be the only requirement for return.

Functional Bracing

Although a hip spica wrap may be used in the early phase of rehabilitation, no support is required once the athlete returns to full participation and motion and strength are restored.

Acetabular Labral Tears

CLINICAL PRESENTATION

History

A history of developmental abnormality or trauma may be reported.
Labral tears may be associated with traumatic dislocation or subluxation.
The patient may report clicking, catching, locking, or popping during movement.
Pain over the anterolateral hip may radiate into the adductor group.
Pain is increased by any one or combination of the following: running/sprinting, torsion/twisting of the hip, prolonged sitting, putting on shoes and socks, and getting in and out of a car.

Observation

Popping or snapping may be palpated during joint motion.

Functional Status

Limping may be noted as the result of shortening of the stance phase of gait.
Catching or locking may be noted as the hip moves from flexion, external rotation, abduction to extension, internal rotation, and adduction.

Physical Examination Findings

The hip scouring, Thomas, and Trendelenberg tests may be positive.
Pain may be elicited during passive hip flexion and internal rotation.
Posterior pain with a FABER (flexion, abduction, and external rotation) test indicates sacroiliac joint pathology, while anterior hip pain in this position is highly suspicious for injury to the labrum, iliopsoas pathology, or injury to the anterior capsule.

The labrum of the hip is a fibrocartilaginous structure that provides stability to the hip and serves as a suction seal to prevent synovial fluid expression from the joint space, thereby protecting the cartilage of the hip.[24] Labral tears in athletes occur frequently as a result of femoroacetabular impingement (FAI), hip instability, internal snapping hip/iliopsoas impingement, and traumatic events that may occur during contact sports (see **Figure 7.10**).

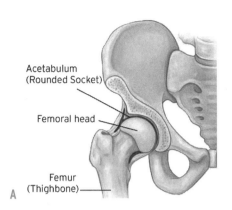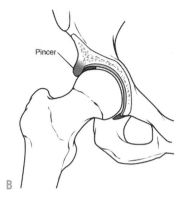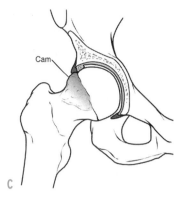

Figure 7.10 Forms of femoroacetabular impingement (FAI). (**A**) Normal anatomy. (**B**) An acetabular pincer. (**C**) Femoral head cam. Both a pincer and cam may be present, creating a mixed FAI causation. *Source:* Reproduce with permission from *Your Orthopaedic Connection.* © American Academy of Orthopaedic Surgeons. http://orthoinfo.aaos.org.

Labral tears are the most common cause of intra-articular hip pain in the athletic population, and FAI is by far the most common cause of these tears. Labral tears associated with cam-type (cam meaning "cog") impingement are more frequently associated with type 1 tears, which entail a detachment at the labral–cartilage junction.[24] Cam impingement refers to an abnormally shaped femoral head, which contacts a normal spherical acetabulum. This condition leads to chondral delamination and detachment of the labrum from the acetabular rim. Cam impingement frequently occurs in hip flexion and internal rotation.

Labral tears that occur with pincer-type impingement are commonly associated with type 2 tears, which entail an intrasubstance tearing of the labrum.[24] Pincer impingement refers to acetabular over-coverage of the femoral head. This overcoverage causes impingement of the labrum between the acetabulum and the femoral neck. Such impingement often leads to a crushing-type injury to the labrum and its eventual degeneration.

Differential Diagnosis
FAI, chondral derangement, synovial disease, instability, dysplasia, arthritis, athletic pubalgia, sports hernia, pelvic floor dysfunction, osteitis pubi, loose bodies, ruptured ligamentum teres, trochanteric bursitis, neurogenic pain secondary to spinal pathology.

Imaging Techniques
Some type of osseous abnormality can be detected on plain radiographs with 87% of patients with labral tears.[24] Commonly used radiographic views include the anteroposterior pelvis and bilateral false profile and Dunn views. Anteroposterior (AP) pelvis and false profile views are useful in detecting pincer lesions, whereas the Dunn view is useful in detecting a cam lesion. A magnetic resonance angiography (MRA) image is useful in evaluating both the labrum and the articular cartilage. Additionally, a fluoroscopically guided intra-articular injection can be used to assess whether the hip pain stems from an intra-articular derangement; pain relief from an intra-articular injection is a reliable indicator of intra-articular injury.

Definitive Diagnosis
The diagnosis is confirmed when a patient has clinical and MRI or MRA evidence of a labral tear and any radiographic evidence of a cam or pincer lesion. Temporary relief in the patient's symptoms with a diagnostic injection confirms the intra-articular source of pain.

Pathomechanics and Functional Limitations
Patients with a labral tear may have difficulty bearing full weight on the involved extremity and ambulate with a Trendelenberg gait. Patients will normally have pain, and therefore difficulty, putting on shoes and socks, sitting for long periods of time, standing or walking for long periods of time, getting in and out of a car, and negotiating stairs. Athletes will have marked pain with sport-specific activities and will likely experience decreased performance, especially those who participate in sports that involve torsion of the hip.

Medications
NSAIDs (e.g., naproxen, ibuprofen, celecoxib, diclofenac sodium) may be prescribed to decrease any associated inflammatory response. A fluoroscopically guided intra-articular injection of cortisone may also be considered as a conservative treatment of a labral tear.

Conservative Management
Conservative measures are first attempted in the treatment of an individual with a diagnosis of a labral tear. This approach consists of activity modification, rehabilitation (which should include a progression of ROM and core strengthening), and medications (NSAIDs and cortisone injection).

Following the initial examination, the patient should be referred for nonoperative treatment consisting of exercises to improve core strength. Often patients can compensate for the lack of a suction seal by increasing core muscle strength—specifically, the strength of the abdominal muscles, lumbopelvic muscles, gluteus medius, and iliopsoas. Single-leg balancing exercises should also be incorporated in the rehabilitation program to facilitate joint proprioception.

Surgical Intervention

FAI and labral tears may be treated by hip arthroscopy. Frayed or degenerative tears of the labrum should be debrided to yield stable edges. When possible, a labral tear at the acetabular margin should be repaired with suture anchors at the acetabular rim. Cam and pincer lesions should also be addressed at the time of arthroscopy. Resection of the pincer lesion (acetabular rim trimming) and resection of the cam lesion (femoral head/neck osteochondroplasty) may help prevent any recurrence of labral tearing.

Practice Tip

If a trial of therapeutic exercise fails and the patient has MRA evidence of a labral tear with concurrent radiographic evidence of a cam or pincer lesion, surgery may be indicated. If MRA is inconclusive for a labral tear and high clinical suspicion for a labral tear exists, an intra-articular injection may be indicated. Such an injection may be given with 1% lidocaine, with or without Depo-Medrol. Fluoroscopy or ultrasound guidance may be used to ensure that the correct location is accessed. Temporary relief in the patient's symptoms with a diagnostic injection confirms the intra-articular source of pain, and the patient may then be a candidate for arthroscopic surgery.

Injury-Specific Treatment and Rehabilitation Concerns

Specific Concerns

Prevent iliopsoas tightness and tendinitis as well as adductor tendinitis.
Avoid sciatica and piriformis syndrome.
Monitor for ilial up-slips and rotations.
Hypertonicity of the quadratus lumborum may cause lower back pain.
Segmental vertebral rotational lesions may develop.

Achievement of a successful outcome of hip arthroscopy is extremely dependent on the postoperative rehabilitation process. Most patients are restricted to 20 lb of foot-flat weight bearing for 10 to 14 days. Patients are instructed to use a continuous passive motion machine to facilitate ROM for the first 4 to

8 weeks after surgery; this exercise should be performed for 2 to 4 hours per day. An alternative way to facilitate ROM is for patients to ride a stationary bike with no resistance for 2 hours per day for the first 4 to 8 weeks operatively. A slow progression to full strength and full activity occurs over a 3- to 4-month time frame.

Estimated Amount of Time Lost

Full return to athletic activity is expected by 4 to 6 months. Patients may continue to note an improvement in their symptoms for as long as a year, however.

Return-to-Play Criteria

Athletes can expect a full return to competition by 4 to 6 months. The return-to-play decision is based on the athlete achieving near to full range of motion with the noninvolved extremity and normal (5/5) manual muscle testing of the hip flexors, extensors, abductors, adductors, and internal/external rotators. In addition, athletes should be almost entirely asymptomatic when completing sport-specific functional drills with the athletic trainer or physical therapist before a full return to play is attempted.

Iliac Crest Contusions

CLINICAL PRESENTATION

History
Direct blow to the iliac crest.
Immediate debilitation because of pain rather than tissue damage.

Observation
Swelling may be localized over the site of injury.
Rapid formation of ecchymosis occurs.
Muscle spasm appears in the abdominal and hip muscles.

Functional Status
Hip and trunk ROM are painful and reduced.
Gait may be antalgic.

Physical Examination Findings
Point tenderness over the iliac crest is noted.
Early onset of a contusion may be followed by widespread ecchymosis.
Pain may be reduced when the patient walks backward.

Athletes who participate in contact and collision sports such as football, ice hockey, and soccer, and female gymnasts who compete on the uneven bars are susceptible to iliac crest contusions. Commonly known as a "hip pointer," this condition can be disabling because of the soft-tissue damage and secondary muscle spasm. The abdominal muscles attached to the iliac crest are crushed between the iliac crest and the object, causing the injury. Both the abdominal muscles and the bone may be injured by the impacting force. If the contusion occurs just below the crest, the hip muscles can be affected as well. Repeated iliac crest trauma or mismanagement of an acute injury to this area can lead to periostitis.

Differential Diagnosis

Stress fracture, muscle strain, iliac crest fracture, iliac crest avulsion fracture, apophysitis (see Box 7.2), bursitis.

Imaging Techniques

Plain radiographs may demonstrate an iliac crest avulsion injury, which can accompany a severe iliac crest contusion (see Figure 7.11). Generally, MRI is

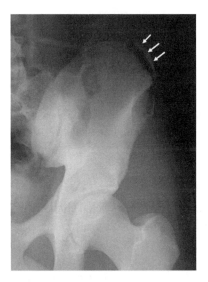

Figure 7.11 Avulsion of the iliac spine with retraction of the fragment indicated by arrows.

7

Box 7.2

Apophysitis

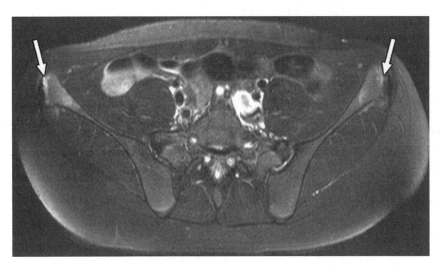

Axial fat-suppressed T2-weighted imaging (TR/TE, 3390/79) of pelvis demonstrates bone marrow edema within iliac the crests bilaterally. Minimal muscle edema is seen in both gluteus medius muscles.

Apophyseal injuries are common in adolescent athletes secondary to the inherent weakness of an open physis resulting from microtrauma or inflammation. The most frequently affected apophyses of the hip are the sartorius attachment to the anterior superior iliac spine (the most common site) and the rectus femoris attachment to the inferior iliac spine. The apophyses at the hamstrings' attachment to the ischial tuberosity and the iliopsoas's attachment to the lesser trochanter may be affected as well. Chronic apophyseal irritation can occur at the ischial and iliac apophyses.

Patients with apophysitis will present with a gradual onset of pain associated with activity, which eventually leads to restricted sports participation. Palpation reveals localized tenderness over the affected area, increased pain with passive stretching of the affected muscle, and pain with resistive manual muscle testing of the involved muscle.

Standard radiographs are useful in assessing whether the patient has an avulsion fracture, but only if ossification is present. Ultrasound may be used to demonstrate changes in the absence of ossification. Further imaging is typically unnecessary.

Most athletes will respond favorably to conservative treatment consisting of rest, ice, and NSAIDs (e.g., naproxen, ibuprofen, celecoxib, diclofenac sodium). Based on the severity of the individual's symptoms, limited weight bearing with the use of crutches may be necessary. ROM exercises may be initiated once symptoms are controlled, followed by a progression of proper stretching and strengthening. A gradual return to sport can be expected when full ROM and baseline strength have been achieved.

Source: © MRI Appearance of Chronic Stress Injury of the Iliac Crest Apophysis in Adolescent Athletes, June 2008 vol. 190 no. 6 1487–1491. American Roentgen Ray Society.

not used to visualize the soft-tissue injury because either the problem is self-limiting or radiographs are adequate.

Definitive Diagnosis

The diagnosis of iliac crest contusion is based on the mechanism of injury, clinical signs, and the patient's functional limitations. Clinical examination alone may not suffice to differentiate an iliac crest contusion from an avulsion of the oblique, latissimus dorsi, or paraspinal muscles or associated fascia.[13]

Pathomechanics and Functional Limitations

Pain and spasm are self-limiting. Spasm makes movement difficult because the abdominal muscles work to stabilize the trunk during extremity movement and work even more during trunk motion. Deep inspirations, coughing, and laughing also cause discomfort as the abdominal muscles are stretched. If the hip abductors are involved in the injury, ambulation is painful and difficult. A hematoma can form over the femoral or lateral femoral cutaneous nerve, increasing pain and resulting in peripheral motor and sensory dysfunction.[13]

■ Immediate Management

Ice and compression may be applied to the injury site to limit inflammation. Electrical stimulation and mild stretching during icing to the muscles help to reduce secondary muscle spasm. If tolerable, passive or active-assisted ROM after electrical stimulation may further relax the muscles, and an elastic wrap for support may extend the muscle relaxation after treatment. If gait is not possible without favoring the involved extremity, crutches with partial weight bearing should be used. Prophylactic crutch use is often prescribed for the first 24 hours to limit irritation and muscle spasm.

■ Medications

Analgesic medications for pain and NSAIDs are used in acute injuries. Injection of a corticosteroid with an anesthetic is very helpful in the early resolution of pain and spasm. Iontophoresis may also be used to deliver these medications.

■ Postinjury Management

An iliac crest contusion does not usually cause long-term disability. The key to reducing disability is limiting the accompanying muscle spasm. Once spasm and pain are relieved and healing is well under way, ROM exercises are initiated to restore lost hip and trunk motion. A brief routine to strengthen the abdominal, hip-flexion, and hip-abduction

muscles and restore trunk stabilization is all that is required before the athlete returns to full sport participation. Padding the injured area during participation reduces the risk of reinjury.

■ Injury-Specific Treatment and Rehabilitation Concerns

> **Specific Concerns**
> Control inflammation.
> Encourage pain-free ROM.

Following an iliac crest contusion, recovery is usually rapid with proper management. If muscle spasm is quickly resolved, pain subsides rapidly. Strength and motion deficits, if present, are minimal; both are recovered in a few days. In contrast, if spasm is prolonged, recovery is also prolonged. Electrical stimulation can be continued if spasm persists, and heat may be administered once the acute inflammation has subsided.

■ Estimated Amount of Time Lost

The amount of time lost from competition ranges from 3 days to 1 week, depending on the force of the impact and resulting injury severity. Development of periostitis can significantly delay healing.

■ Return-to-Play Criteria

The athlete should be able to complete all activities without pain, and muscle spasm should be resolved. Normal gait and the ability to run, jump, and perform all sport-specific activities must be demonstrated.

Functional Bracing

A wrap, girdle, or compression shorts with a protective pad over the injured area reduces the risk of reinjury (see **CT** 7.3).

Hip Dislocation

Traumatic dislocations of the hip (coxofemoral joint) are rare in sport activities, although some cases have been reported to occur in water and snow skiing, jogging, football, and rugby. Posterior dislocations occur more commonly than anterior dislocations in athletic contests. The most common mechanisms of injury are falling onto a flexed knee and being tackled when down on all four limbs.

Hip dislocations are considered a medical emergency because of the potential for neurovascular

CT Clinical Technique 7.3

Protective Padding for Iliac Crest Contusions

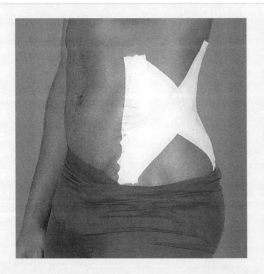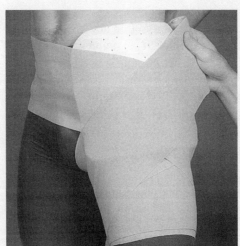

1. Begin with vertical anchor strips 4 in. to 6 in. anterior and posterior to the trauma site.
2. Create an "X" pattern from anchor to anchor using white or elastic tape.
3. Cover the "X" by applying the tape horizontally from anchor to anchor.
4. Pad the area using a commercial or custom-built pad.
5. Secure the pad in place using a hip spica (see CT 7.1), crossing the wrap on the lateral portion of the hip.

CLINICAL PRESENTATION

History

Patients presenting with hip dislocations are in severe distress and discomfort.
The patient may be unable to move the affected hip.
Numbness and tingling throughout the lower extremity may be noted.

Observation

The involved leg may appear to be shortened.
Posterior dislocations will be positioned in flexion, internal rotation, and adduction.
Anterior dislocations will be positioned in marked external rotation, with some degree of flexion and abduction.

Functional Status

The patient is unable to bear weight.

Physical Examination Findings

ROM of the involved hip is restricted or absent.
Lumbosacral plexus injuries are also associated with major pelvic injuries and must be ruled out.
Sciatic nerve injuries are commonly seen with hip dislocations, so care must be taken to check for the presence of a partial or complete tear of the nerve.

compromise. Thus the thorough physical examination conducted should include a careful neurovascular assessment. Particular attention should be paid to the sciatic nerve, which is vulnerable to injury with a posterior dislocation.

Athletes who sustain a dislocation will immediately complain of excruciating pain. Most will be unable to arise from the ground. The athlete's leg will present in a shortened, flexed, internally rotated, and adducted position with a posterior dislocation.

Differential Diagnosis

Acetabular fractures, femoral head and neck fractures, chondral injury of the acetabulum or femoral head, labral tears, sciatic nerve injury, lumbosacral plexus injuries.[7]

Imaging Techniques

Standard anteroposterior and cross-table lateral films should be obtained to assess the exact direction of the dislocation and to identify any associated fracture of the acetabular wall or femoral head. Postreduction radiographs should also be obtained to confirm reduction of the hip.

Definitive Diagnosis

AP pelvis radiographs will confirm the diagnosis of an anterior or posterior hip dislocation. In an alert and cooperative patient who is hemodynamically stable and has no physical findings that suggest an occult pelvic fracture or hip joint injury, an AP pelvis may not be indicated. Once the diagnosis has been made, it is critical to obtain additional radiographs, including AP films of the involved hip as well as internal and external oblique views (Judet views) at 45° of the hip, prior to undertaking any open surgical intervention. CT scans should be routinely ordered following successful closed reduction of a dislocated hip. If a closed reduction is not possible and an open surgical reduction is planned, a CT scan should also be obtained.

Pathomechanics and Functional Limitations

The athlete will be unable to bear weight and will have gross restrictions in range of motion.

The incidence of femoral head osteonecrosis following a traumatic hip dislocation ranges from 10% to 30%.

■ Immediate Management

Prompt reduction of the femoral head is the goal of initial management. The reduction can be attempted with in-line traction with the patient in a supine position, regardless of the direction of the dislocation. The preferred approach is to perform a closed reduction under general anesthesia if readily available. If general anesthesia is not available, a closed reduction with intravenous sedation, using small doses of diazepam (2.5 to 5 mg) and larger doses of morphine (10 to 15 mg), in the emergency department may be attempted.

■ Medications

Narcotic pain medications such as Norco, Vicodin, and tramadol may be used to help manage the patient's pain following the reduction.

■ Postinjury Management

A single attempt at closed reduction can be attempted by applying longitudinal traction with the hip slightly flexed once the patient has been stabilized. If the reduction cannot be easily achieved, the athlete should be given appropriate pain medication and sedation, and radiographs obtained. If the films confirm an uncomplicated dislocation without fracture, additional attempts at closed reduction may be performed with the assistance of an anesthesiologist. The role of the anesthesiologist is to provide sedation and relaxation as well as to ensure patient comfort.

■ Surgical Intervention

Indications for open surgical reduction include an inability to reduce the hip after adequate anesthesia, an intra-articular fracture fragment greater than 2 mm, ipsilateral femoral fracture, neurovascular compromise, and recurrent hip instability following closed reduction. A sciatic nerve injury must be ruled out prior to any attempt at open or closed reduction of the hip.

■ Injury-Specific Treatment and Rehabilitation Concerns

> **Specific Concerns**
>
> Encourage joint motion as tolerated.
> Emphasize progressive weight bearing.
> Restore normal muscle flexibility.
> Implement functional progression exercises specific to the patient's needs.

Rehabilitation starts immediately and begins with a progression of gentle active and active-assisted ROM of the hip. Weight bearing is limited for 3 to 4 weeks. Once full ROM has been achieved and the athlete resumes full weight bearing, strengthening of the pelvic, thigh, and leg muscles may begin. Initial rehabilitation programs should focus on low-impact, isokinetic, full-range strengthening. Once the affected limb is back to nearly normal strength, the patient may begin endurance activities and sport-specific training may resume.

■ Estimated Amount of Time Lost

A return to training may take up to 3 months and a full return to sports may take up to 6 months following an acute hip dislocation.

■ Return-to-Play Criteria

The return-to-play decision is based on the athlete achieving full ROM in the involved extremity as compared to the noninvolved extremity, plus full strength of the hip flexors, extensors, abductors, adductors, and internal/external rotators. Athletes should be almost entirely asymptomatic when completing sport-specific functional drills before a full return to play is attempted.

Functional Bracing

Patients may prefer to use a hip spica brace for added comfort and stability upon their return to play.

Pelvic Fracture

CLINICAL PRESENTATION

History
The patient will be in extreme pain.

Observation
The hip and knee may be flexed to decrease pain.

Functional Status
The patient is often unable to ambulate.

Physical Examination Findings
Pain increases during palpation.
Fracture lines may be palpable.
Laxity and instability of the hip suggest an acetabular fracture with or without an associated fracture of the pelvis.
Distal sensory function may be inhibited.
Vaginal or rectal bleeding may be noted.
Hematuria may be present.
A hematoma may form over the ipsilateral flank, proximal thigh, inguinal ligament, or perineal area.[25]

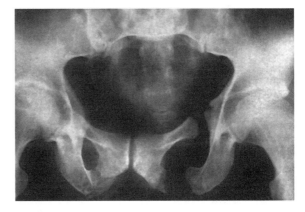

Figure 7.12 Standard anteroposterior pelvic radiograph demonstrating a displaced fracture of the right acetabulum.

The two sides of the pelvis are formed by three bones (the ilium, the ischium, and the pubis) that fuse together to create a ring of bone. Ligaments join the pelvis to the sacrum at the base of the spine, producing a bowl-like cavity below the rib cage. On each side of the pelvis, the acetabulum serves as the socket for the hip joint.

Adolescent athletes are at risk for avulsion fractures of the pelvis. These types of fractures occur as a result of sudden muscle contractions. A small piece of the ischium where the hamstring muscles attach can be torn away by forceful contraction of these muscles.[26]

Elderly individuals with osteoporosis are also at risk for pelvic fractures. The likely mechanism of injury for these individuals is a fall from a standing position. Such injuries typically do not damage the actual structural integrity of the pelvic ring.

Most pelvic fractures involve high-energy forces, such as those sustained in a fall from a significant height, in a crush-type injury, or from a motor vehicle accident.[26] Depending on the degree and direction of the force, these injuries may be life threatening.

Differential Diagnosis
Hip dislocations and fractures, blunt abdominal trauma, lower genitourinary trauma, trauma in pregnancy, hemorrhagic shock, abdominal pain in the elderly.

Imaging Techniques
The standard anteroposterior pelvic radiograph is the most commonly used screening test for pelvic injuries (see **Figure 7.12**). CT scan is the best imaging study for assessment of pelvic anatomy and any associated pelvic, intraperitoneal, and retroperitoneal bleeding. CT also confirms hip dislocations associated with acetabular fractures.[27]

Ultrasonography is used as a part of the Focused Assessment with Sonography for Trauma (FAST) examination to examine the pelvis for intrapelvic bleeding. This imaging modality is also useful in identifying intraperitoneal bleeding.

Retrograde urethrography is indicated for those males with blood at the urethral meatus or with a displaced or boggy prostate. This study is also indicated in females with a vaginal tear or palpable fracture fragments adjacent to the urethra. A cystography may be necessary in those patients with an intact urethra presenting with hematuria.

Definitive Diagnosis
Abnormalities serve as the diagnostic criteria of pelvic fractures and dislocations.

Pathomechanics and Functional Limitations
The individual sustaining a pelvic fracture will not want to bear weight. The patient may also try to keep the hip or knee bent in a specific position to avoid exacerbating the pain.

Potential complications of a pelvic fracture include deep venous thrombosis (DVT), excessive hemorrhaging from the fracture or injury to associated pelvic vasculature, chronic pelvic pain, infection as a result of disruption of the genitourinary or gastrointestinal systems, sexual dysfunction, and genitourinary dysfunction from bladder, prostate, vaginal, or urethral injury.[26]

▧ Immediate Management

The first step in the management of patients with pelvic fracture is to address any acutely life-threatening conditions. Avoid any excessive motion of the pelvis and apply an external compression device to the grossly unstable pelvis. This intervention will provide mechanical stabilization while controlling hemorrhage from the fracture site. Closely monitor the patient's vital signs.

▧ Medications

Narcotic medication (e.g., Vicodin, Tramadol, Norco) is the treatment of choice in the acute setting for a pelvic fracture. Anticoagulant medications such as Coumadin, Lovenox, and aspirin may be used to reduce the risk for DVT secondary to the patient's limited mobility.

▧ Nonoperative Management

Stable fractures, such as avulsion fractures, will normally heal without surgery. With this type of injury, the individual engages in partial weight bearing on one or both of the legs for approximately 3 months, or until the bones are fully healed.[26]

▧ Surgical Intervention

Hemodynamically unstable patients with unstable pelvic fractures require emergent orthopaedic consultation for possible external fixation. An external fixator is a device that has long screws that are inserted into the pelvic bones on each side and connected to a frame outside the body. Each patient must be assessed individually, particularly those with unstable fractures. Some fractures may necessitate traction, while in other cases an external fixator may be sufficient. Patients with unstable pelvic fractures may also require surgical insertion of plates and/or screws.[26]

▧ Injury-Specific Treatment and Rehabilitation Concerns

Stable pelvic fractures heal well, although most patients will need to use crutches for 6 to 12 weeks. Rehabilitation for the first 6 weeks following the injury (or surgery if necessary) consists of gentle ROM and light strengthening exercises. As the fracture heals, achieving full strength of the pelvic muscles and normalizing gait should be of utmost priority in the rehabilitation process.[25]

▧ Estimated Amount of Time Lost

Most individuals who have surgery for a pelvic fracture require at least 3 to 4 months of recovery time.

▧ Return-to-Play Criteria

The prognosis with pelvic fracture varies depending on the severity of the fracture sustained and any associated injuries.

Femoral Fracture

▧ Acute Fractures

The force required to cause an acute fracture is so great that automobile and motorcycle accidents are the most common causes of femoral shaft fractures. The risk of femoral fracture increases in skeletally immature individuals. If a traumatic femoral fracture occurs without significant force in a skeletally mature individual, a precipitating factor such as a bone tumor or osteoporosis should be suspected.

CLINICAL PRESENTATION

History

Significant increases in the frequency, intensity, or duration of exercise may precede the injury.[27]

Gradual, idiopathic onset of symptoms occurs over several weeks' time.

The patient may complain of a "pulling" sensation in the anterior thigh.[28]

Pain or tenderness over the rectus femoris muscle or nondescript anterior hip pain is noted.

Pain increases with activity and decreases with rest.

Female patients may have a history of amenorrhea.

Observation

Mild swelling without ecchymosis.

Functional Status

ROM may be full but uncomfortable in active hip flexion, passive knee flexion, and passive hip extension.

No pain is experienced during hip rotation.

ROM may be limited due to pain rather than physical restriction.

The patient can bear weight but may have an antalgic gait.

Thigh weakness and a slight limp are evident during gait.[28]

Pain may limit running ability.

Physical Examination Findings

The patient has a normal alignment and neurologic examination.

Pain may be experienced when performing a straight-leg raise.

The following special tests may be positive:
- Fist
- Fulcrum
- One-legged hop

Traumatic fractures are often accompanied by shock and neurovascular complications. Because of the extent of possible complications, an acute femoral fracture must be treated as an emergency.

Although the bone is well covered by large muscles, an acute fracture is easily recognized by the patient's severe pain, inability to stand, and deformity. Hallmarks of displaced traumatic femoral fractures include exquisite pain and obvious deformity.

Stress Fractures

Femoral stress fractures occur more frequently than acute fractures in athletes, especially among those in distance running sports. Occasionally, femoral stress fractures are seen in basketball, baseball, or tennis players. Both adolescents and adults may be diagnosed with these fractures.[29] Femoral neck and pubic rami stress fractures have a higher incidence in female endurance runners, who are often amenorrheic and are generally more susceptible to stress fractures, possibly because of lower bone mineral densities.[30] Femoral stress fractures may occur secondary to the female athlete triad (disordered eating, amenorrhea, and osteoporosis).

Stress fractures tend to affect individuals who have been regularly running for at least 2 years and are precipitated by sudden changes in the frequency, intensity, or duration of training.[27] Other factors that predispose individuals to femoral stress fractures include declining fitness levels with age, improperly fitting or worn-out footwear, and poor nutrition.[27] A high degree of suspicion for a stress fracture should be maintained when an athlete presents with unilateral groin pain and limitation in the ROM of the involved hip. It is important to note the trend in pain over time; in particular, pain first noted with training, which then later presents at rest, requires thorough examination. The athlete with a developing stress fracture may not initially experience any symptoms when not training. Later in the progression of the stress fracture, pain is likely experienced with rest. Unfortunately, rest pain may not be felt until the fracture is displaced.

Femoral neck stress fractures are classified as tension fractures, displaced fractures, and compression fractures (see **Figure 7.13**).[27] Tension fractures form on the superior aspect of the femoral neck. Displaced fractures are visible on plain radiographs and frequently require surgical fixation. Compression stress fractures occur on the inferior portion of the femoral neck. Three subclasses have been identified—those with no fatigue line, those with a fatigue line less than 50% of the width of the femoral neck, and those with a fatigue line greater than 50% of the width.

Differential Diagnosis

Muscle strain, tendinitis, bursitis, delayed-onset muscle soreness, bone tumor, bone infection, radiculopathy, osteonecrosis, intra-articular injury (chondral and labral derangement, loose bodies), athletic pubalgia, arthritis, referred pain from the contralateral hip, contusion.[27,31]

Imaging Techniques

It is often difficult to diagnose a stress fracture based on plain radiographs because of the subtle or nonexistent findings on standard radiographs. Anteroposterior (AP) and lateral radiographs are initially negative in 66% of patients with stress fractures. If images are obtained within the first week of

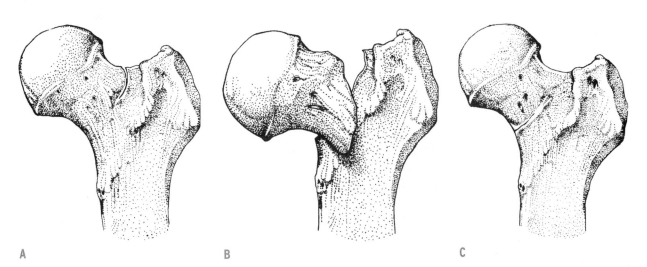

Figure 7.13 Stress fractures of the femoral neck. (**A**) Tension-side stress fracture. (**B**) Displaced femoral stress fracture. (**C**) Compression-side stress fracture. *Source:* Reproduced with permission from Fullerton LR, Snowdy HA. Femoral neck stress fracture. *Am J Sports Med.* 1988;16:365–377.

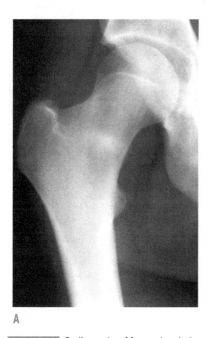
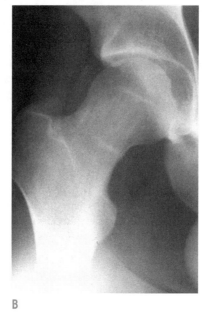
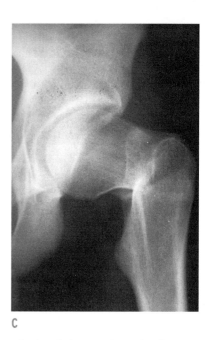

A   B   C

Figure 7.14   Radiographs of femoral neck stress fractures. (**A**) A compression-side femoral neck stress fracture that occurred secondary to overuse (fatigue). Note the periosteal new-bone formation on the inferior femoral neck. Callus formation as the result of healing is also present. (**B**) A complete, nondisplaced stress fracture of the femoral neck. (**C**) A complete, displaced stress fracture of the femoral neck.

symptoms, the accuracy rate is 10% (see **Figure 7.14**).[27] If suspicion is high, a bone scan is often diagnostic within 24 hours of pain onset. If the diagnosis remains unclear after initial radiographic evaluation, CT and/or bone scan should be considered. Nevertheless, MRI is the most specific and sensitive study in the diagnosis of a stress fracture, as it allows for early visualization of marrow changes (see **Figure 7.15**).[30] Traumatic femoral fractures can be diagnosed with radiographs.

Definitive Diagnosis

Traumatic fractures are high-energy injuries, and the deformity associated with them is often obvious. Radiographs or other imaging techniques are positive. Because of the powerful quadriceps and hamstring muscles, femoral shortening is often noted. The patient is unable to ambulate or move the leg without significant pain.

Diagnosing a femoral stress fracture requires a high index of suspicion and is based on positive radiographic studies or the clinical symptoms.

Pathomechanics and Functional Limitations

Frank fractures are usually self-limiting. Nevertheless, improper healing or failed fixation can result in decreased weight-bearing loads, altered gait, and the inability to ambulate.

An undiagnosed stress fracture will progress if high-intensity activity is allowed to continue. The compensatory gait redistributes weight-bearing forces along the extremity and increases the possi-

bility of secondary stress fractures and other overuse conditions.

■ Immediate Management

A traumatic femoral fracture requires stabilization and transport to an emergency room. Shock should be anticipated and appropriate precautions implemented. The extremity is not moved until a traction splint can be applied.

■ Medications

The severe pain associated with a traumatic femoral fracture can only be controlled with narcotic analgesics delivered intravenously, intramuscularly, or orally. Toradol and other injectable anti-inflammatory medications may also aid in pain relief. In contrast, NSAIDs or acetaminophen is usually adequate for pain control of a stress fracture.

■ Postinjury Management

Compression-side stress fracture of the femoral neck presents with increased bone density on the inferior side of the femoral neck. Those injuries that involve less than 50% of the femoral neck can be treated with approximately 4 to 6 weeks of avoidance of weight bearing with crutch walking, based on the patient's signs and symptoms.[28,31] Fractures involving more than 50% of the femoral neck often require surgical correction.

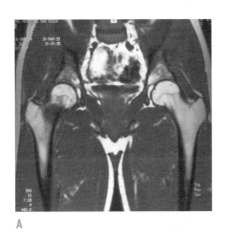

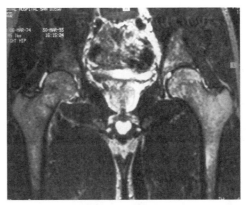

A   B

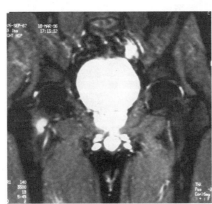

C

Figure 7.15 MRI of femoral neck stress fractures. (**A**) Stress fracture of the posteromedial femoral neck. The darkened area represents a nondisplaced femoral neck fatigue-related stress fracture. (**B**) A stress fracture extending from the cortical surface of the compression side of the femoral neck. (**C**) Compression-side stress fracture of the right hip. The fatigue line is less than 25% of the femoral neck diameter. Note the brightened area on the femoral neck caused by edema.

◾ Surgical Intervention

Traumatic Fractures

Supracondylar (distal femur), intertrochanteric, and subtrochanteric fractures require internal fixation. The surgical approach is usually lateral; the ITB is split, dissection is carried down through muscle tissue to the femur, and the fracture is identified. Stabilization is obtained through plate fixation.

Traumatic femoral fractures require stabilization by various techniques, depending on the fracture location. Midshaft fractures are best treated with intramedullary (IM) rod fixation using a proximal approach with entry through the piriformis fossa, or a distal approach through the intercondylar notch in a retrograde fashion.

IM nailing requires limited dissection, and rehabilitation is faster than that achieved when a lateral approach is needed for plate fixation. Proximal approaches necessitate trunk-stabilization strengthening exercises. Distal retrograde IM nailing involves an **arthrotomy** and patellar mobilization.

Rehabilitation includes ROM and quadriceps strengthening exercises.

Potential complications of traumatic femoral fractures include DVT, pulmonary embolus, nonunion, failure of fixation (especially in unstable comminuted fractures), and infection. Femoral head necrosis can occur if the head is significantly displaced, disrupting the arterial supply.

Stress fractures have fewer complications, but nonunion, displacement of femoral neck stress fractures, and recurrence are possible. Stable compression-side femoral neck stress fractures typically do not require surgery. Patients with compression-side fractures and a fatigue line greater than 50% of the width of the femoral neck are strong candidates for fixation using cannulated screws. Tension-side (superior) stress fractures are stabilized with cannulated screws as well (see **Figure 7.16**). Displaced femoral neck fractures require open reduction and internal fixation to prevent further displacement and avoid osteonecrosis. Surgery should be performed as soon as practical after the diagnosis.

arthrotomy The surgical opening of a joint.

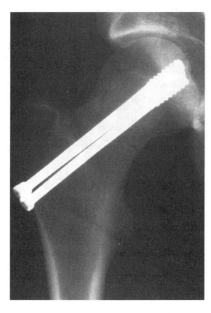

Figure 7.16 A complete, compression-side nondisplaced stress fracture of the femoral neck repaired with three cannulated screws.

Stress Fractures

Those stress fractures involving greater than 50% of the femoral neck and those characterized by cortical separation or callus formation on the superior aspect of the femoral neck are commonly treated with internal fixation. A displaced fracture of the femoral neck is a true medical emergency. Early stabilization with percutaneously placed cannulated screws is vital to decrease the potential for nonunion and osteonecrosis.

Uncomplicated internal fixation of a nondisplaced stress fracture of the femoral neck typically yields a good outcome following pinning and 6 weeks of avoiding weight bearing. Completely displaced stress fractures are associated with nonunion and osteonecrosis rates as high as 25% to 30%; therefore, the outcome in these cases is not as promising.

■ Postoperative Management

Once an acute fracture is surgically repaired, the patient's postoperative weight-bearing status depends on the stabilization technique used and the fracture condition. The more unstable the construct, the less weight bearing that is permitted, and the greater the protection needed with bracing. The IM stabilization generally allows for early weight bearing and ROM exercises; if comminution was severe, however, the initial weight-bearing loads must be limited. Once fracture healing can be documented by serial radiographs, the patient is allowed more liberties with weight bearing. ROM and strengthening exercises while weight bearing can also be initiated.

Athletes will be limited to touch-down weight bearing for approximately 6 weeks. Rehabilitation begins with a goal of full return of both active and passive ROM. Once full ROM has been achieved, a strengthening progression may be initiated, followed by endurance and agility training. Running is typically not introduced until a minimum of 3 months after surgery.

■ Injury-Specific Treatment and Rehabilitation Concerns

> **Specific Concerns**
> Limit stresses on the healing fracture line.
> Maintain cardiovascular fitness.
> Correct biomechanics (with stress fractures).

Although restricted in activities, the patient can maintain cardiovascular fitness and maintain or develop muscle strength in the uninvolved extremities. Swimming and bicycling are commonly used as cardiovascular activities. Open kinetic chain exercises for the hip, knee, and foot of the involved extremity can also be included during the non-weight-bearing phase.

If the thigh fascia or hip joint capsule is restricted, soft-tissue adhesions and joint mobility in the extremity are assessed. In the first few weeks of treatment, electrical stimulation can be used if muscle spasm is present, and heat application can be helpful for relaxation. Gait training involves progressive advancement from no weight bearing to full weight bearing, proceeding from two crutches without weight on the involved extremity, to two crutches with partial weight bearing, to one crutch with partial weight bearing, and finally to elimination of the crutches and an unassisted gait.

Along with gait corrections, progressive exercises for ROM and strength are incorporated early in the rehabilitation program. Before stretching and strengthening exercises, engaging in a cardiovascular activity such as stationary bicycling, swimming, or upper body ergometry for a brief period (10 to 15 minutes) enhances the effects of exercise and joint mobilization. Flexibility exercises should address both the area directly involved by the injury and other lower extremity segments that may have been secondarily affected by the reduced activity. If the patient has been bearing no weight or partial weight, strengthening exercises should target the entire lower extremity from the intrinsic toe muscles to the hip muscles. Once full weight bearing has resumed, proprioceptive and balance exercises such as the Romberg, tandem stance, and stork stand on different surfaces (moving from stable to unstable) can be initiated.

Estimated Amount of Time Lost

An acute fracture with surgical repair requires a long recovery time, approximately 4 to 6 months. A stress fracture may require 8 to 14 weeks for full recovery. The amount of time lost from competition reflects both the fracture severity and the amount of healing required. It is common for stress fractures to heal more slowly than traumatic fractures, but stress fractures generally are more stable.

Return-to-Play Criteria

The patient should be pain free during all activities, including running, hopping, and jumping. Radiographs should demonstrate good healing and an obvious maturing callus at the fracture site. Both ROM and strength in the affected extremity should be comparable with that in the contralateral extremity. Proprioceptive ability, including sport-specific activities, must be adequate before return to full activity, especially if the athlete has not been exposed to the stresses of normal activity for a while.

Piriformis Syndrome

Piriformis syndrome involves compression of the sciatic nerve—usually its peroneal portion. Pain along the course of the sciatic nerve may be misdiagnosed as a lumbosacral lesion. Activities that tend to result in piriformis syndrome include prolonged sitting, especially with the leg in external rotation, the shortened position for the piriformis; stair climbing, walking, and running; and a sudden contraction or overstretching of the muscle. Runners, baseball catchers, and softball catchers commonly develop this syndrome.

Differential Diagnosis

Sciatica, gluteal strain, tendinitis, bursitis, herniated lumbar disk, multifidus syndrome.

Imaging Techniques

Radiographs eliminate other potential diagnoses. In a patient with recalcitrant symptoms, MRI may be helpful to identify or rule out other conditions.

Definitive Diagnosis

The definitive diagnosis is based on positive physical examination findings, negative radiographs,

CLINICAL PRESENTATION

History

The patient may have engaged in stair climbing, running, or repetitive squatting and rising.

The pain may occur with an acute injury, such as falling and landing on the buttocks, causing the piriformis to go into spasm, or a sudden strain of the piriformis while running and slipping or changing directions unexpectedly.

Pain may be reported when turning in bed from one side to the other.[32]

Observation

No visual deformity may be apparent.

If the patient lies in the relaxed supine position, the involved extremity may rest in greater external rotation than the uninvolved leg.

The involved leg may appear shorter than the uninvolved leg.

Functional Status

Pain may be reported with stair climbing, running, squatting, sitting with legs crossed, or prolonged sitting.

Physical Examination Findings

Piriformis palpation reveals tenderness, usually in the junction of either the medial and central third or the central and lateral third of the muscle.

The flexion/adduction/internal rotation position can provoke symptoms.[32,33]

Internal femoral rotation against resistance in the seated position causes pain.

Maximum contraction of the piriformis against resistance (Pace sign) reproduces the pain.

and the exclusion of the conditions described in the "Differential Diagnosis" section.

Pathomechanics and Functional Limitations

Motions that stress the piriformis (e.g., lateral femoral rotation, squatting, stair climbing) are limited. Pressure on the sciatic nerve inhibits sensory and nerve function of the distal leg.

Medications

NSAIDs or acetaminophen may be used to reduce pain and increase function.

Surgical Intervention

Surgery is not normally indicated.

Practice Tip

Most individuals will respond to conservative treatment and rehabilitation. However, if conservative treatment fails and patients continue to have prolonged symptoms (most notably sciatic nerve entrapment), an endoscopic piriformis release can be performed to alleviate the compression of the sciatic nerve as it passes through the piriformis.

Postinjury Management

Relief of muscle spasm and attempts to gain motion in hip internal rotation are initiated. Piriformis syndrome is often accompanied by active trigger points, which can be resolved with myofascial or trigger-point release techniques accompanied by muscle stretching.

Injury-Specific Treatment and Rehabilitation Concerns

Specific Concerns

Control muscle spasm.
Increase internal rotation.

Electrical stimulation for pain and spasm relief and muscle facilitation may be used for the first week of treatment. Trigger-point release over the active area, myofascial release, and deep massage may be used to relieve muscle restriction.

Piriformis stretching is important to relax and lengthen the muscle. Once pain and spasm are relieved, the piriformis and other hip-stabilizing muscles, including the lateral and medial hip muscles and hip extensors, should be strengthened.

Estimated Amount of Time Lost

The amount of time lost from competition is usually not significant. The pain may be nagging and interfere with performance, forcing the patient to report the problem. Pain is the primary limiting factor; once it is relieved, full activity can resume.

Return-to-Play Criteria

The athlete should be able to complete all activities without pain, and muscle spasm and trigger-point tenderness should be resolved.

Sacroiliac Joint Dysfunction

Most "dysfunctions" indicate some loss of mobility. Sacroiliac (SI) joint dysfunction, also referred to as pelvic dysfunction, occurs when sacral motion is less than normal. Several different restrictions can occur, depending on the forces and torques and the locations where they are applied. For example, one side can become elevated, as when stepping off a curb while running and landing with a sharp jolt on one leg or falling and landing on the buttock,

CLINICAL PRESENTATION

History

Pain or a dull ache in the buttocks is noted.
Pain can radiate into the thigh or groin.
The pain increases as the patient attempts to move into the restricted SI motion.

Observation

Usually no swelling, discoloration, or deformity is noted.
Close observation may reveal asymmetry of skin creases in the sacral area.
Pelvic levels and leg lengths may be asymmetric.

Functional Status

The patient may sit or stand away from the involved side.

Physical Examination Findings

Alignment is assessed by comparing right and left sacral sulci and right and left inferior lateral angles (ILAs).
In sacral flexion, the sulci are deeper and the ILA is more posterior; if the sacrum is extended, the sulci are more posterior.
If sacral torsion is present, one of the ILAs is more posterior and the opposite sulcus is more posterior.
Any of the following special tests may be positive:
- FABER
- Quadrant
- Gaenslen
- SI compression
- SI distraction
- Straight-leg raise

restricting the sacrum in flexion. Trunk flexion and rotation activities can result in torsional joint injuries. Pain is often referred to the lower extremity, groin, buttock, or low back.

Differential Diagnosis

Lumbar spine injury, piriformis syndrome, gluteal strain.

Imaging Techniques

Radiographs, CT scan, and MRI may all be negative and are usually not helpful. Nevertheless, such imaging is necessary for working through the differential diagnoses.

Definitive Diagnosis

The definitive diagnosis of SI joint dysfunction is based on the physical examination findings and related special tests.

To assess SI joint mobility, the patient stands, and the clinician's thumbs are placed on each sulcus. When the patient moves into trunk flexion, the sacrum extends; the normal response is for the sulci to drop. If one does and the other does not, the nonmoving side is the restricted side.

Another movement test has the patient standing with the clinician's thumbs over one sulcus and over the midsacrum in line with the sulcus. The patient then raises the leg on that side toward the chest and repeats the lift with the opposite leg. The normal response is for the sacrum to move downward on the side of the lifted leg. If the sacrum does not move down or if it moves up, motion of the SI joint is restricted.

Pathomechanics and Functional Limitations

In patients with normal mechanics, as the lumbar spine flexes, the sacrum extends; as the lumbar spine extends, the sacrum flexes (see **Figure 7.17**). Movement of the sacrum into flexion is called nutation. Movement of the sacrum into extension is termed counternutation. One sacral side moves in the opposite direction from its contralateral side; in ambulation, as the right leg moves forward, the right sacrum rotates posteriorly, and the left sacrum rotates anteriorly. Although the amount of motion allowed in the SI joint is minimal, normal SI mobility during ambulation protects the lower lumbar disks from undue torsional and shearing stresses. If SI motion is restricted, stress applied to the lumbar disks—

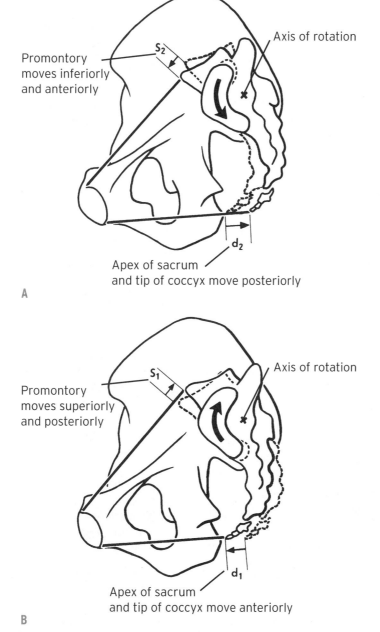

A

B

especially the L5-S1 disk—increases, enhancing the risk of injury.

Several dysfunctions can result from SI joint pathomechanics, which are classified based on the malalignment of either the sacrum on the ilium or the ilium on the sacrum. The more common sacrum-on-ilium (sacroiliac) conditions include sacral flexion, forward torsion, and backward torsion. The more common ilium-on-sacrum (iliosacral) conditions include pubic subluxation, iliac inflare, iliac outflare, and anterior and posterior up-slips. The pathomechanics for each condition vary, as do their causes and treatments.

Medications

NSAIDs or acetaminophen may be used to reduce pain and increase function.

Surgical Intervention

Surgery is performed on the SI joint only after traumatic injury. It is not indicated for conditions with an insidious onset.

Postinjury/Postoperative Management

The restricted SI motions must be identified and resolved. A thorough history of the mechanism of injury and the activities that increase pain plus a complete physical examination are required to diagnose the underlying ailments.

Injury-Specific Treatment and Rehabilitation Concerns

> **Specific Concerns**
> Realign the SI joint and pelvis.
> Reeducate the patient in proper posture and biomechanics.

If the patient has been unable to participate in sports because of SI pain, progressive exercises for ROM and strength can be incorporated early in the rehabilitation program. Stretching exercises are used to correct the SI dysfunction and are similar to the positions in which the patient was placed to resolve the SI dysfunction. A common treatment technique used to treat SI dysfunction is muscle energy. Techniques for addressing the most common dysfunctions are described in this section.

Sacroiliac Joint Muscle-Energy Techniques

Sacral muscle-energy techniques use light isometric muscle contractions. The patient can control the contracting muscles, but the clinician must ensure that joint position is correct and that the muscle contraction is applied in a specific direction with a very light force ("approximately 2 ounces") that is held for 3 to 10 seconds. At the end of the isometric hold, the patient is instructed to relax, and the clinician moves the joint to the point where a new restriction (barrier) is felt. This process is repeated three to five times.

Pubic Subluxation

In the pubic subluxation technique, the patient is placed in the hook-lying position with the knees positioned together, and the clinician's hands are placed on the knees to maintain the position while the patient gently attempts to move the knees apart (see Figure 7.18). In the reverse position, the clinician gently resists the patient's pulling the knees together.

Right Iliac Inflare

In the right iliac inflare technique, the patient is placed in the supine figure-of-four position (see Figure 7.19). A stabilizing hand is placed on the opposite hip, and the resisting hand on top of the knee. The patient is instructed to attempt to move the knee across toward the other leg. The applied stretch pushes down on the knee to move it toward the table. In the home exercise for this dysfunction, the patient lies in a figure-of-four position for several minutes.

Right Iliac Outflare

In the right iliac outflare technique, the patient is supine, and the involved hip is passively moved into internal rotation and adduction with the knee pointed toward the opposite shoulder. The monitoring hand is placed on the patient's sulcus, and the resisting hand is placed over the anterolateral knee. The patient is instructed to provide resistance into hip external rotation and abduction. The stretch is applied to the barrier of internal rotation (see Figure 7.20). In the home exercise for this dysfunction, the patient uses a hold-relax self-technique while supine and hugging the knee toward the opposite shoulder.

Left Up-Slip

In the left up-slip technique, with the patient supine, the clinician grasps the patient's ankle to abduct and flex the hip at 30°. The patient is instructed to take a deep breath in and blow it out slowly. As the patient exhales, the slack in the lower extremity is taken out. The patient is then instructed to perform a couple of quick coughs. The stretch is a sudden thrust performed by suddenly pulling on the leg during the coughs (see Figure 7.21). No home exercise is available for this technique. This procedure is contraindicated in the presence of knee or ankle injury.

---

barrier Restriction of, or resistance to, movement in a joint; the goal of muscle energy is to move the barrier to achieve normal mobility.

muscle energy A manual technique that uses voluntary muscle contraction against a resistive force to achieve desired results.

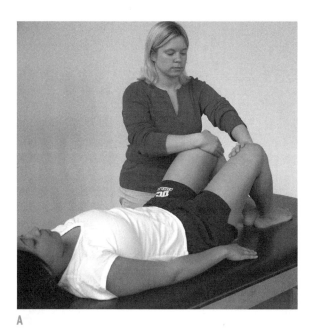

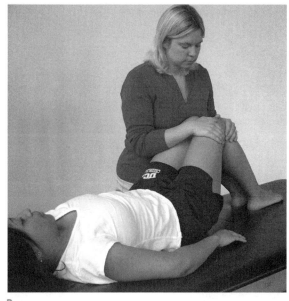

Figure 7.18 Muscle-energy technique for a pubic subluxation. (**A**) Adduction. (**B**) Abduction.

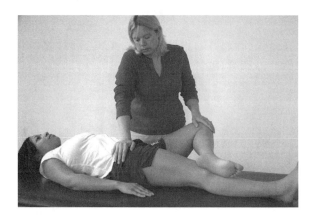

Figure 7.19 Right iliac inflare muscle-energy technique.

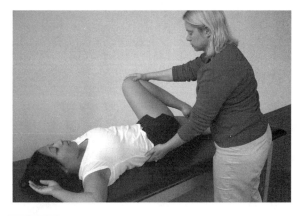

Figure 7.20 Right iliac outflare muscle-energy technique.

The same technique is used in a right up-slip except that the athlete is positioned prone and the leg is abducted and extended to 30°. The instructions for breathing and coughing are the same.

Forward Torsion

With the forward torsion technique, the patient is positioned lying on the involved side. The hips and knees are flexed to 90°, with the knees and legs off the table and the thighs supported on the table. The torso is rotated so that the bottom arm and shoulder are behind the patient, and the top arm is forward and resting comfortably over the table and over its side. The pelvis is monitored by placing one hand over the lumbosacral junction, while the resisting hand grasps the ankles or distal legs. The patient's thighs are supported by the

clinician's thigh. The legs are passively rotated downward to the floor until the resistance (barrier) is met. When rotation of the lumbosacral junction is felt, the barrier is met. The patient applies the isometric force, attempting to push the legs and feet to the ceiling. The stretch force is applied downward at the ankles (see **Figure 7.22**). In the home exercise for this technique, the athlete lies for several minutes on a couch or bed in the position shown in the figure.

Sacroiliac Joint Mobilizations

A nutated sacrum can be treated using postero-anterior (PA) sacral joint mobilization between the inferior lateral angles. Graded mobilizations over the inferior sacrum are used to obtain a counternutated position (see **Figure 7.23A**). In the case of a

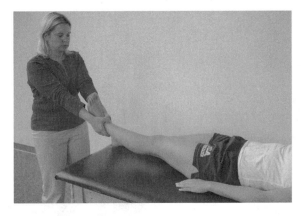

Figure 7.21 Left up-slip muscle-energy technique.

Figure 7.22 Forward torsion muscle-energy technique.

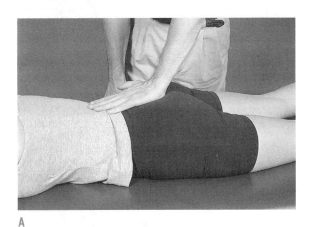

A   B

Figure 7.23 Sacral joint mobilizations. (**A**) Treatment of a nutated sacrum. (**B**) Treatment of a counternutated sacrum.

counternutated sacrum, PA mobilizations are applied over the superior sacrum (see **Figure 7.23B**).

Estimated Amount of Time Lost

The amount of time lost from competition varies depending on the duration of the existing symptoms, the magnitude of pain, and the amount of function lost. Some patients lose no time from activity, whereas others must refrain from participation in their sport for as long as 2 months.

Return-to-Play Criteria

The athlete should be pain free, and examination of the sacroiliac joint should reveal good alignment.

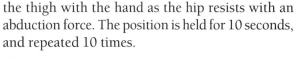

Rehabilitation

This section includes early rehabilitation exercises for the pelvis, hip, and thigh, including flexibility and early strengthening exercises using isometrics and rubber tubing. Other relevant exercises are presented in Chapters 8 and 16.

Flexibility Exercises

Refer to the following exercises in Chapter 8:
- Quadriceps stretch
- Alternate quadriceps stretch
- Hamstring stretch
- Alternate hamstring stretch
- Hip flexor stretch
- Adductor stretch
- Iliotibial band stretch
- Hip internal rotator stretch
- Hip external rotator stretch
- Piriformis stretch

Strengthening Exercises

Advanced exercises for the hip and lower extremity are presented in Chapter 8 and Chapter 16.

Isometrics

Hip Abduction
In a seated position, the patient places the opposite hand against the distal lateral thigh and pushes against the thigh with the hand as the hip resists with an abduction force. The position is held for 10 seconds, and repeated 10 times.

Hip Adduction
In a seated position, the patient places both fists between the distal thighs and attempts to move the thighs together, holding this position for 10 seconds. The exercise is repeated 10 times.

Hip Extension
Standing with the back to the wall and approximately 6 in. from the wall, the patient places the heel of an extended leg to the wall and pushes the leg against the wall, holding the position for 10 seconds. It may be necessary for the patient to hold on to a chair or other secure object for balance. The exercise is repeated 10 times.

Hip Internal Rotation
Seated on a chair with the legs crossed at the ankles and the involved leg crossed under the uninvolved leg, the patient attempts to pull the ankle of the involved leg away from the uninvolved ankle. The position is held for 10 seconds, and repeated 10 times.

Hip External Rotation
Seated on a chair with the legs parallel and the feet touching their medial aspects together, the patient pushes the foot of the involved leg toward the uninvolved extremity, attempting to push the leg into external rotation. The position is held for 10 seconds, and repeated 10 times.

Rubber Tubing Exercises
See Figure 7.24.

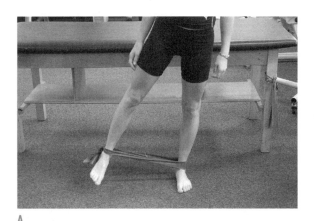
A

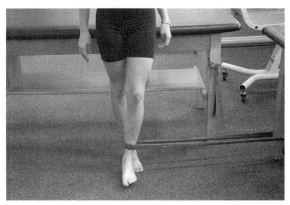
B

Figure 7.24 Resistive hip strengthening exercises. (**A**) *Hip abduction*. With the patient standing, the tubing is wrapped around both ankles. Using large steps, the patient walks sideways toward the involved side. (**B**) *Hip adduction*. With the tubing anchored to a door jamb or an adjacent table, the tubing is wrapped around the patient's involved distal leg. The hip is adducted as far as possible against the tubing. *(continues)*

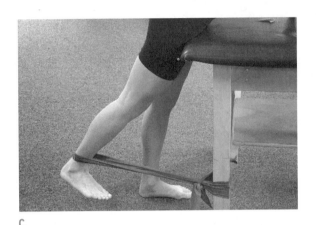

C

D

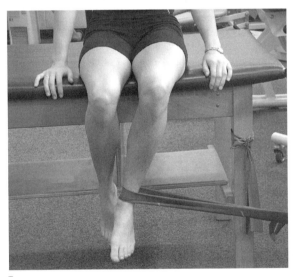

E

Figure 7.24 Continued. Resistive hip strengthening exercises. **(C)** *Hip extension*. With the tubing anchored around the ankle and secured to a table leg, the patient stands at the end of the table and leans to place the trunk on the table. The hip is extended while the knee is kept straight. In a variation of this exercise, the patient stands and grasps a chair for stability while the hip is extended from the neutral position. **(D)** *Hip internal rotation*. With the tubing anchored around a table leg and the patient sitting on the table, the patient attempts to internally rotate the hip against the tubing. **(E)** *Hip external rotation*. With the tubing anchored around a table leg and the patient seated, the patient externally rotates the hip against the tubing.

References

1. Nicholas SJ, Tyler TF. Adductor muscle strains in sport. *Sports Med.* 2002;32:339–344.
2. Morelli V, Smith V. Groin injuries in athletes. *Am Fam Physician.* 2001;64:1405–1414.
3. Tyler TF, Nicholas SJ, Campbell RJ, et al. The effectiveness of a preseason exercise program to prevent adductor muscle strains in professional ice hockey players. *Am J Sports Med.* 2002;30:680–683.
4. Garrett WE Jr. Muscle strain injuries. *Am J Sports Med.* 1996;24(suppl 6):S2–S8.
5. Clanton TO, Coupe KJ. Hamstring strains in athletes: Diagnosis and treatment. *J Am Acad Orthop Surg.* 1998;6:237–248.
6. David HG, Green JT, Grant AJ, Wilson CA. Simultaneous bilateral quadriceps rupture: A complication of anabolic steroid abuse. *J Bone Joint Surg Br.* 1995;77:159–160.
7. Miller MD, Cooper DE, Warner JJP (eds). *Review of Sports Medicine and Arthroscopy.* Philadelphia: W. B. Saunders; 2002.
8. Orchard J, Marsden J, Lord S, Garlick D. Preseason hamstring muscle weakness associated with hamstring muscle injury in Australian footballers. *Am J Sports Med.* 1997;25:81–85.
9. Croisier JL, Forthomme B, Namurois M-H, et al. Hamstring muscle strain recurrence and strength performance disorders. *Am J Sports Med.* 2002;30:199–203.
10. Verrall GM, Slavotinek JP, Barnes PG, et al. Clinical risk factors for hamstring muscle strain injury: A prospective study with correlation of injury by magnetic resonance imaging. *Br J Sports Med.* 2001;35:435–440.
11. Ryan JB, Wheeler JH, Hopkinson WJ, et al. Quadriceps contusions: West Point update. *Am J Sports Med.* 1991;19:299–304.
12. Wieder DL. Treatment of traumatic myositis ossificans with acetic acid iontophoresis. *Phys Ther.* 1992;72:133–137.
13. Anderson K, Strickland SM, Warren R. Hip and groin injuries in athletes. *Am J Sports Med.* 2001;29:521–533.
14. Shbeeb MI, Matteson EL. Trochanteric bursitis (greater trochanter pain syndrome). *Mayo Clin Proc.* 1996;71:565–569.
15. Dobbs MB, Gordon JE, Luhmann SJ, et al. Surgical correction of the snapping iliopsoas tendon in adolescents. *J Bone Joint Surg Am.* 2002;84:420–424.
16. Gruen GS, Scioscia TN, Lowenstein JE. The surgical treatment of internal snapping hip. *Am J Sports Med.* 2002;30:607–613.
17. Pelsser V, Cardinal E, Hobden R, et al. Extraarticular snapping hip: Sonographic findings. *Am J Roentgenol.* 2001;176:67–73.
18. Traycoff RB. Pseudotrochanteric bursitis: The differential diagnosis of lateral hip pain. *J Rheumatol.* 1991;18:1810–1812.
19. Kagan A Jr. Rotator cuff tears of the hip. *Clin Orthop Relat Res.* 1999;368:135–140.
20. Jones DL, Erhard RE. Diagnosis of trochanteric bursitis versus femoral neck stress fracture. *Phys Ther.* 1997;77:58–67.
21. Toohey AK, LaSalle TL, Martinez S, Polisson RP. Iliopsoas bursitis: Clinical features, radiographic findings, and disease associations. *Semin Arthritis Rheum.* 1990;20:41–47.
22. Johnston CAM, Wiley JP, Lindsay DM, Wiseman DA. Iliopsoas bursitis and tendinitis: A review. *Sports Med.* 1998;25:271–283.
23. Johnston CAM, Lindsay DM, Wiley JP. Treatment of iliopsoas syndrome with a hip rotation strengthening program: A retrospective case series. *J Orthop Sports Phys Ther.* 1999;29:218–224.
24. Shindle MK, Domb BG, Kelly BT. Hip and pelvic problems in athletes. *Op Techn Sports Med.* 2007;15:195–203.
25. Mechem CC. Fracture, pelvic. *eMedicine.* September 30, 2009. Available at: http://emedicine.medscape.com/article/825869-overview. Accessed February 13, 2010.
26. American Academy of Orthopaedic Surgeons. Pelvic fractures. Available at: http://orthoinfo.aaos.org/topic.cfm?topic=A00223. Accessed February 13, 2010.
27. Shin AY, Gillingham BL. Fatigue fractures of the femoral neck in athletes. *J Am Acad Orthop Surg.* 1997;5:293–302.
28. Casterline M, Osowski S, Ulrich G. Femoral stress fracture. *J Athl Train.* 1996;31:53–56.
29. Davies AM, Carter SR, Grimer RJ, Sneath RS. Fatigue fractures of the femoral diaphysis in the skeletally immature simulating malignancy. *Br J Radiol.* 1989;62:893–896.
30. Dugowson CE, Drinkwater BL, Clark JM. Nontraumatic femur fracture in an oligomenorrheic athlete. *Med Sci Sports Exerc.* 1991;23:1323–1325.
31. Brukner P, Bennell K. Stress fractures in female athletes: Diagnosis, management and rehabilitation. *Sports Med.* 1997;24:419–429.
32. Beatty RA. The piriformis muscle syndrome: A simple diagnostic maneuver. *Neurosurgery.* 1994;34:512–514.
33. Fishman LM, Dombi GW, Michaelsen C, et al. Piriformis syndrome: Diagnosis, treatment, and outcome: A 10-year study. *Arch Phys Med Rehabil.* 2002;83:295–301.

Additional Lower Extremity Therapeutic Exercises

The exercises and techniques presented in this chapter are adjuncts to those presented in Chapters 4, 5, 6, and 7. Many other exercises can also be incorporated or substituted for those presented here. In addition, most exercises can be modified based on the patient's needs, equipment on hand, or personal preference. To construct a complete rehabilitation program, cross-referencing among these chapters is required.

Flexibility Exercises

The following stretches are held for 10 to 30 seconds and are repeated three or four times.

■ Ankle and Lower Leg

> **Cross-References**
>
> Dorsiflexion stretch for the gastrocnemius (page 121)
> Dorsiflexion stretch for the soleus (page 121)
> Prolonged dorsiflexion stretch (page 122)
> Plantar flexion stretch (page 122)

■ Femoral Muscles

Hamstring Stretch

The patient stands and faces a table about hip height. The foot of the involved leg is placed on the table, with the standing foot facing forward. The patient leans from the hips—not the back—to reach toward the elevated foot with the opposite hand until a stretch is felt. Both knees remain straight during the exercise.

Alternate Hamstring Stretch

The patient lies supine with the nonstretched leg extended. The stretched leg is flexed at the hip, with the hands clasped behind the knee to hold the thigh at 90°. The knee is extended until a stretch is felt in the hamstrings (see Figure 8.1).

Quadriceps Stretch

The side-lying patient bends the knee and grasps the foot behind the buttock. Keeping the hip and back straight, the patient pulls the heel toward the buttock until tension is felt in the anterior thigh (see Figure 8.2).

Alternate Quadriceps Stretch

The patient stands facing a wall, using one hand for support. The opposite hand grasps the foot of the leg being stretched behind the back and, while keeping the knee pointed to the floor and the back straight, the patient pulls the heel toward the buttock until a stretch is felt (see Figure 8.3).

> **Cross-References**
>
> Heel slide (page 179)
> Wall slide (page 179)
> Prone hangs (page 180)
> Prone flexion (page 180)
> Towel propping (page 180)
> Patellar mobilization (page 214)

Figure 8.2 Quadriceps stretch.

Figure 8.3 Alternate quadriceps stretch.

Figure 8.1 Alternate hamstring stretch.

■ Hip Muscles

Hip Flexor Stretch
The patient leans forward, extending one leg backward while keeping the opposite knee flexed. The hips are pushed forward until a stretch is felt in the extended hip (see Figure 8.4).

Adductor Stretch
In the sitting position, the patient flexes both knees and separates the knees to bring the soles of the feet together. With the forearms placed along the legs and the hands at the ankles, the patient pushes the legs down with the forearms until a stretch is felt in the adductors (see Figure 8.5).

Iliotibial Band Stretch
While in a side-lying position on a table, the patient places the top leg over the side of the table and relaxes in this position for approximately 5 minutes. An alternative is to have the clinician apply force to the leg while stabilizing the pelvis (see Figure 8.6).

Hip Internal Rotator Stretch
The patient sits at the edge of a table. The clinician places one hand distal to the flexed knee and applies external rotational force on the hip until the patient feels a stretch in the internal rotators (see Figure 8.7).

Hip External Rotator Stretch
The patient sits at the edge of a table. The clinician places one hand distal to the flexed knee; the opposite hand stabilizes the femur just proximal to the knee. An internal rotational force is applied on the hip until the patient feels a stretch on the external rotators (see Figure 8.8).

Piriformis Stretch
The patient lies supine with the knees and hips flexed and the feet on the floor. The involved leg is crossed over the uninvolved leg. Both knees are brought toward the chest, and the patient grabs the leg to pull the knees closer. As the knees are brought up, the top knee is angled toward the opposite shoulder (see Figure 8.9).

■ Strengthening Exercises

The following isotonic strengthening exercises are used early in the rehabilitation program. When the patient can successfully complete these exercises,

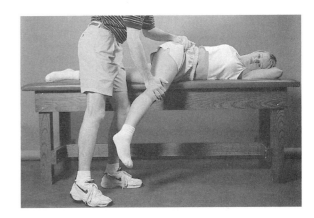

Figure 8.6   Iliotibial band stretch.

Figure 8.4   Hip flexor stretch.

Figure 8.5   Adductor stretch.

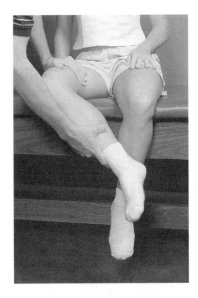

Figure 8.7   Hip internal rotator stretch.

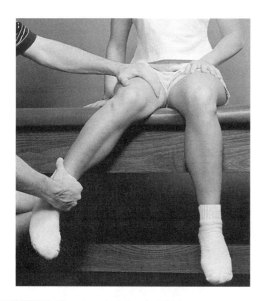

Figure 8.8 Hip external rotator stretch.

Figure 8.9 Piriformis stretch.

weight machines or free weights can be incorporated into the rehabilitation protocol.

Ankle and Lower Leg

Cross-References

Isometrics
  Dorsiflexion (page 122)
  Plantar flexion (page 122)
  Inversion (page 121)
  Eversion (page 121)
Others
  Rubber-tubing exercises (page 123)
  Towel rolls (page 122)
  Marble pickups (page 122)
  Heel raises (page 122)
  Toe raises (page 122)
  Ankle weight exercises (page 122)

Femoral Muscles

Standing Hamstring Curl

The patient stands with the quadriceps pressed against the table and flexes the knee, bringing the heel toward the buttocks. This position is briefly held and the foot is then lowered to the floor, completely extending the knee. The exercise is repeated, beginning with two to three sets of 10 repetitions and progressing to five sets of 10 repetitions. Weights can be added in increments of 5 lb; however, the patient should begin with two sets of 10 repetitions after any increase.

Standing Hip Extension

The patient stands and leans forward with the upper body supported on the table. Keeping the knee extended, the patient extends the hip by raising the leg toward the ceiling, extending the hip only as far as can be done without externally rotating it. The exercise is repeated, beginning with two to three sets of 10 repetitions and progressing to five sets of 10 repetitions. Weights can be added in increments of 5 lb; however, the patient must begin with two sets of 10 repetitions after any increase.

Cross-References

Quadriceps sets (page 180)
Reverse quadriceps sets (page 180)
Hamstring sets (page 181)
Quadriceps/hamstring co-contraction (page 181)
Multiangle isometrics (page 181)
Straight-leg raises (page 181)
Leg curl (page 182)
Leg extension (page 182)
Isokinetics (page 182)

General Lower Extremity Strengthening

Triceps Surae

The patient is seated with resistance placed over the thigh proximal to the knee as the ankle is plantar flexed against the resistance. An alternative position is for the patient to stand with the weight across the shoulders or held in the hands (see **Figure 8.10**). When the knee is extended, the gastrocnemius is emphasized; when the knee is flexed, the soleus is the prime mover.

Step-Up and Step-Down

These exercises begin at low heights and are advanced as range of motion and strength improve. Forward, lateral, and backward vectors of movement can be used. The patient begins by stepping up on a short stool, first with one foot and then the other, then stepping down in the same order (see **Figure 8.11**). The patient should be closely monitored so that substitutions are not made to assist in performing the exercise.

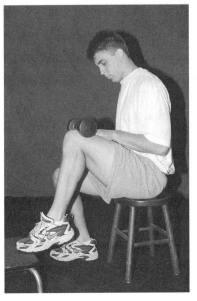

Figure 8.10 Triceps surae.

Squat

The squatting motion can be performed in numerous ways with various devices, including free weights, gym balls, resistive bands, walls, and shuttles. It can be performed in limited range of motion as needed by the individual patient. Hamstring activity is facilitated by trunk flexion.

Single-leg squatting activities can be initiated when the patient is bearing full weight and demonstrates adequate hip and thigh strength to maintain the correct biomechanical position during double-leg squats (see **Figure 8.12**).

Hip Muscles

In this activity, surgical tubing or Thera-Band (The Hygenic Corp., Akron, Ohio) is looped around the leg, just proximal to the knee. The area may be padded with a towel for patient comfort. While standing on the uninvolved leg, the patient moves the involved leg through sets of abduction, adduction, flexion, and extension (see **Figure 8.13**). As the patient advances with this exercise, diagonal motions may be incorporated.

Cross-References

Isometrics
    Hip abduction (page 251)
    Hip adduction (page 251)
    Hip extension (page 251)
    Hip internal rotation (page 251)
    Hip external rotation (page 251)
Others
    Rubber-tubing exercises (page 251)

Figure 8.11 Step-up and step-down.

Figure 8.12 Squat.

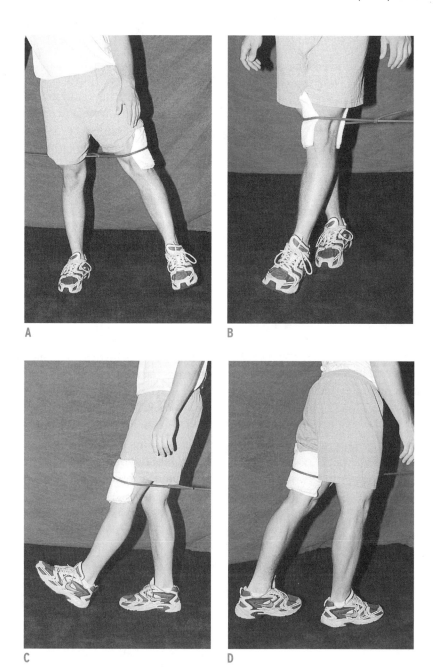

Figure 8.13 Hip muscle exercises. **(A)** Abduction. **(B)** Adduction. **(C)** Flexion. **(D)** Extension.

Proprioception and Functional Exercises

Proprioceptive neuromuscular facilitation (PNF) involves mass movement patterns that incorporate spiral and diagonal motions to facilitate selective irradiation—that is, resisting strong muscle groups at specific times in a pattern to facilitate the contractions of weaker muscle groups in the same pattern. These patterns closely resemble sport and work activity movements. Each spiral and diagonal pattern includes a three-component motion with respect to either all the joints or pivots of action participating in the movement. The three compo-

nents are flexion/extension, adduction/abduction, and rotation. The optimal performance of a pattern involves sequential contractions described as a "chain" of muscles moving in synergy. The agonistic pattern involves components of action that are opposite those of the antagonistic pattern.

Improvements in functional output are achieved when proprioceptive, cutaneous, and auditory inputs are used in the rehabilitative setting. The stretch reflex is the neurophysiologic mechanism on which PNF is based. Autogenic inhibition and reciprocal inhibition are two neurophysiologic phenomena used to describe the neuromuscular system's ability to be stimulated and inhibited.

Rhythmic Initiation

Rhythmic initiation is used to improve the patient's ability to begin movement. This technique involves voluntary relaxation, passive movements, and isotonic contractions of major muscle components of the antagonistic pattern.

Repeated Contractions

The stretch reflex is facilitated and coupled with repetitive voluntary isotonic contractions to enhance the patient's effort to initiate movement. As the patient's ability to produce an isotonic contraction improves, an isometric hold at weaker points in the range may be added to advance the treatment.

Reversal of Antagonists

Stimulation of the agonist contraction occurs when the patient first resists an isometric or isotonic contraction of the antagonist, then resists the agonist movement as the antagonistic pattern is reversed.

- *Slow reversal:* An isotonic contraction of the antagonist is followed by an isotonic contraction of the agonist.
- *Slow reversal hold:* The antagonist performs an isotonic contraction followed by an isometric contraction; the agonist then performs an isotonic contraction followed by an isometric contraction.
- *Rhythmic stabilization:* An isometric contraction of the antagonist is followed by an isometric contraction of the agonist, resulting in co-contraction.

Relaxation Techniques

Relaxation techniques are used to gain range of motion via the relaxation or inhibition of a pattern's antagonist.

Contract–Relax

The patient's body part is passively moved into the agonistic pattern to the point of limitation, when the patient is instructed to contract ("push" or "pull") isotonically in the antagonistic pattern. As the patient then relaxes, the limb is redirected into the agonistic pattern until the patient again feels limitation.

Hold–Relax

The patient's body part is moved in the same sequence as in the contract–relax technique. At the point of limitation, the patient is instructed to perform a maximal isometric contraction and then to voluntarily relax. As the patient feels the relaxation, the limb

is moved into the agonistic pattern to a new point of limitation.

Hold–Contract

The range-limiting (antagonistic) pattern is an isotonic contraction, followed by an isometric contraction of the same pattern against resistance. After a brief, voluntary relaxation, an isotonic contraction of the agonistic pattern is performed.

Lower Extremity PNF Patterns

The two basic PNF patterns for the lower extremity are D1 and D2. These are further divided into two subdivisions (see CT 8.1 and CT 8.2):

- D1 moving into flexion
- D1 moving into extension
- D2 moving into flexion
- D2 moving into extension

These patterns involve diagonal and rotational movements. Each pattern begins when the musculature that will be active is placed in an elongated position and ends when the musculature has obtained a shortened position. Resistance is supplied manually. These patterns incorporate gross muscle activity, rather than individual or isolated muscle activity. It can be beneficial for patients to learn these patterns before using resistance.

Balance Progression

Proprioception is the term used to define the perception of joint position and limb "heaviness." *Kinesthesia* is the term used to define the body's ability to detect positional changes. Although the terms are not interchangeable, they are closely related. Articular mechanoreceptors, Golgi tendon organs, muscle spindles, the vestibular system, the visual system, and cerebellar and cerebral functions all contribute to the body's conscious and unconscious positional awareness.

Many proprioceptive and kinesthetic (balance) activities can be performed with very little equipment. The difficulty of the exercises can be changed by several factors.

Standing Tubing Band Kick

The patient stands single legged on the uninvolved extremity. Tubing or a band is wrapped from the involved ankle and foot to the uninvolved ankle and foot or a secure object, and the patient moves the uninvolved extremity against the tension of the tubing or band while attempting to maintain balance. Patterns of hip flexion, adduction, abduction, extension, or diagonals may be used (see **Figure 8.14**).

CT Clinical Technique 8.1

D1 Lower Extremity PNF Pattern

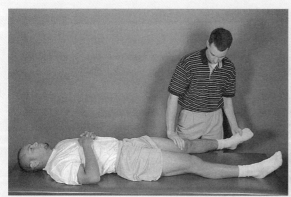
A

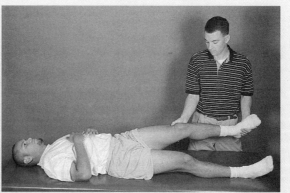
B

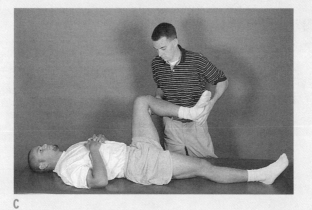
C

(A) Starting position. **(B)** Moving into flexion. **(C)** Terminal flexion.

	Extension into Flexion	Flexion into Extension
Hand Placement (resistance)	One hand is on the dorsal aspect of the medial foot.	One hand is on the plantar aspect of the lateral foot.
	The opposite hand is placed over the anteromedial femur, just proximal to the patella.	The opposite hand is placed on the posterolateral thigh, just proximal to the joint line.
Verbal Command	"Pull against me."	"Push against me."
Motion (in one continuous motion and against resistance)	The hip moves from extension, abduction, and internal rotation to flexion, adduction, and external rotation.	The hip moves from flexion, adduction, and external rotation to extension, abduction, and internal rotation.
	The knee moves from extension to flexion.	The knee moves from flexion to extension.
	The tibia moves from internal rotation to external rotation.	The tibia moves from external rotation to internal rotation.
	The ankle and foot move from plantar flexion and eversion to dorsiflexion and inversion.	The ankle and foot move from dorsiflexion and inversion to plantar flexion and eversion.

8

CT Clinical Technique 8.2

D2 Lower Extremity PNF Pattern

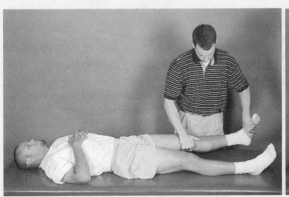
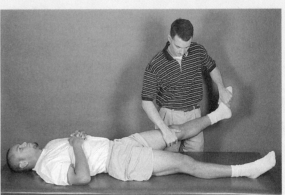
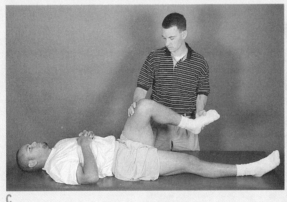
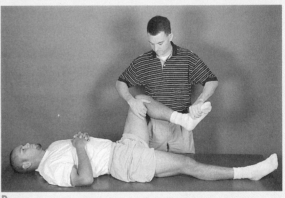

(A) Movement into extension. **(B)** Moving into flexion. **(C)** Hip internal rotation. **(D)** Hip external rotation.

	Extension into Flexion	Flexion into Extension
Hand Placement (resistance)	One hand is on the dorsal aspect of the medial foot. The opposite hand is placed over the anteromedial femur, just proximal to the patella.	One hand is on the plantar aspect of the lateral foot. The opposite hand is placed on the posterolateral thigh, just proximal to the joint line.
Verbal Command	"Pull against me."	"Push against me."
Motion (in one continuous motion and against resistance)	The hip moves from extension, abduction, and external rotation to flexion, adduction, and internal rotation. The knee moves from extension to flexion. The tibia moves from external rotation to internal rotation. The ankle and foot move from plantar flexion and inversion to dorsiflexion and eversion.	The hip moves from flexion, abduction, and internal rotation to extension, adduction, and external rotation. The knee moves from flexion to extension. The tibia moves from internal rotation to external rotation. The ankle and foot move from dorsiflexion and eversion to plantar flexion and inversion.

Figure 8.14 Standing tubing band kick.

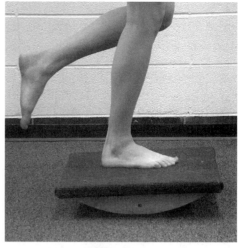

Figure 8.16 Vestibular board.

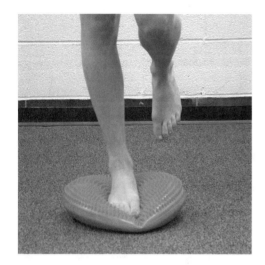

Figure 8.15 Stork stand.

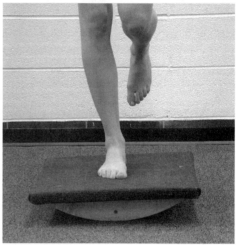

Stork Stand

The patient stands single legged on the involved leg and attempts to maintain balance for as long as possible. The knee can be placed in various angles of flexion depending on the patient's tolerance and restrictions. The patient can perform stork stands while standing on an unstable surface (see Figure 8.15). Ideally, the patient should be able to maintain balance without wavering or losing balance for 30 seconds. To further challenge the patient, progress to performing the exercises with the eyes closed to remove visual cues. Functional activities such as tossing and catching a ball, bouncing a ball, setting a ball, or other upper extremity activity is the next progression.

Balance Beam

The balance beam presents the patient with the difficulty of maneuvering on a narrow base of support. Static and dynamic balance can be challenged by variations of the stork stand and by walking forward, backward, heel to toe, and side stepping.

Vestibular Board

The vestibular board typically challenges the patient in two directions: forward–backward and side to side (see Figure 8.16). Because this board has a larger surface area than other unstable-surface trainers, the patient can perform activities that involve wider stances or kneeling and can focus on controlling two directions of movement.

Proprioception Board

The patient stands on the proprioception or "wobble board" and attempts to balance or trace the edge of the board. Various levels of difficulty can be achieved by changing the height or size of half-balls attached to the proprioception board or by standing on only one leg. The patient also can perform the exercise using front-to-back or side-to-side motions (see Figure 8.17). The number of repetitions can vary.

Mini-trampoline

Several exercises can be performed on the mini-trampoline, including balancing on one foot, stepping on and off the trampoline, hopping on and off the trampoline, and picking up cups positioned from the 3:00 to the 9:00 o'clock positions around the perimeter of the trampoline. Other standard proprioceptive exercises with multiplanar activities and functions such as ball catching while balancing can be performed as well. The number of repetitions can vary.

Single-Leg Squat

The patient squats on one leg and balances for 30 seconds, or longer if possible (see **Figure 8.18**). This exercise should be performed with the affected leg flexed or extended at various joint angles to change the center of gravity. The number of repetitions can vary.

Wall Squats

The patient assumes a squatting position, with the back facing a wall and holding an inflated exercise ball against the wall. The position is held for 30 seconds, or longer if possible (see **Figure 8.19**). The number of repetitions can vary.

Slide Board

The resistance between the surface of the board and the covering placed on the feet decreases friction, allowing the patient to skate-glide on the slide board (see **Figure 8.20**). Repetitions can be counted as the number of times the patient glides from side to side or the number of times the exercise is completed in a specific period.

Rhythmic Stabilization

Rhythmic stabilization can be performed in functional positions such as in a squat, on stairs, or in a downhill skier's tuck. The patient holds the position while the clinician attempts to move him or her from the position with perturbations (see **Figure 8.21**). The force applied is individualized to the patient's tolerance.

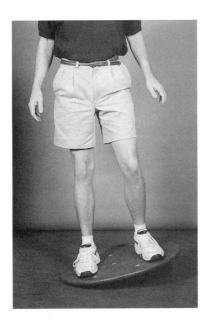

Figure 8.17 Proprioception board.

Figure 8.18 Single-leg squat.

Figure 8.19 Wall squats.

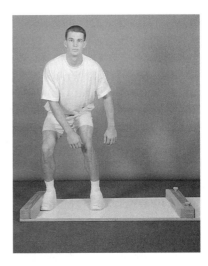

Figure 8.20 Slide board.

Figure 8.21 Rhythmic stabilization.

Half-squat position   Vertical jump

Figure 8.22 Squat jump.

Plyometric Exercises

Plyometrics are exercises that enable a muscle to reach maximum strength in as short a time as possible. These activities are useful in improving strength, speed, and kinesthetic ability. Lower extremity plyometrics typically involve jump training. Thus, before starting plyometric exercises, the patient must have adequate muscular strength and endurance.

Recovery for plyometrics ranges from 5 to 10 seconds between repetitions and from 2 to 3 minutes between sets. The frequency at which the plyometric exercises are performed depends on the patient's level of conditioning and ability and the intensity at which the exercises are performed. High-intensity plyometric exercises should be performed only twice per week to allow adequate recovery.

Plyometric exercises can also be measured by volume, meaning the number of foot contacts made during a workout. Volume for a beginner should be limited to 80 to 100 contacts per session, advancing to 120 to 140 contacts per session. Each activity can be varied in intensity and volume as needed by the patient. Cones, boxes, mats, hurdles, stairs, and medicine balls are used for plyometric activities. Plyometric exercises can also be tailored to be specific for the individual sport demands. Following are examples of plyometric exercises.

▦ Two-Foot Ankle Hop

The patient jumps in place, using only the ankles and jumping as high as possible with only a slight knee bend. As the patient progresses, proprioceptive and kinesthetic challenges can be added by incorporating the hip-twist ankle hop. This exer-cise is similar to the two-foot ankle hop, but this time the patient twists 90° to the left and then to the right while jumping in place. The sequence used is this:

> Jump with both feet together straight up and then land
> Jump again but twist to the right
> Jump and twist to the start position
> Jump and twist to the left
> Jump and twist to the start position

▦ Squat Jump

In this low-intensity plyometric exercise, the patient assumes a half-squat position with hands behind the head, jumps vertically, and, on landing, returns to the half-squat position to repeat the same series without pause (see **Figure 8.22**). At least 10 repetitions per set should be performed.

▦ Split-Squat Jump

In this low-intensity plyometric exercise, the patient assumes a lunge position with one foot forward, jumps vertically to land in a lunge position, and repeats the series without pause (see **Figure 8.23**).

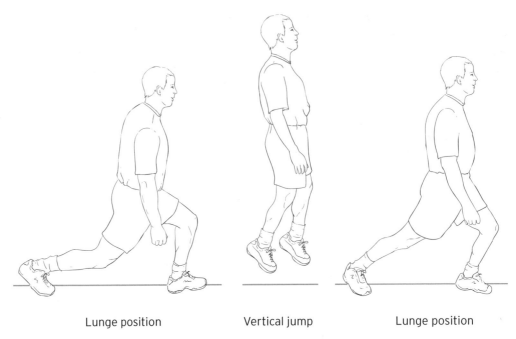

Lunge position   Vertical jump   Lunge position

Figure 8.23 Split-squat jump.

At least 10 repetitions with each foot forward should be performed.

Standing Triple Jump

In this medium-intensity exercise, the patient begins in a partial squat position and jumps horizontally and vertically, using the arms for balance, and lands on one foot. Without pausing, the patient jumps off that foot to land on the opposite foot, and again without pausing, jumps and lands on both feet. Two sets of six jumps each should be performed, with a 30- to 60-second rest period between sets.

Box Jump

In this high-intensity exercise, the patient stands in front of a box in a semi-squatting position, jumps up on a box 1 to 2.5 ft high, and, immediately on contact, jumps off (see **Figure 8.24**). As soon as contact is made with the ground, the patient jumps up or out, using double-arm action. Two to four sets of 5 to 10 repetitions are performed.

Stadium Hop

The patient places the hands on the head and uses both legs to jump stadium steps, one at a time. The movement should be continuous without stopping. The progression can be to jump two steps at a time or increase the number of steps or the speed of the jumps.

Pyramid Box Jump

Three to five boxes are placed from shortest to tallest in series, with space in between. The patient jumps onto the first one, off and onto the floor, and immediately jumps onto the next box, off and onto the ground, and continues through to the final box.

Depth Jump

The patient stands on a 12-in high box and steps off the box, immediately going into a rapid vertical jump. The arms can be used to assist in the jump, and the patient attempts to jump as high as possible. Taller boxes (up to 18 in) can be used as the patient improves.

Functional Agility Exercises

Functional activities are a prelude to sport-specific activities. Some of these functional activities may actually be sport-specific activities, depending on the sport and the functional activity. For example, running and cutting are functional activities but are also sport-specific activities for a basketball player or a football running back. Other lower extremity

Starting position   Jump onto box   Jump from box

Figure 8.24 Box jump.

functional activities include activities such as figure-of-eight runs, timed sprints, side shuffles, backward running, run and jump, and other running activities that involve changes in direction and speed.

Agility exercises combine speed, power, and skill. The patient should begin with simple, well-controlled tasks such as forward and backward running or side shuffling at low intensities. As the patient improves, the agilities can progress to more complex patterns such as figure-of-eights, bag drills, or obstacle courses. As with all other rehabilitation programs, agility activities should be designed to meet the functional requirements of the individual athlete's sport. The following are examples of functional agility exercises:

- The patient jumps over an object on the floor, such as a stepstool or box. This exercise can be done in a forward jump or lateral left-to-right jump sequence. The speed, height, and sequence of the jumps can be varied to increase the difficulty.

- A variety of agility activities can be used to increase performance demands. Examples include running circle-of-eights and running zigzags with sudden changes in running direction (forward, left, right, backward) in response to unpredicted verbal demands, and hopping in different directions (e.g., forward–left, forward–right, left–right).

Endurance

Muscular endurance is the capacity of a muscle group to perform repeated contractions against a load or to sustain a contraction for an extended period. The mechanics of performing an activity often change as the body becomes fatigued. Endurance activities can be performed on treadmills, cycles, skier machines, stair steppers, elliptical runners, and other machines.

Running Progression

Running progressions should begin with low intensities and short distances on smooth, level surfaces such as a treadmill. The degree of activity and the length of rest periods should be determined by the patient's initial fitness level and gradually progress toward the competitive requirements of the individual's sport, whether it be an aerobic activity such as marathon running or an anaerobic activity such as gymnastics. Functional running progressions include everything from walking to sport-specific drills. These exercises are often timed and are limited only by the imagination.

The T-test is a timed functional exercise that uses four cones arranged in a T formation. Cone A, at the base of the T, is the start and finish. Cone B is 10 yards away at the top of the T, cone C is 5 yards to the right of cone B, and cone D is 5 yards to the left. The patient runs from cone A to touch the base of cone B, then shuffles to touch cone C, shuffles back past cone B to touch cone D, returns to cone B, and races for cone A.

Other functional exercises include jogging, running backward, zigzag running, running circles or figure-of-eights, and side shuffles.

Sport-Specific Activities

Sport-specific activities will depend on the athlete's sport and position within the sport. For example, a basketball forward's activities may include forward sprints for the distance of a court length, sprints to a layup or a sudden stop and jump shot, or vertical jumping. A volleyball player's activities would more likely include lateral movements to the left and right with jumps for blocking or hitting, dives, squats for setting, and diagonal sprints for the ball. If the clinician is unfamiliar with the specific sport activities and demands of the athlete's sport and position, he or she should consult with a coach to obtain assistance or instruction in useful activities for this stage of the rehabilitation program. The goal in the final stages of sport-specific activities should be normal performance without signs of favoring or hesitating in using the involved extremity. Observers should not be able to identify which extremity is injured based on the athlete's performance of these tasks.

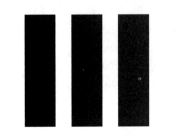

Upper Extremity

Shoulder Injuries

Brady L. Tripp, PhD, ATC
Michael Moser, MD

Sternoclavicular Joint Sprains

CLINICAL PRESENTATION

History

An indirect force to the shoulder girdle or, less commonly, a direct blow.

Pain arising from the SC joint.

The athlete complains of increased pain during shoulder motion and when lying supine.

Observation

In acute injuries, the athlete splints the forearm against the chest, using the opposite arm to provide support.

Dislocations cause the involved shoulder girdle to appear shortened.

Anterior dislocations result in obvious SC joint deformity.

Posterior SC dislocations may produce venous distention in the neck.

Swelling may be localized over the joint.

Functional Status

Pain increases with shoulder girdle motion, especially overhead.

Posterior SC dislocations may produce neurovascular symptoms and/or difficulty breathing or swallowing.

Physical Examination Findings

Simultaneous lateral compression or passive horizontal adduction of both shoulders increases SC joint pain.

With anterior dislocations, the medial clavicle can be palpated anterior to the manubrium.

Posterior dislocations are marked by a palpable manubrium.

Crepitus may be present during palpation or motion of the shoulder girdle.

Hypomobility or frank instability is noted on joint play testing of the medial clavicle.

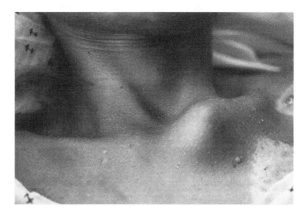

Figure 9.1 Traumatic anterior dislocation of the left sternoclavicular joint.

The motion at the sternoclavicular (SC) joint occurs with most upper extremity motions. During humeral elevation to 140°, the clavicle normally retracts 16°, elevates 6°, and rotates posteriorly 31°.[1] Because of its strong, efficiently designed ligamentous structures, this joint accounts for only a small percentage of all shoulder injuries. During SC sprains, the support structures and disk may be stretched or partially disrupted. In a severe SC joint sprain or dislocation, the capsular and intra-articular ligaments are ruptured. Occasionally, the costoclavicular ligament is intact but stretched, allowing dislocation.

Traumatic SC joint dislocations usually require a mechanism of tremendous direct or indirect force applied to the joint. A direct blow to the medial clavicle may result in posterior displacement of the clavicle. Forceful shoulder retraction may cause the clavicle to pivot on the first rib and dislocate anteriorly (see **Figure 9.1**).

Anterior SC dislocations are 2 to 10 times more common than posterior SC dislocations. The medial clavicle is displaced anteriorly or anterorsuperiorly relative to the sternum. A medial clavicle that is displaced posteriorly or posterior-superiorly is the characteristic finding of a posterior SC dislocation. Although posterior dislocations are rare, they can be life threatening because of the potential for compromise of the underlying trachea and neurovascular structures.

The epiphysis of the medial clavicle does not fuse completely until a person reaches the mid-twenties. Thus it is important to rule out a physeal fracture when examining athletes younger than age 25.

Differential Diagnosis

Fracture of the medial clavicle, sternum, first rib, or hyoid.

Imaging Techniques

Plain radiographs of the SC joint are difficult to interpret. Although special views of the chest have been used, interpretation is difficult because of the distortion of one clavicle over the other. Occasionally, routine anteroposterior (AP), posteranterior (PA), PA oblique, or prone PA radiographs of the chest or SC joint will suggest clavicular injury because the bone appears to be displaced compared with the normal side. Several views can be used to show the SC joint on plain radiographs (see **Figure 9.2**).

A computed tomography (CT) scan is the best imaging technique for all SC joint injuries. It clearly differentiates SC joint injuries from medial clavicular fractures and identifies minor joint subluxations. Ordering CT scans of both SC joints and the medial half of both clavicles allows for bilateral comparison.

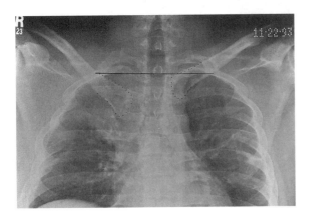

Figure 9.2 Imaging techniques of the sternoclavicular joint. In the serendipity radiographic view, the patient is supine, lying on the film cassette. The x-rays are directed with a 40° cephalic tilt.

Definitive Diagnosis

The diagnosis is based on positive radiographic findings (plain films, CT scan) correlated with positive physical findings. Historically, the diagnosis of SC sprain was made from clinical examination findings, rather than from radiographs. However, CT scans offer excellent visualization of involved structures, often showing small fractures within the joint.

Pathomechanics and Functional Limitations

Because of the associated SC joint motion, shoulder girdle or glenohumeral (GH) joint motion may be inhibited, weak, and produce SC joint pain. In overhead throwers, altered biomechanics may progress to secondary overuse injuries, particularly in the GH joint and medial elbow.

The original SC dislocation may go undetected, spontaneously reduce, or be irreducible; in addition, the physician may decide not to reduce the dislocation. When the stretched or disrupted capsuloligamentous tissues fail to heal, mild to moderate overhead activity may produce recurrent, possibly painless subluxations or dislocations.

■ Immediate Management

Because of potential for compromise of the trachea and neurovascular bundle, posterior dislocations are medical emergencies (see **Figure 9.3**). The involved arm should be immobilized with a sling and figure-of-eight brace. Anterior dislocations can be stabilized by affixing a compression pad over the joint (see **Figure 9.4**). Closed reduction is recommended for both anterior and posterior SC dislocations. Reductions should be performed within 48 hours of the trauma and are typically successful when done early.[1] If a posterior dislocation is suspected, the

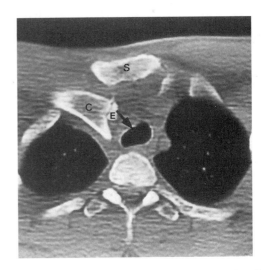

Figure 9.3 CT scan of a posterior sternoclavicular dislocation. The patient was complaining of a "choking sensation" that was increased by lying supine. Note the physeal injury of the medial clavicle and the compression of the trachea (arrow). C, medial clavicle; E, epiphyseal fragment; S, sternum. *Source:* Reproduced with permission from Rockwood CA Jr, Green DP, Bucholz RW, et al (eds). *Rockwood and Green's Fractures in Adults*, ed 4. Philadelphia, PA: Lippincott-Raven; 1996, vol 2, p. 1448.

patient should be transported in a seated position to reduce pressure on the underlying structures.

■ Medications

Nonsteroidal anti-inflammatory drugs (NSAIDs) and narcotic analgesics may be used to control pain. Use of NSAIDs should be constrained to a 3- to 7-day course during the acute inflammation phase of rehabilitation.

■ Postinjury Management

Fractures and dislocations require protective immobilization through either bracing or surgical fixation. Most dislocations are successfully reduced nonsurgically.

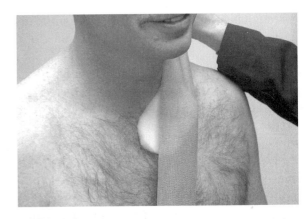

Figure 9.4 Stabilization of anterior sternoclavicular joint dislocations. A pad taped or wrapped over the anterior sternoclavicular joint can maintain joint alignment, thereby allowing for healing or stabilization of the joint prior to surgery.

Anterior Dislocations

The patient lies supine on a table with a 3- to 4-inch-thick pad between the shoulders. Various forms of muscle relaxants or local or general anesthetics are administered. The physician then manually relocates the medial clavicle. In many cases, however, the SC joint may again spontaneously dislocate.

Posterior Dislocations

Three closed reduction techniques are commonly used to manage posterior SC dislocations. A general anesthetic or muscle relaxant is usually administered before the procedure is performed, and access to thoracic surgery should be readily available.

Abduction-Traction Method

The patient lies supine with a sandbag or bolster between the shoulders and the involved arm near the table edge. Abduct the arm and apply traction while gently extending the arm. In some instances, the medial clavicle must be manually moved from behind the posterior sternum.

Adduction-Traction Method

The patient lies supine with a sandbag or bolster between the shoulders. A traction force is applied to the arm as it is moved into adduction and posterior force is applied to both shoulders.

Shoulder Retraction Method

The patient is either supine or seated. Both shoulders are forcefully retracted to realign the SC joint. This technique carries an increased risk of circulatory vessel compromise, nerve tissue impingement, and difficulty swallowing.

■ Postreduction/Postinjury Management

Both shoulders are stabilized using a figure-of-eight brace (see **Figure 9.5**) or commercial shoulder harness, and the involved arm is supported with a sling. A pad may be taped or wrapped over the involved SC joint to prevent anterior displacement during healing. Pain control, rest, and sling immobilization are recommended during the early postoperative or postinjury period.

■ Surgical Intervention

Surgical reduction is most frequently indicated for posterior dislocations, but is rarely undertaken for anterior dislocations. Although closed reduction is often unsuccessful, it should be attempted before surgical reduction.[1] If closed reduction fails, open reduction is performed. Reduction is accomplished with a combination of traction, counter-traction,

Figure 9.5 Figure-of-eight brace. This brace retracts the scapulae and places a traction force on the clavicles.

and careful manipulation. Stable joints are immobilized for healing. Surgical repair is followed by use of a sling and figure-of-eight brace for 6 weeks.

■ Injury-Specific Treatment and Rehabilitation Concerns

> **Specific Concerns**
>
> Stabilize the SC joint.
> Reestablish range of motion and strength.
> Active motion is restricted for 3 weeks for patients with posterior dislocations.

Patients with uncomplicated, stable anterior SC sprains are typically placed in a sling for 1 to 2 weeks. Those with a subluxation should be immobilized in a sling for 3 to 6 weeks, with or without a figure-of-eight brace. Following the closed reduction of a posterior SC dislocation, patients should continue to use a sling and swathe or figure-of-eight brace for 4 to 6 weeks. Motions that exacerbate joint instability must be restricted so these tissues can heal.

During and after immobilization, the joint may be supported by tape if it improves patient comfort. During the active inflammatory phase, cryotherapy may improve patient comfort and create a better environment for healing. Encourage strength and flexibility of the elbow, wrist, and hand during immobilization by engaging the patient in activities that maintain support of the humerus.

For patients with a stable joint, cryotherapy and gentle active-assisted and passive range of motion (ROM) are initiated early to reduce pain, minimize swelling, and avoid the deleterious effects of immobilization. As soon as comfort permits, these patients may begin the exercises requiring minimal cuff activity in the *Shoulder Stability Progression* (see page 464). Scapular clocks, shoulder dumps, and sternal lifts may begin if the patient is still using the sling (see "Shoulder Rehabilitation and Conditioning" in Chapter 12). The isometric stability exercises of this progression may begin by incorporating weight shifts and isometric low rows. Active GH motion is permitted as soon as joint stability is displayed, which may be as early as week 1 depending on the extent of the injury and patient comfort. Patients with joint stability typically progress rapidly, with minimal time lost to their injury.

Patients with SC dislocations are restricted to gentle passive ROM activities for 2 to 3 weeks before active shoulder exercises may begin. Those requiring closed reduction of a posterior SC dislocation are held to the same restrictions as patients with uncomplicated, stable anterior sprains for 3 to 4 weeks. Once the joint is clinically healed and motion is permitted, normal mobility and stability of the shoulder girdle must be reestablished using joint mobilization, therapeutic modalities, and stretching and strengthening exercises. These patients may begin the *Shoulder Stability Progression* while remaining in a sling. Isometric stability exercises may begin with weight shifts, with isometric low rows following shortly thereafter.

Arthrokinematics should be assessed in all patients before active motion is attempted. Reestablish normal arthrokinematics using SC joint mobilization as needed. The active-assisted portion of the *Shoulder Mobility Progression* is begun with table bows and pendulum exercises. Patients with normal SC arthrokinematics typically regain shoulder motion quickly. Strengthening should focus on the muscles that control clavicular motion in a range that does not further stress the joint. The pectoralis muscles are strengthened with the incline press; their sternal fibers are isolated by seated press-ups in limited ROM. Shoulder shrugs target the upper trapezius; however, exercises should avoid shrug-initiated arm movements and subsequent upper trapezius dominance. The closed- and open-chain rhythmic stabilization components of the *Shoulder Stability Progression* are initiated and advanced to include the push-up progression, lawnmowers, functional exercises, and each of the *Foundational Shoulder Exercises* (see page 475) as appropriate for the patient's activities.

Estimated Amount of Time Lost

Stable SC sprains may result in minimal time lost if pain does not interfere with activity. Dislocations may result in 6 to 8 weeks lost from athletics. For posterior SC dislocations, 10 to 12 weeks of recovery is required to allow complete ligament healing, with up to 16 weeks needed before full activities are resumed.

Return-to-Play Criteria

Return-to-play criteria include complete physiologic healing; normal, pain-free shoulder ROM and kinematics, strength, and flexibility; and successful completion of appropriate functional testing demonstrating normal performance of sport-specific tasks.

Functional Bracing

Adhesive taping for the SC joint may assist with pain, swelling reduction, or arthrokinematics during rehabilitation or functional activity.

Clavicular Fractures

CLINICAL PRESENTATION

History

A direct blow to the clavicle or a force transmitted to the clavicle through the humerus.
Pain at the fracture site.

Observation

The athlete splints the forearm against the chest, using the opposite arm to provide support.
To relieve associated sternocleidomastoid spasm, the head and chin are tilted away from the side of the fracture.
The involved shoulder girdle may appear depressed and protracted.
Swelling, skin tenting, or obvious deformity may be present at the fracture site.

Functional Status

Upper extremity and thoracic motion increases pain.

Physical Examination Findings

Gentle clavicular palpation produces localized tenderness and crepitus at the fracture site.

The incidence of clavicular fractures peaks between the ages of 13 and 30 and are most commonly caused by a direct blow or force transmitted through the humerus. Fractures to the lateral clavicle are often displaced inferiorly under the weight of the extremity, with the displaced fragments "button-holing" through the platysma. Clavicular fractures are described based on their type (see Figure 9.6), the group

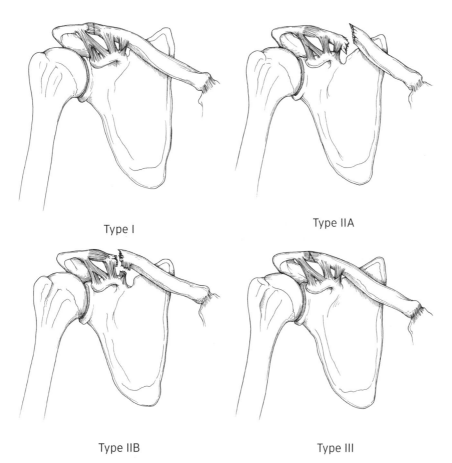

Type I   Type IIA

Type IIB   Type III

Figure 9.6 Types of clavicular fractures. A type I fracture occurs distal to the coracoclavicular ligaments, with little displacement of the fracture fragments. A type IIA fracture occurs medial to the coracoclavicular ligaments, while a type IIB fracture occurs between the coracoclavicular ligaments. Type III, an intra-articular fracture, frequently occurs without ligament disruption. *Source:* Reproduced with permission from Nuber GW, Bowen MK. Acromioclavicular joint injuries and distal clavicle fractures. *J Am Acad Orthop Surg.* 1997;5:11–18.

(fracture location), and the resulting displacement (see **Table 9.1**).[2]

Concomitant injuries associated with acute clavicular fractures depend largely on the magnitude of force and fracture displacement. They include (1) musculoskeletal trauma, (2) lung and pleural injuries, (3) vascular injuries, and (4) brachial plexus injuries. Associated skeletal injuries include SC and acromioclavicular (AC) joint sprains or fracture-dislocations. Lateral clavicle fractures may mimic or coexist with AC joint pathology. Closed reduction of a ligamentous injury is more difficult in the presence of a clavicular fracture.

When assessing clavicular fractures, rule out head and neck injury and examine neurovascular function of the distal extremity during the physical examination. In patients younger than 25 years, medial clavicular fractures are often difficult to distinguish from physeal separations and SC dislocations. With concurrent coracoid process fractures, open reduction and internal fixation may be required. Displaced medial-end fractures may—rarely—compress the mediastinum and subclavian vessels.

Ipsilateral or contralateral first rib fractures may be associated with clavicular fractures but can easily go unnoticed because they are difficult to identify on standard chest radiographs. When undetected, these fractures may injure the lung, brachial plexus, or subclavian vessels.

Neurovascular injuries secondary to clavicular fractures are rare, but brachial plexus trauma can occur. The neurovascular bundle emerges from the thoracic outlet under the clavicle on top of the first rib.[3] Although the underlying plexus is protected by the posterior periosteum, subclavius muscles, and bone, nerves may be directly injured by displaced comminuted bone or any traction produced during the injury. Accordingly, clavicular fractures should not be manipulated without first obtaining radiographs to determine the position of fragments.

Vascular injuries are rare because the subclavius muscle and the thick, deep cervical fascia protect these vessels against direct injury. If the initial fracture displacement has not injured the adjacent vessels, they are unlikely to be injured because the distal fragment is typically displaced inferiorly and anteriorly under the weight of the

Table 9.1

Classification of Clavicular Fractures

Group	Location/Structures Involved
I	Fracture of the middle third of the clavicle
II	Fracture of the distal third of the clavicle
	Type I: Minimal displacement (interligamentous fracture)
	Type II: Displaced secondary to a fracture medial to the coracoclavicular ligaments
	Conoid and trapezoid attached
	Conoid torn, trapezoid attached
	Type III: Fractures of the articular surface
	Type IV: Ligaments intact to the periosteum (in children), with displacement of the proximal fragment
	Type V: Comminuted; ligaments are not attached proximally or distally; ligaments are attached to an inferior, comminuted fragment
III	Fracture of the proximal third of the clavicle
	Type I: Minimally displaced
	Type II: Displaced (ligaments ruptured)
	Type III: Intra-articular fracture
	Type IV: Epiphyseal separation (in children and young adults)
	Type V: Comminuted

Source: Adapted from Craig EV. Fractures of the clavicle, in Rockwood CA Jr, Matsen FA III (eds), *The Shoulder.* Philadelphia: WB Saunders; 1990:367–412.

extremity. The trapezius muscle pulls the proximal segment upward and posteriorly. Suspect vascular injury if the blood pressure between extremities is significantly different.

Differential Diagnosis
AC sprain, SC sprain, first rib fracture.

Imaging Techniques
AP and serendipity radiographic views of the clavicle should be obtained (see Figure 9.2 [SC view]). Some prefer a 15° PA view to assess the amount of shortening. Two views of the clavicle at right angles to each other—a 45° angle superiorly and a 45° angle inferiorly—have been recommended to assess fracture extent and displacement (see **Figure 9.7**).[4]

Spiral CT with three-dimensional reformatted views affords the best view of displacement and is useful in evaluating union of the fracture.[5] The proximal third of the humerus should also be included in the AP view, and the shoulder girdle and upper lung should be imaged to rule out associated injury.[6] An AP view of the cervical or thoracic spine decreases the chance of overlooking rib fractures.[7] If vessel injury is suspected, an arteriogram should be performed.[8]

Fractures of the proximal third of the clavicle can be difficult to detect in radiographs because of the overlapping of the ribs over the vertebrae and mediastinal shadows. A cephalic tilt view of 40° to 45° (serendipity view) often reveals the fracture. In children, medial clavicular fractures are often misdiagnosed as SC dislocations. Tomography or a CT scan can be useful in demonstrating the intra-articular or epiphyseal nature of the injury in this location.

Definitive Diagnosis
The definitive diagnosis of clavicular fracture is often easily made on the clinical finding of clavicular deformity and displacement. Radiographs can

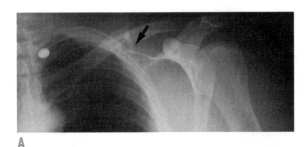
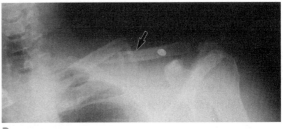

Figure 9.7 Radiographs of a clavicular fracture. (**A**) An AP view of the left shoulder shows a displaced fracture of the middle third of the clavicle (arrow). (**B**) A 45° cephalic tilt view demonstrates a comminuted fracture of the midshaft of the clavicle (arrow).

confirm the fracture location and type and assist in identifying possible compromise to the underlying neurovascular structures. Nondisplaced fractures or isolated fractures of the articular surfaces that do not cause deformity may be overlooked, however. If the diagnosis is in doubt, additional radiographic views or another radiographic series of the clavicle in 7 to 10 days may be helpful in clarifying the clinical picture.

Pathomechanics and Functional Limitations

The patient has pain with upper extremity, thoracic, and neck motion. Because muscles associated with respiration are attached to the clavicle, movement of the fragments may cause pain during deep inspiration. In such patients, exercise should be restricted during the early postinjury and postoperative periods. Upper extremity conditioning may also require restriction to facilitate clinical healing.

■ Immediate Management

A sling is applied for immobilization and protection, and ice should be applied to the joint as comfort permits. If associated lung trauma is suspected, auscultate for symmetric breath sounds. Assessment of distal neurovascular function of the involved extremity should rule out associated neurovascular injury.

■ Medications

Acetaminophen or narcotic analgesics may be used for pain control.

■ Surgical Intervention

Nondisplaced clavicular fractures are best treated conservatively. For displaced fractures, there is no consensus regarding which types should be treated with open reduction. Indications for operative treatment include vascular damage, open fractures, severe skin tenting, complete displacement of fracture segments, or clavicular shortening exceeding 2 centimeters.[9] With a large vessel tear, surgical exploration is mandatory. To gain adequate exposure, as much of the clavicle should be excised as necessary to isolate and repair the injured major vessel. Although in some cases the vessel may be ligated, major vessel ligation in the elderly patient may be dangerous, as remaining circulation to the extremity may be inadequate.[2] Numerous surgical fixation techniques have been described including plate or intramedullary fixation.

■ Postinjury/Postoperative Management

The patient should be placed in a sling until pain subsides and healing is visualized on radiographs. A figure-of-eight brace is sometimes employed to maintain a traction force on the clavicle; however, its use has been associated with less patient satisfaction and greater risk of complication compared with use of the sling alone.[5,10] Rest and acetaminophen or narcotic analgesics for pain control are initially prescribed, followed by ROM exercises. Once the clavicle brace or sling is removed, advanced ROM and strength and conditioning exercises can begin.

■ Injury-Specific Treatment and Rehabilitation Concerns

> **Specific Concerns**
>
> Maintain longitudinal traction on the clavicle during healing.
> Maintain clavicular alignment during healing.
> Figure-of-eight braces are rarely used; instead, postural awareness education is emphasized.
> Avoid stressing the fracture site until healing has occurred.
> Restore ROM and strength when the fracture is resolved.

Nonoperative patients and those with uncomplicated surgical fixation can begin a light maintenance program as pain permits 1 to 4 weeks post injury. Pendulum exercises and active ROM with less than 45° of shoulder elevation in the scapular plane are appropriate for these individuals. All other patients should avoid active shoulder motion until fracture healing is evident. Patients are encouraged to preserve strength and flexibility of the elbow, wrist, and hand during immobilization through activities that maintain support of the humerus.

When clinical or radiographic union is evident, usually at 4 to 6 weeks, patients may begin exercises to restore full active ROM, isometric rotator cuff, trapezius and deltoid strength, and shoulder stability. These patients may begin with the exercises requiring minimal cuff activity in the *Shoulder Stability Progression*. The scapular clocks, shoulder dumps, and sternal lifts may begin safely with the patient in the sling. Isometric stability is restored beginning with weight shifts, isometric low rows, and rhythmic stabilization exercises. Active and active-assisted ROM exercises progress to restore GH motion using the pendulum, T-bar, table wash, and supine press exercises described in the *Shoulder Mobility Progression*.

As active ROM and strength return, conditioning advances to include the push-up progression,

ligated Sutured closed.

9

lawnmowers, functional activities, and each of the *Foundational Shoulder Exercises* as appropriate for the patient's activities.

▇ Estimated Amount of Time Lost

Time lost depends on the rate of healing and the amount of collision required in the sport. Early return to contact sports risks refracture. Athletes may return to noncontact sports in 4 to 6 weeks; those in collision sports may return in 6 to 10 weeks.

▇ Return-to-Play Criteria

Athletes returning to play must demonstrate fracture union and complete physiologic healing; normal shoulder ROM, kinematics, strength, and flexibility; and successful completion of appropriate functional testing demonstrating normal performance of sport-specific tasks.

Functional Bracing

For athletes in contact sports, force-dispersion padding may be placed underneath shoulder pads. Supportive adhesive taping of the distal AC joint may be considered.

Acromioclavicular Joint Sprains

CLINICAL PRESENTATION

History

Direct or indirect trauma to the shoulder.
Pain arising from the AC joint, which may migrate to the upper trapezius.

Observation

In acute injuries, the patient splints the forearm against the chest, using the opposite arm to provide support.
The involved shoulder may be elevated, secondary to trapezius spasm.
Type III AC sprains result in noticeable elevation of the distal clavicle.

Functional Status

Humeral and shoulder girdle movement produce pain.

Physical Examination Findings

Glenohumeral elevation and abduction produce pain.
Scapular dyskinesis.
Localized tenderness of the distal clavicle on palpation.
Possible piano-key sign upon palpation.
Cross-body adduction stress test.
Positive findings on two or more of the following tests help rule in AC pathology; negative findings on all three help rule out AC pathology:[11]
  • Resisted extension test
  • Active compression test
  • AC compression test–may be positive

The acromioclavicular (AC) joint is a diarthrodial joint incompletely divided by a fibrocartilaginous disk (see **Figure 9.8**). Unlike the SC joint, the AC joint has a large perforation in its center. The capsule is thicker on its superior, anterior, and posterior surfaces than on its inferior surface. Normal motion at the AC joint results from scapulothoracic motion and is essential to the scapula's role in providing a stable base on which the humerus can move. The capsular ligaments—mainly the superior AC ligament—provide horizontal stability. The coracoclavicular (CC) ligaments—conoid and trapezoid—provide vertical stability. During arm elevation to 140°, the AC joint moves progressively through 8° of internal rotation (IR), 11° of upward rotation, and 19° of posterior tilting.[12] Hypermobility, hypomobility, instability, or pain with AC joint movement will cause dysfunction along this kinetic chain.

The injury mechanism for AC joint sprain is typically a direct blow to the shoulder point with the humerus adducted; the scapula is driven inferiorly in relation to the clavicle, such as during a fall on the shoulder or in a shoulder-first tackle. The SC ligaments interlock to prevent inferior clavicular displacement, and the clavicle may impinge on the rib cage. Ongoing force on the acromion stretches or tears the AC ligaments (see **Figure 9.9**). With continued acromial displacement, the coracoclavicular

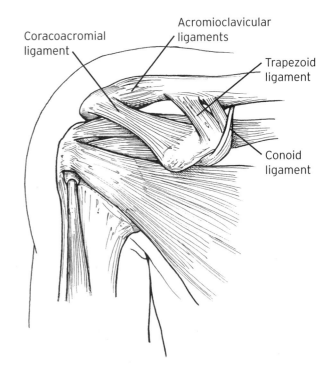

Figure 9.8   The acromioclavicular joint complex is composed of the acromioclavicular ligaments and the coracoclavicular ligaments (conoid and trapezoid). *Source:* Reproduced with permission from Shaffer BS. Painful conditions of the acromioclavicular joint. *J Am Acad Orthop Surg.* 1999;7:176-188.

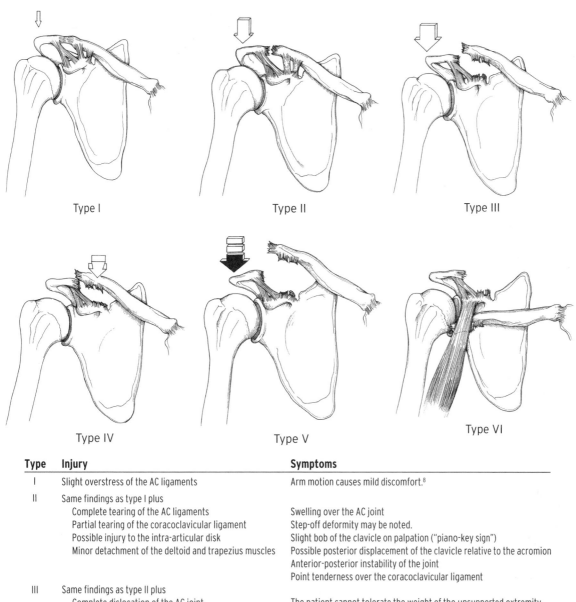

Type I

Type II

Type III

Type IV

Type V

Type VI

Type	Injury	Symptoms
I	Slight overstress of the AC ligaments	Arm motion causes mild discomfort.[8]
II	Same findings as type I plus	
	Complete tearing of the AC ligaments	Swelling over the AC joint
	Partial tearing of the coracoclavicular ligament	Step-off deformity may be noted.
	Possible injury to the intra-articular disk	Slight bob of the clavicle on palpation ("piano-key sign")
	Minor detachment of the deltoid and trapezius muscles	Possible posterior displacement of the clavicle relative to the acromion
		Anterior-posterior instability of the joint
		Point tenderness over the coracoclavicular ligament
III	Same findings as type II plus	
	Complete dislocation of the AC joint	The patient cannot tolerate the weight of the unsupported extremity.
		The distal clavicle is unstable in all directions.
		The distal clavicle is elevated, resulting in "tenting" of the skin.
		Gross bobbing of the clavicle on palpation
IV	Same findings as type III plus	
	Sternoclavicular joint should be evaluated for possible anterior dislocation.[9]	Posterior clavicular displacement
		Possible posterior tenting of the skin
V	Same findings as type IV plus	Upper extremity drooping
	Extensive muscle and soft-tissue disruption	Possible brachial plexus symptoms[9]
	Possible brachial plexus involvement	
VI	Same findings as type IV plus	Superior portion of the shoulder appears flat.
	Possible fracture of the clavicle or ribs	Definitive step-off deformity to the coracoid process

Figure 9.9 Classification of acromioclavicular joint sprains. *Source:* Reproduced with permission from Nuber GW, Bowen MK. Acromioclavicular joint injuries and distal clavicle fractures. *J Am Acad Orthop Surg.* 1997;5:11-18.

distance increases, stretching or tearing the ligaments. Other, less common injury mechanisms include a direct posterior blow to the scapula and a lateral blow to the acromion. On rare occasions, a fall on an outstretched hand or elbow may produce enough indirect force to cause an AC sprain by driving the humerus into the acromion.

Complete AC dislocations are rare in persons younger than 16 years. Visual inspection or palpation may reveal a high-riding clavicle and an apparent AC dislocation. Transperiosteal distal clavicular fracture and periosteal rupture and a distal clavicular fracture in which the CC ligaments remain attached to the periosteum should be ruled out.

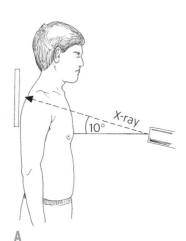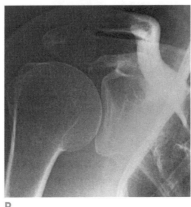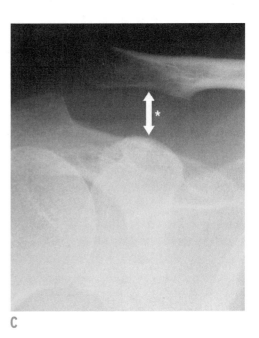

A   B   C

Figure 9.10 Imaging of the acromioclavicular joint. **(A)** The Zanca view is obtained by angling the x-ray beam 10° to 15° in the cephalic direction. **(B)** The AP view of the shoulder demonstrates the glenohumeral anatomy but does not adequately image the acromioclavicular joint. **(C)** The Zanca view provides a better image of the acromioclavicular joint but at the expense of the glenohumeral image. The asterisk indicates the increased distance in coracoclavicular interspace. With CC ligament disruption, the coracoclavicular distance may be increased on the AP or Zanca view. *Source:* (A) Reproduced with permission from Shaffer BS. Painful conditions of the acromioclavicular joint. *J Am Acad Orthop Surg.* 1999;7:176-188.

Differential Diagnosis

Distal clavicular fracture, acromial process fracture, coracoid process fracture, GH internal derangement.

Imaging Techniques

Radiographic evaluation assists in classification of AC injuries. Routine views include an AP view, an AP view with 15° cephalic tilt (Zanca) centered on the coracoid process, an axillary view, and comparison views of the uninjured shoulder (see **Figure 9.10**). An Alexander or "shoulder-forward view" may also be necessary.

> **Practice Tip**
>
> Weighted stress views are no longer routine; they provide little new information, are costly, and cause discomfort.[13]

Definitive Diagnosis

Diagnosis is based on a thorough clinical examination supported by radiographic evaluation. The AC injection test is considered conclusive.[11,14,15] To rule in AC pathology, evidence suggests the combination of a positive bone scan and Paxino's test[16] or positive findings on two or more of the following tests: resisted extension, active compression, and cross-body adduction stress.[11]

Pathomechanics and Functional Limitations

Significant AC ligament disruption causes shoulder girdle dysfunction that affects the entire upper extremity kinetic chain. The stability provided by the involved ligament(s) is reduced, affecting each of the three AC joint motions. Pain and weakness are described with overhead motion and horizontal adduction of the shoulder. Pain and dysfunction occur with contact sports and most activities that load the upper extremity.

■ Immediate Management

Ice and a sling or Kenny-Howard–type AC immobilizer are applied for the first 24 to 48 hours; longer immobilization is required for more severe injuries. A pad and/or shoulder spica wrap can help stabilize the AC joint (see **Figure 9.11**).

■ Medications

Acetaminophen or narcotic analgesics are used for pain control. NSAID use should be constrained to a 3- to 7-day course during the active inflammation phase of rehabilitation.

■ Postinjury Management

Management of AC joint injuries depends on the severity of the injury and the patient's specific situation. Treatment of a pure posterior clavicular dislocation varies, depending on whether the clavicle can be manipulated out of its embedding in the trapezius muscle. Type I and II sprains typically are successfully treated through conservative management; however, the severity of their residual effects

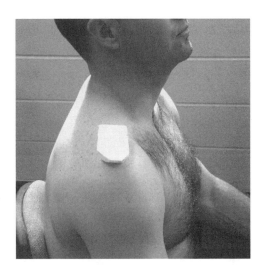

Figure 9.11 Stabilization of acromioclavicular joint sprains. A spica wrap is used to hold a compressive pad over the acromioclavicular joint to maintain alignment. A sling is then applied to reduce traction forces on the joint caused by the weight of the arm.

is underestimated. Short- and long-term outcome studies suggest that 36% to 39% of patients with type I sprains and 48% to 65% of patients with type II sprains experience residual AC joint–related symptoms.[17–21]

Treatment of type III injuries is controversial, with most athletes attempting 3 to 6 months of conservative treatment before considering surgery. Some athletes function well with complete AC joint dislocations. Patients opting for nonsurgical management should be made aware of the possible long-term complications, including osteoarthritis and cosmetic changes caused by displacement of the clavicle, which are typically permanent. While little research exists on this topic, early repair of acute type III injuries may be beneficial for young athletes or those competing in collision or overhead sports.

Conservative management of AC sprains includes ice and a sling or immobilizer until symptoms resolve, usually within 1 to 3 weeks. Patients with sprains that may benefit from additional clavicular support and reduction should be placed in a Kenny-Howard–type AC immobilizer (see **Figure 9.12**). Maintaining joint reduction with 3 to 6 weeks of continuous, uninterrupted pressure downward on the distal clavicle and upward on the acromion (provided indirectly from the elbow through the humerus) is essential. Monitor these patients to ensure the harness provides enough pressure to the distal clavicle to afford its reduction while avoiding complications such as poor patient compliance, skin breakdown, and compression neuropathy. These potential pitfalls of Kenny-Howard–type AC immobilizers necessitate daily examination and readjustment of the device as needed.

Other aggressive forms of treatment can be instituted to emphasize reduction of joint deformity and support the joint during healing, including taping and strapping techniques, compressive bandages, harnesses, plaster casts, and traction.

▒ Surgical Intervention

Because of the severe posterior-distal clavicular displacement that occurs with type IV sprains and the gross displacement and clavicular deformity that occur with type V injuries, surgical repair of these injuries is indicated.[2] Surgery is directed at

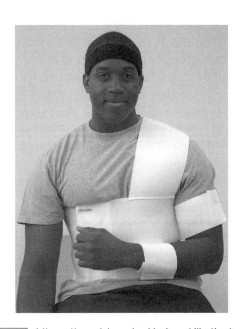

Figure 9.12 A Kenny-Howard–type shoulder immobilization brace used for acromioclavicular joint sprains. This brace decreases the pressure on the joint by supporting the forearm and humerus and providing downward pressure on the distal clavicle to keep the joint structures congruent.

S|T Surgical Technique 9.1

Anatomic AC Joint Reconstruction

Indications

Type IV and V AC joint injuries.

Procedure Overview

1. The patient is placed in a beach chair position.
2. An incision is made just lateral to the axillary skin crease (deltopectoral interval), over the clavicle and coracoid.
3. The underlying fascia is opened in line with the clavicle.
4. Depending on the chronicity of the injury and surgeon's preference, the distal clavicle may be resected.
5. Two small drill holes are made in the clavicle just superior to the coracoid.
6. The graft is passed around the coracoid and the free ends are passed through the drill holes.
7. The shoulder girdle is reduced, and the graft is held with either suture or interference screws.
8. The free ends of the graft can be brought across the AC joint to re-create the AC joint capsule.
9. A secure repair of the overlying fascia is created.

Functional Limitations

The arm is usually immobilized for 6 weeks except for pendulum exercises.

Implications for Rehabilitation

Active motion and strengthening are usually started at 6 weeks and progress slowly to protect the repair.

reconstructing the CC ligaments and excising the distal clavicle (see S|T 9.1). Most type VI injuries are surgically repaired because initial attempts at closed reduction fail. The clavicle may be stabilized by suturing the deltoid and trapezius muscle avulsion and repairing the AC joint capsule. Methods of fixation including the pin, Bosworth screw, and Kirschner wire (K-wire) approaches have been abandoned because of the tendency toward pin migration and continued instability[13]; alternative methods use hook-plate fixations with more success.[22] Distal clavicle resection without reconstruction may be an option for patients with recalcitrant type I or II AC sprains.[23] Little evidence has been published describing long-term outcomes after such anatomic repairs.

■ Postoperative Management

Postoperatively, management of the AC joint depends on the tissue targeted during surgery and physician preference. Both CC and AC ligament reconstructions may be immobilized for 6 weeks, with the patient beginning light ROM in the supine position after 7 to 10 days. Postsurgical immobilization of CC screw fixations varies widely, ranging from no immobilization[24] to 2 weeks[25] to 4 weeks.[26] Following coracoid transfer surgery, elbow flexion may be restricted to 90° and gradually extended starting on day 5.[27]

■ Injury-Specific Treatment and Rehabilitation Concerns

Specific Concerns

Maintain approximation of the distal clavicle and acromion.
Limit stress on the affected tissue or fixation.
Restore shoulder ROM and proper kinematics.
Ensure proper neuromuscular control of the shoulder.

Rehabilitation of type I and II AC sprains includes a sling or immobilizer until symptoms resolve, which usually occurs within 1 to 3 weeks. The immobilization period for type III injuries may be longer or shorter, depending on the desired outcome. If joint reduction is not a goal of treatment, early motion is encouraged and is limited only by pain. If reduction is desired, immobilization may last 3 to 6 weeks. Patients are encouraged to preserve strength and flexibility of the wrist and hand during immobilization as comfort permits. Cryotherapy may improve patient comfort and help create a better environment for the healing process.

The table bows and open- and closed-chain pendulum exercises in the *Shoulder Mobility Progression* may begin as soon as patient comfort allows. Early active-assisted ROM is encouraged through the T-bar and table wash exercises, and then advanced to the active portion including diagonal table wash, wall wash, and supine press exercises as appropriate. Before active motion is progressed, arthrokinematics should be assessed in all patients.

Following immobilization, some patients will benefit from SC joint mobilizations. The *Shoulder Stability Progression* is initiated using scapular clocks, shoulder dumps, and sternal lifts and advanced as comfort permits. Isometric stability is restored beginning with weight shifts, isometric low rows, and closed-chain rhythmic stabilization exercises. Exercises including tubing isometric stability, scapular clocks, and rhythmic stabilization are initiated in pain-free ranges and progressed up to 90° as comfort permits. When the patient displays GH active ROM to 120° with scapular control (no shrug), the dynamic stability portion of the stability progression, manual propriceptive neuromuscular facilitation (PNF), and additional isotonic strengthening may begin. Completing the push-up progression is critical to athletes in overhead or contact sports; however, only those without point tenderness should be advanced to performing these exercises on the floor.

Strengthening exercises should progress to include functional activities and each of the *Foundational Shoulder Exercises* as appropriate for each athlete's activities. Heavy lifting and contact sports are avoided until point tenderness subsides and full pain-free active ROM and neuromuscular control of the shoulder is achieved. Ordinarily, achieving this goal takes 2 weeks for type I and II sprains; however, individual differences, degree of injury, and therapeutic physiologic response may dictate waiting as long as 4 weeks to begin these exercises. Athletes also differ in their ability to tolerate pain. Enough time must be allowed for the soft tissues to heal before beginning exercises that stress the injury; this can take up to 8 to 12 weeks for patients with severe sprains.

Patients undergoing AC stabilization using bioabsorbable material should avoid active GH elevation and horizontal abduction and adduction for the first 5 weeks postoperatively. Isometric and isotonic strengthening in GH abduction and rotations less than 90° of abduction can begin immediately and progress as tolerated. Exercises including the overhead press, bench press, and pectoralis "fly" maneuver may stress the repair and should not be initiated until late in the course of rehabilitation (no earlier than week 8). At this time, patients may also engage in more aggressive isotonic strengthening exercises, such as tubing with greater than 90° of GH abduction, manual PNF, and the dynamic portion of the *Shoulder Stability Progression*.

Estimated Amount of Time Lost

Time lost depends on the injury severity, the surgical procedure, and the nature of the sport. Athletes in contact sports may miss more time than those in non-contact sports. Athletes with type I or II injuries who are treated conservatively may miss 1 to 4 weeks; those with type III injuries may lose 6 to 9 weeks. Type IV to VI sprains result in an extended amount of time lost (4 to 12 months), especially with surgery or associated trauma.

Return-to-Play Criteria

Before returning to activity, the athlete should have full and pain-free shoulder ROM and strength, no tenderness on direct AC joint palpation, and no pain when manual traction is applied to the joint. Athletes should successfully complete appropriate functional tests demonstrating normal performance of sport-specific tasks. For athletes with mild sprains who are participating in contact sports, pain is commonly used to guide the return-to-play decision.

Functional Bracing

A custom thermomoldable plastic pad or commercially available padding system can speed the return to contact sports by dispersing force away from the AC joint (see **CT** 9.1).

Scapular Dyskinesis

Scapular dyskinesis describes dysfunctional motion, position, or stability of the scapula. It is observed in patients suffering from a shoulder disorder such as rotator cuff impingement and other pathology,[28–35] instability,[32,35–37] AC joint injury,[38] and adhesive capsulitis.[39–42]

Scapular function involves three basic roles: (1) The scapula provides a mobile and stable base for the humeral head to afford GH mobility and stability, (2) it controls the position of the glenoid and acromial arch during humeral motion so as to avoid subacromial and posterior (internal) impingement, and (3) it transfers energy safely and efficiently between the upper extremity and the trunk. The collective goal of these scapular functions is to maintain the humeral head's instantaneous center of rotation safely within the glenoid fossa.[43] To support this relationship during humeral motion, the scapulothoracic joint must have adequate mobility, stability, and neuromuscular control. Understanding each of these roles is critical to optimizing the

CT Clinical Technique 9.1

Orthoplast Padding of the AC Joint

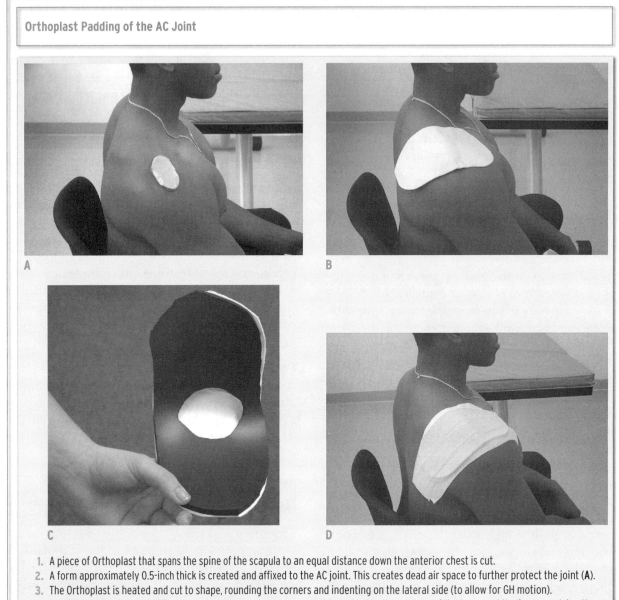

1. A piece of Orthoplast that spans the spine of the scapula to an equal distance down the anterior chest is cut.
2. A form approximately 0.5-inch thick is created and affixed to the AC joint. This creates dead air space to further protect the joint (**A**).
3. The Orthoplast is heated and cut to shape, rounding the corners and indenting on the lateral side (to allow for GH motion).
4. While the Orthoplast is still flexible (reheating may be necessary), it is molded to the contour of the torso and the form overlying the AC joint. The material is trimmed as necessary (**B**).
5. Self-adhesive padding is applied to the anterior and posterior portions of the Orthoplast. The indentation made by the form should not be covered. A bridge is created, providing protection to the AC joint (**C**).
6. The pad is affixed to the shoulder using elastic stretch tape and/or a shoulder spica (**D**).

examination and treatment of shoulder dysfunction and pathology.

Scapular motion involves the complex coordination of multiple translations and rotations, making quantifying and understanding its motion and position difficult. Nevertheless, research employing analysis of six-degrees-of-freedom motion has facilitated understanding of these aspects.[12,44] Scapular position and motion are described relative to the thorax and include rotation around three axes and translation in two planes (superior-inferior and medial-lateral) (see Figure 9.13).[12] Scapular superior translation describes a shrug, whereas lateral translation coupled with scapular IR produces what is commonly described as scapular protraction.

The clinical assessment of scapular function begins with postural observation. At rest, the scapula should be positioned with approximately 5° of

History

Insidious onset or concurrent with other pathology.

Reports of increased or heavy throwing.

Pain over the coracoid process, pectoralis minor, superior and medial borders of the scapula, AC joint, posterior-lateral joint line, or subacromial space.

Posterior cervical pain and trigger points on the dominant side.

Radicular pain or symptoms resembling thoracic outlet syndrome may be reported.

Observation

Thoracic kyphosis, cervical lordosis, and scoliosis may be present.

The scapula may be positioned lower and more protracted relative to the nondominant arm at rest.

Dysfunctional motion, position, or stability of the scapula is observed during arm elevation or lowering or during GH rotation at 90° of abduction.

Functional Status

The patient has poor shoulder function with an associated loss of strength, power, or endurance.

Subsequent biomechanical changes exacerbate symptoms and create further dysfunction.

Physical Examination Findings

The coracoid process, pectoralis minor, and superior and medial scapular borders may be tender to palpation.

Glenohumeral IR deficit (GIRD) may be present in overhead throwers.

The scapular retraction test may be positive.

The scapular assistance test may be positive.

Tests for rotator cuff impingement (subacromial or internal) may be positive.

A relocation test may relieve symptoms of internal (posterior) impingement.

---

upward rotation, 40° of IR, and 15° of anterior tilt. Poor scapular function often presents with poor posture that includes a lower, protracted, and anteriorly tilted dominant-side scapula (see **Figure 9.14**).[45] The overprominence of the medial scapular border and inferior angle are indicative of excessive scapular IR and anterior tilt, respectively—often as the result of thoracic kyphosis, cervical lordosis, scoliosis, tight or shortened pectoralis minor, short head of the biceps, or posterior rotator cuff and capsular tightness.

Dynamic scapular function is assessed by observing multiple repetitions of bilateral forward arm elevation and lowering in the sagittal plane and scapular plane (scaption). Active internal and external GH rotation in 90° of abduction should be observed with overhead-throwing athletes. Scapular motion is classified as "abnormal" if it differs significantly from the "ideal" motion, between sides (asymmetric), or between repetitions (inconsistent). During forward arm elevation, the scapula should rotate upward 40–50° and tilt posteriorly 20–30°. The scapula should translate laterally and internally rotate slightly (protract) as the humerus elevates to 90°, but then rotate externally 10–20° and medially translate (retract) as the humerus continues to full elevation. In healthy shoulders, scapular motions are reversed during arm lowering.[12] To keep the humeral head safely within the glenoid fossa during smooth and controlled humeral elevation and

radicular pain
Pain moving from the torso into the extremities; radiating in a nerve root distribution.

9

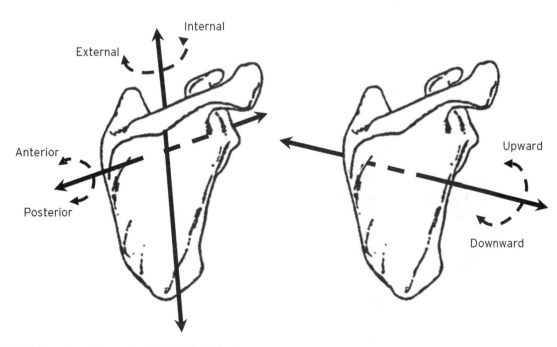

Figure 9.13 Scapular motions are described relative to the thorax.

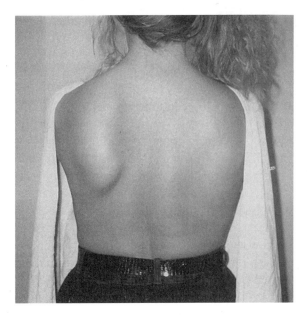

Figure 9.14 Poor scapular posture includes an increase in scapular internal rotation and anterior tilt, as seen in this patient.

lowering, the scapula should rotate with similar control. Deficits in the amount or control of any of these scapular motions result in limited humeral motion, impingement, or poor transfer of force.

Abnormal scapular upward rotation presents as a shrug during arm elevation, as the upper trapezius dominates the scapular rotators in an effort to elevate the acromion. Failure to upwardly rotate the scapula during arm elevation decreases the subacromial space and, therefore, is associated with subacromial impingement.[30,46] An inability to posteriorly tilt the scapula during arm elevation also limits the subacromial space and is observed in patients with subacromial impingement.[28,30,46]

Abnormal scapular IR and posterior tilt may be observed during arm elevation as the medial scapular border and inferior angle lifting away from the thorax ("winging") and failing to externally rotate and tilt posteriorly to retract the scapula during elevation greater than 90° (see Figure 9.14). Poor scapular retraction may be the result of a tight or shortened pectoralis minor or short head of the biceps, or may reflect posterior rotator cuff and capsule tightness. Weakness or poor control of scapular stabilizers—typically the serratus anterior and middle and lower trapezius—also contribute to poor scapular function.

Failure to retract the scapula during arm elevation or GH external rotation (ER) at 90° of abduction causes hyperangulation, consisting of an increased angle between the scapula and the humerus. Hyperangulation, which typically affects

overhead athletes, increases tension on the anterior GH capsule and increases contact between the posterior glenoid labrum and the articular side of the infraspinatus and supraspinatus, leading to internal (posterior) impingement.

The AC joint may become symptomatic due to poor scapular function. Because the clavicle is more rigidly secured at the AC joint than at the sternum, scapular protraction and anterior tilt are imposed at the distal clavicular articulation. In a small number of individuals, thoracic outlet symptoms may emerge due to "closing down" on the neurovascular structures by the unsupported scapula and clavicle.

Because scapular dyskinesis—particularly scapular asymmetry—is observed in a large portion of asymptomatic individuals,[47] the challenge for the practitioner is to recognize the subtle changes in scapular function and to correlate those changes with any symptoms at the GH joint. The role the scapula plays in shoulder dysfunction can be assessed using the scapular assistance test and scapular retraction test.[45] Reduced symptoms during arm elevation with the clinician's manual assistance encouraging proper scapular motion suggest that any conservative or postsurgical rehabilitation should aim to restore normal scapular motion. Similarly, reduced symptoms of impingement or enhanced strength during arm elevation with the clinician applying manual stabilization of scapular retraction suggest that restoring scapular stability should be a primary goal of rehabilitation.

Differential Diagnosis
Cervical radiculopathy, suprascapular nerve syndrome, thoracic outlet syndrome, brachial plexus neuropathy/long thoracic nerve palsy.

Medical Diagnostic Tests
Electromyography and nerve conduction studies may be conducted to rule out palsy of the long thoracic, suprascapular, or other nerves. These tests can also help identify the location and severity of nerve damage.

Imaging Techniques
The orientation of the scapula and the humerus relative to each other and to the thorax is critical in obtaining the optimal radiographic studies to visualize the relationship. Thus the "true" AP radiograph of the GH joint is taken 30° oblique to the sagittal plane, although a 45° view has also been recommended. The scapular Y view is taken at a 30° angle to the frontal plane; the AP radiograph perpendicular to this view is taken at an angle of approximately 60° to the thorax. If further detail of

the scapula is needed, cross-sectional imaging with either MRI or CT scan is ordered.

Definitive Diagnosis

Scapular function is assessed through visual observation of resting scapular posture as well as observation of scapular motion, position, and stability during multiple bilateral repetitions of arm elevation and lowering in forward elevation and scaption. "Abnormal" scapular function is characterized by poor motion, position, or stability between sides (asymmetry), between repetitions (inconsistency), or compared to ideal scapular function. Three-dimensional kinematic assessment may confirm the diagnosis.

Pathomechanics and Functional Limitations

Untreated altered scapular position and motion leads to SC, AC, or GH joint pathology. Glenohumeral elevation, abduction, and overhead activity may be limited by pain or inhibition, diminishing performance during overhead activities. Poor scapular upward rotation and shrugging may lead to or exacerbate symptoms of subacromial impingement and the formation of trigger points and insertional pain in the levator scapulae and upper trapezius. Dysfunctional scapular retraction (ER and posterior tilting) produces hyper-angulation, which in turn increases tension on the anterior GH capsule and contact between the posterior glenoid labrum and the articular side of the rotator cuff, leading to internal (posterior) impingement. Because the components of a malpositioned scapula are inferiorly located, internally rotated, and tilted anteriorly, increased tension is placed on the coracoid by the shortened pectoralis minor tendon and conjoined tendon. With repetitive overhand motions, these shortened tendons encourage tendinopathy, resulting in pain on palpation of the coracoid.

▇ Medications

Analgesics, NSAIDs, and muscle relaxants may help resolve immediate symptoms and facilitate movement. The use of NSAIDs should be constrained to a 3- to 7-day course during the inflammation phase of rehabilitation.

▇ Surgical Intervention

Surgery is not typically indicated for scapular dyskinesis. However, associated neurovascular symptoms or other conditions of the AC or GH joints or the rotator cuff may require surgical correction. If the dyskinesis results from a neurologic condition, nerve repair or transfer may be performed. If the nerve cannot be repaired, muscle transfers can

help improve scapular function. Recalcitrant cases of snapping scapula may require corticosteroid injection, bursectomy, or partial scapular resection.[48] Those patients with posterior capsular tightness that does not respond to conservative treatment may benefit from a posterior capsular release (see ST 9.3 [posterior capsule release]).

▇ Injury-Specific Treatment and Rehabilitation Concerns

Specific Concerns

Decrease muscle spasm.
Correct the scapular malposition.
Facilitate scapular motion, control, and stability.
Strengthen scapular stabilizers and improve flexibility of tight structures.

Improving scapular function should be an integral component of any comprehensive shoulder rehabilitation program. The initial rehabilitation program should focus on the base of the kinetic chain and correction of lumbar and core strength, stability, and flexibility deficits before addressing the scapular component and the upper extremity.[49] (See Chapters 13 and 16 for lumbar spine/core rehabilitation exercises.) Conservative treatment focusing on correction of scapular dysfunction has a high success rate in returning competitive overhead athletes to their preinjury level of performance within 4 months.[50]

Interventions for scapular dyskinesis vary depending on the level of dysfunction, the associated pathology, and the patient's activity level. Discontinuation of activity or a reduced workload may be required in patients with advanced scapular dyskinesia. In other cases, the activity level may be maintained during the rehabilitation process. Assess and monitor isolated GH motion in overhead athletes (see the later section in this chapter, "Overhead Athletes: Adaptations and Pathomechanics").

Painful motions should be avoided during early rehabilitation, with physical agents, manual therapy, and medications being used to reduce pain, trigger points, and inflammation. Rehabilitation focuses on improving scapular position by increasing flexibility and establishing conscious appreciation of the scapular position. Control of the scapula is facilitated through developing strength and endurance of the lower and middle trapezius and serratus anterior. Scapular stability is then developed as a continuum, ranging from static to dynamic to functional, and from single-joint to multiple-joint to functional movements.

Soft-tissue mobilization and stretching of the associated muscles is used to correct associated poor scapular position and spinal posture. Stretching focuses on the pectoralis minor, levator scapulae, upper trapezius, latissimus dorsi, and posterior rotator cuff. The sleeper, cross-body, and corner pectoralis self-stretches and the supine "open book" pectoralis minor manual stretch in the flexibility component of the *Foundational Shoulder Exercises* are initiated early in rehabilitation and continued through the return-to-play point.

Patients may begin with the exercises requiring minimal cuff activity (scapular clocks, shoulder dumps, and sternal lifts) in the *Shoulder Stability Progression* to establish conscious control of the scapula. In the absence of associated GH or AC pathology, rapid progress is typically seen after establishing conscious scapular control. Exercises in the stability progression advance to further activate scapular stabilizers, including ball stability exercises with the arm in 45° of abduction, weight shifts, and low rows. More challenging isometric stability exercises, such as open-chain rhythmic stabilization and tubing isometric stability exercises, incorporate activity of multiple joints and multiple arm positions.

The dynamic stability portion of the *Shoulder Stability Progression* begins when active arm elevation to 120° with scapular control (no shrug) is achieved. These exercises are initiated with hitchhikers and scapular clocks at 90° abduction, before advancing to the tubing retraction, push-up, and lawnmower progressions. Mobility, stability, and strengthening exercises should progress to functional overhead positions and include plyometrics, oscillatory devices, and each of the *Foundational Shoulder Exercises* (including the thrower's portion). Athletes who lost significant time should complete a sport-specific interval strengthening or throwing program.

■ Estimated Amount of Time Lost

Patients are often functional even in the face of scapular dyskinesis. As a consequence, this condition often goes unrecognized until it results in poor performance or further injury. Time lost is based on pain, concurrent injury, risk of further injury, and performance level.

■ Return-to-Play Criteria

Improved scapular motion, position, and stability; normal, pain-free GH ROM; adequate strength; and normal performance of sport-specific activities are the criteria on which the return-to-play decision is made.

Practice Tip

Patients with scapular dyskinesis display reduced serratus anterior activity,[46,51] overactive upper trapezius,[46] and tight pectoralis minor muscles.[52] Exercises that activate key scapular stabilizers with minimal upper trapezius activation should be used in prevention and rehabilitation programs.[53]

The unilateral corner stretch[54] and supine manual stretch effectively lengthen the pectoralis minor.[55] Therapeutic exercises can improve thoracic and scapular posture[56,57] and scapular motion.[57]

Rotator Cuff Pathologies

CLINICAL PRESENTATION

History

Repetitive overhead arm motions result in progressive pain and dysfunction.
Discomfort is noted over the anterior and anterolateral shoulder.

Observation

Poor scapular function, combined with muscle atrophy and wasting, may help diagnose more extensive underlying problems that have manifested as SAIS.
Poor scapular function observed during humeral elevation may include asymmetry and a lack of scapular upward and ER and posterior tilt.[12]

Functional Status

Pain with overhead arm motion.
Pain that increases during internal and external humeral rotation.
Weakness with overhead lifting.

Physical Examination Findings

Discomfort occurs with palpation lateral to the acromion.
The patient has a limited range of humeral IR and posterior capsule tightness.
Pain is reproduced between 60° and 120° of passive or active humeral elevation or abduction (painful arc).
Pain increases with humeral elevation when scapular motion is manually restricted.
Positive findings on two or more of the following tests helps rules in SAIS:[58]
1. Painful arc sign
2. Hawkins-Kennedy impingement sign
3. Weakness in ER
The Hawkins-Kennedy impingement sign may be used to screen for (rule out) subacromial bursitis.[59]
Scapular assistance test and scapular retraction test may be positive.
Symptoms increase in patients with concurrent rotator cuff tears or GH instability.

The supraspinatus, subscapularis, teres minor, and infraspinatus tendons merge with the GH capsule and coracohumeral ligament to form the rotator cuff.

Historically, conditions affecting the rotator cuff have been described as separate pathologies, but researchers are now recognizing the multifactorial nature of rotator cuff pathology. Chronic rotator cuff pathologies are elements of a continuum of bursitis and tendinopathy that includes tendinitis, tendinosis, tenosynovitis, and partial- and full-thickness tears. While the etiology of rotator cuff pathology remains controversial, the three most accepted mechanisms are (1) shear force caused by compressive and tensile stress, (2) impingement (subacromial and internal), and (3) age-related degenerative changes to the tendon. Although rotator cuff tendinopathy, impingements, and labral lesions are presented separately here, they are often associated. Younger athletes typically suffer from rotator cuff injuries associated with shear force or internal impingement. In contrast, subacromial impingement and age-related changes may be factors in development of such injuries in older patients.

The rotator cuff and long head of the biceps provide dynamic stabilization to maintain the humeral head on the glenoid fossa. Large-magnitude and repetitive forces placed on the shoulder may result in fatigue, compressive and tensile overload, inflammation, muscle inhibition, and eventual tissue failure. After injury, the dynamic stability provided by the rotator cuff is compromised. As a consequence, additional injuries—such as capsular lesions, labral tears, and osseous changes—may arise secondary to excessive humeral head displacement.[49]

Symptoms of rotator cuff injury include pain distributed into the deltoid and shoulder stiffness, weakness, instability, and crepitus. ROM measures should isolate GH motion from scapulothoracic motion. Stiffness limits passive GH ROM and causes pain at the motion end point. This symptom is commonly associated with partial-thickness cuff lesions but also can occur with full-thickness lesions. By comparison, weakness or pain with muscle contraction can limit shoulder function. In addition, tendon fibers may be weakened by degeneration and fail without any symptoms, or they may produce only transient symptoms that are interpreted as bursitis or tendinopathy. A more significant force is required to tear the cuff in younger individuals.

Cuff tears often result from a cascade of tendinopathy effects stemming from subacromial impingement syndrome (SAIS); however, this type of impingement typically occurs in older, nonathletic patients. Although SAIS-related rotator cuff disease may exist in the athletic population, other causative factors may be more important in this cohort, including repetitive overuse, GH instability or ligamentous

laxity, soft-tissue contracture (especially of the posterior cuff and capsule), and poor scapular function. Because of these and other mitigating factors, management of rotator cuff disease in athletes can be difficult.

Among athletes, overhead throwers are the most susceptible to rotator cuff injuries, exhibiting a high incidence of partial-thickness and small, complete rotator cuff tears.[60,61] These athletes are often hesitant or unwilling to modify their activities. Consequently, the persistently high demands on the rotator cuff may predispose them to recurrent episodes of cuff-related shoulder pain. Successful management of these patients requires knowledge of the relevant pathoanatomy and an accurate and complete diagnosis.

Rotator Cuff Impingement/Rotator Cuff Tendinopathy

Rotator cuff impingement is categorized as subacromial or internal based on the location of symptoms. Subacromial impingement, outlet or external impingement, describes compression of the subacromial tissues resulting from the narrowing of the subacromial space. Internal impingement, posterior or posterior-superior glenoid impingement, describes pathologic contact between the margin of the glenoid and the underside (internal surface) of the rotator cuff.[60] Whereas SAIS primarily affects older individuals, internal impingement more often affects overhead athletes. Nevertheless, both conditions may coexist in the same individual, and both represent part of the spectrum of rotator cuff disease.

Impingement is increasingly being considered a *symptom* if the patient describes pain during shoulder motion and a *sign* if the pain is elicited upon examination. The diagnosis of "impingement" is losing favor because disorders other than rotator cuff disease can cause shoulder pain when the arm is abducted. In reality, impingement may more accurately be described as a *result,* rather than a *cause,* of shoulder dysfunction. Therefore, the focus of the clinical examination should be identifying the cause of any impingement symptoms rather than emphasizing their classification.

In some cases, SAIS may be differentiated from internal impingement or superior labrum anterior and posterior (SLAP) lesions based on history, clinical examination, and imaging. The location of pain during palpation, the apprehension test, and posterior impingement sign may provide the insight needed to differentiate between subacromial and internal impingement. Diagnostic arthroscopy may be required in some patients. Isolated cases of SAIS may present with pain lateral to the acromion, whereas internal impingement may result in pain along the posterior-superior or and posterior-lateral joint line.

Subacromial Impingement

Subacromial impingement syndrome describes compression of the subacromial tissues resulting from the narrowing of the subacromial space. The subacromial space is demarcated by the undersurface of the anterior third of the acromion, distal clavicle, and AC joint superiorly; the proximal humerus inferiorly; and the coracoacromial ligament anteriorly. The tissues that may be compressed between these confining structures include the rotator cuff, biceps tendon, and accompanying bursa. Subacromial impingement may be differentiated as primary or secondary impingement based on the factors narrowing the subacromial space (see the "Pathomechanics and Functional Limitations" section).

Charles Neer first introduced the term "impingement" in 1972, while paying particular attention to the acromial process.[62] Bone spurs on the undersurface of the acromial process anteriorly were thought to be caused by mechanical irritation of the rotator cuff, the humeral head contacting the acromial undersurface, and traction on the coracoacromial ligament. When the humerus is elevated, the supraspinatus tendon passes under the anterior acromion. In this position, the rotator cuff, biceps tendon, and subacromial bursa can be compressed between the coracoacromial arch and the greater tuberosity. Clinical symptoms were originally labeled "outlet" impingement and "non-outlet impingement" in an older, athletic population; our current understanding of the mechanics of overhead athletes differs considerably from this description. Neer described three stages of impingement syndrome and suggested that 95% of rotator cuff tendon lesions were due to impingement (see **Table 9.2**).

Table 9.2

Neer Stages of Rotator Cuff Impingement

Stage	Pathology	Typical Age Range
I	Reversible edema and hemorrhage	<25 years old
II	Fibrosis and tendinopathy	25 to 40 years old
III	Bone spurs and rotator cuff tendon ruptures	>40 years old

Source: Adapted from Jobe CM. Gross anatomy of the shoulder, in Rockwood CA Jr, Matsen FA III (eds), *The Shoulder*, ed 2. Philadelphia: WB Saunders; 1998:756.

Differential Diagnosis

Rotator cuff tear, internal impingement, AC joint injury, GH instability, glenoid labrum lesions, AC arthrosis, os acromiale, proximal biceps tendinopathy, nerve entrapment, calcific tendinitis, cervical spine disorders, thoracic outlet syndrome.

Medical Diagnostic Tests

Impingement is confirmed when a single injection of 10 mL of 1% lidocaine (Xylocaine) or bupivacaine (Marcaine) into the subacromial space eliminates the pain and allows full, painless shoulder ROM and restoration of strength. If the injection relieves pain but residual strength remains limited, a rotator cuff tear is generally indicated. Both passive and active ROM must be assessed before and after the lidocaine/bupivacaine injection. Although impingement and isolated rotator cuff disease do not generally limit passive motion, such motion may be limited by subacromial scarring and intracapsular and extracapsular contractures. In cases where the injection reduces impingement-related pain and passive motion is limited, ROM must be restored before the patient can resume normal activities.

Published evidence suggests that experienced clinicians are able to accurately inject lidocaine/bupivacaine into the subacromial space in only 29%[63] to 70%[64] of injections. Ultrasound guides are being used more frequently as a cost-effective way to improve the accuracy of diagnostic or therapeutic subacromial injections. Ultrasound-guided injections also improve outcomes in patients with SAIS compared to nonguided injections.[65]

Imaging Techniques

Advances in imaging techniques have led to notable progress in the diagnosis of rotator cuff pathology. Historically, the diagnosis was based on physical examination, plain radiographs, and possibly arthrography. In recent years, diagnostic ultrasound (US), CT arthrography (CTA), MRI, and MR arthrography (MRA) have greatly increased the diagnostic utility of imaging studies. To identify (rule in) or rule out rotator cuff pathology, MRA is the most effective technique, followed closely by MRI, and US in the hands of a skilled technician.[66]

After the clinical examination, a standard series of plain radiographs should be obtained. This series assists in evaluating skeletal structures and gross malalignment and can rule out fractures, dislocations, and calcific tendinitis. Additional imaging modalities are used to confirm the diagnosis.

Table 9.3

Radiographic Series for the Shoulder: Impingement Series Views

View	Description/Use
Anterior-posterior	May be either "routine" or "scapular/Grashey" Both visualize the clavicle, scapular borders, angles and spine, acromion, coracoid, glenoid, AC and SC joints, humeral head, neck, and greater and lesser tuberosities
Scapular outlet Y	A variation of the "scapular Y" view; same projection, but beam angled 5-10° caudally Visualizes the acromial type, subacromial space, and supraspinatus outlet
West Point	A tangential/modified axillary view; beam angled 25° inferiorly and medially Visualizes the anterior-inferior glenoid rim Good view of Bennett's lesion and anterior-inferior glenoid fracture
Rockwood	Anterior-posterior AP view with beam tilted 30° caudally Good view of extension of the acromion relative to the clavicle

A complete shoulder series requires at least four views (see **Table 9.3**).

The standard shoulder series is used to identify arthritis, subacromial spurring, or acromial morphology that predisposes the athlete to impingement inflammatory processes. Primary impingement is correlated with an anterorinferior subacromial spur on the 30° caudal-tilt AP radiograph (see **Figure 9.15**). The scapular Y and outlet views can help the clinician classify acromial morphology and estimate coracoacromial arch narrowing. Radiographs—especially the scapular outlet view—show acromial beaking and subacromial spur formation. MRI may reveal acromial morphology and subacromial

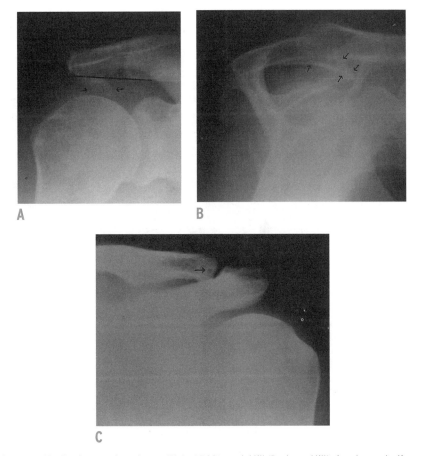

A

B

C

Figure 9.15   Radiographs suggesting impingement syndrome. (**A**) An AP 30° caudal tilt (Rockwood tilt) view demonstrating anterior extension of the acromion (arrows) beyond the anterior border of the clavicle (line). (**B**) A supraspinatus outlet view showing a large anteroinferior osteophyte (arrows). (**C**) A Zanca view demonstrating changes in the distal end of the clavicle (arrow).

bursal inflammation and thickening but is generally more useful in diagnosing rotator cuff disease.[67] Differentiating partial-thickness tears from rotator cuff tendinopathy on MRI can be difficult (see the section "Rotator Cuff Tears" later in this chapter).

Definitive Diagnosis

The history and clinical examination serve as the basis for the clinical diagnosis. Positive findings on two or more tests—painful arc sign, Hawkins-Kennedy impingement sign, and weakness in ER—rule in SAIS.[58] The clinical examination should identify factors leading to secondary impingement including rotator cuff, long head of the biceps, or scapulothoracic muscular weakness or dysfunction; coracoacromial ligament disruption; AC joint instability; or poor core or lower extremity function. Imaging may demonstrate subacromial spurs and variations in acromial process morphology indicative of primary impingement.

Rotator cuff tendinopathy, impingement, and tears are differentiated by a thorough history; detailed physical examination including ROM, joint mobility, and flexibility assessment; and specific tests to indicate functional symptoms related to each type of injury, which are valuable in determining the need for additional imaging. Radiographs and MRI are useful tools in establishing a working differential diagnosis. Rotator cuff tendinopathy is a clinical diagnosis made after rotator cuff tears have been ruled out by MRI, medical diagnostic procedures, history, and other radiographic evaluation. The clinical response to treatment interventions is also helpful in narrowing the diagnosis.

Pathomechanics and Functional Limitations

Subacromial impingement is differentiated as primary or secondary impingement based on the pathomechanics responsible for the narrowing of the subacromial space. During overhead activity, anatomic narrowing of the subacromial space causes repeated compression and gradual degeneration of the rotator cuff. The supraspinatus, which is the most commonly affected muscle, functions to depress the humeral head. During normal shoulder elevation and abduction, humeral depression prevents the greater tuberosity from contacting the acromial arch. When supraspinatus function is inhibited, the humeral head migrates superiorly, creating impingement. Repetitive compression of the rotator cuff tendon against the acromial process or coracoacromial arch injures the tendon and eventually leads to rotator cuff degeneration. The weakened tendon then permits further superior translation of the humeral head, increasing the impingement. This cycle is the source of some controversy: Is impingement the cause or the result of rotator cuff disease?

Primary impingement describes symptoms caused by narrowing of the subacromial space due to anatomical (typically age-related) changes including AC or subacromial spurring, os acromiale, fibrosis, or ossification of the coracoacromial ligament. These changes are rarely observed in an athletic population but may affect a small number of older athletes (usually those older than the age of 35). Acromion morphology can also lead to primary impingement syndrome and rotator cuff injury (see **Figure 9.16**).

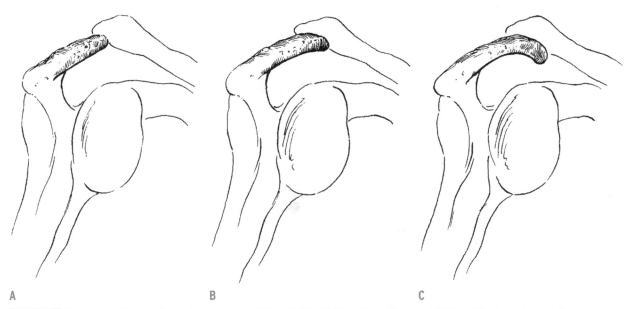

A   B   C

Figure 9.16   Three types (shapes) of acromion processes. (**A**) Type I is flat. (**B**) Type II is gently curved. (**C**) Type III is sharply hooked. *Source:* Reproduced with permission from Jobe CM. Gross anatomy of the shoulder, in Rockwood CA Jr, Matsen FA III (eds), *The Shoulder*, ed 2. Philadelphia: WB Saunders; 1998:45.

The incidence of rotator cuff tears increases in patients with type III acromial processes or anterior acromial spurs.[68,69]

Secondary impingement describes symptoms caused by narrowing of the subacromial space as the result of subtle superior or anterorsuperior GH instability. The humeral head may migrate superiorly due to supraspinatus weakness, or secondary to a number of other causes, including dysfunction or weakness of the rotator cuff, long head of the biceps or scapulothoracic stabilizers, coracoacromial ligament disruption, AC joint instability, or poor core or lower extremity function.

Functionally, patients with SAIS complain of pain and weakness with overhead arm motions. Occasionally these symptoms may increase with humeral ER or IR. Poor scapular function as well as muscle atrophy and wasting may help diagnose an extensive underlying problem that has been manifested as SAIS. During arm elevation, poor scapular function—including asymmetry and decreased scapular upward rotation, posterior tilt, and ER—may be noted.[12] This dyskinesis presents during arm elevation as poor scapulohumeral rhythm and prominence of the medial scapular border and inferior angle. The lack of each scapular motion serves to decrease the subacromial space and, therefore, may either exacerbate or be the origin of the impingement.

Medications

Subacromial corticosteroid injections may relieve pain and increase active motion. Paracetamol (acetaminophen) or NSAIDs are used for short-term symptomatic pain relief. Use of NSAIDs should be constrained to a 3- to 7-day course during the inflammation phase of rehabilitation.

Practice Tip

The best evidence suggests that subacromial corticosteroid injections are not an effective treatment for rotator cuff disease.[70] Individual response to treatment and patient preferences should weigh heavily in the decision to give such injections. If injections are administered, the use of ultrasound to ensure accuracy improves outcomes[71] and no more than two are recommended.

Postinjury Management

Avoid aggravating activities while relying on cryotherapy and medications (if indicated) to control pain and inflammation. Any posterior capsular tightness and IR deficit must be addressed. During rehabilitation, rotator cuff and scapular stabilizer

strengthening exercises are instituted. Closed-chain exercises are implemented for core strength and dynamic scapular stabilization. The best evidence indicates that both surgical and conservative treatment options significantly improve outcomes.[72]

Surgical Intervention

If conservative treatment fails to return the patient to the preinjury level within 3 to 6 months and painful limitation of motion continues, surgical intervention is often recommended. Patients who require surgery may not be able to return to sports involving overhead activity without resolving the anatomical origins of the impingement. During subacromial decompression, the subacromial space, including the bursa, is debrided and an acromioplasty is performed. There is no difference between the long-term outcomes with open[73] versus mini-open[74] acromioplasty. By comparison, arthroscopic subacromial decompression may result in less postoperative morbidity, decreased pain, and an earlier return-to-throwing program (6 to 8 weeks).

Practice Tip

The evidence does not clearly suggest that surgery will improve outcomes regarding pain and shoulder function compared to conservative treatment.[72] Outcomes following arthroscopic acromioplasty do not differ from those obtained with open[73] or mini-open[74] acromioplasty.

Neer recommended anterior-inferior acromioplasty to treat impingement syndrome. His operation consisted of detaching the deltoid muscle from the anterior acromial process and AC joint capsule and splitting the deltoid 5 centimeters distally. An osteotome was used to remove the anterior edge and undersurface of the acromial process and a portion of the coracoacromial ligament so as to decompress the subacromial space. If the clavicular joint was arthritic, the distal 2.5 centimeters of the clavicle was also excised. Neer noted that the anterior acromioplasty operation he described was rarely performed in patients younger than 40 years unless anatomic changes, such as an acromial spur, were present.[75]

Anterior acromioplasty may be accomplished through open or arthroscopic means.[62,76,77] Arthroscopic acromioplasty is often preferred because it may be better tolerated in the early postoperative period, has less potential for deltoid morbidity, and allows for management of concomitant intra-articular injury (see ST 9.2). The technical goal of arthroscopic acromioplasty is to smooth the

S|T Surgical Technique 9.2

Arthroscopic Subacromial Decompression

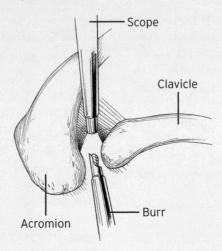

Indications

Many causes of subacromial injury exist, and the primary cause for each patient should be diagnosed before treating subacromial impingement. Decompression is indicated in patients with subacromial impingement who have failed to improve with conservative treatment and activity modification or radiographic evidence of supraspinatus outlet narrowing.

Procedure Overview

1. The affected arm is placed in traction in 15° of abduction with 10 to 15 pounds of longitudinal traction.
2. Arthroscopic portals are created on the lateral and/or superior aspects of the joints.
3. Bursectomy is accomplished with a shaver to improve visualization and partially clear the subacromial space.
4. Subacromial decompression and possible distal clavicular resection are accomplished with a burr and shaver if AC joint arthritis is present. The coracoacromial ligament is released and excised. The distal acromial undersurface is shaved to complete the subacromial decompression, taking care to leave the top of the acromial process intact. A distal claviculectomy is indicated if AC arthritis is significant. Care is taken to avoid debriding the rotator cuff.
5. Further arthroscopic evaluation of the GH joint is performed to determine if additional intra-articular injury must be addressed.

Functional Limitations

Few functional limitations occur with arthroscopic subacromial decompression, which is one of the advantages over open debridement.

Implications for Rehabilitation

Rehabilitation after arthroscopic subacromial decompression can proceed relatively quickly after the initial trauma of the arthroscopy has passed. Because no damage was done to the muscular tissues, ROM and strengthening exercises can be initiated soon (3 to 4 days) after arthroscopy. If the debridement was completed through an open procedure, muscle tissues were violated; in such a case rehabilitation is a longer process.

Potential Complications

Failure of arthroscopic subacromial decompression can occur if an insufficient amount of the acromial process causing the impingement was removed. Similarly, failure can result from a debridement that was too generous, leading to deltoid muscle damage or acromial fracture. Nerve damage can result from the arthroscopy or from an interscalene block, which is often used to augment the anesthesia.

Comments

Arthroscopic subacromial decompression is preferred because it is associated with less morbidity and offers the ability to visualize the GH joint for possible concurrent injury.

Source: Reproduced with permission from Shaffer BS. Painful conditions of the acromioclavicular joint. *J Am Acad Orthop Surg* 1999;7:176-188.

anterior acromial undersurface.[76–79] Although complete anterior acromial flattening relieves rotator cuff impingement, excessive bone removal may result in postoperative acromial stress fracture.[80]

Subacromial decompression alone is ineffective in returning overhead throwers to their prior level of activity.[81] Throwing athletes (particularly those of advanced age) may display irritation and thickening of the bursa with fraying that corresponds with abrasions and hypertrophy of the coracoacromial ligament. In these cases, debridement or repair is indicated if an external partial- or full-thickness rotator cuff tear is present.[82]

Postinjury/Postoperative Management

An appropriate amount of time must be allotted for the tissues to recover. The arm is placed in a sling during the day and at night for comfort during the first 2 weeks. To avoid stressing the acromion, patients should avoid using the shoulder when sitting or rising from a seated position for 6 weeks. After decompression and distal clavicle resection, GH movement is restricted to 135° elevation, 40° ER, and 60° abduction for the first 4 weeks. Abduction with ER and all isotonic strengthening of the GH joint is also avoided during this time. Horizontal adduction across the body is restricted until week 8.

Closed-chain isometrics may begin during week 4 and progress to isotonic strengthening in all GH motions over the following 2 weeks as comfort permits. As GH motion progresses postoperatively, the full pain-free range should be achieved by week 8. More aggressive rotator cuff strengthening exercises are incorporated during week 8. As ROM, mobility, and flexibility are restored, the patient can progress from isotonic to isokinetic and functional resistive exercises as clinical recovery allows.

Injury-Specific Treatment and Rehabilitation Concerns

> **Specific Concerns**
>
> Avoid early overhead activities and using the shoulder when sitting or rising from a seated position.
> Restore GH ROM, strength, and kinematics.
> Identify and address any secondary causes of impingement.

General goals of rehabilitation are to normalize GH and scapulothoracic mobility, strength, kinematics, and dynamic stabilization. Progressive resistance exercise programs improve outcomes, including pain and function, in patients with SAIS.[83] Adding joint mobilizations to exercise programs is more effective than implementing exercise alone.[84]

Early rehabilitation should decrease inflammation and focuses on the initial steps toward normalizing kinematics. Throughout the inflammatory phase, therapeutic modalities seek to improve patient comfort by creating a better environment for the healing process. Patients are encouraged to preserve strength and flexibility of the elbow, wrist, and hand during immobilization using activities that maintain support of the humerus, as comfort permits. Arthrokinematics are facilitated by using inferior, anterior, and posterior glides and stretching the anterior and posterior shoulder as needed. The *Shoulder Mobility Progression* is begun as warranted with open-chain pendulum exercises and table bows. Early exercises start with less than 40° of elevation and should not stress affected tissue. The active-assisted portions begin as patient comfort or postsurgical restrictions permit. Exercises include T-bar–assisted ROM, closed-chain pendulum exercises, table wash, and the supine press. Passive ROM exercises are used only as needed in postsurgical patients.

Nonsurgical patients may begin the exercises requiring minimal cuff activity in the *Shoulder Stability Progression*, with the goal to establish conscious control of the scapula as soon as comfort permits. Postsurgical patients may begin these exercises as early as week 4. Scapular clocks, shoulder dumps, and sternal lifts may begin safely while the patient is still using a sling. Isometric stability is sequentially restored using isometric low rows, rhythmic stabilization, and tubing isometric exercises; avoid weight shifts and bearing weight on the involved arm. Progressive isotonic strengthening, including tubing exercises, for each GH motion begin at 0° of abduction. Elastic tubing allows progression with increasing resistance exercises as tolerated. Horizontal adduction across the body and the Jobe position of abduction (GH abduction in the scapular plane with IR) should be avoided.

To address associated weakness or dysfunction of the supraspinatus, initial strengthening is appropriate with exercises that optimally activate the supraspinatus while inhibiting activation of the deltoid. Motions that activate the serratus anterior and lower trapezius with minimal upper trapezius activation are also advantageous. The exercises addressing each of these goals include side-lying ER, side-lying forward elevation, and prone horizontal abduction with ER (see **Figure 9.17**).[53] These exercises may prove more beneficial for supraspinatus function than the empty or full-can exercises[85]; they help establish

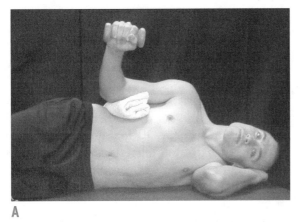

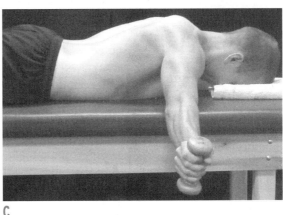

Figure 9.17 Exercises that activate the serratus anterior and lower trapezius with minimal upper trapezius activation. (**A**) Side-lying external rotation. (**B**) Side-lying forward elevation. (**C**) Prone horizontal abduction with external rotation.

strength and muscular balance before introducing more functional positions and motions.

Patients who attain active GH ROM to 120° with scapular control (no shrug) may progress to dynamic stability activities. Exercises start with the arm positioned by the side and progress from isolating the scapulothoracic joint to full body movements. Closed-chain exercises should progress to more than 90° in humeral elevation and introduce greater loads. When symptoms are minimal or absent, strength and endurance approach normal, and motion is not restricted, active ROM and stability exercises may gradually progress to overhead activities, plyometrics, and sport-specific exercises. A sport-specific interval training or throwing program may be initiated as early as week 12.

■ Estimated Amount of Time Lost

Time lost varies depending on the degree of injury and the structures involved, ranging from a few weeks to a year. Patients undergoing acromioplasty typically return to activity after 4 to 6 months, whereas those undergoing distal clavicle resection may return after 6 to 12 months.

■ Return-to-Play Criteria

The patient should achieve normal, asymptomatic GH and scapulothoracic ROM, kinematics, strength, stability, and neuromuscular control. In addition, the athlete must successfully complete appropriate functional testing demonstrating normal performance of sport-specific tasks before returning to athletic activity. Patients with impingement resulting from secondary factors must address those factors to restore normal function.

Practice Tip

Positive findings on two or more of a combination of tests, painful arc sign, Hawkins-Kennedy impingement sign, and weakness in ER help rule in subacromial impingement syndrome.[61]

Internal Impingement

Internal impingement describes pathologic contact between the greater tuberosity, posterior-superior glenoid, and the underside of the rotator cuff during

CLINICAL PRESENTATION

History

Discomfort occurs over the posterior-superior or posterior-lateral joint line.

Repetitive overhead arm motions, including abduction and ER, result in progressive pain and dysfunction.

Throwers initially report shoulder stiffness, but eventually progress to pain during late cocking and decreased throwing velocity, endurance, and control.

Observation

Poor scapular posture and function are evident, as are muscle atrophy and wasting.

The dominant-side scapula is internally rotated at rest (protracted/rounded shoulder).

Poor scapular function is observed during humeral elevation, including a lack of scapular ER and posterior tilt.[86]

Functional Status

Pain with abduction and ER (late cocking phase of throwing).

Poor performance, stiffness, or complaints of "dead arm" in throwers.

Physical Examination Findings

Discomfort is noted with palpation of the posterior-superior or posterior-lateral joint line.

The patient has limited GH IR and a tight posterior capsule.[69,87]

A posterior impingement sign is helpful in ruling this diagnosis in or out, particularly in patients with noncontact mechanisms of injury.[88]

An apprehension test produces posterior-superior joint line pain; a relocation test reduces pain.[89,90]

Symptoms increase in patients with advanced rotator cuff tears, SLAP lesion, or anterior GH instability.

---

humeral abduction and ER.[82] Signs and symptoms of internal impingement are most prevalent in overhead throwers and athletes who participate in racquet sports, but may be reported in anyone whose activity involves repeated abduction and ER. This condition is typically characterized by articular-side rotator cuff tears and posterosuperior labral lesions. It represents a wide spectrum of pathology, however, including partial- and full-thickness rotator cuff tears, anterior and posterior capsular injury, glenoid chondral erosion, chondromalacia of the posterosuperior aspect of the humeral head, and biceps and labral lesions.[88–91] The first clinical evidence of internal impingement was reported in 1992, when Walch et al. described articular-side partial-thickness tears of the posterior supraspinatus tendon and the anterior infraspinatus tendon, posterosuperior glenoid lesions, and osteochondral fractures of the humeral head.[58]

Jobe described a clinical classification system for internal impingement.[92] Throwers with early stage (I) internal impingement describe a need for longer warm-up periods, shoulder stiffness, and discomfort in the late cocking and early acceleration phases of throwing. The intermediate stage (II) includes localized pain over the posterior-superior or posterior-lateral joint line in the late cocking and early acceleration phases of throwing. Throwers with stage II symptoms who do not respond to conservative treatment are considered to have advanced-stage (III) internal impingement.[92]

The etiology of internal impingement in throwers is controversial. The normal and abnormal adaptive changes and glenohumeral IR deficit (GIRD) in overhead athletes play a role in these individuals' development of internal impingement (see "Overhead Athletes: Adaptations and Pathomechanics" later in this chapter). Such chronic adaptations include increased GH ER, humeral head and glenoid retroversion, and anterior capsular laxity. As a result, several compensatory and potentially pathologic anatomic changes may occur—specifically, anterior capsular laxity or microinstability and a posterior capsular contracture that produces a GIRD when the gains in ER are met with greater losses of IR. While evidence regarding the role of anterior instability remains inconclusive, throwers with internal impingement display significantly greater GIRD and posterior capsular tightness compared to asymptomatic throwers.[93]

Patients with internal impingement may present with poor scapular posture and possibly muscle atrophy or wasting. The involved scapula will be internally rotated at rest, presenting as a protracted or rounded shoulder. During repeated active humeral elevation, affected patients display poor scapular control with a lack of scapular ER and posterior tilt.[86] Pain is reported with palpation of the posterior-superior or posterior-lateral joint line. The posterior impingement sign is positive,[88] and posterior pain that is reproduced with an apprehension test is relieved by the relocation test.[89,90] The posterior force applied to the humeral head during the relocation test serves to reduce the contact indicative of internal impingement. Because internal impingement rarely exists in isolation, a full shoulder examination—including measures of active and passive GH ROM, tests for scapular dysfunction, subacromial impingement, labral lesions, and GH instability—should be conducted.

Differential Diagnosis

Rotator cuff tear, subacromial impingement, AC joint injury, GH instability, glenoid labrum lesions, AC arthrosis, proximal biceps tendinitis, nerve

9

entrapment, calcific tendinitis, cervical spine disorders, thoracic outlet syndrome.

Imaging Techniques

Both standard and instability radiographic series should be used to evaluate patients with signs and symptoms of internal impingement. Radiographs of those individuals with internal impingement are often unremarkable; findings that may be associated with internal impingement include Bennett's lesion, rounding of the posterior glenoid rim, and sclerotic changes or osteochondral lesions of the humeral head.

MRI is the gold standard for diagnosing the young overhead thrower with posterior shoulder pain. When labral or partial-thickness cuff pathology is suspected, magnetic resonance arthrography (MRA) may offer improved specificity and sensitivity relative to MRI.[95] For this population, MRI or MRA may be performed with the patient's arm in abduction and ER. Such a position increases tension in the inferior GH ligament, which may help separate the edges of a labral lesion and enhance the sensitivity of the exam.[96] Both MRI and MRA may reveal an articular-side partial-thickness tear of the posterior supraspinatus or infraspinatus, glenoid labral fraying or tear, and contracture of the posterior capsule.[97] Imaging of experienced overhead throwers should be interpreted with caution, however, as 30% of asymptomatic throwers display rotator cuff abnormality and 40% display posterior-superior labral abnormality.[98] In other words, the imaging results should be assessed in the context of the entire clinical presentation. The bony lesions of the posterior glenoid, Bennett's lesions, and humeral head osteochondral lesions commonly associated with internal impingement also may appear on MRI.[97]

Definitive Diagnosis

Definitive diagnosis of internal impingement is based on the correlation of clinical examination findings and imaging. The posterior impingement sign is positive,[89] and pain produced with the apprehension test is reduced by the relocation test.[89,93] MRI or MRA may reveal articular-side rotator cuff tears and posterorsuperior labral lesions. Nevertheless, the complete extent of involved pathology may not be clear until arthroscopy is performed for those patients who do not respond to conservative treatment.[99]

Pathomechanics and Functional Limitations

In patients with internal impingement, the excessive GH ER and horizontal abduction during the arm cocking phase of throwing, coupled with a lack of scapular retraction, results in hyperangulation.[82] Contact between the glenoid and the rotator cuff in this position may be a normal phenomenon in throwers that does not always produce symptoms.[59]

Symptomatic throwing shoulders often have partial rotator cuff tears, SLAP lesions, and laxity.

Among the various mechanisms proposed as underlying development of internal impingement are anterior capsulolabral laxity[89] and contracture of the posterior capsule coupled with a SLAP lesion.[50,100,101] No matter which specific mechanisms are involved, humeral abduction and ER result in repeated or excessive contact between the greater tuberosity, posterorsuperior glenoid, and underside of the rotator cuff. The mechanism becomes pathologic when signs or symptoms of internal impingement develop. In all patients, it is important to investigate and address underlying factors contributing to the condition. In patients who do not respond to conservative treatment, possible contributing factors should be investigated preoperatively under anesthesia and through diagnostic arthroscopy. All underlying factors should be addressed surgically to achieve the optimal outcome.

■ Medications

Acetaminophen or NSAIDs are used for short-term symptomatic pain relief. Use of NSAIDs should be constrained to a 3- to 7-day course during the inflammation phase of rehabilitation.

■ Postinjury Management

Avoidance of aggravating activities, cryotherapy, and medications (if indicated) are all measures used to control pain and inflammation. Overhead throwers with symptoms of early stage I internal impingement, including shoulder stiffness and discomfort in the late cocking and early acceleration phases of throwing, should have 2 weeks of treatment with no throwing. Those with intermediate stage II symptoms, including posterior joint line pain during late cocking or early acceleration, should undergo 4 to 12 weeks of rehabilitation with no throwing.[92]

Any posterior capsular tightness and IR deficit must be addressed with posterior capsule stretching, joint mobilization, and horizontal adduction and sleeper stretches.[69] Rotator cuff and scapular stabilizer strengthening exercises are instituted during the course of rehabilitation. Closed-chain exercises are implemented to enhance core strength and dynamic scapular stabilization.

Conservative treatment should be attempted for 3 to 6 months in patients with internal impingement before considering surgical intervention. Therapy that addresses scapular dysfunction and IR deficit has been shown to improve functional outcomes in patients with internal impingement.[69] Patients who respond to 5 to 9 weeks of therapy with significantly increased posterior capsular mobility also report resolution of their symptoms.[69] In contrast, patients who fail to respond after 12 weeks of therapy (i.e., those with stage III internal impingement) are surgical candidates.[92]

Surgical Intervention

Patients with internal impingement who do not respond after 12 weeks of conservative treatment are surgical candidates.[92] For those not responding to conservative treatment, the final diagnosis and surgical decision are made upon examination under anesthesia or arthroscopic investigation. If patients display significant anterior instability under anesthesia, they undergo capsular plication. A significant deficit in IR displayed under anesthesia suggests a posterior capsular release is appropriate (see **ST** 9.3). Upon diagnostic arthroscopy, patients displaying posterorsuperior labral lesions are candidates for debridement or repair, while rotator cuff tears are repaired accordingly.

Postoperative Management

The rehabilitation progression must respect the healing rate of the tissues addressed surgically; follow the most conservative individual guideline for progression (see "Injury-Specific Treatment and Rehabilitation Concerns" for each appropriate tissue—capsular plication/shift, SLAP lesion, rotator cuff repair/debridement). Because of the multifactorial etiology of most cases of internal impingement, isolated surgical release of the posterior capsule is atypical. Nevertheless, general guidelines are provided here as the related pathologies are presented individually.

The goals of the rehabilitation after surgical release of the posterior capsule are to avoid scarring and contracture of the capsule, and to restore stability and normal kinematics and GH ROM.

Throughout the inflammatory phase, a variety of modalities and cryotherapy are used to improve patient comfort and create a better environment for the healing process. A sling is used sparingly for acute postsurgical pain or if indicated for other surgical procedures. Patients are encouraged to avoid the deleterious effects of immobilization or disuse by actively maintaining the strength and flexibility of the elbow, wrist, and hand as soon as comfort permits. Use of the affected limb for activities of daily living (ADLs) is encouraged as pain

Posterior Capsular Release

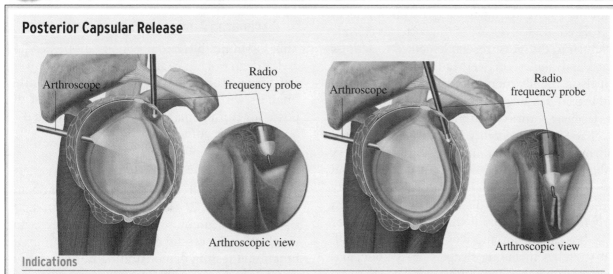

Indications

Failure of conservative treatment with a continued IR contracture or glenohumeral internal rotation deficit (GIRD).

Procedure Overview

1. The patient is placed in the lateral decubitus position.
2. A diagnostic shoulder arthroscopy is completed.
3. The arthroscope is placed in the anterior portal.
4. An electrothermal device is used to selectively cauterize the posterior capsule 1 centimeter from the glenoid rim.

Functional Limitations

Motion may be restricted if posterior capsule adhesions form.

Implications for Rehabilitation

A continual posterior capsular stretching program should be continued until the patient has maximized IR.

allows. Glenohumeral and scapulothoracic passive ROM and active-assisted ROM exercises begin 1 day following surgery and progress to active ROM as tolerated. Any remaining posterior capsular tightness and IR deficit must be monitored and addressed with posterior capsule stretching, joint mobilization, and cross-body and sleeper stretches throughout rehabilitation and during the athlete's return-to-play work. One report suggests that after a posterior capsular release, one can expect an immediate gain of 65° of GH IR.[100]

■ Injury-Specific Treatment and Rehabilitation Concerns

Specific Concerns

Avoid excessive stress on healing tissue (see "Specific Concerns" for each appropriate tissue—capsular plication/shift, SLAP lesion, rotator cuff repair/debridement).

Manage each factor that has been documented clinically or identified and addressed surgically.

For patients who undergo isolated posterior capsular release, early passive and active ROM is encouraged.

Restore GH arthrokinematics, ROM, and strength of the external rotators.

Facilitate scapular motion, control, and stability.

Restore biomechanics (throwing/overhead activity).

The conservative treatment of internal impingement or isolated surgical release of the posterior capsule is similar to the measures implemented to address scapular dyskinesis in overhead athletes. Joint and soft-tissue mobilization and passive ROM exercises within pain-free ranges are begun early to reduce pain and facilitate normal GH arthrokinematics and ROM.

The *Shoulder Mobility Progression* is initiated with open-chain pendulum exercises and table bows at this time and advanced as tolerated. Both active and active-assisted stretching for motion and flexibility of the entire shoulder girdle should be implemented early in rehabilitation. Flexibility of the posterior capsule is paramount, and should be addressed with self-stretches including sleeper, cross-body, and pectoralis stretches 3 to 4 times per day.

The *Shoulder Stability Progression* begins with scapular clocks, shoulder dumps, and sternal lifts and advances quickly into the isometric and dynamic stability exercises within pain-free ranges. Progressive strengthening and aquatic therapy are encouraged as soon as inflammation and patient comfort allows, typically within 1 to 3 weeks. Restoring the strength of GH external rotators and scapular stabilizers is critical. Exercises implemented early in rehabilitation to achieve these goals include side-lying ER

and forward elevation and prone horizontal abduction with ER (see Figure 9.17). Progressive isotonic strengthening, including tubing exercises, for each GH motion begins at 0° of abduction and progresses to functional ranges and GH abduction and ER. Closed-chain exercises are implemented for lower extremity and core strength and dynamic scapular stabilization.

As ROM, joint mobility, and flexibility are restored, the patient can progress to isotonic, isokinetic, and functional resistive exercises as clinical recovery permits. More advanced exercises should include each of the *Foundational Shoulder Exercises*.

Sport-specific and plyometric exercises begin when strength reaches a near-normal level. For those patients with isolated surgical release of the posterior capsule, this is approximately 8 weeks after surgery. The mechanics of throwing/overhead activity should be monitored from this point forward. An interval throwing program (or other activity-specific program) should begin with the goal of returning the athlete to competition. Pitchers with isolated surgical release of the posterior capsule may return to competition 4 to 5 months after surgery.[102] Return to other activities may be appropriate sooner. Priority is placed on maintaining mechanics and posterior capsular flexibility during the athlete's return and throughout his or her career.

■ Estimated Amount of Time Lost

Time lost from athletic competition varies depending on the degree of injury and the structures involved, but ranges from a few weeks to several months. Pitchers with an isolated surgical release of the posterior capsule may return to competition 4 to 5 months after surgery.

■ Return-to-Play Criteria

The athlete should achieve normal, asymptomatic GH and scapulothoracic ROM, kinematics, strength, stability, and neuromuscular control before engaging in athletics. Successful completion of appropriate functional testing demonstrating normal performance of sport-specific tasks is required as part of the return-to-play criteria.

Practice Tip

Internal impingement is often multifactorial in origin. Injury prevention programs that emphasize maintaining posterior capsule flexibility can reduce the prevalence of injury and time lost from competition in overhead athletes.[50,100] Therapy that addresses scapular dysfunction and reduces IR deficit improves symptoms and functional outcomes in overhead athletes.[69]

Rotator Cuff Tears

Rotator cuff tears can be classified based on their onset as acute or chronic, and based on their depth as full thickness (complete) or partial thickness (articular side, bursal side, or interstitial). Full-thickness tears are further described according to their size as massive (more than 5 cm²), large (3–5 cm²), medium (1–3 cm²), or small (less than 1 cm²).[109] Full-thickness rotator cuff tears typically extend through the tendon from the bursal side to the articular side. Partial-thickness tears, which are more common than full-thickness tears, do not extend through the tendon. Partial tears are further classified according to their depth as grade 3 (more than 6 mm), grade 2 (3–6 mm), or grade 1 (less than 3 mm).[110]

CLINICAL PRESENTATION

History
Pain is noted during overhead motions.
Patients with acute tears report a traumatic mechanism with immediate pain and weakness.
Patients with chronic tears report pain and avoidance of overhead motion.
Partial-thickness tears tend to produce more pain than full-thickness tears.

Observation
Atrophy of the supraspinatus and infraspinatus may be noted if the dysfunction has been present for longer than 1 month.

Functional Status
Normal passive ROM and decreased active ROM, especially for overhead motions.
Pain during GH abduction and elevation.

Physical Examination Findings
Crepitus may be felt or heard during GH motion.
Palpable tendon defects may be noted for large or massive tears.
Poor GH flexibility and scapular function are noted; a shrug may be observed during arm elevation.
Positive findings in the following special tests help rule in full-thickness tears:
- Internal rotation lag sign[103] (subscapularis)
- Lift-off test[103] (subscapularis)
- Belly-press test[104] (subscapularis)
- External rotation lag sign[103,105,106] (supraspinatus, infraspinatus, or teres minor)
- Drop sign[103,106] (infraspinatus)
- Empty can test[107] (any rotator cuff)
- Drop-arm test[108] (supraspinatus)
Positive findings on a combination of three tests helps rule in a full-thickness rotator cuff tear:[61]
- Painful arc sign
- Drop-arm sign
- Weakness in ER

Chronic tears may be the end result of a continuum of tendinopathy that begins with tendinitis and progresses to tendinosis. The theories of pathogenesis for both acute and chronic rotator cuff pathology can be synthesized into a unified view. According to this perspective, the cuff is subjected to various types of stress, including tension, compression, shearing, torsion, abrasion, and degeneration. Cuff damage results when the load exceeds the fiber strength, causing immediate or insidious failure. Because these fibers are under tension even when the arm is at rest, they retract after rupture. Each instance of fiber failure has at least four adverse effects:
1. Load is increased on adjacent intact fibers, causing a "zipper" phenomenon.
2. Muscle fibers become detached from bone, diminishing rotator cuff force production.
3. Blood supply to the tendon is compromised, leading to progressive local ischemia.
4. More tendon fibers are exposed to lytic enzymes in joint fluid, removing the hematoma that assists in tendon healing.

Even when a tendon begins the healing process, the initial scar tissue lacks the normal biomechanical properties of the tendon and is at increased risk for failure. These events weaken the cuff substance, impair its function, and diminish its ability to effectively repair itself.

The supraspinatus and infraspinatus are the most commonly torn rotator cuff tendons.[111] Rotator cuff tears may present with weakness on manual muscle testing, although patients with full-thickness defects may still be able to actively elevate or abduct the arm. Interestingly, partial-thickness lesions often produce more pain during manual muscle testing than full-thickness lesions. Patients with bursal-side tears seem to be more symptomatic compared to those with articular-side tears.

Differential Diagnosis
Rotator cuff tendinopathy, GH instability, subacromial impingement syndrome, AC joint arthrosis.

Medical Diagnostic Tests
If an anesthetic injection relieves pain but strength remains poor, a rotator cuff tear is likely. In this case, the weakness is caused by the rotator cuff defect rather than pain.

Imaging Techniques
Suspected rotator cuff tears were once diagnosed through invasive procedures such as arthroscopy or arthrography. More recently, advances in technology have facilitated accurate diagnoses and better visualization of tissues using noninvasive imaging. The ability of imaging techniques to rule in or rule out rotator cuff tears varies depending on the age

of the population and the depth of the tear.[60] For the athletic population (typically persons younger than age 45), for example, ultrasound may be used to rule in a full- or partial-thickness rotator cuff tear. This imaging technology has poor sensitivity, however, so it cannot rule out either pathology.[60] The utility of ultrasound imaging also depends on the skill of the individual reading the image.[112–114]

MRI is useful for ruling full-thickness rotator cuff tears in or out in the athletic population[60] and is superior to arthrography for demonstrating partial tears and tendinopathy.[115–117] MRI and MRA can also illuminate soft-tissue structures not seen on other diagnostic tests. Cuff tears are best demonstrated on fat-suppressed, T2-weighted images. Coronal oblique images afford the best views for evaluating the supraspinatus and infraspinatus tendons. Axial images best visualize the subscapularis and teres minor tendons. Classic findings of a full-thickness tear on MRI include a markedly increased signal intensity within the defect on the T2-weighted cuff images, accompanied by subacromial bursal fluid. Some degree of encroachment may or may not be seen.[67]

With partial tears, an increased signal is noted in the rotator cuff that only partially traverses the substance of the rotator cuff. No significant fluid is present in the subacromial space with these tears. The subdeltoid fat plane is obliterated in complete tears and preserved in partial tears.

The most effective imaging modality for evaluating the rotator cuff in younger patients is a saline- or gadolinium-enhanced MRA. The addition of a contrast medium helps to identify the suspected injury because the medium is found in areas where it does not belong or displaces the tissue into an abnormal position. This technique is effective for ruling in or out full-thickness tears as well as articular-side and bursal-side partial-thickness tears.[95]

Definitive Diagnosis

The definitive diagnosis of rotator cuff tears is based on both the clinical findings and the imaging results. In some cases, larger tendon defects may be palpated by placing the fingers at the anterior corner of the acromion and rotating the humerus. The defect may be palpated posterior to the anterior groove and anterior to the greater tuberosity of the humerus.

Pathomechanics and Functional Limitations

Defects in any rotator cuff tendon often progress to the point that they compromise the integrity of the entire joint. An initial supraspinatus defect typically propagates posteriorly through the remainder of the supraspinatus, then into the infraspinatus. As the tear progresses, the humeral head is displaced superiorly, increasing the load on the long head of the biceps tendon (LHBT). As a result, the width of the LHBT is often greater in the injured shoulder than in the uninjured shoulder. In patients with chronic deficiency of the rotator cuff, the LHBT's pulley system is frequently involved, leading to progressive LHBT tears and eventual rupture. The cuff defect may cross the bicipital groove to involve the subscapularis, beginning at the top of the lesser tuberosity and extending inferiorly. This kind of defect may be associated with disruption of the LHBT pulley system and destabilization of the LHBT leading to medial displacement.

The concavity compression mechanism of GH stability is compromised by cuff disease. Beginning with the early stages of cuff fiber failure, humeral head compression becomes less effective in resisting the upward pull of the deltoid. Partial-thickness cuff tears cause pain on muscle contraction, similar to the pain seen with other partial tendon injuries. The resulting reflex inhibition of the muscle action, combined with the absolute loss of strength from fiber detachment, makes the muscle less effective in maintaining balance and stability. Nevertheless, as long as the glenoid concavity is intact, the compressive action of the residual cuff muscles may continue to stabilize the humeral head. When the weakened cuff can no longer prevent the humeral head from rising under the pull of the deltoid, the remaining cuff becomes compressed between the head and the coracoacromial arch. Under these circumstances, abrasion occurs with GH motion, further contributing to cuff degeneration. Degenerative traction spurs develop in the coracoacromial ligament, which is loaded by humeral head pressure (analogous to the calcaneal traction spur in chronic plantar fascia strains).

Upward humeral head displacement also wears on the upper glenoid lip and labrum, reducing upper glenoid concavity effectiveness. This displacement can lead to cuff deterioration, allowing the tendons to slide down below the center of the humeral head. The cuff tendons then become humeral head elevators rather than depressors. Erosion of the superior glenoid lip may thwart attempts to keep the humeral head centered after cuff repair. Once the full thickness of the cuff has failed, resultant abrasion of the humeral articular cartilage against the coracoacromial arch may lead to secondary degenerative joint disease.

The cuff musculature deterioration that inevitably accompanies chronic cuff tears is one of the most important limiting factors in surgical cuff repair. Atrophy, fatty degeneration, retraction, and loss of excursion are all commonly observed with chronic cuff tendon defects and may be irreversible. These changes progress over time and cannot be rapidly reversed, even after cuff repair.

Immediate Management

The patient must discontinue aggravating activities. Ice should be applied to the shoulder to control inflammation. The patient may find pain relief using a sling.

Medications

NSAIDs may be prescribed to control inflammation and pain. Use of these medications should be constrained to a 3- to 7-day course during the inflammation phase of rehabilitation. Patients with acute tears may require narcotic analgesics for immediate pain control.

Postinjury Management

Initial management is supportive and targets pain control. A minimum of 3 months of conservative treatment is appropriate before considering surgical intervention. A progressive resistance and ROM exercise routine that also targets scapulothoracic, core, and lower extremity stability is implemented, with serial examinations being performed to evaluate cuff tension and symptoms. If the improvement plateau is unacceptable, further diagnostic workup is indicated.

Treatment and prognosis differ for individuals with full-thickness tears, partial-thickness tears, and tendinopathy. Treatment of full-thickness and partial-thickness tears differs based on the size and depth of the tear. Most full- and partial-thickness tears that extend beyond 50% of the tendon thickness are usually repaired surgically. Smaller partial-thickness tears may be surgically debrided or treated conservatively; the same is true for tendinopathies. Any predisposing conditions to shoulder impingement or instability must also be identified and corrected.

Surgical Intervention

Because surgical treatment depends on the size and depth of the tear as well as the quality of the remaining tendon, diagnostic arthroscopy is often appropriate. The rotator cuff insertion is visualized from both the GH joint and the subacromial bursa. A high-grade partial tear may be present on the bursal surface of the rotator cuff with a normal-appearing articular cuff insertion. In patients with bony supraspinatus outlet impingement, diagnostic arthroscopy is followed by arthroscopic acromioplasty.

Partial-thickness tears that extend through less than 50% of the tendon thickness are typically treated with arthroscopic debridement with or without sub-

acromial decompression. Because bursal-side tears may be more symptomatic than articular-side tears of the same size, surgical repair may be considered for bursal-side tears of more than 25% of the tendon thickness.

> **Practice Tip**
>
> Outcomes for young overhead athletes with small partial-thickness tears treated with arthroscopic debridement alone are mixed. In one study, 86% of these individuals (31 out of 36) returned to their preinjury level of athletic activity.[118] Others have reported similar success rates for returning athletes to activity (79% [22 out of 28]) after arthroscopic debridement; however, 91% (20 out of 22) of those returning reported persistent pain with activity.[119]

Patients with rotator cuff tears classified as full-thickness tears, partial-thickness articular-side tears extending through more than 50% of the tendon, and bursal-side tears extending through more than 25% of the tendon are candidates for a repair with or without subacromial decompression[120] (see **ST** 9.4). Most full-thickness rotator cuff tears in throwing athletes are classified as small or medium and require minimal retraction. These tears are frequently amenable to arthroscopic or mini-open repair. Conversely, rotator cuff injuries in contact athletes are occasionally medium to large in size and must be retracted. Under these circumstances, an open repair is preferable.

In small to medium, mobile rotator cuff tears, the arthroscopic and mini-open techniques are indicated. The purely arthroscopic approach—the least invasive option—is associated with decreased subacromial and deltoid trauma. Therefore, in young athletes with good bone and tendon quality and small, mobile cuff tears, arthroscopic repairs are preferred. This procedure may be combined with arthroscopic acromioplasty to treat coexistent supraspinatus outlet narrowing.

In medium to massive, less mobile rotator cuff tears, an open repair is frequently performed. These tears are repaired through a superior, transdeltoid approach. Acromioplasty is performed only if a subacromial spur is present. Tears that are retracted medial to the midportion of the humeral head are protected in an abduction pillow or brace for 2 to 3 weeks after surgery.

Poor outcomes for professional baseball pitchers have been seen following a mini-open rotator cuff repair of small to large tears, with only 8% (1 out of 12) able to return to high-level athletics.[121] What constitutes the "best" surgery for rotator cuff repair

S|T Surgical Technique 9.4

Mini-Open Procedure with Anterior Acromioplasty

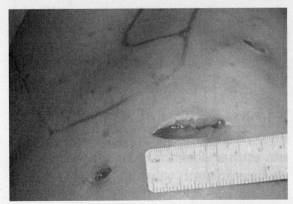

A

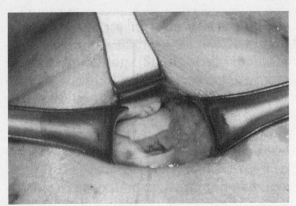

B

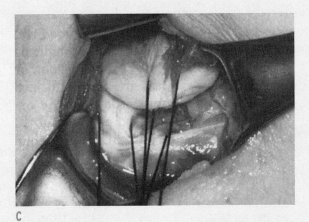

C

Indications

Patients with full- or partial-thickness tears (<0.2 cm) of the supraspinatus or infraspinatus tendon who have failed to improve with conservative treatment.

Procedure Overview

1. The patient is placed in the lateral decubitus or beach chair position.
2. Arthroscopy portals are created over the superior, anterosuperior, and posterosuperior aspects of the joint.
3. An arthroscopic subacromial decompression is performed (see ST 9.2).
4. The deltoid-splitting procedure is performed through an incision across the lateral acromion (**A**).
5. Dissection is carried out to the cuff bluntly and the tear identified (**B**).
6. The proximal aspect of the tear is mobilized, and the humerus is prepared for reattachment (**C**).
7. Various reattachment techniques may be used, including suture anchors and the development of a bony trough and suture reattachment.
8. Tear size, quality of tissue repair, and cuff tension on the repair determine the early postoperative management.

Functional Limitations

The patient's functional limitations depend on the procedure used, tear size, and the degree of mobilization required to repair the rotator cuff.

Implications for Rehabilitation

Rehabilitation speed is determined by the injury and the type of surgical repair. Larger tears require longer healing times.

Potential Complications

Deltoid injury and axillary nerve injury are rare complications.

Comments

The advantage of the mini-open procedure is that it does not require the deltoid origin to be taken down, thereby speeding the rehabilitation process. If the subscapularis is involved in the tear, the more extensive open procedure is more appropriate.

Source: Figures reprinted, with permission, from Bigliani LU. Rotator cuff repair. In: Post M, Bigliani LU, Flatow EL, Pollack RG (eds). *The Shoulder: Operative Technique.* Baltimore: Lippincott Williams and Wilkins; 1998:144.

is controversial. Indeed, these procedures have been performed using both open and arthroscopic techniques (see  9.5). A randomized clinical trial suggested that outcomes after open acromioplasty and rotator cuff repair do not differ from those after arthroscopic acromioplasty and mini-open rotator cuff repair at 1- and 2-year follow-up; however, patients who underwent arthroscopic mini-open repair had significantly better results at 3-month follow-up.[74] These findings are consistent with previous reports indicating that both open and arthroscopic techniques yield good results. The less invasive arthroscopic procedures, however, may facilitate early recovery and progression.

The decision to perform an open versus an arthroscopic rotator cuff repair is made after considering the severity of the patient's pain and dysfunction; symptom duration; tear size and location; and the patient's activity demands, functional limitations, and expectations. A large tear, poor tendon tissue quality, difficulty mobilizing the torn ends, and the presence of a rupture of the long head of the biceps adversely affect postoperative function and patient satisfaction.

S|T Surgical Technique 9.5

Arthroscopic Rotator Cuff Repair

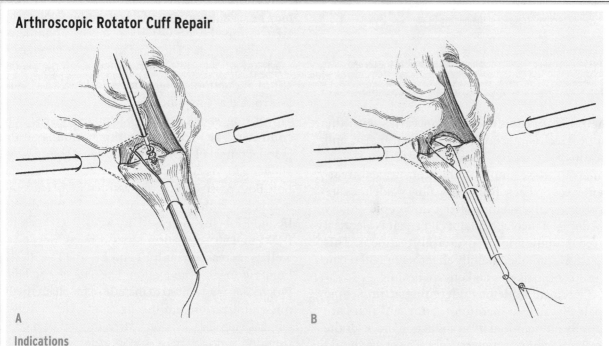

A   B

Indications

A full-thickness rotator cuff tear causing continued dysfunction despite nonoperative treatment.

Procedure Overview

1. The patient is placed in a lateral decubitus position.
2. A standard diagnostic shoulder arthroscopy is completed.
3. The subacromial space is entered, and a bursectomy and acromioplasty are completed as indicated (**A**).
4. The free edge of the tear is debrided.
5. The greater tuberosity is excoriated to expose bleeding bone.
6. Cannulas are placed in the arthroscopic portals to accept instruments that assist in the repair.
7. Depending on the size of tear and surgeon preference, suture anchors are placed in the tuberosity, with the sutures being placed through the rotator cuff tendon (**B**).
8. The sutures are tied using a knot pusher, which reduces the tendon back to the tuberosity, effecting a repair.

Functional Limitations

Active motion and strengthening are usually avoided for the first 6 weeks. Forward elevation progresses slowly during the first 6 weeks to avoid tension on the repair.

Implications for Rehabilitation

Active motion and aggressive strengthening are avoided in the plane of the repaired muscle for at least 6 weeks.

Source: Yamaguchi K, Levine N, Marra G, Galatz L, Klepps S, Flatow E. Transitioning to arthroscopic rotator cuff repair: the pros and cons. *Instructional Course Lectures.* 2003; vol. 52. American Academy of Orthopedic Surgeons.

■ Postoperative Management

An abduction orthosis or sling is used depending on the amount of abduction needed to minimize tension on the repair. The sling or orthosis is used from 1 to 8 weeks, depending on the size of the tear and the tension on the repair. The patient typically returns to the surgeon in 7 to 10 days to have the sutures removed and the shoulder assessed. Some patients are more comfortable sleeping in a recliner for the initial weeks following surgery.

■ Injury-Specific Treatment and Rehabilitation Concerns

> **Specific Concerns**
>
> Avoid excessive stresses on the healing tissue.
> Maintain normal joint osteokinematics.
> Restore full passive ROM as soon as possible.
> Restore dynamic stability and muscular balance of the GH and scapulothoracic joints.

The rehabilitation progression varies with the surgical technique, quality of tissue, tear size, and tension of the repair. The exercises performed are similar to those employed for nonsurgical treatment, except that soft-tissue healing guidelines are respected. Rehabilitation after arthroscopic surgery that does not involve a rotator cuff repair is identical to rehabilitation for nonsurgical treatment. This protocol is modified slightly after rotator cuff repair to protect the tissues and ensure healing.

Overhead athletes undergoing arthroscopic repair of small to medium rotator cuff tears are typically immobilized in an abduction brace for the first 2 to 4 weeks postoperatively. The brace should also be worn at night as directed by the surgeon, typically for the initial 2 weeks. Throughout the inflammatory phase, a variety of modalities and cryotherapy may be used with all patients to improve their comfort and help create a better environment for the healing process. Patients should preserve strength and flexibility of the wrist and hand during immobilization as comfort permits through activities that maintain the elbow in 90° of flexion and support the humerus.

During the first week, the sling is removed, and the patient begins passive GH elevation to tolerance and ER in 45° of abduction. The minimal cuff activity and active-assisted portions of the *Shoulder Mobility Progression* may begin with table bows and pendulum exercises. T-bar–assisted ROM may begin in GH ER in pain-free ranges with the arm in 45° of abduction. Isometric strengthening may begin

toward the end of week 1, with the elbow in 90° of flexion and a bolster or towel placed under the arm. The intensity should remain submaximal; isometrics may include elbow flexion, GH elevation, and IR and ER. Exercises requiring minimal cuff activity in the *Shoulder Stability Progression* are initiated so that the patient can establish conscious control of the scapula as soon as comfort permits. The scapular clocks, shoulder dumps, and sternal lifts may begin safely even with the patient in the sling.

During week 2, GH passive ROM of 120° elevation and increased IR and ER with the arm in 45° of abduction as tolerated should be achieved. T-bar active-assisted GH rotational ROM exercises are continued as tolerated, and GH elevation is initiated. Pendulum, supine press, and table bow exercises may be used to progress GH elevation. Isometrics are continued, with GH extension being initiated as comfort permits. The *Shoulder Stability Progression* is advanced to include ball stability with the arm in 45° of abduction; weight shifts and low rows may be avoided at this time.

During weeks 2 through 6, all exercise should continue. The focus during this period is on the gradual return of ROM and dynamic stability while allowing for tissue healing and avoiding inflammation. Both passive and active-assisted ROM exercises may begin, with the degree of GH abduction during IR and ER being increased. By week 3, GH passive ROM of 150° elevation should be achieved, as well as increase in both IR and ER to 45° with the humerus in 90° of abduction. The *Shoulder Stability Progression* is advanced to include open-chain rhythmic stabilization and tubing isometric exercises emphasizing GH elevation, extension, and IR and ER. Immobilization may be discontinued when appropriate, as early as week 2.

GH passive ROM of 170° elevation and increased IR to 50° and ER to 75° with the humerus in 90° of abduction are the goals of week 5. At this time, isotonic strengthening may begin for elbow flexion and GH IR and ER with the arm in slight abduction (a towel is typically placed under the arm). Manual resistance is used to begin side-lying ER, side-lying forward elevation, and prone horizontal abduction with ER exercises. The supine press is progressed to increase GH elevation ROM as needed. The tubing isometric stability exercises may progress to include additional pain-free ranges.

Week 6 should see a progression of GH passive ROM to full elevation, with an increase in IR to 55° and ER to 90° with the humerus in 90° of abduction. All active-assisted ROM exercises are continued and active motion is initiated. Active GH elevation and abduction are gained through table bows, closed-chain pendulum exercises, and table and wall wash exercises as tolerated. Isotonic strengthening is continued and advanced to include 1-pound dumbbells with side-lying and prone exercises and tubing fencing. The dynamic stability exercises are continued and advanced to include scapular clocks at 90° abduction, hitchhiker exercises, tubing retraction, and the lawnmower progression. Active exercises may progress to more than 90° of GH abduction when the patient displays active elevation to 120° with scapular control (no shrug).

The goal of full active ROM should be achieved between weeks 8 and 10. All isotonic strengthening is advanced; resisted GH abduction may begin in week 10. The isometric and dynamic portions of the *Shoulder Stability Progression* are advanced as tolerated; plyometrics, push-ups, and oscillatory devices are avoided at this time. High-end lawnmowers and tubing punches and dynamic hug exercises are initiated.

During weeks 10 through 12, dynamic stability and isotonic strengthening exercises should begin to progress exercises toward each of the general *Foundational Shoulder Exercises,* beginning with the tubing exercises. All exercises, including passive and active-assisted ROM, are continued as needed to maintain full active ROM.

Mobility, stability, and strengthening exercises should progress to functional overhead positions during week 12. Weeks 12 through 15 should include incremental increases in resistance to improve shoulder strength. Sleeper, cross-body, and pectoralis stretches are initiated at this time and continued through the athlete's return-to-play.

By weeks 16 to 18, exercises should be extended to include plyometrics, wall dribbles, push-ups, use of oscillatory devices, and each of the *Foundational Shoulder Exercises* (including the thrower's portion). A sport-specific interval strengthening or throwing program may begin when appropriate, typically 20 to 22 weeks after surgery. Regular lifting should be resumed, with proper technique being emphasized.

For patients who undergo an acromioplasty with an intact rotator cuff or a partial rotator cuff debridement, active-assisted ROM exercises, including GH extension, and posterior shoulder stretching (sleeper and cross-body stretches) begin at 2 to 4 weeks. The isometric stability exercises of the *Shoulder Stability Progression* may begin by incorporating weight shifts and isometric low rows at this time, as patient comfort permits.

Patients who undergo repairs of large or massive cuff tears and those who require rotator cuff tissue mobilization are more restricted in their activities during the early phase of rehabilitation. Passive ROM is avoided, and these patients are typically placed in an abduction brace. Capsule and tendon release facilitates tendon repair; however, the prognosis for large tears is not as good as for small tears. Initiation of ROM exercises and progression must be individualized based on repair quality.

■ Estimated Amount of Time Lost

Postsurgical rehabilitation of an athlete with a rotator cuff tear requires 6 to 12 months.

■ Return-to-Play Criteria

The athlete should achieve normal, asymptomatic GH and scapulothoracic ROM, kinematics, strength, stability, and neuromuscular control. In addition, the athlete should successfully complete appropriate functional testing demonstrating normal performance of sport-specific tasks before returning to competition.

Long Head of the Biceps Brachii Tendinopathy

CLINICAL PRESENTATION

History

There is a gradual onset with no history of trauma, although acute cases have been reported.

Pain arises from the anterior shoulder, possibly radiating down the biceps or to the deltoid tuberosity, cervical spine, or scapula.

Crepitation or popping may be described in the shoulder during active motion.

Initially, pain is relieved by rest, but becomes more chronic as the condition deteriorates.

Night pain may be described.

Observation

Atrophy may be noted in the biceps brachii and cervical spine.

Functional Status

Pain and weakness increase during overhead arm motions or the arm cocking phase of throwing.

Physical Examination Findings

Pain increases during active GH joint abduction, rotation, and extension; motion often includes a shrug.

Palpable point tenderness and possible crepitus along the LHBT may be found.

The patient may have difficulty elevating the arm above shoulder level or placing the dorsum of the hand against the back.

Yergason's test may help rule in biceps pathology,[122] but in general no special tests are helpful in ruling in or out this condition.[123]

Conditions commonly affecting the long head of the biceps tendon (LHBT) include tendinopathy and SLAP lesions. LHBT tendinopathy is the most common biceps tendon lesion seen in the general population and is a frequent cause of anterior shoulder pain in throwing athletes of all ages. The natural history of degenerative LHBT tendinopathy evolves from tenosynovitis, to tendinosis, to delamination, to pre-rupture, and finally to rupture. Tendinopathy of the LHBT can be classified as primary or secondary.

Primary tendinopathy describes isolated inflammation of the LHBT within the intertubercular groove (tendinitis); it accounts for 5% of all biceps tendinopathies.[124] A condition that presents as primary tendinopathy, but is not readily diagnosed clinically, is the hourglass-shaped thickening of an intra-articular segment of the LHBT.[125] In this condition, the thickened segment of the tendon becomes entrapped and cannot move through the bicipital groove, causing a mechanical block to passive GH elevation synonymous with a trigger-finger mechanism. These patients lack 10–20° of GH elevation, but maintain rotational motion. Over time, the thickening leads to LHBT instability and often requires surgical excision.

The pain associated with LHBT tendinopathy may result from tenosynovitis, which leads to an altered tendon sheath gliding mechanism. Gradual pathologic changes can occur in the tendon, including capillary dilation and tendon edema with progressive cellular infiltration of the tendon sheath and synovium. Filmy adhesions between the tendon and tendon sheath may develop, resulting in crepitus with motion. In the chronic stage, the tendon frays and narrows, and minimal to moderate synovial proliferation and fibrosis develop. Ultimately, the tendon fibers are replaced by fibrous tissue, and dense fibrous adhesions form between the tendon and the bicipital groove. Because the LHBT passes directly under the critical zone of the supraspinatus tendon, microscopic changes consistent with an avascular state occur, including irregular **atrophic** collagen fibers, tendon fiber **fissurization** and shredding, fibroid necrosis, and an inflammatory reaction with an increase in fibrocytes.

Secondary tendinopathy comprises the fraying or rupture of the LHBT due to anatomic or physiologic changes in local tissues. The same mechanism that initiates subacromial impingement syndrome (SAIS) may inflame the LHBT as it passes under the acromion. Inflammatory conditions such as tenosynovitis are also associated with SAIS. Because the biceps sheath is intra-articular, any inflammatory

condition affecting the GH joint affects the biceps as well. Moreover, tumors can affect the shoulder synovium and may involve the tendon's sheath. As a consequence, LHBT tenosynovitis can facilitate development of septic arthritis or rheumatic inflammatory arthritis of the shoulder. The underlying cause of symptoms in these patients is most likely the articular injury. More commonly, LHBT tendinopathy occurs secondary to repetitive wear or stress caused by instability of the tendon during arm motion.

Stability of the LHBT is provided by a pulley system formed by the capsuloligamentous structures of the rotator interval and fibers from the supraspinatus and subscapularis tendons that guide the tendon as it exits the subacromial space. The coracohumeral and superior GH ligaments are primarily responsible for securing the LHBT, with the transverse humeral ligament serving a secondary role. This pulley alters the line of pull of the LHBT by 30–40°.[126,127]

Tear, degeneration, or inflammation of any of the pulley's restraining structures may place added stress on other supportive tissue. Over time, this imbalance results in progressive instability, inflammation, and degeneration of the LHBT and the pulley system. This intricate relationship helps explain why 85% of patients with confirmed LHBT pathology have associated rotator cuff tears.[123] The unstable LHBT typically becomes displaced medially, although this direction depends on the integrity of the rotator interval and subscapularis (see **Figure 9.18**).[128]

The primary function of the biceps is at the elbow; its role at the shoulder is not well understood. A weak contributor to GH abduction, this tendon has been proposed to be a humeral head depressor. The LHBT is involved in throwing athletes with anterior GH instability, who display increased activity during the late cocking phase relative to those throwing athletes without such instability. When the humerus is abducted and externally rotated, the humeral head force is directed anteriorly. In the presence of excessive anterior humeral translation, biceps muscle activity compensates for this hypermobility.[107] The biceps brachii also may provide GH stability during the acceleration and follow-through phases of throwing. Traction forces are conveyed across the GH joint during the follow-through phase via the LHBT, which transmits the tension to the tendon's origin on the superior glenoid labrum. The LHBT also protects the humerus from the tensile stress experienced as the elbow decelerates during the follow-through phase. These forces have been proposed as the mechanism underlying the development of SLAP lesions.

atrophic Characterized by atrophy or wasting.

fissurization The process of forming long, narrow depressions or cracks in the tissue.

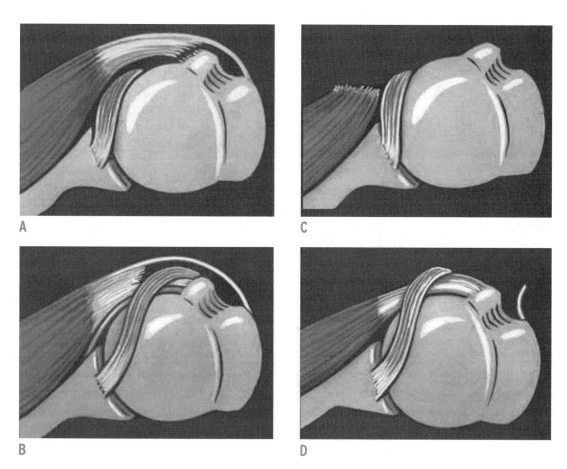

Figure 9.18 Dislocations of the LHBT are classified according to the position of the tendon and the integrity of the supporting structures. **(A)** Intra-articular displacement. **(B)** Intra-articular displacement with a ruptured subscapularis. **(C)** Displacement to the lesser tuberosity, within the subscapularis fibers. **(D)** Extra-articular displacement with a ruptured rotator interval. *Source:* Tonino PM, Gerber C, Itoi E, Porcellini G, Sonnabend D, Walch G. Complex shoulder disorders: evaluation and treatment. *J Am Acad Orthop Surg.* 2009;17:125.

Differential Diagnosis

SLAP lesion, rotator cuff tendinopathy, AC joint disorders, peripheral nerve entrapment, cervical disk herniation, cervical degenerative disk disease, thoracic outlet obstruction.

Medical Diagnostic Tests

A local anesthetic is injected into the bicipital groove. Improved ROM and decreased pain after such injection indicate the presence of LHBT tendinopathy.

Other methods for assessing the patient with suspected bicipital tendinopathy include selective local anesthetic injections in the subacromial space and biceps tendon sheath to differentiate the primary issue from the secondary condition. With this technique, the subacromial space is injected first to eliminate confusion due to anesthetic leakage from the biceps tendon sheath into the rotator cuff area.[129] In recent years, this technique has begun losing favor due to the inaccuracy of injections and because the patient with a rotator cuff tear may feel relief as the anesthetic leaks into the bicipital groove. Ultrasound guidance of

injections into the sheath can improve the accuracy of this technique.

Imaging Techniques

Radiographs are usually normal in patients who have primary bicipital tendinopathy but are occasionally useful in distinguishing biceps tendon lesions from other causes of shoulder pain. Specific radiographic views of the bicipital groove can be obtained if bony abnormalities are suspected.

While costly, MRI and MRA remain the best imaging tools for evaluating soft-tissue abnormalities about the LHBT.[95,130,131] Both of these modalities facilitate the effective examination of the conditions commonly associated with LHBT pathology, including rotator cuff and labrum lesions. The oblique and sagittal views best visualize tendon instability and edema while axial views demonstrate subluxations.[67]

Arthrography in patients with bicipital tendinopathy can show tendon widening and irregularity, loss of the tendon sheath's smooth margin, or groove abnormalities. Notably, the hourglass-shaped thickening of the tendon is best visualized via arthrography.[123] False-negative findings can occur if fluid in the tendon sheath obscures the arthrographic contrast medium or a rotator cuff tear allows the contrast medium to escape and results in failure to fill the sheath.

Ultrasound imaging can demonstrate fluid collection in the tendon sheath and provides a better image of the tendon than arthrography. This modality is an effective, noninvasive, inexpensive, and quick tool to rule in biceps abnormalities[130]; however, it cannot rule out the condition and is much less helpful than MRI in evaluating other conditions commonly associated with LHBT pathology.[95]

Definitive Diagnosis

Definitive diagnosis of LHBT pathology is made via arthroscopy. The tendon is evaluated dynamically during humeral elevation and rotation, and inspected for instability and the hourglass-shaped tendon. The clinical diagnosis of bicipital tendinopathy is based on the clinical findings and exclusion of other possible conditions. Because bicipital tendinopathy is often associated with the presence of other conditions, careful consideration of possible rotator cuff lesions is essential in evaluating and managing the patient with this type of injury.

Pathomechanics and Functional Limitations

Pathologic LHBT changes may result from anatomic constraints, force overload, and aging. The pathomechanics of LHBT instability begin with a lesion or degenerative or inflammatory condition of any component of the tendon's pulley system. Any loss of the pulley's integrity puts extra stress on the remaining supportive tissue. Over time, these pathomechanics become cyclic and result in progressive instability, inflammation, and degeneration of the LHBT and the pulley system. This is particularly true of conditions affecting the supraspinatus and subscapularis, which are commonly associated with biceps tendinopathy.

The bony geometry of the intertubercular groove may promote pathologic tendon changes. For example, a narrow, sharp-walled canal is more apt to cause traumatic or degenerative changes. A shallow groove or oblique wall may precipitate tendon subluxation. A large supratubercular ridge increases tendon susceptibility to mechanical irritation and subluxation. Congenital variations are particularly significant in younger patients. In older patients, long-standing pathologic biceps tendon changes may result in local soft-tissue changes and, eventually, osseous changes that further compromise tendon integrity.

■ Medications

Bicipital tenosynovitis may be treated conservatively with two or three 1-mL hydrocortisone injections directly into the tendon sheath (but not into the tendon itself), followed by 2 to 3 weeks of rest to protect the tendon from further injury. Because corticosteroids may weaken the tendon and have deleterious long-term effects, this treatment should be limited to two or three injections. NSAIDs may be used to control pain and acute inflammation and should be constrained to a 3- to 7-day course during the inflammation phase of rehabilitation.

■ Postinjury Management

Initial treatment of LHBT tendinopathy is conservative, focusing on associated rotator cuff disorders. Activities that exacerbate symptoms should be discontinued and motion restricted to a pain-free range. Cryotherapy, analgesics, anti-inflammatory agents, and occasionally immobilization complement the rest program. Cardiovascular fitness, core and scapulothoracic control, coordination, and strength should be maintained. When the acute symptoms resolve, early supervised therapeutic exercises are performed to address secondary factors leading to irritation of the LHBT and to maintain ROM to the patient's tolerance level. Rotational motion should be emphasized over abduction. Subacromial corticosteroid injections may provide relief while the secondary causes are addressed. Because the intra-articular and subacromial spaces communicate, there may be little need to inject the biceps tendon area.

The *Shoulder Mobility Progression* may begin as needed when symptoms allow. This regimen should advance into the *Foundational Shoulder Exercises* quickly if the LHBT tendinopathy is the sole symptomatic condition. Absence of concomitant shoulder pathology is rare, however. Young patients with LHBT instability often require surgery to address rotator cuff lesions and secure the tendon.

■ Surgical Intervention

Conservative treatment for 4 to 6 months should be attempted before surgical repair is considered. Before surgery, the patient should be informed that function may not be restored to a point such that the individual can return to a high level of activity. Symptoms can recur when the patient resumes rigorous throwing. Thus serious consideration should be given to ceasing activity before contemplating surgery.

Biceps tenotomy and tenodesis are among the surgical options for LHBT pathology, with both open and arthroscopic techniques being used. Various techniques have been promoted for this indication, including suturing the tendon to the lesser tuberosity, suturing the tendon to the coracoid process, anchoring the tendon in the humeral head, the keyhole block method, keyhole tenodesis, anchoring the tendon to the groove using a staple, anchoring the tendon to the deltoid muscle insertion, and anchoring the tendon to the pectoralis major muscle (see **Figure 9.19**).[132,133]

Long-standing bicipital tendinopathy may be the result of other subacromial or rotator cuff conditions that must be addressed for the patient to obtain symptomatic relief. For example, the loss of the LHBT's GH stabilizing function can produce GH instability, allowing the humeral head to translate superiorly or anteriorly. The recent treatment of bicipital tendinopathy has focused on the association of this condition with other conditions involving the rotator cuff, acromial process, coracoacromial ligament, and AC joint. Arthroscopy is useful for evaluating the intra-articular course of the biceps tendon. Mild changes in the biceps tendon can be managed by tendon debridement, acromioplasty, or coracoacromial ligament release, with biceps tenodesis being reserved for severe changes in a frayed tendon and imminent rupture. Other sources recommend open acromioplasty anteriorly and inferiorly, coracoacromial ligament resection, and possibly coracoid osteotomy. On rare occasions, biceps tendon exploration is indicated for severe inflammation. Several longitudinal incisions may be placed in the biceps tendon at the site of symptoms, in hopes that they will stimulate a healing response. Tenolysis is thought to be helpful. When the specific surgical treatment is chosen, great care should be taken to maintain tendon stability within the groove.

tenolysis A surgical procedure performed to remove adhesions from a tendon.

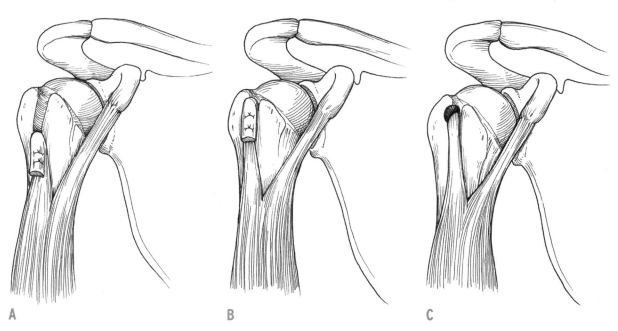

A   B   C

Figure 9.19 Techniques for securing the biceps tendon within its groove. (**A**) In the two-pronged staple technique, the tendon is pulled proximally to the appropriate tension and then secured with a staple. The proximal free edge of the tendon is pulled distally over the staple (not shown) and sewn to itself. (**B**) In the tunnel technique, a burr is used to create a tunnel approximately 2 centimeters in length. The tendon is delivered into the distal hole and pulled out the proximal hole to the appropriate tension. The free edge of the tendon is then sewn back onto itself to secure it. (**C**) In the keyhole technique, the free edge of the tendon is knotted and sutured. A burr is used to create a keyhole, wider proximally to accommodate the knotted tendon and narrowing distally. The knotted tendon is inserted into the keyhole under slight tension, locking it into place. *Source:* Adapted from Hawkins RJ, Bell RH, Lippitt SB (eds), *Atlas of Shoulder Surgery*. St. Louis, MO: Mosby; 1996:145.

Postoperative Management

The postoperative management depends on the injury encountered and the degree of surgical intervention necessary. If rotator cuff damage was addressed or a subacromial decompression was performed, the protocol for this procedure takes precedence. Simple tenodesis can be mobilized with early ROM and gradual addition of progressive resistance exercises in 4 to 6 weeks.

Injury-Specific Treatment and Rehabilitation Concerns

Specific Concerns

Discontinue pain-causing activities early in the program. Emphasize rotational motions.
Post-tenodesis patients:
- Avoid isolated isotonic exercises for the biceps for 4 to 6 weeks per the surgeon's recommendation.
- Avoid heavy lifting and use of the involved arm in rising from a seated position.

Conservative treatment includes avoidance of activities that exacerbate symptoms; motion is restricted to pain-free ranges. While resting from throwing, the athlete can continue exercises that maintain cardiovascular fitness, muscle tone, coordination, and strength. Cryotherapy, analgesics, and anti-inflammatory modalities complement the rest program.

As acute symptoms resolve, exercises in the *Shoulder Mobility Progression* should be performed as needed to maintain or restore ROM; rotational motion is emphasized over abduction. Core and scapular stability and endurance should be evaluated and addressed. When ROM and symptoms permit, the *Shoulder Stability Progression* is initiated and advanced to include plyometrics, functional positions, and the *Foundational Shoulder Exercises*. The coaching staff should identify and correct errors in technique before the patient resumes unrestricted play. An interval throwing or sport-specific conditioning program is used when appropriate.

Early rehabilitation following tenodesis should focus on regaining ROM using the *Shoulder Mobility Progression*. Motion should be limited to less than 90° of GH abduction for the first week and then progressed as symptoms permit. The *Shoulder Stability Progression* may begin during week 1 as soon as symptoms allow; isometric stability exercises that do not isolate or stress the biceps may be ini-

tiated and advanced as tolerated. Humeral extension exercises should not go past the neutral position for 3 weeks. Isolated isometric biceps exercises should begin with light manual resistance during the initial 2 weeks; they may then progress to the tubing isometric stability exercises in GH extension and IR and ER with the elbow at 90° of flexion. Isotonic GH exercises may begin during week 2 or 3, albeit with no resistance. Normal kinematics should be restored using joint mobilizations as needed. Normal ROM should be restored by week 2 or 3. Resistance may be added when the patient demonstrates normal kinematics.

Progression should lead into the *Foundational Shoulder Exercises* by week 5 or 6. Isolated biceps exercises may begin according to the surgeon's recommendation, typically in weeks 8 to 10; isolated isotonics for the biceps are begun 2 to 3 weeks later. Exercises progress with the goal of including plyometrics and sport-specific drills by week 10 or 11. A sport-specific interval training or throwing program is required to return the athlete to competition and may be initiated as early as week 11.

The best way to address bicipital tendinopathy is to prevent its occurrence. Daily stretching and emphasis on strengthening and endurance in the preseason and a maintenance program during the regular season are beneficial, as is a careful warm-up before rehabilitation or participation. Throwing should begin with easy tossing and progress slowly to competitive speed. Older pitchers may incur bicipital injuries more often; thus they require a longer warm-up period than younger pitchers. For any pitcher, the number of innings pitched should be limited, and ice should be applied to the shoulder after pitching.

Estimated Amount of Time Lost

Time lost with conservative treatment ranges from 2 to 4 weeks, depending on the resolution of acute symptoms and full return to normal functional sport-specific activities without pain or weakness. Patients undergoing tenodesis may return in 14 to 22 weeks.

Return-to-Play Criteria

The patient should achieve normal, asymptomatic GH and scapulothoracic ROM, kinematics, strength, stability, and neuromuscular control. Also, successful completion of appropriate functional testing should demonstrate normal performance of sport-specific tasks.

Superior Labrum Anterior and Posterior (SLAP) Lesions

CLINICAL PRESENTATION

History

Insidious onset of pain occurs during or after throwing or after a fall on an outstretched arm, sudden distraction force, or dislocation.

Deep posterior-superior or anterior-superior shoulder pain occurs during overhead motions.

Nonspecific posterior shoulder pain and accompanying "popping" or "click" sensations may be described while throwing or during similar overhead motions.

Observation

Poor scapular function.

Possible hesitancy and wincing during overhead activities.

Functional Status

Patients may have pain and weakness with overhead motions.

Overhead athletes may report a loss of velocity or accuracy.

Physical Examination Findings

Throwers may present with GH IR deficit and scapular dyskinesis. The following special tests may help rule a SLAP lesion in or out:

- Biceps load II[135,136]
- Crank[137,138]
- Biceps load I[139]

The following special tests may help rule in a SLAP lesion:

- Yergason's test[128,136]
- Dynamic labral shear test[140]

Functional instability may be described, although anatomic instability may not be identified.

Lesions to the superior glenoid labrum were first described in 1990 as superior labrum anterior and posterior (SLAP) tears and were classified using a four-type system.[141] The original I–IV classification system remains the most widely used. This system was later expanded with descriptions of SLAP types V–VII,[142] and more recently with types VIII–X (see Figure 9.20).[143]

Mechanisms for SLAP lesions may be either traumatic or chronic. Traumatic SLAP tears may result from a fall on an outstretched arm, a sudden distraction force on the humerus, or GH dislocation. Insidious-onset SLAP tears typically affect overhead athletes. Reports suggest that 88% of confirmed SLAP lesions have coexistent shoulder pathology.[144]

Multiple theories have been proposed regarding the function of the superior labrum and biceps and the associated pathomechanics of these lesions (see "Pathomechanics and Functional Limitations"). The pathomechanics are probably multifactorial and vary between population and type of SLAP lesion. Nevertheless, each theory of pathomechanics suggests the SLAP lesion and the anterior-inferior capsular

laxity observed in overhead athletes are associated. Posterior capsular tightness also plays a critical role in the development of SLAP lesions. A growing body of basic science and outcomes research suggests that these three factors play important roles in the pathomechanics and treatment of SLAP lesions in overhead athletes (see Figure 9.20).

Type I lesions are characterized by fraying of the superior aspect of the labrum along the inner margin. The labral attachment to the glenoid remains solid and the LHBT is not involved. This lesion is typical of the normal degeneration with age and is rarely symptomatic.

Type II lesions involve detachment of the LHBT complex from the superior glenoid tubercle. These tears account for approximately half of all clinically relevant SLAP lesions and have been further discriminated based on the location of the detachment as anterior, posterior, and anterior and posterior. The anterior location is the most common of these lesions. Type II lesions in patients older than 40 years are associated with a supraspinatus tear, while those in patients younger than 40 years are associated with a Bankart lesion and participation in overhead sports.[144]

Type III lesions are bucket-handle tears of the superior labrum that, depending on size, may displace into the joint and create mechanical symptoms. The attachment of the LHBT to the glenoid is not involved. Type IV lesions display the bucket-handle tears of the superior labrum characteristic of type III lesions; however, in this case, the tear extends to split the LHBT.

The reliability of classifying SLAP lesions intraoperatively based on this four-type system has been investigated. Evidence suggests there is significant interrater variability among experienced surgeons in both the classification and choice of treatment.[145]

Types V–VII SLAP lesions are typically the result of trauma. The majority of SLAP lesions of these types are associated with GH instability and a traction mechanism.[142] Type V lesions are anterior-inferior Bankart lesions that extend superiorly into the attachment of the LHBT. Type VI lesions involve a type II tear along with an unstable anterior or posterior labral flap. Type VII lesions include a tear of the middle GH ligament that extends into the attachment of the LHBT.

Type VIII lesions involve a type II tear that extends into the posterior labrum to the 6 o'clock position. Type IX lesions involve a type II tear that extends into the labrum circumferentially. Type X lesions involve a type II tear that extends into the posterior-inferior labrum.

9

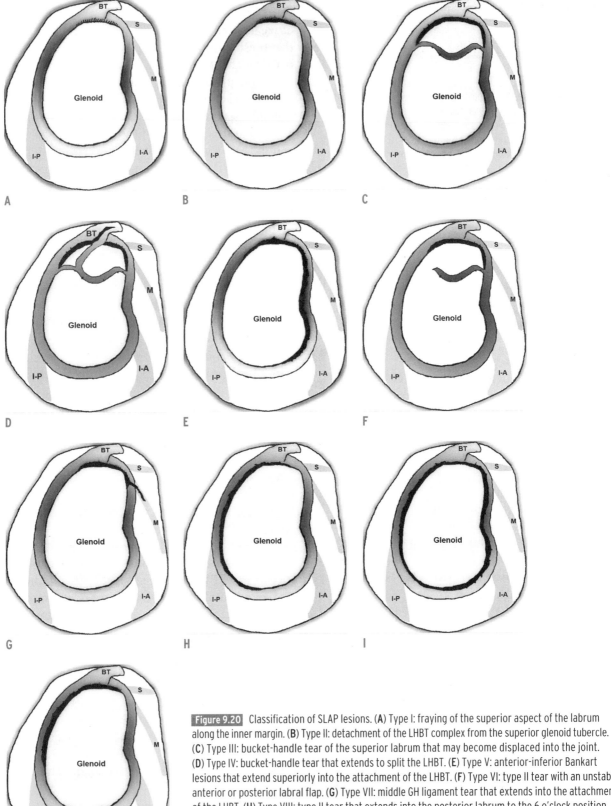

Figure 9.20 Classification of SLAP lesions. (**A**) Type I: fraying of the superior aspect of the labrum along the inner margin. (**B**) Type II: detachment of the LHBT complex from the superior glenoid tubercle. (**C**) Type III: bucket-handle tear of the superior labrum that may become displaced into the joint. (**D**) Type IV: bucket-handle tear that extends to split the LHBT. (**E**) Type V: anterior-inferior Bankart lesions that extend superiorly into the attachment of the LHBT. (**F**) Type VI: type II tear with an unstable anterior or posterior labral flap. (**G**) Type VII: middle GH ligament tear that extends into the attachment of the LHBT. (**H**) Type VIII: type II tear that extends into the posterior labrum to the 6 o'clock position. (**I**) Type IX: type II tear that extends into the labrum circumferentially. (**J**) Type X: type II tear that extends into the posterior-inferior labrum. BT, biceps tendon; S, superior GH ligament; M, middle GH ligament; I-A, anterior band of the inferior GH ligament; I-P, posterior band of the inferior GH ligament. *Source:* Courtesy of Brady Tripp

Differential Diagnosis

LHBT tendinopathy, GH instability, internal impingement, rotator cuff tear, AC joint sprain, AC arthrosis.

Imaging Techniques

Both MRA with a contrast medium such as gadolinium injected into the joint and MRI are more effective than other imaging techniques used to identify labral lesions. MRA is slightly more effective for ruling labral lesions in or out in younger patients.[95] Anterior capsulolabral lesions may be more effectively ruled in or out through MRA performed with the patient's shoulder in abduction and ER.[146] This technique is routinely used in examination of the young overhead thrower, for example. When the labrum is evaluated in all three imaging planes, the presence of a sublabral ganglion cyst is indicative of a SLAP lesion.[147] On coronal images, a type II SLAP tear is identified by high signal intensity and extension of the contrast under the superior labrum (see **Figure 9.21**).[148] The normal anatomic variation in the anterior-superior labrum should be considered during interpretation. This normal variation, along with the radiologist's level of experience, has a significant impact on the value of these diagnostic techniques.[149] Imaging of the shoulder is not diagnostic; instead, the results should be interpreted in association with the clinical presentation.

Definitive Diagnosis

Diagnosis is made through positive MRA or MRI studies and visualization of the lesion during arthroscopy.

Pathomechanics and Functional Limitations

The patient with a SLAP lesion experiences pain, weakness, and reduced function with overhead activities, and/or pain following activity. The athlete may also have difficulty with tasks requiring shoulder

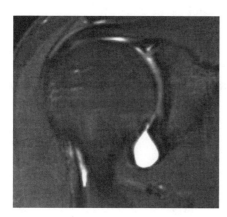

Figure 9.21   An MRA reveals high signal intensity of the contrast dye under the superior labrum, indicative of a type II lesion.

IR and horizontal abduction that stress the biceps–labral complex. Overhead athletes may complain of poor performance and a loss of velocity and control; swimmers may complain of diminished swimming speed. Throwers may also describe pain during the late cocking, acceleration, or ball release phases of throwing.

The roles of the superior labrum, the LHBT, and the subsequent mechanism for SLAP lesions are not well understood. The LHBT has been proposed to act as a static stabilizer of the humeral head, a dynamic depressor, or a dynamic stabilizer of the humerus, although some sources suggest that it is a **vestigial** structure. The most widely accepted mechanisms for development of SLAP lesions in young overhead athletes are classified as being the result of the tension, torsion, or compression forces associated with adaptive changes observed in the GH joint. These changes in experienced throwers include gains in ER, loss of IR, increases in anterior capsular laxity, and contracture of the posterior capsule. Understanding the mechanism proposed in each theory lends insight into both the diagnosis and the treatment of SLAP lesions.

An early theory suggested that the pathomechanics of SLAP lesions are related to the biceps' role as a dynamic humeral head depressor during the follow-through phase of throwing. This proposition arose from electromyography (EMG) studies of biceps activity during this phase.[150] While its function at the GH joint has since been questioned, the biceps' main role during the follow-through phase is to decelerate the elbow.[151] Regardless of the joint at which the biceps is acting, chronic labral tears may result from the repetitive tensile stress placed on the tendon. Although this theory suggests that repetition and throwing mechanics are the root of SLAP lesions, it is not supported in the literature. In a study that attempted to create SLAP lesions through this direct tensile mechanism, researchers had to subluxate the joint inferiorly to produce such a lesion.[152] This finding suggests that sudden inferior traction on the arm may cause type III or IV SLAP lesions but not the type II lesions commonly found in throwers.

More recently, multiple theories have suggested that the pathomechanics of SLAP lesions result from the biceps' role as a humeral head stabilizer. The biceps is believed to act as a dynamic stabilizer during the abduction and extreme ER in the late cocking phase of throwing. Over time, repetitive throwing increases the magnitude of this ER, leading to inferior GH ligament laxity and occult instability as the thrower's arm reaches this position. This mechanism increases the amount of stress placed

vestigial A structure that was once useful, but no longer serves the intended purpose.

on the rotator cuff and biceps tendon as they contract to stabilize the humeral head. Both SLAP and rotator cuff lesions are proposed to result from the repeated tensile force produced by this contraction.[153] The opposite course of pathomechanics has also been proposed—that is, the SLAP tear is hypothesized to be the initial lesion, which then progresses to capsular laxity.[100]

A similar theory suggests that the biceps functions as a static humeral head stabilizer during abduction and ER. In this case, contracture of the posterior GH capsule or subtle anterior GH laxity developed in throwers produces a SLAP lesion as a result of a torsional stress. The posterior contracture or anterior laxity results in the humeral head riding superiorly and posteriorly on the glenoid during the late cocking phase of throwing, instead of assuming its normal posterior-inferior position.[154] Two proposed mechanisms implicate this superior-posterior position of the humeral head as a factor. One theory suggests that this position, when coupled with the normal twisting of the LHBT in abduction and ER, creates torsion that may "peel back" the tendon from the posterior-superior glenoid over time.[155] Other theories suggest that the labrum becomes compressed upon the articular-side of the rotator cuff in this position.[100] Over time, this repetitive compression frays both the rotator cuff and the labrum (see the "Internal Impingement" section earlier in this chapter).

Some research supports the contention that the biceps tendon provides some GH stability. Using cadavers, researchers have found that increasing tension on the biceps tendon in the abducted and externally rotated position enhances GH stability and that simulated SLAP tears increase stress on the inferior GH ligament.[156] Surgeons also report that during arthroscopic repair of the SLAP lesion, anterior-inferior joint laxity is immediately abated.[155]

Physicians address the symptoms of SLAP lesions in athletes by repairing either the anterior capsule or the SLAP lesion. Repairing only the SLAP lesion in athletes with subtle instability does not yield desirable outcomes, however. Notably, residual GH instability is a major reason for failure after surgical repair of SLAP lesions.[157] Likewise, repairing capsular laxity alone does not lead to desirable outcomes in athletes. Initially, some sources recommended treating overhead athletes with these types of tears using an open capsulolabral reconstruction or thermal capsulorrhaphy. The results were disappointing: Fewer than half of the throwers undergoing these procedures returned to play for one or more seasons.[87]

Reflecting on the poor outcomes after surgically addressing either the capsular laxity or the SLAP lesion, physicians have come to recognize the valuable role that each factor may play in pathomechanics. While capsulorrhaphy alone has proved inadequate, thermal capsulorrhaphy along with labral repair yields better functional and long-term outcomes than repairs of the labrum alone.[158,159] Because posterior capsular tightness is commonly found in symptomatic overhead athletes, little evidence exists regarding the outcomes of isolated treatment to address it. Conservative therapy for patients with SLAP lesions and symptoms of internal impingement has been shown to improve functional outcomes in athletes.[69] The patient population of this study, however, was not specific to overhead throwers.

Medications

NSAIDs are used to decrease the initial inflammatory response and should be constrained to a 3- to 7-day course. Acetaminophen or narcotic analgesics may be used for short-term pain relief after surgery.

Postinjury Management

The initial management of SLAP lesions focuses on decreasing pain and inflammation with cryotherapy, NSAIDs, and brief cessation of aggravating activities. Conservative rehabilitation emphasizes posterior capsule stretching, rotator cuff strengthening, and scapular and core stability following the guidelines for scapular dyskinesis (see the "Scapular Dyskinesis" section earlier in this chapter).

Surgical Intervention

Although there is no quality evidence describing SLAP repair outcomes, the recommended treatment for surgical management of a SLAP lesion depends on its severity (see **Table 9.4**). The majority of surgeries to address SLAP tears in athletes involve repairs of type II lesions. Reported outcomes after a type II SLAP repair suggest the percentage of good and excellent results ranges from 40% to 94% in all populations.[160] The percentage of athletes returning to their preinjury level of performance after repair ranges from 20% to 94%.[160] Overhead athletes in particular do not fare as well, with only 64% returning to their preinjury level of performance.[160] Among these individuals, baseball players face the greatest challenge in returning after a type II SLAP repair, with 63% of baseball players returning to their preinjury level of performance compared to 76% to 86% of other overhead athletes.[161,162]

Table 9.4	

Surgical Approaches to SLAP Lesions

Type	Surgical Approach
I	Arthroscopic debridement of unstable and frayed tissue: Care is taken to avoid damaging intact labral tissue and the biceps tendon
II	Arthroscopic debridement of unstable tissue: Repair of stable tissue to an abraded superior glenoid bed with absorbable tack or suture anchor fixation (see S T 9.6)
III	Arthroscopic debridement of an unstable bucket-handle portion: Similar to debridement of a bucket-handle meniscus tear of the knee
IV	Debridement of small unstable labral/biceps fragments: Repair of larger (50% thickness) fragments with suture techniques; tenodesis may be considered
V	Arthroscopic fixation of the superior labrum in the same manner as a type II lesion; the anchors are continued to incorporate the Bankart lesion
VI	Arthroscopic debridement of the flap tear and fixation of the superior labrum in the same manner as a type II lesion
VII	Arthroscopic suturing of the middle GH ligament and repair of the superior labrum in the same manner as a type II lesion
VIII	Arthroscopic repair of the superior labrum in the same manner as a type II lesion; the fixation extends into the posterior labrum
IX	Repair with a capsular shift and anchors in the superior, anterior, and posterior labrum
X	Arthroscopic repair in the same manner as a type VIII lesion

In young athletic populations, the mechanism of injury and any coexistent conditions may affect outcomes after arthroscopic repair of type II SLAP lesions. One study reported 74% of athletes were able to return to their preinjury level of competition, whereas 92% of athletes reporting a discrete traumatic event were able to return to their previous level of competition.[161] Interestingly, repair of a coexistent rotator cuff tear along with repair of a type II SLAP lesion does not diminish the short-term outcome (2.5 years after surgery).[163]

Postoperative Management

Rehabilitation guidelines for surgical patients vary depending on the extent of injury, the tissue repaired, and the fixation method. Those individuals undergoing arthroscopic repair of type II SLAP lesions will be immobilized in a sling at all times while outside of the rehabilitation facility for 3 to 4 weeks. Because the biceps anchor has been repaired, the biceps should not be isolated for strengthening for the first 6 to 8 weeks. Elbow, wrist, and hand exercises are permitted during this time, avoiding stress on the LHBT.

Patients undergoing a posterior-inferior capsulotomy begin the sleeper and cross-body stretches on day 1. During week 1, the sling may be removed for passive elbow flexion and extension, GH elevation to 60°, and rotation in 0° of abduction. The initial three exercises in the *Shoulder Stability Progression* that require minimal rotator cuff activity are then incorporated. Full progression guidelines for those patients undergoing repair of type II SLAP lesions are presented in "Injury-Specific Treatment and Rehabilitation Concerns."

Patients with arthroscopic repairs of type I or type III SLAP lesions typically progress more quickly than those with type II tears. These patients should have a stable biceps anchor and need limited debridement; they should not be immobilized. Rehabilitation may progress more rapidly, although individuals returning to elite levels of throwing may still miss up to one year of competition.[155] The restoration of ROM and function is more aggressive in these patients, with the *Shoulder Stability Progression* and *Shoulder Mobility Progression* beginning when patient comfort permits. Full ROM is often achieved within 10 to 14 days postoperatively. Isotonic IR and ER exercises may be initiated as early as day 10. Patients should progress to the *Foundational Shoulder Exercises* by week 6 or 7 and should begin a sport-specific interval training or throwing program no earlier than week 8.

Injury-Specific Treatment and Rehabilitation Concerns

Specific Concerns

Respect differences in healing rates for repairs of different types of SLAP lesions and using different kinds of fixation methods.

After surgery to repair type II tears, avoid producing undue tension within the biceps muscle or the LHBT.

Avoid early active GH ER after surgery to repair type II tears.

During week 1, the sling is removed to allow passive elbow flexion and extension, GH elevation to 60°, and ER in 0° of abduction. Glenohumeral rotation

9

S T Surgical Technique 9.6

Type II SLAP Lesion Surgery

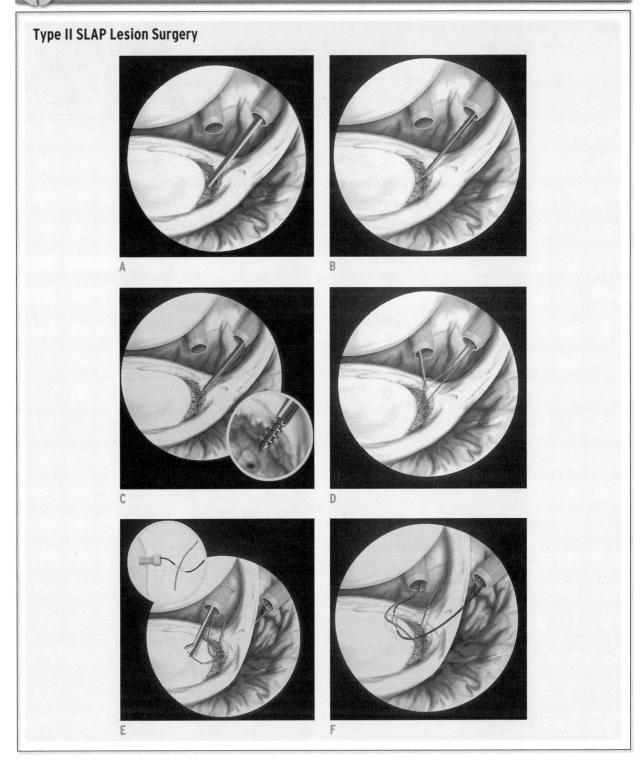

S|T   Surgical Technique   9.6 (Continued)

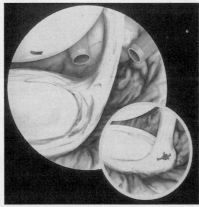

G   H

Indications

Patients with SLAP lesions who have failed to improve on a compressive rehabilitation program.

Procedure Overview

1. The patient is in the lateral decubitus position, and distal traction is applied to the arm.
2. An arthroscopic portal is made posteriorly and two portals are made anteriorly.
3. Diagnostic arthroscopy is performed to confirm the type of SLAP lesion.
4. A burr is used to decorticate exposed bone beneath the superior labrum and the biceps attachment (**A**).
5. A suture anchor is placed directly below the normal biceps tendon insertion (**B** and **C**).
6. The suture is threaded through the labrum and biceps tendon, reduced into anatomic position, and arthroscopically tied by various transport systems (**D, E, F, G,** and **H**).
7. Type IV SLAP lesions may be addressed in the same manner as type II tears, albeit with an additional biceps tenodesis performed for a torn LHBT.

Functional Limitations

Shoulder ROM is limited for 3 to 4 weeks to permit tissue healing if a repair is performed; otherwise, the rehabilitation program is progressive. External rotation beyond neutral and extension of the arm behind the body are avoided for 4 weeks.

Implications for Rehabilitation

Rehabilitation after SLAP debridement can proceed quickly. SLAP repair requires several weeks for tissue healing, followed by progressive ROM and strength exercises. Aggressive biceps muscle contractions should be avoided for 3 months.

Comments

SLAP lesions may be associated with significant damage to the LHBT. If biceps tenodesis is performed, recovery and rehabilitation may be prolonged.

---

is limited to 10° ER and 45° IR for the first week. These ROM exercises are progressed to include gentle active-assisted GH motion during week 2, with motions being limited to 75° elevation, 15° ER, and 45° IR. Submaximal isometrics begin at 0° of abduction during week 2 for GH IR and abduction.

Patients undergoing a posterior-inferior capsulotomy initiate the sleeper and cross-body stretches on day 1 and continue throughout rehabilitation and return to play. During weeks 1 and 2, exercises that require minimal rotator cuff activity such as the scapular clock, shoulder dump, and sternal lift exercises in the *Shoulder Stability Progression* are

used to establish conscious control of the scapula. The isometric stability exercises of this progression may begin by incorporating weight shifts and isometric low rows. No active GH ER, extension, or isolated biceps exercises are permitted at this time.

The use of the sling should be discontinued when appropriate, as early as week 4. Weeks 3 and 4 should include active-assisted GH motion exercises to 90° elevation, 35° ER, and 45° IR. Glenohumeral rotation may begin to incorporate motion in the scapular plane and up to 30° of abduction at this time. The minimal cuff activity and active-assisted portions of the *Shoulder Mobility Progression* may begin with table bows and pendulum exercises. As patient comfort permits, begin the rotator cuff co-contraction and rhythmic stabilization portions of the *Shoulder Stability Progression*. Tubing isometric stability exercises may begin during week 4. These exercises are limited to pain-free positions within the previously mentioned ranges. All exercises should avoid active GH ER, extension, and isolated biceps activity.

During week 5, the active-assisted and T-bar–assisted GH ROM exercises progress to 145° elevation, 45° ER, and 60° IR at 45–50° of abduction. Passive and gentle active-assisted rotational ROM may begin in 90° of abduction. At this time, the *Shoulder Mobility Progression* may advance to include active GH abduction beginning with table washes and then progressing to all exercises in this sequence. The supine press may be used to gain GH elevation as needed. The stretches described in the *Foundational Shoulder Exercises* should be initiated by week 5 and continued throughout the rehabilitation and the patient's return to normal activity. Tubing exercises at this time may include GH IR and ER with minimal abduction (with a bolster placed under the arm). The *Shoulder Stability Progression* should continue to establish isometric stability in all pain-free arm positions (within the previously mentioned ranges) through rhythmic stabilization and tubing isometric stability exercises. When the patient achieves GH active elevation to 120° with scapular control (no shrug), the dynamic stability portion of the *Shoulder Stability Progression* may begin. Manual PNF strengthening also may be initiated during week 5. Isolated biceps strengthening is still avoided at this time, however.

During week 7, GH motion is progressed to 180° elevation, 90° of ER, and 75° of IR with the arm abducted to 90°. Isotonic GH IR and ER strengthening and scapular clock exercises progress to 90° of abduction as patient comfort permits. All exercises in the dynamic stability portion of the *Shoulder Stability Progression* are advanced, including tubing retraction and the push-up and lawnmower progressions. Strengthening exercises should include each of the *Foundational Shoulder Exercises*, beginning with the tubing exercises. Biceps strengthening may begin during weeks 8 to 9.

Full pain-free ROM should be achieved by week 10 or 11. Overhead athletes should extend mobility, stability, and strengthening exercises to functional overhead positions by week 12. Exercises should be progressed to include plyometrics and each of the *Foundational Shoulder Exercises* (including

the thrower's portion) by week 15 or 16. A sport-specific interval strengthening or throwing program may begin when appropriate, typically 16 to 20 weeks after surgery. Strength should be 80% compared bilaterally by week 20 and progress to 100% by week 24. By 24 to 28 weeks, pitchers may begin throwing with full velocity on a level surface; at 28 to 30 weeks, they may begin throwing from the mound.

■ Estimated Amount of Time Lost

Patients treated nonsurgically with rehabilitation may be limited for 2 weeks or up to 4 to 6 months. After surgery, 4 to 12 months of rehabilitation may be required before the patient returns to sport-specific activities. Final return to the previous level of sport activity ultimately depends on many factors, including the sport itself and the level of competition, the patient's adherence to the sport-specific interval training program, the patient's age, and the quality of tissue. Following an interval throwing program, a baseball pitcher may begin throwing at full velocity on a level surface at 6 months and from a mound at 7 months. Return to unrestricted overhead sports is permitted as early as 8 to 9 months postoperatively. Elite overhead athletes may require a longer rehabilitation timeframe before returning to their preinjury level of play compared with other patients.[164]

■ Return-to-Play Criteria

The patient should achieve normal, asymptomatic GH and scapulothoracic ROM, kinematics, strength, stability, and neuromuscular control. The athlete should also successfully complete appropriate functional testing demonstrating normal performance of sport-specific tasks before returning to competition.

Acute Traumatic Glenohumeral Dislocation

An acute traumatic GH dislocation involves the complete dissociation of the joint's articular surfaces, usually associated with considerable soft-tissue injury. The majority of GH dislocations in athletes occur anteriorly, with the most common mechanism being an indirect force caused by excessive humeral abduction and ER. In rare situations, a direct force from the posterior or posterior-lateral shoulder causes an anterior dislocation. The humeral head can dislocate in a subcoracoid direction or, less commonly, in a subclavicular or intrathoracic direction. An anteriorly dislocated GH joint is invariably

CLINICAL PRESENTATION

History

Forced humeral abduction and ER.
A blow to the posterior or posterior-lateral shoulder.
If the neurovascular structures are compromised, radicular symptoms are described.

Observation

If the GH joint is still dislocated:
- The humerus is held in a fixed position, usually slightly abducted and externally rotated.
- A flattened deltoid may be observed with a sulcus above and posterior to the GH joint with fullness anteriorly.

If the GH joint was spontaneously reduced:
- The patient may self-splint the arm using the uninvolved hand to hold the elbow against the trunk to prevent motion.

Functional Status

The patient may be unable or unwilling to move the GH joint.

Physical Examination Findings

Decreased or absent ER.
Guarded or compensated GH joint motion.
After reduction, positive findings on the following tests help rule in anterior instability:
- Apprehension[165-167]
- Relocation[165,168]
- Anterior release[167,169]

A negative anterior release test helps to rule out anterior instability.[167,169]

Dislocations can result in significant soft-tissue or bony lesions that increase the risk of subsequent dislocations. Notably, a Bankart lesion—an avulsion of the anterior-inferior labrum with concurrent stretching of the anterior-inferior capsule—may predispose the patient to recurrent anterior dislocations (see Figure 9.22). Although this type of injury was once thought to be the "essential lesion" to produce anterior dislocations, some recent evidence does not support this theory. Despite the controversy, the incidence of a Bankart lesion in an initial dislocation appears to exceed 85%.[171,172] Bankart lesions are classified based on the integrity of the labrum and glenoid:

- Type I: Intact labrum
- Type II: Simple labral detachment from the glenoid
- Type III: Intrasubstance glenoid labrum tear
- Type IV: Labral detachment with significant fraying or degeneration
- Type V: Complete glenoid labrum degeneration or absence

Occasionally the glenoid periosteum does not become fully detached, resulting in an anterior labroligamentous periosteal sleeve avulsion (ALPSA lesion). Dislocation may also result in a posterior-superior humeral head impaction fracture, known as a Hill-Sachs lesion. Following first-time traumatic dislocations in patients younger than age 24, one report found that 97% (61 out of 63) presented with Bankart lesions and 90% (57/63) displayed Hill-Sachs lesions.[173] Arthroscopy may also reveal defects in the articular cartilage of the posterior-lateral humeral head that are not detectable on radiographs.

positioned in abduction and slight ER. The area just inferior to the acromion takes on a hollow appearance, giving the acromion a more prominent appearance. Incidence of dislocation or subluxation in collegiate athletes is greatest in American football, wrestling, and ice hockey, in that order.[170]

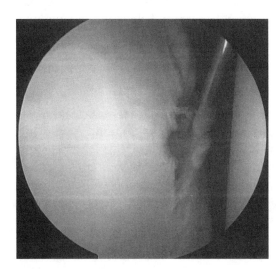
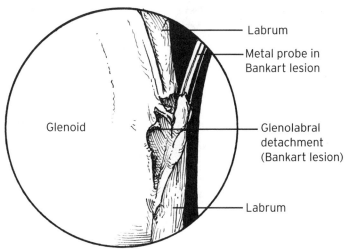

Labrum
Metal probe in Bankart lesion
Glenoid
Glenolabral detachment (Bankart lesion)
Labrum

Figure 9.22 An arthroscopic view from the posterior portion of the glenohumeral joint shows a classic Bankart lesion with detachment of the labrum from the underlying glenoid. *Source:* (**B**) Reproduced with permission from Lintner SA, Speer KP: Traumatic anterior glenohumeral instability: the role of arthroscopy. *J Am Acad Orthop Surg.* 1997;5:233–239.

Differential Diagnosis

Proximal humeral fracture.

Imaging Techniques

Radiographic series for GH instability include AP views with and without GH rotation, and West Point, axillary, and scapular Y views. The presence and direction of a GH dislocation can be identified radiographically using the AP and West Point axillary views (see **Figure 9.23**). Hill-Sachs lesions can be identified via the AP, West Point, or Stryker notch axillary views or via CT scan.[174] Bony Bankart lesions can be identified using a West Point view or CT scan.[174] In younger athletic populations, capsulolabral lesions may be evaluated using CT scan, MRI, or MRA. Both MRI and MRA are recognized as being more effective than CT scan in identifying these lesions, while also offering the ability to detect associated rotator cuff trauma.[95,146]

Definitive Diagnosis

Diagnosis of GH dislocation is based on a thorough radiographic evaluation supported by clinical examination findings. Additional confounding factors may warrant arthroscopic evaluation and establish a more definitive diagnosis of a Hill-Sachs lesion.

Pathomechanics and Functional Limitations

Several factors influence the rate of recurrent shoulder instability after an anterior dislocation. In particular, the recurrence rate is greater in patients who suffer traumatic dislocations from a high-energy mechanism than in patients whose injury is caused by other mechanisms.[175] Age at the time of initial dislocation also influences recurrence: Younger individuals suffering dislocations display greater recurrence rates, with 50% to 64% of those younger than the age of 30 reporting subsequent episodes.[176] Likewise, athletes may have a higher recurrence rate than nonathletes. Methods of postinjury immobilization and choice of treatment (conservative versus surgery) affect recurrence rates as well.

Dislocation can result in Hill-Sachs posterior-lateral humeral fractures or anterior-inferior glenoid rim fractures, potentially releasing chondral debris (loose bodies) within the joint that can abrade the articular surface and accelerate the development of arthritis. Glenoid rim or posterior humeral head fragmentation may release small particles of bone or chondral surface that the synovial lining attempts to absorb. In the process of absorption, lysosomal enzymes are released, which secondarily affect the joint surface, may cause progressive cartilage thinning, and have the potential to trigger chondrolysis.

■ Immediate Management

Dislocations predispose the axillary and musculocutaneous nerves to trauma. A thorough physical examination including sensory, vascular, and motor testing will indicate whether early surgical intervention is warranted. Once the patient's status is determined, the shoulder is placed in a sling for support and partial immobilization. Ice or medications may be prescribed to manage the initial pain, swelling, and muscle guarding. The patient is then transported for radiographic evaluation and possible reduction. Recurrent dislocations often reduce spontaneously, or the patient may have learned particular maneuvers to reduce the dislocation.

■ Medications

Analgesics, anesthetics, or sedatives have been used to assist in reducing GH dislocations. Administration of intra-articular lidocaine is cost-effective, results in fewer complications, and facilitates recovery compared to intravenous sedation, without affecting reduction success rates.[176–178] Narcotic analgesics are prescribed for acute pain management after traumatic dislocations. NSAIDs may be used to decrease the initial inflammatory response but should be constrained to a 3- to 7-day course. Acetaminophen or narcotic analgesics may be used for short-term pain relief after surgery.

chondrolysis
Destruction or atrophy of articular cartilage.

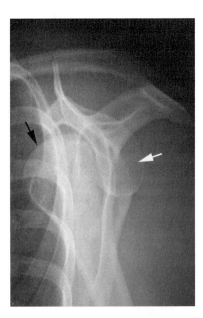

Figure 9.23 Radiographic series for GH instability and CT arthrography help reveal dislocations and associated lesions. The scapular Y view suggests a GH dislocation with the humeral head (black arrow) medial to the glenoid fossa (white arrow).

■ Postinjury Management

The treatment of acute anterior GH dislocations depends on the injury mechanism and the existence of associated injuries. If a physician is present at the time of dislocation, immediate reduction should be considered. Acutely, the patient usually has no muscle spasm, and reduction is typically easily performed. If reduction is not easily achieved using a gentle maneuver, radiographs should be obtained and the reduction performed in a controlled environment.

Many methods of reducing the dislocated shoulder have been described, but very few high-quality reports have compared these methods. Most techniques involve applying longitudinal traction with the arm in slight abduction followed by IR. The Fast, Reliable, and Safe (FARES) reduction technique is more effective, faster, and less painful compared to other commonly used methods.[179]

- **Fast, Reliable, and Safe (FARES) technique:**[179] The patient is supine, with the affected arm at the side, elbow extended, and forearm in a neutral position. The clinician applies gentle traction to the patient's wrist. The clinician then slowly moves the arm into abduction and oscillates the arm horizontally (approximately 5 centimeters above and beneath the horizontal level) using 2 to 3 cycles per second (see **Figure 9.24A**). Once past 90° of abduction, the clinician adds gentle ER to the continued oscillations (see **Figure 9.24B**); the humeral head typically reduces at approximately 120° of abduction.

- **Hippocratic technique:** Variations of this method call for the affected arm to be placed in slight abduction. The clinician applies traction, while a counter-traction is applied using two sheets:[180] The supine patient is stabilized with a sheet tied around the chest and placed in an assistant's hands (counter-traction); a second sheet is then placed around the physician's waist and the patient's flexed forearm. Traction is then applied to the shoulder via the flexed forearm. The patient's arm is flexed, abducted, and internally and externally rotated; care is taken to avoid injury to the brachial plexus, vascular structures, bone, and soft tissue around the shoulder due to excess traction.

- **Kocher technique:**[181] The patient is seated or supine with the elbow flexed to 90°. The clinician presses the affected arm into the side (0° abduction), then slowly externally rotates the arm until resistance is felt (approximately 75°). The clinician then brings the arm into forward elevation as far as possible and reduces the humeral head with IR.

- **Stimson technique:**[182] The patient is positioned prone, with the arm hanging over the edge of the table and 5 pounds of traction applied to the wrist. After the arm has been in traction approximately 10 minutes and the muscles have relaxed, the clinician reduces the shoulder using a gentle IR movement of the arm with simultaneous humeral head compression.

- **Spaso technique:**[183] The patient is supine. The clinician holds the affected arm in 60–80° of forward elevation and applies

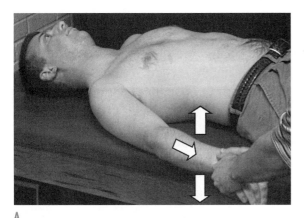
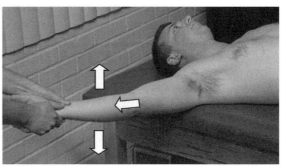

A   B

Figure 9.24 The Fast, Reliable, and Safe (FARES) technique of humeral reduction. **(A)** The clinician provides gentle longitudinal traction and vertical oscillations. **(B)** ER of the arm is slowly added.

gentle traction followed by slight ER; traction is held until the dislocation reduces spontaneously.

There is no consensus regarding the appropriate time frame, position, or value of immobilization after a shoulder dislocation.[184] The shoulder of a young patient who has had a traumatic anterior dislocation is typically immobilized for 3 to 6 weeks. An alternative approach is to immobilize the humerus in 30° of ER for 3 weeks. Recent systematic reviews of the sparse evidence that is available suggest that after a traumatic anterior dislocation, immobilization in ER may reduce the recurrence of dislocation, whereas immobilization in IR does not.[176,177] MRI studies have shown that for those patients with a Bankart lesion, immobilization in ER better approximates the lesion to the glenoid neck than IR.[185] While in some cases compliance may suffer with immobilization in ER, this method may be particularly beneficial for patients younger than age 30.[186]

Surgical Intervention

The discussion regarding treatment options should include the patient's expectations for return to sports and the prognosis considering the extent of tissue damage. Surgical intervention may be required to retrieve the avulsed supraspinatus, infraspinatus, and teres minor from their interposition between the humeral head and the glenoid (see **ST** 9.7). Persistent GH joint subluxation and glenoid rim fracture are additional indications for early surgical intervention. Surgery may also be appropriate for patients who require absolute and complete shoulder stability before returning to their occupation or sport.

Historically, the recurrence rate for young athletes after a first-time anterior dislocation has exceeded 90%.[184] In young overhead athletes, surgical repair may reduce this rate to between 4% and 16%.[184] Reviews of the best available evidence indicate both arthroscopic and open surgery reduce dislocation recurrence rates compared to nonoperative treatment.[176,177] The type of arthroscopic repair of the Bankart lesion also affects recurrence rates.[176] Specifically, patients who undergo arthroscopic repair using transglenoid sutures or staples experience higher recurrence rates compared to patients who are treated with open repair.[176] However, arthroscopic repair using suture anchors yields recurrence rates comparable to those for open repair.[176]

Recurrence rates after arthroscopic Bankart repair are also influenced by the patient's age, sex, and time between first dislocation and surgery.

Higher recurrence rates are reported for males, individuals younger than age 22, and patients waiting longer than 6 months after their initial dislocation to undergo repair.[187] Because current arthroscopic techniques have yielded equivalent outcomes,[188] the decision to perform an arthroscopic procedure as opposed to an open repair depends largely on surgeon experience and patient preference.

The popularity of arthroscopic treatment for shoulder instability has grown in recent years as the techniques and instruments for this procedure have been refined. While arthroscopic repairs are commonly used today, certain pathologies are better treated with open techniques. In particular, patients with bony abnormalities, multiple recurrences, and failed attempts at arthroscopic surgery are typically addressed using open techniques.

Postoperative Management

Progression after arthroscopic Bankart repair is slower in the early phase of rehabilitation compared with rehabilitation after open repairs because of the stabilization method used. The arthroscopic tissue fixation is especially vulnerable during the initial 4 to 6 weeks after the procedure is performed. Consequently, the patient is placed in an immobilizer for the first 2 to 3 weeks and sleeps in the brace for the first 4 weeks. A sling may be used during the day for weeks 2 to 4.

Active-assisted and passive ROM start during the first 2 weeks after surgery. In week 1, ROM is restricted to 70° elevation, and ER and IR to 10° and 45°, respectively, with the arm in 30° of abduction. Submaximal pain-free isometrics and rhythmic stabilization may begin when patient comfort permits. Elevation may be progressed to 90° during week 2. At 4 weeks postoperatively, ROM is increased to 90° elevation and abduction, and 20° of ER and 60° of IR with the arm abducted at 45°. Light isotonic tubing exercises begin in weeks 5 to 6. More aggressive stretching exercises begin at 7 weeks, with the goal of establishing full ROM by week 10. Rotation at 90° abduction is initiated during week 7.

Return to noncontact sports is possible 4 to 5 months after surgery. Return to contact sports requires 5 to 6 months' recovery, and return to throwing may take 7 to 9 months.

Injury-Specific Treatment and Rehabilitation Concerns

Motions that exacerbate joint instability must be restricted so these tissues can heal. Cryotherapy and gentle active-assisted and passive ROM are ini-

S|T Surgical Technique 9.7

Glenohumeral Dislocation: Open Capsular and Bankart Repair

A   B   C

Indications

Recurrent dislocations or irreducible dislocation.

Procedure Overview

1. The patient is placed supine in the modified beach chair position and anesthetized.
2. Physical examination is performed to confirm the diagnosis.
3. Diagnostic arthroscopy is performed to determine the full extent of the injury.
4. A vertical incision is made just inferior to the coracoid process, extending to the anterior midaxillary crease.
5. Full-thickness skin flaps are developed to expose the deltoid and pectoralis fascia.
6. Two choices exist to manage the subscapularis tendon (**A**):
   - A tendon-splitting technique splits the fibers in the line of the muscle fibers. This technique offers limited access to the lateral and superior capsule but is useful in overhead throwing athletes because it leads to quicker rehabilitation.
   - A tendon-separating technique divides the tendon laterally 1 centimeter medial to its insertion.
7. The anterior capsule is incised with a "T" incision beginning at the superior rotator cuff interval, extending inferiorly to the 6 o'clock position. The capsule is then split horizontally just superior to the inferior GH ligament and extending medially to the labrum.
8. A retractor is used to retract the humeral head.
9. The bony surface of the anterior glenoid rim and glenoid neck is decorticated.
10. Three or four drill holes are made on the glenoid articular surface, just posterior to the articular margin. Another option is to use suture anchors for the repair.
11. Drill holes are developed into the prepared glenoid surface.
12. Nonabsorbable sutures are passed through the drill holes and tied to restore the anatomic position of the capsule and labrum.
13. Suture anchors are used to repair the Bankart lesion (**B**).
14. Closure and repair of the capsule are customized to the patient and injury. Care must be taken to avoid overtensioning the repair (**C**).
15. If ROM testing reveals that the capsule is under too much tension, the sutures in the capsule are removed and the closure is repeated, changing the arm position during closure.

Functional Limitations

Limitations are determined by the tension of the capsule repair.

Implications for Rehabilitation

The shoulder is immobilized for the first 2 to 3 weeks and placed in a sling for 4 weeks.

Source: Figures reproduced with permission from Altcheck DW, Dines DM. Shoulder injuries in the throwing athlete. *J Am Acad Orthop Surg.* 1995;3:159–165.

> **Specific Concerns**
>
> Stress on arthroscopic fixations should be minimized for the first 6 weeks, and full ROM is gradually restored by week 10 or 11.
> Avoid early motion into extreme extension, IR, or ER, and activity at more than 90° of abduction.
> Restore dynamic stability and scapular control.

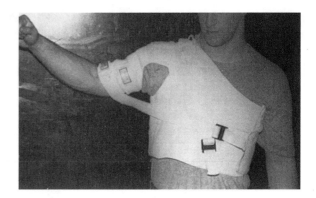

Figure 9.25 An adjustable shoulder brace used to help prevent the glenohumeral joint from reaching provocative positions leading to a dislocation or subluxation.

tiated early to reduce pain and swelling and avoid the deleterious effects of immobilization.

As soon as patient comfort permits, the minimal cuff activity and active-assisted portions of the *Shoulder Mobility Progression* may begin. Shoulder stability is restored using the *Shoulder Stability Progression,* beginning with the minimal cuff activity and isometric portions at this time. These exercises are limited to pain-free positions and 70° of elevation, and ER and IR to 10° and 45°, respectively, for the first 2 weeks. At week 4, these motions are progressed to 90° elevation and abduction, and 20° of ER and 60° of IR with the arm abducted at 45°. The active-cuff portion of the *Shoulder Mobility Progression* may begin at week 5, with the goal of establishing full ROM by week 10. The dynamic stability portion of the *Shoulder Stability Progression* may begin when 120° of active elevation is achieved without a shrug, typically in week 5 or 6.

The stretches described in the *Foundational Shoulder Exercises* should not be initiated until week 7 or 8. Isotonic IR and ER and scapular clock exercises at 90° of abduction begin during week 7, along with the tubing retraction and high-end lawnmower exercises in the dynamic stability portion of the *Shoulder Stability Progression.* Exercises should be progressed to include each of the *Foundational Shoulder Exercises* by week 15. Overhead athletes should progress to include the thrower's component shortly thereafter. A sport-specific interval strengthening or throwing program may begin when appropriate, typically between 16 and 18 weeks after surgery.

▦ Estimated Amount of Time Lost

The injured tissue requires 3 to 6 weeks to heal, with the period for any specific patient depending on the type of injury and its resulting damage. As healing occurs, the tissues need to be mobilized and stretched, the related musculature strengthened, and the involved area put through a functional exercise regimen in preparation for return to activity. This process can take 1 to 3 months, depending on how vigorously the patient maintains the level of physical conditioning in preparation for a return to sport.

▦ Return-to-Play Criteria

The athlete should achieve normal, asymptomatic GH and scapulothoracic ROM, kinematics, strength, stability, and neuromuscular control. In addition, the patient should successfully complete appropriate functional testing demonstrating normal performance of sport-specific tasks and confidence in full use of the extremity. An adjustable shoulder brace may enhance confidence in athletes returning to sports not requiring throwing or catching; however, no evidence suggests use of these devices reduces recurrence rates (see **Figure 9.25**). The recurrence rate for young athletes after a first-time anterior dislocation remains more than 90% for those treated conservatively and between 4% and 16% for those surgically repaired, so each athlete remains at risk of reinjury while playing.[184]

Recurrent Glenohumeral Instability

Glenohumeral instability is classified by frequency (acute or recurrent), mechanism (traumatic or atraumatic), and direction (anterior, posterior, inferior, or multidirectional). Acute traumatic instability occurs when a large-magnitude force tears the GH capsule, ligaments, labrum, or rotator cuff or fractures the humerus or glenoid (see "Acute Traumatic Glenohumeral Dislocation" earlier in this chapter). The compromised structural stability following an initial traumatic event often leads to recurrent instability. Recurrence rates depend on the patient's age, treatment (conservative versus operative), immobilization, and activity level.

Recurrent instability with an atraumatic onset is the result of GH joint laxity. An atraumatic mechanism lacks the force necessary to cause acute

CLINICAL PRESENTATION

History

Patients have a history of traumatic shoulder injury with dislocation or subluxation.

Athletes may describe a "dead arm" or lack of endurance.

Patients with anterior instability:

- Describe pain and apprehension with humeral abduction and ER
- If throwers, describe pain during the arm cocking phase

Patients with posterior instability:

- Describe pain or apprehension with humeral elevation, adduction, and IR such as pushing a door open
- Report a mechanism of a fall on a forward flexed and adducted arm

Patients with inferior instability:

- Describe pain or apprehension when carrying objects[192]
- Describe paresthesia with inferior humeral head translation secondary to traction on the brachial plexus[193]
- If throwers, describe pain during the follow-through phase

Observation

Muscle mass and tone may appear normal or atrophic secondary to nerve involvement.

Dysfunctional motion, position, or stability of the scapula may be noted during humeral motion.

Functional Status

Recurrent pain and weakness may occur related to shoulder motion and function.

Athletes may report loss of throwing velocity, control, or endurance.

Poor function, apprehension, or recurrent instability occurs with activities that place the humerus in abduction and ER (anterior instability) or adduction and IR (posterior instability) or with humeral traction (inferior instability).

Subtle subluxation may occur during the arm cocking (anterior instability) or follow-through phase of throwing (inferior instability).

Physical Examination Findings

Decreased ROM and apprehension are noted during IR and/or ER.

Positive findings on the following tests may help rule in *anterior* instability:

- Apprehension (positive test = apprehension with or without pain)[165-167]
- Relocation (positive test = relief of apprehension)[165,168]
- Surprise/anterior release (positive test = apprehension with or without pain)[167,169]
- Load and shift[194]

A negative surprise/anterior release test may help rule out *anterior* instability.[167,169]

Positive findings on the following tests may help rule in *posterior* instability:

- Posterior apprehension[166,195]
- Jerk[196]

A reproduction of instability symptoms with a sulcus sign may help rule in *multidirectional* instability.[197]

structural damage, yet still results in symptomatic dislocation or subluxation. The etiology for recurrent atraumatic instability includes congenital joint laxity or laxity that has been acquired over time through repetitive GH abduction and ER. Without intervention, the structural damage or joint laxity accompanying either mechanism compromises the patient's ability to stabilize the humeral head in the glenoid, resulting in recurrent dislocations or subluxations.

Anterior Glenohumeral Instability

The anterior band of the inferior GH ligament (AIGHL) is the primary static restraint against anterior humeral head translation when the arm is abducted and externally rotated. The AIGHL also serves as a checkrein for external humeral rotation with the arm abducted and extended. In the late cocking phase of throwing, the humerus is in maximal ER and horizontal abduction, significantly stressing the AIGHL and anterior-inferior joint capsule (see "Overhead Athletes: Adaptations and Pathomechanics" later in this chapter). Repeated microtrauma increases the amount of stress placed on the anterior-inferior joint capsule during the throwing motion, resulting in laxity, excessive humeral translation, and instability or micro-instability. Without intervention, these mechanisms lead to hyperangulation in the late cocking phase, which increases the contact between the articular side of the rotator cuff and the posterior-superior glenoid; this effect has been associated with internal impingement and SLAP lesions (see the "Internal Impingement" section earlier in this chapter). In the anterior drawer or load and shift tests, subtle anterior and even asymmetric laxity may be observed in overhead athletes. Laxity should not cause concern unless it is accompanied by a reproduction of the symptoms of instability.

Posterior Glenohumeral Instability

Posterior instability involves symptomatic dislocation or subluxation that occurs from a direct blow to the anterior shoulder. More typically, however, this type of injury results from an indirect load through the arm with the humerus in elevation, IR, and adduction. Recurrent posterior instability is more common in swimmers, football linemen, and weightlifters who acquire laxity with repetitive microtrauma, have congenital laxity, or have a history of an acute traumatic posterior dislocation. Episodes of posterior instability are rare relative to anterior instability, accounting for 10% of all dislocations in the young athletic population.[189] Posterior laxity may be observed upon examination using the posterior drawer or load-and-shift tests; it should not cause concern unless it is accompanied by a reproduction of the symptoms of instability.

Multidirectional Glenohumeral Instability

Multidirectional instability (MDI) involves symptomatic GH dislocation or subluxation in more than one direction and most frequently occurs in three patterns: (1) anterior-inferior dislocation with posterior subluxation, (2) posterior-inferior dislocation with anterior subluxation, or (3) dislocation in all three directions (anterior, posterior, and inferior). Episodes of multidirectional instability account for less than 10% of all dislocations in the young athletic population.[189]

A number of factors have been implicated in MDI, including congenital or acquired laxity or structural damage due to recurrent trauma. The majority of patients experiencing MDI demonstrate general laxity, including hyperextension at the elbows.[190] When these individuals participate in sports that repeatedly stress the shoulder capsule (such as throwing, gymnastics, or swimming), the capsule may acquire additional laxity. In younger athletes, laxity itself is a frequent finding upon examination using the sulcus sign, anterior and posterior drawer tests, or load-and-shift tests. Laxity should not be a cause for concern unless it is accompanied by a reproduction of the symptoms of instability. Chronic loss of the normal compressive effect of the rotator cuff and capsular support stabilizing effect may contribute to GH instability. This instability is magnified when the glenoid rim is worn, the glenoid lacks normal concavity, the labrum displays one of many anatomic variations, or the normal supportive function of the coracoacromial arch is lost through erosion or surgical removal.

Differential Diagnosis

Impingement syndrome, rotator cuff tear, AC joint arthrosis.

Imaging Techniques

The instability series is helpful in identifying osseous defects in athletes, such as Bankart and Hill-Sachs lesions and tuberosity fractures. Axillary radiographs are critical to rule out a potential posterior dislocation (see **Figure 9.26**).[191] In these cases, if appropriate views are not feasible, a CT scan should be performed. Notably, CT arthrogram and MRI may demonstrate a wide variety of soft-tissue lesions. No specific findings on MRI or MRA are considered diagnostic for atraumatic instability in athletes. Rather, use of each imaging technique may help rule out other significant intra-articular pathology.

Definitive Diagnosis

The diagnosis of recurrent GH instability is based on a positive history of dislocations, the ability of the joint to subluxate or dislocate, radiographic evidence, and physical examination. Clinical diagnosis of MDI is based on a sulcus sign greater than 2 centimeters and instability in more than one direction.

Pathomechanics and Functional Limitations

Anterior instability is expressed with the arm abducted and externally rotated—that is, the position of risk for anterior dislocation. Glenohumeral joints having a history of more than five recurrent dislocations demonstrate anterior articular cartilage erosion; in 20% of patients, subchondral bone is exposed.[198] Posterior capsular contracture, such as that seen with glenohumeral IR deficit (GIRD), may occur to compensate for instability.

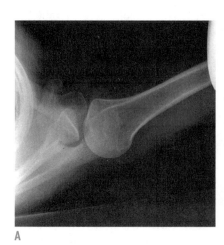
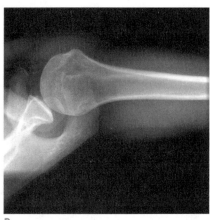

A   B

Figure 9.26 Axillary radiographs help identify dislocations. **(A)** The humeral head is dislocated posteriorly. **(B)** The humeral head is reduced.

Atraumatic instability arises without the trauma necessary to tear the stabilizing soft tissues or to create an osseous lesion. Certain anatomic configurations may predispose the patient to atraumatic instability. For example, a small or functionally flat glenoid fossa may jeopardize the concavity compression, adhesion–cohesion, and glenoid suction cup stability mechanisms. Conversely, an excessively large capsule may allow humeral translation outside the range of balance stability. Weak rotator cuff muscles may provide insufficient compression for the concavity compression stabilizing mechanism. Poor scapulothoracic neuromuscular control may fail to position the scapula in a manner that will balance the net humeral joint reaction force and maintain stability. Once initiated, such instability may be perpetuated by glenoid rim compression resulting from chronically poor humeral head centering. Excessive labral compliance may also predispose patients to this loss of effective glenoid depth.

■ Immediate Management

Immediate management consists of immobilization and ice with transport for radiographic evaluation and possible reduction. There is no consensus regarding the appropriate time frame, position, or value of immobilization following a shoulder dislocation.[184] Anterior dislocations in young patients are immobilized for 3 to 6 weeks. An alternative approach is to immobilize the humerus in 30° of ER for 3 weeks. Posterior dislocations are immobilized for 6 weeks in GH ER with slight extension. In recurrent dislocations, the shoulder often reduces itself spontaneously, or the patient has learned to perform maneuvers that reduce the dislocation. In chronic instability with spontaneous reduction, ice, medications, and limited sling use are commonly employed.

■ Medications

NSAIDs may be used to decrease the initial inflammatory response but should be constrained to a 3- to 7-day course. Acetaminophen or narcotic analgesics may be used for short-term pain relief after surgery.

■ Postinjury Management

The risk of recurrent dislocations is directly related to activity level and inversely related to patient age. Treatment and immobilization for as long as 6 weeks may have little effect on the natural history. Swelling is controlled with appropriate rest, compression, and cryotherapy. Initial treatment for recurrent instability is conservative and combines activity modification (avoiding provocative activities) with a prolonged exercise program to enhance dynamic stability.

The minimal cuff activity and active-assisted portions of the *Shoulder Mobility Progression* may begin with the arm at less than 90° of elevation; table bows and pendulum exercises are undertaken. Patients may also begin the exercises in the *Shoulder Stability Progression* requiring minimal cuff activity, as part of the effort to establish conscious control of the scapula as soon as comfort permits. The scapular clock, shoulder dump, and sternal lift exercises may begin safely even when the patient is using a sling.

Conservative treatment is generally successful in patients with atraumatic MDI. In rare instances, subacromial inflammation develops in a patient with this type of instability. Administering a subacromial corticosteroid injection will reduce symptoms and allow the patient to continue the exercise program.

■ Surgical Intervention

Anterior Glenohumeral Instability

Surgical intervention for initial dislocations is a relatively new concept. Such procedures are being performed in active young adults and adolescents with high recurrence rates because little change in the natural history is effected using conservative management. In these high-risk individuals, visualization and repair of the acute injury can dramatically reduce recurrence rates.[199]

Various surgical techniques have been used to stabilize the shoulder (see ST 9.7). Arthroscopic approaches with transglenoid sutures, stapling, and open capsular shift have been successful. A comprehensive review of the evidence suggests that open and arthroscopic surgeries yield comparable results as treatments for recurrent anterior instability.[200] One study reported 89% of overhead athletes treated with arthroscopic stabilization returned to their desired level of sport.[201]

Posterior Glenohumeral Instability

Surgery is indicated in patients with irreducible posterior dislocations, or those with osseous injuries such as a displaced lesser tuberosity fracture or significant posterior glenoid rim or humeral head fractures (reverse Hill-Sachs lesion). Patients with recurrent instability after 3 to 6 months of focused rehabilitation are considered candidates for surgery. Although surgical treatment for recurrent anterior instability is well accepted, posterior stabilization is more controversial. The posterior-inferior capsular shift is recommended as the standard surgical approach for posterior instability (see **ST** 9.8).

Posterior-Inferior Capsular Shift

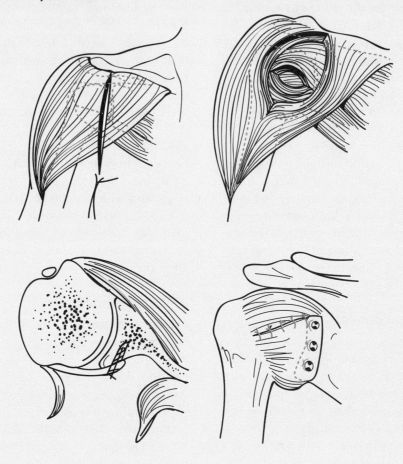

Indications

Failure to reduce posterior dislocation or recurrent posterior instability.

Procedure Overview

1. The patient is placed in the lateral decubitus position.
2. A vertical incision is made from the lateral edge of the acromion toward the axillary crease.
3. A skin flap is developed, exposing the deltoid fascia.
4. The deltoid is split along the length of the fibers from the spine of the scapula inferiorly, exposing the infraspinatus and teres minor and avoiding the axillary nerve.
5. The posterior capsule is identified through the intramuscular division.
6. Beginning at the glenoid edge, a T-shaped capsulotomy is performed, with a horizontal extension occurring directly lateral to the site.
7. A posterior capsulorrhaphy is accomplished by reattaching the capsule to the glenoid. If the labrum is detached or posterior Bankart lesions are present, they are repaired in the same manner as anterior Bankart lesions. Suture anchors can also be used.
8. If the posterior labrum is intact, the capsulorrhaphy can be completed by passing sutures through the labrum.
9. The capsule is advanced medially and superiorly and tensioned with the arm in 20° of abduction and neutral rotation.
10. If inferior laxity is marked, the capsule can be shifted superiorly and laterally at the glenoid.
11. If the bony rim of the posterior glenoid is deficient, a bone block can be placed to augment the bony anatomy.

Functional Limitations

Restrictions of internal rotation past neutral are important to avoid placing excess tension on the repair.

Implications for Rehabilitation

Slow progression with rotational motions and strengthening must be implemented to ensure adequate healing.

Comments

Contraindications to the posterior approach are twofold: (1) significant humeral head involvement of 20% to 50%, which necessitates a subscapular transfer; and (2) total head destruction requiring hemiarthroplasty.

capsulotomy
Cutting of the joint capsule.

Multidirectional Glenohumeral Instability

Surgical repair is indicated for patients who experience traumatic events that lead to MDI and for patients who have been compliant with rehabilitation but whose shoulders remain unstable. An inferior capsular shift with Bankart repair (if needed) yields good results. The goal of surgical intervention is to correct traumatic lesions and decrease capsular volume through either an open or arthroscopic soft-tissue capsular shift procedure. Inferior capsular shift with capsuloligamentous injury repair is the recommended treatment when nonsurgical management has failed. The inferior capsular shift is approached through the most symptomatic site (see **Figure 9.27**). Tensioning the opposite side of the joint is accomplished by overlapping the capsular flaps on the symptomatic side; this technique reduces volume and helps reduce recurrence.

In recent years, the popularity of arthroscopic capsular plication as a treatment for patients with MDI has grown. This technique includes suture plication of the anterior, posterior, and rotator interval capsular structures. While this technique is popular, the surgical treatment of MDI still yields results that are inferior to the treatment of traumatic instability.

Capsular shrinkage also can be performed by electrothermal-assisted capsulorrhaphy and laser-assisted capsular shift techniques. In the past, laser capsulorraphy was the standard for patients with MDI. Although they initially showed some promise, these techniques are probably not indicated in the young, high-demand athlete. While capsulorrhaphy remains an option for recalcitrant MDI cases or as an adjunct to other procedures, it has largely fallen out of favor for these

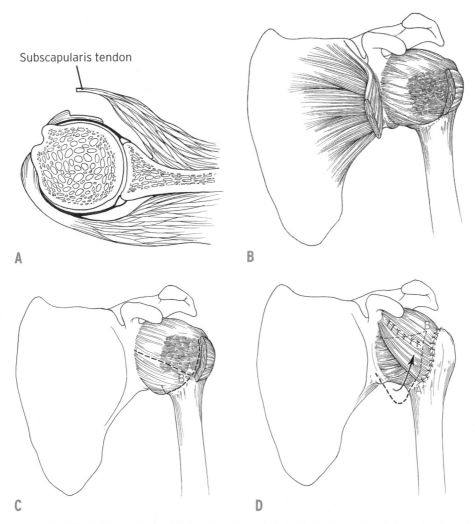

Figure 9.27 Inferior capsular shift. (**A**) The anterior two-thirds of the subscapularis tendon is dissected medially, leaving the posterior portion of the tendon to reinforce the anterior capsule. (**B**) The subscapularis muscle belly and the anterior portion of the tendon are retracted medially. (**C**) The capsule is incised in a "T" fashion, creating superior and inferior leaflets. (**D**) The capsule is advanced and shifted; the superior flap overlaps the inferior flap. *Source:* Reproduced with permission from Schenk TJ, Brems JJ. Multidirectional instability of the shoulder: Pathophysiology, diagnosis, and management. *J Am Acad Orthop Surg.* 1998;6:65-72.

patients, owing to its relatively high failure rate—approaching 40%.[202]

Postoperative Management

Factors affecting the postoperative motion restrictions and the type and length of immobilization include the nature of procedure (open versus arthroscopic), the type of procedure and tissue repaired (e.g., capsular shift, capsulolabral repair), the fixation method (e.g., sutures, suture anchors, bioabsorbable material), and the quality of the tissue.

After capsular plication for anterior instability, the patient is immobilized in 20–30° of abduction and neutral humeral rotation for the first 4 to 6 weeks. The brace should also be worn at night as directed by the surgeon, typically for the initial 4 weeks postoperatively. The arm is removed from the immobilizer to begin active-assisted T-bar and passive ROM during the first 2 weeks after surgery.

In week 1, ROM is restricted to 70° of GH elevation, progressing to 90° during week 2. Humeral ER and IR are restricted to 10° and 20°, respectively, and are addressed with the shoulder in the scapular plane and abducted 30°. Submaximal pain-free isometrics and rhythmic stabilization may begin as soon as patient comfort permits.

At 3 to 4 weeks postoperatively, GH ROM is increased to 100° elevation, 30° of ER, and 45° of IR with the arm abducted to 45°. Light isotonic tubing exercises may begin in pain-free ranges during week 4, as patient comfort permits. During weeks 5 and 6, ROM should progress to 160° elevation, and 65° of IR and ER with the arm abduction angle increased to 90°. By week 9, full elevation may be achieved, as well as 90° of ER and 65° of IR with 90° of abduction. By the end of week 11, full rotational ROM is typically reached. A return to sports is possible 6 to 8 months after surgery, although a return to unrestricted throwing may take 7 to 12 months.

Following a posterior-inferior capsular shift, patients treated for posterior instability may be placed in an immobilizer to maintain GH abduction, neutral rotation, and extension with the elbow positioned posterior to the plane of the body to limit tension on the repair. Immobilization may be maintained for the first 4 to 6 weeks postoperatively, depending on the extent and nature of the repair. Humeral IR is limited to the neutral position in these patients until week 4 after surgery. Progression of rotator cuff activation and other motion is similar to the previously mentioned plications postoperatively.

Injury-Specific Treatment and Rehabilitation Concerns

Specific Concerns

Avoid undue stress on repaired tissue.
Avoid IR past the neutral position.
Avoid provocative motions early in the rehabilitation program.
Encourage joint mobilization and tissue stretching as healing allows.
Reestablish normal neuromuscular control.

Motions that exacerbate joint instability must be restricted so that these tissues can heal. Cryotherapy and gentle active-assisted and passive ROM are initiated early to reduce pain and swelling, and to avoid the deleterious effects of immobilization.

Although management after arthroscopic plication is detailed here, nonoperative treatment follows the same general progression. The timeline for immobilization and motion restrictions varies widely, depending on the patient's age, health, goals, activity, and motivation levels; the demands of the sport; and the preference of the physician. The goal of optimal shoulder stability remains the same.

As soon as patient comfort permits, the minimal cuff activity and active-assisted portions of the *Shoulder Mobility Progression* may begin, including open- and closed-chain pendulum, table bow, and table wash exercises. These exercises are limited to pain-free positions and 90° of elevation, and ER and IR to 10° and 20°, respectively, for the first 2 weeks postoperatively.

Restoration of shoulder stability begins at this time with the *Shoulder Stability Progression*. Conscious control of the scapulothoracic joint is established through the scapular clock, shoulder dump, and sternal lift exercises. Isometric stability may be initiated during the first 2 weeks as well, beginning with the elbow in 90° of flexion and with a small bolster or towel placed under the arm. The intensity should begin at a submaximal level; isometrics may include GH elevation, abduction, and IR and ER. Assuming no SLAP repair was needed, isometric biceps exercises are initiated as well. As patient comfort permits, these activities may advance during the first 2 weeks to include weight shifts, isometric low rows, ball stability, rhythmic stabilization, and tubing isometric stability exercises within pain-free arm positions.

During weeks 3 to 4, all exercises should be continued, with active-assisted and passive ROM exercises being increased to 100° elevation, 30° of ER, and 45° of ER with the arm abducted to 45°. The pendulum, supine press, and table bow exercises may be used to progress GH elevation. At this time, light isotonic tubing exercises may begin in GH IR and ER, with a small towel held between the elbow and the side. Manual resistance is used to begin side-lying ER, side-lying forward elevation, and prone horizontal abduction with ER exercises. The tubing isometric stability and rhythmic stabilization exercises may be extended to include additional pain-free ranges.

By week 6, patients should achieve GH active-assisted and passive ROM of 160° elevation, and 65° of IR and ER with the arm abduction angle increased to 90°. During week 5, light dumbbells should be used with the side-lying ER, side-lying forward elevation, and prone horizontal abduction with ER exercises.

Active GH elevation and abduction are addressed through closed-chain pendulum exercises and diagonal table and wall wash exercises as tolerated. Active exercises may progress to greater than 90° of GH abduction as soon as the patient displays active GH ROM to 120° elevation with scapular control (no shrug). The dynamic stability exercises include the scapular clock at 90° of abduction, the hitchhiker exercise, tubing retraction, and the lawnmower progression.

By week 9, GH ROM should progress to full elevation, plus 90° of ER and 65° IR with 90° of abduction. Tubing isometric stability exercises should move through available pain-free ROM, including GH ER. Dynamic stability exercises should advance to include the high-end lawnmower, tubing punches, dynamic hugs, and high-to-low rows. Stability and isotonic strengthening exercises should begin to extend exercises toward each of the *Foundational Shoulder Exercises,* beginning with the prone and tubing exercises. The push-up progression may begin at this time; however, it should not advance to the floor until week 13 at the earliest.

The goal of full active ROM, including ER, should be achieved between weeks 10 and 11. Stability and strengthening exercises should progress to functional overhead positions during weeks 10 to 12. They should include two-hand plyometrics and incremental increases in resistance to improve shoulder strength. The sleeper, cross-body, and pectoralis stretches described in the *Foundational Shoulder Exercises* are initiated at this time and continued through the athlete's return-to-play.

By weeks 13 to 16, exercises should include one-handed plyometrics, wall dribbles, push-ups (on the floor), and use of oscillatory devices as well as each of the *Foundational Shoulder Exercises*

(including the thrower's portion). Exercises including passive and active-assisted ROM are continued as needed to maintain full active ROM.

A sport-specific interval strengthening program may begin for nonthrowing activities when appropriate, typically 13 to 15 weeks after surgery. Overhead sport or overhead throwing interval strengthening programs may begin 17 to 20 weeks after surgery. Regular lifting should be resumed, with proper technique being emphasized. A return to sports is possible 6 to 8 months after surgery, although a return to unrestricted throwing may take 7 to 12 months.

Estimated Amount of Time Lost

Recovery and rehabilitation can take as long as 3 to 8 months to achieve the required tissue healing and maturation and to reestablish joint mobility, motion, strength, and flexibility.

Return-to-Play Criteria

The athlete should achieve normal, asymptomatic GH and scapulothoracic ROM, kinematics, strength, stability, and neuromuscular control. In addition, the patient should successfully complete appropriate functional testing demonstrating normal performance of sport-specific tasks and confidence in full use of the extremity. An adjustable shoulder brace may enhance confidence in athletes returning to sports not requiring throwing or catching; however, no evidence suggests they affect recurrence rates.

Humeral Fractures

CLINICAL PRESENTATION

History
A fall on the shoulder, elbow, or outstretched arm.
A blow to the arm.
Immediate pain and loss of function.

Observation
Deformity and swelling are usually noted.

Functional Status
Inability to move the arm without significant pain.

Physical Examination Findings
Pain with any motion of the shoulder, elbow, and arm (may be minimal with smaller fractures of the proximal humerus).

The most common mechanism for fractures of the proximal humerus is a fall on the outstretched hand.

In younger patients, a large-magnitude force is more frequently involved, resulting in a more serious fracture. These patients typically present with fracture-dislocations with significant soft-tissue disruption and multiple injuries. Another potential mechanism of injury is excessive humeral rotation, particularly in the abducted position; however, these injuries primarily affect patients with underlying bone deficiencies. Proximal humeral fractures can also occur from a direct lateral blow, a mechanism of injury that may result in a greater tuberosity fracture.

A fracture-dislocation may occur either anteriorly or posteriorly. Metastatic disease may significantly weaken the bone; in such patients, a pathologic fracture may occur via an otherwise trivial mechanism. Whenever a trivial event results in a fracture, consider an underlying pathologic cause.

The force produced during the acceleration phase of throwing can lead to humeral fatigue injuries. Bony and soft-tissue structures are likely to hypertrophy when subjected to gradually increasing loads. If the applied load is greater than the surrounding structures can withstand, a fatigue fracture occurs.

A spontaneous humeral fracture from overhead throwing can have the characteristics of a stress fracture. This phenomenon is due, in part, to the torsion developed during the arm acceleration phase of throwing, which can exceed the torsional stress capacity of the humerus. This torsion may result in chronic widening, demineralization, and fragmentation of the proximal humeral epiphysis and subsequent osteochondrosis of the proximal humeral epiphysis in growing athletes.

Severely displaced proximal humeral fractures typically result from high-velocity blunt trauma. These types of injuries are prevalent in elderly people but rare in athletes. The two-part proximal humeral fractures, including those through the proximal humeral growth plate in young athletes, must be identified and treated.

A four-segment classification of proximal humeral fractures has been developed in which any segment displaced more than 1 centimeter or angulated more than 45°, regardless of the number of fracture lines, is considered a part. One-part fractures account for approximately 80% of all proximal humeral fractures; they include those injuries in which none of the major segments is displaced more than 1 centimeter or rotated more than 45° (see **Figure 9.28**). This section will consider only two-part fractures, which include surgical neck fractures and greater or lesser tuberosity fractures.

Differential Diagnosis
GH dislocation.

Imaging Techniques
In addition to the standard radiographic views, scapular Y views or axillary views are critical to rule out an associated dislocation, which is particularly common with greater and lesser tuberosity fractures (see **Figure 9.29**). Routine radiographs alone may be inadequate to judge displacement of proximal humeral fractures, particularly those involving the tuberosities. For this purpose, CT scan of the proximal humerus is useful.[203]

Definitive Diagnosis
Diagnosis is made by radiographic examination with support from the history and clinical examination.

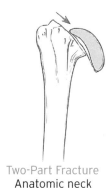

Two-Part Fracture
Anatomic neck

Two-Part Fracture
Surgical neck

Three-Part Fracture
Surgical neck
Greater tuberosity
Shaft

Four-Part Fracture
Humeral head
Greater tuberosity
Lesser tuberosity
Shaft

Figure 9.28 The Neer classification of proximal humeral fractures. *Source:* Reproduced with permission from Neer CS II. Displaced proximal humeral fractures. I: Classification and evaluation. *J Bone Joint Surg Am.* 1970;52:1077-1089.

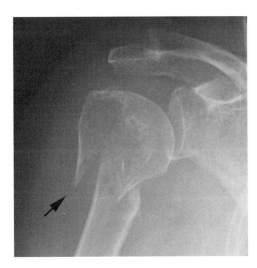

Figure 9.29 An AP radiograph shows a comminuted fracture of the surgical neck (arrow) and head.

Patients who suffer relatively low-force fractures may also need to be evaluated for low bone mineral density and the possibility of metastases.

Pathomechanics and Functional Limitations

By definition, patients with greater tuberosity fractures also have a full-thickness rotator cuff tear. Displacement of the greater tuberosity posteriorly can result in limited ER, whereas superior displacement may restrict abduction and lead to symptoms of impingement. In rare instances, a symptomatic nonunion may occur. In such cases, surgical treatment is necessary; it involves an anatomic reduction and internal fixation of the displaced tuberosity and repair of the rotator cuff tear. Isolated, displaced lesser tuberosity fractures are rare and are associated with subscapularis tendon damage. Some loss of IR may occur and, at least theoretically, a nonunion may develop. In general, however, these fractures do not affect function and require only symptomatic care.

The greater the separation between the fracture segments, the greater the risk of a nonunion. Fractures that are angulated more than 45° and rotated fractures may heal, albeit with significant limitation of humeral motion in one or more directions. Nonsurgical treatment involves closed reduction to correct the angulation, rotation, and impaction of the fracture surfaces. The arm is then immobilized in a sling or a shoulder splint, brace, or spica designed to minimize tension on the healing segments.

■ Immediate Management

The extremity should be immobilized and the patient transported to a medical facility for radiographs. A careful neurovascular examination should be conducted, paying specific attention to radial nerve function.

■ Medications

Paracetamol (acetaminophen) or narcotic analgesics are used for pain control. The use of NSAIDs should be constrained to a 3- to 7-day course during the inflammation phase of rehabilitation.

■ Postinjury Management

Management of one-part fractures consists of immobilizing the arm in a sling and swathe until the entire humerus moves as a unit (approximately 2 weeks). Progressive ROM exercises are employed during the subsequent 4 weeks. Pendulum exercises and ER to a neutral position begin during weeks 3 and 4, with more aggressive ROM exercises beginning in all directions during weeks 5 and 6. When bony healing is clinically solid and demonstrated on radiographs—a point typically reached during week 6—active motion is allowed. Standard shoulder rehabilitation and condition continue until ROM and strength are restored.

Fractures of the surgical neck may be completely immobilized in an orthosis and follow this same timeline. Percutaneous pinning of the fracture after the closed reduction may be considered if the fracture is unstable. Overhead olecranon pin traction may be of use in patients with multiple injuries and those with extensive comminution in the surgical neck region (seen in the most violent sports, such as auto racing). If the fracture remains in an unacceptable position despite all attempts, surgical open reduction and internal fixation are appropriate.

In skeletally immature athletes—particularly pitchers who complain of pain in the proximal humerus of the throwing arm—the possibility of "Little League shoulder" should be considered. This condition, which is usually described as pain in the throwing shoulder of the athlete, comprises epiphysiolysis of the proximal humerus caused by repetitive microtrauma from overhead throwing. These athletes present with diffuse shoulder pain with throwing and typically report a recent increase in throwing volume. Weakness in GH abduction is displayed, along with tenderness and possible swelling over the anterior-lateral shoulder. AP radiographs with ER may suggest proximal physeal widening and possible demineralization, sclerosis, or fragmentation of the proximal humeral metaphysis. These athletes respond favorably to 2 to 3 months of rest, followed by adherence to an interval throwing program.

9

■ Surgical Intervention

Management of proximal humeral fractures typically consists of reduction and percutaneous pin fixation using a fluoroscope to visualize the fracture site. This procedure allows patients to perform early ROM. In pediatric patients, angulation limits are approximately 50% apposition and 45° angulation. Acceptable alignment becomes more precise in older age groups, and the possibility of surgical intervention has increased as the acceptable threshold for displacement has been reduced. In patients aged 10 to 12 years, the least acceptable reduction is 50% displacement and 30° angulation; in those older than age 12, the least acceptable reduction is 30% displacement and 25° angulation. If the position of the fracture is unsatisfactory, closed reduction is appropriate. If closed reduction cannot be achieved, then open reduction is indicated.[204] If closed reduction is achieved but remains unstable, percutaneous pin fixation should be considered.[205]

Displaced proximal humeral fractures are difficult to manage, and a wide spectrum of complications has been reported after both closed and open treatment. Complications may include osteonecrosis, nonunion, malunion, hardware failure, frozen shoulder, infection, neurovascular injury, pneumothorax, and pneumohemothorax.

Greater Tuberosity Fractures

In patients with displaced greater tuberosity fractures, the supraspinatus, infraspinatus, and teres minor muscles cause superior and posterior fragment displacement. This type of fracture is associated with a rotator cuff tear. A significantly displaced fracture is best treated surgically with rotator cuff repair and fracture fixation. Such a fracture may also be associated with anterior GH dislocation.

Lesser Tuberosity Fractures

Surgical fixation is recommended for displaced, isolated lesser tuberosity fractures. The usual mechanism of injury in such cases is a strong ER force when the arm is in maximal ER at 90° of abduction. In adolescents, lesser tuberosity fractures may result from tension on the apophyseal plate. In adults, these fractures are commonly mistaken for pronounced calcific tendinitis. Lesser tuberosity fractures are associated with posterior GH dislocations.

Tension from the subscapularis is responsible for the displacement of the lesser tuberosity. Surgical treatment is not typically required unless the fragment is large enough to prevent IR. In this case, open reduction and internal fixation are appropriate.

■ Postoperative Management

The postoperative management is determined by the extent of the injury, the fixation method, and the resulting stability (if applicable). Once healing is visualized on radiographs or a stable construct is demonstrated, ROM and early progressive resistance exercises can be initiated. In general, ROM exercises can be initiated with pendulum exercises in the first 3 weeks. Healing is usually accomplished in 6 to 8 weeks, and standard shoulder rehabilitation and conditioning are advanced until ROM and strength are restored.

■ Injury-Specific Treatment and Rehabilitation Concerns

> **Specific Concerns**
>
> Maintain stability of the fracture site.
> Restore shoulder ROM and function.

Rehabilitation of proximal humeral fractures seeks to restore adequate motion to permit optimal function. If a fracture or fracture repair is stable, then rehabilitation may be started by days 7 to 10. After surgical repair, gentle passive ROM exercises, including pendulum exercises, can be started within 24 to 48 hours. The *Shoulder Stability Progression* can safely begin with scapular clocks, shoulder dumps, and sternal lifts at this time. Table bows may also be initiated, making sure to avoid bearing weight on the involved arm.

Three weeks after the fracture, the active-assisted portion of the *Shoulder Mobility Progression* begins, including T-bar–assisted ROM, supine press, and table wash exercises. Pulley exercises, significant distraction, and torsional stress should be avoided until radiographic evidence of healing is obtained, usually after 6 weeks. Isometric exercises are generally started at 4 weeks after the fracture, along with the isometric stability portion of the *Shoulder Stability Progression*. Advanced stretching and strengthening exercises, including the more aggressive dynamic stability and *Foundational Shoulder Exercises*, are initiated when appropriate, typically at 3 months.

Timelines and restrictions vary with the fracture type, fracture or fracture repair stability, and patient compliance. Overhead throwers should complete an interval throwing program before returning to play.

Estimated Amount of Time Lost

Four to six months of rehabilitation are usually required before the patient returns to normal activity.

Return-to-Play Criteria

Athletes returning to play must demonstrate fracture union and complete physiologic healing. They should also achieve normal, asymptomatic GH and scapulothoracic ROM, kinematics, strength, stability, and neuromuscular control. In addition, patients should successfully complete appropriate functional testing demonstrating normal performance of sport-specific tasks.

Overhead Athletes: Adaptations and Pathomechanics

The overhead-throwing motion is a complex and sequential whole-body movement designed to produce large-magnitude forces in less than half a second. Throwing is typically described as having six phases.[206] Completing the overhead throw requires the shoulder and elbow to achieve extreme ranges of motion and angular velocities while transmitting forces distally. The production and transfer of force begin as the lead foot contacts the ground. The force follows the kinetic chain in a pattern of precisely timed angular rotation, followed by stabilization at each joint from the ankle, knee, hip, trunk, scapulothoracic, glenohumeral, elbow, wrist, and fingers, and, finally, to the object being propelled. Poor mechanics, sequencing, or fatigue may lead to an inefficient production and transmission of force, poor performance, and eventual injury. Understanding the mechanics, pathomechanics, and chronic adaptations associated with the overhead throw facilitates the diagnosis and treatment of injuries that affect this motion.

Late in the arm cocking phase of the throw, the force transmitted from the lower extremity reaches the shoulder. At this point, the arm is positioned to maximize the length of the muscles that will propel the arm forward—specifically, the latissimus dorsi, pectoralis major, teres major, and subscapularis. The scapulothoracic joint is retracted (externally rotated and posteriorly tilted), while the humerus is abducted to approximately 95°, externally rotated to 180°, and horizontally abducted 20° past the midline as it receives the force and prepares for forward acceleration.[207] The humerus then internally rotates at velocities approaching 6500° per second during the acceleration phase.[207] At the moment of ball release, the shoulder must combat a distraction force that is equivalent to 81%[208] to 108%[209] of body weight while decelerating the arm.

Producing and controlling repetitive large-magnitude forces over a long period may lead to both normal and abnormal physical adaptations. Understanding and recognizing these adaptations are a critical component of evaluating and treating overhead athletes.

Normal Adaptations

Repetitive overhead throwing over time leads to predictable chronic adaptations to soft[100,210] and osseous[211,212] tissues, including version of the glenoid and humeral head (humeral retroversion) and laxity of the anterior-inferior GH joint capsule. These changes result in a shift in the thrower's arc of GH rotational ROM toward ER. While the total arc of motion may remain between 160° and 180°, the magnitude of ER increases, accompanied by an equal decrease in IR.[82,213–215] These normal adaptations afford greater force production during the throw and affect only the throwing shoulder. Such changes are seen in bilateral ROM differences[213–215] and in overhead-throwing athletes as compared to non-overhead-throwing athletes.[100,216] These changes normally develop over years of throwing, which accounts for the differences in ROM noted between throwers in different age ranges; in particular, throwers aged 8 to 12 display less ROM than those aged 15 to 28.[217]

Abnormal Adaptations

Although some changes in a thrower's GH ROM may be normal adaptations, others are associated with pain,[218] decreased performance,[50,100,218] and pathology[91,100] and, therefore, are considered abnormal. These adaptations include excessive laxity of the anterior-inferior GH capsule and contracture of the posterior capsule.

Late in the arm cocking phase, the humerus is abducted 95° and maximally externally rotated (180°) and horizontally abducted 20° past the midline as the scapula is retracted against the thorax. The anterior shear force on the GH joint peaks when the arm is in this position.[219] Anterior GH stability is maintained through compression of the humeral head by the rotator cuff and the anterior-inferior joint capsule, primarily the anterior band of the inferior GH ligament (AIGHL). The AIGHL is also a check-rein for humeral ER. Excessive anterior shear force and ER during this phase, as a result of either an acute traumatic event or repetitive microtrauma, may stretch the AIGHL and lead to anterior-inferior laxity.

During arm deceleration, the posterior rotator cuff and joint capsule must work together to resist the large-magnitude distraction forces while decelerating humeral IR.[219] This tensile stress and forceful eccentric load may result in acute or chronic tears of the rotator cuff. More commonly, however, such cumulative microtrauma leads to scarring and eventual contracture of the posterior joint capsule that can be observed on MRI. Clinicians may observe this contracture through a loss of horizontal adduction or GIRD.

Pathomechanics

Excessive force may be placed on shoulder structures as the result of these abnormal adaptive changes or inefficient throwing mechanics. Throwing mechanics issues in pitchers that increase the force placed on the shoulder include landing with an open stride foot, failing to maintain elbow flexion at the moment of stride-foot contact or at ball release, and poor timing of shoulder ER (either early or late).[220] The aberrant forces produced by these inefficient mechanics, anterior-inferior capsular laxity, or posterior contracture may play a role in the development of internal impingement, rotator cuff tears, SLAP lesions, and micro-instability in overhead athletes.

Poor mechanics, anterior-inferior capsular laxity, or posterior contracture may become pathologic late in the arm cocking phase, when the humerus is abducted 95°, externally rotated to 180°, and horizontally abducted 20° past the midline. It is generally accepted that contact between the posterior-superior glenoid and the articular side of the rotator cuff in this position is a normal phenomenon in throwers, and one that does not always lead to symptoms.[59] When athletes use poor, inefficient throwing mechanics or engage in prolonged bouts of throwing, however, the scapular stabilizers may fail to retract (externally rotate and posteriorly tilt) the scapula sufficiently or the rotator cuff may fail to adequately compress the humeral head in the glenoid. Either mechanism increases stress on the anterior-inferior capsule late in the arm cocking phase and early in the arm acceleration phase; this effect exacerbates laxity and eventual leads to instability or micro-instability. If intervention to correct these erroneous mechanisms is not undertaken, they may result in further hyperangulation in these phases and further humeral translation laxity and instability.[82]

Hyperangulation late in the arm cocking phase increases the amount of contact between the articular side of the rotator cuff and the posterior-superior glenoid, and has been associated with development of internal impingement and SLAP lesions. Originally, Jobe suggested the laxity developed with repeated throwing and the subsequent anterior-inferior instability and hyperangulation were responsible for internal impingement.[86] Supporting this contention were reports that 74% of throwers returned to their previous level of throwing after undergoing anterior capsulolabral reconstruction.[87] More recent investigations suggest a posterior capsular contracture causes the center of rotation of the humeral head to move posterior-superiorly in this position of hyperangulation, further increasing the contact between the glenoid and the rotator cuff and biceps tendon attachments.[50,100,101] The contracture may also exacerbate the peel-back mechanism and increase shear stress on the biceps tendon and rotator cuff in this arm position.[221] This hypothesis is supported by reports that throwers with internal impingement display significantly greater GIRD and posterior capsular tightness compared to asymptomatic throwers.[91]

Isolated Measures of Glenohumeral Motion

Because of the association between pathology and the loss of GH ROM, clinicians should monitor ROM in competitive overhead athletes.[100] Passive rotational ROM for the GH joint is assessed using the standard goniometric technique and arm position.[222] To assess isolated GH as opposed to humeral-thoracic motion, the clinician should control for scapulothoracic motion using the visual inspection technique.[223] Although a goniometer may be used for this purpose, an inclinometer placed on the patient's forearm allows for reliable measurements.[224] The shoulder is passively moved into IR and ER and while visually monitoring the scapula for motion. The position where the acromion begins to rise or a firm capsular end-feel is felt is recorded.

With measures of GH IR and ER, the total arc is calculated (IR + ER) and GIRD is commonly quantified using two different calculations:[100]

Bilateral differences in IR =

$$(\text{nondominant IR} - \text{dominant IR})$$

Bilateral differences in % of total arc =

$$\left(\frac{[\text{nondominant total arc} - \text{dominant total arc}]}{\text{nondominant total arc}} \right)$$

A bilateral difference in IR greater than 20° or a difference in total arc greater than 10% indicates GIRD and is associated with pathology.[100] Evidence suggests that professional pitchers may display an acute loss of IR ROM (approximately 10°) immediately after pitching.[225] These changes are considered normal if motion is restored after 2 to 3 days. One recent study suggests that healthy throwers may display bilateral differences in IR of 11°, whereas those suffering from internal impingement demonstrate a 20° difference.[91]

Posterior Shoulder Tightness

Posterior shoulder tightness and horizontal adduction are measured beginning with the athlete in a side-lying position on the side opposite that being measured. The clinician stabilizes the scapula in the retracted position and restricts motion at the lateral border. The athlete's humerus is abducted to 90° with neutral rotation. The clinician then begins horizontal adduction of the humerus and holds the position at which the scapula begins to move or a firm capsular end-feel is felt. The distance between the medial epicondyle and the bottom of the treatment table is recorded (see **Figure 9.30**).[91] Greater distance reflects less humeral horizontal adduction. The measure is repeated for the opposite shoulder.

One recent study suggests that healthy throwers display 21 ± 6 centimeters of horizontal adduction in their dominant shoulder, whereas those suffering from internal impingement display significantly less,

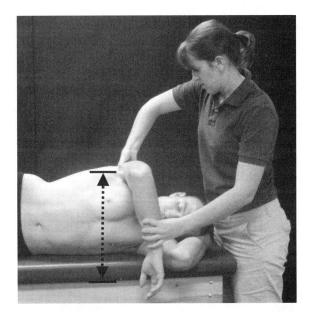

Figure 9.30 Posterior shoulder tightness is measured in this position by manually maintaining scapular retraction and passively lowering the arm into horizontal adduction. The distance between the medial epicondyle and the bottom of the treatment table surface is measured using a tape measure.

in the range of 27 ± 6 centimeters.[91] The measure termed "posterior shoulder tightness" is calculated as the bilateral difference in horizontal adduction (in centimeters). Healthy throwers display less than 1 centimeter of this difference, compared to the 4 centimeters of tightness found in throwers suffering from internal impingement.[91]

9

Rehabilitation

Shoulder rehabilitation and conditioning programs should focus on the base of the kinetic chain and seek to correct lumbar and core strength, stability, and flexibility deficits before addressing the scapular component and the upper extremity.[49] See Chapters 13 and 16 for lumbar spine/core rehabilitation exercises. For most shoulder injuries, the rehabilitation process follows a consistent sequence (see **Table 9.5**). See Chapter 12 for a description of upper extremity therapeutic exercises.

Joint Mobilization Techniques

The following joint mobilization techniques are used to treat pain, stiffness, and reversible joint hypomobility. These exercises are indicated to reestablish the joint-play motion necessary for restoring shoulder complex movement.

Table 9.5

Phases of Shoulder Rehabilitation

Phase I
Rest from painful activity
Reduce pain and inflammation using physical agents, manual therapy, joint mobilizations, and medications
Address core stability, kinetic chain, posture, and postural awareness
Enhance mobility using passive and active-assisted exercises with minimal rotator cuff activity
Improve proximal stability by establishing conscious control of the scapula

Phase II
Progress mobility exercises to include active-assisted and active rotator cuff activity and full ROM
Progress exercises to establish isometric stability with rotator cuff co-contraction
Progress closed-chain isometric exercises to include isotonic multiplanar and open-chain motions
Begin dynamic stability exercises when scapular control is established

Phase III
Progress mobility exercises to include prophylactic flexibility stretches
Progress dynamic stability exercises to include functional, dynamic, multijoint, multiplane, and plyometric strengthening

Phase IV
Return to sport
Continue *Foundational Shoulder Exercises*

Clavicular Glide

Inferior Glide

Inferior glide of the clavicular head is indicated as a component motion for shoulder elevation. The patient is supine, and the clinician stands above the patient's head. The thumb pad contacts the most superior/proximal surface of the clavicle. The opposite thumb is placed on top, and inferior force is exerted diagonally away from the patient's midline.

Posterior Glide

Posterior glide of the clavicular head is indicated as a component motion for shoulder retraction and horizontal abduction. The patient is supine, with the clinician standing to the side of the patient. The thumb pad contacts the anterior/proximal surface of the clavicle. The opposite thumb is placed on top, and posterior force is exerted (see **Figure 9.31**).

Posterosuperior and Anteroinferior Glide of the Clavicle on the Acromion

In this technique, the patient is supine, and the clinician stands facing the patient. The anterior humeral surface is grasped with one hand, while the opposite thumb contacts the anterolateral surface of the clavicle. A force is then exerted in a posterior/superior/medial direction through the thumb, followed by an anterior/inferior/lateral directional force (see **Figure 9.32**).

Scapular Mobilization

Distraction

In this technique, the patient is prone, and the clinician stands facing the patient. The anterior

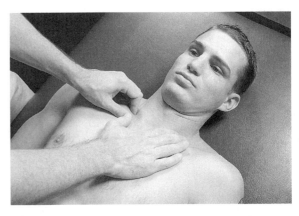

Figure 9.31 Sternoclavicular joint mobilization technique: posterior glide.

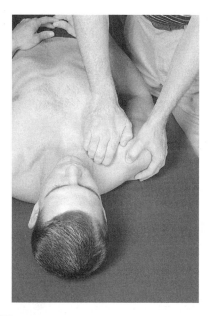

Figure 9.32 Acromioclavicular joint mobilization technique: posterosuperior and anteroinferior glide of the clavicle on the acromion.

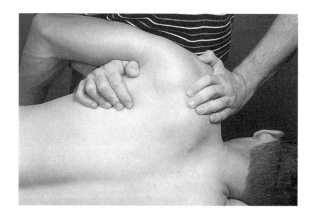

Figure 9.34 Scapular mobilization technique: superior and inferior glide.

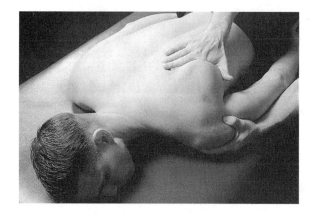

Figure 9.33 Scapular mobilization technique: distraction.

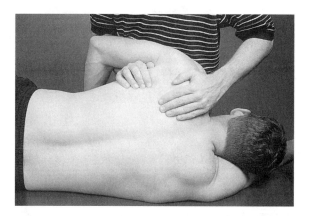

Figure 9.35 Scapular mobilization technique: lateral and medial rotation.

surface of the humerus is grasped with one hand, pulling posteriorly. The opposite second proximal phalanx rests on the thoracic wall, squeezing under and gently lifting the inferior angle of the scapula (see **Figure 9.33**).

Superior and Inferior Glide
In this technique, the patient lies on the side, and the clinician stands facing the patient. The humerus is maintained against the clinician's torso as the scapula is moved superiorly and inferiorly (see **Figure 9.34**).

Lateral and Medial Rotation
In this technique, the patient is side-lying, and the clinician stands facing the patient. The humerus is maintained against the clinician's trunk as the scapula is rotated medially and laterally (see **Figure 9.35**).

■ Glenohumeral Joint Mobilization

Anterior Humeral Glide
Anterior humeral glide is indicated as a component motion for GH external rotation, extension, and abduction. The patient is prone, and the clinician stands facing the patient, holding the patient's arm in a loose-packed position. One hand holds the proximal humerus, while the other hand is placed distal to the acromion. Force is applied in an anterior direction (see **Figure 9.36**).

Inferior Humeral Glide
Inferior humeral glide is indicated as a component motion for flexion and abduction. The patient is supine, and the clinician stands at the patient's side. The proximal phalanx index finger is positioned against the neck of the scapula, while the other hand contacts the lateral/distal surface of the humerus. An inferior force is exerted through the contact on the distal humerus (see **Figure 9.37**).

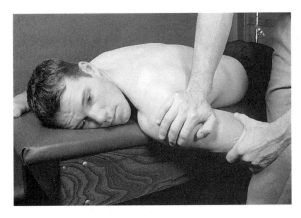

Figure 9.36 Glenohumeral joint mobilization technique: anterior humeral glide.

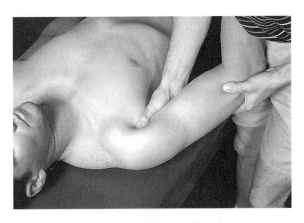

Figure 9.38 Glenohumeral joint mobilization technique: lateral distraction of the humeral head.

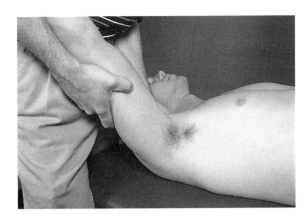

Figure 9.37 Glenohumeral joint mobilization technique: inferior humeral glide.

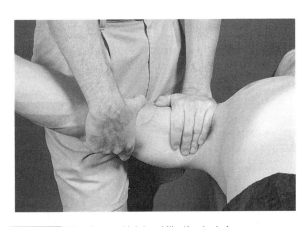

Figure 9.39 Glenohumeral joint mobilization technique: posterior glide of the humeral head.

Lateral Distraction of the Humeral Head

Lateral humeral head distraction is indicated as a joint-play motion for shoulder complex movement. The patient is supine, and the clinician stands at the patient's side. The outside hand grasps the anterior/distal part of the humerus, and the hand nearest the patient is placed so that the proximal phalanx of the index finger and the first web space contact the medial/proximal surface of the humeral neck. A lateral force is exerted with the inside hand's index finger and web space (see Figure 9.38).

Posterior Glide of the Humeral Head

Posterior humeral head glide is indicated as a component motion for internal rotation and flexion. The patient is supine, and the clinician stands at the patient's shoulder facing the patient. The anterior/distal surface of the humerus is grasped with one hand, while the opposite hand contacts the proximal anterior humeral surface, exerting a posterior force (see Figure 9.39).

Self-Mobilization Techniques

Lateral Glide

In this technique, the patient is seated in a chair at the side of the table, with the involved extremity resting in the scapular plane on the table. The uninvolved hand is placed on the medial humerus just below the axilla. The patient applies gentle force in the lateral direction with the uninvolved hand (see Figure 9.40).

Inferior Glide

In this technique, the patient stands at the edge of the table, and the involved hand grasps the edge of the table. The patient leans away from the edge of the table while maintaining the grasp (see Figure 9.41).

Alternative methods include the following:

- The patient sits in a chair, with the involved extremity resting in the coronal plane on a table. The uninvolved hand is placed

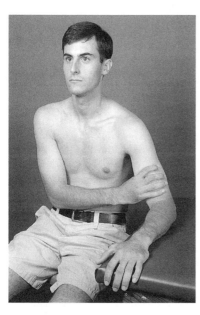

Figure 9.40 Self-mobilization technique: lateral glenohumeral glide.

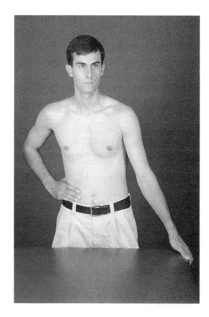

Figure 9.41 Self-mobilization technique: inferior glenohumeral glide.

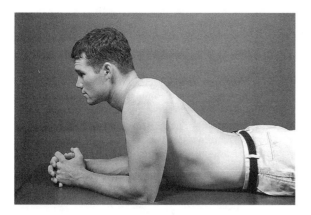

Figure 9.42 Self-mobilization technique: posterior glenohumeral glide.

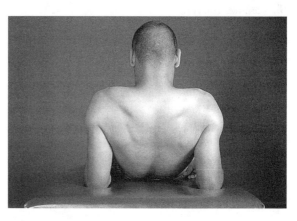

Figure 9.43 Self-mobilization technique: anterior glenohumeral glide.

on the deltoid. The patient applies gentle force in the inferior direction with the uninvolved hand.

■ The patient stands with the involved upper extremity in a neutral position, and the uninvolved hand grasps the humerus just above the epicondyles. The patient then applies gentle force in the inferior direction with the uninvolved hand.

Posterior Glide

In this technique, the patient is prone on the table and rests on the elbows before allowing the body weight to shift downward (see Figure 9.42).

Anterior Glide

In this technique, the patient is supine on the table with shoulders extended and rests on flexed elbows before allowing the body weight to shift downward (see Figure 9.43).

References

1. Wirth MA, Rockwood CA Jr. Acute and chronic traumatic injuries of the sternoclavicular joint. *J Am Acad Orthop Surg.* 1996;4:268–278.

2. Craig EV. Fractures of the clavicle, in Rockwood CA Jr, Matsen FA III (eds), *The Shoulder*. Philadelphia: Saunders; 1990:367–380.

3. Reid J, Kennedy JK. Direct fracture of the clavicle with symptoms simulating a cervical rig. *Br J Sports Med.* 1925; 2:608–609.

4. Quesana F. Technique for the roentgen diagnosis of fractures of the clavicle. *Surg Gynecol Obstet.* 1926;42: 4261–4281.

5. Khan LAK, Bradnock TJ, Scott C, Robinson CM. Fractures of the clavicle. *J Bone Joint Surg Am.* 2009;91A:447–460.

6. Rowe C. An atlas of anatomy and treatment of mid-clavicular fractures. *Clin Orthop Relat Res.* 1968;58:29–42.

7. Dennis S, Harry WD. Fractures of the first rib associated with injuries to the clavicle. *J Trauma.* 1969;9:412–422.

8. Yates DW. Complications of fractures of the clavicle. *Injury.* 1976;7:189–193.

9. Bahk MS, Kuhn JE, Galatz LM, et al. Acromioclavicular and sternoclavicular injuries and clavicular, glenoid, and scapular fractures. *J Bone Joint Surg Am.* 2009;91A: 2492–2510.

10. Andersen K, Jensen P, Lauritzen J. Treatment of clavicular fractures: Figure-of-eight bandage versus a simple sling. *Acta Orthopaedica.* 1987;58:71–74.

11. Chronopoulos E, Kim TK, Park HB, et al. Diagnostic value of physical tests for isolated chronic acromioclavicular lesions. *Am J Sports Med.* 2004;32:655–661.

12. Ludewig PM, Phadke V, Braman JP, et al. Motion of the shoulder complex during multiplanar humeral elevation. *J Bone Joint Surg Am.* 2009;91A:378–389.

13. Simovitch R, Sanders B, Ozbaydar M, et al. Acromioclavicular joint injuries: diagnosis and management. *J Am Acad Orthop Surg.* 2009;17:207–219.

14. Bigliani LU, Nicholson GP, Flatow EL. Arthroscopic resection of the distal clavicle. *Orthop Clin North Am.* 1993;24:133–141.

15. Flatow EL, Duralde XA, Nicholson GP, et al. Arthroscopic resection of the distal clavicle with a superior approach. *J Shoulder Elbow Surg.* 1995;4:41–50.

16. Walton J, Mahajan S, Paxinos A, et al. Diagnostic values of tests for acromioclavicular joint pain. *J Bone Joint Surg Am.* 2004;86:807–812.

17. Mikek M. Long-term shoulder function after type I and II acromioclavicular joint disruption. *Am J Sports Med.* 2008;36:2147–2150.

18. Mouhsine E, Garofalo R, Crevoisier X, Farron A. Grade I and II acromioclavicular dislocations: results of conservative treatment. *J Shoulder Elbow Surg.* 2003;12:599–602.

19. Bergfeld JA, Andrish JT, Clancy WG. Evaluation of the acromioclavicular joint following first- and second-degree sprains. *Am J Sports Med.* 1978;6:153–159.

20. Cox JS. The fate of the acromioclavicular joint in athletic injuries. *Am J Sports Med.* 1981;9:50–53.

21. Gstettner C, Tauber M, Hitzl W, Resch H. Rockwood type III acromioclavicular dislocation: Surgical versus conservative treatment. *J Shoulder Elbow Surg.* 2008;17(2): 220–225.

22. Faraj A, Ketzer B. The use of a hookplate in the management of acromioclavicular injuries: report of ten cases. *Acta Orthop Belg.* 2001;67:448–451.

23. Mazzocca AD, Arciero RA, Bicos J. Evaluation and treatment of acromioclavicular joint injuries. *Am J Sports Med.* 2007;35:316–329.

24. Alldredge RH. Surgical treatment of acromioclavicular dislocations. *J Bone Joint Surg Am.* 1965;47:1278–1283.

25. Bearden JM, Hughston JC, Whatley GS. Acromioclavicular dislocation: method of treatment. *J Sports Med.* 1973;1:5–17.

26. Jay G, Monnet J. The Bosworth screw in acute dislocation of the acromioclavicular joint. Clinical Conference, University of Oklahoma Medical Center; 1969.

27. Brunelli G, Brunelli F. The treatment of acromioclavicular dislocation by transfer of the short head of the biceps. *Int Orthop.* 1988;12:105–108.

28. Hebert LJ, Moffet H, McFadyen BJ, Dionne CE. Scapular behavior in shoulder impingement syndrome. *Arch Phys Med Rehabil.* 2002;83:60–69.

29. Laudner KG, Stanek JM, Meister K. Differences in scapular upward rotation between baseball pitchers and position players. *Am J Sports Med.* 2007;35:2091–2095.

30. Lukasiewicz AC, McClure P, Michener L, et al. Comparison of 3-dimensional scapular position and orientation between subjects with and without shoulder impingement. *J Orthop Sports Phys Ther.* 1999;29:574–586.

31. McClure PW, Michener LA, Karduna AR. Shoulder function and 3-dimensional scapular kinematics in people with and without shoulder impingement syndrome. *Phys Ther.* 2006;86:1075–1090.

32. Warner JJP, Micheli LJ, Arslanian LE, et al. Scapulothoracic motion in normal shoulders and shoulders with glenohumeral instability and impingement syndrome: A study using Moire topographic analysis. *Clin Orthop Relat Res.* 1992;285:191–199.

33. Myers JB, Laudner KG, Pasquale MR, et al. Scapular position and orientation in throwing athletes. *Am J Sports Med.* 2005;33:263–271.

34. Mell AG, LaScalza S, Guffey P, et al. Effect of rotator cuff pathology on shoulder rhythm. *J Shoulder Elbow Surg.* 2001;14:S58–S64.

35. Paletta GA, Warner JJP, Warren RF, et al. Shoulder kinematics with two-plane x-ray evaluation in patients with anterior instability or rotator cuff tearing. *J Shoulder Elbow Surg.* 1997;6:516–527.

36. Ogston JB, Ludewig PM. Differences in 3-dimensional shoulder kinematics between persons with multidirectional instability and asymptomatic controls. *Am J Sports Med.* 2007;35:1361–1370.

37. von Eisenhart-Rothe R, Matsen FA III, Eckstein F, et al. Pathomechanics in atraumatic shoulder instability: Scapular positioning correlates with humeral head centering. *Clin Orthop Relat Res.* 2005;433:82–89.

38. Gumina S, Carbone S, Postacchini F. Scapular dyskinesis and SICK scapula syndrome in patients with chronic type III acromioclavicular dislocation. *Arthroscopy.* 2009;25:40–45.

39. Fayad F, Roby-Brami A, Yazbeck C, et al. Three-dimensional scapular kinematics and scapulohumeral rhythm in patients with glenohumeral osteoarthritis or frozen shoulder. *J Biomech.* 2008;41:326–332.

40. Lin J, Lim HK, Yang JL. Effect of shoulder tightness on glenohumeral translation, scapular kinematics, and scapulohumeral rhythm in subjects with stiff shoulders. *J Orthop Res.* 2006;24:1044–1051.

41. Rundquist PJ, Ludewig PM. Correlation of 3-dimensional shoulder kinematics to function in subjects with idiopathic

loss of shoulder range of motion. *Phys Ther.* 2005;85:636–647.

42. Vermeulen HM, Stokdijk M, Eilers PHC, et al. Measurement of three dimensional shoulder movement patterns with an electromagnetic tracking device in patients with a frozen shoulder. *BMJ.* 2002;61:115–120.

43. Doukas WC, Speer KP. Anatomy, pathophysiology, and biomechanics of shoulder instability. *Oper Tech Sports Med.* 2000;8:179–187.

44. McClure PW, Michener LA, Sennett BJ, Karduna AR. Direct 3-dimensional measurement of scapular kinematics during dynamic movements in vivo. *J Shoulder Elbow Surg.* 2001;10:269–277.

45. Kibler WB, McMullen J. Scapular dyskinesis and its relation to shoulder pain. *J Am Acad Orthop Surg.* 2003;11:142–151.

46. Ludewig PM, Cook TM. Alterations in shoulder kinematics and associated muscle activity in people with symptoms of shoulder impingement. *Phys Ther.* 2000;80:276–291.

47. Uhl TL, Kibler WB, Gecewich B, Tripp BL. Evaluation of clinical assessment methods for scapular dyskinesis. *Arthroscopy.* 2009;25:1240–1248.

48. Lazar MA, Kwon YW, Rokito AS. Snapping scapula syndrome. *J Bone Joint Surg Am.* 2009;91:2251–2262.

49. McMullen J, Uhl TL. A kinetic chain approach for shoulder rehabilitation. *J Athl Train.* 2000;35:329–337.

50. Burkhart SS, Morgan CD, Ben Kibler W. The disabled throwing shoulder: Spectrum of pathology. Part III: the SICK scapula, scapular dyskinesis, the kinetic chain, and rehabilitation. *Arthroscopy.* 2003;19:641–661.

51. Lin J, Hanten WP, Olson SL, et al. Functional activity characteristics of individuals with shoulder dysfunctions. *J Electromyogr Kinesiol.* 2005;15:576–586.

52. Borstad JD, Ludewig PM. The effect of long versus short pectoralis minor resting length on scapular kinematics in healthy individuals. *J Orthop Sports Phys Ther.* 2005;35:227–238.

53. Cools AM, Dewitte V, Lanszweert F, et al. Rehabilitation of scapular muscle balance. *Am J Sports Med.* 2007;35:1744–1751.

54. Borstad JD, Ludewig PM. Comparison of three stretches for the pectoralis minor muscle. *J Shoulder Elbow Surg.* 2006;15:324–330.

55. Ellenbecker TS, Cools A. Rehabilitation of shoulder impingement syndrome and rotator cuff injuries: An evidence-based review. *BMJ.* 2010;44:319–327.

56. Kluemper M, Uhl T, Hazelrigg H. Effect of stretching and strengthening shoulder muscles on forward shoulder posture in competitive swimmers. *J Sport Rehabil.* 2006;15:58–70.

57. Wang CH, McClure P, Pratt NE, Nobilini R. Stretching and strengthening exercises: Their effect on three-dimensional scapular kinematics. *Arch Phys Med Rehabil.* 1999;80:923–929.

58. Park HB, Yokota A, Gill HS, et al. Diagnostic accuracy of clinical tests for the different degrees of subacromial impingement syndrome. *J Bone Joint Surg Am.* 2005;87:1446–1455.

59. MacDonald PB, Clark P, Sutherland K. An analysis of the diagnostic accuracy of the Hawkins and Neer subacromial impingement signs. *J Shoulder Elbow Surg.* 2000;9:299–301.

60. Walch G, Boileau P, Noel E, Donell ST. Impingement of the deep surface of the supraspinatus tendon on the posterosuperior glenoid rim: an arthroscopic study. *J Shoulder Elbow Surg.* 1992;1:238–245.

61. Paley KJ, Jobe FW, Pink MM, et al. Arthroscopic findings in the overhand throwing athlete: evidence for posterior internal impingement of the rotator cuff. *Arthroscopy.* 2000;16:35–40.

62. Neer CS. Anterior acromioplasty for the chronic impingement syndrome in the shoulder: A preliminary report. *J Bone Joint Surg Am.* 1972;54:41–50.

63. Eustace JA, Brophy DP, Gibney RP, et al. Comparison of the accuracy of steroid placement with clinical outcome in patients with shoulder symptoms. *BMJ.* 1997;56:59–63.

64. Yamakado K. The targeting accuracy of subacromial injection to the shoulder: An arthrographic evaluation. *Arthroscopy.* 2002;18:887–891.

65. Chen MJL, Lew HL, Hsu TC, et al. Ultrasound-guided shoulder injections in the treatment of subacromial bursitis. *Am J Phys Med Rehabil.* 2006;85:31–35.

66. Dinnes J, Loveman E, McIntyre L, Waugh N. The effectiveness of diagnostic tests for the assessment of shoulder pain due to soft tissue disorders: A systematic review. *Health Technol Assess.* 2003;7:1–166.

67. Farber A, Fayad L, Johnson T, et al. Magnetic resonance imaging of the shoulder: Current techniques and spectrum of disease. *J Bone Joint Surg Am.* 2006;88:64–79.

68. Banas MP, Miller RJ, Totterman S. Relationship between the lateral acromion angle and rotator cuff disease. *J Shoulder Elbow Surg.* 1995;4:454–461.

69. Tyler TF, Nicholas SJ, Lee SJ, et al. Correction of posterior shoulder tightness is associated with symptom resolution in patients with internal impingement. *Am J Sports Med.* 2010;38:114–119.

70. Koester MC, Dunn WR, Kuhn JE, Spindler KP. The efficacy of subacromial corticosteroid injection in the treatment of rotator cuff disease: A systematic review. *J Am Acad Orthop Surg.* 2007;15:3–11.

71. Naredo E, Cabero F, Beneyto P, et al. A randomized comparative study of short term response to blind injection versus sonographic-guided injection of local corticosteroids in patients with painful shoulder. *J Rheumatol.* 2004;31:308–314.

72. Dorrestijn O, Stevens M, Winters JC, et al. Conservative or surgical treatment for subacromial impingement syndrome? A systematic review. *J Shoulder Elbow Surg.* 2009;18:652–660.

73. Barfield LC, Kuhn JE. Arthroscopic versus open acromioplasty: A systematic review. *Clin Orthop Relat Res.* 2007;455:64–71.

74. Mohtadi NG, Hollinshead RM, Sasyniuk TM, et al. A randomized clinical trial comparing open to arthroscopic acromioplasty with mini-open rotator cuff repair for full-thickness rotator cuff tears. *Am J Sports Med.* 2008;36:1043–1051.

75. Andrews JR, Zarins B, Wilk KE. *Injuries in Baseball.* Philadelphia: Lippincott-Raven; 1998.

76. Ellman H, Kay SP. Arthroscopic subacromial decompression for chronic impingement: two- to five-year results. *J Bone Joint Surg Br.* 1991;73:395–398.

77. Ellman H. Arthroscopic subacromial decompression: Analysis of one- to three-year results. *Arthroscopy.* 1987;3:173–181.

78. Gartsman GM, Blair ME Jr, Noble PC, et al. Arthroscopic subacromial decompression: an anatomical study. *Am J Sports Med.* 1988;16:48–50.

79. Gartsman GM. Arthroscopic acromioplasty for lesions of the rotator cuff. *J Bone Joint Surg Am.* 1990;72:169–180.

80. Matthews LS, Burkhead WZ, Gordon S, et al. Acromial fracture: A complication of arthroscopic subacromial decompression. *J Shoulder Elbow Surg.* 1994;3:256–261.

81. Roye RP, Grana WA, Yates CK. Arthroscopic subacromial decompression: Two- to seven-year follow-up. *Arthroscopy.* 1995;11:301–306.

82. Braun S, Kokmeyer D, Millett PJ. Shoulder injuries in the throwing athlete. *J Shoulder Elbow Surg.* 2009;91:966–978.

83. Lombardi I Jr, Magri AG, Fleury AM, et al. Progressive resistance training in patients with shoulder impingement syndrome: A randomized controlled trial. *Arthritis Rheum.* 2008;59:615–622.

84. Bang M, Deyle G. Comparison of supervised exercise with and without manual physical therapy for patients with shoulder impingement syndrome. *J Orthop Sports Phys Ther.* 2000;30:126–137.

85. Boettcher C, Ginn K, Cathers I. Which is the optimal exercise to strengthen supraspinatus? *Med Sci Sports Exerc.* 2009;41(11):1979–1983.

86. Ludewig PM, Reynolds JF. The association of scapular kinematics and glenohumeral joint pathologies. *J Orthop Sports Phys Ther.* 2009;39:90–104.

87. Tyler TF, Nicholas SJ, Roy T, Gleim GW. Quantification of posterior capsule tightness and motion loss in patients with shoulder impingement. *Am J Sports Med.* 2000;28:668–673.

88. Meister K, Buckley B, Batts J. The posterior impingement sign: Diagnosis of rotator cuff and posterior labral tears secondary to internal impingement in overhand athletes. *Am J Orthop.* 2004;33:412–415.

89. Jobe CM. Superior glenoid impingement. *Orthop Clin North Am.* 1997;28:137–143.

90. Jobe FW, Giangarra CE, Kvitne RS, Glousman RE. Anterior capsulolabral reconstruction of the shoulder in athletes in overhand sports. *Am J Sports Med.* 1991;19:428–434.

91. Davidson PA, El Attrache NS, Jobe CM, Jobe FW. Rotator cuff and posterior-superior glenoid labrum injury associated with increased glenohumeral motion: A new site of impingement. *J Shoulder Elbow Surg.* 1995;4:384–390.

92. McFarland EG, Hsu CY, Neira C, O'Neil O. Internal impingement of the shoulder: A clinical and arthroscopic analysis. *J Shoulder Elbow Surg.* 1999;8:458–460.

93. Jobe CM. Superior glenoid impingement: Current concepts. *Clin Orthop Relat Res.* 1996;330:98–107.

94. Myers JB, Laudner KG, Pasquale MR, et al. Glenohumeral range of motion deficits and posterior shoulder tightness in throwers with pathologic internal impingement. *Am J Sports Med.* 2006;34:385–391.

95. Magee T. 3-T MRI of the shoulder: is MR arthrography necessary? *Am J Roentgenol.* 2009;192:86–92.

96. Meister K, Thesing J, Montgomery WJ, et al. MR arthrography of partial thickness tears of the undersurface of the rotator cuff: An arthroscopic correlation. *Skeletal Radiol.* 2004;33:136–141.

97. Drakos MC, Rudzki JR, Allen AA, et al. Internal impingement of the shoulder in the overhead athlete. *J Bone Joint Surg Am.* 2009;91:2719–2728.

98. Halbrecht JL, Tirman P, Atkin D. Internal impingement of the shoulder: Comparison of findings between the throwing and nonthrowing shoulders of college baseball players. *Arthroscopy.* 1999;15:253–258.

99. Heyworth BE, Williams RJ. Internal impingement of the shoulder. *Am J Sports Med.* 2009;37:1024–1037.

100. Burkhart SS, Morgan CD, Kibler WB. The disabled throwing shoulder: spectrum of pathology. Part I: pathoanatomy and biomechanics. *Arthroscopy.* 2003;19:404–420.

101. Burkhart SS, Morgan CD, Kibler WB. The disabled throwing shoulder: Spectrum of pathology. Part II: Evaluation and treatment of SLAP lesions in throwers. *Arthroscopy.* 2003;19:531–539.

102. Yoneda M, Nakagawa S, Mizuno N, et al. Arthroscopic capsular release for painful throwing shoulder with posterior capsular tightness. *Arthroscopy.* 2006;22:801–805.

103. Hertel R, Ballmer FT, Lambert SM, Gerber C. Lag signs in the diagnosis of rotator cuff rupture. *J Shoulder Elbow Surg.* 1996;5:307–313.

104. Barth JRH, Burkhart SS, De Beer JF. The bear-hug test: a new and sensitive test for diagnosing a subscapularis tear. *Arthroscopy.* 2006;22:1076–1084.

105. Castoldi F, Blonna D, Hertel R. External rotation lag sign revisited: Accuracy for diagnosis of full thickness supraspinatus tear. *J Shoulder Elbow Surg.* 2009;18:529–534.

106. Walch G, Boulahia A, Calderone S, Robinson AHN. The "dropping" and "hornblower's" signs in evaluation of rotator-cuff tears. *J Bone Joint Surg Br.* 1998;80:624–628.

107. Itoi E, Kuechle DK, Newman SR, et al. Stabilising function of the biceps in stable and unstable shoulders. *J Bone Joint Surg Br.* 1993;75:546–550.

108. Calis M, Akgun K, Birtane M, et al. Diagnostic values of clinical diagnostic tests in subacromial impingement syndrome. *BMJ.* 2000;59:44–47.

109. Post M, Silver R, Singh M. Rotator cuff tear: Diagnosis and treatment. *Clin Orthop Relat Res.* 1983;173:78–91.

110. Ellman H. Diagnosis and treatment of incomplete rotator cuff tears. *Clin Orthop Relat Res.* 1990;254:64–74.

111. Jerosch J, Muller T, Castro WH. The incidence of rotator cuff rupture: An anatomic study. *Acta Orthop Belg.* 1991;57:124–129.

112. Soble MG, Kaye AD, Guay RC. Rotator cuff tear: Clinical experience with sonographic detection. *Radiology.* 1989;173:319–321.

113. Brandt TD, Cardone BW, Grant TH, et al. Rotator cuff sonography: A reassessment. *Radiology.* 1989;173:323–327.

114. Vick CW, Bell SA. Rotator cuff tears: Diagnosis with sonography. *Am J Roentgenol.* 1990;154:121–123.

115. Zlatkin MB, Iannotti JP, Roberts MC, et al. Rotator cuff tears: Diagnostic performance of MR imaging. *Radiology.* 1989;172:223–229.

116. Rafii M, Firooznia H, Sherman O, et al. Rotator cuff lesions: Signal patterns at MR imaging. *Radiology.* 1990;177:817–823.

117. Kjellin I, Ho CP, Cervilla V, et al. Alterations in the supraspinatus tendon at MR imaging: Correlation with histopathologic findings in cadavers. *Radiology.* 1991;181:837–841.

118. Andrews JR, Broussard TS, Carson WG. Arthroscopy of the shoulder in the management of partial tears of the rotator cuff: A preliminary report. *Arthroscopy.* 1985;1:117–122.

119. Sonnery-Cottet B, Edwards TB, Noel E, Walch G. Results of arthroscopic treatment of posterosuperior glenoid impingement in tennis players. *Am J Sports Med.* 2002;30:227–232.

120. Weber SC. Arthroscopic debridement and acromioplasty versus mini-open repair in the treatment of significant partial-thickness rotator cuff tears. *Arthroscopy.* 1999;15:126–131.

121. Mazoue CG, Andrews JR. Repair of full-thickness rotator cuff tears in professional baseball players. *Am J Sports Med.* 2006;34:182–189.

122. Nakagawa S, Yoneda M, Hayashida K, et al. Forced shoulder abduction and elbow flexion test: A new simple clinical test to detect superior labral injury in the throwing shoulder. *Arthroscopy.* 2005;21:1290–1295.

123. Gill HS, El Rassi G, Bahk MS, et al. Physical examination for partial tears of the biceps tendon. *Am J Sports Med.* 2007;35:1334–1340.

124. Favorito PJ, Harding WG, Heidt RS. Complete arthroscopic examination of the long head of the biceps tendon. *Arthroscopy.* 2001;17:430–432.

125. Boileau P, Ahrens PM, Hatzidakis AM. Entrapment of the long head of the biceps tendon: The hourglass biceps—a cause of pain and locking of the shoulder. *J Shoulder Elbow Surg.* 2004;13:249–257.

126. Barber FA, Field LD, Ryu RKN. Biceps tendon and superior labrum injuries: Decision-making. *J Bone Joint Surg Am.* 2007;89:1844–1855.

127. Habermeyer P, Magosch P, Pritsch M, et al. Anterosuperior impingement of the shoulder as a result of pulley lesions: A prospective arthroscopic study. *J Shoulder Elbow Surg.* 2004;13:5–12.

128. Tonino PM, Gerber C, Itoi E, et al. Complex shoulder disorders: Evaluation and treatment. *J Am Acad Orthop Surg.* 2009;17:125–136.

129. Burkhead WZ, Arcand MA, Zeman C, et al. The biceps tendon, in Rockwood CA Jr, Matsen FA III (eds), *The Shoulder,* ed 2. Philadelphia: WB Saunders; 1998:1009–1063.

130. Ardic F, Kahraman Y, Kacar M, et al. Shoulder impingement syndrome: Relationships between clinical, functional, and radiologic findings. *Am J Phys Med Rehabil.* 2006;85:53–60.

131. Lee JC, Guy S, Connell D, et al. MRI of the rotator interval of the shoulder. *Clin Radiol.* 2007;62:416–423.

132. Frost A, Zafar MS, Maffulli N. Tenotomy versus tenodesis in the management of pathologic lesions of the tendon of the long head of the biceps brachii. *Am J Sports Med.* 2009;37:828–833.

133. Ahrens PM, Boileau P. The long head of biceps and associated tendinopathy. *J Bone Joint Surg Br.* 2007;89:1001–1009.

134. O'Donoghue D. Subluxating biceps tendon in the athlete. *Clin Orthop.* 1982;164:26–29.

135. Kim SH, Ha KI, Ahn JH, et al. Biceps load test II: A clinical test for SLAP lesions of the shoulder. *Arthroscopy.* 2001; 17:160–164.

136. Oh JH, Kim JY, Kim WS, et al. The evaluation of various physical examinations for the diagnosis of type II superior labrum anterior and posterior lesion. *Am J Sports Med.* 2008;36:353–359.

137. Liu SH, Henry MH, Nuccion S, et al. Diagnosis of glenoid labral tears. *Am J Sports Med.* 1996;24:149–154.

138. Mimori K, Muneta T, Nakagawa T, Shinomiya K. A new pain provocation test for superior labral tears of the shoulder. *Am J Sports Med.* 1999;27:137–142.

139. Kim SH, Ha KI, Han KY. Biceps load test: A clinical test for superior labrum anterior and posterior lesions in shoulders with recurrent anterior dislocations. *Am J Sports Med.* 1999;27:300–303.

140. Kibler WB, Sciascia AD, Hester P, et al. Clinical utility of traditional and new tests in the diagnosis of biceps tendon injuries and superior labrum anterior and posterior lesions in the shoulder. *J Am Acad Orthop Surg.* 2009;37:1840–1847.

141. Snyder SJ, Karzel RP, Pizzo WD, et al. SLAP lesions of the shoulder. *Arthroscopy.* 1990;6:274–279.

142. Maffet MW, Gartsman GM, Moseley B. Superior labrum–biceps tendon complex lesions of the shoulder. *Am J Sports Med.* 1995;23:93.

143. Powell SE, Nord KD, Ryu RKN. The diagnosis, classification, and treatment of SLAP lesions. *Oper Tech Sports Med.* 2004;12:99–110.

144. Kim TK, Queale WS, Cosgarea AJ, McFarland EG. Clinical features of the different types of SLAP lesions: An analysis of one hundred and thirty-nine cases. *J Bone Joint Surg Am.* 2003;85:66–71.

145. Gobezie R, Zurakowski D, Lavery K, et al. Analysis of interobserver and intraobserver variability in the diagnosis and treatment of SLAP tears using the Snyder classification. *Am J Sports Med.* 2008;36:1373–1379.

146. Cvitanic O, Tirman PF, Feller JF, et al. Using abduction and external rotation of the shoulder to increase the sensitivity of MR arthrography in revealing tears of the anterior glenoid labrum. *Am J Roentgenol.* 1997;169:837–844.

147. Westerheide KJ, Karzel RP. Ganglion cysts of the shoulder: Technique of arthroscopic decompression and fixation of associated type II superior labral anterior to posterior lesions. *Orthop Clin North Am.* 2003;34(4):521–528.

148. Keener JD, Brophy RH. Superior labral tears of the shoulder: Pathogenesis, evaluation, and treatment. *J Am Acad Orthop Surg.* 2009;17:627–637.

149. Reuss BL, Schwartzberg R, Zlatkin MB, et al. Magnetic resonance imaging accuracy for the diagnosis of superior labrum anterior-posterior lesions in the community setting: Eighty-three arthroscopically confirmed cases. *J Shoulder Elbow Surg.* 2006;15:580–585.

150. Andrews JR, Carson WG, Mcleod WD. Glenoid labrum tears related to the long head of the biceps. *Am J Sports Med.* 1985;13:337–341.

151. Levy AS, Kelly BT, Lintner SA, et al. Function of the long head of the biceps at the shoulder: Electromyographic analysis. *J Shoulder Elbow Surg.* 2001;10:250–255.

152. Bey MJ, Elders GJ, Huston LJ, et al. The mechanism of creation of superior labrum, anterior, and posterior lesions in a dynamic biomechanical model of the shoulder: The role of inferior subluxation. *J Shoulder Elbow Surg.* 1998; 7:397–401.

153. Jobe CM, Pink MM, Jobe FW, Shaffer B. Anterior shoulder instability, impingement, and rotator cuff tear: Theories and concepts, in *Operative Techniques in Upper Extremity Sports Injuries.* St. Louis, MO: Mosby; 1996:164–176.

154. Grossman MG, Tibone JE, McGarry MH, et al. A cadaveric model of the throwing shoulder: A possible etiology of superior labrum anterior-to-posterior lesions. *J Bone Joint Surg Am.* 2005;87:824–831.

155. Morgan CD, Burkhart SS, Palmeri M, Gillespie M. Type II SLAP lesions: Three subtypes and their relationships to superior instability and rotator cuff tears. *Arthroscopy.* 1998;14:553–565.

156. Rodosky MW, Harner CD, Fu FH. The role of the long head of the biceps muscle and superior glenoid labrum in anterior stability of the shoulder. *Am J Sports Med.* 1994;22:121–130.

157. Cohen DB, Coleman S, Drakos MC, et al. Outcomes of isolated type II SLAP lesions treated with arthroscopic fixation using a bioabsorbable tack. *Arthroscopy.* 2006; 22:136–142.

158. Reinold MM, Wilk KE, Hooks TR, et al. Thermal-assisted capsular shrinkage of the glenohumeral joint in overhead

athletes: A 15- to 47-month follow-up. *J Orthop Sports Phys Ther.* 2003;33:455–467.

159. Andrews JR, Dugas JR. Diagnosis and treatment of shoulder injuries in the throwing athlete: the role of thermal-assisted capsular shrinkage. *Instr Course Lect.* 2001;50:17–21.

160. Gorantla K, Gill C, Wright RW. The outcome of type II SLAP repair: A systematic review. *Arthroscopy.* 2010;26:537–545.

161. Brockmeier SF, Voos JE, Williams RJ III, et al. Outcomes after arthroscopic repair of type-II SLAP lesions. *J Bone Joint Surg Am.* 2009;91:1595–1603.

162. Ide J, Maeda S, Takagi K. Sports activity after arthroscopic superior labral repair using suture anchors in overhead-throwing athletes. *Am J Sports Med.* 2005;33:507–514.

163. Levy HJ, Schachter AK, Hurd JL, et al. The effect of rotator cuff tears on surgical outcomes after type II superior labrum anterior posterior tears in patients younger than 50 years. *Am J Sports Med.* 2010;38(2):318–322.

164. Yung PSH, Fong DTP, Kong MF, et al. Arthroscopic repair of isolated type II superior labrum anterior–posterior lesion. *Knee Surg Sports Traumatol Arthrosc.* 2008;16:1151–1157.

165. Farber AJ, Castillo R, Clough M, et al. Clinical assessment of three common tests for traumatic anterior shoulder instability. *J Bone Joint Surg Am.* 2006;88:1467–1474.

166. Jia X, Petersen SA, Khosravi AH, et al. Examination of the shoulder: The past, the present, and the future. *J Bone Joint Surg Am.* 2009;91:10–14.

167. Lo IKY, Nonweiler B, Woolfrey M, et al. An evaluation of the apprehension, relocation, and surprise tests for anterior shoulder instability. *Am J Sports Med.* 2004;32:301–307.

168. Speer KP, Hannafin JA, Altchek DW, Warren RF. An evaluation of the shoulder relocation test. *Am J Sports Med.* 1994;22:177–183.

169. Gross ML, Distefano MC. Anterior release test: A new test for occult shoulder instability. *Clin Orthop Relat Res.* 1997;339:105–108.

170. Owens BD, Agel J, Mountcastle SB, et al. Incidence of glenohumeral instability in collegiate athletics. *Am J Sports Med.* 2009;37:1750–1754.

171. Owens BD, DeBerardino TM, Nelson BJ, et al. Long-term follow-up of acute arthroscopic Bankart repair for initial anterior shoulder dislocations in young athletes. *Am J Sports Med.* 2009;37:669–673.

172. Baker CL, Uribe JW, Whitman C. Arthroscopic evaluation of acute initial anterior shoulder dislocations. *Am J Sports Med.* 1990;18:25–28.

173. Taylor DC, Arciero RA. Pathologic changes associated with shoulder dislocations. *Am J Sports Med.* 1997;25:306–311.

174. Sanders TG, Morrison WB, Miller MD. Imaging techniques for the evaluation of glenohumeral instability. *Am J Sports Med.* 2000;28:414–434.

175. Robinson CM, Howes J, Murdoch H, et al. Functional outcome and risk of recurrent instability after primary traumatic anterior shoulder dislocation in young patients. *J Bone Joint Surg Am.* 2006;88:2326–2336.

176. Cox CL, Kuhn JE. Operative versus nonoperative treatment of acute shoulder dislocation in the athlete. *Curr Sports Med Rep.* 2008;7:263–268.

177. Kuhn JE. Treating the initial anterior shoulder dislocation: An evidence-based medicine approach. *Sports Med Arthrosc.* 2006;14:192–198.

178. Miller SL, Cleeman E, Auerbach J, Flatow EL. Comparison of intra-articular lidocaine and intravenous sedation for reduction of shoulder dislocations: A randomized, prospective study. *J Bone Joint Surg Am.* 2002;84:2135–2139.

179. Sayegh FE, Kenanidis EI, Papavasiliou KA, et al. Reduction of acute anterior dislocations: A prospective randomized study comparing a new technique with the Hippocratic and Kocher methods. *J Bone Joint Surg Am.* 2009;91:2775–2782.

180. Kocher E. Eine neue reductions methode fur Schultetverrenkung. *Berliner Klin Wehnschr.* 1870;7:101–105.

181. Uglow MG. Kocher's painless reduction of anterior dislocation of the shoulder: A prospective randomised trial. *Injury.* 1998;29:135–137.

182. Stimson L. An easy method of reducing dislocation of the shoulder and the hip. *NY Mecl Rec.* 1900;57:356–357.

183. Ugras AA, Mahirogullari M, Kural C, et al. Reduction of anterior shoulder dislocations by Spaso technique: Clinical results. *J Emerg Med.* 2008;34:383–387.

184. McCarty EC, Ritchie P, Gill HS, McFarland EG. Shoulder instability: Return to play. *Clin Sports Med.* 2004;23:335–351.

185. Itoi E, Sashi R, Minagawa H, et al. Position of immobilization after dislocation of the glenohumeral joint: A study with use of magnetic resonance imaging. *J Bone Joint Surg Am.* 2001;83:661–667.

186. Itoi E, Hatakeyama Y, Sato T, et al. Immobilization in external rotation after shoulder dislocation reduces the risk of recurrence: A randomized controlled trial. *J Bone Joint Surg Am.* 2007;89:2124–2131.

187. Porcellini G, Campi F, Pegreffi F, et al. Predisposing factors for recurrent shoulder dislocation after arthroscopic treatment. *J Bone Joint Surg Am.* 2009;91:2537–2542.

188. Pulavarti RS, Symes TH, Rangan A. Surgical interventions for anterior shoulder instability in adults. *Cochrane Database of Systematic Reviews (Online).* 2009. DOI: 10.1002/14651858.CD005077.pub2.

189. Owens MAJ, Duffey ML, Nelson LTC, et al. The incidence and characteristics of shoulder instability at the United States Military Academy. *Am J Sports Med.* 2007;35:1168–1173.

190. Schenk TJ, Brems JJ. Multidirectional instability of the shoulder: Pathophysiology, diagnosis, and management. *J Am Acad Orthop Surg.* 1998;6:65–72.

191. Millett PJ, Clavert P, Hatch GF III, Warner JJP. Recurrent posterior shoulder instability. *J Am Acad Orthop Surg.* 2006;14:464–476.

192. Cordasco FA. Understanding multidirectional instability of the shoulder. *J Athl Train.* 2000;35:278–285.

193. Satterwhite YE. Evaluation and management of recurrent anterior shoulder instability. *J Athl Train.* 2000;35:273–277.

194. Walton J, Tzannes AJ, Murrell GAC. The predictive value of clinical tests for shoulder instability. *Trans Orthop Res Soc.* 2001;26:288–294.

195. McFarland EG, Kim TK. *Examination of the Shoulder: The Complete Guide.* New York: Thieme Medical Publishing; 2006.

196. Kim SH, Park JS, Jeong WK, Shin SK. The Kim test. *Am J Sports Med.* 2005;33:1188–1192.

197. Tzannes A, Murrell GAC. Clinical examination of the unstable shoulder. *Sports Medicine.* 2002;32:447–457.

198. Harryman DT II. Common surgical approaches to the shoulder. *Instructional Course Lectures.* 1992;41:3–11.

199. Arciero RA, Wheeler JH, Ryan JB, McBride JT. Arthroscopic Bankart repair versus nonoperative treatment for acute, initial anterior shoulder dislocations. *Am J Sports Med.* 1994;22:589–594.

200. Lenters TR, Franta AK, Wolf FM, et al. Arthroscopic compared with open repairs for recurrent anterior shoulder instability: A systematic review and meta-analysis of the literature. *J Bone Joint Surg Am.* 2007;89:244–254.

201. Gartsman GM, Roddey TS, Hammerman SM. Arthroscopic treatment of anterior-inferior glenohumeral instability: Two to five-year follow-up. *J Bone Joint Surg Am.* 2000;82: 991–1003.

202. Joseph TA, Williams JS, Brems JJ. Laser capsulorrhaphy for multidirectional instability of the shoulder. *Am J Sports Med.* 2003;31:26–35.

203. Robinson CM, Akhtar A, Mitchell M, Beavis C. Complex posterior fracture-dislocation of the shoulder: Epidemiology, injury patterns, and results of operative treatment. *J Bone Joint Surg Am.* 2007;89:1454–1466.

204. Nho SJ, Brophy RH, Barker JU, et al. Management of proximal humeral fractures based on current literature. *J Bone Joint Surg Am.* 2007;89:44–58.

205. Taylor DC, Krasinski KL. Adolescent shoulder injuries: Consensus and controversies. *J Bone Joint Surg Am.* 2009; 91:462–473.

206. Escamilla RF, Barrentine SW, Fleisig GS, et al. Pitching biomechanics as a pitcher approaches muscular fatigue during a simulated baseball game. *Am J Sports Med.* 2007;35:23–33.

207. Fleisig GS, Kingsley DS, Loftice JW, et al. Kinetic comparison among the fastball, curveball, change-up, and slider in collegiate baseball pitchers. *Am J Sports Med.* 2006;34: 423–430.

208. Werner SL, Guido JA. Relationships between throwing mechanics and shoulder distraction in collegiate baseball pitchers. *J Shoulder Elbow Surg.* 2007;16:37–42.

209. Werner SL, Gill TJ, Murray TA, et al. Relationships between throwing mechanics and shoulder distraction in professional baseball pitchers. *Am J Sports Med.* 2001;29: 354–358.

210. Bigliani LU, Codd TP, Connor PM, et al. Shoulder motion and laxity in the professional baseball player. *Am J Sports Med.* 1997;25:609–613.

211. Baltaci G, Johnson R, Kohl H III. Shoulder range of motion characteristics in collegiate baseball players. *J Sports Med Phys Fitness.* 2001;41:236–242.

212. Reagan KM, Meister K, Horodyski MB, et al. Humeral retroversion and its relationship to glenohumeral rotation in the shoulder of college baseball players. *Am J Sports Med.* 2002;30:354–360.

213. Borsa PA, Dover GC, Wilk KE, Reinold MM. Glenohumeral range of motion and stiffness in professional baseball pitchers. *Med Sci Sports Exerc.* 2006;38:21–26.

214. Downar JM, Sauers EL. Clinical measures of shoulder mobility in the professional baseball player. *J Athl Train.* 2005;40:23–29.

215. Meister K, Day T, Horodyski M, et al. Rotational motion changes in the glenohumeral joint of the adolescent/Little League baseball player. *Am J Sports Med.* 2005;33:693–698.

216. Burkhart SS, Morgan CD, Kibler WB. Shoulder injuries in overhead athletes: The "dead arm" revisited. *Clin Sports Med.* 2000;19:125–158.

217. Levine WN, Brandon ML, Stein BS, et al. Shoulder adaptive changes in youth baseball players. *J Shoulder Elbow Surg.* 2006;15:562–566.

218. Ruotolo C, Price E, Panchal A. Loss of total arc of motion in collegiate baseball players. *J Shoulder Elbow Surg.* 2006;15:67–71.

219. Fleisig GS, Andrews JR, Dillman CJ, Escamilla RF. Kinetics of baseball pitching with implications about injury mechanisms. *Am J Sports Med.* 1995;23:233–239.

220. Whiteley R. Baseball throwing mechanics as they relate to pathology and performance. *J Sports Sci Med.* 2007;6: 1–20.

221. Burkhart SS, Morgan CD. The peel-back mechanism: Its role in producing and extending posterior type II SLAP lesions and its effect on SLAP repair rehabilitation. *Arthroscopy.* 1998;14:637–640.

222. Norkin CC, White DJ. *Measurement of Joint Motion: A Guide to Goniometry.* Philadelphia: FA Davis Company; 2003.

223. Awan R, Smith J, Boon AJ. Measuring shoulder internal rotation range of motion: A comparison of 3 techniques. *Arch Phys Med Rehabil.* 2002;83:1229–1234.

224. Dwelly PM, Tripp BL, Tripp PA, et al. Glenohumeral rotational range of motion in collegiate overhead-throwing athletes during an athletic season. *J Athl Train.* 2009;44: 611–616.

225. Reinold MM, Wilk KE, Macrina LC, et al. Changes in shoulder and elbow passive range of motion after pitching in professional baseball players. *Am J Sports Med.* 2008;36: 523–527.

9

CHAPTER 10

Elbow Injuries

Lauren J. Stephenson, MA, AT
Jason Reed, DO

Distal Biceps Tendon Rupture

CLINICAL PRESENTATION

History

Acute pain in the antecubital fossa occurs while lifting a heavy object. A "pop" may be reported.

Observation

Marked deformity in the antecubital fossa.
Biceps brachii retracted proximally.
Elbow and forearm ecchymosis.
Increased biceps crease interval (BCI) or biceps crease ratio (BCR).

Functional Status

Marked pain and weakness during elbow flexion and forearm supination.

Physical Examination Findings

Decreased range of motion (ROM), especially during elbow extension, which stretches the unattached tendon.
Palpable biceps tendon defect; the tendon may be absent from the antecubital fossa.
Resisted elbow flexion is weak or absent.
Resisted forearm supination is weak or absent.
Positive biceps squeeze test.
Positive hook test.

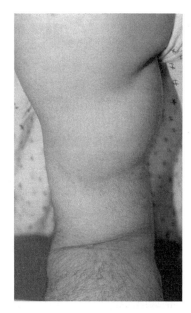

Figure 10.1 Proximal retraction of the biceps muscle belly with attempted elbow flexion.

Complete rupture of the distal biceps brachii tendon accounts for approximately 3% of all biceps injuries. Usually involving the dominant arm, rupture occurs when the patient lifts a heavy object causing a sudden eccentric extension load opposing the contracting biceps while the elbow is in flexion.[1] Although most tendon ruptures occur instrasubstance or at the musculotendinous junction, a complete distal biceps tendon rupture most often occurs at this tendon's insertion into the radial tuberosity.[2] Current theories that support this pathogenesis focus on decreased distal vascularity and impingement of the distal tendon between the radius and ulna during pronation.[3] Most patients are males in their 40s and 50s, and although many injuries are work related, sport-related injuries also occur in activities such as weight lifting.

The patient usually reports sudden pain and weakness while lifting a heavy object. Antecubital fossa palpation reveals a loss of tendon continuity (see **Figure 10.1**). Weakness is demonstrated with elbow flexion and supination. Partial ruptures can be difficult to diagnose based on physical findings alone, and a long delay between injury and examination may make the diagnosis less clear. For these reasons, magnetic resonance imaging (MRI) has become the gold standard in distinguishing between partial and complete ruptures and referral for surgical intervention.

Delays between initial injury and diagnosis can result in muscle retraction, distal tendon shortening, and adhesion formation, which make surgical reinsertion of the original tendon impossible.[1] The use of BCI and BCR as clinical assessment tools can facilitate immediate referral for surgical intervention, thereby increasing the likelihood of a positive outcome. Most surgeons recommend early reattachment of complete distal biceps tendon ruptures. The goal is stable reattachment to allow for early rehabilitation.

Differential Diagnosis
Biceps brachii strain.

Imaging Techniques
The standard elbow radiographic series—anteroposterior (AP), lateral, and oblique—reveals tuberosity avulsion. MRI or ultrasonography can identify a partial rupture or, if the diagnosis is delayed, a ruptured and retracted biceps (see **Figure 10.2**).

Definitive Diagnosis
The definitive diagnosis is based on the clinical findings and supported by MRI findings. A BCI greater than 6.0 cm or a BCR greater than 1.2 cm indicates the need for surgical consultation.

Pathomechanics and Functional Limitations
Pain and loss of mechanical function of the biceps brachii cause difficulty with elbow motion extremes.

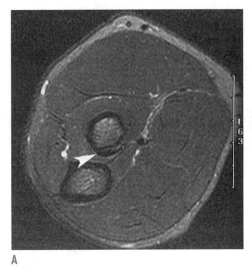 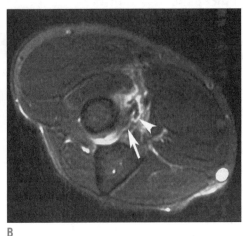

Figure 10.2 MRI of a biceps tendon rupture. **(A)** Normal biceps tendon insertion (arrowhead). **(B)** Partial rupture at the insertion (arrowhead) with degeneration of the distal biceps insertion (arrow).

Resisted elbow flexion with the forearm in neutral results in discomfort, but resisted elbow flexion with the forearm supinated produces frank pain and accentuates deformity.

Pain with active elbow motion may decrease after a few days, but pain and weakness persist with resisted and weight-loaded flexion and supination. Manual laborers, weightlifters, and other individuals who experience distal biceps tendon ruptures have difficulty returning to their previous activities without surgical intervention.

Immediate Management

Immobilize the elbow in flexion and apply ice to decrease local inflammation and muscle spasm.

Medications

Narcotic analgesics may be prescribed for acute pain management. Nonsteroidal anti-inflammatory drugs (NSAIDs) should be avoided with ruptures because of possible platelet dysfunction and the urgent need for tendon repair.

Postinjury Management

Early diagnosis allows for repair to occur within 3 weeks of the injury and produces the best surgical results. The patient is placed in a posterior splint or a hinged ROM brace for comfort, and **palliative** care is provided until surgical repair is performed. Patients with partial ruptures or medical contraindications to surgery should start on a rehabilitation program as soon as swelling decreases.

heterotopic The formation of lamellar bone within soft tissues as the result of osteoblastic activity, similar to myositis ossificans.

palliative Relief of the symptoms without correcting the underlying cause.

Surgical Intervention

Most patients benefit from surgical reattachment of the distal biceps tendon to the radial tuberosity (see **ST** 10.1). The most commonly performed surgical procedures for this purpose are the two-incision technique and a one-incision technique through an anterior approach.[4-6] The two-incision technique is less likely to result in radial nerve injury but is associated with an increased incidence of **heterotopic** bone formation. This risk can be minimized by copious irrigation of the surgical sites and by using a drill and osteotome instead of a burr to excavate the radial tuberosity.

Although the one-incision technique is more likely to cause radial nerve injury from overzealous traction, the incidence of heterotopic bone formation is lower with this approach. Using a single anterior incision to reach the radial tubercle is technically more demanding because of radial nerve proximity. In recent years, advances in the suture anchors used for tendon fixation have limited the need for extensive dissection to expose the cubital fossa.[7,8] An Achilles tendon allograft may be required to repair a chronic distal biceps tendon rupture.[9]

Postoperative Management

After surgical repair, the elbow is splinted in 90° of flexion with the forearm supinated or in neutral position for 7 to 10 days.[10] The sutures are then removed and the patient placed in a hinged flexion-assist splint with a 30° extension block for another 7 weeks. Passive and active-assisted range-of-motion

S|T Surgical Technique 10.1

Repair of a Distal Biceps Tendon Rupture

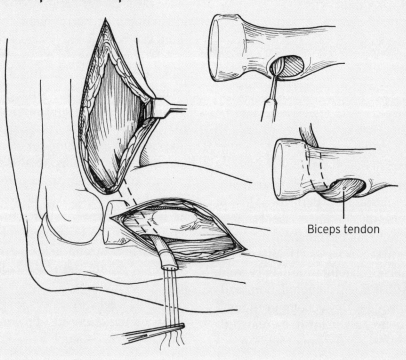

Biceps tendon

Indications

Acute rupture of the distal biceps tendon.

Procedure Overview

Two-Incision Technique

1. A transverse incision is made along the anterior cubital crease.
2. The distal end of the biceps tendon is located.
3. Sutures are placed through the tendon.
4. A second incision is made along the ulnar border of the dorsal forearm to expose the radial tuberosity, where sutures will be secured.
5. A trough with suture tunnels is made in the radial tuberosity.
6. Sutures are passed through the bone tunnels, the tendon is pulled down into the trough, and the sutures are tied, fixating the tendon.
7. The repair is tested in gentle pronation, supination, flexion, and extension.
8. The elbow is placed in a posterior splint in flexion.

One-Incision Technique

1. An anterior incision is made along the cubital crease.
2. The distal end of the biceps tendon is located.
3. Sutures are placed through the tendon.
4. With the forearm supinated, the radial tuberosity is identified in the depth of the anterior cubital exposure.
5. Using two or three suture anchors, the tendon is reattached to the radial tuberosity.
6. The repair is tested in gentle pronation, supination, flexion, and extension.
7. The elbow is placed in a posterior splint in flexion.

Functional Limitations

Radial nerve complications can occur with either procedure but are more frequently observed with the one-incision technique. Early protected ROM is important to attaining good functional outcomes. Long-term strength deficits may occur in elbow flexion and supination but usually are not functionally limiting. Soft-tissue healing of the tendon to a bony bed requires avoiding traction (elbow extension) on the repair in the early postoperative period.

Implications for Rehabilitation

Protected return of motion and strength is necessary to ensure healing of the repair. Initially, the patient's arm is splinted or casted in a neutral forearm position with 90° of elbow flexion.

Source: Figure adapted from the Mayo Clinic.

exercises are progressed with the intent of achieving full extension by 6 weeks postoperatively.[10]

■ Injury-Specific Treatment and Rehabilitation Concerns

> **Specific Concerns**
>
> Protect the healing repair.
> Prevent excessive stress on the biceps brachii tendon based on the healing stage.
> Encourage early ROM to decrease scar tissue formation and prevent functional shortening.

Conservative treatment of distal biceps tendon ruptures can result in considerable permanent loss of strength and endurance of elbow flexion and supination; thus it is typically not recommended.[11]

With advances in secure surgical fixation techniques, postoperative rehabilitation has become more aggressive with this patient population, leading to better outcomes with fewer complications.[12] Some repair techniques allow for immediate initiation of passive ROM exercises in pronation and supination as well as active ROM in activities of daily living as tolerated. Nevertheless, most rehabilitation protocols suggest immobilization for 2 to 3 weeks, followed by controlled passive ROM.[13]

As part of a program that is complementary to the commonly used protocols, ROM is performed within the passive limits so the patient feels no tension at the repair site. The brace is then set to allow this motion. The brace ROM is incrementally advanced as the patient gains motion and healing progresses. The patient can discontinue brace use when full ROM is achieved, albeit no sooner than 8 weeks after surgery so as to protect the repair from reinjury.

Initially, self-ranging (to tolerance) exercises of active extension and passive flexion are performed with the arm supported on a table. Passive pronation and supination are conducted with the elbow in 90° of flexion. The brace is worn while performing the exercises for the first 2 weeks. Properly educating the patient in maintaining motion within pain-free limits is essential, and self-ranging exercises are continued until 6 weeks after surgery. If the patient has not achieved full ROM, passive ROM exercises are instituted. If a contracture appears to be developing, motion is lost, or a plateau lasts longer than a week, passive ROM work may begin sooner.

Moist heat or a warm whirlpool bath may be helpful before ROM exercises to promote relaxation and increase tissue extensibility. Scar massage and mobilization are helpful to minimize excessive scar formation in the cubital crease. Use of an upper body ergometer to actively warm the joint can be initiated 8 weeks after surgery.

Strengthening exercises commence at 4 weeks postoperatively. Initially, they consist of submaximal isometric activities for elbow extension, flexion, pronation, and supination. Shoulder and wrist isotonic exercises are performed by attaching cuff weights around the wrist during the shoulder exercises. Submaximal isotonic exercises to strengthen the elbow musculature may begin 6 weeks after surgery. At 8 weeks, tissue healing to bone is generally sufficient to allow strengthening to progress to patient tolerance. The eccentric phase of strengthening is emphasized at this phase of rehabilitation, to address the original mechanism of injury.

At 12 weeks after surgery, functional activities focus on patient needs. Proprioceptive and plyometric exercises, such as tossing a ball against a backstop or tossing a medicine ball to develop power; occupational activities; and sport-specific drills can be initiated.

■ Estimated Amount of Time Lost

Return to full activities can be achieved after 4 to 6 months of postoperative rehabilitation. Secure tendon fixation to the radial tuberosity allows early rehabilitation. Patients with partial ruptures may return to full activities after 4 to 6 weeks of rehabilitation.

The elbow is prone to stiffness from scar formation within the cubital fossa. In addition, heterotopic ossification has been reported with distal biceps repair. Early recognition and treatment of these conditions should limit their effects on outcomes and return to activity, but any increased joint stiffness postoperatively increases the amount of time lost from competition. Delayed surgical repair also delays the return to play.

■ Return-to-Play Criteria

The patient must have ROM and strength within functional limits to return to activity. Full restoration of ROM and strength is possible after surgical repair. Typically the dominant arm is injured, which must be considered when comparing progress with the contralateral extremity.

Ulnar Collateral Ligament Injury

CLINICAL PRESENTATION

History

Pain is noted during activities that apply a valgus load to the elbow (e.g., throwing).

Chronic instability can occur with repetitive, long-term valgus loading of the elbow.

The patient is often unable to continue with the activity.

A past history of elbow pain may be reported.

Radicular symptoms along the ulnar nerve distribution may be reported.

Observation

Medial elbow swelling may be noted.

Functional Status

ROM is usually full.

Athletes report pain during throwing and decreased throwing velocity and distance.

Physical Examination Findings

Pain during UCL palpation posterior to the medial epicondyle.

Positive valgus stress test with the elbow flexed to 30° and 90°.

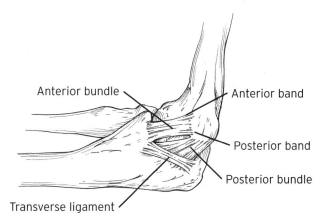

Figure 10.3 The UCL complex consists of the anterior bundle (functionally the most important for valgus stability), the posterior bundle, and the transverse ligament (oblique bundle). The anterior bundle is further subdivided into anterior and posterior bands, which perform reciprocal functions. *Source:* Adapted from Kvitne RS, Jobe FW. Ligamentous and posterior compartment injuries, in Jobe FW (ed), *Techniques in Upper Extremity Sports Injuries.* Philadelphia, PA: Mosby/Year Book; 1996:412.

Injury to the ulnar collateral ligament (UCL) is most commonly encountered in athletes who participate in throwing and overhead sports. Such injuries result from tremendous valgus stress at the elbow during the throwing motion, especially the late cocking and early acceleration phases.

The restraining contribution of bony and soft tissues in valgus stress depends on the elbow position.[14–16] The articulating surfaces, joint capsule, and UCL complex provide almost equal amounts of restraint against valgus stress in elbow extension. The UCL complex has three parts—the anterior and posterior oblique bundles and the transverse ligament (see Figure 10.3). As the joint flexes, the UCL complex assumes more responsibility for the restraining role. The anterior oblique bundle provides almost all of the UCL complex's contribution in restraining valgus stress from full extension through flexion, with the posterior oblique bundle adding support when the elbow exceeds 90° of flexion.[14–17]

Medial elbow biomechanics often are described relative to the pitching motion. Peak angular velocities and valgus stress are greatest during the late cocking and early acceleration phases. These forces can exceed the tensile strength of the medial ligamentous and tendinous structures, at which point the force must be absorbed by the other medial el-

bow structures. The stresses are initially transmitted to the flexor pronator musculature (especially the pronator teres) and then to the deeper UCL. The elbow reaches its most unstable point at approximately 70° of flexion.[18] When the ligamentous and musculature tensile strength is exceeded, injury occurs. With continued repetitive valgus stress, ligament attenuation or frank rupture can occur. Improper mechanics, poor flexibility, and inadequate conditioning can all worsen symptoms and lead to frank ligament rupture. Valgus stress also causes compressive forces on the lateral elbow.

Differential Diagnosis

Medial elbow tendinopathy, ulnar neuropathy, cervical radiculopathy.

Imaging Techniques

Radiographs will reveal any traction osteophytes or avulsion fractures. Stress radiographs can reveal the amount of valgus laxity (see Figure 10.4). MRI is an excellent choice for UCL imaging.

Definitive Diagnosis

The definitive diagnosis is based on the clinical findings and diagnostic imaging results, including radiographs, dynamic ultrasound, and MRI studies.

Pathomechanics and Functional Limitations

Patients with UCL injuries are unable to continue with activities that place a valgus stress on the elbow, such as throwing or swinging a golf club. Many lose significant velocity or distance, and the golf swing is affected by the valgus stress placed on the dominant extremity (i.e., the right arm for right-handed

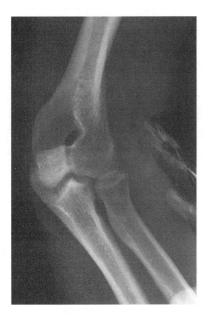

Figure 10.4 Stress radiograph demonstrating UCL deficiency during the application of a valgus load.

golfers). Patients usually do not have difficulty with any other activities.

Immediate Management

In acute ruptures, ice is applied, and the extremity is splinted or placed in a sling as needed for comfort.

Medications

Nonsteroidal anti-inflammatory drugs (NSAIDs) may be prescribed to control pain and inflammation.

Postinjury Management

Postinjury management consists of rest, NSAIDs, and early rehabilitation aimed at helping the patient regain full motion and strength that are lost as a result of inflammatory response in the first 2 to 4 weeks after the initial injury. Any ulnar nerve symptoms that may present must be documented. Once the patient has full ROM and strength, a well-supervised throwing program is initiated. As many as 50% of patients may be able to return to their previous level of activity with nonsurgical management.

Surgical Intervention

Individuals who fail to regain function through a well-supervised exercise program, who do not or cannot modify their activities, who have a complete UCL tear, or who want to return to throwing at a high level are prime candidates for surgical correction.[19,20]

Several different techniques are available for surgical repair or reconstruction, but the results of repair have been inferior to those of reconstruction. Typically, the patient does not present during the acute stage of injury, making repair of the UCL damage more difficult. The ligament is reconstructed using the palmaris longus tendon, if present; alternatively, the plantaris or Achilles tendon may be used for this purpose.[21,22]

The most popular surgical procedure—the Jobe technique—is commonly referred to as "Tommy John surgery," after the major-league baseball pitcher who returned to high-level pitching after this repair. This technique has since undergone several adaptations (see 🅢🅣 10.2).[20,22]

Postoperative Management

A brief period (3 to 7 days) of postoperative immobilization is followed by early rehabilitation. The patient is typically immobilized in a posterior splint and then placed in a hinged ROM brace, which allows immediate wrist and hand movement, including active wrist and hand ROM and squeezing a sponge ball. In weeks 2 to 4 following surgery, motion is limited to 30° of extension and 100° of flexion, which is progressed to 15° of extension and 110° of flexion in the fifth week. At 12 weeks postoperatively, an advanced rehabilitation program is initated.[23] Valgus stress is avoided for 4 months after surgery, at which point a throwing program may begin.

Injury-Specific Treatment and Rehabilitation Concerns

Specific Concerns

Protect the healing graft from valgus stress.
Maintain grip strength.
Allow flexion-extension ROM as tolerated to reduce the formation of scar tissue and other adhesions.

Conservative Management

In most cases of UCL injury and especially in the absence of an acute injury, the patient should pursue a 3- to 6-month course of conservative treatment, especially rest from aggravating activities. If needed, a hinged ROM brace is applied to limit the patient to pain-free ROM. The brace's ROM limits can be increased as symptoms abate.

Conservative management focuses on a well-rounded rehabilitation program including all aspects of the kinetic chain. Posterior shoulder capsule tightness must be addressed. Over time, a tight capsule will limit internal rotation and lead to a

Jobe Technique for UCL Reconstruction ("Tommy John Surgery")

A

B   Frontal View   Medial View — Ulnar nerve

Ulnar nerve

C

D

Indications

Surgical intervention is indicated for those patients who have failed to improve on a proper course of conservative treatment, who cannot or do not wish to modify their activities, who have a complete tear, or who wish to return to throwing at a high level.

Procedure Overview

1. A 10-cm incision is made over the medial epicondyle.
2. The flexor-pronator muscle group is split to provide access to the underlying tissues, and the anterior portion is released from the medial epicondyle (**A**). The ulnar nerve is not exposed unless it is symptomatic.
3. The attachment sites of the UCL are identified.
4. The isometric point of the ligaments is identified, and three tunnels are drilled to form a "lazy Y" in the medial epicondyle (**B**).
5. Anterior and posterior holes are drilled into the proximal ulna near the coronoid tubercle (**C**).
6. A graft approximately 15 cm long is harvested from the contralateral palmaris longus, plantaris, or Achilles tendon (see the "Comments" section).
7. The graft is weaved into a figure-of-eight and then reattached to itself; the graft is tensioned with the elbow flexed to 45° (**D**).
8. Ulnar or medial antebrachial cutaneous nerve transposition is performed only if electromyographic and nerve conduction tests are positive.

Functional Limitations

Postoperative flexion contractures are possible.

Implications for Rehabilitation

Approximately 70% to 85% of athletes who undergo UCL reconstruction can return to their previous level of activity and velocity.

Potential Complications

Ulnar nerve injury is possible with this surgery.

Comments

Results of reconstruction are superior to those achieved with primary repair. If ulnar nerve symptoms exist preoperatively, then a transposition should be performed. Multiple techniques are documented in the literature. Typically the surgeon subcutaneously transposes the nerve anteriorly; the nerve is then held in place by flaps created with the flexor pronator fascia.

Source: Figures reproduced with permission from Chen FS, Rokito AS, Jobe FW. Medial elbow problems in the overhead-throwing athlete. *J Am Acad Orthop Surg.* 2001;9:99-113.

compensatory increase in external rotation, which increases stress along the medial elbow while throwing. All throwers with medial elbow pain should perform stretching exercises for the posterior capsule and musculotendinous tissues. The "sleeper stretch" isolates these tissues (see Chapter 12).

A complete strengthening program is instituted, including leg and pelvic exercises emphasizing gluteal muscles; trunk strengthening emphasizing rotational activity; scapulothoracic control exercises; and exercises targeting rotator cuff function, elbow flexion and extension, pronation and supination, and wrist strengthening.[19,24,25] This program decreases valgus elbow stress. Increased trunk kinetic energy alleviates the need to compensate at the extremity and place valgus stress on the elbow.

Strengthening begins with isolated isometric exercises for the elbow, wrist, and hand to decrease muscle atrophy. Strengthening using isotonics, proprioceptive neuromuscular facilitation (PNF) exercises, and functional activities develops coordinated synergistic activity.

Activities to attain functional dynamic stabilization include PNF, rhythmic stabilization, and plyometrics. Functional stabilization exercises begin with nonprovocative positions, such as two-handed activities with the elbow close to the body. Increasingly provocative positioning with the shoulder and elbow in more functional positions mimicking throwing is incorporated as tolerated.

Most athletes with UCL injuries are throwers, and many different throwing programs exist.[25] Typical progressions initially incorporate an interval program in the which patient throws from flat surfaces, building on the distance, intensity, and number of pitches. As the patient progresses, throwing from a mound is started, and the focus is on a return to normal activity. Advancement during the interval throwing program is highly individualized. The patient must successfully complete the present level and be symptom free before advancing to the next program level. If the patient experiences an increase in symptoms when progressing through program levels, the patient should return to the previously completed level.

Postoperative Rehabilitation

During postoperative rehabilitation, symptoms related to ulnar nerve function should be carefully evaluated and documented. Deteriorating symptoms are cause for concern and warrant referral back to the physician.

After surgery, the patient is guided through a very specific rehabilitation routine. When the hinged ROM brace is applied, motion is set from 30° to 100°. The brace stops are moved to 15° and 110° at week 5, and progress by 5° into extension and 10° into flexion every week after that. This protocol may vary slightly from surgeon to surgeon, but in general, movement into the extremes of motion is a progression with the goal of brace removal by week 6.[26]

Initially, the patient performs pain-free wrist and elbow isometrics and shoulder isometrics, except for external rotation. At week 4, light isotonic exercises for the shoulder, wrist, and elbow begin. Shoulder external rotation is not started until at least 6 weeks after surgery. The patient initially avoids full external rotation but can progress to that point at 8 weeks postoperatively. Exercise resistance steadily advances after week 8, when functional strengthening exercises begin.

As with the conservative treatment of UCL injuries, functional strengthening incorporates a program for the legs, trunk, shoulder girdle, and upper extremity to maximize proper mechanics and alleviate compensatory stress at the medial elbow. Exercises in the form of PNF techniques, isotonics, or resistance tubing are applied in functional activities and incorporated into sport-specific activities. The rehabilitation program emphasizes concentric function of the flexor-pronator group and eccentric function of the scapular stabilizers, posterior rotator cuff, and elbow flexors. Dynamic stabilization exercises using rhythmic stabilization in multiple angles, medicine ball tosses, and Plyoball tosses are incorporated. Initially, the patient should protect the elbow from valgus stress by keeping the arm close to the trunk. Potentially provocative drills with the shoulder in abduction and external rotation are started 3 to 4 months after surgery, before the throwing program begins.

■ Estimated Amount of Time Lost

A period of 3 to 6 weeks is required for recovery from a partial UCL tear. If ligament reconstruction is required, rehabilitation takes 9 to 12 months.[19,27]

■ Return-to-Play Criteria

A throwing program may begin when the patient has achieved full motion and full shoulder and elbow strength, usually 4 to 6 months after surgery. Return to full activity can occur when ROM, strength, and mechanics throughout the trunk and upper extremity are normal and the elbow is symptom free.

Functional Bracing

No brace is used after UCL injury in a thrower. Wrestlers or football players who have sustained an acute injury may use a hinged functional brace.

Posterolateral Rotatory Instability

CLINICAL PRESENTATION

History

Possible prior elbow dislocation may be reported.
A "clunk," giving way, or catching as the elbow moves from extension to flexion or, less commonly, from flexion to extension is described.
Pain may be noted arising from the posterolateral elbow.

Observation

No swelling or deformity.

Functional Status

Apprehension with terminal elbow extension.

Physical Examination Findings

ROM within normal limits.
Positive pivot-shift test.
Positive PLRI test.
Inability to perform a push-up with internal rotation.
Pain or apprehension when performing a lift-off test from a chair.
Negative varus stress test.

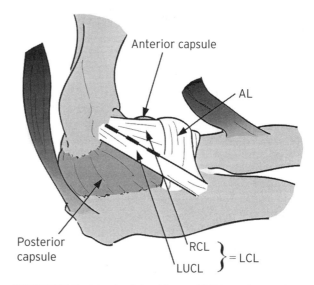

Figure 10.5 The lateral collateral ligament (LCL) complex consists of the radial collateral ligament (RCL), lateral ulnar collateral ligament (LUCL), and annular ligament (AL). The LCL consists of the radial collateral ligament and the LUCL. The dashed line indicates the dividing line used to distinguish the RCL from the LUCL. *Source:* Reproduced with permission from Dunning CE, Zarzour ZDS, Patterson SD, et al. Ligamentous stabilizers against posterolateral rotatory instability of the elbow. *J Bone Joint Surg Am.* 2001;83:1823-1828.

Posterolateral rotatory instability (PLRI)—a deficiency of the lateral ligament complex that produces a subtle instability pattern—is most often the result of a prior acute elbow dislocation.[28] It may also be a result of an unintended consequence after soft-tissue release for lateral elbow tendinopathy,[28] when the lateral ligament complex and a portion of the annular ligament are cut during the procedure (see **Figure 10.5**).[29] PLRI is characterized by a rotatory subluxation of the ulna from the humeral trochlea with concurrent posterolateral dislocation of the radial head from the capitellum.

Clinical findings may be subtle. Patients with PLRI most commonly report a catching sensation as the elbow moves from full extension to flexion, and possibly from flexion to full extension.[22] Occasionally patients may be unable to achieve terminal extension, or may become apprehensive when approaching terminal extension.[30] Pain at the lateral and posterolateral aspects of the elbow during activity may be the primary complaint, because the symptoms associated with instability are masked by pain.

Differential Diagnosis

Radial collateral ligament sprain, synovitis, lateral elbow tendinopathy, osteochondral defect, arthritis.

Imaging Techniques

A standard elbow series (AP, lateral, and oblique radiographs) should be obtained to rule out bony injuries. MRI may demonstrate an attenuated or torn lateral UCL, and a stress radiograph may reveal lateral collateral ligament laxity (see **Figure 10.6**).

Definitive Diagnosis

The definitive diagnosis of PLRI is often based on a positive pivot-shift or PLRI test.

Pathomechanics and Functional Limitations

Patients usually have limitations due to pain from the chronic instability. As the elbow moves from extension to flexion, instability occurs, and the

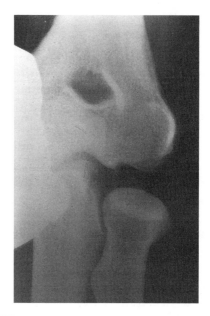

Figure 10.6 Lateral ulnar collateral ligament insufficiency demonstrated with varus stress.

patient is unable to generate forces through the joint distally to the hand.

▨ Medications

Although NSAIDs are often suggested, they do not help the instability symptoms associated with PLRI. If synovitis is present, however, these drugs may decrease the inflammatory response.

▨ Surgical Intervention

Lateral UCL reconstruction—the treatment of choice—is performed to stabilize the elbow (see (ST) 10.3).[22,31] Because of the rotational nature of this injury, most individuals and certainly throwing athletes do not respond favorably to conservative management.

▨ Postoperative Management

The limb is immobilized in 90° of flexion with forearm pronation for 2 weeks, and then a hinged elbow ROM brace is used for an additional 4 to 6 weeks.[30] To decrease stress on the lateral ligaments, the brace holds the forearm in a pronated position. Motion in the brace is set initially to a 60° extension block and is progressed at 2-week intervals to 45° and then to 30°.[30] The brace is removed and extension past 30° is initiated after 6 weeks. The elbow is protected against supination, extension, and varus forces for 4 to 6 months, with full return to activity occurring approximately 9 months after surgery.[16,30]

▨ Injury-Specific Treatment and Rehabilitation Concerns

> **Specific Concerns**
> Avoid stress on the lateral ligaments.
> Encourage gentle, passive ROM between full and 30° of flexion as soon as possible.

Active and active-assisted ROM from full to 30° of flexion is permitted. After 6 weeks, motion into extension can be progressed. Passive ROM is performed into extension only when necessary to address adhesions and scar tissue formation.

Pain-free isometrics for the shoulder, elbow, and wrist muscles are started during the second week. To decrease elbow stress, the resistance is placed proximal to the elbow for shoulder exercises, and wrist and elbow exercises are performed with the forearm pronated. At week 4 after surgery, light isotonic exercises can be steadily progressed.

At 8 weeks, more functional exercises are initiated. Exercises involving rhythmic stabilization, Plyoballs, and tubing at multiple angles are recommended to attain dynamic stabilization. The joint should be protected from varus stress, and progression to more provocative drills is necessary. Early in the functional exercises, the patient performs drills with elbow flexion past 30°. At 6 months postoperatively, the patient may perform all tolerated activities but should avoid varus stress until 9 to 12 months, when all restrictions are lifted.

▨ Estimated Amount of Time Lost

After surgery, 9 to 12 months of rehabilitation is required.

▨ Return-to-Play Criteria

Full, pain-free ROM without any sensation of instability as well as normal strength and function of the trunk, shoulder, elbow, and wrist musculature are required before return to sport is permitted.

Valgus Extension Overload

CLINICAL PRESENTATION

History
Repetitive hyperextension or valgus stress to the elbow is noted.
Pain increases during the acceleration and deceleration phases of throwing or similar activities.
Pain is experienced posteriorly near terminal extension.
Acute symptom onset can frequently be linked to a specific point in time.
The patient may complain of locking or catching.
Chronic UCL injuries have an insidious onset but may progress to frank rupture.

Observation
Medial elbow swelling.

Functional Status
Throwing activities, particularly ball release, are limited by pain and instability.
Osteophyte formation may limit full extension.

Physical Examination Findings
UCL point tenderness.
Pain with valgus testing of the elbow while the forearm is pronated.
Positive valgus extension overload (VEO) test: valgus-testing the elbow while forcefully extending it from 30° of flexion to full extension.

Valgus extension overload syndrome includes a series of symptoms and findings that result from medial elbow laxity with repetitive hyperextension. Notably, the patient has a history of throwing or

Reconstruction of the Lateral UCL

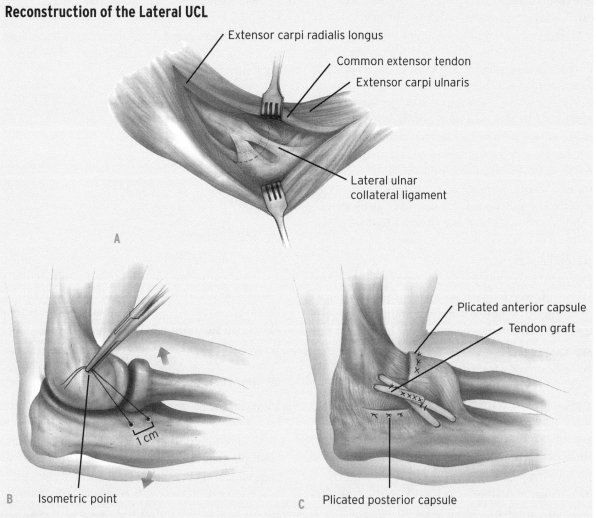

A

Extensor carpi radialis longus

Common extensor tendon

Extensor carpi ulnaris

Lateral ulnar collateral ligament

B   Isometric point

1 cm

Plicated anterior capsule

Tendon graft

C   Plicated posterior capsule

Indications

Demonstrated PLRI by positive pivot-shift test or MRI demonstrating a ruptured lateral UCL.

Procedure Overview

1. A lateral incision is made through the Kocher interval between the anconeus and extensor carpi ulnaris muscle. A subperiosteal reflection of the anconeus muscle distally and exposure of the lateral epicondyle proximally expose the lateral ligament complex (**A**).
2. Two bone tunnels are drilled in the ulna at the lateral UCL insertion site and at the point of isometry of the ligament origin on the lateral column of the humerus. A suture marks the isometric point (**B**).
3. A palmaris longus or other tendon graft is harvested.
4. The graft is passed through the bone tunnels in a figure-of-eight manner (**C**).
5. The graft is sutured to itself in approximately 30° of flexion and pronation.
6. The elbow is immobilized in flexion and pronation.

Functional Limitations

Flexion contractures may be or become permanent.

Implications for Rehabilitation

Extension is limited for 6 weeks. Gentle advancement of ROM and progressive resistance exercise is then instituted.

Potential Complications

Elbow flexion contractures can result from the surgery and may already be present in a throwing athlete. Repair failure can occur with early return to activities or continued prolonged lateral trauma.

Comments

This procedure is approximately 90% effective in restoring stability when no other injuries to the elbow are present.[31]

Source: Figures reproduced with permission from Morrey BF. Acute and chronic instability of the elbow. *J Am Acad Orthop Surg.* 1996;4:117-128.

10

some other activity requiring forceful hyperextension. A wide spectrum of valgus extension injuries may affect the elbow, including muscle inflammation, UCL microtears, frank UCL rupture, and bony changes such as osteophytes, chondromalacia, and osteochondritis.[32] Over time, the repetitive valgus load leads to impingement of the posteromedial olecranon. As the condition progresses, osteophytes and subsequent loose bodies may form.

Chronic valgus overload results in medial elbow pain due to olecranon osteophyte formation. Lateral pain can result from lateral compression injury to the radial head and capitellum, including osteochondral lesions. Over time, the patient loses the ability to effectively perform athletic activities.

Differential Diagnosis

Olecranon osteophyte, olecranon stress fracture, radiocapitellar arthritic changes, osteochondral defect, medial elbow instability, ulnar nerve subluxation/entrapment.

Imaging Techniques

A full elbow series including AP, lateral, and oblique views should be obtained. Radiographs may reveal a posteromedial osteophyte extending off the medial trochlea (see **Figure 10.7**). MRI (with gradient echo sequence) should be performed in patients with acute UCL injuries.

Definitive Diagnosis

The definitive diagnosis is based on the findings of the physical examination and radiographic studies. MRI (with gradient echo sequence) is an excellent choice for revealing acute UCL injury.

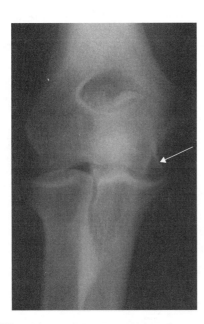

Figure 10.7 Large traction spur on the medial aspect of the ulnar notch. Note the osteophyte formation on the medial trochlea.

Pathomechanics and Functional Limitations

Symptoms include possible valgus instability, resulting in decreased ROM in extension and loss of throwing velocity. Throwing is not possible with an acute injury.

▨ Immediate Management

Acute UCL ruptures are treated with cessation of activity, ice, and a sling for comfort. In contrast, valgus extension overload syndrome without damage to the UCL has an insidious onset and is treated with active rest.

▨ Medications

Narcotic analgesics may be prescribed for acute ligament rupture, and oral NSAIDs are usually recommended. Corticosteroid injection directly into the joint is not advised because of its detrimental effects on the joint cartilage and attenuated structures around the joint capsule.[32]

▨ Postinjury Management

Joints inflamed from valgus extension overload can be managed with a simple sling for several days to a week for comfort. Individuals who have experienced multiple episodes of valgus extension overload may require a longer rest period of 4 to 6 weeks.[33] Conservative care includes therapeutic treatments for the inflammatory condition and active rest. Once the inflammation is controlled, exercises to restore ROM and strength are started.

▨ Surgical Intervention

When UCL insufficiency is the underlying cause of valgus extension overload, consideration should be given to ligament reconstruction. The section on UCL injuries covers ligament reconstruction in detail (see page 357).

A posteromedial olecranon osteophyte can be excised via an open or arthroscopic procedure.[34] For an experienced arthroscopist, elbow arthroscopy is an excellent choice, allowing removal of loose bodies and inflamed synovium and excision of olecranon osteophytes. Pain is usually relieved with osteophyte removal.

▨ Postoperative Management

After removal of olecranon osteophytes, no immobilization is necessary. The goal in the first 2 weeks postoperatively is to reduce edema, and early rehabilitation is aimed at restoring ROM by weeks 3 to 4 and strength and power by weeks 4 to 6.[33] At 6 weeks following surgery, a progressive throwing program may be initiated, and full return to activity may occur between 3 and 6 months after surgery.[33]

Injury-Specific Treatment and Rehabilitation Concerns

Specific Concerns
Protect postsurgical tissue (if applicable).
Decrease inflammation.
Restore forearm muscle strength.
Increase forearm muscle flexibility.
Reeducate dynamic control of the elbow musculature.

Treatment includes rest; NSAIDs; ROM exercises for the shoulder; strengthening of the shoulder, elbow, and wrist musculature; dynamic stabilization exercises; and a gradual return to throwing. The shoulder should be assessed for any internal rotation deficit, which will increase valgus stress on the elbow with throwing. Internal rotation should be increased through passive and self-stretching techniques.

The strengthening and stabilization program focuses on control of rapid elbow extension and decreasing valgus forces. Emphasis is placed on the concentric function of the flexor-pronator group and eccentric function of the scapular stabilizers, posterior rotator cuff, and elbow flexors.[33] Dynamic stabilization exercises with manual techniques or rubber tubing and a Plyoball are used to attain control of the elbow extension and valgus forces.

Postoperative Rehabilitation

Postoperative care after either arthroscopic or open debridement focuses on relief of pain and inflammation and restoration of motion. Active ROM begins as soon as tolerated. No restrictions are placed on motion, except those necessary for surgical wound healing. The clinician may perform gentle, passive extension as necessary, and full motion should be achieved 3 to 4 weeks after surgery. The shoulder should be continually reevaluated to identify and correct any deficits in internal rotation that have occurred over time. Stretching to ensure full internal shoulder rotation must be undertaken to decrease valgus stress upon the patient's return to activity.

The patient may perform pain-free isometric exercises for the shoulder, elbow, and wrist during the first 2 weeks postoperatively. Isotonic ROM exercises begin at weeks 3 to 4. Between weeks 4 and 6, strengthening exercises are incorporated into the rehabilitation program, and more functional exercises are started for the legs, trunk, shoulder girdle, and extremity.[33] As with conservative treatment, the program focuses on developing control of the rapid elbow extension and valgus forces experienced during throwing.

The patient may begin to return to throwing after full ROM is achieved and strength is restored, which should occur approximately 6 weeks after surgery. Throwing athletes should undertake a progressive routine involving incremental increases in duration, frequency, and intensity. Many throwing programs are available that can be adapted to the specific needs of the patient. Return to full activity may take 3 to 6 months. If surgical reconstruction of the medial elbow ligamentous complex was performed, the rehabilitation guidelines in the section on UCL injuries should be followed.

Estimated Amount of Time Lost

The amount of time lost from competition ranges from 3 to 6 weeks for partial ligamentous tears and overuse inflammatory conditions. Surgical osteophyte excision may require 3 to 6 months before full return to activity. Ligament reconstruction requires 9 to 12 months of rehabilitation.

Return-to-Play Criteria

The patient should have a pain-free joint with functional ROM and strength of the shoulder, elbow, and wrist before beginning a sport-specific training or throwing program. A progressive training or throwing program must be successfully completed before full return to play is possible.

Elbow Fractures

Elbow fractures result in a wide spectrum of injuries and, therefore, are handled with a variety of treatment and management techniques. This section focuses on the more common fracture types and general acute fracture treatment. Also, pediatric elbow fractures present unique concerns (see **Box 10.1**).

Approximately half of the elbow's stability is provided by soft tissues and half by bony architecture. Consequently, elbow fractures are likely

CLINICAL PRESENTATION

Radial Head Fractures

History

Valgus stress applied to the elbow.

Axial load applied through an outstretched hand with the forearm in pronation.

Pain reported along the lateral aspect of the elbow.

Observation

Swelling along the lateral elbow.

Function Status

Pain with elbow motion.

Pronation and supination limited by a mechanical block.

Physical Examination Findings

Point tenderness and possible crepitus over the radial head.

Decreased strength during resisted ROM for forearm pronation and supination.

Possible increased varus laxity noted on stress testing.

Olecranon Fractures

History

A direct blow to the elbow.

Elbow hyperextension.

Pain arising from the posterior elbow.

Falling on a partially flexed elbow, causing eccentric loading of triceps and avulsion of olecranon.

Observation

Posterior elbow swelling.

Olecranon deformity.

Functional Status

Pain and crepitus may occur during elbow flexion and extension.

Active elbow extension may be absent.

Physical Examination Findings

Point tenderness over the olecranon process is noted.

The subcutaneous location of the olecranon often makes the fracture line easily palpable.

The strength of resisted ROM against gravity is decreased because of the unstable insertion of the triceps brachii on the olecranon process.

Humeral Fractures

History

A forceful injury such as a fall.

Pain just proximal to the elbow.

Observation

Medial and/or lateral swelling.

Deformity above the elbow.

Functional Status

Pain with elbow motion.

Inability to actively move the elbow secondary to pain.

Physical Examination Findings

Point tenderness and possible crepitus over distal humerus.

Palpable deformity in distal humerus.

Pain with any resisted ROM testing.

to affect joint stability. The section on elbow dislocations covers fractures combined with instability (see page 373). The objective in treating any elbow fracture is to provide a stable joint that allows early motion.

The Müller system, shown in **Figure 10.8**, is used to classify fractures of the distal humerus.[35] Such fractures carry an increased risk of secondary trauma to the neurovascular structures that cross the elbow. Dealing with intra-articular fractures (types B and C) is particularly difficult. The objective of any treatment of distal humeral fracture is to obtain a stable, anatomic reduction of the joint surface so as to allow early motion.

The radial head provides stability against valgus stress (along with the UCL) and affords longitudinal stability to the elbow; fractures to this structure are classified using the Mason system (see **Figure 10.9**). Posterior ulnar translation on the humerus is restricted by the coronoid process, which is frequently fractured during elbow dislocations.[36] The olecranon prevents anterior ulnar translation on the humerus. By virtue of anatomy, olecranon fractures are intra-articular; they are described using the Schatzker classification system (see **Figure 10.10**).[37,38]

Differential Diagnosis

Elbow dislocation, radial collateral ligament sprain, posterolateral complex trauma.

Imaging Techniques

AP, lateral, and oblique radiographs are obtained to show the fracture pattern (see **Figure 10.11**).

Definitive Diagnosis

Radiographs will demonstrate the presence of a fracture about the elbow.

Pathomechanics and Functional Limitations

The extent of biomechanical disruption in the elbow differs by fracture type. Radial head fractures result in decreased strength during pronation and supination and pain during flexion and extension. Unrecognized proximal radius instability can lead to chondromalacia of the radial head and capitellum.[46] Elbow extension strength is decreased in the presence of even minor olecranon process fractures, because the triceps lacks a stable insertion on which to pull. If not properly treated, intra-articular distal humeral fractures lead to reduced ROM, pain, and dysfunction. Fractures to the medial epicondyle result in decreased wrist flexion. Lateral epicondyle fractures result in decreased wrist extension, and possibly impaired pronation and supination.

Box 10.1

Lifespan Concerns: Pediatric Elbow Fractures

Supracondylar Fractures

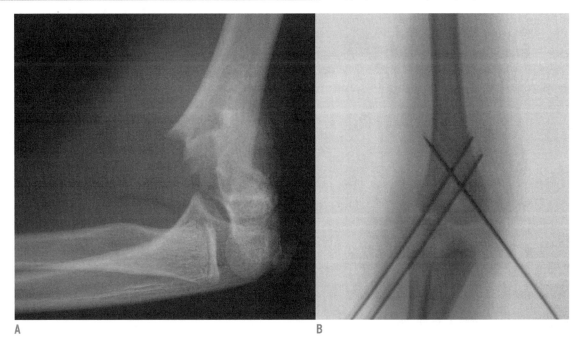

A   B

Supracondylar elbow fracture on radiograph (**A**) and the typical treatment of reduction and pinning for fracture stabilization on fluoroscopic imaging (**B**).

Although rare in adults, fractures of the distal humerus are a concern in pediatric and adolescent athletes. Supracondylar fractures of the humerus are the most common fractures in patients younger than 7 years and account for 60% of elbow fractures in children.[39,40] As many as 70% of these injuries result from a fall on an outstretched hand.[41] Girls are more likely to experience supracondylar elbow fractures, usually to the nondominant hand.

Acute supracondylar fractures are characterized by localized pain and point tenderness over the distal humerus, with possible ecchymosis or deformity. Radiographic assessment is necessary to gauge the severity of the injury and plan treatment. Potential complications include compartment syndrome, neurovascular injury, and malunion, especially with severely displaced fractures. A nondisplaced fracture is treated with casting; a displaced fracture requires surgical reduction in most cases. In children, these fractures heal rapidly, usually without long-term complications.[42,43]

(continues)

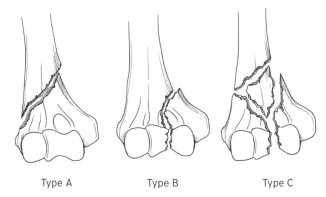

Type A   Type B   Type C

Figure 10.8 Müller's classification of distal humeral fractures. Type A is nonarticular, type B is articular with one articular fragment being continuous with the shaft, and type C is articular with the shaft separated from the articular fragments. *Source:* Reproduced with permission from Webb LX. Distal humerus fractures in adults. *J Am Acad Orthop Surg.* 1996;4:336-344.

▦ Immediate Management

If a fracture is suspected, the extremity should be immobilized and the distal neurovascular status evaluated. The patient should then be transported for radiographs.

> **Practice Tip**
>
> Fractures about the elbow may lead to forearm compartment syndrome. Monitor the patient's neurovascular status before and after splint application.[47]

▦ Medications

Narcotic analgesics may be prescribed to control pain. NSAIDs are typically avoided with fractures because of the possibility of platelet dysfunction and the urgent need for fracture fixation.

10

Box 10.1

Lifespan Concerns: Pediatric Elbow Fractures *(Continued)*

Lateral Condylar Fractures

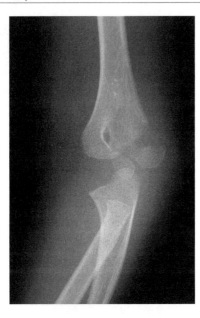

Radiograph of a lateral condylar fracture in a skeletally immature patient.

Lateral condylar fractures account for approximately 12% of elbow fractures seen in children.[39] Although they are less common than supracondylar fractures, these injuries are considered more severe because of the potential for growth plate involvement. They are frequently seen when a child falls on an outstretched hand. Lateral condylar fractures may disrupt the articular surface of the distal humerus or damage the physis. Physeal damage, in turn, can lead to physeal arrest and abnormal growth and deformities.[44]

Displaced fractures usually require surgery.[44] Nondisplaced fractures can be treated with casting, although they can become displaced within the cast because of the anatomic origin of the forearm extensors on the bony fragment. Thus close radiographic and functional follow-up is necessary.[45]

■ Postinjury Management

Distal Humeral Fractures

Stable fractures can be managed nonsurgically. The physician can reduce a displaced fracture by gently applying axial traction while the patient's arm is in the neutral position. The fracture is then immobilized with a cast or rigid splint for 2 weeks, followed by use of a hinged brace to allow early, controlled ROM.[35] Nonsurgical management requires frequent follow-up radiographs. Also, when a hinged brace is used, it must be regularly adjusted. A less than optimal alignment is a common result of conservative management of type A distal humeral fractures.[35]

Radial Head Fractures

Loss of motion, especially terminal extension, is a common result of radial head fracture, even after surgery. The amount of motion lost rarely causes functional disability, however. With conservative treatment, the amount of fracture healing that has occurred must be identified with frequent radiographs, as adequate healing permits more aggressive pursuit of motion and the start of strengthening.

Olecranon Fractures

Nondisplaced olecranon fractures in which the extensor mechanism is still intact may be managed nonsurgically. To improve reduction in displaced fractures, the patient's arm is immobilized with the elbow fully extended; however, this technique can result in a loss of flexion ROM. If the fracture is nondisplaced, the elbow is immobilized in 45° to 90° of flexion for 3 weeks. ROM is limited to 90° until healing is seen on radiographs.[37] Most olecranon fractures are intra-articular and require surgical fixation.

■ Surgical Intervention

Distal Humeral Fractures

Extensive preoperative planning is necessary to ensure an efficient surgery and to obtain the best long-term results.[48] Radiographs are obtained to identify the fracture lines and determine the amount of displacement. Views of the uninvolved elbow are also taken and flipped, thereby providing a silhouette of the expected anatomic alignment.[35] Computed tomography (CT) scans can be helpful in elucidating fracture configurations during preoperative planning.

Surgical management of nonarticular fractures may involve an inverted-V turndown of the triceps brachii tendon, although this technique can result in residual triceps weakness. This risk can be avoided with a medial incision that detaches the

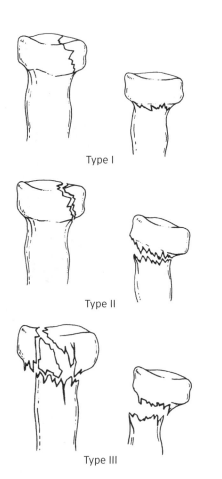

Type	Displacement	Symptoms
I	Minimally displaced (<2 mm)	Forearm pronation/supination is limited by pain.
II	Displaced >2 mm	Motion has a mechanical block secondary to displacement.
	Fracture is angulated, but minimal or no comminution	
III	Displaced >2 mm	Gross deformity
	Severe comminution	Not amenable to surgical repair and requires resection of the radial head

Figure 10.9 Modified Mason classification for radial head fractures. *Source:* Adapted from Browner BD, Jupiter JB, Levine AM, Trafton PG (eds). *Skeletal Trauma.* Philadelphia, PA: WB Saunders; 1992:1137.

triceps from the periosteum. The bony fragments are then reattached using screws, plates, or a combination of these devices.[35]

Intra-articular fractures are managed by using screws to replace the fragments that form the articular surface. The distal segment is then stabilized to the humeral shaft with any of a variety of plates (see **Figure 10.12**). A double-plate fixation is typically employed, in which one plate is fixated directly medially to stabilize the medial humeral column and the other plate is placed posterolaterally to fixate the lateral column. The posterolateral placement decreases the possibility of contact of the ulnar nerve with the plate. If plate placement encroaches on the cubital tunnel, ulnar nerve transposition is required. Other potential complications include stiffness, fibrosis, heterotopic ossification, and nonunion or malunion.[49]

Radial Head Fractures

Indications for surgical fixation of radial head fractures include displaced fractures (> 2.0 mm) and comminution (types II and III; see Figure 10.9).[34] In recent years, more attention has been given to open reduction and internal fixation (ORIF) of radial head and neck fractures.[46] This technique is difficult and should be performed only by surgeons who are very familiar with elbow anatomy. Specific small screw-and-plate sets are excellent choices for radial head or neck ORIF. A lateral Kocher approach will expose the fracture, and the fragments can then be preliminarily reduced with Kirschner wires (K-wires). The type of fixation (screws or plates) depends on the fracture pattern and is beyond the scope of this chapter. The objective is stable fixation that allows early motion. In rare instances, the radial head is excised, although this procedure is not recommended for young, active patients and is contraindicated if the fracture is accompanied by elbow dislocation.[38]

10

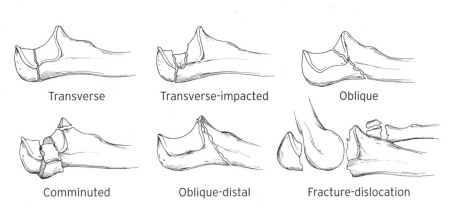

Transverse   Transverse-impacted   Oblique

Comminuted   Oblique-distal   Fracture-dislocation

Figure 10.10 Schatzker classification of olecranon fractures. *Source:* Adapted from Browner BD, Jupiter JB, Levine AM, Trafton PG (eds). *Skeletal Trauma.* Philadelphia, PA: WB Saunders; 1992:1137.

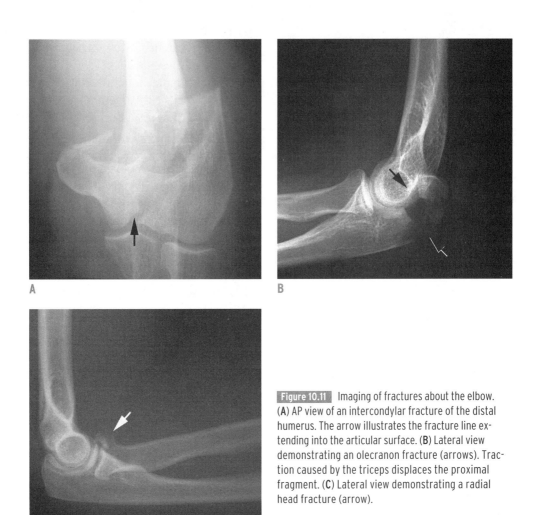

Figure 10.11 Imaging of fractures about the elbow. (**A**) AP view of an intercondylar fracture of the distal humerus. The arrow illustrates the fracture line extending into the articular surface. (**B**) Lateral view demonstrating an olecranon fracture (arrows). Traction caused by the triceps displaces the proximal fragment. (**C**) Lateral view demonstrating a radial head fracture (arrow).

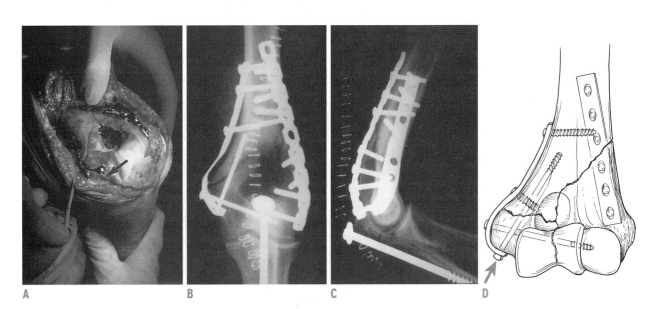

Figure 10.12 Repair of intra-articular distal humeral fracture. (**A**) A flattened one-third tubular plate contoured to fit around the medial epicondyle was used for fixation. Instrumentation imposed on the cubital tunnel (arrow) necessitated transposition of the ulnar nerve. AP (**B**) and lateral (**C**) radiographs depict arrangement of the plates at right angles to each other. (**D**) Illustration of the repairs involved. *Source:* Figure D reproduced with permission from Webb LX. Distal humerus fractures in adults. *J Am Acad Orthop Surg.* 1996;4:336–344.

Olecranon Fractures

A displaced or comminuted olecranon fracture requires ORIF to restore elbow function. A straight posterior approach to the elbow is used.[34] The triceps and anconeus are brought over as a subperiosteal sleeve to expose the fracture fragments. Fixation choices include a large intramedullary screw, tension band, K-wires, plate and screw, or a combination of these devices (see Figure 10.13). The objective is a stable, anatomic reduction of the olecranon and articular surface to allow early motion. Patients with thin arms may be able to feel the plate and screws postoperatively. In some instances, this hardware must be removed after healing has been accomplished.[37] Skeletal immaturity often reduces the need for surgical repair of radius and/or ulnar fractures. The pediatric concerns of forearm fractures are presented in Box 10.2.

◼ Postoperative Management

A short course (5 to 10 days) of immobilization with a posterior splint for comfort is indicated postoperatively. Early motion is begun as soon as the patient is comfortable. A ROM brace may be used early in the course for patient comfort.

Distal Humeral Fractures

The elbow and arm are supported in a sling. Active or active-assisted ROM should be initiated as soon as possible to maintain motion and prevent joint adhesions, and is based on intraoperative assessment of fixation stability.[53] A hinged ROM brace

may be worn at the physician's discretion. Resisted ROM is not begun until the fracture has healed, usually at 8 to 12 weeks.

Radial Head Fractures

After ORIF, the fracture site should be stable enough to allow early passive motion. Typically after approximately 4 weeks, strengthening and more aggressive motion may be initiated.

Olecranon Fractures

Extra caution is needed to identify postoperative wound-healing issues. In particular, the superficial nature of the fixation hardware can create problems with healing. Once stabilized, the olecranon fracture does well with rehabilitation. After an initial 1- to 2-week period to allow adequate wound healing, motion exercises can commence. At 3 to 4 weeks postoperatively, isometric exercises may begin; at 6 to 8 weeks, more aggressive strengthening may be started.

◼ Injury-Specific Treatment and Rehabilitation Concerns

> **Specific Concerns**
>
> Protect the healing fracture.
> Restore functional ROM.
> Restore strength to the surrounding musculature.

Distal Humeral Fractures

Any posterior incision must be thoroughly evaluated for closure problems. The small amount of soft

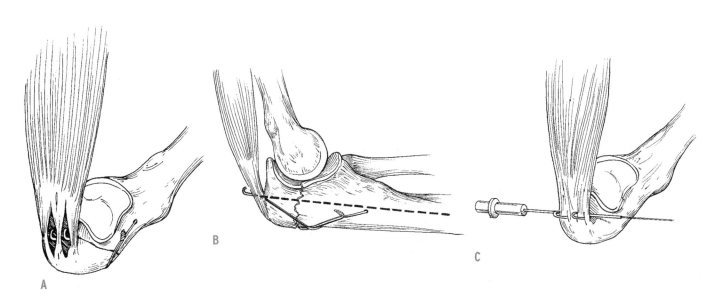

Figure 10.13 Technique for tension-band wiring after an olecranon fracture. (**A**) Fibers of the triceps tendon should be split or moved to allow the bent ends of the K-wires to be impacted firmly against bone. (**B**) If the ends of the K-wires are left superficial to the triceps tendon, elbow extension may cause migration or fatigue failure of the wires. (**C**) A 16-gauge or larger intravenous catheter is used to pass the tension-band wire deep to the triceps fibers. *Source:* Reproduced with permission from Hak DJ, Golladay GJ. Olecranon fractures: Treatment options. *J Am Acad Orthop Surg.* 2000;8:266-275.

Box 10.2

Lifespan Concerns: Pediatric Forearm Fractures

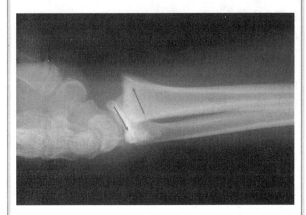

Radiograph of a displaced Salter-Harris II growth-plate fracture of the distal radius.

Fractures of the forearm are frequently seen in young athletes, with the distal radius being the most common site of fracture in children.[40] As with most upper extremity injuries, fractures of the distal radius often involve a fall onto an outstretched hand. With skeletal maturation, the fracture site tends to move from proximal to distal.[50] In younger patients, fractures usually involve the distal metaphysis of the radius and ulna. As patients approach skeletal maturity, however, fractures through the distal radial physis become more common.

The forearm may be deformed with this type of fracture; however, not all forearm fractures are displaced. Skeletal point tenderness also indicates the presence of a fracture. A fracture through the growth plate usually requires surgical reduction and fixation, especially if the amount of displacement is significant.[51] Midshaft fractures of the forearm in younger patients frequently require only closed reduction and casting, but as patients mature, internal fixation often becomes necessary. With growth-plate involvement, abnormal shortening of the radius or ulna is possible. Even so, injuries of the forearm tend to heal well, and serious long-term complications are rare.[52]

tissue between the bone and plates and the skin can lead to healing difficulties. At approximately 1 week after surgery, placing the arm in a hinged ROM brace allows active and active-assisted motion to begin without placing stress along the incision. When the incision is completely closed, ROM progresses unimpeded. Passive ROM begins with radiographic evidence of bone healing at approximately 4 to 6 weeks postoperatively.

Strengthening exercises for the entire extremity begin with isometrics at 2 to 3 weeks. If the surgical procedure requires triceps tendon release and reattachment to gain exposure to the fracture, elbow extension should not commence until 4 weeks. Light isotonic exercises may start at 6 weeks, and the patient can strengthen the arm without restrictions after radiographic evidence of adequate healing is observed, usually around 8 weeks after surgery.

Radial Head Fractures

For a type I radial head fracture, active elbow motion begins immediately. The patient can remain in a sling for comfort. Patients with type II fractures treated without surgery undergo a short period of immobilization. In both cases, formal rehabilitation can start about 3 weeks after injury.

For type I radial head fractures, active motion is begun as early as pain and edema allow, and progressed as tolerated.[54] Passive motion, if needed, is not used until adequate fracture healing is demonstrated on radiographs (approximately weeks 4 to 6). Isometric exercises start at 3 weeks and isotonic exercises at 5 to 6 weeks. Progressive resistive exercises are initiated between weeks 6 and 8, and are progressed as tolerated. Resistance exercises may begin later in the rehabilitation progression if adequate healing is not yet evident in radiographs.

For a type II radial head fracture, the patient performs active wrist and hand ROM immediately, but elbow ROM begins after the joint has been in a splint for 3 to 5 days. Strengthening exercises follow a schedule similar to that employed with conservative treatment for type I injuries.

ROM is started after 3 to 5 days of immobilization for type II fractures managed with ORIF. All motions are accomplished actively or actively assisted, with passive ROM performed only if necessary and then only after adequate fracture healing. Strengthening begins at approximately 3 weeks postoperatively with submaximal isometric exercises and progresses to isotonic exercises at 6 weeks. Heavy resistance is not initiated until after 8 weeks.

Patients with type III fractures treated with radial head excision begin active motion after 3 to 5 days of immobilization. If other tissues were repaired, the repair takes precedence, and rehabilitation follows the course dictated by that procedure.

A hinged elbow brace may be used to assist with stability during early ROM exercises. Patients who are in a hinged brace after surgery should be placed in a forearm position during ROM exercises that is dictated by any associated injuries incurred during the surgical procedure (e.g., with radial collateral ligament reflection, the forearm should be pronated during ROM exercises to reduce stresses on the RCL).[54]

Olecranon Fractures

Patients with olecranon fractures may undergo conservative treatment for nondisplaced or minimally displaced type IA and IB fractures.[34] The elbow is immobilized in the flexion midrange for 7 to 10 days. Radiographs are then repeated; if no further displacement is demonstrated, gentle active flexion with passive extension is attempted. Any increased displacement requires surgical fixation.

Surgical fixation of the olecranon fracture should allow early, protected motion. Because of the superficial nature of the olecranon and the hardware, skin-healing problems may dictate a prolonged period of immobilization. To protect the skin, the patient uses a posterior splint at 90° but can still begin active motion as soon as the first day.[34] The exception involves patients with comminuted or type III fractures, who may require a less aggressive approach. Active and active-assisted motions are used, especially for flexion, but the patient is closely monitored.

Isometric exercises to strengthen the shoulder, elbow, and wrist can begin at 4 weeks. Isotonic exercises can start at 6 to 8 weeks if stable fixation and adequate healing are present.

■ Estimated Amount of Time Lost

The amount of time lost from competition depends on the fracture pattern and the need for surgical fixation (or not). Generally, the patient needs at least 8 to 12 weeks before returning to full activity.

■ Return-to-Play Criteria

The patient can return to sports and physical activities when adequate fracture healing is demonstrated radiographically and clinically. Clinically, patients must have functional ROM of the elbow and superior radioulnar joints and adequate strength compared with the contralateral extremity.

Functional Bracing

No braces, taping, or padding is needed. An athlete with a healed olecranon fracture may find an elbow pad useful for comfort to soften blows to the area.

Elbow Dislocations

Elbow dislocations account for 10% to 25% of all elbow injuries and are second only to the shoulder in upper extremity dislocations among adults.[55] The elbow is the most frequently dislocated upper extremity joint in children (see **Box 10.3**). More than 90% of elbow dislocations occur posteriorly or posterolaterally.

By definition, all dislocations involve ligament trauma. Simple elbow dislocations do not involve a fracture, whereas complex dislocations do involve

---

CLINICAL PRESENTATION

History

Application of a high-energy force to the elbow.
A fall on an outstretched hand while the forearm is supinated.
Exquisite pain.

Observation

Obvious elbow deformity.
Gross elbow swelling that develops rapidly.

Functional Status

Elbow ROM is not possible.
The patient reports decreased or absent grip strength.

Physical Examination Findings

Distal neurovascular function may be compromised.
Point tenderness through the elbow is apparent.
Once the joint is relocated, valgus, varus, and posterolateral instability may be present.

Box 10.3

Lifespan Concerns: Pediatric Elbow Dislocations

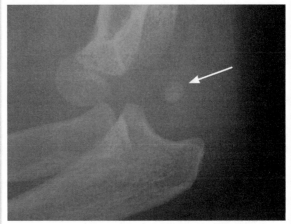

Radiograph of a posterior elbow dislocation. The medial epicondyle (arrow) is displaced and incarcerated in the joint.

An elbow dislocation may appear deformed, and if the medial epicondyle is fractured, the medial aspect of the elbow is typically point-tender.[58-60] Medial epicondyle and medial condylar fractures are commonly seen with posterior elbow dislocations. The radiographic presence of such a fracture increases the suspicion of an elbow dislocation that may have spontaneously reduced. Fractures of the medial epicondyle are more common than dislocations and account for approximately 10% of elbow fractures in children.[61] Because of the physeal anatomy of the skeletally immature elbow, the UCL and flexor muscles frequently avulse a fragment from the medial epicondyle. Elbow dislocations and fractures of the medial epicondyle are usually the result of falling with the forearm supinated and the elbow in full or partial extension. Nearly 50% of medial epicondyle fractures are associated with elbow dislocations, and the displaced fragment may become trapped in the joint,[62,63] preventing closed reduction of the dislocation.

With neurologic compromise or absent distal pulses, an elbow dislocation constitutes an orthopaedic emergency. Treatment of medial epicondyle fractures is controversial, especially for minimally displaced fractures. Nondisplaced fractures are typically treated with casting, whereas displaced fractures may require surgery.[64]

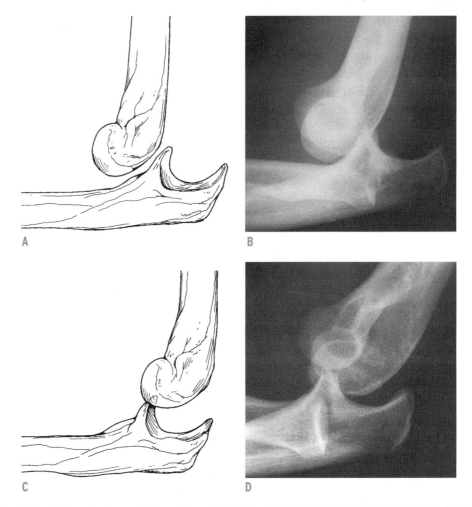

Figure 10.14 (**A** and **B**) Illustration and radiograph of complete posterior dislocation. (**C** and **D**) "Perched" posterior dislocation. *Source:* Reproduced with permission from Morrey BF. Acute and chronic instability of the elbow. *J Am Acad Orthop Surg.* 1996;4:117-128.

fractures. When a fracture does occur, the radial head and coronoid process are most commonly involved; the epicondyles and olecranon can also be involved, however. A shallow olecranon fossa and a prominent olecranon process may increase the risk of a dislocation.[56]

Although radiographs have revealed periarticular fractures in 12% to 60% of all dislocations, in one study surgical exploration revealed a nearly 100% incidence of unrecognized osteochondral injuries in elbow dislocations.[57] Most of these injuries do not require fixation.

Differential Diagnosis

Distal humeral fracture, proximal ulnar fracture, proximal radial fracture, radial head dislocation.

Imaging Techniques

Radiographs confirm the diagnosis and direction of dislocation. AP, lateral, oblique, and true lateral are the most important views (see Figure 10.14). Oblique views or CT are especially helpful in identifying periarticular fractures (see Figure 10.15). MRI evaluation is useful in planning surgical intervention.

Definitive Diagnosis

The definitive diagnosis of elbow dislocation is based on the clinical findings and radiographic images.

Pathomechanics and Functional Limitations

Most patients are unable to move the elbow until it is relocated. Once the displacement is reduced,

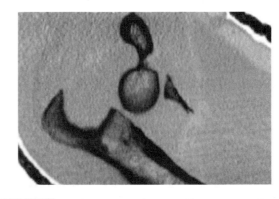

Figure 10.15 A sagittal CT image of a coronoid fracture. *Source:* Reproduced with permission from Ring D, Jupiter JB, Zilberfarb J. Posterior elbow dislocation with radial head and coronoid fractures. *J Bone Joint Surg Am.* 2002;84:547-551.

joint stability must be determined. Many patients can achieve full, stable motion and functional elbow use with conservative care.

Simple dislocations resulting in continued instability and complex dislocations may require surgical intervention to restore stability and repair the fractures. Heterotopic ossification can occur after a dislocation over time, resulting in a debilitating loss of ROM, especially for athletes.

Complex dislocations include injuries to the ligaments and bone and involve articular surfaces.[65] The most common fracture in a complex dislocation is to the coronoid process. The coronoid process serves as a stabilizer of the elbow joint due to its shape and size and is an attachment site of the anterior portion of the UCL.[65] Therefore, any substantial fracture of the coronoid process also compromises the stability of the elbow.

The elbow "terrible triad" involves a dislocation with an associated coronoid process and radial head fracture.[66] This type of injury predominantly occurs in young, active individuals and results in complications including recurrent instability, stiffness, malunion, and nonunion.[65,66]

Immediate Management

The elbow is splinted in the position in which it is found and distal neurovascular status is monitored regularly. The shoulder and wrist must be examined to rule out concomitant injury, which occurs in 10% to 15% of elbow dislocations.[56] The distal radioulnar joint is also examined, to rule out interosseous membrane injury.

> **Practice Tip**
>
> Assess and document the patient's distal neurovascular status prior to closed reduction of elbow dislocations, which should be performed under conscious sedation, preferably in the emergency department.[67]

Medications

Appropriate analgesia, sedation, and muscle relaxants are required for reduction. Minimal sedation is required if the reduction is attempted early, before spasm and swelling develop. Narcotic analgesics may be prescribed after reduction.

Medical Management

Complete neurovascular examination is required before and after reduction. Timely reduction is essential but should be performed in an emergency room or office setting. Sedation and muscle relax-

ation are the keys to reduction. Medial-lateral displacement must be corrected first. This maneuver is followed by forearm traction with the elbow flexed to 20° to unlock the coronoid by application of gentle pressure on the olecranon to bring it distal and anterior. An appreciable "clunk" is a favorable sign for stability.[56]

Surgical Intervention

Although surgical intervention for acute elbow dislocation is rarely needed, two indications for such procedures exist: (1) an elbow that remains unstable in extension between 0° and 50° and (2) unstable fractures, which require fixation.[57] The goal of surgical fixation is stability to allow early motion.

Elbows that are chronically unstable after reduction may require an additional surgical procedure, such as that described in the section on PLRI (see page 361). Complex dislocations need appropriate fracture fixation in the operating room, and sometimes surgical repair of ligamentous structures (see **Figure 10.16**). An associated coronoid process or radial head fracture can cause inherent instability and increase the risk of complications.[36]

Postinjury/Postoperative Management

Postreduction assessment of neurovascular status and stability in extension is critical. Instability in extension after reduction signifies a problematic joint that will likely remain unstable. If the joint is stable after reduction, the elbow is immobilized in 90° of flexion with the forearm in a neutral position for approximately 7 days. Positioning of the proximal radioulnar joint depends on collateral ligament stability.[68] If both collateral ligamentous structures are compromised, the forearm is left in neutral. Injury to the lateral ligaments requires splinting in pronation to tighten any intact medial ligaments and lateral musculotendinous structures. Injury to the medial ligaments requires splinting in supination to tighten any intact lateral ligaments and medial musculotendinous structures.

Once the elbow is relocated and neurovascular status is determined to be satisfactory, the elbow is placed in a posterior splint or hinged ROM brace and the extremity in a sling. A hinged brace can either be locked or allow limited ROM within a stable, pain-free range. The wrist and hand should be free to move. Regular follow-up radiographs should be performed to ensure that reduction has been maintained.

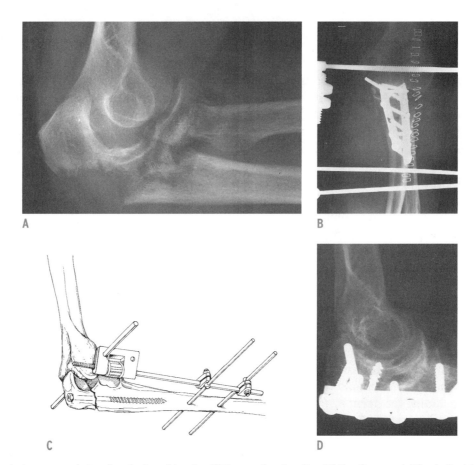

Figure 10.16   Surgical management of an elbow fracture-dislocation. (**A**) Preoperative view. (**B** and **C**) The elbow was stabilized with plates, a transfixing pin in the distal humerus, and a distraction device. (**D**) Satisfactory result after the fracture healed and the device was removed. *Source:* Parts A, B, and D reproduced with permission from Cobb TK, Morrey BF. Use of distraction arthroplasty in unstable fracture dislocations of the elbow. *Clin Orthop.* 1995;312:201-210. Part C reproduced with permission from Morrey BF. Acute and chronic instability of the elbow. *J Am Acad Orthop Surg.* 1996;4:117-128.

Wrist and hand ROM exercises are initiated as soon as possible. Flexion-extension elbow ROM exercises can begin at approximately 1 week after injury, when the patient is fitted with a hyper-extension brace to limit flexion contratures (see **Figure 10.17**).[56,69] Extension is gradually increased over the next 3 to 6 weeks.

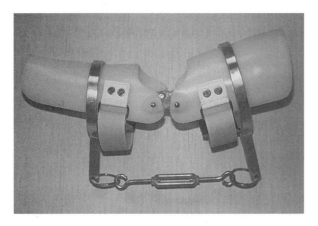

Figure 10.17   Hyperextension brace used to minimize the chance of acquiring a flexion contracture.

■ Injury-Specific Treatment and Rehabilitation Concerns

Specific Concerns

Protect the joint from any forces that would cause further instability.

Maintain grip strength.

Encourage wrist ROM while the elbow is immobilized.

Introduce passive pronation-supination and flexion-extension ROM as allowed.

Determine UCL stability and take corrective measures if necessary.

In uncomplicated dislocations, immobilization for 3 to 7 days is followed by a rehabilitation program aimed at regaining motion while preserving stability. Patients begin rehabilitation 3 to 7 days after injury. Early in the course of rehabilitation, the patient's complaints of elbow instability may increase as the amount of extension is increased. A hinged ROM brace with an extension block can be used to limit the elbow to the stable ranges of motion during activities of daily living. UCL compromise can increase posterolateral elbow instability.[70] If the patient demonstrates UCL laxity, UCL rehabilitation should be incorporated into the program.

Active and active-assisted ROM exercises begin 7 days after injury for the elbow that was easily reduced, remains reduced, and is stable throughout a full ROM. Although a stable joint need not be protected during activities of daily living, a sling may be used for comfort for another 1 or 2 weeks. A patient whose elbow was reduced but is unstable in extension should begin guarded, active ROM approximately 1 week after injury. ROM limits increase as joint stability increases. The goal is to attain full, stable motion in approximately 6 weeks.

As inflammation decreases, modalities such as moist heat packs and whirlpool therapy may promote relaxation and increase tissue viscoelasticity before ROM exercises. An upper body ergometer may be used, with low loads and within stable ROMs, after 3 weeks or as soon as tissue inflammation decreases.

Passive motion, especially into extension, is performed only when necessary in the first 3 to 6 weeks. A progressive loss of ROM is an indication to begin passive motion, albeit only within the stable ROMs. In addition to exercises involving the elbow, early cervical spine, shoulder, wrist, and hand ROM exercises are performed.

The patient may begin squeezing a sponge ball or putty immediately after injury. Submaximal isometrics for the shoulder, elbow, and wrist musculature commence at 2 to 3 weeks. Isotonic strengthening starts at 4 to 5 weeks within stable ranges. Approximately 6 weeks after injury, the patient can progress strengthening exercises as tolerated.

At 4 to 6 weeks, more functional positioning and movements are initiated. Weight bearing through the joint, initially with minimal weight, promotes proprioception and joint stability. Rhythmic stabilization and Plyoball exercises are useful to improve joint dynamic stability.

Postoperative rehabilitation of the unstable joint generally follows the guidelines in the section on PLRI (page 361). Surgical intervention for complex fractures follows the guidelines in the section on fractures (page 365).

Estimated Amount of Time Lost

Many athletes return to sports activity in 5 to 10 weeks following elbow dislocation, depending on the exact nature of the injury. Dislocations requiring surgical intervention for instability and complex dislocations can be debilitating. The amount of time lost from competition varies depending on the amount and type of ligamentous and bony injury.

Complex dislocations require a longer recovery period, and full motion may not be regained.

Return-to-Play Criteria

The joint must remain stable throughout the full ROM. The patient must have a pain-free joint and full strength and be able to perform all functional activities.

Functional Bracing

A brace is typically not required to return to activity. For some athletes who are attempting a quick return to activity, a brace limiting extension may be helpful. However, these athletes must be able to perform their activities safely in this type of brace. For example, a football lineman may be able to return more quickly with a brace that limits full extension.

Osteochondritis Dissecans

CLINICAL PRESENTATION

History

Elbow pain during throwing or similar activities is reported.
Popping and catching may be described.
Loose bodies in the joint can result in elbow locking.

Observation

Mild swelling may be noted on the lateral elbow.

Functional Status

The patient may describe grating or crunching during elbow motion.

Physical Examination Findings

Crepitus may be noted during elbow palpation during flexion and extension.
ROM may be notably decreased.
Loss of terminal extension is observed.
The valgus extension overload stress test may be positive or increase pain on lateral side or increase loss of terminal extension.

Osteochondritis dissecans occurs in younger throwing athletes and usually involves the capitellum of the distal humerus.[71] Increased valgus stress across the elbow during throwing increases contact pressures between the capitellum and the radial head. These contact pressures can also lead to secondary radial head degenerative changes. The sections on UCL and valgus extension overload describe the throwing motion and valgus stress across the elbow in detail. Patients are usually males, age 13 to 16 years, who are involved in throwing activities.[72]

> **Practice Tip**
>
> The diagnosis of osteochondritis dissecans is based on the clinical findings of the loss of terminal elbow extension, posterolateral joint line swelling, and positive valgus extension overload tests. Posteroanterior and lateral radiographs demonstrate **radiolucency** in the central aspect of the capitellum with possible loose bodies. These findings are supported by magnetic resonance (MR) images.[73]

Differential Diagnosis

Valgus extension overload, isolated ligament sprain, overuse tendinopathy arthritis.

Imaging Techniques

Radiographs may reveal the capitellar lesion and any radial head changes. MRI can be used to visualize capitellar lesions and loose bodies, but several views with the elbow in various degrees of flexion may be required to identify the defect (see **Figure 10.18**). Ultrasound imaging has also been used successfully to identify capitellar osteochondritis.[71]

Definitive Diagnosis

The definitive diagnosis is based on radiographic findings.

Pathomechanics and Functional Limitations

During throwing, contact pressure increases laterally in the capitellum and the radial head. Articular cartilage changes can result and lead to early degenerative changes. Loose bodies can form, causing further biomechanical problems.

Athletes with osteochondritis dissecans have throwing limitations secondary to pain and may subsequently change their throwing mechanics. Other than these throwing or similar overhead motions, they may not have any functional limitations.

■ Immediate Management

A short course (3 to 5 days) of immobilization for acute pain may be necessary. Throwing and other aggravating activities should be discontinued until symptoms resolve.

■ Medications

NSAIDs may be prescribed to control pain and inflammation.

■ Postinjury Management

Most patients respond to conservative treatment. The main focus is complete compliance with rest from aggravating activities, as this combined with NSAIDs and ice constitute the initial treatment. In patients whose pain persists even with everyday activities, splinting or casting for 3 to 4 weeks followed by active and active-assisted ROM may be recommended. The patient must continue to restrict activity for 6 to 8 weeks after symptoms are fully relieved.

Before the patient attempts to return to activity, radiographic findings should be stable or improv-

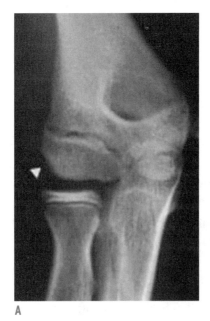

A   B

Figure 10.18 Imaging techniques to identify elbow osteochondritis. (**A**) AP radiograph with the elbow flexed to 45°. Slight flattening and sclerosis of the lateral surface of the capitellum (arrowhead) are seen. (**B**) T1-weighted MRI showing low signal intensity in the superficial aspect of the capitellum. *Source:* Reproduced with permission from Takahara M, Shundo M, Kondo M, Suzuki K, Nambu T, Ogino T. Early detection of osteochondritis dissecans of the capitellum in young baseball players: report of 3 cases. *J Bone Joint Surg Am.* 1998;80:892-897.

ing but need not be normal—normal radiographs may not be observed for years.[72] The return to activity should progress cautiously. Although most athletes return to sport, baseball pitchers have a guarded prognosis.[74]

Educating the patient, coaches, and often parents about avoidance of aggravating activities is essential. Any activity that causes pain results in a prolonged course of treatment and increases the likelihood of an unfavorable outcome.

■ Surgical Intervention

Surgery is indicated in those patients who have failed to improve with an appropriate conservative course of rest, rehabilitation, and a throwing program. Arthroscopy is an excellent tool for visualizing the elbow and removing loose bodies (see **Figure 10.19**). Lesions may be debrided, drilled, repaired, or excised. Results in the literature vary with regard to return to throwing. Open techniques also have produced successful results but do not allow for easy visualization of the rest of the joint.

■ Postoperative Management

Postsurgically, the healing lesion must be respected. Joint motion is beneficial, because it brings fresh synovial fluid to the lesion. Shearing and compressive loading must be avoided in the first 8 weeks postoperatively, so that the healing fibrocartilage clot or osteochondral fragment is not dislodged from the injury site.

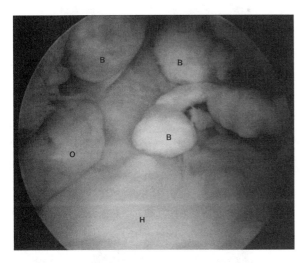

Figure 10.19 Intraoperative photograph demonstrating the presence of loose osteochondral fragments (B) in the posterior elbow compartment of a throwing athlete secondary to valgus extension overload (H, humerus; O, olecranon).

■ Injury-Specific Treatment and Rehabilitation Concerns

Specific Concerns

Protect the capitellum and other load-bearing structures from stress.
After surgery, protect the incision site.
Correct poor biomechanics.

The nonsurgical rehabilitation program is based completely on the patient's symptoms. ROM and strengthening exercises can progress in intensity as tolerated. If symptoms abate for 6 to 8 weeks and the patient has full ROM and strength, a supervised throwing program may be attempted as long as symptoms do not reappear. An off-loading hinged elbow brace may also be used to obstruct the normal valgus motion that occurs with an overhead throwing motion. The brace should be set at a pain-free ROM, with ROM being increased as the patient's symptoms diminish. Normal activities may be resumed approximately 2 weeks after initiating treatment while in the brace, pending the continued absence of symptoms.[75]

After surgery, the elbow is placed in a soft dressing for 1 week. Continuous passive motion stimulates the delivery of nutrition to the area from the synovial fluid. Shearing and heavy compressive forces across the joint must be avoided for at least 8 weeks. With fragment removal, the treatment is once again based completely on the patient's symptoms. ROM and strengthening exercises can progress in intensity as tolerated.

If the fragment is reattached, early motion is used to stimulate healing. Strengthening begins at approximately 3 weeks with submaximal isometrics and progresses to isotonics at about 6 weeks. Heavy resistance should not be applied for at least 8 weeks. After 12 weeks and once the patient has full ROM and strength, a supervised throwing program may begin.

■ Estimated Amount of Time Lost

The amount of time lost from competition is highly variable. Patients with moderate osteochondritis dissecans may lose 4 weeks of activity. By comparison, those with severe damage to the articular surface may never return to throwing activity. After surgery, return to full activity can take as long as 6 months.

■ Return-to-Play Criteria

The patient can return to sports and physical activities when adequate healing is demonstrated clinically. Compared with the contralateral extremity, the athletes must have functional ROM and adequate strength and successfully complete a supervised throwing program.

Osteoarthritis

CLINICAL PRESENTATION

History

A history of heavy labor, weight lifting, and/or throwing is reported.
The patient may describe catching during joint motion.
Pain is noted during joint motion and increases when the joints are loaded (e.g., while weight lifting).
Pain may be most intense in terminal extension.

Observation

A flexion contracture may be noted.
Outward joint deformity may be present in the late disease stages.

Functional Status

The patient is unwilling to use the involved extremity secondary to pain and/or decreased ROM.

Physical Examination Findings

Pain occurs during joint palpation.
Crepitus may be felt during elbow motion.

Although pain is the most common complaint with arthritis of the elbow, patients may also complain of stiffness, weakness, instability, or deformity.[55] Treatment and outcome depend on the type of arthritis, the severity and duration of symptoms, the amount of contracture, and the patient's age.

Osteoarthritis is becoming more frequently recognized, and most cases are in males. Patients usually have a history of heavy labor, weight lifting, or throwing and present in the third to eighth decades of life. Radiographs reveal osteophytes (olecranon, coronoid) and loose bodies.

Posttraumatic arthritis is the result of injury to the elbow articulation, most commonly an intra-articular fracture of the distal humerus. Stiffness is frequently noted after these injuries, and nonunions can lead to chronically unstable, painful elbows.

Differential Diagnosis

Rheumatoid arthritis, osteochondritis, osteochondritis dissecans, medial elbow tendinopathy, lateral elbow tendinopathy.

Medical Diagnostic Tests

A blood test may be ordered to rule out rheumatoid arthritis.

Imaging Techniques

The standard elbow series of AP, lateral, and oblique views is ordered to identify possible decreased joint space, osteophytes, and loose bodies (see **Figure 10.20**).

Definitive Diagnosis

Radiographs demonstrate decreased joint space.

Pathomechanics and Functional Limitations

Patients have gradual onset of pain and loss of motion. Osteoarthritis typically presents with pain during the end ranges of motion. If loose bodies are present, however, the patient will have mechanical symptoms, which may include frank locking. Osteophyte formation may present as decreased ROM, with pain noted through the midrange of motion and a hard end feel. Pain increases when the individual is carrying something at the side with the elbow terminally extended. Patients who are heavy laborers or weightlifters have increased pain with these activities.

■ Medications

A trial of NSAIDs may be prescribed to decrease pain and effusion associated with the destruction of hyaline cartilage and concurrent changes that occur in the subchondral bone.[76] If NSAIDs are tolerated and beneficial, the patient may try an over-the-counter NSAID on a long-term basis. Chondroitin sulfate and glucosamine also may be used. Corticosteroid

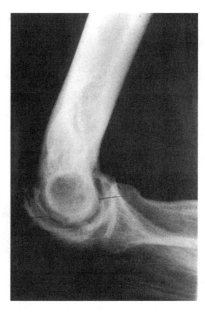

Figure 10.20 Lateral radiograph of an elbow with arthritis.

injections may be administered to help relieve pain in early stages.

Postinjury Management

Most patients are treated conservatively. Initial treatment includes NSAIDs, rehabilitation, and rest from aggravating activities. A corticosteroid injection may be useful in the early disease stages. A carefully designed rehabilitation program should be implemented as well.

Surgical Intervention

Surgery is indicated in those patients who fail to improve with conservative measures and whose symptoms persist. Options include arthroscopy (with loose body removal, synovectomy, and osteophyte excision as appropriate), resection or interposition arthroplasty, arthrodesis, and total elbow arthroplasty. The procedure performed depends on the severity of arthritis and deformity and the patient's age, activity level, and expectations.

Elbow arthroscopy should be performed by a surgeon who is familiar and comfortable with the intricate elbow anatomy, because the portals can be within 3 to 5 mm of a nerve branch. The skilled arthroscopist can address loose bodies and osteophytes and perform a complete synovectomy and capsular releases as necessary. All of these procedures may be helpful in the early to midstages of arthritis, especially in younger, active patients.

When deformity or stiffness is severe, arthroscopic procedures are not indicated. Instead, osteotomy and interposition arthroplasty are viable options. Total elbow arthroplasty is indicated when pain and deformity are significant, conservative and other surgical measures fail, or laxity with deformity is chronic. Most surgeons recommend that a semiconstrained design be followed. The patient must have a good understanding of the realistic functional levels after these procedures. The primary goal is to provide pain relief. Although ROM increases after surgery, full ROM is usually not achieved postoperatively.[77] In particular, the patient will still be limited in activities that require greater degrees of extension and flexion.

Postoperative Management

Postsurgical treatment of arthroscopic conditions requires a soft dressing for about 1 week, followed by rehabilitation. The patient can perform ROM exercises during this time. After the wounds are adequately healed, a program similar to that for the conservative treatment of arthritis should be followed.

After osteotomy or joint replacement surgery, wound care is of the utmost importance. Elbow flexion places stress across most surgical exposures. To assist with incisional healing, the surgeon splints the elbow until the wound is well healed. Semiconstrained implants are splinted in extension, whereas resurfacing implants require a more stable 90° position.

Injury-Specific Treatment and Rehabilitation Concerns

> **Specific Concerns**
> Protect the joint surfaces (after arthroscopic procedures).
> Protect the healing osteotomy or joint replacement.
> Restore function.
> Restore functional ROM.
> Restore pain-free strength to the surrounding musculature.

arthrodesis Fusion of bones across a joint space that limits or restricts joint motion.

Conservative care focuses on controlling pain and inflammation, restoring motion, and strengthening the trunk and entire extremity. ROM is usually best attempted with active or active-assisted exercise to minimize joint irritation. The clinician should be mindful of the end feels with ROM exercises and never force ROM with a hard end feel. Trunk and upper extremity strengthening decreases joint stress. Joint compression should be minimized when the patient with arthritis is engaging in strengthening exercises.

After arthroscopic procedures, ROM and strengthening exercises are based completely on the patient's symptoms. Exercises can progress in intensity as tolerated, but excessive joint loading should be avoided. Return to activity is based on symptoms and ability to perform functional motions, which may take a considerable amount of time to achieve and may require long-term activity modifications.

In rehabilitation after arthroplasty, active ROM begins as soon as the third postoperative day. A splint protects the joint between sessions. More aggressive active-assisted exercises and passive ROM are performed only if necessary. Expectations after surgery must be realistic. The primary goal is to attain pain relief and to have adequate ROM and strength for activities of daily living. The patient typically needs adequate reach for objects during everyday activities, including the head for grooming; approximately 20° of extension and 100° of flexion accomplishes this goal in most individuals.

Although it is important to strengthen the upper extremity after surgery, a permanent lifting restriction of 5 to 10 lb is typically imposed.[78] The patient must understand this restriction before the treatment plan is developed. With a semiconstrained prosthesis, isometric exercises can begin approximately 3 weeks after surgery, with light isotonic exercises starting at 6 weeks. A resurfacing arthroplasty may require a 2- to 3-week delay in initiating these exercises. Strength progression is highly individualized and must be determined in consultation with the surgeon.

Estimated Amount of Time Lost

The amount of time lost from activities depends on the patient's activities and the amount of contracture and deformity. Patients usually modify activities rather than stopping them completely.

Return-to-Play Criteria

The patient can return to sports and physical activities when tolerated. Clinically, the patient must have functional ROM and adequate strength compared with the contralateral extremity. Because of the chronic, progressive nature of this condition, the patient usually modifies activities as needed. After surgical joint replacement, the patient is advised to avoid any activities that may place heavy shear or compressive forces through the joint.

Synovitis

CLINICAL PRESENTATION

History
Generalized elbow pain with an insidious onset.
History of repetitive motion or overuse.

Observation
Swelling may be noted.

Functional Status
ROM limited by pain and swelling.
Decreased strength secondary to pain.

Physical Examination Findings
The elbow may be warm to the touch.

Elbow synovitis can be caused by an inflammatory arthritic process or overuse. In athletes, synovitis almost always results from overuse and is usually self-resolving. This condition, which is common in overhead athletes, weightlifters, and heavy laborers, can occur concomitantly with medial or lateral elbow tendinopathy.

Rheumatoid arthritis—an inflammatory process of the joint's synovial lining—is the most common cause of the inflammatory arthritides. However, it affects the elbow less often than other joints. Patients present with pain and deformity and may have laxity. Unlike patients with primary osteoarthritis, those with rheumatoid arthritis can lose bone stock (and eventually develop periarticular destruction), which can lead to joint laxity. The ulnohumeral articulation is most frequently involved.

Differential Diagnosis
Osteoarthritis, rheumatoid arthritis, tendinopathy.

Medical Diagnostic Tests
Laboratory analysis of aspirated synovial fluid identifies rheumatologic disorders.

Imaging Techniques
Radiographs may show bony destruction on both sides of the articulation if the condition has rheumatologic origins. MRI can reveal synovitis, especially in its earlier stages.

Definitive Diagnosis
The definitive diagnosis is based on the patient's history, physical examination, and radiographic findings.

Pathomechanics and Functional Limitations
Synovitis causes pain, swelling, and an inability to function in sport. The athlete may also have loose bodies or osteophytes in conjunction with the synovitis, which leads to increased pain and swelling and decreased ROM.

Immediate Management

Immediate management consists of rest from aggravating activities, as well as application of ice, compression, and elevation.

Medications

NSAIDs may be prescribed to control synovial inflammation. Corticosteroid injections can temporarily relieve symptoms; however, active joint infection should be ruled out before a corticosteroid is injected.

Postinjury Management

Conservative medical management initially consists of avoiding aggravating activities, NSAIDs, and application of ice to decrease the inflammatory process. As the inflammatory process abates, therapeutic exercise is beneficial to restore normal motion. Corticosteroid injection is indicated in those patients who do not improve on oral NSAIDs.

After injury, the patient is treated with relative rest. During this period, aggravating activities must be avoided. The extremity can be used for activities requiring very low joint loads, but repetitive motions should be eliminated. Therapeutic modalities and gentle ROM exercises with low-load, prolonged stretches are instituted. As inflammation subsides, resistance exercises are initiated.

Surgical Intervention

Surgery is indicated in patients whose symptoms persist despite conservative measures. The procedure selected depends on the severity of the condition and the patient's age, activity level, and expectations. The most commonly used surgical approach is arthroscopic removal of loose bodies and excision of osteophytes. Severe cases with associated arthritis may require resection or interposition arthroplasty, arthrodesis, or total elbow arthroplasty.

Postoperative Management

After surgery, the elbow is placed in a compressive bandage for several days. After this covering is removed, the wounds are bandaged as needed. Movement within tolerable limits is encouraged to limit stiffness. The patient must not use the elbow in the motion extremes, which would stress the healing wounds. Sutures are removed approximately 1 week after surgery, and rehabilitation is started at that point.

Injury-Specific Treatment and Rehabilitation Concerns

> **Specific Concerns**
> Maintain pain-free ROM.
> Control inflammation.
> Avoid short, intense stretches and repetitive motions.

The conservative and postoperative rehabilitation protocols for synovitis are similar. The initial focus is on decreasing inflammation. ROM exercises can be initiated with low-load, prolonged stretches to decrease stiffness and stimulate the synovial lining. In contrast, short, intense stretches and repetitive motions may increase inflammation and must be avoided. ROM should be performed with self-ranging exercises; passive ROM activity is included only out of necessity.

Trunk, shoulder, elbow, and wrist strengthening should be added as the patient attains pain-free, full, active motion. Strengthening the entire kinetic chain minimizes repetitive elbow stresses. Strengthening begins with light resistance and increases as tolerated.

Because synovitis is typically caused by repetitive overuse, a sport-specific program of functional activities is instituted. Low repetitions of drills and activities are initiated. Inflammation is closely monitored and activity duration increased as tolerated. Throwing athletes should be placed on a progressive routine involving incremental increases in throwing duration, frequency, and intensity. Many throwing programs are available that can be adapted to meet the patient's specific needs. For instance, an outfielder will likely focus on longer, less frequent throws. A pitcher will focus on more frequent, high-intensity throws, while a catcher will emphasize frequent, low-intensity throws with intermittent, high-intensity throws.

Estimated Amount of Time Lost

Overuse synovitis can resolve in days to weeks. The ability to truly rest the joint and allow pharmacologic and therapeutic modalities to reduce inflammation has the greatest influence on decreasing time lost to synovitis. Athletes can return to their sports approximately 8 weeks after surgery; however, if the condition existed for a long time before surgery, return may be delayed.

Return-to-Play Criteria

Before returning to competition, the athlete should have a pain-free, swelling-free elbow with full ROM and strength and must complete a sport-specific program of functional activities working up to the normal routine.

Lateral Elbow Tendinopathy

Lateral elbow tendinopathy (also known as lateral epicondylitis or "tennis elbow") is an inflammatory process of the common extensor tendons at their origin on the lateral epicondyle. It is most commonly observed in golfers and tennis players. Electromyographic studies indicate that the greatest amount of elbow muscle activity during tennis ground strokes occurs in the wrist-stabilizing muscles—specifically, the extensor carpi radialis longus and brevis and extensor digitorum communis. As the racquet makes contact with the ball or the golf club makes contact

CLINICAL PRESENTATION

History

There is an insidious onset of pain arising from the lateral epicondyle.

Pain may radiate into the forearm.

The patient has a history of repetitive wrist extension, elbow activity, or overuse.

Observation

Mild swelling may be noted over the lateral epicondyle.

Functional Status

Pain and weakness with lifting or other load-bearing wrist extension.

Possible decreased grip strength.

Physical Examination Findings

Active ROM is not restricted except in extreme cases.

Point tenderness and (possibly) crepitus occur 2 cm distal to the lateral epicondyle.

Pain is noted during lateral epicondyle palpation while resisting wrist extension.

Pain arising from the lateral epicondyle occurs during resisted second and third finger extension while the wrist and elbow are extended.

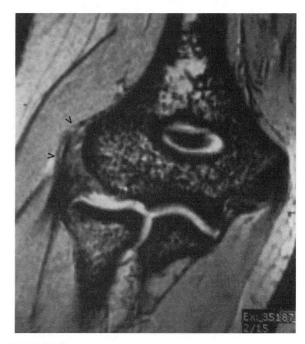

Figure 10.21 Coronal MRI demonstrating lateral elbow tendinopathy (arrowheads).

with the ball and/or ground, torque increases and is transmitted through the tendons.[79]

The common extensors of the wrist originate on the lateral epicondyle. They include the extensor carpi radialis longus and brevis, extensor digitorum communis, and extensor carpi ulnaris. The extensor carpi radialis brevis is most commonly involved in lateral elbow tendinopathy.[80] Although not a wrist extensor, the brachioradialis may be inhibited during elbow flexion. Lateral elbow tendinopathy begins as microtears of the extensor carpi radialis brevis tendon,[80] but the other extensor tendons may also be involved. Lateral elbow tendinopathy typically appears in the fourth and fifth decades of life, and shows equal incidence in men and women.[81,82] Most cases involve the dominant arm.

In surgery, the affected tissue appears grayish and friable; tendon **fibrillation** and a **sinus tract** into the elbow joint may be seen. Characteristic microscopic angiofibroblastic dysplasia of the involved tissue also is noted.[81]

Differential Diagnosis

Radial tunnel syndrome, posterior interosseous nerve syndrome, lateral complex ligament injury, C7 radiculopathy.

Imaging Techniques

Standard elbow radiographs (AP, lateral, and oblique) may be ordered to rule out soft-tissue calcification.

Irritation of the lateral epicondyle and the tendinous attachment may be noted on MRI (see **Figure 10.21**).

Definitive Diagnosis

The definitive diagnosis of lateral elbow tendinopathy is based on the clinical examination findings and the exclusion of ligament injury, nerve entrapment, and cervical radiculopathy.

Pathomechanics and Functional Limitations

Activities involving loaded wrist extension or grip strength are affected. Although grip is primarily provided by the flexors, to attain a strong grip the wrist extensors extend the wrist, thereby creating better length-tension development within the flexor group. Overhand activities also create pain as the wrist extensors hold the wrist in neutral or extension. Repetitive activities exacerbate this condition and further increase pain. The patient may be precluded from engaging in some sport and work activities owing to pain and weakness.

■ Immediate Management

Lateral elbow tendinopathy is initially managed by applying ice and avoiding activities that load the wrist during extension.

■ Medications

A 2-week course of oral NSAIDs may be prescribed to decrease pain and inflammation at the site of the extensor group insertion on the lateral epicondyle,

fibrillation A local, involuntary muscular contraction.

sinus tract A pathway between a pathologic space and a healthy cavity or skin.

with instructions for the patient to take the medication as needed thereafter for any recurrence of symptoms. If the patient fails to respond to conservative treatment and NSAIDs, the physician may opt to inject a corticosteroid deep into the extensor carpi radialis brevis. No more than three injections should be given to control this condition.

Postinjury Management

Most patients respond to conservative treatment in the form of rest, NSAIDs, and therapeutic exercise. Nighttime wrist-neutral splinting may reduce tension on the lateral epicondyle and extensor group.

Surgical Intervention

Surgical treatment involves a small skin incision to expose the common extensor tendons. Any tendon defect is repaired, but the surgeon must take care not to imbricate the tissue, which could lead to decreased elbow extension. Any pathologic tissue is then excised; usually this area includes most of, or the entire origin of, the extensor carpi radialis brevis. The extensor group is then reattached and repaired (see (ST) 10.4).

Postoperative Management

Soft-tissue dressings are applied after surgery. Some surgeons prefer that their patients use a posterior splint for 5 to 7 days postoperatively. The patient can begin moving the elbow within a tolerable ROM at 3 days, and a formal exercise program may begin at 1 week if skin closure is adequate.

Injury-Specific Treatment and Rehabilitation Concerns

Specific Concerns

Protect the healing extensor group.
Control inflammation.
Correct improper biomechanics.

Initial attempts to reduce pain and inflammation involve patient education, treatment, and avoidance of aggravating activities. Typically such activities include gripping or using the hand in a pronated position requiring wrist extensor activity. Use of the extremity for nonaggravating activities is encouraged.

The mechanism of injury can typically be related to poor technique during activities or the improper use of equipment. A careful assessment, correction of poor techniques, and evaluation of all equipment must be performed. Close communication with a knowledgeable coach is helpful in directing the patient in proper techniques, which may include modifications such as a two-handed backhand stroke.

Use of inappropriate equipment is also frequently observed in this patient population. In racquet sports, the racquet grip size is typically too big. The recommended grip size is measured from the proximal palmar crease to the tip of the ring finger, along the radial side of the finger.[80,83] Other racquet modifications may include an increased head size (which increases the "sweet spot"), a lighter racquet (which offers better control), and decreased string tension (which reduces impact forces).

Many patients use a computer workstation that may add to elbow inflammation. Proper workstation design allows the arms to be relaxed at the side and the hands to sit easily on the keyboard.

Initial attempts to reduce the pain and inflammation associated with lateral elbow tendinopathy focus on ice application. Phonophoresis or iontophoresis with anti-inflammatory agents may be attempted. Soft-tissue, deep, or cross-friction massage can help decrease pain and promote blood flow. Continuous ultrasound may be used to increase the tissue's viscoelastic properties before deep friction massage is applied.

The patient should begin flexibility exercises for the wrist extensor group within a pain-free range. Initial attempts may require keeping the elbow in some degree of flexion. Ultimately, the patient progresses to performing flexibility exercises with the elbow extended.

Resistance exercises strengthen the extensor mechanism and should be performed in a pain-free manner. Initial strengthening consists of isometric or light isotonic exercises, with the resistance being increased as tolerated. A comprehensive strengthening program for the entire trunk and upper extremity also is started.

As the patient progresses through the program, more functional activities are included to prepare for the return to full activity. Use of rubber tubes or bands in short concentric and eccentric bursts can mimic the forces placed on the elbow during sport activities. The patient can also practice functional motions with a racquet or club. Resistance can be added by using heavier tubing. The patient performs sport-specific drills and activities, progressing to a gradual return to full activity.

10

Correction of Lateral Elbow Tendinopathy

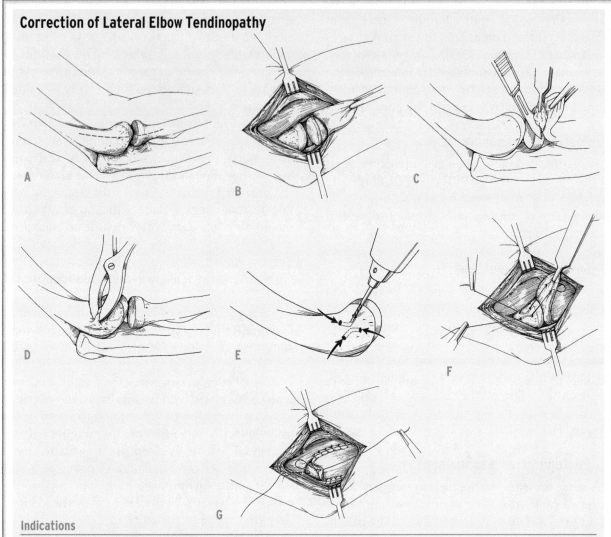

Indications

Pain and symptoms unresponsive to 6 to 12 consecutive months of adequate conservative treatment when other causes have been ruled out.

Procedure Overview

1. An incision is made over the lateral epicondyle (**A**).
2. The common extensor tendon insertion on the lateral epicondyle is identified (**B**).
3. The extensor mechanism is reflected distally.
4. The pathologic tissues are excised from the extensor mechanism (**C**).
5. The lateral epicondyle is decorticated (**D**).
6. V-shaped tunnels are drilled into the epicondyle (**E**).
7. The common extensor tendon origin is reattached to the lateral epicondyle (**F**).
8. The extensor mechanism is reoriented to the surrounding structures using sutures (**G**).

decorticated The surgical removal of the outer layer of a structure.

Functional Limitations

No long-term functional limitations are expected.

Implications for Rehabilitation

These surgical procedures tend to be painful, and early ROM is encouraged. As pain resolves, ROM continues and early progressive resistance exercises are initiated.

Potential Complications

Potential complications include failure to control symptoms and pain.

Comments

Identification of offending biomechanics or activities and subsequent modification of them will help to prevent recurrence of this condition.

Source: Figures reproduced with permission from Jobe FW, Ciccotti MG. Lateral and medial epicondylitis of the elbow. *J Am Acad Orthop Surg.* 1994;2:1–8.

The postoperative rehabilitation program follows a course similar to conservative treatment after initial tissue healing occurs. The patient may perform gentle, active ROM exercises 3 days after surgery. The wrist extensors are gently stretched after suture removal. Strengthening exercises are added at 3 to 4 weeks postoperatively. A counterforce brace is used with strengthening and activities for 2 to 3 months after surgery. After 3 months, the brace is used only with sport and work activities that require prolonged, repetitive use of the extensor mechanism. The patient begins a gradual return to sport and work activities 2 to 3 months after surgery and progresses to full activity as tolerated.

▪ Estimated Amount of Time Lost

The amount of time lost from competition depends on the symptoms' severity and duration. Acute conditions can resolve quickly (2 to 3 days) after short-term treatment. Chronic lateral elbow tendinopathy may have a waxing and waning symptom course, depending on the patient's activity level. Surgical intervention may prolong return to activity to about 4 months.

▪ Return-to-Play Criteria

Before returning to competition, the patient must have full, pain-free ROM and enough strength to progress to more functional activities. Return to full sport participation occurs when functional activities can be performed without pain during or after the activity.

Functional Bracing

A counterforce "tennis elbow strap" may help control symptoms by altering force distribution at the elbow (see **Figure 10.22**).

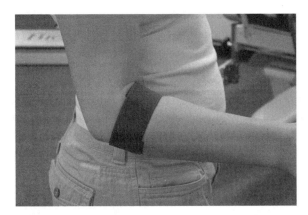

Figure 10.22 Lateral elbow tendinopathy brace. The strap helps reduce tension on the wrist extensor muscles, thereby decreasing symptoms.

Medial Elbow Tendinopathy

CLINICAL PRESENTATION

History

Insidious onset of pain in the medial elbow.
Pain increases during activities that increase valgus stress on the elbow (e.g., golf, throwing).

Observation

Mild swelling of the medial elbow.

Functional Status

Pain and weakness may be reported during functional activities.
Grip strength may be decreased.

Physical Examination Findings

Medial tenderness is noted over the pronator teres and flexor carpi radialis muscles 5 to 10 mm distal and anterior to the medial epicondyle.
Active ROM may not be noticeably limited.
Pain occurs during resisted wrist flexion and pronation.
Flexion contracture may potentially be observed.

Medial elbow tendinopathy (also known as medial epicondylitis or "golfer's elbow") is less common than lateral elbow tendinopathy.[80] It can occur in patients who are involved in sports or occupations that create valgus forces about the elbow. The muscles originating from the medial epicondyle include the pronator teres, flexor carpi radialis, palmaris longus, flexor digitorum superficialis, and flexor carpi ulnaris. The pronator teres and flexor carpi radialis are the muscles most frequently involved in medial elbow tendinopathy.

Although termed "golfer's elbow," this condition can occur with any active endeavor that places valgus force on the elbow.[84–86] Medial elbow biomechanics have been well described with regard to the pitching mechanism. Peak angular velocity and valgus stress are greatest during the acceleration phase, exceeding the tensile strength of the medial ligamentous and tendinous structures (see **Box 10.4**). The stresses are initially transmitted to the flexor pronator musculature (especially the pronator teres), and then to the deeper medial collateral ligament.

Medial elbow tendinopathy typically appears in the fourth and fifth decades of life and has equal incidence in men and women.[80,86] Improper technique, inadequate warm-up, fatigue, and poor conditioning are all factors that can lead to medial elbow inflammation.

Lifespan Concerns: Little League Elbow

Little League elbow can involve either the medial or lateral epicondyle, depending on the specific pathogenesis. Pain over the medial elbow is related to valgus overload and concomitant stress on the medial joint capsule and associated ligaments. The mechanisms of injury involve the early and late cocking phases of the overhand throw.[88] Pain over the lateral elbow region in throwers is associated with compressive forces related to the late cocking and early acceleration phases of the overhand throw.[88] Specific damage may involve osteochondritis of the radial head, the capitellum, or both. Conservative treatment includes rest as well as strengthening and stretching exercises. Limiting both the number of innings per game and the number of pitches thrown per week is the best method of preventing elbow injuries in young pitchers. The number of innings should be limited to three or four per game, and the player's pitch count should be held to fewer than 200 pitches per week.[89] A 10-year study determined that youth (aged 9 to 14) baseball pitchers who threw more than 100 innings a year were three and a half times more likely to be injured than those who did not. The same study indicated there is no evidence that throwing curveballs by athletes younger than 13 years of age significantly increased the risk of injury.[90]

Differential Diagnosis

UCL sprain, medial elbow instability, ulnar neuritis.

Imaging Techniques

Standard elbow (AP, lateral, and oblique) radiographs are taken to rule out soft-tissue calcification, osteophytes, and intra-articular conditions. Electromyographic studies are indicated in patients with neurologic signs and symptoms. MRI and ultrasonography can be helpful in determining whether traumatic tears are present at the insertion of the flexor pronator group.[87]

Definitive Diagnosis

The definitive diagnosis of medial elbow tendinopathy is based on the findings of the clinical examination and the exclusion of ligamentous injury.

Pathomechanics and Functional Limitations

Activities requiring wrist flexion may be affected, such that the patient increases elbow flexion to compensate for this deficit. Activities that apply a valgus force to the elbow may be diminished secondary to pain. Grip may be affected secondary to flexor group pain.

■ Immediate Management

Medial elbow tendinopathy is initially managed by avoiding activities that require repetitive wrist flexion. Ice application can decrease pain and assists in controlling inflammation.

■ Medications

A 2-week course of an oral NSAID may be prescribed, with instructions to take the medication as needed thereafter.

■ Postinjury Management

Most patients with medial elbow tendinopathy respond to conservative treatment. Rest from the aggravating activity, local modalities, rehabilitation, and night wrist-neutral splinting may reduce tension on the tissues.

■ Surgical Intervention

Surgery is indicated for medial elbow tendinopathy if 1 year of conservative management fails to relieve the patient's syndrome. Such surgery may not enable the patient to return to the desired functional level, however. In patients who are not expected to experience considerable valgus load after surgery, debridement with segmental resection of the medial conjoined tendon yields good results. In contrast, in patients who are expected to subject the surgical tissues to significant and continued valgus load, such as throwing athletes, debridement with anatomic repair (instead of resection) of the medial conjoined tendon is performed to reestablish the dynamic valgus stability provided by the flexor pronator mass (see **S T** 10.5). The loss of innervation to the flexor-pronator group can produce debilitating strength deficits.

■ Postoperative Management

The elbow is immobilized in a posterior splint for 5 to 10 days to allow wound healing. Elbow motion is allowed from 45° to 120° for the next 2 weeks. At the end of week 3, the splint is removed and replaced with a neutral wrist splint. Elbow ROM is then performed with the forearm pronated and the wrist flexed. Forearm and wrist ROM is done with the elbow flexed to 90°. No tension is placed on the repair, because tendon relaxation at one joint allows ROM exercises at the other joint. Isometric strengthening for the elbow may also begin at this time. This protocol is maintained for 3 weeks. At week 6, full ROM of all joints is allowed with little regard to the other joint positions. Strengthening exercises can also be initiated 6 to 8 weeks after surgery. A throwing progression can be started when good flexor pronator strength has been regained, usually at 3 to 4 months. Full return to competitive throwing usually requires 6 to 9 months of time and rehabilitation.

Surgical Technique 10.5

Surgical Correction of Medial Elbow Tendinopathy

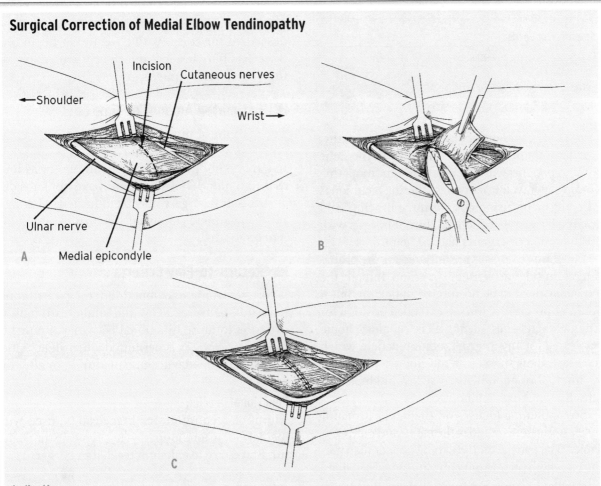

Indications

Pain and symptoms unresponsive to 12 consecutive months of adequate conservative treatment when other causes have been ruled out.

Procedure Overview

1. A 3- to 7-in incision is centered over the medial epicondyle.
2. The medial epicondyle, flexor pronator group, and cutaneous nerves are identified (**A**).
3. The common flexor origin is incised and reflected.
4. The ulnar nerve is identified and protected.
5. Any pathologic tissue is identified and excised.
6. The medial epicondyle is debrided of soft tissue, and a vascular bed is created by drilling several small holes in the epicondyle (**B**).
7. The common flexor group tendons are reattached to the medial epicondyle (**C**).

Functional Limitations

No functional limitations are expected, but the ulnar nerve should be protected posterior to the medial epicondyle.

Implications for Rehabilitation

These surgical procedures tend to be painful, and early ROM is encouraged. As pain resolves, ROM continues and early progressive resistance exercises are initiated.

Potential Complications

Surgery may fail to relieve the patient's pain.

Comments

Identifying and modifying offending biomechanics or activities will help to prevent recurrence.

Source: Figures reproduced with permission from Jobe FW, Ciccotti MG. Lateral and medial epicondylitis of the elbow. *J Am Acad Orthop Surg.* 1994;2:1-8.

■ Injury-Specific Treatment and Rehabilitation Concerns

> **Specific Concerns**
> _____
> Protect the healing flexor pronator group.
> Control inflammation.
> Correct poor biomechanics.

In the early stages of medial elbow tendinopathy, pain and inflammation are controlled in the same way as in patients with lateral elbow tendinopathy. Avoiding aggravating activities, altering techniques and equipment, using counterforce bracing, and applying ice can be beneficial. Iontophoresis with anti-inflammatory agents may be helpful.

Flexibility exercises are initiated for the pronator teres muscle and wrist flexor group. Initially the elbow may need to be positioned in flexion, but it should be progressed into an extended position for flexibility exercises as tolerated. The shoulder should be assessed for any internal rotation deficit, which increases valgus stresses on the elbow with throwing. Internal rotation is increased through passive and self-stretching techniques.

Strengthening focuses on the flexor pronator muscle group and includes the trunk and entire extremity. The patient should exhibit greater than pre-injury strength prior to initiating functional activities, as the patient's baseline strength has already proven to be vulnerable to repetitive valgus injury.[87]

As the patient progresses in the rehabilitation program, more functional activities are incorporated to prepare for the return to full activity. Rubber tubes or bands in short concentric and eccentric bursts can be used to mimic elbow forces during sport activities.

The patient can also practice functional motions with a racquet or club, adding resistance with rubber tubing. Sport-specific drills and activities are included, with the patient progressing to a gradual return to full activity. Functional training usually focuses on endurance activities, because the tissues involved in these exercises usually engage in many short bursts of activity that lead to fatigue.

Postoperative care for medial epicondylar release is similar to that for lateral epicondylar release. Early treatment includes use of a removable posterior splint for approximately 1 week, with gentle wrist and hand ROM exercises beginning about 3 days after surgery. Squeezing a sponge can also begin at 3 days postoperatively, emphasizing submaximal contraction rather than a maximal squeeze. Isometric and submaximal isotonic strengthening exercises start 3 to 4 weeks after surgery, and resistance can be increased at about 6 weeks. Sport-specific and functional activities similar to those described for conservative treatment begin 6 to 8 weeks after surgery, and the patient returns to full activity as tolerated.

■ Estimated Amount of Time Lost

The amount of time lost from competition varies with symptom intensity and duration. A conservative treatment program may continue for as long as 3 to 6 months. If symptoms have not subsided at that point, surgery may be indicated. After surgery, the athlete can usually return to activity in 3 to 6 months.

■ Return-to-Play Criteria

Before returning to competition, the patient must have full, pain-free ROM and enough strength to progress to more functional activities. Return to full sport activities is permitted when all activities can be performed without pain during or after the activity.

Functional Bracing

Although a counterforce brace can be used with medial elbow tendinopathy, it is typically not helpful. Braces are usually not used after surgery.

Elbow Neuropathies

Because of the relatively subcutaneous location of the nerves crossing the elbow, the muscular and ligamentous architecture, and the risk of compromise secondary to other trauma, elbow neuropathies are a frequent occurrence. These neuropathies can produce symptoms in the forearm, wrist, hand, and fingers.

Ulnar Neuropathy

Ulnar nerve compression is second only to the carpal tunnel in the frequency of upper extremity compressive neuropathies. The two most common sites of compression are the epicondylar groove and the area between the heads of the flexor carpi ulnaris (see **Figure 10.23**). Less common sites of compression include the arcade of Struthers, medial intermuscular septum, medial epicondyle, and cubital tunnel (see **Figure 10.24**).[91,92] Compressive neuropathies of other peripheral nerves at the elbow are less common. Neurologic inhibition at the elbow can cause abnormal hand postures (see Chapter 11).

CLINICAL PRESENTATION

Ulnar Neuropathy	Radial Tunnel Syndrome	Posterior Interosseous Nerve Syndrome	Anterior Interosseous Nerve Syndrome
History			
Pain and paresthesia in the ring and little fingers. Medial elbow pain.	Pain in the radial tunnel over the proximal forearm. Aggravation of pain with repetitive pronation and supination. No numbness.	Pain and weakness in the finger extensors and thumb abductors.	Pain and weakness in the thumb flexors, medial flexor digitorum profundus, and pronator quadratus.
Observation			
Wasting of the intrinsic hand muscles (late stages).	No deformity or muscle wasting.	No deformity or muscle wasting.	No deformity or muscle wasting.
Functional Status			
Weakness of the intrinsic hand muscles. Decreased grip strength.	Function limited by pain.	Function limited by pain and weakness.	Inability to flex the thumb interphalangeal joint. Inability to flex the second dorsal interphalangeal joint.
Physical Examination Findings			
Point tenderness over the ulnar nerve. Exacerbation of symptoms when the elbow is flexed. Positive Tinel sign. Positive cubital tunnel compression test.	Point tenderness over the anterior radial neck. Pain with elbow extension, forearm pronation, wrist flexion, third finger extension.	Deviation of the extended wrist ulnarly secondary to the unopposed action of the extensor carpi radialis longus. Inability on affected side to extend fingers or thumb. Weak thumb abduction	During attempted circumduction of the thumb and index finger, persistent extension of the interphalangeal joint (thumb) and dorsal interphalangeal joint (index finger).

10

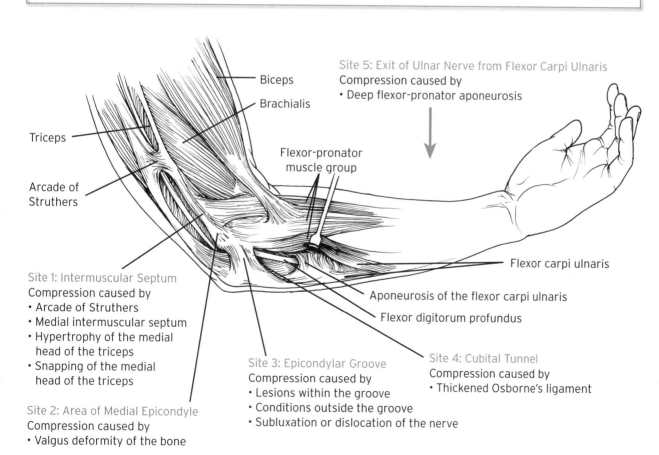

Figure 10.23 Five sites for potential ulnar nerve compression and their associated causes. *Source:* Adapted from Amadio PC. Anatomical basis for a technique of ulnar nerve transposition. *Surg Radiol Anat.* 1986;8:155-161.

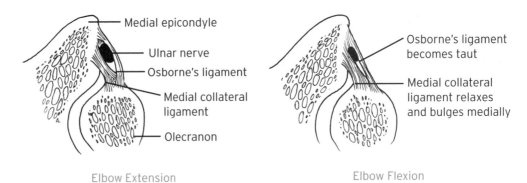

Figure 10.24 Anatomy of the cubital tunnel with the elbow in extension and flexion. *Source:* Adapted from Adelaar RS, Foster WC, McDowell C. The treatment of the cubital tunnel syndrome. *J Hand Surg Am.* 1984;9:90–95.

Radial Tunnel Syndrome

Radial tunnel syndrome causes radial nerve compression. The radial tunnel is located between the radiohumeral joint and the supinator muscle. Compression sites include the fibrous margin of the extensor carpi radialis brevis, fibrous bands at the radiocapitellar joint, the radial recurrent artery, the arcade of Frohse, and a fibrous band at the distal margin of the supinator muscle. Radial tunnel syndrome should be considered in those patients with recalcitrant lateral elbow tendinopathy.

Posterior Interosseous Nerve Syndrome

Posterior interosseous nerve syndrome results from compression of the posterior interosseous nerve (PIN) and causes loss of motor function without sensory deficits. The PIN is a branch of the radial nerve (becoming the PIN as it exits the supinator muscle) and innervates the extensor carpi ulnaris, extensor digiti quinti, extensor digitorum communis, abductor pollicis longus, extensor pollicis longus and brevis, and extensor indicis proprius. PIN syndrome can coexist with, and be confused with, lateral elbow tendinopathy.

Anterior Interosseous Nerve Syndrome

With anterior interosseous nerve compression in the forearm, pain and swelling occur, but no sensory deficits are noted. The anterior interosseous nerve innervates the flexor pollicis longus, radial two-flexor digitorum profundus (thumb and index finger), and pronator quadratus.

Differential Diagnosis

Lateral elbow tendinopathy, medial elbow tendinopathy, cervical abnormality, thoracic outlet syndrome, other neuropathies.

Medical Diagnostic Tests

Electromyographic studies and nerve conduction velocity testing help pinpoint the location of any compressive lesion. Electromyography can map out the affected musculature, thereby identifying the affected nerves. Nerve conduction velocity testing can better determine the location and extent of nerve compression.

Imaging Techniques

Radiographs are usually normal in elbow neuropathies but can confirm the presence of a supracondylar process—a potential site for nerve compression. In the event of posttraumatic neuropathy, radiographs can aid in ruling out nerve injury secondary to bony trauma. Cervical spine radiographs and MRI may be warranted to rule out cervical involvement.

Definitive Diagnosis

The definitive diagnosis of elbow neuropathy is based on the patient's history and the clinical examination findings. Electromyographic findings are especially helpful in making the diagnoses of ulnar neuropathy and anterior interosseous nerve syndrome. Negative findings in the distal humerus and elbow warrant cervical spine and shoulder evaluation for compressive or occlusive neuropathies. **Table 10.1** presents the effects of neuropathy specific to the involved nerve.

Pathomechanics and Functional Limitations

Functional deficits occur along the distribution of the involved nerves and distal branches (see **Figure 10.25**). With careful assessment of motor and sensory status, a more accurate diagnosis of neuropathy can be made and possible causes identified. The pattern of deficits can vary widely, but most defects are exhibited in specific areas of the hand.

Ulnar Neuropathy

Compressive ulnar neuropathy results in numbness and weakness of the hand's intrinsic muscles, which can affect grip and fine motor activities and, therefore, the athlete's performance. The pain can cause functional limitations and is usually exacerbated when the elbow is flexed.

Table 10.1

The Effects of Injury to Specific Peripheral Nerves

Nerve	Sensory Supply	Effect of Injury
Musculocutaneous nerve (C5, C6, C7)	Lateral half of the anterior surface of the fore-arm from the elbow to the thenar eminence	• Severe weakness of elbow flexion • Weakness of supination • Loss of biceps deep tendon reflex • Loss of sensation, cutaneous distribution
Radial nerve (C5, C6, C7, C8, T1)	Back of the arm, forearm, wrist, radial half of the dorsum of the hand, back of the thumb, index finger, and part of the middle finger	• Loss of triceps reflex • Weakness of elbow flexion • Loss of supination (when the elbow is extended) • Loss of wrist extension • Weakness of ulnar and radial deviation • Loss of extension at the metacarpopha-langeal joints • Loss of extension and abduction of the thumb
Median nerve (C5, C6, C7, C8, T1)	Radial half of the palm; palmar surface of the thumb; index, middle, and radial half of the ring finger; and dorsal surfaces of the same fingers	• Loss of complete pronation (brachioradialis can bring the forearm to midpronation but not beyond) • Weakness with flexion and radial deviation (ulnar deviation with wrist flexion) • Loss of flexion at the metacarpophalangeal joints • Loss of thumb opposition or abduction, loss of flexion at the interphalangeal or meta-carpophalangeal joints
Ulnar nerve (C7, C8, T1)	Dorsal and palmar surfaces of the ulnar side of the hand, including the little finger and ulnar half of the ring finger	• Weakness of wrist flexion and ulnar deviation (radial deviation with wrist flexion) • Loss of flexion of dorsal interphalangeal joints of ring and little fingers • Inability to abduct or adduct fingers • Inability to adduct thumb • Loss of flexion of fingers, especially ring and little fingers at the metacarpophalangeal joints • Loss of extension of fingers, especially ring and little fingers at the interphalangeal joint

10

Radial Tunnel Syndrome

Functional limitations occur secondary to pain. Activities requiring repetitive elbow or wrist motions are also affected. Radial nerve compression is most common with passive elbow extension, forearm pronation, and wrist flexion.

Posterior Interosseous Nerve Syndrome

Compression may result in loss of motor function, depending on the specific area of nerve involvement. Although commonly thought of as affecting only motor function, the syndrome produces pain that mimics that associated with lateral elbow tendinopathy. Most PIN compressions resolve spontaneously.

Anterior Interosseous Nerve Syndrome

The patient experiences difficulty pinching with the thumb and index finger (see Figure 10.26). Fine motor skills may also be affected.

■ Immediate Management

With any compressive neuropathy, patients are encouraged to avoid provocative maneuvers that exacerbate symptoms. This restriction is especially important in acute compressive neuropathies.

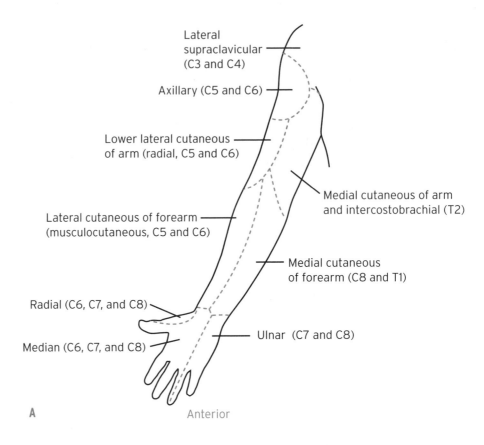

Lateral
supraclavicular
(C3 and C4)

Axillary (C5 and C6)

Lower lateral cutaneous
of arm (radial, C5 and C6)

Medial cutaneous of arm
and intercostobrachial (T2)

Lateral cutaneous of forearm
(musculocutaneous, C5 and C6)

Medial cutaneous
of forearm (C8 and T1)

Radial (C6, C7, and C8)

Median (C6, C7, and C8)

Ulnar (C7 and C8)

A   Anterior

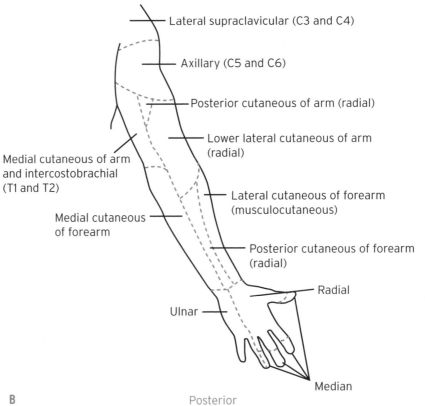

Lateral supraclavicular (C3 and C4)

Axillary (C5 and C6)

Posterior cutaneous of arm (radial)

Lower lateral cutaneous of arm
(radial)

Medial cutaneous of arm
and intercostobrachial
(T1 and T2)

Lateral cutaneous of forearm
(musculocutaneous)

Medial cutaneous
of forearm

Posterior cutaneous of forearm
(radial)

Radial

Ulnar

Median

B   Posterior

Figure 10.25 Sensory function is provided by the C5, C6, T1, and T2 nerve roots. (**A**) Anterior view. (**B**) Posterior view.

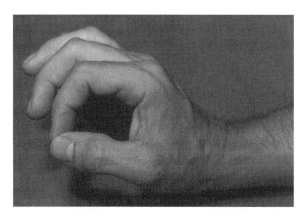

Figure 10.26 Patients with anterior interosseous nerve syndrome are asked to position the hand as shown here. Those with absent profundus and flexor pollicis longus activity flex only the interphalangeal joint of the index finger and the metacarpophalangeal joint of the thumb.

Medications

If the neuropathy is extremely painful, narcotic analgesics may be warranted. The patient may also respond positively to a course of NSAIDs to decrease pain and any inflammation leading to nerve compression. Patients with neuropathies refractory to initial management can be considered for corticosteroid injection. This medication should be carefully injected immediately adjacent to—and not directly into—the nerve.

Postinjury Management

Ulnar Neuropathy

Initial treatment is nonsurgical. Modifying the patient's activities to avoid prolonged elbow flexion, valgus elbow stress, and other offensive activities can relieve symptoms in acute compressive neuropathy. In addition, use of a short course of NSAIDs can speed recovery.

Radial Tunnel Syndrome

Initial treatment focuses on modification of activities so as to avoid provocative maneuvers.

Posterior Interosseous Nerve Syndrome

Initial treatment for PIN syndrome consists of supportive care, as most cases resolve spontaneously.

Anterior Interosseous Nerve Syndrome

Anterior interosseous nerve syndrome is typically related to a neuritis or acute demyelinization within the brachial plexus. Thus most episodes resolve spontaneously.

Surgical Intervention

Ulnar Neuropathy

Surgery is indicated for those patients whose symptoms progress despite, or are refractory to, conservative management. In such individuals, surgical release of Osborne's ligament at the cubital tunnel can relieve symptoms. Medial epicondylectomy has been used in the past but is usually not effective for throwing athletes. Decompression with transposition is the procedure most commonly performed to treat ulnar neuropathy at the elbow. This procedure has the advantage of removing the nerve from the compressive bed; it also effectively lengthens the nerve by transposing it anteriorly. Subcutaneous transposition is the most common strategy, although some surgeons still perform submuscular transpositions. Proximal and distal nerve release must accompany the nerve transposition from its original bed.

Radial Tunnel Syndrome

Before committing to surgery, the physician should make every attempt to confirm that the patient's symptoms are truly due to radial tunnel compression. During a radial tunnel release, care should be taken to ensure that all potential areas of compression are released, including the entire supinator and the distal tissue edge.

Posterior Interosseous Nerve Syndrome

If no clinical evidence of recovery occurs within 90 days, spontaneous recovery is unlikely and surgery should be performed. By the time that this syndrome has been present for 18 months, muscle fibrosis can be irreversible and muscle transfers are necessary. If surgical treatment is attempted, the surgeon must obtain adequate nerve exposure, identify all areas of compression, and perform releases as needed. The extent of decompression varies widely.

Anterior Interosseous Nerve Syndrome

If no improvement occurs with 3 to 6 months of conservative treatment or a space-occupying lesion is present, surgery is indicated. Exposure through an S-shaped incision over the forearm is achieved proximal to the elbow. The median nerve is exposed and traced distally. The most common entrapment area is located under the ulnar head of the pronator teres, which is taken down for exposure and later reattached. Possible areas of entrapment that may need to be released include the pronator teres, lacertus fibrosus, fibrous fascial arches in the pronator teres, and flexor digitorum superficialis.

Postoperative Management

A splint is used for 3 to 7 days after surgery to ensure the patient's comfort, and then rehabilitation begins.

demyelinization
Erosion of a nerve's myelin layer, resulting in decreased nerve function.

■ Injury-Specific Treatment and Rehabilitation Concerns

> **Specific Concerns**
>
> Restore neurologic function.
> Restore patient to full activity.

Typical conservative treatment focuses on avoiding those activities that cause symptoms. Flexibility exercises are performed for any musculature that may be compressing the affected nerve.

Prolonged neuropathy may lead to wasting of the innervated muscles. In such cases, neuromuscular electric stimulation may be useful to prevent or manage disuse atrophy. Therapeutic exercises for gaining active motor function and strengthening should also be performed. A general strengthening program is instituted for the trunk, shoulder girdle, elbow, and wrist muscles, with a more specific program targeting areas affected by the compression.

Functional activities involving fine motor skills should be included in the rehabilitation program. A progressive sport-specific program is instituted once the patient is symptom free. Functional training should be closely monitored for any return of the patient's neurologic symptoms—a development that necessitates activity cessation. A biomechanical evaluation of the athlete's activities is essential to determine any improper mechanics that may contribute to the compression neuropathy.

In patients who undergo surgery, ROM exercises are started at approximately 1 week postoperatively. Nerve-gliding exercises are essential. Strengthening involving isometrics can begin at 2 to 3 weeks, with light resistance started at 3 to 4 weeks. If any musculature was detached to gain exposure to the nerve and then reattached, strengthening begins with submaximal exercises of that muscle at 4 to 5 weeks. Resistance should not be increased until after 6 weeks.

Functional activities involving fine motor tasks can begin as soon as motor function is demonstrated in the previously affected musculature. However, the clinician should be mindful that the musculature may fatigue very quickly. Functional training in sport-specific activities commences at 8 weeks.

■ Estimated Amount of Time Lost

The amount of time lost from competition is highly variable. Symptoms can persist for days to months.

■ Return-to-Play Criteria

Functional strength should be completely restored before the athlete returns to full activity. Full restoration to normal strength may take months, however, and is not an absolute requirement for return to activity.

Rehabilitation

Refer to Chapter 12 for additional therapeutic exercise techniques.

Soft-Tissue Mobilization

The skin, fascia, muscle, tendons, and ligaments around the elbow may be shortened or postsurgical tissues may be adhered, resulting in decreased ROM. Standard massage and myofascial release techniques can be used to increase soft-tissue mobility.

Extensor Group Tendon Cross-Friction Massage

The patient sits with the arm at the end of a table. Using either the thumb or a combination of the index and middle fingers, cross-friction massage is applied to the common extensor tendon approximately 1 to 2 cm distal to the lateral epicondyle.

Range-of-Motion Exercises

Stretching of the shoulder girdle should be emphasized during elbow flexibility routines (see Chapters 9 and 12).

Passive Range of Motion

Obtaining full ROM in the restricted elbow can be difficult. The greatest increases will occur with passive ROM performed for 10 to 15 minutes. The patient is positioned seated or supine, with the affected arm supported with toweling. The clinician slowly moves the patient's arm into the extreme of ROM being treated and holds it there for 20 to 30 seconds. Wrist flexion and extension can be alternately incorporated into every other extension phase of the exercise (see Figure 10.27).

10

A

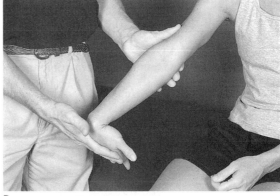
B

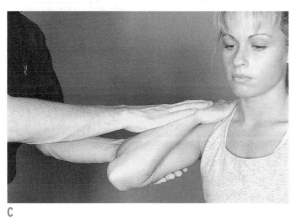
C

Figure 10.27 In passive ROM, the patient stretches the injured extremity against resistance for 10 to 15 minutes. (**A**) Elbow extension, wrist extension. (**B**) Elbow extension, wrist flexion. (**C**) Elbow flexion.

■ Alternative Active-Assisted/ Passive Range of Motion

Flexion

The patient sits with the upper arm supported on a table with the elbow just off the edge. The opposite extremity is used to flex the elbow.

Extension

The patient sits with the upper arm supported on a table with the elbow just off the edge. Using the opposite extremity, the elbow is extended. A small weight (heavy enough to create stretch but not a reflexive muscle contraction) is placed around the wrist to produce passive ROM. The upper extremity is stabilized, and the position is held for a low-load, prolonged stretch.

An alternative stretch for extension involves strapping the weight to the wrist, and having the patient stand against a wall so that the upper arm is stabilized. A towel is placed between the arm and the wall, allowing the elbow to rest in extension.

Pronation and Supination

Seated or standing, the patient holds the end of a 1-foot dowel. The elbow is flexed to approximately 90° and stabilized against the body. The forearm is slowly moved into pronation and held there, and then moved into supination and held there. For slightly more pressure, the patient can use the opposite hand on the upper end of the dowel to apply more force, or a weight can be strapped to the end of the dowel (or a hammer). The patient then controls the upper end with the free hand as the forearm moves in and out of the extremes of motion. This exercise can be performed in various degrees of elbow flexion.

Strengthening Techniques

The following strengthening exercises should be combined with those in Chapters 9, 11, 12, and, when appropriate, 16.

■ Isometric Elbow Exercises

Isometric exercises should be performed with the elbow in different joint positions. Each contraction should be maintained for a minimum of 5 to 10 seconds, depending on the patient's level of strength and endurance. Place emphasis on the gradual increase to maximum tension and subsequent tension decay.

Flexion

Standing with the elbow flexed to the desired angle, the patient provides matching resistance to elbow flexion with the opposite hand placed on the forearm.

Extension

With the patient standing and the elbow flexed to the desired angle, the patient provides matching resistance to elbow extension with the opposite hand placed on the forearm.

Pronation and Supination

Grasping a bar or handle affixed to a wall, the patient attempts to supinate or pronate the forearm.

■ Progressive Resistive Elbow Exercises

Flexion

Standing with the arm at the side and the forearm in a neutral position, the patient flexes the elbow and supinates the forearm in a pain-free arc. Free weights, tubing, or a weight machine designed for elbow flexion can be used for this exercise.

Extension

Lying supine, the patient flexes the shoulder to 90°. The elbow is taken from extension into flexion. Using tubing attached overhead, the patient can stand and pull down, extending the elbow. Resistance can also be applied through the use of a machine.

Pronation and Supination

Standing, the patient holds the lower end of a dowel with a cuff weight attached. The elbow is flexed to 90° and stabilized against the body. The forearm is moved slowly into pronation and then into supination. Resistance can be adjusted by grasping the dowel closer to the weight (decreasing resistance) or closer to the end (increasing resistance). A hammer is a good substitute for a weighted dowel early in the strengthening process.

Proprioceptive Neuromuscular Facilitation Exercise

Refer to Chapter 12 for other upper extremity proprioceptive neuromuscular facilitation exercises.

■ Extension Control Exercises

Patients with extension overload injuries must develop dynamic control in the elbow to limit stress to the posterior structures. While standing and facing tubing that is attached to a wall at about shoulder height, the patient grasps the tubing with the shoulder flexed to approximately 90°. The elbow is concentrically flexed and then extended in a controlled motion through an eccentric flexor contraction. Before the elbow is fully extended, the patient flexes the elbow again, never letting the olecranon process make contact with the olecranon fossa.

Plyometric Exercises

Refer to Chapter 12 for other upper extremity plyometric exercises.

Medicine Ball Exercises

Initially, these exercises are performed with the elbow close to the body in a nonprovocative position. A basketball or weighted medicine ball can be used to perform a two-handed passing motion, throwing to a partner or a trampoline.

Weighted Ball Exercises

As the patient progresses, the arm can be moved out to the side so that more provocative stresses are placed on the elbow and control is developed. Using a small weighted ball, the patient cocks the arm (see Figure 10.28) and tosses the ball at the trampoline using proper throwing mechanics. As the ball returns, the patient catches it, controlling the valgus stress placed on the elbow. As the patient progresses, the full throwing motion is replicated in the exercise.

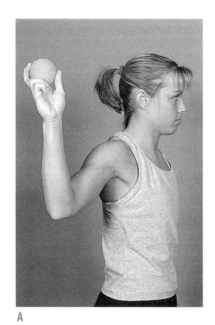

A   B

Figure 10.28   These drills can be used to replicate the throwing motion. (**A**) Overhead throw cocking phase. (**B**) Ball release.

References

1. Wiley WB, Noble JS, Dulaney TD, et al. Late reconstruction of chronic distal biceps tendon ruptures with a semitendinosus autograft technique. *J Shoulder Elbow Surg.* 2006;15(4):440–444.

2. El Maraghy A, Devereaux M, Tsoi K. The biceps crease interval for diagnosing complete distal biceps tendon ruptures. *Clin Orthop Relat Res.* 2008;466(9):2255–2262.

3. Seiler JG 3rd, Parker LM, Chamberland PD, et al. The distal biceps tendon. Two potential mechanisms involved in its rupture: Arterial supply and mechanical impingement. *J Shoulder Elbow Surg.* 1995;4(3):149–156.

4. Boyd MM, Anderson LD. A method of reinsertion of the distal biceps brachii tendon. *J Bone Joint Surg Am.* 1961; 43:1041–1043.

5. Morrey BF. Injury of the flexors of the elbow: Biceps in tendon injury, in Morrey BF (ed), *The Elbow and Its Disorders.* Philadelphia, PA: WB Saunders; 2000:468–478.

6. Norman WH. Repair of avulsion of insertion of biceps brachii tendon. *Clin Orthop.* 1985;193:189–194.

7. Rantanen J, Orava S. Rupture of the distal biceps tendon: A report of 19 patients treated with anatomic reinsertion, and a meta-analysis of 147 cases found in the literature. *Am J Sports Med.* 1999;27:128–132.

8. Ramsey ML. Distal biceps tendon injuries: Diagnosis and management. *J Am Acad Orthop Surg.* 1999;7:199–207.

9. Sanchez-Sotelo J, Morrey BF, Adams RA, O'Driscoll SW. Reconstruction of chronic ruptures of the distal biceps tendon with use of an Achilles tendon allograft. *J Bone Joint Surg Am.* 2002;84:999–1005-2138.

10. Miyamoto RG, Elser F, Millett PJ. Distal biceps tendon injuries. *J Bone Joint Surg Am.* 2010;92:2128–2138.

11. Baker BE, Bierwagen D. Rupture of the distal tendon of the biceps brachii: Operative versus non-operative treatment. *J Bone Joint Surg Am.* 1985;67:414–417.

12. D'Arco P, Sitler M, Kelly J, et al. Clinical, functional, and radiographic assessments of the conventional and modified Boyd-Anderson surgical procedures for repair of distal biceps tendon ruptures. *Am J Sports Med.* 1998;26: 254–261.

13. Cil A, Merten S, Steinmann SP. Immediate active range of motion after modified 2-incision repair in acute distal biceps tendon rupture. *Am J Sports Med.* 2009;37(1): 130–135.

14. Sisto DJ, Jobe FW, Moynes DW, Antonelli DJ. An electromyographic analysis of the elbow in pitching. *Am J Sports Med.* 1987;15:260–263.

15. Morrey BF, An KN. Articular and ligamentous contributions to the stability of the elbow joint. *Am J Sports Med.* 1983;11:315–319.

16. King GJW, Morrey BF, An KN. Stabilizers of the elbow. *J Shoulder Elbow Surg.* 1993;2:165–170.

17. Safran MR. Ulnar collateral ligament injury in the overhead athlete: Diagnosis and treatment. *Clin Sports Med.* 2004;23(4):643–663.

18. Floris S, Olsen BS, Dalstra M, et al. The medial collateral ligament of the elbow joint: Anatomy and kinematics. *J Shoulder Elbow Surg.* 1998;7(4):345–351.

19. Conway JE, Jobe FW, Glousman RE, Pink M. Medial instability of the elbow in throwing athletes: Treatment by repair or reconstruction of the ulnar collateral ligament. *J Bone Joint Surg Am.* 1992;74:67–83.

20. Jobe FW, El Attrache NS. Diagnosis and treatment of ulnar collateral ligament injuries in athletes, in Morrey BF (ed), *The Elbow and Its Disorders.* Philadelphia, PA: WB Saunders; 2000:549–555.

21. Chen FS, Rokito AS, Jobe FW. Medial elbow problems in the overhead-throwing athlete. *J Am Acad Orthop Surg.* 2001;9:99–113.

22. Morrey BF. Acute and chronic instability of the elbow. *J Am Acad Orthop Surg.* 1996;4:117–128.

23. Dodson CC, Thomas A, Dines JS, et al. Medial ulnar collateral ligament reconstruction of the elbow in throwing athletes. *Am J Sports Med.* 2006;34(12):1926–1932.

24. Wilson FD, Andrews JR, Blackburn TA, McCluskey G. Valgus extension overload in the pitching elbow. *Am J Sports Med.* 1983;11:83–88.

25. Azar FM, Wilk KE. Nonoperative treatment of the elbow in throwers. *Oper Techniq Sports Med.* 1996;4:91–99.

26. Azar FM, Andrews JR, Wilk KE, Groh D. Operative treatment of ulnar collateral ligament injuries of the elbow in athletes. *Am J Sports Med.* 2000;28(1):16–23.

27. Wilk KE, Arrigo CA, Andrews JR, Azar FM. Rehabilitation following elbow surgery in the throwing athlete. *Oper Techniq Sports Med.* 1996;4:114–132.

28. O'Driscoll SW, Bell DW, Morrey BF. Posterolateral rotatory instability of the elbow. *J Bone Joint Surg Am.* 1991; 73:440–446.

29. Dunning CE, Zarzour ZDS, Patterson SD, et al. Ligamentous stabilizers against posterolateral rotatory instability of the elbow. *J Bone Joint Surg Am.* 2001;83: 1823–1828.

30. Singleton SB, Conway JE. PLRI: Posterolateral rotatory instability of the elbow. *Clin Sports Med.* 2004;23(4): 629–642, ix–x.

31. Nestor BJ, O'Driscoll SW, Morrey BF. Ligamentous reconstruction for posterolateral rotatory instability of the elbow. *J Bone Joint Surg Am.* 1992;74:1235–1241.

32. Miller CD, Savoie FH 3rd. Valgus extension injuries of the elbow in the throwing athlete. *J Am Acad Orthop Surg.* 1994;2:261–269.

33. Dugas JR. Valgus extension overload: Diagnosis and treatment. *Clin Sports Med.* 2010;29(4):645–654.

34. Bennet JB, Mehlhoff TL. Articular injuries in the athlete, in Morrey BF (ed), *The Elbow and Its Disorders.* Philadelphia, PA: WB Saunders; 2000:563–576.

35. Webb LX. Distal humeral fractures in adults. *J Am Acad Orthop Surg.* 1996;4:336–344.

36. Ring D, Jupiter JB, Zilberfarb J. Posterior dislocation of the elbow with fractures of the radial head and coronoid. *J Bone Joint Surg Am.* 2002;84:547–551.

37. Hak DJ, Golladay GJ. Olecranon fractures: Treatment options. *J Am Acad Orthop Surg.* 2000;8:266–275.

38. Hotchkiss RN. Displaced fractures of the radial head: Internal fixation or excision? *J Am Acad Orthop Surg.* 1997; 5:1–10.

39. Landin LA, Danielsson LG. Elbow fractures in children: An epidemiological analysis of 589 cases. *Acta Orthop Scand.* 1986;57:309–312.

40. Cheng JC, Ng BK, Ying SY, Lam PK. A 10-year study of the changes in the pattern and treatment of 6,493 fractures. *J Pediatr Orthop.* 1999;19:344–350.

41. Farnsworth CL, Silva PD, Mubarak SJ. Etiology of supracondylar humerus fractures. *J Pediatr Orthop.* 1998;18: 38–42.

42. Arino VL, Lluch EE, Ramirez AM, et al. Percutaneous fixation of supracondylar fractures of the humerus in children. *J Bone Joint Surg Am.* 1977;59:914–916.

43. Nacht JL, Ecker ML, Chung SM, et al. Supracondylar fractures of the humerus in children treated by closed reduction and percutaneous pinning. *Clin Orthop.* 1983;177: 203–209.

44. Badelon O, Bensahel H, Mazda K, Vie P. Lateral humeral condylar fractures in children: A report of 47 cases. *J Pediatr Orthop.* 1988;8:31–34.

45. Foster DE, Sullivan JA, Gross RH. Lateral humeral condylar fractures in children. *J Pediatr Orthop.* 1985; 5:16–22.

46. Ring D, Quintero J, Jupiter JB. Open reduction and internal fixation of fractures of the radial head. *J Bone Joint Surg Am.* 2002;84:1811–1815.

47. Brubacher JW, Dodds SD. Pediatric supracondylar fractures of the distal humerus. *Curr Rev Muscuolskelet Med.* 2008;1:190–196.

48. Kuntz DG, Baratz ME. Fractures of the elbow. *Orthop Clin North Am.* 1999;30:37–61.

49. Helfet DL, Kloen P, Anand N, Rosen HS. Open reduction and internal fixation of delayed unions and nonunions of fractures of the distal part of the humerus. *J Bone Joint Surg Am.* 2003;85:33–40.

50. Tredwell SJ, Van Peteghem K, Clough M. Pattern of forearm fractures in children. *J Pediatr Orthop.* 1984;4: 604–608.

51. Gibbons CL, Woods DA, Pailthorpe C, et al. The management of isolated distal radius fractures in children. *J Pediatr Orthop.* 1994;14:207–210.

52. Cannata G, De Maio F, Mancini F, Ippolito E. Physeal fractures of the distal radius and ulna: Long-term prognosis. *J Orthop Trauma.* 2003;17:172–179.

53. Ring D, Jupiter JB, Gulotta L. Articular fractures of the distal part of the humerus. *J Bone Joint Surg Am.* 2003;85(2):232–238.

54. Bano KY, Kahlon RS. Radial head fractures: Advanced techniques in surgical management and rehabilitation. *J Hand Ther.* 2006;19(2):114–135.

55. O'Driscoll SW. Elbow dislocations, in Morrey BF (ed), *The Elbow and Its Disorders.* Philadelphia, PA: WB Saunders; 2000:409–420.

56. Cohen MS, Hastings H 2nd. Acute elbow dislocation: Evaluation and management. *J Am Acad Orthop Surg.* 1998;6:15–23.

57. Durig M, Muller W, Ruedi TP, Gauer EF. The operative treatment of elbow dislocation in the adult. *J Bone Joint Surg Am.* 1979;61:239–244.

58. Wilson NI, Ingram R, Rymaszewski L, Miller JH. Treatment of fractures of the medial epicondyle of the humerus. *Injury.* 1988;19:342–344.

59. Farsetti P, Potenza V, Caterini R, Ippolito E. Long-term results of treatment of fractures of the medial humeral epicondyle in children. *J Bone Joint Surg Am.* 2001;83: 1299–1305.

60. Hines RF, Herndon WA, Evans JP. Operative treatment of medial epicondyle fractures in children. *Clin Orthop. Relat Res.* 1987;223:170–174.

61. Wilkins K. Fractures and dislocations of the elbow region, in Wilkins K (ed), *Fractures in Children.* Philadelphia, PA: JB Lippincott; 1991:509–828.

62. Kilfoyle RM. Fractures of the medial condyle and epicondyle of the elbow in children. *Clin Orthop. Relat Res.* 1965;41:43–50.

63. Tachdjian MO. Fractures of the medial epicondyle of the humerus, in Tachdjian MO (ed), *Pediatric Orthopaedics,* ed 2. Philadelphia, PA: WB Saunders; 1990: 3121–3123.

64. Case SL, Hennrikus W. Surgical treatment of displaced medial epicondyle fractures in adolescent athletes. *Am J Sports Med.* 1997;25:682–686.

65. Jungbluth P, Hakimi M, Linhart W, Windolf J. Current concepts: Simple and complex elbow dislocations: Acute and definitive treatment. *Eur J Trauma Emerg Surg.* 2008;34:120–130.

66. O'Driscoll S, Jupiter JB, King GJ, et al. The unstable elbow. *J Bone Joint Surg Am.* 2000;82(5):724–739.

67. Carter SJ, Germann CA, Dacus AA, et al. Orthopedic pitfalls in the ED: Neurovascular injury associated with posterior elbow dislocations. *Am J Emerg Med.* 2010; 28:960–965.

68. Hildebrand KA, Patterson SD, King GJW. Acute elbow dislocations: Simple and complex. *Orthop Clin North Am.* 1999;30:63–79.

69. Jupiter JB, Ring D. Treatment of unreduced elbow dislocations with hinged external fixation. *J Bone Joint Surg Am.* 2002;84:1630–1635.

70. Uhl TL, Gould M, Gieck JH. Rehabilitation after posterolateral dislocation of the elbow in a collegiate football player: A case report. *J Athl Train.* 2000;3:108–110.

71. Takahara M, Shundo M, Kondo M, et al. Early detection of osteochondritis dissecans of the capitellum in young baseball players: Report of 3 cases. *J Bone Joint Surg Am.* 1998;80:892–897.

72. Shaughnessy WJ. Osteochondritis dissecans, in Morrey BF (ed), *The Elbow and Its Disorders.* Philadelphia, PA: WB Saunders; 2000:255–260.

73. Ruchelsman DE, Hall MP, Youm T. Osteochondritis dissecans of the capitellum: Current concepts. *J Am Acad Orthop Surg.* 2010;18:557–567.

74. Tivnon MC, Anzel, SH, Waugh TR. Surgical management of osteochondritis dissecans of the capitellum. *Am J Sports Med.* 1976;4:121–128.

75. Savoie FH. Osteochondritis dissecans of the elbow. *Oper Techniq Sports Med.* 2008;16(4):187–193.

76. Gramstad GD, Galatz LM. Management of elbow osteoarthritis. *J Bone Joint Surg Am.* 2006;88(2):421–430.

77. Kozak TK, Adams RA, Morrey BF. Total elbow arthroplasty in primary osteoarthritis of the elbow. *J Arthroplasty.* 1998;13:837–842.

78. Lee DH. Posttraumatic elbow arthritis and arthroplasty. *Orthop Clin North Am.* 1999;30:141–162.

79. Morris M, Jobe FW, Perry J, et al. Electromyographic analysis of elbow function in tennis players. *Am J Sports Med.* 1989;17:241–247.

80. Jobe FW, Ciccotti MG. Lateral and medial epicondylitis of the elbow. *J Am Acad Orthop Surg.* 1994;2:1–8.

81. Nirschl RP, Pettrone FA. Tennis elbow: The surgical treatment of lateral epicondylitis. *J Bone Joint Surg.* 1979;61: 832–839.

82. Gruchow HW, Pelletier D. An epidemiologic study of tennis elbow: Incidence, recurrence, and effectiveness of prevention strategies. *Am J Sports Med.* 1979;7: 234–238.

83. Nirschl RP. Elbow tendinosis/tennis elbow. *Clin Sports Med.* 1992;11:851–870.

84. Leach RE, Miller JK. Lateral and medial epicondylitis of the elbow. *Clin Sports Med.* 1987;6:259–272.

10

85. Glousman RE, Barron J, Jobe FW, et al. An electromyographic analysis of the elbow in normal and injured pitchers with medial collateral ligament insufficiency. *Am J Sports Med.* 1992;20:311–317.

86. Plancher KD, Halbrecht J, Lourie GM. Medial and lateral epicondylitis in the athlete. *Clin Sports Med.* 1996;15:283–305.

87. Ciccotti MG, Ramani MN. Medial epicondylitis. *Tech Hand Up Extrem Surg.* 2003;7(4):190–196.

88. Klingele KE, Kocher MS. Little League elbow: Valgus overload injury in the paediatric athlete. *Sports Med.* 2002;32:1005–1015.

89. Adirim TA, Cheng TL. Overview of injuries in the young athlete. *Sports Med.* 2003;33:75–81.

90. Fleisig GS, Andrews JR, Cutter GR, et al. Risk of serious injury for young baseball pitchers: a 10-year prospective study. *Am J Sports Med.* 2011;39:253–257.

91. Posner MA. Compressive ulnar neuropathies at the elbow: I. Etiology and diagnosis. *J Am Acad Orthop Surg.* 1998;6:282–288.

92. Posner MA. Compressive ulnar neuropathies at the elbow: II. Treatment. *J Am Acad Orthop Surg.* 1998;6:289–297.

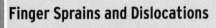
FINGER INJURIES

Finger Sprains and Dislocations

CLINICAL PRESENTATION

History

An axial, valgus, varus, or rotational force to the interphalangeal joint.
Pain localized to the involved joint.

Observation

With an unreduced dislocation, deformity is obvious.
A sprain results in joint swelling and possible discoloration.
A flexion contracture may be present.

Functional Status

Range of motion (ROM) is decreased secondary to pain and
  swelling.

Physical Examination Findings

Joint palpation produces pain.
ROM produces pain.
Anterior-posterior joint glide may reveal instability.
Valgus and/or varus stress testing of the joint may result in pain
  and laxity.

The fingers are easily injured in athletics, and many dislocations are self-reduced by the athlete.[1,2] Often there is no follow-up care or proper treatment because the dislocation appears to be reduced. This lack of attention can result in contractures, missed fractures, instabilities, and malaligned, dysfunctional fingers.

The fingers are designed for mobility and dexterity. Each joint has collateral ligaments and a volar plate to provide palmar stability. The most severe sprain is a dislocation that requires closed or open reduction. The phalangeal architecture can cause a fracture, either from the dislocation or from the reduction. The most common dislocation is either dorsal or palmar at the proximal interphalangeal (PIP) joint (see **Figure 11.1**).

Once a ligament is injured, instability can occur if its integrity cannot be regained. Appropriate treatment is directed at allowing proper healing and regaining joint motion.

Differential Diagnosis
Phalangeal fracture, avulsion fracture.

Imaging Techniques
Anteroposterior (AP), lateral, and oblique plain radiographs help to rule out fractures and ensure proper reduction. Subluxated interphalangeal joints can be identified by the "V" arrangement of the joint sur-

faces (see **Figure 11.2**). Images obtained from unreduced dislocations assist in determining the best reduction method and in identifying intra-articular fractures.

Definitive Diagnosis
The definitive diagnosis is based on pain or instability with ligamentous stress tests and the absence of a fracture on radiographs.

Pathomechanics and Functional Limitations
A tear in a collateral ligament causes lateral instability and may result in recurrent dislocations.[3] Repeated joint trauma causes damage to the articular cartilage and, over time, results in degenerative joint disease. Osteophytes form, reducing ROM and giving the joint a gnarled appearance.

If not adequately treated, an injury to the volar plate on the palmar aspect of the joint results in a flexion contracture. The volar plate contracts, and the PIP joint appears to have a boutonnière deformity; this is commonly termed a pseudobouton-

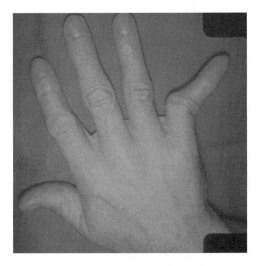

Figure 11.1   An interphalangeal collateral ligament sprain can cause chronic instability, leading to repetitive injury and dysfunction.

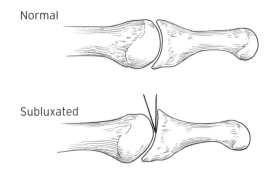

Figure 11.2   A dorsal "V" sign on lateral radiographs can indicate a joint subluxation. The "V" illustrates that the articular surfaces are not congruent or parallel. *Source:* Reproduced with permission from Blazar PE, Steinberg DR. Fractures of the proximal interphalangeal joint. *J Am Acad Orthop Surg.* 2000;8:383-390.

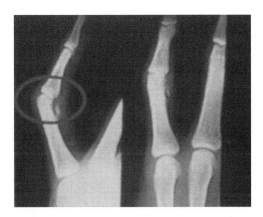

Figure 11.3 An avulsion fracture on the palmar aspect of the interphalangeal joint indicates a volar-plate injury.

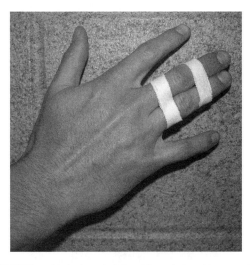

Figure 11.4 Buddy taping. The injured finger is taped to one or both of the neighboring fingers for support and protection.

nière deformity because the central slip of the extensor mechanism remains intact (see **Figure 11.3**).

Immediate Management

After the initial evaluation, ice, compression, and elevation are instituted. The patient is referred for radiographs and joint reduction if necessary.

Medications

Generally pharmacologic agents are unnecessary. However, an athlete taking narcotic pain medicine should not be permitted to participate in competition.

Postinjury Management

When a collateral ligament is injured, a splint should be applied with the PIP joint in 30° of flexion for 2 weeks for comfort, if needed. Buddy taping to the digit adjacent to the collateral ligament injury should continue for an additional 2 to 4 weeks when the athlete is participating in competition (see **Figure 11.4**). In a dorsal PIP dislocation, a collateral ligament injury is associated with a volar-plate injury. In these circumstances, the PIP joint is splinted initially in extension for comfort, and ROM exercises are initiated once swelling improves if the reduction is stable. Joint protection is continued with buddy tape for a total of 6 to 8 weeks for activities.

Taping the injured finger to the adjacent finger helps to protect and further splint the injury from excessive movement, especially rotation and varus/valgus stress.

Surgical Intervention

A torn volar plate can lodge within the joint, requiring an open reduction.[4,5] Recurrent collateral ligament sprains, especially of the fifth finger, may

also require surgery. Surgery is indicated if joint instability results in repeated dislocations or if closed reduction is impaired by soft-tissue interposition.[5] The reduction is made through a midlateral incision over the involved joint. The ligament may be reconstructed with suture anchors when open reduction is required or when chronic instability exists.

After surgery, the joint is often stiff. ROM exercises should be initiated within the limits set by the physician to keep scarring to a minimum. Once activity is resumed, the finger should be buddy taped for protection.

Injury-Specific Treatment and Rehabilitation Concerns

Specific Concerns

Reduce the dislocation.
Decrease pain and swelling while protecting the joint.
Provide support to the affected joint during activity.
Institute early ROM exercises emphasizing flexion and extension.
Avoid valgus and varus joint loading during the early stages of rehabilitation.

If no intra-articular fracture is disrupting joint function, conservative therapy is indicated. Buddy taping can be used for protection, and early, active ROM exercises should be encouraged. The patient is taught to flex and extend each joint independently by blocking the other joints. Passive ROM and aggressive stretching can cause further inflammation. During this time, ice, compression, and elevation are helpful in controlling inflammation. Joint mobilization is often necessary with volar-plate injuries after a few weeks, because those injuries tend to produce more scarring on the palmar aspect and restrict extension.

11

> **Practice Tip**
>
> Evaluate a finger sprain or dislocation for a potential fracture and tendon involvement; radiographs should be obtained prior to reduction of dislocations.

Estimated Amount of Time Lost

Many times, an athlete can participate while using a splint or buddy taping for protection of the injured finger. If a dislocation is open or if open reduction is required, participation should be limited until the wound has closed to prevent infection.

Return-to-Play Criteria

Participation is permitted when pain is controlled sufficiently to allow good function. A splint or tape is used for protection until adequate healing is achieved.

Functional Bracing

An aluminum splint can be customized to immobilize only the affected joint (see **CT** 11.1). Tape may

CT Clinical Technique 11.1

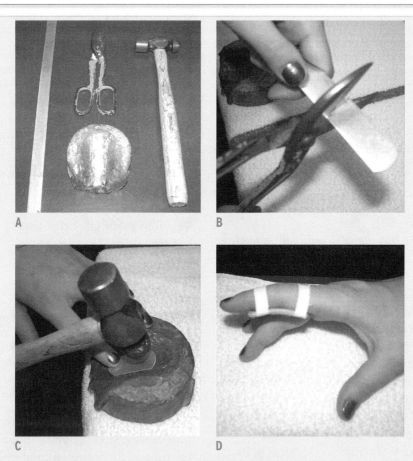

Creating a Custom Aluminum Finger Splint

1. Supplies needed: raw aluminum, lead block (or other form), tin snips, ball-peen hammer (**A**).
2. A thin piece of nonpadded aluminum is cut to the appropriate length, and any sharp edges are filed down (**B**).
3. The ball-peen hammer is used to make a trough in the splint (**C**). The appropriate angle of flexion or extension is pounded in. A block of lead helps to mold the splint when using the hammer. The splint is covered with a thin layer of moleskin to absorb moisture and is taped to the finger.
4. Nonadhesive elastic tape can also be used to secure the splint to help reduce edema (**D**). Further protection is offered by buddy taping to the adjacent finger. The splint can be applied dorsally or to the palmar surface of the finger.

   This type of custom splint is preferred to foam-backed aluminum, which is bulkier and permits more finger movement.

be used to secure the finger to the adjacent one for added protection (see Figure 11.4). In such a case, nonadherent elastic tape helps to control swelling. The splint, brace, or tape support may be discontinued when joint stability and strength return to the preinjury level and active ROM has been restored.

Volar PIP Joint Dislocation (Central Slip Rupture)

CLINICAL PRESENTATION

History

An axial load results in forced flexion of the PIP joint and possibly the DIP joint.

Pain is felt along the finger length but concentrated around the PIP joint.

Observation

The finger is held in a semiflexed position.

Functional Status

Inability to actively extend the PIP joint.

Decreased DIP joint flexion.

Physical Examination Findings

Positive Haines-Zancolli test: Flexion of the DIP joint is not possible with the PIP joint extended.

If passive flexion of the DIP joint is possible with the PIP joint extended, conservative intervention may be possible.

The boutonnière, or "buttonhole," injury is a rupture of the central slip of the extensor tendon at the PIP joint. The lateral slips of the tendon form a buttonhole, and the joint slides through into a fixed, flexed position. Classically, the PIP joint is flexed and the distal interphalangeal (DIP) joint becomes hyperextended because of the pull of the lateral bands of the extensor mechanism.

The extensor tendons in the fingers have a central slip that attaches to the proximal aspect of the middle phalanx, whereas the lateral bands continue to the distal aspect of the finger. When trauma causes a central slip rupture, the delicate balance of the extensor mechanism over the intrinsic muscles of the fingers becomes disrupted. Central slip disruption allows the lateral bands of the extensor tendon to migrate volarly to the axis of rotation of the PIP joint, resulting in flexion (see **Figure 11.5**).

A boutonnière deformity can be caused by either trauma or rheumatoid arthritis. The tendon can rupture when the finger is jammed by forced flexion or axial loading; a laceration can also injure the central slip of the extensor tendon. In rheumatoid arthritis, the PIP joint is slowly forced into flexion by chronic synovitis, which elongates the central slip of the tendon, ultimately rupturing it.[6-8]

The classic deformity does not present until 2 to 3 weeks after the initial injury. If a collateral sprain is misdiagnosed and a splint is applied in 30° of flexion, the deformity will be accentuated. At this point, the PIP joint has a flexion contracture, and surgical management is often necessary.[9-12]

Differential Diagnosis

PIP joint sprain, pseudoboutonnière deformity, phalangeal fracture.

Imaging Techniques

With a history of a traumatic onset, AP, lateral, and oblique radiographs of the finger are obtained to rule out fracture.

Definitive Diagnosis

A boutonnière deformity is diagnosed when the patient is unable to actively extend the PIP joint, and plain films may reveal an avulsion fracture of the dorsum of the middle phalanx.[9] Magnetic resonance

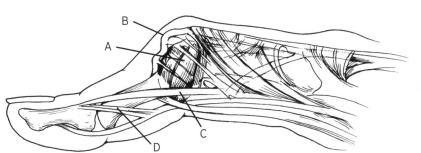
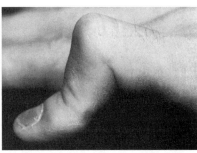

Figure 11.5   A boutonnière deformity. Left: Primary synovitis of the proximal interphalangeal (PIP) joint (A) may lead to attenuation of the overlying central slip (B) and dorsal capsule and increased flexion at the joint. Lateral-band subluxation volar to the axis of rotation to the joint (C) may lead to hyperextension. Contraction of the oblique retinacular ligament (D), which originates from the flexor sheath and inserts into the dorsal base of the distal phalanx, may lead to extension contracture of the distal interphalangeal (DIP) joint. Right: Flexion posture of the PIP joint and hyperextension posture of the DIP joint. *Source:* Part A reproduced with permission from *J Am Acad Orthop Surg.* 1999;7:92-100. © 1999 American Academy of Orthopaedic Surgeons.

imaging (MRI) may show central slip avulsion if radiographs are negative for an avulsion fracture and physical examination findings are not definitive for a central slip injury.

Pathomechanics and Functional Limitations

When the central portion of the extensor tendon is avulsed, the lateral bands continue to exert their force on the DIP joint, causing a flexion deformity at the PIP joint and extension at the DIP joint.[9,11] The lumbrical and interosseous muscles lose their insertion into the middle phalanx due to the incompetent central slip, and their force of action is diverted through the lateral bands. This causes DIP joint hyperextension, accentuated by secondary shortening of the oblique retinacular ligaments. The deformity prevents proper finger function because the PIP joint becomes contracted in the flexed position.

Immediate Management

The digit should be splinted with the PIP and DIP joints extended and treated with ice to reduce inflammation. The patient should also be referred for physician examination and radiographs.

Medications

Nonsteroidal anti-inflammatory drugs (NSAIDs) and analgesics may help with symptom management.

Postinjury Management

The PIP joint must be splinted in extension to approximate the central tendon to the dorsal aspect of the distal phalanx.[8] The splint should allow active DIP joint ROM, and exercise of this joint is encouraged. Splinting should be strictly adhered to for 6 weeks and continued at night an additional 2 to 4 weeks. Dynamic splints are often used to apply a long-duration, low-load force to extend the PIP joint to treat a PIP joint flexion contracture.

Surgical Intervention

If conservative management fails to produce good PIP joint function, surgical reattachment of the central slip is considered. The surgical outcome depends on the severity of the preoperative joint contracture. Surgery is indicated for a chronic boutonnière deformity with a fixed PIP joint flexion contracture and a DIP joint extension contracture.[12,13] Late diagnosis can cause joint contracture, hindering efforts to regain full ROM.

The surgical procedure most commonly performed for a boutonnière deformity is an extensor tenotomy with a release and shift of the lateral bands.[14]

tenotomy
Surgical cutting or division of a tendon.

A tendon graft may be necessary to reattach the central slip.[12] After surgery, the PIP joint is held in extension with a Kirschner wire (K-wire) for at least 10 days, followed by splinting in extension for an additional 2 weeks. The splint may then be removed for activities of daily living, although the joint must be protected during athletics for at least 8 weeks.

Procedures that incorporate a tenotomy require early motion exercises postoperatively. Efforts should be made to avoid extensor tendon stress while mobilizing the finger to prevent lateral band adherence. Possible surgical complications include infection, deformity from contracture, edema, and scar tissue formation.

◼ Injury-Specific Treatment and Rehabilitation Concerns

> **Specific Concerns**
> Reduce the contracture while allowing the central slip to reattach in an acute injury.
> Reduce swelling.
> Encourage lateral band mobility.

For an acute injury, the finger should be splinted continuously in extension for 6 weeks to allow healing of the extensor tendon central slip. The patient should be taught to block the other joints to isolate the DIP joint and encourage active DIP joint ROM throughout the immobilization period. After 6 weeks, active and assisted DIP joint flexion allows mobilization of the lateral bands and helps to prevent their volar migration. If the PIP joint is allowed to flex or if primary healing is not possible, a surgical consultation should be obtained after 6 weeks. Grip exercises can be initiated, and functional stresses may be added. Because of the long immobilization time, the patient should expect the PIP joint to be thick and stiff for several weeks. PIP joint active motion is encouraged, but the finger should be protected during athletic participation during the healing phase.

If surgical management is required, the expected outcome is restoration of full ROM and function. Stiffness should be anticipated for several months as the soft tissue undergoes remodeling; this stiffness often depends on the degree of preoperative contracture.

Postoperative rehabilitation focuses on independent DIP joint function. Active DIP joint ROM exercises with the PIP joint blocked may begin at 2 weeks postoperatively. At 4 weeks, the splint may be removed and gentle, active PIP joint flexion and extension may begin. When the wounds are well healed, gentle soft-tissue mobilization may be initiated. Passive ROM and joint mobilization can be incorporated at 6 to 8 weeks, watching for tissue reaction and edema. The splint can be discontinued after 6 weeks if no flexion contracture is observed. If extension is limited, then a dynamic splint can be applied to encourage ROM. Gradually progressive grip, pinch, and dexterity activities are added after 6 weeks and should continue until function plateaus.

Estimated Amount of Time Lost

When a boutonnière injury is managed conservatively, strict splinting is required for 6 weeks, and the joint should be protected in extension for an additional 4 weeks. The athlete may be able to participate with the splint, but such activity can be difficult with the extended PIP joint.

A concomitant avulsion of the dorsal phalanx or irreducible dislocation of the PIP joint requires primary surgical management. The amount of time lost from competition will be increased if the diagnosis is delayed.

Return-to-Play Criteria

Participation is permitted when the patient understands the consequences of the ruptured tendon and splinting is used. When surgical management is required, the patient must not compete for at least 2 weeks after surgery while the K-wire is in place.

Functional Bracing

PIP joint protection should continue for as long as 8 to 10 weeks during activity. Buddy taping can be used with an aluminum splint during the early phases.

Extensor Tendon Avulsion

The extensor tendon of the finger attaches to the proximal aspect of the distal phalanx. When the finger is extended and struck by an object on the tip, forceful DIP joint flexion can avulse or rupture the extensor tendon. A mallet finger results, and the patient is unable to actively extend the DIP joint (see **Figure 11.6**).

Differential Diagnosis

Phalangeal fracture, extensor tendon rupture.

Imaging Techniques

Standard radiographs include AP, lateral, and posteroanterior (PA) views (see **Figure 11.7**).

CLINICAL PRESENTATION

History

Forced flexion of an extended DIP joint occurs.
A popping sensation in the fingertip may be reported.
Pain is localized to the distal finger.

Observation

Distal phalanx swelling is noted.
The DIP joint remains in a flexed position.

Functional Status

The patient is unable to actively extend the DIP joint.

Physical Examination Findings

Little to no tension is produced during resisted ROM testing of the DIP joint.
The joint can be passively extended.

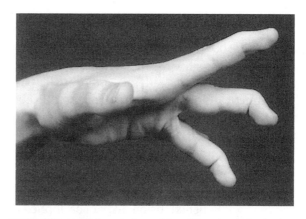

Figure 11.6   Mallet finger is the avulsion of the extensor tendon from the distal phalanx (arrow). The patient would be unable to extend the distal interphalangeal (DIP) joint.

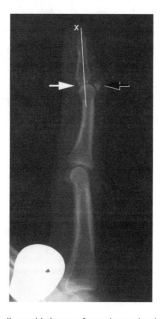

Figure 11.7   Radiographic image of an extensor tendon avulsion. A bone fragment avulsed from the distal phalanx (black arrow) is clearly visible. In this case, the avulsion fracture is intra-articular. The joint space is reduced (white arrow), demonstrated by line X intersecting the midportion of the condyle and proximal middle phalanx.

Definitive Diagnosis

The definitive diagnosis of extensor tendon avulsion fracture is based on the inability to actively extend the DIP joint and radiographic findings indicating an extensor tendon avulsion.

Pathomechanics and Functional Limitations

Rapid tendon loading can rupture the extensor tendon or avulse the bony attachment. When the extensor tendon is no longer attached to the distal phalanx, the patient cannot extend the DIP joint. Except for swelling, passive motion is initially unaffected. Permanent disability, including arthritis, can result when the joint is not kept extended to allow tendon reattachment. When treatment is delayed, the splinting time is much longer because of less inflammation and much slower and less effective **fibroplasia**.[15]

Function is limited with an extensor tendon avulsion fracture because the patient is unable to actively extend the DIP joint. This limitation rarely precludes participation in sports activities, but initially pain limits function. The inability to extend the DIP joint causes more functional deficits in manual dexterity and fine motor skills than in gross sports skills.

fibroplasia Development of fibrous tissues during wound healing.

Immediate Management

The finger is splinted with the DIP joint in extension or slight hyperextension. Ice can be applied to control swelling and reduce pain. The extensor mechanism must be evaluated, and radiographic images assist in differentiating between bony and tendinous involvement. Tendon reattachment to the distal phalanx is required for healing. This generally occurs in conjunction with strict DIP joint splinting in extension for 8 to 10 weeks. Surgical management is usually not necessary. Disrupting healing by allowing the DIP joint to flex can, however, cause a permanent extension lag. Inconsistent splinting also results in poor long-term outcomes.

Medications

NSAIDs may be prescribed to reduce pain and swelling.

Practice Tip

Finger extensor tendon avulsion fractures should be splinted continuously for 8 to 10 weeks.

Postinjury Management

With conservative management, most mallet finger injuries heal with relatively good outcomes.

Mallet finger treatment requires strict splinting of the DIP joint in full extension. With a bony avulsion, splinting should be applied for 6 to 8 weeks. If the injury involves a tendon rupture, splinting should continue for 8 to 10 weeks. Patient education is essential to prevent DIP joint flexion and skin maceration from excessive moisture.[16]

Dorsal and volar splints can be alternated to relieve the constant contact of the splint with the skin. The dorsal splint allows the tactile stimulation that is important in some sport skills.[15] When changing the splint, the patient should hold the finger in the extended position and not let the distal aspect drop into flexion. Stack splints can also be used to maintain DIP joint extension (see **Figure 11.8**).

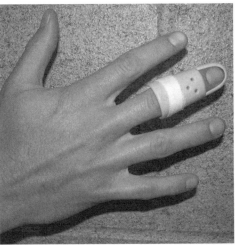

A

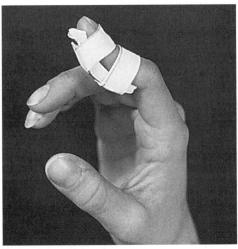

B

Figure 11.8 Mallet finger splints. (**A**) Stack splint. These commercial splints are used to keep the distal interphalangeal joint in extension. They also provide protection to the tip of the finger. (**B**) Volar splint for the management of an extensor tendon avulsion. Because padding on splints holds moisture and can prevent the joint from full extension, the padding may be removed.

Surgical Intervention

Surgery for an extensor tendon avulsion is indicated if the patient cannot, or will not, continuously wear a splint for 8 to 10 weeks.[17] A K-wire can be placed transarticularly to maintain DIP joint extension, although this step is usually necessary only for vocational reasons.[18,19]

In the surgical intervention, a percutaneous K-wire is inserted to hold the DIP joint extended. The pin is inserted under fluoroscopy and maintains full joint extension while the tendon heals. A cork or padding is attached to the tip of the K-wire to minimize injury from the protruding wire. The DIP joint is often stiff after the immobilization, but active extension is the ultimate goal. Athletes cannot participate with K-wires in place. Consequently, surgical treatment does not expedite the healing process and return to competition.

Fingertip pressure that forces the DIP joint into flexion must be avoided for 3 months after surgery. Postoperative complications can include infection, secondary injury from the protruding pin, and loss of DIP joint motion. Patients treated nonsurgically often have better DIP joint motion than those treated surgically.

Injury-Specific Treatment and Rehabilitation Concerns

> **Specific Concerns**
>
> Control flexion ROM to allow healing to occur.
> Obtain full DIP joint extension.

The primary goal in managing a mallet finger is to achieve full DIP joint extension. Arthritic changes may occur over time when good DIP joint function is not restored with the initial immobilization. Compliance with continual splinting is imperative for 9 weeks to ensure good extensor tendon scarring. Because only DIP joint immobilization is necessary, PIP joint motion is unrestricted. Thus PIP joint stiffness is rare.

Once the immobilization period has ended, active DIP joint ROM is encouraged. The patient should be taught how to isolate each joint's function by blocking other joints. Most patients regain function without supervised therapy.

Estimated Amount of Time Lost

Many athletes can participate with the DIP joint splinted in full extension. The PIP joint is not im-

mobilized, which increases function, but care should be taken to prevent the DIP joint from flexing. Poor or inconsistent splinting increases the time for healing.

Return-to-Play Criteria

The athlete can participate with a splint in place if function is not compromised. Full healing must occur before engagement in sports is permitted without splint protection.

Functional Bracing

Either a dorsal or volar splint should be applied in full DIP joint extension. Padding should be minimized, however, because it retains moisture and prevents the splint from maintaining full extension. Stack splints can be used but should fit well; splints that are too loose will allow DIP joint flexion, while those that are too tight can cause skin breakdown (see Figure 11.8).

percutaneous
Through the skin.

Flexor Digitorum Profundus Tendon Avulsion

CLINICAL PRESENTATION

History

Forced extension of the fingers occurred while grasping an object.
The patient may report hearing or feeling a "pop" as the tendon avulsed.
Pain is reported at the distal phalanx and DIP joint.

Observation

DIP joint swelling.
Ecchymosis.
There may be no obvious deformity.

Functional Status

ROM is initially limited by pain.
The patient is unable to actively flex the DIP joint, which is evident when the patient is asked to make a fist.

Physical Examination Findings

The retracted tendon may be felt at the PIP joint or in the palm.
Passive DIP joint ROM is normal; active and resisted ROM is absent.

An avulsion of the flexor digitorum profundus (FDP) tendon can occur with forced DIP joint extension while the athlete is grasping an object. This entity is commonly termed "jersey finger," because it most often results when a player grabs an opponent's jersey or uniform. The fifth finger slides off the jersey and the force is directed to the fourth finger, which has the highest incidence of FDP injury. The tendon rupture site is frequently the bone–tendon attachment at the distal phalanx. The patient is unable to

11

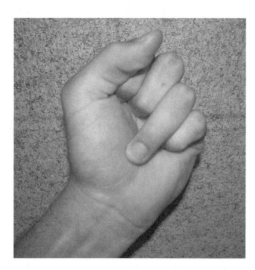

Figure 11.9 Presentation of "jersey finger." The patient is able to flex all fingers except the distal interphalangeal joint of the affected finger.

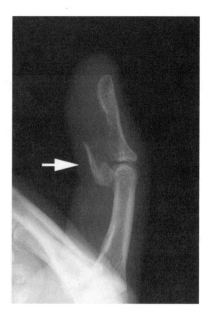

Figure 11.10 Radiographs help determine the presence of an avulsion fracture of the flexor tendon. The site of the bone fragment aids in localizing the tendon end.

fully flex the DIP joint; however, PIP joint motion is unaffected because the flexor digitorum superficialis (FDS) is still intact (see **Figure 11.9**).

Jersey finger is commonly missed; in a cursory evaluation, inability to flex the DIP joint may be assumed to be caused by swelling or pain in the fingertip. When the FDP is avulsed, it retracts to the PIP joint or into the palm if diagnosis is delayed. If retraction is extensive, the tendon can lose blood supply from the vinculae.[20,21] When tendon nutrition has been compromised, direct repair may not be possible. All FDP avulsions should be surgically repaired within 10 to 14 days.

Differential Diagnosis

Phalangeal fracture, DIP joint sprain or dislocation.

Imaging Techniques

Lateral radiographs are used to determine the location of the tendon end. A small piece of bone usually avulses with the tendon (see **Figure 11.10**).

Definitive Diagnosis

A lateral radiograph revealing an avulsion fracture near the middle phalanx and the patient's inability to actively flex the DIP joint indicate a rupture of the FDP. A bony avulsion is not present in all cases; therefore, examination should include active ROM at each interphalangeal (IP) joint.

Pathomechanics and Functional Limitations

The FDS and FDP control flexion of the finger interphalangeal joints. The FDS inserts on the middle phalanx and is responsible only for flexing the PIP joint. The FDP extends to the fingertip and inserts on the distal phalanx.

When the finger is forced into extension while the flexors are contracting, the stress causes the FDP to rupture, most commonly at the distal insertion site. If tendon retraction has not occurred, the avulsed tendon end may be located at the DIP joint. In some cases, the tendon may retract, either to the level of the FDS hiatus at the middle phalanx or into the palm. The tendon's blood supply may be compromised with retraction, placing a time limit on the possibility of direct repair.[21]

The outcome depends on the initial management of the injury, use of good surgical skills to repair the damage, management of scarring, and adherence to a rehabilitation program to restore tendon gliding and joint mobility.

■ Immediate Management

A complete examination should be done to determine whether the tendon is still attached to the distal phalanx. Immediate referral to a hand surgeon is necessary to determine the best course of treatment. If either the referral or the surgery is delayed, a tendon graft may be necessary because of retraction of the FDP.

■ Medications

NSAIDs may be prescribed to reduce pain and swelling.

■ Surgical Intervention

Surgical reattachment of the FDS tendon is necessary with jersey finger (see ⓢⓣ 11.1). The choice of procedure is determined by the level of tendon retraction, which is usually a function of the time elapsed since

Repair of a Flexor Tendon Avulsion

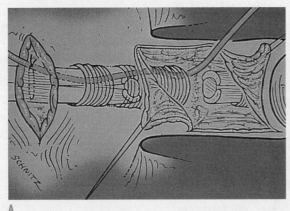

A

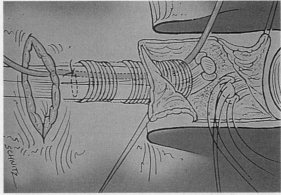

B

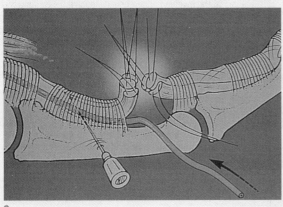

C

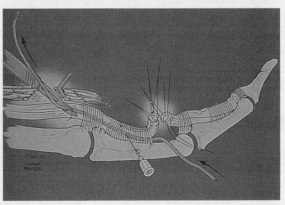

D

Indications

An avulsed FDP tendon.

Procedure Overview

Depending on the level of retraction of the injured tendon and its viability, the tendon may be directly reattached. This is the best option, but the diagnosis and treatment course must be defined early.

1. A midlateral or volar zigzag incision is used, depending on the location of the retracted flexor tendon.
2. The tendon sheath is exposed from the area of the profundus insertion to a point just proximal to the PIP joint. The end of the tendon is identified (**A**).
3. A small catheter is placed in a retrograde position from distal to proximal, passing under the sheath and pulleys to the retraction point of the tendon (**B**).
4. A hypodermic needle is used to temporarily "pin" the proximal tendon in place (**C**).
5. The tendon is drawn up to its attachment site.
6. Using various fixation techniques, the FDP is reattached to the distal phalanx (**D**).
7. If tendon viability has been lost, the tendon must be replaced with either a graft or a Hunter rod. The graft is prepared and pulled through the space the FDP occupied.

Functional Limitations

Tendon retraction can cause necrosis, requiring the use of a tendon graft or Hunter rod staged tendon repair to restore active DIP joint flexion. Delayed repair can cause finger stiffness and contracture, making rehabilitation arduous. Digit dexterity and flexibility may be affected.

Implications for Rehabilitation

Tendon stress should be minimized. Passive flexion is encouraged but not forced, because the tissues react to excessive forces by swelling. The hand should be protected from grasping or using the flexors with resistance until the tendon is well healed. It may take 4 to 6 weeks for the tendon to regain sufficient tensile strength. Gentle active motion is encouraged to facilitate tendon gliding.

Complications

Potential complications include tendon retraction into the palm, stiffness, failure of the tendon graft, and rerupture.

Source: Figures reproduced with permission from Strickland JW. Flexor tendon injuries: II. Operative technique. *J Am Acad Orthop Surg.* 1995;3:55-62.

11

the injury. If the retraction is at the level of the FDS hiatus, the tendon can be reattached if treated within 3 to 6 weeks. If retraction is at the level of the palm, surgery must be performed within 7 to 10 days. If direct repair is not possible, a tendon graft must be used to restore DIP joint function. This graft can be done with the palmaris longus tendon or with a Hunter rod staged tendon reconstruction.[20,21]

Postoperative Management

Postoperatively, the finger is splinted. Once healing has begun, ROM is encouraged to assist in restoration of tendon gliding. Active motion is delayed for 4 weeks to ensure that the repair has healed fully. The athlete is not permitted to participate in sports until the tendon is completely healed.

Injury-Specific Treatment and Rehabilitation Concerns

Specific Concerns

Regain ROM of the affected finger.
Prevent contracture.
Control edema.

Postoperatively, the goals are to allow tendon gliding while minimizing stress on the repair. Passive motion is started 1 week postoperatively and active motion is delayed until 4 weeks after surgery. Grasping with the fingers or stress such as carrying a plastic grocery sack should be avoided for 8 to 10 weeks. At 10 to 12 weeks, more aggressive activities can be tolerated.

Estimated Amount of Time Lost

Surgical repair is necessary to regain DIP joint function. The repair should be protected with splinting for 6 weeks for normal activities and for an additional 4 to 6 weeks during sports activities.

Delayed diagnosis causes the retracted tendon to lose its blood supply, making it unsuitable for reattachment. Furthermore, delayed treatment causes the joint to become stiff from disuse; the DIP joint loses ROM and can become fibrotic. If a tendon graft is required, sports activities are generally restricted for at least 12 weeks.

Return-to-Play Criteria

Once the tendon has healed, the athlete may return to sports. A protective splint should be worn for 4 to 6 weeks after the tendon has healed to reduce DIP and PIP joint stress.[2]

Functional Bracing

The finger should be splinted with a customized aluminum splint in a functional position. The finger is buddy taped for additional support (see Figure 11.4).

Finger Fractures

CLINICAL PRESENTATION

History

Trauma to the involved finger, usually involving a twisting force or direct impact.
Pain.

Observation

Swelling may be observed.
Ecchymosis is common.
Malalignment may be noted with the fingers flexed or extended.
The nail of the involved finger may be malaligned.

Functional Status

ROM is limited by pain.

Physical Examination Findings

Point tenderness over the fracture site.
Crepitus may be present.
Positive percussion test.

Some finger fractures heal well without treatment; however, intra-articular fractures can cause stiff and painful joints, and spiral fractures can cause deformities. Proper examination and treatment help to ensure good alignment and function.

The fingers can be fractured in many ways. The distal phalanx is most commonly fractured with a direct, crushing force and often develops a subungual hematoma. The middle phalanx is often fractured with either a direct force or twisting of the finger.[22–24] The proximal phalanx is usually fractured with torsion and may have a spiral or angular fracture. The tendinous attachment of the muscles that control the phalanges can cause dynamic instability of some finger fractures (see **Figure 11.11**). In each scenario, the fracture location and direction must be considered to determine whether conservative or surgical management is needed to prevent deformity and dysfunction.[24–26]

Differential Diagnosis

Metacarpal fracture, interphalangeal joint dislocation, metacarpophalangeal (MCP) joint dislocation, finger sprain.

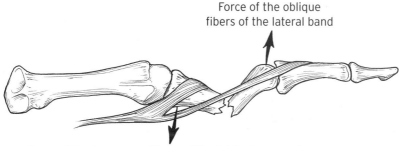

Force of the oblique
fibers of the lateral band

Force of the transverse fibers of the intrinsic apparatus

Central slip

Flexor digitorum superficialis

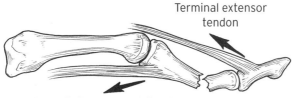

Terminal extensor
tendon

Flexor digitorum superficialis

Figure 11.11 Deforming forces on phalangeal fractures. *Source:* Modified with permission from J. Marlowe.

Imaging Techniques

AP, PA, lateral, and oblique radiographs should be obtained to confirm the diagnosis and identify the presence of an intra-articular fracture (see **Figure 11.12**).

Definitive Diagnosis

The definitive diagnosis is based on radiographic and clinical findings (see **Figure 11.13**).

Pathomechanics and Functional Limitations

Phalangeal fracture stability depends on the location, fracture orientation, and degree of initial displacement. Distal phalanx fractures are usually stable, even though they may be comminuted. Fractures within the diaphyses of the proximal and middle phalanges are typically stable when there is no initial displacement. These fractures generally have good outcomes, especially when the patient complies with splinting restrictions.[22]

When an intra-articular interphalangeal fracture involves the condyles, the fracture is inherently unstable. Similarly, displaced fractures involving the diaphyses of the proximal and middle phalanges are unstable secondary to the pull of the intrinsic muscles and flexor tendons. These fractures require greater care and often surgical management to prevent deformity and ensure that the patient regains joint function.[25–27] Most

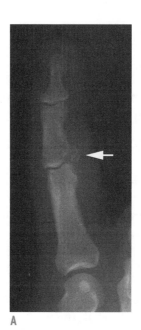
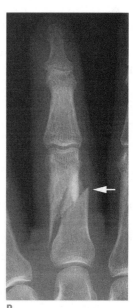

A   B

Figure 11.12 Radiographs of phalangeal fractures. **(A)** Posteroanterior view demonstrating an intra-articular fracture of the proximal interphalangeal joint (arrow) caused by an avulsion of the radial collateral ligament. **(B)** Posteroanterior view showing an oblique fracture of the proximal phalanx (arrow). Clinically, the finger appears shortened.

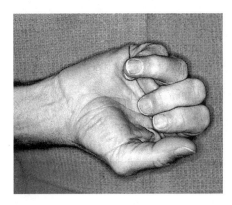

Figure 11.13 Active finger flexion produced overlap in this patient, indicating malrotation associated with a spiral fracture of the proximal phalanx of the ring finger. Alignment appeared normal when the fingers were extended.

fractures heal well with the use of a splint for 3 to 6 weeks.[22] Some fractures require surgical management to prevent deformation or allow a joint to function properly.[25,28]

Immediate Management

Treatment should focus on minimizing pain and swelling. Buddy taping and a splint should be applied, and the patient should be referred to a physician for radiographs.

Medications

NSAIDs may be prescribed for pain relief.

Surgical Intervention

Nondisplaced, stable phalangeal fractures typically heal well with splinting and nonsurgical treatment. Indications for surgical management include open fractures, irreducible fractures, unstable fractures, failed closed reductions, fractures involving more than 25% of the articular surface, and displaced intra-articular fractures. Treatment of avulsion injuries, such as mallet finger or jersey finger, should focus on the soft tissue. All finger surgeries should be performed with minimal incisions and a concerted effort to reduce scar formation between the tendons and bones.

An intra-articular unicondylar and bicondylar fracture is unstable and requires fixation. Such a fracture is reduced and fixated using screws or minicondylar plates.[25,27] Unstable shaft fractures of the middle and proximal phalanges can be fixated with longitudinal K-wires. With longer spiral fractures, percutaneous mini-fragment screws can be used.

Postoperatively, interposition of periosteum within the fracture can cause nonunion, pain, and

deformity. In addition, poor follow-up or noncompliance with splinting can result in deformity. Neglect of intra-articular fractures causes deformity, pain, and degenerative joint disease.

Postinjury/Postoperative Management

Most displaced finger fractures can be treated conservatively with closed reduction and immobilization. Displaced intra-articular fractures require anatomic reduction of the joint surface and sometimes open reduction and internal fixation (ORIF). Once the fracture has been stabilized, early ROM is recommended to prevent adhesions. The splint can be removed as often as 6 times per day to allow passive motion. Generally, K-wires are removed after 3 to 4 weeks and active motion is encouraged.

Most finger fractures heal well with time and protection. The clinician should emphasize that the splinting is not necessarily for pain reduction but rather to ensure good alignment and function later. Unfortunately, many athletes continue to use the splint as long as the finger hurts but then discard the device soon afterward.[22,28,29]

Injury-Specific Treatment and Rehabilitation Concerns

> **Specific Concerns**
>
> Rotational fractures should be followed up to monitor healing.
> Ensure compliance with splinting.
> Restore ROM.

The duration of immobilization depends on the type of fracture but generally is in the range of 3 to 6 weeks. Once the immobilization period has ended, attempts to restore mobility begin. Gentle active motion is encouraged at each joint independently. If digital stiffness or thickening exists, soft-tissue mobilization may begin. Aggressive joint mobilization and passive stretching should start only when the fracture is well healed. Again, this length of this period is dictated by the type of fracture present. Most finger fractures do not require a supervised strengthening program.

Estimated Amount of Time Lost

An athlete may be able to participate with a nondisplaced, extra-articular fracture if splinting and buddy taping are used. If the fracture is intra-articular or displaced, sport participation may be prohibited for 2 weeks to avoid the need for surgery.[22]

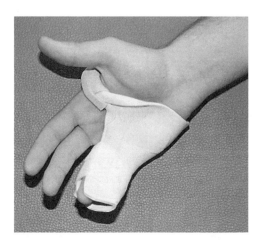

Figure 11.14 Thermoplastic splint used in the treatment of a proximal phalanx fracture.

Finger fractures require 3 to 6 weeks to heal. If the athlete is unable to participate in the sport using a protective splint or taping, then return to competition should be delayed until the fracture is healed. Complicated fractures, especially spiral fractures of the proximal phalanx, can rotate and displace, increasing the amount of time lost from the injury.

■ Return-to-Play Criteria

Return to play is dictated by the physician, because unstable fractures may require surgery if they become displaced during activity. Many athletes with finger fractures can participate in their sports using a splint. All open fractures preclude participation until the wound has healed.

Functional Bracing

An aluminum splint can be cut to the correct size so that the joints above and below the fracture are stabilized (see CT 11.1). If no other soft-tissue injury is present, the interphalangeal joints should be flexed to 30°. Use of nonadherent elastic tape helps to control edema. The finger can be buddy taped to the adjacent finger for added stability (see Figure 11.4). Proximal phalanx fractures can be immobilized with a moldable thermoplastic splint that covers the injured and adjacent fingers (see Figure 11.14).

Trigger Finger

Trigger finger occurs when the flexor tendon becomes caught in the A1 retinacular pulley (see Figure 11.15). Flexor tendons are attached to the bones and volar plates by pulleys that prevent the ten-

---

CLINICAL PRESENTATION

History

Patients tend to be older than 30 years of age; most are 55 to 60 years old.
Complaints of locking, snapping, or catching during finger flexion and extension are reported.
Pain may be in the distal palm, possibly radiating into the finger.
Trigger finger often affects multiple digits.

Observation

Hesitation may be noted during active motion.
Audible snapping may be heard.
Flexion contracture may be present.

Functional Status

ROM is limited secondary to pain.
Nodules may restrict ROM.

Physical Examination Findings

The A1 pulley is tender to palpation.
A nodule may be felt in the FDS tendon.
Triggering or snapping of the fingers may be noted.

---

dons from bowstringing. When the tendon sheath becomes thickened or swollen, it pinches the tendon and prevents it from gliding smoothly (see Figure 11.16). With trigger finger, the finger snaps as it goes through flexion and extension; in the late stages of this defect, the patient may need to manipulate the digit to achieve extension. Although trigger finger may be caused by a collagen vascular disease, such as rheumatoid arthritis, or diabetes,

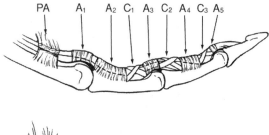
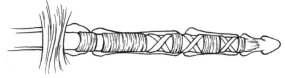

Figure 11.15 Lateral (top) and dorsal (bottom) views of a finger illustrating the components of the digital flexor sheath. The sturdy annular pulleys (A1, A2, A3, A4, and A5) are important biomechanically in keeping the tendons closely applied to the phalanges. The thin, pliable cruciate pulleys (C1, C2, and C3) collapse to allow full digital flexion. A recent addition to the nomenclature is the palmar aponeurosis pulley (PA), which adds to the biomechanical efficiency of the sheath system. *Source:* Reproduced with permission from Strickland JW. Flexor tendon injuries: I. Foundations of treatment. *J Am Acad Orthop Surg.* 1995;3:44-54.

11

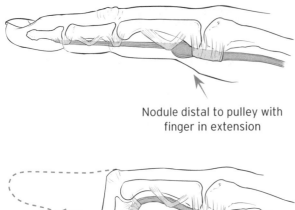

Nodule distal to pulley with finger in extension

Tendon nodule locked proximal to pulley

Figure 11.16 The trigger-finger phenomenon. A nodule or thickening develops in the flexor tendon and strikes the proximal pulley, making finger flexion difficult. *Source:* Reproduced with permission from Greene WB (ed). *Essentials of Musculoskeletal Care,* ed 2. Rosemont, IL: American Academy of Orthopaedic Surgeons; 2000:282.

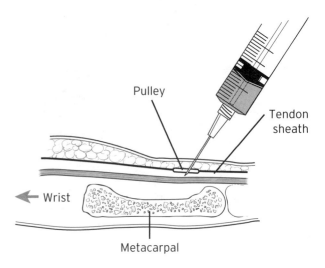

Figure 11.17 Injection site for trigger finger. The needle is carefully passed through the pulley before the medication is injected. *Source:* Reproduced with permission from Greene WB (ed). *Essentials of Musculoskeletal Care,* ed 2. Rosemont, IL: American Academy of Orthopaedic Surgeons; 2000:285.

most cases are idiopathic.[30,31] The occurrence of trigger finger correlates with activities that require pressure in the palm and a high-load power grip. The thumb is most commonly affected, followed by the ring, long, little, and index fingers.

Differential Diagnosis

Dupuytren contracture, sesamoiditis.

Imaging Techniques

Radiologic studies are rarely needed, but views of the hand may help to rule out sesamoiditis.

Definitive Diagnosis

The diagnosis of trigger finger is based on the clinical findings.

Pathomechanics and Functional Limitations

Repetitive activities that require digital flexion and extension are affected. Finger mobility is diminished because of pain.

■ Medications

A corticosteroid may be injected into the tendon sheath[31–35] (see **Figure 11.17**). The patient is encouraged to actively move the digit to disperse the medication. In many cases, the triggering is relieved by this treatment.

■ Surgical Intervention

When one or two corticosteroid injections fail to relieve symptoms, surgical management is recom-

mended to release the A1 pulley. Care is taken to maintain hemostasis and to avoid disrupting the A2 pulley, which may cause tendon bowstringing.[31] The surgical procedure requires a small incision over the metacarpal head of the affected digit and is frequently performed under local anesthesia. The A1 pulley is divided at the midline to release the restriction. The patient is asked to flex and extend the finger to confirm the release.

Active finger ROM is encouraged on the day of surgery, and the wound is protected for approximately 2 weeks. Edema should be managed, but the patient can generally perform many activities of daily living soon after surgery. Sutures are removed in 10 days, and most sports activities can resume at that point.

Practice Tip

To diagnose trigger finger, evaluate tendon gliding for reproduction of the catching. In the presence of catching, conservative treatment consists of steroid injection. If conservative management fails, refer the patient to a hand surgeon.

■ Injury-Specific Treatment and Rehabilitation Concerns

Specific Concerns

Reduce edema and inflammation.
Allow tendon gliding to reduce loss of ROM.

Conservative management involves reducing inflammation and reestablishing function. Night splinting, NSAIDs, and even corticosteroid injections can be used. Early postoperative ROM ensures smooth tendon gliding. Protection of the surgical incision is necessary.

Estimated Amount of Time Lost

The finger may be tender for 2 to 3 days after the corticosteroid injection. Patients who are treated surgically generally require 2 to 4 weeks of protection for the finger, although most sports activities may resume after 10 to 14 days. Extra padding over the incision may be necessary for participating in golf, as an example. Excessive scarring after surgery may increase the duration of dysfunction.

Return-to-Play Criteria

Patients who are treated conservatively may return to play when the finger has full ROM. After surgery or an injection, the athlete may return to competition once pain is controlled and no swelling is present.

Functional Bracing

A silicone-padded glove can be used for golf or other activities that put pressure on the metacarpal heads, which may be sensitive after treatment. The glove is padded in the palm with a shock-absorbent material to relieve pressure from the bony prominences.[29]

Swan-Neck Deformity

CLINICAL PRESENTATION

History

An axial force is applied to the finger, resulting in forced PIP joint flexion.
An associated PIP joint dislocation may have occurred.

Observation

PIP joint hyperextension or dorsal dislocation.
PIP joint swelling.
With time, the finger assumes a posture of PIP joint hyperextension and DIP joint flexion.

Functional Status

Decreased PIP and DIP joint ROM.
Decreased grip strength.

Physical Examination Findings

Decreased resisted ROM for finger flexion and extension is noted.
Joint instability may be noted.

A dorsal dislocation of the PIP joint can rupture the volar plate. The volar plate stabilizes the PIP

Figure 11.18 A swan-neck deformity is characterized by proximal interphalangeal (PIP) joint hyperextension and distal interphalangeal (DIP) joint flexion.

joint and helps to prevent hyperextension. When the PIP joint loses volar stability, the finger hyperextends at the PIP joint, which disrupts the balance of the intrinsic muscles' pull on the DIP joint and causes flexion. When finger extension is attempted, the DIP joint drops into flexion (see **Figure 11.18**).

The volar plate is a thick, fibrocartilaginous structure with a firm attachment on the middle phalanx, where it becomes continuous with the articular cartilage. The volar plate limits PIP joint extension beyond 0°. It is thinner in the proximal direction, which allows the base of the middle phalanx to glide along the articular surface of the proximal phalanx as the finger flexes. Thus the volar plate is both a static stabilizer, limiting hyperextension beyond 0°, and a dynamic stabilizer, influencing the position of the flexor tendons at initiation of PIP joint flexion.[36]

A swan-neck deformity can also result from an unrepaired FDP rupture, intrinsic muscle contracture, or extensor-mechanism disruption at the DIP joint (see **Figure 11.19**). Swan-neck deformities are seen in rheumatoid arthritis, but the mechanism is not the same as with traumatic injuries. Normal laxity in some individuals may result in a swan-neck deformity if the PIP joint can hyperextend, but this need not be immediately repaired if the individual has good finger function.

Differential Diagnosis

PIP joint dislocation, boutonnière deformity, mallet finger.

Imaging Techniques

AP, lateral, and oblique plain radiographs should be obtained to rule out other trauma.

Definitive Diagnosis

PIP joint hyperextension and DIP joint flexion are characteristic of a swan-neck deformity. With a volar-plate injury, the PIP joint is unstable.

Figure 11.19 Swan-neck deformity. Left: Terminal tendon rupture may be associated with synovitis of the distal interphalangeal (DIP) joint, leading to DIP joint flexion and subsequent proximal interphalangeal (PIP) joint hyperextension (A). Flexor digitorum superficialis (FDS) tendon rupture may occur due to infiltrative synovitis, which may lead to decreased volar support of the PIP joint and subsequent hyperextension deformity (B). Right: Lateral-band subluxation dorsal to the axis of rotation of the PIP joint (C), contraction of the triangular ligament (D), and attenuation of the transverse retinacular ligament (E) are depicted. *Source:* Reproduced with permission from Boyer MI, Gelberman RH. Operative correction of swan-neck and boutonnière deformities in the rheumatoid hand. *J Am Acad Orthop Surg.* 1999;7:92-100.

Pathomechanics and Functional Limitations

When the volar plate is ruptured (most often pulled from the distal attachment), the PIP joint loses the ability to prevent hyperextension. As the PIP joint hyperextends, the lateral bands of the extensor mechanism become displaced dorsally, disrupting the extensor force on the DIP joint. Furthermore, the pull of the spiral oblique retinacular ligament becomes volar to the DIP joint axis, causing flexion rather than extension.

■ Immediate Management

The finger should be evaluated for soft-tissue and bony injury, treated with ice to minimize inflammation, and splinted with the PIP joint in extension and the DIP joint in slight flexion. The patient should then be referred to a physician for radiographic evaluation.

■ Medications

NSAIDs may be prescribed to reduce pain and swelling.

■ Surgical Intervention

In the athletic population, this injury rarely requires surgery because splinting facilitates adequate healing. Furthermore, the volar plate often shortens, causing a pseudoboutonnière deformity and a PIP joint flexion contracture. When surgery is indicated in chronic cases or if aesthetics are an issue, the intervention focuses on reattachment of the volar plate using a K-wire to regain PIP joint stability.[36]

■ Postoperative Management

The finger is protected and splinted for 4 weeks after surgical repair. Joint protection should continue while the patient is active until the injury is fully healed.

■ Injury-Specific Treatment and Rehabilitation Concerns

> **Specific Concerns**
> Reduce pain and edema.
> Prevent PIP joint flexion contracture.

During the immobilization period, efforts should focus on reducing edema. After the K-wires are removed, gentle ROM should begin. The athlete should flex and extend each joint independently at least twice daily. Because of the volar-plate disruption, the PIP joint tends to become thickened. Depending on wound healing, soft-tissue mobilization is initiated at 4 to 6 weeks post injury. If the PIP joint shows early signs of contracture, a dynamic splint can be used to help regain extension. Joint mobilization and aggressive ROM techniques should not begin before 8 weeks, and the clinician should be cautious of tissue reaction with passive stretching.

■ Estimated Amount of Time Lost

Surgical repair of the volar plate is necessary to restore volar integrity of the PIP joint. The joint should be protected for 4 weeks for all activities, and splinting is then continued for another 4 weeks while participation in athletics is permitted. Wound healing from surgery can increase the time lost, as can prolonged swelling and stiffness.

■ Return-to-Play Criteria

The surgeon dictates when the athlete is allowed to participate in sport activities after surgery, typically at 4 to 6 weeks postoperatively. Splinting and buddy taping are required during sports while the athlete is rehabilitating the finger (see Figure 11.4).

Functional Bracing

A customized aluminum splint can be fabricated to protect the PIP and DIP joints (see CT 11.1). The injured finger should be taped to the adjacent finger for added stability.

THUMB INJURIES

Thumb Ulnar Collateral Ligament Sprain

CLINICAL PRESENTATION

History

Forceful thumb abduction while the MCP joint is extended.
Pain arising from the ulnar side of the joint.
Functional thumb instability.

Observation

MCP joint swelling and ecchymosis.

Functional Status

Decreased grip and pinch strength.

Physical Examination Findings

The valgus stress test reveals pain and instability.
Pain and swelling may prohibit a thorough examination of the thumb.

A sprain of the thumb's ulnar collateral ligament (UCL) is commonly known as gamekeeper thumb. Historically, this type of injury occurred as gamekeepers sacrificed rabbits by breaking their necks using the ground and their thumbs and index fingers. The thumb is injured as a result of the valgus force on an abducted MCP joint, spraining the UCL.[37-39] If sufficient force is applied, MCP joint dislocation occurs (see **Figure 11.20**). In modern times, a UCL sprain or dislocation is more likely to occur when a person falls while holding a ski pole with the band improperly wrapped around the wrist (skier's thumb)[40] or when an athlete strikes an opponent or object with an open hand. Because thumb stability is important for prehension, treatment is directed to optimize ligament healing so as to restore full ligament function.

A Stener lesion occurs when the adductor aponeurosis becomes interposed between the ruptured UCL and its insertion site at the base of the proximal phalanx, and either the distal portion or the ligament retracts superficially and proximally.[39] The UCL is no longer in contact with the insertion

area and cannot heal. Therefore, the ligament must be reattached to provide joint stability.

Differential Diagnosis

Bennett's fracture, UCL avulsion fracture, phalangeal fracture.

Imaging Techniques

AP, lateral, and oblique radiographic views of the thumb are taken. Magnetic resonance imaging (MRI) can be used to determine the presence of any intact fibers. A stress radiograph may also be performed (see **Figure 11.21**). The joint is anesthetized and imaged while a valgus force is applied. However,

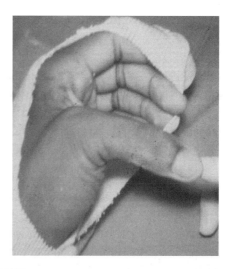

Figure 11.20 An ulnar collateral stress test shows laxity at the metacarpophalangeal (MCP) joint with valgus stress. The test is applied in 0° and 30° of flexion, and the results are compared bilaterally.

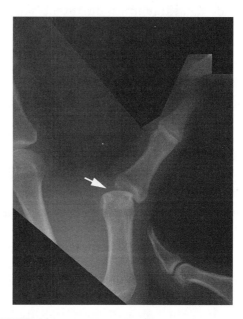

Figure 11.21 Stress radiograph demonstrating a grade III sprain of the ulnar collateral ligament (UCL). The metacarpophalangeal (MCP) joint opens on the ulnar side when stress is applied (arrow). A Stener lesion also may be present.

11

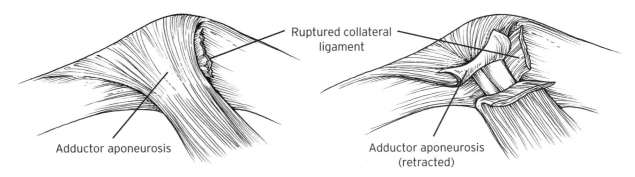

Figure 11.22 Left: When a complete rupture of the ulnar collateral ligament (UCL) occurs, the distal end of the torn ligament is usually displaced proximal and superficial to the proximal edge of the intact adductor aponeurosis. Right: Division of the adductor aponeurosis is required for repair of the ligament. *Source:* Reproduced with permission from Heyman P. Injuries to the ulnar collateral ligament of the thumb metacarpophalangeal joint. *J Am Acad Orthop Surg.* 1997;5:224-229.

this technique may encourage a partial tear to become complete.[41,42]

Definitive Diagnosis

The definitive diagnosis is based on clinical findings or MRI demonstrating a UCL tear and the absence of bony injury.

Pathomechanics and Functional Limitations

A UCL injury causes MCP joint instability, resulting in disability in grasp. Pinch strength and grip strength with the thumb abducted are also weakened. As long as a few fibers of the ligament remain intact, the ligament can heal. However, if a complete tear occurs, the intrinsic aponeurosis, which lies between the ends of the UCL, will block healing[37,39,42,43] (see **Figure 11.22**).

■ Immediate Management

For grade I and II injuries, the thumb should be splinted with an ulnar gutter splint or thumb-spica splint.

■ Medications

NSAIDs may be prescribed to control postinjury or postoperative pain and inflammation.

■ Postinjury Management

Valgus stress to the thumb with an empty end feel indicates a complete ligament tear, and the patient should be referred to a hand surgeon. Grade I and II sprains can be treated with splinting. Grade III sprains usually require surgical correction.[37]

When the patient is at rest, the splint should include the thumb interphalangeal joint and extend onto the forearm for greater pain control. The athlete may participate with the thumb MCP joint immobilized with a thermoplastic splint and tape. In a grade III injury, the UCL tear is complete, and surgical repair is necessary.

■ Surgical Intervention

The torn UCL may retract under the adductor aponeurosis. With an acute injury, the ligament ends may be reapproximated with a direct repair, or the ligament may be reattached to the periosteum (see **ST 11.2**). Chronic injuries may require a ligament reconstruction, usually with the abductor pollicis longus (APL) tendon.

■ Postoperative Management

After surgery, the thumb is placed in a spica splint or cast for 3 to 4 weeks. The patient may begin carefully monitored interphalangeal and MCP joint ROM exercises. At 4 weeks postoperatively, the patient can progress to a removable thumb-spica splint. The splint should be removed only for exercises and hygiene for an additional 2 weeks. At that point, a decision can be made regarding athletic participation with a protective splint. The joint should be protected during sports activities for 3 months after surgery.[37]

Practice Tip

Evaluate the thumb and wrist for potential fracture; evaluate the laxity in the UCL. If there is an empty end feel, refer the patient to a hand surgeon. In contrast, injuries with an end point can be treated conservatively with a splint.

■ Injury-Specific Treatment and Rehabilitation Concerns

Specific Concerns

Protect the joint from stress to allow healing.
Restore full ROM and attain equal grip and pinch strength.

When the immobilization period has ended, efforts focus on regaining wrist and grip strength. Resistive exercise is initiated 6 weeks after surgery. Multi-

S|T Surgical Technique 11.2

Repair of a UCL Sprain/Dislocation

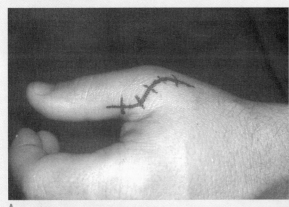
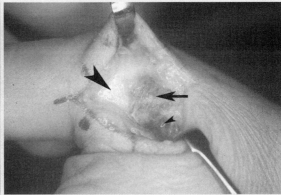

A   B

Indications

Complete tear of the UCL (Stener lesion).

Procedure Overview

1. A chevron, straight, or S-shaped incision is made over the dorsal MCP joint with the apex directed toward the UCL and the broad base toward the thumb's dorsal aspect (**A**).
2. The adductor aponeurosis is identified, detached from the extensor pollicis longus, and reflected; it is repaired at closing.
3. The injury is identified (**B**).
4. If the stump is adequate, the ligament is prepared.
5. If the stump will not hold a suture, the avulsed ligament is reattached using a pull-out wire technique. The wire reinforces the attachment and is removed percutaneously after 4 weeks. If the ligament has been torn in its midportion, sutures are placed with the MCP joint flexed to 15° to 20° and the area is immobilized in a thumb-spica cast for 5 weeks.
6. For chronic instability, a reconstruction can be done using a slip of the APL tendon. The surgical approach is the same as that described earlier.
7. The tendon graft is fed through drill holes about the joint and secured.

Functional Limitations

No limitations are anticipated.

Implications for Rehabilitation

Partial tears should be protected to allow closed healing. Efforts should be made to minimize ligament stress, even with examination, to prevent a complete tear. If a Stener lesion exists, surgical management is required for adequate stability.

Potential Complications

Early stress can cause instability. Immobilization after repair is required, and protection during athletic activity is necessary to prevent reinjury. Sensory nerve loss at the incision site may occur.

---

planar wrist curls are performed with dumbbells. Grip exercise begins with light therapeutic putty or a sponge and progresses to thicker putty.

Thumb ROM is usually regained by allowing normal daily activities, but the range should be compared by placing both hands palm up on a hard surface. Flexion, abduction, adduction, extension, and opposition are evaluated. Any deficiency is noted and addressed. The dexterity of the involved thumb also can be restored by playing handheld computer games, because most games require extensive thumb use.

■ Estimated Amount of Time Lost

Depending on the injury grade, the ligament may require as long as 4 weeks to heal. After surgical repair, the athlete may be able to participate with the thumb immobilized.

■ Return-to-Play Criteria

The thumb should be protected until full, pain-free ROM is attained. All swelling and tenderness should be resolved before the athlete returns to competition, and valgus stress must not reproduce pain.

CT Clinical Technique 11.2

Constructing a Moldable Thermoplastic Splint

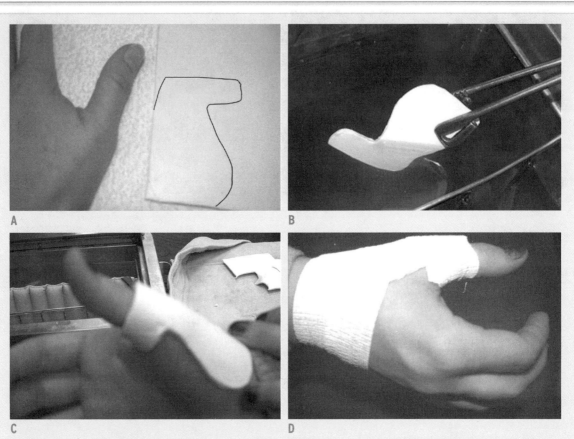

A   B

C   D

This technique demonstrates construction of an ulnar-side carpometacarpal (CMC) thumb splint for a UCL injury. Because the splint minimizes the amount of material in the palm, skilled players are more likely to use the device during sports participation. The mold shape and location of splint application vary with the injury being treated. Several different types of thermoplastic splinting materials are available in varying thicknesses.

1. A pattern is drawn onto the material, which is heated for cutting (**A**).
2. The splint is heated in warm water until malleable (**B**).
3. The plastic is then dried to prevent a burn to the athlete during molding, applied to the injured part, and positioned correctly (**C**).
4. Nonadhesive elastic tape is used to secure the splint and apply even pressure during molding (**D**). The athlete can hold a sport implement, such as a bat or stick, during molding and must maintain the correct position until the splint cools and hardens. Any rough edges can be reheated with a heat gun or padded with moleskin.

During athletic participation, the splint is held in place with athletic tape. During daily activities, the splint can be secured with a hook-and-loop strap glued to the plastic.

Grip strength should be equal bilaterally. Reinjury may cause chronic MCP joint instability, resulting in pain and dysfunction.

Functional Bracing

Thumb-spica taping or a thermoplastic, removable splint can be used (see **CT** 11.2). Full interphalangeal joint motion should be allowed, and the splint should not cause pinching at the wrist.[29] Nonadherent tape can be applied to secure the splint.

To protect the joint after injury, a thumb-spica wrist splint is often used. This device immobilizes the wrist and carpometacarpal (CMC) and MCP joints, making it ideal for enhancing healing. On the downside, this kind of splint makes it difficult for the athlete to participate in sports. When sufficient healing has taken place, a smaller splint only on the MCP joint can be used.

Bennett's Fracture

A Bennett's fracture occurs at the first CMC joint and results from axial and abduction forces to the thumb. The fracture is associated with a subluxa-

History

An axial load and forced abduction of the thumb, causing CMC joint subluxation.

Intense pain arising from the CMC joint.

Observation

Swelling and possible deformity may be observed.

Functional Status

Abduction and flexion ROM are decreased or absent.

Decreased grip strength is noted.

Physical Examination Findings

Crepitus is found over the CMC joint.

Resisted ROM produces pain and weakness.

The following special tests are positive:

· Bump test
· Teeter-totter test, in which pressure is applied to the distal metacarpal, and the clinician feels the metacarpal sublux when pressure is released

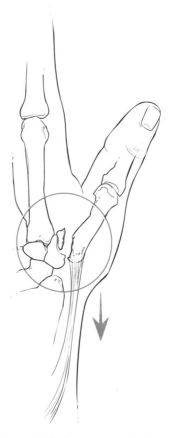

Figure 11.23 A Bennett's fracture causes a retraction of the first metacarpal (arrow). This fracture is unstable and requires surgical management. *Source:* Reproduced with permission from Greene WB (ed). *Essentials of Musculoskeletal Care,* ed 2. Rosemont, IL: American Academy of Orthopaedic Surgeons; 2000:259.

tion of the metacarpal on the trapezium from the pull of the APL tendon (see **Figure 11.23**). Early diagnosis and treatment are imperative to prevent loss of function of this highly mobile joint.[44–46] Unless properly recognized and treated, this intra-articular fracture–subluxation injury can result in an unstable, arthritic joint with secondary loss of motion and pain.[47] Because the thumb CMC joint is critical for pinch and opposition, Bennett's fractures may severely affect thumb function.

Differential Diagnosis

CMC joint sprain, carpal fracture, metacarpal fracture, phalangeal fracture.

Imaging Techniques

Standard PA, lateral, and oblique radiographs should be obtained in patients with suspected thumb fractures or dislocations. Traction radiographs may be used to assess the degree of comminution (see **Figure 11.24**). Computed tomography (CT) or tomograms can help define both the degree of comminution within a fracture and the suspected impaction of the articular surface.

Definitive Diagnosis

The definitive diagnosis is based on radiographic findings.

Pathomechanics and Functional Limitations

The fracture is unstable because the APL tendon places tension on the fractured bone fragment. The CMC joint becomes dysfunctional, and all thumb motions are affected.[46,47]

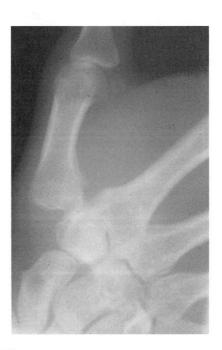

Figure 11.24 A Bennett's fracture usually consists of a triangular piece from the first metacarpal, which remains in its anatomic position, while most of this bone tends to draw proximally.

Immediate Management

The thumb is splinted; ice is applied to control swelling; and the athlete is immediately referred to a hand or orthopaedic surgeon.

Medications

Narcotic analgesics may be required to control acute pain. NSAIDs may be prescribed to control post-injury or postoperative pain and inflammation.

Postinjury Management

Bennett's fractures require either closed reduction with percutaneous pinning or an ORIF if the fragment is long enough. The strong pull of the APL frequently leads to displacement; as a consequence, stabilization of the fracture is required.[45] A thumb-spica cast is applied for 2 to 6 weeks, depending on the stability achieved at surgery. A thermoplastic splint (see CT 11.2) can be used after the cast is removed, and rehabilitation may begin.

Surgical Intervention

The strong pull of the APL frequently causes displacement, which requires repair consisting of either ORIF or closed reduction with percutaneous pinning (see ST 11.3). Generally, closed reduction followed by percutaneous K-wire fixation is successful in maintaining reduction. In this procedure, wires are drilled through the dorsal radial thumb metacarpal base into the reduced volar ulnar fragment. If the fragment is very small, reduction may be maintained by placing the K-wire from the thumb metacarpal into the trapezium or the index metacarpal.

Injury-Specific Treatment and Rehabilitation Concerns

> **Specific Concerns**
>
> Stabilize the CMC joint.
> Reduce edema.
> Regain thumb ROM.
> Increase grip strength.

Gentle mobility of the thumb interphalangeal joint begins within 2 weeks of surgery to help manage edema and prevent adhesion formation. Depending on fracture stability, immobilization using a thumb-spica cast may last from 2 to 6 weeks. When the immobilization period ends and all pins have been removed, wrist strengthening may begin with multi-planar dumbbell curls. Grip strength may also be addressed by having the patient squeeze a sponge at first, with resistance being gradually increased with use of therapeutic putty. Active motion is en-couraged for the first 8 weeks postoperatively, and then passive motion and joint mobilization if needed. Dexterity is regained using coordination drills or handheld video games.

Estimated Amount of Time Lost

Fracture healing requires 4 to 6 weeks, depending on the amount of stability achieved. Surgical management will affect the amount of time lost from sport. The athlete may not participate with percutaneous pins in place.

Return-to-Play Criteria

Full thumb strength and flexibility are required for participation without a protective device. Early participation may be allowed if bone healing is complete and function with a splint is good.

Functional Bracing

Thumb-spica taping improves stability, and a thermoplastic splint can be worn during play (see CT 11.3).

---

de Quervain Tenosynovitis

CLINICAL PRESENTATION

> **History**
>
> Pain arising from the thumb during thumb and wrist motion.
>
> **Observation**
>
> APL or EPB tendon swelling may be noted on the radial side of the wrist.
>
> **Functional Status**
>
> Thumb motion becomes painful and restricted.
>
> **Physical Examination Findings**
>
> On palpation, thickening and crepitus may be noted in the tendons.
> Tendon palpation causes pain.
> The Finkelstein test is positive (but has poor diagnostic accuracy).
> Passive CMC joint manipulation does not produce pain.

In de Quervain tenosynovitis, the tendons of the APL and extensor pollicis brevis (EPB) become thickened, restricting tendon gliding within their sheath (see **Figure 11.25**). The APL and EPB are held against the radial styloid process by the extensor retinaculum. Acute trauma or repetitive motion can cause swelling, and thumb motion causes pain, especially when the wrist is ulnarly deviated.[48,49]

The patient reports pain with thumb and wrist motion. This injury is frequently seen in baseball players who have increased their batting-practice repetitions but can occur in a variety of sports in

Repair of a Bennett's Fracture

Indications

When articular incongruity is more than 1 mm after closed reduction, surgical intervention is indicated.

Procedure Overview

1. The procedure may be performed under local or general anesthesia.
2. Efforts are made to pin percutaneously under fluoroscopy; this strategy is usually very successful.
3. Fracture reduction is accomplished under fluoroscopy with traction on the thumb in palmar abduction. The subluxated metacarpal is reduced medially toward the palm.
4. K-wires are drilled through the dorsal radial thumb metacarpal base and into the reduced volar ulnar fragment. If the fragment is very small, reduction may be maintained by placing the K-wire from the thumb metacarpal into the trapezium or the index metacarpal (**A**).
5. Splinting or casting may also be performed to help protect the K-wire stabilization (**B**).

Functional Limitations

Degenerative joint disease and loss of motion after immobilization can affect the outcome.

Implications for Rehabilitation

Percutaneous pins should be removed before athletic activity is accelerated. Thumb abduction should not be stressed too early to help stabilize the CMC joint.

Potential Complications

Displaced intra-articular fractures predispose the patient to arthritis and loss of motion within the affected joints. Unfortunately, even after restoration of articular congruity, some patients develop posttraumatic arthritis secondary to the osteocartilaginous injury sustained in the initial trauma. Loss of motion also occurs after prolonged immobilization. Other complications can include thumb infection and instability.[45,47]

Source: Figure reproduced with permission from Soyer AD. Fractures of the base of the first metacarpal: Current treatment options. *J Am Acad Orthop Surg.* 1999;7:403-412.

which repetitive wrist motion is common, such as rowing and tennis.

Differential Diagnosis

CMC joint arthritis.

Imaging Techniques

Radiographic evaluation of the CMC joint and wrist helps to rule out other joint abnormalities.

Definitive Diagnosis

The definitive diagnosis is based on a positive Finkelstein test as demonstrated by pain over the APL and EPB, but the rate of false-positive results is high.

Pathomechanics and Functional Limitations

de Quervain syndrome is an overuse injury that is exacerbated by repetition. When the tenosynovitis

CT **Clinical Technique** 11.3

Thumb-Spica Taping

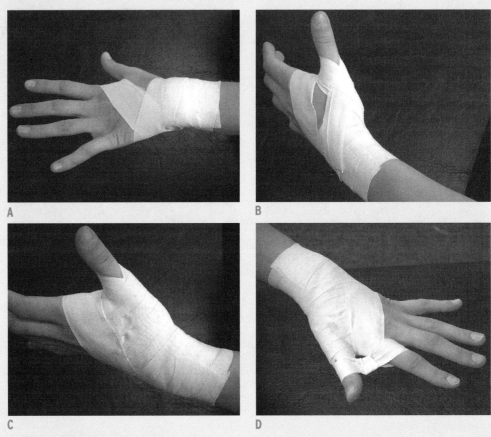

1. Prewrap is applied to the wrist, hand, and thumb.
2. Anchors are placed just proximal to the wrist and across the hand using 1- or 1.5-in. tape (**A**).
3. Two or three figure-of-eight strips are placed over the MCP and CMC joints (**B**).
4. Either individual or continuous spicas are made around the base of the thumb, metacarpal, and CMC joint.
5. "U" strips are used around the metacarpal, and the wrap is finished with closing anchors (**C**).
6. An optional checkrein may be used to further limit mobility by buddy taping to the index finger (**D**).

---

is in an acute inflammatory stage, the patient has functional limitations due to pain with all thumb and wrist motions. As the syndrome becomes chronic, functional problems increase. If the tenosynovitis remains untreated, the edema within the tendon sheath becomes exudative and eventually can become calcific.[49] The longer the inflammatory process is allowed to cycle due to repeated injury, the longer it will take to resolve once rest and rehabilitation have begun.

■ Medications

NSAIDs control the inflammatory process and are effective when used in conjunction with splinting and restricted activities. A corticosteroid injection into the sheath of the first dorsal compartment may reduce tendon thickening and improve gliding.

■ Postinjury Management

A resting splint is used to reduce the inflammation. Once pain has subsided during nonstressful activities, the splint can be removed for strengthening exercises. Active ROM should be performed daily.

■ Surgical Intervention

If conservative management fails, the first dorsal compartment can be surgically released. An incision is made over the thickened area, and blunt dissection is performed to release the compartment.[50] Care is taken to avoid the superficial radial nerve. Tendon gliding must be regained to prevent the structures from scarring down.

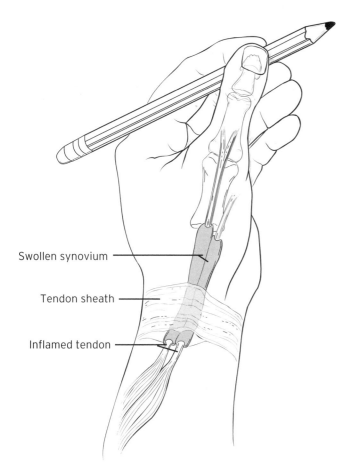

Swollen synovium —

Tendon sheath —

Inflamed tendon —

Figure 11.25 de Quervain tenosynovitis of the first extensor compartment. *Source:* Reproduced with permission from Greene WB (ed). *Essentials of Musculoskeletal Care,* ed 2. Rosemont, IL: American Academy of Orthopaedic Surgeons; 2000:232.

Postoperative Management

After surgery, postoperative splinting is used for 10 to 14 days. Patients are encouraged to undertake normal activities and engage in active thumb exercises to improve tendon gliding.

Injury-Specific Treatment and Rehabilitation Concerns

Specific Concerns

Reduce swelling within the tendon sheath, which can cause stenosis.
Improve tendon gliding by maintaining ROM.

Because de Quervain tenosynovitis is an overuse injury, therapy can begin immediately after the examination. Multiple modalities may be used to help relieve the pain and inflammation. Splinting during activities of daily living can protect the tendons,

but controlled activity and active ROM help to keep the tendons gliding.

The time required for splinting depends on the patient's response. If the symptoms are not relieved with splinting, removal of the patient from the aggravating position, and use of various therapeutic modalities and NSAIDs, then reevaluation may be necessary. If the first dorsal compartment must be surgically released, continual splinting is used for 10 to 14 days. At that time, the splint may be removed for gentle wrist, hand, and thumb active ROM twice daily. At 6 weeks, the splint may be removed for daily activities, and wrist strengthening may begin. Multiplanar curls, pronation, supination, and grip exercises can be taught to the patient. Exercises should be well tolerated and should continue until all symptoms resolve.

Estimated Amount of Time Lost

Limitations in athletic activities are dictated by pain, and the athlete should not participate if the ability to perform is decreased. Consequently, no strict prohibition on participating in a sport with de Quervain syndrome exists. In an acute flare-up, the tenosynovitis may require 2 to 3 days of protected rest to resolve.

Return-to-Play Criteria

The athlete can participate when pain, swelling, and crepitus are controlled. Splinting during participation may allow an early return to sports.

Functional Bracing

An ulnar gutter splint reduces thumb and wrist motions. Commercial braces, as well as tape, offer protection by restricting wrist ulnar and radial deviation and thumb mobility.

HAND AND WRIST PATHOLOGIES

Metacarpophalangeal Joint Dislocation

Forced hyperextension disrupts the volar plate and palmar stability of the MCP joint. The dislocation is typically in the dorsal direction and can be either complex or simple. With a complex dislocation, the metacarpal head becomes buttonholed between the palmar fascia and lumbrical and flexor tendons, making closed reduction impossible (see **Figure 11.26**).

The palmar fascia tightens around the metacarpal head when the lumbrical and flexor muscles are active. This tightening tends to strangle the metacarpal

11

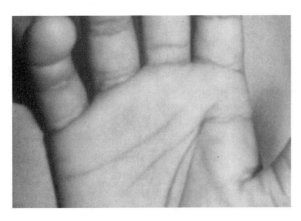

Figure 11.26 Metacarpophalangeal joint dislocation. The patient has immobility, pain, and deformity in the palm.

CLINICAL PRESENTATION

History

Hyperextension of the MCP joint.
Pain arising from the knuckles.

Observation

Obvious MCP joint deformity.
Alteration of the palmar crease.
Marked swelling.

Functional Status

Inability to move the knuckles.

Physical Examination Findings

The metacarpal head can be palpated in the palm.
ROM tests cannot be performed.

head, making it impossible to reduce the dislocation. The problem is referred to as a "Chinese finger puzzle" because the more it is manipulated, the tighter the palmar fascia becomes around the metacarpal head.[29,51] Open reduction is recommended if the initial closed attempt fails.

Differential Diagnosis

Phalangeal fracture, metacarpal fracture.

Imaging Techniques

AP and lateral radiographs of the hand are used to rule out fractures and to confirm proper relocation following closed reduction.

Definitive Diagnosis

The definitive diagnosis is made from joint observation, but radiographs are needed to rule out associated fracture.

Pathomechanics and Functional Limitations

Forced MCP joint hyperextension can cause a dislocation. The joints are typically very stable, but when a force is applied while the intrinsic muscles are contracting, the proximal phalanx may be pried from the metacarpal head. The affected joint is unable to function properly, and any movement tightens the palmar fascia around the metacarpal head.

■ Immediate Management

Neurovascular function should be monitored, the proximal and distal joints splinted, and the patient immediately referred for evaluation and reduction.

■ Medications

NSAIDs and analgesics are used after injury and/or surgery.

■ Postinjury Management

If the dislocation is treated immediately, the reduction technique involves manipulating the MCP joint so as to slide the phalanx back into place, followed by flexing and applying pressure to the MCP joint. Traction on the MCP joint during attempted reduction tends to entrap the ruptured palmar plate between the joint surfaces and make closed reduction impossible. If closed reduction fails, immediate open reduction is recommended. The hand should be splinted in an intrinsic-plus position where the MCP joints are in flexion and the fingers are straight. Early, active finger motion is encouraged.[51]

■ Surgical Intervention

If closed reduction is not possible, open reduction is necessary because the palmar fascia tightens around the metacarpal head. Although a volar approach is most commonly used, this technique puts the digital nerves at risk. A retractor is inserted to manipulate the soft tissue, and the surgeon can then move the structures to reduce the dislocation. Once reduction is accomplished, the joint is often very stable. Care must be taken to minimize scar formation in the palm. Scar-tissue formation from an incision through the palmar fascia can cause pain and decrease MCP joint extension.

■ Postoperative Management

After surgery, scar tissue should be minimized with compression. Hyperextension is avoided for 5 weeks. A splint is used for 2 weeks, and then rehabilitation may begin.

■ Injury-Specific Treatment and Rehabilitation Concerns

Specific Concerns

Maintain active interphalangeal joint ROM during immobilization.
Reduce scar-tissue formation in the palm.

Good functional outcomes are obtained in most patients. Rehabilitation is directed toward maintaining finger ROM, minimizing scar formation in the palm, and preventing MCP joint hyperextension.

The hand is immobilized for 2 weeks after injury or surgery. During this time, the patient is taught gentle active motion of all fingers, incorporating light gripping. Hyperextension is avoided, and protection may be necessary during athletics to prevent this stress. If needed, soft-tissue mobilization may begin at 3 weeks. For most patients, passive mobility and joint mobilization are not necessary to gain function. Restoration of grip strength is emphasized approximately 6 weeks after surgery.

Estimated Amount of Time Lost

The athlete can generally return to play 3 to 4 weeks after a closed reduction or 6 to 8 weeks after an open reduction.[51] When open reduction is required, return to play is delayed for 6 to 8 weeks, depending on wound healing, scar management, and the return of strength and motion. Return to play may be possible in a cast or a protective splint earlier as long as the wound is healed. Minimization of scarring merits special attention, because scar-tissue formation in the palm can restrict function.

Return-to-Play Criteria

The patient should demonstrate the functional ROM required for sport-specific skills. In some cases, the patient can return to competition earlier if the joint can be protected with bracing or padding. If an open reduction was performed, the wound and underlying tissue should be healed before participation resumes.

Functional Bracing

The finger should be taped to the adjacent finger for stability (see Figure 11.4); most athletes are unable to tolerate a splint at the MCP joint. Use of silicone padding or a gel-filled glove can reduce the pressure at the metacarpal head if this area is sensitive to pressure.

Metacarpal Fractures

Hand trauma often results in a fracture to one of the metacarpals. The first and fifth metacarpals are most commonly injured—the fifth metacarpal is especially vulnerable because of the increased mobility of these bones. First metacarpal fractures and fracture–dislocations are covered in the section on thumb injuries. The second and third metacarpals are rigidly fixed at their bases and stable, with little motion at the CMC joints. The fourth and fifth metacarpals

CLINICAL PRESENTATION

History

An axial force delivered to the metacarpals, such as improper punching.
A rotational or crushing force to the hand.
Pain localized to the involved metacarpals.

Observation

Deformity, swelling, and discoloration may be present.
Knuckle asymmetry may be observed, and the knuckle may appear to be missing.
The fingernail of the involved metacarpal may be rotated relative to the other nails.
Finger malalignment may be noted. During metacarpal and PIP joint flexion, the fingers should point to the scaphoid.

Functional Status

Decreased finger ROM secondary to pain and possible deformity.
Decreased grip strength.

Physical Examination Findings

Metacarpal palpation may reveal crepitus, tenderness, and deformity along the injured part of bone.
Pain radiates through the affected finger.

move more freely, with 15° and 25° of motion in the CMC joints, respectively.[52–54]

Metacarpal fractures account for 30% to 40% of all hand fractures and result from either a direct force or indirect trauma through axial loading.[55,56] Torsional stress on the digits can also produce a metacarpal fracture. A "boxer fracture" is the most common type of injury, in which the neck of the fifth metacarpal is damaged by a compressive force as the fist makes contact with another object.

The metacarpal fracture pattern often describes the mechanism of injury. Direct or axial trauma leads to transverse or oblique fractures, whereas torsional injury leads to spiral fractures. The fractures can be stable or unstable, depending on whether shortening, rotation, or angulation is present.[52,53,55] Malrotation can cause the fingers to overlap when the hand is made into a fist. Efforts should be made to prevent even small amounts of rotation, as they can cause permanent disability.

Most metacarpal fractures can be treated conservatively with immobilization of the hand, wrist, and involved fingers. Articular fractures of the fifth metacarpal between the metacarpal ligament insertion and the insertion of the extensor carpi ulnaris (ECU) tendon may cause migration of the proximal fractured portion, however; thus they often require ORIF or closed reduction with percutaneous pinning.[56]

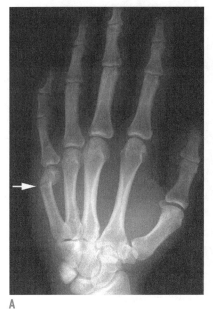
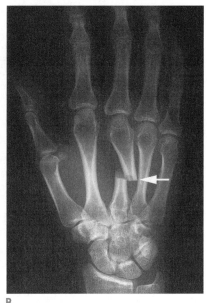

Figure 11.27 Radiographs of metacarpal fractures. (**A**) Fracture of the fifth metacarpal ("boxer fracture"). (**B**) Fracture of the third metacarpal. The fracture displacement warrants closed reduction before casting.

Differential Diagnosis
MCP joint dislocation, CMC dislocation, phalangeal fracture, carpal dislocation.

Imaging Techniques
AP, lateral, and oblique radiographs should be obtained (see **Figure 11.27**). A CT scan is helpful when an intra-articular fracture is present.

Definitive Diagnosis
Radiographs are used to definitively diagnose a metacarpal fracture.

Pathomechanics and Functional Limitations
Metacarpal fractures usually heal without consequence. However, neglect or improper immobilization can result in a nonunion or malunion and subsequent decreased grip strength.

▦ Immediate Management
A suspected metacarpal fracture should be immobilized with a splint and the patient referred for radiographs. Taping the fingers also prevents rotation and displacement of a spiral fracture.

▦ Medications
Analgesics may provide relief from pain in the acute or postoperative period.

▦ Postinjury Management
The fracture is reduced (if necessary) and a cast applied. The metacarpal bone is difficult to immobilize; although a short arm cast can effectively restrict wrist and hand ROM, this bone invariably moves when the finger moves. Accordingly, the generally accepted treatment is to apply a cast and tape the fingers together to restrict metacarpal motion.

The cast is worn for 4 weeks, after which gradual hand and wrist ROM and strengthening exercises are implemented. Active finger motion is encouraged early to prevent stiffness and help reduce edema. Rehabilitation is started when the immobilization phase has ended. Efforts are made to regain ROM and strength in the wrist, hand, and fingers.

▦ Surgical Intervention
Surgical treatment of metacarpal fractures is indicated with intra-articular disruption, severe angulation that cannot be reduced by a closed method, an unstable rotational deformity, and multiple fractures. Most often, the closed reduction can be stabilized using percutaneous pinning that minimizes the disruption of normal tissue. Depending on the orientation, rotation, and stability of the fracture, small screws may be necessary to maintain appropriate reduction and facilitate proper healing. These devices are inserted through a dorsal incision over the fracture site.

Percutaneous pinning with K-wires may help stabilize the fracture. Comminution of the metacarpal shaft can be treated with pinning, mini-fragment screws, plate-and-screw fixation, or a tension band (see **Figure 11.28**).[53,57] Percutaneous pins are left in place for approximately 4 weeks, at which point healing should be confirmed by radiography.

Functional limitations may arise with metacarpal malrotation. If fracture fixation and stability are

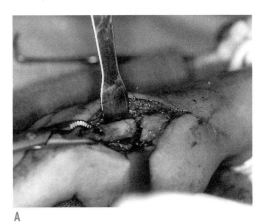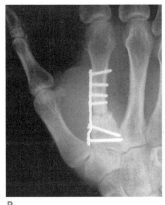

A   B

Figure 11.28 Plate-and-screw fixation of a displaced metacarpal fracture. (**A**) Exposure of nonunion site in preparation for curettage, bone grafting, and internal fixation. (**B**) Internal fixation accomplished with a mini-condylar blade-plate device to achieve skeletal stability.

lost, the bone's tendency is to return to its original deformity. Open reduction of a metacarpal shaft fracture can compromise the bone's blood supply or cause fibrosis of the interosseus muscles, adherence of the extensor tendons, or a local infection.

With closed reduction, as much as 40° of angulation is acceptable in the fourth or fifth metacarpal. It is not necessary to hold the MCP or PIP joints flexed, as this positioning often results in excessive stiffness.

■ Injury-Specific Treatment and Rehabilitation Concerns

Specific Concerns

Maintain stability of the fracture site.
Promote and restore ROM.

Rehabilitation is initiated as soon as the immobilization period ends. Generally, active ROM of all fingers should be normal if the cast was applied properly. If the cast extended beyond the distal palmar crease in the hand, motion may be impaired until the MCP joints can be stretched. Wrist strength is addressed with multiplanar dumbbell curls, pronation, and supination. Grip exercises are gradually increased in intensity using therapeutic putty. All exercises progress at the patient's tolerance. Sport-specific tasks such as palming a basketball can be employed for hand strengthening.

■ Estimated Amount of Time Lost

A metacarpal fracture requires 4 to 6 weeks to heal, after which a gradual return to sport participation is permitted. A displaced fracture requires a longer healing time and possibly ORIF. Hand weakness and pain may restrict participation in athletic activities.

■ Return-to-Play Criteria

The fracture should be healed before the athlete returns to participation in sports in which playing with a padded cast or splint on the hand is prohibited (e.g., wrestling). However, early return to athletics is possible when the fracture is stable and adequate protection is provided in the form of thermoplastic materials, padding, and casts. The athlete may participate without protection when the fracture is healed and full strength and mobility have returned to the upper extremity.

Functional Bracing

Fractures to the second through fourth metacarpals can often be padded and protected with thermoplastic materials and gel padding. The fingers should remain taped together to prevent rotation. Depending on the fracture location and stability, the physician may permit play with a custom-fabricated silicon splint.

Lunate Dislocations

The lunate is the most commonly dislocated of all the carpal bones. Perilunate dislocations result from a dislocation of the distal carpal row. In a lunate dislocation, the space between the distal and proximal carpal bones is forced open. The lunate cup is commonly directed volarly in dislocation because of the mechanism of injury, which is a fall on an outstretched hand.[58,59] Because of the stresses involved, a scaphoid fracture often accompanies a perilunate dislocation.[60,61] The intercarpals supinate, placing

11

History

A fall or other mechanism that results in forceful hand rotation or wrist hyperextension and/or ulnar deviation.
Pain arising from the palmar or dorsal aspect of the hand, proximal to the wrist.

Observation

When the patient makes a fist, the third metacarpal is at the same level as the other knuckles (Murphy sign).
Diffuse swelling can occur.
In some patients, lunate displacement is observed.

Functional Status

Pain occurs with all wrist motions.
Wrist and finger flexion may be limited by swelling.

Physical Examination Findings

Pressure on the median nerve can result in flexor muscle numbness or paralysis.
Diffuse pain occurs during palpation.
The displaced lunate may be detected during palpation.

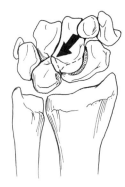

Stage I   Stage II

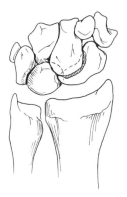
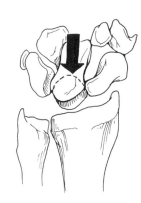

Stage III   Stage IV

Figure 11.29 Stages of progression of perilunar instability. Stage I: Disruption of the scapholunate ligamentous complex. Stage II: The force propagates through the space of Poirier and interrupts the lunocapitate connection. Stage III: The lunotriquetral connection is violated, and the entire carpus separates from the lunate. Stage IV: The lunate dislocates from its fossa into the carpal tunnel, the lunate rotates into the carpal tunnel, and the capitate becomes aligned with the radius. *Source:* Reproduced with permission from Kozin SH. Perilunate injuries: Diagnosis and treatment. *J Am Acad Orthop Surg.* 1998;6:114-120.

stress on the carpals and causing either a lunate or perilunate dislocation. If the scapholunate ligament remains intact, the scaphoid may be fractured.[62]

Carpal instability can take many forms and represents a spectrum of injury, including scapholunate dissociation, lunate and perilunate dislocations, scaphoid fracture, and other intercarpal instabilities (see **Figure 11.29**). This injury, which is often misdiagnosed as a wrist sprain, may lead to chronic wrist pain and instability.

Differential Diagnosis

Scapholunate sprain, scaphoid fracture, triangular fibrocartilage complex (TFCC) tear.

Imaging Techniques

AP and lateral radiographs of the wrist are required to diagnose a lunate dislocation or other carpal instability (see **Figure 11.30**). On the AP view, two arcs should be identified. The first proximal arc is the radiocarpal row, which should be smooth and continuous; disruption suggests a lunate dislocation.[63,64] The second arc is the midcarpal row, which also should be smooth and continuous; disruption suggests a perilunate dislocation. The lunate is normally quadrangular; when dislocated, however, it appears triangular on the AP view—an additional clue to the presence of a dislocation.

On the lateral view, the column formed by the radius, lunate, and capitate in a series of "C" shapes provides evidence of a lunate dislocation. The lunate

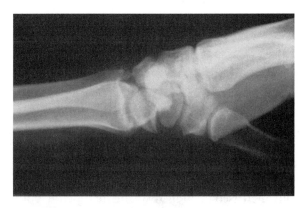

Figure 11.30 This lateral radiograph depicts a dorsal perilunate dislocation, with the capitate and scaphoid dorsal to the lunate.

should lie within the radius cup, and the capitate should rest within the lunate cup. Loss of this normal column implies lunate or perilunate dislocation.

Stress radiographs of the wrist may be necessary to demonstrate intercarpal ligamentous instability when no evidence of wrist dislocation is apparent on plain films. Stress radiographs obtained with radial and ulnar deviation of the hand may demonstrate scapholunate dissociation (see "Scapholunate Dissociations" later in this chapter).

Definitive Diagnosis

The definitive diagnosis is based on the radiographic findings.

Pathomechanics and Functional Limitations

Carpal dislocations often result in carpal instability, which causes chronic pain and loss of function. Failure to diagnose and treat the injury promptly contributes to this problem. Median nerve inhibition can lead to signs and symptoms similar to those associated with carpal tunnel syndrome (CTS).

If the dislocation is not identified early, the lunate may deteriorate to the point that it must be surgically removed. The lunate may also rotate around the dorsal ligament, interfering with the blood supply and resulting in Kienböck's disease (see **Figure 11.31**).[63-65] Early reduction and reconstruction can prevent these complications.

Immediate Management

The wrist should be assessed for the entire spectrum of injuries. If a carpal dislocation is suspected, the wrist, forearm, and hand should be splinted. Attempts to reduce a dislocation should not be made without a radiograph, even when symptoms of median nerve compromise are noted during the on-field evaluation. A lunate dislocation injury may be mistaken for a distal radius fracture, which is difficult to reduce.

A patient with a lunate dislocation should be referred to a hand specialist or a physician trained in carpal instabilities immediately. A hand surgeon

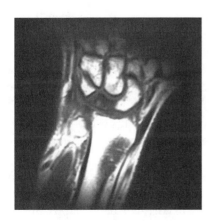

may decide to immobilize the elbow to reduce pronation and supination.

Medications

Pain medication may be needed to allow closed reduction.

Postinjury Management

Carpal instability can exist even in the presence of negative radiographs; consequently, immobilizing the wrist in a cast for 2 weeks and then reevaluating it is often advised. Cast immobilization is required after both surgical and nonsurgical reduction. Gentle finger ROM is initiated after 3 days to prevent a contracture. Once the cast is removed, aggressive ROM tactics and strengthening are initiated.

Surgical Intervention

Surgery is indicated for an acute dislocation if scapholunate instability exists. Maintaining scapholunate function is the goal of surgical management for a lunate dislocation. Generally, percutaneous K-wires are used to manipulate the carpals and secure them at the proper locations during immobilization.[65] Ligament repair or reconstruction is necessary to treat or prevent carpal instability patterns.

Stability of the carpal articulations often is traded for mobility. The midcarpal joints frequently are stiff, and ROM is limited. Because of the complexity of the carpal biomechanics and the potential for osteoarthritic changes, this injury should be managed by a hand surgeon. Wrist ROM is often limited, especially in extension, but a pain-free outcome is anticipated. Failure to treat carpal instability leads to arthritis in most cases.

Injury-Specific Treatment and Rehabilitation Concerns

> **Specific Concerns**
>
> Reduce the dislocation and remove pressure from the median nerve.
> Prevent osteonecrosis and lunate collapse (Kienböck's disease).

Rehabilitation may be extensive with carpal dislocations, because a long immobilization period is often necessary, often 2 to 3 months after surgery. Wrist flexion and extension and ulnar and radial deviation, pronation, and supination are often limited postoperatively. When the pins are removed, aggressive ROM techniques may begin. The clinician should direct passive stress and joint mobilization to both the radiocarpal joints and the midcarpal joints. Long-duration, low-load stretches to promote supination can be applied by the patient sitting on his or her own hand.

Hand and wrist strengthening is done with resistive exercise. Wrist curls, grip exercises, and upper body strengthening apply this stress to the involved hand. Resistance exercises should be performed after mobility exercises to take advantage of any newly gained range. Therapeutic exercise is generally done 4 to 5 times per week.

■ Estimated Amount of Time Lost

Cast immobilization is usually required for 2 to 3 months. The length of the disability period depends on the presence of concomitant injury and carpal instability. Lunate and perilunate dislocations can result in significant time lost from athletics, especially when weight bearing on the hand is required. Brace support or taping is often needed as the athlete is reintroduced to the sport.

■ Return-to-Play Criteria

Return to play is permitted when ROM and strength are good and healing is complete. If ROM is affected, modifications in technique or the use of a brace may be necessary.

Functional Bracing

Athletic tape or a commercially available brace can be used to protect the hand and wrist during sport participation (see **Figure 11.32**).

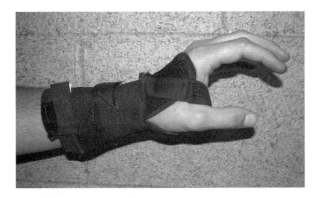

Figure 11.32 Commercially available braces often provide enough support in patients with lunate dislocations to permit them to engage in daily activities and participation in some sports.

Scaphoid Fractures

CLINICAL PRESENTATION

History

Forced extension of the wrist, such as falling on an outstretched arm.
Pain originating from the "anatomic snuffbox."

Observation

Little deformity from the scaphoid fracture is noted.
Secondary swelling from contusive forces may be observed.

Functional Status

Decreased grip strength.
Decreased ROM in all directions, but most notably during flexion, extension, and ulnar deviation.

Physical Examination Findings

Pain, point tenderness, and possible crepitus are noted during palpation of the anatomic snuffbox.
Pain is significantly increased during active and passive radial deviation.

The wrist comprises an intricate network of eight carpal bones arranged in two rows that articulate with the radius and fibrocartilaginous end of the ulna proximally and the metacarpals distally. The carpal frame stabilizes the wrist and allows the hand and fingers to move. The hand muscles primarily originate in the forearm and pass over the wrist. The flexor carpi ulnaris, which inserts into the pisiform bone, is the only muscle that inserts into the wrist complex.

The carpal bones move in concert during flexion, extension, ulnar and radial deviation, and pronation and supination. With wrist extension and radial deviation, the radius impinges on the scaphoid; because of its narrow midportion (waist), the scaphoid is predisposed to injury[66,67] (see **Figure 11.33**). A carpal fracture can occur with compression and shearing of the bone, as when a person falls on an outstretched hand, compressing the scaphoid between the radius and the second row of carpal bones, particularly the capitate. The scaphoid can also be injured in a weight-bearing position (e.g., in gymnasts), when the hand is stabilized and the forearm rotates abruptly.

The scaphoid bone is the most frequently fractured carpal bone. Because healing depends on the presence of an adequate blood supply and the blood enters the scaphoid along the dorsal surface near

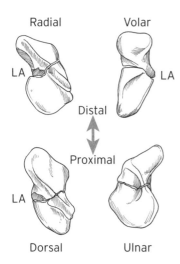

Figure 11.33 Four views of a right scaphoid demonstrate its complex shape. The surface is predominantly articular, and most of the blood supply enters through the nonarticular dorsal ridge (LA = lateral apex of the dorsal ridge). The fracture line depicts the pattern of so-called waist fractures. *Source:* Adapted from Compson JP. The anatomy of acute scaphoid fractures: A three-dimensional analysis of patterns. *J Bone Joint Surg Br.* 1998;80:218-224.

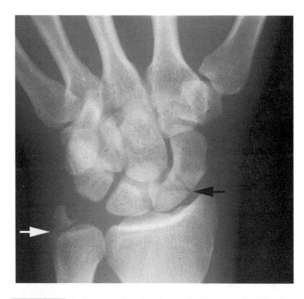

Figure 11.34 Posteroanterior view demonstrating a scaphoid fracture (black arrow). Note the associated fracture of the ulnar styloid process (white arrow).

its midportion, this bone is prone to osteonecrosis and nonunion.[63,68,69] A scaphoid fracture is often missed and mistaken for a wrist sprain on an early radiograph.

Differential Diagnosis

Wrist sprain, radial or ulnar fracture, thumb sprain, metacarpal fracture.

Imaging Techniques

A scaphoid fracture can be diagnosed with high-quality AP and lateral radiographic images. A PA view of the scaphoid with the wrist in ulnar deviation may distract the fragments and make the fracture more apparent. Many times, however, the fracture cannot be visualized on initial plain films (see **Figure 11.34**).

An MRI or CT scan may be necessary to detect an occult fracture that is not visible on plain films (see **Figure 11.35**). MRI is the most sensitive imaging modality for detecting an occult fracture of the scaphoid.

Definitive Diagnosis

The definitive diagnosis is based on positive findings on plain radiographs or MRI. If the initial radiograph does not show the fracture when a strong clinical suspicion for this condition exists, the wrist should be placed in a thumb-spica cast for 2 weeks and then reevaluated. Positive clinical findings and a mechanism of forced wrist extension may warrant the initial diagnosis of a scaphoid fracture until it can

be definitively ruled out.[66,67,70] MRI or radiographs repeated after 2 weeks should identify the fracture.

Pathomechanics and Functional Limitations

Most scaphoid fractures occur at the narrow midpoint of the waist. This aspect of the scaphoid can be impinged upon by the styloid process of the radius during forced radial deviation. This type of fracture is usually associated with a force applied to the distal pole of the scaphoid, often with wrist hyperextension. The radial styloid process functions as a fulcrum against the center of the scaphoid, resulting in the predominance of fractures at the waist. The mechanism of injury usually is a fall on an outstretched hand. On clinical examination, pain is elicited when pressure is exerted on the distal pole or on the scaphoid at the anatomic snuffbox on the radial aspect of the wrist.

A gap or fracture offset of 1 mm or more indicates instability, with the potential for nonunion or malunion, and internal fixation should be performed.[63,70,71] Internal fixation may also be considered routinely for proximal-pole fractures, regardless of the degree of displacement, in view of the long healing time and high risk of nonunion despite cast treatment.

■ Immediate Management

If a scaphoid fracture is suspected, ice should be applied immediately to prevent edema. A splint should be placed to immobilize the wrist, elbow, and thumb. Given the mechanism of injury (wrist

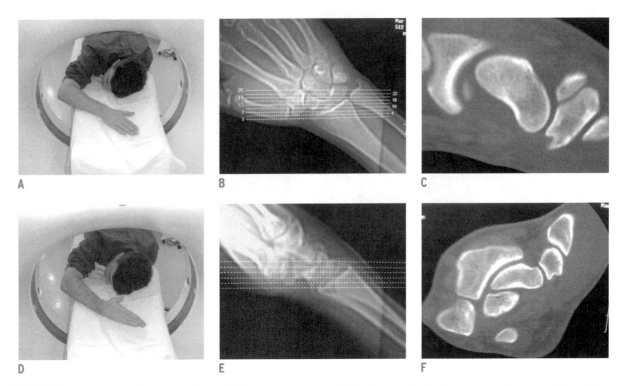

Figure 11.35 CT of the scaphoid is easier to interpret if the images are obtained in the planes defined by the long axis of the scaphoid. To achieve this imaging, the patient lies prone on the table with the arm overhead. (**A**) For sagittal-plane images, the forearm is held pronated, and the hand lies flat on the table. The forearm crosses the gantry at an angle of approximately 45° (roughly in line with the abducted thumb metacarpal). (**B**) Scout images are obtained to confirm appropriate orientation and to ensure that the entire scaphoid is imaged. Sections are obtained at 1-mm intervals. (**C**) Images obtained in the sagittal plane are the best choice for measuring the intrascaphoid angle. (**D**) For coronal-plane images, the forearm is in neutral rotation. (**E**) Scout images demonstrate the alignment of the wrist through the gantry of the scanner. (**F**) Interpretation of images obtained in the coronal plane is straightforward.

hyperextension) and pain over the scaphoid, care should proceed as if a scaphoid fracture is present.

Medications

Analgesic medication or NSAIDs may be prescribed to control the athlete's pain and inflammation.

Surgical Intervention

In managing acute scaphoid fractures, the fracture stability, ease of reduction, associated ligamentous injury, and risk of impaired blood supply must be considered, rather than the direction of the fracture line or location of the fracture within the scaphoid. Nonunion and osteonecrosis are common sequelae of acute fractures. Because the risk of impaired vascularity is greater with fractures located in the proximal third of the scaphoid, stable internal fixation may be indicated to provide mechanical stability and fracture-surface contact to enhance revascularization. The faster healing rates and earlier rehabilitation that are possible with percutaneous techniques of internal fixation have caused healthcare providers to largely abandon the

classic conservative treatment in favor of internal fixation (see **ST** 11.4). The fracture location may be a poor prognosticator of the outcome, because the architecture of the blood supply can be variable and unpredictable. Vascularized bone grafting may be required for proximal pole nonunions and osteonecrosis.

Postinjury/Postoperative Management

Conservative management is the first option in treating a presumed scaphoid fracture. The wrist and thumb should be immobilized for 2 weeks using a short or long arm cast, even if a fracture is not definitively identified. Follow-up radiographs can help determine whether the immobilization needs to continue. Once union has been established, wrist strengthening exercises may begin, but additional protection should be provided against impact loading for another 3 months. Postoperative management of a scaphoid fracture with bone graft also requires extensive healing time. A thumb-spica cast is used for 6 to 12 weeks, and then strengthening exercises are initiated.

S|T Surgical Technique 11.4

Repair of the Scaphoid: Vascularized Bone Graft Inlay

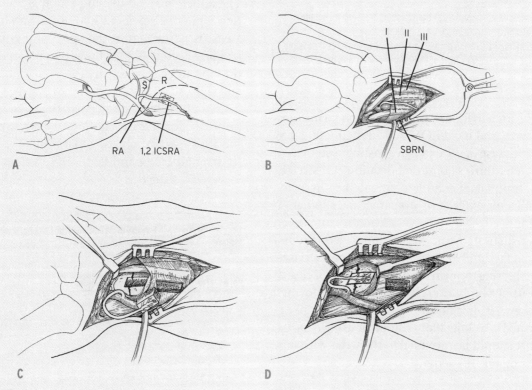

Terminology

RA, radial artery; S, scaphoid; R, radius; 1, 2 ICSRA, first and second vessels, intercompartmental supraretinacular artery; I, II, III, superficial branches of the radial nerve (SBRN).

Indications

Unstable, displaced scaphoid fractures need primary ORIF and sometimes primary grafting. Fractures at the proximal pole or waist of the scaphoid require long immobilization periods; if nonunion or osteonecrosis occurs, surgical intervention is indicated.

Procedure Overview

1. A curvilinear incision is made over the dorsolateral scaphoid (**A**).
2. The arteries 1, 2 ICSRA and the superficial branches of the radial nerve (I, II, III) are identified and protected (**B**).
3. The bone graft is harvested with an intact arteriole, and the graft-site vascularity is confirmed (**C**).
4. A notch is made in the two halves of the scaphoid to accept the graft.
5. The graft bone (with its arterial blood supply) is fitted into the notch in the scaphoid (**D**).
6. Additional fixation using K-wires or scaphoid screws may be performed at this time.

Functional Limitations

Surgical intervention with bone grafts may cause midcarpal stiffness, resulting in a permanent loss of wrist motion. In most cases, the athlete can adapt to the loss of motion, even when participating in a skill position. In contrast, an athlete who bears weight on the upper extremity, such as a gymnast, may not be able to gain enough pain-free wrist extension to perform.

Implications for Rehabilitation

The patient is fitted with a long arm thumb-spica splint for 10 to 14 days, followed by a long arm thumb-spica cast for up to 6 weeks. The long immobilization period required for bone healing causes wrist and hand weakness and stiffness.

Potential Complications

Potential complications include nonunion of the scaphoid, scapholunate dissociation, and instability.

Comments

Osteogenic ultrasonic or electromagnetic bone stimulators can be used to assist healing.

Source: Figures adapted from the Mayo Foundation, Rochester, MN.

Injury-Specific Treatment and Rehabilitation Concerns

> **Specific Concerns**
>
> Promptly diagnose and treat the scaphoid fracture with immobilization to allow primary bone healing.
>
> Maintain immobilization during participation in athletics if possible.
>
> Achieve full, pain-free ROM of the affected wrist and hand.

After the immobilization period for scaphoid fractures ends, wrist and hand ROM and strengthening may begin. Because of the extensive casting system used with such injuries, joint mobilization and stretching techniques may be implemented right away. Wrist flexion, extension, pronation, and supination are addressed.

Wrist strengthening is accomplished through multiplanar dumbbell curls and gripping exercises. Weight bearing through the involved wrist for closed-chain upper body exercise should be performed with the wrist in a neutral position. Push-ups are performed in a "knuckle" position or using handles. Support should be provided to the wrist with tape or bracing for this activity.

Estimated Amount of Time Lost

Depending on the sport's requirements, an athlete may be incapacitated from 2 to 6 months, barring complications. Immobilization of the wrist with a thumb-spica cast for 6 weeks remains the treatment of choice for stable fractures of the scaphoid midportion and distal pole. If a fracture is suspected but plain films are negative, the wrist should be immobilized for 2 weeks. Reevaluation and more extensive diagnostic testing such as MRI may be performed at that time. If the sport's rules permit and the athlete is functional, participation in athletics can proceed with cast immobilization and appropriate padding. Many scaphoid fractures require 8 weeks of immobilization for union to occur. Follow-up radiographs should be taken to monitor the patient for signs of nonunion or osteonecrosis.

Return-to-Play Criteria

The key to treating a scaphoid fracture is to facilitate primary healing. Many scaphoid fractures are missed on initial examination and, consequently, result in nonunion or osteonecrosis. Treatment requires extensive immobilization, which can result in wrist and hand weakness. Rehabilitation, therefore, should focus on increasing upper extremity strength. Protection should be used for wrist support and to prevent stress when the bone has healed enough for the athlete to return to play.

Functional Bracing

The athlete may be able to participate in competition while the scaphoid fracture is immobilized if a cast is permitted in the sport and appropriate padding is used. A wrist brace that incorporates the thumb can be used during the transitional period, and tape can offer support in the later stages of healing. Once the bone has healed, the wrist should be protected for at least another 2 weeks, especially if the athlete is participating in a contact sport. Gentle strengthening and flexibility exercises can be initiated during this period.

Scapholunate Dissociations

CLINICAL PRESENTATION

History

Forced wrist extension.
Forced wrist rotation.
Pain and crepitus.

Observation

Swelling.

Functional Status

Decreased grip strength.
Decreased ROM in all planes secondary to pain.

Physical Examination Findings

A "pop" and pain may be experienced during pronation and ulnar deviation, indicating midcarpal instability.
The following special tests may be positive:
- Watson test for scapholunate instability[73]
- Lunotriquetral ballottement test

The wrist is an intercalated segment based on the configuration of multiple joint segments and ligamentous stabilizing elements. The carpal bones shift in concert when the wrist moves from flexion, extension, and radial and ulnar deviation. Because the scapholunate articulation creates a stable column for wrist function, even a partial ligament tear can result in instability in this area[72] (see **Figure 11.36**). The most common pattern of carpal instability is dorsal intercalated segment instability (DISI), in which the lunate is displaced volarly and flexed dorsally. The volar intercalated segment instability (VISI) pattern occurs when the lunate is displaced dorsally and flexed into the volar position.[72,73]

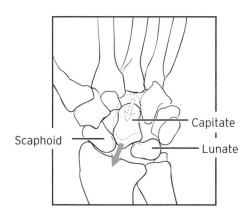

Figure 11.36 Compression of the capitate between the scaphoid and lunate can rupture the scapholunate ligament and/or the lunotriquetral ligament, causing instability.

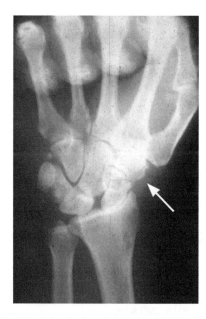

Figure 11.37 Scapholunate dissociation. When this injury is suspected, radiographs are taken with the fist clenched. The space between the scaphoid and lunate indicates a ligament disruption.

The scaphoid bone is important to wrist stability because it bridges both the radiocarpal and midcarpal joints. The carpal bones flex and rotate to produce wrist extension, flexion, and radial and ulnar deviation. These bones function at two primary articulations—the radiocarpal joint between the distal radius and proximal carpal row, and the midcarpal joint between the proximal and distal carpal rows. The strongest and most important wrist ligaments are located intracapsularly on the palmar side. These ligaments are configured in a double "V," whose apex points distally.[29] A site of potential weakness exists between the "V" formations near the lunate-capitate articulation at the space of Poirier, where carpal dislocations occur most commonly.[72]

A scapholunate dissociation generally occurs after wrist trauma, such as a fall on the hand, forcing the wrist into extension; rotational forces may cause shearing. Pain and inability to use the wrist are usually noted immediately after the injury.

Differential Diagnosis
Lunate dislocation, scaphoid fracture, wrist sprain.

Imaging Techniques
AP and lateral views are taken first, and additional images in ulnar and radial deviation and clenched views are ordered as necessary to determine carpal instability, especially when the DISI and VISI patterns are suspected (see **Figure 11.37**). The clenched-fist view is helpful in accentuating a scapholunate gap. MRI can distinguish tears in the scapholunate ligament and determine the presence of occult fractures. Wrist arthroscopy is the "gold standard" for diagnosing carpal ligament injuries and may be required to make a definitive diagnosis.

Definitive Diagnosis
The normal scapholunate angle is 30° to 60°; an angle greater than 70° is diagnostic for carpal in-

stability. A capitolunate angle greater than 20° also suggests carpal instability. A scapholunate space of more than 3 mm is abnormal.[72,74–76]

Pathomechanics and Functional Limitations
Wrist instability occurs when the scapholunate ligament stabilizing the proximal scaphoid pole or the interosseous ligament between the individual carpal bones is torn. The scaphoid may subluxate in a rotational manner, and the lunate may flex or dorsiflex with wrist motion. Pain and weakness ultimately limit the athlete's function.

▧ Immediate Management
Neurovascular status should be monitored. A splint is used to immobilize the wrist in a position of comfort.

▧ Medications
Narcotic pain medicine is prescribed after surgery.

▧ Surgical Intervention
Carpal instability is treated with reduction and immobilization in radial deviation and extension. Partial injuries without instability may be treated with casting, whereas complete injuries require surgical management. The scapholunate gap should be closed, and the lunate and capitate must be realigned. In acute injuries, open reduction is necessary with ligament repair. A short arm cast is worn for 6 to 8 weeks, followed by a removable splint for

an additional 4 weeks. The dorsal interosseous ligaments are repaired by reattaching the ligaments directly or by roughening the bone and attaching the ligaments through drill holes with a reefing of the dorsal capsule.

Postinjury/Postoperative Management

After injury, the wrist is splinted in a position of function until proper clinical and radiologic examination can be made. After surgery, a short arm cast is used for 6 to 8 weeks. Percutaneous K-wires can then be removed, and active motion begins. Joint mobilization is often necessary because of the lengthy immobilization period.

Injury-Specific Treatment and Rehabilitation Concerns

> **Specific Concerns**
>
> Protect the healing bone during healing.
> Restore wrist ROM.
> Restore thumb ROM, especially in opposition.

Rehabilitation begins after the immobilization period ends, when the percutaneous K-wires are removed. Active wrist ROM in all planes is encouraged, and strengthening of the entire upper extremity is incorporated as indicated. Generally, finger ROM is unaffected, but the thumb may be stiff, especially in opposition.

Passive motion and aggressive joint mobilization of the wrist may begin after 8 weeks. The patient may have difficulty achieving full supination. Grip, all planes of wrist activity, and supination and pronation should be strengthened in addition to the elbow and shoulder.

Full strength and flexibility are the goals of rehabilitation, but a functional, pain-free result is ideal. The athlete is generally advised to avoid excessive stresses and weight bearing on the involved wrist for several months to a year after the injury.

Estimated Amount of Time Lost

The wrist requires 8 to 12 weeks of immobilization after surgery. Further protection is required for the individual who wishes to engage in sports activities while rehabilitating. The patient may be able to participate in athletics while immobilized, but not if percutaneous pins are in place. Once the pins are removed, conditioning exercises and limited participation with a cast are permitted. The amount of time lost from competition is influenced by the type of surgical reconstruction and the rules of the athlete's sport—specifically, whether they allow participation of an athlete while wearing a cast.

Return-to-Play Criteria

The injured wrist should be protected from falls and excessive stress until its ROM and strength are similar to the contralateral side; this restoration of functionality may take several months. Again, the ability to participate in athletics is generally dictated by the acceptance of and ability to perform using a protective device.

Functional Bracing

A commercial wrist splint is often used to protect the wrist from excessive stress during sports. Athletic tape can also be used for this purpose, being placed either circumferentially to help stabilize the wrist or through the hand to help control motion.

Hamate Fractures

CLINICAL PRESENTATION

History

A fall on the hand or an impact while holding an implement such as a racquet or bat.
Generalized wrist and hand pain.

Observation

Outward deformity is rarely noted.

Functional Status

Pain is produced during abduction and adduction of the fifth finger.
Grip strength is diminished.

Physical Examination Findings

Pain occurs during resisted flexion or abduction of the fifth finger.
Pain is produced during palpation of the hook of the hamate.

The hamate can be injured in a variety of ways in athletes. The body of the hamate is fractured less frequently than its "hook," which projects into the palm. Fractures of the body of the hamate are usually associated with fourth and fifth CMC fracture–dislocations. The hook of the hamate serves as a muscular attachment for the flexor digiti minimi brevis and the opponens digiti minimi and as a ligamentous attachment for the transverse carpal and pisohamate ligaments (see **Figure 11.38**). A fracture of the hamate body or hook causes grip instability, and excessive movement can result in ulnar nerve motor and sensory deficits.[77,78]

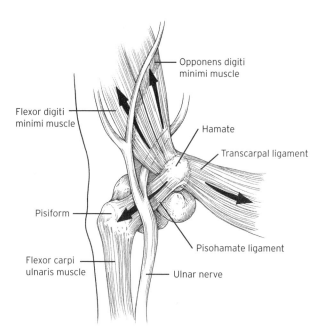

Figure 11.38 Intrinsic forces acting on the hook of the hamate. *Source:* Modified with permission from J. Marlowe.

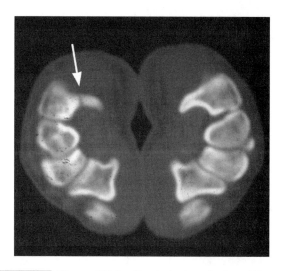

Figure 11.39 CT scan of bilateral hands showing a fracture of the hook of the hamate.

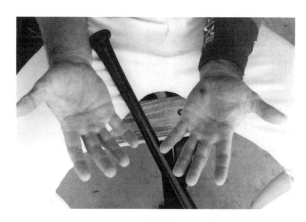

Figure 11.40 Mark over the hook of a hamate in a professional baseball player.

Fractures of the body of the hamate can result from an axial force through the metacarpals or a direct blow to the ulnar aspect of the wrist. Although the hook of the hamate can be fractured by a fall, fractures are more common in sports that require holding an implement, such as a softball or baseball bat, golf club, hockey or lacrosse stick, or tennis racquet. The fracture can also occur from repetitive stress or a direct blow when the club or racquet strikes the ground.

The hook of the hamate is located by identifying the pisiform and then palpating along a line from the pisiform to the head of the second metacarpal. Although firm pressure over a fractured hook generally causes discomfort, mild to moderate pressure may cause little pain. As a consequence, many fractures are overlooked.

Differential Diagnosis
CMC fracture, CMC dislocation, false aneurysm of the ulnar artery.

Imaging Techniques
Radiographs should include the carpal-tunnel view and a view with the wrist supinated to visualize the hook of the hamate and pisiform. A CT scan should be considered when clinical findings suggest the presence of a fracture that is not visible on routine radiographs[79,80] (see **Figure 11.39**).

Definitive Diagnosis
Imaging studies are performed to identify the presence or absence of a hamate fracture. Follow-up studies are used to determine whether a nonunion has occurred.

Pathomechanics and Functional Limitations
If the diagnosis is not made promptly, the ulnar nerve within the Guyon canal can be damaged, resulting in palsy, or the fifth flexor digitorum profundus tendon can rupture.[79,80] Over time, a definite protrusion over the hamate becomes sensitive during gripping (see **Figure 11.40**). The athlete may have a functional disability because of grip weakness and pain when using the sport implement.

▬ Immediate Management
Immediate management consists of immobilization, application of ice, and referral for radiographs.

▬ Medications
Pain medications are not often needed, but NSAIDs can be used to control inflammation.

■ Surgical Intervention

Fractures of the hamate hook and body are usually nondisplaced and can be treated with cast immobilization. In contrast, intra-articular fractures of the hamate body with displacement of more than 1 mm are best treated with ORIF. Displaced fractures that involve the distal aspect of the hook often result in nonunion if they are not treated with ORIF. The simplest procedure that allows an early return to athletics is removal of the fractured portion of the bone.[80] This surgery is often done with painless nonunions to prevent a later tendon rupture. Surgical intervention generally does not affect long-term hand strength or motion.

■ Postinjury/Postoperative Management

Compression is applied to the hand to minimize edema formation in the palm. Finger ROM is initiated after 3 days. Power grips that stress the flexor tendons are avoided for 2 weeks.

■ Injury-Specific Treatment and Rehabilitation Concerns

> **Specific Concerns**
> Protect the hamate from pressure.
> After surgery, avoid gripping activities.

Treatment focuses on reducing pain while allowing surgical incisions to heal (if applicable). A supervised rehabilitation program is not generally required after this procedure. Efforts should target decreasing edema formation, which may lead to scar formation in the palm. Active finger ROM is encouraged early, and grip and wrist exercises may begin at 2 to 4 weeks, when the immobilization period has ended.

When the patient is ready to participate in athletics, excessive pressure on the Guyon canal must be avoided; such pressure can cause ulnar nerve symptoms. Wearing gloves with silicone padding can reduce stress on this area.

■ Estimated Amount of Time Lost

After 4 weeks of cast immobilization, the patient may be able to return to sport with the hook of the hamate padded. Early diagnosis influences the amount of time lost from competition, because the severity of soft-tissue damage increases if the hand is not immobilized.

■ Return-to-Play Criteria

Return to sport is allowed when the athlete can grasp the stick, bat, or racquet without pain and has pain-free function of the fifth finger.

Functional Bracing

A doughnut or relief pad can be used over the sensitive area. Silicone or gel-padded gloves can be worn to minimize the amount of restrictive material in the palm.

Triangular Fibrocartilage Complex Injuries

CLINICAL PRESENTATION

History
Wrist hyperextension and ulnar deviation.
Repetitive stress.
Increased pain with wrist extension and ulnar deviation.
Grinding, clicking, and/or general wrist weakness.

Observation
On rare occasions, the distal ulna is diffusely swollen.

Functional Status
Active, passive, and resistive ROM of the wrist is decreased, especially in extension.
Load bearing on the hands, such as performing a push-up or bench press, is limited by pain.

Physical Examination Findings
Wrist crepitus, popping, locking, or clicking may be felt during active ROM.
Wrist and grip strength are diminished.
The piano-key sign of the distal ulna is found.
Point tenderness is noted on the medial wrist.
Tenderness of the UCL may be noted.
Ulnar collateral stress test produces pain, but no laxity is noted.
Ulnar deviation and compression of the wrist produce pain.

The triangular fibrocartilage complex (TFCC) comprises the ligamentous and cartilaginous structures that suspend the distal radius and ulnar carpus from the distal ulna. The TFCC is the primary ligamentous stabilizer of the distal radioulnar joint (DRUJ) and the articulation of the ulna and carpal bones. The TFCC provides a continuous gliding surface that allows three degrees of freedom in the wrist (flexion/extension, ulnar/radial deviation, supination/pronation).[81–83] Similar to the knee menisci, the TFCC is a shock absorber that absorbs approximately 40% of the force applied to the wrist; the other 60% is absorbed by the radius. Also similar to the meniscus, the TFCC can be injured with a shearing force, impact to the hand, or repetitive stress.[83,84] Acute TFCC tears are difficult to diagnose and are often associated with wrist sprains.

A distal radius fracture should raise suspicion for a TFCC injury. TFCC tears are present in 35% of intra-articular fractures and 53% of extra-articular fractures.[81,85] The TFCC can suffer degenerative damage, especially if the athlete is more than 30 years old and the area has been chronically stressed. Degenerative injuries are difficult to treat because fibrocartilage heals poorly, and activity modifications may be required to reduce pain.[83,84] A TFCC injury can be debilitating for some athletes, and surgical intervention may be needed after an acute injury if function is limited despite efforts to facilitate proper healing and rehabilitation.[86,87]

Differential Diagnosis
Ulnar fracture, carpal fracture.

Imaging Techniques
Radiographs help to rule out fractures and other carpal instabilities. Patients with a torn TFCC display average ulnar variance (radial shortening) of 4.6 mm versus 2.5 mm for those with no tear; dorsal angulation of 24° is associated with such an injury versus 12° for no tear.[83,84] MRI is beneficial in diagnosing TFCC tears, although degeneration may be difficult to identify. A magnetic resonance arthrogram can also be used to diagnose a TFCC tear (see **Figure 11.41**).

Definitive Diagnosis
The piano-key sign—that is, a prominent and ballotable distal ulna with full forearm pronation—may be present. Lunotriquetral ballottement and extensor carpi ulnaris (ECU) tendon subluxation may also be demonstrated. The definitive diagnosis of TFCC injury can be made arthroscopically if surgical intervention is indicated.

Pathomechanics and Functional Limitations
The TFCC helps to absorb shock and provide stability at the wrist. Degenerative disease or shearing of the joint can cause a tear in this complex, resulting in pain and loss of motion. Pain and weakness may reflect DRUJ instability. Gymnasts and weightlifters who bear weight on the upper extremities are often affected by such injuries, for example. Basketball shooting may cause pain because of the hyperflexed and pronated position during follow-through.

▨ Immediate Management
Immediate management includes rest, ice, compression, and elevation. The patient may engage in nonpainful activity with the wrist protected.

▨ Medications
NSAIDs can be used to decrease pain and swelling.

▨ Postinjury Management
If a TFCC injury is suspected without an associated fracture, cast immobilization should be applied in slight flexion for 4 to 6 weeks. Failure to treat the injury appropriately can lead to degeneration, ulnar chondromalacia, impingement, or calcification. Conservative management should be attempted before surgical intervention, because the patient will continue to require protection and will probably have pain with many activities, even after surgery.

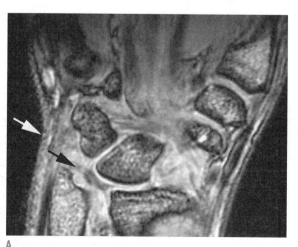 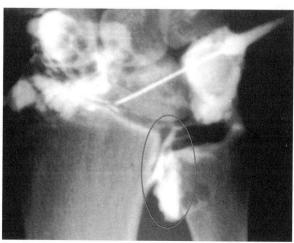

Figure 11.41 Imaging of triangular fibrocartilage complex trauma. (**A**) Coronal MRI showing disruption of the complex (black arrow) and the area of maximum tenderness on palpation (white arrow). (**B**) Arthrogram demonstrating a complex tear.

■ Surgical Intervention

Surgical treatment is indicated if the DRUJ is unstable or if a Galeazzi fracture–dislocation is present.[85,87] In addition to repairing the TFCC using sutures, K-wire stabilization just proximal to the DRUJ is recommended for 4 to 6 weeks.

Some surgeons prefer to perform wrist arthroscopy rather than an open procedure in the setting of a TFCC injury, even though visualization is difficult and the arthroscopic instruments are large in relation to the joint size. General principles include debriding the area to create a stable, smooth rim of tissue; maintaining a 2-mm peripheral rim; and limiting the debridement to less than two-thirds of the central TFCC. Variations on this procedure, including stabilization, can be performed, depending on the findings during arthroscopy and the involvement of the ECU tendon.

An ulnar-shortening osteotomy may be considered for patients with ulnar-positive variance or a failed debridement. Arthroscopic techniques have become more popular strategies for the treatment of TFCC injuries. Debriding only the degenerative tissue while leaving most of the tissue can alleviate the pain in some patients.[87–90]

An open procedure requires a longer immobilization period postoperatively, but the surgeon can usually visualize and debride the area better. Activity should be minimized when the K-wire is in place. Wrist pronation and supination are affected by this injury, and stabilization procedures can result in further loss of motion. Degenerative disease of the TFCC and DRUJ can also affect the outcome, producing continued pain and loss of motion, especially with weight-bearing functions.

■ Injury-Specific Treatment and Rehabilitation Concerns

> **Specific Concerns**
> Stabilize and protect the wrist during healing.
> Encourage ROM.

The athlete is encouraged to rest the wrist and to reduce stress by using a brace or tape during everyday activities and athletics. Any modality that is indicated for an inflamed condition can also be used.[86] Specific exercises include active and passive wrist ROM. Long-duration stretches with the elbow extended help to lengthen the wrist flexors and extensors. Strengthening is done in all wrist planes and for grip and the elbow. Although pronation and supination are also resisted, these exercises should be pursued within pain-free limits.

Postoperative rehabilitation mirrors the preoperative phase, while respecting the acute phase in the 2 to 4 weeks after surgery. The time period for immobilization varies, depending on the presence of a fracture and the degree of damage. The surgeon dictates the aggressiveness of the early rehabilitation phase, because the surgical procedure may range from an endoscopic debridement to an open repair.

■ Estimated Amount of Time Lost

Depending on the severity of the injury and the presence of an associated fracture (or not), immobilization ranges from 4 to 10 weeks, with a gradual adaptation to stress occurring throughout the rehabilitation program. The amount of damage and the demands of the sport dictate the time lost with a TFCC injury. Some athletes, depending on their sport position, may participate during the immobilization period if adequately protected. Treatment should not be compromised to permit participation, although an interior lineman in football, for example, may be able to play with a fiberglass cast. If symptoms do not improve with immobilization and rehabilitation, some patients may require arthroscopic or open surgical intervention.

■ Return-to-Play Criteria

The athlete may return to play using a protective brace or tape if pain-free participation is assured. Full ROM and strength are long-term goals that must be met before participation without protection is permitted.

Functional Bracing

Commercial wrist braces offer protection and limit ROM. Athletic tape applied circumferentially can also protect the wrist with a TFCC injury.

Colles' Fractures

Fractures of the distal third of the forearm and wrist are common in both elderly and youth populations. These extra-articular fractures, involving the radius and/or ulna, are termed Colles' fractures. With this type of injury, compression and torsion across the articular surfaces result in a variety of patterns of intra-articular displacement.[91] Typically, the fracture occurs in the distal end of the radius, where it widens. The displaced portion is wider than the

History

Fall on an outstretched arm or other forceful wrist extension. Exquisite pain.

Observation

Dorsal wrist displacement is obvious.
The wrist and forearm may have a "dinner-fork" appearance.

Functional Status

The involved wrist and arm are incapacitated.

Physical Examination Findings

Wrist motions are impaired.

rest of the bone, making it difficult to fit together. Improper reduction can cause early degenerative wrist changes and deformity.

A strong force, such as a hard fall on an outstretched hand, can push the hand into the forearm, causing a Colles' fracture. This injury is common among inline skaters because of their higher velocity at the time of the fall.

Differential Diagnosis

Carpal ligament disruption.

Imaging Techniques

Lateral and AP radiographs are obtained to identify a transverse fracture of the distal radius approximately 2.5 cm from the wrist. The fragment is commonly tilted and shifted backward and radially, with proximal impaction[91-93] (see **Figure 11.42**). Occa-

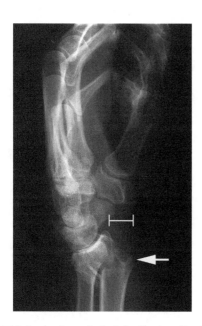

Figure 11.42 Lateral radiograph of a Colles' fracture. The distal radius is displaced dorsally by approximately 50% of the metaphyseal diameter (lines) and is dorsally angulated by approximately 30° (arrow).

sionally, the distal fragment is severely comminuted or crushed. An ulnar styloid fracture may also be present.

Definitive Diagnosis

The findings on the clinical examination are confirmed by radiographs.

Pathomechanics and Functional Limitations

While the fracture is healing, wrist, hand, and finger motions are limited. The fracture may also impair the median, radial, or ulnar nerves.

■ Immediate Management

The forearm should be splinted as found, with the hand placed in a functional position. Neurovascular function should be checked before and after splinting. Ice may be applied, and the extremity should be elevated with a sling (see **Figure 11.43**).

■ Surgical Intervention

The fracture should be reduced to anatomic alignment. Colles' fracture reduction is achieved with longitudinal traction, palmar tilt, and ulnar deviation. If adequate reduction is not possible, ORIF with a plate is necessary to achieve a good outcome. Generally, if the DRUJ is in good alignment, wrist ROM and strength are expected to return to normal.

■ Postinjury/Postoperative Management

A short arm cast is applied for 6 weeks, although a long arm cast may be recommended depending on the fracture position. Early finger motion is encouraged, and elbow and shoulder strengthening may begin as pain subsides. Rehabilitation commences when the cast is removed.

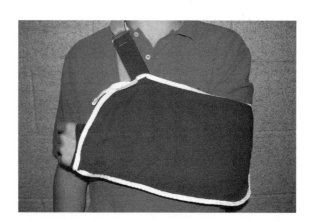

Figure 11.43 Postinjury management of a forearm fracture. The wrist should be splinted and placed in a sling that elevates the hand.

11

Injury-Specific Treatment and Rehabilitation Concerns

Specific Concerns

Obtain suitable reduction, fixation, and stabilization.
Maintain upper extremity strength and ROM during the wrist immobilization period.
Maintain general cardiovascular conditioning.

Immediately after surgery, the extremity is immobilized in a splint. Efforts should be undertaken to reduce edema formation. Active finger ROM is encouraged early during this phase. Once the immobilization period ends, wrist ROM and strengthening may begin. Wrist ROM may be slow to return and, depending on the reactivity of the tissues, aggressive joint mobilization may be used. Supination is most difficult to achieve. Long-duration stretches may be accomplished by having the athlete sit on his or her hand with the palm up. Wrist curls and pronation and supination resistance can be performed, as well as grip exercises.

Estimated Amount of Time Lost

Cast immobilization for at least 6 to 8 weeks is required for healing. If closed reduction is not adequate, ORIF may be necessary.[92] After the period of immobilization ends, regaining strength and flexibility may take an additional 4 weeks.

Radial shortening causes malunion. Associated DRUJ injury further incapacitates the patient. Concomitant injury to the median nerve or excessive swelling results in carpal tunnel syndrome.

Return-to-Play Criteria

Before returning to competition, the athlete should have full strength and ROM on the injured side, matching that of the uninjured side. Bracing during participation may allow an early return once the fracture is healed and the athlete has demonstrated good functional skills.

Functional Bracing

A wrist brace can be used. Circumferential tape around the wrist may provide some functional support.

Carpal Tunnel Syndrome

Carpal tunnel syndrome—the most common entrapment neuropathy—is characterized by pain, weakness, and paresthesia in the median nerve dis-

History

Repetitive stress to the wrist and hand.
Recent other trauma to the wrist and hand.
Numbness or paresthesia in the median nerve distribution (thumb, index, and middle fingers; palm of the hand).
Symptoms may increase at night.
The patient may report dropping items.

Observation

Chronic CTS may lead to thenar eminence atrophy.

Functional Status

Pain or paresthesia increases during wrist extension or hyperflexion.
Wrist strength and ROM are usually within normal limits.
Grip strength, especially thumb opposition, may be decreased.

Physical Examination Findings

Sensory and motor deficits are noted in the median nerve distribution. The following special tests may be positive:
- Phalen test
- Tinel sign
- Carpal-compression test

tribution of the hand. The carpal tunnel is located on the anterior wrist. Its floor is formed by the carpal bones, and its roof by the transverse carpal ligament. Eight finger flexor tendons, their synovial sheaths, and the median nerve course through this small space (see **Figure 11.44**). If the median nerve is compressed under the flexor retinaculum at the wrist, CTS results.[94–96]

CTS may have an acute onset after wrist trauma, but it is more commonly associated with repetitive

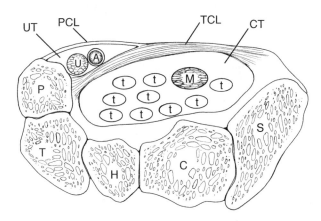

Figure 11.44 Cross-section of the wrist demonstrating the relationship of the carpal tunnel (CT) and the ulnar tunnel (UT). *Abbreviations:* A, ulnar artery; C, capitate; H, hamate; M, median nerve; P, pisiform; PCL, palmar carpal ligament; S, scaphoid; t, flexor tendon; T, triquetrum; TCL, transverse carpal ligament; U, ulnar nerve. *Source:* Reproduced with permission from Szabo RM, Steinberg DR. Nerve entrapment syndromes in the wrist. *J Am Acad Orthop Surg.* 1994;2:115-123.

stress that results in inflammation of the tendons and synovial sheaths within this space, leading to median nerve compression. Compression can follow trauma (e.g., a Colles' fracture or lunate dislocation), and decompression should be performed as soon as possible to reduce the potential for permanent nerve damage. The tightness of splints should always be checked and vascular function monitored after an acute injury of the wrist, hand, or arm to avoid nerve damage.

Flexor tendon tenosynovitis, a ganglion, and osteoarthritis or rheumatoid arthritis can be associated with CTS. This condition can arise in athletes who perform repeated wrist-flexion activities and most frequently is unilateral, affecting the dominant hand. It is also commonly seen in younger patients who use their wrists a great deal in repetitive manual labor or are exposed to vibration.[95]

Differential Diagnosis
Cervical spine trauma; C5, C6, or C7 nerve-root impingement trauma along the path of the median nerve.

Medical Diagnostic Tests
Electromyography or nerve conduction tests can be performed on the median nerve distribution (see **Figure 11.45**).

Imaging Techniques
Radiographs are performed to rule out bony changes in the wrist.

Definitive Diagnosis
Although electromyography may be performed to determine median nerve function, most diagnoses are based on clinical findings.

Pathomechanics and Functional Limitations
Repetitive finger activity, especially when the wrist is not supported in a slightly extended position, causes mild swelling within the tendon compartments.[96,97] Any volume change in the area constrained by the transverse carpal ligament can place pressure on its contents. The structure most vulnerable to this kind of subtle increase in pressure is the median nerve. The nerve becomes demyelinated, causing the symptoms associated with CTS. In severe cases, secondary axonal loss may occur.

■ Medications
A corticosteroid is injected into the tendon sheath to decrease inflammation.[97]

■ Postinjury/Postoperative Management
Initially, CTS is treated conservatively with rest, immobilization, and NSAIDs. The wrist is immobilized in 10° of extension using a commercial or thermoplastic cock-up splint, which is worn at night. If symptoms persist, corticosteroid injection or surgical decompression of the transverse carpal ligament may be necessary.

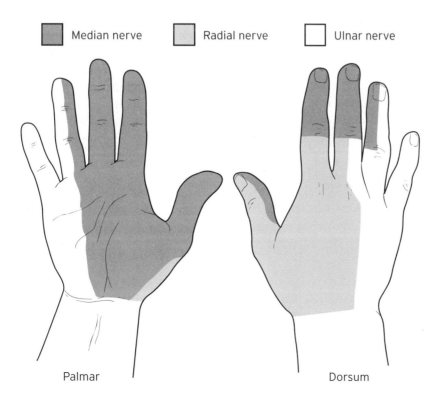

Median nerve   Radial nerve   Ulnar nerve

Palmar

Dorsum

Figure 11.45 The median, radial, and ulnar nerve distributions in the hand.

Surgical Intervention

Surgery for CTS is directed at releasing the transverse carpal ligament. Endoscopic techniques are available, but most patients who undergo open procedures heal quickly. The median nerve is more easily visualized with an open procedure.[98–101]

Injury-Specific Treatment and Rehabilitation Concerns

Specific Concerns
Encourage extension activities.
Limit early flexion posture.

Pressure is applied to control edema, and the hand is splinted for 10 days to 2 weeks. Finger ROM is encouraged early. Gentle wrist ROM is initiated at 2 weeks, and progressive strengthening is begun at 3 weeks. A night splint or a functional brace is used during activity to help support the wrist. Generally a commercial device, this support should be used during the activity that precipitated the development of CTS, such as keyboard use. Supervised rehabilitation programs are often unnecessary after surgical procedures for CTS. Unless there is actual damage to the median nerve, full function should return in 6 to 8 weeks, when the soft tissue heals.

Estimated Amount of Time Lost

Because CTS is a chronic inflammatory condition, efforts are made to change the individual's biomechanics so as to reduce pressure on the wrist. The athlete may continue to participate in athletics while altering techniques, using splints, and beginning a rehabilitation program. If the symptoms cannot be controlled, the precipitating activity must be ceased. Generally, the longer the patient has had the condition, the longer it will take for the symptoms to resolve. If surgical management is necessary, the athlete typically needs 4 to 6 weeks of healing before protected return to activity is tolerated.[100]

Return-to-Play Criteria

The athlete is permitted to participate when the neurologic symptoms have subsided. Postoperatively, sport participation is allowed when wrist strength and flexibility are normal. Use of supports can help to reduce the CTS-related symptoms. However, if these symptoms persist, activity should be discontinued. Once the nerve has healed, the ath-

lete may return to sport when the progressive addition of stressful activities can be tolerated.

Functional Bracing

Braces are used to help support the wrist in a functional position, minimize pressure, and aid posture.

Ulnar Nerve Injuries in the Hand

CLINICAL PRESENTATION

History
Compression along the ulnar nerve, especially at the Guyon canal.
Weakness and numbness after a long bicycle ride, particularly on a bumpy surface.
Fracture of the radius, ulna, or carpal bones, especially the pisiform or hamate, which compresses the nerve.
Numbness or paresthesia over the ulnar nerve distribution.

Observation
The fourth and fifth fingers are flexed (bishop's palsy).

Functional Status
Inability to extend the fourth and fifth fingers.
Decreased grip strength.

Physical Examination Findings
Paresthesia or other neurologic impairment over the ulnar nerve distribution.
Positive Tinel sign over the Guyon canal.

The hand is innervated by three distinct nerves—ulnar, radial, and median (see Figure 11.45). Each of these nerves has a sensory component and a motor component. The ulnar nerve is the most commonly injured nerve in the upper extremity. Nerve injury results in weakness, paralysis, and sensory dysfunction. The site of the nerve injury must be identified; it may be at the cervical spine, thoracic outlet, elbow region, wrist, or hand.

Anatomically, the Guyon canal is divided into three zones. Zone 1 is the area proximal to the ulnar nerve bifurcation. Compression in zone 1 causes combined motor and sensory loss and is most commonly caused by a fracture of the hook of the hamate or a ganglion. Zone 2 encompasses the motor branch of the nerve after it has bifurcated. Compression of this area causes pure loss of motor function to all of the ulnar-innervated muscles in the hand. A ganglion and fracture of the hook of the hamate are the most common causative factors. Zone 3 encompasses the superficial or sensory branch of the bifurcated nerve. Compression here causes sensory loss to the hypothenar eminence, the small finger, and part of the ring finger, but no motor deficits. Common causes of such injuries include an ulnar artery aneurysm, thrombosis, and synovial inflammation.[29]

Ulnar-nerve entrapment in athletes is usually attributable to compression in the Guyon canal, which is formed by the hook of the hamate and the pisiform.[102,103] The median nerve may become compressed in the carpal tunnel, whereas the radial nerve is typically injured in the shoulder or upper arm. The presentation is often that of a motor lesion, due to the isolated involvement of the deep motor branch as it courses around the hook of the hamate. Nerve compression, either from swelling or from body weight, can cause injury as well. Within the hand and wrist, repetitive stress or compression can injure the nerve. Such an injury is often termed "bishop's palsy," because the motor involvement causes an inability to extend the fourth and fifth fingers (see **Figure 11.46**). The resultant hand posture resembles that of a clergyman giving a blessing. Bicyclists often develop bishop's palsy caused by ulnar nerve compression from the weight on the handlebars. The pressure may be relieved by wearing cycling gloves and using thickly padded handlebars.[104]

Differential Diagnosis

Nerve entrapment syndrome in the upper extremity or cervical spine.

Medical Diagnostic Tests

Electromyographic and nerve conduction studies are used to identify the site of the nerve compression.

Imaging Techniques

To determine the presence of a carpal fracture, hand radiographs are taken. The carpal tunnel view is helpful in visualizing the hook of the hamate and pisiform. If the patient's condition does not resolve on its own, MRI is used to determine the presence of scar tissue or edema in the canal of Guyon.

Definitive Diagnosis

The definitive diagnosis is based on the nerve conduction study and clinical findings.

Pathomechanics and Functional Limitations

Generally when pressure is reduced, nerve function returns. If a neurapraxia is caused by chronic or repetitive stress, the nerve may require several weeks to regain full function. However, if rest does not relieve nerve pressure, the ligament overlying the Guyon canal can be surgically released.[105]

■ Immediate Management

The hand is splinted in a functional position that relieves pressure from the proximal palm.

■ Medications

To reduce swelling that puts pressure on the nerve, 0.5 cc of triamcinolone is injected into the canal.

■ Surgical Intervention

If a fracture of the hook of the hamate is noted, cast immobilization or splinting is required for 4 to 6 weeks. The Guyon canal is decompressed by releasing the retinaculum.[106] The surgeon should minimize the palm dissection, because scar tissue can produce similar symptoms. Scarring can restrict flexor tendon function, especially in the fourth and fifth fingers. When surgery is performed, early active ROM helps to prevent adhesion formation.

■ Postoperative Management

The postoperative dressing should apply even pressure in the palm to minimize swelling. Pressure dressings are applied immediately after surgery and removed after 3 to 4 days.

■ Injury-Specific Treatment and Rehabilitation Concerns

Specific Concerns

Support the wrist during healing.
Encourage early finger ROM.

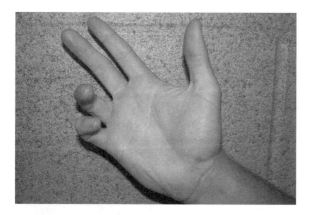

Figure 11.46 Presentation of motor involvement of ulnar nerve compression in the hand. Wasting and inability to extend the fourth and fifth fingers are seen.

Smaller dressings are applied to cover the wound, and a commercial wrist brace can be employed to support the hand and reduce use of the affected upper extremity during the acute healing phase.

Wrist and finger ROM is encouraged early and often. After 2 weeks, the patient may discard the brace and resume normal activities. If pressure must be placed on the palm, the area should be padded to distribute and absorb the force. Generally no supervised rehabilitation program is required after this procedure.

Estimated Amount of Time Lost

When the acute nerve pressure is eliminated, the deformity typically resolves in 24 to 72 hours. If equipment can be modified, the problem may resolve and participation can resume. If the injury is due to chronic stress and the development of scar tissue within the canal, however, symptom resolution will require more time. For example, a neurapraxia may require 2 to 6 weeks to resolve.[100] Similarly, if the nerve injury is caused by a carpal fracture, immobilization and healing time are affected by the fracture.

The amount of time lost from sport increases if scar tissue forms within the Guyon canal or if a fracture of the pisiform or the hook of the hamate occurs concomitantly.

Return-to-Play Criteria

Participation is permitted when motor and sensory nerve functions return.

Functional Bracing

Shock-absorbing gloves should be worn to reduce pressure on the palm. If the injury occurred from bicycling, padding may also be applied to the handlebars.

Rehabilitation

Wrist and Hand Rehabilitation

The goal of wrist and hand rehabilitation is to restore complete extremity function, but return to sport is always a secondary consideration to long-term recovery. For many patients, early return to sport may be safely accomplished while wearing a protective brace, cast, or tape. Some leagues and sports, however, place restrictions on the types of protective equipment permitted, especially for the hand. These rules must be consulted before clearing the athlete for sport participation. Ultimately, the umpire or referee decides whether to allow use of a protective device in competition. The clinician also should be knowledgeable about the functional requirements of the specific sport and should ensure that athletes—and, in the case of minors, parents—understand the consequences of an early return to activity.

The functional goals of wrist rehabilitation vary with the demands of the individual's sport. For example, a gymnast bears weight on the upper extremity, placing increased stress on the wrist's supportive structures, and requires increased ROM. This situation stands in sharp contrast to that of a football lineman, who can participate with minimal limitations despite wrist immobilization. Athletes can generally return to their sports when strength and ROM are adequate to participate effectively and enough tissue healing has occurred to prevent reinjury, pain, and a poor outcome. Young athletes should be protected from early degenerative changes, and older athletes must accept that longer healing times, loss of motion, and prolonged discomfort are the result of acute injury compounded by normal degeneration. Some injuries may cause a permanent loss of motion and reduced function. The expectations given each individual's situation should be explained, and activities should be modified and therapeutic exercises prescribed while the patient is in the healing phase to maximize functional outcome.

Wrist rehabilitation is divided into four phases: (1) acute management, (2) rehabilitation with activity restriction, (3) progressive rehabilitation, and (4) sport reintegration. The general rehabilitation goals include decreasing pain; minimizing the inflammatory response; reducing swelling; increasing ROM and strength; improving general conditioning; and maximizing muscle control, coordination, and sport-specific skills to allow a safe return to activity. Guidelines and timelines for protection and immobilization should always be clearly dictated by the physician so that this information is understood by the athletic trainer, physical therapist, coach, parent, and athlete.

Objective Evidence of Rehabilitation Goals

Goniometric measurement is used to determine wrist ROM. Although normal ROM is, of course, the goal of rehabilitation, this outcome is not always possible due to the complex nature of many wrist injuries. Depending on the nature of the injury, an estimation should be made of the expected ROM. For example, scapholunate injuries cause changes in the intercalated motion of the carpals and a loss of motion; therefore, motion may be limited to 60% to 80% of normal in athletes who experience such injuries. Furthermore, because normal variances may exist due to sport stress or genetics, motion should be compared with the opposite side and expectations adjusted accordingly.

Normal wrist ROM is characterized as follows:
- Flexion = 80°
  (32° = radiocarpal, 48° = midcarpal)
- Extension = 70°
  (47° = radiocarpal, 23° = midcarpal)
- Radioulnar deviation = 50°
  (20° = radiocarpal, 30° = midcarpal)
- Pronation = 80°
- Supination = 90°

Functional motion can be measured according to the activity requirement of the sport. For example, is motion adequate for push-ups, follow-through in basketball, or batting a ball? If not, modifications are necessary to prevent injury when the athlete is ready to reintegrate these activities into the training program.

Ideally, following rehabilitation, the athlete should have normal strength on the injured side compared with the opposite side. Strength can be measured by manual muscle testing in flexion, extension, pronation, and supination. Grip strength can be measured using a dynamometer. Most people normally have greater strength on the dominant side, and rehabilitation goals should take this

11

difference into consideration. Functional strength and endurance can be measured by weight bearing and tolerance to repetitive activities, such as throwing and catching balls of different sizes and weights.

Therapeutic Exercises

Therapeutic exercises are designed to meet the rehabilitation goals, depending on the healing phase. Generally, exercises are prescribed to increase ROM, strengthen the extremity, and promote function.

Phase 1 of wrist rehabilitation—acute management—may involve immobilization with a fiberglass or plaster cast, splint, or brace. The physician should clearly dictate the immobilization period, especially with removable appliances. Casts should be used for athletes who require strict immobilization, and the athlete should be taught finger ROM exercises and edema precautions. Removable appliances should be reserved for injuries that need rest from daily activities and for patients who perform gentle, therapeutic exercise at certain times during the day. During the acute management phase, therapeutic exercise is directed at pain and edema reduction and tissue healing. All activity should be pain free, and ROM should be active or done by the patient. Passive motion at this stage could cause increased swelling or pain.

Phase 2 of wrist rehabilitation incorporates strengthening exercises and more aggressive ROM therapy. The wrist may continue to require protection from stress of daily activity in the form of a supportive brace, which should be removed for exercise. Resistance can be added with weights or resistive bands. Although weights are more easily controlled by the patient and help prevent substitution patterns, bands are portable and easy to use.

Exercises include the following activities:

- Passive and active stretching (done first to warm up the joint and to ensure that resistance is performed over a greater ROM)
- Wrist extension
- Wrist flexion
- Radial deviation
- Biceps curl
- Triceps elbow extension
- Pronation/supination with hammer
- Grip exercise

All exercise should be pain-free, and the weight chosen should cause fatigue at the end of the set but not result in a substitution pattern. The joint should be isolated as much as possible. Joint mobilization

may begin in this stage but is limited to grade 1 and 2 mobilization forces.

Phase 3 of wrist rehabilitation incorporates progressive functional training. Strength-training exercises similar to phase 2 should be done, but sport-specific drills may be added. Polyurethane-covered medicine balls can be used in a traditional throw-and-catch exercise. Additionally, balls can be used for weight bearing. Traditional strength-training exercises can be integrated into the program, but the wrist should be supported with taping or bracing to minimize motion and increase stability. Joint mobilization can be more aggressive, and efforts should be made to increase motion to full range. The patient should sit on the hand, both in pronated and supinated positions, for a long-duration stretch.

Phase 4 of wrist rehabilitation comprises sport reintegration. By this time, the tissues should have healed enough to withstand the rigors of sports participation. The patient should continue to perform maintenance exercises for isolated upper extremity strengthening. Both active and passive ROM exercises should continue, and the clinician should pay close attention to tissue reaction from overexertion or stress.

Finger Rehabilitation

Injuries to the fingers are often overlooked or neglected with respect to rehabilitation. Sprains and some fractures may go untreated because the injury rarely prevents the athlete from competing. Unfortunately, poor care often leads to the crooked, contracted knuckles that are the war wounds of old injuries. Proper treatment with protection and rehabilitation can prevent deformities while improving function.

The fingers are highly innervated and produce a tremendous amount of pain when injured. Despite this issue, most athletes can participate with splints and tape on the fingers, even if the sport requires the use of the hands. Yet some injuries and surgical interventions preclude sport participation, even with adequate protection. Restrictions on the return to competition should be clearly outlined.

The goal of rehabilitation for the fingers is to reduce edema and pain while promoting full ROM. Full PIP joint extension is difficult and can be compared with the opposite side. Flexion is measured by goniometry or by the proximity of the fingertip to the distal palmar crease. Finger flexion also should be checked with the MCP joint extended by having the patient attempt to touch the fingertip to the point where the finger meets the hand.

The fingers are very reactive to stress, and strict attention should be paid to increased swelling and pain after passive therapies and therapeutic exercise. The network of tendons and ligaments is intricate, and the joint capsules are very vascular. Aggressive joint mobilization can be more detrimental than helpful in some patients.

Although the goals of rehabilitation are swelling control and full ROM, most athletes are able to participate in their sport early in the rehabilitation program. Splinting is performed in positions of function, and often an injured finger is buddy taped to another for added support. Once the immobilization phase has ended, protection should continue during sports activities.

Therapeutic Exercises

Therapeutic exercises for the fingers should concentrate largely on active rather than passive exercise. Active exercise causes the tendons to slide within their sheaths, decreases swelling, and is limited by patient tolerance, resulting in less tissue reaction. The patient should emphasize full ROM, and the clinician should teach the patient to block other joints to isolate DIP and PIP joint function. Long-duration passive stretching can be done with splints or gentle joint mobilization.

Thumb Rehabilitation

The goal of thumb rehabilitation is to restore compete function. Although the athlete's goal may be to return to competition as quickly as possible, the clinician must consider the safety of sport participation during injury healing and the consequences of secondary injury. Return to sport is always a secondary concern, after long-term recovery. Early return to sport may be safely accomplished with protective braces, casts, or tape in many patients.

The functional goals of thumb rehabilitation are for the athlete to effectively use the hand in the sport. The thumb should have good interphalangeal, MCP, and CMC joint motion. Flexion, extension, abduc-

tion, adduction, and opposition should be exercised. The clinician often must teach the patient to move the thumb in each direction and to block unwanted motion so as to isolate joint function and allow the appropriate tendons to glide. Creative techniques, including the use of handheld games, can promote good thumb mobility and strength.

Thumb rehabilitation begins after a protective phase during acute inflammation or when immobilization is required for proper healing. Many immobilization devices are easily removed, but this step should be taken only on the advice of the physician directing the patient's care. Too many splints are discarded too early, resulting in a poor longer-term outcome. As with the fingers, active exercise is preferred because the tissues in the small joints react negatively to stress, and increased swelling and pain may result from overly aggressive exercise.

Objective Evidence of Rehabilitation Goals

Goniometric measurement is performed to determine thumb ROM. The patient is encouraged to touch the thumb tip to each finger to promote and measure thumb opposition. Strength can be determined using a grip dynamometer and by manual muscle testing of individual motions, which are then compared to the strength of the uninvolved side. Function can be determined by the patient's ability to perform complex tasks.

Therapeutic Exercises

Therapeutic exercises for the thumb are designed to meet the rehabilitation goals, depending on the phase of healing. Generally, exercises are prescribed to increase ROM, strengthen the thumb, and promote function.

Exercises include the following activities:

- Interphalangeal flexion/extension
- MCP and CMC flexion, extension, abduction, adduction, and opposition

The final phase of thumb rehabilitation is sport reintegration. The patient should continue to perform maintenance exercises for isolated upper extremity strengthening. Ball skills and use of sports implements such as sticks and bats are addressed during this phase.

11

References

1. McCue FC, Andrews JR, Hakala M, Gieck JH. The coach's finger. *J Sports Med.* 1974;2:270–275.

2. McCue FC, Garroway RY. Sports injuries to the hand and wrist, in Schneider RC, Kennedy JC, Plant ML (eds), *Sports Injuries: Mechanisms, Prevention and Treatment.* Baltimore, MD: Williams & Wilkins; 1985:743–763.

3. Lairmore JR, Engber WD. Serious, often subtle, finger injuries: Avoiding diagnosis and treatment pitfalls. *Physician Sportsmed.* 1998;26:57–73.

4. Harrison BP, Hilliard MW. Emergency department evaluation and treatment of hand injuries. *Emerg Med Clin North Am.* 1999;17:793–822.

5. McCue FC, Honner R, Johnson MC, Gieck JH. Athletic injuries of the proximal interphalangeal joint requiring surgical treatment. *J Bone Joint Surg Am.* 1970;52:937–956.

6. Souter WA. The problem of boutonnière deformity. *Clin Orthop.* 1974;104:116–133.

7. Aronowitz ER, Leddy JP. Closed tendon injuries of the hand and wrist in athletes. *Clin Sports Med.* 1998;17:449–467.

8. Coons MS, Green SM. Boutonnière deformity. *Hand Clin.* 1995;11:387–402.

9. Hurlbut PT, Adams BD. Analysis of finger extensor mechanism strains. *J Hand Surg Am.* 1995;20:832–840.

10. Massengill JB. The boutonnière deformity. *Hand Clin.* 1992;8:787–801.

11. Palmer RE. Joint injuries of the hand in athletes. *Clin Sports Med.* 1998;17:513–531.

12. Pratt AL, Burr N, Grobbelaar AO. A prospective review of open central slip laceration repair and rehabilitation. *J Hand Surgery (European Volume).* 2002:27:530–534.

13. Hester PW, Blazar PE. Complications of hand and wrist surgery in the athlete. *Clin Sports Med.* 1999;18:811–829.

14. Wehbe MA, Schneider LH. Mallet fractures. *J Bone Joint Surg Am.* 1984;66:658–669.

15. McCue FC III, Meister K. Common sports hand injuries: An overview of aetiology, management and prevention. *Sports Med.* 1993;15:281–289.

16. Rayan GM, Mullins PT. Skin necrosis complicating mallet finger splinting and vascularity of the distal interphalangeal joint overlying skin. *J Hand Surg Am.* 1987;12:548–552.

17. Garberman SF, Diao E, Peimer CA. Mallet finger: results of early versus delayed closed treatment. *J Hand Surg Am.* 1994;19:850–852.

18. Lubahn JD. Mallet finger fractures: A comparison of open and closed technique. *J Hand Surg Am.* 1989;14:394–396.

19. Stern PJ, Kastrup JJ. Complications and prognosis of treatment of mallet finger. *J Hand Surg Am.* 1988;13:329–334.

20. Leddy JP, Packer JW. Avulsion of the profundus tendon insertion in athletes. *J Hand Surg Am.* 1977;2:66–69.

21. McCue FC III, Wooten SL. Closed tendon injuries of the hand in athletes. *Clin Sports Med.* 1986;5:741–755.

22. McCue FC III, Meister K. Common sports hand injuries: An overview of aetiology, management and prevention. *Sports Med.* 1993;15:281–289.

23. Lubahn JD, Hood JM. Fractures of the distal interphalangeal joint. *Clin Orthop.* 1996;327:12–20.

24. Strickland JW, Steichen JB, Kleinman WB. Phalangeal fractures: Factors influencing performance. *Orthop Rev.* 1982;1:39.

25. Baratz ME, Divelbiss B. Fixation of phalangeal fractures. *Hand Clin.* 1997;13:541–555.

26. Creighton JJ Jr, Steichen JB. Complications in phalangeal and metacarpal fracture management: Results of extensor tenolysis. *Hand Clin.* 1994;10:111–116.

27. Freeland AE, Benoist LA, Melancon KP. Parallel miniature screw fixation of spiral and long oblique hand phalangeal fractures. *Orthopedics.* 1994;17:199–200.

28. Schenck RR. Dynamic traction and early passive movement for fractures of the proximal interphalangeal joint. *J Hand Surg Am.* 1986;11:850–858.

29. McCue FC III, Mayer V. Rehabilitation of common athletic injuries of the hand and wrist. *Clin Sports Med.* 1989;8:731–776.

30. Freiberg A, Mulholland RS, Levine R. Nonoperative treatment of trigger fingers and thumbs. *J Hand Surg Am.* 1989;14:553–558.

31. Green DP, Wolfe SW. Tenosynovitis, in Green DP, Hotchkiss RN, Pederson WC (eds), *Green's Operative Hand Surgery, Vol. 4,* ed 4. New York: Churchill Livingstone; 1999:2029.

32. Carlson CS Jr, Curtis RM. Steroid injection for flexor tenosynovitis. *J Hand Surg Am.* 1984;9:286–287.

33. Murphy D, Failla JM, Koniuch MP, et al. Steroid versus placebo injection for trigger finger. *J Hand Surg Am.* 1995;20:628–631.

34. Marks MR, Gunther SF. Efficacy of cortisone injection in treatment of trigger fingers and thumbs. *J Hand Surg Am.* 1989;14:722–727.

35. Rhoades CE, Gelberman RH, Manjarris JF. Stenosing tenosynovitis of the fingers and thumb: Results of a prospective trial of steroid injection and splinting. *Clin Orthop.* 1984;190:236–238.

36. Boyer MI, Gelberman RH. Operative correction of swanneck and boutonniere deformities in the rheumatoid hand. *J Am Acad Orthop Surg.* 1999;7:92–100.

37. McCue FC III, Hakala MW, Andrews JR, Gieck JH. Ulnar collateral ligament injuries of the thumb in athletes. *J Sports Med.* 1974;2:70–80.

38. Campbell CS. Gamekeeper's thumb. *J Bone Joint Surg Br.* 1955;37:148–149.

39. Stener B. Displacement of the ruptured ulnar collateral ligament of the metacarpophalangeal joint. *J Bone Joint Surg Br.* 1962;44:869–879.

40. Gerber C, Senn E, Matter P. Skier's thumb: Surgical treatment of recent injuries to the ulnar collateral ligament of the thumb's metacarpophalangeal joint. *Am J Sports Med.* 1981;9:171–177.

41. Heyman P. Injuries to the ulnar collateral ligament of the thumb metacarpophalangeal joint. *J Am Acad Orthop Surg.* 1997;5:224–229.

42. Kozin SH, Bishop AT. Gamekeeper's thumb: Early diagnosis and treatment. *Orthop Rev.* 1994;23:797–804.

43. Glickel SZ, Malerich M, Pearce SM, Littler JW. Ligament replacement for chronic instability of the ulnar collateral ligament of the metacarpophalangeal joint of the thumb. *J Hand Surg Am.* 1993;18:930–941.

44. Green DP, Stern PJ. Fractures of the metacarpals and phalanges, in Green DP, Hotchkiss RN, Pederson WC (eds), *Green's Operative Hand Surgery, Vol. 2,* ed 4. New York: Churchill Livingstone; 1999:711–772.

45. Soyer AD. Fractures of the base of the first metacarpal: Current treatment options. *J Am Acad Orthop Surg.* 1999;7:403–412.

46. Metacarpal and carpometacarpal trauma, in Peimer CA, Wolfe SW, Elliot AJ (eds), *Hand and Upper Extremity.* New York: McGraw-Hill; 1996:883–920.

47. Rockwood CA, Green DP, Butler TE Jr. Fractures and dislocations of the hand, in Rockwood CA Jr, Green DP, Bucholtz RW, Heckman JD (eds), *Rockwood and Green's Fractures in Adults.* Philadelphia, PA: Lippincott-Raven; 1996:607–744.

48. Arons MS. De Quervain's release in working women: A report of failures, complications, and associated diagnoses. *J Hand Surg Am.* 1987;12:540–544.

49. Weiss AP, Akelman E, Tabatabai M. Treatment of de Quervain's disease. *J Hand Surg Am.* 1994;19:595–598.

50. Louis DS. Incomplete release of the first dorsal compartment: A diagnostic test. *J Hand Surg Am.* 1987;12:87–88.

51. Kahler DM, McCue FC III. Metacarpophalangeal and proximal interphalangeal joint injuries of the hand, including the thumb. *Clin Sports Med.* 1992;11:57–76.

52. Stern PJ. Fractures of the metacarpals and phalanges, in Green DP, Hotchkiss RN, Pederson WC (eds), *Green's Operative Hand Surgery, Vol. 1,* ed 4. New York: Churchill Livingstone; 1999:711–771.

53. Green DP, Butler TE. Fractures and dislocations in the hand, in Rockwood CA Jr, Green DP, Bucholtz RW, Heckman JD (eds), *Rockwood and Green's Fractures in Adults, Vol. 1,* ed 4. Philadelphia, PA: Lippincott Williams & Wilkins; 1996:607–744.

54. Ashkenaze DM, Ruby LK. Metacarpal fractures and dislocations. *Orthop Clin North Am.* 1992;23:19–33.

55. Axelrod TS. Metacarpal fractures, in Light T (ed), *Hand Surgery Update,* ed 2. Rosemont, IL: American Academy of Orthopaedic Surgeons; 1999:11–17.

56. de Jonge JJ, Kingma J, van der Lei B, Klasen HJ. Fractures of the metacarpals: A retrospective analysis of incidence and aetiology and a review of the English-language literature. *Injury.* 1994;25:365–369.

57. Maruyama T, Saha S, Mongiano DO, Mudge K. Metacarpal fracture fixation with absorbable polyglycolide rods and stainless steel K wires: A biomechanical comparison. *J Biomed Mater Res.* 1996;33:9–12.

58. Berger RA. The gross and histologic anatomy of the scapholunate interosseous ligament. *J Hand Surg Am.* 1996;21:170–178.

59. Campbell RD Jr, Lance EM, Yeoh CB. Lunate and perilunate dislocations. *J Bone Joint Surg Br.* 1964;46:55–72.

60. Cooney WP, Linscheid RL, Dobyns JH. Fractures and dislocation of the wrist, in Rockwood CA Jr, Green DP, Bucholtz RW, Heckman JD (eds), *Rockwood and Green's Fractures in Adults, Vol. 1.* Philadelphia, PA: Lippincott Williams & Wilkins; 1996:745–867.

61. Herzberg G, Comtet JJ, Linscheid RL, et al. Perilunate dislocations and fracture–dislocations: A multicenter study. *J Hand Surg Am.* 1993;18:768–779.

62. Kobayashi M, Berger RA, Linscheid RL, An KN. Intercarpal kinematics during wrist motion. *Hand Clin.* 1997;13:143–149.

63. Redler MR, McCue FC III. Injuries of the hand in athletes. *VA Med.* 1988;115:331–336.

64. Minami A, Kaneda K. Repair and/or reconstruction of scapholunate interosseous ligament in lunate and perilunate dislocations. *J Hand Surg Am.* 1993;18:1099–1106.

65. Sotereanos DG, Mitsionis GJ, Giannakopoulos PN, et al. Perilunate dislocation and fracture dislocation: A critical analysis of the volar-dorsal approach. *J Hand Surg Am.* 1997;22:49–56.

66. Barnaby W. Fractures and dislocations of the wrist. *Emerg Med Clin North Am.* 1992;10:133–149.

67. Calandra JJ, Goldner RD, Hardaker WT Jr. Scaphoid fractures: Assessment and treatment. *Orthopedics.* 1992;15:931–937.

68. Adolfsson L, Lindau T, Arner M. Acutrak screw fixation versus cast immobilisation for undisplaced scaphoid waist fractures. *J Hand Surg Br.* 2001;26:192–195.

69. Geissler WB. Carpal fractures in athletes. *Clin Sports Med.* 2001;20:167–188.

70. Seitz WH, Papandrea RF. Fractures and dislocations of the wrist, in Bucholz RW, Heckman JD (eds), *Rockwood and Green's Fractures in Adults,* ed 5. Philadelphia, PA: Lippincott Williams & Wilkins; 2001:749–799.

71. Simank HG, Schiltenwolf M, Krempien W. The etiology of Kienbock's disease: A histopathologic study. *J Hand Surg.* 1998;3:63–69.

72. Taleisnik J. Scapholunate dissociation, in Strickland JW, Steichen JB (eds), *Difficult Problems in Hand Surgery.* St Louis, MO: CV Mosby; 1982:341–348.

73. Watson HK, Weinzweig J. Physical examination of the wrist. *Hand Clin.* 1997;13:17–34.

74. Mayfield JK, Johnson RP, Kilcoyne RK. Carpal dislocations: Pathomechanics and progressive perilunar instability. *J Hand Surg Am.* 1980;5:226–241.

75. Lavernia CJ, Cohen MS, Taleisnik J. Treatment of scapholunate dissociation by ligamentous repair and capsulodesis. *J Hand Surg Am.* 1992;17:354–359.

76. Watson HK, Ryu J. Evolution of arthritis of the wrist. *Clin Orthop Relat Res.* 1986;202:57–67.

77. Rettig AC. Athletic injuries of the wrist and hand: Part I. Traumatic injuries of the wrist. *Am J Sports Med.* 2003;31:1038–1048.

78. Aldridge JM III, Mallon WJ. Hook of the hamate fractures in competitive golfers: Results of treatment by excision of the fractured hook of the hamate. *Orthopedics.* 2003;26:717–719.

79. David TS, Zemel NP, Mathews PV. Symptomatic, partial union of the hook of the hamate fracture in athletes. *Am J Sports Med.* 2003;31:106–111.

80. McCue FC III, Faltaous AA, Baumgarten TE. Bilateral hook of the hamate fractures. *Orthopedics.* 1997;20:470–472.

81. Palmer AK, Werner FW. The triangular fibrocartilage complex of the wrist: Anatomy and function. *J Hand Surg Am.* 1981;6:153–162.

82. Cooney WP, Linscheid RL, Dobyns JH. Triangular fibrocartilage tears. *J Hand Surg Am.* 1994;19:143–154.

83. Nakamura T, Yabe Y, Horiuchi Y. Functional anatomy of the triangular fibrocartilage complex. *J Hand Surg Br.* 1996;21:581–586.

84. Palmer AK. Triangular fibrocartilage complex lesions: A classification. *J Hand Surg Am.* 1989;14:594–606.

85. Bowers WH. The distal radioulnar joint, in Green DP, Hatchkiss RN, Pederson WC (eds), *Green's Operative Hand Surgery.* New York: Churchill Livingstone; 1999:989–995.

86. Nguyen DT, McCue FC III, Urch SE. Evaluation of the injured wrist on the field and in the office. *Clin Sports Med.* 1998;17:421–432.

87. Adams BD. Partial excision of the triangular fibrocartilage complex articular disk: A biomechanical study. *J Hand Surg Am.* 1993;18:334–340.

88. Bednar JM. Arthroscopic treatment of triangular fibrocartilage tears. *Hand Clin.* 1999;15:479–488.

89. Lucey SD, Poehling GG. Arthroscopic treatment of triangular fibrocartilage complex tears. *Techniq Hand Upper Extrem Surg.* 1997;1:228–236.

90. Minami A, Ishikawa J, Suenaga N, Kasashima T. Clinical results of treatment of triangular fibrocartilage complex

tears by arthroscopic debridement. *J Hand Surg Am.* 1996; 21:406–411.

91. Dekkers M, Soballe K. Activities and impairments in the early stage of rehabilitation after Colles' fracture. *Disabil Rehabil.* 2004;26:662–668.

92. Raisbeck CC. Closed reduction of Colles fractures. *J Bone Joint Surg Am.* 2003;85:1614.

93. Fernandez DL, Palmer AK. Fractures of the distal radius, in Green DP, Hatchkiss RN, Pederson WC (eds), *Green's Operative Hand Surgery.* New York: Churchill Livingstone; 1999:930–933.

94. Pfeffer GB, Gelberman RH, Boyes JH, Rydevik B. The history of carpal tunnel syndrome. *J Hand Surg Br.* 1988; 13:28–34.

95. Atroshi I, Gummesson C, Johnsson R, et al. Prevalence of carpal tunnel syndrome in a general population. *JAMA.* 1999;282:153–158.

96. Bindra RR, Evanoff BA, Chough LY, et al. The use of routine wrist radiography in the evaluation of patients with carpal tunnel syndrome. *J Hand Surg Am.* 1997;22: 115–119.

97. Dammers JW, Veering MM, Vermeulen M. Injection with methylprednisolone proximal to the carpal tunnel: Randomised double blind trial. *BMJ.* 1999;319:884–886.

98. Bozentka DJ, Osterman AL. Complications of endoscopic carpal tunnel release. *Hand Clin.* 1995;11:91–95.

99. Cook AC, Szabo RM, Birkholz SW, King EF. Early mobilization following carpal tunnel release: A prospective randomized study. *J Hand Surg Br.* 1995;20:228–230.

100. Lundborg G, Dahlin LB. The pathophysiology of nerve compression. *Hand Clin.* 1992;8:215–227.

101. Palmer AK, Toivonen DA. Complications of endoscopic and open carpal tunnel release. *J Hand Surg Am.* 1999;24: 561–565.

102. Posner MA. Compressive ulnar neuropathies at the elbow: I. Etiology and diagnosis. *J Am Acad Orthop Surg.* 1998;6:282–288.

103. Edmonson AS, Crenshaw AH. Ulnar nerve, in Canale ST (ed), *Campbell's Operative Orthopaedics,* ed 6. St. Louis, MO: Mosby; 1980:1679–1684.

104. Sicuranza MJ, McCue FC III. Compressive neuropathies in the upper extremity of athletes. *Hand Clin.* 1992;8: 263–273.

105. Kleinman WB. Cubital tunnel syndrome: Anterior transposition as a logical approach to complete nerve decompression. *J Hand Surg Am.* 1999;24:886–897.

106. Szabo RM, Steinberg DR. Nerve entrapment syndromes in the wrist. *J Am Acad Orthop Surg.* 1994;2:115–123.

Upper Extremity Therapeutic Exercises

Brady L. Tripp, PhD, ATC

The exercises and techniques presented in this chapter are adjuncts to those described in Chapters 9, 10, and 11. Many other exercises can also be incorporated or substituted for those presented here. In addition, most exercises can be modified based on the patient's needs, the equipment on hand, or personal preference. To construct a complete rehabilitation program, cross-referencing among chapters is required.

Mobility Exercises

Mobility is developed through a progression of closed- and open-chain exercises that require increasing levels of rotator cuff activity—from passive, to active-assisted, to active. Early rehabilitation should maintain pain-free range of motion (ROM) and begin restoring mobility by incorporating physical agents, manual therapy, joint mobilizations (see "Joint Mobilization Techniques" in Chapter 9), and medications to reduce pain, trigger points, soft-tissue restrictions, and inflammation as appropriate. Thoracic spine motion may be limited, with or without obvious kyphosis, and should be addressed with joint mobilization. Specific postoperative restrictions in ROM, muscle activity, and weight bearing must be respected during mobility activities. Most progressions establish mobility through closed- and open-chain exercises that require increasing levels of muscular activity.

Shoulder

Isolate glenohumeral (GH) motion from humeral-thoracic motion to identify GH ROM deficits. Measures include GH internal rotation (IR) and external rotation (ER) and posterior shoulder tightness (see "Overhead Athletes: Adaptations and Pathomechanics" in Chapter 9). Soft-tissue mobilization and stretching of the associated muscles helps correct the poor scapular position and spinal posture associated with dysfunctional shoulders. Muscles that typically lack flexibility include the pectoralis minor, levator scapulae, upper trapezius, latissimus dorsi, and posterior rotator cuff.

The development of shoulder mobility progresses through closed- and open-chain exercises that require increasing levels of rotator cuff activity. The progression begins with open-chain pendulum exercises and table bows in pain-free ranges; these exercises require minimal rotator cuff activity. The active-assisted exercises begin as patient comfort or postsurgical restrictions afford. Exercises include

Cross-References

Clavicular mobilization:
  Inferior glide (page 342)
  Posterior glide (page 342)
  Posterosuperior and anteroinferior glide (page 342)
Scapular mobilization:
  Distraction (page 342)
  Superior and inferior glide (page 343)
  Lateral and medial rotation (page 343)
Glenohumeral mobilization:
  Anterior humeral glide (page 343)
  Inferior humeral glide (page 343)
  Lateral distraction (page 344)
  Posterior glide (page 344)
Self-mobilization techniques:
  Lateral glide (page 344)
  Inferior glide (page 344)
  Posterior glide (page 345)
  Anterior glide (page 345)

T-bar–assisted ROM, closed-chain pendulum exercises, table washes, and the supine press. Glenohumeral motion should be restored and maintained as needed. Shoulder motion and GH rotation are restored and maintained through the flexibility portion of the *Foundational Shoulder Exercises*.

Joint mobilization and horizontal adduction and sleeper stretches can effectively address a tight posterior capsule.[1] Stretching the entire upper arm without first ensuring proper GH osteokinematics motion may further exacerbate the patient's symptoms.[2]

Shoulder Pendulum Exercises (Codman Exercises; Minimal Rotator Cuff Activity)

The patient stands flexed at the waist and supports the uninvolved side by leaning on the table. The involved extremity is allowed to hang in a relaxed position, free from support. Using a rocking motion of the entire body, the patient oscillates the involved extremity through elevation, extension, horizontal adduction, horizontal abduction, and circumduction (see **Figure 12.1**). This exercise should not be performed with weights because the resulting joint distraction stretches the static stabilizers.

Table Bows (Minimal Rotator Cuff Activity)

The patient stands with the palm on a towel, flat on the table. The patient performs a bow toward the table, letting the hand slide on the table, and returns to the starting position. This exercise progresses to increase GH elevation ROM and is also performed with lateral trunk flexion to increase GH abduction ROM. Alternatively, the patient can move the trunk (forward or lateral flexion) over a fixed hand to improve elevation and abduction ROM (see **Figure 12.2**).

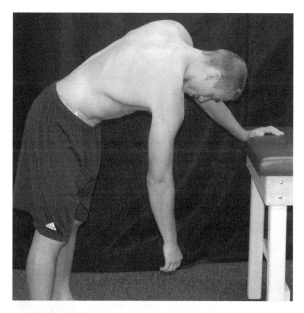

Figure 12.1 Pendulum exercises allow the arm to hang in a relaxed position, free from support. The patient oscillates the arm in each direction, using a rocking motion of the entire body, to passively move the GH joint.

Cross-Body Self-Stretch

For the self-stretch, the patient stands with back against the wall, stabilizing the involved scapula against the wall. The patient pulls the humerus across the chest in horizontal adduction (see **Figure 12.3**).

Sleeper Stretch

The patient lies on the involved side with the humerus and elbow flexed to 90° (a pillow may be placed under the patient's head for comfort). The opposite hand is used to internally rotate the humerus (see **Figure 12.4**).

Figure 12.3 The cross-body self-stretch is used to address a tight posterior capsule and rotator cuff.

T-Bar–Assisted ROM (Active-Assisted Rotator Cuff)

The following ROM exercises are performed using a T-bar, wand, or cane.

Shoulder Elevation

The patient stands or is supine, holding the wand at waist level with palms pronated. Both upper extremities are lifted directly overhead in the sagittal plane, guiding the involved extremity with the uninvolved extremity (see **Figure 12.5**).

Shoulder Abduction

The patient stands or is supine, holding the wand at waist level with the involved hand supinated and the uninvolved hand pronated. The patient guides the involved upper extremity with the uninvolved extremity and moves it overhead in a lateral direction in the coronal plane (see **Figure 12.6**).

12

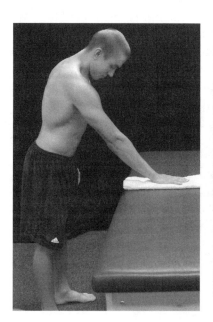
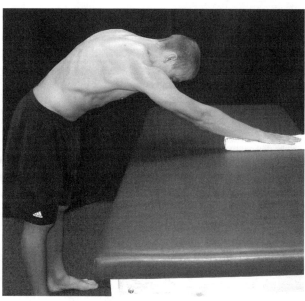

Figure 12.2 Table bows are used to gain GH elevation with minimal rotator cuff activity.

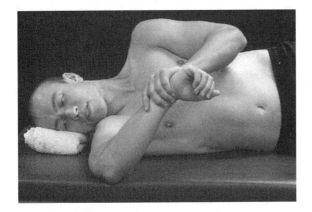

Figure 12.4 The sleeper self-stretch is used to increase flexibility of the posterior capsule and rotator cuff.

Figure 12.5 Range of motion exercise: shoulder elevation.

Figure 12.6 Range of motion exercise: shoulder abduction.

Shoulder Internal Rotation

The patient stands or is supine, holding the wand at the umbilical level with elbows flexed to 90°. The involved arm is guided medially (see **Figure 12.7**).

Shoulder External Rotation

The patient stands or is supine, holding the wand at chest level with shoulders abducted to 90° and

Figure 12.7 Range of motion exercise: shoulder internal rotation.

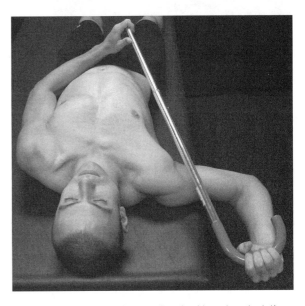

Figure 12.8 Range of motion exercise: shoulder external rotation.

elbows flexed to 90°. The patient guides the involved hand with the uninvolved hand to move it inferiorly and superiorly from the waist to the overhead position, with the forearm moving in the sagittal plane (see **Figure 12.8**).

Shoulder Horizontal Abduction

The patient stands or is supine and holds the wand at chest level with the involved hand supinated. The patient guides the involved hand with the uninvolved hand to move it laterally and medially in the transverse plane.

Shoulder Extension

The patient sits or stands, holding the wand on the involved side at waist level with the hand in a neutral position. The uninvolved hand is held in horizontal adduction with the hand at waist level. The patient guides the involved hand with the uninvolved hand to move it posteriorly in the sagittal plane (see **Figure 12.9**).

Table Wash and Diagonal Table Wash (Active Rotator Cuff)

The patient stands with the palm on a towel, flat on the table. The patient actively slides the hand forward on the table into GH elevation, abduction, diagonal, circles, and other positions (see **Figure 12.10**). This exercise progresses to an inclined table to increase resistance and GH ROM.

Wall Wash (Active Rotator Cuff)

The patient assumes an athletic stance with the palm on a towel, placed flat on the wall in front of the hip. The patient slides the hand diagonally across the wall while extending the contralateral hip (see **Figure 12.11**).

Supine Press (Active Rotator Cuff)

The supine press is used to gain GH elevation. The hands are close together on a wand; the patient presses the wand toward the ceiling. Glenohumeral elevation range is progressed by increasing the elevation angle of the table; the distance between the hands is progressed as well (see **Figure 12.12**).

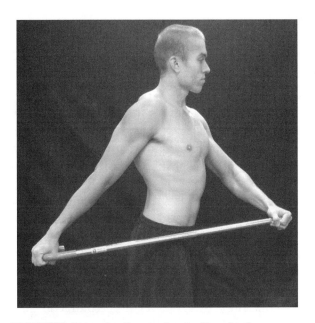

Figure 12.9 Range of motion exercise: shoulder extension.

Figure 12.11 The wall wash is a closed-chain progression from the table wash that incorporates the entire kinetic chain.

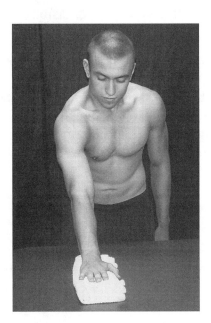

Figure 12.10 The table wash is a closed-chain exercise that can safely progress the active ROM in multiple planes.

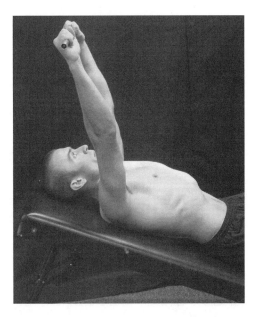

Figure 12.12 The supine press with a wand progresses from a flat table to an incline to safely gain active shoulder elevation.

12

Supine "Open Book" Pectoralis Minor Manual Stretch

The scapula is passively retracted (scapular ER and posterior tilt) while maintaining GH ER to stretch the pectoralis minor (see **Figure 12.13**).

Pectoralis Self-Stretch

The patient stands with the arm abducted to 90°, elbow flexed to 90°, and palm and forearm held flat against a wall or door frame. The patient rotates the trunk away from the abducted arm, increasing GH horizontal abduction. This stretch is appropriate only for those individuals with no anterior GH instability (see **Figure 12.14**).

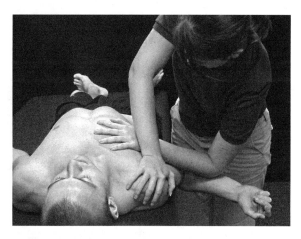

Figure 12.13 The supine "open book" pectoralis minor manual stretch facilitates scapular external rotation and posterior tilt.

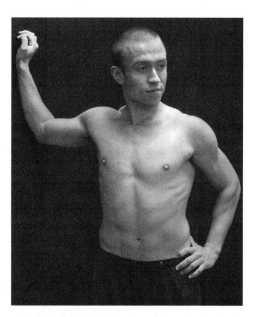

Figure 12.14 The pectoralis self-stretch is performed by rotating the trunk away from the stationary arm. The angle of glenohumeral abduction is adjusted to address additional fibers.

Elbow, Forearm, Wrist, and Hand

With the elbow extended, passively flexing the wrist and fingers stretches the posterior forearm muscles (wrist and finger extensors); passively extending the wrist and fingers stretches the anterior forearm muscles (wrist and finger flexors).

> **Cross-References**
>
> Flexion (page 398)
> Extension (page 398)
> Pronation/supination (page 398)

Developing Shoulder Stability

Shoulder stability is developed as a continuum, from static to dynamic to functional, and from single-joint to multiple-joint to functional movements. Early shoulder stability exercises should establish conscious control of scapulothoracic position and focus on improving postural awareness and scapular stability. This progression should start during immobilization. Patients can safely perform the first three exercises described in this section while confined to a sling. The exercises emphasize thoracic spine mobility and scapular retraction, elevation, and depression. Isometric stability is initiated at the proximal shoulder through closed-chain exercises that emphasize rotator cuff co-contraction and is advanced through rhythmic stabilization.

Shoulder Stability Progression

Establishing Conscious Control

- Scapular clocks in sling or 0° of abduction (minimal rotator cuff activity)
- Shoulder dumps in sling or 0° of abduction (minimal rotator cuff activity)
- Sternal lifts in sling or 0° of abduction (minimal rotator cuff activity)

Isometric Stability

These exercises are progressed when rotator cuff muscle activity is permitted.

- Weight shifts (rotator cuff co-contraction)
- Isometric low rows, with hip/thoracic extension (rotator cuff co-contraction)
- Ball stability (rotator cuff co-contraction)
- Open-chain rhythmic stabilization (rotator cuff co-contraction)
- Tubing isometric stability (rotator cuff co-contraction)

Dynamic Stability

These exercises are progressed when GH active elevation to 120° with scapular control (no shrug) is established.

- Scapular clocks at 90° of abduction
- Push-up progression
- Hitchhiker
- Tubing retraction progression
- Lawnmower progression

Scapular Clocks in Sling or 0° of Abduction (Minimal Rotator Cuff Activity)

The patient actively moves the scapula in four directions: 12 and 6 o'clock = superior and inferior translation; 3 and 9 o'clock = protraction and retraction (see Figure 12.15).

Shoulder Dumps in Sling or 0° of Abduction (Minimal Rotator Cuff Activity)

The patient begins with a contralateral-side lunge, protracting the involved scapula and flexing and rotating the trunk toward the contralateral knee. The patient is instructed to move as if "you are dumping out a glass of water that is fixed to the top of your shoulder." The patient then returns to the starting position and completes the movement with retraction (scapular ER and posterior tilt) as if bringing the scapula to the back pocket (see Figure 12.16).

Sternal Lifts in Sling or 0° of Abduction (Minimal Rotator Cuff Activity)

The patient corrects any forward head posture with a chin tuck and extends the thoracic spine as if lifted by a string attached to the sternum (see Figure 12.17).

Weight Shifts (Rotator Cuff Co-contraction)

The patient stands with both palms on a table. The patient shifts weight on and off of the involved shoulder, applying an appropriate percentage of weight. This exercise progresses in terms of the amount of weight placed on the limb and to greater levels of humeral elevation, to unstable surfaces, and to the wall and floor (see Figure 12.18).

Isometric Low Rows with Hip/Thoracic Extension (Rotator Cuff Co-contraction)

The patient pushes a palm against a fixed table as if pushing it away. The scapula should retract

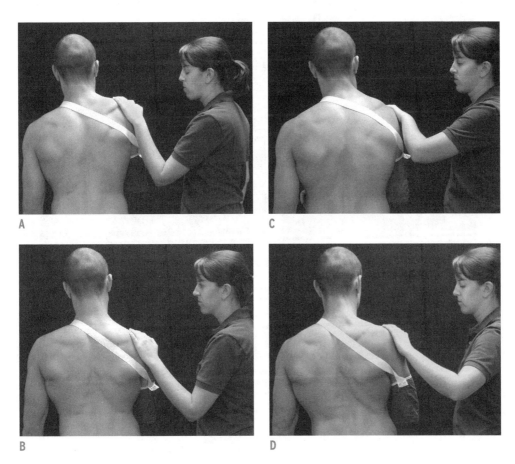

Figure 12.15 Scapular clocks can be used to develop neuromuscular control while in a sling. The patient moves the scapula to the 12, 6, 3, and 9 o'clock positions following the clinician's cues. **(A)** Scapular elevation. **(B)** Depression. **(C)** Protraction. **(D)** Retraction.

Figure 12.16   Shoulder dumps develop scapular neuromuscular control and incorporate the entire kinetic chain.

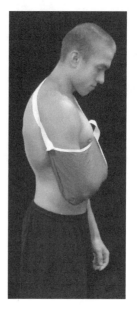
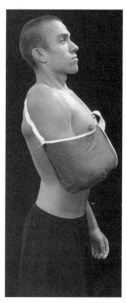

Figure 12.17   Sternal lifts are used to enhance postural awareness and activate the lower trapezius to facilitate scapular external rotation and posterior tilt.

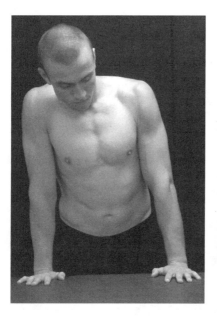
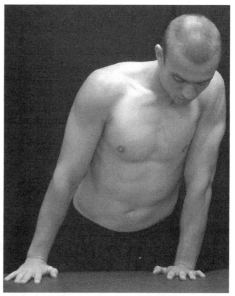

Figure 12.18   Weight shifts allow a safe progression of force through the shoulder to encourage rotator cuff co-contraction.

(scapular ER and posterior tilt) as the lower trapezius is activated (see **Figure 12.19**).

Ball Stability (Rotator Cuff Co-contraction)

The patient stands, with a medicine ball placed on a table under the involved hand. The clinician provides perturbations in varying directions as the patient maintains stability. This exercise progresses to include additional positions and levels of stability (see **Figure 12.20**).

Open-chain rhythmic stabilization and tubing exercises are used to progress isometric stability to include variable resistance over multiple joints, arm positions, and planes of motion.

Open-Chain Rhythmic Stabilization (Rotator Cuff Co-contraction)

The patient is supine with the arm in the desired position. The clinician provides perturbations in varying directions as the patient maintains stabil-

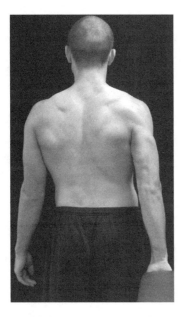

Figure 12.19 Isometric low rows are used to activate the lower trapezius early in rehabilitation.

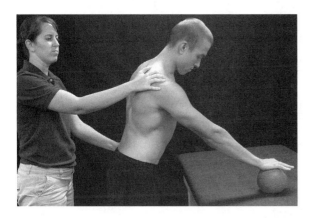

Figure 12.20 Ball stability exercises help develop reactive neuro-muscular control and stability in safe closed-chain positions. The clinician provides perturbations in varying directions as the patient maintains stability.

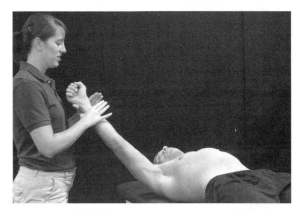

Figure 12.21 Rhythmic stabilization progresses to include open-chain and functional arm positions and variable resistance.

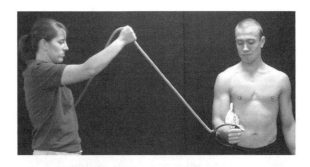

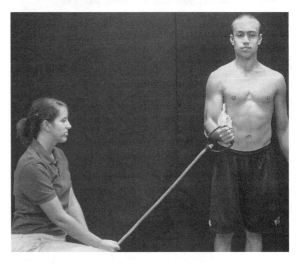

Figure 12.22 Isometric stability exercises can use varying arm positions to enhance co-contraction of the rotator cuff in response to resistance controlled by the clinician.

ity. This exercise progresses to include additional arm positions, additional resistance (e.g., tubing, dumbbell, oscillatory device), active movement (proprioceptive neuromuscular facilitation [PNF] patterns), and decreasing stability provided (e.g., inflated ball, seated, supine) (see **Figure 12.21**).

Tubing Isometric Stability (Rotator Cuff Co-contraction)

The patient stands with the elbow flexed to 90° with a towel or small bolster under the arm. The desired position of humeral rotation is held. The patient steps or rotates away from the fixed end of the tubing to stress humeral IR, ER, elevation, and extension while maintaining the humeral position. The patient returns to the starting position while maintaining the arm position. The clinician may provide manual resistance to tubing to control the direction and application of resistance. This exercise progresses to include additional arm positions and levels of stability (see **Figure 12.22**).

Rehabilitation and conditioning programs for the shoulder should also begin with exercises that activate the lower and middle trapezius and the serratus anterior while avoiding dominance by the upper trapezius. These exercises include side-lying ER, side-lying forward elevation, and prone horizontal abduction with ER.[3] These exercises effectively isolate critical muscles and help establish strength and muscular balance before introducing more functional positions and motions.

When patients achieve GH elevation to 120° with scapular control (no shrug), the dynamic stability portion of the *Shoulder Stability Progression* may begin. Dynamic stability is developed beginning with the arm positioned by the side and advances from isolating the scapulothoracic joint to full body movements. Closed-chain exercises should progress in humeral elevation to positions above 90°, introduce greater loads, and provide less stability. Exercises include scapular clocks with the hand on the wall at 90° of elevation and then at 90° of abduction. The push-up progression begins with the hands on the wall, then advances to the table, and eventually moves to the floor. This progression evolves into a test of core and full-body stability and advances to a plyometric and endurance power exercise.

Scapular retraction and activation of the scapular stabilizers are facilitated using trunk and hip extension and rotation in more functional positions through the hitchhiker exercise and the tubing retraction and lawnmower progressions. As shoulder stability and mobility progress, these exercises move toward 90° of humeral elevation and abduction and functional positions while emphasizing endurance.

Scapular Clocks at 90° of Abduction

The patient stands with the arm at 90° of abduction and the involved hand on the wall. The patient actively moves the scapula in four directions: 12 and 6 o'clock = superior and inferior translation; 3 and 9 o'clock = protraction and retraction. This exercise can also be performed with 90° of shoulder elevation (see **Figure 12.23**).

Push-up Progression

The push-up with a plus (protraction) exercise progresses from being performed on a wall, to being performed on a table, and to being performed on the floor. A medicine ball can be placed under one or both hands. Floor push-ups are progressed to single-leg versions, unstable surfaces, and box "step-up-and-over" movements from the plank position.

In the push-up–to–plank row, the patient grasps dumbbells in each hand and performs a standard push-up with protraction. While holding the plank, the patient performs a unilateral row with scapu-

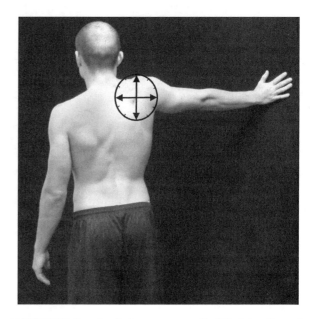

Figure 12.23 Scapular clocks are progressed to 90° of elevation and abduction as shoulder motion is restored.

lar retraction (scapular ER and posterior tilt). This exercise progresses to lifting the dumbbell to point it toward the ceiling (see **Figure 12.24**).

Hitchhiker

The patient stands with both elbows flexed to 90°, with neutral GH rotation (thumbs-up). The patient holds the tubing in both hands, facing the fixed end of the tubing. The patient externally rotates both shoulders, lifts the sternum, retracts both scapulas (ER and posterior tilt), and supinates both wrists (points the thumbs posteriorly) (see **Figure 12.25**).

Tubing Retraction
Fencing

The patient stands perpendicular to the fixed end of the tubing, with the involved elbow flexed to 90° and with 90° of GH ER. The patient performs a lateral lunge toward the fixed end of the tubing while pointing the hand toward the fixed end of the tubing as if performing an attack in fencing. The patient then returns to the starting position and completes the movement with retraction (scapular ER and posterior tilt) (see **Figure 12.26**).

Punches and Dynamic Hug

The patient assumes an athletic stance with both elbows flexed to 90°, tubing held in both hands, neutral GH rotation, and facing away from the fixed end of the tubing. The patient performs a forward punch with scapular protraction with one arm, followed by the other (see **Figure 12.27**).

In the dynamic hug, the patient assumes an athletic stance with both arms abducted to 70° to 80°, elbows flexed 10° to 20°, tubing held in both hands, and facing away from the fixed end of the tubing. The

A

B

C

Figure 12.24 Push-ups are progressed to include scapular protraction ("plus"). Single-leg planks and push-ups (**A**), plank dumbbell rows (**B**), and plank trunk rotations (**C**) are repeated bilaterally.

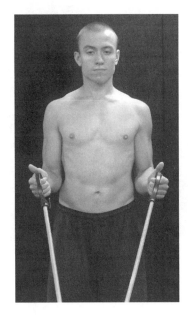

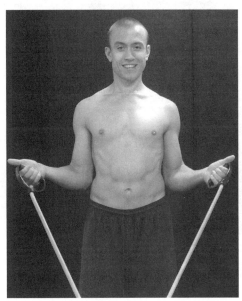

Figure 12.25 Hitchhiker exercises help engrain the movement pattern of coupled humeral external rotation with scapular external rotation and posterior tilt by activating the lower and middle trapezius.

12

patient performs horizontal adduction and scapular protraction with both arms as in a bear hug. This exercise progresses in resistance and through the use of unstable surfaces.

Mini-Squat Rows

The patient is in an athletic, mini-squat stance, holding tubing in each hand, and facing the fixed end of the tubing. The patient performs a bilateral row, end-ing with the hands at waist level while extending the hips (standing upright). The hands end at waist height to avoid upper trapezius substitution.

Lawnmower Progression

The lawnmower progression is a continuation of the shoulder dump exercise. The patient begins with a contralateral lunge, protracting the involved scapula, and flexing and rotating the trunk toward

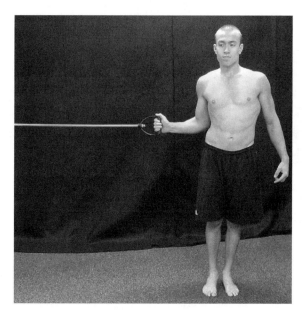

Figure 12.26 Fencing incorporates the entire kinetic chain to activate the middle and lower trapezius and serratus anterior and facilitate scapular external rotation and posterior tilt.

Figure 12.27 Standing punches with tubing emphasize lower extremity and trunk stability while developing functional scapular mobility and stability through protraction and serratus anterior activity.

the contralateral knee. The patient reaches the extended hand over the contralateral knee as if grabbing the pull cord of a lawnmower. The patient returns to the starting position as if pulling the cord, thereby starting the lawnmower. When performing the "low-end lawnmower," the patient ends the motion with the hand at the hip. The "high-end lawnmower" exercise ends with the arm in abduction and ER. Each exercise is completed with scapular retraction (scapular ER and posterior tilt) as if bringing the scapula to the patient's back pocket. This exercise progresses in resist-

ance, adding tubing or dumbbells and introducing various levels of stability.

Strengthening Exercises

Each exercise should be performed in 3 sets of 5, progressing to 3 sets of 10 with the same weight before increasing weight. The weight should be easy to lift and cause no discomfort or radiculopathy. Patients should be certain to slowly lower the weights against resistance, and always release air (breathe) when performing the concentric phase of the exercise. Proper posture is essential to enable the target muscles to work most effectively. If the patient cannot maintain proper form or posture throughout an entire set, reduce the amount of resistance.

◼ Shoulder Girdle and Arm Exercises

Exercises should be progressed to include each of the *Foundational Shoulder Exercises*. When dynamic stability through full GH range of motion is achieved, additional plyometric and sport-specific exercises are used to enhance reactive and functional stability and endurance. Activities should continue to emphasize the kinetic chain and proximal stability, while increasing demands through progressive variation of the tasks by increasing the load, lever arm, and speed and including variable resistance exercises (see **Table 12.1**).

Exercises include medicine ball tosses and wall dribbles, diagonal patterns, and functional positions with tubing or an oscillatory device

Tubing/Oscillatory Device IR/ER at 0° of Abduction (with a Bolster) and 90° of Abduction

Holding the tubing with the shoulder abducted to 90° and the elbow flexed to 90°, the patient rotates the arm while maintaining the shoulder abduction. Standing facing the direction of the resistance, the patient strengthens the external rotators; facing away from the resistance strengthens the internal rotators (see **Figure 12.28**). For shoulder IR/ER with minimal abduction, a towel or small bolster is held under the arm.

Wall Dribbles

The patient stands facing the wall with the arm abducted to 90°. The patient repeatedly bounces a ball against the wall, moving the arm in an overhead arc across the body with and without elbow flexion. This exercise progresses to use a weighted, medicine, or sport-specific ball, and completing larger and faster arcs (see **Figure 12.29**).

Prone Horizontal Abduction

The patient lies prone on a table, with the involved extremity hanging off the side, and holding a dumbbell parallel to the body. The arm is brought level with the tabletop, held for 2 seconds, and slowly lowered to the starting position. The exercise is then repeated with the humerus externally rotated.

Prone Row

The patient lies prone on the table, with the involved arm holding a dumbbell off the edge of the table. The weight is lifted by horizontally adducting the shoulder and flexing the elbow, raising the weight as high as possible while keeping the chest on the table. The ending position is held for 2 seconds and slowly lowered to the starting position.

Lateral Raise

The patient stands with the feet shoulder width apart and the knees slightly bent, abducting the arms to raise the weights from the thighs to shoulder height (see **Figure 12.30**).

Table 12.1		
Exercise Variables the Clinician Manipulates to Progress the Demands		
Variable	**Progression**	
Joints included	Proximal → 2-proximal → entire extremity → functional	
Plane of motion	Single-plane → multi-plane → functional	
Kinetic chain	Closed → open → variable → functional	
Lever arm	Short → long → variable → functional	
Muscle contraction	Isometric → isotonic → plyometric → functional	
Resistance applied	Single-plane→ multi-plane → functional	
Resistance intensity	Low → high → variable → functional	
Task speed	Slow → fast → variable → functional	
Environment	Stable → unstable → variable → functional	
Visual input	Eyes open → eyes closed → functional	

Source: Adapted from Tripp BL. Integrating sensorimotor control into rehabilitation. *Athl Ther Today.* 2006;11:24.

Figure 12.28 Glenohumeral internal rotation using tubing is performed while maintaining 90° of abduction and elevation.

Figure 12.29   Wall dribbles are performed standing close to the wall by quickly bouncing and catching a medicine ball. The patient dribbles the ball through an arc or circle on the wall.

Figure 12.30   Lateral raise.

Figure 12.31   Bent lateral raise.

Figure 12.32   Upright row.

Bent Lateral Raise

The patient bends forward, with knees slightly flexed and feet placed shoulder width apart, raising each weight to nearly shoulder height laterally and then slowly lowering the weight to the front of the body (see Figure 12.31). An incline bench may be used to support the trunk if needed. This exercise should not be performed with a patient in the early stages of lumbar disk disease.

Supraspinatus Press

The patient stands with the shoulders abducted in the scapular plane to 90°, externally rotated to 90°, and the elbows flexed to 90°, and holds a weight in each hand. The patient moves the weights in a short arc from chin height to head height.

Upright Row

The patient stands with the feet placed shoulder width apart and the knees slightly bent, gripping a barbell using an overhand grasp. The bar is raised to the chin, lifting the elbows as high as possible (see Figure 12.32).

Seated Row

The patient is seated with the feet braced on the floor, shoulder width apart. The hands are placed in an overhand grip to work the upper trapezius, rhomboids, and latissimus dorsi. The bar is raised to the chest and then slowly returned to the starting position (see Figure 12.33).

Bent Row

The patient stands with the feet placed shoulder width apart and the knees slightly flexed, bending the trunk to approximately 45° with the spine straight. Using an overhand grip, the patient pulls the barbell to the chest by raising the elbows laterally away from the body and moving the scapulae together. The abdominal muscles are contracted during the lift and the subsequent return to the starting position (see Figure 12.34).

Figure 12.34 Bent row.

Figure 12.33 Seated row.

Shrug

The patient stands with the feet placed shoulder width apart. Using an overhand grip on the bar, the patient shrugs the shoulders to lift the weight, holds the position for 3 seconds, and then slowly returns to the starting position. Proper posture should be maintained during the lift.

Bench Press

The bench press can be used in the standard form or in limited (elbows do not go behind shoulder) ranges of motion. Range limits can be set by using spotting racks or padded rolls on the bar itself. Chest-press machines or dumbbells can be used for unilateral motions.

▪ Elbow Exercises

Biceps Curl

Biceps curls may be performed in several different positions, including standing, sitting, and reclin-

ing. The position of the forearm and hand affects the primary elbow mover:

- Pronated (moving into supination during flexion): biceps brachii
- Neutral: brachioradialis
- Supinated: brachialis

Although these exercises primarily focus on the muscles acting on the forearm, wrist, and finger flexors, extensors are also strengthened.

Triceps Extension

The patient sits or stands holding a dumbbell overhead by abducting the humerus to 180° and internally rotating it. The opposite hand can be used to support the arm just proximal to the elbow. The weight is slowly lowered by flexing the elbow and then returned to the starting overhead position.

Cross-References

Elbow isometric exercises:
  Flexion (page 398)
  Extension (page 398)
  Pronation/supination (page 398)
Elbow isotonic exercises:
  Flexion (page 398)
  Extension (page 398)
  Pronation/supination (page 398)

▪ Wrist and Hand

Putty Exercises

Commercial putty such as TheraPutty can be used to strengthen the finger, hand, and forearm muscles. Putty is available in various viscosities, each of which provides a different resistance to deformity. Depending on the grip, isolated finger flexion, abduction, adduction, and gripping exercises can

12

be performed. The amount of putty used should be adequate for the size of the patient's hand and the particular exercise being performed.

Rubber Band Exercises

Standard office rubber bands can be used to re-educate the intrinsic muscles of the hand and fingers. For finger abduction and adduction exercises, loop the band around the contiguous fingers.

Grip Strength

Putty, spring-loaded hand grips, or dynamometers can be used to restore the patient's grip strength. Initially, putty should be used to restore neuromuscular control because it does not entail an eccentric component. The patient can then progress to isotonic exercises using the grips. Progress can be quantified by using the dynamometer.

Wrist Flexion and Extension

The pronated forearm is supported on a table, holding the weight off the edge of the table. The forearm and hand are pronated for wrist extension exercises and supinated for flexion exercises.

Pronation and Supination

The forearm is supported on a table with the forearm and wrist in the neutral position. The patient holds one end of a dumbbell, alternately slowly lowering and raising the weight by pronating and supinating the forearm and returning to the starting position.

Towel Roll/Wrist Roll

The patient grasps a rolled towel with both hands. One wrist is extended and the other flexed as if wringing out the towel (see **Figure 12.35**). This position is held for 5 seconds and then repeated in the opposite direction. An alternative method is to tie a weight to the center of a 2-ft dowel using a 2- or 3-ft rope or strap. With the shoulders flexed to 90° and the elbow straight, the patient winds the dowel to lift the weight and reverses direction to slowly lower the weight.

Proprioception and Functional Exercises

Drop/Catch Ball

The patient stands and uses the involved upper extremity to drop and catch a ball or weighted medicine ball as quickly and with as little motion as possible while maintaining a stable position (see **Figure 12.36**). To increase the difficulty, the patient progresses from positions of 0° of flexion and abduction into flexion and abduction.

Inflated Exercise Ball Walkout

The patient lies prone over an inflated exercise ball. The patient walks forward and backward using his or her hands, maintaining balance and stability as the body rolls across the ball. To increase stability, the patient should hold the lower extremities and trunk rigid (see **Figure 12.37**). Balancing on a single arm adds an isometric stability component to this exercise.

Inflated Exercise Ball Push-Up

The patient performs standard or modified push-ups while the hands are supported on the inflated exercise ball, mini-trampoline, or other unstable surface (see **Figure 12.38**). The mobility of the ball increases the stabilization demand on the shoulders. When the hands are spread shoulder width or farther apart, the shoulder muscles are empha-

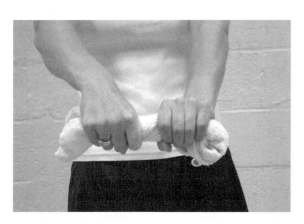

Figure 12.35 Towel roll/wrist roll.

Figure 12.36 Ball drop/catch.

Figure 12.37 Inflated exercise ball walkout.

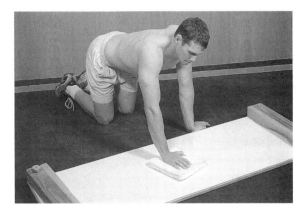

Figure 12.39 Slide board movements.

Figure 12.38 Inflated exercise ball push-up. A mini-trampoline or other unstable surface can be substituted in lieu of the exercise ball.

sized. When the hands are close together, the triceps are emphasized.

Slide Board Movements

The patient is in a quadruped position with the involved extremity bearing weight as tolerated on the slide board. While wearing a slide board slipper on the involved hand, the patient performs rapid, small circles in clockwise and counter-clockwise directions (see **Figure 12.39**). The initial position of the exercise is below shoulder level (less than 90° of flexion) and progresses by increasing time, weight bearing, circle circumference, and positions (to more than 90° of flexion).

Upper Extremity Proprioceptive Neuromuscular Facilitation Patterns

The two primary proprioceptive neuromuscular facilitation (PNF) patterns for the upper extremity are the D1 (see **CT 12.1**) and D2 (see **CT 12.2**). These exercises are particularly useful because they move the extremity across the cardinal planes in a functional manner.

Plyometrics

Plyometrics are exercises that enable a muscle to reach maximum strength in as short a time as possible. Implements such as weighted balls, basketballs, elastic bands, and rebounders can be used for various catching or throwing drills. Exercises such as power drops, backward throws, overhead throws, pullover passes, and side throws can increase the shoulder girdle response to functional demands. Sport-specific programs are recommended, and patterns can be mixed with jumping and catching drills. Some of these programs include interval throwing, mound pitching, golf, tennis, and swimming.

> **Cross-References**
> Medicine ball exercises (page 399)
> Weighted-ball exercises (page 399)

Foundational Shoulder Exercises

The *Foundational Shoulder Exercises* develop and maintain the basis of general kinetic chain function in athletics. These exercises help establish and maintain a solid foundation of flexibility, strength, and neuromuscular control for athletic movement. Clinicians may use these exercises as goals as they advance individual rehabilitation and conditioning programs. Athletes should continue these exercises throughout their return to sport as part of a comprehensive conditioning program.

Flexibility (completed daily):

1. Sleeper self-stretch (see Figure 12.4)
2. Cross-body self-stretch (see Figure 12.3)
3. Supine "open book" pectoralis minor manual stretch (see Figure 12.13)

12

CT Clinical Technique 12.1

D1 Upper Extremity PNF Pattern

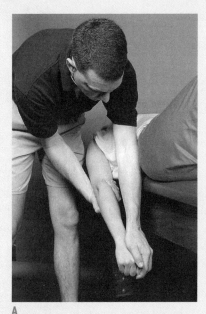

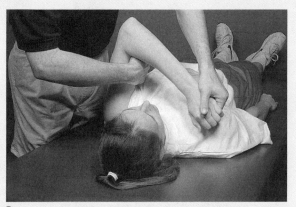

A
Flexion component

B
Extension component

	Extension into Flexion	**Flexion into Extension**
Hand Placement (resistance)	One hand is in the palm of the patient's hand, with the patient grasping the clinician's hand. The opposite hand is placed on the distal humerus, just proximal to the elbow.	One hand resists against the patient's hand, wrist, and fingers. The opposite hand is placed on the distal posterolateral aspect of the humerus, just proximal to the elbow.
Verbal Command	"Pull against me; squeeze my hand; turn against me; bend your elbow; pull across your face."	"Push against me; open your hand; turn against me; straighten your elbow; push toward me."
Motion (movement occurs synchronously from distal to proximal)	The fingers move from flexion and adduction to extension and abduction. The thumb moves from flexion and abduction to extension and adduction. The wrist and forearm move from flexion and pronation to extension and supination. The elbow moves from extension to flexion. The glenohumeral joint moves from extension, adduction, and internal rotation to flexion, abduction, and external rotation. The scapula moves from retraction and depression to protraction and elevation.	The fingers move from extension and abduction to flexion and adduction. The thumb moves from extension and adduction to flexion and abduction. The wrist and forearm move from extension and supination to flexion and pronation. The elbow moves from flexion to extension. The glenohumeral joint moves from flexion, abduction, and external rotation to extension, adduction, and internal rotation. The scapula moves from protraction and elevation to retraction and depression.

CT **Clinical Technique** 12.2

D2 Upper Extremity PNF Pattern

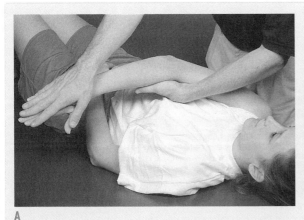

A
Starting position

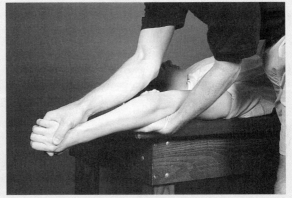

B
Terminal extension

	Extension into Flexion	Flexion into Extension
Hand Placement (resistance)	One hand grasps the radial side of the fingers, hand, and wrist. The opposite hand resists against the distal anteromedial humerus.	One hand is in the palm of the patient's hand, with the patient grasping the clinician's hand. The opposite hand resists against the distal posterolateral humerus.
Verbal Command	"Lift against me; open your hand; turn against me; keep your elbow straight; lift towards me."	"Pull against me; squeeze my hand; turn against me; keep your elbow straight; pull towards your opposite hip."
Motion (movement occurs synchronously from distal to proximal)	The fingers move from extension and abduction to flexion and adduction. The thumb moves from extension and abduction to flexion and adduction. The wrist and forearm move from extension and pronation to flexion and supination. The elbow moves from extension to slight flexion. The glenohumeral joint moves from extension, abduction, and internal rotation to flexion, adduction, and external rotation. The scapula moves from retraction and depression to protraction and elevation.	The fingers move from flexion and adduction to extension and abduction. The thumb moves from flexion and adduction to extension and abduction. The wrist and forearm move from flexion and supination to extension and pronation. The elbow moves from slightly flexed to extension. The glenohumeral joint moves from flexion, adduction, and external rotation to extension, abduction, and internal rotation. The scapula moves from protraction and elevation to retraction and depression.

12

Table 12.2

Interval Throwing Program: Phase 1

45-ft Phase

Step 1 A. Warm-up throwing

        B. 45 ft (25 throws)

        C. Rest 15 minutes

        D. Warm-up throwing

        E. 45 ft (25 throws)

Step 2 A. Warm-up throwing

        B. 45 ft (25 throws)

        C. Rest 10 minutes

        D. Warm-up throwing

        E. 45 ft (25 throws)

        F. Rest 10 minutes

        G. Warm-up throwing

        H. 45 ft (25 throws)

60-ft Phase

Step 3 A. Warm-up throwing

        B. 60 ft (25 throws)

        C. Rest 15 minutes

        D. Warm-up throwing

        E. 60 ft (25 throws)

Step 4 A. Warm-up throwing

        B. 60 ft (25 throws)

        C. Rest 10 minutes

        D. Warm-up throwing

        E. 60 ft (25 throws)

        F. Rest 10 minutes

        G. Warm-up throwing

        H. 60 ft (25 throws)

90-ft Phase

Step 5 A. Warm-up throwing

        B. 90 ft (25 throws)

        C. Rest 15 minutes

        D. Warm-up throwing

        E. 90 ft (25 throws)

Step 6 A. Warm-up throwing

        B. 90 ft (25 throws)

        C. Rest 10 minutes

        D. Warm-up throwing

        E. 90 ft (25 throws)

        F. Rest 10 minutes

        G. Warm-up throwing

        H. 90 ft (25 throws)

120-ft Phase

Step 7 A. Warm-up throwing

        B. 120 ft (25 throws)

        C. Rest 15 minutes

        D. Warm-up throwing

        E. 120 ft (25 throws)

Table 12.2

Interval Throwing Program: Phase 1 (*Continued*)

Step 8 A. Warm-up throwing

      B. 120 ft (25 throws)

      C. Rest 10 minutes

      D. Warm-up throwing

      E. 120 ft (25 throws)

      F. Rest 10 minutes

      G. Warm-up throwing

      H. 120 ft (25 throws)

150-ft Phase*

Step 9 A. Warm-up throwing

      B. 150 ft (25 throws)

      C. Rest 15 minutes

      D. Warm-up throwing

      E. 150 ft (25 throws)

Step 10 A. Warm-up throwing

      B. 150 ft (25 throws)

      C. Rest 10 minutes

      D. Warm-up throwing

      E. 150 ft (25 throws)

      F. Rest 10 minutes

      G. Warm-up throwing

      H. 150 ft (25 throws)

180-ft Phase

Step 11 A. Warm-up throwing

      B. 180 ft (25 throws)

      C. Rest 15 minutes

      D. Warm-up throwing

      E. 180 ft (25 throws)

Step 12 A. Warm-up throwing

      B. 180 ft (25 throws)

      C. Rest 10 minutes

      D. Warm-up throwing

      E. 180 ft (25 throws)

      F. Rest 10 minutes

      G. Warm-up throwing

      H. 180 ft (25 throws)

Step 13 A. Warm-up throwing

      B. 180 ft (25 throws)

      C. Rest 10 minutes

      D. Warm-up throwing

      E. 180 ft (25 throws)

      F. Rest 10 minutes

      G. Warm-up throwing

      H. 180 ft (25 throws)

Step 14 Begin throwing off the mound or return to respective position

*Pitchers progress to flat-ground throwing from wind-up at 60 ft, then progress to phase 2 of the interval throwing program.

12

4. Corner pectoralis self-stretch (for those with no anterior GH instability) (see Figure 12.14)

Strengthening (completed 3 to 4 times per week):

1. Tubing/oscillatory device IR/ER at 0° of abduction (with a bolster) and 90° of abduction
2. Tubing punches and dynamic hug (see Figure 12.27)
3. Tubing fencing (see Figure 12.26)
4. Tubing hitchhiker (see Figure 12.25)
5. Push-up–to–plank row and single-leg push-up (alternating hip extensions) (see Figure 12.24)
6. High-end lawnmower (see the "Lawnmower Progression" section)
7. Wall dribbles (see Figure 12.29)

Throwers add:

8. Plyometric medicine ball toss in internal/external rotation
9. Wall dribbles (one or two medicine balls for 30 seconds)
10. Wrist series (seated with forearm on table)
    - Flexion medicine ball plyometrics
    - Extension (medicine ball or dumbbell wrapped in towel)
    - Pronation/supination and radial/ulnar deviation (e.g., dumbbell, rubber mallet, towel-weight)

Throwing Protocol

The patient is allowed to initiate a throwing program if the following criteria are met:

- Full range of motion with no pain
- Satisfactory results on the clinical examination with no neurologic symptoms and with adequate medial stability
- Satisfactory muscular performance
- Proper throwing mechanics

Once the patient fulfills these criteria, the throwing program can be initiated. **Table 12.2** presents the first phase of an interval throwing program. Throwers are started on an interval long-toss program beginning with light tossing from 45 ft. Progression of the throwing program is based on the distance, intensity, and number of throws, which are increased gradually during the next several weeks. Once throwers successfully complete step 8 of phase 1, they may begin phase 2, throwing from the pitching mound.

Table 12.3 presents the second phase in the interval throwing program. During this return-to-activity phase, the thrower begins the strengthening program referred to as the "thrower's 10 program." Once the throwing program is successfully completed, the patient may gradually return to play.

Table 12.3

Interval Throwing Program: Phase 2, Throwing Off the Mound

Stage 1: Fastball Only	Stage 2: Fastball Only
Step 1: Interval throwing; 15 throws off mound at 50%	Step 9: 45 throws off mound at 75%; 15 throws in batting practice
Step 2: Interval throwing; 30 throws off mound at 50%	Step 10: 45 throws off mound at 75%; 30 throws in batting practice
Step 3: Interval throwing; 45 throws off mound at 50%	Step 11: 45 throws off mound at 75%; 45 throws in batting practice
Step 4: Interval throwing; 60 throws off mound at 50%	**Stage 3: Fastballs and Breaking Balls**
Step 5: Interval throwing; 30 throws off mound at 75%	Step 12: 30 throws off mound at 75%; 15 throws off mound at 50% with breaking balls; 45 to 60 throws off mound at 75%
Step 6: 30 throws off mound at 75%; 45 throws off mound at 50%	Step 13: 30 throws in batting practice (fastball only); 30 breaking balls at 75%; 30 throws in batting practice
Step 7: 45 throws off mound at 75%; 15 throws off mound at 50%	Step 14: 30 throws off mound at 75%; 60 to 90 throws off mound at 75%
Step 8: 60 throws off mound at 75%	Step 15: Simulated game: progressing by 15 throws per workout (use interval throwing to 120 ft as warm-up). All throwing off the mound should be done in the presence of the pitching coach to stress proper throwing mechanics (use of a speed gun may aid in effort control).

A complete throwing rehabilitation program focuses on the entire kinetic chain. Throwers develop power from their legs and pelvis and transmit it through the trunk and scapulothoracic complex to the upper extremity. The thrower with a decreased ability to generate power from below compensates by attempting to generate the power within the upper extremity, which increases stresses throughout the joints. A well-rounded rehabilitation program focuses on all aspects of the kinetic chain, including the legs, hips, and trunk. As part of the evaluation of a thrower's shoulder or elbow, clinicians should assess stability of the trunk and lead leg through a single-leg squat.

References

1. Tyler TF, Nicholas SJ, Lee SJ, et al. Correction of posterior shoulder tightness is associated with symptom resolution in patients with internal impingement. *Am J Sports Med.* 2010;38:114–119.
2. McMullen J, Uhl TL. A kinetic chain approach for shoulder rehabilitation. *J Athl Train.* 2000;35:329–337.
3. Cools AM, Dewitte V, Lanszweert F, et al. Rehabilitation of scapular muscle balance. *Am J Sports Med.* 2007; 35:1744–1751.

12

IV Spine and Torso

Lumbar Spine Injuries
Charles Thompson, MS, AT
Jeff Bechler, MD

Facet Joint Dysfunction

CLINICAL PRESENTATION

History

Sudden or repetitive lumbar extension, lateral bending, or rotation may be noted.

Sciatic-like symptoms in the lower extremity may be described, although no sciatic impingement is present and there are no other neurologic complaints.

Observation

Alterations in walking gait and alteration of functional movements (lowering the body to sit in a chair, lying on a table, clothing removal) may be noted.

Asymmetry of anatomic structures is present.

The patient may stand in the position producing the least discomfort (e.g., lateral bending away from the impingement).

Rotation is not always as obvious as lateral bending.

Functional Status

Loss of normal lumbar motion in flexion/extension, side bending, and rotation.

Pain with any of the above mentioned motions.

The patient may report decreased symptoms when sitting or during lumbar flexion.

Physical Examination Findings

Point tenderness may be found over the involved joint.

Muscle spasm, soft-tissue or bony asymmetry, or change in tissue texture may be noted.

The quadrant test may be positive.

Tests for sciatic nerve involvement are negative.

"Dysfunction" describes an abnormal condition. Facet joint dysfunction is the loss of normal function caused by either hypermobility or hypomobility of the facets. Hypomobility is the most common cause of facet joint pain.

Facet joint dysfunction is common after trauma; other causes of such damage include inflammation and facet joint degeneration. During facet trauma, the richly innervated facet capsule that contains encapsulated, unencapsulated, and free nerve endings may be impinged between the two facet surfaces or become irritated secondary to an inflammatory response.[1] Facet joint impingement falls along the same continuum as facet joint sprain, but sprains are more severe injuries, produce more severe symptoms, and are managed with extended nonoperative care. A full muscle energy evaluation should be initiated in the case of facet joint dysfunction.

Facet joints (also known as zygapophyseal joints, Z joints, apophyseal joints, and posterior intervertebral joints) are synovial diarthrodial articulations with a rich supply of various nerve endings, including proprioceptive and nociceptive receptors. As such, the surrounding capsule can become inflamed and produce pain during motion. Because the joint surfaces are covered with hyaline cartilage, repetitive stress and osteoarthritic degeneration can produce facet hypertrophy, degeneration, inflammation, and pain with joint movement.

> **Practice Tip**
>
> The presence of lumbar disk degeneration is not predictive of facet joint arthritis. In contrast, the presence of facet joint arthritis is strongly associated with disk degeneration.[2]

Each vertebra has four facet surfaces that form two inferior and two superior facet joints. These two articulations plus the presence of the intervertebral disk create a three-joint complex.[2] One superior and one inferior facet joint are found on each side, posterior and lateral to the vertebral body (see **Figure 13.1**). One facet joint is created by the posterolateral articulation between the inferior articular process of a vertebra and the superior articular process of the vertebra immediately below it. The superior articular process is slightly concave and faces anterolaterally. The inferior articular process is slightly convex and faces posteromedially. In the upper lumbar spine, the facets are initially aligned in a sagittal arrangement, but the alignment gradually changes to a frontal plane orientation. The facets are interdependent with the intervertebral disks and vertebral bodies between which they are aligned. Alteration of the normal mechanics of a facet joint or the diskal interface will result in biomechanical changes within the entire complex.[2]

Because of their positions, the facets resist both axial and vertical stress and shearing forces directed at the spine. In the lumbar spine, the facet joints

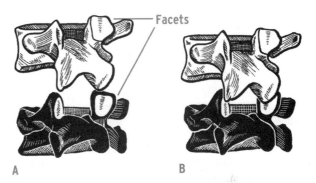

Figure 13.1 Articulation of facet joints. **(A)** The vertebrae are shown separated to illustrate how the articular surfaces fit together. **(B)** Normal appearance of the vertebrae. *Source:* Reproduced with permission from Kapanji A. *The Physiology of the Joints: Annotated Diagrams of the Mechanics of Human Joints,* ed 3. New York: Churchill Livingstone; 1974.

13

are the primary check against vertebral rotation, protecting the disk from these forces.[2] If the disk between the vertebrae becomes narrowed, the facet's ability to withstand vertical forces is decreased. If loads on the facets become greater than the joints can tolerate, the inferior facet rotates posteriorly and the joint's neurally enriched capsule is stretched, causing facet pain.

Although facet pain can occur from many causes—including degenerative changes, nerve irritation, nerve-root entrapment, and frank joint and capsule injury—facet "locking" is a more common source of facet pain (see **Box 13.1**). A locked segment may potentially be a hypomobile facet. The mechanism of injury for this dysfunction can be extension, side bending, rotation, or some combination of these forces. A locked facet is typically more painful at rest and becomes less painful with movement. Pain and restricted range of motion (ROM) may be significant in the acute stages of such an injury.[3] The patient may be able to point to the exact spot of the facet pain, which is usually found approximately a thumb's-width lateral to the spinous processes. Although decreased motor function and radiating pain are not normally considered facet symptoms, the joint has been implicated in radiculopathy. Radiating sensory symptoms during a straight-leg raise test do not necessarily indicate that intervertebral disk material is pressing on a nerve root; some clinicians require motor involvement in the extremity to declare that the nerve root is the source of the problem.[3]

Facet joint syndrome is associated with articular cartilage damage characteristic of chondromalacia. Because other clinical studies have been unable to determine a clear pathoanatomic cause, however, this diagnosis is questionable.

Differential Diagnosis

Herniated disk, spondylolysis or spondylolisthesis, arthritis, stress or compression fracture, lumbar disk disease, **spinal stenosis**, hip conditions, sacroiliac conditions, posterior element overuse syndrome, vertebral endplate fracture.

spinal stenosis
Developmental narrowing of the spinal canal that can affect either the spinal cord or the peripheral nerve roots.

Box 13.1

Posterior Element Overuse Syndrome

Posterior element overuse syndrome (PEOS) is caused by repetitive extension and rotation of the lumbar spine. This condition is associated with symptoms similar to those found in spondylolysis. PEOS involves the intrinsic muscle-tendon units, the facet joints, and the joint capsule and ligaments. This condition is second only to spondylolysis as the most frequent cause of low back pain in young athletes.

Medical Diagnostic Tests

Facet joint diagnostic blockade is indicated for painful lumbar disorders.[4,5] A facet diagnostic injection is accomplished with the aid of fluoroscopy. The symptomatic facet is approached and visualized fluoroscopically, and the joint is injected with a long-acting anesthetic such as bupivacaine HCl. Pain relief is temporary, and recent studies have shown that this intervention has limited long-term therapeutic benefits. Failure of the injection to relieve the pain should typically rule out the presence of facet joint dysfunction.

Several clinical characteristics are useful in identifying patients whose low back pain will be relieved by facet joint anesthesia: age older than 65 years; pain not exacerbated by coughing, hyperextension, flexion, rising from flexion, or extension rotation; and pain relieved by recumbency.[4]

Imaging Techniques

The ambiguous definitions of facet joint dysfunction reduce the usefulness of radiographic imaging in making a definitive diagnosis.[5] Although an anteroposterior (AP) radiographic projection shows the facet joints, they are best profiled with oblique views that are obtained if specific conditions are suspected. The oblique views best profile the facet joints and the pars interarticularis. In these views, the facet joints can be examined for asymmetry or degenerative changes (see **Figure 13.2**). Facet osteoarthritis is best identified using computed tomography (CT) scans[5] while fat-saturation magnetic resonance

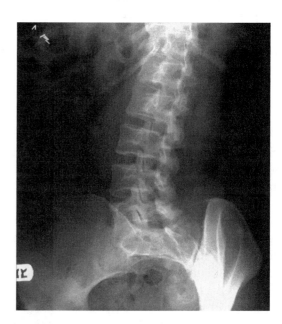

Figure 13.2 Oblique view of the lumbar vertebral facet joints and the pars interarticularis. Note the characteristic "Scotty dog" shape formed by these structures.

imaging (MRI) is the imaging modality of choice for facet synovitis.[6]

Definitive Diagnosis

No specific diagnostic criteria or pathognomonic sign exists for facet-related pain. In fact, the facet is likely to be an overlooked source of pain in the lumbar spine. Facet joint syndrome is diagnosed primarily based on the mechanism of injury, patient reports of pain location, and movements. The diagnosis of facet joint dysfunction may be based on the clinical finding of nonradicular low back pain that increases when the patient is standing or during lumbar extension and/or rotation.[1]

Pathomechanics and Functional Limitations

Because the coupled motions of lateral bending and rotation occur on opposite sides in the lumbar spine, except when the patient is in full flexion or extension, where the motion occurs on the same side (Fryette's laws), the patient with facet joint dysfunction usually has restricted lateral bending to the side opposite the involved facet and restricted rotation to the same side. A left facet impingement presents with a loss of motion in right-side bending and rotation to the left side. The restricted side bending is on the side opposite the locked facet because the pain with impingement stops motion from occurring. Although this presentation is not always the case in the lumbar spine, it is the most common.

Immediate Management

Immediate ice and reduced stress on the involved facet will minimize the effects of the injury. The patient often feels the injury is minor and may not report it right away. As a consequence, significant time may elapse before the clinician is informed of the injury; such notification often occurs when the pain interferes with performance.

Medications

Medications should play a secondary role in the treatment of facet joint disorders. Aspirin, acetaminophen, and nonsteroidal anti-inflammatory drugs (NSAIDs) are useful for analgesic and anti-inflammatory effects. Opioids and muscle relaxants should not be routinely used for this injury.

> **Practice Tip**
> The success of intra-articular injections in relieving facet joint pain is significantly improved in older patients who report a history of low back pain, have nonradicular pain during spinal extension, are free from muscle spasm, and deny Valsalva-related symptoms.[1]

Postinjury Management

Aggressive rehabilitation with active treatment is indicated and should include aerobic training.

Surgical Intervention

Surgical intervention is rarely indicated for facet joint dysfunction in chronic lower back pain or degenerative conditions. In acute trauma, facet joint disruption combined with an anterior column injury may suggest three-column instability and require surgical intervention. Surgical decompression of the facet joints may be indicated in obese patients with recurrent facet pain.[7]

Radiofrequency neurotomy may be used to treat chronic low back pain by interrupting the pain pathways. Evidence suggests that radiofrequency facet joint denervation can provide short-term improvement.[8,9]

Injury-Specific Treatment and Rehabilitation Concerns

> **Specific Concerns**
> Avoid extension early in the rehabilitation process.
> Alleviate spasm if present.
> Increase mobility of the hypomobile segment.

If the facet joints are hypomobile, grade I and II joint mobilizations should be performed. Grade III and IV mobilizations are contraindicated for hypermobile joints; consequently, each joint must be carefully examined before such treatment is considered. Finding a hypermobile joint adjacent to a hypomobile joint is common; therefore, mobility at each spinal level must be evaluated before using joint mobilization. Once pain and spasm are under control, the more aggressive grade III and IV mobilizations can facilitate increased motion gains if the joints are still restricted.

Therapeutic modalities are used in the early phases of rehabilitation to relieve pain and spasm. They may include gentle traction with lateral bending to open the facet joint and a variety of thermal modalities based on the clinician's preference.

Gentle rotation and side bending in the pain-free ROM can be followed by progressive exercises into the less comfortable ROM to tolerance. Extension motions are initially avoided to eliminate the application of high compressive forces to the recovering tissue. Strengthening exercises are incorporated as early as tolerated in the program once

ROM is normal and neutral spine techniques are initiated. The next course of exercises follows the routine for extremity injuries. Because the capsule and its neural structures are likely damaged, proprioception must be restored using static balance activities when the patient can move freely without pain. The patient then progresses to more dynamic exercises, evolving into more complex proprioceptive coordination and, finally, to agility activities. Functional activities are initiated before the final phase of the rehabilitation program, in which sport-specific drills and skill executions are performed.

After any lumbar injury, the patient should be instructed in pelvic-neutral positioning, pelvic stabilization, and proper body mechanics. To perform these activities, the patient may first need to improve proprioception and body awareness, flexibility, strength, and endurance; any deficiencies in these areas, including muscle imbalances, should be addressed with exercises in the rehabilitation program.

A strength and endurance program directed toward the transverse abdominis, lower internal obliques, and multifidus muscles should be included in all lumbar injury rehabilitation programs, because these structures are stabilizers for the lumbar spine.

■ Estimated Amount of Time Lost

The amount of time lost from competition varies, depending on whether the injury is an impingement or a sprain. Sprains resolve more slowly. Secondary effects such as pain, muscle spasm, and weakness may delay the recovery time.

■ Return-to-Play Criteria

The patient should be pain free during all activities. Full lumbar spine ROM—especially extension with rotation—should be restored before return to full participation. Core-muscle strength (especially the transverse abdominis, multifidus, and trunk rotators) and sufficient muscle endurance are necessary to allow the patient to maintain proper trunk position and movement throughout the sport's specific requirements. Because strength and flexibility muscle imbalances (e.g., tight hip flexors, tight paraspinals, weak hip extensors, weak core abdominals) are often found in patients with lumbar spine injuries, these defects should be corrected before return to full sport participation. Trunk proprioception should be restored to preinjury levels as required by body position and movement during agility and sport-specific activities.

Lumbosacral Dysfunction

CLINICAL PRESENTATION

History

Sudden flexion, twisting, and/or lifting mechanism.
Sudden impact force (blunt force trauma, fall to the ground).
Sudden onset of pain.
Muscle spasm may prevent normal posture or motion. Finding a comfortable position is difficult because of pain, which can radiate into the buttock.

Observation

The patient is in obvious discomfort, frequently changing positions or standing or sitting in an abnormal posture to either guard or relieve the pain.
Paraspinal muscle spasm.
Posterior pelvic rotation.[10]

Functional Status

ROM is limited by pain and spasm.
Forward flexion is often reduced, whereas extension is less painful.
If the injury is unilateral, lateral bending to the uninvolved side is more painful as the muscle on the injured side is stretched.
Extension ROM is often normal and painless.

Physical Examination Findings

Palpation may reveal muscle spasm, soft-tissue or bony asymmetry, or change in tissue texture.
Neurologic tests for sensory and motor function and reflexes are normal.
Although the straight-leg raise test may be painful as the lumbar muscles are stretched during the maneuver, there is no radiating neurologic pain.

Lumbar strains, which are among the most common low back injuries, involve injury to the inert back support structures. A low back strain is an injury to the paraspinal muscles traversing the spinal column (see **Figure 13.3**). "Lumbar spine sprains" are sometimes returned as a diagnosis. Under normal circumstances, the amount of lumbar spine motion is not sufficient to cause a sprain. Despite the distinct difference in definitions, the terms "sprain" and "strain" are commonly misused. A sprain or strain has come to describe a soft-tissue injury of the back that does not involve the intervertebral disks or spinal nerves.

Differential Diagnosis

Differential diagnoses include herniated disk, painful Schmorl nodes (vertebral endplate compression), and nondisplaced vertebral fracture. Examination for lumbar spine dysfunctions (extended/flexed and rotated vertebrae), iliosacral dysfunctions (up/down-slips, innominate rotations, and in/out flares), sacral

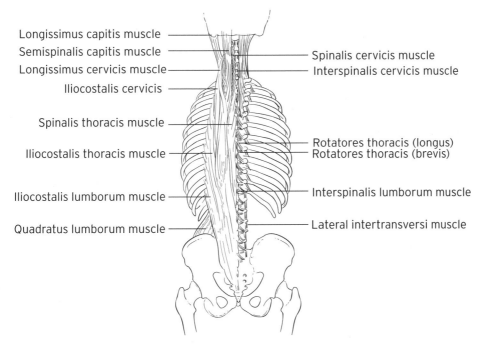

Longissimus capitis muscle
Semispinalis capitis muscle
Longissimus cervicis muscle
Iliocostalis cervicis

Spinalis thoracis muscle

Iliocostalis thoracis muscle

Iliocostalis lumborum muscle

Quadratus lumborum muscle

Spinalis cervicis muscle
Interspinalis cervicis muscle

Rotatores thoracis (longus)
Rotatores thoracis (brevis)

Interspinalis lumborum muscle

Lateral intertransversi muscle

Figure 13.3 The paraspinal muscles.

iliac dysfunctions (extended/flexed, vertical rotations, and torsions) should be completed to eliminate these problems as a part of the differential diagnoses. Complications from arthritis and ankylosing spondylitis can be considered but may be eliminated from the differential diagnosis depending on the history (i.e., acute trauma versus chronic or insidious onset).

Imaging Techniques
Radiographs are negative, although standing radiographs and flamingo stance radiographs are helpful in determining if there are pelvic or leg-length abnormalities, either of which can contribute to low back dysfunctions. In patients older than 30 years, some intervertebral disk-space narrowing is normal and expected.

Definitive Diagnosis
Lumbar sprain or strain is frequently a diagnosis of exclusion based on the physical examination and normal radiographs.

Pathomechanics and Functional Limitations
Pain and spasm restrict the patient's movements and abilities, but first-time events are self-limiting. A patient who experiences repeated episodes may develop chronic low back pain. Poor posture and body mechanics, combined with muscle imbalances, especially in the trunk and hip muscle groups, often predispose the patient to the initial injury. If these factors are not corrected, they can be sources of repeated episodes of low back pain.

▦ Immediate Management
Immediate management consists of ice; splinting with a brace (see **Figure 13.4**), tape, or elastic wrap; rest; and mild stretching to reduce spasm.[10]

▦ Medications
Aspirin, acetaminophen, and NSAIDs are useful for analgesic and anti-inflammatory effects. Opioids and muscle relaxants should not be used routinely for this condition.

ankylosing (ankylosis) Immobility of a joint, often progressive in nature.

13

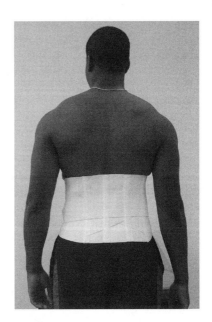

Figure 13.4 Lumbar brace used to stabilize the lumbar spine and sacroiliac joint.

■ Postinjury Management

Once pain and spasm are controlled, treatment includes various techniques to help the patient regain pain-free ROM. Posture and biomechanics must be evaluated so that dysfunctions can be corrected before the patient returns to activity, so as to reduce the risk of recurring injury.

■ Injury-Specific Treatment and Rehabilitation Concerns

> **Specific Concerns**
>
> Relieve pain and muscle spasm.
> Regain ROM, soft-tissue mobility, strength, endurance, and proprioception.
> Restore functional abilities to preinjury levels.

All lumbar injury recovery programs should include cardiovascular exercise, which is an important aspect of total recovery in patients with low back disability.[11] Before stretching and strengthening exercises, a brief period (10 to 15 minutes) of cardiovascular activity, such as stationary bicycling or upper body ergometry, enhances the effects of exercise and joint mobilizations.

Soft-tissue restriction and joint mobility in the back and hips should be assessed, especially if the patient has a history of back injuries or pain. Both soft-tissue scarring and restricted movement contribute to the risk of future injuries; myofascial release and instrument-assisted soft-tissue mobilization (Graston technique) can be used in these cases. Grade I and II joint mobilizations can help to relieve pain and spasm in the very early days of treatment as long as spondylosis, spondylitis, spondyolysis, and spondylolisthesis have been eliminated as diagnoses. Other modalities, such as electrical stimulation for pain and swelling relief and muscle facilitation, may provide early symptomatic relief.

Balance of the trunk and hip muscles—in particular, the abdominals (including the transverse abdominis, obliques, hip flexors, hip extensors, multifidus, and erector spinae)—must be emphasized because both tight and lengthened muscles display weakness. The transverse abdominis, lower internal obliques, and multifidus are especially important for pelvic and spinal stabilization and should be emphasized early in the rehabilitation program. The psoas muscle group often is ignored but is important because it is the only hip flexor that attaches to the spine.

Flexibility exercises should address the area directly involved in the injury and other segments that influence trunk stability and activity. If facet joint restriction is present between the vertebrae, grade III and IV mobilizations can improve mobility. Standing static exercises increase trunk and hip strength and stability and also provide early proprioceptive and balance activities. From these static exercises, the patient progresses to more dynamic exercises that evolve into coordination activities and, finally, to agility activities. The patient then moves to functional activities before beginning the final phase of the rehabilitation program, in which sport-specific drills and skills are performed.

■ Estimated Amount of Time Lost

The amount of time lost from competition may vary from a few days to 4 weeks or more. It is influenced by injury severity, the injury history (initial or chronic), the patient's age and physical condition, and the specific stress applied to the back during sport participation.

■ Return-to-Play Criteria

Before returning to competition, the patient should be pain free in all lumbar motions—flexion, extension, lateral flexion, and rotation—both actively and with overpressure. All functional and sport-specific activities should also be pain free, and soft-tissue mobility should be sufficient. Good balance in flexibility and strength of the opposing muscle groups (lumbar muscles and hip flexors, abdominal muscles and hip extensors) is necessary. Appropriate endurance and strength of the multifidus, lower internal obliques, and transverse abdominis stabilize the lumbar spine throughout all activities. Proprioception, agility, and sport performance should all be within normal limits and allow the patient to execute any sport-specific activity in a manner equivalent to the preinjury performance.

Vertebral Fractures

Vertebral fractures can involve either the vertebral body or the posterior structures (see **Figure 13.5**). Vertebral body fractures are most often attributable to axial loading or compression, tend to occur between the T11 and L1 levels, and are rare in athletics.[12] Body fractures are usually stable, without fragment displacement. These types of injuries are seen more often in older individuals with osteoporosis, in younger individuals with a history of steroid use, or after high-energy trauma. Posterior vertebral fractures occur during high-impact flexion injuries. They can disrupt bony alignment and result in fracture fragment dis-

axial loading
A load directed vertically along the axis of the spine creating a compression force.

History

A sudden flexion force is experienced.
Unstable fractures can impinge on the spinal cord, causing numbness, weakness, or paralysis.
If only the bone and/or its ligaments are affected and paralysis is not present, the patient may report severe back pain that increases with movement and decreases with rest.

Observation

Pain and muscle spasm are apparent.
Discoloration may not be visible immediately, but swelling or deformity may be evident.

Functional Status

ROM is severely restricted by pain and muscle spasm.
The patient may not be able to walk secondary to pain. If the spinal cord has been affected, motor, sensory, and reflex deficiencies may exist.

Physical Examination Findings

Palpation may reveal spasm, swelling, or deformity.
Tenderness to palpation over the fracture site is present.
A step-off deformity or a gap between the spinous processes may be present.
Appropriate neurologic tests are performed to identify associated spinal cord injury.
The patient is questioned regarding difficulty with urination or bowel evacuation or reduced perianal sensations.

location, ligamentous instability, and secondary spinal cord injury.

Spinous process fractures and transverse process fractures occur more frequently in the athletic population than fractures of the vertebral body.[13] Spinous process fractures result in time lost from athletic activities until the defect is healed, as such a fracture weakens the posterior aspect of the ring that

protects the spinal cord (cauda equina). Tension placed on the middle layer of the lumbar fascia can result in fracture of the transverse process.[14]

Stress fractures can also occur in the lumbar spine; such injuries usually affect older individuals and females whose health is influenced by the female athlete triad.[15,16] The most common site of all lumbar fractures, the pars interarticularis, is described in the Spondylolisthesis section.

Differential Diagnosis

Herniated lumbar disk, muscle strain, internal organ injuries.

Medical Diagnostic Tests

Patients with vertebral fractures should also be evaluated for their risk of osteoporosis. If a low-energy mechanism of injury was involved, the physician should consider bone-density evaluation with dual-energy x-ray absorptiometry. If osteoporosis is detected, a treatment protocol should be initiated.

Imaging Techniques

Lateral, AP, and oblique lumbar spine radiographs are obtained to identify fractures and dislocations (see **Figure 13.6**). Compression and burst fractures will reveal decreased anterior-border vertebral body height, especially on lateral views (see **Figure 13.7**). A kyphotic deformity may also be noted. Increased space between spinous processes may indicate an unstable flexion-distraction injury.

Computed tomography best visualizes the bony architecture of the fracture. CT imaging allows coronal and sagittal reconstructed images to identify overall spinal alignment. MRI is best suited for identification of marrow changes consistent with early fracture, ligamentous and other soft-tissue injury, and neural element impingement.

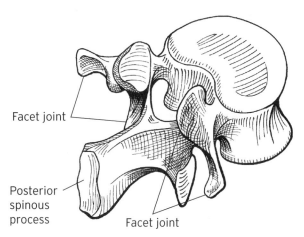

Figure 13.5 The posterior division of the vertebral column includes the facet joints on either side of the arch and the posterior spinous process. *Source:* Reproduced with permission from Kapanji A. *The Physiology of the Joints: Annotated Diagrams of the Mechanics of the Human Joints*, ed 3. New York: Churchill Livingstone; 1974.

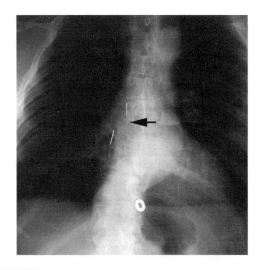

Figure 13.6 Anteroposterior view of a comminuted fracture-dislocation of T9.

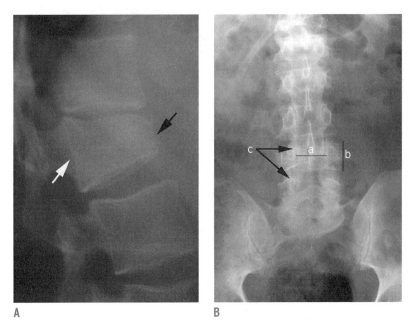

A   B

Figure 13.7   Radiographs of compression and burst fractures. (**A**) Lateral radiograph of a compression fracture. Note that the anterior aspect of the vertebral body (black arrow) is less than the posterior aspect (white arrow). (**B**) AP view of a burst fracture of a lumbar vertebra shows the characteristic widening of the interpedicular distance (**a**) associated with the loss of vertebral height (**b**). The facet joints appear to be normally aligned (**c**).

Active dynamic radiographs (flexion-extension) should be avoided during the acute postinjury phase if a fracture has been identified, as muscle guarding in this phase may obscure evidence of instability. Passive dynamic images are not indicated.

Definitive Diagnosis
A fracture may be suspected after signs and symptoms are investigated but can be confirmed only with radiographic examination.

Pathomechanics and Functional Limitations
The location of the trauma can be classified based on the columnar anatomy of the spinal column[17,18] (see **Figure 13.8**). Trauma involving the middle or posterior column has the greatest risk of producing neurologic problems. After a fracture or dislocation, the patient may experience persistent back pain, especially if the fracture is unstable. If nerve damage has also occurred, paralysis or sensation loss is likely to persist.

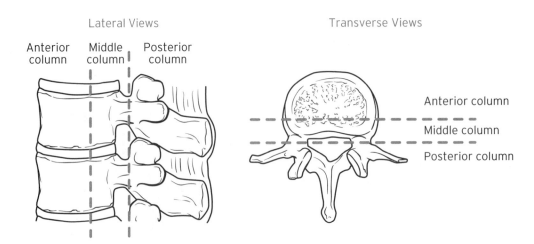

Figure 13.8   The three-column theory of spinal anatomy. The anterior column consists of the anterior two-thirds of the vertebral body and annulus fibrosus and the anterior longitudinal ligament. The middle column is formed by the posterior third of the vertebral body and the annulus fibrosus and the posterior longitudinal ligament. The posterior column is formed by the neural arch, the ligamentum flavum, intraspinous ligament, and the supraspinous ligament. *Source:* Reproduced with permission from Spivak JM, Vaccaro AR, Cotler JM. Thoracolumbar spine trauma: I. Evaluation and treatment. *J Am Acad Orthop Surg.* 1995;3:345-352.

Immediate Management

The emergency medical plan is enacted, with immobilization and transport to an emergency facility via a backboard for further medical examination.

Medications

NSAIDs and opioid analgesics are effective in pain management. However, patients undergoing fusion surgery should avoid NSAIDs, which may inhibit bone fusion.

Postinjury Management

The initial postinjury management goal is to assess the extent of injury and plan for stabilization of the involved structures. Transverse process fractures may need only bracing or relative rest to resolve, whereas a burst fracture may require surgical stabilization, although closed reduction and immobilization may sometimes yield good results.[12] The immediate management is designed to relieve pain and spasms associated with the injury while providing protection from further injury.

Lumbar fractures involving the posterior elements without instability can be treated with bracing. Lumbar burst fractures are high-energy injuries, for which treatment options include nonoperative bracing, casting, or surgical intervention. Surgical treatment is considered in patients with neurologic deficits, canal compromise, and instability. Nonoperative treatment may be selected for neurologically intact patients with burst fractures. Transverse process fractures are treated symptomatically, and activity can be resumed when the athlete is functional.

Surgical Intervention

Surgery is indicated for instability, progressive neurologic dysfunction, persistent pain despite nonoperative management, and unstable spinal fractures. The techniques employed in these procedures, which are often referred to as "fusions," can be performed using either a posterior (see (ST) 13.1) or anterior (see (ST) 13.2) approach. Brace or cast immobilization can be effective for some patients with stable fractures, but a fracture–dislocation often requires reduction and surgical fixation.

Posterior segmental instrumentation provides fixation of the anterior, middle, and posterior columns using pedicle screw constructs. The pedicle screw can stabilize all three columns via a posterior approach. A short construct using pedicle screw fixation maintains lordosis, while avoiding more complication-inducing long distraction constructs such as hooks and rods.

A patient with a lumbar burst fracture without neurologic deficit who was initially treated with nonoperative management, but who now has the onset of neurologic deficits, including increased canal impingement, may require surgical correction. Anterior decompression with instrumentation is indicated when the anterior column has failed and the middle-column fragments have retropulsed into the canal. Adequate decompression in the subacute time frame often requires exposure of the anterior and middle columns with direct decompression via a retroperitoneal approach.

Postoperative Management

Functional limitations are related to injury severity and the presence (or absence) of neurologic involvement. These limitations are influenced by the extent of the surgical intervention required to stabilize the condition. Once the segment has been stabilized, treatment includes provisions to ensure no further neurologic compromise occur and to maximize functional outcomes. Rehabilitation concerns and implications are determined by the extent of the injury, the surgery required, and the patient's neurologic status. A postoperative bracing regimen is used to limit trunk flexion; a gradual progressive rehabilitation program is instituted. Compression fractures may be immobilized in a brace with restricted flexion and rotation. During this time, cardiovascular activities and exercises to maintain extremity strength may be undertaken, pending a physician's clearance.

Injury-Specific Treatment and Rehabilitation Concerns

> **Specific Concerns**
>
> Limit spinal flexion.
> Relieve pain, muscle spasm, and soft-tissue restrictions.
> Restore muscle balance, trunk and hip flexibility and strength, and muscle endurance.
> Establish core-stabilization strength with application for functional activities.

Symptomatic relief of muscle spasm and pain can begin while the patient is still wearing the brace. The physician may permit removal of the brace to facilitate such passive treatments. Because stability with minimal joint movement is desired, joint mobilization is contraindicated. Thermal modalities and electrical stimulation for symptomatic relief and strengthening may be employed, however.

13

S T Surgical Technique 13.1

Posterior Stabilization (Fusion) of the Lumbar Spine

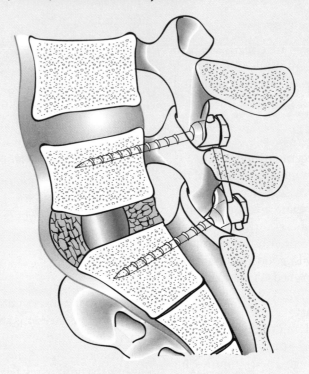

Indications

Unstable fractures involving the anterior and middle column with neurologic involvement (radicular symptoms).

Procedure Overview

1. The patient is positioned prone on a lumbar spine table.
2. The posterior elements are exposed using subperiosteal dissection. The capsules of the facets above and below the fusion are not violated.
3. The transverse processes are cleared of muscular attachments and the transverse process and pars are identified, providing the landmarks for pedicle screw placement.
4. Pedicle screws are directed along the pedicle, while using a probe to palpate all quadrants of the pedicle to ensure there are no pedicle wall violations.
5. Radiographs assist in the placement of screws. The pedicle path is tapped, and a pedicle screw is placed.
6. Electromyographic (EMG) testing is performed to ensure that no nerve encroachment has occurred.
7. After the pedicle screw is inserted appropriately into the pedicle, a bone graft is placed over the decorticated facet and transverse process, providing the posterolateral fusion.
8. The fracture fragments are indirectly decompressed with distraction during the acute posttraumatic period.

Functional Limitations

Limitations are determined by the degree and level of neurologic function. Trunk flexion must be restricted in the early postoperative phase. The functional limitations created by this surgical approach affect trunk- and core-stabilization musculature. Many spine surgeons discourage their patients from participating in contact athletics after undergoing an instrumented lumbar fusion.

Implications for Rehabilitation

Postoperative bracing protects the stable construct during the healing phase (3 to 6 months). Trunk- and core-stabilization strengthening exercises are initiated.

Complications

This procedure carries a slight risk of rod or screw failure or nerve root damage. EMG testing can determine whether nerve damage occurred during the pedicle screw fixation. Other potential complications include damage to nerves and vessels, malalignment of the hardware resulting in neurologic impingement, failure or loosening of hardware, and adjacent-segment disease. Degeneration of the segment often takes place over a period of time and is not necessarily a result of the surgery.

S|T Surgical Technique 13.2

Anterior Posterior Stabilization (Fusion) of the Lumbar Spine

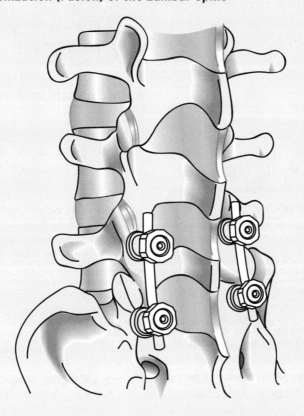

Indications

Unstable fractures involving the anterior and middle columns without neurologic involvement.

Procedure Overview

1. The patient is positioned on the surgical table in a lateral position for a thoracic or thoracolumbar approach. The table is flexed to facilitate exposure of the target structures.
2. An incision is made lateral to the body's midline.
3. The muscles, internal organs, inferior vena cava, and abdominal aorta are retracted to expose the anterior vertebral body.
4. The disk's superior and inferior vertebral endplate attachment are dissected, and the disk is removed.
5. If applicable, displaced bony fragments are reduced.
6. The endplates are scarified to cause bleeding in the subchondral bone.
7. Notches are made in the superior and inferior vertebral bodies that will accept the graft.
8. The graft is harvested from the donor site (typically the iliac crest).
9. The disk space is spread, and the graft is inserted between the vertebrae. A shim may be inserted to hold the graft in place.
10. A fixation plate (rod) is positioned over the anterior surface of the fractured vertebra, extending one or two segments above and below this vertebra.
11. Holes are drilled into the vertebrae, and the plate is fixated.
12. The incision site is closed.

Functional Limitations

Limitations are ultimately determined by the degree and level of neurologic function. Trunk flexion must be restricted in the early postoperative period. Functional limitations created by this surgical approach affect trunk- and core-stabilization musculature.

Implications for Rehabilitation

Postoperative bracing is instituted to protect the stable construct during the healing phase. Trunk- and core-stabilization strengthening exercises are initiated.

13

The physician may permit mild exercises during the later stages of the brace period. Although trunk and hip exercises may be difficult, open-chain strengthening exercises for the extremities can be used. The patient must be instructed to isometrically contract the core muscles to aid in stabilizing the trunk during these exercises, thereby placing less stress on the injury site and preparing the trunk muscles for later exercises. Once the patient is out of the brace, mild flexibility exercises and early strengthening exercises can be initiated. Flexibility exercises should be accompanied by soft-tissue mobilization to restore motion, especially of the back. Strengthening exercises begin as isometrics, progressing to early stabilization with upper and lower extremity motion activities, and then to active motion exercises for the back extensors, abdominal, and oblique muscles.

Special attention should be paid to developing strength and muscle endurance in the transverse abdominis, lower internal obliques, and multifidus muscles (primary stabilizers of the trunk), in addition to the larger, more peripheral trunk muscle groups. The hip extensors, abductors, and adductors also contribute to trunk stabilization and can be rehabilitated once the patient is ambulating in the brace. Standing balance activities for proprioception can begin in the brace and continue in a more aggressive progression once the brace is removed. From these static exercises, the patient advances to more dynamic exercises that evolve into coordination and finally agility activities. Functional activities begin before the final phase of the rehabilitation program, in which sport-specific drills and skill executions are performed.

■ Estimated Amount of Time Lost

In patients without neural involvement, disability may last as long as 3 to 6 months. Neural damage, general health, and degree of fracture instability or dislocation all affect the amount of time lost from activities. After spinal fusion, many surgeons do not allow patients to return to contact athletics.

■ Return-to-Play Criteria

If no permanent neurologic damage is present, the patient may return to full sport participation provided there is no pain during motion and activity, appropriate core stability is maintained throughout all activities, functional motion and strength are adequate to meet the sport stresses, performance of functional and sport-specific activities is normal, and the physician provides a release to participate.

Functional Bracing

Initial back bracing may be required (see Figure 13.4) but is no longer needed once the patient has completed a full rehabilitation course.

Disk Pathologies and Nerve-Root Impingement

CLINICAL PRESENTATION

History

A single incident that produces an acute onset of pain, usually a bending and/or twisting motion, is often described, but the actual degeneration is more insidious.

Low back pain or unilateral referred leg pain may be reported.

The patient may have difficulty finding a position of comfort, especially if the disk is herniated.

The patient may assume a hook-lying position to relieve pain.

The preferred sleep position (stomach, side, or back) can be used to aid in the diagnosis, as can symptom changes while reclining.

Determine if symptoms change during or after prolonged sitting.

Determine if symptoms radiate from the back down through the buttock and down the leg.

Observation

A lateral shift of the spine away from the site of pain may be observed in standing.

Observe for walking gait, alteration of functional movements (sitting to a chair, lying on a table, clothing removal).

Loss of lordosis is noted.

Muscle spasm occurs secondary to pain.

The patient must change positions frequently during the examination.

Functional Status

Lumbar ROM is restricted, especially in trunk flexion.

Straight-leg raising is usually limited by pain to less than 45°.

The patient changes positions frequently.

Physical Examination Findings

Pain may lessen when the back is extended or the patient lies prone on the elbows.

Neurologic testing for motor and sensory function and reflexes identifies deficiencies according to the neural level involved.

The following special tests may be positive:
- Well-leg straight-leg raise
- Straight-leg raise
- Milgram

The intervertebral disks lie between the vertebrae and function to separate them, thereby permitting motion and absorbing shock. The central area, known as the nucleus pulposus (formed by type II collagen fibers), is surrounded by a fibrous outer shell of several concentric layers, known as the annulus fibrosis (formed by type I collagen fibers) (see **Figure 13.9**).[2] This anatomic arrangement gives the disk properties similar to those of a ligament,

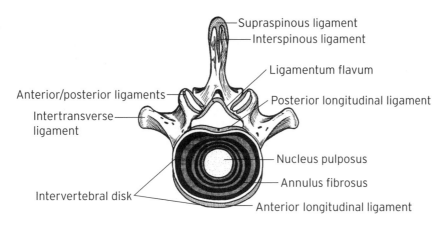

Figure 13.9   Anatomy of an intervertebral disk. *Source:* Reproduced with permission from Kapanji A. *The Physiology of the Joints: Annotated Diagrams of the Mechanics of the Human Joints,* ed 3. New York: Churchill Livingstone; 1974.

in that it resists tension and articular cartilage within the disk resists compression.[2]

The various levels of disk derangement lie along a continuum that ranges from pressure of the nucleus pulposus without annulus fibrosis rupture to annulus fibrosis fragmentation with portions of the nucleus pulposus lying outside the intervertebral disk (see Figure 13.10). Most disk derangements begin in the nucleus and progress outwardly.[2] These

defects can be classified as a bulge, herniation, or prolapse (rupture of the annulus with disk material escaping).

Although the cause of disk derangement is not completely known, any activity that affects inherent segment stability may affect the disk. Possible results of instability include facet synovitis, annulus breakdown, and nuclear material migration beyond the confines of the disk and surrounding

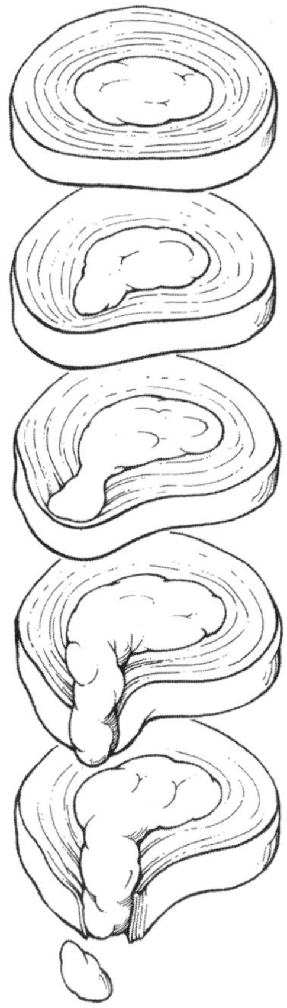

Illustration	Classification	Description
	A. Normal	
	B. Protrusion	Some of the fibers of the annulus fibrosus are damaged. The nucleus pulposus bulges into the annulus fibrosis.
	C. Prolapse	Pressure from the nucleus pulposus pushes the outer annulus fibrosis fibers toward the spinal canal.
	D. Extrusion	Tearing of the outer layers of the annulus fibrosis; the intact nucleus pulposus moves into the spinal canal
	E. Sequestration	Fragments of the annulus fibrosus and/or the nucleus pulposus break off and are outside the disk in the spinal canal, or in the intervertebral foramen, where pressure on the nerve roots may result.

Figure 13.10   Classifications of disk pathology. *Source:* Reproduced with permission from Gill K. Percutaneous lumbar diskectomy. *J Am Acad Orthop Surg.* 1993;1:33-40.

ligaments. The presence of a disk protein primarily found in males, cartilage intermediate-layer protein (CILP) single-nucleotide polymorphism, may also increase the risk of disk degeneration in males.[19]

These developments may produce a mechanical or chemical irritation of the nerve roots or spinal cord.[17] When the nucleus pulposus herniates into the spinal column, the spinal nerves experience both mechanical pain and chemical irritation from the nucleus pulposus. This condition, which is more severe, causes intractable pain.

The most common sites for disk derangements in the lumbar spine are at L4–L5 and L5–S1, the locations of the greatest stress on the lumbar spine in forward-bending and rotation movements.

Differential Diagnosis

Muscle spasm, active trigger points, fracture, facet syndrome, spinal stenosis (in older patients).

Medical Diagnostic Tests

Neurophysiologic EMG testing can be helpful in determining chronicity or permanent nerve injury. These tests are also helpful in differentiating polyneuropathy and other systemic neurologic disorders from radiculopathy.

Imaging Techniques

AP and lateral radiographs may demonstrate intervertebral space narrowing, indicating reduced height of the intervertebral disks. Sagittal and axial MRI may indicate a herniated or ruptured intervertebral disk. Compression on the spinal cord, lumbar nerve root, and cauda equina also may be noted (see **Figure 13.11**). A myelogram identifies spinal cord impingement caused by a herniated lumbar disk (see **Figure 13.12**).

Diskography, which entails the injection of an opaque contrast medium into an intervertebral disk,

polyneuropathy
A disease that affects a number of peripheral nerves.

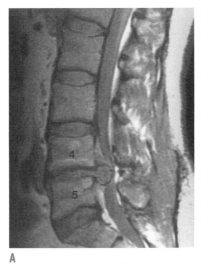
A

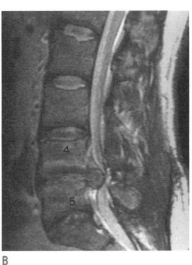
B

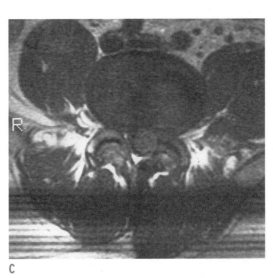
C

Figure 13.11 MRI demonstrating intervertebral disk lesions. **(A)** Sagittal T1-weighted image demonstrating a herniation at L4-L5 with cauda equina compression. **(B)** Sagittal T2-weighted image demonstrating the herniated disk and decreased disk signal intensity at several lumbar levels. **(C)** Axial image demonstrating a large disk fragment that could be misinterpreted as the thecal sac.

has been used to characterize small tears in the annulus fibrosis (see **Figure 13.13**). The use and reliability of diskography remain controversial, however.[20]

Definitive Diagnosis

Clinical findings are not always accurate in diagnosis of disk disease. The traditionally accepted symptom comprises radiating sensory or motor symptoms within a dermatomal distribution. Motor findings may include weakness in foot dorsiflexion and great toe extension and flexion, indicating impairment

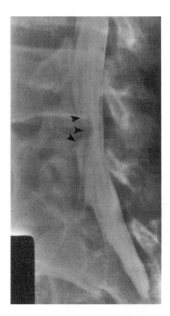

Figure 13.12 Lumbar myelogram demonstrating an extradural defect around the exiting nerve root and a curved or deflected path of the exiting root secondary to a herniated disk.

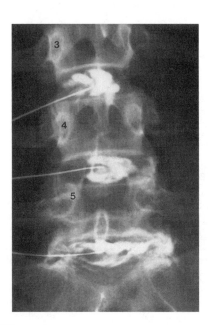

Figure 13.13 Lumbar diskogram. The L4-L5 disk demonstrates an annular fissure on the left side without external extravasation. The L5-S1 disk has a posterolateral tear that communicates with the epidural space.

of the nerves that exit the intervertebral foramen at L4 to L5 and L5 to S1, the levels most commonly affected by lumbar disk disease. Radicular symptoms are typically what brings the patient to the clinician and are usually the reason for removal from sports activities. At one time radicular symptoms were a primary diagnostic tool; more recently, however, the introduction of the MRI has significantly enhanced the diagnostic process. Asymptomatic individuals often have disk changes identified on MRI, suggesting that radiographic impingement does not indicate the presence of clinical symptoms.[17]

> **Practice Tip**
>
> Diskography is not indicated to diagnose lumbar disk herniation with radiculopathy. Its reliability remains a source of dispute in the diagnosis of diskogenic low back pain. Even after the diagnosis is certain, traditional conservative rehabilitation measures are effective in 95% of patients.[21,22]

Pathomechanics and Functional Limitations

Pain is the primary factor restricting function and can be debilitating until it resolves. Patients should avoid positions that place increased pressure on the irritated disk. Forward bending, flexion, and rotation all substantially increase posterior disk pressure. Rotation also increases pressure on the weakened and irritated disk. The symptoms of disk injury, unless at the sequestration stage, can often be resolved with appropriate conservative care.

■ Immediate Management

This situation is not emergent unless evidence of cauda equina syndrome exists (see **Box 13.2**). The patient should initially be treated symptomatically, and then the extent of the injury should be determined.

■ Medications

NSAIDs and oral corticosteroids are standard pharmacologic treatments for radiculopathy. Selective nerve root blocks have both diagnostic and therapeutic utility. In contrast, narcotics and muscle relaxants have not been shown to improve the long-term outcome of patients with lumbar radiculopathy, and such medicines should be judiciously used in individuals with this condition.

■ Postinjury Management

To determine the extent of the disk disease, physician referral for MRI often is required. Pain relief

13

Cauda Equina Syndrome

The cauda equina is formed by the L2 to S4 nerve roots, below the level where the spinal cord terminates. Compression of the cauda equina is a medical emergency; patients may be predisposed to develop this condition because of disk herniation or compressive trauma to the lumbar spine. With cauda equina syndrome present, the patient has difficulty walking, may be unable to rise from a chair, and loses bowel and/or bladder control. Symptoms may occur acutely or gradually over time.

Suspected cases of cauda equina syndrome should be immediately referred for medical examination. Beyond 48 hours after neural compromise, the surgical success rate is dramatically reduced. Because nerve roots from the left and right sides of the spinal cord emerge in the cauda equina below L2, symptoms include bilateral loss of sensation and motor innervation. Autonomic retroperineal nerves innervating the bladder, bowel, and sexual organs also pass through the cauda equina; thus they are at risk for permanent damage if surgical decompression is not performed soon after symptom onset.

is an immediate concern. It can frequently be accomplished in the short term with electric stimulation to relieve muscle spasm and by placing the patient in a supine, hook-lying position or prone with "hips away" from the side of the pain, much like the posture the patient may have in ambulation, and the trunk in extension.

■ Surgical Intervention

Surgical intervention is indicated for patients whose intractable pain persists despite 4 to 6 weeks of non-operative treatment. Decompressive laminectomy is the standard surgical procedure for spinal stenosis that causes radicular symptoms. In this procedure, the lamina and ligamentum flavum are removed on both sides of the vertebra (bilateral laminectomy) or unilaterally (hemilaminectomy) (see **ST** 13.3). Lumbar disk herniations may be corrected using the microdiskectomy technique, especially if radicular symptoms are present (see **ST** 13.4).

S|T Surgical Technique 13.3

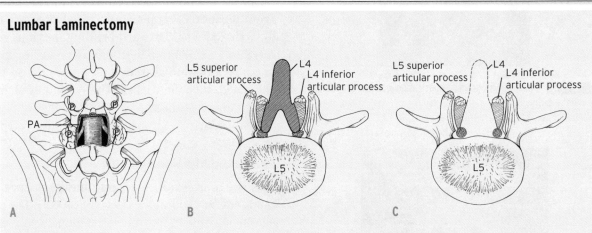

Lumbar Laminectomy

Indications

Failure of conservative management for 4 to 6 weeks; cauda equina syndrome with bowel and bladder dysfunction.

Procedure Overview

1. The patient is positioned prone on a frame to maximize lumbar flexion and increase the space between the laminae.
2. The lamina is exposed using subperiosteal dissection (**A**).
3. The lamina is thinned with a high-speed burr and removed with a punch, protecting the underlying dural tissues (**B**).
4. The integrity of the facet capsules and pars interarticularis must be maintained to avoid iatrogenic postdecompressive instability (**C**).

Functional Limitations

Although overnight hospitalization is often not required, some patients may require hospitalization for as long as 72 hours. Walking is encouraged as soon as possible. Lumbar flexion and rotation are limited to protect the healing tissues.

Implications for Rehabilitation

Heavy lifting and exertional activities may be restricted for as long as 6 weeks.

Source: Reproduced with permission from Frymoyer JW. Degenerative spondylolisthesis: Diagnosis and treatment. *J Am Acad Orthop Surg.* 1994;2:9-15.

S|T Surgical Technique 13.4

Microdiskectomy

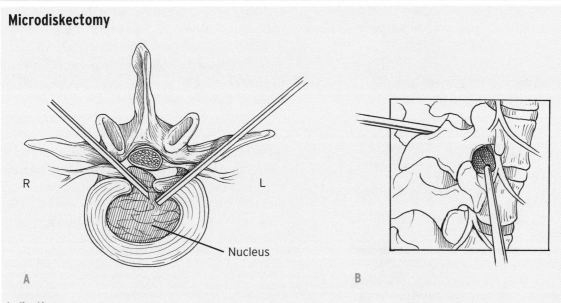

Nucleus

A   B

Indications

Failure of conservative management for 4 to 6 weeks; unilateral radicular symptoms with foot pain greater than back pain.

Procedure Overview

1. The patient is positioned prone on a frame to maximize lumbar flexion and increase the space between the laminae, thereby allowing access to the ligamentum flavum.
2. A small (approximately 1-in) incision is made over the spinous process(es).
3. A high-speed burr is used to thin the lamina inferiorly and superiorly at the affected level. A small portion of the facet joint may be removed to relieve pressure on the nerve root.
4. The ligamentum flavum is dissected free from the dura.
5. The nerve root is identified and gently retracted, allowing access to the disk herniation (**A**).
6. The disk herniation is removed using minimal annular incisions to decrease the incidence of disk reherniation. The endplates of the intervertebral disk are not violated during the removal of the herniated disk fragment (**B**).

Functional Limitations

Sitting, bending, and lifting are restricted for the first 1 to 2 weeks postoperatively.

Implications for Rehabilitation

Formal rehabilitation focusing on abdominal and core strengthening does not begin until 3 to 4 weeks after surgery.

Comments

A microsurgical technique using a microscope or loupe and headlight offers decreased postoperative pain because of the smaller surgical incisions required. The use of tubular retractors also offers decreased postoperative pain because less subperiosteal dissection of muscles is necessary to access the affected intervertebral disk. Hospitalization is rarely required following this procedure.

Source: Reproduced with permission from Mathews HH, Long BH. Minimally invasive techniques for the treatment of intervertebral disk herniation. *J Am Acad Orthop Surg.* 2002;10:80-85.

13

Some physicians suggest that the optimal time for surgical intervention in disk pathologies is during the first 3 to 4 months after symptoms appear. Surgery should be performed sooner if muscle weakness is significant or if bowel or bladder dysfunction is present. In the case of bowel or bladder dysfunction, emergency surgery is indicated (see Box 13.2).

▇ Postoperative Management

Postoperative management depends on the type of surgery performed. Bed rest may be recommended for 1 to 3 days following surgery. Provocative positions, especially lumbar flexion and rotation, should be avoided while the tissues are healing. An advantage of the microdiskectomy is that it enables a faster rehabilitation progression, allowing rehabilitation to begin at 3 to 4 weeks.

▓ Injury-Specific Treatment and Rehabilitation Concerns

> #### Specific Concerns
>
> Centralize the patient's pain.
> Begin teaching the mechanics of daily living activities while the patient is still symptomatic.
> Improve the patient's posture, body mechanics, and general fitness level.
> Teach the patient to move into and maintain a pelvic-neutral position.
> Restore muscle balance, flexibility, endurance, and strength, especially for the muscles controlling the trunk, pelvis, and hips.
> Relieve pain and muscle spasm.

Exercises can be used initially to relieve pain from the disk protrusion if surgery is not performed. These exercises may consist of prone positioning of the patient to "centralize" the pain from the lower extremity to the central low back. In theory, this positioning reduces the posterior disk pressure by allowing gravity to pull the bulge back toward the disk's center (refer to "Williams' Flexion and McKenzie Extension Exercises" in the Rehabilitation section later in this chapter).

If the patient is unable to lie flat in the prone position, one or more pillows can be placed under the low back and hips, with the pillow height being gradually reduced as the patient's tolerance improves. When the patient is able to lie in the prone position, add pillows or blankets under the chest to increase extension. This can be done at home for activities including reading, watching television, or working on a laptop. The next progression includes "press-up" activities with the patient in the push-up position and pressing only the trunk off the floor or plinth.

A standing trunk-extension exercise is performed as a home exercise throughout the day. The patient is instructed in finding a pelvic-neutral position, and then exercises to improve the flexibility and strength of the muscles required to hold this position are gradually introduced according to tolerance. Once the pain has become more cen-

tralized, the patient may advance first to flexibility exercises for the hips and other lower extremity joints and then to strengthening exercises. These strengthening exercises must include the abdominals, especially the transverse abdominis and obliques, hip and back extensors (particularly the hip extensors and abductors and the multifidus), and the lower extremities if weakness has developed secondary to the injury.

Hip- and trunk-stabilization exercises should be a part of the strengthening program and are presented at the end of this chapter. Static balance activities beginning with a stork stand, first with eyes open and then with eyes closed, are also incorporated. The patient then proceeds to more dynamic exercises that evolve into coordination and agility activities. Functional activities are started before the final phase of the rehabilitation program, in which sport-specific drills and skill executions are performed.

▓ Estimated Amount of Time Lost

The amount of time lost from competition varies but can range from 2 weeks to 2 months. If surgery has been performed, the size of the herniation, the intensity and prolongation of pain, neural deficits, the degree of motor deficiency (if neural innervation has been impaired), and the extent of the surgery will all affect the disability time. Single-level microdiskectomy allows 90% of elite athletes to return to competitive sports. Unfortunately, athletes who undergo surgical intervention for multilevel disk herniations are less likely to resume high-level activity.

▓ Return-to-Play Criteria

Before returning to competition, the patient should be pain free during all activities. Soft-tissue and joint mobility should be normal, and the patient should be strong enough to tolerate all stresses applied to the lumbar spine. The patient should have good pelvic (trunk) stability and be able to maintain pelvic-neutral position during sport activities. Hip, abdominal, and back strength and endurance should be sufficient to provide adequate support during sport performance.

Spondylolysis and Spondylolisthesis

Spondylolysis is a defect in the pars interarticularis of the vertebral arch, usually at the L5–S1 level in athletes. In older patients, the L4–L5 level is most

CLINICAL PRESENTATION

History

The patient reports participation in activities where the lumbar spine is repeatedly hyperextended.

The patient may present with back pain radiating into the buttocks or down to the knee, but the pain is usually localized along the belt line, either unilaterally or bilaterally.

Pain is dull, aching, and/or cramping in the low back.

Pain is aggravated with standing, trunk extension, and trunk rotation.

Observation

The patient often demonstrates an excessive lumbar lordosis.

To relieve the low back pain, the patient may stand with the hips and knees flexed and the pelvis tilted posteriorly, creating flattened buttocks.

Functional Status

Hamstrings and paraspinal muscle tightness and spasm may occur. ROM is usually full but painful in lumbar extension and rotation.

Physical Examination Findings

Passive straight-leg raising may reproduce the patient's symptoms. If the patient stands on the ipsilateral leg and extends the trunk, pain during the maneuver constitutes a positive test.

affected secondary to a degenerative process. Spondylolisthesis is diagnosed when the vertebral body below the lesion slips anteriorly. Both spondylolysis and spondylolisthesis cause low back pain, particularly in adolescent athletes.[23] Of the five classifications of these conditions (see **Table 13.1**), types I and II occur only in children and adolescents.[24]

The amount of slippage associated with spondylolisthesis is described based on the percentage of disk displacement relative to the caudal segment (see **Table 13.2**).[25] Significant slippage can narrow

Table 13.1

Classification of Spondylolysis and Spondylolisthesis

Type	Onset	Description
I	Dysplastic	Congenital abnormalities
II	Isthmic	Fatigue fracture of the pars interarticularis
III	Degenerative	Associated with long-term instability
		Occurs more often in women older than 40 years of age
IV	Traumatic	Acute fracture of the neural arch other than the pars interarticularis
V	Pathologic	Associated with bone disease

Table 13.2

Grading of Spondylolisthesis

Grade	Percent Slip*
I	0 to 25%
II	25% to 50%
III	50% to 75%
IV	>75%

*Percentage of forward translation of the vertebrae relative to the one above them.
Source: Adapted from Purcell L, Micheli L. Low back pain in young athletes. *Sports Health: A Multidisciplinary Approach.* 2009;1:212-221.

the spinal canal and increase the possibility of spinal cord damage.[26,27] These conditions can occur at any lumbar level, but defects and possible impingement as a result of slippage are most common at the L4 and L5 levels.[28] Although the cause of these conditions remains unknown, some believe that a stress fracture may result, at least in part, from the repetitive hyperextension commonly noted in sports such as gymnastics, weight lifting, football, and hockey.[26,29]

The clinical examination of patients with these conditions is frequently unremarkable. Nonspecific low back pain is often the major complaint; the pars defect itself has been implicated in producing pain.[29] Passive intervertebral motion findings include significant hypermobility at the segment in question. Imaging studies such as a bone scan may be indicated.[26]

Differential Diagnosis

Ankylosing spondylitis, central disk derangement, herniated nucleus pulposus, tumor, posterior element overuse syndrome.

Imaging Techniques

To establish the diagnosis, AP and weight-bearing oblique radiographs of the lumbar spine are obtained. Although weight-bearing views increase the anterior displacement of the vertebral body as identified by their posterior alignment, only one-third of stress defects are identified using these kinds of plain radiographs (see **Figure 13.14**).[25] The characteristic "Scotty dog" deformity may be identified during radiographs of a patient with advanced spondylolysis; a "decapitated Scotty dog" deformity is indicative of spondylolisthesis. Sufficient anterolisthesis can compress the associated nerve roots or cauda equina (see Box 13.2).

Practice Tip

Because of the relatively high amount of radiation used and the low sensitivity of the procedure, the routine use of oblique radiographs in young athletes is discouraged.[25]

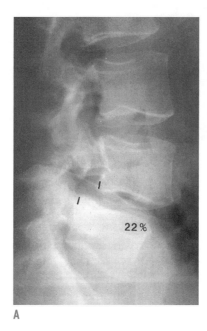
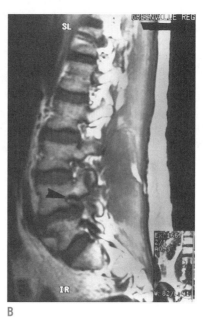

Figure 13.14   Imaging of spondylolisthesis. (**A**) Lateral radiograph demonstrating anterior slippage of L4 on L5. (**B**) Sagittal MRI revealing stenosis of the foramen (arrow) and flattening of the nerve root.

Single-photon emission computed tomography (SPECT) can be used to identify injury of the pars that may not be detectable on plain radiographs.[25] Serial SPECT evaluations may be recommended after therapeutic treatment or resolution of uptake with brace therapy. A CT myelogram may be performed to verify the diagnosis of a pars defect based on SPECT scanning (see **Figure 13.15**).

Definitive Diagnosis

For spondylolisthesis, lateral radiographs will demonstrate the malalignment. In the case of spondylolysis, the diagnosis is made with the radiographic techniques described earlier in this section.

Pathomechanics and Functional Limitations

In the early phases of degeneration of the pars, back hyperextension and twisting motions should be eliminated or modified as much as possible, especially in spondylolisthesis. As the condition progresses, the patient will develop segmental instability secondary to a loss of the locking mechanism.[28] Over time, slippage of the vertebra can compress the caudal sac or compress the lumbar nerve roots[30] or result in stenosis of the spinal foramen[28] (see **Figure 13.16**).

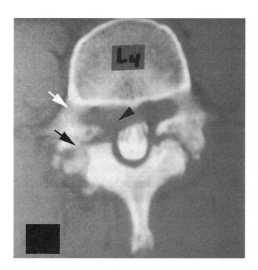

Figure 13.15   CT myelogram of the L4 pars interarticularis. The left black arrow indicates a pars interarticularis defect at the level of the pedicle (white arrow). Nerve root compression is identified by the right black arrow.

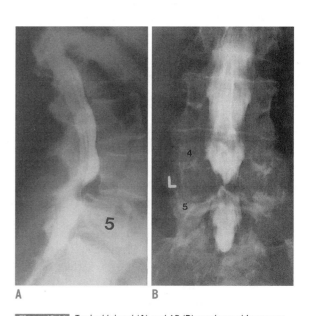

Figure 13.16   Typical lateral (**A**) and AP (**B**) myelographic appearance of degenerative spondylolisthesis. Significant constriction is apparent on the caudal sac at L4-L5.

Medications

NSAIDs or acetaminophen may be prescribed to control pain and inflammation.

Postinjury Management

Limiting extension is key in controlling pain with either spondylolisthesis or spondylolysis. Rest and an extension-limiting brace may be used for 3 to 6 weeks, or even longer, to facilitate healing. In severe cases, a rigid brace may be used for 6 months; however, this treatment method is not universally accepted by orthopaedic surgeons.[23,25] Behavioral modifications to prevent the patient from extending the lumbar spine should be initiated in all cases.

Surgical Intervention

Surgery is indicated in the presence of intractable pain, neurologic deficits, or instability of the segment, or in patients who have failed to improve with nonoperative management (including bracing).[23]

For an isolated pars defect without significant neurologic deficits, a surgical option is repair of the pars defect with bone grafting and instrumentation. This is not a fusion procedure; rather, the pars defect is grafted with bone and secured with either screw fixation or a pedicle screw rod-hook construct. If neurologic symptoms are present and decompression is indicated, however, a fusion is also warranted because decompression alone is associated with poor outcomes in comparison to decompression and fusion (see **Figure 13.17**). Although the fusion procedure can be performed with or without instrumentation, instrumentation is thought to improve fusion rates. On the downside, use of instrumentation increases the risk of surgical complications as well as the cost of the procedure. The fusion options include posterolateral fusion with bone placed over the decorticated transverse process and a combined posterior fusion with transforaminal or posterior lumbar interbody fusion. These techniques allow anterior interbody fusion from a posterior approach.

Postoperative Management

Patients are often braced depending on the technique used for fusion. When bony fusion is confirmed using radiographic criteria, patients are allowed to increase their activity without limitations.

Injury-Specific Treatment and Rehabilitation Concerns

> **Specific Concerns**
>
> Limit lumbar extension and rotation in the early stages of rehabilitation.
> Restore normal lumbar mobility.
> Regain normal trunk and extremity strength, balance, and agility.
> Achieve adequate strength and endurance of the trunk and hip stabilizers during functional activities.
> Properly perform functional and sport-specific activities in the posterior pelvic-tilt position.
> Obtain pain-free lumbar extension and rotation.

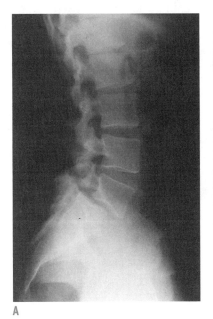
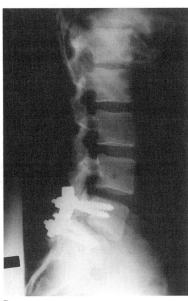

A   B

Figure 13.17   L5-S1 spondylolisthesis. (**A**) Lateral radiograph demonstrating vertebral displacement. (**B**) Following resection of the arch, bilateral foraminotomies, and decompression of the L5 nerve roots, the vertebrae were fused and fixated with pedicle screw instrumentation at L5-S1.

In young athletes with spondylolisthesis, surgical repair may be the treatment of choice. Older athletes and those with spondylolysis are generally treated conservatively, with instruction in proper positioning (posterior pelvic tilt), cardiovascular exercises, and strength and muscle endurance exercises. Williams' flexion exercises can be initiated early, and the importance of maintaining a posterior pelvic tilt must be stressed. Exercises may need to be performed in the brace (for postoperative patients), especially in the early phases of rehabilitation. During the healing phase, symptoms will dictate the need for the brace during exercises.

Flexibility of the hips (including the hamstrings and hip flexors) and the back, along with strengthening of the abdominal (especially the transverse abdominis and obliques) and paraspinal muscles (especially the multifidus), is important to establish a good base for subsequent stability during functional activities and exercises. Balance activities begin in the brace with static stork standing or tandem standing, then advance to performance out of the brace. From these static exercises, the patient progresses to more dynamic exercises that evolve into coordination activities and, finally, agility activities.

The duration of the rehabilitation process depends on the length of time for which activity is restricted; the loss of flexibility, strength, and muscle endurance during the immobilization period; and the amount of general deconditioning that has occurred. If the patient is required to maintain restricted activity in the brace for 6 months, rehabilitation may take at least that long.

Estimated Amount of Time Lost

The amount of time lost from competition is influenced by a number of factors. Recovery time from spondylolisthesis—the more severe injury—can be prolonged, with severe cases extending into months of time lost. Athletes with minor cases of spondylolysis may lose only a few days from their sport, with minimal or no interference with activity. The physician is likely to place restrictions on participation until both signs and symptoms are resolved and radiographs no longer indicate a need for activity restriction.

Return-to-Play Criteria

Patients with asymptomatic spondylolisthesis may participate in competitive sports. A patient whose symptoms have subsided may practice in the brace but should avoid activities that overstress the lumbar spine. If pain continues for 9 months after the injury (at which point results are unlikely to improve), the patient is allowed to resume full sport participation if able to perform despite pain. If full sport participation is not possible because of pain, surgery and reduced activity are the available options.[31]

Functional Bracing

A slip between the vertebrae is most likely in patients 9 to 15 years of age, and females are twice as likely to experience a slip as males.[31] If the patient is not a candidate for surgical intervention, bracing is advantageous to promote healing. Rigid bracing to limit trunk mobility entirely or limit only trunk extension is likely to be used during the first 3 to 6 weeks up to 6 months, depending on the amount of slippage and the physician's recommendation. A brace may also be worn during the first half of rehabilitation and perhaps even after the patient has returned to activity. The physician's instructions and the patient's symptoms are the key guiding elements.

Rehabilitation

Bed rest was once the primary treatment for low back injuries. Recently, however, the routine care of patients with low back injuries has changed dramatically. Treatment has become dynamic, with the recommended regimen including starting exercises early in the program, restricting rest to extreme cases only, and encompassing more aggressive protocols. This approach yields longer-lasting favorable results, with less residual disability.

Rehabilitation guidelines should be based on a treatment-based classification system (see **Table 13.3**). The Delitto lumbar spine treatment-based classification system, for example, relies on spinal movement and forces that decrease (centralize) symptoms, in-

Table 13.3

Delitto Treatment-Based Classification System

Classification	Primary History and Clinical Findings	Treatment Approach
Exercise		
Extension syndrome	Patient stands in extension	Emphasize extension exercises
	Spinal flexion increases pain	Avoid flexion motions
	Pain is centralized during lumbar extension	
	Pain and peripheralization of symptoms increase during flexion testing	
Flexion syndrome	Patient assumes a flexed spinal posture	Emphasize flexion exercise
	Extension activities increase pain	Avoid extension motions
	Symptoms are centralized during lumbar flexion testing	
	Pain and peripheralization of symptoms increase during extension testing	
Lateral shift syndrome	Shoulders are out of line with the pelvis in the frontal plane	Pelvic translocation exercises
	The spine is side bent, restricting lumbar motion testing	
	Symptoms are centralized during pelvic translocation (shear force)	
Mobilization		
Lumbar mobilization	Local, unilateral low back pain is noted	Lumbar mobilization/manipulation
	An "opening pattern" is evident during lumbar movement testing	Lumbar range-of-motion exercises
	A "closing pattern" is evident during lumbar movement testing	
Sacroiliac mobilization	The patient reports local pain at the posterior superior iliac spine, buttock, or lateral thigh	Sacroiliac manipulation
		Sacroiliac muscle energy
	Positive results are obtained for 75% of the sacroiliac test cluster	Lumbar range-of-motion exercises
Immobilization		
Immobilization syndrome	The patient has repeated prior episodes of low back pain with minimal perturbation	Trunk-strengthening exercises
	A history of trauma is reported	
	Generalized ligamentous laxity is present	
	"Instability catch" occurs during lumbar flexion lumbar movement testing	
Traction		
Traction syndrome	Signs and symptoms of nerve root compression are evident	Intermittent mechanical traction
	No improvement (centralization) occurs with lumbar movement testing	Autotraction
Lateral shift syndrome	The shoulders are out of line with the pelvis in the frontal plane	Autotraction
	Unilateral side-bending restriction occurs during lumbar movement testing	
	The patient's status worsens with pelvic translocation	

Source: Adapted from George SZ, Delitto A. Clinical examination variables discriminate among treatment-based classification groups: A study of construct validity in patients with acute low back pain. *Phys Ther*. 2005;85:308-309.

13

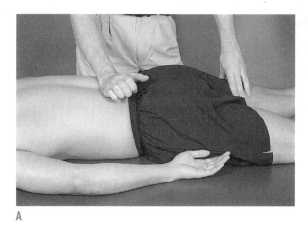
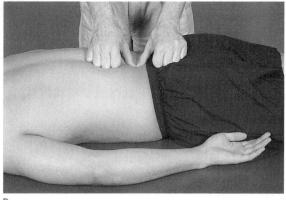

A   B

Figure 13.18   Lumbar spine mobilization techniques. (**A**) Unilateral posteroanterior (PA) glide. (**B**) Transverse glide. Central PA glide is not shown here.

crease pain, and increase radicular symptoms (peripheralization). Forces that centralize pain are emphasized; forces that increase pain or peripheralization are avoided. In testing, motions are evaluated in the following order: spinal flexion, extension, and pelvic translocation (a shear force applied across the pelvis and lumbar spine). The examination is conducted with the patient in the seated, supine, prone, and kneeling positions.[32,33]

Exercises for ROM and strength are incorporated early in a low back injury rehabilitation program. Before stretching and strengthening exercises begin, a brief period (10 to 15 minutes) of cardiovascular activity, such as on a stationary bicycle or upper body ergometer, will enhance the effects of exercise and joint mobilization.

Lumbar Spine Mobilization Techniques

Manual therapy interventions that focus on facilitating normal joint motion should be used with caution as an intervention for segmental hypomobility (see **Figure 13.18**). Mobilizations are typically graded from I through IV.[34] (Grade V represents a high-velocity thrust, a manipulation, and is not covered here.) The mobilization grade is selected based on the desired amount and range of passive motion to be gained at the segment. Grades I and II are helpful for the more acute conditions to relieve pain, and grades III and IV are appropriate for chronic conditions, in which the goal is to increase mobility.

Patients can be instructed in self-mobilization techniques to help relieve facet pain. In this type of exercise, the patient lies in the supine, hook-lying position with knees together and then rocks the hips to the side, rolling the knees from one side to the other, while the shoulders remain on the surface. Additional facet joint motion may be obtained through passive rotation of the involved joints.

With the patient in a side–lying position, the clinician places the fingers on the superior and inferior aspects of the spinous process of the involved level and gently rocks it back and forth to introduce motion to the segment (see **Figure 13.19**).

The Maitland technique employs specific degrees of oscillation or sustained holds to eliminate reproducible signs of pain (see **Figure 13.20**). Graded oscillations of I through IV are directed at pain relief or ROM gains: Grades I and II focus solely on reducing pain, and grades III through IV are used to increase mobility. The oscillations fire both type I postural and type II dynamic mechanoreceptors (position- or pressure-sensitive neurons) to reduce pain and muscle guarding.

Flexibility Exercises

Because the hip and thigh muscles originate in the back and pelvis, flexibility exercises that target these muscles are just as important as those directed at the lumbar muscles. Any hip or thigh muscle with restricted motion that attaches to the pelvis or spine

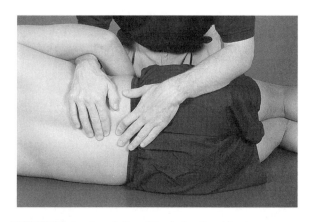

Figure 13.19   Passive rotation of the dysfunctional facet may increase motion and decrease pain.

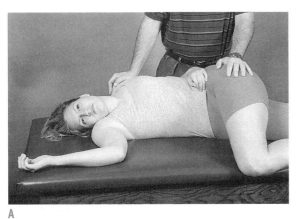 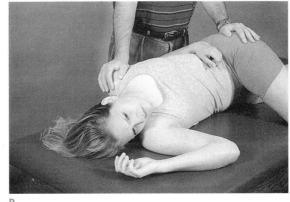

A   B

Figure 13.20 The Maitland technique. (**A**) The left hand rotates the pelvis forward and indirectly applies an axial torque to the thoracic and lumbar spine. The right hand steadies the thorax. (**B**) The same procedure seen from a different angle.

should be included in a lumbar spine rehabilitation program.

Also see the discussion of the following exercises in Chapter 8:

- Hamstring stretch (page 255)
- Quadriceps stretch (page 255)
- Hip flexor stretch (page 256)
- Adductor stretch (page 256)
- Iliotibial band stretch (page 256)

Active Lumbar Rotation Stretch

In the supine position, the patient bends both knees and hips with the feet flat. The knees are then rotated to the same side, while the shoulders remain in contact with the surface (see Figure 13.21). A stretch should be felt in the low back on the side opposite the knees. The position is held for about 20 seconds, and then the stretch is relaxed. This exercise is repeated 3 to 4 times on the same side, and then repeated on the opposite side.

Cat-Cow Stretch

In a quadruped position, the patient arches the back upward as high as possible (see Figure 13.22A) and then sinks the low back down toward the floor as low as possible (see Figure 13.22B).

Stabilization Exercises

The patient must be able to stabilize the pelvis to reduce lumbar spine stresses and allow lower extremity forces (rather than back forces) to produce power during sport activity (see **Table 13.4**). These kinds of stabilization exercises should be incorporated early in the program and be mastered before the patient progresses to agility, functional, or sport-specific activities. They range from simple

A

B

Figure 13.21 Active lumbar rotation stretch.

Figure 13.22 Cat-cow stretch (back press and release).

Table 13.4

Basic Progression of Lumbar Stabilization Exercise

1. Determine the full excursion of lumbar-pelvic motion.
2. Identify and maintain a pelvic-neutral position.
3. Practice extremity motions in a pelvic-neutral position.
4. Superimpose mass body movements.
5. Maintain stabilization during functional and sport-specific activities.

to complex. The exercises employed early in the rehabilitation program focus primarily on body awareness and pelvic positioning. Later exercises emphasize maintenance of the correct pelvic position while performing upper and lower extremity activities.

Pelvic-Neutral Position

The patient is instructed in finding and maintaining a pelvic-neutral position—that is, a midmotion position between the extremes of full anterior and full posterior pelvic tilt. This is the least stressful and most desirable position for the pelvis throughout any activity. The patient rocks the pelvis between anterior and posterior tilts, slowly diminishing the excursion until the pelvis settles into the midposition.

The patient can be instructed in how to find the pelvic-neutral position in the supine, seated, and standing positions. A supine or seated position may be easier for the patient at first. Once comfortable in locating the pelvic-neutral position in one attitude, however, the patient should be instructed in finding this position in the other stances. Once the pelvic-neutral position is found, it should be maintained while performing all activities (see **Figure 13.23**).

Arm and Leg Motions

Exercises involving arm and leg motions include a series of stabilization activities to increase trunk

Figure 13.23 Finding the pelvic-neutral position while supine. The neutral position is the midpoint between full anterior pelvic tilt and posterior pelvic tilt.

stability and control the core muscles during upper and lower extremity movement through reeducation (see **Figure 13.24**). The pelvic-neutral position must be maintained throughout the exercise, a process that is simplified by use of a mirror. The patient should not be allowed to perform any of these exercises unassisted until the pelvic-neutral position can be maintained without either verbal cueing or tactile feedback. The first series of exercises is performed in the supine, hook-lying position.

The second series of stabilization activities is performed in a quadruped position (see **Figure 13.25**). As in the supine, hook-lying exercises, a pelvic-neutral position must be maintained throughout the activity. If the pelvic-neutral position is lost or the patient rolls the hips to the side, the clinician should use verbal and tactile cueing to correct the position. This exercise should be performed on a firm surface; a soft tabletop requires excessive movement of the body.

A further progression of these stabilization activities can be performed while sitting on a Swiss ball. The erect position and the unstable surface of the Swiss ball increase the degree of difficulty.

If additional progression is desired, the same sequence of exercises can be performed in a standing position. Once the patient can perform these exercises, the next advance is to simple functional activities, such as kicking or throwing a ball while maintaining a pelvic-neutral position.

Williams' Flexion and McKenzie Extension Exercises

During the 1950s, Williams' flexion exercises were introduced for the treatment of low back pain. These exercises were the predominant choice for exercise treatment of low back pain until the 1980s, when McKenzie presented his approach to back pain. Although both of these clinicians used exercise to relieve back pain and believed that such pain resulted from stress on the intervertebral disks, their theories, philosophies, and approaches differed radically.

Current trends call for development of an individualized program based on the patient's examination findings. Neither Williams' flexion exercises nor McKenzie's program currently predominates. In fact, specific references to Williams' flexion exercises or McKenzie exercises are now rare. Many clinicians find these exercises to be rather low level, so they advance patients to other exercises that present more of a challenge.

Figure 13.24 Stabilization activities to increase trunk stability. **(A)** Upper extremity movement. The arms start at the sides. One arm is raised overhead, then returned to the start position; the opposite arm is raised overhead, then returned to the start position in alternating windmill fashion. **(B)** Lower extremity movement. The legs start in the hook-lying position. The patient raises one knee toward the chest and then returns it to the start position. The exercise is repeated in an alternating manner with the opposite leg. **(C)** Upper and lower extremity movement. As the left leg is brought toward the chest, the right arm is simultaneously raised overhead. Both extremities are then returned to the start position, and the exercise is repeated with the opposite extremities. **(D)** Once these activities have been mastered without losing the pelvic-neutral position, a further progression in the hook-lying position can include extending one leg fully, then returning it to the start position, and repeating the exercise on the opposite side. **(E)** The next exercise can include extension of both legs simultaneously, followed by return to the start position. Caution must be exercised with each progression to ensure that the patient does not lose the pelvic-neutral position and arch the back.

13

◼ Williams' Flexion Exercises

Williams believed that back pain was the result of human evolution in movement from a quadruped to an upright position; thus he proposed that the standing position was the cause of back pain because it placed the low back in a lordotic curve. He theorized that this increased lordosis was the source of low back pain and suggested that relief could be obtained by stretching the hip flexors and erector spinae and strengthening the abdominal and gluteal muscles. Williams advocated seven exercises to minimize the lumbar curve—pelvic-tilt exercises, partial sit-ups, single knee-to-chest and

bilateral knee-to-chest, hamstring stretching, standing lunges, seated trunk flexion, and full squat (see **Figure 13.26**).

◼ McKenzie Exercises

McKenzie suggested that people spent too much time in a lumbar-flexed position—a primary cause of low back pain. Although McKenzie incorporated some flexion exercises into his programs, his main emphasis was extension. McKenzie's approach to lumbar pain, which was more flexible (no pun intended) than Williams', was based on three primary classifications of pain—postural syndromes,

Figure 13.25 Quadruped stabilization exercises. **(A)** In the proper quadruped position, the shoulders are directly over the hands, which are spread about shoulders'-width apart, and the knees are directly under the hips. **(B)** While the patient maintains a pelvic-neutral position, one arm is raised and returned to start position. The exercise is repeated with the opposite arm. **(C)** One leg is extended off the surface and behind the body, and then returned to the start position. The exercise is repeated with the opposite leg. **(D)** The left leg and right arm are lifted simultaneously and then returned to the start position. The exercise is repeated with the opposite extremities.

derangement syndromes, and dysfunction syndromes. Postural syndromes are the mildest of the lumbar conditions and essentially represent soft-tissue–related lumbar pain that remains localized. Numbness and tingling are absent, and pain is intermittent. Derangement syndromes involve some changes in the intervertebral disk and are associated with more severe symptoms, with possible pain referral into the lower extremity. Changes in motion are seen, and the pain can be either constant or intermittent. A dysfunction is the most severe condition, with the patient demonstrating vertebral position changes that increase disk pressure.

McKenzie advocated six different exercises to relieve low back pain: prone lying flat for 5 minutes, prone lying on elbows, prone press-ups, standing trunk extensions, seated lumbar flexion-extensions, and both knees to chest in supine position (see **Figure 13.27**). The precise regimen is based on the patient's pain complaints.

These exercises emphasize trunk-extension activities. McKenzie theorized that with a disk bulge or herniation, gravity could pull the fragment into proper position, thereby relieving the symptoms and reducing the bulge or herniation. He also proposed that individuals too often sustained a flexed position, which aggravates the lumbar disks, and believed that an extended position is necessary to counteract these abuses.

Balance Progression, Agility Exercises, and Plyometric Exercises

Chapter 8 provides a progression of proprioception, balance, coordination, agility, and plyometric exercises. At the outset, they may not appear to be balance activities for the trunk. Because the trunk depends on the lower extremities for stability, however, these activities are appropriate for low back rehabilitation (see **Table 13.5**). The patient must maintain a pelvic-neutral position during all exercises. Verbal cueing for this activity may be necessary, especially as the patient starts a new activity.

A

B

C1

C2

D

E

F

G

Figure 13.26 Williams' flexion exercises. (**A**) Pelvic tilt. (**B**) Sit-up in knee flexion. (**C**) Single knees to chest (C1) and double knees to chest (C2) to stretch the erector spinae. (**D**) Seated reach to toes to stretch the hamstrings and erector spinae. (**E**) Forward crouch to stretch the iliofemoral ligament. (**F**) Seated flexion. (**G**) Standing squat to strengthen the quadriceps.

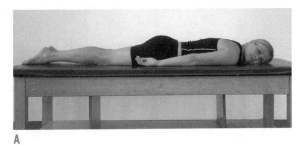

A

B

C

D

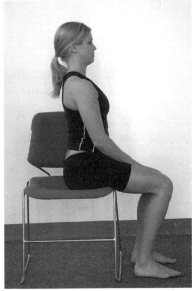

E

F

Figure 13.27 McKenzie exercises. (**A**) Prone lying for 5 minutes. (**B**) Prone lying on elbows for 5 minutes. (**C**) Prone press-ups (10 repetitions, 6 to 8 times per day). (**D**) Trunk extension in standing (10 repetitions, 6 to 8 times a day). The hands are placed in the low back area and extended backward from the trunk. Knees are not flexed. (**E**) Seated lordosis (15 to 20 repetitions, 3 times a day). The lumbar spine is moved from flexion to extension. (**F**) Both knees to chest (10 repetitions). One knee is brought to the chest at a time, and one knee is lowered at a time. This prevents excessive lumbar lordosis during the exercise.

Table 13.5

Sample Early Lumbar Stabilization Program

The patient advances to higher levels if he or she can complete a predetermined number of repetitions in lower levels without difficulty.

Supine Progression

Start position: The patient is supine with knees bent and feet flat on support surface. The patient finds and maintains a neutral spine position throughout the exercise.

Levels	Action
1	Contract abdominal muscles; hold and release
2	Contract gluteal muscles†; hold and release
3	Co-contract gluteal and abdominal muscles; hold and release
4	Co-contract muscles, alternate sides; raise and lower heels
5	Co-contract muscles, alternate sides; raise and lower toes
6	Co-contract muscles, lift both legs off surface and alternately extend knees
7	Co-contract muscles, lift both arms together over head and back down
8	Co-contract muscles, alternate sides; lift arms up over head and back down
9	Co-contract muscles, lift both legs together, combine arm motions from level 8 with alternating knee extension

Prone Progression

Start position: The patient is prone with a pillow placed for support under the pelvis and abdomen and arms resting overhead. The patient finds and maintains a neutral spine position throughout the exercise.

Levels	Action
1	Contract abdominal muscles, hold and release; contract gluteal muscles, hold and release
2	Co-contract abdominal and gluteal muscles; hold and release
3	Co-contract abdominal and gluteal muscles, contract adductors; hold and release
4	Co-contract abdominal and gluteal muscles, first contract adductors and then hip extensors to alternately raise legs
5	Co-contract abdominal and gluteal muscles, first contract adductors and then bilateral hip extensors to raise both legs at once
6	Co-contract abdominal and gluteal muscles, alternate sides; lift one arm up overhead and lower, then the other arm
7	Co-contract abdominal and gluteal muscles, combine levels 5 and 6; the arm and leg on opposite sides are raised and lowered together (raise left arm and right leg and lower, then raise right arm and left leg and lower)

Quadruped Progression

Start position: The patient is on hands and knees and finds and maintains a neutral spine position throughout the exercise.

Levels	Action
1	Contract abdominal muscles; hold and release
2	Contract gluteal muscles; hold and release
3	Co-contract gluteal and abdominal muscles; hold and release
4	Co-contract abdominal and gluteal muscles, shift weight anterior and posterior
5	Co-contract abdominal and gluteal muscles, alternate sides; straighten and extend one leg and return to start position, then the other leg
6	Co-contract abdominal and gluteal muscles, alternate sides; straighten and extend one arm in front, then the other
7	Co-contract abdominal and gluteal muscles, alternate sides; extend and straighten opposite arm and leg simultaneously

Bridging Progression

Start position: The patient is supine with knees bent and feet flat on support surface. The patient lifts the pelvis off the surface (the abdomen and pelvis should form a "flat" surface) and finds and maintains a neutral spine position throughout the exercise.

Levels	Action
1	Contract abdominal muscles; hold and release
2	Contract gluteal muscles; hold and release
3	Co-contract abdominal and gluteal muscles; hold and release
4	Co-contract abdominal and gluteal muscles, alternate sides; lift heels off surface and lower
5	Co-contract abdominal and gluteal muscles, alternate sides; lift toes off surface and lower
6	Co-contract abdominal and gluteal muscles, alternate sides; lift foot off surface and lower
7	Co-contract abdominal and gluteal muscles, alternate sides; extend knee, lower leg to surface, slide heel back to start position
8	Same as for level 7, but without letting the leg touch the floor

(continues)

13

Table 13.5

Sample Early Lumbar Stabilization Program *(Continued)*

Standing Progression

Start position: The patient stands with the feet shoulder width apart and finds and maintains a neutral spine position throughout the exercise.

Levels	Action
1	Contract abdominals; hold and release
2	Contract gluteals; hold and release
3	Co-contract abdominal and gluteal muscles—hold and release
4	Maintain co-contraction in walking
5	Maintain co-contraction while performing semisquats (no more than 30° to 40° of hip flexion)

Note: When alternating sides, the patient performs the action first on one side and then on the other.

* Use the command "Pull your navel to your spine."

† Use the command "Tighten your muscles as if stopping urination midflow."

Source: Adapted with permission from the Dynamic Lumbar Stabilization Program, The San Francisco Spine Institute, 1989.

Reproduced with permission from Dynamic Lumbar Stabilization Program, The San Francisco Spine Institute, Daly City, CA 1989.

References

1. Bresford ZM, Kendall RW, Willick SE. Lumbar facet syndromes. *Curr Sports Med Rep.* 2010;9:50–56.

2. Varlotta GP, Lefkowitz TR, Schweitzer M, et al. The lumbar facet joint: A review of current knowledge: Part 1: Anatomy, biomechanics, and grading. *Skeletal Radiol.* 2011;40:13–23.

3. Mooney V, Robertson J. The facet syndrome. *Clin Orthop. Relat Res.* 1976;115:149–156.

4. Revel M, Poiraudeau S, Auleley GR, et al. Capacity of the clinical picture to characterize low back pain relieved by facet joint anesthesia: Proposed criteria to identify patients with painful facet joints. *Spine.* 1998;23:1972–1976.

5. Varlotta GP, Lefkowitz TR, Schweitzer M, et al. The lumbar facet joint: A review of current knowledge: Part II: Diagnosis and management. *Skeletal Radiol.* 2011;40: 149–157.

6. Czervionke LF, Fenton DS. Fat-saturated MR imaging in the detection of inflammatory facet arthropathy (facet synovitis) in the lumbar spine. *Pain Med.* 2008;9:400–406.

7. Cabraja M, Abbushi A, Woiciechowsky C, Kroppenstedt S. The short- and mid-term effect of dynamic interspinous distraction in the treatment of recurrent lumbar facet joint pain. *Eur Spine J.* 2009;18:1686–1694.

8. Leclaire R, Fortin L, Lambert R, et al. Radiofrequency facet joint denervation in the treatment of low back pain: A placebo-controlled clinical trial to assess efficacy. *Spine.* 2001;26:1411–1417.

9. Cohen SP, Williams, KA, Kurihara C, et al. Multicenter, randomized, comparative cost-effectiveness study comparing 0, 1, and 2 diagnostic medial branch (facet joint nerve) block treatment paradigms before lumbar facet radiofrequency denervation. *Anesthesiol.* 2010;113:395–405.

10. Snijders CJ, Hermans PFG, Niesing R, et al. The influence of slouching and lumbar support on iliolumbar ligaments, intervertebral discs, and sacroiliac joints. *Clin Biomech.* 2004;19:323–329.

11. Feuerstein M, Berkowitz SM, Huang GD. Predictors of occupational low back disability: Implications for secondary prevention. *J Occup Environ Med.* 1999;41:1024–1031.

12. Weininger P, Schultz A, Hertz H. Conservative management of thoracolumbar and lumbar spine compression and burst fractures: Functional and radiographic outcomes in 136 cases treated by closed reduction and casting. *Arch Orthop Trauma Surg.* 2009;129:207–219.

13. Arregui-Dalmases C, Ash JH, Del Pozo E, et al. Characterization of the transverse and spinous processes: Fracture forces under quasi-static and dynamic loading. *Biomed Sci Instrum.* 2010;46:154–159.

14. Barker PJ, Freeman AD, Urquhart DM, et al. The middle layer of lumbar fascia can transmit tensile forces capable of fracturing the lumbar transverse process: An experimental study. *Clin Biomech.* 2010;25:505–509.

15. Ganiyusufoglu AK, Onat L, Karatoprak O, et al. Diagnostic accuracy of magnetic resonance imaging versus computed tomography in stress fractures of the lumbar spine. *Clin Radiol.* 2010;65:902–907.

16. Mudd LM, Fornetti W, Pivarnik JM. Bone mineral density in collegiate female athletes: Comparisons among sports. *J Athl Train.* 2007;42:403–408.

17. Spivak JM, Vaccaro AR, Colter JM. Thoracolumbar spine trauma: II. Principles of management. *J Am Acad Orthop Surg.* 1995;3:353–360.

18. Spivak JM, Vaccaro AR, Colter JM. Thoracolumbar spine trauma: I. Evaluation and classification. *J Am Acad Orthop Surg.* 1995;3:345–352.

19. Min S, Nakazato K, Yamamoto Y, et al. Cartilage intermediate layer protein gene is associated with lumbar disc degeneration in male, but not female, collegiate athletes. *Am J Sports Med.* 2010;38:2552–2557.

20. Boden SD, Wiesel SW. Lumbar spine imaging: Role in clinical decision making. *J Am Acad Orthop Surg.* 1996;4:238–248.

21. Young JL, Press JM, Herring SA. The disc at risk in athletes: Perspectives on operative and nonoperative care. *Med Sci Sports Exerc.* 1997;29(suppl 7):S222–S232.

22. Wheeler AH. Diagnosis and management of low back pain and sciatica. *Am Fam Physician.* 1995;52:1333–1341, 1347–1348.

23. Standaert CJ, Herring SA, Halpern B, King O. Spondylolysis. *Phys Med Rehabil Clin N Am.* 2000;11:785–803.

24. Lonstein JE. Spondylolisthesis in children: Cause, natural history, and management. *Spine.* 1999;24:2640–2648.

25. Purcell L, Micheli L. Low back in young athletes. *Sports Health: A Multidisciplinary Approach.* 2009;1:212–221.

26. Skinner HB. *Diagnosis and Treatment in Orthopedics.* Norwalk, CT: Appleton & Lange; 1995.

27. Schneiderman GA, McLain RF, Hambly MF, Nielsen SL. The pars defect as a pain source: A histologic study. *Spine.* 1995;20:1761–1764.

28. Kalichman L, Hunter DJ. Degenerative lumbar spondylolisthesis: Anatomy, biomechanics and risk factors. *J Back Musculoskelet Rehabil.* 2008;21:1–12.

29. Letts M, Smallman T, Afanasiev R, Gouw G. Fracture of the pars interarticularis in adolescent athletes: A clinical–biomechanical analysis. *J Pediatr Orthop.* 1986; 6:40–46.

30. Frymoyer JW. Degenerative spondylolisthesis: Diagnosis and treatment. *J Am Acad Orthop Surg.* 1994;2:9–15.

31. Hambly MF, Wiltse LL, Peek RD. Spondylolisthesis, in Watkins RG (ed), *The Spine in Sports.* St. Louis, MO: Mosby-Year Book; 1996:157–163.

32. Manal TJ, Claytor R. The Delitto classification scheme and the management of lumbar-spine dysfunction. *Athl Ther Today.* 2005;10:6–12.

33. George SZ, Delitto A. Clinical examination variables discriminate among treatment-based classification groups: A study of construct validity in patients with acute low back pain. *Phys Ther.* 2005;85:306–314.

34. Edmond SL. *Manipulation and Mobilization: Extremity and Spinal Techniques.* St. Louis, MO: Mosby-Year Book; 1993.

13

Abdominal and Thorax Injuries

Erin M. Rosenberg, MS, ATC
William Rosenberg, MD

Cardiac Tamponade

CLINICAL PRESENTATION

History

Blunt trauma to the chest.
Feeling of impending doom.

Observation

Distended neck veins.
Severe agitation.
Anxiety.

Functional Status

The patient may display the signs and symptoms of shock.

Physical Examination Findings

Distant or muffled heart sounds.
Tachycardia.
Hypotension.
Paradoxical pulse.

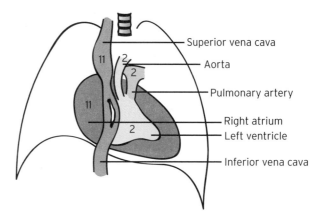

Figure 14.1 Cardiac tamponade. As effusion develops, both atria and ventricles are compressed. Inflow pressure in the superior and inferior vena cavae decreases, right atrium ventricular volume falls, and arterial pressure is reduced. *Source*: Reproduced with permission from Henry MM, Thompson JN (eds). *Clinical Surgery*. Philadelphia, PA: WB Saunders; 2001.

Cardiac tamponade is most commonly the result of a penetrating torso wound, which is exceedingly rare in athletics. However, it can also be caused by blunt trauma. Injury to the inelastic pericardium allows blood to fill the pericardial cavity; as the pressure builds, the heart muscle becomes compressed. The thin walls of the atria collapse, causing decreased end-diastolic volume.[1] Further increases in pressure affect the ventricular wall, increasing end-diastolic pressure. With reduced blood volume entering and leaving the heart, cardiac output falls, and hypotension and shock occur. A lethal condition can rapidly develop. Adults can accommodate only about 100 mL of pericardial blood without experiencing shock.

Penetrating trauma causes pericardial bleeding due to a hole in the pericardium that is too small to vent blood. In contrast, blunt trauma disrupts epicardial vessels or ruptures the heart. The signs and symptoms of cardiac tamponade can be delayed for days to weeks after injury. Symptoms then develop as a result of rebleeding or effusions from pericarditis (see **Figure 14.1**).

Differential Diagnosis

Myocardial contusion, pulmonary contusion, rib or sternal fracture.

Medical Diagnostic Tests

The pressure within the superior vena cava, the central venous pressure, is greater than 15 mm Hg. A paradoxical pulse also suggests tamponade.

Imaging Techniques

Cardiac ultrasound enables rapid and accurate diagnosis of cardiac tamponade. Echocardiography can reveal characteristic features of this condition, such as right atrial compression and right ventricular diastolic collapse. Rapid-imaging spiral computed tomography (CT) scans are accurate in diagnosing tamponade.

Definitive Diagnosis

The definitive diagnosis is based on clinical examination followed by cardiac ultrasound or CT scans revealing a fluid-filled pericardial cavity.

Pathomechanics and Functional Limitations

Once the patient begins to demonstrate the signs and symptoms of cardiac tamponade, signs of shock and a rapid decline in vital signs occur rapidly. Immediate definitive treatment is necessary to save the patient's life.

Immediate Management

The patient is treated for shock and immediately transported for medical care.

Medical Management

A patient in severe shock with suspected tamponade requires immediate pericardial decompression. This can be accomplished through a subxiphoid pericardial window, thoracotomy, or sternotomy. Controversy exists regarding the value of therapeutic pericardiocentesis. Aspiration may be warranted in those patients with urgent signs of severe tamponade. Aspiration and pericardial windows increase the patient's viability, but surgical decompression of the thorax is necessary.

In those individuals whose conditions appear nonemergent, IV fluids are begun with close cardiac and hemodynamic monitoring. The need for intubation and oxygenation is assessed. Small changes

paradoxical pulse A pulse that becomes weaker during inspiration and stronger during expiration.

14

pericardiocentesis A diagnostic procedure in which a needle is used to draw fluid from the pericardium.

in pericardial blood volume can result in significant hemodynamic changes.

■ Estimated Amount of Time Lost

The amount of time lost from sport depends on the severity of the heart-muscle damage, which is determined by a thorough cardiac evaluation. The patient may have a complete recovery or may experience long-term disability.

■ Return-to-Play Criteria

Recovery from surgery and return to physical activity are closely monitored. Upon complete recovery from the surgical decompression, physical activity is progressed gradually under close medical supervision.

Myocardial Contusion

CLINICAL PRESENTATION

History

Blunt impact to the sternum.
Mild to severe chest pain.

Observation

Pallor.

Functional Status

Shock is possible.
The patient may be unconscious.

Physical Examination Findings

Tachycardia.
Irregular heart rate.
Hypotension.

---

volume expanders Benign IV agents that allow temporary restoration of blood volume without having to wait for blood type matching.

Myocardial contusion occurs when blunt trauma creates forces that compress the heart between the sternum and the thoracic vertebrae. It can also occur from rapid chest-wall deceleration. The heart rebounds against the sternum, and the ensuing cardiac-muscle damage can cause death. Life-threatening ventricular dysfunction or ventricular arrhythmia may develop. Myocardial contusions can occur in contact sports; baseball (being hit by a pitched ball); lacrosse; and activities such as cycling, skiing, rock climbing, and motor sports.[2]

Most cases of myocardial contusion are minor. Severe contusions are unusual in contact sports, and most result in sudden death. The affected individuals die of heart-muscle laceration, valve disruption, transmural hematoma, or, in rare situations,

main coronary artery occlusion. Death occurs from hemodynamic decompensation.

Differential Diagnosis

Cardiac tamponade, pulmonary contusion, rib or sternal fracture.

Imaging Techniques

Echocardiography provides an image of ventricular hypokinesis.

Definitive Diagnosis

Along with echocardiography, 24-hour cardiac rhythm monitoring, serial measurements of troponins, and creatine phosphokinase enzyme monitoring confirm the diagnosis.[2]

Pathomechanics and Functional Limitations

Patients with minor contusions do very well, typically having no long-term problems. Patients with severe contusions have high death rates.

■ Immediate Management

If the signs and symptoms of cardiac involvement are present (e.g., tachycardia, irregular heart rate, hypotension), the patient must be immediately transported for medical care.

■ Medications

Ionotropic agents, peripheral vascular drugs, and **volume expanders** are used for emergent care.

■ Medical Management

The primary goal in minor cardiac injury is to monitor cardiac function and intervene appropriately to prevent hemodynamic collapse. In severe injury, hemodynamic support is necessary during and after surgical intervention. In patients with myocardial contusions, cardiac monitoring (electrocardiogram) and hemodynamic monitoring of blood pressure, pulse, and neck venous distention are important and may identify more serious injury. After 24 hours of normal results, the patient may be discharged.

> **Practice Tip**
>
> Hospitalization with cardiac monitoring is necessary for patients with mild myocardial contusions. Most dysrhythmias occur within the first 24 hours after trauma occurs.[2]

■ Estimated Amount of Time Lost

The amount of time lost from competition depends on cardiac-muscle damage and recovery as demonstrated by cardiac function. Mild contusions are expected to result in little time lost. Severe cardiac-muscle damage may result in permanent cardiac-muscle dysfunction and long-term participation loss.

◾ Return-to-Play Criteria

Progressive aerobic exercise and strengthening are permitted, with progression to full sport participation as tolerated by the cardiovascular system.

Pulmonary Contusion

CLINICAL PRESENTATION

History

Blunt blow to the chest.
Severe chest pain.
Dyspnea.

Observation

Cough.
Hemoptysis.

Physical Examination Findings

Tachypnea.
Diminished breath sounds.
Rales.
Respiratory distress.

A pulmonary contusion comprises a bruise of the lung that is associated with hemorrhage and edema into the lung parenchyma.[2] This injury occurs from blunt trauma, which results in rib fractures that displace and penetrate the lung parenchyma. Pulmonary contusions also occur with rapid chest-wall deceleration. In this case, the lung rebounds against the chest wall, resulting in a contusion. Children are more prone to pulmonary contusions because their chest walls are compressed and less force is dissipated by their ribs.

The lung insult results in interstitial bleeding, followed by edema and alveolar thickening. The injured lung develops decreased blood flow with increased pulmonary vascular resistance. Ventilation–perfusion mismatch occurs from edema and pulmonary pressure changes. Depending on the contusion size, respiratory distress is mild to severe. Symptoms may not become significant until 24 to 48 hours after injury.

Differential Diagnosis

Myocardial contusion, cardiac tamponade, rib or sternal fracture, pneumothorax.

Imaging Techniques

Chest radiography should be obtained initially. Findings include focal or patchy infiltrates, although they are often not present until 4 to 6 hours after injury and may take as long as 48 hours to appear.

CT scan allows imaging of a pulmonary contusion immediately after injury and is more sensitive than radiography.

> **Practice Tip**
>
> CT scan of the chest is superior to chest x-ray in identifying pulmonary contusions and in determining the extent of injury. In two published cases of athletic-related pulmonary contusions, chest radiographs revealed no abnormalities while CT scans detected areas of opacification consistent with pulmonary contusions.[3]

Definitive Diagnosis

Diagnosis is based on physical findings and confirmed by chest radiographs and/or CT scan.

Pathomechanics and Functional Limitations

The shortness of breath and chest pain associated with pulmonary contusion can be debilitating. In addition, symptom onset can be delayed after initial injury. Failure to recognize progressive respiratory compromise can result in loss of respiratory function and death.

hemoptysis
Coughing up blood.

◾ Immediate Management

The first priority is to ensure an open airway, breathing, and circulation. Immediate transport to the hospital should be arranged.

◾ Medications

Aggressive pain control is initiated using oral or injectable narcotic analgesics.

parenchyma The internal functional tissues of an organ.

◾ Medical Intervention

Mild pulmonary contusions can be managed on an outpatient basis with supportive care and close observation for 7 to 10 days after injury. Hospitalization is necessary for observation when severe lung contusion is suspected or diagnosed. Observation with monitoring of vital signs and serial chest radiographs may be all that is necessary. However, with significant respiratory distress, intensive care unit admission is necessary. Large-bore IV lines are required for fluid resuscitation and tissue perfusion in the presence of shock. Because the lung damage is very sensitive to fluid balance, judicious fluid management is necessary, including the possible use of diuretics once the patient's tissue perfusion and urine output are restored.

Intercostal anesthetic blocks for rib fractures are helpful for pain relief. Epidural catheters may be used for prolonged pain control. A chest tube may need to be placed if a hemothorax or pneumothorax exists. Aggressive pulmonary drainage

14

with vigorous suctioning, chest physiotherapy, and postural drainage is important to maintain the patient's airway and remove excessive secretions. Intubation and ventilatory support are necessary in patients with severe respiratory distress and ventilatory failure.

Injury-Specific Treatment and Rehabilitation Concerns

The gradual return to exercise training involves an aerobic program, weight training, and functional training after symptom resolution.

Estimated Amount of Time Lost

Return to activity is based on the injury severity, with the amount of time lost from competition ranging from 1 to 4 weeks.

Return-to-Play Criteria

Return is based on exercise tolerance and the ability to progress through functional exercises.

Spontaneous Pneumomediastinum

CLINICAL PRESENTATION

History
Retrosternal chest pain.
Neck pain.

Observation
The patient often appears anxious.

Functional Status
Shortness of breath.
Dysphagia.
Dysphonia.

Physical Examination Findings
Subcutaneous emphysema over the supraclavicular area.
Hoarseness.
Hamman sign (precordial crackles or crunching sounds with each heartbeat).

occult Hidden or not readily detectable by laboratory tests or physical examination.

In spontaneous pneumomediastinum, free air enters the mediastinum as a result of alveolar rupture, which occurs because of elevated alveolar pressure. This pressure may result from decompression diving, coughing, vomiting, or sudden exertion. It is often associated with the Valsalva maneuver.[4]

Differential Diagnosis
Pneumothorax, hemothorax, lung contusion, rib fracture, myocardial contusion, pleural effusion.

Imaging Techniques
Chest and cervical spine radiographs are typically diagnostic for spontaneous pneumomediastinum, revealing free air within the mediastinal tissue. Lateral cervical spine films may demonstrate free air in the deep cervical tissues and behind the trachea and larynx. CT scan may be helpful in the diagnosis, but the priority is to identify the underlying cause, such as pneumothorax. Imaging with a Hypaque swallow may be necessary to exclude an esophageal injury.

Definitive Diagnosis
Diagnosis is confirmed by a chest radiograph showing mediastinal air.

Pathomechanics and Functional Limitations
This condition is typically self-limiting and does not lead to any long-term functional deficits.

Immediate Management

Activity is discontinued, and medical attention sought immediately. The patient's airway is maintained, and respiration and circulation are regularly monitored. Associated injuries are excluded (see the "Differential Diagnosis" section).

Medications

Pain medications may be necessary.

Medical Management

Medical management includes rest and pain management. No evidence-based medical guidelines for this condition have been developed yet, so the treatment administered varies.[4] Some sources advocate hospitalization for patients with spontaneous pneumomediastinum because of the potential for complications (e.g., pneumothorax). Others believe that no restrictions are necessary. A CT scan may be prudent to evaluate for occult pneumothorax, which occurs in 18% of patients with spontaneous pneumomediastinum.

Injury-Specific Treatment and Rehabilitation Concerns

Progression to aerobic activities and weight training are permitted as tolerated. The patient must be counseled against performing the Valsalva maneuver.

Estimated Amount of Time Lost

Full activity can usually be resumed 7 to 10 days after injury.

Return-to-Play Criteria

The patient must demonstrate symptom-free, sport-specific training levels.

Pneumothorax

CLINICAL PRESENTATION

History

Sudden, unrelieved shortness of breath.
Mild to severe chest pain localized to the affected lung, which is often pleuritic.

Observation

Dyspnea, especially on exertion.
Dry cough.
Asymmetric chest-wall expansion.

Functional Status

Altered breathing pattern.

Physical Examination Findings

Possible chest-wall tenderness.
Tachypnea.
Tachycardia.
Decreased fremitus.
Hyperresonance.
Diminished breath sounds.
Patient complaints can vary greatly.

Pneumothorax is the result of air leakage from the lung into the pleural space, usually from lung parenchyma disruption. Greater air pressure in the pleural cavity than in the lung causes lung collapse and respiratory compromise, with the degree of compromise depending on the air volume in the pleural cavity. Pneumothorax can be either spontaneous or traumatic (see **Figure 14.2**). Spontaneous pneumothorax occurs predominantly in men 20 to 40 years old.

Spontaneous Pneumothorax

Spontaneous pneumothorax typically occurs without trauma. Although its cause is not fully under-

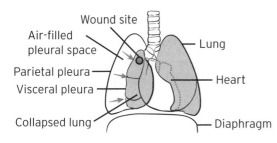

Figure 14.2 Pneumothorax occurs when air enters the pleura from an opening in the chest wall and causes intrapleural pressure to increase.

stood, the most widely accepted explanation cites rupture of subpleural blebs.[5] The origin of these blebs is unknown. They are thought to be congenital, but associated factors such as a tall and thin body build, tobacco smoking, or abuse of substances such as "ecstasy" may increase the risk of occurrence. Activities that increase intrathoracic pressure have also been postulated as a contributing factor. Most cases, however, are unrelated to exercise and sports. Recurrence rates vary from 20% to 50%.[5]

Traumatic Pneumothorax

Traumatic pneumothorax can result from either blunt or penetrating trauma and is the most common intrathoracic injury after blunt trauma.[2] Pneumothorax may result from a rib fracture penetrating the lung, a decelerating injury resulting in a lung tear, a crush injury disrupting alveoli, or a sudden increase in intrathoracic pressure.[6] Multiple injury mechanisms warrant a high index of suspicion for this condition.

Differential Diagnosis

Hemothorax, spontaneous pneumomediastinum, rib fracture, myocardial contusion, pulmonary embolus.

Imaging Techniques

Posteroanterior and lateral chest radiographs are obtained to diagnose pneumothorax.

Definitive Diagnosis

Clinical findings are confirmed with chest radiographs that reveal loss of lung volume and air in the pleural space.

Pathomechanics and Functional Limitations

Loss of usable lung volume results in diminished oxygen exchange and shortness of breath. Tension pneumothorax can occur if this condition is left untreated, with resultant shock and death.

Immediate Management

The patient's airway, breathing, and circulation must be monitored and vital signs checked every 5 minutes. Oxygen should be administered if the patient is experiencing shortness of breath or is tachypneic. If the patient is unstable and a tension pneumothorax is suspected, qualified personnel may perform needle decompression via the second intercostal space at the midclavicular line. If onsite facilities are available and the patient is stable, a chest radiograph should be obtained. The patient should be transported to the hospital (via ambulance if markedly symptomatic) for appropriate definitive diagnostic examination and management.

Immediate care is important, but emergent care is not always necessary. Patients with suspected

fremitus Palpable vibration, as felt when placing the hand on the chest or throat during speaking.

embolus Solid, liquid, or gaseous mass blocking a passageway.

14

pneumothorax should not be left unattended and should be continually monitored until the medical examination is complete. Individuals with a suspected pneumothorax should not be allowed to travel by airplane, as changes in cabin pressure have the potential to acutely exacerbate the pneumothorax.

Medications

Oral, intramuscular, or IV analgesics are required during and for a short period after hospitalization with chest-tube placement. Nonsurgical treatment requires few or no medications.

Medical Management and Surgical Intervention

Pneumothorax is typically managed with placement of a chest tube (see **ST** 14.1). However, a small, asymptomatic pneumothorax can occasionally be managed with serial chest radiographs and close observation. Daily chest radiographs are recommended until resolution is achieved.

Injury-Specific Treatment and Rehabilitation Concerns

Advancement through aerobic activities, strength training, and sport-specific functional progression is permitted as tolerated.

Estimated Amount of Time Lost

Return to play is allowed 3 to 4 weeks after symptoms resolve.

Return-to-Play Criteria

The patient must delay normal sport activities until chest radiographs demonstrate that the pneumothorax has completely resolved.

Tension Pneumothorax

Tension pneumothorax is characterized by the rapid development of large air volumes that are trapped within the pleural space. This condition can result from blunt trauma, a penetrating chest wound, or a spontaneous pneumothorax.

The defect in the lung parenchyma or bronchus may act as a flap valve, allowing air to enter the pleural space with each breath but not escape back through the lung or tracheobronchial tree. As intrapleural pressure increases, the lung collapses and the mediastinal structures shift away from the side of the pneumothorax. The large veins (vena cava)

CLINICAL PRESENTATION

History

Blunt trauma and/or penetrating chest wound that may involve the lung itself.

Observation

Difficulty breathing.
Bulging of the chest-wall intercostal muscles and supraclavicular area.
Neck-vein distention.
Cyanosis.
Tracheal deviation to the side opposite the pneumothorax.

Functional Status

Severe, rapid, progressive respiratory distress.
Increasing air hunger.

Physical Examination Findings

Weak pulse.
Drop in blood pressure.
Chest hyperresonance on the side of the pneumothorax but with decreased breath sounds.
These findings vary and are not consistently present.

---

in the mediastinum collapse, venous return to the heart is compromised, and hemodynamic instability ensues (see **Figure 14.3**).

Sucking Chest Wound (Open Chest Injury)

An open chest-wall injury may allow air to enter the pleural space directly due to negative intrathoracic pressure; this outcome occurs most commonly after a shotgun blast or impalement injury. Pneumothorax or hemothorax may also be present. Immediate treatment consists of placement of an occlusive dressing that is taped on three sides. This arrangement allows air to escape through the open side but prevents air from being sucked back into the chest with inspiration. A full, four-sided occlusion dressing may exacerbate or increase the pneumothorax. A sucking chest wound is a medical emergency that can result in death if untreated.

Differential Diagnosis

Pneumothorax, hemothorax, myocardial injury, pulmonary embolus, cardiac tamponade.

Definitive Diagnosis

Clinical findings, response to emergency treatment, and chest radiographs indicate the diagnosis.

Pathomechanics and Functional Limitations

Rapid respiratory and circulatory collapse occurs because of increased intrathoracic pressure on the lung, heart, and major vessels. If function is restored, no long-term functional loss typically occurs. Conversely, failure to recognize and treat the condition is life threatening.

Chest-Tube Placement

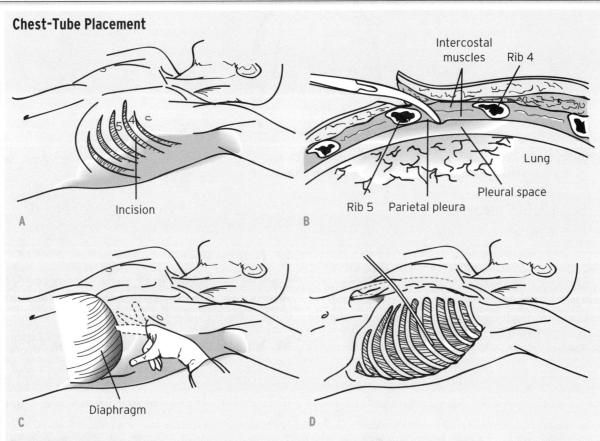

A — Incision

B — Intercostal muscles, Rib 4, Lung, Pleural space, Rib 5, Parietal pleura

C — Diaphragm

D

Indications

Greater than 20% pneumothorax with respiratory distress.

Procedure Overview

1. A local anesthetic is administered.
2. A 20- to 22-French diameter tube or 16-French Thal tube is inserted in the fifth intercostal space at the anterior or midaxillary line. The tube is passed through the skin and subcutaneous tissue and over the top of the rib. It is then passed through the intercostal muscle and into the pleural space.
3. The opposite end of the tube is connected to an underwater seal with negative suction.
4. Negative pressure (suction) should be maintained at a water level of approximately 20 cm to obtain adequate drainage.
5. The chest tube is maintained until the air leak has sealed (no water-level fluctuation with inspiration) and no air is leaking, with fluid drainage of less than 100 mL per 24 hours.
6. A chest radiograph is taken at the end of the procedure to evaluate lung reexpansion and tube location.

Functional Limitations

While the tube is in place, hospitalization is required. The tube is removed when it has stopped functioning (no water-level fluctuation). Daily radiographs are performed to document improvement. Upon discharge, the patient rests and follows up with radiographs to confirm progressive resolution of the pneumothorax.

Implications for Rehabilitation

Because of the significant recurrence rate for pneumothorax, the patient and athletic trainer must be educated in signs and symptoms that signal reemergence of this condition. Slow, conservative return to activity is suggested.

Potential Complications

Potential complications include unilateral pulmonary edema from rapid reexpansion, lung injury, chest-wall bleeding, air leak, tube occlusion, persistent pneumothorax, subcutaneous emphysema, diaphragm laceration, infection, extrapleural tube positioning, and cardiac arrhythmia.

Comments

Tube placement and size vary with respect to the diagnosis. For example, to treat a hemothorax, a 36-French diameter tube is placed in the fifth or sixth intercostal space at the midaxillary line.

Source: Reproduced with permission from Pearson FG, Cooper JD, Deslauriers J, et al. *Thoracic Surgery*, ed 2. New York, NY: Churchill Livingstone; 2002.

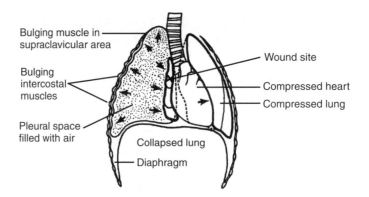

Figure 14.3 Tension pneumothorax. When air enters the pleural space but cannot exit, a tension pneumothorax develops. Continued leaking of air from the lung into the pleural space causes the lung to collapse until it is reduced to 2 to 3 in. diameter.

■ Immediate Management

Placement of a partially sealed occlusive dressing allows air to exit through the unsealed dressing side, while preventing air from reentering during breathing (see **Figure 14.4**). Complete occlusion may increase the pneumothorax.

Qualified personnel can decompress the pleural space by inserting a large-bore (14-gauge) needle through the anterior chest wall in the second intercostal space at the midclavicular line.[6] This technique is a quick method for decompressing the pleural space by allowing trapped air to flow out through the needle and can be life-saving. It must be followed by formal chest-tube placement.

■ Medications

Oral, intramuscular, or IV analgesics are required during and for a short period after hospitalization with chest-tube placement.

■ Medical and Surgical Intervention

When the patient reaches the emergency room, a large-bore chest tube (24 French) is placed into the fifth or sixth intercostal space at the midaxillary

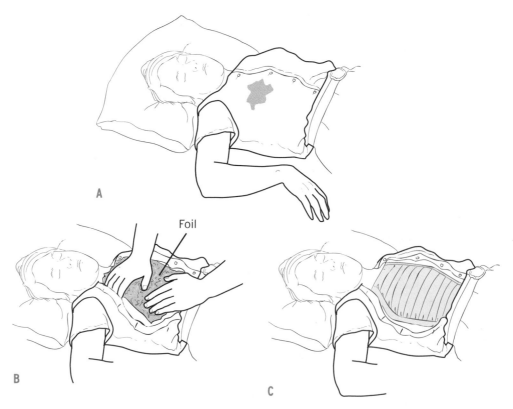

Figure 14.4 In an open chest injury, air moves in and out of the wound, remaining in the pleural space and causing a tension pneumothorax. (**A**) This partially sealed occlusive dressing allows air to exit through the unsealed side, while preventing air from reentering during breathing. Complete occlusion might increase the pneumothorax. (**B**) One side of the dressing should be left untaped so that air can exit the wound during breathing; however, the dressing should be snug enough so that air does not enter the wound from the untaped side (**C**).

line. A larger tube (36 to 40 French) should be placed if the patient has an associated hemothorax. The tube is connected to an underwater seal with negative suction. A chest radiograph is obtained to ensure adequate lung expansion, and vital signs and blood oxygen levels are closely monitored.

■ Postinjury/Postoperative Management

Once the patient is stabilized, serial chest radiographs are taken to monitor pneumothorax resolution. The chest-tube removal criteria are the same as for a pneumothorax.

■ Injury-Specific Treatment and Rehabilitation Concerns

Advancement through aerobic activities, strength training, and sport-specific functional progression is permitted as tolerated.

■ Estimated Amount of Time Lost

Return to play is permitted 3 to 4 weeks after symptoms resolve.

■ Return-to-Play Criteria

The patient must delay normal activities until chest radiographs indicate that the pneumothorax has completely resolved.

Hemothorax

CLINICAL PRESENTATION

History

Blunt trauma or a penetrating chest-wall injury.
Sudden, unrelieved shortness of breath.
Mild to severe chest pain localized to the affected lung, which is often pleuritic.

Observation

Dyspnea, especially on exertion.
Dry cough.
Asymmetric chest-wall expansion.

Functional Status

Shock manifestations: apprehension, thirst, cold, clammy, chills, pallor, weak pulse, decreased blood pressure.

Physical Examination Findings

Possible chest-wall tenderness.
Tachypnea.
Tachycardia.
Diminished breath sounds.

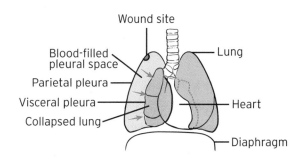

Figure 14.5 A hemothorax occurs when major blood vessels are lacerated and blood is present in the pleural space outside the lung.

A hemothorax is the result of either blunt chest-wall trauma or a penetrating chest-wall injury; it often occurs in combination with a pneumothorax. In this condition, blood occupies the pleural space solely or in combination with air, resulting in respiratory compromise (see **Figure 14.5**). The blood source can be the lung, chest wall, major or lesser vessels, diaphragm, or abdominal organs. With major blood loss, shock may occur. A significant hemothorax is unlikely to result from athletic competition.

Differential Diagnosis

Pneumothorax, tension pneumothorax, myocardial trauma, pulmonary embolus.

Imaging Techniques

Chest radiographs are taken while the patient is in the supine and lateral supine positions. If the films are not diagnostic, lateral or decubitus films can help to differentiate pleural fluid from contusion or intraparenchymal hemorrhage. Ultrasound may be beneficial in identifying pleural fluid. CT scan is also useful in differentiating pleural fluid from parenchymal fluid.

Definitive Diagnosis

The diagnosis is based on clinical signs and chest radiographs; CT is helpful in establishing the type of fluid present.

Pathomechanics and Functional Limitations

Loss of usable lung volume results in diminished oxygen exchange and shortness of breath. Tension pneumothorax can occur if a hemothorax is left untreated, with resultant shock and death.

■ Immediate Management

Airway, breathing, and circulation should be monitored and a possible need for cardiopulmonary resuscitation (CPR) anticipated. Any external bleeding must be controlled, vital signs recorded every 5 minutes, and the emergency medical system (EMS) activated when appropriate. Symptoms can

14

range from mild to severe, including shock. The patient must be continually monitored until the medical examination is complete.

Surgical Intervention

Surgical management focuses on draining the pleural space and controlling bleeding.[6] Most bleeding responds well to chest-tube evacuation and lung reexpansion. Placement of a 32- to 36-French chest tube in the fifth or sixth intercostal space with underwater seal is required. The chest tube remains in place until air no longer leaks from the lung and less than 100 to 150 mL of fluid drains in 24 hours (see ST 14.1). Approximately 10% of patients with traumatic hemothorax require thoracotomy to control bleeding.

Chest radiographs must be taken immediately after chest-tube placement to confirm its correct positioning and reveal fluid and air evacuation. If fluid remains after chest-tube placement, a second tube may be required. If fluid persists, thoracotomy may be necessary. Daily chest radiographs are necessary until the fluid buildup is fully resolved. Thoracotomy indications include the immediate removal of more than 1200 mL of blood or 200 mL/h or more of bloody output for more than 4 hours after chest-tube placement.[6]

Postinjury/Postoperative Management

Serial chest radiographs are taken to evaluate for hemothorax resolution; chest-wound healing is monitored. The patient is initially limited to bed rest due to respiratory distress. Many activities of daily living (ADLs) can be resumed when the chest tube is removed. With hospital discharge, the patient can slowly and progressively return to daily living habits. No long-term functional loss is expected.

Injury-Specific Treatment and Rehabilitation Concerns

Advancement through aerobic activities, strength training, and sport-specific functional progression is permitted as tolerated.

Estimated Amount of Time Lost

Return to play is allowed 3 to 4 weeks after symptoms resolve.

Return-to-Play Criteria

The patient must delay normal activities until chest radiographs demonstrate that the hemothorax has completely resolved.

Commotio Cordis (Cardiac Concussion)

CLINICAL PRESENTATION

History
Blunt trauma to the chest.

Observation
Collapse and loss of consciousness.

Functional Status
Unconscious.

Physical Examination Findings
Absent pulse.

Commotio cordis is a cause of sudden death due to blunt trauma to the chest wall. The blow most commonly occurs to the left precordial area and usually involves individuals who are 5 to 15 years of age. Trauma is related to the speed and force of impact against the chest wall and most often results from a blow due to a projectile (e.g., baseball, hockey puck, lacrosse ball, physical hit). Adolescents have a narrower anteroposterior chest diameter and greater chest-wall compliance, which are thought to contribute to greater force transmission to the heart. Usually the heart and chest wall do not experience any structural damage.

Chest protectors and equipment modifications may protect the heart against forces that might otherwise trigger commotio cordis. In studies involving pigs, the use of a soft baseball reduced the risk of ventricular fibrillation due to blunt trauma.[7]

Differential Diagnosis
Myocardial infarction, respiratory arrest, ruptured aneurysm.

Definitive Diagnosis
Because of the high mortality rate associated with this condition, the definitive diagnosis is often made posthumously.

Pathomechanics and Functional Limitations
Commotio cordis is caused by blunt trauma to the chest wall that occurs 15 to 30 milliseconds prior to the T-wave peak during cardiac repolarization. This results in significant electrical disarray and cardiac arrhythmias. Ventricular fibrillation is the most common arrhythmia, but complete heart block and idioventricular rhythms have also been described. The arrhythmia may be refractory to standard resuscitation measures, including defibrillation.

The survival rate of commotio cordis is approximately 15%.[8] The probability of survival increases with early cardiopulmonary resuscitation and defibrillation.

■ Immediate Management

The patient is assessed for the presence of a pulse; if absent, CPR and Advanced Cardiac Life Support protocol are initiated. If an automated external defibrillator is available, the heart is defibrillated. EMS is activated immediately.

■ Postinjury/Postoperative Management

A cardiology workup is necessary to rule out possible underlying disease. The workup should include an electrocardiogram, echocardiogram, and ambulatory Holter monitor.

■ Injury-Specific Treatment and Rehabilitation Concerns

Autopsy studies have revealed no cardiac injury. Patients who survive the condition typically return to full activity if no other cardiac conditions are discovered during the postinjury workup.

■ Estimated Amount of Time Lost

Time loss is determined by cardiology workup.

■ Return-to-Play Criteria

Individuals who have recovered (spontaneously or with resuscitation) from apparent commotio cordis should undergo cardiac examination to determine underlying cardiac abnormalities. The patient may return to competition once recovery is complete and underlying cardiac disease has been excluded or controlled. Data are lacking on the risk of recurrent events with return to sport.

Costochondritis

Costochondritis is an inflammatory process that involves the cartilaginous junction between the ribs and sternum. Its onset may be related to repetitive direct trauma or indirect trauma, but is often unrelated to activity. In some individuals, chronic inflammation develops and ongoing treatment is necessary.

Differential Diagnosis

Costochondral separation, fractured rib, fractured sternum, bone tumor.

CLINICAL PRESENTATION

History

Pain localized to the sternal border and costal angle.

Observation

Swelling may be visible but is rare.

Functional Status

Deep breathing may be limited.
The Valsalva maneuver may cause pain.
Pain occurs when exerting the thoracic musculature.

Physical Examination Findings

Tenderness along the sternal border.
Tenderness along the costal angles.

Imaging Techniques

Radiographs are used to rule out rib fractures.

Definitive Diagnosis

Clinical findings, together with radiographic studies and occasionally bone scans for exclusion of differential diagnoses, determine the presence of costochondritis.

Pathomechanics and Functional Limitations

Pain with deep inspiration may slow the conditioning process.

■ Immediate Management

Ice and support such as a rib belt help reduce the pain (see **Figure 14.6**).

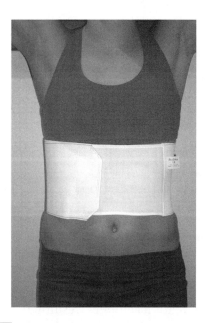

Figure 14.6 Rib belt offering support to rib cage.

14

■ Medications

Prescription or over-the-counter nonsteroidal anti-inflammatory drugs (NSAIDs) may be prescribed.

■ Postinjury Management

The inflammatory process is decreased with immediate care and the area supported with wrapping during the healing process.

■ Injury-Specific Treatment and Rehabilitation Concerns

Modalities of ice or heat (depending on the inflammatory process) and stretching exercises are instituted. Limitations are dictated by pain. Deep inspiration may be painful, and conditioning may be impaired.

■ Estimated Amount of Time Lost

This condition tends to be self-limiting, and return to full activities is possible.

■ Return-to-Play Criteria

Activity limitation is dictated by pain only, with no restrictions. A rib belt or chest protector (in contact sports) may reduce the patient's pain (see Figure 14.6).

Rib Stress Fractures

CLINICAL PRESENTATION

History

Insidious onset of aching, often localized at the site of injury.
Sudden-onset chest pain may be described.
A sudden, sometimes audible "snap" may be described.

Observation

A guarding posture may be assumed.

Functional Status

Pain may occur during deep inspiration.

Physical Examination Findings

Palpable tenderness may or may not be present over the fracture site.
Pain is possible with respiration, but respiration is normal.
Other physical findings may be normal.

Rib stress fractures are an uncommon response to repetitive-motion activities, resulting in muscle-distraction forces that cause bone fatigue. Although rib stress fractures are relatively rare in athletics, the onset is often sport specific and position related.

Baseball pitchers may develop a stress fracture of the first rib from maximal distraction between the upward and downward muscular forces on the rib.[9] The scalenus anticus and medius muscles appear to oppose the intercostal and upper serratus anterior muscles, generating sufficient force to stress the first rib.[10] This process most commonly involves the nonthrowing arm but can affect either side.

Rowers most often fracture the fourth and fifth ribs as the result of forces generated by the serratus anterior muscle (see **Figure 14.7**). Lower rib fractures have been observed in golfers and from batting in baseball players. These injuries also appear to be related to repetitive muscle-contraction forces.

Differential Diagnosis

Costochondritis, muscle strain.

Imaging Techniques

Chest and rib radiographs are typically normal in stress fractures. Bone scan is the test of choice when radiographs are normal and the index of suspicion is high. Such studies are very sensitive for fractures but are not specific. Although both sensitive and specific for fractures, CT scan is rarely necessary.

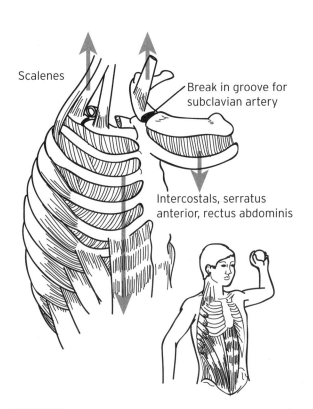

Scalenes

Break in groove for subclavian artery

Intercostals, serratus anterior, rectus abdominis

Figure 14.7 Rib stress fracture. Activities such as pitching may result in a stress fracture of the first rib. *Source*: Reproduced with permission from DeLee JC, Drez D (eds). *DeLee and Drez's Orthopaedic Sports Medicine: Principles and Practices*. Philadelphia, PA: WB Saunders; 1994:577.

Definitive Diagnosis

A positive bone scan confirms the diagnosis.

Pathomechanics and Functional Limitations

Deep breathing and exertion of the thoracic muscles may produce pain.

◼ Immediate Management

Immediate management consists of discontinuing participation, seeking medical attention, and pursuing diagnostic testing.

◼ Medications

Narcotics are rarely required for pain; NSAIDs are often useful for short periods. Intercostal nerve blocks are not warranted.

◼ Medical Management

Rest and analgesic care are necessary until full pain relief is realized. Often rest without medication is sufficient to remedy the problem.

◼ Postinjury/Postoperative Management

Rest and NSAIDs with support during the healing process are indicated. Activities are permitted as pain allows; the condition tends to be self-limiting.

◼ Injury-Specific Treatment and Rehabilitation Concerns

Aerobic activities and light-resistance upper extremity exercises are performed as pain allows. For pitchers, throwing rehabilitation should begin with a short-toss and long-toss program. Advancement to the mound occurs with a throwing progression after a time of rest to allow fracture healing, typically 4 to 6 weeks.

◼ Estimated Amount of Time Lost

Recovery takes approximately 4 to 6 weeks. The functional activities progression must be closely monitored. Any recurrent symptoms require activity modification to restore a pain-free mode. Fractures of the first rib in pitchers can be slow to respond to rehabilitation.

◼ Return-to-Play Criteria

The patient must be pain-free, both to palpation and the activity stresses that caused the fracture.

Rib Fractures

CLINICAL PRESENTATION

History

Blow to the chest.
Chest pain.
Pain increased with inspiration and forced exhalation.

Observation

Respiratory muscle splinting.
Possible ecchymosis.
Possible swelling.

Functional Status

Trunk motion reduced secondary to pain.

Physical Examination Findings

Point tenderness over the fracture site.
Pain with the rib compression test.

Simple rib fractures are the most common injury after blunt chest trauma. In this situation, direct force to the chest wall results in nondisplaced or minimally displaced fractures at or near the point of impact. In addition, force transmission can result in a fracture anywhere along the rib.

The most frequent fracture sites are ribs 4 through 9. Fractures involving ribs 1 and 2 require considerable force and often result in injury to the underlying neurovascular structures. The flexibility of young children's rib cages makes them far less likely to fracture ribs than adults.

Rib fractures to athletes occur primarily in contact and high-velocity sports. Such fractures must always be considered as a possible indication of underlying organ injury. The number, location, and severity of the fractures must lead to a high index of suspicion; multiple fractures indicate greater force, and concomitantly greater risk of underlying injury. Children require high forces to fracture ribs—an event that increases the potential for underlying organ damage.

Differential Diagnosis

Pneumothorax, myocardial contusion, pulmonary contusion, cardiac tamponade, costochondritis.

Imaging Techniques

Chest radiographs will reveal most rib fractures. Detailed rib radiographs are rarely needed but may be helpful in detecting fractures to ribs 1 and 2 and ribs 8 through 12. The possibility of a pneumothorax is increased when multiple ribs are fractured (see **Figure 14.8**).

14

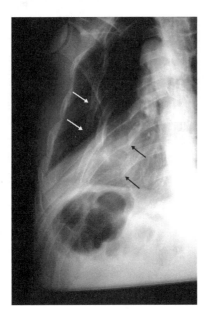

Figure 14.8 Rib fractures in a football player. The arrows indicate some of the fracture sites (not all fractures are labeled).

Chest radiographs repeated 2 to 3 days after the initial injury may demonstrate the late development of intrathoracic injuries. Notably, pneumothorax onset may be delayed for hours to days after the injury. Repeated chest radiographs are recommended only when the patient's clinical symptoms continue to suggest a rib fracture.

Definitive Diagnosis
The diagnosis is based on positive radiographic studies.

Pathomechanics and Functional Limitations
Pain limits activity. If the condition is the result of significant trauma, the patient's cardiovascular and pulmonary status must be monitored on an ongoing basis.

◼ Immediate Management
The rate and quality of respiration are evaluated, and the pulse rate is documented. All athletic activity should be discontinued. The patient is monitored closely, with particular attention paid to the chest wall, looking for paradoxical motion that could indicate a flail chest. Physician examination is arranged.

◼ Medications
Mild to moderate analgesics are usually all that is needed for pain management. Appropriate pain relief allows rest and helps normalize breathing. On occasion, intercostal nerve blocks can be administered to relieve pain.

◼ Postinjury Management
Rest and pain relief are typically sufficient. A rib belt may be helpful in relieving pain (see Figure 14.6), although some patients find the belt more irritating than helpful. If the patient feels the rib belt compromises breathing, its use should be discontinued.

◼ Injury-Specific Treatment and Rehabilitation Concerns
General conditioning can resume as pain subsides. Typically aerobic activities are tolerated initially, followed by a progression of strength training, including trunk-stabilization exercises.

◼ Estimated Amount of Time Lost
Pain relief is usually complete in 2 to 3 weeks. Noncontact sports may resume when pain relief is sufficient. Contact sports can normally be resumed after 3 weeks, but the patient will require rib-cage protection for 6 to 8 weeks after injury (see Figure 14.9).

◼ Return-to-Play Criteria
Return to activity must always be individualized according to the physical examination findings.

Sternal Fractures

Sternal injuries can occur from direct forces, such as contact with a football helmet or steering wheel, or indirect forces, which result from cervical and upper thoracic spine hyperflexion. The chin may strike the manubrium, driving it posteriorly.[10] Most sternal fractures involve the manubrium and midsternal

Figure 14.9 Protective rib vest. These devices can be used prophylactically to prevent rib and costochondral injuries or to prevent reinjury to these structures.

History

Direct blow to the sternum.
Cervical and thoracic spine hyperflexion.
Complaints of sternal pain.

Observation

Difficulty breathing.
Swelling.

Functional Status

Pain that increases with respiration.
Initial shortness of breath.

Physical Examination Findings

Anterior chest-wall tenderness is noted.
Crepitus with palpable deformity indicates displacement.

body. Cervical, upper thoracic, and rib fractures and underlying soft-tissue damage may accompany this injury. Sternal fractures are extremely painful.

Differential Diagnosis

Myocardial contusion, pulmonary contusion, cardiac tamponade, rib fracture, costochondritis.

Imaging Techniques

Posteroanterior and lateral chest radiographs with sternal views are usually diagnostic. Mediastinal widening on chest radiographs may indicate underlying great-vessel injury and mandate aortography.

Definitive Diagnosis

Diagnosis is based on positive radiographic findings.

Pathomechanics and Functional Limitations

This significant injury needs attentive monitoring. Activity restrictions are necessary, and functional progression is slow.

■ Immediate Management

Participation in the sport or other activity ceases, and the patient's pulse and respiration are monitored. Immediate medical attention is required, with diagnostic studies being performed as needed.

■ Medications

Analgesics may be prescribed for pain management; initial management may require narcotics for this extremely painful injury. Later in the course of care, NSAIDs may be helpful to relieve discomfort.

■ Medical Management

Nondisplaced sternal fractures typically respond to conservative management. Displaced fractures can be reduced using postural reduction. In this technique, with the patient supine, a sandbag is placed transversely under the shoulders, slightly below the scapula.[10] The torso is hyperextended, and traction is then applied by pulling on the patient's arms (see **Figure 14.10**). This reduction method is used only in individuals with posterior manubrial displacement. With nondisplaced fractures and fractures that have been reduced, rest and analgesics are required. However, if underlying myocardial injury is suspected, appropriate testing should be instituted.

■ Postinjury Management

Conservative care requires serial lateral chest radiographs approximately every 3 weeks until healing is complete. Noncontact activities are allowed as the patient's level of comfort permits.

■ Surgical Intervention

Surgical intervention is extremely rare and is reserved for individuals having gross displacement, with compromised respiratory function, severe pain, or nonunion. In this procedure, the surgeon makes a midline incision over the sternum, and the fracture is reduced and fixated with Kirschner wires (K-wires) or a plate and screws.

■ Postoperative Management

Surgical treatment also requires serial chest radiographs for evaluation of fracture healing and positioning. The wires or pin and plate also must be monitored.

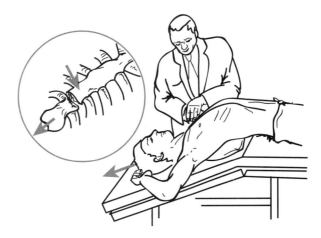

Figure 14.10 Reduction of a sternal fracture. If necessary, an assistant may apply traction by grasping the patient's arm at the axilla and pulling cephalad. The inset view shows details of the forces applied in reduction. *Source*: Reproduced with permission from DeLee JC, Drez D (eds). *DeLee and Drez's Orthopedic Sports Medicine: Principles and Practices*. Philadelphia, PA: WB Saunders; 1994:576.

14

Injury-Specific Treatment and Rehabilitation Concerns

Aerobic exercise is permitted as tolerated. Initially, noncontact activities such as stationary bicycling are appropriate; they are followed by running activities. Strength training as tolerated begins with the lower extremities, followed by trunk and upper extremity strengthening as healing allows.

Estimated Amount of Time Lost

Depending on the treatment method used, 6 to 12 weeks may be required before the patient can return to competition. Internal fixation, especially with K-wires, necessitates closer follow-up. No contact activities are permitted until these wires are removed.

Return-to-Play Criteria

Noncontact sports are allowed as tolerated. Patients will require 6 to 12 weeks of recovery before returning to contact sports, depending on their pain relief and radiographic evidence of healing. Contact-sport athletes need protection similar to that described for rib fractures (e.g., flak jacket; see Figure 14.9).

Flail Chest

CLINICAL PRESENTATION

History
High-velocity blunt impact to the ribs.
Chest pain.

Observation
Chest-wall deformity.

Functional Status
Labored breathing.

Physical Examination Findings
Chest-wall tenderness.
Abnormal, segmented chest-wall motion (paradoxical breathing).
Flail-chest findings can be delayed as long as 10 days after injury.

Flail chest is the result of a severe, direct impact to the rib cage with fractures of four or more ribs in two or more places (see **Figure 14.11**).[11] Because of the resulting paradoxical motion of the fractured segment of ribs, it is the most serious chest-wall injury. During inspiration and expiration, the fractured section of the ribs moves separately and in the opposite direction from the rest of the rib cage. This causes

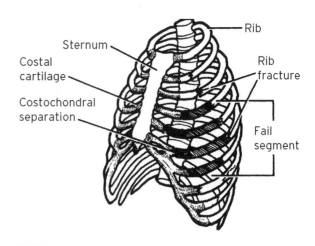

Figure 14.11 Flail chest occurs when four or more consecutive ribs are fractured in two or more places.

difficulty in breathing, due to diminished chest expansion with increased energy expenditure.

Because of the severe trauma associated with flail chest, underlying lung injury is common. Pulmonary contusion occurs in approximately half of all patients with flail chest. Pneumothorax and hemothorax occur in more than 70% of patients.[12]

Imaging Techniques
Chest radiographs are necessary to evaluate rib fractures and lung fields. Rib radiographs may provide better detail of the fracture sites. CT scan is more accurate than plain films and may be necessary to further evaluate the lung parenchyma.

Definitive Diagnosis
Diagnosis is based on clinical evaluation supported by chest radiographs.

Pathomechanics and Functional Limitations
Flail chest results in loss of rib-cage integrity, which compromises the ability to protect thoracic organs and maintain respiratory function. Long-term functional respiratory loss and chest deformity are common.

Immediate Management

Immediate management consists of maintaining the patient's airway and monitoring vital signs. A pillow placed over the flail segment may relieve pain and ease breathing.[11] The patient must be immediately transported to the hospital by EMS.

Medications

Pain management is paramount for successful conservative management; IV narcotics and NSAIDs are most effective. Intercostal blocks, intrapleural analgesia, and patient-controlled analgesia methods such as procedural sedation and analgesia (PSA) pumps are all helpful.

Medical Management

Medical treatment requires aggressive pulmonary therapy with suctioning, incentive spirometry, early mobilization, and air humidification.[12] Effective analgesia is also important. Close observation is required to detect possible respiratory decompensation, which is an indication for endotracheal intubation and positive-pressure mechanical ventilation. Oxygen supplementation is provided to keep oxygen saturation greater than 90%.

Surgical Intervention

Surgical fixation with K-wires, plates, and screws to stabilize the fractures is rarely indicated.

Postinjury/Postoperative Management

Chest-wall protection is required for return to contact sports. A flak jacket or some other form of protection is adequate for this purpose.

Injury-Specific Treatment and Rehabilitation Concerns

Slow progression of aerobic activity begins upon hospital discharge. The progression occurs in accordance with patient tolerance and fracture healing.

Estimated Amount of Time Lost

Fracture healing requires approximately 8 weeks. Contact sports may resume approximately 3 months after injury or once complete healing is verified.

Return-to-Play Criteria

The patient may return to competition after clinical and radiographic evidence of complete fracture healing along with adequate sport-specific conditioning have been attained.

Spleen Injury

Spleen injury usually results from direct abdominal force but can also occur secondary to rapid acceleration or deceleration. Most commonly, the left upper quadrant is injured by a deceleration mechanism or by displacement of left lower rib fractures, most commonly the fifth through ninth ribs. This mechanism of injury is seen primarily in contact sports and high-speed, noncontact sports.[2]

CLINICAL PRESENTATION

History

Mechanism of direct trauma to the abdomen or left upper quadrant.
Pain in the upper left quadrant and left shoulder (Kehr's sign).
A recent history of mononucleosis increases the risk of splenic trauma.

Observation

Contusion over the point of contact.
Abdominal guarding.

Functional Status

Lightheadedness.
Malaise.
Fatigue.

Physical Examination Findings

Point tenderness of the ribs overlying the spleen.
Tenderness in the left upper abdomen.
Abdominal rigidity.
Hypotension.
Tachycardia.
Ecchymosis in the periumbilical area (Cullen's sign).
Ecchymosis in the lateral abdominal wall (Turner's sign).

Injury results in spleen contusion, subcapsular hematoma, rupture, or laceration. Hematoma with delayed rupture at an interval of days to weeks after injury occurs in 10% to 15% of patients. The spleen is a very vascular organ, receiving 5% of the cardiac output, primarily via the splenic artery. Accordingly, immediate and serious bleeding is commonly observed after splenic trauma.

The spleen is at particular risk when mononucleosis or another viral-related splenomegaly develops. Splenomegaly makes the spleen much more vulnerable to injury and to rupture. Therefore, patients with splenomegaly should be prohibited from contact sports until the spleen has returned to normal size.

splenomegaly
Enlargement of the spleen.

Differential Diagnosis

Abdominal wall contusion; rib fracture; intercostal muscle strain; liver, kidney, intestine, and diaphragm injuries.

Medical Diagnostic Tests

Diagnostic peritoneal lavage (DPL) may be considered in hemodynamically unstable patients. DPL is an invasive procedure in which a catheter is placed within the peritoneal cavity. Aspiration of peritoneal blood indicates abdominal bleeding, but this finding is nonspecific and does not indicate which organ is the source of the bleeding.

Imaging Techniques

Improved imaging techniques have greatly contributed to the nonsurgical treatment of splenic injury. CT scan is the imaging modality of choice in hemodynamically stable patients. This type of study can be performed quickly with current-generation scanners. IV contrast should be used to facilitate the detection of splenic injury. CT scan is an excellent choice for imaging both large and small volumes of intra-abdominal blood and can be very specific for detecting splenic contusion, rupture, or laceration. Its widespread use has been instrumental in reducing the number of laparotomies in stable patients with low-grade spleen injuries, allowing surgeons to assess and reassess these injuries in a noninvasive manner.

Abdominal ultrasound can be performed quickly to detect hemoperitoneum. The usefulness of this technique is limited by its poor specificity, especially in children.[13] A negative ultrasound does not rule out abdominal bleeding, however, and further imaging with CT scan is necessary to detect hemoperitoneum.[14]

Definitive Diagnosis

The definitive diagnosis of spleen injury is based on a positive CT scan in a hemodynamically stable patient. Exploratory laparotomy is used to establish the definitive diagnosis of splenic trauma in the unstable patient.[14]

Pathomechanics and Functional Limitations

Pneumococcal, meningococcal, and *Haemophilus influenzae* type B vaccinations are recommended for patients who have had their spleen removed.[14] A heightened awareness of the immune-compromised state of these individuals is important, as they may require quicker implementation of antibiotic coverage for potential bacterial illness.

■ Immediate Management

The patient's abdomen should be evaluated and checked thoroughly for signs of injury. Pulse rate, respiration rate, and blood pressure should be monitored and recorded. If an injury is suspected, the patient should be immediately transported to an emergency room. On the field, CPR protocol must be followed until EMS transport is available. The patient is placed in the Trendelenburg position if tachycardia or hypotension is noted (see **Figure 14.12**).

■ Medications

Postoperative pain management with narcotics will likely be required. The routine use of long-term prophylactic antibiotics after splenectomy is controversial. Antibiotics (e.g., amoxicillin) should be administered to any asplenic individual with the first sign of infection (e.g., fever, sore throat) to re-

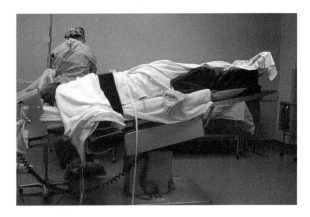

Figure 14.12   The Trendelenburg position.

duce the risk of developing postsplenectomy sepsis. Vaccinations for pneumococcus, *Haemophilus influenzae* type B, and meningococcus should also be given to a patient after splenectomy to minimize the risk of infection.

■ Medical Management

The management goal is to stop the internal bleeding and preserve the spleen.[10] Nonsurgical management is successful in 90% of children and as many as 70% of adults. Although failure of conservative management most often occurs within 48 to 72 hours after the initial injury, late ruptures occur and have been reported 2 weeks to several months later.

For nonsurgical management to be feasible, the patient must be hemodynamically stable, without hypotension, hypovolemia, head injury, or coagulopathy. The best candidate for conservative management is a young, hemodynamically stable patient with an isolated splenic injury. Hypotension is an indication for surgical intervention.

A large-bore IV line should be placed in every patient. Ideally, monitoring will occur in the intensive care unit. Initial laboratory tests include complete blood count, urinalysis, and chemistry panel with liver enzymes. Hemoglobin and hematocrit (H/H) assessments should be ordered every 6 hours for 24 hours. If the patient remains stable, the H/H should then be checked every 12 hours. A stable H/H and decreased abdominal pain can be expected in the first 12 hours after the initial injury. Strict bed rest is maintained for 2 to 3 days. The patient must refrain from oral intake until the need for surgery has been definitively ruled out and there is no sign of ileus. The patient should be admitted to the hospital and observed for 2 to 6 days.

coagulopathy A disorder of the blood-clotting mechanism.

> **Practice Tip**
>
> Nonoperative management for spleen injury is preferred in hemodynamically stable patients due to the high risk of postsplenectomy infection. The mortality rate of postsplenectomy infection is approximately 50%.[14]

Surgical Intervention

Surgical intervention is necessary if the patient presents to the emergency room as hemodynamically unstable or becomes unstable after attempts at conservative management. Other indications for surgery include a decreasing hemoglobin level, increasing abdominal tenderness, and persistent hypotension, tachycardia, and hypovolemia. Patients older than 55 years are more likely to require splenectomy than younger individuals.

Two large-bore, peripheral IVs must be placed; prophylactic antibiotics are commonly administered perioperatively. A generous upper midline abdominal incision is typically used, with extension as needed to evaluate for other injuries. Spleen mobilization allows full spleen inspection. Laparoscopic splenectomy may be an option for the hemodynamically stable patient and allows an earlier return to athletic competition.

Surgical treatment may include suture repair (splenorrhaphy), topical and intraparenchymal application of clotting agents, and wrapping the spleen in mesh with partial resection. If the bleeding persists or the spleen is shattered, it should be removed without attempts at preservation (see **Table 14.1**).

Postinjury/Postoperative Management

Hospitalization lasts approximately 5 to 10 days. The patient's hemodynamic status is followed closely postoperatively. After the patient returns home, rest is recommended, with slow progression of ADLs. No exertional activities—such as lifting, pushing, or pulling—are permitted until cleared by the surgeon.

Injury-Specific Treatment and Rehabilitation Concerns

With nonsurgical treatment, the primary concern is rebleeding. Close monitoring of activities is important, with the patient instructed to report symptoms and complaints promptly. Both nonsurgical management and surgical care require an extended convalescence, which causes cardiovascular and musculoskeletal detraining. Consequently, endurance training and trunk strengthening must be emphasized once the patient recovers sufficiently.

Surgical treatment requires observation and management of the incision, with sutures removed at 7 to 10 days post surgery. Daily living activities are allowed with slow progression, as with conservative management.

Estimated Amount of Time Lost

With a mild splenic contusion, the patient is withheld from sports activity for 2 to 3 weeks. Patients with a significant injury who are treated conservatively should refrain from strenuous activity for 3 months, with no contact sports for as long as

Table 14.1

Spleen Injury Scale

Grade*		Injury Description
I	Hematoma	Subcapsular, nonexpanding, less than 10% surface area
	Laceration	Capsular tear, nonbleeding, less than 1 cm parenchymal depth
II	Hematoma	Subcapsular, nonexpanding, 10% to 50% surface area; intraparenchymal, nonexpanding, less than 5 cm in diameter
	Laceration	Capsular tear, active bleeding, 1 to 3 cm parenchymal depth that does not involve a trabecular vessel
III	Hematoma	Subcapsular, more than 50% surface area or expanding; ruptured subcapsular hematoma with active bleeding; intraparenchymal hematoma more than 5 cm or expanding
	Laceration	More than 3 cm parenchymal depth or involving trabecular vessels
IV	Hematoma	Ruptured intraparenchymal hematoma with active bleeding
	Laceration	Laceration involving segmental or hilar vessels producing major devascularization (more than 25% of the spleen)
V	Laceration	Comminuted spleen
	Vascular	Hilar vascular injury that devascularizes the spleen

* Advance one grade for multiple injuries up to grade III.
Source: Reproduced with permission from Moore EE, Cogbill TH, Jurkovich GL, et al. Organ injury scaling: Spleen and liver. *J Trauma.* 1995;38:323.

4 months. Patients who undergo a laparatomy are not allowed strenuous activity for 3 to 6 weeks after surgery. Athletes who undergo a splenectomy may return to contact sports as soon as postoperative healing is complete.[14]

Return-to-Play Criteria

Return-to-play guidelines after splenic injury are controversial due to the inability to predict full recovery and the potential complication of delayed splenic rupture. Patients treated conservatively should avoid strenuous activity for 3 months. Athletes may then gradually return to full activity.[14] Surgical patients are prohibited from strenuous activity during the early postoperative period to ensure healing. Patients treated with splenectomy usually return to contact sports sooner than those treated conservatively. Contact should be restricted until postoperative healing is complete, which can range from 3 to 6 weeks. Conditioning should be maintained once strenuous activities are allowed.[14]

Renal Trauma

CLINICAL PRESENTATION

History

Blunt or penetrating trauma over the area of either kidney.
Abdominal pain.
Flank pain.

Observation

Flank contusion or ecchymosis.

Functional Status

Pain with trunk motion.

Physical Examination Findings

Costovertebral angle tenderness.
Abdominal mass.
Urinalysis revealing gross or microscopic hematuria.
Hypotension.

Blunt force causes 80% of renal trauma. Approximately 30% of all renal injuries are sport-related. Blunt trauma is more prevalent in males, which appears to be related to their greater contact-sport participation. As in other types of abdominal trauma, injury mechanisms include a direct blow to the flank from rapid deceleration or a penetrating rib fracture.[2] The degree of renal injury depends on the amount of applied force.

Children have a higher rate of injury to the kidneys than to the spleen or liver. The explanation for this difference may be that children have less protective tissue and a large kidney size relative to trunk size. In blunt trauma, left kidney injury coexists with spleen injury roughly 30% of the time. Right kidney injury coexists with liver injury approximately 40% of the time.

Differential Diagnosis

Urinary tract infection, rib fractures, lumbar strain, muscle contusion, intrinsic renal disease, kidney stones, urethra or prostate injury (specifically in cyclists).

Medical Diagnostic Tests

Urinalysis often reveals gross or microscopic hematuria, but 25% to 40% of patients have normal urinalyses.

Imaging Techniques

Improved imaging and staging have resulted in a trend toward conservative management of renal injury. Chest radiographs may reveal lower rib fractures. Lumbar spine radiographs help to evaluate possible transverse-process fractures, which are commonly associated with renal trauma. An abdominal flat-plate radiograph (also known as a KUB—kidney, ureter, bladder) may reveal a psoas shadow or loss of the renal outline.

A CT scan with IV contrast enhancement is the gold standard for evaluating renal trauma. Its diagnostic accuracy is 98%, and this imaging modality is an excellent choice for identifying the extent of injury and assessing urinary extravasation.

Renal arteriograms are rarely needed. The main indication for their use is a grade IV or V injury with planned partial nephrectomy or selective embolization. Intravenous pyelography has been largely replaced by CT studies. Nevertheless, pyelography can be very helpful in evaluating kidney function and gross urinary extravasation in the patient who requires emergency laparotomy for other intra-abdominal injuries.

Definitive Diagnosis

A positive CT scan provides the definitive diagnosis of renal injury.

Pathomechanics and Functional Limitations

Renal trauma results in mild to severe pain; physical limitations will likewise vary. Because of the potentially adverse prognosis, the patient must limit all activities and be monitored closely until bleeding resolves.

Immediate Management

When renal injury is suspected, the patient's abdomen should be evaluated and checked thoroughly

hematuria Microscopic or macroscopic blood in the urine.

nephrectomy Surgical removal of a kidney.

embolization Blocking an artery or vein by use of a foreign material.

pyelography Radiographs of the kidney and ureter after the injection of a radiopaque dye.

for signs of trauma. Pulse rate, respiration rate, and blood pressure should be monitored and recorded. If an injury is suspected, the patient should be immediately transported to an emergency room. On the field, CPR protocol must be followed until EMS transport is available. The patient is placed in the Trendelenburg position if tachycardia or hypotension is noted (see Figure 14.12).

Medical Management

Approximately 80% of all patients with renal trauma can be treated conservatively. The kidney has a great capacity for spontaneous healing, and late complications are rare. Also, the successful use of embolization procedures, stenting, and percutaneous drainage has decreased the need for surgery. Renal lacerations, even with wide fragment separation, may exhibit spontaneous resolution.[15] However, surgical intervention is necessary in hemodynamically unstable patients with hilar or pedicle injuries.

Hematuria is the key indicator of renal trauma. Gross hematuria is a sign of significant injury, but microscopic hematuria should not be disregarded and deserves appropriate follow-up and workup. Significant vascular renal injury can occur without hematuria.

As with all abdominal injuries, adequate hemodynamic stability must be maintained through IV fluid replacement and maintenance. Typical routine laboratory tests should be performed, including a urinalysis, complete blood count, electrolytes, liver function tests, creatinine, glucose, amylase, and lipase.[16] Treatment regimens for renal injury are categorized by grade (see **Table 14.2**). All athletes with grade I or II renal injuries and most athletes with grade III or IV injuries are managed nonoperatively. Indications for operative exploration include grade V renal injury, hypotension, and penetrating trauma.[16]

Postinjury/Postoperative Management

If surgery is performed, wound care is necessary. Athletes with renal injuries managed nonoperatively should not return to sports until the hematuria has completely resolved, which usually occurs within 2 to 6 weeks.[16]

Injury-Specific Treatment and Rehabilitation Concerns

Return to activity should be graduated, with aerobic exercise followed by strength training and specific trunk-stabilization exercises.

Estimated Amount of Time Lost

A patient who has sustained a mild renal injury may return to activity in 2 to 6 weeks if hematuria has subsided. A severe renal injury usually resolves in 6 to 8 weeks; however, renal lacerations may require 6 to 12 months to heal.[16] Return to sport activities requires complete healing with no microscopic hematuria and CT evidence of full resolution.

Return-to-Play Criteria

After surgery, 8 to 12 weeks of recovery may be needed before the patient can return to contact sports. Prior to resumption of full sport activities, no microscopic hematuria should be present, and a CT scan should be obtained to document full healing. Conservatively managed renal trauma can re-

14

Table 14.2

Renal Injury Scale

Grade*		Injury Description
I	Contusion	Microscopic or gross hematuria; urologic studies normal
	Hematoma	Subcapsular, nonexpanding without parenchymal laceration
II	Hematoma	Nonexpanding perirenal hematoma confined to the renal retroperitoneum
	Laceration	Less than 1 cm parenchymal depth of renal cortex without urinary extravasation
III	Laceration	More than 1 cm parenchymal depth of renal cortex without collecting-system rupture or urinary extravasation
IV	Laceration	Parenchymal laceration extending through the renal cortex, medulla, and collecting system
	Vascular	Main renal artery or vein injury with contained hemorrhage
V	Laceration	Comminuted kidney
	Vascular	Avulsion of renal hilum with devascularized kidney

*Advance one grade for multiple injuries to the same organ.
Source: Reproduced with permission from Moore EE, Shackford SR, Pachter HL, et al. Organ injury scaling: Spleen, liver, and kidney. *J Trauma.* 1989;29:1664.

sult in full resolution of microscopic hematuria, along with a normal CT scan, allowing return to sport activity in 4 to 6 weeks.

Abdominal Sports Hernia

CLINICAL PRESENTATION

History

Pain in lower abdominal, medial inguinal, and pubic region.
Symptoms aggravated by sudden propulsive movements such as kicking.

Observation

No visible abnormalities.

Functional Status

Pain and tenderness with resisted sit-ups or resisted trunk rotation.

Physical Examination Findings

Tender medial inguinal canal, lower rectus abdominus, and pubic tubercle.
Dilated external inguinal ring.
Absence of hernia bulge.

Groin injuries that involve the lower abdominal and inguinal region may result in a syndrome of chronic exertional pain that has been termed abdominal sports hernia, athletic hernia, and athletic pubalgia. These injuries occur most commonly in sports associated with repetitive twisting or turning motions, such as soccer and ice hockey. Pathologic findings in the groin at surgical exploration have included a torn external oblique aponeurosis (see **Figure 14.13**), torn conjoined tendon, torn conjoined tendon from the pubic tubercle, torn internal oblique muscle, disrupted posterior inguinal floor but without a direct hernia, and ilioinguinal nerve entrapment by scar tissue.

Symptom onset in athletic pubalgia may be either acute or insidious without a specific precipitating event. The pain is usually noted in the

Figure 14.13 Attenuated external oblique aponeurosis in the left inguinal canal in a patient with an abdominal sports hernia.

medial inguinal and pubic regions, occurring principally with the initial propulsive movements in running or skating. Associated adductor symptoms and adductor strain are common. Examination findings are subtle and variable but may include any or all of the features described in the following subsections. It is important to exclude an inguinal hernia on examination.

Differential Diagnosis

Muscle strain, femoral hernia, inguinal hernia, osteitis pubis, pelvic stress fracture, hip arthritis, hip adductor muscle strain.

Imaging Techniques

If symptoms persist, pelvic magnetic resonance imaging (MRI) should be obtained to exclude other abnormalities. Plain pelvic radiographs may be done initially. Bone scan may be performed as an alternative to MRI to evaluate for osteitis pubis.

Definitive Diagnosis

The diagnosis is usually one of exclusion, based on history, physical examination, and imaging studies. Radiographs, MRI, and bone scan of the pelvis help to exclude other possible diagnoses.

Pathomechanics and Functional Limitations

Initially, the patient may complain of discomfort with squatting, walking stairs, and torso rotation. Most commonly, daily activities are asymptomatic, and the patient complains only with sport-specific activities (e.g., agility activities, kicking, sprinting).

■ Immediate Management

Rest, NSAIDs, and avoidance of aggravating activities are recommended.

Medications

NSAIDs may be helpful for pain relief.

Postinjury Management

Initial treatment is conservative—rest, NSAIDs, and ultrasound. Conservative management focuses on trunk stabilization and lower abdominal and adductor strength and flexibility. Athletes with a sports hernia will frequently have recurrent groin pain with resumption of strenuous activity. Surgical intervention is commonly required and should be considered in those patients whose limiting symptoms persist despite conservative treatment.

Surgical Intervention

Surgical options include primary pelvic-floor repair, open mesh repair, and laparoscopic posterior mesh repair (see **Figure 14.14**). Other procedures carried out in some patients in conjunction with pelvic-floor repair include ilioinguinal neurolysis and adductor release.

Postoperative Management

In the early postoperative period, patients should be observed for wound healing and signs of infection. Active abdominal exercises and heavy lifting should be avoided for 4 to 6 weeks to allow adequate tissue healing. Rehabilitation can begin in approximately 2 weeks, when the patient is relatively pain free and wound healing is complete.

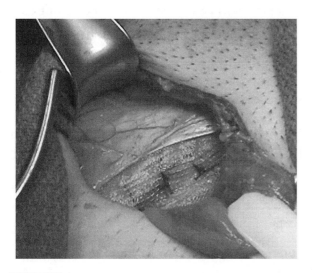

Figure 14.14 The reconstructed inguinal floor is shown, with polypropylene mesh placed deep to the external oblique layer.

Injury-Specific Treatment and Rehabilitation Concerns

After surgical repair, rest and normal light activities are recommended for 2 weeks. At that point, the patient can start walking on a treadmill, progressing gradually to jogging, stationary bicycling, and pool walking. Ice should be applied to the surgical site after each workout. At 3 to 4 weeks postoperatively, ultrasound and active release techniques for scar tissue at the groin site are used as needed. If necessary, NSAIDs may be continued. Progression to full activity and strength training should be as tolerated during weeks 4 through 8. Individuals who have had an athletic pubalgia-type injury should undergo off-season sport-specific training annually, with attention to lower abdominal and adductor strength and flexibility work to prevent recurrence or injury to the contralateral groin.

Estimated Amount of Time Lost

Approximately 16 weeks of activity is usually missed. A trial of conservative management should be instituted for 8 weeks, followed by 8 weeks of postoperative management if surgery is required.

Return-to-Play Criteria

With conservative management, return to play is allowed after symptoms have resolved. After surgery, play can resume once rehabilitation has been completed and the patient can perform normal sport activity without symptoms, usually 7 to 10 weeks after surgery.

Functional Bracing

Use of compression shorts may be warranted for approximately 1 year after injury (see Figure 7.3).

Inguinal Hernia

Herniations in this region can occur as congenital or acquired defects and are classified as indirect inguinal, direct inguinal, or femoral hernias (see **Figure 14.15**). Most groin hernias that occur in children and young adults are indirect hernias, in which the internal inguinal ring is dilated with peritoneal protrusion into the inguinal canal. Direct hernias are the result of an acquired weakness in the transversalis fascia and floor of the inguinal canal. Femoral hernias occur almost exclusively in women and are uncommon before age 30 years; they have a high rate of **incarceration**.

14

incarceration A confined or restricted hernia that is difficult to reduce.

History

Pain may be described as arising from the inguinal canal area, although pain may not be described by all patients.

Pain may radiate into the testicles of male athletes and discomfort may get worse as the day progresses.[18]

Observation

A visible bulge around the inguinal ligament is apparent.

The bulge increases with exertion and reduces with relaxation or recumbency.

Functional Status

Aching pain is exacerbated by physical exertion.

Physical Examination Findings

Tenderness and a palpable mass in the lower abdomen and/or scrotum are noted; the mass increases with coughing and diminishes when the patient is in the supine position.

A history of groin pain in combination with a noticeable bulge is present in most individuals with inguinal hernias. Some patients, however, may have only an asymptomatic bulge or pain without a visible bulge. Symptoms may be aggravated by strenuous physical activity. If present, the hernia bulge usually disappears when the individual is in the recumbent position. Incarceration or strangulation is a risk of any groin hernia but is not a common occurrence in young, athletically active individuals. Risk factors for hernia development, such as chronic cough or constipation, should be considered.

Differential Diagnosis

Hydrocele, lipoma, appendicitis, testicular torsion, testicular or scrotal disease.

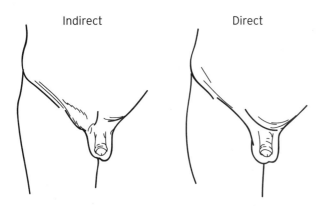

Indirect   Direct

Figure 14.15 Direct and indirect hernia. Differentiation between these hernias is not always clinically possible. Understanding their features, however, improves your observation. *Source*: Reproduced with permission from Bates B. *A Guide to Physical Examination*, ed 3. Philadelphia, PA: JB Lippincott; 1983:272.

Definitive Diagnosis

The definitive diagnosis is based on the clinical findings and in difficult cases may require ultrasound or MRI assessment.[18]

Pathomechanics and Functional Limitations

Inguinal hernia results in weakness or tearing of the pelvic-wall or pelvic-floor musculature, with permanent or recurrent intestinal protrusion through the opening. Physical activity, coughing, straining, and heavy lifting can increase abdominal pressure, and pain limits function.[19]

■ Immediate Management

Physical examination should be performed to confirm the presence of a hernia and to determine whether it is reducible. Patients with suspected groin hernias should be referred to a general surgeon for further examination. An acutely symptomatic patient with increased pain and an incarcerated hernia should be seen emergently by a general surgeon.

■ Medications

The patient requires postoperative pain management, typically the short-term use of narcotics.

■ Surgical Intervention

Asymptomatic inguinal hernias may require only observation,[18] but an inguinal hernia in an athlete should be surgically repaired. The repair may be carried out on an elective basis (i.e., in the off-season) unless the hernia is incarcerated or symptoms limit activity. If the repair is delayed, athletic activity can continue as tolerated. An athletic truss, which provides external support, may provide some temporary symptomatic benefit, but currently there is no research to support its effectiveness in preventing hernia progression or enlargement.[18]

Surgical options include both open repair and laparoscopic repair. Most inguinal hernia repairs in adults are performed using a tension-free, mesh-repair technique. In children and teenagers who are still growing, primary tissue repair is usually preferred.

Active abdominal exercises and heavy lifting should be avoided for 2 to 3 weeks after laparoscopic procedures and 4 to 6 weeks after open procedures to allow adequate tissue healing. Forceful Valsalva maneuvers should also be avoided during the first 7 to 14 days.

Postinjury/Postoperative Management

The patient should be monitored for wound healing, infection, hematoma, and return of bowel function the first week.

Injury-Specific Treatment and Rehabilitation Concerns

Light activities are permitted for the first 7 to 14 days after repair. Return to exercise can begin after 7 to 15 days, starting with cardiovascular conditioning and progressing to strength and functional training over 3 to 4 weeks, according to comfort level. The patient must avoid all strenuous activity, such as heavy lifting, pushing, and pulling, for 2 to 3 weeks. A slow, progressive trunk-stabilization program can begin 3 weeks after surgery. The patient should apply ice after activity and use NSAIDs as needed.

Estimated Amount of Time Lost

The amount of time lost from competition varies but can range from 4 to 7 weeks, depending on the type of repair. Laparoscopic repair may result in a more rapid return to unrestricted exercise and competitive play, as early as 3 to 4 weeks after surgery.

Return-to-Play Criteria

Return to sport is based on exercise tolerance and ability to progress with pain-free exercise.

References

1. Mullins RJ. Management of shock, in Mattox KL, Feliciano DV, Moore EE (eds), *Trauma*, ed 4. New York: McGraw-Hill; 2000:195–232.
2. Amaral JF. Thoracoabdominal injuries in the athlete. *Clin Sports Med.* 1997;16:739–753.
3. Lively MW, Stone D. Pulmonary contusion in football players. *Clin J Sport Med.* 2006;16:177–178.
4. Ferro RT, McKeag DB. Neck pain and dyspnea in a swimmer. *Physician Sportsmed.* 1999;27:67–71.
5. Curtin SM, Tucker AM, Gens DR. Pneumothorax in sports. *Physician Sportsmed.* 2000;28:23–32.
6. Richardson JD, Spain DA. Injury to the lung and pleura, in Mattox KL, Feliciano CV, Moore EE (eds), *Trauma*, ed 4. New York: McGraw-Hill; 2000:523–547.
7. Links MS, Wang PJ, Pandian NG, et al. An experimental model of sudden death due to low energy chest-wall impact (commotio cordis). *N Engl J Med.* 1998;338:1805–1811.
8. Maron BJ, Gohman TE, Kyle SB, et al. Clinical profile and spectrum of commotio cordis. *JAMA.* 2002;287:1142–1146.
9. Brukner P, Khan K, Sutton J. *Clinical Sports Medicine.* New York: McGraw-Hill; 1993:258–264.
10. Lyons FR. *Orthopaedic Sports Medicine: Principles and Practice.* Philadelphia, PA: WB Saunders; 1994:572–579.
11. Martin SL, Stewart RM. Chest and thorax injuries, in Schenck RC Jr (ed), *Athletic Training and Sports Medicine*, ed 3. Rosemont, IL: American Academy of Orthopaedic Surgeons; 1999:356–377.
12. Cogbill TH, Landercasper J. Injury to the chest wall, in Mattox KL, Feliciano DV, Moore EE (eds), *Trauma*, ed 4. New York: McGraw-Hill; 2000:483–505.
13. Gaines BA. Intra-abdominal solid organ injury in children: Diagnosis and treatment. *J Trauma.* 2009;67:135–138.
14. Gannon EH, Howard T. Splenic injuries in athletes: A review. *Curr Sports Med Rep.* 2010;9:111–114.
15. Peterson NE. Genitourinary trauma, in Mattox KL, Feliciano DV, Moore EE (eds), *Trauma*, ed 4. New York, NY: McGraw-Hill; 2000:839–874.
16. Bernard JJ. Renal trauma: Evaluation, management, and return to play. *Curr Sports Med Rep.* 2009;8:98–103.
17. Committee on Sports Medicine and Fitness. American Academy of Pediatrics: Medical conditions affecting sports participation. *Pediatrics.* 2001;107:1205.
18. Ouellette LR, Dexter WW. Inguinal hernias: Value of preparticipation examination, activity restriction decisions, and timing of surgery. *Curr Sports Med Rep.* 2006;5:89–92.
19. Fitzgibbons RJ Jr, Filipi CJ, Quinn TH. Inguinal hernias. In Brunicardi FC (ed), *Schwartz's Principles of Surgery.* New York: McGraw-Hill; 2005:1366.

14

Cervical Spine Injuries

Jeff G. Konin, PhD, ATC,
PT, FACSM, FNATA
Sean T. Bryan, MD, FAAFP
Adam Shimer, MD

Cervical Spine Fractures and Dislocations

Unsupervised sports such as diving, surfing, and downhill skiing present the greatest risk for cervical spine fractures and dislocations. Even so, spinal injuries that occur during organized activities such as football, rugby, soccer, and ice hockey receive greater attention despite their relative infrequency. Cervical spine fractures may or may not be associated with spinal cord injury.

The nature and treatment of cervical spine fractures depend on their location. Fractures and dislocations of the upper cervical spine (C1 and C2) are unique because of the anatomy of the craniocervical junction (C0–C1) and the atlantoaxial junction (C1–C2). Trauma to these structures must be considered separately from trauma of the lower cervical spine. Fractures of the spinous or transverse processes produce significant pain and may limit the range of motion (ROM) but do not often carry the threat of permanent disability associated with fractures or dislocations of the vertebral body.

The standard on-field and clinical examination techniques of palpation and ROM testing must be undertaken with caution in a patient with acute cervical spine trauma. Using too much pressure while palpating can dislodge a bony fragment and cause more severe trauma. In the presence of unstable vertebral segments or fracture, ROM testing can further traumatize the spinal cord. At the first sign of injury to a cervical vertebra or the spinal cord, the patient should be immediately immobilized and transported to an appropriate medical facility.

> **Practice Tip**
>
> All potential emergency responders must be familiar with the types of equipment worn by athletes and be aware of their special considerations during the immediate management during immediate care. All personnel responsible for immediate care of potentially catastrophic injuries (i.e., athletic trainers, physicians, emergency medical technicians, coaches) must conduct regular rehearsals of their facility's emergency action plan.[1]

The general description of the immediate, on-field management of cervical spine injuries is provided in this chapter. Also refer to Chapter 17 for information regarding the management of head injuries.

C1 Fractures and Dislocations

CLINICAL PRESENTATION

History

Significant neck pain is associated with any attempt to rotate the head.

Observation

The patient may posture the cervical spine and skull for comfort. Dislocation may result in an involuntary tilt or rotation of the cervical spine.

No visible sign of injury may be noted along the cervical spine.

Functional Status

Because this injury does not always present as traumatically as a lower cervical spine fracture, the patient may attempt to return to play. Any patient with a history of spearing and subsequent neck pain should be fully examined before a return-to-play decision is made.

Physical Examination Findings

Most fractures of C1 do not cause neurologic deficit because of the large spinal canal at this level; the nature of these fractures tends to actually enlarge the spinal canal.

ROM and clinical provocation and alleviation tests should not be performed in patients with suspected cervical spine fractures or dislocations.

Fractures of the atlas (C1) account for 1% to 2% of all spinal fractures.[2,3] Jefferson fractures are the most common C1 fracture; they involve a bilateral fracture of the C1 ring caused by a blow to the top of the head producing an axial load in the cervical vertebrae (see **Figure 15.1**). This type of fracture can occur in diving injuries or in football, particularly when "spear tackling."

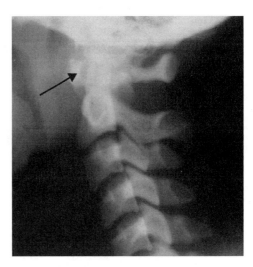

Figure 15.1 Lateral cervical spine radiograph showing a fracture of the arch of C1.

15

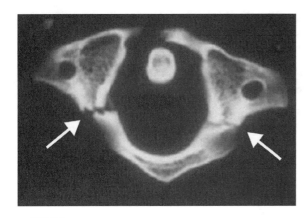

Figure 15.2 Axial CT image highlighting bilateral C1 ring fractures.

Differential Diagnosis

Neck strain, cervical sprain, cervical spasm.

Imaging Techniques

The role of imaging in the diagnosis of C1 fractures has changed over time. Historically, the diagnosis and management of C1 fractures have been based on cervical spine radiographs, particularly the open-mouth odontoid view. If the sum of the lateral overhang of the lateral masses of C1 over C2 is greater than 8.1 mm, taking into account the magnification of the film, rupture of the transverse ligament is likely and the fracture is considered unstable.[3] Fractures with less lateral displacement of C1 over C2 are considered relatively stable.

The definitive diagnosis of C1 fractures has been significantly aided by computed tomography (CT) and magnetic resonance imaging (MRI).[4] The ring of C1 and the fracture can be imaged with CT scans (see **Figure 15.2**). With the advent of CT tech-

nology, unilateral fractures of C1 have been shown to be more common than previously thought. The three-dimensional reconstructions available with CT allow excellent visualization of the displacement of the lateral masses of C1 over C2. MRI is useful in the diagnosis of C1 fractures to determine if the transverse ligament of the atlas is disrupted, which serves as a determinant of fracture stability.

Definitive Diagnosis

Diagnosis of C1 fracture is made based on positive findings on radiographs, CT, or MRI (for soft-tissue and spinal cord injuries).

Pathomechanics and Functional Limitations

The loss of integrity of the C1 vertebral arch creates potential rotational instability between the C1 and C2 vertebrae. Subsequent force to the cervical spine can result in a dislocation and cause permanent spinal cord injury or death.

The patient experiences severe pain on cervical motion, especially rotation or flexion. Spasm of the cervical spine muscles limits motion. Trunk rotation substitutes for cervical and capital rotation.

■ Postinjury Management

The treatment of most C1 fractures is a rigid collar, such as an Aspen or Miami J collar (see **Figure 15.3**), worn for 8 to 12 weeks, with follow-up radiographs being performed every 2 to 4 weeks to evaluate fracture healing and determine whether the amount of dislocation has increased.

In patients whose fractures are deemed unstable, with probable disruption of the transverse ligament (based on MRI or displacement of the lateral masses

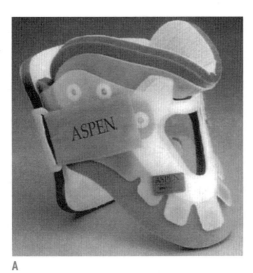

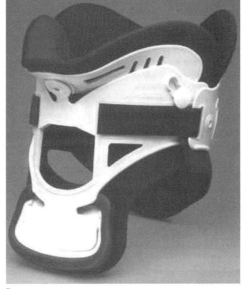

A B

Figure 15.3 Cervical collars. **(A)** Aspen collar. **(B)** Miami collar.

of C1 on C2), halo immobilization is recommended for 8 to 12 weeks, followed by a period of time in a rigid collar.

Medications

Acute pain management is achieved by the use of nonsteroidal anti-inflammatory drugs (NSAIDs) and narcotic analgesics as needed. Muscle relaxants may be prescribed to treat acute muscle spasm.

Surgical Intervention

Surgical intervention is rarely necessary for C1 fractures. The patient may require the fitting of a halo brace to maintain constant traction on the skull, allowing C1 to reassume proper alignment with C2.[2] This brace is named for its resemblance to a halo as it surrounds the head. The purpose of the halo brace is to provide stability in the cervical spine above and below the injury without allowing cervical movement in any plane while the fracture or surgical site is healing (see **S T** 15.1). Treatment duration for an unstable Jefferson fracture can range anywhere from 3 to 5 months.

Intolerance of the halo brace or halo failure (residual instability) has been traditionally treated with a posterior occipitocervical fusion to C2. This treatment results in an obligate reduction of cervical rotation and flexion/extension of at least 50%. Recently, fracture repair has been obtained using paired screws in the C1 lateral masses and posterior cross-link.[5]

Postoperative Management

Attendant postoperative care of the surgical wounds is critical because the patient cannot view several of the portals. The patient is typically hospitalized for 2 to 3 days (if neurologically intact) after the halo is positioned for close monitoring of postoperative status. The halo pins should be retensioned to 8 in-lb at 24 hours and again 1 week after placement, as many studies have demonstrated pin loosening as much as 70% due to carbon fiber halo ring relaxation.[6] Pin site loosening, drainage, and infection are the most common complications of prolonged halo use. The pin sites should be closely monitored and routinely, gently cleaned with either peroxide, saline, or a soap-and-water solution.[6]

Once discharged, the patient must be aware of pressure sores that can be caused by the vest. During postoperative home care, a relative or friend should be assigned to regularly check the areas that are not visible to the patient. A proper hygiene routine, consisting of checking for chafing under the vest and applying absorbent powder such as cornstarch, can reduce moisture and prevent pressure sores.

Injury-Specific Treatment and Rehabilitation Concerns

> **Specific Concerns**
>
> Maintain the hygiene of the halo fixation sites.
> Maintain functional levels of activity as permitted by the physician.
> Restrict ROM after halo removal.
> Focus on restoration of ADLs.

The patient must first master ADLs within the confines of the halo. After halo removal, the patient is placed in a rigid collar for at least 3 months, followed by use of a soft collar for an additional 2 to 3 months. As the cervical spine regains muscular strength and endurance through rehabilitation exercises, the patient will require no additional support.

Estimated Amount of Time Lost

Patients who sustain C1 fractures do not return to contact or collision sports. Ultimately, the rehabilitation goal is to return the patient to a functional lifestyle. Depending on the severity of the trauma and residual instability and in the absence of spinal cord trauma, the patient may be able to return to select recreational activities such as golf or tennis with the physician's consent.

C2 Fractures and Dislocations

CLINICAL PRESENTATION

> **History**
>
> Cervical hyperextension.
> Possible neurologic, cardiac, and respiratory deficits.
>
> **Observation**
>
> Cervical spasm may be present.
> Motion may be guarded.
> Observed findings may be unremarkable.
>
> **Functional Status**
>
> Pain occurs with rotational movements of the cervical spine.
> ROM should not be evaluated in patients with suspected cervical spine trauma.
>
> **Physical Examination Findings**
>
> Pain at the cervical spine just below the occiput.
> Possible neurologic, cardiac, and respiratory deficits.

15

S|T Surgical Technique 15.1

Application of a Halo Brace

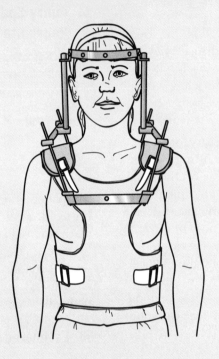

Indications

Upper cervical spine fracture or instability.

Procedure for Halo Application

1. The size of the crown (halo) and vest are determined.
2. Pin sites are determined while the ring/crown is held in place.
3. Pins are tightened at increments of 2 in-lb in a diagonal fashion until 8 in-lb of torque is achieved.
4. The crown is connected to the vest via four upright supports.
5. Tools are taped to the vest or kept at the bedside for emergency vest removal.
6. Forty-eight hours after halo application, the pins are retightened to 8 in-lb.
7. Pin sites are left uncovered and cleansed with hydrogen peroxide every other day or as needed.

Functional Limitations

Activities of daily living (ADLs) are difficult and cumbersome. The patient must sleep in a seated or semireclined position.

Implications for Rehabilitation

Muscular contractions and limited ADLs are maintained per physician's orders while the patient is in the halo. After removal of the halo, rotation between C1 and C2 is limited or absent. The attending physician should be consulted to determine the anticipated level of function.

Potential Complications

Potential complications include loosening of the pins, rings, and crowns; infection; pressure sores beneath the vest; loss of reduction secondary to a poorly fitting vest or unwanted motion; bleeding at the pin sites; and difficulty swallowing. (The halo will be repositioned with less extension in this situation.[2])

C2 fractures are characterized and managed based on the unique anatomy of the C2 odontoid process, which allows for rotation of the head (see **Figure 15.4**). Fractures of C2 are grouped into three categories—odontoid fractures, hangman's fractures (traumatic spondylolisthesis of the axis), and miscellaneous fractures such as vertebral body fractures.[7]

Fractures of the odontoid are classified into three types (see **Figure 15.5**). Type I fractures are oblique fractures of the very tip or upper portion of the odontoid process. Relatively uncommon injuries, they should always raise suspicion for possible occipital-cervical dissociation—a potentially life-threatening injury that can easily be overlooked.

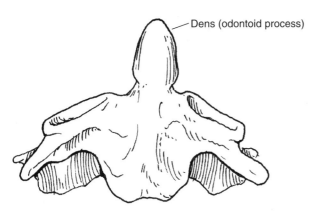

- Dens (odontoid process)

Figure 15.4 The odontoid process (dens) is a bony projection from C2 that sits posterior to C1. The articulation between the odontoid process and C1 allows for capital rotation. *Source:* Adapted from Chutkan NB, King AG, Harris MB. Odontoid fractures: evaluation and management. *J Am Acad Orthop Surg.* 1997; 5:199-204.

Type II fractures are the most common fracture of the odontoid process. Type III fractures extend into the vertebral body.

A hangman's fracture affects the posterior elements of C2, resulting in traumatic spondylolisthesis of the axis. The mechanism of injury is usually

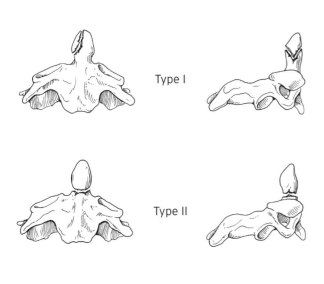

Type I

Type II

Type III

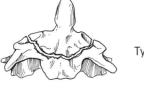

Figure 15.5 The Anderson and d'Alonzo classification system for odontoid fractures. Type I fractures are avulsion fractures of the tip of the odontoid process. Type II fractures occur at the junction of the odontoid process and the body of the axis. In the type III pattern, the fracture extends into the body of the axis through the cancellous bone. *Source:* Reproduced with permission from Chutkan NB, King AG, Harris MB. Odontoid fractures: evaluation and management. *J Am Acad Orthop Surg.* 1997;5:199-204.

hyperextension.[8] This hyperextension of the neck and subsequent fracture are similar to the injury caused by judicial hangings—hence the name "hangman's fracture." Most low-velocity hangman's fractures seen clinically are not associated with spinal cord injury because the low velocity causes a bilateral fracture, which in turn opens the spinal canal. High-velocity fractures sever the spinal cord and result in almost instantaneous death. Patients who survive the first few minutes after fracturing C2 have a good chance of recovery if the spinal cord is not involved, although return to contact or collision sports is often unlikely.

The classification of hangman's fractures is not well defined or accepted. One classification system describes a type I hangman's fracture as a fracture of the posterior elements of C2 without displacement of C2 on C3; a type II fracture consists of subluxation of C2 on C3. Another classification of hangman's fractures identifies a type I fracture as a posterior element fracture of C2 with 3 mm or less subluxation of C2 on C3. Type II fractures have a subluxation of C2 on C3 of 4 mm or angulation of more than 11°. Type III fractures are rare, may be associated with severe neurologic injury or death, and are confirmed with the disruption of the C2–C3 facet joints and possible locked facets.[7]

Differential Diagnosis

Cervical muscle strain, cervical sprain, spasm, other cervical fractures, degenerative osteoarthritis.

Imaging Techniques

The imaging and diagnosis of C2 fractures begin with plain cervical radiographs (see **Figure 15.6**). However, CT scanning—particularly with sagittal and coronal reconstructions—allows for definitive diagnosis of

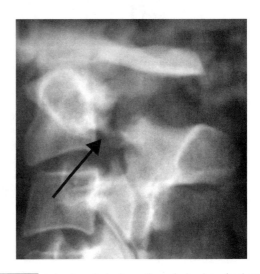

Figure 15.6 Lateral cervical spine radiograph showing a fracture of the posterior arch of C2 (hangman's fracture).

15

the fracture and better evaluation of the fracture subtype (see **Figure 15.7**). MRI is rarely necessary in a neurologically intact patient with a C2 fracture.

Definitive Diagnosis

Diagnosis of C2 fracture is made based on conclusive findings on radiographs, CT scan, or MRI.

Pathomechanics and Functional Limitations

Cervical rotation is limited and painful, and muscle spasm further limits motion. Trunk rotation substitutes for cervical and capital rotation. Instability of the vertebra can jeopardize the integrity of the spinal cord and the associated spinal nerve roots.

■ Postinjury Management

The treatment of odontoid fractures depends on the fracture pattern. Type I fractures can usually be treated with a rigid collar. Type II fractures generally require halo immobilization for 8 to 12 weeks (see ST 15.1). However, the incidence of nonunion in type II fractures increases significantly when the patient is older than age 40 years; cervical fusion may be necessary in such cases. Type III fractures have been reported to heal in a rigid collar in as many as 65% of individuals, but some of these patients may require halo immobilization.

The management of a hangman's fracture almost always consists of immobilization. Fractures without dislocation can usually be managed with a rigid collar. Cervical traction and subsequent halo immobilization may be required for patients with fractures and significant dislocations at C2–C3. A type II hangman's fracture with acute kyphotic angulation due to an intact anterior longitudinal ligament is further subtyped as a type IIA. The distinction between type II and type IIA fractures is very important, in that traction is often used to achieve reduction in a type II fracture but should be avoided in a type IIA fracture because it can result in worsening of deformity and possible iatrogenic neurologic injury.

■ Surgical Intervention

If surgery is necessary for an odontoid fracture (generally a type II fracture), posterior fusion is often performed with a C1–C2 fusion or, more recently, with transarticular stabilization at C1–C2. Any planned posterior screw instrumentation of the atlantoaxis demands careful study of associated vertebral artery anatomy and patient-to-patient variation. Anterior screw fixation of the odontoid can be performed in certain cases but is technically more demanding than posterior fusion (see **Figure 15.8**).[9] Surgery is occasionally necessary for a hangman's fracture when dislocation is significant or when satisfactory alignment cannot be maintained with a halo brace. The rare hangman's fractures that require surgery can be managed with either an anterior C2–C3 fusion with instrumentation or a posterior C1–C3 fusion.[9] Miscellaneous fractures of C2 include mild fractures of the vertebral body or lateral masses of C2 that can usually be managed with rigid-collar immobilization (see **ST 15.2**).

■ Postsurgical Management

After a fusion of C1–C2, the patient may be put in a rigid collar for up to 3 months. Rehabilitation is

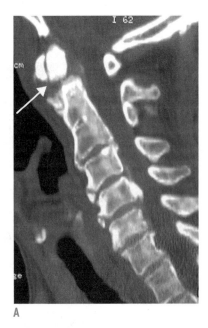 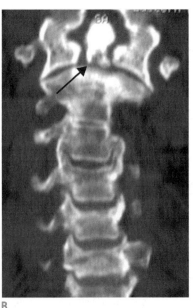

A   B

Figure 15.7 CT scans of type II odontoid fractures. (**A**) Sagittal view. (**B**) Coronal view.

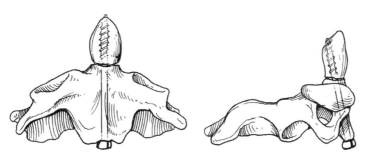

Figure 15.8   Anterior single-screw fixation of an odontoid process fracture. *Source:* Reproduced with permission from Chutkan NB, King AG, Harris MB. Odontoid fractures: Evaluation and management. *J Am Acad Orthop Surg.* 1997;5:199–204.

S|**T** Surgical Technique **15.2**

Posterior Atlantoaxial Fusion (Goel-Harms Fusion)

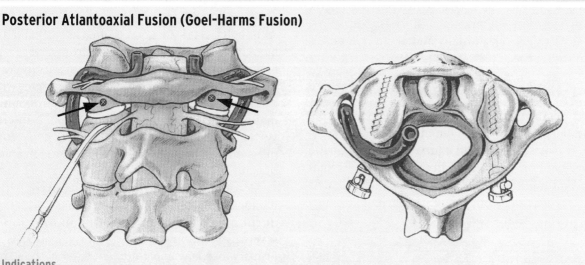

Indications

Significant instability of C1–C2 including rupture of the transverse ligament; type II odontoid fracture; recalcitrant C1-C2 rotary subluxation; if satisfactory reduction cannot be achieved or maintained with a halo brace.

Procedure Overview

Although Goel-Harms fusion (C1 lateral mass screws and C2 pedicle screws) is described here, the Brooks and Gallie techniques employing posterior-element wiring and structural bone grafting remain acceptable alternatives.

1. The patient is positioned prone, and a midline incision is made in the upper posterior neck from lower occiput to C4. The paraspinal muscles are dissected off the spine to expose the lateral extent of the posterior elements of C1 and C2. Care is taken to preserve the C2-C3 facet.
2. The lateral undersurface of the C1 ring is bluntly and subperiosteally dissected down to the posterior aspect of the lateral masses. This dissection is above the exiting C2 or greater occipital nerve root.
3. Using the middle of the lateral mass as a starting point, a hand drill is advanced toward the anterior C1 ring, guided by lateral fluoroscopic imaging. A beaded probe is use to palpate and assure a safe bony pathway. An appropriate-length polyaxial screw is placed.
4. The superomedial border of the C2 pedicle is bluntly dissected and visualized. This medial border is used to direct a screw path approximately 15° medial within the C2 pedicle. Again, a beaded probe is used to palpate the bony pathway. An appropriate-length screw is placed.
5. The paired C1-C2 screws are connected using a rod between the polyaxial heads.
6. A bone graft harvested from the posterior iliac crest is affixed between the C1 and C2 posterior elements using nonabsorbable suture or wire.

Functional Limitations

Rotation of C1 on C2 is lost.

Implications for Rehabilitation

Rotational motions are avoided until the surgical repair has fully healed.

Comments

Patients are prohibited from engaging in future contact and collision sports.

Source: Figures reproduced from Bransford RJ, Lee MJ, Reis A. Posterior fixation of the upper cervical spine: contemporary techniques. *J Am Acad Orthop Surg.* 2011; (19):67.

15

limited to ADLs, and the ultimate rehabilitation goal is to return the patient to a functional lifestyle.

Injury-Specific Treatment and Rehabilitation Concerns

Specific Concerns

Prevent rotation between C1 and C2 during healing.
Limit flexion and extension activities.
Maintain cardiovascular fitness as permitted by the physician.

Some surgeons prefer to be more progressive and will place the patient in a hard collar only for a week or two at most. Others may opt to use a soft collar for 1 to 2 weeks initially and begin rehabilitation right away.

Estimated Amount of Time Lost

The amount of time lost depends on the type of fracture, but an athlete rarely continues in contact or collision sports after such an injury. Depending on the severity of the trauma and in the absence of spinal cord trauma, the patient may be able to return to select recreational activities (e.g., golf, tennis) pending the physician's consent.

Subaxial Cervical Spine Fractures and Dislocations

CLINICAL PRESENTATION

History

Axial loading and hyperflexion are the predominant mechanisms of history for these fractures.

Observation

The patient is typically down, and unwilling or unable to move.

Functional Status

The patient may or may not display radicular signs and symptoms.
Muscular weakness or inability to function is demonstrated.
Cardiovascular and respiratory systems may be compromised.
ROM testing should not be performed on patients suspected of suffering a cervical spine injury.

Physical Examination Findings

Cervical spine pain at the level of injury.
Typically bilateral weakness and loss of motor function below the injury site.
Usually bilateral deficit and loss of sensation below the injury site.
Severe spasm and neck pain.
Priapism in males.

priapism Abnormal, painful, continued erection of the penis, often the result of a spinal cord lesion.

Because of the significant variety of cervical spine fractures and dislocations involving the lower cervical spine (C3 to C7), no uniform classification of these injuries is accepted. A broad way to categorize these lower cervical spine injuries is to separate the injuries with facet dislocation from those without facet dislocation.

Cervical spine injuries with either unilateral or bilateral facet dislocation are common.[10] Injuries with unilateral facet dislocation are usually accompanied by cervical radiculopathy (single-level root syndrome from compression of the nerve root by the dislocated facet). Injuries with bilateral facet dislocation result in approximately 50% narrowing of the spinal canal and are almost always associated with acute spinal cord injury (see **Figure 15.9**). Although facet dislocation is often accompanied by facet fracture, it can also occur from severe ligamentous injury and without any obvious fracture. Lower cervical spine fractures and dislocations without facet dislocation include a number of abnormalities, such as teardrop fractures to the anterior vertebral body, significant vertebral body compression fractures or burst fractures, and ligamentous injury with subluxation of the cervical spine.

Most of these injuries are due to severe hyperflexion of the cervical spine with possible subsequent hyperextension, resulting in fractures or severe ligamentous injuries.[10,11] Axial loading is the primary mechanism of injury for cervical spine fractures with spinal cord insult.[12] Torg and associates[12] discovered that a cervical spine in a slightly flexed position converts the natural lordotic curve into a straight column, predisposing it to injury.

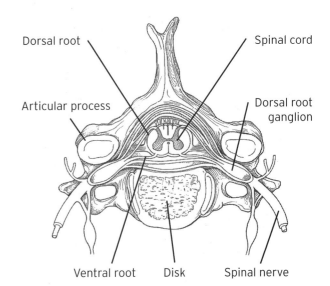

Figure 15.9 Cross-sectional view of the neural structures of the lower cervical spine. *Source:* Reproduced with permission from Levine MJ, Albert TJ, Smith MD. Cervical radiculopathy: Diagnosis and nonoperative management. *J Am Acad Orthop Surg.* 1996;4:305-316.

The clinical presentation of patients with lower cervical spine injuries with fracture and/or dislocation includes severe neck pain and neurologic deficit with either radiculopathy or evidence of acute spinal cord injury. Spinal cord syndromes are described in the "Spinal Cord Injury" section later in this chapter.

Differential Diagnosis

Neck strain, cervical sprain, cervical spasm.

Imaging Techniques

Imaging of lower cervical spine injuries is similar to imaging of upper cervical spine (C1 and C2) injuries. Plain lateral radiographs usually demonstrate fracture or dislocation, although they may sometimes be normal (see **Figure 15.10**). CT scan is optimal; such studies should be taken as soon as possible because of better fracture delineation and the ability to obtain sagittal and coronal reconstructions (see **Figure 15.11**). Cervical CT scan also identifies narrowing of the spinal canal caused by retropulsed bone fragments or vertebral subluxation. MRI is useful to evaluate the spinal cord for hemorrhage and edema and can help identify ligamentous disruption and the presence of a herniated cervical disk.[10]

Definitive Diagnosis

Radiographs, CT scan, or MRI will confirm the presence of a fracture.

Pathomechanics and Functional Limitations

Pain with cervical movement and neck spasm can prohibit movement. Dynamic impact of the spinal cord can result in paralysis of the lower extremities and possibly the upper extremities, depending on the location of the injury. The role of residual compression of the spinal cord from bony fragments or space-occupying hematoma relative to further neural element insult is unclear.

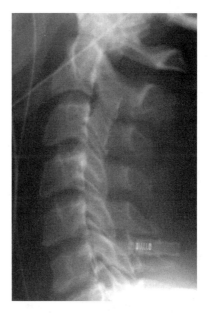

Figure 15.10 Normal lateral cervical spine radiograph of a patient subsequently found to have multiple cervical fractures.

retropulsed Displaced posteriorly.

■ Postinjury Management

If dislocation is significant, the immediate management is to reduce the dislocation and restore normal spinal canal and foraminal anatomy. This reduction is generally performed using cervical skeletal traction with either a halo brace or Gardner-Wells tongs. Dislocations may be difficult to reduce with skeletal traction and may require open reduction.

Some lower cervical spine fractures that do not jeopardize the spinal cord, such as transverse or spinous process fractures, can be managed simply with a rigid collar, such as a Miami or Aspen collar (see Figure 15.3). These injuries include single-level, stable vertebral body fractures and facet

15

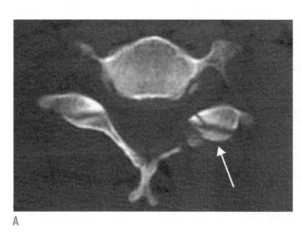

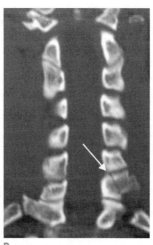

A   B

Figure 15.11 CT scan of the same patient shown in Figure 15.10. **(A)** Axial view of a left C6–C7 facet fracture. **(B)** Coronal view of a fracture of the C7 facet.

fractures without subluxation or dislocation. The rigid collar is generally applied for 8 to 12 weeks; the patient then spends a period of time in a soft collar. In the past, many severe injuries of the lower cervical spine were managed with initial reduction and long-term halo immobilization. Significant morbidity is noted with 3 to 4 months of halo immobilization, however, so long-term immobilization is used less commonly today than in the past. Nevertheless, halo traction and even long-term halo immobilization continue to be used in the management of some fractures (see ST 15.1).

Surgical Intervention

Surgical stabilization, particularly with cervical instrumentation, has become more widely used for lower cervical spine fractures and dislocations. The most commonly performed procedure for stabilization of these injuries is the anterior cervical decompression (either diskectomy or partial/total corpectomy) with fusion (see ⓢⓣ 15.3). The introduction of various anterior instrumentation systems has improved fusion rates and decreased the time for which patients must wear an external orthosis postoperatively. Anterior cervical diskectomy and

---

ⓢⓣ Surgical Technique   15.3

Anterior Cervical Diskectomy and Fusion

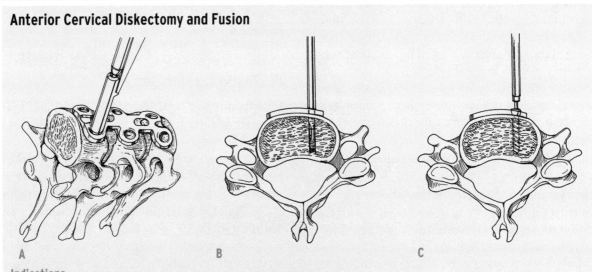

A   B   C

Indications

Failure to achieve satisfactory closed reduction or inability to maintain reduction with an external orthosis; significant ligamentous injury with evidence of severe facet instability; angulation of the spine of more than 15°; more than 40% compression of a vertebral body; subluxation of 20% or more of one vertebral body on another.

Procedure Overview

1. The patient is placed supine with the head slightly turned to one side.
2. Cervical traction is maintained during the procedure.
3. A transverse or longitudinal incision is made in the anterior neck, and dissection is carried down through the platysma and along the medial border of the sternocleidomastoid muscle to the spine.
4. An anterior cervical diskectomy at the affected level is performed, and the bone graft is placed in the disk space.
5. The appropriate anterior plate is selected and held in place. Holes are drilled into the vertebral bodies above and below the bone graft, and then screws are placed with a special locking system unique to the plate used (**A, B,** and **C**).

Functional Limitations

Decreased cervical ROM is noted following this surgery. The presence of an associated spinal cord injury determines the patient's overall level of function.

Implications for Rehabilitation

The patient is placed in a rigid protective collar for 4 to 6 weeks, followed by use of a soft collar.

Complications

Potential complications include hardware failure, bone graft displacement, injury to the trachea or esophagus with swallowing problems or hoarseness, and neurologic deficit related to spinal cord manipulation.

Source: Figures reproduced with permission from An HS. Internal fixation of the cervical spine: Current indications and techniques. *J Am Acad Orthop Surg.* 1995;3:194-206.

fusion are performed with a bone graft placed in the disk space. Although iliac crest bone can be harvested from the patient, it is now more common practice to use processed allograft bone. The use of banked bone results in decreased morbidity from pain due to an incision in the iliac crest. Once the bone graft is placed, a decision must be made about anterior instrumentation, which is generally used in the setting of acute trauma.

Posterior cervical fusion is also often used for fractures and dislocations of the cervical spine (see ST 15.4). Occasionally a patient has such severe ligamentous injury that both anterior and posterior cervical fusions are necessary to maintain adequate stability and alignment of the cervical spine. These procedures can be performed on the same day or as a staged procedure, depending on the medical condition of the patient.

Surgical Technique 15.4

Posterior Cervical Fusion with Lateral Mass Instrumentation

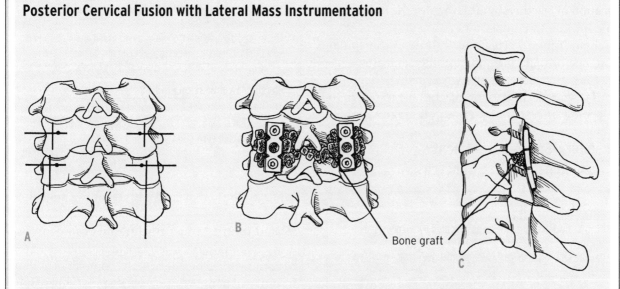

Bone graft

Indications

Fracture and/or dislocation of the cervical spine involving the posterior ligaments; irreducible facet dislocations; severe anteroposterior ligamentous injury in which a posterior fusion may be used to supplement an anterior fusion; severe anterior soft-tissue trauma, swelling, or presence of a tracheotomy.

Procedure Overview

1. The patient is placed prone.
2. A midline cervical incision is made, and the cervical paraspinous muscles are dissected off the lamina and facets bilaterally.
3. Fusion is carried out one segment above and below the affected level.
4. Drill holes are made in the lateral masses of the involved segments bilaterally (**A**).
5. Screws are placed in the holes and attached to titanium rods or plates for stabilization (depending on the instrumentation used) (**B**).
6. Posterior instrumentation is supplemented with fusion of the facets, and bone can be laid along the facets and lamina bilaterally (**C**).

Functional Limitations

Mild loss of cervical flexion and extension is experienced. The total amount of ROM decrease is related to the number of segments fused; an increased number of fusions results in a greater ROM deficit.

Implications for Rehabilitation

The patient is placed in a rigid protective collar for 4 to 6 weeks, followed by use of a soft collar. Weight lifting is limited to 10 lb for 6 weeks.

Complications

Potential complications include hardware failure, bone graft displacement, and neurologic deficit related to the manipulation of the spinal cord.

Source: Figures reproduced with permission from An HS. Internal fixation of the cervical spine: Current indications and techniques. *J Am Acad Orthop Surg.* 1995;3:194-206.

■ Postoperative Management

The postoperative management is determined by the bony injury and associated spinal cord trauma. In the absence of neurologic deficit, protected cervical motion and generalized upper and lower extremity exercises may be initiated to prevent muscular atrophy and maintain cardiovascular and respiratory function. If spinal cord injury is significant, the patient will require extensive care and rehabilitation.

■ Estimated Amount of Time Lost

The amount of time lost depends on the type and location of fracture, but it is rare for the individual to continue in contact and collision sports after such an injury. Permanent trauma to the spinal cord results in permanent disability, and all too often the patient depends on a wheelchair. If the spinal cord is spared, the patient may be able to return to select low-risk sports, such as golf or tennis.

■ Injury-Specific Treatment and Rehabilitation Concerns

> **Specific Concerns**
>
> Restrict flexion and extension as indicated by the physician.
> Maintain cardiovascular levels during convalescence.
> Restore strength and gain available ROM (may be restricted by the surgical technique used).

Generally, absent neurologic involvement, lower extremity cardiovascular conditioning (e.g., stationary bicycling, elliptical machines) may begin soon after the initial protective period. Cardiovascular equipment involving the upper extremities, such as stair steppers and cross-country ski machines, should be used more cautiously because of the potential for stressing the cervical musculature and causing pain or spasm. After the fracture heals completely, gentle ROM and strengthening exercises may begin with the physician's approval (see the "Rehabilitation" section later in this chapter).

■ Return-to-Activity Criteria

If the surgery was the result of trauma, return to competitive sport is unlikely. In contrast, if the surgery was necessitated by degenerative arthritis or disk disease, the patient's outcome depends on the quality of the surgery and subsequent rehabilitation. Overall, the time lost due to lower cervical spine fractures without spinal cord injury generally ranges from 6 to 18 months.

Spinal Cord Injury

CLINICAL PRESENTATION

History

Axial loading and/or hyperflexion.

Observation

The patient may be unable or reluctant to move unassisted. There may be no residual movement of the extremities. Decorticate or decerebrate postures may be noted.

Functional Status

Bilateral neuromuscular involvement, including muscular weakness/paralysis and radicular symptoms below the injury, may be present.
Airway and cardiac function must be assessed and maintained.
ROM or clinical orthopaedic tests should not be performed in the presence of suspected cervical spine injury.

Physical Examination Findings

Pain may be noted with palpation of the cervical spine—but palpation should not be performed on patients with known or suspected vertebral fractures.
Neuromuscular involvement ranges from weakness to paralysis.

Injury to the spinal cord with resulting neurologic deficit is perhaps the most feared of any athletic-related injury. Spinal cord trauma can cause significant temporary or permanent disability and may be accompanied by injury to the bony cervical spine. In older patients with cervical spondylosis, however, significant spinal cord injury may occur without obvious spinal fracture. Cervical spine injuries resulting in permanent paralysis have significantly declined since the antispearing rule was implemented for football in 1976.[11]

The clinical presentation of spinal cord injury varies. Complete spinal cord injury results in a total loss of spinal function below the level of the injury. Trauma to the spinal cord itself is rarely reversible, but occasionally neurologic function improves some with reduction of a severe dislocation, such as in a patient with bilateral dislocated facets.

A number of patterns of incomplete spinal cord injury are seen clinically (see **Figure 15.12**). The most commonly observed incomplete spinal cord injury is central spinal cord syndrome. It results in incomplete loss of motor function, with upper extremity weakness being more pronounced than lower extremity weakness. This disproportionate weakness is due to the anatomy of the spinal cord; the fibers in the corticospinal tract that supply the cervical nerve roots are more central in the spinal cord than those supplying the lower extremities.[11] Central

Name (Figure Element)	Description	Deficit Patterns
Central spinal cord syndrome (**A**)	Hemorrhage and ischemia of the corticospinal tracts	Weakness of the upper extremities more pronounced than the lower extremities
	Trauma to the cells within the anterior horn of the cervical spinal cord	
Anterior spinal cord syndrome (**B**)	Trauma to the anterior two-thirds of the spinal cord	Loss of motor function and pain and temperature sensation below the level of the injury
		Touch, pressure, and proprioceptive function are usually present
Brown-Séquard syndrome (**C**)	Hemisection of the spinal cord involving the spinothalamic tracts	Loss or weakness of motor function on the side of the trauma
		Loss of pain and temperature sensation on the side opposite the trauma

Source: Adapted with permission from Spivak JM, Vaccaro AR, Cotler JM. Thoracolumbar spine trauma: I. Evaluation and classification. *J Am Acad Orthop Surg.* 1995;3:345–352.

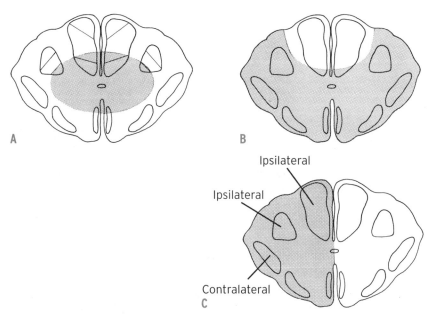

Figure 15.12 Patterns of neurologic deficit associated with incomplete lesions of the spinal cord. Injury is indicated by shaded area.

spinal cord syndrome results in hemorrhage and ischemia of the corticospinal tracts, with a disproportionate injury to the more central nerve fibers supplying the upper extremities.[11,13] This syndrome may also be due to actual damage to anterior horn cells in the gray matter of the cervical spinal cord. Central spinal cord syndrome has historically been described in older patients with cervical spondylosis and osteophytic ridges who suffer a hyperextension injury of the cervical spine. Transient compression results in hemorrhage and ischemia in the spinal cord. However, central spinal cord syndrome is often seen in young patients with spinal trauma and incomplete spinal cord injury.

Brown-Séquard syndrome is a hemisection of the spinal cord, with loss of motor function on the side of the injury and loss of pain and temperature on the side contralateral to the injury. This syndrome occurs because of the decussation of the spinothalamic tracts one or two segments above their entry into the spinal cord. The corticospinal tracts, which supply motor function, have already crossed in the medulla and maintain an ipsilateral course throughout the spinal cord. Classic Brown-Séquard syndrome is rarely seen in the absence of penetrating trauma, such as a bony fragment. Instead, this condition usually takes the form of a "modified" Brown-Séquard syndrome, in which the patient has some motor weakness on one side of the body and decreased pain and temperature on the opposite side. Central spinal cord syndrome may be seen with a modified Brown-Séquard syndrome in which weakness is more pronounced in the upper extremities than the lower extremities.

Anterior spinal cord syndrome is an injury to the anterior two-thirds of the spinal cord in the

decussation The crossing of one structure over the other.

15

hemisection Cutting into two; bisecting.

region of the anterior spinal artery. The neurologic deficit consists of loss of all motor function below the level of the injury and loss of pain and temperature sensation below the level of injury (the spinothalamic tracts). The motor deficit in this condition is usually equal in the upper and lower extremities, unlike in central spinal cord syndrome. Touch, pressure, and proprioceptive function are typically preserved due to sparing of the dorsal columns.

Differential Diagnosis

Cervical radiculopathy, cervical disk disease, cervical fracture, primary or metastatic tumor, brachial plexus injury, neurapraxia, hysterical paralysis.

Imaging Techniques

A lateral cervical spine radiograph is indicated when the neurologic examination suggests a spinal cord injury. All patients with suspected spinal cord injury should undergo CT scanning to evaluate the cervical spine for fracture, dislocation, or compromise of the spinal canal (see **Figure 15.13**). MRI is useful for evaluating hemorrhage or edema within the spinal cord itself and for identifying a disk herniation, which may compress or sever the spinal cord (see **Figure 15.14**).[4]

Definitive Diagnosis

The definitive diagnosis is based on the clinical examination, possible neurologic findings, and confirmation by MRI or CT scans.

Pathomechanics and Functional Limitations

The patient may experience quadriplegia or paraplegia, depending on the level of spinal cord involvement. The degree of spinal cord trauma determines the patient's functional limitations. Complete trauma to the spinal cord results in the loss of all sensory, motor, and reflex function distal to the site of the lesion. When the lesion occurs above the C4 level, the phrenic nerve, which controls

metastatic The spreading of a cancerous growth from one body area to another.

hysterical paralysis The inability to move brought on by fear and/or anxiety.

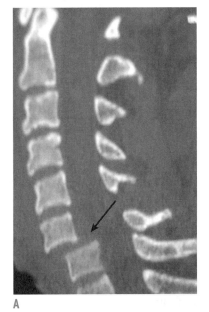

A

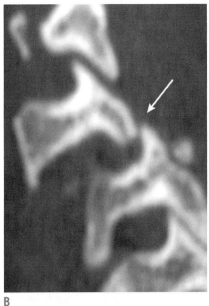

B

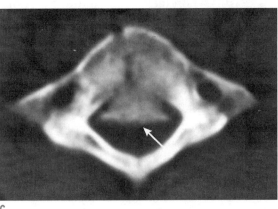

C

Figure 15.13   CT scans of the cervical spine. (**A**) Sagittal image demonstrating significant subluxation of C6 on C7 and bilateral facet dislocation. (**B**) Scan of a dislocation of the right C6–C7 facet joint. (**C**) Axial scan demonstrating vertebral body fracture with bone displaced into the spinal canal.

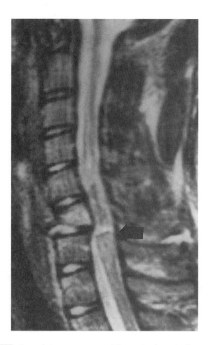

Figure 15.14 Complete severance of the spinal cord after a severe C6 fracture-subluxation. The 18-year-old male patient sustained a diving injury and immediate C6 quadriplegia. This MRI scan, obtained 90 minutes after the injury, depicts complete severance of the cord at the base of the C6 vertebra and hemorrhage into the cord **cephalad** to the C6 level (arrow).

breathing, is impaired and the patient is placed on a respirator. Incomplete spinal cord trauma may result in the selective loss of motor, sensory, or reflex function (see Figure 15.12).

Medications

Drug treatment for acute spinal cord injury remains quite controversial. A number of medications, including corticosteroids, naloxone (an opioid antagonist), and GM-1 ganglioside, have been tested for this indication.[14–27]

The medications that have undergone the most rigorous human investigation in acute spinal cord injury include corticosteroids, predominantly methylprednisolone (see **Box 15.1**).[11,28–31] The results of the National Acute Spinal Cord Injury Study II (NASCIS 2), which were published in 1990, indicated statistically significant improvement in motor function and sensation at 6 months post injury in patients who received high-dose methylprednisolone within 8 hours of trauma.[29] The dose of methylprednisolone used in this study was 30 mg/kg as a loading dose and 5.4 mg/kg/h constant infusion for 23 hours.

The NASCIS 3, published in 1997, compared the efficacy of methylprednisolone administered for 24 hours and 48 hours, depending on the timing of administration of the drug. The authors concluded that patients with spinal cord injury who receive

Box 15.1

Corticosteroids for Acute Spinal Cord Trauma

The anti-inflammatory corticosteroid methylprednisolone has been used to minimize disability associated with acute spinal cord injury. In the National Acute Spinal Cord Injury Study II (NASCIS 2), a subset of patients who were treated within 8 hours of injury with methylprednisolone demonstrated improvement in motor and sensory function at 6 weeks and 6 months when compared with other groups in the trial. The 24-hour dosing protocol of methylprednisolone 30 mg/kg intravenously over 15 minutes, followed by a 5.4 mg/kg/h infusion for 23 hours, when administered within the 8-hour window, has become the standard treatment for acute spinal cord injury.

A follow-up study, the National Acute Spinal Cord Injury Study III (NASCIS 3), confirmed the findings of NASCIS 2 and suggested that individuals receiving therapy between 3 and 8 hours after suffering the acute spinal cord injury have improved outcomes when the infusion of methylprednisolone lasts for 48 hours instead of 24 hours.

methylprednisolone within 3 hours of injury should be given a 24-hour infusion, whereas patients who received methylprednisolone from 3 to 8 hours after injury should be given a 48-hour infusion.[30]

For a number of years after these studies were published, the use of methylprednisolone in acute spinal cord injury was considered standard practice. However, critiques of both studies and recent reports have suggested that the available evidence does not warrant the routine use of methylprednisolone in the treatment of acute spinal cord injury. The risk of harmful side effects from such high-dose corticosteroid administration may be greater than any demonstrated clinical benefit obtained from the drug.[31] The administration of methylprednisolone is now regarded as an option in treating a patient with acute spinal cord injury, which should be considered on an individual basis.[28]

The use of naloxone was evaluated in NASCIS 2 and has also been tested in other studies. To date, this drug has not shown clear efficacy in the management of acute spinal cord injury. Similarly, no evidence demonstrates clinical benefit from the use of GM-1 ganglioside in the treatment of acute spinal cord injury.[28]

Surgical Techniques/Medical Intervention

Although surgical techniques cannot repair an injured spinal cord, the procedures described elsewhere in this chapter may be necessary to treat the bony cervical spine injuries that often accompany acute spinal cord injury. In those patients with cervical spine dislocations, immediate reduction is

cephalad Toward the head.

15

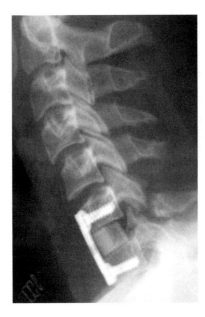

Figure 15.15 Immediate postoperative lateral cervical spine radiograph demonstrating normal alignment with fixation.

indicated to restore spinal canal diameter and decompress the spinal cord.[11,32] Stabilization, either with an external orthosis or surgery (see, for example, ST 15.4) may be necessary to prevent secondary injury due to cervical spine instability (see Figure 15.15). If a disk herniation is causing spinal cord compression, diskectomy is necessary.

With no definitive treatment for a spinal cord injury, the treatment is primarily supportive. Prevention of secondary injury and early initiation of mobilization and rehabilitation are the goals. Because of the poor prognosis, efforts to prevent cervical spinal cord injuries from athletic participation are of paramount importance.

Postoperative Management

Patients with acute cervical spinal cord injury (particularly of the upper cervical spinal cord) may develop respiratory failure and require intubation and ventilatory support.[11,13] Patients with cervical spinal cord injuries may also have significant hypotension due to neurogenic shock and may need vasopressors to maintain adequate circulation to the spinal cord. Maintenance of mean arterial blood pressure of 85 to 90 mm Hg for the first 7 days after acute spinal cord injury has been advocated to improve spinal cord perfusion.[33]

Patients with acute spinal cord injury are perhaps the population at the highest risk of deep venous thrombosis (DVT) and pulmonary embolus. In fact, in the absence of prophylaxis, the majority (more than 60%) of these patients will develop DVT. Pulmonary embolus is the third most com-

mon cause of death in these patients and generally occurs without warning. Mechanical prophylaxis alone, using intermittent pneumatic compression (IPC) or other devices, does not provide adequate protection against thrombosis in patients with acute spinal cord injury.[34] Currently, good evidence supports chemical anticoagulation in patients with complete spinal cord injuries who are at increased risk for DVT and pulmonary embolus; these recommendations are based on a large number of randomized controlled studies as well as published clinical guidelines.[35] Diligent precautions against formation of decubitus ulcers should be implemented, including regular turning and use of air mattresses. Available motion to the extremities should be exploited as early as possible to preserve the intact motor units, maintain sensory function, and prevent flexion contractures.

Injury-Specific Treatment and Rehabilitation Concerns

Rehabilitation for patients with spinal cord injury traditionally is directed at regaining functional ADLs. There are no universal exercises or protocols for these injuries, and most patients with severe and lasting neurologic deficits spend posthospital time at a spinal cord rehabilitation center.

Spinal cord injury rehabilitation centers are available for patients with significant neurologic injury who have profound sequelae. These centers are equipped with the personnel, modalities, and exercise equipment necessary to assist such patients in regaining their ability to perform ADLs. The centers attend to the patient's physical, mental, and emotional health, and some facilities also offer educational seminars for family members to help them adjust to the patient's limitations. More information about these centers can be obtained from the American Spinal Injury Association (http://www.asiaspinalinjury.org).

Estimated Amount of Time Lost

Trauma to the spinal cord results in permanent disability. The total amount of lost function reflects the proportion of the spinal cord that is injured and the spinal level at which the injury occurs. Some patients are unable to resume any level of physical activity; others may be able to participate in wheelchair sports or similar activities.

The amount of time lost due to a spinal cord injury depends on the severity of injury, the completeness of recovery, and the type of activity desired after recovery. Those patients who fully recuperate from such trauma do not usually return to contact or collision sports but may engage in noncontact activities and sports as soon as they regain sufficient muscular endurance, strength, ROM, and neurologic soundness.

Return-to-Play Criteria

Typically, patients with a spinal cord injury do not return to their prior level of competition. Select activities may be possible, pending the approval of the attending physician.

Transient Quadriparesis (Cervical Spinal Cord Neurapraxia)

CLINICAL PRESENTATION

History

An episode of bilateral muscular weakness/paresis.
Bilateral neurologic symptoms associated with areas of muscular involvement.

Observation

The patient may be unable or reluctant to move unassisted.
There may be no residual movement from the extremities.
Decorticate or decerebrate postures may be noted.

Functional Status

Neurologic and muscular weakness symptoms are self-limiting.

Physical Examination Findings

The cervical spine is pain free and has no deformities.
Bilateral neurologic and muscular weakness symptoms resolve on their own.
No activity is allowed until the patient recovers full, bilaterally equal strength, ROM, and sensation, and is pain and symptom free.

Transient quadriparesis (cervical spinal cord neurapraxia) is a type of spinal cord injury that results from the effect of transient compression of the spinal cord. Clinical manifestations include dysesthesia (burning pain), numbness, tingling of the extremities, and weakness or complete motor paralysis of the upper or lower extremities. An episode of transient quadriparesis generally resolves within 10 to 15 minutes, although residual sensory symptoms may persist for 24 to 48 hours (see **Table 15.1**).[36,37] This condition is considered a spinal cord syndrome because it is bilateral and often involves all four extremities. Transient quadriparesis should not be confused with brachial plexus injury.

Spinal stenosis—that is, narrowing of the spinal column—has long been thought to be the culprit in several spinal neurologic conditions. However, current evidence suggests stenosis of the spinal

Table 15.1

Grading System for Neurapraxia

Grade	Duration of Symptoms
1	All neurologic symptoms resolve in less than 15 minutes
2	All neurologic symptoms resolve in more than 15 minutes but less than 24 hours
3	Neurologic symptoms persist for more than 24 hours

Source: Adapted from Torg JS, Guille JT, Jaffe S. Injuries to the cervical spine in American football players. *J Bone Joint Surg Am.* 2002;84:112-122.

foramen does not predict neurologic injury.[38] Cervical stenosis without instability may not be a strong predictor of neurologic susceptibility.

Differential Diagnosis

Cervical radiculopathy, cervical disk disease, tumor (primary or metastatic), brachial plexus injury, brachial plexus neurapraxia, hysterical paralysis (conversion disorder).

Imaging Techniques

Cervical spine radiographs in a patient with cervical spinal cord neurapraxia are negative for vertebral fracture or dislocation. Often, narrowing of the spinal canal is congenital (see **Figure 15.16**). The Torg ratio has been developed for determining the diameter of the spinal canal based on the anterior-to-posterior width of the spinal canal divided by the anterior-to-posterior width of the vertebral body at the same level.[38] This ratio was devised before the widespread use of MRI, which now allows for direct measurement of spinal canal diameter.

A patient with suspected cervical spinal cord neurapraxia must be assumed to have a cervical fracture or ligamentous injury until proven otherwise and should undergo CT scanning to rule out fractures. MRI should be used to evaluate the patient for cervical disk herniation and degenerative changes of the cervical spine and to assess spinal canal diameter. If these studies are negative, flexion-extension radiographs of the lateral cervical spine should be obtained to rule out any evidence of instability.

Definitive Diagnosis

Diagnosis is based on findings of the clinical examination, symptoms indicating the condition, significant imaging findings, and exclusion of other possible conditions.

Pathomechanics and Functional Limitations

Initially, the patient with transient quadriparesis displays the signs and symptoms of a frank spinal

15

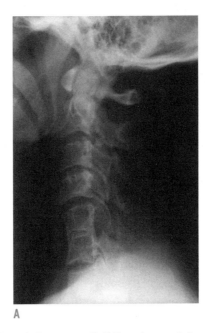
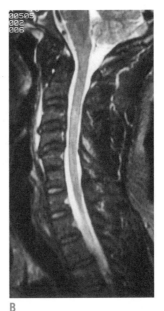

A   B

Figure 15.16 **(A)** Lateral radiograph shows congenital failure of segmentation at C5-C6 (Torg type II) with no acute fractures or subluxations. **(B)** Sagittal T2-weighted MRI demonstrates signal change within the cord. Subsequent flexion-extension radiographs showed a stable spine. The patient was permanently restricted from contact sports.

cord injury. These symptoms are temporary, and full function gradually returns. Repeated episodes of transient quadriparesis can indicate significant spinal stenosis and increase the risk of permanent neurologic damage with each episode.

Immediate Management

The immediate management of a patient with cervical spinal cord neurapraxia is the same on the field as that for all suspected spinal injuries. The spine should be immobilized and the patient's respiratory or circulatory function monitored. By the time the patient reaches the hospital, the symptoms have usually resolved except for mild sensory symptoms. The neurologic examination is typically normal.

> **Practice Tip**
> Manual cervical spine stabilization must be immediately applied in all cases of cervical spine trauma. Maintain neutral spine alignment with minimal cervical motion during the management of the injury.[1]

Postinjury/Postoperative Management

Cervical spinal cord neurapraxia is a reversible phenomenon that generally does not require postinjury treatment. In some instances, high-dose methylprednisolone has been used to limit edema formation, but the need for this approach is questionable and somewhat controversial.[28,31]

The patient should undergo a thorough orthopaedic and neurologic examination to identify predisposing factors to transient neurapraxia (e.g., cervical stenosis, cervical disk disease). Often such a finding is incidental after the injury, but its identification could serve as a predictor of further episodes.

Estimated Amount of Time Lost

The patient cannot return to play while still symptomatic. The severity and duration of the symptoms are good indicators of how quickly participation can resume. The longer and more severe the symptoms, the greater the amount of time lost. If the recovery is lengthy or anatomic anomalies are present, then any possible return to play is contingent on the ultimate recovery and findings.

Injury-Specific Treatment and Rehabilitation Concerns

> **Specific Concerns**
> Provide palliative treatment for pain and muscle spasm.
> Restore ROM.
> Strengthen cervical muscles.

By definition, neurapraxia is a 24- to 48-hour transient quadriparesis; however, neurologic symptoms may persist much longer.[37] Rehabilitation depends on cessation of symptoms and gradual muscular reconditioning. If the episode completely resolves in hours, specific rehabilitation may not be necessary. If the episode has long-lasting symptoms, an exercise program beginning with isometric cervical exercises and progressing to isotonic training can be beneficial. Examples of these exercises and specific targeted muscles are found later in this chapter (see the "Brachial Plexus Injury" section) and in Chapter 16.

■ Return-to-Play Criteria

A single episode of transient quadriparesis in the presence of a congenitally narrow spinal canal does not reflect a particular predisposition to permanent neurologic deficit.[36,37] Although the patient can return to contact sports, such an episode of transient and severe neurologic deficit is likely to be frightening to both the patient and the patient's family. Return to competition after an episode of transient quadriparesis should be thoroughly discussed with the patient and the patient's family. The importance of returning to athletic competition (e.g., for a professional athlete versus a high school athlete who will not participate in sports after high school) must be considered.

Patients who have spinal cord dysfunction and ligamentous instability, significant degenerative disease, cervical disk disease with cord compression, symptoms that last more than 36 hours, or more than one recurrence of transient quadriparesis should not be allowed to participate again in collision sports. **Table 15.2** presents guidelines for return to competition after transient neurapraxia.[36]

Table 15.2

Return-to-Play Guidelines for Cervical Neurapraxia

No Contraindications

Asymptomatic with a spinal canal-to-vertebral body ratio of less than 0.8

Relative Contraindications

One episode of neurapraxia with a spinal canal-to-vertebral body ratio of more than 0.8

Documented episode of cervical cord neurapraxia (CCN) associated with intervertebral disk disease or degenerative changes

Documented episode of CCN associated with MRI evidence of cord deformation

Absolute Contraindications

Documented episode of CCN associated with MRI evidence of cord defect or cord edema

Documented episode of CCN associated with ligamentous instability, neurologic symptoms lasting more than 36 hours, or multiple episodes

Source: Reproduced with permission from Torg JS, Guille JT, Jaffe S. Injuries to the cervical spine in American football players. *J Bone Joint Surg Am.* 2002;84:112-122.

Cervical Disk Disease and Herniation (Cervical Degenerative Disk Disease)

CLINICAL PRESENTATION

History

Neck and/or unilateral arm pain, numbness, paresthesia, or weakness.

Observation

The cervical spine may be postured to relieve radicular symptoms.
Muscle spasm may occur in the cervical spine and possibly the associated myotomes.
In prolonged cases, atrophy of the associated muscles may be noted.

Functional Status

Unilateral muscular weakness is noted, perhaps associated with one or more myotomes.
Radicular symptoms occur along associated dermatomes.
Strength and ROM may be limited secondary to pain and muscle spasm.

Physical Examination Findings

The patient may have associated muscle weakness.
Sensory impairment along the associated dermatomes is possible.
Associated reflexes may be diminished or absent.
Upper-quarter screen produces the findings described in **Table 15.3**.
The following special tests may be positive:
- Shoulder abduction test
- Cervical compression test
- Cervical distraction test
- Spurling test

Cervical disk herniation is less common than lumbar disk herniation.[39–41] Its lower incidence is related to the fact that the cervical disks are smaller and under less stress from weight bearing than the lumbar disks.

Most cervical disk pathologies are related to degenerative disease. Acute injury is relatively uncommon; in fact, a herniation that presents after acute trauma is likely related to previous disk degeneration.[42] The prevalence of cervical disk disease increases with age and may be related to activity.[41,42] The levels most affected by cervical disk disease are C5–C6 and C6–C7.

Most cervical disk herniations occur posterolaterally, which explains the usual clinical syndrome of neck and unilateral arm pain (cervical radiculopathy). Other disks may protrude centrally and posteriorly through the posterior longitudinal ligament to compress the spinal cord but do not affect the spinal nerve roots (see **Figure 15.17**). These central disks can result in profound myelopathy and acute spinal cord syndromes.

Table 15.3

Single Cervical Nerve Root Syndrome

	Cervical Disk			
	C4-C5	C5-C6	C6-C7	C7-T1
Compressed root	C5	C6	C7	C8
Percentage of cervical disks involved at this level	2%	19%	69%	10%
Reflex(es) diminished	Deltoid, pectoralis	Biceps, brachioradialis	Triceps	Finger jerk
Motor weakness	Deltoid	Forearm flexion	Forearm extension (wrist drop)	Hand intrinsic muscles
Paresthesia and hypesthesia	Shoulder	Upper arm, thumb, radial forearm	Fingers 2 and 3, all fingertips	Fingers 4 and 5

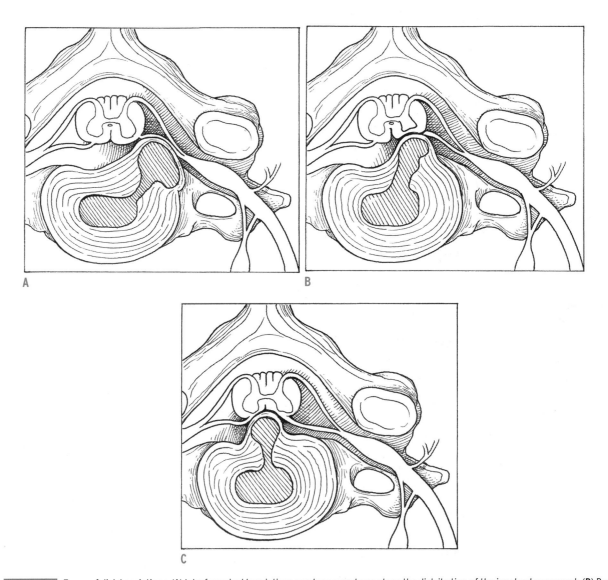

Figure 15.17   Types of disk herniations. (**A**) Intraforaminal herniations produce symptoms along the distribution of the involved nerve root. (**B**) Posterolateral radicular symptoms occur in a more diffuse pattern but tend to remain on one side of the body. (**C**) Midline herniations produce diffuse radicular symptoms on both sides of the body. *Source:* Reproduced with permission from Levine MJ, Albert TJ, Smith MD. Cervical radiculopathy: Diagnosis and nonoperative management. *J Am Acad Orthop Surg.* 1996;4:305-316.

The clinical symptoms most commonly associated with a herniated cervical disk are neck pain and unilateral arm pain that may be accompanied by numbness, paresthesias, and weakness (see Table 15.3). In a patient with obvious cervical radiculopathy with weakness, numbness, and reflex changes, the diagnosis of cervical disk disease can be made by clinical examination alone.

Differential Diagnosis

Cervical spondylolysis, cervical strain, degenerative osteoarthritis, tumor (primary or metastatic).

Imaging Techniques

Imaging studies may be obtained for patients with signs and symptoms of cervical disk herniations that are not improved with conservative therapy. Cervical spine radiographs may demonstrate degenerative change such as disk-space narrowing or vertebral "beaking" caused by osteophytes but do not provide visualization of a herniated disk (see **Figure 15.18**). MRI is the most useful test in the evaluation of a cervical herniated disk, allowing visualization of the disks and compression of the nerve roots or the spinal cord.

Despite the usefulness of MRI, cervical myelography with postmyelogram CT scans may still be necessary (see **Figure 15.19**). Myelography and CT are particularly useful in patients who have multilevel abnormalities on MRI or have previously undergone cervical surgery.

Definitive Diagnosis

The definitive diagnosis of cervical disk disease is based on the clinical findings and a positive radiograph, MRI, or CT myelogram.

myelography A radiographic technology for recording the activity of the spinal cord and nerves.

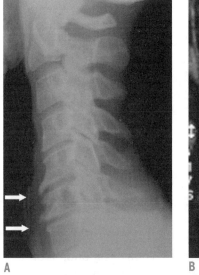
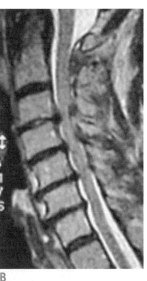

A

B

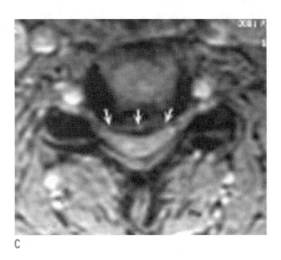

C

Figure 15.18 Imaging studies of cervical degenerative disk disease. (**A**) Lateral radiograph indicating narrowing of the intervertebral space and osteophyte formation consistent with degenerative disk disease. Note the "beaked" formation of the vertebrae (arrows). (**B**) Sagittal MRI demonstrating degenerative disk disease at multiple levels. (**C**) Axial MRI showing a bulge of the cervical disk (arrows). *Source:* Parts B and C are reproduced with permission from Khanna AJ, Carbone JJ, Kebaish KM, et al. Magnetic resonance imaging of the cervical spine: current techniques and spectrum of disease. *J Bone Joint Surg Am.* 2002;84(suppl 2);70-80.

15

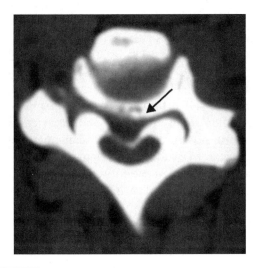

Figure 15.19 Postmyelogram axial CT image of large central disk herniation causing spinal cord compression.

Pathomechanics and Functional Limitations

The patient's functional status is related to the amount of pain and arm weakness experienced but is typically self-regulated by patient tolerance. Advanced cases of disk degeneration create a neuropathy in the involved nerve roots and can paralyze the associated muscles. Secondary muscle spasm may develop in the scapular and cervical muscles.

Immediate Management

The initial management of a patient with a suspected cervical herniated disk is conservative. Cervical pain and muscle spasm can be treated with cold packs, and a soft collar may be applied to reduce pressure on the cervical vertebrae. The patient may experience reduced symptoms when lying down or reclining.

Medications

In patients with severe, acute pain, a course of an oral corticosteroid, such as methylprednisolone or dexamethasone, may be used. The course of corticosteroids is followed by NSAIDs, such as ibuprofen. In patients with acute and intense pain, narcotics may be necessary for at least the first 5 to 7 days.

Postinjury Management

Approximately 60% to 70% of patients with a cervical herniated disk improve significantly or recover completely without surgical intervention.[41] The patient continues with palliative treatments and collar use and segues into more specific rehabilitation.

Surgical Techniques

The decision of which surgical technique to use for a herniated cervical disk (i.e., an anterior or posterior approach) is based on whether the disk herniation occurs (central or lateral), whether the cervical spine is unstable, and whether contralateral disk disease is present (even if asymptomatic). Some surgeons operate on all herniated cervical disks using an anterior approach.

The posterior cervical laminectomy and foraminotomy can be performed at more than one level if adjacent symptomatic disk disease or spondylosis is present (see (ST) 15.5). The posterior approach is less disruptive of normal anatomy and motion of the cervical spine than an anterior cervical diskectomy with or without fusion.

In the presence of cervical disk disease, some surgeons elect to perform an anterior cervical diskectomy without a bone graft; in most instances, the spine goes on to fuse spontaneously at the affected level (see (ST) 15.6). Other surgeons always place a bone graft, with or without anterior cervical instrumentation. The technique of anterior cervical diskectomy for cervical disk disease is the same as that described for cervical spine stabilization after fractures and dislocations.

In patients who have a posterior laminotomy or anterior cervical diskectomy with or without fusion, the hospital stay is usually one night. Some patients can be discharged on the same day as surgery.

Postoperative Management

Range of motion is protected and lifting is restricted for 2 to 3 weeks after surgery. The patient may wear an external orthosis such as an Aspen or Miami J collar for several weeks or several months (see Figure 15.3). If internal hardware is used, the patient may wear a soft collar for several weeks to decrease pain and prevent muscle spasm.

Injury-Specific Treatment and Rehabilitation Concerns

> **Specific Concerns**
>
> Control inflammation.
> Provide symptomatic treatment for radicular pain and muscle spasm.
> Decrease the compressive forces on the cervical nerve roots.
> Increase facet joint motion.

A treatment protocol including heat, massage, and gentle ROM exercises may be helpful for symptomatic management of cervical disk disease. A period of soft-collar immobilization may reduce the

S|T Surgical Technique 15.5

Posterior Cervical Laminectomy and Foraminotomy

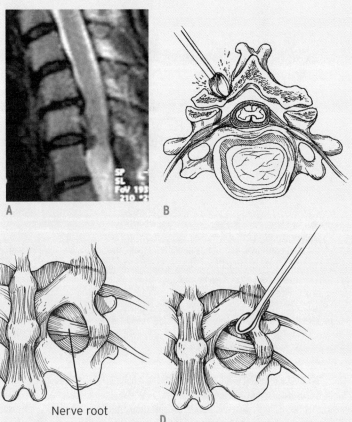

Nerve root

Indications

A documented cervical herniated disk that continues to produce significant pain after 4 to 6 weeks of conservative therapy (**A**); patients with significant weakness or spinal cord dysfunction; lateral herniated disk causing unilateral nerve root compression without evidence of spinal cord compression.

Procedure Overview

1. The patient is placed prone in a fixed head holder.
2. A midline skin incision is made, and the paraspinous muscles are dissected off the laminae and facet joints on the appropriate side (**B**).
3. Laminectomy is performed, and the nerve root is identified and decompressed laterally as it enters the foramen (**C**).
4. The herniated disk fragment or fragments are generally found in the axilla of the nerve root and are removed (**D**).

Functional Limitations

ROM and strengthening exercises are necessary, especially with a preoperative neurologic deficit. Lifting is limited to less than 10 to 15 lb (4.50 to 6.75 kg) postoperatively for 2 to 3 weeks and no more than 25 lb (11.25 kg) for 6 to 8 weeks.

Implications for Rehabilitation

For patient comfort, a soft collar may be worn for a few days (if a single-level laminectomy is performed).

Comments

Normal activities may resume within 2 to 3 months of surgery.

Source: Figures reproduced with permission from Albert TJ, Murrell SE. Surgical management of cervical radiculopathy. *J Am Acad Orthop Surg.* 1999;7:368-376.

muscle spasms associated with the injury.[42] Cervical traction is often advocated for these patients as well. Although it can be helpful for chronic cervical spondylotic radiculopathy, this modality is usually not helpful with an acute herniated cervical disk and may actually aggravate the patient's pain.[42] Cervical epidural steroids may be helpful in the management of these patients but probably should be given only after imaging techniques confirm the presence of a cervical disk herniation.

Anterior Cervical Diskectomy

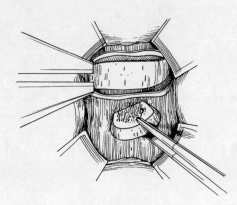

Indications

A documented cervical herniated disk that continues to produce debilitating pain after 4 to 6 weeks of conservative therapy, or earlier in patients with significant weakness or spinal cord dysfunction surgery; central disk herniation with spinal cord compression; possibly patients with bilateral disk herniations, even if one side is asymptomatic.

Procedure Overview

1. The patient is placed supine with the head slightly turned to one side.
2. A longitudinal incision is made in the anterior neck, and dissection is carried down through the platysma and along the anterior border of the sternocleidomastoid muscle to the spine.
3. A bone graft is harvested, often from the patient's iliac crest.
4. An anterior cervical diskectomy at the affected level is performed, and a bone graft is placed in the disk space.
5. An anterior plate may be used to secure the graft (see ST 15.3).

   This procedure is the same as that performed for cervical spine stabilization after fracture-dislocation, as described for anterior cervical diskectomy and fusion; with disk disease, however, hardware is not always used. The use of hardware/fixation depends on the activity level of the patient and the preference of the surgeon. For example, athletes are more likely to have fixation than sedentary workers.

Functional Limitations

Many patients require ROM and strengthening exercises, especially those who have preoperative neurologic deficits.

Implications for Rehabilitation

Lifting is limited to less than 10 to 15 lb (4.50 to 6.75 kg) postoperatively for 2 to 3 weeks and no more than 25 lb (11.25 kg) for 6 to 8 weeks.

Comments

Normal activities may resume within 2 to 3 months of surgery.

Source: Figure reproduced with permission from Albert TJ, Murrell SE. Surgical management of cervical radiculopathy. *J Am Acad Orthop Surg.* 1999;7:368-376.

If conservative measures fail to decrease the patient's symptoms after several weeks of treatment or if the patient develops significant weakness of the arm or signs and symptoms of cervical spinal cord dysfunction (cervical myelopathy), surgical intervention should be considered.

■ Estimated Amount of Time Lost

After surgery, 6 to 8 weeks of activity may be lost, but the type of injury and surgical technique dictate whether patient can return to contact and collision sports. Patients treated conservatively lose variable amounts of time from activity. A patient who re-

covers quickly from an acute episode and does not require surgery may be allowed to return to diving, for example, but not if the episode resulted in a large herniation, surgical intervention, or fusion. Return to activity is contingent on the severity of the injury, the type and extensiveness of treatment, the amount of invasion, and the success of rehabilitation.

■ Return-to-Play Criteria

The presence of a symptomatic herniated disk with spinal cord or nerve root compression causing significant pain, weakness, or numbness is an absolute contraindication to athletic activity. In a patient who has had a posterolateral laminectomy and foraminotomy for a lateral herniated disk, return to contact and collision sports is possible after sufficient recovery, provided there is no residual neurologic deficit and no abnormal ROM of the cervical spine.

Patients who have undergone anterior cervical diskectomy and fusion for symptomatic cervical disk herniation should not be allowed to return to contact or collision sports because of the possibility of altered biomechanics surrounding the fused segments. Depending on the severity of injury and surgical intervention, patients who regain full preinjury strength and functional status may return to sports. However, it is unlikely that those with hardware will return to contact and collision sports. It is also unlikely that a surgeon would allow an athlete who has sustained an axial load-type force to return to sports such as football, ice hockey, gymnastics, soccer, cheerleading, or wrestling. The level of risk, age of the patient, and specific position played (in football) all factor into the return-to-play decision.

Brachial Plexus Injury

CLINICAL PRESENTATION

History

Cervical spine forced laterally away from the shoulder.
Forcible depression of the shoulder while the cervical spine remains neutral or slightly lateral to the shoulder.
Rotation of the cervical spine away from the affected shoulder.
Compression of the Erb point.
The combination of any of these mechanisms.

Observation

The patient most often carries the affected arm hanging loosely at the side, with the body leaning toward the affected shoulder.
Typically no signs of this injury are visible; the most characteristic aspects of this condition are the mechanism of injury and the symptoms described by the patient.

Functional Status

Radicular neurologic symptoms of numbness and tingling throughout the brachial plexus dermatomes immediately after insult.
Muscular weakness or transient paralysis along the myotomes.

Physical Examination Findings

Unilateral muscular weakness and radicular symptoms along the C5 to T1 myotomes and dermatomes.
Subjective neurologic assessment of dermatomes.
Pain-free cervical spine on palpation and ROM.
The following special tests may be positive:
· Brachial plexus traction/compression test
· Spurling test
· Shoulder abduction test

The brachial plexus is formed by the C5 to T1 nerve roots. These roots exit the cervical spine and pass through the cervicoaxillary canal under the clavicle to provide innervation to the upper extremity. Trauma to the brachial plexus occurs when the cervical spine moves away from the shoulder in a forcible fashion, often when the head or shoulder hits an unyielding object or an opponent. This mechanism primarily occurs in football players when the helmet and neck are hyperextended or moved laterally away from a depressed shoulder, such as during a tackle.[37,43]

The resulting force can either stretch the nerves on the opposite side of the motion or compress the nerves on the side toward which the cervical spine is bending. Another mechanism for brachial plexus trauma is compression of the Erb point—the most superficial aspect of the brachial plexus, located 2 to 3 cm superior to the clavicle. The typically brief, transient motion stresses the brachial plexus, and the resulting condition includes radicular symptoms and muscular weakness along the path of the neurologic cords to the affected hand and fingers (see **Figure 15.20**).

The unilateral radicular symptoms—often referred to as a "stinger" or "burner"—are the result of trauma to the brachial plexus or its associated nerve roots.[44] The unilateral symptoms of brachial plexus neuropathy must be differentiated from the bilateral symptoms associated with spinal cord injury. In athletes, brachial plexus neuropathy is typically traumatic, but symptoms have been reported from activity as simple as carrying a heavy backpack on one shoulder, which depresses it to the point of causing chronic but steady traction on the brachial plexus of the ipsilateral shoulder. Chronic brachial plexus neuropathy may be the result of decreased subaxial cervical space available for the spinal cord and cervical nerve roots.[45]

A complete rupture of the brachial plexus from a traction injury is rare and must be recognized in a timely fashion to prevent permanent disability. A delay of 6 months or longer is the most significant negative prognostic factor in recovery via a surgical graft.[46]

Differential Diagnosis

Spinal cord trauma, subluxated or dislocated humerus, abnormally shaped clavicle compressing the thoracic outlet.

Imaging Techniques

It is rare for true brachial plexus injuries to require further testing or imaging, let alone surgical intervention. If the injury is not limited to a few episodes over time but instead becomes chronic, further diagnostic evaluation should be initiated. Plain radiography or CT scan can rule out stenosis or osteophytes

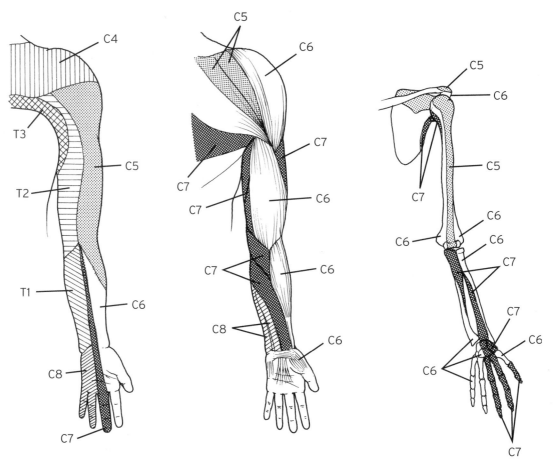

Figure 15.20 Dermatomes, myotomes, and sclerotomes of the upper extremity. The patient will have sensory and/or motor nerve symptoms within these regions corresponding with the associated spinal nerve root(s) involved. *Source:* Reproduced with permission from Levine MJ, Albert TJ, Smith MD. Cervical radiculopathy: Diagnosis and nonoperative management. *J Am Acad Orthop Surg.* 1996;4:305-316.

of the intervertebral foramen that impinge on the cervical nerve roots; MRI is used to identify injury to the spinal cord and associated nerve roots.

Definitive Diagnosis

Diagnosis of brachial plexus injury is made based on identification of the mechanism of injury, symptoms limited to the involved dermatomes (in most cases, symptoms are unilateral), rapid fading of symptoms, and the exclusion of the conditions identified in the "Differential Diagnosis" section. Repeated episodes of brachial plexus trauma warrant radiographs and/or MRI to rule out a structural predisposition to this condition.

Chronic episodes of brachial plexus neuropathy without trauma may be caused by cervical stenosis, breast or lung carcinoma, regional hematoma, or thoracic outlet syndrome.

Pathomechanics and Functional Limitations

Neuropathy of the involved nerve roots results in paresthesia of the associated dermatomes and muscle weakness of the associated myotomes (see Figure 15.20). Associated spasm of the upper trapezius, sternocleidomastoid, levator scapulae, or scalene

muscles can cause pain and restrict ROM in the cervical spine.

■ Immediate Management

If cervical spine instability or spinal cord injury is a possibility, the patient must be splinted and placed on a backboard. If the mechanism and resulting symptoms indicate brachial plexus injury, the paresthesia and muscular weakness typically resolve within a few seconds to several minutes.

■ Postinjury/Postoperative Management

The primary goal with postacute brachial plexus insult is to return the patient to full functional and neurologic status as quickly as possible. Immediate treatment of brachial plexus neuropathy should include ice and physical agents (such as electric stimulation) that are designed to decrease muscle spasm in the upper back and shoulder area. These modalities are simply palliative, however; they should not be the focus of long-term treatment of this or any other cervical spine condition. Rest and a soft cervical collar may also be indicated.

Injury-Specific Treatment and Rehabilitation Concerns

> **Specific Concerns**
>
> Control pain and muscle spasm.
> Strengthen cervical muscles.
> Restore ROM.

The primary goals of rehabilitation after a brachial plexus injury are to strengthen and condition the musculature affiliated with the cervical spine. Determination of the patient's neurologic status largely depends on subjective information obtained during the examination. Muscular strength and coordination can be ascertained through exercises specific to maintaining cervical stability. The muscles that provide support and protection to the cervical spine—including the trapezius, sternocleidomastoid, levator scapulae, scalene, splenius, and longissimus groups—must be strengthened to lessen the likelihood of reinjury. Additionally, the patient must have regained full functional ROM before a return to competition is contemplated. Manual interventions should focus on general manual traction while the patient is in a comfortable position—for example, with some lateral cervical flexion, usually to the side of the injury.

Brachial plexus neuropathy occasionally returns after the initial episode and may become chronic. A treatment scheme based on the Maitland approach to treatment of acute and chronic nerve root abnormality is indicated.[47] In this approach, manual traction is initially performed at the angle in which the cervical spine is postured with little additional motion. The cervical spine is generally found laterally flexed to the side of the injury. As time elapses and symptoms permit (i.e., the patient has less pain with ROM), lateral flexion and rotation to the opposite side are indicated. For example, if the injury is on the left side, then a slow progression to right lateral flexion and right rotation is appropriate. As the condition becomes chronic, palliative measures can progress to moist heat rather than ice and, as pain allows, traction should progress to the neutral position. In addition, rotation away from the side of the injury is initiated and continued until the patient has full, pain-free motion, rotation, and lateral flexion away from the affected side.

Estimated Amount of Time Lost

Brachial plexus neuropathy can result in only a few minutes of playing time being lost or, depending on the magnitude of the symptoms and the underlying injury, may result in several months of absence from contact or collision sports.

Return-to-Play Criteria

Two criteria must be met before the patient can return to participation. First, cervical spine abnormality must be ruled out. Any patient suspected of having a cervical spine injury should not be allowed to return to play until potentially catastrophic conditions have been ruled out. Second, both dermatomes and ROM should be evaluated. The patient may return to competition when cervical ROM is full and pain free and when strength and sensation of the upper extremity are equal bilaterally. Strength of shoulder abduction (deltoids), elbow flexion (biceps), elbow extension (triceps), wrist extension, wrist flexion, and finger abduction and adduction must be ascertained.

Functional Bracing

Cervical collars alone do not provide protection from brachial plexus trauma, and collars custom-made by nonprofessionals may increase the chance of injury to the cervical spine and should be avoided. Wearing a collar does not preclude an athlete from the obligation to use proper tackling technique or maintain cervical strength and conditioning. Athletes who sustain multiple brachial plexus injuries should be evaluated for other cervical conditions, tackling technique, and a cervical conditioning program before a decision is made to recommend a cervical collar.

Cervical Strains

CLINICAL PRESENTATION

History

Sudden contraction or overstretching of the muscles.
Pain over the involved muscles.
Muscle spasm placing pressure on nerves, producing radicular symptoms.

Observation

The head is postured for comfort.
Muscle spasm causes the head and cervical spine to tilt along the muscle's line of pull.

Functional Status

Active and resisted ROM in the muscle's antagonistic pattern produces pain.
Passive ROM in the muscle's antagonistic pattern produces pain.
Strength is decreased.
Motion is limited.

Physical Examination Findings

Palpable tenderness over the injured site.
Confirmation of the findings noted in the "Functional Status" section.

A cervical strain can be identified largely based on the history of injury and reproducible pain with muscular contraction. It is rare, although possible, for a muscular injury to cause radicular symptoms, but muscle spasm or edema may impinge on specific nerves as they pass by the affected muscle.

The patient's functional status following a cervical strain depends on the severity of the strain. Pain following a cervical muscle strain peaks between 24 and 72 hours, followed by a gradual decrease in intensity. Six weeks may be required for resolution of pain. A minor strain may be merely annoying, while function is still possible; a muscular tear, by comparison, may prohibit participation in athletics. Full cervical ROM in addition to functional strength should be ascertained before making any determination on activity.

Differential Diagnosis

Cervical sprain, brachial plexus injury, disk injury, infectious illness (e.g., meningitis).

Imaging Techniques

An abnormal radiograph can confirm the presence of muscular injury. Although this type of imaging is not typically performed, MRI indicates muscular damage.

Definitive Diagnosis

Diagnosis is made based on the limited ROM and strength deficit for the affected muscle.

Pathomechanics and Functional Testing

Specific muscle testing is performed to determine the exact muscle afflicted or motion involved, as well as strength testing of that muscle to assess the injury severity.

■ Immediate Management

Any underlying injury should be ruled out. Application of ice and stretching may retard additional spasm and swelling. A soft collar may be warranted in the acute stages to decrease pain and spasm.

■ Medications

NSAIDs may be used to alleviate pain and inflammation. If spasm is severe, muscle relaxants and antianxiety medications may be helpful.

■ Surgical Intervention

It is unusual for a cervical strain to require surgical repair. Most muscles in the neck have reciprocal muscles that provide a similar function; consequently, the loss of a specific muscle, although cosmetically damaging, may not affect overall cervical function.

■ Postinjury/Postoperative Management

Ice is administered while the inflammatory response is still active, followed by heat and gentle exercises specific to the injured and complementary muscles. Use of a soft collar should be discontinued as soon as practical.

■ Injury-Specific Treatment and Rehabilitation Concerns

Specific Concerns

Control muscle spasm.
Maintain ROM.
Strengthen cervical muscles.

Management of a cervical strain focuses on limiting swelling and spasm. Once these issues are under control, early ROM should be initiated, followed by gentle strengthening. ROM includes working on cervical flexion and extension, rotation, and lateral bending. Strengthening exercises can begin with isometric cervical exercises in all directions, increasing to free weights using the shoulder and cervical musculature. All major muscles must be strengthened, not merely the affected ones.

■ Estimated Amount of Time Lost

The amount of time lost from competition due to a cervical strain may vary from no time lost to 6 weeks or longer in the event of a complete muscle tear. The time lost depends on how quickly the patient regains ROM and functional strength.

■ Return-to-Play Criteria

Return to play can occur when full ROM is regained and the athlete can see and protect himself or herself in competition.

Functional Bracing

Bracing is not indicated for a cervical strain. Cervical braces are intended for postsurgical or postinjury protection, not for use during competition.

Immediate Management of On-Field Cervical Spine Injuries

A cervical spine injury should be assumed when the patient is unconscious on the playing field. If the athlete is conscious but down on the field, a complete physical examination of the cervical spine and the associated myotomes and dermatomes should be conducted before the athlete is removed from the field. Any athlete with signs or symptoms indicating trauma to the cervical spine or spinal cord should be placed on a backboard and transported immediately to a hospital.[48] If the airway is obstructed, as little motion as possible should occur to the athlete, and a jaw-thrust maneuver is recommended over the head-tilt technique.[1] If the athlete is prone, a log-roll method of transferring the patient to a stretcher is preferred while maintaining appropriate spinal stabilization.

Considerable debate has focused on when and where to remove equipment such as a helmet and shoulder pads. The football helmet assists in stabilizing the cervical spine, and shoulder pads help to maintain a slight degree of extension. As such, both should be kept in place while removing the face mask and anterior aspects of chest and shoulder pads. The football helmet and shoulder pads should not be removed until radiographs are ob-

tained, but the need for cardiopulmonary resuscitation (CPR) warrants removal of the helmet and shoulder pads. If CPR is indicated, the athlete's airway should be exposed (the face mask must be removed), while the jersey and lacing/padding can be cut to allow for administration of CPR manually or with the implementation of an automated external defibrillator. Established guidelines specific to certain sports (e.g., football, ice hockey, lacrosse) address the efficacy of helmet removal; the common theme among these recommendations is to leave the helmet on because its removal can cause further cervical insult.[48,49]

General guidelines for appropriate care of the spine-injured athlete are outlined in **Table 15.4**.

Table 15.4

Guidelines for Appropriate Care of the Spine-Injured Athlete

General Guidelines

Any athlete suspected of having a spinal injury should not be moved and should be managed as though a spinal injury exists.

The athlete's airway, breathing, circulation, neurologic status, and level of consciousness should be assessed.

The athlete should not be moved unless absolutely essential to maintain the airway, breathing, and circulation.

An athlete who must be moved to maintain the airway, breathing, or circulation should be placed in a supine position while maintaining spinal immobilization. When moving an athlete with a suspected spine injury, the head and trunk should be moved as a unit. The emergency medical services (EMS) system should be activated as soon as it is ascertained that the athlete is either unconscious or has a suspected spinal injury.

Face Mask Removal

The face mask should be removed immediately with appropriate face-mask removal instruments regardless of the patient's current respiratory status.

Instruments used for this purpose may include a powered cordless screwdriver or cutting tools designed for sport-specific equipment. Those involved in the prehospital care of injured football players should have the tools for safely removing face masks readily available and regularly rehearse the psychomotor process of removing the face mask in a competent and timely manner.

Football Helmet Removal

The athletic football helmet and chin strap should be removed only in the following circumstances:

- If the helmet and chin strap do not hold the head securely, such that immobilization of the helmet does not also immobilize the head
- If the design of the helmet and chin strap is such that even after removal of the face mask, the airway cannot be controlled or ventilation cannot be provided
- If the face mask cannot be removed after a reasonable period of time
- If the helmet prevents immobilization for transportation in an appropriate position
- If the shoulder pads are also being removed (independent removal of either the helmet or the shoulder pads is not recommended)

Helmet Removal

Spinal immobilization must be maintained while removing the helmet.

Helmet removal should be frequently practiced under proper supervision in a controlled environment.

Specific guidelines for helmet removal need to be developed. In most circumstances, it may be helpful to remove cheek padding and/or deflate air padding, and cut the chin straps before helmet removal.

Equipment

Appropriate spinal alignment must be maintained.

The fact that the football helmet and shoulder pads elevate an athlete's trunk when in the supine position should be recognized.

If the football helmet is to be removed, the shoulder pads must also be removed at the same time.

The front of the shoulder pads can be opened without helmet removal to allow access for CPR and defibrillation.

15

Practice Tip

An electric screwdriver is the most efficient tool for face-mask removal. A second removal tool must also be available in case of failure or malfunction of the first one. The face mask should be removed in the case of suspected cervical spine injury that will require transportation. Even if the patient is breathing upon initial assessment, the individual's condition may later deteriorate, making airway access an emergent issue.[1]

The development, planning, and rehearsal of an emergency plan for the prehospital care of the athlete with a suspected spinal cord injury are essential. Such a plan should include communication with the institution's administration and those personnel directly involved with the assessment and transportation of the injured athlete.[46] All providers of prehospital care should practice and be competent in all of the skills identified in these guidelines before they are needed in an emergency situation. Rehearsal should include venue-specific considerations, including the possibility of inclement weather environments.[50]

Rehabilitation

The key premise underlying rehabilitation of cervical spine injuries is the need to continue to protect the cervical spine and help the patient regain normal strength. The achievable ROM depends on the surgical procedure performed, because some repair techniques permanently limit ROM. The initiation of ROM activities may be delayed as long as 3 months to allow complete healing to occur.

Typically, the first goals of rehabilitation are to protect the repair or injury from further harm and decrease swelling and pain. Gradually, with the physician's permission, exercises to strengthen and protect the cervical spine can be initiated. The muscles primarily involved in these functions are the trapezius, latissimus dorsi, levator scapulae, sternocleidomastoid, and scalene. In addition, the rotator cuff, scapular stabilizers, and pectoralis muscles may be stretched and strengthened to facilitate proper posture and ROM and to encourage balance among muscle groups. Finally, core stabilization exercises are paramount to maintaining a healthy cervical spine.

Other aspects of cervical rehabilitation include teaching correct lifting techniques, proper posture (while sitting, standing, and walking), and balance. Challenges to this rehabilitation program begin at the onset of therapy, when limitations (e.g., ROM, weight restrictions) are put in place to protect the injury.

Chapter 13 describes more spinal-stabilization techniques. Manual therapy and ROM exercises should not be performed in the presence of an unhealed fracture.

Manual Therapies

Massage

Soft-tissue massage can be used to reduce muscle spasm and break up scar tissue. Deep pétrissage and effleurage increase circulation, decrease pain, and help to resolve muscle spasm (see **Figure 15.21**). Cross-friction massage and myofascial release techniques can be used to help reduce soft-tissue restrictions that limit ROM. Cross-friction massage is performed by positioning the cervical spine so that the muscle is lax. Pressure is then applied to the muscle perpendicular to the direction of its fibers.

Cervical Traction

Manual or mechanical cervical traction can be used to decrease the weight-bearing forces on the facet joints, reduce pressure on the intervertebral disks and the cervical nerve roots, and elongate the cervical musculature (see **Figure 15.22**). Laterally bending the cervical spine during traction opens the facet joints and stretches the soft tissues, while simultaneously compressing the structures on the side toward the bend. Flexing the cervical spine stretches the posterior structures, and extending it targets the anterior structures.

Vertebral Glides

Vertebral glides are used to restore normal joint motion to a hypomobile segment. Typically, mobilizations are graded from I to V. The mobilization grade

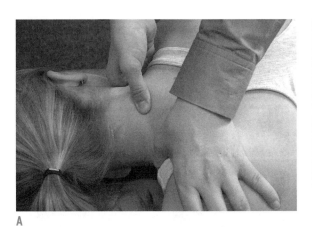 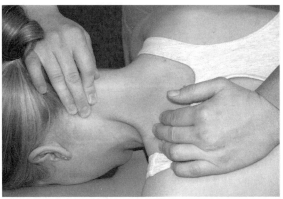

A B

Figure 15.21 Soft-tissue mobilization techniques for the cervical spine musculature. (**A**) Cross-friction massage of the upper trapezius muscle. (**B**) Myofascial release.

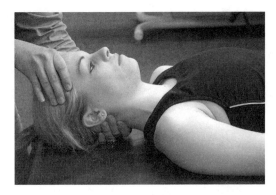

Manual traction to the cervical spine. This technique can reduce pressure on the disks, facets, and nerve roots. Changing the angle of pull allows specificity of the structures being stressed.

selected for use is based on the amount of passive ROM needed at the segment (see **Figure 15.23**).

The central posteroanterior (PA) glide, which is simply the spring test applied with grades of mobilization, is commonly used to treat facet hypomobility (see Figure 15.23A). To mobilize the entire segment, the thumbs are placed over the spinous process and pressure is exerted in an anterosuperior direction. To isolate individual facets, pressure is applied directly over the target joint.

The thumbs are placed over the spinous process of the segment in question to introduce rotation. Lower mobilization grades are used for more acute dysfunctions. Transverse glides introduce a rotational force to the segment by moving the spinous process laterally (see Figure 15.23B).

Flexibility Exercises

Flexibility, including ROM exercises, is critical for cervical spine rehabilitation, particularly for those patients with disk disease and brachial plexus

trauma. Some cervical spine conditions, however, are in a rare group for which ROM exercises are contraindicated for safe recovery; these conditions include many surgical corrections, spinal cord injury, and some fractures. As with any rehabilitation program, the physician must be consulted before exercises are initiated after injury or surgery. The following exercises focus on stretching specific muscles associated with the cervical spine; performing these stretches will enhance the ROM of the particular muscle or group.

The average ROM of the cervical spine is 0° to 45° of flexion, extension, and lateral flexion and 60° of rotation. The most effective method of stretching the cervical spine is manual resistance. Only the force necessary to achieve a gentle, pain-free stretch is applied (see **Figure 15.24**). An alternative is to have the patient apply his or her own resistance to the stretch. Using elastic bands or weights to assist stretching is not recommended for the cervical spine. For all of these stretches, the patient sits or lies down; force is applied in a steady fashion for 15 to 20 seconds and repeated 3 to 4 times.

Strengthening Exercises

The patient can progress through a range of isotonic strengthening exercises, including flexion, extension, left and right lateral bending, and left and right rotation. Initially, motion against gravity may provide sufficient resistance to strengthen the muscle for flexion-extension and lateral bending. As the patient progresses, manual resistance can be used to strengthen the cervical muscles. The techniques used for manual resistance exercises are similar to those used for flexibility, except that the patient now moves against the resistance (see Figure 15.24).

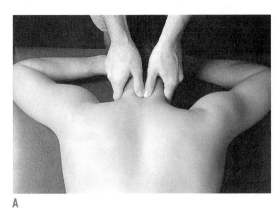

A

B

Figure 15.23 Cervical vertebral glides. (**A**) Central posteroanterior glide, which applies pressure to the spinous process in an anterior direction. (**B**) Transverse glide, in which the spinous process is gently mobilized left and right.

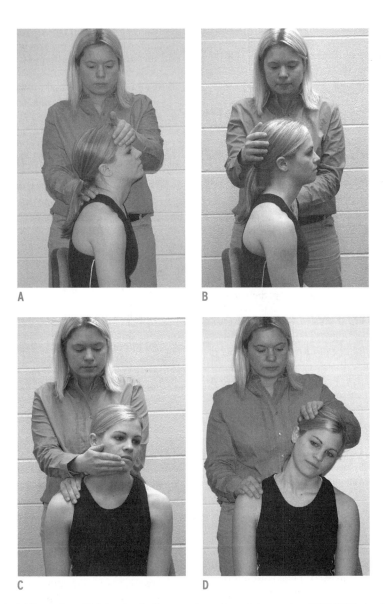

Figure 15.24 Cervical passive ROM exercises. (**A**) Extension for the upper trapezius, rotators, and multifidi. (**B**) Flexion for the sternocleidomastoid and multifidi. (**C**) Rotation for the sternocleidomastoid on the side toward the motion, scalenes, rotators, and multifidi. The exercise is repeated in each direction. (**D**) Lateral bending for the upper trapezius, sternocleidomastoid, and scalenes. Adding cervical flexion to the lateral bending targets the levator scapulae. The exercise is repeated in each direction.

15

Options are limited for free-weight or weight-machine training of the cervical muscles. Some commercial isotonic weight machines provide options for cervical flexion, extension, and lateral bending motions. Although free weights can be attached to a belt that fits around the patient's head, these techniques are not advocated for rehabilitation because of the risk of further traumatizing the area. Refer to Chapter 16 for a description of strengthening techniques for the extrinsic cervical spine muscles.

Core Stabilization Exercises

Exercise programs designed to strengthen stabilizing muscles are crucial for the proper treatment of hypermobile spinal segments. These programs should also be a part of spinal rehabilitation after hypomobile segments have been effectively mobilized and the patient has normal ROM. Refer to Chapter 16 for a description of spinal core stabilization exercises.

■ References

1. Swartz EE, Boden BP, Courson RW, et al. National Athletic Trainers' Association Position Statement: Acute management of the cervical spine-injured athlete. *J Athl Train.* 2009;44:306.

2. Botte MJ, Byrne TP, Abrams RA, Garfin SR. Halo skeletal fixation: Techniques of application and prevention of complications. *J Am Acad Orthop Surg.* 1996;4:44–53.

3. Joint Section on Disorders of the Spine and Peripheral Nerves of the American Association of Neurological Surgeons and the Congress of Neurological Surgeons. Management of acute cervical spine and spinal cord injuries: Isolated fractures of the atlas in adults. *Neurosurgery.* 2002;50(suppl 3):S120–S124.

4. Khanna AJ, Carbone JJ, Kebaish KM, et al. Magnetic resonance imaging of the cervical spine: Current techniques and spectrum of disease. *J Bone Joint Surg Am.* 2002; 84(suppl 2):70–80.

5. Tan J, Li L, Sun G, et al. C1 lateral mass–C2 pedicle screws and crosslink compression fixation for unstable atlas fracture. *Spine.* 2009;34:2505–2509.

6. Kerwin GA, Chou KL, White DB, et al. Investigation of how different halos influence pin forces. *Spine.* 1994; 19:1078–1081.

7. Anderson LD, d'Alonzo RT. Fractures of the odontoid process of the axis. *J Bone Joint Surg Am.* 1974;56:1663–1674.

8. Chutkan NB, King AG, Harris MB. Odontoid fractures: Evaluation and management. *J Am Acad Orthop Surg.* 1997;5:199–204.

9. Joint Section on Disorders of the Spine and Peripheral Nerves of the American Association of Neurological Surgeons and the Congress of Neurological Surgeons. Management of acute cervical spine and spinal cord injuries: Isolated fractures of the axis in adults. *Neurosurgery.* 2002;50(suppl 3):S125–S139.

10. Joint Section on Disorders of the Spine and Peripheral Nerves of the American Association of Neurological Surgeons and the Congress of Neurological Surgeons. Management of acute cervical spine and spinal cord injuries: Treatment of subaxial cervical spine injuries. *Neurosurgery.* 2002;50(suppl 3):S156–S165.

11. Delamarter RB, Coyle J. Acute management of spinal cord injury. *J Am Acad Orthop Surg.* 1999;7:166–175.

12. Torg J, Vegso JJ, O'Neill MJ, Sennett B. The epidemiologic, pathologic, biomechanical, and cinematographic analysis of football-induced cervical spine trauma. *Am J Sports Med.* 1990;18:50–57.

13. Joint Section on Disorders of the Spine and Peripheral Nerves of the American Association of Neurological Surgeons and the Congress of Neurological Surgeons. Management of acute cervical spine and spinal cord injuries: Management of acute spinal cord injuries in an intensive care unit or other monitored setting. *Neurosurgery.* 2002; 50(suppl 3):S51–S57.

14. *American Hospital Formulary Science Drug Information,* ed 2003. Bethesda, MD: American Society of Health-System Pharmacists; 2003.

15. *Drug Facts and Comparisons,* ed 56. St. Louis, MO: Facts & Comparisons; 2001.

16. Dipiro JT, Talbert RL, Yee GC, Matzke GR, Well BG, Posey LM (eds). *Pharmacotherapy: A Pathophysiologic Approach,* ed 5. New York, NY: McGraw-Hill Medical Publishing Division; 2002.

17. *Physicians' Desk Reference 2003,* ed 57. Montvale, NJ: Medical Economics; 2002.

18. Barkin RL, Barkin D. Pharmacologic management of acute and chronic pain: Focus on drug interactions and patient-specific pharmacotherapeutic selection. *South Med J.* 2001;94:756–770.

19. McCarthy DM. Comparative toxicity of nonsteroidal anti-inflammatory drugs. *Am J Med.* 1999;107:37S–47S.

20. Rainsford KD. Profile and mechanisms of gastrointestinal and other side effects of nonsteroidal anti-inflammatory drugs (NSAIDs). *Am J Med.* 1999;107:27S–36S.

21. Jackson LM, Hawkey CJ. COX-2 selective nonsteroidal anti-inflammatory drugs: Do they really offer any advantages? *Drugs.* 2000;59:1207–1216.

22. Urban MK. COX-2 specific inhibitors offer improved advantages over traditional NSAIDs. *Orthopedics.* 2000; 23(suppl):761S–764S.

23. Goodman S, Ma T, Trindade M, et al. COX-2 selective NSAID decreases bone ingrowth in vivo. *J Orthop Res.* 2002;20:1164–1169.

24. Brown C, Mazzula JP, Mok MS, et al. Comparison of repeat doses of intramuscular ketorolac tromethamine and morphine sulfate for analgesia after major surgery. *Pharmacotherapy.* 1990;10(6 Pt 2):45S–50S.

25. Zimmerman HJ, Maddrey WC. Acetaminophen (paracetamol) hepatotoxicity with regular intake of alcohol: Analysis of instances of therapeutic misadventure. *Hepatology.* 1995;22:767–773.

26. Nesathurai S. Steroids and spinal cord injury: Revisiting the NASCIS 2 and NASCIS 3 trials. *J Trauma.* 1998;45: 1088–1093.

27. Walker J, Criddle LM. Methylprednisolone in acute spinal cord injury: Fact or fantasy? *J Emerg Nurs.* 2001;27: 401–403.

28. Joint Section on Disorders of the Spine and Peripheral Nerves of the American Association of Neurological Surgeons and the Congress of Neurological Surgeons. Pharmacologic therapy after acute cervical spinal cord injury. *Neurosurgery.* 2002;50(suppl 3):S63–S72.

29. Bracken MB, Shepard MJ, Collins WF, et al. A randomized, controlled trial of methylprednisolone or naloxone in the treatment of acute spinal-cord injury: Results of the Second National Acute Spinal Cord Injury Study. *N Engl J Med.* 1990;322:1405–1411.

30. Bracken MB, Shepard MJ, Holford TR, et al. Administration of methylprednisolone for 24 or 48 hours or tirilazad mesylate for 48 hours in the treatment of acute spinal cord injury: Results of the Third National Acute Spinal Cord Injury Randomized Controlled Trial. National Acute Spinal Cord Injury Study. *JAMA.* 1997;277:1597–1604.

31. Carlson GD, Gorden CD, Oliff HS, et al. Sustained spinal cord compression: Part I. Time-dependent effect on long-term pathophysiology. *J Bone Joint Surg Am.* 2003;85:86–94.

32. Carlson GD, Gorden CD, Nakazawa A, et al. Sustained spinal cord compression: Part II. Effect of methyprednisolone on regional blood flow and recovery of somatosensory evoked potentials. *J Bone Joint Surg Am.* 2003;85:95–101.

33. Joint Section on Disorders of the Spine and Peripheral Nerves of the American Association of Neurological Surgeons and the Congress of Neurological Surgeons. Blood pressure management after acute spinal cord injury. *Neurosurgery.* 2002;50(suppl 3):S58–S62.

34. Green D, Rossi EC, Yao JS, et al. Deep vein thrombosis in spinal cord injury: Effect of prophylaxis with calf compression, aspirin, and dipyridamole. *Paraplegia.* 1982;20:227–234.

35. Spinal Cord Injury Thromboprophylaxis Investigators. Prevention of venous thromboembolism in the acute

treatment phase after spinal cord injury: A randomized, multicenter trial comparing low-dose heparin plus intermittent pneumatic compression with enoxaparin. *J Trauma.* 2003;54:1116–1124; discussion 25–26.

36. Torg JS, Guille JT, Jaffe S. Injuries to the cervical spine in American football players. *J Bone Joint Surg Am.* 2002; 84:112–122.

37. Thomas BE, McCullen AGM, Yuan HA. Cervical spine injuries in football players. *J Am Acad Orthop Surg.* 1999; 7:338–347.

38. Torg JS, Naranja RJ, Pavlov H, et al. The relationship of developmental narrowing of the cervical spinal canal to reversible and irreversible injury of the cervical spine cord in football players: An epidemiological study. *J Bone Joint Surg Am.* 1996;78:1308–1314.

39. Mundt DJ, Kelsey JL, Golden AL, et al. An epidemiologic study of sports and weight lifting as possible risk factors for herniated lumbar and cervical discs: The Northeast Collaborative Group on Low Back Pain. *Am J Sports Med.* 1993;21:854–860.

40. Rao R. Neck pain, cervical radiculopathy, and cervical myelopathy: Pathophysiology, natural history, and clinical evaluation. *J Bone Joint Surg Am.* 2002;84:1872–1881.

41. Levine MJ, Albert TJ, Smith MD. Cervical radiculopathy: Diagnosis and nonoperative management. *J Am Acad Orthop Surg.* 1996;4:305–316.

42. Fager CA. Cervical disc herniation, in Long DM (ed), *Current Therapy in Neurological Surgery.* Toronto, Ontario: BC Decker; 1985:164–167.

43. Torg J. The cervical spine, spinal cord, and brachial plexus, in Scuderi GR, McCann PD, Burno PJ (eds), *Sports Medicine: Principles of Primary Care.* St. Louis, MO: Mosby; 1997:186–201.

44. Standaert CJ, Herring SA. Expert opinion and controversies in musculoskeletal and sports medicine: Stingers. *Arch Phys Med Rehabil.* 2009;90:402–406.

45. Presciutti SM, DeLuca P, Marchetto P, et al. Mean subaxial space available for the cord index as a novel method of measuring cervical spine geometry to predict the chronic stinger syndrome in American football players. *J Neurosurg Spine.* 2009;11:264–271.

46. Bentolila V, Nizard R, Bizot P, Sedel L. Complete traumatic brachial plexus palsy: Treatment and outcome after repair. *J Bone Joint Surg Am.* 1999;81:20–28.

47. Maitland GD. *Vertebral Manipulation*, ed 4. London: Butterworths; 1977.

48. Intra-Association Task Force for Appropriate Care of the Spine-Injured Athlete. *Prehospital Care of the Spine-Injured Athlete.* Dallas, TX: National Athletic Trainers' Association; 2000.

49. Laprade RF, Schnetzler KA, Broxterman RJ, et al. Cervical spine alignment in the immobilized ice hockey player: A computed tomographic analysis of effects of helmet removal. *Am J Sports Med.* 2000;28:800–803.

50. Anderson JC, Courson RW, Kleiner DM, McLoda TA. NATA position statement: Emergency action planning in athletics. *J Athl Train.* 2002;37:990.

15

Additional Spine and Torso Therapeutic Exercises

The exercises and techniques presented in this chapter are adjuncts to those presented in Chapter 13 (Lumbar Spine Injuries), Chapter 14 (Abdominal and Thorax Injuries), and Chapter 15 (Cervical Spine Injuries). These exercises are also needed for developing core stability to correct certain lower extremity and upper extremity injuries. Other exercises can also be incorporated or substituted for those presented here. Additionally, most exercises can be modified based on the patient's needs, equipment on hand, or personal preference. To construct a complete rehabilitation program, cross-referencing among these chapters may be required.

Flexibility Exercises

Refer to Chapters 4, 5, 6, and 7 for lower extremity flexibility exercises and Chapters 9 and 12 for upper extremity flexibility exercises.

Cross-References

Lumbar Spine
    Lumbar spine joint mobilization (page 508)
    Lumbar rotation stretch (page 509)
    Cat-cow stretch (page 509)
    Williams' flexion exercises (page 511)
    McKenzie extension exercises (page 511)
Cervical Spine
    Cervical spine vertebral glides (page 575)
    Cervical range of motion (ROM) exercises (page 576)

Seated Sun Salutation

The patient is seated on a large inflatable ball with the knees flexed to 90°. The exercise is begun by the patient rolling forward with the cervical spine relaxed (see **Figure 16.1A**). The spine is then extended and the arms brought over the head as the patient inhales. If tolerated, at the end of the motion the spine is arched slightly and held for 1 to 2 seconds (see **Figure 16.1B**). The patient exhales while returning to the starting position. This exercise is repeated five times. To focus on the pectorals and anterior deltoid, the arms are brought down and back.

Thoracolumbar Stretch

To focus on the thoracic and upper lumbar spine, the patient kneels with the forearm across a foam roller; the forearm is in the neutral or supinated position (see **Figure 16.2A**). The foam roller is used to assist in the rotation of the thoracic spine, stretching the interscapular muscles (see **Figure 16.2B**). The end

A

B

Figure 16.1 Seated sun salutation. (**A**) Flexion component. (**B**) Extension component.

A

B

Figure 16.2 Midback roller stretch. (**A**) Starting position. (**B**) Ending position.

position is held for 2 to 3 seconds and the exercise is repeated five or six times. Repeat with the opposite arm. The thoracolumbar stretch can be modified to isolate the latissimus dorsi by rolling across the body.

■ Pectoralis/Lateral Muscle Stretch

The patient begins by lying on an inflatable ball, while holding a wand across the waist with both hands (see **Figure 16.3A**). The patient extends the hips and moves the wand over and behind the head (see **Figure 16.3B**). If pain is experienced, the patient can widen the grip on the wand. The patients hold the position for 5 to 10 seconds. The stretch is repeated five times.

■ Inflatable Ball Lateral Stretch

The patient begins in a side-lying position over the inflatable ball, grasping the wand with both hands over the head. While using the feet to stabilize the lower extremity, the patient moves the body over the ball, lowering the wand toward the ground, while stretching the costal muscles and latissimus dorsi (see **Figure 16.4**). The position is held for 2 to 3 seconds and is repeated five times.

This exercise can be modified by the patient assuming a kneeling position with one hand on the

Figure 16.4   Inflatable ball lateral stretch with wand.

floor and the opposite hand positioned on the ball diagonally across the body (see **Figure 16.5A**). While relaxing the shoulder muscles, the patient reaches out to stretch the latissimus dorsi (see **Figure 16.5B**). The ending position is held for 2 to 3 seconds for five repetitions. Repeat for the opposite side.

■ Standing Latissimus Dorsi Stretch

An inflatable ball is placed on a table so that the patient's arm is abducted to 90° (see **Figure 16.6A**). While keeping the hand on the ball, the patient

A

B

Figure 16.3   Pectoralis/lateral muscle stretch. (**A**) Starting position. (**B**) Ending position.

A

B

Figure 16.5   Latissimus dorsi stretch. (**A**) Starting position. (**B**) Ending position.

squats to lengthen the spine and stretch the latissimus dorsi (see Figure 16.6B). Pain in the shoulder can indicate rotator cuff impingement and should be avoided.

Core Strengthening Exercises

Core muscles are centrally located to the core of the body and provide stability to the spine. The larger muscles on the periphery enable spine and trunk movement. The core muscles include the transverse abdominis, lower internal obliques, and multifidus; the trunk muscles include the erector spinae, external obliques, and rectus abdominis. The core muscles co-contract to provide stiffness and stability to the lumbar spine and pelvis during static and dynamic activities. Multifidus recovery after low back injury does not occur without specific strengthening exercises, and the most important abdominal muscle providing stabilization is the transverse abdominis. For these reasons, the exercises in this section should be taught to patients with low back pain or sacroiliac instability. Refer to Chapter 13 for a description of pelvic-neutral exercises.

Transverse Abdominis Strengthening

In the supine, hook-lying position, the patient actively pulls the umbilicus to the spine as far as possible and holds this position for 5 to 10 seconds. The patient should be instructed to breathe while performing this exercise.

Abdominal Draw-In

This exercise can be performed with the patient standing, bent forward with the hands on the table (see Figure 16.7A) or advanced to the quadruped position (see Figure 16.7B). With the spine and pelvis in the neutral position, the patient exhales while drawing the stomach up and in. The ending maneuver is held for 3 to 5 seconds and repeated 10 times.

Lumbar Multifidus Strengthening

The multifidus is recruited when the pelvic floor muscles are tensed, so the best way to facilitate strengthening is to have the patient tense the pelvic floor muscles. Instructions given to the patient include this admonition: "Tighten your muscles as if stopping urination midstream." The patient holds this position for 5 to 10 seconds.

A

B

Figure 16.6 Standing latissimus dorsi stretch. (**A**) Starting position. (**B**) Ending position.

A

B

Figure 16.7 Abdominal draw-in. (**A**) Initial (easier) position. (**B**) Advanced position.

16

Co-Contraction

Once the patient can perform each of the prior exercises correctly, the next step is to perform an isometric co-contraction of both muscles. These activities are repeated to build strength and muscle endurance. The patient progresses from performing co-contraction while sitting, then standing, and then during functional activities.

Abdominal Muscle Strengthening

Crunches

In the supine, hook-lying position with the feet unanchored, the patient performs a curl-up until the scapulae are off the floor (see Figure 16.8). The patient can progress from the arms being crossed over the chest to the hands held behind the head.

Straight-Leg Curls

In the supine position with the legs extended but not anchored, the patient performs a sit-up in a smooth, continuous motion.

Obliques

In the hook-lying position with the hips and knees rotated to one side and the shoulders flat on the floor, the patient lifts the upper trunk toward the upper hip (see Figure 16.9). When the repetitions are completed on this side, the patient reverses the position, so that the hips and knees are rotated to the opposite side, and repeats the exercise.

Paraspinal Muscle Strengthening

The patient can progress each of these exercises to performing them on an inflatable ball. The unstable surface of the ball makes the exercise more difficult.

Cobras

The patient is prone on the table with the arms at the side. The exercise begins with the patient retracting the scapulae, followed by lifting the chest off the table while keeping the cervical spine in line with the spine (see Figure 16.10). The legs remain on

Figure 16.9 Obliques.

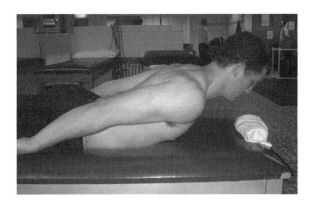

Figure 16.10 Cobras.

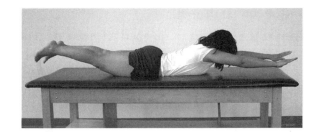

Figure 16.11 Superman.

the table during this exercise, which is repeated 10 to 15 times.

Superman

In the prone position, the patient maintains the pelvic-neutral position, tightens the gluteals, and raises the arms and legs upward for a count of five (see Figure 16.11).

Figure 16.8 Crunches.

Prone Leg Lifts

Lying on the end of a table with both feet on the floor and the hands grasping the table, the patient tightens the abdominals and gluteals and raises both legs until they are level with the trunk (see **Figure 16.12**). A Roman chair can also be used for this exercise.

Prone Trunk Lifts

Lying prone on the end of a table with the legs on the table and the trunk extended over the end and inclined toward the floor, no more than about 30°, the patient contracts the gluteal and paraspinal muscles to elevate the trunk until it is level with the lower extremities (see **Figure 16.13**). This exercise can also be performed on a Roman chair. The patient should not bend too far forward; this position would place undue stress on the lumbar disks.

Bridging Exercises

Lying supine with the knees bent and the feet flat on the surface, the patient tightens the abdomen and buttocks, pressing the small of the back into the surface. While keeping the abdomen and buttocks contracted, the back straight, and the body in a straight line from the knees to the shoulders, the patient lifts the hips off the surface. This position is held for a count of three to five and then released.

■ Medicine Ball Exercises

Crunch Toss

While in the hook-lying position on the floor, the patient positions the arms overhead. Standing approximately 10 ft from the patient, the clinician tosses a medicine ball to the patient so that the ball is caught with the arms extended overhead as the patient performs an abdominal crunch (see **Figure 16.14**). The patient returns the ball to the clinician and returns to the starting position on the floor. A pelvic-neutral position should be maintained throughout this exercise.

Standing Rotations

Standing about an arm's length apart with backs to each other, the patient and partner rotate to the side with the shoulders flexed and abducted to 90°. The medicine ball is passed back and forth, and the exercise is then repeated on the opposite side (see **Figure 16.15**).

Figure 16.14 Crunch toss.

Figure 16.12 Prone leg lifts.

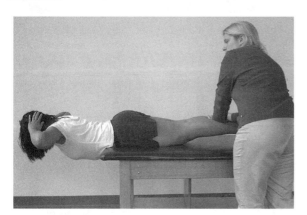

Figure 16.13 Prone trunk lifts.

Figure 16.15 Standing rotations.

16

Spinal Stabilization Exercises

Exercise programs designed to strengthen stabilizing muscles are crucial to the proper treatment of hypermobile spinal segments. These programs should also be an integral part of proper follow-up care, after hypomobile segments have been effectively mobilized by the clinician and the patient is able to achieve normal ROM.

When the patient can maintain a neutral spine, movement of the arms and legs is introduced (see **Figure 16.16**). This is a difficult maneuver for the patient in the early stages of any stabilization program; however, with minimal training, the patient can generally learn to maintain a neutral spine while in motion. Once this skill is mastered, the stabilization program is relatively straightforward. The patient begins by superimposing easy movements over the neutral spine and progresses in sequence to more difficult maneuvers. Stabilization exercises for the cervical spine require movements of the upper extremities. In one exercise, the patient assumes a prone position on an inflated exercise ball while slowly rotating the shoulders (see **Figure 16.17**).

The spinal stabilization exercises presented in Chapter 13 can be performed on foam or inflatable rollers (see **Figure 16.18**). The perturbating surface requires paraspinal and core muscle activation to maintain balance and stabilize the kinetic segment.

Cardiovascular Exercises

Cardiovascular fitness should be maintained throughout the rehabilitation process. In the early stages of rehabilitation, a patient with a lower extremity injury to the pelvis, hip, or thigh may not be able to use the injured extremity to condition. Many cardiovascular exercises also improve ROM and strength. Given the patient's unique situation, the best methods to maintain or improve cardiovascular function must be determined. A patient's cardiovascular system can be exercised during

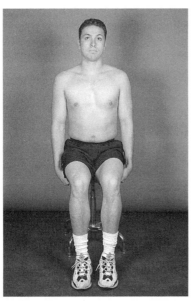

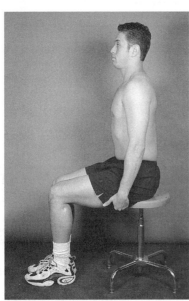

Figure 16.16 Spinal stabilization exercises. Movement of the arms and legs is introduced when the patient achieves a neutral spine.

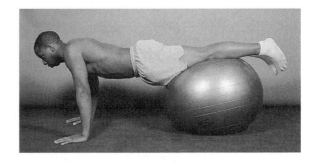

Figure 16.17 Stabilization exercise for the cervical spine.

Figure 16.18 Foam or inflatable rollers can be used for spinal stabilization exercises.

different stages of the rehabilitation process by using a stationary bicycle, upper body exerciser, stair stepper, or rowing machine. Swimming or other water-supported exercises are also useful.

Sport-Specific Activities

Sport-specific activities will depend on the patient's sport and position within the sport. For example, a basketball forward's activities may include forward sprints for the distance of a court length, sprints to a lay-up, a sudden stop and jump shot, or vertical jumping. A volleyball player's activities would more likely include lateral movements to the left and right with jumps for blocking or hitting, dives, squats for setting, and diagonal sprints for the ball. Each of these activities should be performed in pelvic-neutral position. If the clinician is unfamiliar with the specific activities and demands of the patient's sport and position, a coach should be consulted to obtain assistance or instruction in useful activities for this stage of the rehabilitation program. The goal in the final stages of sport-specific activities should be normal performance without signs of hesitation in performing any activity.

16

V Head and Systemic

Head Injuries

Jake E. Resch, PhD, ATC

Traumatic Brain Injury

Unlike most injuries sustained in sport, traumatic brain injuries (TBIs) have the potential for catastrophic outcomes if managed inappropriately. These injuries must be managed cautiously, with awareness of the potential dangers and the potential long-term consequences of prematurely returning an athlete to competition after injury. The sports medicine team should work together to develop a head injury policy so that each member of the team understands his or her role in the event that an athlete experiences a concussion or potentially life-threatening injury. The examination process relies on the practitioner's ability to identify the signs and symptoms associated with a TBI, including the ability to recognize deteriorating conditions that indicate a more serious situation. Clinical decision making should follow an assessment plan that uses a multifactorial and multidisciplinary approach, including objective measures of symptoms, cognitive function, and postural stability.[1-25]

Mechanics of Traumatic Brain Injury

During closed-head impact, the skull is accelerated, which rapidly displaces and rotates the cranium. Depending on the velocity change and trajectory, the brain displaces within the skull and deforms. The speed of loading—either static or dynamic—and extent of deformation are factors in the severity of injury.[26] In sport, a common brain injury is concussion, which is the result of dynamic loading. The resulting motion within the cranium results in three potential stresses that may injure the brain: compressive, tensile, and shearing (see Figure 3.5).

Compression is a crushing force that the tissue cannot absorb. Tension is the pulling or stretching of tissue. Shearing involves a force that moves across the parallel organization of the tissue. Uniform compressive stresses are fairly well tolerated by neural tissue, but shearing stresses are poorly tolerated.[2,27,28] The biomechanical mechanisms responsible for concussion may be divided into two categories: those related to head-contact injuries and those related to head-movement injuries.[29]

A forceful blow to a resting, moveable head usually produces maximum brain injury beneath the point of cranial impact (coup injury). A moving head hitting an unyielding object usually produces maximum brain injury opposite the site of cranial impact, as the brain shifts within the cranium (contrecoup injury).[30] When the head is accelerated before impact, the brain lags toward the trailing surface, squeezing away the cerebrospinal fluid (CSF) and producing maximal shearing forces at this site (see Figure 17.1).[30] This brain lag thickens the layer of CSF under the point of impact, which explains the absence of coup injuries when

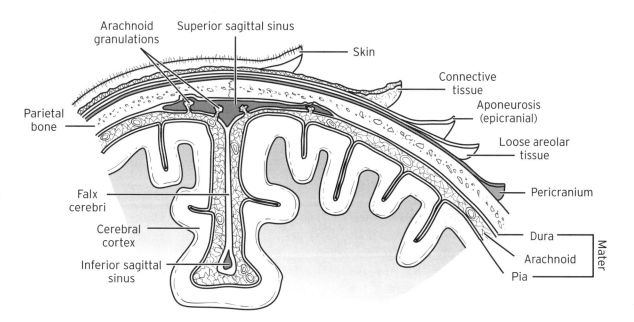

Figure 17.1 Cross-section of the skull. The outer layer is formed by the skin and its subcomponents, the middle layer by the cranium, and the inner layer by the meninges (dura mater, arachnoid mater, and pia mater). The cerebrospinal fluid is located in the subarachnoid space, between the arachnoid mater and the pia mater.

the head is moving. However, when the head is stationary before impact, neither brain lag nor disproportionate CSF distribution occurs, accounting for the absence of contrecoup injury and the presence of coup injury.

During the past several years, researchers have investigated the forces responsible for a concussive injury utilizing accelerometers placed inside helmets to measure both head acceleration and the point of impact. Depending on the study, the range of forces measured in g (weight per unit mass) in football range from 21 g to 230 g.[31–35] Concussive injuries have been recorded between approximately 70 g and 102 g. Re-creation of professional American football game footage revealed impacts occurring between approximately 9 mph and 26 mph with concussive injuries occurring between 16 mph and 26 mph.[35]

Pathology

Perhaps the most challenging aspect of TBI management is recognizing the injury, especially when there are no observable signs an injury has occurred. TBI can be classified into two types: focal and diffuse. Focal brain injuries, also known as posttraumatic intracranial mass lesions, include subdural hematomas, epidural hematomas, cerebral contusions, and intracerebral hemorrhages and hematomas. Diffuse brain injuries can result in widespread or global disruption of neurologic function and are not usually associated with macroscopically visible brain lesions (although cerebral edema may be noted). Most diffuse injuries involve an acceleration–deceleration motion, either within a linear plane or along a rotational model. In both cases, lesions are caused by the brain being shaken within the skull. For example, with a linear acceleration–deceleration mechanism, the head experiences a violent movement (side to side or front to back) before impact.

The resulting trauma to the head reflects how fast the head moves (acceleration and deceleration speeds), what the rate of deceleration is, and how much force has occurred.[4,36] Rotational or rotational acceleration–deceleration injuries are believed to be the primary injury mechanism for diffuse brain injuries. Structural diffuse brain injury (diffuse/traumatic axonal injury [DAI]) is the most severe type of diffuse injury because the mechanical stretching of axonal membranes results

in ionic flux, diffuse depolarization, calcium influx, and mitochondrial swelling.[37] Such injuries can disrupt the centers of the brain responsible for breathing, heart rate, consciousness, memory, and cognition. Nonstructural diffuse injuries, such as cerebral concussions, are typically less severe than structural brain lesions because the anatomic integrity of the central nervous system is maintained. Although these injuries are less severe, they can still result in disrupted consciousness, memory, or cognition and can place the individual at higher risk for second-impact syndrome.[36]

Studies in basic neuroscience have demonstrated that mild TBI, or concussion, is followed by a complex cascade of ionic, metabolic, and physiologic events that can adversely affect cerebral function for several days to weeks depending on the affected individual's age and injury severity.[38,39] Concussive brain injuries trigger a pathophysiologic sequence characterized in the early stages by an indiscriminate release of excitatory amino acids, particularly glutamate. Glutamate subsequently binds to kainate, N-methyl-D-aspartate (NMDA), and D-amino-3-hydroxy-5-methyl-4-isoxazolepropionic acid (AMPA) ionic channels, adding to massive ionic flux. The ionic flux is corrected by adenosine triphosphate (ATP) dependent Na^+/K^+ pumps, which acquire the needed ATP through anaerobic/rapid glycolysis. A byproduct of anaerobic glycolysis is lactate, which also may be utilized for energy production. This period of hyperglycolysis has been shown to last 30 minutes to approximately 4 hours in moderate to severe brain injured rodents.[37,39] This transient metabolic dysfunction is accompanied by persistent metabolic instability, mitochondrial dysfunction, diminished cerebral glucose metabolism, reduced cerebral blood flow, and altered neurotransmission. These events culminate in axonal injury and neuronal dysfunction and a hypometabolic state.[38] Approximately 80% to 90% of concussions resolve within a 7- to 10-day period in adults.[29] Repeated injury may result in a chronic pathobiologic condition.[37] Clinically, concussion results in neurologic deficits, cognitive impairment, and somatic symptoms.[40]

All medical personnel must understand the immediate, delayed, and associated findings and the known complications of TBI. An injury that initially appears minor may gradually worsen and reveal the signs and symptoms of a more serious condition.

Cerebral Concussion

CLINICAL PRESENTATION

History

Direct or rotational blow to the head or body.
Complaints of headache, feeling as if in a "fog," dizziness, visual disturbances, concentration difficulties, and similar problems.
Distinct changes in personality may be noted (e.g., sadness, impulsivity, aggressiveness).

Observation

Light and noise sensitivity.
Poor balance and coordination.
Dizziness.
Nausea and vomiting.
Memory loss or disorientation.

Functional Status

Altered level of consciousness (loss of consciousness is not a prerequisite finding).
Vision disturbances.
Concentration difficulties.
Inability to maintain balance.

Physical Examination Findings

Positive findings on neuropsychological tests.
The following special tests may be positive:
· Balance Error Scoring System (BESS)
· Romberg test
· Tandem walk

These findings vary with the severity of the injury.

Concussion is defined as a complex pathophysiological process affecting the brain and induced by traumatic biomechanical forces.[41] This impaired pathophysiological process results in an altered mental status and one or more of the following symptoms: headache, nausea, vomiting, dizziness, balance problems, fatigue, trouble sleeping, drowsiness, sensitivity to light or noise, blurred vision, difficulty remembering, and difficulty concentrating.[42] The onset of symptoms may occur either immediately after the injury or after several hours following the insult.[41] Loss of consciousness (LOC) does not have to occur for the patient to be diagnosed with a concussion; likewise, LOC has been shown not be a predictor of time to recovery.[6,30]

Concussion Recognition

The varying presentations of the concussed athlete make this injury potentially difficult to recognize and diagnose.[27] Unfortunately, many concussions are not reported until after the practice or game.[43–45] The force of a concussive impact causes a transient irregularity in the electrophysiology of the brain substance, altering mental status. Although concussions may

not involve LOC, patients may experience impaired cognitive function, especially in remembering recent events (posttraumatic amnesia) for a short or prolonged period of time, and in assimilating and interpreting new information.[6,17,27,28] Two types of posttraumatic amnesia (PTA) are distinguished: anterograde and retrograde. Anterograde amnesia is having difficulty remembering events that occurred after the concussion. Retrograde amnesia is having difficulty remembering events leading up to the injury. Either form of PTA may last for varying amounts of time.

Since 2000, symptomology has gained increasing attention in regard to recognition and diagnosis of concussion. Symptoms such as headache, dizziness, drowsiness, difficulty concentrating, fatigue, "feeling as if in a fog," and balance disturbance may occur. The presence of a headache, which tends to occur with nearly all concussions, should not be underestimated.[43] Athletes who experience a postconcussion headache are significantly more likely to experience PTA and four times more likely to experience three or four abnormal on-field markers of concussion severity.[46] The intensity and duration of the headache or any other symptom may indicate whether the injury is improving or worsening with time. Other well-documented signs and symptoms include transient mental confusion, lack of coordination, irrational behavior, and others. Serial observations for signs and symptoms should be conducted every 5 minutes to identify progressive underlying brain damage.[30]

Differential Diagnosis

Subdural hematoma, epidural hematoma, intracerebral hemorrhage, second-impact syndrome, skull fracture.

Medical Diagnostic Tests

A sideline physical and neurologic assessment coupled with a systematic assessment may reveal significant postconcussive symptoms. Sideline instruments, such as the Sport Concussion Assessment Tool 2 (SCAT2), are suggested for use in the acute phase of the injury.[41] Neuropsychological tests can identify subtle changes in the patient's cognitive status, reaction time, attention span, and concentration. Postural-stability tests may reveal motor deficits or sensory-integration problems that indicate a concussion has been sustained.

Imaging Techniques

Radiographic imaging, computed tomography (CT), or magnetic resonance imaging (MRI) may be performed to rule out the presence of a cerebral hematoma, hemorrhagic lesion, or other traumatic injury that would indicate a medical emergency but are not diagnostic for a concussion.

anterograde amnesia Memory loss of events occurring after injury.

retrograde amnesia Memory loss of events occurring prior to injury.

serial observation Repeated assessment of the same injury.

17

Definitive Diagnosis

A systematic multifaceted approach should be employed to diagnose a concussion. If an athlete exhibits any symptoms or physical signs (e.g., loss of consciousness, amnesia, lack of coordination, behavioral changes, and/or cognitive impairments), a concussion should be suspected (see **Table 17.1**). Serial assessments following the injury may discern between the concussed state or a more serious injury.

■ Immediate Management

Management of concussive injuries consists of removal from participation and serial evaluations. In the event of LOC (even brief), the patient should be evaluated by a physician, with consideration given to neuroimaging of the brain. Do not leave the athlete alone following the injury due to potential deterioration during the initial hours after the injury.[41] No athlete should return to participation while still experiencing symptoms or displaying signs associated with a concussed state and no athlete with a concussion should return to play without a full neurocognitive assessment. More specific assessment guidelines are presented in the "Management of Sport-Related Head Injuries" section of this chapter.

■ Medications

Most physicians advise against the use of pain medications immediately after a cerebral concussion, as their use may mask symptoms. Once it is evident that a more serious head injury has not occurred, acet-aminophen may be considered to treat headache symptoms associated with the concussion. Medications containing aspirin or nonsteroidal anti-inflammatory drugs (NSAIDs) that decrease platelet function and may increase intracranial bleeding should be avoided, as they can accelerate hematoma formation.

Cerebral Hematoma

The skull fits the brain like a custom-made helmet, leaving little room for space-occupying hematomas. Two primary types of hematomas can occur after head trauma: epidural and subdural. Epidural hematomas are located outside the dura mater; subdural hematomas are found inside the dura mater (see **Figure 17.2**). Each type can increase intracranial pressure and shift the cerebral hemispheres away from the hematoma. As the hematoma develops, intracranial pressure increases, and the patient's neurologic signs deteriorate.

■ Epidural Hematoma

An epidural hematoma is an accumulation of blood between the dura mater and the inner surface of the skull as a result of arterial bleeding, most often from the middle meningeal artery. The accumulation of blood typically leads to a rapid degradation in the patient's neurologic status. The patient may lose consciousness from the concussive force, then have a period of altered consciousness, and subsequently appear asymptomatic with normal neurologic examination results.[2]

The problem arises when the injury leads to a slow accumulation of blood in the epidural space, causing the patient to initially appear asymptomatic until the hematoma reaches a critically large size and begins to compress the underlying brain.[47] Immediate surgery may be required to decompress the hematoma and control the hemorrhage. The clinical manifestations of an epidural hematoma depend on the type and amount of energy transferred, the time course of the hematoma formation, and the presence of simultaneous brain injuries. Often the size of the hematoma determines its clinical effects.[48,49]

■ Subdural Hematoma

The mechanism of a subdural hematoma is more complex than that of an epidural hematoma. The force of a blow to the skull thrusts the brain against the point of impact. The subdural vessels stretch and tear, resulting in development of a hematoma within the subdural space. Subdural hematomas are

---

Table 17.1

Graded Symptom Checklist for Concussion*

Symptom	Grade
Balance problems/dizziness	
Drowsiness	
Difficulty concentrating	
Fatigue	
Feel "in a fog"	
Headache	
Difficulty remembering	
Nausea	
Sensitivity to light	
Sensitivity to noise	

*A graded symptom checklist is used not only for the initial examination, but also for subsequent follow-up assessments. It is periodically repeated until all post concussion signs and symptoms have returned to baseline or cleared at rest and during physical exertion. The items can be either checked as "present" or scored on a scale of 0 to 6, with 0 representing "not present" and 6 representing "severe."[48]

CLINICAL PRESENTATION

Epidural Hematoma	Subdural Hematoma	Intracerebral Hemorrhage/ Cerebral Contusion
History		
Coup or contrecoup mechanism (acceleration-deceleration) resulting in inward deformity	Coup or contrecoup mechanism	Direct blow to an immoveable head or coup or contrecoup mechanism (acceleration-deceleration) and inward deformation of the skull at the site of impact
Pathology		
Dural detachment from inner table of skull; middle meningeal artery is usually ruptured	Subdural venous bleeding resulting from stretching or tearing of subdural veins; if acute, presents within 48 to 72 hours after trauma; if chronic, presents at 3 weeks after trauma	Cerebral contusions of underlying brain tissue at the site of impact; multiple small areas of contusions may coalesce into a large area resembling a lesion
Observation		
Size of hematoma determines the clinical presentation; patient can demonstrate lucid intervals or persistent unconsciousness	Acute presentation can vary, from patients who are awake and alert with no focal neurologic deficits to those with altered consciousness and often a state of coma with major focal neurologic deficits; chronic presentation typically involves symptoms suggestive of increased intracranial pressure	Normal function or any type of neurologic deterioration, including coma
Functional Status		
Neurologic status deteriorates within 10 minutes to 2 hours	Neurologic status deteriorates within hours to days (acute) or weeks to months (chronic)	Rapid deterioration of neurologic status
Physical Examination Findings		
Skull fracture may be noted on radiographs	Skull fracture less common; usually involves slower bleeding causing altered consciousness	Possible depressed skull fracture

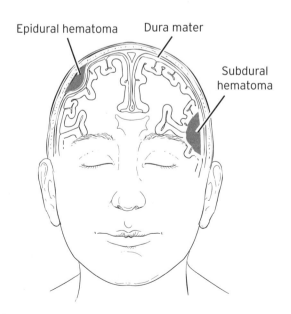

Figure 17.2 Types of cerebral hematoma. Epidural hematomas form between the dura mater and the skull. Subdural hematomas form between the dura mater and the brain.

classified as acute, when symptoms present 48 to 72 hours after injury, and chronic, with more variable clinical manifestations that occurr in a later time frame.[2] Low pressure causes the clot to form slowly, delaying the onset of symptoms for hours or days (acute) or even weeks or months (chronic) after the actual trauma, when the clot may absorb fluid and expand. The clinical presentation of an acute subdural hematoma varies. Although the individual may be awake and alert with no focal neurologic deficits, more typically persons with any sizable acute subdural hematoma have significant neurologic deficits, including altered states of consciousness.[2]

■ Intracerebral Hemorrhage

A cerebral contusion is a heterogeneous zone of brain damage that consists of hemorrhage, cerebral infarction, necrosis, and edema. Cerebral contusion

17

is a frequent sequela of head injury and is often considered the most common traumatic lesion of the brain visualized on radiographic evaluation.[2,50] This injury usually results from an inward deformation of the skull at the impact site. Contusions can vary from small, localized areas of injury to large, extensive areas of involvement. An intracerebral hematoma is similar in pathophysiology and radiographic appearance to a cerebral contusion. The intracerebral hematoma—a localized collection of blood within the brain tissue itself—is usually caused by a torn artery from a depressed skull fracture, penetrating wound, or acceleration–deceleration mechanism. These injuries are rarely associated with a lucid interval, but rather are often rapidly progressive; however, the formation of a traumatic intracerebral hematoma can be delayed. Intracerebral hematomas and subdural hematomas are the most common causes of lethal sport-related brain injuries.[2]

The brain substance may suffer a cerebral contusion (bruising) when an object hits the skull, or vice versa. The impact causes injured vessels to bleed internally, and consciousness is lost. A cerebral contusion may be associated with partial paralysis (hemiplegia), one-sided pupil dilation, or altered vital signs and may persist for a prolonged period. Progressive swelling can further compromise brain tissue not injured in the original trauma. Even with a severe contusion, however, eventual recovery without intracranial surgery can occur. The prognosis often is determined by the supportive care delivered from the moment of injury, including adequate ventilation and cardiopulmonary resuscitation, proper transport techniques (if necessary), and prompt expert evaluation.

Differential Diagnosis

Concussion, second-impact syndrome, skull fracture.

Medical Diagnostic Tests

Thorough neurologic examination for cerebral hematoma involves special tests for cognitive function and postural stability, cranial nerve assessment, and neuroimaging (CT or MRI).

Imaging Techniques

An epidural hematoma results in the classic appearance of a biconvex or lenticular shape of the hematoma on CT scans (see **Figure 17.3**).[2] A subdural hematoma is confirmed by MRI demonstrating extra-axial, low-density fluid collection in the subdural space. An intracerebral hemorrhage results from inward deformation of the skull, leading to transient compression of the brain against the skull and hemorrhagic contusions present on CT scan.

hemiplegia Paralysis of one side of the body.

Definitive Diagnosis

The definitive diagnosis is based on the findings of the neurologic examination and cognitive and postural-stability testing. Although CT and MRI scans can help rule out a more serious injury such as a hemorrhage, these tests do not indicate the severity of a cerebral concussion. A variety of cognitive and motor tests must be employed to obtain an accurate diagnosis, because deficits may be present in one area but not another.

■ Immediate Management

When symptoms present acutely, the patient must be provided with adequate ventilation, including intubation and cardiopulmonary resuscitation (CPR) if necessary. Cranial nerve inhibition is a sign of increased intracranial pressure (see **Figure 17.4**). The patient must be transported to the nearest appropriate hospital in the event that surgical decompression of the brain is necessary.

Because of the latent symptoms associated with a subdural hematoma, a patient demonstrating early neurologic symptoms should be monitored closely. If the cause or magnitude of the injury is in doubt, immediately refer the patient to a physician. Even with delayed onset, any signs of rapid deterioration in neurologic status should be addressed emergently. More specific assessment guidelines are presented in the "Management of Sport-Related Head Injuries" section of this chapter.

■ Medications

Aspirin and NSAIDs should not be administered while a person is experiencing postconcussion symptoms. These medications and other cyclooxygenase-1 inhibitors prevent blood coagulation and can exacerbate intracranial hemorrhage. Dexamethasone or another corticosteroid may be administered to minimize cerebral edema. Emergency antiseizure and anticonvulsive medications may be prescribed based on the patient's symptoms. These medications can affect the patient's apparent neurologic status, causing slurred speech, lethargy, and poor psychomotor control.

■ Surgical Intervention

If pharmacologic attempts to control intracranial hemorrhage are not successful or if the rate of hematoma formation is too rapid, surgical decompression of the skull may be required. The mechanical release of pressure is often sufficient to save the patient's life, but permanent neurologic deficit may still result.

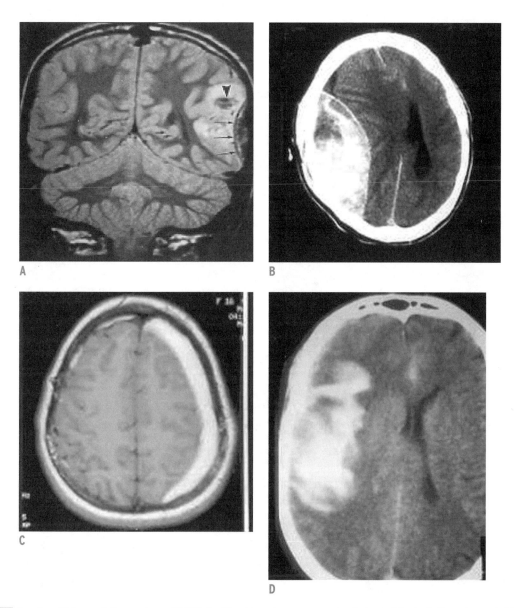

Figure 17.3 Imaging of intracranial hemorrhage. (**A**) MRI of epidural hematoma compressing the underlying brain tissue (arrows). (**B**) CT scan of a large epidural hematoma. (**C**) MRI of a subdural hematoma. (**D**) CT scan of an intracranial hematoma.

▇ Postinjury/Postoperative Management

The treatment for any athlete who has suffered loss of consciousness or altered mental status should include prolonged observation and monitoring for several days, because slow bleeding can cause subsequent deterioration of mental status. In such a case, surgical intervention may be necessary to evacuate (drain) the hematoma and decompress the brain.

Second-Impact Syndrome

Second-impact syndrome (SIS) occurs when a patient who has sustained an initial head trauma, most often a concussion, experiences a second injury before symptoms associated with the first have totally resolved. During the past two decades, sport-related SIS has been the topic of much discussion and debate.[27,28,51–57]

Often, the first injury goes unreported or unrecognized. The SIS usually occurs within 1 week of the initial injury, resulting in cerebral edema. Though controversial, the underlying mechanism for SIS may be due to an increased vulnerability to brain injury as a result from metabolic perturbations, altered blood flow, axonal injury, and abnormal neural activation.[37] Brainstem failure develops in 2 to 5 minutes, eventually leading to coma and respiratory failure. Unfortunately, the mortality rate of SIS is 50%, and the morbidity rate is 100%. Although the number of reported cases is relatively low, the potential for SIS in an athlete with a mild

17

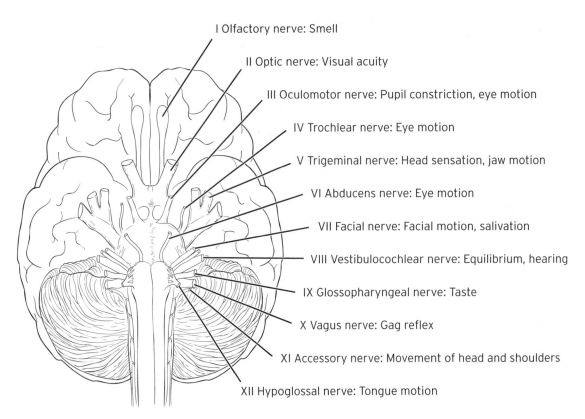

I Olfactory nerve: Smell

II Optic nerve: Visual acuity

III Oculomotor nerve: Pupil constriction, eye motion

IV Trochlear nerve: Eye motion

V Trigeminal nerve: Head sensation, jaw motion

VI Abducens nerve: Eye motion

VII Facial nerve: Facial motion, salivation

VIII Vestibulocochlear nerve: Equilibrium, hearing

IX Glossopharyngeal nerve: Taste

X Vagus nerve: Gag reflex

XI Accessory nerve: Movement of head and shoulders

XII Hypoglossal nerve: Tongue motion

Figure 17.4   The cranial nerves comprise 12 pairs of nerves that have specific sensory and motor functions.

CLINICAL PRESENTATION

History

The patient experiences a second blow to the head, typically within a short period of time (up to 10 days) after a concussion,
Symptoms from the original concussion were unresolved at the time of the second impact.
LOC may or may not occur.

Observation

The patient typically collapses within seconds to 1 minute of impact.
Rapid onset of pupil dilation and loss of eye movement occur.
Respiratory failure is evident.

Functional Status

Control of eye motion is lost.
Respiratory failure occurs.
Coma occurs rapidly.

Physical Examination Findings

Inhibited cranial nerve function.
Impaired cognition progressing to eventual LOC.
Loss of motor function.
Rapid deterioration in vital signs.

entation of signs and symptoms and recommended care follow a standard course, however.

Differential Diagnosis

Subdural hematoma, epidural hematoma, intracerebral hemorrhage, concussion, skull fracture.

Imaging Techniques

MRI is more sensitive in identifying cranial edema than CT (see Figure 17.3).

Definitive Diagnosis

The definitive diagnosis is based on the history of two substantial concussive forces within a 1-week period or sustaining a second concussion while the symptoms of a prior concussion are still present. Cerebral imaging, intracranial pressure tests, and neurologic status also contribute to the final diagnosis.

■ Immediate Management

Following a head injury, especially with an unconscious victim, assume a C-spine injury might have occurred. Stabilize the cervical spine and remove the face mask for access to the airway (unless the face mask cannot be removed), but leave the helmet and shoulder pads in place for transport (see **Figure 17.5**). Transport by ambulance to the nearest emergency room for further evaluation. More specific assessment guidelines are presented in the "Management of Sport-Related Head Injuries" section of this chapter.

head injury should be a major consideration when making a return-to-play decision.[58]

The structures involved in these head injuries vary depending on the impact acceleration–deceleration forces and the mechanism. The pres-

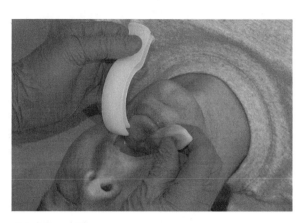

Figure 17.5 To maintain an open airway, qualified personnel may be required to use an adjunct (oropharyngeal or nasophyrngeal) airway for an athlete with a head injury. This technique can be performed with the helmet on and the face mask pulled back.

■ Medications

If the condition worsens, the patient may be managed pharmacologically as described for cerebral hematoma.

■ Surgical Intervention

Surgical decompression and/or cranial clot removal may be necessary.

Skull Fractures

CLINICAL PRESENTATION

History

The patient experiences blunt trauma or high-velocity blow to the skull.
LOC may have occurred after the injury.

Observation

Bleeding may be present.
Deformity of the skull may be noted.
Posterior auricular ecchymosis (Battle's sign) may be evident.
Periorbital ecchymosis ("raccoon eyes") may indicate a fracture of the anterior portion of the skull.
Otorrhea may be present with basilar skull fractures.
Rhinorrhea is possible.

Functional Status

The signs and symptoms of a TBI also may be noted.
Skull fractures may affect the inner or middle ear and result in hearing loss.
Anterior skull fractures may affect cranial nerves V, VI, VII, and VIII.

Physical Examination Findings

Note: Do not palpate open wounds.
Point tenderness over the site of injury.
Possible crepitus over the fracture line.
The "halo test" confirms CSF leakage from the nose or ears.

With a skull fracture, coup and contrecoup mechanisms of brain injury frequently do not occur because the bone itself, which is either transiently (linear skull fracture) or permanently (depressed skull fracture) displaced at the moment of impact, absorbs much of the trauma energy or directly injures the brain tissue (see **Figure 17.6**). The bones of the skull are relatively thick, but thin areas of bone in the parietal and temporal regions and the inherently thin bones of the sphenoid sinus, foramen magnum, and sphenoid wings forming the base of the skull increase the risk of fracture at these sites. Focal lesions are most common at the anterior tips and the inferior surfaces of the frontal and temporal lobes because the associated cranial bones have irregular surfaces.[2,28]

Linear skull fractures and basilar skull fractures tend to result when a wide area of the skull receives a low-energy force during a fall to the turf or court or from contact with another stationary object. These injuries carry the risk of a concurrent epidural hematoma, thrombosis of the venous sinus, or dysunion of the cranial sutures. Basilar fractures may also cause damage to the dura mater.

Skull fractures may be difficult to diagnose clinically. Clinically, a depressed skull fracture may be confused with a deep scalp hematoma. Therefore, radiographic evaluation is needed for the prompt detection and proper management of skull fractures. An associated brain injury must always be considered when evaluating skull fractures.

High-energy trauma to a limited area of the skull, such as being struck by a moving bat, causes

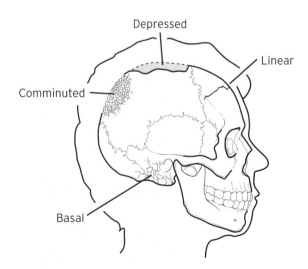

Figure 17.6 Types of skull fractures. *Depressed:* Portion of the skull is indented toward the brain. *Nondepressed:* Minimal indentation of the skull toward the brain. *Linear:* Fracture line runs circumferentially with no indentation of the skull. *Comminuted:* Multiple fracture fragments. *Basal/basilar:* Involves the base of the skull.

17

otorrhea Cerebral spinal fluid draining from the ear canal as a result of a skull facture/TBI.

rhinorrhea Cerebral spinal fluid draining from the nose as a result of a skull fracture/TBI.

a depressed fracture. The rounded nature of the skull results in the comminution of depressed skull fractures. Open depressed or comminuted fractures may expose the underlying meninges and allow foreign matter to be introduced into the cranial vault.

Differential Diagnosis

Subdural hematoma, epidural hematoma, intracerebral hemorrhage, concussion, SIS.

Imaging Techniques

The imaging technique of choice for identifying most types of skull fractures is CT; plain-film radiographs are not sensitive enough to identify most linear fractures. With CT, the sagittal and helical views are the preferred images (see **Figure 17.7**).

Definitive Diagnosis

The definitive diagnosis of the type of skull fracture is based on imaging findings, preferably a CT scan.

Pathomechanics and Functional Limitations

Closed skull fractures (e.g., linear fractures) create weakened areas that diminish the skull's ability to absorb and dissipate force, thereby increasing the risk of the fracture line expanding and the skull losing its ability to protect the brain from concussive forces. However, as long as the patient is not subjected to concussive forces while the skull is healing, activities of daily living (ADLs) are not normally inhibited.

Depressed skull fractures decrease the volume of the cranial vault—and any loss of volume reduces the space available for the brain. As the volume of the vault decreases, the forces placed on the brain increase, potentially fatally inhibiting its function.

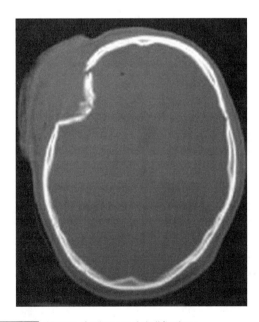

Figure 17.7 CT scan of a depressed skull fracture.

Bony segments of the fracture can also lacerate the underlying brain, vascular, and meningeal tissue. Open fractures can result in profuse blood loss and expose the underlying tissue to contaminants.

◼ Immediate Management

Patients with suspected or known skull fractures should be transported in a reclining position. Open fractures and associated skin wounds should be covered with a sterile gauze bandage. (*Note:* A suspected cervical fracture must take precedence in the management options.) More specific assessment guidelines are presented in the "Management of Sport-Related Head Injuries" section of this chapter.

◼ Medications

Pharmacologic options are based on the suspicion of underlying brain trauma. In the absence of brain injury, narcotic analgesics, aspirin, ibuprofen, or acetaminophen may be prescribed for pain. A patient with an open fracture is prescribed a course of prophylactic antibiotics.

◼ Surgical Intervention

Surgery is required if the bony segments of a depressed fracture are displaced more than 5 mm, if a cerebral hematoma has formed, or if the dura mater or venous sinus is torn. With a depressed fracture, the surgeon cleans and manually realigns the displaced fragments of bone. Large pieces of bones may be wired together. The bony fixation may be improved through the use of a titanium mesh or bone cement.

◼ Postinjury/Postoperative Management

Signs of underlying brain trauma must be evaluated. Many skull fractures are treated conservatively, including linear fractures and simple depressed skull fractures. With time, most fragments of depressed skull fractures become realigned, and the normal contour of the skull returns. The physician may elect to treat occipital and basilar condyle fractures with a hard cervical collar. The patient is restricted to bed rest for a few days after injury and then restricted to modified activity until healing occurs.

◼ Estimated Amount of Time Lost

Simple linear fractures usually heal in 4 to 6 weeks, but the patient should remain out of sports participation for a lengthier recovery period once the fracture is stable. The amount of time lost increases as the complexity of the fracture increases.

Return-to-Play Criteria

The fracture must be stable and completely healed on radiographic evaluation. Any underlying injury such as brain trauma or inner ear disruption also must be resolved.

Protective Headgear

Patients should be encouraged to wear appropriate helmets when returning to competition, especially in sports not mandating headwear, such as roller blading, bicycling, and skiing.

Management of Sport-Related Head Injuries

Management of sport-related head injuries has improved vastly over the past two decades. This improvement has been due to introduction of clinical tests and publication of research allowing for evidence-based practice. In addition, policies put forth by the National Athletic Trainers' Association,[30] the International Concussion in Sport documents,[1,41,59] and most recently the National Collegiate Athletic Association (see **Table 17.2**) have led to increased awareness and improved management of sport-related concussion. Recognition of a concussion is straightforward if the athlete has LOC. However, 90% to 95% of all cerebral concussions involve no LOC—only a transient loss of alertness or the presence of mental confusion. The patient appears dazed, dizzy, or disoriented, making the injury potentially more difficult to recognize.

The primary objectives for managing head injuries are as follows:

- Recognize the injury and its severity
- Determine whether the athlete requires emergency medical attention
- Monitor neurocognitive and balance deficits, and changes related to symptomology
- Decide when the athlete may return to sport activity

This section focuses on the important findings of the initial examination after head injury.

Table 17.2

National Collegiate Athletic Association Concussion Management Plan Legislation

An active member institution shall have a concussion management plan for its student-athletes. The plan shall include, but is not limited to, the following:

1. An annual process ensures that student-athletes are educated about the signs and symptoms of concussions. Student-athletes must acknowledge that they have received information about the signs and symptoms of concussions and that they have a responsibility to report concussion-related injuries and illnesses to a medical staff member.

2. A process ensures that a student-athlete who exhibits signs, symptoms, or behaviors consistent with a concussion shall be removed from athletics activities (e.g., competition, practice, conditioning sessions) and evaluated by a medical staff member (e.g., sports medicine staff, team physician) with experience in the evaluation and management of concussions.

3. A policy precludes a student-athlete who is diagnosed with a concussion from returning to activity (e.g., competition, practice, conditioning sessions) for at least the remainder of that calendar day.

4. A policy requires medical clearance for a student-athlete who is diagnosed with a concussion to return to athletics activity (e.g., competition, practice, conditioning sessions) as determined by a physician (e.g., team physician) or the physician's designee.

Source: © National Collegiate Athletic Association 2011. All Rights Reserved.

Practice Tip

A comprehensive concussion or head injury policy should include the following elements:

1. A written document is distributed among the sports medicine team, organizational safety personnel, institutional and organizational administrators, and coaches.

2. The policy must identify personnel involved in carrying out the policy and outline the qualifications of those executing the plan.

3. The policy should specify equipment needed to carry out tasks required in the event of a head injury.

4. A clear mechanism for communication among the involved personnel should be established.

5. The policy should specify the necessary documentation supporting the implementation and evaluation of the policy.

6. The policy should be reviewed by the administration and legal counsel of the sponsoring organization or institution.[60]

Initial On-Site Assessment

Head trauma in an athletic situation requires immediate assessment for appropriate emergency action by an athletic trainer and/or physician; if at all possible, the initial examination should be performed with the patient at the site where the injury occurred.

Primary Survey

The primary survey takes only 10 to 15 seconds, as respiratory and cardiac status are assessed to rule out a life-threatening condition. A patient who is unconscious or is regaining consciousness but is still disoriented and confused should be managed as if a cervical spine injury is present (see Chapter 15). An unconscious patient should be transported from the field or court on a spine board with his or her head and neck immobilized.

17

Vital signs should be monitored at regular intervals (every 5 minutes) while talking to the patient in an attempt to help bring about full consciousness. Any athlete who experiences LOC for any amount of time requires immobilization and transfer to an emergency facility so the patient can undergo a thorough neurologic examination. This decision may change depending on the medical staff available at the time of injury.

Secondary Survey

A thorough history is the most important part of the examination because it can quickly narrow down the assessment. The presence of LOC, mental confusion, amnesia, or one or more symptoms associated with sport-related concussion such as headache and dizziness are evaluated. Confusion can be determined rather quickly by noting the patient's facial expression (e.g., dazed, stunned, "glassy eyed") and any inappropriate behavior, such as running the wrong play or returning to the wrong huddle.

Amnesia testing is conducted by first asking simple questions directed toward recent memory and then progressing to more involved questions. Asking the patient what the first thing he or she remembered after the injury tests for length of anterograde amnesia. Asking what the play was before the injury or who the opponent was last week tests for retrograde amnesia, which is generally associated with a more serious head injury. It is important to note that the clinician should ask only those questions for which he or she can validate the athlete's responses. Questions of orientation (name, date, time, and place) may be asked; however, research suggests that they are not good discriminators between injured and uninjured athletes.[41,61] Facing the patient away from the field and asking the name of the opposing team may be helpful. Questions should be posed to determine if tinnitus, blurred vision, or nausea is being experienced. A concussion symptom checklist similar to that found in Table 17.1 may be used to facilitate the follow-up assessment of signs and symptoms.

Portions of the observation and palpation plan should take place during the initial on-site examination. While the history is obtained, any deformities or abnormal facial expressions (cranial nerve VII), speech patterns, respirations, or extremity movements should be noted. Additionally, gentle palpation of the skull and cervical spine should be performed to rule out an associated fracture. The athlete who is conscious or who was momentarily unconscious should be transported to the sideline or locker room for further evaluation after the initial on-site examination. **Table 17.3** highlights the primary and secondary survey.

■ Sideline Assessment

A more detailed examination can be conducted on the sideline or in the athletic training clinic once the helmet has been removed and once the cervical spine has been evaluated and found to be without injury. A quick cranial nerve assessment should be performed first. Visual acuity (cranial nerve II: optic) can be checked by asking the patient to read or identify selected objects (at near range and far range). Eye movement (cranial nerves III and IV: oculomotor and trochlear) should be checked for coordination and a purposeful appearance by asking the patient to track a moving object. The pupils should be equal in size and reactive to light; they should constrict when light is shined into their eyes. Observation of the pupils also assesses the oculomotor nerve. Abnormal movement of the eyes or changes in pupil size or reaction to light often indi-

---

Table 17.3

On-Site Assessment

Primary Survey	Secondary Survey	
Rule out life-threatening condition	History	Mental confusion
Check respirations (breathing)		Loss of consciousness
Check cardiac status		Amnesia
	Observation	Monitor eyes
		Graded symptom checklist
		Deformities, abnormal facial expressions, speech patterns, respirations, extremity movement
	Palpation	Skull and cervical spine abnormalities
		Pulse and blood pressure (if condition is deteriorating)

cate increased intracranial pressure. The possibility of a skull fracture should also be ruled out, especially if the patient was not wearing a helmet at the time of injury.

If the patient's outward condition appears to worsen, the pulse rate and blood pressure should be assessed. An unusually slow heart rate or increased pulse pressure (increased systolic and decreased diastolic pressures) after the individual has calmed down may be signs of increasing intracranial pressure. Most individuals with cerebral concussions do not have abnormal findings; however, vital signs are important considerations for detecting a more serious injury such as an epidural or subdural hematoma. Significant deviations in the patient's vital signs require referral for more extensive evaluation and possible life support.

Special Tests for the Assessment of Coordination

The use of a quantifiable clinical balance test, such as the Balance Error Scoring System (BESS), is recommended over the standard Romberg test, which for years has been used as a subjective tool to assess balance. The BESS provides a quick, cost-effective method of objectively assessing postural stability in athletes on the sideline or in the athletic training clinic after a concussion and has been found to be a reliable and valid assessment tool for managing sport-related concussion.[12,62,63] Balance test results during injury recovery are most reliable when they are compared with baseline measurements. Clinicians who work with athletes or patients on a regular basis should attempt to obtain baseline measurements before competition.

Practice Tip

A detailed concussion history is helpful in identifying individuals who may be at increased risk for sport-related concussion. The detailed history should include the following items:

- The number of prior concussions
- Previous symptoms associated with sport-related concussion
- All previous head, face, or cervical spine injuries
- Questions regarding the mechanisms of prior injuries
- Any protective equipment worn at the time injury (inappropriate use might have caused a prior injury)

Conduct formal neuropsychological testing if possible as well as a balance assessment utilizing the BESS or a more sophisticated measure. Also conduct a physical/neurologic assessment including assessment of cervical spine and cranial nerves.[30,41]

More sophisticated balance assessment using computerized forceplate systems have identified

deficits as long as 3 to 5 days after a concussion.[12,64,65] These tests are recommended for making return-to-play decisions, especially when preseason baseline measurements are available for comparison.

Special Tests for Assessment of Cognition

A brief mental status examination should be conducted to evaluate any deficits in orientation, memory, concentration, and general coherence after injury. Recently, attention has focused on developing more systematic methods to evaluate mental status on the sideline, beyond the traditional questions of "Where are we?" and "How many fingers?"

The Standardized Assessment of Concussion (SAC) is a brief screening instrument designed for the neurocognitive assessment of concussion by a medical professional with no prior expertise in neuropsychological testing.[65,66] Several prospective studies have demonstrated the psychometric properties and clinical sensitivity of the SAC in assessing concussion and tracking postinjury recovery.[19–21,67] This instrument takes approximately 5 minutes to administer and assesses four domains of cognition: orientation, immediate memory, concentration, and delayed recall. A composite total score (out of 30 possible points) is calculated to provide an overall index of cognitive impairment and injury severity. The SAC also contains a brief neurologic screen and documentation of injury-related factors (e.g., LOC, posttraumatic amnesia, retrograde amnesia). Equivalent alternative forms of the SAC are available and should be used to minimize practice effects from serial testing after an injury.

Another standardized brief screening tool used for concussion assessment is the Sport Concussion Assessment Tool 2 (SCAT2), which was released with the 2008 Consensus Statement on Concussion in Sport (see **Figure 17.8**).[41] The SCAT2 is a revision of the original SCAT published in the 2004 Consensus Statement on Concussion in Sport. It is derived from the sideline evaluation for concussion, the Management of Concussion in Sports palm card, the SAC, the sideline concussion check, and the SCAT. The components of the assessment include measures of self-reported symptoms, memory function, and balance testing. In comparison to the SCAT, the SCAT2 incorporates a modified version of the BESS to assess postural stability, more clearly defined tests of memory and concentration, and overall ease of administration for clinicians. As with the SCAT and any other test utilized for concussion assessment, baseline testing is recommended.[41]

SCAT2

Sport Concussion Assessment Tool 2

Name

Sport/team

Date/time of injury

Date/time of assessment

Age _____   Gender ☐ M ☐ F

Years of education completed

Examiner

What is the SCAT2?[1]

This tool represents a standardized method of evaluating injured athletes for concussion and can be used in athletes aged from 10 years and older. It supersedes the original SCAT published in 2005[2]. This tool also enables the calculation of the Standardized Assessment of Concussion (SAC)[3,4] score and the Maddocks questions[5] for sideline concussion assessment.

Instructions for using the SCAT2

The SCAT2 is designed for the use of medical and health professionals. Preseason baseline testing with the SCAT2 can be helpful for interpreting post-injury test scores. Words in Italics throughout the SCAT2 are the instructions given to the athlete by the tester.

This tool may be freely copied for distribution to individuals, teams, groups and organizations.

What is a concussion?

A concussion is a disturbance in brain function caused by a direct or indirect force to the head. It results in a variety of non-specific symptoms (like those listed below) and often does not involve loss of consciousness. Concussion should be suspected in the presence of **any one or more** of the following:

- Symptoms (such as headache), or
- Physical signs (such as unsteadiness), or
- Impaired brain function (e.g. confusion) or
- Abnormal behaviour.

Any athlete with a suspected concussion should be REMOVED FROM PLAY, medically assessed, monitored for deterioration (i.e., should not be left alone) and should not drive a motor vehicle.

Symptom Evaluation

How do you feel?

You should score yourself on the following symptoms, based on how you feel now.

	none	mild		moderate		severe	
Headache	0	1	2	3	4	5	6
"Pressure in head"	0	1	2	3	4	5	6
Neck Pain	0	1	2	3	4	5	6
Nausea or vomiting	0	1	2	3	4	5	6
Dizziness	0	1	2	3	4	5	6
Blurred vision	0	1	2	3	4	5	6
Balance problems	0	1	2	3	4	5	6
Sensitivity to light	0	1	2	3	4	5	6
Sensitivity to noise	0	1	2	3	4	5	6
Feeling slowed down	0	1	2	3	4	5	6
Feeling like "in a fog"	0	1	2	3	4	5	6
"Don't feel right"	0	1	2	3	4	5	6
Difficulty concentrating	0	1	2	3	4	5	6
Difficulty remembering	0	1	2	3	4	5	6
Fatigue or low energy	0	1	2	3	4	5	6
Confusion	0	1	2	3	4	5	6
Drowsiness	0	1	2	3	4	5	6
Trouble falling asleep (if applicable)	0	1	2	3	4	5	6
More emotional	0	1	2	3	4	5	6
Irritability	0	1	2	3	4	5	6
Sadness	0	1	2	3	4	5	6
Nervous or Anxious	0	1	2	3	4	5	6

Total number of symptoms (Maximum possible 22) ▢

Symptom severity score ▢
(Add all scores in table, maximum possible: 22 x 6 = 132)

Do the symptoms get worse with physical activity? ☐ Y   ☐ N
Do the symptoms get worse with mental activity? ☐ Y   ☐ N

Overall rating

If you know the athlete well prior to the injury, how different is the athlete acting compared to his / her usual self? Please circle one response.

no different	very different	unsure

Figure 17.8   Sport Concussion Assessment Tool 2 (SCAT2). *Source:* Reprinted from McCrory P, Meeuwisse W, Johnston K, et al. Consensus statement on concussion in sport: the Third International Conference on Concussion in Sport held in Zurich, November 2008. *Clin J Sport Med.* 2009;19(3):185-200.

Cognitive & Physical Evaluation

1 **Symptom score** (from page 1)
22 **minus** number of symptoms

| | of 22 |

2 **Physical signs score**
Was there loss of consciousness or unresponsiveness?   Y   N
If yes, how long? _____ minutes
Was there a balance problem/unsteadiness?   Y   N

Physical signs score (1 point for each negative response)   of 2

3 **Glasgow coma scale (GCS)**

Best eye response (E)

No eye opening	1
Eye opening in response to pain	2
Eye opening to speech	3
Eyes opening spontaneously	4

Best verbal response (V)

No verbal response	1
Incomprehensible sounds	2
Inappropriate words	3
Confused	4
Oriented	5

Best motor response (M)

No motor response	1
Extension to pain	2
Abnormal flexion to pain	3
Flexion/Withdrawal to pain	4
Localizes to pain	5
Obeys commands	6

Glasgow Coma score (E + V + M)   of 15

GCS should be recorded for all athletes in case of subsequent deterioration.

4 **Sideline Assessment – Maddocks Score**

"I am going to ask you a few questions, please listen carefully and give your best effort."

Modified Maddocks questions (1 point for each correct answer)

At what venue are we at today?	0	1
Which half is it now?	0	1
Who scored last in this match?	0	1
What team did you play last week/game?	0	1
Did your team win the last game?	0	1

Maddocks score   of 5

Maddocks score is validated for sideline diagnosis of concussion only and is not included in SCAT 2 summary score for serial testing.

[1] This tool has been developed by a group of international experts at the 3rd International Consensus meeting on Concussion in Sport held in Zurich, Switzerland in November 2008. The full details of the conference outcomes and the authors of the tool are published in British Journal of Sports Medicine, 2009, volume 43, supplement 1.
The outcome paper will also be simultaneously co-published in the May 2009 issues of Clinical Journal of Sports Medicine, Physical Medicine & Rehabilitation, Journal of Athletic Training, Journal of Clinical Neuroscience, Journal of Science & Medicine in Sport, Neurosurgery, Scandinavian Journal of Science & Medicine in Sport and the Journal of Clinical Sports Medicine.

[2] McCrory P et al. Summary and agreement statement of the 2nd International Conference on Concussion in Sport, Prague 2004. British Journal of Sports Medicine. 2005; 39: 196-204

5 **Cognitive assessment**
Standardized Assessment of Concussion (SAC)
Orientation (1 point for each correct answer)

What month is it?	0	1
What is the date today?	0	1
What is the day of the week?	0	1
What year is it?	0	1
What time is it right now? (within 1 hour)	0	1

Orientation score   of 5

Immediate memory
"I am going to test your memory. I will read you a list of words and when I am done, repeat back as many words as you can remember, in any order."

Trials 2 & 3:
"I am going to repeat the same list again. Repeat back as many words as you can remember in any order, even if you said the word before."

Complete all 3 trials regardless of score on trial 1 & 2. Read the words at a rate of one per second. Score 1 pt. for each correct response. Total score equals sum across all 3 trials. Do not inform the athlete that delayed recall will be tested.

List	Trial 1	Trial 2	Trial 3	Alternative word list		
elbow	0 1	0 1	0 1	candle	baby	finger
apple	0 1	0 1	0 1	paper	monkey	penny
carpet	0 1	0 1	0 1	sugar	perfume	blanket
saddle	0 1	0 1	0 1	sandwich	sunset	lemon
bubble	0 1	0 1	0 1	wagon	iron	insect
Total						

Immediate memory score   of 15

Concentration
Digits Backward:
"I am going to read you a string of numbers and when I am done, you repeat them back to me backwards, in reverse order of how I read them to you. For example, if I say 7-1-9, you would say 9-1-7."

If correct, go to next string length. If incorrect, read trial 2. One point possible for each string length. Stop after incorrect on both trials. The digits should be read at the rate of one per second.

		Alternative digit lists	
4-9-3	0 1	6-2-9 5-2-6	4-1-5
3-8-1-4	0 1	3-2-7-9 1-7-9-5	4-9-6-8
6-2-9-7-1	0 1	1-5-2-8-6 3-8-5-2-7	6-1-8-4-3
7-1-8-4-6-2	0 1	5-3-9-1-4-8 8-3-1-9-6-4	7-2-4-8-5-6

Months in Reverse Order:
"Now tell me the months of the year in reverse order. Start with the last month and go backward. So you'll say December, November ... Go ahead"

1 pt. for entire sequence correct

Dec-Nov-Oct-Sept-Aug-Jul-Jun-May-Apr-Mar-Feb-Jan   0   1

Concentration score   of 5

[3] McCrea M. Standardized mental status testing of acute concussion. Clinical Journal of Sports Medicine. 2001; 11: 176-181

[4] McCrea M, Randolph C, Kelly J. Standardized Assessment of Concussion: Manual for administration, scoring and interpretation. Waukesha, Wisconsin, USA.

[5] Maddocks, DL; Dicker, GD; Saling, MM. The assessment of orientation following concussion in athletes. Clin J Sport Med. 1995;5(1):32–3

[6] Guskiewicz KM. Assessment of postural stability following sport-related concussion. Current Sports Medicine Reports. 2003; 2: 24-30

17

Figure 17.8 Continued.

(continues)

6 Balance examination

This balance testing is based on a modified version of the Balance Error Scoring System (BESS)[6]. A stopwatch or watch with a second hand is required for this testing.

Balance testing

"I am now going to test your balance. Please take your shoes off, roll up your pant legs above ankle (if applicable), and remove any ankle taping (if applicable). This test will consist of three twenty second tests with different stances."

(a) Double leg stance:

"The first stance is standing with your feet together with your hands on your hips and with your eyes closed. You should try to maintain stability in that position for 20 seconds. I will be counting the number of times you move out of this position. I will start timing when you are set and have closed your eyes."

(b) Single leg stance:

"If you were to kick a ball, which foot would you use? [This will be the dominant foot] Now stand on your non-dominant foot. The dominant leg should be held in approximately 30 degrees of hip flexion and 45 degrees of knee flexion. Again, you should try to maintain stability for 20 seconds with your hands on your hips and your eyes closed. I will be counting the number of times you move out of this position. If you stumble out of this position, open your eyes and return to the start position and continue balancing. I will start timing when you are set and have closed your eyes."

(c) Tandem stance:

*"Now stand heel-to-toe with your **non-dominant foot** in back. Your weight should be evenly distributed across both feet. Again, you should try to maintain stability for 20 seconds with your hands on your hips and your eyes closed. I will be counting the number of times you move out of this position. If you stumble out of this position, open your eyes and return to the start position and continue balancing. I will start timing when you are set and have closed your eyes."*

Balance testing – types of errors

1. Hands lifted off iliac crest
2. Opening eyes
3. Step, stumble, or fall
4. Moving hip into > 30 degrees abduction
5. Lifting forefoot or heel
6. Remaining out of test position > 5 sec

Each of the 20-second trials is scored by counting the errors, or deviations from the proper stance, accumulated by the athlete. The examiner will begin counting errors only after the individual has assumed the proper start position. **The modified BESS is calculated by adding one error point for each error during the three 20-second tests. The maximum total number of errors for any single condition is 10.** If an athlete commits multiple errors simultaneously, only one error is recorded but the athlete should quickly return to the testing position, and counting should resume once subject is set. Subjects that are unable to maintain the testing procedure for a minimum of **five seconds** at the start are assigned the highest possible score, ten, for that testing condition.

Which foot was tested: ☐ Left   ☐ Right
(i.e. which is the **non-dominant** foot)

Condition	Total errors
Double Leg Stance (feet together)	of 10
Single leg stance (non-dominant foot)	of 10
Tandem stance (non-dominant foot at back)	of 10
Balance examination score (30 **minus** total errors)	of 30

7 Coordination examination

Upper limb coordination

Finger-to-nose (FTN) task: *"I am going to test your coordination now. Please sit comfortably on the chair with your eyes open and your arm (either right or left) outstretched (shoulder flexed to 90 degrees and elbow and fingers extended). When I give a start signal, I would like you to perform five successive finger to nose repetitions using your index finger to touch the tip of the nose as quickly and as accurately as possible."*

Which arm was tested: ☐ Left   ☐ Right

Scoring: 5 correct repetitions in < 4 seconds = 1

Note for testers: Athletes fail the test if they do not touch their nose, do not fully extend their elbow or do not perform five repetitions. Failure should be scored as 0.

Coordination score   of 1

8 Cognitive assessment

Standardized Assessment of Concussion (SAC)

Delayed recall

"Do you remember that list of words I read a few times earlier? Tell me as many words from the list as you can remember in any order."

Circle each word correctly recalled. Total score equals number of words recalled.

List		Alternative word list	
elbow	candle	baby	finger
apple	paper	monkey	penny
carpet	sugar	perfume	blanket
saddle	sandwich	sunset	lemon
bubble	wagon	iron	insect

Delayed recall score   of 5

Overall score

Test domain	Score
Symptom score	of 22
Physical signs score	of 2
Glasgow Coma score (E + V + M)	of 15
Balance examination score	of 30
Coordination score	of 1
Subtotal	**of 70**
Orientation score	of 5
Immediate memory score	of 15
Concentration score	of 5
Delayed recall score	of 5
SAC subtotal	**of 30**
SCAT2 total	**of 100**
Maddocks Score	**of 5**

Definitive normative data for a SCAT2 "cut-off" score is not available at this time and will be developed in prospective studies. Embedded within the SCAT2 is the SAC score that can be utilized separately in concussion management. The scoring system also takes on particular clinical significance during serial assessment where it can be used to document either a decline or an improvement in neurological functioning.

Scoring data from the SCAT2 or SAC should not be used as a stand alone method to diagnose concussion, measure recovery or make decisions about an athlete's readiness to return to competition after concussion.

Figure 17.8   Continued.

Athlete Information

Any athlete suspected of having a concussion should be removed from play, and then seek medical evaluation.

Signs to watch for
Problems could arise over the first 24-48 hours. You should not be left alone and must go to a hospital at once if you:
- Have a headache that gets worse
- Are very drowsy or can't be awakened (woken up)
- Can't recognize people or places
- Have repeated vomiting
- Behave unusually or seem confused; are very irritable
- Have seizures (arms and legs jerk uncontrollably)
- Have weak or numb arms or legs
- Are unsteady on your feet; have slurred speech

Remember, it is better to be safe.
Consult your doctor after a suspected concussion.

Return to play
Athletes should not be returned to play the same day of injury. When returning athletes to play, they should follow a stepwise symptom-limited program, with stages of progression. For example:
1. rest until asymptomatic (physical and mental rest)
2. light aerobic exercise (e.g. stationary cycle)
3. sport-specific exercise
4. non-contact training drills (start light resistance training)
5. full contact training after medical clearance
6. return to competition (game play)

There should be approximately 24 hours (or longer) for each stage and the athlete should drop back to the previous asymptomatic level if any post-concussive symptoms recur. Resistance training should only be added in the later stages.
Medical clearance should be given before return to play.

Tool	Test domain	Time	Score			
		Date tested				
		Days post injury				
SCAT2	Symptom score					
	Physical signs score					
	Glasgow Coma score (E + V + M)					
	Balance examination score					
	Coordination score					
SAC	Orientation score					
	Immediate memory score					
	Concentration score					
	Delayed recall score					
	SAC Score					
Total	SCAT2					
Symptom severity score (max possible 132)						
Return to play			Y N	Y N	Y N	Y N

Additional comments

Figure 17.8 Continued.

(continues)

Concussion injury advice (To be given to concussed athlete)

This patient has received an injury to the head. A careful medical examination has been carried out and no sign of any serious complications has been found. It is expected that recovery will be rapid, but the patient will need monitoring for a further period by a responsible adult. Your treating physician will provide guidance as to this timeframe.

If you notice any change in behaviour, vomiting, dizziness, worsening headache, double vision or excessive drowsiness, please telephone the clinic or the nearest hospital emergency department immediately.

Other important points:
- **Rest and avoid strenuous activity for at least 24 hours**
- **No alcohol**
- **No sleeping tablets**
- **Use paracetamol or codeine for headache. Do not use aspirin or anti-inflammatory medication**
- **Do not drive until medically cleared**
- **Do not train or play sport until medically cleared**

Clinic phone number

Patient's name

Date/time of injury

Date/time of medical review

Treating physician

Contact details or stamp

Figure 17.8   Continued.

Table 17.4

Tests of Concentration

Questions	Correct Response?
Recite the days of the week backward beginning with today.	
Recite the months of the year backward beginning with this month.	
Serial 3s: count backward from 100 by 3 until you get to single digits.	
Serial 7s: count backward from 100 by 7 until you get to single digits.	

Table 17.5

Tests of Recent Memory

Questions	Correct Response?
Where are we playing (name of field or site)?	
Which quarter (period, inning, etc) is it?	
Who scored last?	
Who did we play last week?	
Who won last week?	
Repeat the words used to determine anterograde amnesia.	

Table 17.6

Selected Neuropsychological Tests and Abilities Evaluated

Tests	Ability Evaluated
Hopkins Verbal Learning Test (HVLT)	Verbal memory
Trail Making Test: A and B	Visual scanning, mental flexibility, attention
Brief Visuospatial Memory Test (BVMT)	Visual memory
Stroop Color-Word Test	Mental flexibility, attention
Wechsler Digit Span Test	Attention span
Symbol Digit Modalities Test	Visual scanning, attention
Grooved Pegboard Test	Motor speed, coordination
Paced Auditory Serial Addition Test	Attention, concentration, immediate memory recall, rapid mental processing

In lieu of the SAC or SCAT2, a series of questions to properly evaluate concentration (see **Table 17.4**) and recent memory (see **Table 17.5**) can be asked.

Neuropsychological tests have also been used to identify and manage TBI in athletes.[12,13,63,64,68] Although most of these tests are difficult to administer as part of a sideline examination, they are useful for baseline and postconcussion assessments in the clinical setting. The two varieties of neuropsychological tests are the paper-and-pencil format and the computerized format. On most paper-and-pencil neuropsychological tests, young, healthy, well-motivated athletes who experience mild cerebral concussion will demonstrate significant cognitive decline immediately after injury.[12,57,68,69] **Table 17.6** lists examples of paper-and-pencil tests used by neuropsychologists in cooperative efforts with athletic trainers and team physicians to evaluate recovery of neurocognitive function in symptomatic players.

Computerized Neuropsychological Testing

As neuropsychological testing has become more popular in the sports medicine setting, experts have attempted to find more practical assessment tools.

Several factors have greatly limited the widespread application of formal neuropsychological testing at the secondary school and collegiate levels. Notably, the time and financial costs typically required for conventional neuropsychological testing are often not feasible in a sports setting. Additionally, many institutions lack the necessary personnel to implement the recommended model of individual preseason baseline neuropsychological testing of all athletes for comparison with postinjury test results.

Neuropsychologists have made recent advancements in the development of computerized applications for the assessment of concussion and TBI. In particular, computerized test modules have been designed specifically to assess sport-related concussion. This kind of computerized testing may offer several scientific and practical advantages over conventional paper-and-pencil batteries. Most computerized batteries require 20 to 30 minutes per athlete. To save time, computerized testing can be conducted in large group settings, with several athletes being tested simultaneously on separate computers. Computerized neuropsychological testing thereby greatly reduces the time, cost, and personnel demands associated with baseline testing of one athlete at a time with traditional tests.

Computerized testing allows a more precise measurement of subtle deficits associated with concussion, including reaction time, cognitive processing speed, and response latency. For example, computerized neuropsychological tests permit highly accurate measurement of simple and complex reaction time, with near-millisecond timing accuracy.[70,71] This level of timing resolution has become increasingly important to neuropsychological research, especially in the areas of concussion and TBI. Finally, these newer methods allow the individual's data to be stored and easily accessed for clinical management after a concussion and large data sets to be archived for research purposes.

Computerized testing offers several practical and methodologic advantages, especially related to baseline testing of large numbers of athletes. Despite the widespread use of computerized neuropsychological programs by high school, collegiate, and professional sports, questions still exist regarding the psychometric properties of such programs—namely, their reliability and validity.[72-75] If a test demonstrates reliability, an athlete will perform equally on the same test on two or more days.[73] Research that addresses this issue has shown poor to good reliability for computerized neuropsychological tests, falling below what is recommended for clinical decision making.[72,73,75] Validity is the extent to which the scores of an instrument measure what the instrument is intended to measure. To collect evidence of validity, satisfactory evidence of reliability is needed.[73] Further research is required to provide evidence of clinical validity on computerized neuropsychological tests and to determine how these measures compare with one another. Issues related to user qualifications for administration and interpretation of computerized neuropsychological testing results also require further consideration.

Due to these and other issues associated with computerized neuropsychological testing, it is important for the clinician to realize that such measures should not be utilized as the sole basis of management decisions. Instead, such testing represents an aid to the clinical decision-making process, to be used in conjunction with a range of clinical domains and investigational results.[41]

■ The Importance of Using a Battery of Tests

One important concept when utilizing an instrument to determine clinical utility is the measure's sensitivity. Sensitivity is defined as the extent to which a test can differentiate between clinical patients (in this context, those patients diagnosed as concussed) and normal controls. For instance, if a measure has a sensitivity of 86%, it should correctly classify 86% of known clinical patients. Research has shown that a battery of tests including self-reported symptoms, computerized neuropsychological testing, and a computerized balance assessment possesses a sensitivity of 91% to 96%, depending on the computerized neuropsychological test utilized. When delivered independently, any one of these tests had a sensitivity of approximately 62% to 81.3%.[73] This research emphasizes the importance of using multiple tests to manage sport-related concussion, rather than relying on a single measure.

Practice Tip

The goal of the baseline assessment is to identify an individual's "normal," pre-injury performance, which provides a reliable benchmark against which to measure postinjury recovery.[30] A proper baseline assessment consists of the following elements:

- Use of objective assessment tools such as computerized neuropsychological tests, the BESS or another objective measure of balance, or a self-reported symptom inventory to determine deficits and measure recovery.
- A combination of brief screening tools used for sideline assessment.

Before employing computerized neuropsychological testing into a concussion management protocol, know the test's user requirements, copyright restrictions, and standardized instructions for administration and scoring. In addition, all evaluators should be appropriately trained prior to test administration.

In the event that the appropriate resources (such as a neuropsychologist) are not available, the clinician should use screening instruments such as the SAC, SCAT2, BESS, and self-reported symptom checklists that have been developed for use in athletics. Only those tests with evidence-based, population-specific normative data, test-retest reliability, clinical validity, and sufficient sensitivity and specificity should be used.

Provide a quiet setting free from distraction to allow the individual being tested to provide a maximal effort. Make sure the individual understands the instructions for each clinical test prior to beginning the test. Be available throughout testing in case the individual has any questions about the instructions. Results of clinical tests should be combined with a graded exercise protocol and clinical evaluation to ensure the most effective approach to injury management and making return-to-play decisions.

Rehabilitation

Rehabilitation After Cerebral Concussion

The literature on medical treatment and rehabilitative therapies for sport-related concussion is sparse. During the emergence of sport-concussion research, most researchers have focused on measuring acute effects and recovery, with little emphasis on treatment interventions. The current standard of care involves a period of rest during the acute postinjury period, followed by a gradual return to noncontact exercise without risk for reinjury and eventual return to full participation once the athlete has been symptom free under exertional conditions for several days.[41] An emphasis on wellness is also critical during the acute recovery period, especially with regard to a regulated sleep cycle, limited physical exertion, and avoidance of alcohol, recreational drugs, and medications that have not been approved by the attending physician.

A developing area of research is the effects of cognitive rest and rehabilitation. A strong recommendation is that athletes recovering from sport-related concussion should limit their exertion with activities of daily living and limit their scholastic and other cognitive stressors.[41] Activities such as attending class or extracurricular activities and social activities such as playing video games, texting, and excessive computer use should be limited to facilitate recovery to avoid exacerbation of symptoms.[41] Concussed athletes should also be discouraged from driving to and from school and other appointments. Research has shown that concussed individuals when compared to individuals with other orthopaedic trauma due to activities of daily living had a 0.45-second slower response time associated with braking. This difference is equivalent to a 7.5-m difference when driving a car at 60 miles per hour.[76]

The need is clear for prospective studies examining the potential benefit from pharmacologic agents and rehabilitation techniques with regard to the rate and completeness of recovery after concussion. In the general brain injury literature, the efficacy of cognitive rehabilitation remains a topic of great debate. Similar to recent studies on methods of assessing sport concussion, this type of research in a sports medicine setting may elucidate effective treatments for head injury in a general trauma setting.

Return to Competition After Sport-Related Concussion

The question of return to competition after a head injury is handled on an individual basis, although conservatism seems the wisest course in all cases. A multifaceted approach is suggested when making a return-to-play decision. One component of this approach is tracking self-reported symptomology.

Caution is warranted when assessing an athlete in regard to self-reported symptoms. In a study conducted in 2004, approximately 53% of concussions went unreported based on symptomology experienced by the athlete. The rationales cited for this under-reporting included not thinking a concussion was serious enough to be held out of competition, not wanting to be held out of competition, and a lack of awareness of having a concussion.[45] It is important to educate and stress the seriousness and potential implications of this injury to athletes of all ages, coaches, parents, and the entirety of the sports medicine team. Ultimately, employing a battery of tests along with a physical and neurologic examination will help to reduce the potential for a premature return-to-play decision.

For adult athletes who have access to experienced team physicians and sufficient resources (e.g., neuropsychologists, consultants, neuroimaging), a return to play may be made more rapidly.[30,41] Experts agree that when making a return-to-play decision after a diagnosed concussion, a stepwise or graded approach is best (see **Table 17.7**). Each step of the protocol should take approximately 24 hours, although this may change with the sports medicine staff's experience with sport-related concussion. The graduated return-to-play protocol should be activated only after the athlete reports being asymptomatic. If a return of any symptom occurs at any step of the protocol, the athlete must rest an additional 24 or more hours prior to restarting the protocol to ensure the resolution of the returning symptom.

The following factors should be considered when making decisions regarding an athlete's readiness to return after head injury:

- History of concussion, including the frequency and severity of each episode, should be determined.
- The sport of participation (contact versus noncontact).

17

Table 17.7

A Graduated Return-to-Play Protocol for Sport-Related Concussion

Rehabilitation Stage	Functional Exercise	Objective
No activity	Complete physical and cognitive rest	Recovery
Light aerobic exercise	Walking, swimming, or stationary cycling, while keeping the intensity at less than 70% of the maximum predicted heart rate	Increase heart rate
Sport-specific exercise	Skating drills in ice hockey; running drills in soccer No head-impact activities	Add movement
Noncontact training drills	Progression to more complex training drills, such as passing drills in football and ice hockey May start progressive resistance training	Exercise, coordination, and cognitive load
Full-contact practice	Following medical clearance, participation in normal training activities	Restore confidence and assess functional skills by coaching staff
Return to play		Normal game play

Source: McCrory P, Meeuwisse W, Johnston K, et al. Consensus statement on concussion in sport: The 3rd International Conference on Concussion in Sport held in Zurich, November 2008. *J Athl Train.* 2009;44(4):434-448.

- Availability of experienced personnel to observe and monitor the athlete during recovery.
- Repeated assessment utilizing a battery of tests (physical/neurologic assessment, neuropsychological and balance testing) along with a graded return-to-play protocol.

Ultimately, the athletic trainer and team physician and other potential members of the sports medicine team (i.e. neuropsychologist) need to work together to ensure the appropriate return-to-play decision. The return-to-play decision should be based on evidence derived from a thorough clinical evaluation, neuropsychological testing, symptomology, postural stability, and prior history of head injury.

Education Regarding Sport-Related Concussion

One of the most important tools the athletic trainer can use to prevent sport-related concussion is education. Education of athletes, coaches, administrators, parents, and the general public is vital for effective prevention and management of sport-related concussions. Education regarding sport-related concussion should include information about the detection of concussion, its clinical features, assessment techniques, and principles of safe return to play. Since 2000, multiple educational materials have been created and disseminated by organizations including the Centers for Disease Control and Prevention, National Athletic Trainers' Association, National Collegiate Athletic Association, National Hockey League, and National Football League, among others. The focus of these media has been on helping individuals recognize the signs and symptoms of concussion and the seriousness of the injury—because any brain injury is potentially serious. For the athletic trainer, it is important not only to know how to recognize and manage sport-related concussion, but also to be aware of these media and educate individuals about this injury.

Legislation Regarding Sport-Related Concussion

Since 2008, many states have enacted laws related to the management of sport-related concussions. Washington was the first state to pass such legislation, which is known as the Zachary Lystedt law in that state. The Zachary Lystedt law, which has been used as a model by some other states for their own legislation, requires removal from competition of any athlete who shows signs or symptoms of concussion; education of coaches, athletes, and parents about concussion; the signed acknowledgment of parents and athletes that they recognize the possibility of concussion and head injury prior to the start of a sport season; and a return-to-play decision by a licensed healthcare provider trained in the evaluation and management of concussion. Although many states have similar laws, it is important to realize that each state's legislation may include some unique provisions that the athletic trainer must be aware of. As with any medical practice, it is important that the athletic trainer adheres to the standard of practice under the direction of a medical doctor.[77]

References

1. Aubry M, Cantu RC, Dvorak J, et al. Summary and agreement statement of the 1st International Symposium on Concussion in Sport, Vienna 2001. *Clin J Sport Med.* 2002;12:6–11.
2. Bailes JE, Hudson V. Classification of sport-related head trauma: A spectrum of mild to severe injury. *J Athl Train.* 2001;36:236–243.
3. Barr WB. Methodologic issues in neuropsychological testing. *J Athl Train.* 2001;36:297–302.
4. Barr WB, McCrea M. Sensitivity and specificity of standardized neurocognitive testing immediately following sports concussion. *J Int Neuropsychol Soc.* 2001;7:693–702.
5. Bleiberg J, Halpern EL, Reeves D, Daniel JC. Future directions for neuropsychological assessment of sports concussion. *J Head Trauma Rehabil.* 1998;13:36–44.
6. Cantu RC. Posttraumatic retrograde and anterograde amnesia: Pathophysiology and implications in grading and safe return to play. *J Athl Train.* 2001;36:244–248.
7. Collins MW, Lovell MR, Iverson GL, et al. Cumulative effects of concussion in high school athletes. *Neurosurgery.* 2002;51:1175–1181.
8. Erlanger D, Saliba E, Barth JT, et al. Monitoring resolution of postconcussion symptoms in athletes: Preliminary results of a web-based neuropsychological test protocol. *J Athl Train.* 2001;36:280–287.
9. Ferrara MS, McCrea M, Peterson CL, Guskiewicz KM. A survey of practice patterns in concussion assessment and management. *J Athl Train.* 2001;36:145–149.
10. Giza CC, Hovda DA. The neurometabolic cascade of concussion. *J Athl Train.* 2001;36:228–235.
11. Grindel SH, Lovell MR, Collins MW. The assessment of sport-related concussion: The evidence behind neuropsychological testing and management. *Clin J Sport Med.* 2001;11:134–143.
12. Guskiewicz KM, Ross SE, Marshall SW. Postural stability and neuropsychological deficits after concussion in collegiate athletes. *J Athl Train.* 2001;36:263–273.
13. Macciocchi SN, Barth JT, Littlefield LM, Cantu RC. Multiple concussions and neuropsychological functioning in collegiate football players. *J Athl Train.* 2001;36:303–306.
14. Halstead DP. Performance testing updates in head, face, and eye protection. *J Athl Train.* 2001;36:322–327.
15. Kelly JP. Loss of consciousness: Pathophysiology and implications in grading and safe return to play. *J Athl Train.* 2001;36:249–252.
16. Lovell MR, Collins MW, Iverson GL, et al. Recovery from mild concussion in high school athletes. *J Neurosurg.* 2003;98:296–301.
17. Lovell MR, Iverson GL, Collins MW, et al. Does loss of consciousness predict neuropsychological decrements of concussion? *Clin J Sport Med.* 1999;9:193–198.
18. Maroon JC, Lovell MR, Norwig J, et al. Cerebral concussion in athletes: Evaluation and neuropsychological testing. *Neurosurgery.* 2000;47:659–669.
19. McCrea M. Standardized mental status assessment of sports concussion. *Clin J Sport Med.* 2001;11:176–181.
20. McCrea M. Standardized mental status testing on the sideline after sport-related concussion. *J Athl Train.* 2001;36:274–279.
21. McCrea M, Kelly JP, Randolph C, et al. Immediate neurocognitive effects of concussion. *Neurosurgery.* 2002;50:1032–1042.
22. Oliaro S, Anderson S, Hooker D. Management of cerebral concussion in sports: The athletic trainer's perspective. *J Athl Train.* 2001;36:257–262.

23. Osborne B. Principles of liability for athletic trainers: Managing sport-related concussion. *J Athl Train.* 2001;36:316–321.

24. Powell JW. Cerebral concussion: Causes, effects, and risks in sports. *J Athl Train.* 2001;36:307–311.

25. Randolph C. Implementation of neuropsychological testing models for the high school, collegiate, and professional sport settings. *J Athl Train.* 2001;36:288–296.

26. Viano DC, Lovsund P. Biomechanics of brain and spinal cord injury: Analysis of neuropathologic and neurophysiologic experiments. *J Crash Prevent Injury Control.* 1999;1(1):35–43.

27. Cantu RC. Athletic head injuries. *Clin J Sports Med.* 1997;16:531–542.

28. Cantu RC. Reflections on head injuries in sport and the concussion controversy. *Clin J Sports Med.* 1997;7:83–84.

29. Guskiewicz KM, Mihalik JP, Shankar V, et al. Measurement of head impacts in collegiate football players: Relationship between head impact biomechanics and acute clinical outcome after concussion. *Neurosurgery.* 2007;61(6):1244–1252.

30. Guskiewicz KM, Bruce SL, Cantu RC, et al. National Athletic Trainers' Association position statement: Management of sport-related concussion. *J Athl Train.* 2004;39(3):280–297.

31. Broglio SP, Sosnoff JJ, SungHoon S, et al. Head impacts during high school football: A biomechanical assessment. *J Athl Train.* 2009;44(4):342–349.

32. Dumas SM, Manoogian SJ, Bussone WR, et al. Analysis of real-time head accelerations in collegiate football players. *Clin J Sport Med.* 2005;15(1):3–7.

33. Milhalik JP, Bell DR, Marshall SW, Guskiewicz KM. Measurement of head impacts in collegiate football players: An investigation of positional and event-type differences. *Neurosurgery.* 2007;61(6):1229–1235.

34. Schnebel B, Gwin JT, Anderson S, Gatlin R. In vivo study of head impacts in football: A comparison of National Collegiate Athletic Association D1 versus high school impacts. *Neurosurgery.* 2007;60(3):490–496.

35. Pellman EJ, Viano DC, Tucker AM, et al. Concussion in professional football: Reconstruction of game impacts and injuries. *Neurosurgery.* 2003;53(4):799–812.

36. Ommaya A. Biomechanical aspects of head injuries in sports, in Jordan B, Tsairis P, Warren R (eds), *Sports Neurology.* Rockville, MD: Aspen Publishers; 1990:75–83.

37. Barkhoudarian G, Hovda DA, Giza CC. The molecular pathophysiology of concussive brain injury. *Clinics in Sports Medicine.* 2011;30(1):33–48.

38. Hovda DA, Prins M, Becker DP, et al. Neurobiology of concussion, in Bailes JE, Lovell MR, Maroon JC (eds), *Sports-Related Concussion.* St. Louis, MO: Quality Medical Publishing; 1999:12–51.

39. Giza CC, Hovda DA. The neurometabolic cascade of concussion. *J Athl Train.* 2001;36:228–235.

40. Alexander MP. Mild traumatic brain injury: Pathophysiology, natural history, and clinical management. *Neurology.* 1995;45:1253–1260.

41. McCrory P, Meeuwisse W, Johnston K, et al. Consensus statement on concussion in sport: The 3rd International Conference on Concussion in Sport held in Zurich, November 2008. *J Athl Train.* 2009;44(4):434–448.

42. Committee on Head Injury Nomenclature of the Congress of Neurological Surgeons. Glossary of head injury including some definitions of injury to the cervical spine. *Clin Neurosurg.* 1966;12:386–394.

43. Guskiewicz KM, Weaver NL, Padua DA, Garrett WE Jr. Epidemiology of concussion in collegiate and high school football players. *Am J Sports Med.* 2000;28:643–650.

44. Guskiewicz KM, McCrea M, Marshall SW, et al. Cumulative effects of recurrent concussion in collegiate football players: The NCAA Concussion Study. *JAMA.* 2003;290:2549–2555.

45. McCrea M, Hammeke T, Olsen G, et al. Unreported concussion in high school football players: Implications for prevention. *Clin J Sport Med.* 2004;14(1):13–27

46. Collins MW, Field M, Lovell MR, et al. Relationship between postconcussion headache and neuropsychological test performance in high school athletes. *Am J Sports Med.* 2003;31(2):168–173.

47. Jamieson KG, Yelland JDN. Extradural hematoma: Report of 167 cases. *J Neurosurg.* 1968;29:13–23.

48. Bricolo AP, Pasut LM. Extradural hematoma: Toward zero mortality, a prospective study. *Neurosurgery.* 1984;14:8–12.

49. Servadei F. Prognostic factors in severely head injured adult patients with epidural haematomas. *Acta Neurochir (Wien).* 1997;139:273–278.

50. Schonauer M, Schisano G, Cimino R, Viola L. Space occupying contusions of cerebral lobes after closed brain injury: Considerations about 51 cases. *J Neurosurg Sci.* 1979;23:279–288.

51. Practice parameter: The management of concussion in sports (summary statement). Report of the Quality Standards Subcommittee of the American Association of Neurology. *Neurology.* 1997;48:581–585.

52. Roberts W. Who plays? Who sits? Managing concussion on the sidelines. *Physician Sportsmed.* 1992;20:66–72.

53. Wilberger JJ, Maroon J. Head injuries in athletes. *Clin Sports Med.* 1989;8:1–9.

54. Mueller FO. Catastrophic head injuries in high school and collegiate sports. *J Athl Train.* 2001;36:312–315.

55. Kelly JP, Nichols JS, Filley CM, et al. Concussion in sports: Guidelines for the prevention of catastrophic outcome. *JAMA.* 1991;226:2867–2869.

56. Saunders RL, Harbaugh RE. The second impact in catastrophic contact-sports head injuries. *JAMA.* 1984;252:538–539.

57. Hugenholtz H, Richard MT. Return to athletic competition following concussion. *CMAJ.* 1982;127:827–829.

58. Cantu RC. Guidelines for return to contact sports after a cerebral concussion. *Physician Sportsmed.* 1986;14:75–83.

59. McCrory P, Johnston K, Meeuwisse W, et al. Summary and agreement statement of the 2nd International Conference on Concussion in Sport, Prague 2004. *Br J Sports Med.* 2005;39(4):196–204.

60. Anderson JC, Courson RW, Kleiner DM, McLoda TA. National Athletic Trainers' Association position statement: Emergency planning in athletics. *J Athl Train.* 2002;37(1):99–104.

61. Maddocks D, Saling M. Neuropsychological sequelae following concussion in Australian rules footballers. *J Clin Exp Neuropsychol.* 1991;13:439–442.

62. Riemann BL, Guskiewicz KM, Shields EW. Relationship between clinical and forceplate measures of postural stability. *J Sport Rehabil.* 1998;8:71–82.

63. Riemann BL, Guskiewicz KM. Objective assessment of mild head injury using a clinical battery of postural stability tests. *J Athl Train.* 2000;35:19–25.

64. Guskiewicz KM, Riemann BL, Perrin DH, Nashner LM. Alternative approaches to the assessment of mild head

injuries in athletes. *Med Sci Sports Exerc.* 1997;29 (7 suppl):S213–S221.

65. McCrea M, Kelly JP, Randolph C, et al. Standardized Assessment of Concussion (SAC): On-site mental status evaluation of the athlete. *J Head Trauma Rehabil.* 1998;13:27–35.

66. McCrea M, Randolph C, Kelly JP. *Standardized Assessment of Concussion (SAC): Manual for Administration, Scoring and Interpretation.* Waukesha, WI: CNS, Inc.; 1997.

67. McCrea M, Kelly JP, Kluge J, et al. Standardized assessment of concussion in football players. *Neurology.* 1997;48:586–588.

68. Barth JT, Alves WM, Ryan TV, et al. Mild head injury in sports: Neuropsychological sequelae and recovery of function, in Levin HS, Eisenberg HA, Benton AL (eds), *Mild Head Injury in Sport.* New York: Oxford University Press; 1989:257–275.

69. Collins MW, Grindel SH, Lovell MR, et al. Relationship between concussion and neuropsychological performance in college football players. *JAMA.* 1999;282:964–970.

70. Kane RL, Kay GG. Computerized assessment in neuropsychology: A review of tests and test batteries. *Neuropsychol Rev.* 1992;3:1–117.

71. Kane RL, Reeves DL. Computerized test batteries, in Horton A (ed), *The Neuropsychology Handbook, Vol. 2.* New York: Springer; 1997:426–467.

72. Randolph C, McCrea M, Barr WB. Is neuropsychological testing useful in the management of sport-related concussion? *J Athl Train.* 2005;40(3):139–152.

73. Broglio SP, Ferrara MS, Macciocchi SN, et al. Test–retest reliability of computerized concussion assessment programs. *J Athl Train.* 2007;42(4):509–514.

74. Broglio SP, Macciocchi SN, Ferrara MS. Sensitivity of the concussion assessment battery. *Neurosurgery.* 2007;60(6):1050–1057; discussion 1057–1058.

75. Schatz P. Long-term test–retest reliability of baseline cognitive assessments using ImPACT. *Am J Sports Med.* 2009;38(1):47–53.

76. Preece MS, Horswill MS, Geffen GM. Driving after concussion: The acute effect of mild traumatic brain injury on drivers' hazard perception. *Neuropsych.* 2010;24(4):493–503.

77. The Zachary Lystedt Bill of 2009. House Bill 1824 (2009). Available at: http://apps.leg.wa.gov/documents/billdocs/2009-10/Pdf/Bills/House%20Bills/1824.pdf. Accessed June 22, 2011.

17

Face and Related Structures Pathologies

Zygomatic Fractures

CLINICAL PRESENTATION

History

Direct blow to the face, especially the zygoma.

Observation

Bruising may be seen at the site of impact.
Depression of the zygomatic bone may be observed before swelling develops.
The eye above the fracture may have a downward slant.
Enophthalmos may be observed.

Functional Status

Disruption of the bony contour of the eye may restrict eye motility.

Physical Examination Findings

A step-off deformity may be palpated at the fracture site.
Extraoral or intraoral palpation may reveal crepitus at the fracture site.
If numbness is present, it follows the distribution of the infra-orbital nerve.

The facial skeleton is formed by a series of bony horizontal and vertical buttresses that serve as shock absorbers for the craniofacial complex. These relatively dense, bony pillars are surrounded by more delicate areas of bone that form the bony sinuses in the face. The facial buttresses absorb and dissipate the force of an impact, preventing injury to the underlying structures such as the brain, eyes, and other neurovascular structures. Fractures of the facial bones have unique risks and complications, such as blood from a hemorrhage collecting in the pharynx and obstructing the airway.[1]

The zygomatic bone articulates with the frontal bone, maxilla, temporal bone, and wing of the sphenoid (see **Figure 18.1**). Fractures of the zygomaticomaxillary complex (ZMC) usually involve several of these articulations and account for approximately 10% of sport-related facial fractures.[2]

Zygomatic fractures occur when significant force is applied to the prominent cheekbone. Upon impact, the bony complex is forced posteriorly and rotates laterally and inferiorly. The medial and lateral canthal tendons that support the eye attach to the medial and lateral orbital rims, respectively. Thus any malalignment of the rim bones changes the axis of the intercanthal line, giving the eye a downward-sloping appearance (see **Figure 18.2**).

The Manson system can be used to classify ZMC fractures based on the findings of computed tomography (CT) scans (see **Table 18.1**). Most sport-related zygomatic fractures are low- or medium-velocity injuries, such as being "elbowed" in the ZMC.

enophthalmos
A protruding globe.

Differential Diagnosis

Orbital fracture, malar fracture, mandible fracture, facial contusion.

Imaging Techniques

CT scan is the most accurate imaging technique for identifying ZMC fractures (see **Figure 18.3**).[3] In many cases, subtle fractures are not visible on standard

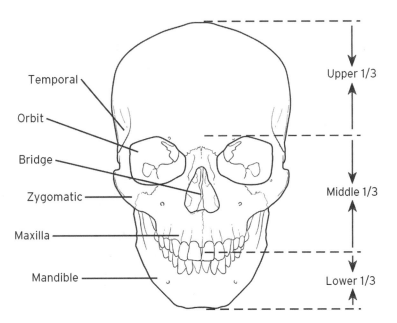

Figure 18.1   The craniofacial skeleton can be divided into upper, middle, and lower components.

18

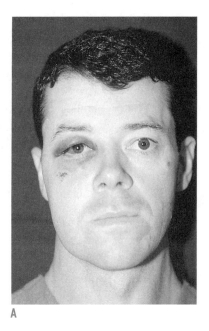

A   B

Figure 18.2   Clinical findings associated with a ZMC fracture include periorbital ecchymosis, downward slant of the lateral canthus, and a depressed cheekbone (**A**). Compare this view with the underlying bony injury (**B**).

radiographs. The type of zygomatic fracture observed on CT imaging can be classified using the Manson system (see Table 18.1).

Definitive Diagnosis

The definitive diagnosis and subsequent management approach for zygomatic fractures are based on the findings of radiographs or CT scans (or both).

Pathomechanics and Functional Limitations

Derangement of the periorbital architecture can disrupt the normal alignment of the eyes, causing diplopia and other vision deficits. Surgical repair is required to correct the vision disturbance. Unfortunately, rigid internal fixation is not as strong as the patient's own intact facial skeleton. If a similar blow occurs to the repaired fracture site before bone healing is complete, the patient is at risk for a more severe fracture pattern than the initial injury. The

second injury is likely to damage the underlying vital structures.

■ Immediate Management

Because facial trauma may disrupt the airway, the patient's airway, breathing, and circulation (ABCs) must be evaluated and continually monitored. If the ABCs have been compromised, their management takes precedence. If the ABCs are normal and a fracture is suspected, remove the athlete from competition and evaluate for trauma to the brain and cervical spine. Treat the injured area with ice to control the formation of edema and refer the patient to a specialist.

Table 18.1

Manson Classification System for Zygomatic Fractures

Classification	Description
Low energy	No displacement
	No instability of the fragment
Moderate energy	Complete fracture
	Moderate displacement
	Comminution
High energy	Fracture line extends through the glenoid fossa of the temporomandibular joint

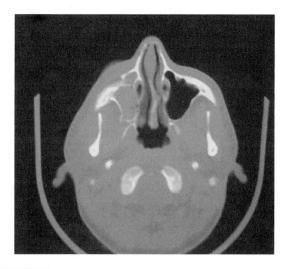

Figure 18.3   CT scan demonstrating a fracture of the left zygomatic bone. Note the absence of the sinus, which appears as a large, dark area on the right side of the image.

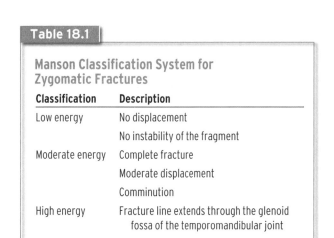

Medications

Acetaminophen or narcotic analgesics can be started for pain relief after a closed head injury has been ruled out. Although nonsteroidal anti-inflammatory drugs (NSAIDs) are a treatment option, they may increase bleeding in acute injuries and have been implicated in increasing bone healing time.

Surgical Intervention

If indicated, surgical repair should be performed within 7 to 10 days to prevent early fracture consolidation. Rigid fixation of these fractures is usually obtained with titanium mini-plates and screws specifically designed for facial bones. The surgical approach helps to minimize facial scars by internally fixating the plates and screws under the eyelid (see **Figure 18.4**). The use of rigid fixation has decreased the need for extended intermaxillary fixation (wiring the jaws together) and resulted in more predictable, stable, long-term results and fewer nutrition-related difficulties postoperatively.[4]

Postinjury/Postoperative Management

The goals for managing all facial fractures are the same: make an accurate diagnosis; obtain precise anatomic reduction of the fracture; stabilize the fracture to achieve facial contour, symmetry, and primary healing of the bones; and, if applicable, reestablish the pretraumatic dental occlusion.

Estimated Amount of Time Lost

A minimum of 6 to 8 weeks is required for fracture healing. Athletes who are prohibited from wearing facial protection (e.g., boxers) may be withheld from competition for as long as 3 months.

Return-to-Play Criteria

The patient can return to competition when the fracture site is stable and no residual vision deficit exists.

Functional Bracing

Properly constructed protective facial devices may allow the patient to return to competition earlier.

Nasal Fractures

CLINICAL PRESENTATION

History

Direct blow to the nose.
Often associated with multiple trauma to the face and head.[5]

Observation

Epistaxis.
Possible deformity.
Edema may hinder the initial examination and delay repair.[5]
With time, suborbital ecchymosis ("raccoon eyes") may develop.

Functional Status

The patient often is unable to breathe through the nose, especially during inspiration.

Physical Examination Findings

Pain and possible crepitus may occur during palpation of the nasal bone.
Intranasal inspection may identify the presence of a septal hematoma, deviated septum, or fracture that occludes the airway.

Nasal fractures account for approximately half of all sport-related facial fractures, with 15% of these injuries being recurrent fractures.[6] Because these fractures occur so frequently, their severity may be

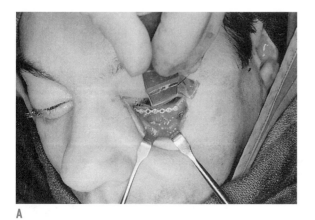

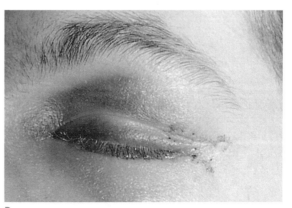

A   B

Figure 18.4 Surgical treatment of a ZMC fracture. (**A**) Rigid fixation is obtained using titanium mini-plates and screws. (**B**) Early postoperative results of the fracture reduction and fixation.

18

underestimated and, therefore, they may be under-treated.[6] Nasal factures are sometimes missed when they occur secondary to other head and face trauma.[5]

The nasal bones can be fractured from an anterior (frontal) or lateral force. The thinner lower portion of the nasal bone is more likely to be fractured than the denser bone that interfaces with the maxilla.[5] A frontal blow causes the nasal bones to splay apart, much like the pages of an open book, giving the nose a wide, flat appearance. More commonly, a nasal fracture occurs when the impact comes from a lateral direction, causing the nose to deviate to the side away from the direction of the blow. The nasal bone on the side of the impact is forced inward; also, if the blow is severe enough, the opposite nasal bone is pushed outward (see **Figure 18.5**). Because of the intimate relationship between the septum and the nasal bones, if the nasal bones fracture, the septum may deviate and fracture.

Epistaxis (Nosebleed)

Several blood vessels that supply the nose join at the anterior septum in a confluence known as the *Little area* or *Kiesselbach plexus*. This confluence of blood vessels is readily subject to environmental insults such as excessive heat and dryness and trauma; 90% of all nosebleeds occur in the anterior portion of the septum.[7]

Differential Diagnosis

Epistaxis, septal hematoma, nasal cartilage separation.

Imaging Techniques

> **Practice Tip**
>
> Radiographs have limited value in diagnosing nasal fractures and should not be heavily weighted in the management decision-making process. The course of treatment should be based on the results of the clinical examination and, if warranted, nasal endoscopy.[5,8]

A CT scan may identify the bony anatomy and the fracture configurations. Radiographs have limited to no value in diagnosing nasal fractures, as they yield a 60% false-negative rate on interpretation, and suture lines are sometimes incorrectly interpreted as fractures (see **Figure 18.6**).[5,6] Sagittal multi-planar reconstruction (MPR) CT images provide for better radiographic interpretation.[9]

Definitive Diagnosis

The diagnosis of a nasal fracture is frequently based entirely on the clinical findings, especially intra-nasal observation, palpation of asymmetric nasal bones, and visible deviation of the nasal septum. Radiographs add little predictive value to diagnosing a nasal fracture.[5]

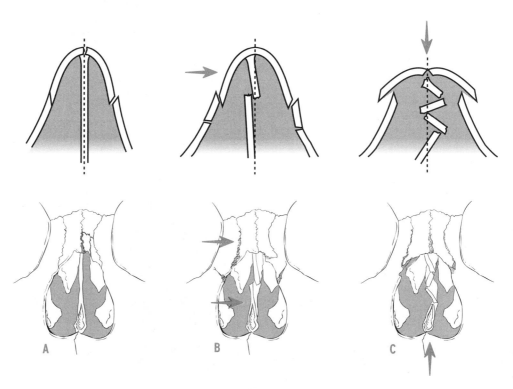

Figure 18.5 Trauma to the nasal bones can take on a variety of forms. (**A**) Isolated nasal bone fracture with no septal displacement. (**B**) Lateral forces that result in a fracture of nasal bones and septal deformation. (**C**) Frontal blow that results in splayed fractures of the nasal bones and septum.

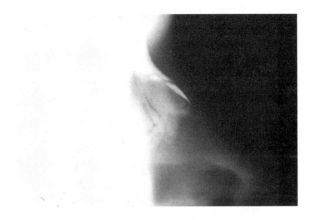

Figure 18.6 Lateral radiograph depicting a nasal fracture.

Figure 18.7 Swelling and gross deviation of the nasal dorsum indicate a possible nasal fracture.

Nasal injuries produce rapid swelling that can mask the underlying tissues. This factor and the relative unreliability of radiographic findings increase the importance of performing a thorough examination of the nose as soon as possible after the injury occurs. Prompt diagnosis is also required to obtain a closed reduction; conversely, delaying the diagnosis may necessitate an open reduction.

The intranasal examination should be conducted with proper lighting, a nasal speculum, and, if necessary, suction. The intranasal structures are sprayed with a vasoconstrictor such as phenylephrine to control epistaxis. The septum is inspected for deviation or fractures severe enough to occlude or obstruct the airway and to identify intranasal lacerations. Small amounts of blood in the saliva are commonly encountered with nasal fractures.[10] A slow, steady unilateral drip is considered traumatic (rather than spontaneous) epistaxis.

Particular emphasis should be placed on diagnosing a septal hematoma. Trauma to the nose can cause blood to accumulate between the septal cartilage and the overlying mucoperichondrium, similar to what occurs with a hematoma of the ear. The septum bulges outward and may appear darker than the surrounding nasal mucosa as a result of the accumulated blood. A suspected septal hematoma demands immediate attention.

Pathomechanics and Functional Limitations

The late effects of poorly managed nasal fractures can include functional breathing difficulties and an unacceptable cosmetic appearance; the latter can ultimately have a negative psychological effect on the patient (see Figure 18.7). Trauma to the septum is highly predictive of nasal deformity and airway obstruction.[5]

Although the cosmetic effects of nasal injury are the most outwardly notable, the risk of secondary complications is also significant with this type of damage. The external nose and nasal passages are intricately associated with the sebaceous glands, Eustachian tubes, and nasal sinuses. Deviation of the septum, nasal bones, or lateral cartilages can have a profound effect on nasal airflow.

An untreated fracture or deviated septum can decrease nasal airflow, causing the patient to rely on breathing through the mouth. Permanent deformity may result. If a septal hematoma is not diagnosed, the cartilage can become ischemic and necrotic, leading to collapse of the nasal dorsum with a resultant "saddlenose" deformity. Edema within the nasal passage can block one or both Eustachian tubes, thereby affecting hearing or balance, or both.

■ Immediate Management

The nose should be evaluated for asymmetry or other deformity as soon as possible after the injury occurs and before edema forms. Associated injury to the head, mouth, and the eye's bony orbit should be ruled out at this time. The nose should be treated with ice to limit swelling and control epistaxis. An open wound that exposes cartilage or bone should be treated in the same way as an open fracture—that is, the wound should be thoroughly irrigated and the patient placed on appropriate antibiotics.

Epistaxis as a result of nasal trauma is usually of a limited nature and can almost always be controlled by exerting digital pressure on the anterior nose and placing the patient in a seated position

mucoperichondrium The structure overlying the nasal cartilage that provides it with blood supply and nutrients.

18

with the head upright. Nasal packing is required only when severe bleeding cannot be controlled using external pressure.

The anterior nasal chamber can be packed using commercially available nose packs, a sectioned tampon, or, less preferably, sterile gauze. A physician may elect to soak the pack in thrombin to further control the bleeding. The pack should not be forced deep into the nasal cavity, and care must be used to prevent overpacking. The posterior nasal chamber should be packed only by healthcare providers in an emergency department. Nasal packs should not be left in place for more than 72 hours. Keeping the nose packed for a longer period of time increases the risk of infection, including meningitis.

If the nasal injury has occurred within 7 days, and septal deviation or nasal airway obstruction is present, the patient should receive a direct referral to an ear, nose, and throat (ENT) specialist. Likewise, if the patient does not immediately demonstrate nasal deviation or nasal airway obstruction but over the next 21 days has cosmetic concerns regarding the appearance of the nose or has develops difficulty breathing through the nose, referral should be made to an ENT specialist.[8]

Medications

NSAIDs or narcotic analgesics can be started for pain relief after a closed head injury has been ruled out. If closed reduction is required, a local or mild general anesthetic or sedative may be administered.

> **Practice Tip**
>
> Closed reduction of nasal fractures can be performed using a local anesthetic such as tetracaine gel while still yielding equivalent results to manipulations performed under general anesthesia.[11]

Surgical Intervention

In managing a septal hematoma, the physician incises the affected mucosa and evacuates the hematoma. The nasal passage is then packed with gauze impregnated with petrolatum or a vasoconstrictor (such as Lacrilube).

Repair can be limited to a simple closed reduction of the nasal bones using topical and local anesthesia in the physician's office or may comprise a more involved open reduction of a fractured or severely dislocated septum in the operating room.[11] The realigned nasal bones or septum are then splinted externally and internally (see **Figure 18.8**). The splints are usually removed in 7 to 10 days.

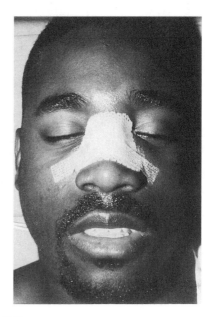

Figure 18.8 The displaced nasal bones and septum are realigned and splinted to maintain proper alignment during the healing process.

Postinjury/Postoperative Management

The indications for treatment of nasal injuries by a physician are nasal airway obstruction or obvious external nasal deformity. Acute fractures or displacements should be managed as soon as possible after injury. Swelling that occurs over time may obscure the deformity and make proper repair difficult. If swelling has occurred, it is usually prudent to wait at least 4 to 7 days in adults and 4 days in children for the swelling to subside. The patient can then be reexamined and definitive repair performed if needed.

A septal hematoma must be identified and drained early to prevent a saddlenose deformity. Drainage can be performed under local anesthesia, such as lidocaine without epinephrine, with subsequent drainage using an 18-gauge needle and packing of the passage. Alternatively, the area may require anesthesia for incision, drain insertion, and packing of the area to ensure the hematoma does not return.

Recurrent epistaxis can be decreased with use of a humidifier or vaporizer at night while sleeping. Petrolatum gel is applied twice daily to control bleeding until the injury is completely healed.

Estimated Amount of Time Lost

Depending on the amount of protection that can be provided to the nose, the patient may lose no time from activity. A surgically repaired nasal fracture may keep the patient from activity for 7 to 10 days.

Figure 18.9 A custom-designed protective facial mask can protect the nose and allow the athlete to resume competition. This device can also protect the nasal structures from repetitive injury.

CLINICAL PRESENTATION

History

Direct blow to the mandible.

Observation

Swelling forms over the fracture site.
Malocclusion of the teeth may be noted.
Intraoral bleeding is possible.
Ecchymosis may be visible on the floor of the mouth.
A step deformity (malalignment of the teeth) may be noted between the teeth on each side of the fracture site.

Functional Status

Difficulty opening the mouth.
Pain with biting down or inability to bite down.
Possible maltracking of the mandible during motion.

Physical Examination Findings

Intraoral examination may reveal a step deformity.
Intraoral or extraoral palpation may reveal pain and crepitus along the fracture site.
Pain is produced when stressing the mandible.
The tongue-blade test may be positive.
Anterior distraction of the mandible produces pain.

malocclusion
Improper alignment of the teeth when the mouth is closed.

Return-to-Play Criteria

The decision to return the athlete to competition and the need for nasal protection should be carefully weighed. The nasal bones generally heal sufficiently within 4 to 8 weeks, allowing the athlete to return to competition in contact sports.

Functional Bracing

A protective facial device of sufficient strength to prevent further injury should be used if the athlete resumes competition soon after repair (see **Figure 18.9**). Because repeated nasal injuries are possible, prophylactic use of a protective facial device should be considered after the athlete experiences a nasal fracture.

Mandible Fractures

The horseshoe-shaped mandible articulates with the base of the skull at the temporomandibular joints (TMJs). It is a strong cortical bone but is relatively weak at its angles, the neck of the condyles, and the distal body, where the long root of the canine tooth and the mental foramen are located (see **Figure 18.10**). Because of the mandible's arched shape and the presence of several weak, thin areas, the lower jaw often fractures in two places during this kind of injury.

The subcondylar regions are the most commonly fractured areas of the lower jaw. These areas are thinner than the rest of the mandible; therefore, forces generated at impact are transmitted to these areas. A subcondylar fracture can have devastating, long-term functional and cosmetic sequelae.

The condylar region of the mandible is a growth center, and suspected fractures to this region in young patients require extraordinary attention. Trauma to an immature epiphysis may result in shortened mandible height and lead to occlusion problems. Injuries to this region can also result in hemorrhage into the TMJ, potentially leading to fibrosis and ankylosis.

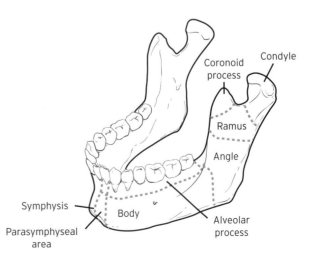

Figure 18.10 The bony mandible and its associated dental structures.

18

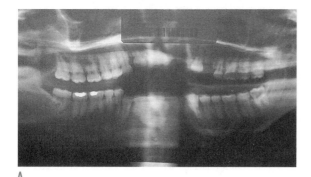

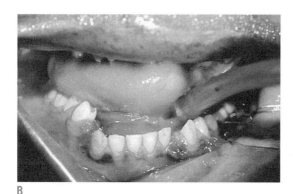

Figure 18.11 Methods used to evaluate step-off deformities. **(A)** Panorex-type radiograph demonstrating a right mandibular body fracture with a step-off deformity of the teeth. **(B)** The clinical view reveals intraoral bleeding from a mucosal tear and the step-off deformity of the teeth.

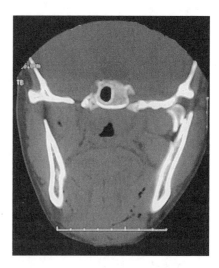

Figure 18.12 A CT scan demonstrating a left subcondylar fracture.

Differential Diagnosis

TMJ sprain or dislocation, tooth fracture.

Imaging Techniques

Simple anteroposterior radiographs, such as the modified Towne view, Walter view, or an orthopantograph, usually reveal condylar head, mandibular arch, and subcondylar fractures (see Figure 18.11). A CT scan can reveal more subtle fractures and provide valuable information about displacement of the fractured segments and possible intracranial injuries (see Figure 18.12).

Definitive Diagnosis

Positive physical and radiographic findings are used to make the diagnosis of a mandible fracture.

Pathomechanics and Functional Limitations

The patient has difficulty opening and closing the mouth, and chewing is painful. Functional limitations are created by the malocclusions and instability of the fracture. Over time, asymmetry of the mandible can create unequal pressures within the TMJ, resulting in degenerative changes and dysfunction.

■ Immediate Management

Fractures that occur on both sides of the jaw can become unstable. At the time of injury, the anterior segment can shift backward, causing the tongue to block the airway. Pulling the tongue or the anterior jaw forward can open the airway. The tongue or jaw should be stabilized in this position and the patient transported to the emergency department, with proper cervical spine immobilization if necessary. Refer to the discussion of immediate management of zygomatic fractures for more information on appropriate measures in case of airway compromise.

A secondary survey should be conducted to rule out trauma to the brain, cervical spine, face, teeth, and eyes. A hard cervical collar or Barton bandage should be applied to limit jaw motion while the patient is referred for further medical attention (see Figure 18.13).

■ Medications

NSAIDs or narcotic analgesics can be administered for pain relief once a closed head injury has been ruled out.

■ Surgical Intervention

Displaced fractures must be reduced, either by placing the patient in maxillomandibular fixation with the jaws wired together for 4 to 6 weeks or by rigidly fixing the segments with plates and screws using an open technique. Rigid fixation has the advantage of allowing the patient to open and close the jaws, thereby preventing long-term injury to the TMJs

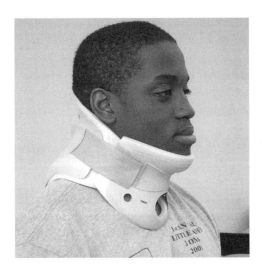

Figure 18.13 A hard cervical collar used for immobilizing the cervical spine can also be used to immobilize the mandible.

through early motion and allowing for improved nutritional status (see **Figure 18.14**).

■ Postinjury/Postoperative Management

Nondisplaced fractures with easily reproducible occlusion can be managed with close observation and a diet of soft foods. If the patient's jaw has been fixated, the diet should be modified to ensure sufficient caloric intake and a proper nutritional balance. Several commercially available supplements can be used to achieve these goals.

■ Estimated Amount of Time Lost

An athlete with a jaw fracture should not be allowed to return to play until healing has occurred, which generally takes 6 to 8 weeks. Use of protective devices can permit an earlier return, however (see the "Functional Bracing" section).

■ Return-to-Play Criteria

Return-to-play criteria depend on the sport and fixation techniques. Generally, the more rigid the internal fixation technique, the quicker the return to play. Wiring of the jaw can compromise nutritional status and make it difficult and time consuming to take in adequate oxygen to satisfy the energy demands created by high-intensity activity.

Functional Bracing

A protective cage or helmet with a jaw extension can allow athletes in selected sports to return to competition earlier.

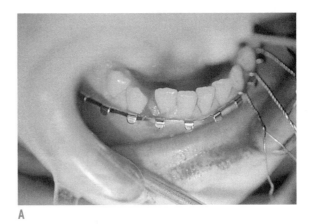

A

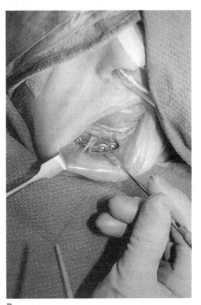

B

Figure 18.14 The management of a displaced fracture includes maxillomandibular fixation. (**A**) Arch bars and wires can be placed on the upper and lower teeth to fixate the jaws into proper occlusion and allow for healing of minimally displaced or nondisplaced fractures over a 4- to 8-week period. (**B**) Rigid fixation of the fracture with titanium plates and screws allows for immediate postsurgical jaw motion.

Temporomandibular Joint Dislocations

The TMJ is the only synovial joint in the skull and is surrounded by a loose capsule. The articular surfaces are covered with a fibrous cartilage rather than the hyaline cartilage found in other joints. A cartilaginous disk divides the joints into upper and lower compartments. The superior temporal articulation is formed by the articular tubercle, articular eminence, glenoid fossa, and posterior glenoid spine.

The TMJ subluxates during normal opening and closing of the mouth. Traumatic dislocations tend to occur when the TMJ muscles are relaxed and the individual sustains a lateral blow to the mandible. In addition, dislocations can occur nontraumatically, during sneezing, eating, or other times when the mouth is opened widely. Progressive joint degeneration can lead to a chronically dislocating TMJ.[12]

Simple dislocations are marked by the mandible displacing anteriorly relative to the joint and most frequently occur unilaterally. Complex dislocations are characterized by an upward displacement, commonly involving a fracture of the skull, or posterior displacement, fracturing the auditory canal.

Differential Diagnosis

Mandibular fracture.

Imaging Techniques

Obtaining precise images of the TMJ is a daunting challenge. Historically, CT and magnetic resonance imaging (MRI) have been used, but are subject to several limitations. The best images of this joint are obtained using helical CT scans.[13]

Definitive Diagnosis

The definitive diagnosis is based on the clinical symptom of the TMJ locking or catching. It is confirmed through radiographic studies.

Pathomechanics and Functional Limitations

The TMJ subluxates anteriorly each time the mouth is opened and closed. Chronic TMJ disorders can interfere with the patient's ability to chew, speak, yawn, and sneeze. Embarrassing moments can occur when the TMJ locks in social situations.

Unrecognized TMJ pathology can lead to chronic headaches and neck pain. Patients who have sus-

tained a traumatic posterior TMJ dislocation may experience hearing deficits.[14] The auditory canal can be fractured when the condyle displaces posteriorly; narrowing of the canal and the subsequent inflammatory response can reduce hearing temporarily or permanently.

◼ Immediate Management

A Barton bandage should be applied to limit jaw motion while the patient is referred for further medical attention. A physician should attempt to reduce a frank dislocation as soon as possible after the injury (see the "Postinjury/Postoperative Management" section).

◼ Medications

Mild sedatives or anesthetics may be required to reduce the dislocation. NSAIDs or narcotic analgesics can be started for pain relief after a closed head injury has been ruled out.

◼ Surgical Intervention

Reducing an anterior TMJ dislocation is relatively easy if the patient is relaxed; such relaxation is made easier if mild sedatives or anesthetics are administered. The physician grasps the lower molars with the thumbs and the symphysis of the mandible with the index fingers. The thumbs on the molars then apply downward pressure while the fingers rotate the anterior portion of the mandible upwardly.

◼ Postinjury/Postoperative Management

After reduction, the patient must be restricted from widely opening the mouth for as long as 2 months. Ideally, the patient will make a conscious effort to avoid yawning or chewing large, hard foods and will voluntarily abide by this restriction. With a severe or recurrent dislocation or if the patient is unwilling or unable to restrict mandibular motion, the jaw may need to be wired shut.

Like patients with mandibular fractures, patients sustaining a TMJ dislocation eat a modified diet emphasizing soft, nutritional foods. If the patient's jaw has been fixated, the diet should be modified to include sufficient caloric intake while maintaining the proper nutritional balance.

◼ Estimated Amount of Time Lost

An athlete with a TMJ dislocation treated conservatively normally does not lose time from competition, although a first-time dislocation may require 4 to 14 days of healing before returning to competition. Surgical repair extends the amount of time lost.

Return-to-Play Criteria

The TMJ should be properly located, and the patient should be able to open the mouth to the point necessary to breathe and speak without recurrent locking.

Functional Bracing

Facial protection similar to that used for mandibular fractures can help to prevent recurrent traumatic dislocations. Custom-designed mouthpieces may also be effective in reducing the frequency of dislocations in a chronically dislocating TMJ.

Tooth Fractures

CLINICAL PRESENTATION

History

A blow to the teeth.
Biting on a hard object.
Depending on the nature of the injury, discomfort may vary from minimal pain to constant pain (see Table 18.2).

Observation

Fractures to the crown may produce obvious defects, although type I fractures may be less visible.
The tooth may be luxated.
Bleeding may be noted with type III fractures.

Functional Status

Depending on the type of fracture, the patient may be unable to eat or drink without pain.

Physical Examination Findings

Palpation of the teeth may reveal deformity.

Tooth fractures can involve either the crown or the root. A fracture of the crown usually does not require urgent attention unless it involves the neurovascular tissue or the pulp of the tooth (see **Figure 18.15**). Fractures that expose the tooth's nerves can be extremely painful (see **Table 18.2**).

Root fractures are more difficult to diagnose. Any mobility of a tooth, pain on palpation, or movement suggests a root fracture. These fractures are described by their location—that is, cervical third, middle third, or apical third.

A dentoalveolar fracture is a fracture of the alveolar bone and the associated teeth. The involved teeth may or may not have associated fractures of the crown or root, or they may be subluxated or avulsed. Dentoalveolar fractures should be treated as open fractures. Eighty percent of dental injuries involve the four anterior teeth.[15]

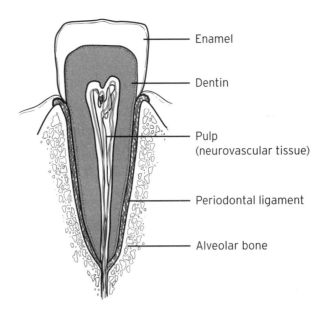

Figure 18.15 The dentoalveolar process includes the tooth, alveolar bone, and the periodontal ligament.

Differential Diagnosis

Tooth luxation, tooth avulsion, mandible fracture, maxillary fracture, TMJ dislocation or sprain.

Imaging Techniques

Radiographs are used to identify fracture lines, especially of the root, and the depth of the fracture. They also serve as a reference for future procedures.

Definitive Diagnosis

The definitive diagnosis is based on gross observation or dental radiographic findings.

Pathomechanics and Functional Limitations

The fracture type and the associated pain limit the patient's ability to eat and drink. A type I crown fracture may simply cause irritation as the tongue passes over the fracture site. Other fractures of the crown or root must be evaluated by a dentist as soon as possible to prevent infection and decrease the risk of losing the tooth.

Immediate Management

Inspect the mouth for lost pieces of the tooth, some of which may be embedded within the lips, cheek, or gum. Recovered segments of a tooth fracture should be managed in the same way as a tooth avulsion. To reduce the risk of aspiration, the mouth should be thoroughly inspected for residual tooth fragments. If the tooth is fragmented, transport the segment using a commercially available kit or place it in milk or a saline solution. To prevent infection of a fractured crown or root, have the patient gargle with saline solution.

18

Table 18.2

Fractures of the Crown

Type	Portion Involved	Symptoms
I	Only the enamel is fractured.	Pain is minimal, but the patient may report irritation of the tongue as it rubs across the fracture site.
II	The dentin is fractured, but the pulp is not exposed.	The tooth is sensitive to cold.
III	The fracture exposes the pulp.	Pain is constant.

▦ Medications

NSAIDs or narcotic analgesics may be started for pain relief after a closed head injury has been ruled out. The dentist will also determine the need for tetanus prophylaxis and antibiotic medications.

▦ Postinjury Management

Type I fractures most often present cosmetic concerns, especially when the front teeth are involved. Treatment of tooth fractures includes covering the exposed pulp and dentin with calcium hydroxide paste supported by an acid-etched composite resin, which alleviates discomfort and allows healing to begin.[16] If the crown is superficially fractured and has a resultant sharp edge that bothers the patient, the edge can be gently filed down with an emery board.

▦ Estimated Amount of Time Lost

Athletes sustaining type I and II fractures of the crown may return to competition but should be evaluated by a dentist immediately after the game. Type III fractures must be evaluated by a dentist before the patient is cleared to play.

▦ Return-to-Play Criteria

The tooth should be stable, with no risk of dislodging and becoming trapped in the airway during competition.

Functional Bracing

The incidence of injury or reinjury of the teeth when athletes are wearing intraoral mouthguards is low.

Tooth Luxations and Tooth Avulsions

Tooth Luxation

Luxation or dislocation of a tooth has occurred when the tooth is malpositioned in its bone socket. Malposition generally indicates some damage to the periodontal ligaments and neurovascular structures. The tooth should be gently manipulated into the proper position, the surrounding alveolar bone

CLINICAL PRESENTATION

History

A direct blow to the mouth or teeth.
Complaints of pain, discomfort, or an abnormal sensation when biting.

Observation

The tooth may be visibly malaligned; with an avulsion, the tooth is completely dislodged from the gum.
Bleeding may be present.

Functional Status

The patient is unable to bite down.

Physical Examination Findings

A luxated tooth is mobile during palpation.

palpated for fractures, and the patient referred to a dentist. An intruded tooth is characterized by the displacement of the root into the bone, resulting in a fracture of the mandible or maxilla and the possible rupture of the periodontal ligament. An extruded tooth involves the displacement of the tooth out of its socket, jeopardizing the neurovascular supply and tearing the periodontal ligaments. The prognosis for long-term damage depends on the amount of displacement from the tooth's normal position.[15]

Tooth Avulsion

An avulsion injury is described as a partial or total separation of the tooth from the alveolus, creating damage similar to that observed with an extruded tooth. Tooth avulsion is an urgent situation, however. The prognosis for viability of the tooth and its successful replantation is inversely proportional to the length of time the tooth is out of its socket. Generally, the tooth should be replanted within 20 minutes to 2 hours.

Differential Diagnosis

Tooth fracture, mandible fracture, maxillary fracture, TMJ dislocation or sprain.

Imaging Techniques

Radiographs are used to identify concomitant injury to the root or socket. They also serve as a reference for future procedures.

Definitive Diagnosis

The diagnosis of a tooth luxation or avulsion can be made based on the patient's signs and symptoms. However, radiographs are required to identify possible fracture of the root or bony socket.

Pathomechanics and Functional Limitations

If the periodontal ligament fibers undergo desiccation or are removed as a result of rough handling, the tooth may undergo resorption or ankylosis to the surrounding bone and ultimately be lost.

▣ Immediate Management

The keys to successful replantation are maintaining the tooth's nourishment and preserving its periodontal ligament. As such, prompt attention by a dentist is imperative to save the tooth.

Tooth Luxation

The patient can be asked to gently bite down on a piece of folded sterile gauze to stabilize the tooth during transport.

Tooth Avulsion

The root of the tooth, where the ligaments are attached, should be handled carefully. Do not scrub or brush the root of the avulsed tooth. Instead, gently handle the tooth by the crown and irrigate it with normal saline. If the tooth cannot be immediately replanted into its socket, it should be cleansed with care and simply placed in the buccal vestibule of the mouth (between the cheek and gum), and the patient should be transported immediately to a dentist. If the patient is unable to hold the tooth in the cheek, it should be placed in fresh cold milk, sterile saline, the patient's saliva, or cool tap water. Milk is an ideal storage medium; activity in periodontal cells has been maintained for as long as 6 hours when a tooth is stored in milk. Commercially available transport systems for avulsed teeth also may be used.

▣ Medications

NSAIDs and narcotic analgesics can be started for pain relief after a closed head injury has been ruled out.

▣ Surgical Intervention

For a tooth luxation, the dentist will replant the tooth into its socket, splint the tooth, prescribe analgesics and antibiotics and a diet of soft foods, and follow the athlete closely. Often the tooth requires endodontic therapy (root canal treatment) for ultimate salvage.

▣ Postinjury/Postoperative Management

Treatment of a tooth luxation may involve splinting the affected tooth with bonded acrylic and monofilament nylon or wiring by a dentist.[16] A diet consisting of soft foods may be necessary during the healing process for both surgical and nonsurgical management.

▣ Estimated Amount of Time Lost

The amount of time lost from activities will vary from the immediate return to competition to 2 to 3 days missed if oral surgery is required.

▣ Return-to-Play Criteria

A player should not return to competition if the tooth is displaced 3 mm or more.

Functional Bracing

The incidence of injury or reinjury of the teeth is quite low when athletes wear intraoral mouthguards.

Orbital Fractures ("Blowout" Fractures)

The bony orbit of the eye is formed by portions of the frontal, maxillary, and zygomatic bones and the wings of the sphenoid, lacrimal, and ethmoid bones (see **Figure 18.16**). The orbit serves to support the globe. A strong orbital rim is created by thickened portions of the frontal, maxillary, and zygomatic bones, thereby protecting the eye from large, solid objects.

Orbital fractures can occur independently or in combination with interior wall fractures; interior wall fractures can also occur alone. A direct blow to the orbital rim may be insufficient to fracture the bony rim, but it may increase the intraorbital pressure sufficiently to fracture the thin interior bones. The interior bones most commonly fractured are those of the inferior medial portion, or the floor of the orbit—an injury known as a "blowout" fracture (see **Figure 18.17**).[17] Comminuted fractures are the most common type of blowout fracture.[18] The rate of orbital fractures is highest in young males (20 to 29 years). Although comminuted fractures are more common in adults, the "trapdoor" type fracture is the most common in younger patients. Trapdoor fractures result in the capture of the inferior rectus muscle between the fragmented floor.[18]

A circumferential bony framework protects the vital structures of the orbital complex. The aperture

desiccation The process of tissue dehydration or drying out.

18

CLINICAL PRESENTATION

History

A blow to the orbital rim or periorbital region.
Pain when opening the mouth.

Observation

Infraorbital ecchymosis.
Enophthalmos.
Vertical dystopia.
Possible hyphema.
An eyelid retractor may be necessary to view the eye, especially
in the presence of swelling.

Functional Status

Entrapment of the inferior rectus muscle can limit upward gaze
of the affected eye.
If the fracture involves the sinus, air may escape from the
lower portion of the globe when the patient attempts to blow
the nose.

Physical Examination Findings

Numbness in the cheek can result from inhibition of the infra-
orbital nerve.
The globe may appear to be slightly displaced relative to the
unaffected eye.
The patient may describe nausea and vomiting.

of the bony rim does not allow objects with diameters greater than 10 cm to penetrate to the globe.[19] The circumferential bony rim should be palpated during the examination. Although fractures of the orbital rim can occur at any point, fractures of the inferior rim are the most common type.

Differential Diagnosis

Differential diagnoses include zygomatic fracture, neuropathy of the ocular motor nerves, subcon-

junctival hemorrhage, commotio retinae, and concussion. The presence of concurrent conditions such as hyphema and ruptured globe may be masked by the patient's symptoms and must be ruled out.

Medical Diagnostic Tests

A forced duction test is used to determine whether limited ocular movements are caused by entrapped soft tissues, edema, or a contused motor nerve or muscle. First, the affected eye is anesthetized with a topical anesthetic. Next, the sclera is grasped with a fine-toothed forceps at the level of the inferior rectus muscle insertion. Last, the eye is gently moved in the superior and inferior directions. If the globe moves easily, entrapment of the ocular contents can be ruled out.

Imaging Techniques

A multislice CT scan from the coronal (bird's eye) view is ideal for evaluating the interior walls of the orbit and can accurately reveal a blowout fracture (see **Figure 18.18**).

Definitive Diagnosis

The diagnosis of an orbital fracture can be made based on the patient's signs and symptoms, especially enophthalmos or exophthalmos, and is confirmed through radiographs or CT scan, or both (see **Figure 18.19**). The diagnosis of orbital fractures may be delayed because many of the initial signs and symptoms—a blow to the head, nausea, and vomiting—may initially resemble those of a concussion.[17]

Pathomechanics and Functional Limitations

Diplopia on upward gaze can be due to restricted movement of the eye from direct entrapment of the inferior rectus muscle or swelling or contusion of the muscle. Delayed recognition may result in ischemia and entrapment of the ocular muscles, causing permanent damage, restriction of motion, and vision irregularities.[17] Orbital fractures may also violate the maxillary and frontal sinuses.

■ Immediate Management

Shield the affected eye, and transport the patient to the hospital for appropriate medical care. Because of the possibility of surgery, withhold food and fluids until an ophthalmologist evaluates the patient. The patient should also be advised not to blow the nose.

■ Medications

NSAIDs and narcotic analgesics can be started for pain relief once a closed head injury has been ruled out. In some cases, oral antibiotics may be prescribed.

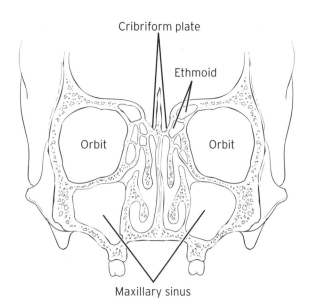

Figure 18.16   The orbital walls separate the orbit and its contents from the various sinuses of the face.

A

B

Fractured
floor
of orbit

Antrum   Periorbital fat

Figure 18.17   Orbital rim fracture. (**A**) The opening of the periorbital rim does not allow objects with a diameter greater than 10 cm to penetrate. (**B**) The force generated at impact causes a blowout fracture of the thin, bony walls of the orbital floor.

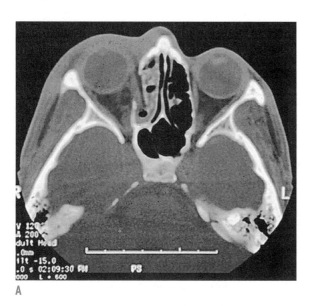

A

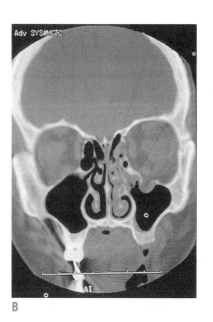

B

Figure 18.18   (**A**) A CT scan demonstrates a fracture of the medial wall of the orbit, showing its contents communicating with the ethmoid sinus. (**B**) A CT scan showing an orbital floor fracture with displacement of the orbital soft tissues into the maxillary sinus.

18

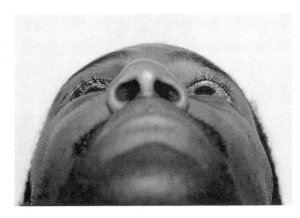

Figure 18.19 A worm's-eye view demonstrating enophthalmos of the patient's right eye after a fracture of the orbital floor.

Surgical Intervention

Because soft-tissue swelling, hemorrhage, or damage to the oculomotor nerves can mimic the signs and symptoms of an orbital floor fracture, the surgical correction of a blowout fracture is controversial.[2] Immediate repair is indicated when the patient presents with diplopia, radiographic (CT scan) evidence of muscle or soft-tissue entrapment, and altered ocular reflex. Aggressive timing of surgical repair is also indicated for patients younger than the age of 18. Orbital rim fractures are repaired with open reduction techniques through aesthetic incisions and stabilized with mini-plates and screws.

> **Practice Tip**
> Orbital fractures that are repaired within 2 weeks have better outcomes than those with delayed repair, but delay is a safe option in pediatric patients.[20]

Postinjury/Postoperative Management

Patients should be restricted from forcibly blowing the nose until the fracture site is healed. The associated pressure can cause motion in the fractured bone separating the orbit and the facial sinuses and delay the healing process. If eye motion causes pain, the patient may be instructed to use a forward gaze and rely on head motion to obtain the needed field of view.

Estimated Amount of Time Lost

Protective facial devices sufficient to prevent reinjury should be used if the player returns to competition before 4 to 8 weeks have passed.

Return-to-Play Criteria

Radiographic evidence of healing of the involved bones is usually required before the athlete returns to competition. The patient's vision must be adequate to safely participate in sport.

Functional Bracing

Protective eyewear can prevent both acute injury and reinjury.

References

1. Crow RW. Diagnosis and management of sports-related injuries to the face. *Dent Clin North Am.* 1991;35:719–732.
2. Torg JS (ed). *Athletic Injuries to the Head, Neck and Face*, ed 2. Philadelphia, PA: Lea & Febiger; 1991:611–649.
3. Manson PN, Markowitz B, Mirvis S, et al. Toward CT-based facial fracture treatment. *Plast Reconstr Surg.* 1990;85:202–214.
4. Garza JR, Baratta RV, Odinet K, et al. Impact intolerances of the rigidly fixated maxillofacial skeleton. *Ann Plast Surg.* 1993;30:212–216.
5. Mondin V, Rinaldo A, Ferlito A. Management of nasal bone fractures. *Am J Otolaryngol.* 2005;26:181–185.
6. Schendel SA. Sport-related nasal injuries. *Physician Sportsmed.* 1990;18:59–74.
7. Friedrich C. Therapy of recurring epistaxis of the anterior nasal septum. *Arch Otorhinolaryngol.* 1982;236:131–134.
8. Karagama YG, Newton JR, Clayton MGG. Are nasal fractures being referred appropriately from the accident and emergency department to ENT? *Injury.* 2004;35:968–971.
9. Kim BH, Seo HS, Kim A-Y, et al. The diagnostic value of the sagittal multiplanar reconstruction CT images for nasal bone fractures. *Clin Radiol.* 2010;65:308–314.
10. Linn LW, Vrijhoef MM, de Wijn JR, et al. Facial injuries sustained during sports and games. *J Maxillofac Surg.* 1986;14:83–88.
11. Chadja NK, Repanos C, Carswell AJ. Local anaesthesia for manipulation of nasal fractures: Systematic review. *J Laryngol Otol.* 2009;123:830–836.
12. Kafas P, Chiotaki N, Stavrianos C, Stavrianou I. Temporomandibular joint pain: Diagnostic characteristics of chronicity. *J Med Sci.* 2007;7:1088–1092.
13. Meng F, Liu Y, Zhao Y, et al. A comparative study of the skeletal morphology of the temporo-mandibular joint of children and adults. *J Postgrad Med.* 2008; 54:191–194.
14. Reychler H, Tovaru S. Current recommendations for the diagnosis of temporo-mandibular joint disorders: Review paper (part one). *Medica.* 2008;3:52–53.
15. Padilla RR, Felsenfeld AL. Treatment and prevention of alveolar fractures and related injuries. *J Craniomaxillofac Trauma.* 1997;3:22–27.
16. Camp JH. Diagnosis and management of sports-related injuries to the teeth. *Dent Clin North Am.* 1991;35:733–756.
17. Lane L, Penne RB, Bilyk JR. Evaluation and management of pediatric orbital fractures in a primary care setting. *Orbit.* 2007;26:183–191.
18. Chi MJ, Ku M, Shin KH, Baek S. An analysis of 733 surgically treated blowout fractures. *Int J Ophthalmol.* 2010; 224:167–175.
19. Guyette RF. Facial injuries in basketball players. *Clin Sports Med.* 1993;12:247–264.
20. Gonzalez MO, Durairaj VD. Indirect orbital floor fractures: A meta-analysis. *Middle East Afr J Ophthalmol.* 2010;17:138–141.

CHAPTER 19

Environmental Conditions

Brendon P. McDermott,
PhD, ATC
Douglas J. Casa, PhD,
ATC, FACSM,
FNATA
E. Randy Eichner, MD

Heat Cramps

CLINICAL PRESENTATION

History

Recent history of intense exercise in a hot environment.
Lack of heat acclimatization.
Insufficient sodium intake during meals and practices.
Inadequate rest between exercise bouts.
Irregular access to meals and fluids.
Previous history of cramping.
Chronic dehydration.

Observation

Profuse sweating.
Obvious muscle cramping (involuntary full muscle contractions).

Functional Status

Increased fatigue.
Cramping inhibits routine muscle activity and function.

Physical Examination Findings

Dehydration.
Skin turgor.
Decreased body weight.
Thirst.
Sweat that is high in salt content.

turgor The skin's resistance to being deformed. It is tested by lifting a small nap of skin on the hand and noting how quickly it returns to normal. In dehydrated individuals, the skin will slowly return to normal.

Recent evidence suggests that heat cramps are related to an electrolyte deficit.[1,2] A sodium deficiency—whether caused by inadequate intake of sodium or excessive amounts of sodium lost in sweat or, most likely, a combination of the two—increases the risk of heat cramps.[1] Individuals who experience heat cramps should have their rehydration and dietary protocols analyzed to determine if their sodium intake is insufficient.[3,4] Increasing the amount of sodium in the diet and rehydration beverages during practices and games decrease the incidence of heat cramping.[1,3] Extra sodium intake early in practice may ward off heat cramps later in the session—for example, adding 0.5 to 1.0 g of sodium to the first 30 to 40 oz (0.9 to 1.18 L) of a sports drink consumed during a practice, with a regular sports drink consumed for the remainder of the practice. These considerations become even more relevant during periods of two or three practices per day in the heat, when sweat sodium losses are exacerbated and replacement time is limited.[1] Consumption of additional sodium without proper dilution in a rehydration beverage is not recommended.[3,5,6]

Neuromuscular fatigue has recently been proposed as a cause of heat cramps.[7] Most likely, heat cramps have a multifactorial origin that includes at least three of the following conditions: decreased blood sodium, muscular fatigue, hypohydration, decreased pH, and decreased blood glucose. Athletes prone to cramping have been studied in the field and laboratory without initiating heat cramps.[3,8] This inability to re-create heat cramps in an artificial setting has changed the focus to cramp research with electrically induced cramps. Recent evidence supports the correlation between the activity of these cramps and actual heat cramps. Future research is necessary to verify research surrounding electrically induced cramping as related to heat cramps, however.

Regardless of the cause of heat cramps, these responses often present in athletes who perform strenuous exercise in the heat, who become dehydrated or fatigued, and who have decreased blood sodium concentrations.[1,5–12] Conversely, cramps can also occur in the absence of warm or hot conditions (e.g., in ice hockey players).[5]

Cramps tend to occur later in an activity in conjunction with muscle fatigue and after fluid and electrolyte imbalances have reached critical levels, such as during a conditioning session at the conclusion of practice. Dehydration, consumption of a diet containing insufficient electrolytes, and large losses of sodium and other electrolytes in sweat appear to increase the risk of severe, often whole-body, muscle cramps.[12] Muscle cramps can often be avoided with adequate conditioning, acclimatization, rehydration, and electrolyte replacement and appropriate dietary practices.[3,10,13–17]

The current hydration and electrolyte status of athletes who experience heat cramps should be identified to develop conditioning and acclimatization strategies.[4] If problems persist, the athlete should be referred to the team physician, registered dietitian, or both.

Differential Diagnosis

Muscle strain, exertional sickling.

Definitive Diagnosis

The most critical criteria are intense pain (not associated with acute muscle strain) and persistent involuntary muscle contractions in working muscles during and after prolonged exercise and most often associated with exercise in heat.[5,11]

Pathomechanics and Functional Limitations

The presence of muscle spasm interferes with the athlete's ability to ambulate or compete.

■ Immediate Management

The following procedures are recommended if heat cramps are suspected:[19,20]

- ■ Reestablish normal hydration status and replace some sodium losses with an electrolyte sports drink.

- Some additional sodium may be needed (especially in athletes with a history of heat cramps) earlier in the activity (before cramps begin) and is best administered by dilution in a sports drink.[1,3] For example, 0.5 to 1 g of sodium dissolved in 1 L of a sports drink early in the exercise session provides ample fluids and sodium and is palatable.
- Light stretching, relaxation, and massage of the involved muscle may help relieve the acute pain of a muscle cramp.
- Ice can help relieve cramping pain, especially when combined with massage.
- Refer the patient to the supervising physician if the condition does not improve with the recommended course of action.

Medications

Intravenous (IV) normal saline may be given by the medical staff (see **Figure 19.1**). The IV amount and sodium concentration are dictated by the supervising physician, with the aims of ameliorating fluid deficit and replacing electrolyte losses.[5,11]

Postinjury Management

Acutely, the athlete should be treated for muscle pain similar to that of a muscle strain to avoid further injury. Modify the athlete's electrolyte intake to avoid future episodes of heat cramps. Weight charts and urine specific gravity may be used to monitor hydration and rehydration (see "Identifying the Level of Hydration or Dehydration" later in this chapter).[5,11]

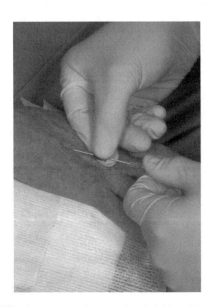

Figure 19.1 Intravenous sodium may be administered by qualified personnel to rehydrate the patient and replace electrolytes.

Estimated Amount of Time Lost

The amount of time lost from competition is dictated by the severity of the condition and the length of time it took to initiate treatment. Generally, athletes can return to play within a few hours or by the next day.[5,11]

Return-to-Play Criteria

Athletes should be assessed to determine if they can perform at the level needed for safe and successful participation. After an acute episode of heat cramps, diet, rehydration practices, electrolyte consumption, fitness status, level of acclimatization, and use of dietary supplements should be reviewed and possibly modified to decrease the risk of recurrence.[5,11] Hydration status can be assessed with weight charts and physical examination.

Heat Exhaustion

CLINICAL PRESENTATION

History

Intense exercise in a hot environment.
Dehydration and/or electrolyte depletion.

Observation

Physical fatigue and dizziness.
Profuse sweating.
Pallor.
Nausea, vomiting, or diarrhea.
Central nervous system (CNS) inhibition (e.g., confusion, slurred speech, ataxia).

Functional Status

The patient is unable to continue exercise or has difficulty exercising in a hot environment.
Persistent muscle cramps may be present.

Physical Examination Findings

Ataxia and coordination problems.
Syncope.

ameliorating
Improving a condition.

Heat exhaustion is a moderate illness characterized by the inability to sustain adequate cardiac output as a result of strenuous physical exercise and environmental heat stress. Inherent needs to maintain blood pressure and essential organ function, combined with a loss of fluid due to acute dehydration, create a challenge the body cannot sustain.[5,18]

Intense exercise in the heat challenges the cardiovascular system to deliver blood adequately to the working muscles, sweat glands, organs, and brain

19

while attempting to maintain exercise intensity. When cardiac output becomes compromised due to hypovolemia, exercise intensity likewise becomes compromised. Additionally, the body must work hard to keep itself cool, primarily by shunting heat via warm blood to the skin, where it is cooled by the atmosphere. Ultimately, a safe body temperature is maintained by evaporating sweat or by losing heat through a thermal gradient via convection and radiation. If the air temperature is extremely hot, the only means of losing heat may be through the evaporation of sweat.

In some cases when the intensity of exercise and environmental conditions are extreme, the cardiovascular system cannot meet the demands of blood supply to the muscles and skin while also maintaining blood pressure.[14] This situation can be exacerbated by dehydration and sodium loss from profuse sweating or robust sweat sodium concentrations.[18] The consequence may be cardiovascular insufficiency and slowing or cessation of activity.[18]

Differential Diagnosis
Exertional heat stroke, exertional hyponatremia, heat syncope, postural hypotension, exercise-associated collapse.[10–12]

Definitive Diagnosis
The most critical criteria are obvious difficulty continuing intense exercise in the heat; lack of severe hyperthermia (usually less than 104°F [40°C]), although mild hyperthermia is common (100°F to 103°F [37.7°C to 39.4°C]); and lack of severe CNS dysfunction. If any CNS dysfunctions (see those described for exertional heat stroke later in this chapter) are present, they are mild and subside quickly with treatment and rest.[5,11,12]

■ Immediate Management
The following procedures are recommended for heat exhaustion:[5,11,12,19,20]

- Remove the athlete from play and immediately move to a shaded or air-conditioned area.
- Remove excess clothing and equipment.
- Cool the athlete until the rectal temperature is approximately 101°F (38.3°C).
- Have the athlete lie comfortably with the legs propped above heart level.
- If the athlete is not nauseated, vomiting, or experiencing CNS dysfunction, rehydrate orally with chilled water or a sports drink.

- If the athlete is unable to take oral fluids, start a normal saline IV.
- Monitor heart rate, blood pressure, respiratory rate, core temperature, and CNS status.
- Transport to an emergency facility if rapid improvement (within 10 minutes) is not noted with the prescribed treatment.

■ Medications
An IV may be recommended if consciousness is altered or if the patient is nauseated or vomiting and dehydrated. Note that this treatment is not appropriate for exertional hyponatremia; these patients require high-sodium foods or hypertonic IV.[12]

■ Postinjury Management
The athlete should work with the medical staff to optimize hydration, acclimatization, fitness level, and other possible contributing factors to reduce the likelihood of another episode.[10–12,21–25]

■ Injury-Specific Treatment and Rehabilitation Concerns

> **Specific Concerns**
> Maintain cardiovascular status.
> Ensure adequate hydration.
> Confirm resolution of all symptoms.

If the underlying cause of heat exhaustion was a lack of acclimatization or a poor fitness level (or both), correct the problem before the athlete returns to full-intensity training in heat (especially in sports where equipment is worn on the body).[5,11,12]

■ Estimated Amount of Time Lost
Avoid intense practice in heat until at least the next day to ensure recovery from fatigue and dehydration. In severe cases, intense practice in heat should be delayed for more than 1 day.[5]

■ Return-to-Play Criteria
Physician clearance or, at minimum, a discussion with the supervising physician is recommended before the athlete returns to intense exercise. Any underlying conditions that might predispose the patient to continued problems—such as improper nutrition, cardiovascular condition, or a disease state—must be ruled out.[5,11]

Exertional Heat Stroke

CLINICAL PRESENTATION

History

Recent history of intense or endurance exercise in a warm or hot environment.

Observation

The patient may be experiencing nausea, vomiting, or diarrhea; each of these conditions further dehydrates the body.

The skin is hot and may be either wet or dry.

The patient may demonstrate obvious CNS dysfunction or altered consciousness. Many patients will become combative and act "out-of-sorts."

Functional Status

The patient is unable to function normally.

Cognitive impairments may hinder normal communication with the patient.

Physical Examination Findings

Rectal temperature greater than 104°F (40°C).
CNS dysfunction.
Increased heart rate.
Decreased blood pressure.
Increased respiratory rate.
Dehydration.
Combativeness.

During exercise (usually intense) in warm and hot environments (especially when humidity is high), body temperature increases can exceed the physiologic capacity to dissipate heat. If this increase is sustained, hyperthermia may result, and exertional heat stroke (EHS) can be the consequence. As thermoregulatory capacity is exceeded, body temperature rises, and extreme circulatory and metabolic stresses can produce tissue damage and severe physiologic dysfunction, leading to EHS and possible death. Exertional heat stroke is a leading killer of high school and collegiate athletes in the United States.[26–30]

Prevention and early identification of EHS are key to avoiding deaths from this cause.[30] Incipient EHS can resemble less serious conditions, such as heat exhaustion or exercise-related collapse.[12,30] As such, the immediate medical examination must differentiate among these potential diagnoses. Many cases of fatal EHS can be attributed to delayed recognition and treatment. The first half-hour appears to be the critical period in which aggressive treatment is lifesaving.[30]

Practice Tip

Temperature assessment for athletes who have been exercising in the heat requires use of a valid method. The only methods demonstrating consistently reliable results include rectal, intestinal, and esophageal temperature assessment. However, neither intestinal nor esophageal measurement is feasible following exercise. Therefore, rectal temperature assessment is imperative when core temperature assessment is warranted during or immediately following exercise in the heat or cold. Oral, axillary, forehead skin, and aural temperatures do not provide valid or reliable body temperatures under these conditions.[5,10,11,30-37]

Prompt assessment of the core body temperature and CNS function is critical to the appropriate evaluation of EHS. Axillary, oral, temporal artery, and tympanic (aural canal) temperatures are not valid measurements of core temperature for this purpose.[31–37] Instead, the medical staff should be trained and equipped to assess core temperature via rectal thermometer or an ingestible thermistor (see **Figure 19.2**).[5,30–32,37] If the measuring device can be kept in place while whole-body cooling is conducted (i.e., a rectal thermistor), the point at which body cooling can be halted can be objectively determined. An additional benefit is that the continuous monitoring of core temperature allows for cooling to continue unimpeded (i.e., the patient need not be removed from the bath to check body temperature).[30] If rectal temperature cannot be measured accurately, the medical staff should rely on CNS alterations to discriminate between heat exhaustion and EHS and not on potentially inaccurate oral, axillary, or tympanic measurements. Relying on an inaccurate temperature

Figure 19.2 Core temperature using an ingestible thermistor. Before competition, the athlete swallows a capsule-sized thermistor. As the thermistor passes through the digestive tract, core temperature is transmitted via radio waves to a handheld unit that displays and records the information. The thermistor passes naturally through the digestive tract and is not reusable.

19

measurement may cause death if treatment is delayed as a result.[12,30]

If hyperthermia is untreated, physiologic changes will likely occur within vital organ systems (e.g., muscle, heart, brain) and result in fatal consequences (multiple organ failure). Aggressive and immediate whole-body cooling is the key to optimal treatment.[30]

Differential Diagnosis

Heat exhaustion, seizure, syncope, exercise-associated collapse, hyponatremia, postural hypotension.[30]

Definitive Diagnosis

The most critical criteria for the definitive diagnosis of EHS are hyperthermia, usually defined as a rectal temperature greater than 104°F (40°C) immediately postincident, and CNS dysfunction, such as altered consciousness, coma, convulsions, disorientation, irrational behavior, decreased mental acuity, irritability, emotional instability, confusion, hysteria, or apathy.[5,9,11,12,30,38–41]

■ Immediate Management

heat capacity
The quantity of heat required to raise the temperature of a unit of mass by a specific unit change in temperature; thermal capacity.

If rapid on-site cooling is possible (i.e., appropriate medical staff such as a licensed athletic trainer [AT] or physician are on-site and the patient's airway, breathing, and circulation [ABCs] are stable), the patient should be cooled first and transported later. Immediate whole-body cooling (ice water immersion) is considered the "gold standard" treatment for EHS and should be initiated within minutes after an incident (see **Figure 19.3**).[42] Increasing the rate of cooling minimizes the mortality and recovery rate, because the likelihood of organ failure is directly correlated with the length and degree of hyperthermia. Anecdotal and textbook reports of full-body cold immersion therapy not being recommended for EHS due to the risk of inducing cardiovascular shock, peripheral vasoconstriction, or hypothermic overshoot are unfounded. Medical

Figure 19.3   Full-body cooling station. These ice-filled and water-filled tubs, which should be maintained in a shaded area, are used to immerse the athlete's body and rapidly lower the core temperature.

organizations that oversee the education of athletic trainers, emergency medical technicians, nurses, and physicians should ensure that curricula teach ice-water immersion for EHS and rectal temperature assessment to provide the public they serve with optimal care.[5,11,30,42–53]

> **Practice Tip**
>
> Because the long-term recovery following exertional heat stroke depends on the severity and duration of extreme core temperature (more than 105°F [40.6°C]), whole-body cooling should begin immediately. The goal is to cool the body as fast as possible. The "gold standard" in whole-body cooling is ice-water immersion. Other acceptable modalities for body cooling include cold-water immersion, rotating wet ice-towels, and a cold shower. There have been no deaths following exertional heat stroke when patients were immediately treated with cold- or ice-water immersion.[5,10,11,42–52]

Immersion therapy produces the best cooling rates due to thermal conductivity and the volume-specific heat capacity of the water. The lower the temperature, the faster the cooling occurs.[50] If conditions allow, immersion in water at a temperature of 35°F (1.7°C) is recommended for the acute treatment of EHS. This temperature may not be feasible to attain or maintain in hot conditions, in which case the immersion bath should simply be kept as cold as possible.

Cooling can be successfully verified by measurement of the patient's rectal temperature. If on-site cooling is not an option, the patient must be immediately transported to the nearest medical facility that can cool the individual appropriately.

The following procedures are recommended for the immediate treatment of a patient with EHS (assuming ABCs have been assessed and appropriate medical staff are on-site):

- Remove clothing and equipment.
- Immediately immerse the athlete in a tub of cold water in the range of 35°F to 58°F (1.7°C to 14.5°C).
- Constantly monitor the patient's core temperature by rectal thermistor or thermometer during immersion therapy.
- If immersion is not possible, alternative cooling strategies must be implemented. Immediately move the patient to a shaded area or air-conditioned facility. Cooling techniques such as cold-water spraying, fans, ice bags, or ice over as much of the body as possible and cold towels (replaced frequently) must be used. Simply placing ice bags on the major arteries of the body

offers extremely limited body cooling and is not recommended.[42]

- As the patient is being cooled, continue to monitor the ABCs, rectal temperature, and CNS function (e.g., cognition, convulsions, orientation, consciousness). Once the patient's rectal temperature reaches 102°F (38.9°C), cooling can be stopped, but the patient's vital signs, including rectal temperature, must continue to be monitored. Transport the patient to a medical facility for further evaluation.

Medications

Normal saline via IV may be given if medical staff are available and dehydration confirmed.[12,30]

Postinjury Management

Physiologic changes can occur after an episode of EHS. For example, the athlete's heat tolerance may be temporarily or permanently compromised. A careful return-to-play strategy should be developed by the athlete's physician and implemented with the assistance of the AT or other qualified healthcare professional.[5,11,12,30,54–59]

Injury-Specific Treatment and Rehabilitation Concerns

> **Specific Concerns**
> Rule out secondary injury to the body's organ systems, especially the renal and cardiovascular systems.
> Ensure adequate hydration.
> Reacclimatize the athlete and ensure appropriate physical fitness.

Physician clearance is required before the athlete who has experienced exertional heat stroke returns to exercise. The athlete should avoid all exercise until completely asymptomatic and laboratory test results (blood creatine kinase concentration) are normal. The athlete should cautiously begin a gradual return to physical activity to regain peak fitness and acclimatization under the supervision of the AT and team physician. The type and length of exercise should be determined by the athlete's physician. Consideration must be given to three conditions that may exist following an EHS episode: temporary heat intolerance, predisposition to heat illness, and impaired physical fitness or acclimatization due to time loss from activity. The following is a suggested exercise pattern leading to the return to full activity in a 5- to 7-day period following physician clearance:[5,30,58,59]

1. Easy to moderate exercise in a climate-controlled environment, followed by strenuous exercise in a climate-controlled environment.
2. Easy to moderate exercise in heat, followed by strenuous exercise in heat.
3. (If applicable) Easy to moderate exercise in heat with equipment, followed by strenuous exercise in heat with equipment. Ideally, the athlete's core temperature should be monitored.

Estimated Amount of Time Lost

The severity of the incident dictates the length of recovery time. The patient should avoid exercise for at least 1 week after release from medical care. A much longer time may be required in severe cases or in athletes with residual heat intolerance. See the rehabilitation concerns discussed earlier in this chapter.[5,30,58,59]

Return-to-Play Criteria

Physician clearance is required before the patient returns to activity. The patient should have no residual effects from EHS, restoration of the body's thermoregulatory system, and adequate rehydration and nutrition.[5,30,58,59] The athlete must also be reacclimatized to the environmental conditions.[58,59] See the rehabilitation concerns discussed previously.

Exertional Hyponatremia

CLINICAL PRESENTATION

History

Overconsumption of fluids.
Salty sweat.
Inadequate sodium intake in the diet or during prolonged activity more than 2 hours.

Observation

Nausea, vomiting (often repeated).
Swelling of extremities (hands and feet).
CNS dysfunction.
Respiratory distress.
Dizziness/lightheadedness.
Headache.

Functional Status

Lethargy.
Increasing headache.
Extreme fatigue.
Apathy.
Agitation.

Physical Examination Findings

Urine (if present) has low specific gravity.
CNS dysfunction develops as the condition progresses.

19

When an athlete consumes more fluids (especially water) than necessary, sodium in the bloodstream can become diluted, resulting in exertional hyponatremia. Ultimately, if the decrease in blood sodium is severe enough, complications such as cerebral and pulmonary edema can arise and prove fatal.[10,12] Exertional hyponatremia tends to occur during activities that last for 4 hours or longer in warm or hot weather.[60] This condition is considered serious when plasma sodium levels decrease to less than 130 mmol/L. The more pronounced or lengthy the decrease, the greater the risk of medical consequences.[5,12,60] Sodium lost through sweat and urine, coupled with inadequate sodium intake during lengthy events, increases the rate at which hyponatremia develops.[5]

Although excessive fluid intake is likely the most common cause of exertional hyponatremia, especially in marathon runners and athletes participating in shorter events, this condition can also occur in the absence of overhydration in athletes who do not adequately replace sodium (see **Table 19.1**).[5,11,12,60–62] In fact, in long, hot races such as the Hawaii Ironman Triathlon, exertional hyponatremia can occur even in athletes who are also volume depleted (hypohydrated).[60,63] Athletes need adequate sodium in the diet before an event or long practice session. Also, ingesting fluids and foods that contain sodium during long-duration activities helps to replace lost sodium.[5,64] In certain circumstances, individuals who lose a great deal of sodium in sweat may need to specifically supplement sodium during the event by using electrolyte pills or electrolytes diluted in a sports drink or pediatric electrolyte solution.

The risk of developing hyponatremia is significantly reduced when fluid consumption during activity does not exceed fluid losses.[12] Because exercise dehydration compromises thermoregulatory function, athletes must be aware of their individual fluid needs to protect against both dehydration and overhydration.[5,10,12]

Fluid needs can be determined by establishing an athlete's sweat rate (L/h) during a given intensity of activity, while wearing a given amount of clothing and equipment, for a given set of environmental conditions.[10] Large variability exists in sweat rates (0.5 to 3.9 L/h), so individual assessment is vital.[10] When fluid needs are being established, it is best to mimic the conditions of a specific athletic event to establish an accurate sweat rate[5] (see "Developing an Individualized Hydration Protocol" later in this chapter).

Although significant attention has been devoted to the need to rehydrate athletes, caution must also be taken to prevent overhydrating athletes. Several deaths have occurred from exertional hyponatremia.[60,61,65,66] However, simply prescribing or promoting dehydration as a means of hyponatremia prevention is strongly discouraged.

Differential Diagnosis

Heat stroke, heat exhaustion, postural hypotension, heat syncope, exercise-associated collapse.[12,60]

Definitive Diagnosis

The definitive diagnosis of exertional hyponatremia is made based on blood sodium concentrations less than 130 mmol/L.[65,66] Urine with low specific gravity is produced during the event and tends to appear after activity—for example, in the medical tent. In some cases, high levels of antidiuretic hormone with minimal urine production seem to be a contributing factor.[67] If the condition progresses, CNS changes (e.g., altered consciousness, confusion, coma, convulsions, altered cognitive functioning) and respiratory changes result from cerebral and pulmonary edema, respectively.

Exertional hyponatremia is more likely to occur during physical activity that lasts for longer than

Table 19.1	
Factors Leading to Exertional Hyponatremia	
Factor*	**Cause**
Excessive fluid intake	More fluid is ingested than is lost through sweat and urine over a given period of time, resulting in hyperhydration and decreased blood sodium levels.
Sodium intake/output imbalance (e.g., high sweat sodium levels, low sodium levels in fluids and foods)	Sodium is lost in sweat during lengthy exercise sessions, especially in athletes with salty sweat.
	The individual has low sodium levels in the diet leading up to the event, or low sodium levels in fluids and foods during the event.

*The combination of these two conditions exacerbates the patient's condition.

4 hours, providing enough time for the athlete to both consume fluids and lose large amounts of fluids through sweating. This condition may also be more likely to develop during lower-intensity endurance exercises when the athlete has extra opportunity to consume a large volume of fluid.[5,11,12,60,61,65]

The most critical criteria for determination of exertional hyponatremia are as follows:[5,12]

- The absence of severe hyperthermia (temperature most commonly is less than 104°F [40°C])
- Low blood sodium levels (less than 130 mmol/L)—the severity of the condition increases as sodium levels decrease
- The likelihood of excessive fluid consumption before, during, and after exercise (weight gain during activity)
- Low sodium intake
- Indications of sodium deficits before, during, and after exercise
- Progressively worsening headache

Immediate Management

The possibility of heat stroke or heat exhaustion must be ruled out. If either condition is present, treat the patient appropriately.[5,11,12,60] If exertional hyponatremia is confirmed, treatment via hypertonic (3% to 7% NaCl) intravenous saline is necessary to correct the hypotonicity. On-site evaluation of blood sodium concentrations is recommended, especially if EHS is ruled out. This step necessitates transport to an advanced medical facility, after or simultaneously with placement of an IV delivering a hypertonic solution.[65,66]

Practice Tip

Effective treatment for moderate or severe exertional hyponatremia includes hypertonic saline given in 100-mL intervals. This IV treatment mitigates abnormal sodium concentrations and fluid volume compartmentalization within the body within minutes. Normal IV saline administration is contraindicated, and blood sodium concentrations should be confirmed prior to, and serially throughout, treatment.[10,11,59-66]

Symptoms that complicate the diagnosis are the patient feeling dizzy or weak and collapsing. When this response occurs after the athlete has stopped competition, rather than during competition, the likely cause is postural hypotension—that is, a pooling of blood in the legs and inadequate blood supply to the upper body.[17] This problem

can be avoided by walking or flexing the legs when standing in place. When an athlete collapses from postural hypotension, the legs should be raised above the head and held there for 3 to 4 minutes to relieve symptoms.[12]

The following procedures are recommended for exertional hyponatremia:

- If blood sodium levels cannot be determined on-site, delay rehydrating the patient (which may worsen the condition) and transport the individual immediately to a medical facility. If the athlete is able to eat, encourage consumption of high-sodium foods (potato chips, pretzels, or three to five bouillon cubes dissolved in water).[61]
- The administration of sodium, certain diuretics, or IV solutions may be necessary. Administration should be monitored by the physician on-site or in the emergency department to ensure that no complications develop.

Medications

An IV of a hypertonic sodium replacement, diuretic (if hyperhydrated), and/or anticonvulsive drug (if the patient has seizures) may be administered by a physician on-site or in the hospital.[12,61,65,66]

Postinjury Management

Physician clearance before return to competition is strongly recommended for all patients and is required for patients who were hospitalized.[5,11,12]

Estimated Amount of Time Lost

In minor cases of exertional hyponatremia, activity can resume a few days after the athlete completes an educational session on establishing an individual hydration protocol. This will ensure that the proper amounts and types of beverages and meals are consumed before, during, and after physical activity.[5,11]

Return-to-Play Criteria

In minor cases of exertional hyponatremia, participation can resume in a few days, assuming actions have been taken to modify fluid intake and sodium ingestion. In extreme cases in which system damage occurred, the physician must dictate an appropriate and gradual return to participation when recovery is complete.[5,11]

19

Hydration Needs for Athletes

Proper hydration influences the quality of athletic performance.[6,9,11,13–16,18] The evaporation of sweat from the skin's surface is a powerful cooling mechanism that releases the heat being produced by the working muscles. Replenishing the body's fluids is an important consideration in any type of physical exertion. Athletes have sometimes been told to consume "as much fluid as possible" to ward off the dangers of dehydration. More recently, athletes and medical staff have been told to limit hydration due to the potential dangers associated with over-hydrating. Not drinking enough during activity and thus inducing dehydration can impair performance and health. Yet overdrinking beyond what is lost can cause exertional hyponatremia.

How does the competitive athlete balance the risks of dehydration and hyponatremia? The answer lies in individualizing fluid needs and tailoring a hydration plan to personal differences. This is a simple process that can maximize performance and minimize risk. The following is an overview of dehydration, with guidelines to determine an individual's fluid needs.

■ Dehydration

Dehydration is the acute change in fluid stores from a steady-state condition of normal body water (euhydration) to something less than normal body water (hypohydration).[18] Dehydration is caused by two distinct factors that may occur during exercise (see **Table 19.2**): (1) the loss of fluids by sweating, urinating, and respiration, and (2) fluid intake that is less than fluid losses.[1,2,6,9–16,60,68–75]

If the body remains in a state of decreased body water stores for an extended period of time, the individual is said to be hypohydrated—a steady-state condition of decreased body water.[18] Because the human body is approximately 65% water, a significant decrease (approximately 2%) in body water stores alters normal physiologic function. For example, cardiovascular function (heart rate), thermoregulatory capacity (sweating), and muscle function (endurance capacity) can be impaired if dehydration reaches critical thresholds, altering the physiologic function of these processes.[5,6,9,14,16,18]

Table 19.2

Factors Leading to Dehydration

Condition	Effect
During moderate and intense activity	Sweat rate increases proportionally to the intensity of the activity. At high-intensity levels (e.g., >75% $\dot{V}_{O_{2max}}$), the rate at which fluid can be processed by the stomach and intestines and emptied into the bloodstream is decreased. Increasing intensity likely decreases the amount of time the individual can focus on rehydration.
During activity in warm and hot conditions	As the temperature increases, the sweat rate increases.
Individuals with high sweat rates	High sweat levels signal a need to consistently replenish fluids.
Inadequately hydrated at the start of exertion	Dangerous levels of dehydration can be reached more rapidly.
Multiple practices on the same day	As the number of daily exercise sessions increases, the amount of fluid needed during the course of the day increases.
Improper eating	Most fluid consumption occurs during mealtimes, so a disturbance in normal meals may alter the ability to maintain proper hydration.
Inadequate access to fluids	Low fluid intake significantly increases the risk of dehydration.
Poor vigilance	Athletes do not follow, or are unaware of, directions for proper hydration before, during, and after exercise.
Somatotype	A person's size influences the sweat rate; larger individuals generally have a higher sweat rate than smaller individuals.
Characteristics of the rehydration fluid	If the temperature of the rehydration fluid is too hot or cold, if it consists of nonideal compounds, or if the person dislikes the flavor, the degree of voluntary rehydration may be altered.
Individual fluid tolerance	Some individuals cannot comfortably handle the amounts of fluid needed to approximate fluid losses during activity; one solution may be to gradually drink small amounts of fluids over time rather than larger amounts of fluid in a shorter time frame.
	Athletes may be able to alter the amount when the hydration protocol is practiced during training sessions.

When fluid consumption is less than fluid losses, dehydration occurs. Fluid can be lost in sweat, urine, and feces and during respiration. During exercise, most fluid loss occurs in the form of sweat. Fluid losses can be replaced by fluids consumed either orally or intravenously and those produced during metabolism (a small amount of water is formed by the metabolic pathways that allow muscles to contract). Most fluid intake occurs from the oral consumption of fluids or fluids in food products. Generally speaking, during exercise, when sweat losses exceed oral fluid intake, dehydration occurs. Mild dehydration, consisting of approximately 1% to 2% of total body weight, is likely to occur and is not a great concern, but losses beyond this point should be avoided if possible.[10]

Recognizing Dehydration

Although dehydration is an important factor that contributes to hyperthermia associated with exercise, other factors play roles in this process. For example, intensity of activity, environmental conditions (humidity, temperature, shade or cloud cover), level of fitness, degree of heat acclimatization, amount of clothing and equipment worn, and illness all contribute to the rate of rise in body temperature. Athletes should consider these factors when trying to decrease the risk associated with exercise in warm and hot conditions.[5,10–12]

Athletes, coaches, and the medical staff must be adept at recognizing and treating hyperthermia. If it is mild, the runner needs to slow down or stop, depending on the symptoms. If the symptoms are more severe, an immediate effort must be made to reduce core body temperature. Athletes should be able to recognize the basic signs and symptoms of heat illness, for which dehydration may be a cause—irritability and general discomfort, headache, weakness, dizziness, cramps, chills, vomiting, nausea, head or neck heat sensations, disorientation, and decreased performance.

Treating Dehydration

A dehydrated athlete should be moved to a cooler environment (e.g., indoor air conditioning, shaded area), if possible, and appropriately rehydrated. A conscious, cognizant, dehydrated athlete without gastrointestinal distress can aggressively rehydrate orally. Patients who are experiencing mental deterioration from dehydration or gastrointestinal distress should be transported to a medical facility for IV rehydration. If an exertional heat illness beyond dehydration is suspected, medical treatment is necessary. Additionally, dehydration itself, if severe, may require medical assistance.[6]

An athlete who has CNS dysfunction or who is nauseated or vomiting may have EHS or hyponatremia and should be treated or transported for immediate medical attention and laboratory evaluation. If an athlete's weight loss is greater than 2% within a given day or on consecutive days, the athlete should return to normal hydration status before being allowed to practice.[5,6] If the degree of dehydration is minor and the athlete is symptom free, continued participation is acceptable. The athlete must maintain adequate hydration status and should receive periodic checks from on-site medical personnel.[5,6]

■ Developing an Individualized Hydration Protocol

Optimal hydration is based on the premise that fluid intake should approximate fluid losses. When these processes are synchronized, the hazards of underhydrating or overhydrating are reduced, and the likelihood of a safe and productive exercise session is enhanced.[6]

Determining Sweat Rates

Hydration strategies must take into account the sweat rate, sport dynamics (e.g., rest breaks, fluid access), environmental factors, heat acclimatization state, exercise duration, exercise intensity, and individual preferences or limits. To assess an individual's rehydration needs, the individual's sweat rate must be determined using the following calculation:[6]

Sweat rate = body weight prepractice − body weight post practice + fluid intake − urine ÷ exercise time (in hours)

A single measure of body weight may not be representative of a euhydrated athlete. This value represents a single measure along a continuum, and the athlete may be hypohydrated or hyperhydrated at that point in time. Future determinations of percent dehydration, or baseline body weight, should not be based on a single measure, but rather on an average of daily measures.[76,77]

The most valuable sweat rate measurements are those obtained during a representative range of environmental conditions, intensities, practices, and competitions.[6] **Table 19.3** presents a sample worksheet for calculating sweat rates.

Sweat rate calculation is the most fundamental consideration when establishing a hydration protocol. Average sweat rates from the scientific literature or other athletes can vary from 0.5 L/h to more than 2.5 L/h (1.1 lb/h to 5.5 lb/h) and are not

19

Table 19.3

Example Fluid Replacement Calculations

Name	Date	Pre-exercise Body Mass	Post-exercise Body Mass	Δ Body Mass	Fluid Consumed	Urine Volume	Sweat Loss	Exercise Duration	Sweat Rate
Johnny Athlete	8/2	173.4 kg	171.4 kg	−2 kg	2 L	0 L	4 L	2 hr	2 L/hr
Samantha Player	7/3	60.2 kg	60.1 kg	−0.1 kg	3 L	0 L	3.1 L	1.5 hr	2.07 L/hr
Sammy Cyclist	9/27	81.3 kg	81.5 kg	+0.2 kg	4 L	0.2 L	3.6 L	3 hr	1.2 L/hr

Athletes should replace 125–150% of body weight lost during exercise within an hour of the end of an exercise session. If an athlete loses 1.5 kilograms during exercise, they should consume 1.88 to 2.25 liters of fluid to adequately replace fluids lost during exercise. The "Sweat Rate" column above represents the recommended rate of fluid consumption for athletes during activity.

Source: Data from Casa DJ, Armstrong LE, Hillman SK, et al. National Athletic Trainers' Association position statement: Fluid replacement for athletes. *J Athl Train.* 2000;35:212-224.

accurate enough to use as a basis for individual hydration plans.[6]

When calculating an individual's sweat rate for application during competition, have the athlete practice at a similar intensity in a 1-hour training session in climatic conditions that are similar to the expected conditions.[6] The following procedure is recommended to determine the sweat rate:[6]

- Perform a warm-up until perspiration is generated.
- Urinate if necessary.
- Disrobe and have a weight reading taken on an accurate scale.
- Conduct practice for 1 hour at an intensity similar to that of the targeted competition.
- Drink a measured amount of a beverage of choice during the practice.
- Do not urinate during the practice (unless the amount of urine is measured).
- Disrobe and have a second weight reading taken on the same scale after the practice.
- Enter the data into Table 19.3.

Metabolism of carbohydrates, fats, and protein during exercise accounts for a small amount of the weight lost during activity, so weight changes after an activity can largely be attributed to sweat losses. Thus the previously described calculation of fluid needs is a viable option for determining hydration requirements.

When sweat rate is not known or measurement is not feasible, the easiest way to monitor and enhance behavior is to weigh athletes before and after practice. Athletes who lose weight during the practice should be encouraged to drink more during the next practice. Conversely, if they gain weight

during the practice, encourage them to drink less during the next practice.[5,78] To maximize performance and reduce the risk of heat illness or overhydration, athletes should lose between 1% and 2% body weight during practices and competitions.

Heat acclimatization produces dramatic physiologic changes that can enhance an athlete's ability to tolerate exercise in the heat, but it may also alter individual fluid-replacement considerations (see **Table 19.4**).[9] The sweat rate generally increases after 10 to 14 days of heat exposure, requiring a greater fluid intake for a similar bout of exercise. An athlete's sweat rate should be reassessed after acclimatization.[6] Also, moving from a cool environment to a warmer one increases the overall sweat rate during exercise (independent of the sweat changes associated with heat acclimatization). Athletes must closely monitor their hydration status for the first week of exercise in a warm environment. Increased sodium intake is recommended during the first 3 to 5 days of heat exposure, because the increased thermal strain and sweat rate increase the sodium lost in sweat. Adequate sodium intake optimizes fluid palatability and absorption during the first few days and may decrease exercise-associated muscle cramping. After 5 to 10 days, sweat sodium concentration decreases, but the overall sweat rate is higher, so the athlete should still be conscientious about sodium ingestion.[6]

Fluid replacement beverages should be easily accessible in individual fluid containers and flavored to the athlete's preference. Individual containers permit easier monitoring of fluid intake.[6] Clear water bottles marked in 100-mL (3.4-oz) increments provide visual reminders to help athletes gauge proper amounts.[6] Carrying water bottles or other hydration systems during activity when access to fluid is limited encourages greater fluid volume ingestion.[6]

Table 19.4

Strategies for a Successful Heat Acclimatization Program

1. Attain adequate fitness in cool environments before attempting to heat acclimatize.

2. Exercise at higher intensities (more than 50% $\dot{V}_{O_{2max}}$) and gradually increase the duration (up to 90 min/d) and intensity of the exercise sessions during the first 2 weeks.

3. Initially, perform the highest-intensity workouts during the cooler morning or evening hours and other training during the hottest time of the day. After 10 to 14 days of exercise in the heat, most of the benefits of acclimatization will have occurred, and some of the intense exercise should then take place during the hotter times of the day.

4. Monitor body weight to ensure that proper hydration is maintained as sweat rate increases.

5. When necessary, monitor rectal temperature so that body temperature stays within safe limits.

6. Athletes who live in a cool environment but will travel to a hot environment for competition can induce partial acclimatization by wearing insulated clothing, although they should leave some skin surface uncovered and monitor rectal temperature to avoid hyperthermia. Additionally, if the athlete can arrive 3 to 5 days before competition in a hot environment, many of the benefits of acclimatization can be attained.

7. Ensure intake of ample sodium in the diet and rehydration beverages in the initial week of practices in a hot environment, because sweat sodium losses are greater than before training commenced or while training in a cooler environment. Extra sodium also ensures optimal expansion of plasma volume, a cardinal component of acclimatization.

Source: Adapted from Casa DJ. Exercise in the heat: II. Critical concepts in rehydration, exertional heat illness, and maximizing athletic performance. *J Athl Train.* 1999;34:253-262.

Athletes should begin exercise sessions in a well-hydrated state. Hydration status can be monitored by athletes in several ways. Assuming proper hydration, pre-exercise body weight should be relatively consistent across exercise sessions. However, body weight is dynamic. Frequent exercise sessions can induce non–fluid-related weight loss influenced by timing of meals and defecation, time of day, and calories expended in exercise.[5,6]

■ Identifying the Level of Hydration or Dehydration

The simplest way to assess hydration status is by comparing urine color (from a sample in a container) to a urine color chart. A urine color of 1 to 3 indicates sufficient hydration, whereas a color of 5 or greater indicates dehydration. A color of 8 indicates rhabdomyolysis with myoglobin in the urine and is much more severe than dehydration alone.[5,6,79–81] Urine volume is another general indicator of hydration status. An athlete should need to urinate frequently during the course of the day. Remember that body weight changes during exercise give the best, and practical, indication of hydration needs.[6]

A more objective way to assess hydration status than urine color is with urine-specific gravity. **Table 19.5** indicates how urine-specific gravity correlates with hydration status. If the athlete's hydration status is unclear at the time of the baseline body weight before a practice (especially in at-risk individuals), it would be wise to also assess urine-specific gravity at that time to ensure this weight reflects a hydrated condition. If not, the athlete should be hydrated before practice and a new baseline body weight obtained or, at a minimum, the athlete should be monitored (if minimally dehydrated) more closely.[5,6]

To ensure proper pre-exercise hydration, the athlete should consume approximately 500 to 600 mL (17 to 20 oz) of water or a sports drink 2 to 3 hours before exercise and 200 to 300 mL (7 to 10 oz) of water or a sports drink 10 to 20 minutes before exercise.[5] These pre-exercise amounts should be less if the individual has a small frame and low body mass (i.e., a female marathon runner). Furthermore, it is recommended that fluid recommenda-

Table 19.5

Indices of Hydration Status

	Percentage of Body Weight Change*	Urine Color	Urine-Specific Gravity
Well hydrated	+1 to −21	1, 2, or 3	<1.020
Minimal dehydration	−1 to −3	4 or 5	1.020–1.024
Significant dehydration	−3 to −5	5 or 6	1.025–1.029
Serious dehydration	>5	6, 7, or 8	>1.030

*Percent (%) body weight change = pre-exercise body weight − post-exercise body weight × 100 ÷ pre-exercise body weight

Note: A seriously dehydrated athlete may not be able to provide a urine sample. Also, these entities are physiologically independent, and the numbers provided are only general guidelines.

Source: Adapted from Casa DJ, Armstrong LE, Hillman SK, et al. National Athletic Trainers' Association position statement: Fluid replacement for athletes. *J Athl Train.* 2000;35:212-224.

19

tions most often be based on individual sweat rates rather than the general guidelines, although the guidelines can serve as a reference. Fluid temperature influences the amount consumed. Although individual preferences exist, a cool beverage at 10°C to 15°C (50°F to 59°F) is recommended.[6]

Post-exercise hydration should aim to correct any fluid loss occurring during the practice or event and encourage the rapid restoration of physiologic function. Ideally, the rehydration process should be completed within 2 hours to speed recovery. If not, the athlete can freely rehydrate throughout the course of the day. Rehydration fluids should contain water to improve the hydration status, carbohydrates to replenish glycogen stores, and electrolytes to speed rehydration. Additionally, a small amount of protein after exercise in the rehydration beverage can enhance muscle recovery.[82]

When rehydration must be rapid, the athlete should compensate for obligatory urine losses incurred during the rehydration process and drink 25% to 50% more than sweat losses to ensure optimal hydration 4 to 6 hours after the event (see Table 19.5).[5,6] When the rehydration must occur during a brief period between two exercise sessions (i.e., between events, halftime), it is critical to educate athletes that full rehydration may not be possible given the time constraints and gastrointestinal intolerance for large quantities of fluids. In these circumstances, partial rehydration is absolutely necessary. Rehydrating only 50% of the fluid deficit during a 20-minute period provides a number of performance and physiologic advantages during the next exercise session.[83] The goal, therefore, to begin the next exercise session properly hydrated may not be feasible, but drinking the maximal tolerable amount (never to exceed fluid losses) in a process of partial rehydration can still be an effective hydration strategy.

Sports Drinks

In many situations, athletes benefit from including carbohydrates (CHOs) and electrolytes (i.e., sodium and potassium) in their rehydration drinks. Rehydration fluids should contain CHOs if the exercise session lasts more than 45 to 50 minutes or is intense. An ingestion rate of approximately 1 g/min (0.04 oz/min) maintains optimal carbohydrate metabolism; this equates to 1 L of a 6% carbohydrate drink per hour of exercise, or less for those who have sweat rates less than 1 L/h.[5] Carbohydrate concentrations greater than 8% increase the rate of CHO delivery to the body but compromise the rate of fluid emptying from the stomach and absorption from the

intestine. Fruit juices, CHO gels, sodas, and some sports drinks have CHO concentrations greater than the 8% threshold and are not recommended as the sole source of fluids during an exercise session.[5]

Athletes should consume CHOs at least 30 minutes before the normal onset of fatigue, and earlier if the environmental conditions are unusually extreme, although this may not apply for very intense, short-term exercise, which may require earlier intake of CHOs.[5] Most CHO forms (i.e., glucose, sucrose, maltodextrins) are suitable for this purpose, and the absorption rate is maximized when multiple forms are consumed simultaneously. Substances to be limited include fructose (which may cause gastrointestinal distress), and athletes should avoid alcohol, very high amounts of caffeine (which may decrease focus), and carbonated beverages (which may decrease voluntary fluid intake due to stomach fullness).[6] Modest amounts of caffeine have demonstrated performance benefits without compromised hydration and, therefore, should not be discouraged owing to their "diuretic effects."[84]

A modest amount of sodium (0.5 to 0.7 g/L) is an acceptable addition to all hydration beverages because salt stimulates thirst, increases voluntary fluid intake, may decrease the risk of hyponatremia, and causes no harm.[6] More sodium should be added to the athlete's fluid intake when there is a history of poor nutrition (meals not eaten) or heat cramps, the duration of physical activity exceeds 4 hours, and the activity occurs in notably hot weather. Under these conditions, adding modest amounts of sodium (0.5 to 0.7 g/L) can offset sodium lost in sweat and minimize the physiologic events associated with electrolyte imbalances (e.g., muscle cramps, hyponatremia).[6]

Strategies for Preventing Exertional Heat Illnesses

Each athletic organization should establish an emergency plan related to exertional heat illnesses. A thorough plan includes steps to reduce the risk of heat illness, identify the signs and symptoms of the early stages of exertional heat illnesses, and describe the immediate care protocol should these conditions arise

Some factors leading to the onset of heat illness, such as fitness level, can be optimized to reduce the individual's predisposition to these conditions. Other factors, such as intrinsic metabolic disorders, cannot (see **Table 19.6**).[1,5,9,11,12,17,30,69,79,85–94] The medical staff must educate coaches, athletes, and parents regard-

Table 19.6

Intrinsic and Extrinsic Factors Predisposing Heat Illness

Intrinsic Factors	Extrinsic Factors
History of exertional heat illnesses	Intense or prolonged exercise (several hours) with minimal breaks
Inadequate heat acclimatization	Limited access to fluids before and during practice and rest breaks
Lower level of fitness status	High ambient temperature, humidity, or sun exposure
High percentage of body fat	Recent exposure to heat and humidity
Dehydration	High wet-bulb globe temperature
Overhydration	Inappropriate clothing or equipment for climatic conditions (i.e., amount of football gear can be minimized during initial days when practices occur twice a day)
Fever	
Gastrointestinal illness	
Salt deficiency	Inappropriate work/rest ratios based on exercise intensity
Inadequate meals or insufficient calorie intake	No shaded areas to escape environmental conditions
Skin condition (e.g., sunburn, rash)	Lack of education and awareness of heat illnesses among coaches, athletes, and medical staff
Certain medications (e.g., antihistamines, diuretics)	No emergency plan to identify and treat exertional heat illnesses
Dietary supplements (e.g., ephedra)	A delay in recognition of early warning signs
Motivation to push oneself ("warrior mentality")	
Reluctance to report problems, issues, or illness	
Prepubescence	

ing the basic signs and symptoms of the exertional heat illnesses, so problems can be identified and referred to the team's AT as soon as possible.[5,6,11]

Medical personnel can predict when complications will arise while athletes exercise in hot environments. The rate of core temperature increase is influenced by several factors (see **Table 19.7**).[1,5,6,11,12,17,30,75,79,82,85,90,95–105] Prevention is best augmented by the early identification of heat-related problems. Headaches, dizziness, and nausea, for example, are not normal responses to exercise in the heat and may provide early warnings of a problem. Athletes should be encouraged to report

any abnormal symptoms early to coaches and the medical staff.

Some individual athletes may have predispositions to heat illness. Awareness allows closer monitoring of such an athlete's status. For example, athletes who are overweight, not acclimatized, ill, lacking sleep or rest, or "overmotivated" and those with extremely high sweat rates may be at increased risk and require more attention on the part of the medical staff (see **Table 19.8**).[5,11,12,60]

The wet-bulb globe temperature is a good measure of the environmental risks during exercise (see **Figure 19.4**). **Table 19.9** shows a conservative approach

Table 19.7

Critical Factors Influencing Core Temperature Increase: Key Factors to Consider for Reducing Risk of Exertional Heat Illness

Factor	Modification in Hot/Humid Environment
Intensity of exercise	Decrease intensity of exercise Decrease work/rest ratio
Heat acclimatization status and fitness level	Institute a fitness/acclimatization program before the start of formal practices Exclude from participating in two-a-day practices those athletes who have not attained an adequate level of fitness and/or acclimatization
Hydration status (see Table 19.5)	Monitor hydration status before, during, and after activity
Amount of equipment and clothing	Wear less equipment or clothing, especially during initial days of exercise in the heat
Wet-bulb globe temperature (especially level of humidity)	Exercise during times of day when wet-bulb globe temperature is lower or at least have shade during rest breaks

19

Table 19.8

Preventing Heat-Related Illness and Exertional Hyponatremia

Provide education and implement rehydration strategies that ensure athletes drink fluids based on their own fluid losses and do not exceed the amount of fluids lost in sweat and urine.

Encourage athletes to be well acclimatized to the heat because this is an effective way to decrease sweat sodium losses.

Encourage athletes to maintain normal meal patterns and not restrict dietary sodium intake, so sodium levels are normal before the event starts.

Encourage athletes to consume a little extra sodium with meals and snacks during continuous days of exercise in hot weather to help maintain blood sodium levels.

Figure 19.4 Recording the wet-bulb globe temperature (WBGT). The WBGT produces an index based on the air temperature, relative humidity, and radiant heat. WBGT measurements should be recorded before practice or competition and repeated at regular intervals during the activity.

that may be appropriate for athletes who are not accustomed to extreme heat (i.e., those who live in the northern climates of the United States).[106] **Table 19.10** shows a slightly more liberal approach, which may be more appropriate for athletes who are accustomed to living and exercising in hot environments.[107]

If the medical staff does not have access to a wet-bulb globe thermometer, another option for determining practice schedules is to use heat and humidity measures, which can be ascertained with a simple sling psychrometer (see **Figure 19.5**). EHS risk rises with increasing heat and relative humidity. Fluid breaks should be scheduled for all practices, and more frequently as the heat stress rises. With reference to **Figure 19.6**, add 5°F to the temperature between 10 A.M. and 4 P.M. from mid-May to mid-September on bright, sunny days. Practices should be modified to reflect heat stress conditions. Regular practices with full practice gear can be conducted for conditions that plot to the left of the triangles.[108,109] Cancel all practices when the temperature and relative humidity plot to the right of the circles; practices can be moved

into air-conditioned spaces or held as walk-through sessions with no conditioning activities.

Hypothermia

Mild hypothermia is defined as a core temperature between 98.6°F and 95°F (37°C and 35°C), moderate hypothermia as a core temperature between 94°F and 90°F (34°C and 32°C), and severe hypothermia as a core temperatures less than 90°F (32°C).[110–114] Hypothermic risk increases as duration and intensity of cold, wet, windy conditions increases. Activities presenting the greatest potential for risk include endurance events (e.g., marathons, triathlons) as well as outdoor activities of increased duration (e.g., American football, distance hiking).

Differential Diagnosis

Hyponatremia, traumatic brain injury.

Table 19.9

Wet-Bulb Globe Temperature (WGBT) Risk Chart

WBGT	Flag Color	Level of Risk	Comments
<18°C (<65°F)	Green	Low	Risk is low but still present.
18°C–23°C (65°F–73°F)	Yellow	Moderate	Risk level increases as the event progresses throughout the day.
23°C–28°C (73°F–82°F)	Red	High	Everyone should be aware of injury potential; individuals at risk should not compete.
>28°C (>82°F)	Black	Extreme or hazardous	Consider rescheduling or delaying the event until conditions are safer; if the event must take place, be on high alert. Take steps to reduce risk factors (e.g., more and longer rest breaks, reduced practice time, reduced exercise intensity, access to shade, minimal clothing and equipment, and cold tubs at practice site).

Source: Adapted from Roberts WO. Medical management and administration manual for long distance road racing, in Brown CH, Gudjonsson B (eds), *IAAF Medical Manual for Athletics and Road Racing Competitions: A Practice Guide.* Monaco: International Amateur Athletic Federation Publications; 1998:39–75.

Table 19.10

Activity Restrictions for Outdoor Physical Conditioning in Hot Weather

Wet-Bulb Globe Temperature* (°F)	Flag Color	Guidance for Nonacclimatized Personnel *Guidance for Fully Acclimatized Personnel in Italics*
<78.0°F	No flag	Extreme exertion may precipitate heat illness. *Normal activity.*
78.1°F–82.0°F	Green	Use discretion in planning intense exercise. *Normal activity.* However, pay special attention to at-risk individuals in both cases.
82.1°F–86.0°F	Yellow	Limit intense exercise to 1 hour, limit total outdoor exercise to 2.5 hours. *Use discretion in planning intense physical activity.* However, pay special attention to at-risk individuals in both cases. Be on high alert: Watch for early signs and symptoms in both cases.
86.1°F–89.9°F	Red	Stop outdoor practice sessions and outdoor physical conditioning. *Limit intense exercise to 1 hour, limit total outdoor exercise to 4 hours. Be on high alert: Watch for early signs and symptoms throughout.*
≥90°F	Black	Cancel all outdoor exercise requiring physical exertion. *Cancel all outdoor exercise involving physical exertion.*

*Calculation of wet-bulb globe temperature (WBGT): 0.7 Twb ± 0.2 Tbg ± 0.1 Tdb, where Twb indicates wet-bulb temperature, Tbg is black-globe thermometer temperature, and Tdb is dry-bulb temperature. Guidelines assume that personnel are wearing summer-weight clothing; all activities require constant supervision (i.e., via athletic trainer) to ensure early detection of problems. When equipment must be worn, as in football, use the guidelines for one flag color level below. For example, if WBGT is 86°F (yellow), use the guidelines for red.

Source: Adapted from Nunnelly SA, Reardon MJ. Prevention of heat illness, in Pandolf KB, Burr RE (eds), *Medical Aspects of Harsh Environments, Vol 1.* Washington, DC: Borden Institute, Office of the Surgeon General, US Army; 2002:223.

Definitive Diagnosis

The diagnosis of hypothermia is made when the individual's core temperature is less than 98.6°F (37°C). Core temperature assessment when thermal injuries (hot or cold) are suspected must be completed with the use of a rectal thermometer.

Pathomechanics and Functional Limitations

Hypothermia prevents normal nerve conduction and, therefore, normal muscle function by reducing motor control and coordination. Obvious CNS

Figure 19.5 Sling psychrometer. Although not as comprehensive as a wet-bulb globe temperature, a sling psychrometer can be used to measure the ambient conditions.

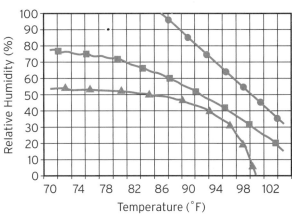

Figure 19.6 Heat stress risk temperature and humidity graph. *Conditions that plot between squares and circles:* Use a work/rest ratio with 15 to 20 minutes of activity followed by 5- to 10-minute rest and fluid breaks; practice should be in shorts only (with all protective equipment removed, if used for activity). *Conditions that plot between triangles and squares:* Use a work/rest ratio with 20 to 25 minutes of activity followed by 5- to 10-minute rest and fluid breaks; practice should be in shorts (with helmets and shoulder pads only, not full equipment if used for activity). *Conditions that plot beneath triangles:* Use a work/rest ratio with 25 to 30 minutes of activity followed by 5- to 10-minute rest and fluid breaks.

19

History

Recent history in a cold, or cold and wet, environment.
Previous history of cold injury.
Low body fat and muscle mass.
Inadequate clothing worn.
Lack of cold acclimatization.
Limited caloric and/or fluid intake.
Alcohol or drug use.

Observation

Shivering (if mild).
Slow breathing (see **Table 19.11**).

Functional Status

Impaired fine or gross motor control (depending on severity).
Muscle rigidity.

Physical Findings

Bradycardia.
Decreasing blood pressure.
Depressed respiration.
Cyanosis.
Dilated pupils.

dysfunction sets in at body temperatures less than 92.3°F (34°C).[114,115]

Immediate Management

The first step in acute management is to remove wet or damp clothing, and wrap the entire victim in dry, warm clothing or blankets. Emergency medical transport action plans should be activated for moderate and severe hypothermia. Gentle heating should target the trunk (core) of the body.[116,117] This approach helps avoid afterdrop, which may occur if heating is limited to the extremities.[118,119] Warm fluids should be provided if the patient is able to tolerate oral fluids; examples of such fluids

include heated broth or tea. Some external heating mechanisms are available in most large-scale events and in emergency rooms that are constructed to treat hypothermia. Vital signs should be monitored at regular intervals during recovery. Transport is necessary for any moderate to severe hypothermia situation to prevent post-hypothermia complications, such as kidney failure, infection, or cardiac arrhythmia.[120]

Medications

Intravenous fluid administration can expedite recovery only if dehydration is confirmed as a major factor in hypothermia onset. There is no known medication that helps speed body heat production to treat hypothermia.

Postinjury Management

The medical staff should make every attempt to identify any known causes of the hypothermia episode. This information will help to reduce future risk.[110]

Estimated Amount of Time Lost

The amount of time lost from activities following hypothermia is directly related to the severity and duration of the original episode.

Return-to-Play Criteria

There is no known published recommendation for the return-to-play decision following hypothermia. Because the affected individual has an increased risk of recurrence following an initial episode, emphasis should be placed on preventive practices and acclimatization whenever possible. Following moderate to severe hypothermia, physician clearance should be followed with gradual return-to-play and gradual increases in cold exposure.

Table 19.11

Signs and Symptoms of Hypothermia

	Mild	Moderate	Severe
Body temperature	98.6°F–95°F (37°C–35°C)	94°F–90°F (34°C–32°C)	<90°F (32°C)
Shivering	Vigorous	Vigorous to absent	Absent
Muscle coordination	Impaired fine motor control	Impaired gross motor control	None
Skin color	Pallor, cold skin	Cyanosis	Severe cyanosis
Mental function	Slight amnesia, lethargy	Slurred speech, dilated pupils	Unconscious, comatose
Cardiac signs	Normal heart rate	Bradycardia and potential arrhythmia	Arrhythmia or fibrillation
Blood pressure			Hypotension
Other	Rhinorhea, polyuria	Depressed respiration, muscle rigidity	Potential pulmonary edema or cardiac arrest

Source: Adapted from Cappaert TA, Stone JA, Castellani JW, Krause BA, Smith D, Stephens BA. National Athletic Trainers' Association position statement: Environmental cold injuries. *J Athl Train.* 2008;43:640-658.

Frostbite

CLINICAL PRESENTATION

History

Localized exposure to freezing temperatures.
Previous frostnip.
Tingling or burning in the area.
Alcohol or nicotine use.

Observation

Edema.
Red, waxy, or mottled gray skin appearance.

Functional Status

The potential for hypothermia exists.
Any friction on affected tissues is contraindicated and should be avoided.

Physical Examination Findings

Edema.
Hardened peripheral tissue that does not rebound.
Anesthesia in the skin.

Frostbite occurs when the skin and local tissue freeze (tissue temperature is less than 28°F [−2.2°C]), which induces necrosis within minutes. Frostbite can occur in cool, dry environments but also may be expedited when environments are moist, such as inside shoes or clothing.[110] Initial episodes of frostnip (a precursor to frostbite) may predispose the patient to future frostnip or frostbite.[110–112] Because the environments that cause hypothermia and frostbite are similar, core temperature must be assessed to confirm the diagnosis.[121,122]

Differential Diagnosis

Hypothermia, Raynaud's phenomenon.

Immediate Management

Immediate rewarming of the affected tissue can facilitate recovery but should be performed slowly. Rewarming should occur in a warm, dry environment, or the extremity can be placed in a lukewarm bath (water temperature greater than 98°F [36.7°C] is contraindicated).[110] Dry heat or steam should be avoided for rewarming.[110,121,123] When tissue returns to a normal color and is pliable, thawing can cease. Any friction to tissue can further necrosis and must be avoided.[110–112] Any potential refreezing of tissue will most likely result in further damage and should be prevented once rewarming begins. Regardless of the severity of the frostbite, the patient should be transported as soon as possible to an advanced medical facility to avoid further complications.

Practice Tip

The NATA position statement on cold injuries recommends prompt treatment of recognized frostbite to include rewarming of tissues slowly. Recommended methods of rewarming include contact with warm skin and immersion in lukewarm water. Tissue aggravation is contraindicated because it can further tissue damage.[110,121-124]

Medications

Analgesic medications may be prescribed to reduce the painful sensations felt during rewarming. If dehydration is confirmed, IV normal saline may be administered as well. Depending on the severity of the frostbite, tissue plasminogen activators may be prescribed to promote tissue healing.[124]

Postinjury Management

Following rewarming, debridement and infection control are of utmost importance to limit damage to the affected tissue from the initial episode. Secondary injury due to infection accounts for considerable tissue loss following frostbite.[110]

Estimated Amount of Time Lost

The amount of time lost from activities following frostbite is directly related to the amount and severity of tissue damage. In extreme cases, limb loss is possible. In mild cases, there may be no time lost due to only superficial tissue damage.

Return-to-Play Criteria

Frostbite causes no systemic or complicated damage. Once tissue integrity is verified following frostbite, the patient should be allowed to return to play. The only lasting sequela following frostbite is a potential susceptibility to future injury. Any potential predisposition should be mitigated, and a prevention plan should be in place upon return to play.

References

1. Bergeron MF. Exertional heat cramps, in Armstrong LE (ed), *Exertional Heat Illnesses.* Champaign, IL: Human Kinetics; 2003:91–102, 230–234.
2. Horswill CA, Stofan JR, Lacambra M, et al. Sodium balance during U.S. football training in the heat: cramp-prone vs. reference players. *Int J Sports Med.* 2009;30:789–794.
3. Bergeron MF. Heat cramps during tennis: A case report. *Int J Sport Nutr.* 1996;6:62–68.
4. Armstrong LE, Casa DJ. Methods to evaluate electrolyte and water turnover of athletes. *Athl Train Sports Health Care.* 2009;1(4):1–11.
5. Casa DJ, Almquist J, Anderson S, et al. Inter-association task force on exertional heat illnesses consensus statement. *NATA News.* June 2003;24–29.

19

6. Casa DJ, Armstrong LE, Hillman SK, et al. National Athletic Trainers' Association position statement: Fluid replacement for athletes. *J Athl Train.* 2000;35:212–224.

7. Schwellnus MP. Cause of exercise associated muscle cramps (EAMC): Altered neuromuscular control, dehydration or electrolyte depletion? *Br J Sports Med.* 2009;43:401–408.

8. Jung AP, Bishop PA, Al-Nawwas A, Dale RB. Influence of hydration and electrolyte supplementation on incidence and time to onset of exercise-associated muscle cramps. *J Athl Train.* 2005;40:71–75.

9. Casa DJ. Exercise in the heat: II. Critical concepts in rehydration, exertional heat illnesses, and maximizing athletic performance. *J Athl Train.* 1999;34:253–262.

10. Sawka MN, Burke LM, Eichner ER, et al. American College of Sports Medicine position stand: Exercise and fluid replacement. *Med Sci Sports Exerc.* 2007;39:377–390.

11. Binkley HM, Beckett J, Casa DJ, et al. National Athletic Trainers' Association position statement: Exertional heat illnesses. *J Athl Train.* 2002;37:329–343.

12. Casa DJ, Roberts WO. Considerations for the medical staff: Preventing, identifying and treating exertional heat illnesses, in Armstrong LE (ed.), *Exertional Heat Illnesses.* Champaign, IL: Human Kinetics; 2003:169–196, 255–259.

13. Armstrong LE, Epstein Y. Fluid–electrolyte balance during labor and exercise: Concepts and misconceptions. *Int J Sport Nutr.* 1999;9:1–12.

14. Gisolfi CV. Fluid balance for optimal performance. *Nutr Rev.* 1996;54(4 Pt 2):S159–S168.

15. Maughan RJ. Optimizing hydration for competitive sport, in Lamb DR, Murray R (eds.), *Optimizing Sport Performance.* Carmel, IN: Cooper Publishing; 1997:139–183.

16. Murray R. Fluid needs in hot and cold environments. *Int J Sports Nutr.* 1995;5(suppl):S62–S73.

17. Armstrong LE, Anderson JM. Heat exhaustion, exercise-associated collapse, and heat syncope, in Armstrong LE (ed.), *Exertional Heat Illnesses.* Champaign, IL: Human Kinetics; 2003:57–90, 234–241.

18. Casa DJ. Exercise in the heat: I. Fundamentals of thermal physiology, performance implications, and dehydration. *J Athl Train.* 1999;34:246–252.

19. Armstrong LE, Epstein Y, Greenleaf JE, et al. American College of Sports Medicine position stand: Heat and cold illnesses during distance running. *Med Sci Sports Exerc.* 1996;28:i–x.

20. Armstrong LE, Hubbard RW, Kraemer WJ, et al. Signs and symptoms of heat exhaustion during strenuous exercise. *Ann Sports Med.* 1987;3:182–189.

21. Armstrong LE, Maresh CM. The induction and decay of heat acclimatisation in trained athletes. *Sports Med.* 1991;12:302–312.

22. Gisolfi C, Robinson S. Relations between physical training, acclimatization, and heat tolerance. *J Appl Physiol.* 1969;26:530–534.

23. Kenney WL. Physiological correlates of heat intolerance. *Sports Med.* 1985;2:279–286.

24. Mitchell D, Senay LC, Wyndham CH, et al. Acclimatization in a hot, humid environment: Energy exchange, body temperature, and sweating. *J Appl Physiol.* 1976;40:768–778.

25. Piwonka RW, Robinson S, Gay VL, Manalis RS. Preacclimatization of men to heat by training. *J Appl Physiol.* 1965;20:379–384.

26. Armstrong LE. Classification, nomenclature, and incidence of the exertional heat illnesses, in Armstrong LE (ed.), *Exertional Heat Illnesses.* Champaign, IL: Human Kinetics; 2003:17–28, 227–230.

27. Bijur PE, Trumble A, Harel Y, et al. Sports and recreation injuries in US children and adolescents. *Arch Pediatr Adolesc Med.* 1995;149:1009–1016.

28. Hawley DA, Slentz K, Clark MA, et al. Athletic fatalities. *Am J Forensic Med Pathol.* 1990;11:124–129.

29. Mueller FO, Schindler RD. Annual survey of football injury research, 1931–1984. *Athl Train J Natl Athl Train Assoc.* 1985;20:213–218.

30. Casa DJ, Armstrong LE. Heatstroke: A medical emergency, in Armstrong LE (ed.), *Exertional Heat Illnesses.* Champaign, IL: Human Kinetics; 2003:26–56, 230–234.

31. Ganio MS, Brown DM, Casa DJ, et al. Validity and reliability of devices that assess body temperature during indoor exercise in the heat. *J Athl Train.* 2009;44:124–135.

32. Casa DJ, Becker SM, Ganio MS, et al. Validity of devices that assess body temperature during outdoor exercise in the heat. *J Athl Train.* 2007;42:333–342.

33. Low DA, Vu A, Brown M, et al. Temporal thermometry fails to track body core temperature during heat stress. *Med Sci Sports Exerc.* 2007;39:1029–1035.

34. Armstrong LE, Maresh CM, Crago AE, et al. Interpretation of aural temperatures during exercise, hyperthermia, and cooling therapy. *Med Exerc Nutr Health.* 1994;3:9–16.

35. Deschamps A, Levy RD, Coslo MG, et al. Tympanic temperature should not be used to assess exercise-induced hyperthermia. *Clin J Sport Med.* 1992;2:27–32.

36. Knight JC, Casa DJ, McClung JM, et al. Assessing if two tympanic temperature instruments are valid predictors of core temperature in hyperthermic runners and does drying the ear canal help [abstract]. *J Athl Train.* 2000;35:S21.

37. Roberts WO. Assessing core temperature in collapsed athletes: What's the best method? *Physician Sportsmed.* 1994;22(8):49–55.

38. Epstein Y. Exertional heatstroke: Lessons we tend to forget. *Am J Med Sports.* 2000;2:143–152.

39. Knochel JP. Environmental heat illness: An eclectic review. *Arch Intern Med.* 1974;133:841–864.

40. Roberts WO. Exercise-associated collapse in endurance events: A classification system. *Physician Sportsmed.* 1989;17(5):49–55.

41. Shapiro Y, Seidman DS. Field and clinical observations of exertional heat stroke patients. *Med Sci Sports Exerc.* 1990;22:6–14.

42. Casa DJ, McDermott BP, Lee EC, et al. Cold water immersion: The gold standard for exertional heatstroke treatment. *Exerc Sport Sci Rev.* 2007;35:141–149.

43. Armstrong LE, Crago AE, Adams R, et al. Whole-body cooling of hyperthermic runners: Comparison to two field therapies. *Am J Emerg Med.* 1996;14:355–358.

44. Brodeur VB, Dennett SR, Griffin LS. Exertional hyperthermia, ice baths, and emergency care at the Falmouth Road Race. *J Emerg Nurs.* 1989;15:304–312.

45. Clements JM, Casa DJ, Knight JC, et al. Ice-water immersion and cold-water immersion provide similar cooling rates in runners with exercise-induced hyperthermia. *J Athl Train.* 2002;37:146–150.

46. Golden F, Tipton M. *Essentials of Sea Survival.* Champaign, IL: Human Kinetics; 2002.

47. Hayward JS, Collis M, Eckerson JD. Thermographic evaluation of relative heat loss areas of man during cold water immersion. *Aerosp Med.* 1973;44:708–711.

48. Marino F, Booth J. Whole body cooling by immersion in water at moderate temperature. *J Sci Med Sport.* 1998;1:73–82.

49. McDermott BP, Casa DJ, O'Connor FG, et al. Cold-water dousing with ice massage to treat exertional heat stroke: A case series. *Aviat Space Environ Med.* 2009;80:720–722.

50. Proulx CI, Ducharme MB, Kenny GP. Effect of water temperature on cooling efficiency during hyperthermia in humans. *J Appl Physiol.* 2003;94:1317–1323.

51. Sandor RP. Heat illness: On-site diagnosis and cooling. *Physician Sportsmed.* 1997;25(6):35–40.

52. Gagnon D, Lemire BB, Casa DJ, Kenny GP. Cold-water immersion and the treatment of hyperthermia: Using 38.6°C as a safe rectal temperature cooling limit. *J Athl Train.* 2010;45:439–444.

53. Wyndham C, Strydom N, Cooks H, et al. Methods of cooling subjects with hyperpyrexia. *J Appl Physiol.* 1959;14:771–776.

54. Armstrong LE, De Luca JP, Hubbard RW. Time course of recovery and heat acclimation ability of prior exertional heatstroke patients. *Med Sci Sports Exerc.* 1990;22:36–48.

55. Epstein Y. Heat intolerance: Predisposing factor or residual injury? *Med Sci Sports Exerc.* 1990;22:29–35.

56. Mehta AC, Baker RN. Persistent neurological deficits in heat stroke. *Neurology.* 1970;20:336–340.

57. Royburt M, Epstein Y, Solomon Z, Shemer J. Long-term psychological and physiological effects of heat stroke. *Physiol Behav.* 1993;54:265–267.

58. McDermott BP, Casa DJ, Ganio MS, et al. Recovery and return to activity following exertional heat stroke: Considerations for the sports medicine staff. *J Sport Rehabil.* 2007;16:163–181.

59. O'Connor FG, Casa DJ, Bergeron MF, et al. American College of Sports Medicine roundtable on exertional heat stroke: Return to duty/return to play: conference proceedings. *Curr Sports Med Rep.* 2010;9:314–321.

60. Armstrong LE. Exertional hyponatremia, in Armstrong LE (ed.), *Exertional Heat Illnesses.* Champaign, IL: Human Kinetics; 2003:103–136, 244–249.

61. Speedy DB, Noakes TD, Schneider C. Exercise-associated hyponatremia: A review. *Emerg Med.* 2001;13:17–27.

62. Speedy DB, Rogers IR, Noakes TD, et al. Exercise-induced hyponatremia in ultradistance triathletes is caused by inappropriate fluid retention. *Clin J Sports Med.* 2000;10:272–278.

63. Hiller WDB, O'Toole ML, Massimino F, et al. Plasma electrolyte and glucose changes during the Hawaiian Ironman Triathlon. *Med Sci Sports Exerc.* 1985;17:S219.

64. Montain SJ, Cheuvront SN, Sawka MN. Exercise associated hyponatremia: Quantitative analysis to understand the aetiology. *Br J Sports Med.* 2006;40:98–106.

65. Hew-Butler T, Anley C, Schwartz P, Noakes T. The treatment of symptomatic hyponatremia with hypertonic saline in an Ironman triathlete. *Clin J Sport Med.* 2007;17:68–69.

66. Hew-Butler T, Ayus JC, Kipps C, et al. Statement of the Second International Exercise-Associated Hyponatremia Consensus Development Conference, New Zealand, 2007. *Clin J Sport Med.* 2008;18:111–121.

67. Armstrong LE, Curtis WC, Hubbard RW, et al. Symptomatic hyponatremia during prolonged exercise in heat. *Med Sci Sports Exerc.* 1993;25(5):543–549.

68. Sawka MN, Young AJ, Francesconi RP, et al. Thermoregulatory and blood responses during exercise at graded hypohydration levels. *J Appl Physiol.* 1985;59:1394–1401.

69. Armstrong LE. *Keeping Your Cool in Barcelona: The Effects of Heat, Humidity and Dehydration on Athletic Performance, Strength and Endurance.* Colorado Springs, CO: United States Olympic Committee Sports Sciences Division; 1992:1–29.

70. Armstrong LE, Hubbard RW, Szlyk PC, et al. Voluntary dehydration and electrolyte losses during prolonged exercise in the heat. *Aviat Space Environ Med.* 1985;56:765–770.

71. Bijlani R, Sharma KN. Effect of dehydration and a few regimes of rehydration on human performance. *Indian J Physiol Pharmacol.* 1980;24:255–266.

72. Cheung SS, McLellan TM. Heat acclimation, aerobic fitness, and hydration effects on tolerance during uncompensable heat stress. *J Appl Physiol.* 1998;84:1731–1739.

73. Morimoto T, Miki K, Nose H, et al. Changes in body fluid and its composition during heavy sweating and effect of fluid and electrolyte replacement. *Jpn J Biometeorol.* 1981;18:31–39.

74. Murray R. Dehydration, hyperthermia, and athletes: Science and practice. *J Athl Train.* 1996;31:248–252.

75. Nadel ER, Fortney SM, Wenger CB. Effect of hydration state on circulatory and thermal regulations. *J Appl Physiol.* 1980;49:715–721.

76. Baker LB, Lang JA, Kenney WL. Change in body mass accurately and reliably predicts change in body water after endurance exercise. *Eur J Appl Physiol.* 2009;105:959–967.

77. Armstrong LE. Assessing hydration status: The elusive gold standard. *J Am Coll Nutr.* 2007;26:575–584.

78. Murray R. Determining sweat rate. *Sports Sci Exch.* 1996;9 (suppl):63.

79. Armstrong LE. *Performing in Extreme Environments.* Champaign, IL: Human Kinetics; 2000.

80. Armstrong LE, Maresh CM, Castellani JW, et al. Urinary indices of hydration status. *Int J Sport Nutr.* 1994;4:265–279.

81. Armstrong LE, Soto JA, Hacker FT Jr, et al. Urinary indices during dehydration, exercise, and rehydration. *Int J Sport Nutr.* 1997;8:345–355.

82. Ivy JL, Goforth HW, Damon BM, et al. Early postexercise muscle glycogen recovery is enhanced with a carbohydrate–protein supplement. *J Appl Physiol.* 2002;93:1337–2002.

83. Casa DJ, Maresh CM, Armstrong LE, et al. Intravenous versus oral rehydration during a brief period: Responses to subsequent exercise in the heat. *Med Sci Sports Exerc.* 2000;32:124–133.

84. Ganio MS, Klau JF, Lee EC, et al. Effect of various carbohydrate–electrolyte fluids on cycling performance and maximal voluntary contraction. *IJSNEM.* 2010;20:104–114.

85. Armstrong LE, Casa DJ. Predisposing factors for exertional heat illnesses, in Armstrong LE (ed.), *Exertional Heat Illnesses.* Champaign, IL: Human Kinetics; 2003:151–168, 250–255.

86. Armstrong LE, Hubbard RW, Askew EW, et al. Responses to moderate and low sodium diets during exercise–heat acclimation. *Int J Sport Nutr.* 1993;3:207–221.

87. Armstrong LE, Maresh CM. Exercise–heat tolerance of children and adolescents. *Pediatr Exerc Sci.* 1995;7:239–252.

88. Armstrong LE, Szlyk PC, DeLuca JP, et al. Fluid–electrolyte losses in uniforms during prolonged exercise at 30 degrees C. *Aviat Space Environ Med.* 1992;63:351–355.

89. Bar-Or O. Thermoregulation in females from a life span perspective, in Bar-Or O, Lamb DR, Clarkson PM (eds), *Exercise and the Female: A Life Span Approach.* Carmel, IN: Cooper Publishing; 1996:249–284.

90. Cadarette BS, Sawka MN, Toner MM, Pandolf KB. Aerobic fitness and the hypohydration response to exercise-heat stress. *Aviat Space Environ Med.* 1984;55:507–512.

91. Chung NK, Pin CH. Obesity and the occurrence of heat disorders. *Mil Med.* 1996;161:739–742.

19

92. Dawson B. Exercise training in sweat clothing in cool conditions to improve heat tolerance. *Sports Med.* 1994;17:233–244.

93. Fortney SM, Vroman NB. Exercise, performance and temperature control: Temperature regulation during exercise and implications for sports performance and training. *Sports Med.* 1985;2:8–20.

94. Gardner JW, Kark JA, Karnei K, et al. Risk factors predicting exertional heat illness in male Marine Corps recruits. *Med Sci Sports Exerc.* 1996;28:939–944.

95. Kark JA, Burr PQ, Wenger CB, et al. Exertional heat illness in Marine Corps recruit training. *Aviat Space Environ Med.* 1996;67:354–360.

96. Montain SJ, Sawka MN, Cadarette BS, et al. Physiological tolerance to uncompensable heat stress: Effects of exercise intensity, protective clothing, and climate. *J Appl Physiol.* 1994;77:216–222.

97. Nadel ER, Pandolf KB, Roberts MF, Stolwijk JA. Mechanisms of thermal acclimation to exercise and heat. *J Appl Physiol.* 1974;37:515–520.

98. Nielsen B. Solar heat load: Heat balance during exercise in clothed subjects. *Eur J Appl Physiol Occup Physiol.* 1990;60:452–456.

99. Pandolf KB, Burse RL, Goldman RF. Role of physical fitness in heat acclimatisation, decay and reinduction. *Ergonomics.* 1977;20:399–408.

100. Pascoe DD, Shanley LA, Smith EW. Clothing and exercise: I. Biophysics of heat transfer between the individual clothing and environment. *Sports Med.* 1994;18:38–54.

101. Shapiro Y, Pandolf KB, Goldman RF. Predicting sweat loss response to exercise, environment and clothing. *Eur J Appl Physiol Occup Physiol.* 1982;48:83–96.

102. Francis K, Feinstein R, Brasher J. Optimal practice times for the reduction of the risk of heat illness during fall football practice in the southeastern United States. *Athl Train J Natl Athl Train Assoc.* 1991;26:76–78, 80.

103. Pandolf KB, Cadarette BS, Sawka MN, et al. Thermoregulatory responses of middle-aged and young men during dry-heat acclimation. *J Appl Physiol.* 1998;65:65–71.

104. Maughan RJ, Shirreffs SM. Preparing athletes for competition in the heat: Developing an effective acclimatization strategy. *Sports Sci Exch.* 1997;10:1–4.

105. Tilley RI, Standerwick JM, Long GJ. Ability of the wet bulb globe temperature index to predict heat stress in men wearing NBC protective clothing. *Mil Med.* 1987;152:554–556.

106. Roberts WO. Medical management and administration manual for long distance road racing, in Brown CH, Gudjonsson B (eds.), *IAAF Medical Manual for Athletics and Road Racing Competitions: A Practical Guide.* Monaco: International Amateur Athletic Federation Publications; 1998:39–75.

107. Nunnelly SA, Reardon MJ. Prevention of heat illness, in Pandolf KB, Burr RE (eds.), *Medical Aspects of Harsh Environments.* Washington, DC: TMM Publications; 2002:209–230.

108. Kulka J, Kenney WL. Heat balance limits in football uniforms: How different uniform ensembles alter the equation. *Physician Sportsmed.* 2002;30(7):29–39.

109. Armstrong LE, Johnson EC, Casa DJ, et al. The American football uniform: Uncompensable heat stress and hyperthermic exhaustion. *J Athl Train.* 2010;45:117–127.

110. Cappaert TA, Stone JA, Castellani JW, et al. National Athletic Trainers' Association position statement: Environmental cold injuries. *J Athl Train.* 2008;43:640–658.

111. Sallis R, Chassay CM. Recognizing and treating common cold-induced injury in outdoor sports. *Med Sci Sports Exerc.* 1999;31:1367–1373.

112. Hamlet MP. Human cold injuries, in Pandolf KB, Sawka MN, Gonzalez RR (eds.), *Human Performance Physiology and Environmental Medicine at Terrestrial Extremes.* Indianapolis, IN: Benchmark Press; 1998:435–466.

113. Ulrich AS, Rathlev NK. Hypothermia and localized cold injuries. *Emerg Med Clin North Am.* 2004;22:281–298.

114. Danzl DF. Accidental hypothermia, in Marx JA (ed.), *Rosen's Emergency Medicine: Concepts and Clinical Practice, Vol. 3.* St. Louis, MO: Mosby; 2006:2236–2254.

115. Savage MV, Brengelmann GL. Control of skin blood flow in the neutral zone of human body temperature regulation. *J Appl Physiol.* 1996;80:1249–1257.

116. Kempainen RR, Brunette DD. The evaluation and management of accidental hypothermia. *Respir Care.* 2004;49:192–205.

117. Danzl DF, Lloyd EL. Treatment of accidental hypothermia, in Pandolf KB, Burr RE (eds.), *Textbooks of Military Medicine: Medical Aspects of Harsh Environments, Vol. 1.* Falls Church, VA: Office of the Surgeon General, US Army; 2002:491–529.

118. Delaney KA, Howland MA, Vassallo S, Goldfrank LR. Assessment of acid–base disturbances in hypothermia and their physiologic consequences. *Ann Emerg Med.* 1989;18:72–82.

119. Giesbrecht GG, Bristow GK, Uin A, et al. Effectiveness of three field treatments for induced mild (33.0 degrees C) hypothermia. *J Appl Physiol.* 1987;63:2375–2379.

120. Collins AM, Danzl DF. Hypothermia with profound anemia and pancreatitis. *Wilderness Environ Med.* 2006;17:31–35.

121. Murphy JV, Banwell PE, Roberts AHN, McGrouther DA. Frostbite: Pathogenesis and treatment. *J Trauma.* 2000;48:171–178.

122. Hassi J. Frostbite, a common cold injury: Challenges in treatment and prevention. *Int J Circumpolar Health.* 2000;59:90–91.

123. Biem J, Koehncke N, Classen D, Dosman J. Out of the cold: Management of hypothermia and frostbite. *CMAJ.* 2003;168:305–311.

124. Bruen KJ, Ballard JR, Morris SE, et al. Reduction of the incidence of amputation in frostbite injury with thrombolytic therapy. *Arch Surg.* 2007;142:546–551.

GLOSSARY

allogenic graft Graft tissue obtained from the same species but not from the patient (e.g., from a cadaver).

alta An abnormally high position.

analgesic Pain-relieving without the loss of consciousness.

anastomose To join or connect two structures such as blood vessels.

anesthetic Loss of sensation; may be local or general (body-wide).

ankylosing (ankylosis) Immobility of a joint, often progressive in nature.

anterograde amnesia Memory loss of events occurring after injury.

anteversion The femoral neck is anterior relative to the long axis of the femur.

antibiotic Used to kill bacteria that cause infection.

antiseptic Inhibits the growth of disease-producing organisms.

ameliorating Improving a condition.

arteriogram A radiograph of a blood vessel after the injection of a radiopaque dye into the bloodstream.

arthrodesis Fusion of bones across a joint space that limits or restricts joint motion.

arthrofibrosis Abnormal formation of fibrous tissue within a joint.

arthroplasty Joint replacement surgery.

arthrotomy The surgical opening of a joint.

autogenic graft Graft tissue transplanted from one part of the patient's body to another part.

atrophic Characterized by atrophy or wasting.

axial loading A load directed vertically along the axis of the spine creating a compression force.

baja An unexpectedly low position.

barrier Restriction of, or resistance to, movement in a joint; the goal of muscle energy is to move the barrier to achieve normal mobility.

bifurcated Made up of, or divided into, two parts.

bipartite A congenital or traumatic splitting of a structure into two parts.

bone scintigraphy A nuclear bone scan in which a radioactive substance is injected into the patient's body and the amount of absorption is identified. Increased ab-sorption may indicate a stress fracture or periosteal inflammation.

capsulotomy Cutting of the joint capsule.

cauterized Sealed off by using heat.

cephalad Toward the head.

cerclage Encircling a structure with a ring or loop.

cheilectomy Surgical removal of bone spurs.

chondrocyte A cell that forms the matrix of bone cartilage.

chondrolysis Destruction or atrophy of articular cartilage.

coagulopathy A disorder of the blood-clotting mechanism.

compensation Changes in biomechanical function to overcome muscular weakness or joint dysfunction.

core muscles The muscles closest to the center of the body in the trunk that provide stability of the spine during movement, including the lower internal obliques, transverse abdominis, and multifidus.

corticocancellous graft An autograft of bone, usually harvested from the iliac crest, that consists of both cortical bone and bony callus.

curette A scoop-shaped surgical instrument used to remove tissue.

decorticated The surgical removal of the outer layer of a structure.

decussation The crossing of one structure over the other.

dehiscence Opening of the wound.

dehiscing Tearing of the repaired tissue.

demyelinization Erosion of a nerve's myelin layer, resulting in decreased nerve function.

desiccation The process of tissue dehydration or drying out.

dystopia Change in the position of the pupil relative to the unaffected side.

ecchymosis A bluish discoloration of the skin caused by bleeding under the skin; a bruise.

ectopic A structure that is in an anatomically incorrect place.

embolization Blocking an artery or vein by use of a foreign material.

embolus Solid, liquid, or gaseous mass blocking a passageway.

enophthalmos A protruding globe.

epitenon A glistening, synovial-like membrane that envelops the tendon surface.

exostosis A bone spur or bony overgrowth.

extravasate To escape from the blood or lymph vessels into the tissues.

false-negative Results incorrectly indicating the absence of trauma or disease.

fasciotome A device used to split subcutaneous or intramuscular fascia.

fasciotomy Surgical incision of the fascia.

fibrillation A local, involuntary muscular contraction.

fibrocartilage A mesh of collagen fibers, proteoglycans, and glycoproteins, interspersed with fibrochondrocytes.

fibroplasia Development of fibrous tissues during wound healing.

fissurization The process of forming long, narrow depressions or cracks in the tissue.

frank Clearly or visibly evident.

fremitus Palpable vibration, as felt when placing the hand on the chest or throat during speaking.

harvest morbidity The death, failure, or rejection of implanted tissue.

heat capacity The quantity of heat required to raise the temperature of a unit of mass by a specific unit change in temperature; thermal capacity.

hemarthrosis A collection of blood within a joint.

hematuria Microscopic or macroscopic blood in the urine.

hemiplegia Paralysis of one side of the body.

hemisection Cutting into two; bisecting.

hemoptysis Coughing up blood.

heterotopic The formation of lamellar bone within soft tissues as the result of osteoblastic activity, similar to myositis ossificans.

histology Microscopic study of healthy tissue.

hysterical paralysis The inability to move brought on by fear and/or anxiety.

idiopathic Of unknown cause or origin.

incarceration A confined or restricted hernia that is difficult to reduce.

intimal Relating to the innermost membrane of the vessel.

kinetic chain A series of body parts linked together by joints and muscles through which action/reaction forces are transmitted.

lavage The washing or cleansing of a hollow tissue space with water.

ligated Sutured closed.

lipohemarthrosis Fatty cells within the synovial membrane.

malocclusion Improper alignment of the teeth when the mouth is closed.

malunion Healing of a bone in a faulty position, creating an imperfect union.

metastatic The spreading of a cancerous growth from one body area to another.

morphology Pertaining to a tissue's structure and form without regard to function.

mucoperichondrium The structure overlying the nasal cartilage that provides it with blood supply and nutrients.

muscle energy A manual technique that uses voluntary muscle contraction against a resistive force to achieve desired results.

myelography A radiographic technology for recording the activity of the spinal cord and nerves.

nephrectomy Surgical removal of a kidney.

nonunion Failure of a bone to heal within 9 months following the initial fracture.

notchplasty A surgical enlargement of the intercondylar notch to increase the space available to the ACL.

occult Hidden or not readily detectable by laboratory tests or physical examination.

osteonecrosis Bone death secondary to a decreased blood supply; avascular necrosis.

otorrhea Cerebral spinal fluid draining from the ear canal as a result of a skull facture/TBI.

palliative Relief of the symptoms without correcting the underlying cause.

paradoxical pulse A pulse that becomes weaker during inspiration and stronger during expiration.

parenchyma The internal functional tissues of an organ.

pathognomonic Specifically distinctive for some disease or disease process; absolutely diagnostic.

percutaneous Through the skin.

pericardiocentesis A diagnostic procedure in which a needle is used to draw fluid from the pericardium.

pluripotential cells Embryonic cells that can develop into many different types of cells, having a number of different actions.

polyneuropathy A disease that affects a number of peripheral nerves.

premorbid Before the onset of the condition.

priapism Abnormal, painful, continued erection of the penis, often the result of a spinal cord lesion.

pseudopodia "Fake feet;" extensions from a cell that allow it to move.

pyelography Radiographs of the kidney and ureter after the injection of a radiopaque dye.

radicular pain Pain moving from the torso into the extremities; radiating in a nerve root distribution.

radiolucency Transparent to x-rays.

reef (reefing) A folding or tucking of tissues.

retrograde amnesia Memory loss of events occurring prior to injury.

retropulsed Displaced posteriorly.

rhinorrhea Cerebral spinal fluid draining from the nose as a result of a skull facture/TBI.

secondary intention Healing that occurs secondary to the formation of a scar or other indirect union.

sepsis The spread of an infection into the bloodstream, creating a systemic condition.

sequelae Conditions resulting from an injury or disease.

serial observation Repeated assessment of the same injury.

seronegative spondyloarthropathy An inflammatory condition of the spine that progresses to affect tendinous insertions throughout the body.

sinus tract A pathway between a pathologic space and a healthy cavity or skin.

spinal stenosis Developmental narrowing of the spinal canal that can affect either the spinal cord or the peripheral nerve roots.

splenomegaly Enlargement of the spleen.

sports hernia The combination of an adductor strain, abdominal strain, and osteitis pubis.

stasis Slowing or blockage of blood flow.

substitution A secondary muscle or muscle group performing the action that would otherwise be performed by a primary muscle.

tenodesis The surgical relocation and fixation of a tendon.

tenolysis A surgical procedure performed to remove adhesions from a tendon.

tenotomy Surgical cutting or division of a tendon.

turgor The skin's resistance to being deformed. It is tested by lifting a small nap of skin on the hand and noting how quickly it returns to normal. In dehydrated individuals, the skin will slowly return to normal.

vestigial A structure that was once useful, but no longer serves the intended purpose.

viscoelastic Having the ability to flow or deform and return to the original state.

volume expanders Benign IV agents that allow temporary restoration of blood volume without having to wait for blood type matching.

INDEX

PHOTO CREDITS

Openers
© Bocos Benedict/ShutterStock, Inc.

Chapter 1
1.1A–C Reproduced with permission from Johnson TR, Steinbach LS (eds). *Essentials of Musculoskeletal Imaging.* Rosemont, IL: American Academy of Orthopaedic Surgeons; 2004:9, 435; **1.2A–C** Reproduced with permission from Johnson TR, Steinbach LS (eds). *Essentials of Musculoskeletal Imaging.* Rosemont, IL: American Academy of Orthopaedic Surgeons; 2004:488, 489, 496; **1.3A,B** Reproduced with permission from Johnson TR, Steinbach LS (eds). *Essentials of Musculoskeletal Imaging.* Rosemont, IL: American Academy of Orthopaedic Surgeons; 2004:243.

Chapter 2
2.3 © Biophoto Associates/Photo Researchers, Inc.; **2.6** Reprinted with permission from Arendt EA (ed). *Orthopaedic Knowledge Update: Sports Medicine*, ed 2. Rosemont, IL: American Academy of Orthopaedic Surgeons; 1999:32; **2.10** Reproduced with permission from Johnson TR, Steinbach LS (eds). *Essentials of Musculoskeletal Imaging.* Rosemont, IL: American Academy of Orthopaedic Surgeons; 2004:556; **2.11** Reproduced with permission from Johnson TR, Steinbach LS (eds). *Essentials of Musculoskeletal Imaging.* Rosemont, IL: American Academy of Orthopaedic Surgeons; 2004:49.

Chapter 3
3.1 Courtesy of Smith & Nephew; **3.8A–C** Reproduced with permission from Sarmiento A, Latta LL. Functional fracture bracing. *J Am Acad Orthop Surg.* 1999;7:66–75; **3.11A–C** Reproduced with permission from Sarmiento A, Latta LL. Functional fracture bracing. *J Am Acad Orthop Surg.* 1999;7:66–75; **3.13A–C** Reproduced with permission from Sarmiento A, Latta LL. Functional fracture bracing. *J Am Acad Orthop Surg.* 1999;7:66–75; **3.15A,B** Reproduced with permission from Naranja RJ Jr, Iannotti JP. Displaced three- and four-part proximal humerus fractures: evaluation and management. *J Am Acad Orthop Surg.* 2000;8:373–382; **3.17** Reproduced with permission from Shin AY, Gillingham BL. Fatigue fractures of the femoral neck in athletes. *J Am Acad Orthop Surg.* 1997;5:293–302.

Chapter 4
4.1A–C Reproduced with permission from Anderson RB, Hunt KJ, McCormick JJ. Management of common sports-related injuries about the foot and ankle. *J Am Acad Orthop Surg.* 2010 Sep; 18(9):546–56; **4.3A–D** Reproduced with permission from Richardson EG. Hallucal sesamoid pain: causes and surgical treatment. *J Am Acad Orthop Surg.* 1999;7:270–278; **4.4A,B, 4.5A,B, 4.6A–D** Reproduced with permission from Richardson EG. Hallucal sesamoid pain: causes and surgical treatment. *J Am Acad Orthop Surg.* 1999;7:270–278; **4.7, 4.8A,B** Reproduced with permission from Mann RA. Disorders of the first metatarsophalangeal joint. *J Am Acad Orthop Surg.* 1995;3:34–43; **4.10A,B** Reproduced with permission from Mann RA. Hallux rigidus, in Greene WB (ed), *Instructional Course Lectures XXXIX.* Park Ridge, IL: American Academy of Orthopaedic Surgeons; 1990:15–21; **4.11** Reproduced with permission from Johnson TR, Steinbach LS (eds). *Essentials of Musculoskeletal Imaging.* Rosemont, IL: American Academy of Orthopaedic Surgeons; 2004:631; **4.13** Reproduced with permission from Johnson TR, Steinbach LS (eds). *Essentials of Musculoskeletal Imaging.* Rosemont, IL: American Academy of Orthopaedic Surgeons; 2004:567; **4.14A,B** Reproduced with permission from Recht MP, Donley BG. Magnetic resonance imaging of the foot and ankle. *J Am Acad Orthp Surg.* 2001;9: 187–199; **4.19** Reproduced with permission from Johnson TR, Steinbach LS (eds). *Essentials of Musculoskeletal Imaging.* Rosemont, IL: American Academy of Orthopaedic Surgeons; 2004:623; **4.20A–C** Reproduced from Thompson MC, Mormino MA. Injury to the tarsometatarsal joint complex. *J Am Acad Orthop Surg.* 2003;11: 260–267; **4.21** Reproduced with permission from Greene WB (ed). *Essentials of Musculoskeletal Care*, ed 2. Rosemont, IL: American Academy of Orthopaedic Surgeons; 2000:602; **4.22A,B** Reproduced with permission from Johnson TR, Steinbach LS (eds). *Essentials of Musculoskeletal Imaging.* Rosemont, IL: American Academy of Orthopaedic Surgeons; 2004:595–596; **4.25** Reproduced with permission from Johnson TR, Steinbach LS (eds). *Essentials of Musculoskeletal Imaging.* Rosemont, IL: American Academy of Orthopaedic Surgeons; 2004:645; **4.28A,B** Reproduced with permission from Zalavaras C,

Thordarson D. Ankle syndesmotic injury. *J Am Acd Orthop Surg.* 2007;15(6):330–339; **4.30A–C** Reproduced with permission from Recht MP, Donley BG. Magnetic resonance imaging of the foot and ankle. *J Am Acad Orthp Surg.* 2001;9: 187–199; **4.31A,B** Reproduced with permission from Johnson TR, Steinbach LS (eds). *Essentials of Musculoskeletal Imaging.* Rosemont, IL: American Academy of Orthopaedic Surgeons; 2004:650; **4.32A–E** Reproduced with permission from Kay RM, Matthys GA. Pediatric ankle fractures: evaluation and treatment. *J Am Acad Orthop Surg.* 2001;9:268–278; **4.34** Reproduced with permission from Jones DC. Tendon disorders of the foot and ankle. *J Am Acad Orthop Surg.* 1993;1:87–94; **4.35** Reproduced with permission from Paavola MP et al. Current concepts review: Achilles tendinopathy. *J Bone Joint Surg Am.* 2002;84:2062–2076; **4.36A** Reproduced with permission from Jones DC. Tendon disorders of the foot and ankle. *J Am Acad Orthop Surg.* 1993;1:87–94; **4.36B** Reproduced with permission from Johnson TR, Steinbach LS (eds). *Essentials of Musculoskeletal Imaging.* Rosemont, IL: American Academy of Orthopaedic Surgeons; 2004:641; **4.38** Reproduced with permission from Saltzman CL, Tearse DS. Achilles tendon injuries. *J Am Acad Orthop Surg.* 1998;6:316–325; **4.40A,B** Reproduced with permission from Johnson TR, Steinbach LS (eds). *Essentials of Musculoskeletal Imaging.* Rosemont, IL: American Academy of Orthopaedic Surgeons; 2004:572; **4.41** Reproduced with permission from Johnson TR, Steinbach LS (eds). *Essentials of Musculoskeletal Imaging.* Rosemont, IL: American Academy of Orthopaedic Surgeons; 2004:650; **4.45A** Reproduced with permission from Sullivan JA, Anderson SJ (eds). *Care of the Young Athlete.* Rosemont, IL: American Academy of Orthopaedic Surgeons and American Academy of Pediatrics; 1999:308; **4.45B** Reproduced with permission from Johnson TR, Steinbach LS (eds). *Essentials of Musculoskeletal Imaging.* Rosemont, IL: American Academy of Orthopaedic Surgeons; 2004:519; **4.46** Reproduced with permission from Johnson TR, Steinbach LS (eds). *Essentials of Musculoskeletal Imaging.* Rosemont, IL: American Academy of Orthopaedic Surgeons; 2004:647; **4.48** Reproduced with permission from Johnson TR, Steinbach LS (eds). *Essentials of Musculoskeletal Imaging.* Rosemont, IL: American Academy of Orthopaedic Surgeons; 2004:504

Chapter 5

5.3 Reproduced with permission from Johnson TR, Steinbach LS (eds). *Essentials of Musculoskeletal Imaging.* Rosemont, IL: American Academy of Orthopaedic Surgeons; 2004:548; **5.4**

Reproduced with permission from Johnson TR, Steinbach LS (eds). *Essentials of Musculoskeletal Imaging.* Rosemont, IL: American Academy of Orthopaedic Surgeons; 2004:485; **5.9A** Reproduced with permission from Cosgarea AJ, Jay PR. Posterior cruciate ligament injuries: evaluation and management. *J Am Acad Orthop Surg.* 2001;9:297–307; **5.9B** Reproduced with permission from Johnson TR, Steinbach LS (eds). *Essentials of Musculoskeletal Imaging.* Rosemont, IL: American Academy of Orthopaedic Surgeons; 2004:550; **5.12** Reproduced with permission from Cosgarea AJ, Jay PR. Posterior cruciate ligament injuries: Evaluation and management. *J Am Acad Orthop Surg.* 2001;9:297–307; **5.13** Reproduced with permission from Johnson TR, Steinbach LS (eds). *Essentials of Musculoskeletal Imaging.* Rosemont, IL: American Academy of Orthopaedic Surgeons; 2004:550; **5.15A,B** Reproduced with permission from Cosgarea AJ, Jay PR. Posterior cruciate ligament injuries: evaluation and management. *J Am Acad Orthop Surg.* 2001;9:297–307; **5.20A,B** Reproduced with permission from Johnson TR, Steinbach LS (eds). *Essentials of Musculoskeletal Imaging.* Rosemont, IL: American Academy of Orthopaedic Surgeons; 2004:553; **5.23A,B** Reproduced with permission from Johnson TR, Steinbach LS (eds). *Essentials of Musculoskeletal Imaging.* Rosemont, IL: American Academy of Orthopaedic Surgeons; 2004:501; **5.23C** Reproduced with permission from Johnson TR, Steinbach LS (eds). *Essentials of Musculoskeletal Imaging.* Rosemont, IL: American Academy of Orthopaedic Surgeons; 2004:521; **5.24, 5.25** Reproduced with permission from Good L, Johnson RJ. The dislocated knee. *J Am Acad Orthop Surg.* 1995;3:284–292; **5.27A,B** Reproduced with permission from Johnson TR, Steinbach LS (eds). *Essentials of Musculoskeletal Imaging.* Rosemont, IL: American Academy of Orthopaedic Surgeons; 2004: 511–513; **5.28** Reproduced with permission from Johnson TR, Steinbach LS (eds). *Essentials of Musculoskeletal Imaging.* Rosemont, IL: American Academy of Orthopaedic Surgeons; 2004:531; **5.29B,C** Reproduced with permission from Cole BJ, Harner CD. Degenerative arthritis of the knee in active patients: evaluation and management. *J Am Acad Orthop Surg.* 1999;7:389–402.

Chapter 6

6.3 Reproduced with permission from Johnson TR, Steinbach LS (eds). *Essentials of Musculoskeletal Imaging.* Rosemont, IL: American Academy of Orthopaedic Surgeons; 2004:483; **6.4B** Reproduced with permission from Fulkerson JP. Patellofemoral pain disorders: evaluation and management. *J Am Acad Orthop Surg.* 1994;

2:124–132; **6.5** Reproduced with permission from Crosby LA, Lewallen DG (eds). *Emergency Care and Transportation of the Sick and Injured,* ed 6. Rosemont, IL: American Academy of Orthopaedic Surgeons; 1995:555; **6.7A,B** Reproduced with permission from Boden BP, Pearsall AW, Garrett WE, Feagin JA Jr. Patellofemoral instability: evaluation and management. *J Am Acad Orthop Surg.* 1997;5:47–57; **6.9** Reproduced with permission from Johnson TR, Steinbach LS (eds). *Essentials of Musculoskeletal Imaging.* Rosemont, IL: American Academy of Orthopaedic Surgeons; 2004:488; **6.11A–C** Reproduced with permission from Matava MJ. Patellar tendon ruptures. J *Am Acad Orthop Surg.* 1996;4:287–296; **6.13A,B** Reproduced with permission from Johnson TR, Steinbach LS (eds). *Essentials of Musculoskeletal Imaging.* Rosemont, IL: American Academy of Orthopaedic Surgeons; 2004:495.

Chapter 7
7.1 Reproduced with permission from Clanton TO, Coupe KJ. Hamstring strains in athletes: diagnosis and treatment. *J Am Acad Orthop Surg.* 1998;6:237–248; **page 221** © John C. Hunter, M.D., U.C. Davis Medical Center, Sacramento, CA; **7.2** Reproduced with permission from Clanton TO, Coupe KJ. Hamstring strains in athletes: diagnosis and treatment. *J Am Acad Orthop Surg.* 1998;6:237–248; **7.12** © BSIP/Photo Researchers, Inc; **7.14A-C, 7.15A-C,7.16** Reproduced with permission from Shin AY, Gillingham BL. Fatigue fractures of the femoral neck in athletes. *J Am Acad Orthop Surg.* 1997;5:293–302.

Chapter 9
9.1, 9.2 Reproduced with permission from Wirth MA, Rockwood CA Jr. Acute and chronic traumatic injuries of the sternoclavicular joint. *J Am Acad Orthop Surg.* 1996;4:268–278; **9.3** Reproduced with permission from Rockwood CA Jr, Green DP, Bucholz RW, et al (eds). *Rockwood and Green's Fractures in Adults,* ed 4. Philadelphia, PA: Lippincott-Raven;1996:vol 2, 1448; **9.7A,B** Reproduced with permission from Johnson TR, Steinbach LS (eds). *Essentials of Musculoskeletal Imaging.* Rosemont, IL: American Academy of Orthopaedic Surgeons; 2004:181; **9.10B** Reproduced with permission from Shaffer BS. Painful conditions of the acromioclavicular joint. *J Am Acad Orthop Surg.* 1999;7:176–188; **9.10C** Simovitch R, Sanders B, Ozbaydar M, Lavery K, Warner JJP. Acromioclavicular joint injuries: diagnosis and management. *J Am Acad Orthop Surg.* 2009;17:207–219; **9.14** Reproduced with permission from Kibler WB, McMullen J. Scapular dyskinesis and its relation to shoulder pain. *J Am Acad Orthop Surg.* 2003;11:142;

9.15A–C Reproduced with permission from Iannotti JP. *Rotator Cuff Disorders: Evaluation and Treatment.* Rosemont, IL: American Academy of Orthopaedic Surgeons; 1991:5; **page 301** © shoulderdoc.co.uk; **9.18** Reproduced with permission from Tonino PM, Gerber C, Itoi E, Porcellini G, Sonnabend D, Walch G. Complex dhoulder disorders: evaluation and rreatment. *J Am Acad Orthop Surg.* 2009;17:125; **9.21** Keener JD, Brophy RH. Superior labral tears of the shoulder: pathogenesis, evaluation, and treatment. *J Am Acad Orthop Surg.* 2009;17:627; **page 320, 231** © Stephen J. Snyder, MD; **9.22A,B** Reproduced with permission from Lintner SA, Speer KP. Traumatic anterior glenohumeral instability: the role of arthroscopy. *J Am Acad Orthop Surg.* 1997;5:233–239; **9.25** Reprinted with permission from Griffin LY (ed) *Orthopaedic Knowledge Update: Sports Medicine.* Rosemont, IL: American Academy of Orthopaedic Surgeons; 1994:102; **9.26A,B** Reproduced with permission from Millett PJ, Clavert P, Hatch III GF, Warner JJP. Recurrent posterior shoulder instability. *J Am Acad Orthop Surg.* 2006;14:464

Chapter 10
10.1, 10.2A,B Reproduced with permission from Ramsey ML. Distal biceps tendon injuries: diagnosis and management. *J Am Acad Orthop Surg.* 1999;7:199–207; **10.4, 10.6** Reproduced with permission from Morrey BF. Acute and chronic instability of the elbow. *J Am Acad Orthop Surg.* 1996;4:117–128; **10.7** Reproduced with permission from Miller CD, Savoie FH. Valgus extension injuries of the elbow in the throwing athlete. *J Am Acad Orthop Surg.* 1994;2:261–269; **10.11A–C** Reproduced with permission from Johnson TR, Steinbach LS (eds). *Essentials of Musculoskeletal Imaging.* Rosemont, IL: American Academy of Orthopaedic Surgeons; 2004:270, 274, 278; **10.12A–C** Reproduced with permission from Webb LX. Distal humerus fractures in adults. *J Am Acad Orthop Surg.* 1996;4:336–344; **10.14B,D** Reproduced with permission from Morrey BF. Acute and chronic instability of the elbow. *J Am Acad Orthop Surg.* 1996;4:117–128; **10.17** Reproduced with permission from Morrey BF. Acute and chronic instability of the elbow. *J Am Acad Orthop Surg.* 1996;4:117–128; **10.19** Reproduced with permission from Williams RJ, Altchek DW.Atraumatic injuries of the elbow in athletes, in Arendt EA (ed), *Orthopaedic Knowledge Update: Sports Medicine,* ed 2. Rosemont, IL: American Academy of Orthopaedic Surgeons; 1999:226; **10.20** Reproduced with permission from Norberg FB, Savoie FH III, Field LD. Arthroscopic treatment of arthritis of the elbow. *Instr Course Lect.* 2000;49:247–253; **10.21** Reproduced with permission from Williams RJ,

Altchek DW. Atraumatic injuries of the elbow in athletes, in Arendt EA (ed), *Orthopaedic Knowledge Update: Sports Medicine*, ed 2. Rosemont, IL: American Academy of Orthopaedic Surgeons; 1999:228; **10.26** Reproduced with permission from Lubahn JD, Cermak MB. Uncommon nerve compression syndromes of the upper extremity. *J Am Acad Orthop Surg*. 1998;6:378–386.

Chapter 11
11.5B Reproduced with permission from *J Am Acad Orthop Surg*. 1999;7:92–100. © 1999 American Academy of Orthopaedic Surgeons; **11.7** Reproduced with permission from Johnson TR, Steinbach LS (eds). *Essentials of Musculoskeletal Imaging*. Rosemont, IL: American Academy of Orthopaedic Surgeons; 2004:369; **11.10** Reproduced with permission from Johnson TR, Steinbach LS (eds). *Essentials of Musculoskeletal Imaging*. Rosemont, IL: American Academy of Orthopaedic Surgeons; 2004:318; **11.12A,B** Reproduced with permission from Johnson TR, Steinbach LS (eds). *Essentials of Musculoskeletal Imaging*. Rosemont, IL: American Academy of Orthopaedic Surgeons; 2004:350–351; **11.13** Reproduced with permission from Kozin SH, Thoder JJ, Liberman G. Operative treatment of metacarpal and phalangeal shaft fractures. *J Am Acad Orthop Surg*. 2000;8:111–121; **11.18** Reprinted with permission from Boyer MI, Gelberman RH. Operative correction of swan-neck and boutonniere deformities in the rheumatoid hand. *J Am Acad Orthop Surg*. 1999;7:92–100; **11.21** Reproduced with permission from Johnson TR, Steinbach LS (eds). *Essentials of Musculoskeletal Imaging*. Rosemont, IL: American Academy of Orthopaedic Surgeons; 2004:378; **page 423** Figures reproduced with permission from Heyman P. Injuries to the ulnar collateral ligament of the thumb metacarpophalangeal joint. *J Am Acad Orthop Surg*. 1997;5:224–229; **11.27A,B** Reproduced with permission from Johnson TR, Steinbach LS (eds). *Essentials of Musculoskeletal Imaging*. Rosemont, IL: American Academy of Orthopaedic Surgeons; 2004:347; **11.28A,B** Reproduced with permission from Kozin SH, Thoder JJ, Lieberman G. Operative treatment of metacarpal and phalangeal shaft fractures. *J Am Acad Orthop Surg*. 2000;8: 111–121; **11.30** Reproduced with permission from Kozin SH. Perilunate injuries: diagnosis and treatment. *J Am Acad Orthop Surg*. 1998;6: 114–120; **11.31** Reproduced with permission from Allan CH, Lichtman DM. Kienböck's disease: diagnosis and treatment. *J Am Acad Orthop Surg*. 2001;9:128–136; **11.34** Reproduced with permission from Johnson TR, Steinbach LS (eds). *Essentials of Musculoskeletal Imaging*. Rosemont, IL: American Academy of Orthopaedic Surgeons;

2004:356; **11.35A–F** © 1999 by Jesse B. Jupiter, MD; **11.40** Reproduced with permission from *J Am Acad Orthop Surg*. 2001;9:389–400. © 2001 American Academy of Orthopaedic Surgeons; **11.41A** Reproduced with permission from Johnson TR, Steinbach LS (eds). *Essentials of Musculoskeletal Imaging*. Rosemont, IL: American Academy of Orthopaedic Surgeons; 2004:333; **11.41B** Reproduced with permission from Nagle DJ. Evaluation of chronic wrist pain. *J Am Acad Orthop Surg*. 2000;8:45–55; **11.42** Reproduced with permission from Johnson TR, Steinbach LS (eds). *Essentials of Musculoskeletal Imaging*. Rosemont, IL: American Academy of Orthopaedic Surgeons; 2004:340.

Chapter 13
3.2 © Neil Borden/Photo Researchers, Inc.; **13.6** Reproduced with permission from Johnson TR, Steinbach LS (eds). *Essentials of Musculoskeletal Imaging*. Rosemont, IL: American Academy of Orthopaedic Surgeons; 2004:697; **13.7A,B** Reproduced with permission from Johnson TR, Steinbach LS (eds). *Essentials of Musculoskeletal Imaging*. Rosemont, IL: American Academy of Orthopaedic Surgeons; 2004:691, 711; **13.11A–C**, **13.12**, **13.13** Reproduced with permission from Boden SD, Wiesel SW. Lumbar spine imaging: role in clinical decision making. *J Am Acad Orthop Surg*. 1996;4:238–248; **13.14A,B** Reproduced with permission from Lauerman WC, Cain JE. Isthmic spondylolisthesis in the adult. *J Am Acad Orthop Surg*. 1996;4:201–208; **13.15** Reproduced with permission from Johnson TR, Steinbach LS (eds). *Essentials of Musculoskeletal Imaging*. Rosemont, IL: American Academy of Orthopaedic Surgeons; 2004:687; **13.16A,B** Reproduced with permission from Frymoyer JW: Degenerative spondylolisthesis: diagnosis and treatment. *J Am Acad Orthop Surg*. 1994;2:9–15; **13.17A,B** Reproduced with permission from Lauerman WC, Cain JE. Isthmic spondylolisthesis in the adult. *J Am Acad Orthop Surg*. 1996;4: 201–208.

Chapter 15
15.14 Reproduced with permission from Delamarter RB, Coyle J. Acute management of spinal cord injury. *J Am Acad Orthop Surg*. 1999;7: 166–175; **15.16A,B** Reproduced with permission from Thomas BE, McCullen GM, Yuan HA. Cervical spine injuries in football players. *J Am Acad Orthop Surg*. 1999;7:338–347.

Unless otherwise indicated, all photographs and illustrations are under copyright of Jones & Bartlett Learning, have been provided by the American Academy of Orthopaedic Surgeons; or have been provided by the authors.